Botanica's Pocket

ANNUALS &
PERENNIALS

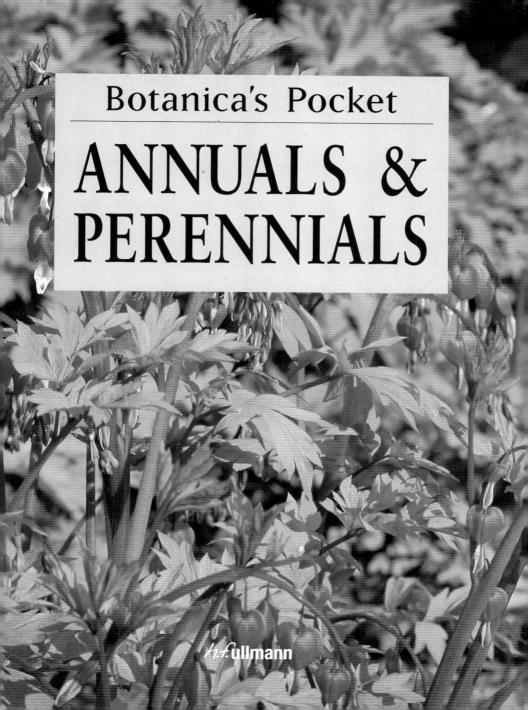

Botanica's Pocket

ANNUALS &
PERENNIALS

h.f.ullmann

Copyright © Random House Australia 2004

Photos © Random House Australia Pty Ltd 1999
from the Random House Photo Library

Text © Random House Australia Pty Ltd 1999

Original ISBN 0 091 83809 6

Consultants: **Geoff Bryant, Tony Rodd and
Dr Gerlinde von Berg**

Publisher: **Gordon Cheers**

Associate Publisher: **Margaret Olds**

Managing Editor: **James Young**

Editors: **Anna Cheifetz, Clare Double, Loretta Barnard
and Denise Imwold**

Design: **Stan Lamond**

Cover Design: **Bob Mitchell**

Photolibrarian: **Susan Page**

Index: **Glenda Browne**

Production Manager: **Linda Watchorn**

Publishing Coordinator: **Sarah Sherlock**

Copyright © 2006/2007 for this edition:

Tandem Verlag GmbH

h.f.ullmann is an imprint
of Tandem Verlag GmbH

Printed in China

ISBN 978-3-8331-4459-2

10 9 8 7 6 5 4 3 2 1
X IX VIII VII VI V IV III II I

Contents

Introduction

People often think of annuals and perennials simply as a way to provide quick garden color. However, they should not be underestimated; they encompass an enormous diversity of foliage forms, textures and growth habits. Certainly, they can be short lived and sometimes they become untidy well before the end of the growing season, but unlike more permanent plants, they are relatively cheap, easily propagated, tough, adaptable and above all, versatile.

Trees and shrubs will probably remain the framework of your garden, yet on their own they can seem staid and uninteresting. Annuals and perennials brighten the garden and provide continuous variety of flower, foliage and form. Think of them as the color palette for your garden, to be used to fill in the broad lines of the more permanent features. Use the pastel shades of *Impatiens* in broad washes as you would watercolors, or the vivid oil paint colors of marigolds for intense spots of brightness.

Whatever the design of your garden and regardless of the climate it experiences, there is such a wide range of annuals and perennials in this book that you need never be short of choice. However, ornamental grasses and bulbs, corms and tubers are not included here.

What are annuals and perennials?

The difference between annuals, biennials and perennials relates to the life cycles of the plants. Annuals grow from seed to full maturity within one growing season. Marigolds, ageratums and zinnias are

Anticlockwise from bottom left:
Lychnis coronaria, Salvia nemorosa 'Primavera', *Phlomis russeliana* and a *Verbascum* cultivar

Ajania 'Bess' and 'Benny' make a striking pot planting

typical annuals. They flower, set seed and die, all within a single year. Biennials, such as Canterbury bells and some foxgloves, complete their life cycles over two years, sometimes producing a few flowers in the first season, but most often just making foliage growth and establishing their root systems. Perennials live longer than two seasons and may outlive many shrubs. In fact, strictly speaking, shrubs and trees are perennials, but when gardeners talk of perennials they generally mean plants that don't develop permanent woody stems.

Perennials occur in several types. Some, such as *Acanthus,* are evergreen and don't have a period of total dormancy, though few flower continually except in very mild climates. Herbaceous perennials—those most common in temperate climate gardens—usually have a period of dormancy when they die back to a permanent rootstock. Most commonly this is during winter, but plants from hot dry areas may be dormant in sum-

mer or during periods of very low rainfall.

Some herbaceous perennials have developed the ability to use their roots or stems as food storage organs to enable them to survive extended periods of dormancy. Known as rhizomes and tubers, these storage roots can often be separated from the parent plant and grown on as new plants, in much the same way as bulbs and corms. Dahlias and alstroemerias are well-known tuberous plants, while bearded irises are probably the most widely grown rhizomatous plants. Some plants have specialized rhizomes known as stolons, which spread across the surface of the ground, or just below the surface, taking root as they spread.

Some perennials are treated as annuals, either because they cease to be attractive as they age, or because they are incapable of surviving cold winters. Petunias and impatiens, for example, may live for several seasons if protected from frost, but they become leggy and untidy, so they are usually replaced annually.

It is not uncommon for a genus to contain both annual and perennial species, such as the annual and perennial cosmos, or species with differing growth habits, like the fibrous and tuberous rooted irises and begonias. In cultivation, the differences between annuals, biennials and the various types of perennials tend to become blurred. The important thing is how you use the plants, and with annuals and perennials you can give free rein to your imagination.

Obtaining plants

When first establishing a perennial garden you will probably buy all of your plants from a nursery or garden center. However, one of the great advantages of perennials is their ease of propagation. By the end of the first season you will have quite a few large plants ready for

Anticlockwise from left:

Raising annuals from seed: fill the seed tray with a good soil mix; lightly sprinkle the seed over the surface; cover the seeds with a little seed-raising mixture; cover with clear plastic or glass; remove the cover once the seedlings have germinated and grow on until large enough to transplant.

Anticlockwise from left:

**Transplanting seedlings: make holes with an
old pencil or 'dibble'; loosen soil around the
seedling and separate the roots; place the
seedling in the hole, firm the soil down and
water immediately.**

dividing. Some, such as peonies, will
grow for many years without needing to
be divided, and may not recover quickly
once broken up, but to maintain their
vigor most perennials need dividing at
least every three years. Many can also be
grown from cuttings, usually of the fast-
growing spring shoots.

Annuals must be raised from seed.
You can do this yourself or buy ready-
to-plant seedlings from a garden center.
For small quantities, raising your own
seed is seldom cheaper than buying
seedlings, but if you have large beds to
plant out, raising your own plants often
represents a considerable saving. If you
need large quantities of seedlings it's
best to find a nursery that will order for
you from commercial growers' seed
catalogs. Not only will you make greater
financial savings this way, you'll also
find that the commercial seed selection

is usually better than garden center
stock in range, quality and price.

Seed sowing and germination are
usually very straightforward procedures.
In many cases the seed may be sown
directly where it is to grow, although it is
more common to sow in trays and then
plant out. The only complication is
timing: you don't want to sow too early
as your seed may fail to germinate or the
seedlings may be frost damaged; too late
and they may not mature before cold
stops their growth.

Climate adaptability

Most of the traditional garden perennials
are hardy and very adaptable. However,
those from southern Africa, Central and
South America and parts of Australia
tend to be less cold-tolerant and may
not be suited to frosty areas, especially
where late frosts can be expected.

Annuals such as this *Gerbera jamesonii* cultivar can be brought indoors during the flowering period.

If you live in a cool-temperate climate you may still be able to grow these plants. Often the problem is not so much the cold, but a combination of cold and wet conditions. Plants such as *Gerbera* will tolerate quite hard frosts if they are kept dry but will rot when cold and wet. Most gardens have a few areas that are protected and remain dry in winter; these are the places to plant the Southern African daisies and the tender novelties like *Alonsoa*. Some tender perennials, such as *Heliotrope* and the 'Butterfly' *Impatiens*, demand complete frost protection. Treat them as annuals, grow them in containers that can be moved under cover for the winter, or take cuttings in the autumn and keep them indoors until spring.

Annuals are usually grown to provide color. Because they are only temporary plants and always treated as such they succeed everywhere. They permit gardeners in cold areas to briefly ignore the prospect of winter bleakness and inject a touch of tropical summer color into their gardens.

Annuals are subject to all the normal climatic considerations—wind, salt spray and summer heat—but they are remarkably resilient plants that carry on flowering under most conditions, except severe cold.

Tender annuals must be planted in spring, after the last frosts, with a view to summer and autumn flowering. However, the so-called hardy annuals are often planted in the autumn and left to over-winter for spring flowering. Pansies, sweet William and Iceland poppies are among the best known hardy annuals. With careful planning it is possible to have bloom almost all year round.

Garden design

Although annuals allow far more scope for design changes and mixing and matching than permanent plants, many people prefer to work to some sort of garden design. If you're keen on cottage gardens, perennials may make up the bulk of your planting; conversely if large rose beds are your preference you may need just a few annuals as fillers. Every garden has a place for annuals and perennials and there are many ways to use them.

Below: A semi-formal garden of petunias, pelargoniums, roses, lavender, potato vine and clipped *Buxus*

Below: This garden makes good use of water, trees, shrubs and annuals and perennials: *Papaver orientale, Stachys macrantha* and a *Hemerocallis* cultivar

Annual flower bed

Think of annuals and the chances are you'll think of vivid flower beds. While the massed plantings seen in botanic gardens and large private gardens are beyond most of us, a bed or two of annuals does not look out of place, even in a small garden. Of course, lawns and flower beds go well together. A velvety green sward is offset to perfection by a bed of riotous color, and the flower beds are easy to view and walk around when surrounded by lawn. It's hard not to be impressed by the effect of all that color in such a small space. However, massed bedding demands a considerable amount of time and effort for a fairly brief display, and the effort has to be repeated at least twice a year. This eventually loses its novelty for all but the most dedicated gardeners, which is why really impressive flower beds tend to be restricted to botanic or corporate gardens and private show gardens.

Making a good flower bed requires that the soil be worked to a fine tilth and regularly fertilized. To keep up the color as long as possible may mean replanting up to three times a year. The main summer display must be planted by mid-spring and removed by late summer, to be replaced by an autumn selection; this is then replaced in early winter by hardy annuals that will flower from late winter to mid-spring.

The bold display we expect from massed annuals allows the gardener to get away with some pretty unusual color combinations. Beds composed of many clashing colors certainly create an immediate impact, but they can be hard to live with. Careful color planning and consideration of height will result in a bed that is just as colorful, but far more harmonious and relaxing.

Massed bedding doesn't have to be rigidly planned. The readily available wildflower seed mixes offer an easier alternative: just scatter the seed, rake it in lightly and wait. Provided the seed bed has been well prepared and you keep the weeds down, the plants will do

Helichrysum petiolare 'Goring Silver', *Verbena* 'Temari Scarlet' and *Argyranthemum frutescens* 'Summer Melody'

A herbaceous border featuring *Lychnis coronaria* and *Salvia* × *sylvestris* cultivars

the rest. The seed companies have done all the color mixing and size gradation for you, although there's nothing to stop you making up your own seed mixtures and scattering them to the wind. Quite often the effects of such random sowing are better than anything you could have planned—which just goes to show that nature is still the best gardener!

Beds of annuals are not just about flowers; some very interesting effects can be created by foliage alone. Silverleaf, bloodleaf, *Coleus* and many other bedding plants don't need flowers to make an impact. Others, such as *Celosia* and the red leaf begonias, combine interesting foliage with bright flowers.

Herbaceous border

Perennials too, are often best grown in large beds, which provide bold impact when planted in color groups, and allow the plants to be viewed from all angles, often emphasizing the foliage forms. Because these perennial beds are often used as an edging to a lawn, driveway or wall, they are usually called herbaceous borders, even when they are not really borders.

Herbaceous perennials blend well with other garden plants, especially annuals, but because they are regularly lifted and divided, it's often more convenient to cultivate them separately in large beds. Lifting the plants and dividing and removing the waste is greatly simplified when there are no permanent shrubs or trees in the way.

The herbaceous border requires no special construction techniques: it is just a large garden bed. It can be edged with a low hedge or some form of retainer, such as bricks, or it may just be cut from a lawn. The soil should be thoroughly prepared by digging in plenty of compost and applying supplementary fertilizers. Beds cut from lawns will benefit from a light dressing of lime, otherwise a general garden fertilizer will be adequate. Most large perennials grow rapidly, and with their fairly deep roots they feed heavily; the more you can loosen the soil to allow the roots to spread, the better they will grow. It's not possible to add too much compost, provided it's well rotted down.

The skill in developing a herbaceous border is in the planting. A good planting is the peak of garden excellence; a poor one is just an assortment of mismatched plants. Decide on an overall theme before you begin. There should be some sense of direction or emphasis, for example plantings within a restricted color range; groups of compatible foliage, such as all silver-leafed plants; or plants with similar flower types, such as a bed composed entirely of daisies. Remember to consider the varying heights of the plants, keeping the taller ones to the back and making sure they don't hide one another in a jumble of foliage. You can also use variations in size to highlight particular plants by exposing their best features. Less attractive parts can be strategically hidden.

This may seem a rather rigid way of planting, and indeed it can be. The best gardeners know when to break the rules with effects like brightly contrasting colors or foliage, and they know when to hold back too. Growing a successful herbaceous border demands that you know your plants.

Ornamental grasses can be combined with annuals and perennials to great effect. *Festuca mairei, Lychnis coronaria, Coreopsis verticillata* and *Achillea millefolium* are featured here.

Cottage garden

The cottage garden aims for seemingly natural randomness and attractive plant associations. By planting simple flowers and rambling old fashioned shrubs, particularly roses and others with fragrance, it's possible to create a charming effect. A cottage garden should make you want to explore; it should be filled with interesting little novelties waiting to be found. Night-scented stocks, small pansies, cornflowers and larkspur are annuals that are perfect for the cottage look. Among the biennials and perennials, consider foxgloves, *Coreopsis, Scabiosa, Dianthus,* all the various primulas, and peonies.

If your aim is to create a garden reminiscent of the past, avoid using too many plants with large double flowers and vibrant colors. If the semi-wild look is what you're after, any color is acceptable, but once again avoid flowers that look 'overdeveloped'. Cottage and semi-wild gardens should have a light, airy feel; single flowers on rather open

bushes are often more appropriate than compact bushes with large double blooms.

Cottage gardens and semi-wild gardens are often promoted as an easy-care alternative, but don't be fooled. They require just as much planning as any other garden style and probably more maintenance. Planning a cottage garden depends largely on the layout of your site. Large open areas lend themselves to extensive beds and drifts of plants, the wildflower seed mixes are very useful here. If large beds don't appeal, dividing

A classic cottage garden at Great Dixter in Kent, UK

The gray foliage of *Artemisia* makes a pleasant foil for peonies and penstemons.

up a big garden into several small theme gardens is a good way to maintain interest. Try to design the garden so there's always something new around every corner; the prospect of a pleasant surprise keeps people looking and adds to your own pleasure. Compact gardens are usually better suited to small pockets of flowers and containers full of color.

Woodland garden

Recreating a natural effect is the prime aim of the woodland garden, and the closely associated bog garden. However, such freedom doesn't mean that you can ignore the rules: the natural look and the randomness are only apparent, not real. The great paradox of gardening is that the more natural the effect, the more planning it requires. However, making mistakes is one of the best ways to learn,

so accept occasional setbacks by putting your new-found knowledge to work.

Of course, you can't plant a woodland from scratch—first you need trees. Initial appearances may suggest that foliage dominates in the woodland garden (think of all those hostas and ferns) but careful study will reveal a subtle blend of foliage and flowers, and give you an idea of the proportions of the plants. Novice gardeners are inclined to think that a woodland garden must be absolutely full of plants, when in reality a better understanding of plant sizes and growth forms enables the gardener to create an illusion of abundance even with relatively few plants.

The advantage of not cramming everything in is that you have room for little treasures: those plants that you forget about for most of the year, then all of a sudden, much to your delight, they're there again. Woodlands tend to be spring gardens, but there are enough late-flowering small perennials and shrubs to maintain year-round interest. It's also acceptable to plant a few shade-loving summer annuals, such as impatiens and mimulus, to add a dash of color. However, be discreet, tranquillity is important in the woodland garden.

Rock gardens

Rock gardens, more than most other garden styles, attempt to recreate natural features in the garden and as is often the case, the more natural and simple the finished product appears, the more difficult it is to create. It should therefore come as no surprise that rockeries are one of the most difficult areas of garden design. Indeed, they are often viewed as the height of the gardener's art.

The secret lies in creating a sense of scale. The plants must be in proportion to size of the rocks and the garden as a whole. A large rock garden with sizeable rocks allows larger plants to be used; creating a successful small rock garden demands more skill as it is difficult to maintain realistic proportions on a small scale. It requires a knowledgeable gardener with an artistic touch.

Above right: **Pulsatilla halleri** subsp. *slavica*
Right: *Calceolaria,* Herbeohybrida Group cultivar

Before building your rock garden, visit some of the natural rockeries that can be found in hills and mountains. Look at how time and the forces of nature have acted on the rocks. In stable areas where the rocks have settled and plants have started to grow, you will usually find that the rocks are well embedded and their grain tends to run in the same direction. Jumbled piles of loose rocks are unstable and liable to move, and few plants will be found there. Keep these natural variations in mind when designing your rockery and you will be able to create changes of mood in the design. You will also be better able to cater for the particular needs of the plants.

Rockeries are all about slopes and changes in level, so they are an excellent way of developing a naturally sloping site. On flat ground there are no natural slopes, so positioning the rockery becomes critical. A small rockery in the middle of a flat expanse of lawn is bound to look unnatural. Flat sites require large rocks or extensive contouring to provide the necessary variations in level.

Ground cover plants

Ground covers are not just ornamental, they also serve to bind the soil with their roots, preventing erosion by heavy rains. By covering the surface of soil they also prevent the sun drying the ground and stop the wind blowing away the topsoil. They are, in effect, living mulches.

Some ground covers, such as *Dichondra*, can be used as lawn substitutes while others are an easy way of adding quick color or foliage variation. Massed annuals and many perennials may be used as ground covers even if they are not usually grown for the purpose.

Lysimachia nummularia (yellow) intertwined with *Duchesnia indica*

Clockwise from top:
Chrysanthemum
'Dreamstar Deborah',
Salvia officinalis
'Ictarina', *a Hedera*
helix cultivar and
Heuchera 'Rachel' in a
striking container
planting

Container growing

Annuals and perennials often make
excellent container plants because they
provide plenty of color, yet don't take up
a lot of room. Many, such as pelargoniums
and *Portulaca* are also drought tolerant,
which can be a lifesaver when you forget
to water.

Use window boxes and tubs planted
with vivid annuals to brighten up dark
areas in summer, then replace them with
polyanthus and violas for winter color.
If you have a greenhouse, conservatory
or covered patio, you can grow your
tender perennials in containers and
move them under cover for the winter.

Always use a good potting mix in
containers and remember to add some
slow-release fertilizer. Add a wetting
agent too, or you may find the mix very
difficult to re-wet if it dries out completely. Your potting mix will probably
contain fertilizers, but regular watering
leaches them out. Container plants
demand regular feeding—liquid fertilizers
are usually the most convenient to apply.

Don't be afraid to innovate and
improvise with shocking color combinations or novelty containers, such as
boots, teapots and old commodes.
There are endless ways of using annuals
and perennials in containers.

Soil and planting

The plant and the climate in which it
evolves are inextricably entwined. Most
things about a plant—its soil preference,
flower type, flowering time, pollination
strategy, germination requirements and
even its lifespan—are determined by its
natural environment. With few exceptions, these things usually remain the
same even when the plant is growing in
garden conditions that are nothing like

Tulips and *Aubrietia*
× *cultorum* (purple edge)
seen through an arbor
covered in *Mahonia*
species

its natural environment. You may experience cool moist summers but that
will not make the belladonnas bloom in
mid-summer. You may experience mild
winters but the hellebores will not
germinate in autumn. Once evolved it
usually takes many generations for a
successful survival characteristic to be
adapted or bred out.

Generally, plants perform better if the
garden conditions are slightly easier
than those they may experience in the
wild. A little extra water, slightly richer
soil and more shelter usually result in
better growth, but there are limits. When
in doubt, you can't go too far wrong by
trying to emulate the plant's natural
conditions.

When growing plants from arid
regions, bear in mind that in the wild
these plants usually start life as tiny
seedlings. They often develop large tap
roots or storage organs below ground
before much above-ground growth is

apparent. When you plant one of these
species, it will most likely have been
container-grown under good conditions
and may not have the root system or
reserves necessary to allow it to
immediately cope with drought or other
adversity. In such cases you will need to
provide ample moisture to establish new
plants, even though they will ultimately
be very drought tolerant.

Most large herbaceous perennials
thrive on soil with ample humus, as do
woodland plants. When growing such
plants, incorporate as much compost as
possible. Genuine leaf mold from around
deciduous trees is best, but well-rotted
garden composts and commercially
available soil conditioners are satisfactory.

Alpine plants are more likely to prefer
a scree soil. Scree is a term that is often
misunderstood—it does not mean pure
shingle. That may be the dictionary
definition, but in a gardening sense it
means a soil composed of fine gritty

stone chips and organic matter, as if you had mixed potting soil with shingle.

This type of soil is free draining but fairly moisture retentive at depth. Most surface hugging alpines will rot if the soil surface remains wet for long periods; a scree soil helps prevent this problem, as does a thin layer of fine stone chips around the crown of the plant.

Scree soils are usually suitable for dry climate plants too. Very few plants, even those that are very drought tolerant, actually demand a sandy soil. In most cases additional humus is beneficial but some plants, particularly those from dry winter climates, require very sharp drainage. To achieve this add stone chips rather than sand. Sand drains well but results in soils that can be hard to re-wet once dry; shingle improves the soil porosity and drainage while remaining easy to dampen.

Most annuals and perennials are planted either when very small or as divisions of larger plants. There is nothing very tricky about the planting. Simply plant seedlings at the same level as they were in their seed trays and avoid burying the crowns of herbaceous perennials

too deeply. The top of a perennial's crown usually sits at or just below soil level.

Care and cultivation
FEEDING

Annuals and perennials pack a lot of growth into a short period of time and consequently often have high nutrient demands. Thorough preparation with plenty of compost and supplementary fertilizer is preferable to trying to correct problems later. Additional fertilizers incorporated in mulches, or in organic, powdered chemical or liquid forms can be used to keep the plants growing steadily, but they can't make up for inadequate preparation.

The vivid orange calyces that surround the ripening fruit of *Physalis alkekengi*

Precise nutrient requirements vary depending on the plant, but the conditions under which they grow in the wild should give you some idea. However, don't take the native conditions as the final guide—many garden plants are far removed from the wild species and often require more care and attention to feeding and watering.

Avoid using very high nitrogen fertilizers or you may find that you get plenty of foliage but few flowers. A balanced fertilizer with a little extra potash is usually best. Some perennials, notably the southern African daisies, prefer fairly poor soils, so yet again it pays to know your plants.

When establishing large flower beds and herbaceous borders take the time to work in plenty of nutrient-rich humus. Your own garden compost is the best choice but well-rotted stable manure and other farmyard residues will also be beneficial. Rotted sawdust, peat and bark-based soil conditioners will help to improve the structure of the soil but as they contain few nutrients, you will need to add fertilizers to supplement them.

Whatever you use, make sure it is thoroughly decomposed. If it has to break down further after incorporation it will inevitably rob the soil of nitrogen.

If you have areas that are regularly used for flower beds repeat the composting every year, several weeks prior to planting. Likewise, whenever you lift your perennials for division incorporate plenty of compost before replanting.

Inevitably some experimentation will be necessary until you become familiar with your plants' requirements but don't neglect fertilizing simply because you're a bit worried about over-doing it. It is better to kill a few plants with kindness (and learn from your mistakes) than to stunt them all through neglect.

Pink phlox, white lilies, white erigeron daisies and dark blue delphiniums in a herbaceous border

Another herbaceous border featuring *Canna* species, *Dahlia* 'Bishop of Landaff', *Salvia microphylla, Miscanthus* species and *Cortaderia* species

WATERING

Regular watering is also important. It's no good having great soil if the plants are too wilted to use it.

Watering annuals and perennials from above with sprinklers can damage the flowers and beat the plants down to the ground. It also causes puddling, which can result in the development of a hard crust on the soil surface. Perforated soak hoses and drip lines are preferable, as well as being more water-efficient. If you must use sprinklers, choose the finest mist you can get. Containers demand regular watering, often daily in summer, and hanging baskets dry out particularly quickly.

Annuals should be watered as often as is necessary to ensure steady growth and flowering. On the whole you should err on the dry side. Most annuals will tolerate short dry periods but few will tolerate excess moisture without rotting or developing fungus diseases.

The establishment period, immediately after the planting out of seedlings, is when water is most needed. Seedlings grown *in situ* develop at a rate determined by the growing conditions, but young plants transplanted into new conditions need assistance to get established.

Ensure the young plants are moist before taking them out of their seedling trays and handle them carefully to lessen any root disturbance or transplant shock. This is particularly important with plants such as larkspur that resent any root disturbance. They may struggle on for quite some time but they rarely recover fully after an initial setback.

When to water perennials largely depends on their growing and flowering seasons. Those that bloom in early spring can usually get by with natural rainfall unless the spring weather is very dry. As the summer heats up they can be left to dry off naturally. Summer flowering perennials need even moisture throughout the growing season to be at their best.

Maintenance

Routine maintenance will keep your plants blooming longer. Remove any spent flowers and developing seed heads (unless you want the plants to self-sow), as once a plant sets seed it may cease flowering. Remove any damaged foliage or stems and stake tall plants, such as delphiniums. If producing the largest flowers is important, it pays to disbud plants like chrysanthemums, dahlias and tuberous begonias. This means removing the small lateral flower buds to produce larger terminal buds. You will need to consult specialist publications for the precise methods for each genus.

Provided they are kept growing steadily, annuals and perennials are remarkably free of pests and diseases. Of course, they can fall foul of all the regular pests, such as aphids, mites and various caterpillars, but these problems can usually be traced back to the growing conditions. Established plants in good growing conditions can cope with minor pests and diseases, but those in poor growing conditions will succumb.

The annual and perennial borders curve through lush lawn to create an inviting garden retreat.

Above: Tip pruning encourages bushiness and greater flower production.

Right: Annuals and perennials in this very formal garden provide year-round color and variation.

Young seedlings are far more vulnerable regardless of the conditions. They are likely to be attacked by slugs, snails, cutworms, earwigs, slaters and birds, although losses from anything other than slugs and snails are seldom significant. Seedlings are also prone to the fungal disease known as damping off. Damping off rots the seed leaves and stems, causing the seedling to collapse. Good hygiene lessens the problem but damping off can occur at any time, so it's a good idea to regularly drench young seedlings with a fungicide solution.

Because the range of pests and diseases varies depending on your climate and location, only general advice is offered here. Consult your nursery or garden center for specialized information.

At the end of the summer season you will need to remove the spent annuals and tidy up dead growth on the perennials. If you intend to replant with overwintering hardy annuals remove the summer plants when they show noticeable signs of deterioration, otherwise leave them for some late color. Getting your winter and spring annuals planted early ensures they are well established before the really cold weather arrives.

Success with annuals and perennials requires more gardening effort than growing shrubs and trees, but this is repaid by a garden with more seasonal change and greater interest and color.

Top 20 annuals and perennials for special purposes

FOR COASTAL GARDENS
Arctotis (many)
Armeria maritima
Aurinia saxatilis
Centaurea cyanus
Cerastium tomentosum
Convolvulus cneorum
Crambe maritima
Dorotheanthus bellidiformis
Erysimum (many)
Eschscholzia californica
Felicia amelloides
Euryops (many)
Gazania (many)
Hesperis matrionalis
Limonium perezii
Lobularia maritima
Pelargonium (many)
Silene uniflora
Tanacetum coccineum
Xeronema callistemon

FOR ROCK GARDENS
Aethionema grandiflorum
Anagallis monellii
Androsace sarmentosa
Arabis caucasica
Aubrieta deltoidea
Campanula (many)
Dianthus (many)
Eschscholzia californica
Gazania (many)
Gentiana (many)
Iberis sempervirens
Lewisia cotyledon
Papaver alpinum
Phlox (ground covers)
Primula (many)
Pulsatilla vulgaris
Saxifraga (many)
Soldanella montana
Thymus (many)
Veronica austriaca and cultivars

FOR SHADY SITUATIONS
Acanthus mollis
Aconitum napellus
Ajuga reptans and cultivars
Anemone nemorosa
Aquilegia (many)
Bergenia cordifolia
Campanula (many)
Clivia miniata
Convallaria majalis
Dicentra (many)
Epimedium (many)
Helleborus (many)
Hosta (many)
Meconopsis betonicifolia
Myosotis sylvatica
Primula (many)
Rodgersia (many)
Streptocarpus capensis
Tricyrtis (many)
Trillium (many)

FOR DROUGHT TOLERANCE
Achillea (many)
Arctotis (many)
Baptisia australis
Coreopsis verticillata
Cosmos bipinnatus
Dorotheanthus bellidiformis
Eryngium (many)
Eschscholzia californica
Euphorbia (many)
Gazania (many)
Limonium perezii
Pelargonium (many)
Portulaca grandiflora
Romneya coulteri
Sedum (many)
Sempervivum (many)
Tithonia rotundifolia
Verbena (most)
Yucca (many)
Zauschneria (many)

FOR FRAGRANCE
Convallaria majalis
Dianthus (many)
Galium odoratum
Gypsophila paniculata
Hedychium gardnerianum
Heliotropium arborescens
Hesperis matrionalis
Hosta plantaginea
Iberis amara
Lathyrus odorata
Lobularia maritima
Matthiola incana
Melissa officinalis
Mentha (many)
Nicotiana sylvestris
Paeonia lactiflora hybrids (several)
Phlox paniculata cultivars
Reseda odorata
Thymus (many)
Viola odorata

Clockwise from top: **Papaver orientale** 'China Boy', **Paeonia officinalis** cultivar, **Tanacetum coccineum** cultivar, **Papaver orientale** cultivar

HARDINESS ZONE MAPS

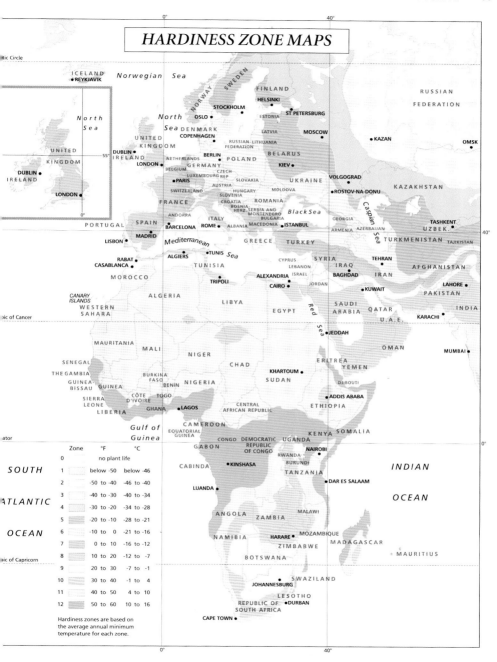

Zone	°F	°C
0	no plant life	
1	below -50	below -46
2	-50 to -40	-46 to -40
3	-40 to -30	-40 to -34
4	-30 to -20	-34 to -28
5	-20 to -10	-28 to -21
6	-10 to 0	-21 to -16
7	0 to 10	-16 to -12
8	10 to 20	-12 to -7
9	20 to 30	-7 to -1
10	30 to 40	-1 to 4
11	40 to 50	4 to 10
12	50 to 60	10 to 16

Hardiness zones are based on
the average annual minimum
temperature for each zone.

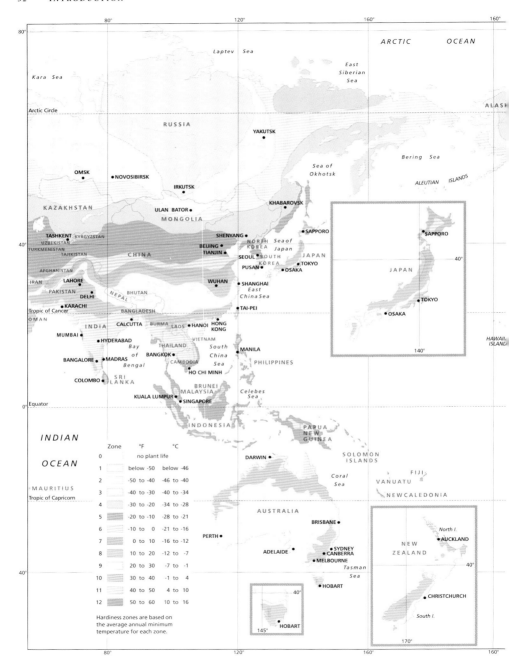

Zone	°F	°C
0	no plant life
1	below -50	below -46
2	-50 to -40	-46 to -40
3	-40 to -30	-40 to -34
4	-30 to -20	-34 to -28
5	-20 to -10	-28 to -21
6	-10 to 0	-21 to -16
7	0 to 10	-16 to -12
8	10 to 20	-12 to -7
9	20 to 30	-7 to -1
10	30 to 40	-1 to 4
11	40 to 50	4 to 10
12	50 to 60	10 to 16

Hardiness zones are based on
the average annual minimum
temperature for each zone.

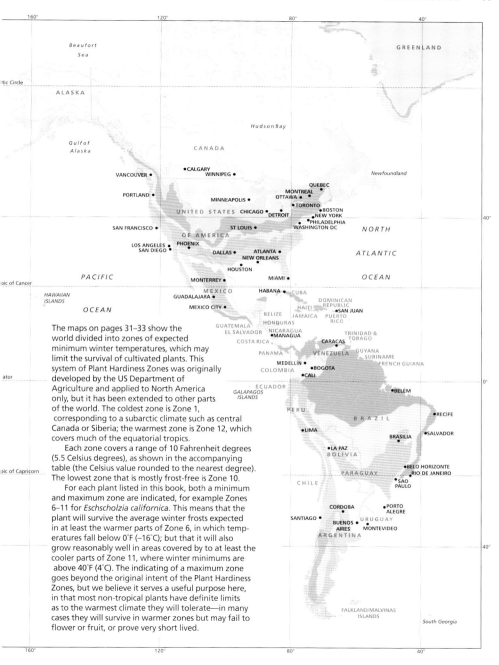

160°   120°   80°   40°

Beaufort Sea

GREENLAND

tic Circle

ALASKA

Gulf of Alaska

Hudson Bay

CANADA

•CALGARY
WINNIPEG •

VANCOUVER •

Newfoundland

PORTLAND •

QUEBEC
MONTREAL •
OTTAWA •
•TORONTO
MINNEAPOLIS •

UNITED STATES CHICAGO •
DETROIT •   •BOSTON
•NEW YORK
•PHILADELPHIA

SAN FRANCISCO •   ST LOUIS •   WASHINGTON DC

NORTH

OF AMERICA

LOS ANGELES • PHOENIX •
SAN DIEGO •

ATLANTIC

DALLAS •   ATLANTA •
NEW ORLEANS •

HOUSTON •

OCEAN

ic of Cancer   PACIFIC

MONTERREY •   MIAMI •

HAWAIIAN
ISLANDS

MEXICO
GUADALAJARA •

HABANA • CUBA

DOMINICAN
REPUBLIC
HAITI
JAMAICA •SAN JUAN
PUERTO
RICO

OCEAN

MEXICO CITY •

BELIZE

The maps on pages 31–33 show the
world divided into zones of expected
minimum winter temperatures, which may
limit the survival of cultivated plants. This
system of Plant Hardiness Zones was originally
developed by the US Department of
Agriculture and applied to North America
only, but it has been extended to other parts
of the world. The coldest zone is Zone 1,
corresponding to a subarctic climate such as central
Canada or Siberia; the warmest zone is Zone 12, which
covers much of the equatorial tropics.

GUATEMALA
EL SALVADOR NICARAGUA
COSTA RICA •MANAGUA

HONDURAS

TRINIDAD &
TOBAGO

PANAMA   CARACAS •

VENEZUELA GUYANA
SURINAME
MEDELLIN •   FRENCH GUIANA
COLOMBIA •BOGOTA
•CALI

ator   ECUADOR
GALAPAGOS
ISLANDS

•BELÉM

PERU   B R A Z I L   •RECIFE

Each zone covers a range of 10 Fahrenheit degrees
(5.5 Celsius degrees), as shown in the accompanying
table (the Celsius value rounded to the nearest degree).
The lowest zone that is mostly frost-free is Zone 10.

•LIMA

•LA PAZ
BOLIVIA

BRASILIA •   •SALVADOR

For each plant listed in this book, both a minimum
and maximum zone are indicated, for example Zones
6–11 for *Eschscholzia californica*. This means that the
plant will survive the average winter frosts expected
in at least the warmer parts of Zone 6, in which temperatures fall below 0°F (–16°C); but that it will also
grow reasonably well in areas covered by to at least the
cooler parts of Zone 11, where winter minimums are
above 40°F (4°C). The indicating of a maximum zone
goes beyond the original intent of the Plant Hardiness
Zones, but we believe it serves a useful purpose here,
in that most non-tropical plants have definite limits
as to the warmest climate they will tolerate—in many
cases they will survive in warmer zones but may fail to
flower or fruit, or prove very short lived.

ic of Capricorn

•BELO HORIZONTE
•RIO DE JANEIRO
PARAGUAY   •SAO
PAULO

CHILE

CORDOBA •   •PORTO
ALEGRE

SANTIAGO •   URUGUAY
BUENOS • •MONTEVIDEO
AIRES
ARGENTINA

FALKLAND/MALVINAS
ISLANDS   South Georgia

160°   120°   80°   40°

A

ABELMOSCHUS

This genus of around 15 species is from tropical Africa and Asia. In older books all the species were included in the larger genus *Hibiscus*. They are annuals, biennials or short-lived perennials with tough bark (sometimes used for fiber) and maple-like leaves. Some species die back to a large tuber in the tropical dry season. The hibiscus-like flowers occur in shades of yellow, pink, orange or red. Several species make attractive ornamentals and the vegetable okra or gumbo *(Abelmoschus esculentus)* is grown for its edible young pods.

CULTIVATION

They are mostly grown as summer annuals, requiring fertile, well-drained soil, a sheltered position in full sun, and plentiful water. Propagate from seed in spring. Rust disease can be a problem: spray with a fungicide.

Abelmoschus moschatus
MUSK MALLOW

This tropical Asian species is very variable, with many wild and cultivated races. Some are used for fiber and the seeds (musk seeds) yield oils and fats (ambrette) used medicinally and in perfumery. The whole plant has a slight musky smell. The hairs on the leaves are often bristly and the large flowers are typically pale yellow with a purple eye. Ornamental cultivars have a range of flower colors. The compact cultivar **'Mischief'** grows well in pots or can be naturalized in a sunny sheltered position; red, pink or white flowers are borne in summer and autumn. **'Pacific Light Pink'** is an 18 in (45 cm) dwarf cultivar with 2-tone pink flowers up to 4 in (10 cm) wide. **'Pacific Orange Scarlet'** (syn. 'Oriental Red') is also very popular. ZONES 8–12.

Abelmoschus moschatus
'Pacific Orange Scarlet'
(below)

Acaena argentea
(right)

This species from Peru and Chile has prostrate stems that spread to form a 24 in (60 cm) wide mat. The leaves, which are up to 6 in (15 cm) long, are pinnate with 9 to 15 leaflets, blue-gray above with silvery undersides. The flower and seed heads are purple. **ZONES 7–10.**

ACAENA

Around 100 species make up this genus of low-growing evergreen perennials. Those grown in gardens all have thin, creeping stems or buried rhizomes that bear, at intervals, tufts of small pinnate leaves with toothed margins. Flowers are rather insignificant, green or purple-brown, in dense stalked heads or spikes, but are followed by small dry fruit with barbed hooks that cling to socks at the slightest touch. Acaenas are grown as rock garden plants or sometimes as ground covers, valued for their pretty, intricate foliage. Some more vigorous species are regarded as weeds, even in their native countries.

CULTIVATION

They are tough little plants, thriving in exposed places and poor soil, but do demand good drainage and summer moisture. Propagate from seed or by division.

Acaena novae-zelandiae *(above)*

This species from New Zealand, southeast Australia and New Guinea may be prostrate or mounding with wiry stems from 6–24 in (15–60 cm) long. The bright green leaves (sometimes tinted red) are up to 4 in (10 cm) long and composed of 9 to 15 leaflets. The flowerhead is cream and the immature fruiting heads have bright red spines on the burrs. It is a vigorous grower, sometimes becoming a nuisance. **ZONES 5–10.**

A

ACANTHUS
BEAR'S BREECHES

Around 30 species of perennials and shrubs from tropical Africa and Asia as well as Mediterranean Europe make up this genus. The genus name goes back to ancient Greek, and the large and colorful family Acanthaceae (mainly tropical) takes its name from the genus. The deeply lobed and toothed leaves of *Acanthus mollis* and *A. spinosus* have lent their shape to the carved motifs used to decorate the capitals of Corinthian columns. It is only the more temperate perennial species that have been much cultivated, valued for their erect spikes of bracted, curiously shaped flowers, as well as their handsome foliage. The flowers appear in spring and early summer, after which the leaves may die back but sprout again before winter.

CULTIVATION
Frost hardy, they do best in full sun or light shade. They prefer a rich, well-drained soil with adequate moisture in winter and spring. Spent flower stems and leaves can be removed if they offend. Snails and caterpillars can damage the new leaves. Propagate by division in autumn, or from seed.

Acanthus mollis
(below left)

Occurring on both sides of the Mediterranean, this well-known species is somewhat variable, the form grown in gardens having broader, softer leaves and taller flowering stems than most wild plants. It is more of a woodland plant than other acanthuses, appreciating shelter and deep, moist soil. The large leaves are a deep, glossy green and rather soft, inclined to droop in hot dry weather. Flower spikes can be over 6 ft (1.8 m) tall, the purple-pink bracts contrasting sharply with the crinkled white flowers. Spreading by deeply buried rhizomes, it can be hard to eradicate once established. **'Candelabrus'** is one of several cultivars of *Acanthus mollis*.
ZONES 7–10.

Acanthus hungaricus *(above)*
syn. *Acanthus balcanicus*

Despite its species name, this plant does not occur wild in present-day Hungary, though some of the Balkan countries to which it is native were once part of the Austro-Hungarian Empire. It forms dense tufts of pinnately divided, soft, rather narrow leaves. The flower spikes may be up to 5 ft (1.5 m) tall, with vertical rows of white flowers almost hidden beneath dull pinkish bracts. It prefers a hot sunny position.
ZONES 7–10.

Acanthus mollis
'Candelabrus' *(above)*

Acanthus spinosus
(left)

This eastern Mediterranean species has large leaves that are deeply divided, the segments having coarse, spine-tipped teeth. In summer it sends up flower spikes to about 4 ft (1.2 m) high, the individual flowers and bracts being very similar to those of *Acanthus mollis.*
ZONES 7–10.

A

Achillea 'Coronation Gold'
(left & below)

This vigorous hybrid cultivar originated as a cross between *Achillea clypeolata* and *A. filipendulina*. It has luxuriant grayish green foliage and flowering stems up to 3 ft (1 m) tall with large heads of deep golden yellow in summer and early autumn. ZONES 4–10.

ACHILLEA
YARROW, MILFOIL, SNEEZEWORT

There are about 85 species of *Achillea*, most native to Europe and temperate Asia, with a handful in North America. Foliage is fern-like, aromatic and often hairy. Most species bear masses of large, flat heads of tiny daisy flowers from late spring to autumn in shades of white, yellow, orange, pink or red. They are suitable for massed border planting and rockeries. The flowerheads can be dried and retain their color for winter decoration.

CULTIVATION
These hardy perennials are easily grown and tolerant of poor soils, but they do best in sunny, well-drained sites in temperate climates. They multiply rapidly by deep rhizomes and are easily propagated by division in late winter or from cuttings in early summer. Flowering stems may be cut when spent or left to die down naturally in winter, when the clumps should be pruned to stimulate strong spring growth. Fertilize in spring.

A

Achillea filipendulina

This species, native to the Caucasus, bears brilliant, deep yellow flowers over a long summer season. It grows to 4 ft (1.2 m) with flowerheads up to 6 in (15 cm) wide and is one of the most drought resistant of summer flowers. **'Gold Plate'**, a strong-growing, erect cultivar reaching 4 ft (1.2 m), has aromatic, bright green foliage, and flat, rounded heads of golden yellow flowers, 4–6 in (10–15 cm) wide. **'Parker's Variety'** has yellow flowers. ZONES 3–10.

Achillea 'Great Expectations' *(left)*
syn. *Achillea* 'Hoffnung'

Often listed as a cultivar of *A. millefolium*, 'Great Expectations' is a hybrid between *A. millefolium* and *A.* 'Taygetea', a cultivar of uncertain origin. 'Great Expectations' is a vigorous 30 in (75 cm) high plant that produces a prolific display of butter yellow flowerheads. ZONES 2–10.

Achillea filipendulina
'Cloth of Gold' *(below)*

Achillea filipendulina
'Gold Plate' *(right)*

Achillea × kellereri
(right)

This unusual achillea is a hybrid between *Achillea clypeolata* and the rarely cultivated *A. ageratifolia*. It is a mat-forming plant, no more than 8 in (20 cm) tall even when flowering. It has massed rosettes of narrow gray-green leaves with comb-like toothing. In summer it produces on loosely branched stems daisy-like cream flowerheads ³/₄ in (18 mm) across, with a darker disc. **ZONES 5–10.**

Achillea 'Lachsschönheit'
(right)
syn. *Achillea* 'Salmon Beauty'

This is one of the recently developed Galaxy hybrids. A cross between *Achillea mille-folium* and *A.* 'Taygetea', this cultivar resembles the former in growth habit. In summer it produces masses of salmon pink heads which fade to paler pink, then almost to white. **ZONES 3–10.**

Achillea millefolium *(left)*
MILFOIL, YARROW

Widely distributed in Europe and temperate Asia, this common species is hardy and vigorous to the point of weediness, and natural-izes freely. It grows to 24 in (60 cm) tall with soft, feathery, dark green foliage and white to pink flowers in summer. Cultivars include **'Cerise Queen'**, cherry red with pale

Achillea millefolium
'Apfelblüte' *(above)*

Achillea millefolium
'Red Beauty' *(right)*

colors; **'Fanal'** (syn.
'The Beacon'), bright
red; **'Red Beauty'**,
silvery leaves and rose
red flowers; the pink
'Rosea'; and **'Apfelblüte'**, which is deep
rose pink. Once
established, plants can
be difficult to eradicate.
Most *Achillea* hybrids
have this species as one
parent. **'Paprika'** has
orange-red flowerheads
that fade with age.
ZONES 3–10.

Achillea millefolium
'Fanal' *(right)*

A

Achillea
'Moonshine' (above)

A cultivar of hybrid origin, this plant bears pretty flattened heads of pale sulfur yellow to bright yellow flowers throughout summer. It is a good species for cut flowers. It has delicate, feathery, silvery gray leaves and an upright habit, reaching a height of 24 in (60 cm). It should be divided regularly in spring to promote strong growth. ZONES 3–10.

Achillea ptarmica
'The Pearl' (right)

Achillea ptarmica
SNEEZEWORT

This plant has upright stems springing from long-running rhizomes and in spring bears large heads of small white flowers among the dark green leaves which are unusual among achilleas, not being dissected, but merely toothed. It reaches a height of 30 in (75 cm), providing a quick-growing cover in a sunny situation. 'The Pearl' is a double cultivar, widely grown. ZONES 3–10.

Achillea 'Taygetea' *(above)*

This popular achillea is known by the above for want of a better name. The true *Achillea taygetea* is a little known species from southern Greece (Taygetos Mountains), now treated as a synonym of *A. aegyptiaca,* whereas our *A.* 'Taygetea' is now thought to be a garden hybrid, its parents possibly *A. millefolium* and *A. clypeolata.* It is a vigorous grower with flowering stems about 24 in (60 cm) tall, the flowerheads pale creamy yellow in large flat plates. **ZONES 4–10.**

Achillea tomentosa *(below)*
WOOLLY YARROW

Native to southwestern Europe, this is a low, spreading plant with woolly or silky-haired, finely divided gray-green leaves and flowerheads of bright yellow on 12 in (30 cm) stems. Tolerating dry conditions and hot sun, it is excellent in the rock garden or as an edging plant. **ZONES 4–10.**

Achillea
'Schwellenberg'
(right)

A distinctive hybrid cultivar of spreading habit and grayish foliage, the leaf divisions are broad and overlapping. Tight heads of yellow flowers appear on short stalks through summer and into autumn. **ZONES 3–10.**

ACINOS
CALAMINT

This genus of 10 species of annuals and woody, evergreen perennials gets its name from the Greek word *akinos,* the name of a small aromatic plant. Usually small, tufted, bushy or spreading plants growing to 8 in (20 cm), they come from central and southern Europe and western Asia. The 2-lipped, tubular flowers are borne on erect spikes in mid-summer.

CULTIVATION
Mostly quite frost hardy, they will grow in poor soil as long as it is well drained (they do not like wet conditions) and need full sun. Propagate from seed or cuttings in spring.

Acinos alpinus
(above)
syn. *Calamintha alpina*
ALPINE CALAMINT

Spikes of violet flowers 1 in (25 mm) wide and with white marks on the lower lips are borne on this spreading, short-lived perennial, a native of central and southern Europe. Growing from 4–8 in (10–20 cm) in height, it has rounded leaves with either pointed or blunt tips. ZONES 6–9.

ACIPHYLLA
SPEARGRASS, SPANIARD

This genus consists of 40 or so species of stiff-leafed perennials in the carrot family, mainly native to New Zealand with a few species in Australia. They are found primarily in alpine areas or windswept open grasslands at lower altitudes. Despite the common name speargrass, they are quite unrelated to grasses. They have deep tap roots that give rise to clusters of deeply divided basal leaves with long, narrow leaflets, often ochre in color with vicious spines at their tips. Strong, long-spined flower stems develop in summer and extend beyond the foliage clump. They carry masses of small white or yellow-green flowers. There are separate male and female flower stems.

CULTIVATION
The small to medium-sized species are not too difficult to cultivate but the larger species are liable to sudden collapse outside their natural environment. Plant in full sun with moist, well-drained soil deep enough to allow the tap root to develop. Do not remove the insulating thatch of dead leaves. Propagate from seed, or small suckers used as cuttings, or by division.

Aciphylla aurea
(below)
GOLDEN SPANIARD, TARAMEA
Found in drier conditions than most, this species from New Zealand's South Island forms a foliage clump around 3 ft (1 m) tall by 5 ft (1.5 m) wide. Its golden fan-shaped leaves have narrow 24 in (60 cm) long leaflets. The flower stems grow to around 4 ft (1.2 m) tall. ZONES 7–9.

A

Aciphylla montana (left)

Found in the southern half of the South Island of New Zealand, this species forms a clump of finely divided olive green leaves about 12 in (45 cm) high by 18 in (45 cm) wide. The flower stems, which are up to 18 in (45 cm) tall, are topped with a branched head of pale yellow flowers. Conspicuous sheath-like bracts surround the base of the flowerhead. ZONES 7–9.

Aciphylla hectori (above)

A tiny species found in the southwest of the South Island of New Zealand, this plant consists of a tuft of stiff olive green foliage up to 4 in (10 cm) high and wide. The flower stem is up to 10 in (25 cm) tall; flowers are pale yellow to white. ZONES 7–9.

Aconitum carmichaelii (above)
syn. *Aconitum fischeri*

A native of northern and western China, this has become one of the most popular monkshoods by virtue of the rich violet-blue flowers, which are densely packed on the spikes in late summer. The leaves, thick, glossy and deeply veined, grow on rather woody stems. Several races and selections are cultivated, varying in stature from 3–6 ft (1–1.8 m). These include the **Wilsonii Group,** which contains, among others, the award-winning **'Kelmscott'; 'Arendsii'** (syn. 'Arends') is another striking blue-flowered cultivar. ZONES 4–9.

ACONITUM
ACONITE, MONKSHOOD, WOLFSBANE

Consisting of around 100 species of perennials scattered across temperate regions of the northern hemisphere, this genus is renowned for the virulent poisons contained in the sap of many. From ancient times until quite recently they were widely employed for deliberate poisoning, from execution of criminals to baiting wolves, or placing in an enemy's water supply. The poison has also been used medicinally in carefully controlled doses and continues to attract the interest of

Aconitum carmichaelii
'Arendsii' *(above)*

pharmaceutical researchers. The plants themselves are instantly recognizable by their flowers, mostly in shades of deep blue or purple or less commonly white, pink or yellow, with 5 petals of which the upper one bulges up into a prominent helmet-like shape. In growth habit and leaves, the monkshoods show a strong resemblance to their relatives the delphiniums.

CULTIVATION

Monkshoods make attractive additions to herbaceous borders and woodland gardens. They prefer deep, moist soil and a sheltered position, partly shaded if summers are hot and dry. Propagate by division after the leaves die back in autumn, or from seed.

Aconitum napellus
(right)
ACONITE, MONKSHOOD

Of wide distribution in
Europe and temperate
Asia, this is also the
monkshood species
most widely grown in
gardens and is as hand-
some as any when well
grown. The stems are
erect, to 4 ft (1.2 m)
high, with large leaves
divided into very
narrow segments and a
tall, open spike of
deep blue to purplish
blooms. A vigorous
grower, it likes damp
woodland or stream
bank conditions.
ZONES 5–9.

Aconitum 'Ivorine'
(below)

This hybrid cultivar
grows to about 3 ft
(1 m) tall with dense
foliage. The many spikes
of pale ivory-yellow
flowers rise a short
distance above the
foliage. ZONES 4–9.

Aconitum vulparia *(left)*
syn. *Aconitum lycoctonum* subsp. *vulparia*
WOLFSBANE

Growing to over 3 ft (1 m) in height, this species
has tall, erect stems and rounded, hairy leaves that
are 6–8 in (15–20 cm) wide. Rather open spikes of
pale yellow flowers, longer and narrower than
those of most other species, are borne in summer.
It is native to central and southern Europe.
ZONES 4–9.

ACORUS

SWEET FLAG

This unusual genus consists of only 2 species of grass-like evergreen perennials from stream banks and marshes in the northern hemisphere. They are in fact highly atypical members of the arum family, lacking the large bract (spathe) that characteristically encloses the fleshy spike (spadix) of minute flowers. The flower spikes are inconspicuous and the plants are grown mainly for their foliage. The leaves are in flattened fans like those of irises, crowded along short rhizomes. Both leaves and rhizomes are sweet-scented, most noticeably as they dry, and have been used in folk medicine, perfumery and food flavorings.

CULTIVATION

Sweet flags are easily grown in any boggy spot or in shallow water at pond edges, needing no maintenance except cutting back to limit their spread. They are fully frost hardy. Propagate by division.

Acorus gramineus

Native to Japan, this species has soft, curved leaves under 12 in (30 cm) long and about ¼ in (6 mm) wide. The flower spikes are about 1 in (25 mm) long and emerge in spring and summer. **'Pusillus'**, popular in aquariums, is only about 4 in (10 cm) high; **'Variegatus'** has cream-striped leaves; **'Ogon'**, more recently introduced from Japan, has chartreuse and cream variegated leaves. ZONES 3–11.

Acorus gramineus
'Ogon' *(above)*

A

ACTAEA
BANEBERRY

Only 8 species of frost-hardy perennials belong to this genus, which occurs in Europe, temperate Asia and North America, mostly in damp woodlands and on limestone outcrops. They are attractive plants with large compound leaves springing from a root-crown, the leaflets thin and broad with strong veining and sharp teeth. Flowers are in short, feathery spikes or heads, the individual flowers smallish with many white stamens among which the narrow petals are hardly detectable. The fruits are white, red or black berries, often on a stalk of contrasting color. All parts of the plants are very poisonous but particularly the berries, which may be attractive to small children.

CULTIVATION

Requiring a cool, moist climate, these plants grow best in sheltered woodland conditions or in a damp, cool spot in a rock garden. Propagate from seed or by division.

Actaea alba (below)
WHITE BANEBERRY

From eastern USA, this summer-flowering perennial is most notable for its handsome berries, though its flowers and foliage are also attractive. It forms a clump of fresh green, divided leaves with a spread of 18 in (45 cm), from which rise the fluffy white flowers on stems up to 3 ft (1 m) high. By late summer they have developed into spires of small, gleaming white berries on red stalks. ZONES 3–9.

Actaea rubra (above)
RED BANEBERRY, SNAKEBERRY

This North American species grows to 24–30 in (60–75 cm) tall and wide and its leaves are 6–18 in (15–45 cm) wide. The mauve-tinted white flowers are about ¼ in (6 mm) in diameter and clustered in round heads on wiry stems. The berries are bright red. **Actaea rubra f. neglecta** is a taller growing form with white berries. ZONES 3–9.

A

Actinotus helianthi
(left)
FLANNEL FLOWER
This biennial or short-lived, evergreen perennial grows 12 in–3 ft (30–90 cm) high with a spread of 24 in (60 cm). It has deeply divided gray-green foliage. Furry erect stems appear in spring and summer, topped by star-like flowerheads which consist of a cluster of pink-stamened, greenish florets surrounded by flannel-textured dull white bracts with grayish green tips. Flannel flowers prefer a well-drained soil in full sun and grow especially well in arid situations. **ZONES 9–10.**

ACTINOTUS

There are 11 species in the Australian genus *Actinotus*, of which the best known is *Actinotus helianthi*—a favorite wild-flower native to the open woodlands of the sandstone country around Sydney where it makes a great display in late spring and summer. In the structure of their flowerheads, members of this genus mimic those of the daisy (composite) family, but in fact they belong to the carrot (umbellifer) family. The leaves and flowerheads are both felted with dense hairs which help *Actinotus* species reduce moisture loss in a dry climate and grow in poor, scarcely water-retentive soils.

CULTIVATION

They demand light shade, a mild climate and very good drainage. Plants are usually treated as biennials. Propagate from seed or stem cuttings in spring or summer.

A

ADENOPHORA

A genus of around 40 species of herbaceous perennials closely related to *Campanula,* in fact distinguished from it only by an internal feature of flower structure. Most are native to eastern Asia but 2 species occur wild in Europe. One species is grown in Japan for its edible roots.

CULTIVATION

Cultivation requirements and mode of propagation are the same as for *Campanula.*

Adenophora uehatae (below)

Native to eastern Asia, this is a charming dwarf species with large, pendulous pale mauve-blue bells borne on short leafy stems. It makes a fine rock garden subject. ZONES 5–9.

A

Adonis annua
(right)
PHEASANT'S EYE

Quite different from most species, this is a summer-flowering annual with finely divided foliage and branching stems 12–15 in (30–38 cm) tall. The bright red, 5 to 8-petalled flowers are about 1 in (25 mm) wide with black centers. It occurs naturally in southern Europe and southwest Asia. ZONES 6–9.

ADONIS

This genus consists of 20 species of annuals and perennials from Europe and cooler parts of Asia, with brightly colored flowers similar to *Anemone*, to which it is closely related. The Greek god Adonis, beloved of Aphrodite, gave his name to the original annual species; its red flowers were said to have sprung from drops of his blood when he was killed by a boar. The leaves are mostly finely divided, the uppermost ones on each stem forming a sort of 'nest' on which the single bowl-shaped flower rests. It is only the perennial species that are much cultivated, used in herbaceous borders and rock gardens.

CULTIVATION

Adonis require a cool climate with warm dry summers. They are best grown in a sheltered spot in full sun, and in moist, fertile soil with a high humus content. Propagate from fresh seed or by division of clumps.

Adonis vernalis *(above)*

This European perennial species has very narrow, almost needle-like, finely divided leaflets. Its 12- to 20-petalled, bright yellow flowers are large, up to 3 in (8 cm) across, and open in early spring. Both this species and *A. annua* have been used medicinally, but are now regarded as too toxic for general use. ZONES 3–9.

A

AECHMEA

Take your pick in pronouncing this name, which is of Greek origin. Regardless of whether you call it ike-maya, eek-mee-a, aitch-mee-a, ak-mee-a, or ek-mee-a, you will have company! It is one of the largest and most diverse bromeliad genera, as well as being one of the most popular among indoor plant growers. *Aechmea* consists of over 170 species from Central and South America. Most are epiphytes or rock-dwellers, conserving water in the vase-like structure formed by the rosette of stiff leaves, which may be barred, striped or otherwise patterned, and prickly margined in some such as *Aechmea agavifolia.* The flowers are small but often intensely colored, in dense spikes that vary greatly in size and structure but always with numerous overlapping bracts that usually contrast in color with the flowers: a typical example is *Aechmea* 'Mary Brett'. The berry-like fruits that follow are often colorful as well.

Aechmea agavifolia
(above)

CULTIVATION

How aechmeas are treated depends very much on the climate. In the humid tropics and subtropics they grow happily outdoors, most preferring filtered sun. Despite being epiphytes, they will grow on the ground as long as soil is open and high in humus, and the bed is raised slightly. Some tolerate surprisingly cool condi-tions and can be grown outdoors well into the temperate zones, so long as frost is absent. In more severe climates they are grown as indoor or con-servatory plants, potted in a coarse medium just like many orchids. Propagate by division (separating 'pups' with a sharp knife), or from seed.

Aechmea 'Mary Brett'
(below)

Aechmea fasciata
(right)
SILVER VASE

Reminiscent of a formal flower arrangement, this Brazilian species has a 'vase' of silvery gray leaves irregularly barred green, from which emerges in summer a short, broad cluster of violet-blue flowers among crowded, spiky bracts of a most delicate clear pink. The rosettes, up to about 18 in (45 cm) high, do not clump up much. **ZONES 10–12.**

Aechmea chantinii *(left)*

Known as the Queen of the Aechmeas, this species from northwestern South America has vivid red and yellow flowers rising above long, drooping, salmon-orange bracts. The rosettes consist of olive green leaves often with silvery gray dark green or almost black banding. The flowers appear in summer, followed by blue or white berries. It has an upright, urn-like habit and reaches a height and spread of 12–24 in (30–60 cm). **'Black'** is one of several cultivars of *Aechmea chantinii.* Ensure that growing conditions are not too moist in winter. This species is very cold sensitive. **ZONES 11–12.**

Aechmea chantinii 'Black' *(right)*

A

Aechmea nidularioides (left)

This species has strap-like leaves about 24 in (60 cm) long; the flowering stalk terminates in a rosette of red bracts at the center of which sit yellow flowers in an eye-catching display. **ZONES 10–12.**

Aechmea 'Shining Light' (left)

This hybrid cultivar has a broad rosette of leaves that are glossy, pale green above and wine red on the undersides. It produces a large, about 24 in (60 cm) high, much-branched panicle, with bright red bracts and numerous small red flowers in summer. **ZONES 11–12.**

Aechmea pineliana (above)

Attractive grown in bright light or full sun where the foliage takes on a deep rose color, this south Brazilian species grows to a height and spread of 12–15 in (30–38 cm). It has a dense upright habit with stiff, pointed gray-green leaves edged with red spines. The yellow flowers form a short, cylindrical head and are borne above the scarlet stems and bracts from winter through to spring. On maturity the flowers turn black. It is sun and cold tolerant and adapts well to outdoor conditions. **ZONES 10–12.**

Aechmea 'Royal Wine' (below)

This popular hybrid cultivar, well adapted to indoor culture, has strap-like, bronze-green leaves with red bases and a slightly branched, pendent inflorescence with dark blue petals. The fruits that follow the flowers are scarlet. **ZONES 11–12.**

*Aegopodium
podagraria*
GROUND ELDER, GOUTWEED

Spreading to an indefi-
nite width, and up to
3 ft (1 m) high, ground
elder sends up its pure
white umbels of bloom
during summer.
'Variegatum' is some-
times grown as a ground
cover: its leaflets are
neatly edged white and
it is slightly smaller and
less aggressive than the
normal green form.
ZONES 3–9.

*Aegopodium
podograria* 'Variegata'
(below)

AEGOPODIUM

Consisting of 5 species of perennials in the carrot family, native to
Europe and Asia, this genus is known in cool-temperate gardens
only in the form of the common ground elder or goutweed—
admittedly a moderately handsome plant, but detested by most for
its rampant spread by underground rhizomes and the virtual
impossibility of eradicating it. Resembling a lower-growing version
of parsnip, it has compound leaves with large, toothed leaflets and
rounded umbels of white flowers. Ground elder was for a long time
used in herbal medicine, once thought effective against gout, and
its young shoots can be used as a green vegetable.

CULTIVATION

Growing ground elder is far easier than stopping it, and it is
difficult to see why anyone would wish to do so. However, it is
undoubtedly an effective ground cover where space allows,
smothering other weeds. It does best in moist soil and partial
shade. Any piece of root will grow.

A

Aethionema
grandiflorum *(left)*
syn. *Aethionema pulchellum*

PERSIAN STONE CRESS

Grown for its sprays of dainty, phlox-like, pale pink to rose pink flowers in spring, this Middle Eastern species is a short-lived perennial. It has a loose habit, narrow, bluish green leaves and reaches a height of 12 in (30 cm). It makes a good rock garden specimen.
ZONES 7–9.

AETHIONEMA

Ranging through the Mediterranean region and into western Asia, the 30 or more species of this genus include evergreen perennials, subshrubs and low shrubs, all with small, narrow leaves and producing spikes or clusters of 4-petalled pink to white flowers in spring and summer. The genus belongs to the mustard family, falling into the same tribe as *Arabis* and *Alyssum*. A number of species are cultivated, prized mainly by rock garden enthusiasts for their compact habit and profuse display of blooms such as the mauve-pink cultivar '**Mavis Holmes**'.

Aethionema
'Mavis Holmes' *(below)*

CULTIVATION

Aethionemas thrive best in a climate with cool, moist winter and a warm, dry summer. They should be grown in raised beds or rockeries in gritty, free-draining soil and exposed to full sun. Propagate from seed or cuttings.

AGAPANTHUS
AFRICAN LILY, AGAPANTHUS, LILY-OF-THE-NILE

Native to southern Africa, these strong-growing perennials are popular for their fine foliage and showy flowers produced in abundance over summer. Arching, strap-shaped leaves spring from short rhizomes with dense, fleshy roots. Flowers are various shades of blue (white in some cultivars) in many flowered umbels, borne on a long erect stem, often 3 ft (1 m) or more tall. Agapanthus are ideal for background plants or for edging along a wall, fence or driveway. Some hybrid examples are **'Irving Cantor'** and **'Storm Cloud'**. **Headbourne Hybrids** are especially vigorous and hardy. They grow to 3 ft (1 m) and come in a range of bright colors.

CULTIVATION
Agapanthus can thrive in conditions of neglect, on sites such as dry slopes and near the coast. They enjoy full sun but will tolerate some shade, and will grow in any soil as long as they get water in spring and summer. They naturalize readily, soon forming large clumps; they also make excellent tub and container specimens. Remove spent flower stems and dead leaves at the end of winter. Agapanthus are frost hardy to marginally frost hardy. Propagate by division in late winter, or from seed in spring or autumn.

Agapanthus africanus (above)
This species from western Cape Province is moderately frost tolerant, but is not common in gardens. Often plants sold under this name turn out to be *Agapanthus praecox*. It produces blue flowers on 18 in (45 cm) stems from mid-summer to early autumn; each flowerhead contains 20 to 50 individual blossoms, the color varying from pale to deep blue. The leaves are shorter than on *A. praecox*. ZONES 8–10.

Agapanthus 'Irving Cantor' (left)

A

Agapanthus campanulatus *(left)*

Native to Natal in South Africa, this species makes a large clump of narrow, grayish leaves that die back in autumn. In mid- to late summer, crowded umbels of pale blue flowers with broadly spreading petals are borne on 3 ft (1 m) stems. It is the most frost-hardy agapanthus. ***Agapanthus campanulatus* var. *patens,*** smaller and more slender, is one of the daintiest of all the agapanthus. ZONES 7–11.

Agapanthus praecox

This is the most popular agapanthus. Its glorious starbursts of lavender blue flowers appear in summer, and its densely clumped evergreen foliage is handsome in the garden all year round. It is also available in white. ***Agapanthus praecox* subsp. *orientalis*** has large dense umbels of blue flowers. It prefers full sun, moist soil and is marginally frost hardy. ZONES 9–11.

Agapanthus 'Loch Hope' *(above)*

A late-flowering agapanthus, this cultivar grows to a height of 4 ft (1.2 m) and has abundant, large dark violet blue flowerheads. ZONES 9–11.

Agapanthus praecox subsp. *orientalis (left)*

AGASTACHE

This is a genus of some 20 species of perennials found in China, Japan and North America. Most species are upright with stiff, angular stems clothed in toothed-edged, lance-shaped leaves from ½–6 in (1.2–15 cm) long depending on the species. Heights range from 18 in–6 ft (45 cm–1.8 m) tall. Upright spikes of tubular, 2-lipped flowers develop at the stem tips in summer. The flower color is usually white, pink, mauve or purple with the bracts that back the flowers being of the same or a slightly contrasting color.

CULTIVATION

Species are easily grown in moist, well-drained soil and prefer a sunny position. Hardiness varies, but most species will tolerate occasional frosts down to 20°F (–7°C). Propagate from seed or cuttings.

Agastache rugosa (above)

This species from China and Japan grows to 4 ft (1.2 m) tall with branching stems that make it more shrubby than most species. The leaves are around 3 in (8 cm) long and rather sticky. The flower spikes are up to 4 in (10 cm) long with small pink or mauve flowers that have white lobes.
ZONES 8–10.

Agastache foeniculum (right)
syn. *Agastache anethiodora*
ANISE HYSSOP

This 18 in–4 ft (45 cm–1.2 m) tall, soft-stemmed North American species makes a clump of upright stems with 3 in (8 cm) leaves. Often treated as an annual, it is primarily grown for the ornamental value of its purple flower spikes. The anise-scented and flavored foliage is used to make a herbal tea or as a flavoring.
ZONES 8–10.

AGERATINA

This is just one of many genera, predominantly American, that has been split off the large and unwieldy *Eupatorium*. Although composites, that is, members of the daisy family, they have inflorescences consisting of many small fluffy heads without ray florets, and hence are quite un-daisy-like in appearance. *Ageratina* consists of over 200 species from warmer parts of the Americas, a small number extending to somewhat cooler parts of eastern USA. Two Mexican species have become bad weeds in parts of Australia. The genus includes annuals, perennials and soft-wooded shrubs. Leaves are in opposite pairs on the cane-like stems and have a musky, slightly unpleasant smell. The small, soft flowerheads are in terminal panicles and are either white or pale pink.

CULTIVATION

They are easily grown in any sheltered spot in moist soil. The species from the USA are fairly frost hardy, others hardly at all. Propagate from seed, cuttings or by division.

Ageratina altissima (below)
syn. *Eupatorium altissimum*

Native over a wide area of eastern and central USA, this perennial is one of the taller species, growing to about 8 ft (2.4 m) high. Its leaves are up to 5 in (12 cm) long, toothed in the upper part, and the numerous small white flowerheads appear in late summer. ZONES 6–9.

A

***Ageratina
ligustrina*** *(right)*
syn. *Eupatorium
ligustrinum*

A very distinctive
shrubby species native
to Central America,
Ageratina ligustrina
can reach as much as
15 ft (4.5 m) tall, with
densely massed
branches and glossy
evergreen leaves
reminiscent of privet
leaves (hence *ligustrina,*
'privet-like'). The white
flowerheads with
pinkish enclosing bracts
are borne in large
panicles in autumn.
ZONES 9–11.

***Ageratina
occidentalis*** *(left)*
syn. *Eupatorium
occidentale*

Native to the north-
western states of the
USA, this is a many-
stemmed perennial
about 30 in (75 cm)
high, with small almost
triangular leaves. The
fluffy flowerheads,
borne in late summer
in numerous small
panicles, vary in color
from white to pink or
purple. ZONES 6–9.

A

***Ageratum
houstonianum*** *(left)*
Native to Central
America and the West
Indies, this annual
ageratum is popular as
a summer bedding
plant. Available in tall
(12 in [30 cm]), me-
dium (8 in [20 cm])
and dwarf (6 in [15 cm])
sizes, they form clumps
of foliage with fluffy
flowers in an unusual
dusky blue that blends
effectively with many
other bedding plants.
Also available are pink
and white forms.
ZONES 9–12.

AGERATUM
FLOSS FLOWER

While undoubtedly best known for the annual bedding plants that
are derived from *Ageratum houstonianum,* this genus includes
some 43 species of annuals and perennials mostly native to warmer
regions of the Americas. They are clump-forming or mounding
plants up to 30 in (75 cm) tall with felted or hairy, roughly oval to
heart-shaped leaves with shallowly toothed or serrated edges.
Flowerheads are a mass of fine filaments, usually dusky blue,
lavender or pink and crowded in terminal clusters.

CULTIVATION
Best grown in full sun in moist, well-drained soil. Regular deadheading is essential to prolong the flowering. Propagate by
spring-sown seed, either raised indoors in containers or sown
directly in the garden.

AGLAONEMA

This genus of about 20 species of perennial subshrubs comes from the humid tropics of Southeast Asia. In growth form they are the old world counterparts of the tropical American *Dieffenbachia* and can be used for indoor decoration in a similar way. Some species are renowned for their tenacious hold on life and ability to grow in conditions of poor light and soil. The somewhat fleshy stems branch from the base and may root where they touch the ground. The broad, oblong leaves are often mottled or barred with cream. Tiny flowers are borne in a short fleshy spike within a furled spathe, an arrangement typical of the arum family. The spikes are more conspicuous in the fruiting stage, displaying oval berries that can be quite colorful.

CULTIVATION

In the tropics aglaonemas are easily grown in any moist, shady area beneath trees but in temperate regions they are grown indoors in containers. Propagation is normally by cuttings or offsets, which are easily rooted.

Aglaonema 'Silver Queen' *(above)*

This *A. nitidum* 'Curtisii' × *A. pictum* 'Tricolor' hybrid branches freely from the base, eventually forming a large clump of foliage. It has narrow, 12 in (30 cm) long leaves marbled and flecked with silvery white. ZONES 11–12.

Aglaonema 'Parrot Jungle' *(right)*

This hybrid has *A. nitidum* as one of its parents; the other is unknown. It is an upright, 3 ft (1 m) high plant with 18 in (45 cm) long, leathery dull green, lance-shaped leaves with silvery markings on the upper surfaces. The spathes are creamy white. ZONES 11–12.

A

AGRIMONIA
AGRIMONY

About 15 species of perennials belong in this genus, occurring in temperate regions of the northern hemisphere. It is related to *Potentilla* but has its small yellow flowers in elongated spikes, opening progressively from the base, and its fruits are small spiny burrs. The pinnate leaves with thin, toothed leaflets are mainly basal. Agrimonias are plants of woodland verges and meadows and have little ornamental value, but they have a long history of medicinal use, the leaves and flowers making an infusion with astringent and diuretic properties due to their tannin content. They also yield a yellow dye.

CULTIVATION
They are very easily grown in any moist fertile soil, in full sun or light shade. Seed is difficult to germinate so propagation is usually by division of the rhizome.

Agrimonia eupatoria (below)
COMMON AGRIMONY
Native to Europe, western Asia and North Africa, this species makes a sparse clump of foliage from a deeply buried rhizome; leaves consist of up to 13 leaflets, white-haired on the undersides, and the weak flowering stem is up to about 24 in (60 cm) tall. ZONES 6–10.

Agrostemma
githago *(right)*
CORN COCKLE

This fast-growing
showy annual reaches
a height of 24–36 in
(60–90 cm), making it
ideal for planting at the
back of an annual
border. It has a slender,
few-branched, willowy
habit with long narrow
leaves in opposite pairs.
Broadly funnel-shaped
pink flowers about 2 in
(5 cm) in diameter
appear on long hairy
stalks from late spring
to early autumn. The
tiny dark brown seeds
are poisonous.
ZONES 8–10.

AGROSTEMMA

Two or possibly more species of slender annuals from the Mediterranean region belong to this genus, related to *Lychnis* and *Silene*.
One of them is well known as a weed of crops in Europe, but is
still a pretty plant with large rose-pink flowers and is sometimes
used in meadow plantings and cottage gardens. Distinctive features
of the genus are the long silky hairs on the leaves and the calyx
consisting of 5 very long, leaf-like sepals radiating well beyond
the petals.

CULTIVATION
They are very frost hardy, growing best in full sun in a well-drained
soil. Young plants should be thinned to about 10 in (25 cm) spacing
and may need light staking if growing in exposed areas. Propagate
from seed sown in early spring or autumn.

A

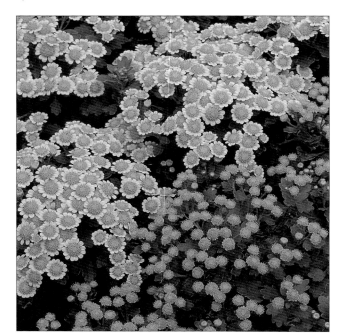

Ajania 'Bess' and
A. 'Benny' *(left)*

AJANIA

This genus, consisting of 30 or so species from eastern and central
Asia, is one of a number of genera now recognized in place of
Chrysanthemum in its older, broader sense. *Ajania* is closest to
Dendranthema and its species have similar bluntly lobed leaves
usually with whitish woolly hairs on the undersides. Flowerheads
are small and button-like, lacking ray florets and arranged in
flattish panicles at the branch tips. The plants have extensively
branching underground rhizomes, sending up numerous tough,
wiry stems. Only *Ajania pacifica* is widely cultivated for ornament
in gardens and parks. *Ajania* 'Bess' differs in having small white
ray florets on the flowers and *A.* '**Benny**' has flowers typical of
the genus.

CULTIVATION
The plants are very hardy and easily grown in a wide range of
situations, thriving in both poor and fertile soils, though preferring
good drainage and full sun. If not cut back hard after flowering,
including the rhizome, they may rapidly smother adjacent plants.
Propagate from rhizome divisions.

A

Ajania pacifica *(right)*
syns *Chrysanthemum pacificum,*
Dendranthema pacificum

An attractive plant, occurring wild
in far eastern Asia, this species
makes a spreading, loose mound of
evergreen foliage up to about 18 in
(45 cm) high. The leaves are deep
green on the upper side and clothed
in dense white hairs beneath; the
white shows at the coarsely scalloped
edges, making a striking contrast
with the green. Sprays of brilliant
gold flowerheads in autumn further
enhance the effect. **Ajania pacifica**
'Silver and Gold' has silver-edged
leaves and bright golden yellow
button-like flowers. **ZONES 4–10.**

Ajania pacifica 'Silver and Gold' *(below)*

A

AJUGA
BUGLE

About 50 species of low-growing annuals and perennials make up this genus, which ranges through Europe, Asia, Africa and Australia, mainly in cooler regions. Although belonging to the mint family, their foliage is hardly aromatic. Rosettes of soft, spatulate leaves lengthen into spikes of blue, purple or pink (rarely yellow) 2-lipped flowers. In most perennial species the plants spread by runners or underground rhizomes, some forming extensive carpets. They make attractive ground covers, especially for shady places such as corners of courtyards.

Ajuga pyramidalis 'Metallica Crispa' *(below)*

CULTIVATION
These are frost-hardy, trouble-free plants requiring little but moist soil and shelter from strong sun, though the bronze and variegated forms develop best color in sun. The commonly grown species thrive in a range of climates, from severe cold to subtropical. Snails and slugs can damage foliage. Propagate by division.

Ajuga pyramidalis *(left)*
PYRAMIDAL BUGLE

Widely distributed in Europe including parts of the UK, this attractive species makes a compact mat of rosettes, spreading by short underground rhizomes. The hairy dark green rosette leaves grade into the broad leafy bracts of the flowering stem to give it a narrowly pyramidal form, usually about 8 in (20 cm) tall. Flowers are mostly blue or mauve, and open from spring to mid-summer. **'Metallica Crispa'** is a curious miniature form, with rounded and somewhat contorted leaves showing a metallic purple sheen. ZONES 5–9.

Ajuga reptans
(bottom)

EUROPEAN BUGLE,
COMMON BUGLE, BLUE BUGLE

The commonly grown ajuga, native to Europe, spreads by surface runners like a strawberry plant, making a mat of leafy rosettes only 2–3 in (5–8 cm) high and indefinite spread. In spring it sends up spikes of deep blue flowers, up to 8 in (20 cm) high in some cultivars. The most familiar versions are: **'Atropurpurea'** (syn. 'Purpurea'), which has dull purple to bronzy green leaves; **'Burgundy Glow'**, with cream and maroon variegated leaves; **'Multicolor'**, with white, pink and purple leaves; and **'Variegata'**, with light green and cream leaves. Rather different is **'Jungle Beauty'**, which is much larger, spreads more rapidly, and has dark green leaves tinged with purple. **'Catlin's Giant'** has much larger leaves and longer, to 8 in (20 cm), inflorescences. **'Pink Elf'** is a compact form with dark pink flowers. ZONES 3–10.

Ajuga reptans 'Atropurpurea' *(above)*

Ajuga reptans 'Jungle Beauty' *(right)*

A

ALCEA
HOLLYHOCK

The botanical name *Alcea* is the old Roman one; Linnaeus adopted it although he also used the name *Althaea,* from the Greek *altheo,* to cure, in allusion to the plant's use in traditional medicine. Native to the eastern Mediterranean, hollyhocks were originally called holy hock or holy mallow; it is said that plants were taken to England from the Holy Land during the Crusades. There are about 60 species in the genus, all from western and central Asia. They bear flowers on spikes which may be 6 ft (1.8 m) or more high, making them far too tall for the average flowerbed; even 'dwarf' cultivars grow to 3 ft (1 m) tall.

CULTIVATION
Hollyhocks are quite frost hardy but need shelter from wind, benefiting from staking in exposed positions. They prefer sun, a rich, heavy well-drained soil and frequent watering in dry weather. Propagate from seed in late summer or spring. Rust disease can be a problem; spray with fungicide.

Alcea rosea *(above & above right)*
syn. *Althaea rosea*
HOLLYHOCK

This biennial, believed originally to have come from Turkey or Palestine, is popular for its tall spikes of flowers which appear in summer and early autumn, and come in a range of colors including pink, purple, cream and yellow; they can be either single, flat circles of color 4 in (10 cm) across, or so lavishly double that they are like spheres of ruffled petals. Foliage is roundish and rough and the plants may be as much as 10 ft (3 m) tall, erect and generally unbranched. The **Chater's Double Group** of cultivars have peony-shaped, double flowers that may be any color from purple-blue, purple, red, yellow and white to pink or apricot. There are many other cultivars and series, which include **Pinafore Mixed** and **Majorette Mixed** with lacy, semi-double flowers in pastel shades. ZONES 4–10.

ALCHEMILLA
LADY'S MANTLE

A

There are around 300 species of herbaceous perennials in this Eurasian genus. There are also a few alpine species in Australia and New Zealand, but it is not clear if they are natives or naturalized introductions. They form clumps of palmate (hand-shaped) or rounded, lobed, gray-green leaves often covered with fine hairs. Their spreading stems often root as they grow. Branched inflorescences of tiny yellow-green flowers develop in summer. Their sizes range from 6–30 in (15–75 cm) tall and wide. Many species have styptic and other medicinal properties.

CULTIVATION
They are very hardy and easily grown in any well-drained soil in afternoon shade. They may be grown in sun but the foliage will deteriorate in the summer heat. Propagate from seed or division in late winter to early spring.

Alchemilla conjuncta (below)
Native to the French and Swiss Alps, this 12 in (30 cm) tall species has 7 to 9 lobed, pale green leaves with toothed edges and a dense covering of silvery hairs on the undersides. The flowering stems are up to 15 in (38 cm) tall. ZONES 5–9.

Alchemilla rohdii
(left)

One of the numerous European species that have at times been included under the name *Alchemilla vulgaris,* this makes a low spreading plant less than 8 in (20 cm) high with fresh green leaves, their short rounded lobes finely toothed. The greenish yellow flowers are not very showy. **ZONES 6–9.**

Alchemilla mollis
(center left)
LADY'S MANTLE

Sometimes sold as *Alchemilla vulgaris,* this is the most widely cultivated species in the genus. It is a low-growing perennial ideal for ground cover, the front of borders or for rock gardens. It is clump forming, growing to a height and spread of 16 in (40 cm). It has decorative, wavy edged leaves which hold dew or raindrops to give a sparkling effect. In summer, it bears masses of small sprays of greenish yellow flowers, similar to *Gypsophila.* **Alchemilla speciosa** is very like *A. mollis* except that its leaves are more deeply lobed and the leaf stems have a covering of fine hairs. **ZONES 4–9.**

Alchemilla speciosa *(right)*

Very similar in general appearance to the commonly grown *Alchemilla mollis,* this Caucasian species has slightly more deeply divided leaves with narrower, sharper teeth. It also differs in minor floral details. **ZONES 6–10.**

ALONSOA
MASK FLOWER

This genus consists of some 12 species of perennials and subshrubs found in tropical western America from Mexico to Peru. Named for Alonzo Zanoni, an eighteenth-century Colombian Secretary of State, they are commonly known as mask flowers because the shape of the flower bears a fancied resemblance to a carnival mask. The flowers are usually small, but often vividly colored and open through most of the year.

CULTIVATION
Provided they receive some sun, mask flowers are very easily grown in any free-draining soil. They are propagated from seed, cuttings or by layering the stems. Only very light frosts are tolerated, though young plants can be propagated in autumn and over-wintered under cover.

Alonsoa warscewiczii (above)

An evergreen perennial that in some climates (zones 5–9) is short-lived and treated as an annual, this native of Peru can form a 24 in (60 cm) high subshrub in a frost-free climate. Named after Joseph Warscewicz (1812–66), a botanist who collected in South America, it bears clusters of small, vivid orange-red flowers. In suitably mild conditions these appear throughout the year. There are several cultivars with flowers in various shades of pink and orange.
ZONES 9–11.

ALPINIA
ORNAMENTAL GINGER

Of Asian and Pacific origin, these plants are widely cultivated in tropical and subtropical gardens, for their showy blooms, some as commercial cut flowers. They grow from fleshy rhizomes to form large clumps. The aboveground shoots are in fact pseudostems consisting of tightly furled leaf bases as in cannas and bananas. The large thin leaves form 2 rows. Although strictly speaking perennials, they do not die back and can be used in the garden like a shrub.

CULTIVATION

Although frost tender, many will tolerate winter temperatures just above freezing as long as summers are warm and humid. They like part-shade, a warm, moist atmosphere and rich soil. Propagate by division.

Alpinia galanga
(left)
GALANGAL, THAI GINGER

Although most alpinias are grown for ornament and are not regarded as edible, this Southeast Asian species is the source of an important spice, a vital ingredient of Thai cooking in particular. It is the thick, white-fleshed rhizome that is used, either freshly grated, dried or powdered ('laos powder'), to add a subtle piquancy to dishes such as curries. The plant makes a clump of leafy stems 6 ft (1.8 m) high. The flowers, white with pink markings, are not very showy.
ZONES 11–12.

Alpinia zerumbet *(above)*
syns *Alpinia nutans, A. speciosa*
SHELL GINGER

This evergreen, clump-forming perennial grows to
around 10 ft (3 m) with a spread of 5–10 ft
(1.5–3 m). It has long, densely massed stems with
broad, green leaves. The drooping sprays of flowers
appear in spring and intermittently in other
seasons, starting as waxy white or ivory buds,
opening one at a time to reveal yellow lips with
pink- or red-marked throats. **'Variegata'** has
leaves irregularly striped yellow; it tends to be
lower growing. ZONES 10–12.

Alpinia purpurata *(right)*
RED GINGER

This Pacific Islands species produces showy spikes
of small white flowers among vivid scarlet bracts
throughout the year. The glossy leaves are narrow
and lance-shaped. New plantlets sprout among
the flower bracts and take root when the dying
flower stems fall to the ground under the weight
of the growing plantlets. The plants grow to 10 ft
(3 m) tall. ZONES 11–12.

ALSTROEMERIA

PERUVIAN LILY

Native to South America where they occur mostly in the Andes, these tuberous and rhizomatous plants with about 50 species are among the finest perennials for cutting, but they do drop their petals. Erect, wiry stems bear scattered, thin, twisted leaves concentrated on the upper half, and terminate in umbels of outward-facing flowers, usually with flaring petals that are variously spotted or streaked. They flower profusely from spring to summer.

CULTIVATION

All grow well in sun or light shade in a well-enriched, well-drained acidic soil. They soon form large clumps, bearing dozens of flowerheads. Propagate from seed or by division in early spring. They are frost hardy, but in cold winters protect the dormant tubers by covering with loose peat or dry bracken. They are best left undisturbed when established, but one-year-old seedlings transplant well. They do well naturalized under trees or on sloping banks.

Alstroemeria aurea

(left)

syn. *Alstroemeria aurantiaca*

Native to Chile, this is the most common and easily grown species of *Alstroemeria*. It has heads of orange flowers, tipped with green and streaked with maroon. The leaves are twisted, narrow and lance-shaped. Several cultivars exist, which include 'Majestic' and 'Bronze Beauty'. Both have deep orange or bronzy orange flowers; they grow to 2–3 ft (0.6–1 m) with a similar spread. ZONES 7–9.

Alstroemeria, Dr Salter's Hybrids

This group of hybrid cultivars includes a wide range of colors. The flowerheads are more compact than in the Ligtu Hybrids, the flowers open more widely, and the 3 inner petals are more heavily marked. 'Walter Fleming' has flowering stems up to 3 ft (1 m) tall and cream and gold flowers tinged with purple, the inner petals spotted red-purple. ZONES 7–9.

Alstroemeria,
Dr Salter's Hybrid,
'Walter Fleming' *(left)*

Alstroemeria, Dutch Hybrid, 'Yellow Friendship' *(above)*

Alstroemeria, Dutch Hybrid cultivar *(right)*

Alstroemeria, Dutch Hybrids

These are the alstroemerias that now dominate the cut-flower trade in many countries. They are bred mainly by one Dutch firm, and some of the newer cultivars are only made available to commercial cut-flower growers, who grow them under glass to avoid any rain damage to the blooms. The flowers, in compact umbels, are broad petalled and have heavily marked upper petals often in strongly contrasting colors. **'Yellow Friendship'** and **'Mirella'** are examples of this type of hybrid.
ZONES 8–10.

Alstroemeria, Dutch Hybrid, 'Mirella' *(right)*

Alstroemeria psittacina (right)
syn. *Alstroemeria pulchella*
NEW ZEALAND CHRISTMAS BELL

Though native to Brazil, *Alstroemeria psittacina* gets its common name from its popularity in New Zealand, where its narrow, crimson and green flowers are borne at Christmas. The well-spaced stems, about 24 in (60 cm) high, spring from tuberous roots. Easily grown in warm-temperate climates, it can spread rapidly and prove difficult to eradicate. ZONES 8–10.

Alstroemeria haemantha (left)
HERB LILY

This Chilean species has green leaves with a slightly hairy margin. The stiff flower stems up to 3 ft (1 m) tall carry up to 15 orange to dull red flowers during early summer, their upper petals splashed with yellow. The plants can spread by their fleshy rhizomes to form quite large patches. ZONES 7–9.

Alstroemeria, Ligtu Hybrids

The well-known Ligtu Hybrids first appeared in Britain in the late 1920s, when *Alstroemeria ligtu* was crossed with *A. haemantha*. They come in a range of colors from cream to orange, red and yellow, but have been overshadowed in recent years as cut flowers by other hybrid strains derived from *A. aurea*. The plants die down soon after flowering. ZONES 7–9.

Alstroemeria, Ligtu
Hybrid cultivar *(left)*

A

ALYSSUM
MADWORT

The commonly grown bedding alyssum is now classified under *Lobularia,* but there are still some 170 species of annuals, perennials and subshrubs in this genus and many of them are superb rockery plants. They are mainly low spreaders with small elliptical leaves. In spring and early summer they are smothered in heads of tiny white, cream, yellow or pink flowers. Most are less than 8 in (20 cm) tall with a few of the shrubbier species reaching 24 in (60 cm).

CULTIVATION
Plant in full sun with gritty, well-drained soil. Alyssums are ideal for growing in rock crevices and as dry-stone wall plants, though it is important that they are given an occasional soaking in spring and summer. Most species are fairly frost hardy and are propagated from seed or small cuttings.

Alyssum chalcidicum *(above)*

Considered by some authorities to be simply a form of *A. murale,* this Turkish perennial forms a tufted gray-green mound up to 15 in (45 cm) high. The individual leaves are around 1/2 in (12 mm) long and are very densely packed. From mid-spring the mound is covered in tiny yellow flowers. ZONES 7–10.

Alyssum murale *(above)*
YELLOW TUFT

One of the taller species, this native of southeastern Europe grows to around 18 in (45 cm) tall. Its leaves are gray-green and 1/2–1 in (12–25 mm) long. The flowers are yellow. ZONES 7–9.

A

AMARANTHUS

The 60 or so species of annuals and short-lived perennials that make up this genus range through most warmer parts of the world and include weeds, leaf vegetables and grain crops as well as a few ornamentals, grown for their brilliant foliage, curious flowers and adaptability to hot, dry conditions. They are popular bedding plants, with large and attractively colored leaves and minute flowers borne in drooping tassel-like spikes.

CULTIVATION

A sunny, dry position with protection from strong winds is essential, and they enjoy a fertile, well-drained soil, mulched during hot weather. They are marginally frost hardy and in cool climates are usually brought on under glass before planting out in late spring. Prune when young to thicken growth. Prepare soil for planting with plenty of manure, and water seedlings regularly. Protect from snails when young and watch for caterpillars and aphids. Propagate from seed.

Amaranthus caudatus (left)
LOVE-LIES-BLEEDING, TASSEL FLOWER

This species, growing to 4 ft (1.2 m) or more high, has oval, dull green leaves and dark red flowers in long, drooping cords, their ends often touching the ground. Flowers appear in summer through to autumn. In many old gardens this plant was used to give height in the center of circular beds. ZONES 8–11.

Amaranthus tricolor

Native to tropical Africa and Asia, this quick-growing annual has given rise to many cultivated strains, some used as leaf vegetables (Chinese spinach), others as bedding plants with brilliantly colored leaves. They are bushy and reach about 3 ft (1 m) high and 18 in (45 cm) wide. Tiny red flowers appear in summer. **'Flaming Fountain'** has leaves that are deep green at the base, bronze tinted higher up, and entirely blood red at the top. **'Joseph's Coat'**, has brilliant bronze, gold, orange and red variegated 8 in (20 cm) long leaves which retain their coloring into late autumn. ZONES 8–11.

Amaranthus tricolor 'Flaming Fountain' *(above)*

Amaranthus tricolor 'Joseph's Coat' *(left)*

A

AMMI

Six species of carrot-like perennials belong to this genus, occurring wild in the Mediterranean region, western Asia and the Canary Islands. They are fairly typical umbellifers with large, ferny basal leaves and flowering stems bearing large umbels of numerous small white flowers. One species (*Ammi majus*) is sometimes grown for cut flowers or as a 'cottage garden' plant, and a second (*A. visnaga*) has long been used medicinally in the Middle East. *Ammi* was the classical Greek and Latin name for a plant of this type, though its exact identity is uncertain.

CULTIVATION

Usually treated as annuals, they are easily grown in a sheltered but sunny position in any reasonable garden soil, kept fairly moist. Propagate from seed in spring. They will usually self-seed once established.

Ammi majus (above)
BISHOP'S WEED

Native to the Mediterranean region and western Asia, this species has become widely naturalized on other continents. It grows to about 24–36 in (60–90 cm) tall, producing a succession of large, lacy flowering heads in summer and autumn. The cut flowers are sometimes sold in florists' shops.
ZONES 6–10.

AMSONIA
BLUE STAR

A genus of around 20 species of perennials and subshrubs native to southern Europe, western Asia, Japan and North America. They grow to around 3 ft (1 m) tall and have bright to deep green, narrow, lance-shaped leaves. Stems and leaves bleed milky sap when cut. The flowers, borne mainly in summer, are tubular with widely flared mouths. They are carried in phlox-like heads at the stem tips.

CULTIVATION
Amsonias are easily grown in any moist, well-drained soil that does not dry out in summer. Plant in full sun or part-shade. They are moderately to very frost hardy and generally die back to the rootstock in winter. Propagation is from seed, early summer cuttings or by division in late winter.

Amsonia tabernaemontana
(right)
BLUE STAR, BLUE DOGBANE

Amsonia tabernaemontana is a delightful perennial from north-eastern and central USA. Stiff stems, 24–36 in (60–90 cm) tall, are topped by pyramidal clusters of small, star-shaped flowers of pale blue from late spring to summer, flowering along with peonies and irises. The leaves are narrow to elliptical and about 2¹/₂ in (6 cm) long. This species needs minimal care if given a moist, fertile soil in full sun to light shade. It is good in the perennial border or in a damp wildflower meadow. The species name commemorates a famous sixteenth-century German herbalist, who latinized his name as *Tabernaemontanus*. ZONES 3–9.

A

Anagallis tenella
(left)
BOG PIMPERNEL

Found in western Europe, this prostrate perennial has stems up to 6 in (15 cm) long that root as they grow. It is seldom over 1 in (25 mm) high and has a spread of around 12 in (30 cm). The funnel-shaped flowers are soft pink, occasionally white, and are borne in summer. Growing in boggy spots in the wild, it is best suited to the edges of ponds and other damp, sheltered spots. **'Studland'** has scented, deeper pink flowers. ZONES 8–10.

ANAGALLIS
PIMPERNEL

These are low-growing, often mat-forming annuals and perennials with small, heart-shaped to elliptical, bright green leaves arranged in opposite pairs. In spring and summer small, 5-petalled flowers appear in profusion on short stems. The flowers usually arise from the leaf axils or occasionally in small racemes at the stem tips. They come in a variety of colors including pink, orange, red, blue and white.

CULTIVATION
Plant in full sun in any well-drained soil that does not dry out entirely in summer. The more attractive, less vigorous species are excellent rockery plants. Propagate annuals from seed; perennials from seed, by division or from small tip cuttings. Some of the weedy species self-sow only too readily.

Anagallis monellii *(below)*
syns *Anagallis linifolia, A. collina*

This charming little plant is grown for its brilliant blue or scarlet flowers of ½ in (12 mm) diameter, which appear during summer. This species grows to under 18 in (45 cm), with a spread of 6 in (15 cm) or more. ZONES 7–10.

ANAPHALIS
PEARLY EVERLASTING

A genus of around 100 species of gray-foliaged perennials. They occur over most of the northern temperate regions and at high altitudes in the tropics. The narrow, lance-shaped leaves are often clothed in cobwebby hairs attached directly to upright stems. Panicles on clusters of papery white flowerheads terminate the stems in summer or autumn. The flowerheads may be small, resembling some achilleas, or large, with large papery bracts resembling helichrysums. Heights range from 6–30 in (15–75 cm) depending on the species. Like other ever-lastings they are useful for cut flowers, and the foliage and flowers are just as decorative when dried.

CULTIVATION
Plant in light, gritty, well-drained soil in full sun. They do not like being wet but when in active growth the soil should not be allowed to dry out completely. Prune back hard in winter. Propagate from seed or division.

Anaphalis triplinervis (above)

This is a Himalayan species that grows to 30 in (75 cm) tall. It has daisy-like white bracts and leaves that are pale green above with felted undersides, broader towards the apex and usually with 3 prominent veins diverging from the base. **'Sommerschnee'** ('Summer Snow') grows only to a height of 12 in (30 cm) and has shorter, more heavily felted leaves. It may be, in fact, a hybrid with *Anaphalis nepalensis*. ZONES 5–9.

Anaphalis javanica (above)

From higher mountains of the Malay archipelago, this is a somewhat shrubby, evergreen species with a very dense coating of silver-gray hairs on the narrow leaves. It grows to about 18 in (45 cm) high and bears clusters of small, white flowerheads in summer. ZONES 9–10.

Anaphalis triplinervis
'Sommerschnee' (above)

A

Anchusa azurea
'Loddon Royalist' *(left)*

ANCHUSA
ALKANET, SUMMER FORGET-ME-NOT

This genus consists of about 50 species of annuals, biennials and perennials occurring in Europe, North and South Africa and western Asia. Many have a rather weedy habit and undistinguished foliage, but they bear flowers of a wonderful sapphire blue. Though individually not large, they are carried in clusters over a long spring and early summer season and do not fade easily. They are popular with bees, and are suitable for beds, borders and containers. The dwarf perennials are at home in a rock garden.

CULTIVATION

Frost hardy, they grow best in a sunny position in deep, rich, well-drained soil. In very hot areas, planting in part-shade helps maintain the flower color. Feed sparingly and water generously. Taller species benefit from staking and the plants require plenty of room as they make large root systems. Cut flower stalks back after blooming to promote new growth. Propagate perennials by division in winter, annuals and biennials from seed in autumn or spring. Transplant perennials when dormant in winter.

Anchusa azurea
(center right)
syn. *Anchusa italica*

ITALIAN ALKANET

Native to the Mediter-
ranean and Black Sea
areas, this species is an
upright perennial 3–4 ft
(1–1.2 m) high and
24 in (60 cm) wide. It
has coarse, hairy leaves
and an erect habit with
tiers of brilliant blue
flowers borne in spring
to summer. Its several
cultivars differ in their
precise shade of blue:
deep blue, tinted purple
'Dropmore'; purple
'Dropmore Purple';
rich blue **'Morning
Glory'**; light blue
'Opal'; and the intense
deep blue of **'Loddon
Royalist'**. ZONES 3–9.

Anchusa azurea
'Dropmore Purple' *(above)*

Anchusa azurea
'Dropmore' *(below)*

A

Anchusa capensis
'Blue Angel' *(left)*

Anchusa capensis
(center left)
CAPE FORGET-ME-NOT

This southern African species is biennial in cool climates, but in warm-temperate gardens it can be sown very early in spring to bear intense blue flowers in summer. It grows to 15 in (40 cm) tall and wide. As an annual, **'Blue Angel'** reaches a height and spread of 8 in (20 cm), and forms a compact pyramid of shallow, bowl-shaped, sky blue flowers in early summer. **'Blue Bird'** is taller, 24 in (60 cm), but equally striking. ZONES 8–10.

Anchusa granatensis *(below)*

This low-growing species from southwestern Europe is unusual in having flowers of a bright purplish red rather than the usual blue of other anchusas. The epithet *granatensis* means 'of Granada' referring in this case to the southern Spanish city. ZONES 6–9.

Androsace sarmentosa
'Brilliant' *(right)*

Androsace
sarmentosa *(below)*

This is another
Himalayan perennial
species that spreads by
runners. It forms
patches of rosettes of
small, oval leaves with a
covering of fine silvery
hairs. Large heads of
yellow-centered, pink
flowers on 4 in (10 cm)
stalks are borne in
spring. **'Brilliant'** has
darker mauve-pink
flowers. ZONES 3–8.

ANDROSACE
ROCK JASMINE

This genus consists of around 100 species of annuals and perennials
from cooler regions of the northern hemisphere. It is mainly the
low-growing perennials that are valued as garden plants, forming
dense mats or cushions no more than 4 in (10 cm) high. Favorites
for rock garden planting, they are rarely spectacular but are
appealing. Most species have light green or silvery gray, loose
rosettes of foliage crowded along prostrate stems, topped with
umbels of small, white or pink, 5-petalled flowers in spring and
summer.

CULTIVATION
They grow best in sunny, well-drained scree
or rockery conditions with free-draining,
gravel-based soil and additional humus.
Most are quite frost hardy, but some may
require alpine-house conditions in areas
subject to heavy winter rains. Propagate
from seed, cuttings or self-rooted layers.

A

ANEMONE
WINDFLOWER

This genus of over 100 species of perennials occurs widely in the northern hemisphere, but with the majority in temperate Asia. Species include a diverse range of woodland plants as well as the common florist's anemone *(Anemone coronaria)*. All have tufts of basal leaves that are divided in palmate fashion into few to many leaflets. The starry or bowl-shaped flowers have 5 or more petals, their colors covering almost the whole range of flower colors. Anemones can be divided into the autumn flowering species with fibrous roots, such as *A. hupehensis* and *A. × hybrida,* and the tuberous and rhizomatous types, usually spring flowering, which include the ground-hugging *A. blanda* and *A. nemorosa.* There are other rhizomatous species which tolerate less moisture and more open conditions. Given the right conditions and left undisturbed for many years, many of these will form wonderful carpets of both leaf texture and color through their delicate flowers. The tuberous-rooted types, of which *A. coronaria* is best known, flower in spring and are best replaced every 1–2 years.

CULTIVATION

Most woodland species are very frost hardy and do well in rich, moist yet well-drained soil in a lightly shaded position. Propagate from seed planted in summer or divide established clumps in early winter when the plant is dormant. The tuberous-rooted types appreciate full sun and well-drained soil, and welcome a dry dormancy period. However, they are more prone to frost damage and the tubers tend to become weakened after blooming. For this reason, they are often treated as annuals.

Anemone appenina *(left)*

A 6 in (15 cm) tall, rhizomatous species from southern Europe, it has a clump of basal leaves, each divided into 3 segments which are themselves further divided. Pinkish flowers about 1 in (25 mm) wide on short stems open in spring. **'Petrovac'** is a vigorous cultivar with many-petalled, deep blue flowers. **'Purpurea'** has pinkish purple flowers, while *Anemone appenina* var. *albiflora* has all-white flowers. ZONES 6–9.

Anemone blanda
'Radar' *(right)*

Anemone hupehensis
JAPANESE WIND FLOWER

A perennial with fibrous roots, this species from central and western China (long cultivated in Japan), can be almost evergreen in milder climates where, if conditions are to its liking, it may spread and provide good ground cover, producing its single white to mauve flowers on tall, openly branched stems during the early autumn. The cultivar **'Hadspen Abundance'** has deep pink petals edged with pale pink to almost white. **'September Charm'** has large pale pink flowers with 5 to 6 petals, while *Anemone hupehensis* var. *japonica* is the Japanese cultivated race, taller and with more petals than the wild Chinese plants. It includes **'Prinz Heinrich'** ('Prince Henry') with 10 or more deep rose pink petals, paler on the undersides. Most of the cultivars ascribed to this species are now placed under *Anemone* × *hybrida*. ZONES 6–10.

Anemone hupehensis 'Hadspen Abundance' *(right)*

Anemone blanda

This delicate-looking tuberous species is frost hardy. Native to Greece and Turkey, it grows to 8 in (20 cm) with crowded tufts of ferny leaves. White, pink or blue star-shaped flowers, $1^{1}/_{2}$ in (35 mm) wide, appear in spring. It self-seeds freely and, given moist, slightly shaded conditions, should spread into a beautiful display of flowers. Popular cultivars include the large-flowered **'White Splendour'**; **'Atrocaerulea'**, with deep blue flowers; **'Blue Star'**, with pale blue flowers; and **'Radar'** with white-centered magenta flowers. ZONES 6–9.

Anemone blanda 'White Splendour' *(left)*

Anemone × *hybrida* 'Honorine Jobert' *(above)*

Anemone × hybrida

These popular hybrids are believed to have arisen as crosses between *Anemone hupehensis* and its close relative the Himalayan *A. vitifolia*, the latter distinguished by the dense woolly hair on its leaf undersides and usually white flowers. The hybrids generally have leaves that are hairier beneath than in *A. hupehensis*, and flowers in all shades from white to deepest rose, the petals numbering from 5 to over 30. They generally lack fertile pollen. The robust plants may reach heights of 5 ft (1.5 m) in flower. There are over 30 cultivars, among the most common being '**Honorine Jobert**' with pure white, 6–9-petalled flowers and very dark green leaves. Most nurseries do not list cultivar names but just sell the plants in flower, when they are easy to select both for color and flower type. **ZONES 6–10.**

Anemone × **hybrida** cultivar *(left)*

A

Anemone nemorosa *(below)*
WOOD ANEMONE

As its common name implies, this European species is happiest in a moist, shaded position where its delicate creamy white early spring flowers delight the passer by. Usually under 4 in (10 cm) high, it has fine creeping rhizomes that will quickly cover a wanted area if conditions are suitable. Many named cultivars exist including **'Allenii'**, a rich lilac blue on the outside of the petals and pale lilac on the insides; **'Robinsoniana'**, with lavender-blue petals; and **'Vestal'**, a late-blooming white variety. ZONES 5–9.

Anemone nemorosa 'Robinsoniana' *(above)*

A

Anemone sylvestris
(left)

SNOWDROP ANEMONE

From Europe, this fibrous-rooted species is usually about 8 in (20 cm) tall, with deeply dissected glossy dark green leaves. The solitary, fragrant, single white flowers have prominent yellow stamens and are borne over a long season in spring and early summer. Cultivars include **'Grandiflora'**, with large nodding flowers and **'Elisa Fellmann'**, with semi-double flowers.
ZONES 4–9.

Anemone rivularis
(right)

Ranging from India to western China and flowering in late to mid summer, this fibrous-rooted species has leaves with broader, more rounded divisions than most anemones. It grows to around 24 in (60 cm) tall, with white cup-shaped flowers tinted blue on the outside, and purple stamens. ZONES 6–9.

Anemone trullifolia *(right)*

Originating from the eastern Himalayas and western China, this fibrous-rooted anemone grows to around 12 in (30 cm) high with broadly lobed basal leaves. Delicate, long-stalked bluish, white or yellow flowers appear in summer. ZONES 5–9.

ANEMONELLA
RUE ANEMONE

The name is a diminutive of *Anemone* and in fact the sole species of this North American genus is a more diminutive plant than most anemones, but in foliage and flowers it is more reminiscent of a *Thalictrum*. It is a tuberous-rooted perennial forming a small, dense clump of foliage, the compound leaves with few but rather large leaflets. The flowers are large for the size of the plant and few to each short flowering stem, with a variable number of over-lapping petals in shades of white to pale mauve.

CULTIVATION
It makes a charming rock garden plant but also adapts to moist, undisturbed spots in a woodland garden. It requires moist but very well-drained, humus-rich soil, and a semi-shaded position. Growth is slow and skilful management is needed to keep plants healthy for many years. Propagate by careful division of mature plants in autumn or from seed in spring.

Anemonella thalictroides (below)
This beautiful plant occurs wild in eastern USA and southeastern Canada, in mountain woodlands. Usually 8 in (20 cm) or less in height, it has smooth blue-green leaves. In spring and early summer it bears delicate bowl-shaped flowers about ³/₄ in (18 mm) wide with 5 to 10 petals. ZONES 4–9.

A

ANEMOPSIS
YERBA MANSA

Although its name means 'anemone-like', this genus of a single species from western USA and Mexico is quite unrelated to anemones, but related rather to the lizard's-tail genera *Saururus* and *Houttuynia*. The 'flowers' that look like those of some of the anemones with elongated receptacles are in fact inflorescences, with a group of petal-like white bracts at the base of a spike of tiny, fleshy greenish flowers. It is a creeping evergreen perennial that spreads both by thick underground rhizomes and surface runners that develop rosettes of leaves at intervals. The rhizome is used medicinally by Native Americans, who also use the small, hard fruits for beadwork.

CULTIVATION
It will grow equally well in boggy ground or in a well-drained raised bed or rockery, preferably in full sun. Although quite ornamental and unusual, it is a vigorous grower and can quickly become invasive, and is difficult to eradicate due to its tenacious rhizomes. A boggy stream or pond edge is perhaps its most appropriate placement. Propagate by division or from cuttings.

Anemopsis californica *(above)*
YERBA MANSA

Occurring wild in the southwestern states of the USA and adjacent Baja, California (Mexico), yerba mansa can rapidly spread over a very large area when conditions suit it, mounding sometimes to about 18 in (45 cm) high. The spoon-shaped leaves become purple-tinged in the sun, and the curious white-bracted flower spikes develop over a long season in spring, summer and autumn. ZONES 8–11.

A

Angelica sylvestris
(right)

WILD ANGELICA, WOOD
ANGELICA

This 7 ft (2 m) tall biennial is a European native found in woods and damp meadows. It has bipinnate or tripinnate leaves up to 2 ft (60 cm) long, each segment of which can be 3 in (8 cm) long. The leaves are covered with small bristly hairs and have serrated edges. The flowers may be white or pink. This species is seldom used for culinary or herbal purposes. ZONES 7–10.

ANGELICA

This genus of 50 or so species is mainly indigenous to the cooler parts of the northern hemisphere. They are valued for the bold palm-like structure of their leaves, the bunches of pale green flowers on tall stems and the pleasant aroma.

CULTIVATION
They prefer moist, well-drained, rich soil in sun or shade. Plants die after flowering and setting seed and should then be removed. Angelica will self-sow or can be propagated from seed.

Angelica pachycarpa (right)

A species that has recently come into cultivation as an ornamental, this is semi-evergreen and remarkable for the succulence and glossiness of its compact foliage. The flowering branches barely rise above the foliage and rapidly develop clusters of small thick fruits. ZONES 8–10.

A

ANIGOZANTHOS
KANGAROO PAW

Native to southwestern Australia, these evergreen perennials are noted for their unique bird-attracting tubular flowers, the outsides coated with dense shaggy hairs and opening at the apex into 6 'claws', the whole resembling an animal's paw. Foliage is somewhat grass-like, and the various species can range in height from 1–6 ft (0.3–1.8 m). Flowers come in many colors including green, gold, deep red and orange-red; some species and hybrids are bi-colored. In recent years many hybrids have been produced, meeting the demands of the cut-flower industry and the florists' trade in potted flowers, although most will grow outdoors equally well. An example is *Anigozanthos* 'Red Cross'.

Anigozanthos
'Red Cross' *(below)*

CULTIVATION
They prefer warm, very well-drained sandy or gravelly soil and a hot, sunny, open position. Water well during dry seasons. Most will tolerate very light frosts and do well in coastal regions. Most tolerate drought, although flowering will be prolonged with summer water. Propagate by division in spring or from fresh seed. Plants are often affected by ink disease, a fungus which blackens the foliage. Watch for snails which can shred younger leaves overnight.

A

Anigozanthos, Bush Gems Series

The best of the kangaroo paws for their resistance to ink disease, the Bush Gems hybrids are mostly of compact size, with flowers ranging from yellow, gold and green through to orange, red and burgundy. '**Bush Heritage**' is a small cultivar of 12–20 in (30–50 cm) in height with flowers of burnt terracotta and olive green. '**Bush Twilight**' grows 8–15 in (20–40 cm) tall. Its prolific flowers in muted orange, yellow and green tones appear mainly in spring above the dull green, very narrow leaves. Other popular cultivars in the series are '**Bush Glow**', sunset red, and '**Bush Gold**', golden yellow. ZONES 9–11.

Anigozanthos, Bush Gems Series, 'Bush Heritage' *(below)*

Anigozanthos, Bush Gems Series, 'Bush Glow' *(left)*

Anigozanthos flavidus *(center)*
YELLOW KANGAROO PAW

Regarded as the hardiest of the kangaroo paws, this species has a vigorous clumping growth habit to 3 ft (1 m) across. With long, dull green leaves, flowering stems 3–5 ft (1–1.5 m) tall, and flowers in green, yellow or soft red tones, this species has proved adaptable to a range of soils and climates. Native to the far south-western corner of Australia, where it is attractive to native birds, it is used extensively in hybridization programs. ZONES 9–11.

Anigozanthos, Bush Gems Series, 'Bush Twilight' *(below)*

A

Anigozanthos humilis (left)

This is a low, clumping perennial, growing no taller than 15 in (40 cm) but spreading anything up to 3 ft (1 m) if conditions are favorable. It can die back in summer and autumn, so should be positioned so that it will not be overgrown while dormant. The flowering stems, often twice the height of the foliage, carry blooms in a wide range of colors from cream through dull orange to red. It prefers full sun. ZONES 9-11.

Anigozanthos
'Regal Claw' (right)

One of the many striking cultivars with parents listed as *Anigozanthos preissii* and *A. flavidus*, 'Regal Claw' is a dwarf plant with flowers of orange with a red felted overlay. ZONES 9–11.

Anigozanthos
manglesii (right)
RED-AND-GREEN KANGAROO PAW

This striking plant has blue-green, strap-like leaves. The deep green flowers contrast vividly with a red base and stem, and appear mainly in spring. Flowering stems are 18–36 in (45–90 cm) in height and the plant has a spread at the base of about 18 in (45 cm). Unfortunately this spectacular species is one of the most difficult to cultivate, being very susceptible to ink disease as well as summer root rot. ZONES 9–10.

ANTENNARIA

CAT'S EARS, LADIES' TOBACCO

A genus of around 45 species of evergreen to near-evergreen perennials of the daisy family from temperate regions of the northern hemisphere, most species form dense mats of leaf rosettes that root as they spread; a few are mounding and up to 15 in (38 cm) tall. The narrow, crowded leaves are usually silver gray and hairy. The summer-borne flowerheads are of the 'everlasting' type with dry, papery bracts surrounding a disc of petal-less florets, the heads clustered on short stems that hold them clear of the foliage mat.

CULTIVATION

Most species are very frost hardy and are best grown in moist, well-drained soil in full sun or morning shade. They can be used in perennial borders or as rockery plants. Propagate from seed or division.

Antennaria dioica (below right)
CATSFOOT

Antennaria dioica 'Australis' (above)

A stoloniferous perennial occurring wild in the colder parts of the northern hemisphere. It forms a mat of rosettes of narrow spatula- to lance-shaped leaves, dark green above but white-woolly on the undersides. In summer, strong 8 in (20 cm) tall flower stems develop bearing clusters of white, pink or yellow flowerheads. Catsfoot is unusual among composites (daisies) in having different sexes on different plants (dioecious), the female flowerheads larger than the male. An attractive ground cover or rock garden plant, it also has some medicinal uses. *Antennaria dioica* **'Rosea'** has deep pink flowerheads; and **'Australis'** silvery gray stems topped with clusters of white flowers. ZONES 5–9.

A

Anthemis 'Moonlight' *(above)*

ANTHEMIS

In suitable conditions the 100 or so species of this genus of annuals and perennials from Mediterranean regions and western Asia flower prolifically, and this is what prompted the name, from the Greek anthemon. Belonging to the larger daisy family, the flowerheads have the typical daisy shape and are generally white, cream or yellow with distinctive contrasting disc florets; a typical example is *Anthemis* 'Moonlight'. Even when not in flower most species have somewhat aromatic, finely dissected foliage in shades of green or silver gray, which can be used to advantage in the mixed border or rockery. Formerly *Anthemis* was taken in a broader sense to include the herb chamomile, which belongs to the genus *Chamaemelum*.

CULTIVATION

These plants flower best in full sun and like well-drained soil. The perennials can be short-lived and often become untidy, but cutting back after flowering in the autumn ensures a more shapely plant. They are easily replaced by cuttings taken in the warmer months or by division in autumn or spring. Annual species can be grown from seed.

Anthemis cretica *(below)*

A mound-forming perennial from southern Europe and Turkey, often with a gray down on its leaves, this species has white flowerheads with yellow discs held on solitary stems up to 12 in (30 cm) high during the spring and summer months. ZONES 5–9.

Anthemis tinctoria *(below)*
DYER'S CHAMOMILE, GOLDEN MARGUERITE

Native to Europe and western Asia, this is a very hardy, easily grown perennial that is covered in late spring and summer with a dazzling display of daisy flowers above fern-like, crinkled green leaves. The plant mounds to as much as 3 ft (1 m) high if supported on a rockery or a bank. The epithet *tinctoria* signifies a dye plant, and indeed the flowers of this species were once used to make a yellow dye. The typical form with bright golden flowers is now less popular than some of the cultivars, notably **'E. C. Buxton'** with subtle soft yellow blooms blending beautifully with the fine foliage. ZONES 4–10.

ANTHERICUM

SPIDER PLANT

A genus of some 50 species of fleshy-rooted perennial lilies that form clumps of narrow, grass-like leaves. The flower stems are wiry and up to 3 ft (1 m) tall and by mid-summer are bearing their small, starry, 6-petalled, white flowers. They are natives of Europe, northern Africa and Asia Minor.

CULTIVATION

Plant in moist, well-drained soil in full sun or morning shade. Moderately frost hardy, they are propagated by sowing fresh seed or by division in late winter to early spring.

Anthericum liliago 'Major' *(below)*

Anthericum liliago
(right)
ST BERNARD'S LILY

This European species has 15 in (38 cm) long, gray-green leaves and in summer develops 3 ft (1 m) tall spikes of narrow-petalled, 1 in (25 mm) wide white flowers, each petal with a greenish mid-vein. **'Major'** has larger, pure white flowers.
ZONES 7–10.

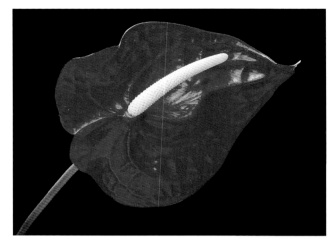

Anthurium andraeanum (left)

Grown for its large, brilliantly colored spathe with raised veining, this species grows to about 24 in (60 cm) high, with large heart-shaped leaves. The plants only produce one or two flowers at a time but they bloom all year. The spathes, so glossy they appear varnished, are typically bright red, but other colors have been bred including pink, and green marbled with red. ZONES 11–12.

ANTHURIUM
FLAMINGO FLOWER

This is a huge and diverse genus of evergreen, clumping or climbing epiphytes in the arum family, all from tropical America. Familiar as florists' plants and cut flowers are 2 to 3 species with typically brilliant red, flat spathes held above broad leathery leaves; selection and breeding has broadened the range of colors to include white, pink and orange. The actual flowers are the tiny bumps gathered around the central spadix.

CULTIVATION

Anthuriums are easy to grow in a tropical climate but elsewhere they are more likely to flourish in a greenhouse or indoors in containers. Indoors, they need bright light, high humidity and constant warmth and moisture to flower. Plant outdoors in a humid position, in well-drained, peaty soil in full or part-shade out of the wind. Keep soil moist but not soggy. Daytime temperatures should not fall below about 60°F (15°C). Propagate from rhizomes in early spring. Potted plants need dividing and repotting every few years.

Anthurium scherzerianum (above)
FLAMINGO FLOWER

Growing to 24–30 in (60–75 cm) this species typically has red spathes, with curled spadices but cultivars vary from white to pink to very dark red, sometimes with paler spots. The elongated, rather dull green leaves are very thick and leathery. Although this is one of the more cold-hardy species, it must be protected from frost. ZONES 10–12.

A

ANTHYLLIS

This is a genus of around 25 species of annuals, perennials and small shrubs. The leaves are pinnate but the leaflets are often small and closely crowded, creating the appearance of coarsely serrated leaves. The individual flowers are small and pea-like but borne abundantly in dense, rounded heads from spring to summer. Flower colors include yellows, reds and pinks.

CULTIVATION

Easily grown in any well-drained soil in full sun. Cold hardiness varies with the species but most will tolerate moderate frosts. Propagate from seed or small cuttings.

Anthyllis montana
'Atrorubens' *(above right)*

Anthyllis vulneraria
var. *alpestris (below)*

Anthyllis montana

This perennial species from the mountains of southern Europe has ferny pinnate leaves and spreads to form a mat of foliage up to 10 in (25 cm) tall and 3 ft (1 m) wide. From late spring the plant is studded with profuse $^1/_2$ in (12 mm) wide heads of pink and white flowers that from a distance resemble pink clover. **'Atrorubens'** has deeper pink to purplish flowers. ZONES 7–9.

Anthyllis vulneraria
KIDNEY VETCH, LADIES' FINGERS

This spreading, short-lived perennial ground cover is native to Europe and North Africa. It forms crowded rosettes of silky-haired foliage and may sometimes mound up to about 18 in (45 cm) tall. The flowers, in $^1/_2$ in (12 mm) wide heads, are cream and yellow, often with red or purple tints. The species is used medicinally as an astringent, laxative and cough remedy. It is also dried for use in flower arrangements. *Anthyllis vulneraria* **var. alpestris** is a variety from mountainous areas. ZONES 7–9.

A

ANTIRRHINUM
SNAPDRAGON

The resemblance of snapdragon flowers to the face of a beast was noted by the ancient Greeks, who called them Antirrhinon, nose-like. In French they are gueule de loup, wolf's mouth, and in German and Italian the name means lion's mouth. Closely related to the toadflaxes *(Linaria)*, the genus consists of about 40 species, most from the western Mediterranean region but with a few from western North America. They are annuals, perennials and evergreen subshrubs. The common snapdragon *(Antirrhinum majus)* is a perennial but it is normally treated as an annual in gardens.

CULTIVATION
They prefer fertile, well-drained soil in full sun. Propagate the garden snapdragon from seed in spring or early autumn.

Antirrhinum hispanicum (left)

This short-lived peren-nial from Spain is a very pretty miniature species, 10 in (25 cm) tall with flowers about half the size of the garden snapdragon. Mauve-pink is its only color. ZONES 7–10.

A

Antirrhinum majus *(above)*
GARDEN SNAPDRAGON

This bushy, short-lived perennial is valued for its showy flowers, borne over a long period from spring to autumn. The many named cultivars, usually grown as annuals, spread 12–18 in (30–45 cm) and may be tall, 30 in (75 cm); medium, 18 in (45 cm); or dwarf, 10 in (25 cm). Plant breeders have developed snapdragons with wide open or double flowers, but none have the charm of the traditional form, as exemplified by the strain called **Liberty**. Treat these garden snapdragons as annuals—they rarely flower well after the first year, and old plants are apt to succumb to the fungus, antirrhinum rust. Deadhead to prolong flowering and pinch out early buds to increase branching. The **Coronette Series** of F1 hybrids, bred as bedding plants, exemplifies some of the qualities plant geneticists are injecting into their breeding programs. These include tolerance of bad weather, extra large blooms on heavy spikes and uniformity from seedling stage. They can grow to 24 in (60 cm) or more tall and a number of individual colors are available, from bronze through shades of pink to deep red to yellows and white. Two popular cultivars are **'Flower Carpet'** and **'Madame Butterfly'**. ZONES 6–10.

Antirrhinum majus, Liberty Series cultivar *(above)*

A

APONOGETON
WATER HAWTHORN

This genus of aquatic plants consists of 40-odd species, found wild in streams and lakes through tropical and subtropical regions of Africa, Asia and Australasia, but with the greatest concentration in Madagascar. The leaves are long-stalked, oval to narrowly oblong, with a close network of veining; they may be fully submerged, or most of the leaves may float on the surface. Long-stalked flowering heads emerge just above water, branched into short fleshy spikes of curious small white, pink or purplish flowers. The tuberous roots and flower buds are sometimes eaten in their native countries.

CULTIVATION

Aponogetons fall into 2 groups as far as cultivation is concerned. The larger group consists of choice subjects for the tropical aquarium, notably the magnificent Madagascar lace plant *(Aponogeton madagascariensis)* with its large lattice-like submerged leaves. Although not quite typical of this group, its requirements are very specialized. This group requires a fairly deep tank, the water kept to at least 60°F (16°C) in winter, higher in summer. The smaller group, typified by *A. distachyos,* is more cold hardy and vigorous. These plants can be grown outdoors in temperate climates so long as the water has no more than a thin crust of ice from time to time in winter. They are easily grown, planted into the bottom mud or sand. Propagate by division of the tubers, or from seed.

Aponogeton
distachyos *(below left)*
WATER HAWTHORN

From southern Africa, this plant makes an interesting ornamental for garden ponds, but is best not grown too close to waterlilies *(Nymphaea)*, as its densely massed foliage tends to smother them. Hawthorn-scented white flower spikes, 2–4 in (5–10 cm) long and of a curious Y-shape, are produced from late spring to autumn and sometimes into winter, turning green as they age and bend into the water, where the fruit ripens. It will grow in temperate climates provided the water does not freeze. **ZONES 8–10.**

Aquilegia caerulea *(right)*
BLUE COLUMBINE, ROCKY MOUNTAIN
COLUMBINE

This short-lived, upright,
alpine species from the Rocky
Mountains grows to 24 in
(60 cm) or more in height with
a rather narrow growth habit.
It is Colorado's state flower and
arguably the finest of the wild
columbines. Large, powdery
blue and white nodding flowers
on branching stems appear in
late spring and early summer.
It sometimes produces a few
blooms in autumn. It does
best in rich soil. ZONES 3–9.

Aquilegia atrata *(above)*
DARK COLUMBINE

Native to the alpine woodlands of Europe but
tolerant of milder conditions, this species closely
resembles the common columbine *(Aquilegia
vulgaris)* but has dark violet-purple flowers with
protruding yellow stamens, borne in late spring
and early summer. Preferring part-shade in
warmer areas, it grows to around 18 in (45 cm)
tall. ZONES 3–9.

AQUILEGIA
COLUMBINE

The common name comes from the Latin
for dove, as the flowers were thought to
resemble a cluster of doves. Native to
Europe, North America and temperate
regions of Asia, these graceful, clump-
forming perennials are grown for their
spurred, bell-shaped—single and double
forms—flowers in a varied color range, and
for their fern-like foliage. Some are also
useful as cut flowers, and the dwarf and
alpine species make good rock garden
plants. They flower mostly in late spring and
early summer, and look best in bold clumps
with a foreground planting of annuals.

CULTIVATION
Frost hardy, they prefer well-drained light
soil, enriched with manure, and a sunny site
protected from strong winds and with
some shade in hot areas. In cold climates
columbines are perennials and need to be
cut to the ground in late winter, but growing
larger-flowered cultivars as annuals usually
gives best results. Propagate by division or
from seed in autumn and spring; many of
them self-seed readily.

Aquilegia elegantula *(below)*

This species from the Rocky Mountains and northern Mexico is closely allied to *Aquilegia formosa* but is smaller, to 24 in (60 cm), and the pale orange or yellow flowers are slightly longer-spurred. **ZONES 5–9.**

Aquilegia canadensis *(right)*
AMERICAN WILD COLUMBINE

This native of eastern North America produces masses of nodding, red and yellow flowers with medium-length spurs, on 18–24 in (45–60 cm) stems in late spring and early summer. It is tolerant of full sun, provided there is plenty of moisture. It will also tolerate heat if some shade is provided. Hummingbirds love the nectar-rich flowers. **ZONES 3–9.**

Aquilegia 'Crimson Star' *(left)*

These long-spurred aquilegias usually face their flowers upwards to the viewer, in contrast to the pendent flowers of the short-spurred granny's bonnets. The nectar spurs, which in other aquilegias normally match the color of the petals of which they are a prolongation, match the crimson of the sepals in this cultivar. **ZONES 3–10.**

Aquilegia chrysantha *(below)*
GOLDEN COLUMBINE

This is among the showiest of the North American columbines, with large, long-spurred, fragrant yellow flowers on stems often exceeding 3 ft (1 m) in height. Native to southwestern North America, it is more tolerant of sun and heat than most. White and double-flowered cultivars are available. **ZONES 3–10.**

Aquilegia flabellata *(right)*

This hardy alpine species from Japan and Korea has soft, blue-green, ferny leaves and nodding, blue-purple flowers with short hooked spurs. A summer-flowering species, it grows to about 18 in (45 cm) high. ZONE 5.

Aquilegia, McKana Hybrid cultivar *(below)*

Aquilegia, McKana Hybrids

This best-known strain of long-spurred columbines is derived from North American species, chiefly *Aquilegia caerulea, A. chrysantha* and *A. formosa.* They bear flowers in a wide range of colors in late spring and early summer. Whatever the color of the sepals, the 5 petals that carry the spurs are usually white or yellow. Pinching off spent flowers will prolong the season. The plants grow to 3 ft (1 m) or more. ZONES 3–10.

Aquilegia formosa
(left)

WESTERN COLUMBINE

This attractive species with long-spurred, nodding, pale scarlet flowers and protruding stamens comes from the Pacific Northwest of North America and is the parent of many popular garden cultivars. The flowering stems reach up to 3 ft (1 m) and are held above ferny leaflets. Its main flowering season is late spring and early summer. ZONES 5–9.

A

Aquilegia vulgaris
GRANNY'S BONNETS, COLUMBINE

This is the true columbine of Europe, one of the parents of many hybrids. It grows to 3 ft (1 m) high with a spread of 18 in (45 cm) or more. On long stems from the center of a loose rosette of gray-green foliage, it bears funnel-shaped, short-spurred flowers, typically dull blue in wild plants but ranging through pink, crimson, white and purple in garden varieties. The cultivar **'Nora Barlow'** has double flowers of a curious form, with many narrow, greenish sepals and pink petals that lack spurs. ZONES 3–10.

Aquilegia vulgaris,
double form *(left)*

Aquilegia vulgaris
'Nora Barlow' *(below left)*

Aquilegia vulgaris
cultivar *(below)*

A

ARABIS
ROCK CRESS

Over 120 species make up this northern hemisphere genus of annuals and perennials, the latter mostly evergreen. Although some can reach as much as 3 ft (1 m) in height, species grown in gardens are dwarf, often mat-forming perennials suited to the rock garden, dry walls and crevices. They spread by short rhizomes, producing crowded tufts of spatula-shaped leaves. Short sprays of delicate, 4-petalled flowers are held above the foliage in spring and summer.

CULTIVATION

They grow best in very well-drained soil in a sunny position. Propagation is from seed or from cuttings taken in summer, or by division.

Arabis caucasica
var. *brevifolia* (right)

Arabis caucasica
(below right)
syn. *Arabis albida*
WALL ROCK CRESS

This tough, evergreen perennial is sometimes used to overplant spring-flowering bulbs. Easily grown, it forms dense clusters of thick foliage up to 6 in (15 cm) high and 18 in (45 cm) wide. In spring it has white flowers on loose racemes above gray-green leaf rosettes. There are various forms of *Arabis caucasica* such as **'Pinkie'**, **A. c. var. brevifolia** and double-flowered forms such as **'Flore Pleno'** (syn. 'Plena'). ZONES 4–10.

Arabis blepharophylla (above)
CALIFORNIA ROCK CRESS

This moderately frost-hardy Californian native, which grows at low altitudes, forms a compact clump 4–6 in (10–15 cm) high. It has tufts of toothed green leaves that extend into short, leafy spikes of pink to purple flowers during spring. It is best in a rockery or crevice where it will not be overrun. The most available cultivar is **'Frühlingzauber'** (syn. 'Spring Charm'), with rich rose purple flowers. ZONES 7–10.

A

ARCTOTHECA

This is a South African genus composed of 5 species of rosette-forming perennials, some with prostrate short stems, others lacking any aboveground stem. The growth form is dandelion-like, with flower stems emerging from the center of the foliage rosette. The toothed or lobed leaves are densely coated in downy, white hairs, on the undersides only in some species and on both sides in others. The daisy-like flowerheads are borne singly on short stems. They are usually pale yellow or brownish yellow. In warmer temperate climates some species naturalize freely, in places becoming troublesome weeds.

CULTIVATION

Arctotheca species are very easily grown in any well-drained soil in full sun. They are marginally frost hardy and are propagated from seed or by removing small offset rosettes from established clumps.

Arctotheca calendula (right)
CAPE DANDELION, CAPE WEED

A short-lived species that often pops up in lawns, Cape dandelion can be cultivated as a ground cover. In some parts of the world it is regarded as a trouble-some weed, choking vegetable crops and tainting cows' milk. Its leaves are around 6 in (15 cm) long and the light yellow flower-heads, about 2 in (5 cm) in diameter, appear in continuous succession on short stems from the center of the rosette from spring to autumn. Plants that are sub-jected to frequent mowing are far smaller than those that are left to develop naturally.
ZONES 8–11.

Arctotheca populifolia (below)

This species occurs naturally on beaches and coastal dunes, its prostrate stems becoming buried by loose sand. It has become naturalized along coasts of southern Australia. Its 3 in (8 cm) long leaves are often elliptical in shape and unlobed with a dense felty coating of white hairs on both sides. The yellow flowerheads are small, $^{1}/_{2}$–1 in (12–25 mm) in diameter on very short stalks, and appear from summer to autumn.
ZONES 9–11.

Arctotis cumbletonii
(right)

A

Arctotis fastuosa
(below)
syn. *Venidium fastuosum*
CAPE DAISY, MONARCH OF THE VELD

A perennial from the open veld in South Africa's western Cape Province, this is an adaptable plant and can be treated as an annual in colder regions. It will grow 24 in (60 cm) high, with silvery green, lobed leaves and glistening orange flowerheads with purple zones at the base of each of the many ray petals and a black central disc. It is a colorful choice for a sunny position in the garden. ZONES 9–11.

ARCTOTIS
syns *Venidium,* × *Venidioarctotis*
AFRICAN DAISY

This genus consists of about 50 species of annuals and evergreen perennials from South Africa. The stems and leaves are to varying degrees coated in matted downy hairs, giving them a gray-green or silvery gray color. The showy flowers are typical of the daisy family. They rely on the sun to open fully and come in a range of colors from creamy yellow often through orange to deep pinks and claret reds. Many hybrids are now available, their blooms with rings of darker color towards the center. Growth habit varies from compact and shrubby to quite prostrate, plants of the latter type making a faster-spreading and colorful ground cover. Some of the more distinctive *Arctotis* species include *A. arctotoides,* with narrow, deeply lobed leaves, and *A. cumbletonii* with narrow disc florets.

CULTIVATION
Given plenty of space in full sun and well-drained, sandy soil, arctotises may be used as bedding plants or to cover a large area of dry bank. Flowering can be prolonged if blooms are deadheaded after the first flush in early summer. Propagate from seed or cuttings, which can be rooted at any time of year.

A

Arctotis hirsuta
(left)

This annual species of
Arctotis has lobed,
hairy, gray-green leaves.
The flowers, in shades
of orange and yellow to
white, are borne in
spring to mid-summer.
Arctotis hirsuta is best
propagated from seeds
sown in early autumn.
ZONES 9–11.

Arctotis Hybrid,
'Apricot' *(left)*

Arctotis Hybrid,
'Dream Coat' *(below)*

Arctotis Hybrids

These plants were
known until recently as
× *Venidioarctotis*
hybrids, one of the main
parent species having
being placed in the
genus *Venidium* (now
combined with *Arctotis*).
They are grown as
annual bedding plants
in frost-prone areas but
will overwinter in milder
climates. Growing to a
height and spread of
around 18 in (45 cm),
they have gray, lobed
leaves that are quite
downy beneath. In
summer and autumn
they produce a long
succession of showy
blooms, to 3 in (8 cm)
across in a very wide
range of colors, often
2-toned. **'Gold Bi-
Color', 'Apricot',
'Flame', 'Dream Coat'**
and **'Wine'** are among
the more popular
named hybrids.
ZONES 9–11.

A

Arctotis Hybrid,
'Flame' *(right)*

Arctotis Hybrid,
'Wine' *(right)*

Arctotis Hybrid,
'Gold Bi-Color' *(below)*

A

ARENARIA
SANDWORT

This genus is composed of around 160 species of mainly mound-forming or ground cover perennials, some of which become shrubby with age. They are widespread in the northern hemisphere, with a few southern hemisphere species too. The plants commonly develop a dense mass of fine stems clothed with tiny, deep green or gray-green leaves and small, usually white, flowers in spring or summer. The flowers may be borne singly or in small clusters.

CULTIVATION
They are easily grown in any moist, well-drained soil in full sun. They are ideal rockery or tub plants and are generally very frost hardy. Propagate from seed, self-rooted layers or small tip cuttings.

Arenaria balearica
(left)

Native to the islands of the western Mediterranean, this miniature species forms a mat of stems that root as they spread. The shiny, bright green leaves are less than ¹/₄ in (6 mm) long and are almost circular. The plant is dotted profusely with ¹/₄ in (6 mm) wide, green-centered, white flowers in spring and summer. ZONES 7–9.

Arenaria montana
(below)

This species from south-west Europe is larger than most arenarias in both leaves and flowers. It has gray-green leaves up to 1¹/₂ in (35 mm) long and mounds to about 6 in (15 cm) tall. Its flowering stems tend to be rather upright and extend slightly above the foliage clump. The abundant flowers are nearly 1 in (25 mm) in diameter, pure white with yellow-green centers. ZONES 4–9.

Arenaria tetraquetra *(below)*

This is a densely foliaged, 1–2 in (2.5–5 cm) high, cushion plant from the mountains of southwest Europe. It has tiny overlapping leaves that give it a heather-like appearance. Small, white flowers are massed at the stem tips in spring. ZONES 6–9.

ARGEMONE
PRICKLY POPPY

This is a genus of 29 species of poppy-like plants native to the Americas, occurring mostly in drier subtropical regions. Most are annuals or perennials, but one is a shrub. They tend to be upright growers, many reaching 4 ft (1.2 m) or more tall, with strong stems and lobed leaves. In many species the stems, leaves and flowerbuds are a pale blue-gray and are covered in sharp prickles. The flowers, mainly yellow or orange, are from 2–6 in (5–15 cm) in diameter, usually 6-petalled and appearing throughout the warmer months. Several species, first grown as ornamentals, have become troublesome weeds of crops and waste places. They are all poisonous.

CULTIVATION
They are very easily grown in any well-drained soil in full sun. Hardiness varies with the species, though most will tolerate moderate frosts. Propagate from seed. Some species self-sow and become invasive.

Argemone mexicana (below)
This annual species is native to Mexico and nearby areas of the Caribbean but has spread widely through warmer parts of the world as a weed of crops and waste ground. It has prickly, white-marked, grayish green leaves and fragrant, yellow, poppy-like flowers about 2 in (5 cm) wide appearing in summer. It has an erect habit, growing to 3 ft (1 m) high. ZONES 8–11.

A

Aristea ecklonii
(left)

This vigorous, ever-
green from southeastern
Africa is 18–24 in
(45–60 cm) tall. It
forms tangled clumps
of long, lanceolate
green leaves, above
which starry, deep blue
flowers appear rather
sparsely in summer.
ZONES 9–11.

ARISTEA

This genus contains around 50 species of mainly evergreen,
rhizomatous, iris-like perennials from tropical and southern
Africa and Madagascar. They form clumps of sword-shaped leaves
from 8–36 in (20–90 cm) tall depending on the species. The ½–1 in
(12–25 mm) wide, 6-petalled flowers are clustered along erect,
cane-like stems and are usually in shades of blue or purple. The
flowering season ranges from late winter to summer.

CULTIVATION

Aristeas thrive on stream banks, in moist, sandy, humus-rich soil in
full sun or light shade. Most species are hardy to about 25°F (−4°C)
but are damaged if subjected to frequent frosts. Older plants do not
transplant well, so division may not always be successful. Propagation
from seed in autumn or spring usually produces an abundance.

ARISTOLOCHIA
DUTCHMAN'S PIPE, BIRTHWORT

A

This large genus of over 500 species comprises evergreen and deciduous, twining climbers and some herbaceous perennials, native to many different climatic regions. The climbers are most often cultivated, chosen for their heart-shaped leaves and unusually shaped tubular flowers, which have a swelling at the base and a hood above, usually with a sharply bent tube between them. Insects are attracted into the mouth of the flowers by a strong scent, and pollen is scattered over their bodies. The fruit are also curiously shaped, dangling from slender stalks and splitting at maturity to spill fine seed as they rock in the breeze.

CULTIVATION
The plants require well-drained, humus-rich soil in a sunny position with some shade in summer, and support for their climbing habit. Many have some degree of frost tolerance and will grow vigorously in warm-temperate climates. In spring, prune the previous year's growth to 2 to 3 nodes. Propagate from seed in spring or from cuttings in summer. Watch out for spider mites.

Aristolochia clematitis (below)
BIRTHWORT

Now seldom grown in gardens, this European species was used by medieval midwives, following the medieval Doctrine of Signatures—a belief that the Creator had marked plants in such a way that doctors could recognize diseases they were intended to cure. The womb-like shape of the birthwort flower indicated that the plant would help in problems of childbirth.
ZONES 5–9.

A

ARMERIA
THRIFT, SEA PINK

This genus of about 35 species of low-growing, tufted, early summer-flowering perennials grows in a wide variety of environments in the temperate zones of Eurasia, Africa and the Americas—from salt marshes and storm-swept headlands to alpine meadows. The crowded, narrow, mostly evergreen leaves usually form a dense mound, and atop each slender stalk are small flowers crowded into globular heads.

CULTIVATION
They are suitable for rock gardens or borders and prefer exposed, sunny positions and rather dry soil with good drainage. They are generally frost hardy. Propagate from seed or cuttings in spring or autumn.

Armeria alliacea
(left)

Occurring widely in the western half of Europe, this is one of the more robust species, with large tufts of long, soft, flat, deep green leaves and numerous bright reddish purple flower-heads on stems up to 18 in (45 cm) tall. **ZONES 5–9.**

A

Armeria leucocephala 'Corsica' *(right)*

Armeria leucocephala

A dwarf, densely mound-forming
perennial from the Mediterranean
islands of Corsica and Sardinia, this
attractive species has tangled, fine,
linear leaves up to 4 in (10 cm) long,
often finely hairy, as are the fine flower
stalks, up to 15 in (38 cm) tall. The
small flowerheads vary in color; it is
usually **'Corsica'** with brick-red summer flowers that is seen in gardens.
ZONES 7–9.

Armeria maritima *(below)*
COMMON THRIFT, SEA PINK

Native around much of the northern
hemisphere, thrift grows to 4 in
(10 cm) high and to 8 in (20 cm)
wide, and forms a mound-like mass
of narrow, dark green leaves. Dense
flowerheads of small, white to pink
flowers are produced in spring and
summer. Most *Armeria* cultivars are
derived from this species. **'Vindictive'**
has vibrant rose pink flowers. **'Alba'**
has small white flowers. ZONES 4–9.

ARTEMISIA
WORMWOOD

This large genus of evergreen and deciduous perennials and shrubs from temperate regions of the northern hemisphere has many species from arid and semi-arid environments. They are grown for their decorative foliage, which is often aromatic, sometimes repellent to insects and may be coated with whitish hairs. Attractive in a flower border, the feathery foliage provides year-round interest. The small yellowish flowerheads are not showy.

CULTIVATION

Mostly quite frost hardy, they prefer an open, sunny situation with light, well-drained soil. Prune back lightly in spring to stimulate growth. Propagate from cuttings in summer or by division in spring. Transplant during winter.

Artemisia arborescens *(below)*

This spreading, evergreen perennial from the Mediterranean region reaches a height of 4 ft (1.2 m) with a rounded habit and lacy, silver-gray foliage. Small, yellowish blooms are borne in summer and early autumn. Only moderately frost hardy, it is a good plant for the back of a border. ZONES 8–11.

Artemisia absinthium *(left)*
COMMON WORMWOOD, ABSINTHE

Of wide natural occurrence in Europe and temperate Asia, common wormwood grows to 3 ft (1 m) though often rather lower, with much divided, dull gray foliage. It is a perennial that spreads by rhizomes, the tangled, flopping stems also rooting as they spread. Inconspicuous, dull yellow flowerheads are borne in late summer. Trim after flowering to keep neat. **'Lambrook Silver'**, with its tidy habit is considered one of the better silver-leaved shrubs, and provides a restful contrast to brightly colored flowers in a herbaceous border. ZONES 4–10.

Artemisia caucasica (right)
syns *Artemisia lanata,*
A. pedemontana

Widely distributed through southern European mountains from Spain to the Ukraine and the Caucasus, this is a semi-deciduous or evergreen perennial less than 12 in (30 cm) high and of spreading habit, with soft, silvery grayish leaves divided into very narrow lobes. In summer it produces short spikes of dull yellow flowerheads. ZONES 5–9.

Artemisia dracunculus (left)
TARRAGON

Native to central and eastern Europe and grown for its narrow, aromatic, green leaves which have a delicate, peppery aniseed flavor, tarragon grows up to 3 ft (1 m) in the warmer months, dying back to a perennial rootstock over winter. As it does not produce seed, propagate by division in early spring. The tarragon seed sometimes offered is the flavorless *Artemisia dracunculoides,* known as Russian tarragon. ZONES 6–9.

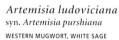

Artemisia ludoviciana
syn. *Artemisia purshiana*
WESTERN MUGWORT, WHITE SAGE

Native to western North America and Mexico, this rhizomatous species is grown for its lance-shaped, sometimes coarsely toothed leaves, which are densely white-felted beneath and gray- to white-haired above. Bell-shaped, grayish flowerheads are produced in summer. A spreading, invasive species, it reaches 4 ft (1.2 m) high and is very frost hardy. **'Valerie Finnis'**, with its jagged leaf margins, together with **'Silver Queen'** are 2 of several popular cultivars. ZONES 4–10.

Artemisia ludoviciana
'Silver Queen' (right)

A

Arthropodium cirratum *(left)*
RENGA RENGA LILY

This New Zealand species bears graceful sprays of starry white flowers on a 24 in (60 cm) stem above tufts of broad, handsome leaves in late spring. It looks a little like a hosta and is a good substitute in the hot-summer climates in which hostas languish. The Maoris used the fleshy roots in medicine. **ZONES 8–10.**

ARTHROPODIUM

The ungainly name *Arthropodium* is from the Greek and means having a jointed foot, referring to the way the footstalk of each flower has a joint in the middle. Of this genus of a dozen or so perennials from Australasia, only 2 or 3 are seen in gardens, the most ornamental being the New Zealand renga renga, *A. cirratum.*

CULTIVATION
Essentially warm-temperate plants, in cool areas they need a sheltered spot in fertile, well-drained soil. Propagate from seed or by division.

Arthropodium milleflorum *(right)*
Native to Australia, this deciduous species with tuberous roots has long, narrow leaves and in late spring bears numerous, small, pale lilac flowers on 24 in (60 cm) tall stems. The effect is rather like an ornamental grass and it would be a good choice for this role in warm-temperate flowerbeds. The species name means 'thousand-flowers', which is perhaps an exaggeration. **ZONES 8–11.**

ARUNCUS
GOAT'S BEARD

A

There are 3 species in this genus of rhizomatous perennials, occurring widely over temperate and subarctic regions of the northern hemisphere. Their appearance is very much that of a giant astilbe, with ferny basal leaves up to 3 ft (1 m) long and summer plumes of tiny cream flowers in 8–18 in (20–45 cm) long, pyramidal panicles carried on wiry stems that hold them well above the foliage.

CULTIVATION
They are best grown in sun or part-shade in moist, humus-rich, well-drained soil around edges of ponds. Goat's beard is very frost hardy and is propagated from seed or by division.

Aruncus dioicus
'Kneiffii' *(below)*

Aruncus dioicus
(above)
syns *Aruncus sylvestris, Spiraea aruncus*

A graceful, woodland perennial, this clump-forming plant produces a mass of rich green, fern-like foliage and arching plumes of tiny, greenish or creamy white flowers in summer. It grows 6 ft (1.8 m) tall and 4 ft (1.2 m) wide. Cut flowering stems back hard in autumn. **'Kneiffii'** reaches about 3 ft (1 m) and has cream-colored flowers. ZONES 3–9.

A

Asarum arifolium
(left)

This is a variable, evergreen species from southeastern USA with large, elongated, heart-shaped leaves up to about 6 in (15 cm) long, marked with lighter green between the prominent veins. **ZONES 7–9.**

ASARUM
WILD GINGER

This genus, belonging to the same family as *Aristolochia* (Dutchman's pipe), consists of over 70 species of rhizomatous perennials, both evergreen and deciduous, distributed widely through temperate areas of the northern hemisphere but most numerous in Japan and the USA. They are better known for their use in traditional medicine than as ornamental plants, though the foliage can make an attractive ground cover in shaded woodland gardens. The leaves are either kidney- or heart-shaped, and the small, bell-shaped flowers, which are usually hidden below the leaves, are mostly dull brownish or purplish and open at the mouth into 3 sharply reflexed sepals. Some examples include *Asarum chinense, A. maximum, A. muramatui* and *A. sieboldii.* All 4 species have very attractive foliage.

Asarum muramatui
(below)

CULTIVATION
These plants prefer a shady site in moist, well-drained soil and can be planted out any time between autumn and spring. They spread rapidly; divide the clumps every few years in spring. They can also be propagated from seed. They are prone to attack from slugs and snails.

Asarum canadense *(right)*
CANADIAN SNAKEROOT

This deciduous perennial native to the woodlands
of eastern North America forms tufted mats with
fleshy, creeping rhizomes and coarse-textured,
heart-shaped leaves, 2–3 in (5–8 cm) wide rising
on hairy stalks to 8 in (20 cm) high. Hidden
beneath in spring are inconspicuous, brown, bell-
shaped flowers. Decoctions of the rhizomes were
used medicinally by Native Americans and white
settlers. ZONES 3–8.

Asarum caudatum *(left)*
BRITISH COLUMBIA WILD GINGER

Native to the coastal mountains of western North
America, this ground-hugging, evergreen perennial
grows in relatively deep shade on the forest floor.
Spreading by rhizomes, it forms irregular, open
patches and flowers from late spring into summer.
Large, 6 in (15 cm) long, kidney-shaped leaves rise
to 8 in (20 cm) above ground, hiding the brownish
purple blooms. ZONES 6–9.

Asarum europaeum *(right)*
ASARABACCA

Widely distributed in European woodlands, this
species has conspicuous shaggy hairs on both the
creeping rhizomes and the 4–6 in (10–15 cm) long
leaf stalks. The deep-green, glossy leaves are
kidney-shaped to almost circular, up to 3 in (8 cm)
wide. The dull purplish flowers, hidden under the
leaves, are insignificant, only about ¹/₂ in (12 mm)
long. Asarabacca was formerly used medicinally
and as an ingredient in snuff powders, but is
moderately toxic. ZONES 6–9.

Asarum maximum *(left)*

Native to China, this species has the heart-shaped
leaves typical of many within the genus, but they
are characterized by gray mottling, which contrasts well with the dark green base color. In
spring it produces 2 in (5 cm) wide pear-shaped
red-purple flowers with white or yellow markings.
ZONES 7–10.

ASCLEPIAS
MILKWEED

Found naturally in the Americas, this genus consists of over
100 species of perennials, subshrubs and (rarely) shrubs and includes
both evergreen and deciduous plants. Most have narrow, pointed
elliptical to lance-shaped leaves and all have milky white sap. The
flowers are borne in stalked clusters arising from the upper leaf
axils. They are small, with 5 reflexed petals below a waxy corona, a
feature characteristic of the milkwood family (see also *Hoya*).
Elongated seed pods follow; the seeds have silky plumes and are
dispersed on the breeze. Their sap is acrid and poisonous, and the
butterfly larvae that feed on them are toxic to predators such as
birds. A few species have become widespread weeds of warmer
regions. Some African species with inflated, prickly pods are now
placed in the genus *Physocarpus*.

CULTIVATION
They are easily grown in any
well-drained soil in full sun.
Hardiness varies considerably
with the species. Some of the
shorter-lived perennials may
be treated as annuals, and
are usually raised from seed.
Some hardier North American
species require a cool climate
and will not survive in the
dormant state where winters
are too warm. Propagate
from seed or semi-ripe
cuttings.

Asclepias speciosa
(below)

A 3 ft (1 m) tall peren-
nial from eastern North
America, this species
has oval leaves up to
6 in (15 cm) long. The
flowers are dull pinkish
red and white and up
to 1 in (25 mm) in
diameter. The fruit
have soft spines.
ZONES 2–9.

A

Asperula setosa
(right)

Native to Turkey, this annual species grows to about 12 in (30 cm) high with very narrow, small leaves and lilac flowers arranged in dense clusters at the branch tips. ZONES 5–9.

ASPERULA
WOODRUFF

There are around 100 species of annuals, perennials and small, twiggy subshrubs in this genus, distinguished from the closely related *Galium* by the generally longer tube of the small flowers. They occur mainly in temperate regions of Europe, Asia and Australasia. Most are densely foliaged mat- or tuft-forming perennials with tiny, narrow leaves arranged in whorls of 4 or more on the fine stems. In spring and summer the plants may be smothered in tiny flowers, usually white, pale pink or occasionally yellow. Most species spread by underground runners and a few of the woodland species grow to around 24 in (60 cm) high, with larger, bright green leaves. Like galiums, asperulas often develop fragrance as the cut foliage dries and some were once used as strewing herbs; at least one species yields a dye.

CULTIVATION
The small species generally do best in rockery conditions with gritty, well-drained soil in full sun. They can be raised from seed, from small rooted pieces removed from the clump, or by division.

Asperula arcadiensis *(below)*

This perennial Greek species makes a woody based tuft of foliage to 6 in (15 cm) high. The narrow leaves are gray and downy, about ½ in (12 mm) long. The tiny flowers are pink to pale purple. ZONES 5–9.

A

Asphodeline lutea
(left)

ASPHODEL, KING'S SPEAR

A native of the Mediterranean region eastward from Italy, this fragrant, frost-hardy plant can grow to 5 ft (1.5 m), though usually rather less so. Tufts of narrow, glossy leaves appear below spear-like stems bearing spikes of yellow, star-shaped flowers, some $1^1/4$ in (30 mm) wide. The plants should be kept moist before the flowering period in spring. **ZONES 6–10.**

ASPHODELINE
JACOB'S ROD

This is a genus of some 20 species of biennial and perennial lilies, native to the Mediterranean region and Asia Minor. The name indicates their close similarity to *Asphodelus*. They have thick, fleshy roots, from which sprout narrow, grassy to spear-shaped leaves that are usually bright green, sometimes with a bluish tint. Stiffly upright flower spikes up to 5 ft (1.5 m) tall develop in summer. They carry large numbers of star-shaped yellow, white or pale pink flowers on the upper half of the stem.

CULTIVATION
These plants are very frost hardy and easily grown in any well-drained soil in full sun. Propagate from seed or by division in winter or early spring. Try to avoid damaging the roots or they may rot.

ASPHODELUS

When Tennyson's lotus eaters 'rested weary
limbs at last on beds of asphodel', it was the
plant now known as *Asphodelus albus* on which
they probably reclined—the name *asphodelos*
goes back to the ancient Greeks. The genus
consists of 12 species of fleshy-rooted annual
and perennial lilies, native to the Mediterranean
region and to western Asia as far as the
Himalayas. They have basal tufts of narrow,
grass-like leaves and 6-petalled, starry, white,
green or pink flowers borne along stiff, upright
stems, which may be branched. Spring and
summer are the main flowering seasons.

CULTIVATION

Hardiness varies with the species, though most
will tolerate moderate frosts. They require
reasonably sunny, warm, dry summer conditions
to flower well and prefer a light, sandy, humus-rich
soil with good drainage. Propagate by division
immediately after flowering or from seed.

Asphodelus aestivus *(left)*

Widely distributed
around the Mediterra-
nean, this species grows
to a height of about 3 ft
(1 m), with broad,
leathery basal leaves.
The branched panicles,
elongating in spring,
bear white to very pale
pink flowers as much as
3 in (8 cm) across, the
petals with darker
mid-lines. ZONES 6–10.

Asphodelus albus *(above)*

Native to Europe and
North Africa, *Asphodelus
albus* is probably the
most commonly culti-
vated species in the
genus. It has thick,
fleshy roots and sword-
shaped leaves up to
24 in (60 cm) long. The
12–36 in (30–90 cm)
tall flower stems bear
pinkish brown striped,
white flowers along
most of their length in
spring, those at the base
opening first. The
variable bracts—white
or brown—are especially
noticeable before the
star-shaped flowers
open. ZONES 5–10.

A

ASTELIA

This genus of some 25 species of rhizomatous, evergreen perennials has a scattered distribution around the southern hemisphere including the Falkland Islands, Mauritius and Réunion, southeastern Australia and New Zealand, the latter being the richest in species. The bold, sword-shaped leaves are arranged in rosettes or tufts and the plants vary in stature from about 2 in (5 cm) to 8 ft (2.4 m) or even more. Most have a silvery coating of fine, silky hairs on the leaves, though this may be confined to the undersides. Habitats vary from alpine bogs to temperate rainforests, the larger-growing species generally in the latter, sometimes as epiphytes. Inconspicuous flowers are often hidden by the foliage but in many species are followed by showy clusters of brightly colored berries. There are separate male and female flowers, on the same plant in some species, on separate plants in others.

CULTIVATION

They are easily grown in moist, peaty, well-drained soil in full sun or part-shade; a few species will grow in boggy soil. Hardiness varies, though most species will tolerate light frosts. Propagate from seed or by division.

Astelia nervosa
(above)
KAKAHA

Spreading 6 ft (1.8 m) or more and up to 36 in (90 cm) high, this vigorously clumping, New Zealand species is valued for its narrow arching leaves thinly coated with silvery hairs and growing 2–6 ft (0.6–1.8 m) long. In summer, starry, light brown fragrant flowers form in clusters on the ends of long, slender stems. These are followed by small green fruit, which turn orange-red when ripe.
ZONES 9–10.

A

Aster 'Coombe's Violet'
(right)

ASTER
MICHAELMAS OR EASTER DAISY, ASTER

Native to temperate regions of the northern hemisphere (most numerous in North America), this large genus of perennials and deciduous or evergreen subshrubs has over 250 species, ranging from miniatures suitable for rock gardens to 6 ft (1.8 m) giants. The simple leaves are mostly smooth edged, sometimes hairy, often quite small. Showy, daisy-like flowerheads are usually produced in late summer or autumn in a wide range of colors, including blue, violet, purple, pink, red and white, all with a central disc of yellow or purple. There are many aster cultivars once listed under the parent species, but this has become too complex and many now stand alone. A typical example is *Aster* 'Coombe's Violet'. The 'China asters' grown as bedding annuals are now placed in the genus *Callistephus*.

CULTIVATION
Easily grown, they prefer sun (or part-shade in hot areas) in a well-drained soil, preferably enriched with compost. Keep moist at all times and shelter from strong winds and stake the taller species. Cut the long stems down to ground level and tidy the clumps when the flowers have faded. Propagate by division in spring or late autumn, or from softwood cuttings in spring. Divide plants every 2 to 3 years, using the most vigorous outer part. Powdery mildew, rust, aphids and snails can be a problem.

Aster alpinus *(below)*
From the higher mountains of Europe, this clump-forming plant, usually about 6–12 in (15–30 cm) high and 18 in (45 cm) wide, bears large, violet-blue, daisy flowers with yellow centers from late spring until midsummer; the foliage is dark green. It is a popular rock garden plant and is fully frost hardy. There are a number of named cultivars. **'Trimix'** grows to 8 in (20 cm) and has flowers that are a tricolor mix of pink, blue and white. ZONES 3–9.

A

Aster amellus 'Breslau'
(left)

Aster amellus
'Blutendecke' *(below)*

Aster amellus
ITALIAN ASTER

The Italian aster, actually a native of the eastern half of Europe and also Turkey, is usually represented in gardens by its many cultivars. In its typical form it grows to 18–24 in (45–60 cm) with oblong basal leaves that can be somewhat hairy and erect stems which can become floppy if grown in too much shade. Although spreading by underground rhizomes, it is not considered invasive and is especially disease resistant. The large, fragrant flower-heads are pink and purple-blue, while popular cultivars are stronger in color and include **'King George'**, a deep violet, **'Violet Queen'**, somewhat paler, and the bright pink **'Sonia'**. **'Bluten-decke'** is a German Foerster selection dating from 1950. It grows to 18 in (45 cm) tall with silvery violet-blue flowers. **'Breslau'** was introduced by Kock of Germany in 1960 and is 18 in (45 cm) tall with violet-blue flowers. **'Sternkugel'** has paler flowers. ZONES 4–9.

Aster amellus
'Violet Queen'
(left)

A

Aster amellus
'Sternkugel' *(above)*

Aster amellus 'Sonia'
(below)

Aster amellus 'King
George' *(above)*

A

Aster divaricatus *(right)*
WHITE WOOD ASTER

Also from eastern North America, this is a distinctive species with slender, wiry, dark mahogany stems to about 24 in (60 cm) tall that tend to twist and wander, broad-based leaves tapering to fine points, and delicate, open sprays of small, white flowerheads. Spreading by rhizomes to form loose clumps, it is essentially a plant for the woodland garden. Some forms are taller and more robust. ZONES 3–9.

Aster ericoides *(left)*
HEATH ASTER

The specific name means 'with leaves like those of *Erica*', the heath genus, and indeed this species from eastern and central USA and northern Mexico has very small, narrow leaves, at least on the upper stems. With flowering stems rising up to 3 ft (1 m) high from tufted basal shoots towards mid-summer and into autumn, it provides a wonderful display of massed, small, white flowerheads as does one of its more compact cultivars, **'White Heather'**. There are a number of cultivars of varied heights, mostly with pale pinkish or yellowish blooms. The cut flowers are popular with florists. ZONES 4–10.

Aster ericoides
'White Heather'
(right)

Aster linosyris ×
A. sedifolius (right)

Aster linosyris
GOLDILOCKS ASTER

Very different from the
usual concept of an
aster, this species from
Europe, North Africa
and western Asia is a
rather insignificant
plant, but good for
areas where summers
are hot and dry.
Goldilocks aster grows
to 24 in (60 cm) in
height with very fine,
dull gray-green foliage
and erect sprays of
small yellow flower-
heads in late summer.
The heads lack the
usual ray florets—this
trait has dominated in
its hybrid with *Aster
sedifolius* (*A. linosyris* ×
A. sedifolius).
ZONES 4–10.

Aster novae-angliae
'Andenken an Alma
Pötschke' (left)

Aster novae-angliae
NEW ENGLAND ASTER

Originally native over a
wide area of the eastern
and central USA, this
species is represented
in cultivation by many
cultivars, showing
much variation in form
and color of blooms.
Vigorous clumps of
mostly vertical, 3–5 ft
(1–1.5 m) stems may
lean with the weight of
large, loose clusters of
daisies, making staking
necessary. Cultivars
include the late-
blooming, clear pink
'Harrington's Pink';
the rose pink, mildew-
resistant 'Barr's Pink';
the cerise 'September
Ruby'; and 'Hella
Lacy'. 'Andenken an
Alma Pötschke', often
shortened to 'Alma
Pötschke', is a com-
pact-growing, though
4 ft (1.2 m) tall plant
with bright rose pink
blooms. 'Dauerblau'
was introduced in 1950
by Foerster of Germany.
Its flowers open late
and it grows to 4 ft
(1.2 m) tall. They all
prefer moist, rich soil
in full sun. ZONES 4–9.

Aster novae-angliae
cultivar (left)

A

Aster novae-angliae
'Dauerblau' *(left)*

Aster novae-angliae
'Barr's Pink' *(below)*

A

Aster novi-belgii
NEW YORK ASTER

Novi-belgii is Linnaeus' attempt to translate New Amsterdam (now New York) into Latin; the Belgii were the tribe encountered by Julius Caesar in the Low Countries. The New York aster in its wild form is native to the east coast, from Newfoundland to Georgia. It has given rise to innumerable garden forms in colors ranging from the palest mauve to violet and deep pink, and with varying degrees of 'doubling' of the flowerheads. They are among the most useful plants for the perennial border in cooler-temperate climates, responding to generous feeding and watering in spring and summer. Watch for mildew. Cultivars include **'Court Herald'**; **'Mulberry'** has large, semi-double, rich mulberry red blooms. **'Ernest Ballard'**, named for a leading aster breeder, grows to 3 ft (1 m) with large, purple-red blooms. **'Audrey'** grows to a compact 12 in (30 cm) with double, lavender blue autumn flowers. **'Schone von Dietlikon'** has deep violet-blue flowers and grows to 4 ft (1.2 m) tall. ZONES 3–9.

Aster novi-belgii 'Ernest Ballard' *(above right)*

Aster novi-belgii 'Audrey' *(right)*

Aster novi-belgii 'Court Herald' *(below)*

A

Aster umbellatus *(below)*
FLAT-TOPPED ASTER

From eastern USA, this robust
aster can grow up to 4 ft
(1.2 m). By flowering time its
rather broad basal leaves have
withered, leaving only the
smaller stem leaves. In summer
it produces densely clustered
white flowerheads ³/₄–1 in
(18–25 mm) in diameter.
ZONES 3–9.

Aster novi-belgii
'Schone von Dietlikon'
(above)

Aster sedifolius
(right)

Native to central and
southern Europe, this
vigorous, spreading
perennial, sometimes
treated as an annual,
grows to 3 ft (1 m)
high. It has tiny leaves
and masses of pink,
violet-blue or purple
flowerheads over a long
flowering season that
can extend from late
spring through summer
to autumn. **ZONES 5–9.**

Astilbe, Arendsii Hybrid, 'Europa' *(above)*

Astilbe, Arendsii Hybrid, 'Brautschleier' *(above)*

Astilbe, **Arendsii Hybrids**
(above & right)

This hybrid group, derived from four east Asian species, *Astilbe astilboides*, *A. japonica*, *A. davidii* and *A. thunbergii*, is named after German horticulturalist Georg Arends (1863–1952) to whom many of the finest cultivars are credited. Heights vary from 18–48 in (0.45–1.2 m), with a spread of 18–30 in (45–75 cm). They produce feathery spikes from late spring to early summer. Cultivars are available in a range of colors from red through pink to white and include **'Amethyst'**, with pale purple to pink flowers; **'Fanal'** with long-lasting scarlet flowers; **'Brautschleier'** ('Bridal Veil'), white; **'Professor van der Wielen'**, white; **'Rheinland'**, deep rose; and **'Europa'**, pale pink flowers. ZONES 6–10.

ASTILBE
FALSE SPIRAEA

This genus of 14 species of pretty, early to late summer perennials comes mostly from eastern Asia, where they grow in the moist ground beside woodland streams though there are also 2 species occurring in the eastern USA. All astilbes have basal tufts of ferny, compound leaves, the leaflets usually sharply toothed. Pointed, plume-like panicles of tiny, white to pink or red flowers rise well above the foliage. Most usual in cultivation are the hybrids grouped under the name *Astilbe × arendsii*, though there are many recent hybrid cultivars of different parentage. The name 'spiraea' was mistakenly attached to this genus when they were introduced to England in the 1820s.

CULTIVATION
They need a lightly shaded place with rich, leafy soil that never dries out, though they do not like being actually flooded, especially in winter. Cooler climates suit them best; in hot summers they need constant watering to keep their roots cool. Good cut flowers, they also make pretty pot plants for bringing indoors for a while when the blooms are at their best. In a heated greenhouse they will flower early. Propagate by division in winter.

A

Astilbe, Arendsii Hybrid,
'Professor van der Wielen'
(above)

Astilbe 'Betsy Cuperus' (above)

One of the larger hybrid cultivars, this plant grows to over 3 ft (1 m) and has deep green foliage and arching sprays of pale peachy pink flowers. ZONES 6–10.

Astilbe, Arendsii Hybrid, 'Fanal' (left)

Astilbe chinensis

A late-summer-flower-
ing species native to
China, Korea and
eastern Siberia, this
attractive, clump-
forming plant reaches
24 in (60 cm) with
toothed, hairy, dark
green leaflets and dense,
fluffy flower spikes of
tiny, star-shaped, white,
flushed with pink
blooms. **'Pumila'**, a
dwarf form growing to
12 in (30 cm) with
pinkish mauve flowers,
will tolerate heavier
clay soils and will
spread quickly if
conditions are to its
liking. ***Astilbe chinensis***
var. *davidii,* to 6 ft
(1.8 m) with purple-
pink flowers crowded
on long, slender
panicles, has the added
interest of bronze-
toned new foliage. ***A. c.***
var. *taquetti* has
lavender-pink flowers
on a plant about 3 ft
(1 m) tall. ZONES 6–10.

Astilbe chinensis
'Pumila' *(above)*

Astilbe chinensis var.
davidii *(left)*

A

Astilbe 'Straussenfeder'
(right)

Bred in Germany, 'Straussenfeder' grows to 3 ft (1 m) tall, with decorative leaves and distinctive flowering panicles with drooping branches, the blooms rose pink. The name is German for 'ostrich feather'. ZONES 6–10.

Astilbe 'Serenade'
(below)

Often listed under *Astilbe chinensis*, but probably a hybrid, 'Serenade' has pinkish red flowers on stems up to 15 in (40 cm) high. Otherwise, it is very similar to *A. chinensis*. ZONES 5–10.

ASTRAGALUS
MILK VETCH

There are some 2,000 species of annuals, perennials and shrubs in this legume genus and they are found over much of the temperate zone of the northern hemisphere. The leaves are usually pinnate with up to 45 leaflets. A few have trifoliate leaves. Size varies considerably, from small cushion plants through to plants 5 ft (1.5 m) tall. The flowers are pea-like and are carried in spikes or racemes in the leaf axils near the top of the plant. A number of the west Asian species including *Astragalus gummifer* are the traditional source of gum tragacanth, a gelatinous gum used in cosmetics, pharmaceutical products and ice-creams, among other uses.

CULTIVATION,3
Plant in moist, well-drained soil in full sun. Most species will tolerate moderate to severe frosts. Propagate the annuals from seed, the perennials and shrubs from seed or small cuttings.

Astragalus
angustifolius *(above)*
A native of Greece and the Middle East, this species is an 18 in (45 cm) high, cushion-forming shrub with spiny stems. The leaves are pinnate with 5 to 12 pairs of leaflets. Racemes of 1 in (25 mm), cream to light purple flowers open in summer.
ZONES 7–9.

A

ASTRANTIA
MASTERWORT

All 10 species of this genus, an unusual member of the carrot family, are herbaceous perennials that occur in mountain meadows and woodlands of Europe and western Asia. Gardeners delight in their delicate flowerheads surrounded by a collar of pointed bracts, carried on wiry stems above clumps of deeply toothed, lobed foliage of soft mid-green.

CULTIVATION

Keeping in mind their natural habitat, these plants are best suited to moist, fertile, woodland conditions, or near the edges of streams or ponds where the soil is always moist. As long as the roots are kept moist they will tolerate full sun, indeed the variegated species color much better in such a position. In a suitable situation they will build up clumps. Propagate by division in early spring or from seed.

Astrantia major
(above)

Astrantia major
'Sunningdale Variegated'
(below)

Native to central and eastern Europe, this species has deeply lobed, palmate leaves forming a loose mound of foliage 18 in (45 cm) tall from which rise nearly bare stems to 24 in (60 cm) or more, each topped by intricately formed, soft pink or white, daisy-like flowerheads, surrounded by petal-like bracts in the same colors. The flowers are produced almost throughout summer. **'Rosea'** is slightly taller, with blooms of rich rose pink. **'Sunningdale Variegated'** is grown for the rich tapestry of its large yellow- and cream-marked leaves and for its delicate, pink-flushed white blooms.
ZONES 6–9.

Aubrieta × cultorum
'Cobalt Violet' *(left)*

Aubrieta × cultorum

There are many garden hybrids that come under this heading, plants with unknown parentage and with a wide range of growth and flowering habit. The flower color varies from white through pinks and purples to almost violet, some double, and some with variegated foliage. Some examples include **'Cobalt Violet'**, **'Purple Gem'** and **'Doctor Mules'**, which has rich blue-violet flowers. ZONES 4–9.

AUBRIETA
ROCK CRESS

Although mountain flowers, aubrietas are not diminutive and temperamental as are many alpine plants. Rather they make carpets of color at the front of flowerbeds, or down retaining walls. Not very tall—6 in (15 cm) or so at most—they will happily sprawl to several times their height and in spring cover themselves with 4-petalled flowers, mainly in shades of purple. About a dozen species are native to stony hillsides and mountains from the Mediterranean area to as far east as Iran. The plants most often seen in gardens are hybrids mainly derived from *Aubrieta deltoidea*. The genus name honors the French botanical painter Claude Aubriet (1668–1743); it has sometimes been spelt *Aubrietia*.

CULTIVATION
They are easy to grow in cool-temperate climates (flowering is erratic in warm ones), asking only for sunshine or a little shade and fertile, well-drained soil. They are short lived and it is wise to take a few cuttings in summer every 3 or 4 years; they are readily propagated also by division of the rhizomatous rootstock.

Aubrieta deltoidea
(below left)

Native to southeastern Europe and Turkey, this compact, mat-forming perennial has greenish gray leaves and masses of starry, mauve-pink flowers borne over a long period in spring. The species is now rare in gardens, most cultivated aubrietas being hybrids now known collectively as *Aubrieta × cultorum*, though they are commonly listed as *A. deltoidea*. ZONES 4–9.

Aubrieta gracilis
(right)

A delicate species form-
ing thin mats, *Aubrieta
gracilis* comes from
Greece and Albania. The
leaves are tiny and
narrow and the slender
3–4 in (8–10 cm)
flowering stems bear
$^1/_2$–$^3/_4$ in (12–18 mm)
wide purple flowers in
summer. **A. macedonica**
is a very similar species.
ZONES 5–9.

Aubrieta macedonica
(below)

A

Aurinia saxatilis
(right)
syn. *Alyssum saxatile*
BASKET OF GOLD, YELLOW
ALYSSUM

This native of central and southeastern Europe is the only commonly grown species. It has hairy, gray-green leaves, forms rather loose mounds to 10 in (25 cm) high and is smothered in bright yellow flowers in spring and early summer. It is very popular as a rockery or wall plant. There are a number of cultivars, including **'Argentea'** with very silvery leaves; **'Citrina'** with lemon yellow flowers; **'Gold Dust'**, up to 12 in (30 cm) mounds with deep golden yellow flowers; **'Sulphurea'** with glowing yellow flowers; and **'Tom Thumb'**, a 4 in (10 cm) high dwarf with small leaves. ZONES 4–9.

AURINIA

This is a genus of 7 species of biennials and evergreen perennials, formerly included in *Alyssum*, found from central and southern Europe to the Ukraine and Turkey. They are mainly small, spreading, mound-forming plants. The leaves are initially in basal rosettes, mostly fairly narrow. They bear elongated sprays of tiny yellow or white flowers in spring and early summer.

CULTIVATION
Plant in light, gritty, well-drained soil in full sun. They are ideal for rockeries, rock crevices or dry-stone walls. Most species are very frost hardy and are propagated from seed or small tip cuttings; they will self-sow in suitable locations.

BAPTISIA
FALSE INDIGO

Baptisia is a genus of 20–30 species of pea-flowered perennials that grow naturally among the tall grasses of the prairies and woodlands of eastern and central USA. The common name arises from the former use of some species by dyers as a substitute for true indigo *(Indigofera)*. Few of the species are grown much in gardens. Most are somewhat shrubby in habit, and the leaves are divided into 3 leaflets like a clover or a medic. The blue, purple, yellow or white pea-flowers are borne in terminal spikes over a fairly long summer season.

CULTIVATION
The plants prefer full sun and neutral, well-drained soil. They are not bothered by frost, nor do they resent very dry conditions in summer. As they have a deep root system they should not be transplanted or disturbed. Propagation is best done from seed in autumn or by division.

Baptisia alba *(above)*

This bushy, upright species grows to around 5 ft (1.5 m). Its bluish green foliage provides a backdrop to the sprays of pea-like blooms, white sometimes streaked with purple, borne during early summer. ZONES 7–10.

Baptisia australis
(left)
FALSE INDIGO

This summer-flowering perennial is attractive in both flower and foliage. The leaves are blue-green and form a loose mound up to about 4 ft (1.2 m) high and 3 ft (1 m) across. The lupin-like flowers are borne on erect spikes from early to mid-summer and are an unusual shade of purplish blue. The seed pods can be dried for indoor decoration. ZONES 3–10.

Begonia
'Cleopatra' *(right)*

This rhizomatous begonia is a popular, easy-to-grow plant with a dense mass of shortly creeping rhizomes that support crowded, sharply lobed, yellow-green and purplish brown leaves. Profuse, long-stalked sprays of pale pink flowers bloom in early spring. In warm climates it is a popular balcony plant, thriving in hot sun. **ZONES 10–12.**

BEGONIA

BEGONIA

Begonias are native to moist tropical and subtropical regions of all continents except Australia, and are most diverse in South America. There are over 1500 known species, ranging from rhizomatous perennials a few inches (centimeters) high to 10 ft (3 m) shrubs. Many are grown indoors, prized for their beautifully colored and textured foliage or showy flowers, sometimes both present on the one species or cultivar. Mostly evergreen, their broad, usually asymmetrical leaves have a rather brittle and waxy texture. Female flowers, as distinct from male flowers that are on the same plant, have broad, colored flanges on the ovaries, which develop into winged fruits. Begonia enthusiasts divide the species and cultivars into a number of classes depending on growth habit and type of rootstock. The **cane-stemmed** begonias are erect growers, sometimes quite tall, with straight stems, fibrous roots, and usually pendent clusters of showy flowers; somewhat similar are some **shrubby** begonias, with a more closely branched habit (the bedding begonias belong here); another similar group but with lower, softer stems are known as the **winter-flowering** begonias, grown for their profuse and colorful flowers that peak in winter; the **rhizomatous** begonias are a large and varied class, with leaves arising directly from creeping, knotty rhizomes—they include the **Rex** begonias with colorfully variegated leaves and many others grown for foliage; finally the **tuberous** begonias, now largely represented by hybrids of the **Tuberhybrida** Group, which die back to tubers in winter and bear large, showy, often double flowers in summer, for example, 'Mandy Henscke'.

B

Begonia fuchsioides
'Vesuv' *(left)*

Begonia fuchsioides

Native to Venezuela, this shrubby
begonia has small, crowded, oval leaves,
flushed pink on new growths. Small
coral red to pale pink flowers are borne
in numerous short sprays over a long
season from autumn to spring. Suitable
for outdoor use, it grows to 3 ft (1 m)
tall with an erect, closely branched
habit and gracefully drooping branchlets.
It prefers good light. The cultivar
'Vesuv' is a good example. ZONES 10–12.

CULTIVATION

Many of the cane-stemmed, winter-flowering, shrubby
and rhizomatous types can be grown outdoors in
frost-free climates and make fine garden plants, though
rhizomatous kinds in particular are prone to slug and
snail attack. As indoor plants they do well in standard
potting mix with peat moss or leafmold added to
increase acidity. Grow in bright to moderate light, with
good ventilation and above-average humidity, which
can be maintained by standing pots on a tray of pebbles
and water. Pinch back young plants of the shrubby type
to keep them compact and to encourage flowers.
Tuberous begonias require special treatment: tubers
must be forced into growth in early spring at a
temperature of 65°F (18°C) in peat moss or sphagnum,
and kept in a cool, well-ventilated greenhouse for the
summer flowering season. After flowering, plants die
back and tubers are lifted in mid-autumn and stored
dry. Propagate from tubers in the case of tuberous
begonias. Other begonias may be propagated from stem
or leaf cuttings (laying the cut leaf blades flat on damp
sand and weighing them down with pebbles), or by
division of rhizomes, or from seed. Begonias are
susceptible to gray mold, powdery mildew and botrytis
in the warmer part of the year if conditions are too
damp.

Begonia × hiemalis (above)
syn. *Begonia × elatior*
WINTER-FLOWERING BEGONIA

This name applies to a group of
winter-flowering hybrid cultivars
originating from crosses between
Begonia socotrana and Tuberhybrida
Group begonias, resulting in a range
of easily grown plants with single or
double blooms in subtle colors from
white through yellow and orange to
red and pink. They have fibrous
rather than tuberous root systems
and tend to die after flowering,
though some newer cultivars have
overcome this drawback.
ZONES 10–11.

Begonia, Semperflorens-cultorum Group

(right & center)

BEDDING BEGONIA, WAX BEGONIA

Derived largely from the Brazilian ***Begonia semperflorens,*** the dwarf, shrubby begonias of this group are often grown as bedding annuals, for example, '**Ernst Benary**', or for borders in shaded gardens. They are also popular as potted plants for window boxes or patio tubs. Freely branching with soft, succulent stems, their rounded, glossy green (bronze or variegated in some cultivars) leaves are about 2 in (5 cm) long. The flowers are profuse, opening progressively at the branch tips over a long summer and early autumn season (most of the year in warmer climates). The numerous cultivars include singles and doubles in colors of bright rose pink, light pink, white or red; they are generally released as a series, with mixed colors. They are grown from seed or stem cuttings and planted out in late spring in cooler climates; pinch out growing tips to encourage bushy growth. **Cocktail Series** are bushy miniatures with bronzy foliage and single flowers: '**Gin**' has metallic black-green leaves and deep pink flowers; '**Vodka**' produces deep red flowers against very dark green leaves; and the pale bronze leaves of '**Whiskey**' are offset by white flowers. **Thousand Wonders** is an older series consisting of compact, sun-hardy plants in mixed shades of pink and white. ZONES 9–11.

Begonia 'Pink Shasta' *(above)*

One of the 'angel-wing' type of cane-stemmed begonias, 'Pink Shasta' grows to 3–4 ft (1–1.2 m) high with branching stems and leaves slightly silver spotted. It produces pendulous panicles of light salmon-pink flowers through spring, summer and autumn. It originated as a seedling of '**Shasta**', which is derived from *Begonia coccinea.* ZONES 10–12.

Begonia, Semperflorens-cultorum Group, 'Ernst Benary' used as a border *(left)*

B

Belamcanda chinensis *(left)*
LEOPARD LILY, BLACKBERRY LILY

This 24–36 in (60–90 cm) tall plant has something of the habit of an iris but the summer flowers are quite un-iris-like in appearance. Up to 2 in (5 cm) across, they come in a range of colors from cream to yellow, apricot or deep orange-red, usually with darker spotting, hence the common name leopard lily. The seed pods open to reveal tight clusters of seeds resembling the fruitlets of a blackberry, hence their other common name.
ZONES 8–11.

BELAMCANDA

This genus, native to southern and eastern Asia and belonging to the iris family, contains only 2 species. The plants are perennials but of weak growth and tending to be short lived, with flattened fans of thin-textured leaves arising from thin rhizomes. Slender flowering stems terminate in a few rather small flowers with 6 narrow petals; these are followed by seed pods which split widely to reveal rows of shiny black seeds, like small berries— these are popular for dried flower arrangements.

CULTIVATION

These are warm-temperate plants that require sunshine and rich, well-drained soil. Water well in summer. In a cold climate the dormant plants will need protection from heavy frosts. Propagate by division or from seed, which should be sown every second or third year to ensure the plants' survival.

BELLIS
DAISY

The little white flower that spangles lawns in spring is one of the best loved of European wildflowers. These, the true daisies, consist of 15 species of small perennials that occur wild in Europe, North Africa and Turkey. *Bellis* is from the Latin *bellus* which means 'pretty' or 'charming', while the English 'daisy' is a corruption of 'day's eye', arising from the way the flower closes up at night, opening again to greet the sunrise. The plants form rosettes with small oval to spoon-shaped leaves; each rosette produces a succession of flowerheads on individual stalks in shades of white, pink, blue or crimson. Only one of the species is widely cultivated, mostly in the form of improved strains.

CULTIVATION

Daisies are favorite flowers for edging flowerbeds in spring and, while they are perennial in cool-temperate climates, it is usual to treat them as annuals or biennials, sowing seed in autumn. They thrive in any good garden soil in sun or part-shade; keep soil moist in winter and spring. Propagate from seed or by division.

Bellis perennis
'Medici's White' *(below)*

Bellis perennis,
Pomponette Series cultivar *(above)*

Bellis perennis
(below)
ENGLISH DAISY, COMMON DAISY

This daisy has become widely naturalized in temperate parts of most continents. The wild plants are small, form- ing carpets of crowded rosettes that spread through lawns by run- ners. The 1 in (25 mm) wide flowerheads, appearing from late winter to early summer, are white with golden centers and pale purplish undersides. **'Medici's White'** is a white cultivar. The garden strains mostly have double flowerheads of red, crimson, pink or white, all with a gold center. **'Alba Plena'** is an old double white cultivar, very different from the Pomponette Series daisies now popular as bedding plants and cut flowers; these are a far cry from the wild flowers, making neat hemispherical flowerheads 1½ in (35 mm) wide with curled petals, on stems up to 10 in (25 cm) high, in mixed colors. ZONES 3–10.

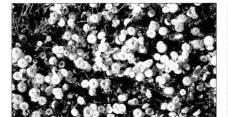

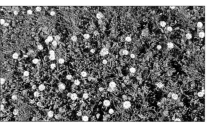

B

BELLIUM

This is a genus of 3 species of annual and perennial, trailing or mounding daisies native to southern Europe. The botanical name was intended to indicate their close similarity to *Bellis*, though in fine details of floral structure they are quite distinct. They are delightful miniature plants with very small, crowded, spatula-shaped leaves and tiny white flowerheads borne in profusion.

CULTIVATION

They prefer a sunnier, drier position than English daisies and thrive in well-drained rockeries. They should be mulched with fine gravel to prevent the foliage becoming mud-splashed during rain. All species will tolerate light to moderate frosts. Propagate from seed or by division.

Bellium minutum *(above)*

A summer-flowering annual from the islands of the Mediterranean, this species has leaves that are slightly over $1/4$ in (6 mm) long. Its white flower-heads, which are carried on 2 in (5 cm) stems, are equally tiny, just over $1/2$ in (12 mm) wide with purplish undersides. ZONES 6–9.

Bergenia cordifolia (right)
HEARTLEAF SAXIFRAGE

Native to Siberia's Altai Mountains, this tough perennial has crinkly edged, more or less heart-shaped leaves up to 8 in (20 cm) wide, and produces panicles of drooping purple-pink flowers on 12–15 in (30–38 cm) stems in late winter and early spring. It is long flowering and its leaves remain green in winter. **'Purpurea'** has magenta-pink flowers and leaves tinged purple. ZONES 3–9.

BERGENIA

Consisting of 6 or 7 species of rhizomatous, semi-evergreen perennials in the saxifrage family from eastern and central Asia, this genus is characterized by large, handsome, paddle-shaped leaves, arising from the ground on short stalks to form loose clumps. There are also many garden hybrids that have been developed over the last 100 years or so. Large clusters of flowers—mostly pale pink, but also white and dark pink—are borne on short, stout stems in winter and spring. An example is **'Eroica'**, with deep pink flowers. The foliage often develops attractive red tints in winter.

CULTIVATION

Bergenias make excellent rockery plants, thriving in sun or shade and tolerant of exposed sites as well as moist ground beside streams or ponds, but leaves color most strongly when plants are grown under drier conditions. Some are good as ground cover when planted *en masse*. Water well in hot weather and remove spent flowerheads to prolong flowering. Propagate by division in spring after flowering, when plants become crowded.

Bergenia 'Eroica'
(below)

B

Bergenia
'Morgenröte' *(left)*
syn. *Bergenia*
'Morning Red'

This small-growing cultivar has plain green leaves under 6 in (15 cm) and produces dense small clusters of largish orchid pink flowers on deep red stalks in late spring, sometimes blooming again in the summer. ZONES 4–9.

Bergenia
purpurascens *(below)*
syn. *Bergenia beesiana*

The large fleshy, oval, purple-tinted leaves of this species develop a deeper color in winter, especially in a cold climate where frost occurs. Bright pink to reddish purple flowers are borne in late winter and spring on stems up to 18 in (45 cm) tall. ZONES 5–9.

Bergenia × schmidtii *(left)*

Arguably the most vigorous and most widely planted bergenia, this old hybrid between *Bergenia ciliata* and *B. crassifolia* has large, rounded, fleshy, dull green leaves. Set among the foliage are rose pink blooms on stalks up to 12 in (30 cm) long. The main flush of flowers occurs in late winter and early spring; frosts may damage blooms, but it often flowers sporadically at other times. The plant spreads to make a fine ground cover, and adapts well to warm-temperate humid climates. ZONES 5–10.

B

Bergenia 'Silberlicht' *(above)*
syn. *Bergenia* 'Silver Light'

This hybrid cultivar forms compact clumps of glossy green leaves up to 8 in (20 cm) long with scalloped margins. The large, pure white to palest pink flowers appear in late spring in compact clusters on a succession of flower stalks up to 18 in (45 cm) high.
ZONES 5–9.

Bergenia stracheyi *(right)*
syn. *Bergenia milesii*

This species has relatively small leaves with hairs lining the edges and wedge-shaped at the base. Forming extensive clumps with age, it produces tight clusters of nodding, cup-shaped, deep pink to white flowers in early spring on stalks 10 in (25 cm) high.
ZONES 6–9.

B

Bidens ferulifolia 'Gold Marie' *(above)*

Bidens ferulifolia

Native to Mexico and Arizona, *Bidens ferulifolia* is a bushy, evergreen perennial 18–24 in (45–60 cm) tall, usually short lived. The leaves are small and fern-like, divided into narrow segments, and it bears golden-yellow, few-rayed flowerheads 1–1½ in (25–35 mm) wide in a long succession from late spring to autumn. Cultivars available include **'Arizona'**, **'Gold Marie'**, **'Golden Goddess'** and **'Peter's Goldteppich'**. ZONES 8–10.

Bidens aequisquamea (below)

BIDENS
TICKSEED, BEGGAR'S TICKS, BURR-MARIGOLD

This is a genus of around 200 species of annuals, perennials, subshrubs and shrubs that is closely related to *Cosmos* and occurs in most parts of the world except very cold regions. In most countries this genus is represented only by a weedy species. The majority are native to Mexico and adjacent regions of the Americas. The plants have erect leafy stems, usually much branched, with opposite pairs of leaves that are generally compound or deeply divided. Yellow daisy flowers (occasionally red to purple, for example, the purplish pink *Bidens aequisquamea*), mostly with very few but broad ray florets, open in a long succession and are followed by burr-like seed heads containing narrow seeds, each tipped with 2-barbed bristles (*Bidens* means '2-toothed') that can stick to clothing and fur.

CULTIVATION

These plants are very easily grown in any well-drained soil. Plant in full sun or morning shade, and water well in summer. Although hardiness varies with the species, most will withstand moderate frosts. Propagate from seed or cuttings, or by division, depending on the growth form.

Bidens ferulifolia 'Peter's Goldteppich' *(below)*

Billbergia amoena *(left)*

The species name is Latin for 'delightful to the eye' and this Brazilian bromeliad is eye-catching when well grown. Its loosely clustered leaf rosettes consist of rather few, broad leaves up to 24 in (60 cm) long, making large 'tanks', and may be pale gray-green or various shades of purple with cream or green spotting. The flower spikes may rise as high as 3 ft (1 m) with very large dark pink bracts and a few chalky blue-green flowers about 2 in (5 cm) long. **ZONES 11–12.**

Billbergia nutans
(left)
QUEEN'S TEARS, FRIENDSHIP PLANT

This popular species from southern Brazil and Argentina can be grown outdoors in sheltered rockeries or tubs, even in full sun and in places with occasional light frosts. Indoors it likes coarse potting mix and good light. Reaching a height of 24 in (60 cm) and spreading to make large dense clumps, its pale olive green leaves are grass-like, tapering into long thread-like, recurving tips, and pendent clusters of flowers appear in spring on long arching spikes. The curled-back petals are pale green and navy blue, but the long pink bracts are more eye-catching. **ZONES 10–12.**

BILLBERGIA
VASE PLANT

This genus of bromeliads consists of around 50 species of evergreen perennials from Central and South America. Most species are 'tank epiphytes', plants that perch on trees with the bases of their broad, strap-like leaves tightly overlapping around a central hollow that fills with rainwater, providing a reservoir for the plant between rainfalls. The horny-textured leaves, often edged with small teeth, in many species have a coating of mealy, grayish white scales interrupted by greener bands. Showy, stalked flower clusters appear at any time of year from the centers of the leaf rosettes, with pink or red bracts often more conspicuous than the tubular flowers.

CULTIVATION

Easy to grow, they make ideal indoor plants, or can be planted outdoors in subtropical or tropical climates in sheltered, humid spots. A porous, fast-draining soil mix suits them, or plant them on a mound of stones. Some species soon form quite large clumps and can be propagated by division after flowering; propagate the slower-growing ones by cutting off the basal 'pups' and treat as cuttings. Scale insects and mealybugs can be a problem; brown leaves may result from too much sun.

B

Blandfordia grandiflora (left)
syn. *Blandfordia flammea*

This is the most colorful species and the one most prized for cut flowers. Its leaves are very narrow and rather rigid, and flowering stems are 24–36 in (60–90 cm) tall, carrying 3 to 10 flowers; these are up to 2½ in (6 cm) long, flared toward the mouth, and vary from deep pinkish red to red with yellow tips or sometimes pure yellow, always with a thin waxy bloom. **ZONES 9–11.**

BLANDFORDIA
CHRISTMAS BELLS

This is an eastern Australian genus of 4 species of grassy leaved perennials with deeply buried corm-like rhizomes. They are prized for their beautiful, waxy red or red-and-yellow flowers that appear around Christmas in the southern hemisphere. The plants are long lived, with tough, narrow basal leaves in sparse to dense tufts, from which arise one to several stiff flowering stems, bearing near the top semi-pendent flowers; these are bell-shaped and up to 3 in (8 cm) long, the 6 petals fused for most of their length.

CULTIVATION
Coming mainly from peaty coastal swamps in the wild, these are not easy plants to maintain in cultivation—they are prone to root-rot and are sensitive to nutrient imbalances. Plant in moist, peaty soil in full sun or light shade. Keep consistently moist. They tolerate light frosts and may be propagated by division or raised from seed. Both develop slowly.

BOLTONIA
FALSE CHAMOMILE

This is a genus of 8 species of perennial daisies, all from eastern and central USA except for one species which comes from temperate East Asia. Very much like tall asters, they have in recent years become popular as background plants for perennial borders and as cut flowers. Over winter they die back to a clump of simple, narrow leaves. In late spring, tall flowering stems begin to develop and by late summer they carry hundreds of small daisies in shades of white, pink, lilac, violet or purple.

CULTIVATION
They are very easily grown in moist, well-drained soil in any sunny position. However, like many of the asters, they are prone to mildew from late summer, which cuts short the flower display. Frost hardy, they are propagated from seed or cuttings or by division.

Boltonia asteroides
(below)

This is the best known boltonia in gardens. It is widely distributed in northeastern USA. The flowering stems may be as much as 8 ft (2.4 m) tall, with the ³/₄ in (20 mm) flowerheads ranging in color from white through pale pink to mauve. **'Snowbank'** is a white-flowered selection with stems growing up to 6 ft (1.8 m) tall. ***Boltonia asteroides* var. *latisquama*** differs in its larger flowerheads, which are up to 1¹/₄ in (3 cm) across in shades of mauve or purple. ZONES 4–9.

B

BORAGO

This is a European genus of 3 species of annuals and short-lived perennials. The plants are generally erect with rather coarse growth and are covered with bristly hairs. They form clumps of lance-shaped basal leaves that rapidly develop in spring into branched, leafy flowering stems. By late spring the plants bear semi-pendulous, starry purple-blue or white flowers, which are quite ornamental. The flowers are a rich source of nectar and are popular with beekeepers.

CULTIVATION

These plants are easily grown in any light, moist, well-drained soil in full sun. Usually they are propagated from seed, which often self-sows, so plants may become slightly invasive. Seed of the annual species can be sown in late winter for an early crop. Protect from snails.

Borago officinalis
(below)
BORAGE

This annual herb is grown for its cucumber-flavored leaves and pretty, purplish blue star-shaped flowers. The plant grows to around 30 in (75 cm) high with clusters of flowers in spring and summer. The fresh young leaves are used raw in salads and cool drinks or cooked with vegetables. The edible flowers have long been used to decorate salads.
ZONES 5–10.

B

BOYKINIA
syn. *Telesonix*

A North American and Japanese genus of 9 species of woodland and alpine perennials, these plants spread by shortly creeping rhizomes. They resemble the closely related genera *Heuchera* and *Tiarella*, and have lobed and toothed, roughly heart- or kidney-shaped hairy leaves, varying in size depending on the species. Stalked panicles of small, 5-petalled, white, cream or reddish flowers open through spring or summer. While not spectacular, they are graceful plants that help to lighten shady corners. Botanists differ on the question of whether *Telesonix* should be united with *Boykinia*.

CULTIVATION
Plant in moist, humus-rich, well-drained soil in dappled shade. Hardiness varies, though all species will tolerate at least moderate frosts. Propagate by division in late winter.

Boykinia jamesii *(above)*
syns *Boykinia heucheriformis, Telesonix jamesii*

A native of Colorado, this is one of the more cold-hardy species and also among the smallest. Its kidney-shaped leaves are usually less than 2 in (5 cm) wide and the plant forms a compact mound of fresh green foliage around 4 in (10 cm) high and up to 6 in (15 cm) in diameter. Its narrow 6 in (15 cm) stems bear purple-red flowers, larger than those of other boykinias, and it needs to be treated as an alpine. ZONES 5–8.

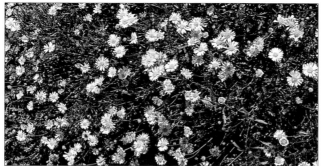

Brachycome 'Sunburst'
(left)

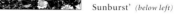

Brachycome 'Outback
Sunburst' *(below left)*

Brachycome 'Amethyst' *(below)*

A long-flowering perennial with purple-blue
flowers, this recent hybrid grows to about 12 in
(30 cm) tall and wide. ZONES 9–11.

BRACHYCOME
syn. *Brachyscome*

Native to Australia, the low-growing annuals
and evergreen perennials of this genus are
attractive ground cover or rockery plants.
Many of the perennials are mound-forming,
spreading by underground runners and
having finely divided, soft, fern-like foliage.
They bear a profusion of daisy-like flowerheads in shades of blue, mauve, pink and
yellow, with orange or brownish centers or
yellow as in the hybrids **'Sunburst'** and
'Outback Sunburst', both with white ray florets.
Australian botanists have disputed over the
spelling of this genus, the debate hingeing on
whether the nineteenth-century botanist who
spelt it *Brachyscome* had the right to subsequently correct his bad Greek, as he did
(it combines *brachys,* short, with *kome,* hair,
referring to a seed feature, but the 's' is
dropped when they are joined).

CULTIVATION
They require a sunny situation and a light,
well-drained garden soil. Many are moderately
frost hardy and some will tolerate coastal salt
spray. Do not over-water as they prefer dry
conditions. Pinch out early shoots to encourage
branching and propagate from ripe seed or
stem cuttings or by division in spring or
autumn.

Brachycome multifida (right)

This perennial species is a charming ground cover in warm-temperate climates, though it is not long lived and should be renewed every few years. It grows 4–6 in (10–15 cm) high and spreads to about 18 in (45 cm). The mauve-pink flowerheads bloom for weeks in late spring and summer. It likes sunshine and perfect drainage and is propagated by layers or from cuttings. **'Break O' Day'** is a selected form with finer leaves, profuse mauve-blue flowers and a very compact habit. ZONES 9–11.

Brachycome iberidifolia 'Blue Star' (below)

Brachycome iberidifolia
SWAN RIVER DAISY

This daisy is a weak-stemmed annual, long grown as a bedding or border plant, that grows to a height and spread of around 12 in (30 cm), sometimes taller. It has deeply dissected leaves with very narrow segments. Small, fragrant, daisy-like flowerheads, normally mauve-blue but sometimes white, pink or purple, appear in great profusion in summer and early autumn. **'Blue Star'** is a cultivar with massed flowers that are small and mauve to purple-blue. ZONES 9–11.

B

BRACTEANTHA
syn. *Helichrysum*
STRAWFLOWER, EVERLASTING DAISY

This Australian genus of 7 species of annuals and perennials, until recently classified in *Helichrysum,* differs from true helichrysums in their large, decorative flowerheads carried singly or a few together at the end of the flowering branches, each consisting of golden yellow to white bracts of straw-like texture surrounding a disc of tiny yellow or brownish florets. The leaves, mostly broad and thin, are often downy on their undersides, or can be very sticky in some species. Most of the cultivated forms and seedling strains are treated as forms of *Bracteantha bracteata,* but further botanical study is likely to result in new species being recognized.

CULTIVATION
Plant in moist, well-drained soil in full sun. The summer-flowering annuals may be planted from late winter for an early display. Provided they are not waterlogged, most species will tolerate light to moderate frosts. Propagate annuals from seed and perennials from seed or tip cuttings.

Bracteantha bracteata
'Dargon Hill Monarch'
(center right)

Bracteantha bracteata
cultivar *(top right)*

Bracteantha bracteata
'Diamond Head' *(right)*

Bracteantha bracteata *(left)*
syn. *Helichrysum bracteatum*

This annual or short-lived perennial has an erect habit and grows to a height of around 3 ft (1 m). It has weak, hollow stems, thin green leaves and from summer to early autumn bears golden yellow blooms up to 2 in (5 cm) in diameter at the branch tips. In the mid-nineteenth century annual strains with larger flowerheads in shades of pink, bronze red, cream, purple and yellow were developed; these plants were generally more vigorous; **Bright Bikinis Series** is a modern descendant of these. Some more spreading, shrubby perennial plants from eastern Australia, which may be recognized as distinct species, have been named as cultivars. These include the popular '**Dargan Hill Monarch**', with rich yellow blooms up to 3 in (8 cm) across that emerge over several months; and '**Diamond Head**', which is similar but lower and more compact. ZONES 8–11.

B

BROMELIA

This genus gives its name to the large family Bromeliaceae (the bromeliads). The 50 or so species of *Bromelia* are scattered widely through South America and parts of Central America and the West Indies. They are mostly ground-dwelling perennials resembling pineapple plants, with strong, hooked spines along the margins of their long, stiff leaves which generally turn a bronzy color in strong sun. The leaves form large rosettes, which in some species can multiply by sending out long rhizomes to make extensive clumps. A stout flower spike arises from the center of the rosette surrounded by leaf-like bracts that may be brilliantly colored; the flowers are tubular and densely packed and give way to large fleshy yellow fruits, which in some species are used medicinally.

CULTIVATION

Bromelia species are mostly grown outdoors in frost-free climates, thriving in full sun and well-drained soil. They are relatively free from diseases and pests. Propagate from offsets or seeds, keeping seedlings well ventilated to discourage damping off fungus.

Bromelia balansae
(above)
HEART OF FLAME
This vigorous species reaches a height of 5 ft (1.5 m) and can spread extensively. Its flower spike is up to 3 ft (1 m) tall and is surrounded by glossy, brilliant scarlet, spiny-edged bracts, the longer, lower ones only colored at the base. The purple flowers, borne in late summer, are in a series of dense heads among shorter whitish bracts. The dull orange-yellow berries can form very large clusters, taking almost a year to ripen. This plant has been used in South America as an impenetrable living fence.
ZONES 10–12.

B

BRUNNERA

This is a genus of 3 species of perennials closely related to the forget-me-not (*Myosotis*) and *Anchusa*. They range in the wild from eastern Europe to western Siberia and form clumps of heart-shaped to rather narrow basal leaves on long stalks. Leafy, branched flowering stems bear panicles of tiny 5-petalled purple or blue flowers in spring and early summer. There are cultivated forms with white flowers and variegated foliage.

CULTIVATION

Essentially woodland plants, they prefer humus-rich, moist soil with a leafy mulch and a position in dappled shade. They are very cold hardy and in suitable conditions will self-sow and naturalize. Propagate from seed, by removing small rooted pieces or by taking cuttings of the soft spring shoots.

Brunnera macrophylla (above)
SIBERIAN BUGLOSS

The small violet flowers of this species show their relationship to the forget-me-nots; they are held on slender stems 18–24 in (45–60 cm) tall above the bold mounds of heart-shaped leaves. When the flowers appear the new leaves grow to their full length of 4–6 in (10–15 cm). Clumps spread slowly underground but self-seed readily, making excellent ground cover under trees and large shrubs. 'Hadspen Cream' has paler green leaves prettily edged with cream, and paler blue flowers. ZONES 3–9.

BULBINELLA

This southern hemisphere genus has an unusual distribution, with 6 species endemic to New Zealand and the remainder of its 20 or so species native to southern Africa. They are fleshy-rooted perennial lilies similar to the related *Bulbine* but with mostly broader, thinner leaves and crowded spikes of golden yellow flowers terminating the long, hollow stems. They form clumps of somewhat untidy foliage. Some of the larger South African species, such as *Bulbinella floribunda,* make excellent cut flowers. The alpine species are much smaller but not so easily grown.

CULTIVATION

In the wild, many species grow in very damp areas and in cultivation they demand moist, humus-rich soil that never dries out entirely in summer. A position in sun or semi-shade is best. Most species are at least slightly frost hardy and are propagated from seed or by dividing established clumps. The fleshy roots should be planted with the root-crown at soil level.

B

Bulbinella floribunda (above)
CAT'S-TAIL

This native of South Africa produces 24–36 in (60–90 cm) tall flower stalks from late winter to mid-spring. Each stalk is topped with a broad, 4 in (10 cm) spike crammed with tiny orange-yellow flowers and terminating in tight green buds. Long, narrow basal leaves appear in winter, forming a large tangled clump. The plant dies back in summer and autumn. It is excellent as a long-lasting cut flower. ZONES 8–10.

Bulbinella hookeri (left)

Found in the subalpine grasslands of both the main islands of New Zealand, this species has very narrow, grassy leaves and develops into a thick clump of foliage. The flower stems are around 24 in (60 cm) tall, half of which is the densely packed spike of ¼ in (6 mm) wide flowers. ZONES 8–10.

CALAMINTHA
CALAMINT

Seven species make up this genus of aromatic perennial herbs, occurring as natives mainly in Europe and temperate Asia but with 2 species confined to the USA. In growth habit they are quite like the true mints *(Mentha)*, with creeping rhizomes and leaves in opposite pairs on square stems, but the white, pink or purplish flowers are mostly larger and are borne in looser terminal sprays. The leaves of several species are used in herbal medicine, as well as being infused to make herbal teas. The name *Calamintha* (beautiful mint) goes back to ancient Greek, referring originally to an aromatic herb of this general kind but now not identifiable.

CULTIVATION
Mostly fairly frost hardy, calaminthas are easily grown in moist but well-drained soil in a sheltered position; some species prefer woodland conditions in part-shade, others thrive best in full sun. Propagate by division of rhizomes or from seed sown in spring.

Calamintha nepeta
LESSER CALAMINT

Native to much of Europe, also North Africa and western Asia, this unassuming plant to 12–24 in (30–60 cm) tall favors dry, well-drained conditions in full sun. Its small leaves are hardly toothed and the small summer flowers, held in long, erect, rather open sprays, are pale mauve or almost white. The epithet *nepeta* was presumably given to indicate its resemblance to the catmint genus *Nepeta*. *Calamintha nepeta* subsp. *glandulosa* 'White Cloud' and 'Blue Cloud' are popular cultivars. ZONES 4–10.

Calamintha nepeta subsp. *glandulosa* 'White Cloud' *(left)*

Calathea makoyana *(below)*
PEACOCK PLANT, CATHEDRAL-WINDOWS

From eastern Brazil, this dwarf species grows to no more than 18 in (45 cm) but has the most gorgeously patterned leaves, well justifying its common name; they are broadly oval, with a feathery design of dark green markings on a pale creamy background grading to mid-green at the margins. The undersides have the same markings in purple. Makoy, after whom the species is named, was a renowned nineteenth-century Belgian grower of hothouse plants. ZONES 11–12.

CALATHEA

Consisting of 300 or so species of evergreen perennials of the arrowroot family, native to Central and South America and the West Indies, this genus is prized for its decorative foliage. At least one species is grown as a food crop, yielding small starchy tubers. The long-stalked, mostly upright leaves are usually large and often beautifully variegated in shades of green, white, pink, purple and maroon, and usually purplish on the undersides. The flowers are interesting but rarely showy, in short dense spikes with overlapping bracts that may be white or variously colored and often partly hidden beneath the foliage.

CULTIVATION

In the wet tropics and subtropics calatheas make attractive foliage plants for outdoor landscaping in shaded areas beneath trees or in courtyards. In colder parts of the world they are grown indoors. Many will thrive in low light levels. Plant in humus-rich, moist but well-drained soil. Water freely in warmer weather and fertilize regularly. Propagate by division of rhizomes. The sheathing leaf bases often harbor mealybugs, and the foliage is affected by aphids, spider mites and thrips.

Calathea burle-marxii
(above)

Named in honor of the renowned Brazilian landscape designer, Roberto Burle Marx, whose gardens featured dramatic swathes of plants such as calatheas, this east Brazilian species grows rapidly up to 5 ft (1.5 m) high, with short bamboo-like stems growing erect from the rhizomes. The leaves may be over 24 in (60 cm) long and half as wide, bright green with a yellowish central stripe on the upper surface, duller gray-green beneath. The $^3/_4$ in (20 mm) long pale violet flowers emerge from waxy white bracts grouped in a large spike. ZONES 11–12.

Calathea veitchiana (left)

One of the taller growing calatheas, to 3 ft (1 m) or more in height, this species from Peru has leaves blotched light green along the center, the blotches bordered by scalloped bands of dull green, these in turn are bordered greenish yellow, while on the underside the dark green areas become purple. The small white flowers are borne in a club-shaped spike with green bracts. This species is named after a horticulturalist, James Veitch, whose famous English nursery continued throughout the nineteenth century. **ZONES 11–12.**

Calathea zebrina (right)
ZEBRA PLANT

This vigorous species from Brazil is usually 24–36 in (60–90 cm) tall, and can develop into a broad clump of crowded stems, its habit reminiscent of a dwarf canna except that the large, velvety, deep green leaves are marked by parallel stripes or bars of pale chartreuse; the undersides are purplish red. It will thrive in somewhat cooler climates than most calatheas, making a fine ground cover plant, though the leaves turn yellowish in winter; they can be trimmed away to reveal clusters of chocolate brown bracts which protect the spring flowers. **ZONES 10–12.**

CALCEOLARIA
LADIES' PURSE, SLIPPER FLOWER, POCKETBOOK FLOWER

C

Gardeners who know this genus only in the form of the gaudy 'slipper flowers' sold by florists may be surprised to learn that it contains upward of 300 species, ranging from tiny annuals to herbaceous perennials and even scrambling climbers and quite woody shrubs. All are native to the Americas, from Mexico southward to Tierra del Fuego, and all share the same curious flower structure, with a lower lip inflated like a rather bulbous slipper. Flower colors are mainly yellows and oranges, often with red or purple spots.

CULTIVATION
Calceolarias come from a wide range of natural habitats and vary greatly in cold hardiness. When grown outdoors they prefer a shady, cool site in moist, well-drained soil with added compost. Provide shelter from heavy winds as the flowers are easily damaged. Shrubby species may benefit from being pruned back by half in winter. Propagate from seed or softwood cuttings in summer or late spring. The Herbeohybrida Group, grown mainly in cool greenhouses, are fed and watered liberally in the summer growing season; they are subject to a number of diseases and pest infestations.

Calceolaria,
Herbeohybrida Group
cultivar *(below)*

Calceolaria, Herbeohybrida Group

These are the popular florists' calceolarias, a group of hybrids derived from 3 Chilean species. They are soft-stemmed, compact, bushy biennials often treated as annuals, producing in spring and summer blooms in a range of bright colors from yellow to deep red and so densely massed they almost hide the soft green foliage. Innumerable named varieties have appeared over the years, and they are now mostly sold as mixed-color seedling strains and series. Marginally frost hardy, they can be used for summer bedding but do not tolerate very hot, dry weather. Normally 12–18 in (30–45 cm) tall, dwarf strains can be as small as 6 in (15 cm). **'Sunset Mixed'** are bushy F1 hybrids 12 in (30 cm) tall with flowers in vibrant shades of red, orange and mixes of these two; they are useful in massed bedding. **'Sunshine'** is also an F1 hybrid of compact form around 10 in (25 cm) high, with bright golden yellow blooms, bred for planting in massed displays or for use in borders. ZONES 9–11.

C

Calceolaria,
Herbeohybrida Group
cultivar *(left)*

Calceolaria tomentosa
(left)

A native of Peru, this soft-
stemmed perennial species
grows to about 3 ft (1 m) with
broad, soft, heart-shaped leaves
with toothed margins. The
golden-yellow flowers have an
almost globular 'slipper' about
1¹/₂ in (35 mm) wide.
ZONES 9–10.

Calceolaria,
Herbeohybrida Group,
'Sunset Mixed' *(left)*

CALENDULA
MARIGOLD

It is thought that St Hildegard of Bingen (1098–1179) dedicated *Calendula officinalis* to the Virgin Mary and gave the flowers the name Mary's gold, or marigold. To gardeners of today 'marigold' generally signifies the unrelated *Tagetes* from Mexico (the so-called 'African' and 'French' marigolds). In the Middle Ages marigolds were considered a certain remedy for all sorts of ills ranging from smallpox to indigestion and 'evil humors of the head', and even today the marigold is a favorite of herbalists. The genus *Calendula* consists of 20-odd species of bushy annuals and evergreen perennials, occurring wild from the Canary Islands through the Mediterranean region to Iran in the east. They have simple, somewhat aromatic leaves and daisy-like, orange or yellow flowers.

CULTIVATION

Calendulas are mostly fairly frost-hardy plants and are readily grown in well-drained soil of any quality in sun or part-shade. Flowering will be prolonged with regular deadheading. Propagate from seed, and watch for aphids and powdery mildew.

Calendula arvensis
(below)
FIELD MARIGOLD

This sprawling annual is a common wildflower in Mediterranean countries, where it grows among the long grass of fields and displays its golden flowers from spring to autumn and on into winter if the weather is mild. The name *Calendula* comes from the same root as calendar and refers to the almost all-year blooming. It is rarely cultivated but, transplanted to gardens, it can make a bright show. ZONES 6–10.

C

Calendula officinalis *(left)*
POT MARIGOLD, ENGLISH MARIGOLD

Originally native to southern Europe and long valued for its medicinal qualities, this species is known in gardens only by its many cultivars and seedling strains, popular winter- and spring-flowering annuals that remain in bloom for a long time. There are tall and dwarf forms, all of bushy habit, the tall growing to a height and spread of 24 in (60 cm) and the dwarf to 12 in (30 cm). All forms have lance-shaped, strongly scented, pale green leaves and single or double flowerheads. Tall cultivars include **'Geisha Girl'** with double orange flowers; the **Pacific Beauty Series** with double flowers in a number of different colors including bicolors; **'Princess'** with crested orange, gold or yellow flowers; and the **Touch of Red Series** with double flowers in tones of deep orange-red. Dwarf cultivars include **'Fiesta Gitana'** with double flowers in colors ranging from cream to orange, and **'Honey Babe'** with apricot, yellow and orange flowers. ZONES 6–10.

Calendula officinalis
'Fiesta Gitana' *(below)*

Calendula officinalis,
Pacific Beauty Series *(right)*

Callistephus chinensis (right)
syn. *Aster chinensis*

This erect, bushy, fast-growing annual has oval, toothed, mid-green leaves and long-stalked flowerheads. There are many seedling strains available, ranging from tall, up to 3 ft (1 m), to dwarf, about 8 in (20 cm). Stake tall cultivars and remove spent flowers regularly. The **Milady Series** are vigorous cultivars to 12 in (30 cm) in height with double flowerheads in pinks, reds, white, purplish blue and mixed colors. ZONES 6–10.

CALLISTEPHUS
CHINA ASTER

This genus contains one annual species, native to China and once included in the genus *Aster*. It is a colorful garden flower, with summer blooms in a wonderful array of shades from white to pink, blue, red and purple, popular both for bedding and as a cut flower. Long cultivation has given rise to many variants, and plant breeders add new strains almost every year. The 3–4 in (8–10 cm) flower-heads can be either yellow-centered single daisies or fully double. The doubles can have petals that are plume-like and shaggy, more formal and straight or very short, making the blooms like perfect pompons.

CULTIVATION
China aster is usually sown in spring to flower during summer, but the season of bloom is not long and it is usual to make successive sowings to prolong it. It is superlative for cutting and will grow in any climate, from the coolest temperate to subtropical. Give it sunshine and fertile, well-drained soil, and do not plant it in the same bed 2 years in a row—a rest of 2 or 3 years between plantings is desirable to guard against aster wilt, a soil-borne fungus.

C

CALTHA

There are about 10 species of moisture-loving perennials in this
genus of the ranunculus family, all occurring in cold marshlands
and alpine bogs of the cool-temperate zones in both northern and
southern hemispheres. With their cup-shaped, white or yellow
flowers and kidney- or heart-shaped leaves, they bring bright color
to the edges of garden ponds or to mixed borders in moist soil.
They spread by thick rhizomes and often come into leaf and flower
very early, appearing from beneath melting snow.

CULTIVATION

These frost-hardy plants prefer full
sun and rich, damp soil at the water's
edge or in any damp spot. Propagate
by division in autumn or early spring,
or from seed in autumn. Watch for
rust fungus, which should be treated
with a fungicide.

Caltha palustris
MARSH MARIGOLD, KINGCUP

Occurring widely in
temperate regions of the
northern hemisphere,
this semi-aquatic or
bog plant is sometimes
grown for its attractive
flowers. It is deciduous
or semi-evergreen with
dark green, rounded
leaves and glistening
buttercup-like, golden
yellow flowers borne
from early spring to
mid-summer. It grows
to a height and spread
of 18 in (45 cm). The
cultivars **'Monstrosa'**
and **'Flore Pleno'** both
have double flowers,
while **Caltha palustris
var. *alba*** has single
white flowers with
yellow stamens.
ZONES 3–8.

Caltha palustris
'Flore Pleno' *(left)*

Caltha palustris
'Monstrosa' *(below)*

Campanula carpatica *(below)*

CARPATHIAN BELLFLOWER, TUSSOCK BELLFLOWER

The slowly spreading clumps of basal leaves of this species make it well suited for use as an edging or rock garden plant. From late spring through summer, 8–12 in (20–30 cm) stems rise above the foliage, carrying upward-facing, 1–2 in (2.5 –5 cm) wide, bowl-shaped flowers in blue, lavender or white. The most common cultivars available are the compact-growing **'Blue Clips'** and **'White Clips'**, and the bright violet blue **'Wedgwood Blue'**. ZONES 3–9.

Campanula 'Burghaltii' *(above)*

This cross between *Campanula latifolia* and *C. punctata* has interesting flowers, up to 3 in (8 cm) long and amethyst purple in the bud stage opening to pale gray-mauve. Rhizomes do not creep to any great degree. It grows to about 24 in (60 cm) in height. ZONES 4–9.

Campanula 'Birch Hybrid' *(above right)*

A hybrid between *Campanula portenschlagiana* and *C. poscharskyana*, this delightful miniature campanula grows up to 6 in (15 cm) high with blooms of a light blue color. ZONES 4–9.

CAMPANULA

BELLFLOWER, BLUEBELL

Native to temperate parts of the northern hemisphere, this large genus includes about 250 species of showy herbaceous plants, mostly perennials but a few annual or biennial. The leaves vary in shape and size, mainly arising from upright stems or sometimes only in basal clusters. The flowers are mostly bell-shaped but in some species are more tubular, urn-shaped or star- shaped, and come mainly in shades of blue and purple with some pinks and whites.

CULTIVATION

Campanulas are useful for rockeries, borders, wild gardens and hanging baskets. All do best in a moderately rich, moist, well-drained soil. They grow in sun or shade, but flower color remains brightest in shady situations. Protect from drying winds and stake taller varieties, which make good cut flowers. Remove spent flower stems. Propagate from seed in spring (sow alpines in autumn), by division in spring or autumn, or from basal cuttings in spring. They are very frost hardy to frost tender. Transplant during winter and watch for slugs.

Campanula glomerata
'Superba' *(above)*

Campanula isophylla
'Krystal Weiss' *(right)*

Campanula glomerata
CLUSTERED BELLFLOWER

This variable species is found throughout Europe and temperate Asia. The violet-blue flowers are grouped in almost globular clusters on 10–15 in (25–38 cm) tall stems in early summer and again later if the old flower stems are removed. **'Superba'** grows to 24 in (60 cm); *Campanula glomerata* **var. *dahurica*** is a deeper violet than the species. There are also double-flowered and white versions. **ZONES 3–9.**

Campanula isophylla
ITALIAN BELLFLOWER

This dwarf evergreen trailing perennial grows to 4 in (10 cm) high with a spread of 12 in (30 cm) or more. It is only moderately frost hardy and is commonly grown indoors. It bears large star-shaped blue or white flowers in summer. The leaves are small and heart-shaped. **'Alba'** has white flowers. The so-called *Campanula isophylla* Kristal hybrids, **'Kristal Blau'** and **'Krystal Weiss'**, are not really hybrids but selected forms with particularly showy blue and white flowers respectively. **ZONES 8–10.**

Campanula isophylla
'Kristal Blau' *(below)*

Campanula lactiflora
MILKY BELLFLOWER

Native to the Caucasus region and eastern Turkey, this popular strong-growing perennial reaches a height of 5 ft (1.5 m) and spreads into a broad clump. The strong stems bear many narrow oval leaves. In summer it produces very large and dense panicles of bell-shaped lilac-blue flowers (occasionally pink or white). If the flowering stem is cut back after flowering, side shoots may bear blooms in late autumn. **'Loddon Anna'** has lilac-pink flowers; **'Pritchard's Variety'** has deep violet-blue flowers. ZONES 5–9.

Campanula lactiflora cultivar (above right)
Campanula lactiflora 'Pritchard's Variety' *(right)*

Campanula latifolia *(above)*
GREAT BELLFLOWER

Widely distributed in Europe and temperate Asia, this attractive species grows to 3 ft (1 m) tall with long-stalked basal leaves and strong leafy stems ascending from a compact rootstock. The upper leaves grade into bracts with lilac to white flowers arising from the axils; the flowers are up to 2 in (5 cm) across, bell-shaped and with elegantly recurved petals. ZONES 5–9.

Campanula medium *(below)*
CANTERBURY BELL

A biennial species from southern Europe, this is a slow-growing, erect plant with narrow basal leaves. In spring and early summer it has stout spires up to 4 ft (1.2 m) tall of crowded, white, pink or blue, bell-shaped flowers with recurved rims and prominent large green calyces. Dwarf cultivars grow to 24 in (60 cm), and double forms have a colored calyx like a second petal tube. Grow as border plants in part-shade. ZONES 6–10.

C

Campanula rotundifolia (below)
HAREBELL, SCOTTISH BLUEBELL

This variable species, widely distributed around the temperate northern hemisphere, has a hardy nature. Loose rosettes of rounded, long-stalked leaves arise from creeping rhizomes, followed by slender, wiry stems holding nodding lilac-blue to white bells during the summer months. ZONES 3–9.

Campanula persicifolia (left)
PEACH-LEAFED BELLFLOWER

Native to southern and eastern Europe and temperate Asia, this well-known species has large, nodding, bowl-shaped purplish blue or white flowers borne above narrow, lance-shaped, bright green leaves in summer. It is a rosette-forming perennial spreading by rhizomes and reaching a height of 3 ft (1 m). Pinch individual blooms off upright stems as soon as they fade. 'Alba' has white flowers; 'Boule de Neige' and 'Fleur de Neige' have double white flowers. ZONES 3–9.

Campanula portenschlagiana
(below)

syn. *Campanula muralis*
DALMATIAN BELLFLOWER

Native to a small area of the Dalmatian lime-stone mountains of Croatia, this is a dwarf, evergreen perennial growing to a maximum height of 6 in (15 cm) with an indefinite spread. It has crowded small violet-like leaves and a profusion of small, star-shaped, violet flowers in late spring and early summer. Best suited to rockeries and wall crevices, it likes a cool, partially shaded site with good drainage. ZONES 5–10.

Campanula rapunculoides (left)
CREEPING BELLFLOWER, ROVER BELLFLOWER

Considered by some a weed on account of the difficulty of eradicating its long rhizomes, this common European native may conversely be useful for the wild woodland garden as it spreads and self-seeds easily. It sends up widely spaced stems to about 3 ft (1 m) tall with serrated nettle-like leaves and nodding violet-blue bell-shaped flowers during the summer months. ZONES 4–10.

C

Campanula vidalii
(above)

syn. *Azorina vidalii*

AZORES BELLFLOWER

Campanula vidalii is so
different from other
campanulas that some
botanists place it in a
genus of its own
(*Azorina*). A shrubby
evergreen perennial, it
has crowded, narrow,
fleshy leaves and bears
nodding flesh pink or
white bells of a
remarkable waxy textu-
re in early summer on
18 in (45 cm) tall stems.
It is a garden plant for
warm-temperate
climates only—in cool
climates it is best
grown in a mildly
warmed greenhouse.
ZONES 9–11.

Campanula takesimana (top right)

A native of Korea, this striking perennial has
unusually long bell-shaped flowers, satiny creamy
white to lilac-pink outside but spotted with darker
purple-brown inside. The large leaves form loose
basal rosettes, and the roots tend to spread so the
plant forms a large clump. The flowering stems are
up to 3 ft (1 m) long but are usually weak and
reclining. The cultivar **'Alba'** has white flowers.
ZONES 5–9.

Campanula takesimana
'Alba' *(above)*

C

CANISTRUM

This bromeliad genus has 7 species, all native to eastern Brazil where they grow as epiphytes or rock dwellers. They are rosette plants rather like neoregelias, the rosette funnel-shaped and holding water in the base. In the center of the rosette appears a short flowerhead, consisting of a tight clump of small flowers enclosed by a neat ring of short but colorful bracts.

CULTIVATION

Usually grown as indoor plants in cooler climates, in the wet tropics and subtropics canistrums do well outdoors in a partially shaded position planted in low forks of trees or on rock piles, or in raised beds in a very open, humus-rich soil mixture. In dry summer weather, mist-spray frequently. Propagate from offsets or seed; protect seedlings from fungus and scale insects.

Canistrum lindenii
(below)
syns *Aechmea rosea,
Canistrum roseum*

The stemless rosettes of this species consist of broad, spiny edged leaves up to 18 in (45 cm) long, green with silvery scales on the undersides. The crowded small flowers are white and the surrounding bracts are pale green to white (pink or reddish in **'Roseum'**); it blooms in summer. ZONES 11–12.

CANNA

This genus of robust rhizomatous perennials consists of about 25 species, all native to tropical and South America. Belonging to the same broad grouping as gingers and bananas, they resemble these in that their apparent aboveground stems are not true stems but collections of tightly furled leaf bases, rising from the thick knotty rhizomes. Slender flowering stems grow up through the centers of these false stems, emerging at the top with showy flowers of asymmetrical structure. Most of the wild species have rather narrow-petalled flowers in shades of yellow, red or purple. All garden cannas are hybrids with much broader petals, originating as crosses between several species in the mid-nineteenth century. Early hybrids had fairly smooth petals in single colors but the addition of *Canna flaccida* genes resulted in larger, crumpled flowers with striking variegations ('orchid-flowered cannas'). The colors of cannas range from the common reds, oranges and yellows through to apricots, creams and pinks. The leaves can be green, bronze or purple, or sometimes white or yellow striped. Plants range in height from 18 in (45 cm) to 8 ft (2.4 m).

CULTIVATION

Cannas thrive outdoors in frost-free, warm climates but if grown outside in colder areas the roots need to be protected with thick mulch in winter, or else the rhizomes may be lifted in autumn and stored until spring—alternatively they can be grown in containers in a conservatory or greenhouse. They are sun-loving plants and thrive in hot dry weather as long as water can be kept up to the roots, and they respond well to heavy feeding. Cut back to the ground after flowers finish. Propagate in spring by division.

Canna × *generalis* cultivars
(top, center & right)

C

Canna × generalis

Canna × generalis is a large, highly variable group of canna hybrids of unknown or complex parentage. Plants are extremely variable, ranging from dwarfs less than 3 ft (1 m) to large growers that reach 6 ft (1.8 m). Foliage is also variable and may be plain green, reddish, purple or variegated. Flowers come in all the warm shades, either in plain single colors like the orange-red **'Brandywine'** or spotted or streaked as in the yellow and red **'King Numbert'**. **'Königin Charlotte'** has dazzling red flowers. **'Lenape'** is a dwarf hybrid with bright yellow flowers with a red throat and brownish red spots; it grows to a height of only 30 in (75 cm). **'Lucifer'** is a most attractive hybrid with yellow-edged red petals and purple-toned leaves. It is one of the newer dwarf types, growing to 3 ft (1 m). ZONES 9–12.

Canna × generalis
'Lucifer' *(left)*

Canna × generalis
'Königin Charlotte'   *Canna × generalis*
(below left)   'Brandywine' *(below)*

Canna × *generalis*
'Lenape' *(right)*

Canna indica
(below right)
syn. *Canna edulis*
INDIAN SHOT

Despite the common name, this species is native to northern South America, although it is commonly naturalized in warm regions elsewhere. Growing to about 8 ft (2.4 m) tall, it has dark green leaves with purple tones and in summer bears dark red to yellow flowers with very narrow petals, followed shortly by fleshy spined capsules containing black seeds—their hardness and smooth spherical shape allowed them to be substituted for shotgun pellets, hence the common name. Some strains, once distinguished as *Canna edulis*, have been cultivated for the edible starch in their rhizomes, known as 'Queensland arrowroot'. ZONES 9–12.

CARDAMINE
BITTERCRESS

This genus of the mustard family includes 150 or more species of annuals and perennials from most parts of the world, usually with dissected or compound leaves forming basal tufts and on lower parts of the flowering stems. Small, 4-petalled, white, pink or purple flowers like small stocks open progressively up the stem and are followed by slender pods that split apart suddenly, flinging the minute seeds a short distance. They are found in shady, moist habitats, some forming large mats, but the genus also includes several common small weeds, for example Cardamine hirsuta which can be eaten like watercress.

CULTIVATION
Given moist soil and full or part shade, these soft-leafed plants can be planted in a woodland garden or in an informal border, where their foliage makes an attractive ground cover.

Cardamine raphanifolia
(above)
syn. *Cardamine latifolia*

The botanical name of this species, native to southern Europe and western Asia, means 'radish-leafed' and its leaves do resemble those of a small radish plant. It is a perennial of up to about 24 in (60 cm) in height, the stems springing from a creeping rhizome. The flowers are pinkish purple and are borne from late spring to mid-summer. Coming from stream banks and damp woodland, the plant will take sun as long as its roots are kept moist.
ZONES 7–9.

CARTHAMUS

This genus of prickly composites of the thistle tribe consists of
14 species of annuals and perennials from the Mediterranean
region and western Asia. Some are nuisance weeds but one species,
safflower, is of commercial importance as an oil seed, and was also
the source of red and yellow dyes used for rouge and food coloring.
They are plants of upright growth with very sharp spines bordering
the parchment-textured leaves; the thistle-like flowerheads are
smallish, mostly with yellow florets surrounded by a ring of fiercely
spiny bracts.

CULTIVATION

Not fussy as to soil but enjoying a full sun position, these plants
need little care and their flowers make good, though not long
lasting, cut flowers that can be easily dried. Propagate from seed in
spring.

Carthamus tinctorius (left)
SAFFLOWER, FALSE SAFFRON

A fast-growing annual
24–36 in (60–90 cm)
tall, this thistle is
valued for its orange-
yellow flowers in
summer and for the oil
contained in its seeds.
Its leaves are spiny and
oblong, running down
the stems. Safflower is
frost hardy and grows
best in fertile, well-
drained soil.
ZONES 7–11.

C

CATHARANTHUS
MADAGASCAR PERIWINKLE

Although still referred to as *Vinca* by many gardeners, this genus is in fact quite distinct. It consists of 8 species of annuals and evergreen perennials or subshrubs, all originally from Madagascar though one widespread and often weedy species, *Catharanthus roseus,* has spread throughout warmer regions of the world. It has given rise to many horticultural selections, grown as bedding and border plants or sold in pots by florists. They are plants with repeatedly branched, rather fleshy stems and plain, smooth-edged leaves. The flowers are clustered in the upper leaf axils and are somewhat oleander-like, with a short tube opening by a very narrow mouth into 5 flat, radiating petals, the whole effect being very neat and star-like.

CULTIVATION
In cooler areas *Catharanthus* can be grown in a sunny conservatory or as summer bedding plants. In warm climates they are moderately tolerant of deep shade, the fiercest sun, and a dry atmosphere. Grow in free-draining soil, which should be kept moist in the growing period. Tip prune to keep bushy, but not so heavily as to inhibit flowering. They can be propagated from seed or from cuttings in summer.

Catharanthus roseus
syns *Lochnera rosea, Vinca rosea*
PINK PERIWINKLE

In its original form this shrubby perennial is a rather slender plant about 24 in (60 cm) high, with white to rose pink flowers shading to a darker red eye in the center. Garden forms are generally lower and more compact with larger flowers in a wider range of colors, blooming almost throughout the year in warm climates but mainly in spring and summer in cooler climates. Some mixed color series have flowers ranging from purple through pink to white, while others have pale colors (or are white) with prominent red eyes. All plant parts contain poisonous alkaloids from which drugs of value in the treatment of leukaemia have been refined.
ZONES 9–12.

Catharanthus roseus
cultivar *(left)*

C

Celmisia
asteliifolia *(right)*
SILVER SNOW DAISY

This species is native to Tasmania and south-eastern mainland Australia, forming large swathes of silvery gray foliage over grassy mountain slopes above the treeline. A dense network of woody rhizomes connects tangled rosettes of narrow, curving leaves that are white-felty on the undersides and dark gray-green on the upper. In mid-summer appear profuse 2–3 in (5–8 cm) wide flower-heads with white ray florets that are purplish on the reverse, on stalks 8–12 in (20–30 cm) tall. **ZONES 6–9.**

CELMISIA
SNOW DAISY, MOUNTAIN DAISY, NEW ZEALAND DAISY

Sixty or so species of rhizomatous perennials and subshrubs with white daisy-like flowerheads make up this genus, the majority native to New Zealand but with a smaller number native to Tasmania and south-eastern mainland Australia. Mostly occurring in higher mountain grasslands, meadows and rocky places, they are attractive evergreen plants with tufts of narrow silvery gray leaves and a profuse display of yellow-centered white flowers, mostly solitary on scaly stalks. The leaf undersides of most species are covered with a thick silvery white fur.

CULTIVATION
Most celmisias are true alpine plants that resent lowland conditions, but a few will grow successfully in rockeries, peat beds or scree gardens in temperate climates. Plant in full sun or part-shade and in moist, well-drained, gritty, acid soil. Protect from hot sun in drier areas and from excessive moisture in cool climates. Propagate from seed in autumn or by division in late spring.

C

Celmisia hookeri (below)

From the South Island of New Zealand, where it occurs in dry grasslands from the coast to lower mountain slopes, this larger-leaved species bears leaves to 12 in (30 cm) long and 3 in (8 cm) wide, glossy deep green above, thick white felty beneath. Flowerheads are up to 4 in (10 cm) across on short, thick stems, with a wide disc and a narrow rim of ray florets. ZONES 7–9.

Celmisia semicordata (above)
syn. *Celmisia coriacea*

This is one of the largest-growing species, also from low to medium altitudes on the South Island of New Zealand. Forming with age large mounds of rosettes, the striking silvery leaves are stiff and straight, up to 18 in (45 cm) long and 1–3 in (2.5–8 cm) wide. The white flowerheads are up to 4 in (10 cm) across, on slender stems to 15 in (38 cm) long. Generally regarded as the easiest celmisia to grow, *Celmisia semicordata* is more tolerant than most of heat and dry conditions but likes ample summer moisture. ZONES 7–9.

CELOSIA
COCKSCOMB, CHINESE WOOLFLOWER

This genus of erect annuals, perennials and shrubs in the amaranthus family contains 50 or more species from warmer parts of the Americas, Asia and Africa, but only *Celosia argentea* is widely cultivated as a bedding annual and for cut flowers. It has evolved in cultivation into numerous forms, hardly recognizable as belonging to the one species. It has simple, soft, strongly veined leaves; the variation is almost wholly in the structure of the heads of the small flowers, which have undergone proliferation and deformation in the two major cultivated races.

Celosia argentea, Plumosa Group cultivar *(above)*

CULTIVATION
In cool climates celosias are treated as conservatory plants, or planted out for summer bedding after raising seedlings under glass in spring. Better adapted to hot climates, they can withstand the fiercest summer heat. They require full sun, rich, well-drained soil and constant moisture. Propagate from seed in spring.

Celosia argentea
syns *Celosia cristata, C. pyramidalis*

Probably native to tropical Asia, this erect, summer-flowering annual reaches 3 ft (1 m) high or more. The leaves are mid-green; the silvery white flowers appear in summer in dense, erect, pointed spikes with a silvery sheen. The species is best known in the guise of two strikingly different cultivar groups, which are hardly recognizable as belonging to the species. These are the **Plumosa Group**, with erect, plume-like heads of tiny deformed flowers in a range of hot colors, and the **Cristata Group** (cockscombs), with bizarre wavy crests of fused flower stalks also in many colors. Both have been developed in cultivation with a range of seedling strains, differing in height as well as size and the color of the flowerheads. The Plumosa Group in particular are favored for cut flowers and sale in pots for indoor decoration. Some dwarf strains are no more than 6 in (15 cm) tall, while the old-fashioned bedding strains are about 24 in (60 cm). Most strains are sold as mixed colors. ZONES 10–12.

Celosia argentea, Cristata Group cultivars *(above & below)*

C

Celosia spicata *(left)*

Of uncertain origin, this annual species has appeared in recent years as a cut flower. Growing to 24 in (60 cm) or more, it has an erect, slender habit and much narrower leaves than *Celosia argentea*. The summer flowers are neatly crowded onto terminal spikes, opening progressively from the base with the buds purplish pink and the flowers ageing to pale silvery pink as the spikes elongate. The flowers last well when dried. There are many cultivars available. **'Caracas'** is an example. ZONES 10–12.

Celosia spicata 'Caracas' *(above)*

CENIA

These low-growing annuals and perennials in the daisy family are closely related to *Cotula,* in which they were formerly included. The plants have rather the aspect of *Anthemis* but the yellow flowerheads lack ray florets, appearing like large buttons, borne singly on slender stalks. The finely divided leaves are softly hairy and slightly aromatic.

CULTIVATION

Easily grown as rock garden or edging plants, they produce a succession of cheerful blooms, though the plants can become straggly as they age. Sow seed in autumn, and plant out in a sunny spot when seedlings are about 1 in (25 mm) high.

Cenia turbinata (below)
syn. *Cotula turbinata*
BACHELOR'S BUTTONS

Native to coastal areas of South Africa's Cape Province, this species is a short-lived perennial but in the garden is most often treated as an annual. The sprawling stems radiate from a central rootstock, concealed beneath the pale green, dissected, hairy foliage. In spring it produces a succession of bright yellow 'buttons' about 1¼ in (30 mm) in diameter on short, weak stalks. The plant grows 4–6 in (10–15 cm) high and spreads to about 24 in (60 cm).
ZONES 8–10.

C

Centaurea cineraria *(above)*
syns *Centaurea candidissima* of gardens,
C. gymnocarpa
DUSTY MILLER

A shrubby perennial from the Mediterranean
region, *Centaurea cineraria* is grown mainly for its
beautiful, much divided silvery white foliage.
When not in flower the plant is easily mistaken for
the unrelated *Senecio cineraria,* also known as
dusty miller. Small thistle-like, lilac-pink flowerheads held on much-branched flower stems reveal
delicate symmetry and color. The silveriness of the
foliage can vary from plant to plant, the best being
selected for propagation. ZONES 7–10.

CENTAUREA
CORNFLOWER, KNAPWEED

This genus, belonging to the thistle tribe of
composites, is a huge one with around
450 species scattered all over the temperate,
grassy regions of Eurasia and north Africa,
with one or two in America. It includes
annuals, biennials and perennials. Some
spiny-leafed species are troublesome weeds
in some parts of the world. Apart from the
common annual cornflower, some of the
perennial species are desirable garden
plants; they come in various colors, from
white through shades of blue, red, pink,
purple and yellow. The flowerheads typically
have an urn-shaped receptacle of fringed or
spiny bracts, from the mouth of which
radiate the quite large florets, each deeply
divided into 5 colored petals; smaller florets
occupy the center of the head, but do not
form a distinct disc as in other members of
the daisy or Compositae family.

CULTIVATION
Cornflowers do well in well-drained soil in
a sunny position. Propagate from seed in
spring or autumn; perennials can also be
divided in spring or autumn.

Centaurea cyanus *(left)*
BLUE-BOTTLE, BACHELOR'S BUTTON, CORNFLOWER

One of the best known wildflowers of Europe and
northern Asia, this species is also a common weed
of cereal crops. It is a weak-stemmed erect annual
24–36 in (60–90 cm) tall with very narrow leaves
and small, rather untidy flowerheads that are
typically a slightly purplish shade of blue. Garden
varieties have been developed with larger flowers
in shades of pale and deep pink, cerise, crimson,
white, purple and blue, some of them dwarf and
more compact. Best displayed in large clumps, it
will flower for months if deadheads are removed
regularly. ZONES 5–10.

C

Centaurea montana (above left)
PERENNIAL CORNFLOWER, MOUNTAIN BLUET

From the mountains of Europe, this long-cultivated perennial species is up to 30 in (75 cm) high and has creeping rhizomes; it may form large clumps when conditions are to its liking. The leaves are usually smooth edged and green, and the 2 in (5 cm) wide violet flowerheads, borne in early summer, are distinctive for their widely spaced florets, giving them a delicate lacy effect. ZONES 3–9.

Centaurea hypoleuca 'John Coutts' (above)

Centaurea hypoleuca

Also from the Caucasus and Iran as well as eastern Turkey, this spreading perennial has fragrant pale to deep pink flowerheads, produced singly on stalks up to 24 in (60 cm) high in early summer often with a second flush in autumn. It has long, lobed leaves, green on top and gray underneath, and forms a clump 18 in (45 cm) across. 'John Coutts' bears deep rose pink flowers. ZONES 5–9.

Centaurea dealbata (above)
PERSIAN CORNFLOWER

Native to the Caucasus region and northern Iran, this very leafy perennial has deeply cut foliage that is grayish green underneath. Lilac-purple to lilac-pink flowerheads appear from late spring onwards. An erect plant, *Centaurea dealbeata* grows to 3 ft (1 m) high. 'Steenbergii' has larger, deep pink blooms. ZONES 4–9.

Centaurea macrocephala (right)
GLOBE CORNFLOWER

With foliage a bit like a large dandelion, this perennial comes from the subalpine fields of Armenia and nearby parts of Turkey. In summer, stout leafy stems, up to 3 ft (1 m) tall, carry yellow flowerheads 2 in (5 cm) across with a club-like base of shiny brown bracts. ZONES 4–9.

CENTRANTHUS
VALERIAN

Around 10 species belong to this genus of annual and perennial herbs closely related to *Valeriana*, native to the Mediterranean region and western Asia, but only one, *Centranthus ruber*, is widely planted for ornament. They make tufts of soft leaves that may be simple and smooth edged or less commonly dissected, and the leafy, branched flowering stems bear many irregular heads of tiny tubular flowers.

CULTIVATION
Grow in full sun in moderately fertile, chalk or lime soil that is well drained. Deadhead regularly. These plants are not long lived and are best divided every 3 years to ensure a good display. Propagate from seed or by division.

Centranthus ruber
(left)
RED VALERIAN, JUPITER'S
BEARD, KISS-ME-QUICK

This perennial is often seen as a naturalized plant on dry banks and is ideal for dry rock gardens as well as borders. It forms loose clumps of somewhat fleshy leaves and grows to a height of 24–36 in (60–90 cm). From late spring to autumn it produces dense clusters of small, star-shaped, deep reddish pink to pale pink flowers that last for a long time. The cultivar **'Albus'** has white flowers. One of the easiest plants to grow, it requires sun and good drainage and will tolerate exposed positions and poor alkaline soil.
ZONES 5–10.

C

Cerastium alpinum (right)
ALPINE MOUSE-EAR

This cold-loving perennial species is widely distributed across subarctic regions of the northern hemisphere, coming south in Europe in the mountains. Forming a mat or small hummock, *Cerastium alpinum* has hairy rounded leaves and in summer bears conspicuous white flowers with broad petals purplelined in the throat, singly or in 2s or 3s on short, erect stalks. It does not adapt well to cultivation in warmer climates, requiring cool, humid summers. ZONES 2–8.

Cerastium boissieri (below)

CERASTIUM

Sixty or so species of low-growing annuals and perennials belong to this genus. They occur in most temperate regions of the world though mainly in the northern hemisphere, where some extend into arctic regions. The annuals include some common weeds of lawns (mouse-eared chickweeds), proliferating in winter and spring, but some of the perennials are useful garden plants grown as ground covers or rock garden subjects, for example, *Cerastium boissieri.* They have very weak stems from a network of thin rhizomes, and small leaves, usually clothed in whitish hairs, tapering to narrow bases. The flowers are white with 5 petals, each notched at the apex, held in stalked clusters above the leaves.

CULTIVATION

Easily cultivated, some cerastiums can be invasive if planted in confined spaces in a rock garden. All are frost hardy and like full sun and well-drained soil. Their foliage should, if possible, be kept dry both in winter and during humid summer weather, as the fine hairs on the leaves tend to retain moisture and become mildewed. They are easily propagated by division of rhizomes.

C

Ceratostigma plumbaginoides (left)
syn. *Plumbago larpentae*

CHINESE PLUMBAGO, PERENNIAL
LEADWORT, DWARF PLUMBAGO

Native to western China, this bushy perennial grows to 18 in (45 cm) high with rather erect, crowded stems arising from much-branched rhizomes. It has oval, mid-green leaves that turn a rich orange and red in autumn. The flowers are plumbago-like, with small clusters of single cornflower blue blooms appearing on reddish, branched stems in late summer and autumn. **ZONES 6–9.**

CERATOSTIGMA

This genus of 8 species of herbaceous perennials and small shrubs is primarily of Himalayan and East Asian origin, with one species endemic to the Horn of Africa. Most of the species grown in gardens are small deciduous shrubs and from spring to autumn they produce loose heads of blue flowers that indicate the genus's relationship with *Plumbago*. The small leaves are deep green, turning to bronze or crimson in autumn before dropping.

CULTIVATION
Ceratostigma species will grow in any moist, well-drained soil in sun or part-shade. Propagate from seed or semi-ripe cuttings, or by division. In cold climates they will reshoot from the roots even though the top growth may die back to ground level.

CHELIDONIUM
GREATER CELANDINE, SWALLOWWORT

A single species of short-lived perennial belongs to this genus of the poppy family, native to Europe and western Asia. It forms a clump of leafy stems, the slightly brittle leaves divided into several irregular leaflets with scalloped edges. Short sprays of small 4-petalled bright yellow flowers are produced over a long season, each flower soon succeeded by a slender pod that splits to release tiny black seeds. Broken leaves and stems bleed an orange latex which is irritating to the skin and has been used to cure warts; the plant has many other traditional medicinal uses but is quite poisonous.

Chelidonium majus 'Flore Pleno' *(above)*

CULTIVATION

The plant is very frost hardy and is easily grown in sun or light shade, adapting to all except very wet soils. Its duration may be only biennial, but it self-seeds readily and can become invasive. Propagate from seed or by division in autumn and cut back after flowering to keep under control.

Chelidonium majus *(right)*

This quick-growing perennial can form an effective ground cover if a number of seedlings are planted closely together. It is an erect to rather sprawling plant about 2–4 ft (0.6–1.2 m) high and wide, with attractive pale green foliage. From mid-spring to mid-autumn it produces a continuous scatter of bright golden yellow flowers about 1 in (25 mm) across; the slender seed capsules are 2 in (5 cm) long. **'Flore Pleno'** has double flowers. ZONES 6–9.

C

CHELONE
TURTLEHEAD

This genus of 6 species of rather coarse
but showy perennials from North America
is related to *Penstemon,* which they
resemble in growth habit and foliage.
The name comes from the Greek *kelone*
meaning a tortoise or turtle, and refers to
the hooded, gaping flowers, borne in
short terminal spikes. Leaves are toothed
and shiny in most species.

CULTIVATION

They are best along streams or pond
edges, but also adapt to a moist border
planting with rich soil in full sun or part-
shade. Propagate by dividing clumps in
early spring, from cuttings in summer or
from seed in spring or autumn.

Chelone lyonii (left)
PINK TURTLEHEAD

This species from the
mountains of south-
eastern USA grows to a
height of at least 3 ft
(1 m), with erect,
angled stems and dark
green leaves up to 6 in
(15 cm) long. The
summer flowers are
rosy purple and are
produced in axillary
and terminal spikes
terminating the stems,
and in upper leaf axils.
ZONES 6–9.

Chelone obliqua
(above)
ROSE TURTLEHEAD

Also from southeastern
USA, this is the showiest
of the turtleheads and
the best as a garden
plant. Pairs of rich
green leaves line 3 ft
(1 m) tall vertical stems
topped with short
spikes of rosy-purple
flowers in late summer
and autumn.
ZONES 6–9.

C

CHIASTOPHYLLUM

This genus in the crassula family consists of a single species of somewhat succulent evergreen perennial native to the Caucasus Mountains. It has leafy stems arising from a rootstock, the rounded, blunt-toothed leaves arranged in opposite pairs. The stems terminate in branched, drooping spikes of small yellow, bell-shaped flowers.

CULTIVATION

Its natural habitat is cool, moist crevices among rocks, and this should be simulated in the garden, for example on the shady side of a stone wall or bank, or a cool position in the rock garden. Watch for snails and slugs. Propagate from seed in autumn or by division in summer.

Chiastophyllum oppositifolium
(above)
syn. *Cotyledon simplicifolia*

This plant grows to no more than 8 in (20 cm) high but can spread by rhizomes to make a mat of indefinite width. The leaves are rather like some of the herbaceous sedums, pale green and thinly succulent with scalloped margins, the rusty red lower ones about 1 1/2 in (38 mm) long. The golden yellow flowers are 1/4 in (6 mm) long, appearing in late spring and early summer.
ZONES 7–9.

CHRYSANTHEMUM
CHRYSANTHEMUM

C

Although the garden (or florist's) chrysan-themums are so well known, the history of *Chrysanthemum* as a botanical name is very confusing. At one time this was used by botanists in a very broad sense to include not only the florist's chrysanthemums but several other related groups such as the Shasta daisies, marguerites, tansies and pyrethrums. After World War II the scientific evidence against this broad view began to mount, and a number of genera were split off *Chrysanthemum* to contain these rather distinct groups. For a while the florist's chrysanthemums themselves were given another genus name *(Dendranthema)* but a recent decision by an international committee on botanical nomenclature has brought their scientific name back into line with popular usage and they are now treated as the rightful claimants to the name *Chrysanthemum.*

The genus in this present, redefined sense consists of 37 species of perennials occurring wild mostly in eastern Asia, though two extend into northern Europe. They have lobed, somewhat aromatic leaves and panicles of daisy-like flowerheads in shades of red, purple, pink, yellow or white. Some of the species were taken into cultivation in China, possibly over 1000 years ago, and by the seventeenth century hundreds of named cultivars were recorded. News of these gorgeous flowers reached the West and by the early nineteenth century a number of cultivars had been introduced to Europe. Breeding continued in both China and western countries to produce the extra-ordinary array of forms and colors available today. The largest and most striking cultivars are grown only for exhibition by

chrysanthemum enthusiasts, but commercial growers raise other varieties by the millions for sale either as cut flowers or as flowering pot plants; their normal late summer-autumn flowering season is frequently extended by manipulation of day length and temperature in greenhouses.

Genera listed elsewhere in this book whose species were once classified under *Chrysanthemum* are: *Argyranthemum,* the marguerites, evergreen subshrubs from the Canary Islands and Madeira; *Leucanthemum,* white-flowered perennials from the Medi-terranean and Europe, including the ox-eye and Shasta daisies; *Tanacetum,* perennials and subshrubs from temperate Eurasia and North Africa, with very aromatic foliage and yellow, red or white flowers—they include the insecticidal pyrethrum, tansy and feverfew; *Ajania,* perennials from eastern and northern Asia rather like the florist's chrysanthemums but with flowers in numerous yellow button-like heads. And finally, 'Chrysanthemum' in the sense recognized before the recent decision, is the group of 5 annuals from Europe and North Africa including the crown daisy, corn marigold and painted daisy. The correct genus name for this group is still uncertain, so they are listed hereunder but with the genus in quotes, indicating they are no longer true *Chrysanthemums.*

CULTIVATION
Chrysanthemums are generally frost-hardy, though some forms are a little more tender than others. They can be grown outdoors in most temperate climates but, for indoor use, exhibition purposes or choice cut flowers, are usually raised under glass. Plant

outdoors in full sun in a well-drained, slightly acid soil improved with compost and well-rotted manure. For pot culture, use a rich, organic growing medium. Avoid excessive watering and in early summer feed with low-nitrogen, high-potassium fertilizer. Pinching out stem tips when they are 6–12 in (15–30 cm) high promotes flowering lateral stems with many flowers (known as 'sprays'), but for the largest exhibition blooms all lateral buds are removed at an early stage, leaving a single terminal bud—a 'disbudded chrysanthemum'. Stake tall plants with canes. Propagate bedding types from seed, named varieties from root divisions or basal cuttings of late autumn shoots. The annual species of 'Chrysanthemum' are easily grown in any good garden soil in a sunny position, by sowing seed in spring in cool climates or in autumn in warmer climates.

Chrysanthemum × grandiflorum

syns *Chrysanthemum morifolium, Dendranthema × grandiflorum*

FLORISTS' CHRYSANTHEMUM

Thought to be derived mainly from the Chinese species *Chrysanthemum indicum*, this hybrid group includes most of the cultivated chrysanthemums, and all of those with large double blooms. A more recent development is the breeding of the 'Korean chrysanthemums', introducing genes from *C. zawadskii* for more compact plants with smaller single heads, good for bedding. The chrysanthemum plant can be up to 5 ft (1.5 m) tall though mostly smaller; it has rather woody stems rising from a mass of creeping rhizomes, bluntly lobed leaves up to 3 in (8 cm) long with gray felted undersides; flowerheads may be anywhere from 1 to 6 in (2.5–15 cm) across, borne on a broad panicle and ranging from white, pink or yellow through various bronze colors to deep red or purple. Most of the larger types are 'double' lacking disc florets.

Chrysanthemum × grandiflorum, Single Form cultivar *(right)*

C

Chrysanthemum enthusiasts and societies have classified the thousands of cultivars into 10 groups, based on the overall form of the blooms and the shape and orientation of the florets. The full range of colors is represented in each group. The groups are:

Chrysanthemum × grandiflorum 'Elizabeth Shoesmith' *(above left)*

Chrysanthemum × grandiflorum 'Jane Sharpe' *(above)*

Chrysanthemum × grandiflorum 'Yellow Nightingale' *(below)*

Anemone-centered: daisy-like but with a pin-cushion center and a single or double row of radiating flat florets; normally grown as sprays rather than single blooms.

Incurved: fully double globular blooms with firm-textured florets curving inward and packed closely together, used for cut flowers as well as exhibition, long-lasting when cut. Cream **'Gillette'** and yellow **'Max Riley'** are examples.

Intermediate: falling somewhat between incurved and reflexed, these have ball-like blooms, some-times with recurving florets at the base. Pale bronze **'Crimson Tide'** and deep pink **'Elizabeth Shoesmith'** are examples. Another Intermediate is **'Jane Sharpe'**, which has salmon florets and a deep pink reverse.

Pompon: globular double blooms formed of numerous, tightly packed florets; normally grown as sprays rather than single blooms, they make excellent cut flowers.

Quill-shaped: double blooms with narrow tubular florets that open out at the tips. **'Yellow Nightingale'** is an example.

Chrysanthemum × *grandiflorum* 'Flame Symbol' *(right)*

Reflexed: rounded or dome-shaped, fully double blooms, the florets curved out and down, often with a curl or twist. Burnt-orange **'Flame Symbol'**, deep pink **'Matthew Scaelle'**, mid-pink **'Debonair'** and **'Yellow Symbol'** are examples.

Fully reflexed: perfectly rounded double blooms with florets that curve out and down, lowermost florets touching the stem.

Single: daisy-like blooms with up to 5 rows of radiating florets around a flattened yellow disc; excellent for massed planting.

Spider: double blooms with long narrow tubular florets that spread out in all directions, usually curled or twisted at the end. Golden-orange **'Dusky Queen'** and white **'Sterling Silver'** are examples.

Spoon-shaped: double blooms with radiating narrow, tubular florets with the tips expanded to form spoon shapes. **'Spears'** is an example. ZONES 4–10.

Chrysanthemum × *grandiflorum* 'Matthew Scaelle' *(above)*

Chrysanthemum × *grandiflorum* 'Yellow Symbol' *(above)*

Chrysanthemum × *grandiflorum* 'Dusky Queen' *(below)*

Chrysanthemum × *grandiflorum* 'Sterling Silver' *(below)*

C

'Chrysanthemum' carinatum *(left)*
syn. *Chrysanthemum tricolor*

PAINTED DAISY, SUMMER CHRYSANTHEMUM, TRICOLOR
CHRYSANTHEMUM

This and some of the following species are considered to belong to a separate genus from the florists' chrysanthemums but its name is yet to be determined, hence the quotes. It is a colorful garden flower from Morocco that grows to 24 in (60 cm), spreading to about 12 in (30 cm) with much-divided, fleshy leaves and banded, multi-colored flowers in spring and early summer. **'Monarch Court Jesters'** comes in red with yellow centers or white with red centers, and the **Tricolor Series** has many color combinations. They are excellent as bedding plants and cut flowers. ZONES 8–10.

'Chrysanthemum' coronarium *(left)*
CROWN DAISY

This is a fast-growing annual from the Mediterranean that will grow to a height of about 3 ft (1 m). The light green leaves are deeply divided and feathery. Daisy-like flowerheads are single or semi-double, very pale to deep yellow and up to 2 in (5 cm) across. The tender young shoots of selected strains are used in oriental cooking, where they are known as *shungiku* or chop suey greens; they can also be used raw in salads but have a strong aromatic taste.
ZONES 7–11.

Chrysanthemum ×
grandiflorum
'Spears' *(above)*

'Chrysanthemum' segetum (below)
CORN MARIGOLD

Originating from the eastern Mediterranean area and North Africa, this fast-growing annual is now widely naturalized in temperate regions. Up to about 24 in (60 cm) tall, it has gray-green leaves that are toothed or, on the lower stem, deeply cut. The daisy-like flowerheads, 1¹/₂–2¹/₂ in (4–6 cm) across, appear in summer and early autumn in various shades of yellow. They make good cut flowers. **'Zebra'** has brick red outer florets. **ZONES 7–10.**

'Chrysanthemum' segetum 'Zebra' (right)

C

Chrysocephalum apiculatum
(above)
syn. *Helichrysum apiculatum*
YELLOW BUTTONS, COMMON EVERLASTING

Occurring over a large part of the Australian continent and also Tasmania, this species is highly variable in growth habit and foliage characters. Some forms are up to 24 in (60 cm) high, others much lower, some make compact clumps of basal rosettes, others spread extensively. The simple, flat leaves vary from gray-felted to green and only slightly hairy. Flowerheads are golden yellow, in small to large clusters, appearing mainly in spring or summer but can appear at any time of year. Some very attractive forms have been introduced to cultivation. ZONES 8–11.

CHRYSOCEPHALUM

All 8 species of this Australian genus of perennials were formerly included in *Helichrysum*, a genus of the daisy family that botanists are still in the process of redefining and narrowing in scope. *Chrysocephalum* species are mostly evergreens, with slender leafy stems arising from wiry rhizomes by which the plants may spread extensively, though some species have more compact rootstocks. The small 'everlasting' type flowerheads are mostly clustered at the stem apex, and have many rows of tiny yellow or white chaffy bracts surrounding a small group of orange discflorets. Some species are vigorous growers and make useful ground covers, as well as providing a fine display of spring and summer blooms.

CULTIVATION
These plants prefer a climate with warm, dry summers but are nonetheless fairly adaptable if grown in well-drained, open soil of moderate fertility and in a sunny spot. Propagate from seed, rhizome division, or cuttings from lower stems.

Chrysocephalum baxteri (left)
syn. *Helichrysum baxteri*
FRINGED EVERLASTING, WHITE EVERLASTING

Native mainly to Victoria, Australia, this compact perennial has narrow, almost grass-like dark green leaves, woolly white underneath, forming a mound to about 6 in (15 cm) high. The 4–8 in (10–20 cm) flowering stems each carry a single daisy-like flowerhead, with showy white or cream (sometimes buff or pinkish) papery bracts surrounding yellow discflorets. It can flower at any time but peaks in spring. This species makes an attractive rock garden plant. ZONES 8–10.

*Chrysogonum
virginianum* (above)

This low growing,
mat-forming perennial
suitable for a rock
garden spreads by
underground runners,
but is not normally
invasive. It bears yellow
daisy-like flowerheads
through summer into
autumn. ZONES 6–9.

CHRYSOGONUM
GOLDEN KNEE, GOLDEN STAR

This genus of only a single species of herbaceous perennial from
eastern USA belongs to the sunflower tribe of the very large daisy
or composite family. The botanical name is Latinized Greek for
'golden knee', alluding to the joint-like stem nodes from which the
flower stalks arise. Plants spread by long-running rhizomes,
sending up short erect stems with heart-shaped leaves arranged in
opposite pairs. The bright yellow flowerheads have only 5 broad
ray-florets and are produced over a very long flowering season in
spring and summer.

CULTIVATION
Easy to grow, *Chrysogonum* can spread over a large area of ground
but prefers light shade and a rather peaty, moist soil. Propagate
from seed or by division.

C

CHRYSOSPLENIUM
GOLDEN SAXIFRAGE

A genus of 50 or more species of low-growing perennials of the saxifrage family, native in temperate regions of the northern hemisphere except for a handful in temperate South America. They are interesting little plants with creeping fleshy stems and round or kidney-shaped leaves, and little flat heads of golden yellow flowers sitting in a circle of leaf-like bracts which may be yellow at the base but are usually green tipped.

CULTIVATION
They prefer moist, sheltered spots in semi-shade and grow well in boggy edges of streams or ponds. Propagate from seed or by division.

Chrysosplenium davidianum (below)
Native to western China, this species forms low carpets of hairy stems and rounded leaves that are hairy on the undersides and have strongly scalloped edges. The flattened heads of tiny yellow flowers with yellow-tinted bracts are borne from late spring to early summer. ZONES 5–9.

CIMICIFUGA
BUGBANE

This genus of about 15 species of perennials in the ranunculus family, native to cooler regions of the northern hemisphere. The name literally means 'bug repellent', from the Latin *cimex,* the bedbug, and *fugare,* to repel, reflecting an early use of one species. The foliage is reminiscent of astilbes, having large compound leaves with toothed leaflets, but the branched flowering stems terminate in long, erect spikes of small white, cream or pinkish flowers, the many stamens being the conspicuous part of each flower. Some North American species are important in herbal medicine.

CULTIVATION

These plants are bold additions to the summer garden, at the back of borders or in open woodland situations. They prefer part-shade and a deep, rich soil and need regular watering but otherwise need little attention. Plant rhizome divisions in spring or autumn, but do not disturb the root; they flower best when established, and seldom need staking.

Cimicifuga japonica var. *acerina* (below)

Cimicifuga simplex 'Hanse Herms' *(above)*

Cimicifuga simplex (below)
KAMCHATKA BUGBANE

From Japan and far eastern Siberia, this species is the latest to flower of the whole genus, the flowers coming in late autumn. It is also smaller, reaching a height of about 4 ft (1.2 m). The flowers are white, carried on long arching wands, and the foliage is much divided. **'Elstead'** has purplish buds opening to pure white and is a very graceful plant. **'Hanse Herms'** is another popular cultivar. ZONES 3–9.

Cimicifuga japonica
JAPANESE BUGBANE

From woodlands of Japan, this species is distin-guished by its very long stalked leaves with shallowly lobed leaflets up to 4 in (10 cm) wide. The flower-ing stems are slender and leafless, up to 4 ft (1.2 m) high, bearing rather undistinguished small white flowers from mid-summer to early autumn. *Cimicifuga japonica* **var. *acerina*** (syn. *C. acerina*) has long drawn-out points on the leaf lobes. ZONES 5–9.

C

CINERARIA

This name has been the source of much confusion. The true *Cineraria*, as botanists understand it, is a genus of about 50 species from southern Africa and Madagascar, little known in gardens. The florist's 'cinerarias' are a colorful group of hybrids of Canary Island origin now referred to as *Pericallis* × *hybrida* though once placed in the genus *Senecio;* and the gray-leafed *Cineraria maritima* of gardens is correctly *Senecio cineraria,* a Mediterranean plant. The true (African) cinerarias are perennials and subshrubs with broad, rather fleshy leaves that are often heart-shaped or kidney-shaped and may be hairy or woolly. They produce numerous stalked flowerheads with yellow ray-florets, like small daisies.

CULTIVATION

Only a few South African species have ever been cultivated, making attractive low plants for rockeries or banks, or used as ground covers. They are not very frost hardy and like well-drained, humus-rich soil and plenty of sun. Propagate from seed, cuttings, or by root divisions.

Cineraria saxifraga (above)

This South African perennial is broadly spreading and usually about 8 in (20 cm) high, with prostrate branches that root into the soil. The pale green somewhat succulent leaves, to about 1½ in (38 mm) long, are almost kidney-shaped and coarsely toothed. Numerous small, yellow, daisy-like flowerheads appear through spring, summer and autumn, on weak slender stalks. ZONES 9–11.

CIRSIUM

This name of this genus of 200 species of thistles from the cooler parts of the northern hemisphere comes from the Greek *kirsos* (swollen vein). Several species are cursed by farmers as noxious weeds, but others make attractive ornamentals. There are both annual and perennial species. They are mostly very spiny plants, with a basal leaf rosette and branched flowering stems bearing spiny flowerheads of typical thistle form.

CULTIVATION

They can be grown in average garden soil but like good drainage. They are easily raised from seed, but care must be taken when planting them in situations where seed may escape into surrounding areas.

C

Cirsium occidentale (below)
COBWEB THISTLE

Native to central western and south-western California, this biennial grows to 3 ft (1 m) tall with leaves that are deeply divided, rather hairy and armed with numerous needle-like spines. The clustered flowerheads, borne in spring and summer, are enclosed in striking white woolly bracts and the florets are scarlet in color. ZONES 9–11.

CLARKIA
syn. *Godetia*

This genus, allied to the evening primroses *(Oenothera)* and consisting of about 36 species, was named in honor of Captain William Clark, of the famous Lewis and Clark expedition that crossed the American continent in 1806. They are bushy annuals, undistinguished in foliage but spectacular in their all too short flowering season when they are covered in showy funnel-shaped flowers in various shades of pink, white and carmine. The flowers can be 4 in (10 cm) across, and they look a little like azaleas—in Germany they are called *Sommerazalee,* the summer azalea. They are very good as cut flowers, borne on long stems and lasting a week in water.

CULTIVATION
They are easily grown in full sun in any temperate climate. They prefer moist but well-drained, slightly acid soil; soil that is too fertile will see good foliage but poor flower production. Propagate from seed in autumn or spring.

Clarkia unguiculata *(above)*
syn. *Clarkia elegans*
MOUNTAIN GARLAND

This species is usually taller than its fellow-Californian *Clarkia amoena* but with smaller flowers, only 1 in (25 mm) across, often frilled and doubled. The flowers, produced at the tops of slender, reddish stems 3 ft (1 m) or more in height, have a broader color range, including orange and purple. ZONES 7–11.

Clarkia amoena
(left)
syn. *Clarkia grandiflora*
FAREWELL-TO-SPRING

A free-flowering annual, this Californian native is fast growing to a height of 24 in (60 cm) and spread of 12 in (30 cm). It has lance-shaped, mid-green leaves, thin upright stems, and in summer bears spikes of open, cup-like, single or double flowers in shades of pink; a number of cultivars have been produced from this species. Allow it to dry out between waterings and watch for signs of botrytis. ZONES 7–11.

Clematis integrifolia *(right)*

From southern Europe, this herbaceous clematis is hardly recognizable as belonging to this genus, at least until it flowers. It forms a gradually expanding clump with masses of stems arising from the base each spring, each one ending in a single, nodding flower of four 1 in (25 mm) long petals. It is normally purple-blue, deeper in the center. The stamens are creamy white and tightly packed. The flower stalks tend to flop and may need support. Improved forms like **'Hendersonii'**, **'Rosea'** and **'Tapestry'** are rather more reliable in this regard than the species. ZONES 3–9.

CLEMATIS
VIRGIN'S BOWER, TRAVELLER'S JOY

The 200 or more species of deciduous or evergreen woody climbers or woody-based perennials in this genus are scattered throughout the world's temperate regions, but most of the popular, larger-flowered garden plants have come from Japan and China. They climb by twisting their leaf-stalk tendrils about a support and are ideal for training on verandah posts, arbors, bowers and trellises. Showy bell-shaped or flattish flowers with 4 to 8 petals (*sepals* really) are followed by masses of fluffy seed heads, often lasting well into winter.

CULTIVATION

The most important requirement for successful cultivation is a well-drained, humus-rich, permanently cool soil with good moisture retention. The plants like to climb up to the sun with their roots in the shade. Prune old twiggy growth in spring and propagate from cuttings or by layering in summer. In some areas where growing clematis is a problem, plants are often grafted. Clematis wilt can be a problem.

Clematis mandshurica *(above)*
syn. *Clematis recta* var. *mandshurica*

A native of China and Japan, this herbaceous perennial species has a sprawling habit or may climb to about 3–6 ft (1–1.8 m) in height. The small white flowers, about 1¼ in (3 cm) across, are borne in erect terminal umbels, while the smooth dark brown seeds have long yellowish tails. Plant in a protected, part-shaded position. ZONES 7–9.

C

Cleome hassleriana (left)
syn. *Cleome spinosa* of gardens

Native to subtropical South America, this fast-growing, bushy annual is valued for its unusual spidery flowers. An erect plant, it grows to 4 ft (1.2 m) tall with a spread of 18 in (45 cm). It has large palmate leaves and the hairy, slightly prickly stems are topped in summer with heads of airy, pink and white flowers with long, protruding stamens. Several cultivars are available as seed, and these range in color from pure white to purple. ZONES 9–11.

CLEOME
SPIDER FLOWER, SPIDER PLANT

This genus of 150 species of bushy annuals and short-lived evergreen shrubs, from subtropical and tropical zones all over the world, is characterized by its spidery flowers with 4 petals that narrow into basal stalks and mostly long, spidery stamens and styles. The leaves are composed of from 5 to 7 palmate leaflets. One species is widely grown as a background bedding plant, useful for its rapid growth and delicate floral effect.

CULTIVATION
Marginally frost hardy, they require full sun and fertile, well-drained soil, regular water and shelter from strong winds. Taller growth can be encouraged by removing side branches, and dead flowers should also be removed. Propagate from seed in spring or early summer. Check for aphids.

CLINTONIA

Five species of woodland lilies from North America and eastern Asia make up this genus, all rhizomatous perennials with rich green smooth foliage rather like that of *Convallaria*, and erect spikes or umbels (solitary in one species) of small, starry 6-petalled flowers.

CULTIVATION

All species need a cool, peaty, lime-free soil and a shaded, humid position, and so are best suited to a woodland garden. Winter mulching will protect from frost. Propagate from seed or division of rhizomes.

Clintonia borealis
(below)
CORN LILY, BLUEBEARD

From eastern and central North America, this species has loose clusters of yellowish white flowers with recurving petals and protruding stamens, followed by blue berries. It reaches a height of 6–12 in (15–30 cm) and blooms in late spring and early summer. **ZONES 3–9.**

Clintonia umbellulata (above)
SPECKLED WOOD-LILY

From eastern USA, this is one of the prettiest species with dense umbels of fragrant white flowers, often speckled green or purplish, rising on stems up to 15 in (40 cm) tall above dense patches of luxuriant foliage. The flowers appear in late spring and early summer and are followed by black berries. **ZONES 4–9.**

Clintonia andrewsiana (right)

A native of northern California and Oregon, this species has small bell-like flowers that are poised in a cluster at the top of the stems; they are colored a rich carmine red, the three inner petals with a central creamy vein. The flowers are followed by violet-blue berries. This plant increases slowly, reaching a height of about 24 in (60 cm). **ZONES 7–9.**

CLIVIA
KAFFIR LILY

This genus of southern African lilies was named after Lady Clive, Duchess of Northumberland, whose grandfather was the famous Clive of India. She was a patron of gardening and *Clivia nobilis* first flowered in the UK in her greenhouses. The genus consists of 4 species of evergreen perennials with thick, strap-like, deep green leaves springing from short rhizomes with thick roots. Flowers are borne in dense umbels terminating somewhat flattened stems and are funnel-shaped to trumpet-shaped, with 6 red to orange, sometimes green-tipped petals that are partially fused into a tube. They are sometimes followed by quite conspicuous, deep red, berry-like fruits.

CULTIVATION
They will grow well outdoors in a mild, frost-free climate, or in a conservatory or greenhouse in regions with colder climates. Plant in a shaded or part-shaded, position in friable, well-drained soil. They are surface-rooting, however, and dislike soil disturbance. Keep fairly dry in winter and increase watering in spring and summer. Propagate by division after flowering. Clivias may also be grown from seed, but can be slow to flower.

Clivia miniata
(below left)
BUSH LILY, FIRE LILY

This most commonly cultivated and showiest species is distributed widely in eastern South Africa. About 18 in (45 cm) in height, it has broad leaves, sometimes up to 3 in (8 cm) wide and bears clusters of broadly funnel-shaped flowers up to 3 in (8 cm) long, mostly orange to scarlet with a yellow throat, usually in spring but with the occasional bloom at other times. Many cultivars have been selected over the years, including yellow and cream forms. There is a group of especially prized forms commonly called 'hybrids' with tulip-shaped, deep, rich scarlet blooms. ZONES 10–11.

C

Codonopsis
convolvulacea 'Alba'
(left)

CODONOPSIS

Native to eastern Asia and higher mountains of the Malay region, this genus allied to *Campanula* consists of about 30 species of perennials with swollen roots, some with scrambling or climbing stems, and simple, broad to narrow leaves that smell slightly unpleasant when bruised. The flowers are pendent or nodding, basically bell-shaped but with many variations, and in many cases prettily veined.

CULTIVATION

They require a moist, cool-temperate climate and most species grow best in a light, well-drained soil in part or complete shade. For best effect, plant in a raised bed or on a bank where the insides of the nodding flowers can be seen. Propagate from seed or by division with care.

Codonopsis convolvulacea

This species from the Himalayas and Western China sends up twining stems to as much as 8 ft (2.4 m) high if a suitable support is available or it may hang down a bank or wall. The broadly bell-shaped flowers are up to 2 in (5 cm) across, range in color from violet to almost white and are carried singly on long stalks at ends of lateral branches. **'Alba'** has white flowers.
Codonopsis clematidea from central Asia is very similar to *C. convolvulacea*, but has nodding flowers with purple veining.
ZONES 5–9.

Codonopsis clematidea
(right)

C

Columnea arguta
(left)

A native of Panama, this is one of the most beautiful species which is at its best grown in a large hanging basket in a humid conservatory. The pendulous stems grow up to 6 ft (1.8 m) long, forming a dense curtain of foliage; the small, crowded leaves are dark green on their convex uppersides with velvety purplish hairs, and the strongly hooded flowers, about 3 in (8 cm) long, make a display of brilliant color. ZONES 11–12.

COLUMNEA

With over 150 species of shrubs, subshrubs and climbers from tropical America, this is one of the largest genera of the African violet and gloxinia family, as well as being one of the most important in terms of ornamental indoor plants. Coming from regions of high rainfall and humidity, many grow as epiphytes, with long trailing stems and rather fleshy leaves. The beautiful and unusual flowers, mostly in colors of red, orange and yellow, have a long tube and often a hooded or helmet-shaped upper lip; they are adapted to pollination by hummingbirds, which hover under the flower and brush pollen from anthers beneath the hood onto their heads while sipping nectar from the tube.

CULTIVATION
Some species demand constant high humidity, but many can grow outdoors in warm climates in a suitably sheltered spot in filtered light; in cooler climates they need the protection of a greenhouse or conservatory. Hanging baskets are ideal for most columneas, whether they are of the type with quite pendulous stems or more erect, scrambling plants. Grow in an open, fibrous compost, including, for example, sphagnum moss, peat and charcoal. Water freely in summer, reducing water as the weather cools. Propagate from cuttings.

CONSOLIDA

LARKSPUR

Botanists in the past often treated these annuals as species of *Delphinium,* but the consensus now is that the 40 or so species constitute a distinct genus, occurring in the Mediterranean region and west and central Asia. The name *Consolida* was bestowed in the Middle Ages in recognition of the plants' use in the healing of wounds; they were believed to help the clotting (consolidating) of the blood. The larkspurs grown in gardens are mostly derived from the one species, *Consolida ajacis,* and include many strains, mostly grown as mixed colors. The flowers of the taller kinds will last a long time when cut. They have finely divided, feather-like leaves and poisonous seeds.

CULTIVATION

They are not difficult to grow, succeeding in any temperate or even mildly sub-tropical climate and liking full sun and rich, well-drained soil. Tall cultivars need to be staked. Propagate from seed and watch for snails and slugs and for powdery mildew.

Consolida ajacis (below)
syns *Consolida ambigua, Delphinium consolida*

The name larkspur comes from the nectar spur at the back of the flowers, hidden in the open blooms but clearly visible on the unopened buds. This Mediterranean species originally had blue flowers. Present-day garden larkspurs are the result of hybridizing this species with *Consolida orientalis* to give the 'rocket larkspurs', or may be derived mainly from *C. regalis* in the case of the 'forking larkspurs'. Their blooms may be pink, white or purple and are usually double, borne mainly in summer. Some can reach a height of 4 ft (1.2 m). ZONES 7–11.

C

CONVALLARIA
LILY-OF-THE-VALLEY

Some botanists have recognized several species of *Convallaria,* but most believe there is only one, occurring wild in forests from France to Siberia, also cooler parts of North America. The plant spreads over the forest floor by slender underground rhizomes which at intervals send up pointed oval leaves and slender flowering stems adorned with little white bells, shining like pearls against the dull green of the foliage. The red berries that follow have their uses in medicine, but they are poisonous—dangerously so, as they are sweet enough to tempt children to eat them.

CULTIVATION

The rhizomes, or 'pips' as they are commonly known from their growing tips, should be planted in autumn in a part-shaded position. Given the right conditions, lily-of-the-valley spreads freely and in a confined space sometimes becomes overcrowded, when it will benefit from lifting and thinning. Grow in fertile, humus-rich, moist soil. They can be potted for display indoors, then replanted outdoors after flowering. Propagate from seed or by division.

Convallaria majalis (below)

Renowned for its glorious perfume, this beautiful plant does best in cool climates. It is low growing, 8–12 in (20–30 cm) high but of indefinite spread, with mid-green leaves. The dainty white bell-shaped flowers, $1/4–1/2$ in (6–12 mm) across, appear in spring. Pink-flowered variants are known, collectively referred to as *Convallaria majalis* var. *rosea,* and there are several cultivars with variegated or gold foliage. ZONES 3–9.

CONVOLVULUS

Found in many temperate regions of the world, this genus consists mainly of slender, twining creepers (the bindweeds) and small herbaceous plants. Only a few species are shrubby, and even these are soft stemmed and renewed by shooting from the base. They have simple, thin-textured, usually narrow leaves, and flowers like morning glories, with a strongly flared tube that opens by unfurling 'pleats'. However, *Convolvulus* species differ from morning glories (*Ipomoea*) in having flowers that stay open all day, rather than shrivelling by mid-morning or early afternoon; they usually open in succession over a long season.

CULTIVATION

These easily grown plants adapt to most soils and exposed as well as sheltered positions, but prefer full sun. Cut back hard after flowering to promote thicker growth. Propagation is from cuttings.

Convolvulus althaeoides (above)

Native to the Mediterranean region, this is a perennial which can spread by underground rhizomes. It has trailing or twining stems and oval to heart-shaped leaves that may be strongly lobed and slightly overlaid with silver. The profuse bright pink flowers are 1–1½ in (25–38 mm) across, and they are borne in late spring and summer. In a mild climate the plants may become invasive. If not supported, they will mound untidily to about 6 in (15 cm) high. ZONES 8–10.

C

Convolvulus tricolor
syn. *Convolvulus minor*

This bedding annual from the Mediterranean bears profuse deep purple-blue or white flowers with banded yellow and white throats. The small leaves are lance-shaped and mid-green. A slender, few-branched plant, it grows to a height of 8–12 in (20–30 cm) and blooms from late spring to early autumn, but each flower lasts only one day. '**Blue Ensign**' has very deep blue flowers with pale yellow centers. ZONES 8–11.

Convolvulus tricolor 'Blue Ensign' *(above left)*

Convolvulus tricolor, mixed *(left)*

Convolvulus cneorum *(below left)*
BUSH MORNING GLORY

This attractive plant from Mediterranean Europe has crowded, weak, upcurving stems sprouting from the base to 1–2 ft (0.3–0.6 m). The leaves, in tufts along the stems, are soft and narrow with a coating of silky hairs, giving them a silvery sheen. The stems terminate in dense clusters of silky buds, each producing a long succession of flowers through spring and summer, flesh pink in bud opening pure dazzling white with a small yellow 'eye'. ZONES 8–10.

COREOPSIS

These 80 species of annuals and perennials from cooler or drier regions of the Americas make up this genus of the daisy family. The flowerheads, borne on slender stems mainly in summer, are mostly shades of gold or yellow, some bicolored. Leaves vary from simple, narrow and toothed, to deeply divided. They may be basal or scattered up the stems. *Coreopsis rosea* 'American Queen' is a popular cultivar.

Coreopsis rosea 'American Queen' *(above)*

Coreopsis auriculata 'Nana' *(below)*

CULTIVATION

The annuals are grown as bedding plants, while the perennials are excellent for herbaceous borders. Perennials prefer full sun and a fertile, well-drained soil but also grow well in coastal regions and in poor, stony soil. Propagate by dividing old clumps in winter or spring, or by spring cuttings. Annuals also prefer full sun and a fertile, well-drained soil; they will not tolerate heavy clay soil. Stake tall varieties. Propagate from seed in spring or autumn.

Coreopsis grandiflora

(below right)

TICKSEED

Among the easiest of perennials, this golden yellow daisy from southeastern and central USA provides color from late spring to mid-summer. Somewhat hairy leaves and stems form a loose mound to 12–24 in (30–60 cm) tall and wide, the flower stems rising to nearly 24 in (60 cm) or usually flopping on their neighbors. Best suited to a meadow garden, it can be treated as an annual and self-seeds freely. More compact cultivars such as **'Badengold'**, **'Sunray'** or **'Early Sunrise'** are the best choices for the well-maintained border. ZONES 6–10.

Coreopsis auriculata

This is a frost-hardy but short-lived perennial from southeastern USA that will grow to a height of 18 in (45 cm). The flowerheads are a rich yellow, produced through summer. The leaves are oval or lance-shaped. There are several improved forms, such as **'Perry's Variety'**, which has semi-double flowers. **'Nana'** is a compact form growing to 6 in (15 cm) tall. ZONES 4–9.

C

Coreopsis verticillata

This perennial produces crowded erect stems to 30 in (75 cm) tall from a tangled mass of thin rhizomes. The leaves, in whorls of 3, are divided into very narrow segments. The abundant bright yellow flower-heads appear from late spring until autumn. It does best in light soil of low fertility. **'Moonbeam'** is slightly lower and more com-pact with lemon yellow blooms. **ZONES 6–10.**

Coreopsis verticillata 'Moonbeam' *(above left)*

Coreopsis lanceolata 'Baby Sun' *(left)*

Coreopsis lanceolata *(below)*

This is a tufted peren-nial with long-stalked, lance-shaped basal leaves and bright golden yellow flowerheads on leafy stems up to about 24 in (60 cm) high. It is extremely floriferous and when mass planted can make sheets of gold in spring and early summer. Short lived, it is very free-seeding, and is a weed in parts of Australia. Double forms are sometimes grown. **'Baby Sun'** is a compact long bloom-ing cultivar about 12 in (30 cm) high; suitable for bedding. **ZONES 3–11.**

Coreopsis tinctoria *(left)*
TICKSEED, PLAINS COREOPSIS, CALLIOPSIS

This fast-growing, showy annual produces clusters of bright yellow flowerheads with red centers during summer and autumn. Of slender, weak habit, and 24–36 in (60–90 cm) tall, the plants tend to incline over and may need staking. It provides good cut flowers. **ZONES 4–10.**

CORONILLA
CROWN VETCH

A legume genus of 20 or so species of annuals, perennials and low, wiry shrubs, native to Europe, western Asia and northern Africa. They have pinnate leaves with small, thin or somewhat fleshy leaflets, and stalked umbels of small pea-flowers a little like some clover or medic flowers. Certain perennial and shrub species are grown as ornamentals, valued for their profuse flowers blooming over a long season, though not especially showy. *Coronilla* is Latin for 'little crown', referring to the neat circular umbels of some species.

CULTIVATION
They need full sun, moderately fertile, well-drained soil and protection from cold winds. Cut leggy plants back to the base in spring. Propagate from seed, cuttings, or division of rootstock.

Coronilla varia (below)
syn. *Securigera varia*
CROWN VETCH

A sprawling perennial from Europe, crown vetch has run wild in some parts of the USA. It can spread quite rapidly by a deep network of thin rhizomes, the weak leafy stems rising to about 24 in (60 cm) tall. The soft pinnate leaves resemble those of the true vetches (*Vicia*) and the clover-like heads of pink to lilac-pink flowers appear throughout summer. Not suited to a formal garden, it can be rather invasive, but makes a good soil-binding plant for a sunny bank, stopping erosion while slower plants take hold. Some botanists now place it in the genus *Securigera*.
ZONES 6–10.

C

CORYDALIS

The 300 or so species in this genus, allied to the fumitories *(Fumaria)*, occur in temperate regions of the northern hemisphere. Mostly perennials, but with some annuals, their basal tufts of ferny, deeply dissected leaves spring from fleshy rhizomes or tubers. The smallish tubular flowers, with a short backward-pointing spur that may be curved, are usually in short spikes. They are mostly creams, yellows, pinks and purples, and a few have clear blue flowers.

CULTIVATION

The sun-loving species do well in rock gardens, while the shade lovers are best beneath border shrubs or in a woodland garden. Soil should be moist but well drained, and rich in humus for woodland species. Several, such as *Corydalis lutea,* self-seed freely in cracks between paving or on walls. Propagate from seed or by division.

Corydalis lutea *(left)*
YELLOW CORYDALIS

The most easily grown species, this native of Europe's southern Alps is widely naturalized in temperate climates around the world. A rhizomatous perennial, it makes broad clumps or mounds of fresh green foliage to 12 in (30 cm) high, and is dotted from spring to autumn with short sprays of soft yellow flowers. It will grow in many situations but often self-seeds in wall crevices or moist chinks in rockeries. In a woodland garden it makes an attractive ground cover.
ZONES 6–10.

Corydalis flexuosa
(above)

This species forms a small clump of green foliage around 12 in (30 cm) tall. During late spring and early summer, short spikes of long-spurred, tubular, clear blue flowers, each about 1 in (25 mm) long, appear above the foliage. It requires a cool spot in part-shade and moist soil.
ZONES 5–9.

Corydalis solida (right)
FUMEWORT

This species from northern Europe and Asia is similar to *Corydalis cava* differing, as its name suggests, in having a solid, not hollow, tuber and stem base. Each 6–10 in (15–25 cm) erect stem has only 2 or 3 dissected leaves, one at the base, and terminates in a dense spike of pink to purplish red flowers in spring. It dies back in summer. The cultivar **'George Baker'** has rich salmon-red flowers. ZONES 6–9.

Corydalis wilsonii
(below)

This species from China forms low mounds of blue-green foliage to 8 in (20 cm) high and wide. Loose spikes of bright yellow flowers are borne in spring. ZONES 7–9.

C

Cosmos bipinnatus
cultivar *(left)*

Cosmos bipinnatus
(below far left)
COMMON COSMOS, MEXICAN ASTER

This feathery-leafed annual from Mexico and far southern USA reaches 5–6 ft (1.5–1.8 m) in height with showy daisy-like flowerheads in summer and autumn, in shades of pink, red, purple or white. Taller plants may need staking. Newer strains are usually more compact and can have double flowers and striped petals. 'Sea Shells' has usually pink, sometimes crimson or white flowerheads with edges of ray-florets curled into a tube. ZONES 8–11.

Cosmos atrosanguineus *(left)*
BLACK COSMOS, CHOCOLATE COSMOS

A tuberous-rooted, clump-forming perennial growing to 24 in (60 cm) in height and spread, the unusual black cosmos from Mexico has long-stalked, very dark maroon flowerheads that have a chocolate scent, most noticeable on warm days. It flowers from summer to autumn. The leaves are rather few-lobed and tinged dull purplish. It normally dies back in autumn and requires fairly dry soil if the rootstock is not to rot; alternatively the roots can be lifted and stored for the winter like dahlias. ZONES 8–10.

COSMOS
MEXICAN ASTER

This genus of 25 annuals and perennials allied to *Dahlia,* contains a couple of well-known garden flowers. They have erect but weak, leafy stems and the leaves are variously lobed or deeply and finely dissected. Flowerheads, on slender stalks that terminate branches, are daisy-like with showy, broad ray-florets surrounding a small disc; they range in color from white through pinks, yellows, oranges, reds and purples to deep maroon.

CULTIVATION

They are only moderately frost hardy and in cold climates need protection in winter. Seedlings should be planted out only after all danger of frost has passed. They require a sunny situation with protection from strong winds and will grow in any well-drained soil as long as it is not over-rich. Mulch with compost and water well in hot, dry weather. Propagate annuals from seed in spring or autumn, the perennials from basal cuttings in spring. Deadhead regularly, and in humid weather check for insect pests and mildew.

COSTUS
SPIRAL FLAG, SPIRAL GINGER

Belonging to the ginger family, this genus of clump-forming ever-green perennials consists of some 150 species scattered throughout the wet tropics, though concentrated mainly in tropical America and West Africa. The ginger-like leaves are arranged in an ascending spiral around the stem, and attractive terminal flowerheads with overlapping bracts, rather like a pine cone. The flowers which emerge between the bracts are orange, yellow, pink, red or white.

CULTIVATION
They are suitable for planting outdoors only in tropical or sub-tropical regions. In cooler climates they make showy indoor plants but require high humidity and a heated greenhouse or conservatory in winter. Grow in humus-rich soil in a well-lit position, but not direct sunlight. Propagate by division or from seed in spring. Plants grown indoors may be affected by red spider mite.

Costus speciosus
CREPE GINGER, SPIRAL GINGER

Of wide distribution in tropical Asia, this tall-growing species has short elliptic leaves running in a conspi-cuous spiral up the slender cane-like stems that are themselves gently twisted into a spiral, and up to 8 ft (2.4 m) tall. The large flowerheads consist of tightly overlapping green bracts tinged reddish, and white, sometimes pinkish flowers with yellow centers and petals like silky crêpe, emerging one or two at a time over much of the year.
ZONES 11–12.

Costus speciosus cultivar *(right)*

C

CRAMBE

This genus, related to *Brassica,* consists of 20 species of annuals and perennials, ranging in the wild from central Europe to central Asia, also in parts of Africa. They have large, cabbage-like basal leaves that are shallowly to very deeply lobed, and large panicles of small, 4-petalled white flowers with a somewhat cabbage-like smell. They are attractive to bees.

CULTIVATION

Mostly very frost hardy, they will grow in any well-drained soil and prefer an open, sunny position, although they will tolerate some shade. Propagation is by division in early spring or from seed sown in spring or autumn.

Crambe cordifolia
(below left & far left)
COLEWORT

From the Caucasus region, this very spectacular perennial has lobed leaves up to about 18 in (45 cm) long and almost as wide, forming a broad but untidy rosette. The stout, much-branched flowering stem bursts into a cloud of small, white, starry flowers, the whole measuring 4 ft (1.2 m) across with a total height of 6 ft (1.8 m). It is very deep rooted and will produce numerous offsets.
ZONES 6–9.

Crambe maritima
(below left)
SEA KALE

Occurring wild along cooler European coastlines, this robust small perennial forms a mound of broad bluish green or even purplish, cabbage-like leaves with curled and crisped margins. In late spring and summer it produces dense, erect panicles of honey-scented white flowers, as much as 2½ ft (75 cm) tall. The young leafy shoots are used as a green vegetable, often blanched to lessen the bitterness.
ZONES 5–9.

Cryptanthus zonatus (right)
ZEBRA PLANT

This species is presumed to be native to Brazil but has not been found in the wild. It forms flattish rosettes of rather irregular shape and up to about 12 in (30 cm) in diameter. The attractive wavy-edged leaves are dark green to somewhat purplish and banded crosswise with silvery gray or pale brownish markings. In summer a cluster of tubular white flowers appears in the center of each rosette. 'Zebrinus' has more highly colored leaves with a chocolate-brown background color.
ZONES 10–12.

CRYPTANTHUS
EARTH STAR

One of the most distinctive and easily recognized genera of bromeliads, *Cryptanthus* consists of 20 or more species of rosette-forming perennials, all native to eastern Brazil where they reportedly grow on the ground, though in cultivation they are quite happy when treated as epiphytes. They have shortly creeping rhizomes that branch into small, flat rosettes of star-like form, usually with a small central funnel. The leaves have finely toothed, wavy edges and in many species and cultivars are striped or barred with white or red. Small white flowers emerge from the center of the rosettes.

CULTIVATION
They require similar growing conditions to most of the epiphytic bromeliads, but their compact size makes them especially suitable as indoor plants. Ensure a position in weak sun or partial shade, planting in a standard potting mix with some sphagnum moss or peat added. All need protection from frost and like a high level of humidity. They are susceptible to scale insect and mealybug. Propagate from seed or offsets.

Cryptanthus bivittatus 'Pink Starlight' *(above)*

Cryptanthus bivittatus *(top right)*

This species has not been found in the wild since its introduction to cultivation. The rosette is 12 in (30 cm) or more across, the dark green leaves each with longitudinal yellow stripes and very rippled edges. *Cryptanthus bivittatus* var. *atropurpureus* has leaves suffused with red and the stripes pale red, turning purple in full sun. 'Pink Starlight' has pinkish white leaves with an olive green central stripe. ZONES 10–12.

C

CTENANTHE

The ancient Greeks, it seems, could pronounce the 2 consonants that begin words such as this (*kteis,* comb; *anthos,* flower), but present-day English speakers normally pretend that the 'c' is not there. Around 15 species belong to this genus of tropical plants closely related to *Maranta* and *Calathea,* all but one of them native to Brazil (the exception is a native of Costa Rica). They are evergreen perennials or subshrubs with short rhizomes; the taller species produce forking, somewhat bamboo-like aerial stems with a single leaf at each node. The rather leathery, lance-shaped or almost oblong leaves are borne on slender stalks which broaden into sheathing bases. The flowers are borne in spikes with tightly overlapping bracts and are not showy.

CULTIVATION

Several species are widely grown as indoor foliage plants, or in frost-free climates they are easily grown outdoors in the shade of trees, protected from drying winds. Indoors they require bright to moderate light but direct sunlight may cause the leaves to curl. They need ample water during the growing season and dislike low humidity. Propagation is usually from basal offshoots.

Ctenanthe lubbersiana (left)
BAMBURANTA

Endemic to Brazil, this most commonly grown ctenanthe is a splendidly marked foliage plant, growing to 30 in (75 cm) with branching stems that spread laterally. The oblong green leaves are patterned in irregularly shaded bands of pale yellow-green, with pale green undersides. Small, white flowers on one-sided spikes are produced intermittently. ZONES 10–12.

Ctenanthe oppenheimiana (below left)

From Brazil, this widely grown species is normally about 18 in (45 cm) high but can grow taller under good conditions. Its 10–12 in (25–30 cm) long leaves are oblong and have a herringbone pattern of broad grayish bars on a dull green background, with dull red undersides. Most commonly grown is the cultivar **'Tricolor'** with irregular blotches of creamy yellow on its leaves; the red undersides give it a reddish glow from above. ZONES 10–12.

CYNOGLOSSUM

A genus of 55 species of annuals, biennials and perennials from most temperate regions of the world. All species are frost hardy and valued for their long flowering period. They are related to the common forget-me-not, which many resemble.

CULTIVATION

All species need a fertile but not over-rich soil; if over-nourished the plants tend to flop over. Propagation is from seed sown in autumn or spring or, in the case of perennial species, by division.

Cynoglossum amabile (right)
CHINESE FORGET-ME-NOT

This upright annual or biennial, growing to a height of about 20 in (50 cm) has dull green hairy lanceolate leaves and flowers in racemes, generally blue although white and pink forms can occur. Flowers are produced in spring and early summer. It self-seeds very readily. **'Firmament'** has pendulous sky blue flowers. ZONES 5–9.

Cynoglossum amabile
'Firmament' *(below)*

D

D

The following are the 10 main classification groups of Dahlia hybrids.

Single-flowered (Group 1): As the name of this group suggests, these hybrids have a single ring of ray petals (sometimes 2) with an open center. Most singles are small plants usually growing no more than 18 in (45 cm) high, so they are ideal for bedding and are often sold as seed strains. **'Yellow Hammer'** is a popular bedding variety with bronze foliage and rich yellow flowers. **'Schneekönigin'** has pure white flowers.

Dahlia, Group 1, 'Schneekönigin'
(left)

DAHLIA

This comparatively small genus of about 30 species from Mexico and Central America has had as much impact on gardens as almost any other group of herbaceous perennials. Of this number only 2 or 3 species were used to create the thousands of named varieties of the past and present. Progeny of *Dahlia coccinea* and *D. pinnata* originally formed the nucleus of the modern hybrid dahlias. Others are derived from forms of *D. hortensis* such as the popular cultivar **'Ellen Huston'**. So many different flower forms have been developed that the hybrids are classified into about 10 different groups, determined by the size and type of their flowerheads. Some authorities suggest that there should be more, as group 10 consists of disparate classes as yet too small to give groupings of their own, known as the miscellaneous group. Most groups have small-, medium- and large-flowered subdivisions.

CULTIVATION

Dahlias are not particularly frost resistant so in cold climates the tubers are usually lifted each year and stored in a frost-free place to be split and replanted in spring. Most prefer a sunny, sheltered position in well-fertilized, well-drained soil. Feed monthly and water well when in flower. Increase flower size by pinching out the 2 buds alongside each center bud. All, apart from bedding forms, need staking. Propagate bedding forms from seed, others from seed, cuttings from tubers or by division.

Anemone-flowered (Group 2): This group includes fewer cultivars than most of the others. They have one or more rows of outer ray florets; instead of the yellow center, these tiny flowers have mutated into outward-pointing tubular florets.

Collarette (Group 3): This group, once again becoming popular, has a single row of 8 outer large florets which are usually flat and rounded at the tips. Then comes a row of shorter tubular, wavy florets often in a contrasting color and finally the normally yellow center.

Waterlily or nymphaea-flowered (Group 4): These fully double-flowered dahlias have slightly cupped petals that have a more than passing resemblance to their namesakes, the waterlilies. The overall effect is of a flattish flower. **'Cameo'** has white flowers with a cream base; **'Gerrie Hoek'** has pink waterlily flowers on strong stems and is popular as a cut flower. **'Emanuel Friediirkeit'** has bright red flowers.

Decorative (Group 5): This group are fully double-flowered dahlias with no central disc showing. The petals are more numerous and slightly twisted making the flower look fuller than the waterlily types. This group, which can produce some truly giant forms, may be subdivided into formal decoratives and informal ones. Informal decoratives have petals that are twisted or pointed and of an irregular arrangement. **'Hamari Gold'** is a giant decorative with golden-bronze flowers. **'Evening Mail'** is also a giant decorative. **'Majuba'** is a very free-flowering compact, medium-sized decorative dahlia bearing deep red blooms on strong stems. Large informal decorative types include **'Almand's Climax'** which has lavender blooms with paler tips; **'Alva's Supreme'** with yellow flowers; **'Golden Ballade'** with deep golden flowers and **'Suffolk Punch'** with rich purple flowers.

Dahlia, Group 4, 'Emanuel Friediirkeit' *(below)*

Dahlia, Group 4, 'Gerrie Hoek' *(above)*

Dahlia, Group 5, 'Golden Ballade' *(below left)*

Dahlia, Group 5, 'Majuba' *(below)*

D

Dahlia, Group 5, 'Suffolk Punch' *(above)*

Dahlia, Group 6, 'Rose Cupid' *(below)*

Ball (Group 6): As the name suggests these dahlias are full doubles and almost ball-shaped. Miniature, small, medium and large forms are available. **'Rose Cupid'** is a medium-sized ball dahlia with salmon pink blooms; **'Wotton Cupid'** is a dark pink miniature.

Pompon (Group 7): These are similar to ball dahlias but even more globose and usually not much more than 2 in (5 cm) across. They are sometimes called 'Drum Stick' dahlias. **'Buttercup'** is a yellow pompon form.

Cactus-flowered (Group 8): This group of fully double-flowered dahlias have long, narrow rolled petals giving the flowers a spidery look. This group can be divided further by size as well as into classes with straight petals, incurved petals or recurved petals. **'Hamari Bride'** is a medium-sized white form.

Semi-cactus (Group 9): As the name suggests this group is close to Group 8 but the petals are broader at the base and less rolled back at the edges. **'So Dainty'** is a miniature with golden bronze and apricot flowers; **'Brandaris'** is a medium form with soft orange and golden yellow flowers; **'Hayley Jane'** is a small form with purplish pink flowers and white bases; and **'Salmon Keene'** has large salmon pink to golden flowers. **'Dankbarkeit'** has pale salmon pink flowers and **'Vulkan'** has orange-red.

Dahlia, Group 9, 'Brandaris' *(below left)*

Dahlia, Group 9, 'Dankbarkeit' *(below)*

Miscellaneous (Group 10): This category consists of small groups and unique forms of dahlias that do not fit into any of the above groups. If breeders increase the numbers in any of the forms in this category, they will probably be split off to form new groups. Under this heading can be found such forms as orchid types which are single with revolute petals: **'Giraffe'** with its banded yellow and bronze flowers is an example. The star dahlias are also single in appearance and produce very pointed, widely spaced petals. Peony-flowered dahlias, which are still kept as a separate group in some countries, usually have one or two rows of flat petals with a center which can be open or partly covered by small twisted petals; examples of this form include **'Bishop of Llandaff'** with its brilliant scarlet blooms above its beautiful deep burgundy leaves, **'Fascination'** with light pinkish purple flowers and dark bronze foliage, and **'Tally Ho'** with deep orange flowers and gray-green leaves, tinged with purple.

Dahlia, Group 9, 'Vulkan' *(above)*

Dahlia, Group 10, 'Bishop of Llandaff' *(right)*

Dahlia, Group 10, 'Tally Ho' *(right)*

D

DARMERA
syn. *Peltiphyllum*

UMBRELLA PLANT, INDIAN RHUBARB

A genus of only one species, this is a herbaceous perennial with very large handsome leaves that follow the flowers in spring. The flowers, usually white or pink and in clusters on unbranched stems, are followed by attractive inedible fruit. It is native to northwestern California and southwestern Oregon.

CULTIVATION
As this plant comes from cool areas and damp to wet situations, it makes a good specimen in muddy banks and by streams. It is frost tolerant but not drought resistant. Propagation is by division or from seed.

Darmera peltata *(above & below)*
syn. *Peltiphyllum peltatum*

This dramatic foliage plant can have leaves up to 24 in (60 cm) across on 6 ft (1.8 m) stalks. It bears attractive pink to white flowers in early spring. The dwarf form called '**Nana**' only grows to 12 in (30 cm). ZONES 5–9.

D

Datura innoxia
(right)

syn. *Datura meteloides*

Though sometimes classed with *Brugmansia*, this bushy perennial from Central America is in fact a true *Datura*. It has pink or white flowers, the latter resembling those of *Datura stramonium*, but it is less poisonous, as its specific name suggests. If grown as an annual it makes a bush just under 3 ft (1 m) tall. ZONES 9–11.

DATURA
ANGEL'S TRUMPET

The tropical and subtropical genera *Brugmansia* and *Datura* are closely related; the taller, woody species with pendulous flowers are now included in *Brugmansia*. The genus contains 8 species of annuals or short-lived perennials, grown for their large, handsome and usually fragrant flowers. They bloom throughout summer and are white, sometimes blotched with purple, yellow or violet-purple. The foliage has an unpleasant odor, and all parts of the plants are narcotic and poisonous.

CULTIVATION
They need full sun and fertile, moist but well-drained soil. Propagate from seed.

Datura stramonium *(right)*
JIMSON WEED, JAMESTOWN WEED, COMMON THORN APPLE

This American annual is a common weed in many countries. It grows to 6 ft (1.8 m) and its 3 in (8 cm) long trumpets, which are produced throughout summer and autumn, can be white or purple. ZONES 7–11.

D

Delphinium elatum
(above)

Delphinium, Belladonna Group
(below right)

These perennials
(*Delphinium elatum* ×
D. grandiflorum) have
an upright, loosely
branching form and are
frost-hardy. Their
widely-spaced blue or
white flowers, 1 in
(25 mm) or more wide,
are single or sometimes
semi-double and borne
on loose spikes up to
4 ft (1.2 m) tall. They
bloom in summer.
Propagate by division
or from basal cuttings
in spring. ZONES 3–9.

DELPHINIUM

This genus contains 250 or so species native
to mainly northern hemisphere temperate
zones, with a few found in scattered, high-
altitude areas of Africa. They range from
attractive self-seeding annuals or dwarf
alpine plants up to statuesque perennials
that can exceed 8 ft (2.4 m) in height. Nearly
all start growth as a tuft of long-stalked
basal leaves, their blades divided into 3 to
7 radiating lobes or segments. The tufts
elongate into erect, sometimes branched
flowering stems that bear stalked, 5-petalled
flowers each with a backward-pointing
nectar spur. Garden delphiniums are mainly
derived from *Delphinium elatum* and its
hybrids. Recognized groups include the
Belladonna, Elatum and Pacific hybrids.
Many other hybrids are available. An example
is *Delphinium* 'Polarnacht'. The annual
larkspurs have now been placed in the genus
Consolida.

CULTIVATION

Very frost hardy, most like a cool to cold winter. They prefer full
sun with shelter from strong winds, and well-drained, fertile soil
with plenty of organic matter. Stake tall cultivars. Apply a liquid
fertilizer at 2–3 weekly intervals. To maintain type, propagate from
cuttings or by division though some species have been bred to come
true from seed.

D

Delphinium, Pacific Hybrids

These short-lived perennials, usually grown as biennials, were bred in California with the main parent being the perennial *Delphinium elatum*. They are stately plants to 5 ft (1.5 m) or more in height with star-like single, semi-double or double flowers of mostly blue, purple or white, clustered on erect rigid spikes. Some of the named cultivars are: **'Astolat'**, a perennial with lavender-mauve flowers with dark eyes; **'Black Knight'**, with deep rich purple flowers with black eyes; **'Galahad'** has pure white flowers. **'Guinevere'** bears pale purple flowers with a pinkish tinge and white eyes; **'King Arthur'** has purple flowers with white eyes; and **'Summer Skies'** has pale sky blue flowers. ZONES 7–9.

Delphinium grandiflorum

syn. *Delphinium chinense*

BUTTERFLY DELPHINIUM, CHINESE DELPHINIUM

Native to China, Siberia, Japan and Mongolia, this tufted perennial grows to a height of 18 in (45 cm) and a spread of 12 in (30 cm), the leaf segments further divided into narrow lobes. Its large bright blue flowers, with the long spurs finely warted, bloom over a long period in summer. It is fully frost hardy. **'Azure Fairy'** has pale blue flowers; **'Blue Butterfly'** has bright blue flowers. ZONES 3–9.

Delphinium, Pacific Hybrid 'Black Knight' *(below)*

Delphinium grandiflorum 'Blue Butterfly' *(above)*

Delphinium cardinale *(below)*

SCARLET LARKSPUR

This short-lived upright perennial to 6 ft (2 m) tall is native to California and Mexico. It has finely divided leaves and bears slender loose spikes of small, single red blooms with yellow centers in summer. Provide a rich, moist soil and a little shade. ZONES 8–9.

D

Delphinium
'Polarnacht' *(above)*

Delphinium, Pacific Hybrid
'Galahad' *(below)*

Delphinium semibarbatum *(below)*
syn. *Delphinium zalil*

This short-lived, tuberous delphinium is indigenous to Iran and central Asia, where its flowers are used to dye silk. It is a rare plant of great beauty, producing spikes of sulfur yellow flowers with orange tips from spring to mid-summer. It grows to a height of 3 ft (1 m) with a 10 in (25 cm) spread.
ZONES 6–9.

Delphinium 'Tempelgong' *(right)*
syn. *Delphinium* 'Temple Gong'

This Delphinium elatum hybrid was raised by Foerster of Germany in 1936. It has deep-centered violet-blue flowers and grows 5–6 ft (1.5–1.8 m) tall. ZONES 3–10.

DIANELLA

FLAX LILY

This genus of small-flowered lilies is named after Diana, the ancient Roman goddess of hunting. It consists of 25 to 30 species of ever-green, clump-forming perennials from Australia, New Zealand and the Pacific Islands; they grow in woodlands and are delightful plants for a shaded place in a warm-temperate garden. They are mostly under 3 ft (1 m) tall and are alike in their long leaves and sprays of small, deep or bright blue flowers in spring and early summer. Long-lasting, bright blue berries follow the flowers.

CULTIVATION

They prefer sun or part-shade and a moderately fertile, humus-rich, well-drained, neutral to acidic soil. Propagate by division, or rooted offsets, or from seed in spring and autumn. They naturalize in mild climates.

Dianella caerulea
(right)
BLUE FLAX-LILY

The evergreen foliage of this species from eastern Australia arises in clumps from a creeping rhizome often with elongated, cane-like aerial stems. The grass-like leaves, up to 3 ft (1 m) long, have rough margins and the open panicles, up to 24 in (60 cm) tall, sup-port small starry blue or, rarely, white flowers in spring and summer. These are followed in autumn by deep purple-blue berries which are sometimes more ornamental than the flowers. ZONES 9–11.

D

DIANTHUS
CARNATION, PINK

This large genus of some 300 species occurs mostly in Europe and Asia with one species in Arctic North America and a few in southern Africa. Most are rock garden or edging plants. Much hybridizing has bred pinks and carnations for specific purposes. Border Carnations, annuals or perennials up to 24 in (60 cm), are used in borders and for cut flowers. Perpetual-flowering Carnations are mainly grown in the open but may be grown under cover to produce unblemished blooms; these are often disbudded leaving only the top bud to develop. American Spray Carnations are treated like perpetuals except that no disbudding is carried out. Malmaison Carnations, now undergoing a revival in popularity, are so-called because of their supposed resemblance to the Bourbon rose 'Souvenir de la Malmaison'; highly perfumed, they are grown in the same way as the perpetuals but need more care. Other groups of hybrids for the garden and cutting are the Modern Pinks and the Old-fashioned Pinks. Finally comes the Alpine or Rock Pinks bred from alpine species and used mostly in rock gardens. In all groups, some cultivars are all the same color (self-colored), and others are flecked, picotee or laced; the latter two types have petals narrowly edged with a different color.

CULTIVATION
Ranging from fully to marginally frost hardy, Dianthus species like a sunny position, protection from strong winds, and well-drained, slightly alkaline soil. Stake taller varieties. Prune stems after flowering. Propagate perennials by layering or from cuttings in summer; annuals and biennials from seed in autumn or early spring. Watch for aphids, thrips and caterpillars, rust and virus infections.

Dianthus barbatus
(below)
SWEET WILLIAM

A slow-growing, frost-hardy perennial often treated as a biennial, sweet William self-sows readily and grows 18 in (45 cm) high and 6 in (15 cm) wide. The crowded, flattened heads of fragrant flowers range from white through pinks to carmine and crimson-purple and are often zoned in two tones. They flower in late spring and early summer and are ideal for massed planting. The dwarf cultivars, about 4 in (10 cm) tall, are usually treated as annuals. It has been crossed with Modern Pinks to produce a strain of hybrids, known as 'Sweet Wivelsfield'. ZONES 4–10.

Dianthus caryophyllus *(right)*
WILD CARNATION, CLOVE PINK

The wild carnation is a loosely tufted woody-based perennial species from the Mediterranean area with a history of cultivation dating back to classical times. It has pink-purple, pink or white flowers in summer, their perfume is sweet with a spicy overtone somewhat like cloves, and grows to about 30 in (75 cm) tall by 9 in (23 cm) wide or more. From this species have been raised over the years many varieties of Annual or Marguerite Carnations and the hardy Border Carnations, in addition to the modern Perpetual-flowering Carnations commonly grown for the cut-flower trade. ZONES 8–10.

D

Dianthus erinaceus
(right)

This attractive cushion-forming species from Turkey forms a lovely rock garden plant that will trail over the top of rocks. It rarely grows more than 2 in (5 cm) tall but can exceed 24 in (60 cm) in spread and its gray-green foliage is surprisingly prickly. The small single pink flowers are produced on short stems not much above the mat in summer. ZONES 7–9.

Dianthus chinensis
CHINESE PINK, INDIAN PINK

This popular annual, originally from China, has a short, tufted growth habit, and gray-green, lance-shaped leaves. In late spring and summer it bears masses of single or double, sweetly scented flowers in shades of pink, red, lavender and white. It is slow growing to a height and spread of 6–12 in (15–30 cm), and is frost hardy. **'Strawberry Parfait'** has single pink flowers, lightly fringed with deep red centers. ZONES 7–10.

Dianthus chinensis
'Strawberry Parfait' *(left)*

D

Dianthus gratiano-politanus 'Tiny Rubies'
(bottom right)

Dianthus giganteus *(below)*

As its name implies this
is a comparatively tall
species reaching up to
3 ft (1 m) tall. It comes
from the Balkan Penin-
sula. In summer it
produces dense heads
of purple-pink flowers.
ZONES 5–9.

Dianthus gratianopolitanus *(above)*
syn. *Dianthus caesius*

CHEDDAR PINK

The English common name comes about because in the UK
this species is only known from the limestone of Cheddar
Gorge, but in fact it is widely distributed in continental
Europe. It makes tidy mounds of blue-gray, linear leaves
developing into broad mats 12 in (30 cm) or more wide.
Delightfully fragrant, purplish pink blossoms with toothed
('pinked') petals are borne on 6–8 in (15–20 cm) wiry stems
in spring; the flowers will often continue until frost. It
requires a very well-drained, alkaline soil and full sun. **'Tiny
Rubies'** is ideal as a neat compact ground cover. **'Tiny Tim'**
has ¹/₂ in (12 mm), double, deep pink flowers on 4 in
(10 cm) stems. ZONES 5–9.

Dianthus 'First Love' *(right)*

There are many an-
nual strains of Pinks,
some descended
from the Chinese
Pink, *Dianthus
chinensis*, others
from sweet William
(*D. barbatus*). **'First
Love'**, a low grower
at 6 in (15 cm), may
be a cross between
these groups. The
fringed magenta and
white flowers, often
bicolored, are
scented. ZONES 6–10.

Dianthus plumarius
(right)
GARDEN OR COTTAGE PINK

A loosely tufted, evergreen perennial with pale pink or white flowers with strongly fringed petals, this species grows 12–18 in (30–45 cm) high and spreads to 10 in (25 cm) across. A native of Europe, this is one of the main parents of the Old-fashioned Pinks and Modern Pinks. There are many named cultivars, bearing sprays of single or fully double, sweetly scented flowers in red, pink, purple-red, mauve and white. Many have fringed petals and a contrasting eye. **ZONES 3–10.**

Dianthus pavonius
(above)
syn. *Dianthus neglectus*

This is usually a tufted or mat-forming perennial to 6 in (15 cm) tall and up to 10 in (25 cm) across. It comes from the Alps of France and Italy. The flowers are usually solitary occasionally up to 3, pale pink with toothed petals. **ZONES 4–9.**

Dianthus superbus 'Rainbow Loveliness' *(above)*

Dianthus superbus
(left)

Native to mountains in Europe and temperate Asia, this species is a loosely tufted perennial sometimes as much as 3 ft (1 m) high. Its leaves are mid-green and about 3 in (8 cm) long. The rich purple-pink fragrant flowers, produced singly or in pairs through summer, have petals deeply divided giving flowers a loosely fringed appearance. Seldom grown, it has been used in producing garden hybrids. It is better known as a parent of the Loveliness Strain which includes **'Rainbow Loveliness'**, with deeply fringed single flowers of mauve and pink shades carried on slender stems in spring. **ZONES 4–10.**

D

D

Dianthus, Alpine Pinks

Also known as Rock Pinks, the cultivars of this hybrid group are compact plants forming mounds or mats of crowded fine leaves. The flowers come in many colors and shapes and are usually held 6–12 in (15–30 cm) above the foliage. **'La Bourboule'** (syn. 'La Bourbille') bears a profusion of single clove-scented pink flowers with fringed petals; **'Pike's Pink'** has gray-green foliage and rounded double pink flowers with a darker zone at the base; **'Nancy Colman'** is very similar but without the darker zone. ZONES 4–9.

Dianthus, Alpine Pink, 'Pike's Pink' *(left)*

Dianthus, Alpine Pink, 'Nancy Colman' *(below)*

Dianthus, Ideal Series

These short-lived perennial hybrids between *Dianthus barbatus* and *D. chinensis,* are usually grown as annuals or biennials, flowering in the first season. They grow to 14 in (35 cm) and have bright green leaves. They bear clusters of fringed, 5-petalled flowers in shades of deep violet, purple, deep pink and red in summer. **'Ideal Violet'** has deep purple-pink flowers with paler margins. ZONES 5–10.

Dianthus, Ideal Series, 'Ideal Violet' *(left)*

Dianthus, Modern Pink, 'Allwoodii' *(above)*

Dianthus, Modern Pink
cultivar *(right)*

Dianthus, Modern Pinks

These densely leaved, mound-forming perennials are derived from crosses between cultivars of *Dianthus plumarius* and *D. caryophyllus*. Early hybrids were called *D. × allwoodii*, but these hardly stand apart from the rest of the Modern Pinks now. Modern Pinks have gray-green foliage and many erect flowering stems, each carrying 4 to 6 fragrant, single to fully double flowers in shades of white, pink or crimson, often with dark centers and with plain or fringed petals. Most are 12–18 in (30–45 cm) tall, spreading 18 in (45 cm) and flowering from late spring until early autumn; some are clove-scented. '**Allwoodii**' bears fringed, pale purple-pink flowers with deep red central zones; '**Becky Robinson**' bears laced pink, clove-scented double blooms with ruby centers and margins; '**Dick Portman**' bears double crimson flowers with pinkish cream centers and margins; '**Doris**' is a scented pale pink double with deep pink centers; '**Gran's Favourite**' is a sweetly scented, short-stemmed double, white with maroon centers and margins; '**Joy**' has semi-double carmine-pink flowers on strong upright stems; '**Laced Monarch**' bears deep pink to cerise double flowers with pale pink markings; '**Monica Wyatt**' has full double clove-scented pale pink flowers with dark centers; '**Valda Wyatt**' has clove-scented, rich pink double flowers with darker centers; and '**Warrior**' has double pink flowers with deep red centers and margins. ZONES 5–10.

Dianthus, Modern Pink, '**Dick Portman**' *(above)*

Dianthus, Modern Pink, '**Doris**' *(below)*

D

Dianthus, Modern
Pink, 'Laced Monarch'
(top)

Dianthus, Modern
Pink, 'Gran's Favourite'
(above left)

Dianthus, Modern
Pink, 'Joy' *(above)*

Dianthus, Modern
Pink, 'Warrior' *(left)*

Dianthus, Old-Fashioned Pink, 'Clare'
(above)

Dianthus, Old-Fashioned Pinks

These are tuft-forming perennials that grow to 18 in (45 cm) high. In late spring and early summer they bear single to fully double, clove-scented flowers to 2½ in (6 cm) across in colors varying from white, through pale pink and magenta to red, often fringed and with contrasting centers. **'Mrs Sinkins'** is a famous Old-fashioned Pink with pure white shaggy flowers prone to split at the calyx; it is highly perfumed. **'Pink Mrs Sinkins'** is a pale pink form of **'Mrs Sinkins'**. Other Old-fashioned Pinks include **'Clare'**, which produces bicolored clove-scented double pink fringed flowers with maroon centers, and **'Rose de Mai'**, which bears clove-scented single pink flowers with deep pink eyes. ZONES 5–9.

Dianthus,
Old-Fashioned Pink,
'Mrs Sinkins' and 'Pink
Mrs Sinkins' *(center)*

Dianthus,
Old-Fashioned Pink,
'Rose de Mai' *(right)*

D

Dianthus, Perpetual-flowering Carnation, 'Charlotte' *(above)*

Dianthus, Perpetual-flowering Carnations

These popular flowers are marginally frost hardy perennials that reach at least 3 ft (1 m) high with a spread of 12 in (30 cm). Their stems will need support. Fully double flowers, usually fringed, are produced all year. Disbud large-flowered varieties; spray types produce about 5 flowers per stem and do not need disbudding. Cultivars include **'Charlotte'** which bears cream flowers striped salmon pink; **'Malaga'** has salmon pink flowers; **'Olivia'** has salmon pink flowers with fringed petals; **'Raggio di Sole'** has bright orange flowers with red specks; **'Sofia'** bears white flowers with clear red stripes. ZONES 8–11.

Dianthus, P-fC, 'Malaga' *(above)*

Dianthus, P-fC, 'Olivia' *(above left)*

Dianthus, P-fC, 'Raggio di Sole' *(below)*

Dianthus, P-fC, 'Sofia' *(above)*

DIASCIA

TWINSPUR

This genus of about 50 species of delicate but long-blooming perennials from South Africa is popular in rockeries, borders and as potted specimens. They bear terminal racemes of flat, generally pink flowers with double nectar spurs on the back, and have erect or prostrate stems with toothed, mid-green leaves. A number of attractive cultivars are available including **'Kelly's Eye'**, and **'Rose Queen'**, which is an excellent bedding plant.

CULTIVATION

Full sun is best, with afternoon shade in hot areas; most are frost hardy, but they dislike humidity. A fertile, moist but well-drained soil and regular summer watering are vital. Pinch out tips to increase bushiness and cut back old stems after flowering. Propagate from seed in autumn, or cuttings in autumn, to over-winter in a cool greenhouse.

Diascia barberae

(below)

This low-growing, rather fragile perennial has small, heart-shaped, pale green leaves; it bears clusters of twin-spurred, salmon pink flowers from spring to early autumn. It grows 6–12 in (15–30 cm) tall with a spread of 8 in (20 cm). **'Ruby Field'** bears salmon pink, wide-lipped flowers that are produced over a long period from summer to autumn. ZONES 8–10.

D

Diascia 'Rose Queen'
(above)

Diascia barberae
'Ruby Field' *(right)*

Diascia 'Rupert Lambert' *(left)*

This cultivar grows to about 10 in (25 cm) tall by 20 in (50 cm) wide and has narrow, shallowly toothed pointed leaves. The deep pink flowers with parallel spurs are produced during summer and autumn. ZONES 8–10.

Diascia 'Blackthorn Apricot' *(above)*

This is probably another selection from *Diascia barberae*. It grows to 16 in (25 cm) tall by at least 20 in (50 cm) wide and its apricot pink flowers, with downward-pointing spurs, are produced on loose spikes from summer well into autumn. ZONES 8–10.

Diascia fetcaniensis *(left)*
syn. *Diascia felthamii*

Indigenous to the Drakensburg Mountains, this fairly compact plant with ovate hairy leaves to 1 in (25 mm) long grows to a height of 12 in (30 cm) and spreads about 3–4 ft (1–1.2 m). It produces loose racemes of rose pink flowers with downward-curved spurs from summer well into autumn. ZONES 8–10.

D

Diascia stachyoides
(above)

Growing to 16 in (40 cm) tall, this perennial has slightly serrated leaves decreasing in size up the flower stems, which are sparsely clad in deep rose pink flowers in summer, their spurs pointing down and outwards. ZONES 8–10.

Diascia vigilis *(right)*
syn. *Diascia elegans*

A vigorous plant with a strongly stoloniferous habit, it grows to 20 in (50 cm) tall. The foliage is light green and glossy. It produces loose racemes of clear pink flowers from summer into early winter with incurved spurs. This is one of the most frost hardy and floriferous species. ZONES 8–10.

D

Dicentra spectabilis *(left)*
BLEEDING HEART

This popular garden perennial grows 24–36 in (60–90 cm) tall with a spread of 18–24 in (45–60 cm). Pink and white heart-shaped flowers on long arching stems appear in late spring and summer. After flowering, the foliage usually dies down to the ground. **'Alba'** is a pure white form with green-yellow markings and pale green leaves that will grow true from seed. ZONES 2–9.

Dicentra formosa
WESTERN BLEEDING HEART

This spreading plant grows to about 18 in (45 cm) high with a spread of 12 in (30 cm). Dainty pink and red flowers appear on slender arching stems during spring and summer. **'Alba'** is a white-flowered form. ZONES 3–9.

Dicentra formosa 'Alba' *(below)*

DICENTRA
BLEEDING HEART

This genus consists of about 20 species of annuals and perennials much admired for their feathery leaves and the graceful carriage of their flowers, although they do not grow or flower well without a period of winter chill. The flowers, pendent and heart-shaped, come in red, pink, white, purple and yellow. They flower from mid-spring into early summer, though potted plants can be gently forced into early spring bloom if taken into a mildly warmed greenhouse at mid-winter. From Asia and North America, they are usually found in woodland and mountainous areas.

CULTIVATION
Mostly quite frost hardy, dicentras love humus-rich, moist but well-drained soil and some light shade. Propagate from seed in autumn or by division in late winter.

Dicentra spectabilis 'Alba' *(below left)*

Dicentra formosa *(below)*

DICHORISANDRA

This genus of about 25 species from Central and South America is related to the common wandering Jew *(Tradescantia)*. The foliage of these soft-stemmed perennials may be glossy green or banded or striped with cream. The small cup-shaped flowers are purple or blue and are followed by fleshy orange fruits.

CULTIVATION

In warm-temperate climates they can be grown in well-drained, shady spots; however, they cannot survive frost and must be overwintered in a greenhouse in colder climates. They require adequate moisture at all times and high humidity in summer. Propagate by division in early spring or from cuttings in summer.

Dichorisandra reginae *(below)*

This soft-stemmed clump-forming perennial to 12 in (30 cm) high has erect stems and dark green leaves to 7 in (18 cm) long that are purplish beneath and are often flecked with silver. Small dense spikes of purple-blue flowers are produced from summer to autumn. ZONES 11–12.

Dichorisandra thyrsiflora *(right)*
BLUE GINGER, BRAZILIAN GINGER

The common name for this species is a misnomer, arising from its ginger-like stems covered in tightly sheathing leaf bases. This perennial has glossy, dark green leaves 12 in (30 cm) long that are spirally arranged along the upright stems. It produces dense terminal clusters of deep purple-blue flowers in autumn, and grows to a height of 8 ft (2.4 m) and spread of 3 ft (1 m). ZONES 10–12.

DICLIPTERA

This genus of the acanthus family consists of some 150 species of
annuals, perennials, subshrubs or scrambling climbers. The simple,
smooth-edged leaves are arranged in opposite pairs. The tubular
flowers are in terminal or sometimes axillary clusters. They range
in the wild through most tropical and subtropical regions of the
world.

CULTIVATION

In frosty areas lift and store in greenhouses for the winter or take
cuttings which can then be held over indoors until after spring
frosts. Propagate from cuttings.

*Dicliptera
suberecta* (left)
syns *Jacobinia suberecta,
Justicia suberecta*

This is the only species
commonly found in
cultivation. It comes
from Uruguay and
makes a soft-wooded,
sprawling perennial up
to about 24 in (60 cm)
and sometimes wider.
Its stems and leaves are
covered with velvety
gray felt which makes a
dramatic setting for the
tubular orange-red
flowers, which are
produced through late
summer and autumn.
It is a good pot plant
and somewhat shade
tolerant. ZONES 8–11.

Dictamnus albus
(*right*)
syn. *Dictamnus fraxinella*

BURNING BUSH, DITTANY, GAS PLANT

This herbaceous, woody-stemmed perennial bears early summer spikes of fragrant, star-shaped, white, pink or lilac flowers with long stamens. It grows to 3 ft (1.2 m) tall with a spread of 36 in (90 cm) and has glossy light green leaves. It is quite frost hardy. **Dictamnus albus var. purpureus** (syn. *D. a.* var. *rubra*) bears purple-pink flowers with purple veins. **ZONES 3–9.**

D

DICTAMNUS
BURNING BUSH

The Book of Exodus tells how God spoke to Moses on Mount Sinai from a bush that burned yet was not consumed by the fire. Theologians point out that since this was a miracle the species is irrelevant. Gardeners insist that it must have been *Dictamnus albus,* the only species in its genus and indeed indigenous to the Mediterranean and temperate Asia. In still, warm conditions so much aromatic oil evaporates from the leaves that if you strike a match near it the vapor ignites and the bush is engulfed in flame, but so briefly that it is not damaged.

CULTIVATION
This perennial needs full sun and fertile, well-drained soil. It resents disturbance. Propagate from fresh seed in summer.

D

Dierama pendulum
syn. *Dierama ensifolium*

This perennial from South Africa has flower stems up to 4 ft (1.2 m) high and grass-like leaves to 20 in (50 cm) or more long. The open bell-shaped flowers in shades of pink or magenta are produced on wiry pendulous stems in summer. **'Album'** produces white flowers. ZONES 8–10.

Dierama pendulum 'Album' *(left)*

DIERAMA

This genus of about 40 species of evergreen perennials of the iris family is indigenous to tropical Africa and South Africa. Growing from corms, the plants produce tufts of upright, grass-like leaves up to 3 ft (1 m) long, and fine wiry flower stems which bend like fishing rods under the weight of the flower clusters. These charming plants thrive and also look good near a pool or water feature. Several fine hybrid cultivars have been raised.

CULTIVATION
These warm-temperate plants demand a sheltered, sunny spot in cool areas, and rich, moist, well-drained soil. They are marginally frost hardy and dislike being disturbed. Propagate by corm division in spring, or from seed in spring and autumn.

DIETES
FORTNIGHT LILY

Native to southern Africa and to Lord Howe
Island off eastern Australia, this genus
contains 6 species of evergreen rhizomatous
perennials that are grown for their attractive,
iris-like flowers. The flowers usually last
only for a day but new buds open over a
long period in spring and summer. They
have leathery, erect, sword-like leaves which
form large clumps. In the past the species
were included in the genus *Moraea,* from
which they differ in being rhizomatous.

CULTIVATION

All species thrive in part-shade or full sun,
and prefer humus-rich, well-drained soil
that does not dry out too quickly.
Marginally frost hardy, they are tough
enough to serve as low hedges and, once
established, self-seed readily. Propagate
from seed in spring or autumn or by
division in spring.

Dietes iridioides (above)
SYNS DIETES VEGETA, MORAEA IRIDIOIDES

This species has branching, wiry stems that carry
2½–3 in (6–8 cm) wide, iris-like flowers that are
white with central yellow marks. It grows to a
height of 24 in (60 cm) and a spread of 12–24 in
(30–60 cm), forming dense clumps of basal leaves
in a spreading fan. Its preferred habitat is in semi-
shade under tall, open trees. **ZONES 8–11.**

Dietes bicolor (left)
syn. *Moraea bicolor*

Sometimes called the
Spanish iris, though it
is neither an iris nor
Spanish (it comes from
South Africa), *Dietes
bicolor* has pale green
sword-shaped basal
leaves and pale yellow
flowers that appear
from spring to summer.
Each of the 3 larger
petals has a central
brown mark. It grows
to around 3 ft (1 m) in
height. **ZONES 9–11.**

D

Digitalis lanata *(above)*
GRECIAN FOXGLOVE

A clump-forming biennial or short-lived perennial, this subtle species produces flowers in mid- to late summer on stems up to 36 in (90 cm) tall. The flowers are strange but appealing: they are pale cream to fawn, finely veined with brown inside and a lighter cream lower lip. ZONES 4–9.

Digitalis grandiflora
syns *Digitalis ambigua,
D. orientalis*

YELLOW FOXGLOVE

A charming pale lemon-flowered foxglove, this species grows to 3 ft (1 m) when in flower from early to mid-summer and has rich green, prominently veined leaves. It can be a biennial or a short-lived perennial. **'Dwarf Temple Bells'** (syn. 'Temple Bells') is a smaller form but with larger pale yellow flowers. ZONES 4–9.

Digitalis grandiflora
'Dwarf Temple Bells' *(right)*

DIGITALIS
FOXGLOVE

Natives of Europe, northern Africa and western Asia, these 22 species of biennials and perennials, some of them evergreen, are grown for their tall spikes of tubular, 2-lipped flowers which come in many colors including magenta, purple, white, cream, yellow, pink and lavender. The leaves are simple, mid-green and entire or toothed. The medicinal properties of digitalis have been known since ancient times, and these plants are still used in the treatment of heart ailments.

CULTIVATION
Marginally frost hardy to fully frost hardy, they grow in most sheltered conditions, doing best in cool climates in part-shade and humus-rich, well-drained soil. Cut flowering stems down to the ground after spring flowering to encourage secondary spikes. Propagate from seed in autumn or by division; they self-seed readily.

Digitalis ferruginea *(above)*
RUSTY FOXGLOVE

A biennial or short-lived perennial, this robust plant can reach 4 ft (1.2 m) or so tall. The leaves are comparatively narrow and rich green. The trumpet-shaped flowers are golden brown with darker red-brown veins and are produced in summer. ZONES 7–10.

Digitalis lutea *(right)*

This foxglove is a 24 in (60 cm) tall, clump-forming, summer-flowering perennial from Europe. It is admired for its elegance and unusual color, which varies from almost white to canary yellow, and there are usually purple spots in the flowers' throats. It has hairless, glossy, dark green leaves and is sometimes cultivated for medicinal use. ZONES 4–9.

Digitalis purpurea f. *albiflora (above)*

Digitalis × mertonensis

(above center)

A hybrid of *Digitalis grandiflora* and *D. purpurea*, this frost-hardy perennial forms a clump about 3 ft (1 m) tall and 12 in (30 cm) wide. Summer flowering, it bears spikes of tubular, pink to salmon flowers above a rosette of soft, hairy, oval leaves. Divide after flowering. ZONES 4–9.

Digitalis purpurea *(right)*

This is the common foxglove, a short-lived, frost-hardy perennial with an upright habit, a height of 3–5 ft (1–1.5 m) and a spread of 24 in (60 cm). The flowers come in purple, pink, rosy magenta, white or pale yellow, above a rosette of rough, oval, deep green leaves. All parts of the plant, especially the leaves, are poisonous. Many seedling strains are available, grown as bedding annuals, the **Excelsior Hybrids** in mixed colors being very popular. ***Digitalis purpurea* f. *albiflora*** has pure white flowers sometimes lightly spotted brown inside; it will usually come true from seed especially if it is isolated from other colored forms. ZONES 5–10.

DIMORPHOTHECA
AFRICAN DAISY, CAPE MARIGOLD

These 7 species of annuals, perennials and evergreen subshrubs from South Africa have colorful, daisy-like flowers from late winter. Related to *Osteospermum,* they are useful for rock gardens and borders.

CULTIVATION
They need an open sunny situation and fertile, well-drained soil; they are salt tolerant. The flowers only open in sunshine. Prune lightly after flowering; deadheading prolongs flowering. Propagate annuals from seed in spring and perennials from cuttings in summer. Watch for fungal diseases in summer rainfall areas.

Dimorphotheca pluvialis (below) syn. *Dimorphotheca annua*
RAIN DAISY

This bedding annual produces small flowerheads in late winter and spring that are snow white above and purple beneath, with brownish purple centers. Low growing, it reaches 8–12 in (20–30 cm) in height with a similar spread. ZONES 8–10.

D

DIONAEA
VENUS FLYTRAP

This genus contains only one species, the best known of all carnivorous plants, though it is quite small. The rosettes of leaves
rarely exceed 8 in (20 cm) across, while the flower stems reach
about 12 in (30 cm) high; and the white, 5-petalled flowers are
about ½ in (12 mm) wide. Each leaf has 2 flattened lobes with stiff
spines along the margins. Minute glands secrete insect-attracting
nectar; when the insect alights, it stimulates 3 hairs on each lobe,
and the trap closes shut. The nectar digests the insect by liquefying
it. When only the hard bits are left, the leaf opens and the remains
are blown away.

CULTIVATION
Marginally frost hardy, grow in peat kept saturated by standing the
pot in a saucer of rainwater in full sun. Pinching out emerging
flower stems and removing dead traps will encourage new traps to
grow. Feed plants tiny pieces of meat or cheese and watch the
flytrap in action. Without some animal protein, it will not flower.
Propagate from seed or leaf cuttings or by division in spring.

*Dionaea
muscipula* *(above)*

This rosette-forming
perennial comes from
southeastern USA,
where it grows in mossy
bogs. The rounded
leaves are yellow-green
or red and have winged
stalks. Like so many
carnivorous plants, it
is very sensitive to
pollution and is
becoming rare in the
wild. ZONES 8–10.

D

DIONYSIA

A genus of 42 species in the primula family from the arid mountains of southwestern and central Asia, these tufted or cushion-forming alpine plants, much admired by alpine plant enthusiasts, usually grow in moist shaded crevices. The flowers are tubular and flared out nearly flat at the end.

CULTIVATION

Only grown in climates with cool to cold winters and needing protection from excessive damp on the foliage, these plants are normally grown under cover in pots or in the hollows of tufa rocks. Make sure that the cushions are sitting up on a bed of coarse gravel to stop crown rot. Propagate from seed or by division.

Dionysia involucrata (above)

Considered to be relatively easy to grow, this species forms a dense cushion of rich green foliage from which are borne in early summer masses of violet to violet-purple flowers with white eyes that darken with age.
ZONES 4–9.

DIPSACUS
TEASEL

Related to *Scabiosa,* this genus consists of 15 species of biennials and short-lived perennials from Europe, North Africa and temperate Asia. They have harsh bristly or prickly leaves arranged in opposite pairs on the strong stems, which branch into long-stalked, erect, barrel-shaped flowerheads. At the base of each flowerhead is a circle of long, springy, spine-like bracts. The small white, pink or purple flowers open progressively from the base of the head; an additional short springy bract accompanies each small flower. Apart from fuller's teasel, they are known as wildflowers or weeds. They are popular with landscape designers because of their statuesque habit.

CULTIVATION

Teasels are happy in well-drained garden soil of moderate fertility, in sun or light shade. They are frost hardy and will generally self-seed freely in the garden. Propagate from seed.

Dipsacus fullonum *(below)*
syn. *Dipsacus sylvestris*
WILD TEASEL

D

Native to Europe and western Asia, this common wildflower is a prickly biennial up to 6 ft (1.8 m) tall, initially with a basal rosette of long, pointed leaves though these shrivel by the time the plant flowers; the stem leaves are shorter. The long-stalked flowerheads, borne mid- to late summer, are about 3 in (8 cm) long, with mauve-pink flowers emerging between small, curved, springy bracts which persist long after the flowers are gone. In more recent times *Dipsacus sativus* has been the species principally used for fulling—the dressing of cloth after it is woven. **ZONES 4–10.**

Dipsacus sativus *(above)*
syn. *Dipsacus fullonum* subsp. *sativus*
FULLER'S TEASEL

This biennial species is known only as a cultivated plant, though botanists now believe it may be derived from the wild Mediterranean species *Dipsacus ferox.* It is similar in most respects to *D. fullonum* but the small bracts that cover the flowerheads are shorter and broader and slightly hooked at the apex—it is the dried heads of this teasel, gathered after flowering, that are used to 'card' woollen cloth, the springy hooks raising the nap as the cloth is dragged past. It is also grown as a curiosity and for dried flowers. **ZONES 5–10.**

DISPORUM

FAIRY BELLS

Disporum is a genus of between 10 and 20 species of elegant and attractive woodland plants related to and similar to Solomon's seal *(Polygonatum)*. Species are native to the USA, eastern Asia and the Himalayas. They have creeping rhizomes that can travel some distance but they are not invasive. The arching stems are often slightly branched and clothed with attractive alternating leaves. The flowers are bell-shaped and hang under the stems. They can be white to green-yellow.

CULTIVATION

As these are woodland plants give them a cool part-shaded position with ample organic material like leafmold. They are definitely not for tropical or arid zones. Propagate from seed or by division.

Disporum flavens *(above)*

This Korean woodland perennial grows in neat clumps to 30 in (75 cm) high by 12 in (30 cm) across. It has attractive lance-shaped leaves and in early spring will produce up to 3 drooping soft yellow flowers per stem. These are followed in autumn by small black berries. **ZONES 5–9.**

Disporum smilacinum *(left)*

Also from Korea aswell as Japan, this species grows to about 16 in (40 cm) tall and will spread to at least 12 in (30 cm) wide. It is sparsely branched with oval and oblong-shaped leaves to 3 in (7 cm) long. It produces one or two drooping cup-shaped white flowers per stem in mid- to late spring. **ZONES 5–9.**

DODECATHEON
SHOOTING STAR

The shooting stars (about 14 species) are western North America's equivalent to Europe's cyclamens and, like them, they are perennials and cousins of the primrose. Most are rosette-forming and grow to about 15 in (38 cm) high, with pink or white flower clusters. They have swept-back petals and protruding stamens.

CULTIVATION
Fully frost hardy, they prefer part-shade in moist, well-drained acidic soil. Most require a dry dormant summer period after flowering. They resent disturbance. Propagate from seed in autumn or by division in winter.

Dodecatheon pulchellum
'Red Wings' *(right)*

Dodecatheon pulchellum
syns *Dodecatheon amethystinum, D. pauciflorum, D. radicatum*

Native to the mountains of western North America, this clump-forming perennial has mid-green 8 in (20 cm) long leaves in rosettes and produces up to 30 deep cerise to lilac flowers per stem. White forms are known as well as a form named **'Red Wings'** which has magenta-pink flowers on strong stems in late spring and early summer. ZONES 4–9.

Dodecatheon meadia *(right)*
From eastern North America, this is the best-known species, bearing white, rose pink or cyclamen pink, nodding flowers. It has primula-like, clumped rosettes of pale green leaves, and ranges from 6–18 in (15–45 cm) high with a spread of 18 in (45 cm). It was named for the English scientist Richard Mead (1673–1754), a patron of American botanical studies. ZONES 3–9.

Dodecatheon jeffreyi *(below right)*
SIERRA SHOOTING STAR

Occurring from California to Alaska, this plant grows to about 18 in (45 cm) tall. Its flower spike is topped with many red-purple flowers with deep purple stamens. Its leaves are slightly sticky and about 12 in (30 cm) long. ZONES 5–9.

Doronicum orientale 'Magnificum' *(left)*

This clump-forming perennial grows to about 20 in (50 cm) tall and has bright green ovate leaves. The flowers, up to 2 in (5 cm) across, are produced in mid- to late spring. This cultivar apparently comes true from seed. ZONES 4–9.

Doronicum columnae 'Miss Mason' *(below left)*

This is a large-flowered selection with blooms about 3 in (8 cm) across in mid- to late spring. Its bright yellow daisies are held well above its heart-shaped leaves on stems up to 24 in (60 cm) tall. ZONES 5–9.

DORONICUM
LEOPARD'S BANE

The 35 species of herbaceous perennials that make up this genus extend from Europe through western Asia to Siberia. Species are grown for their attractive, bright yellow daisy-like flowers which are produced in spring and summer above fresh bright green foliage. Most species make attractive border plants of restrained habit and are also good as cut flowers.

CULTIVATION

Doronicums will cope with a range of habitats, but for best results give them a moisture-retentive but not wet soil, high in humus; part-shade or morning sun is preferred but never heavy dark shade. Propagate from seed or by division.

Doronicum pardalianches *(above)*
syn. *Doronicum cordatum*
LEOPARD'S BANE

Doronicum pardalianches is a spreading, clump-forming perennial to 3 ft (1 m) tall and wide. The oval basal leaves, to 5 in (12 cm) long, have heart-shaped bases. Bright yellow daisy-like flowers are borne on slender, branching stems from late spring to mid-summer. ZONES 5–9.

Dorotheanthus
bellidiformis (below)
ICE PLANT, LIVINGSTONE DAISY,
BOKBAAI VYGIE

This small succulent
annual has daisy-like
flowerheads in dazzling
shades of yellow, white,
red or pink in summer
sun, although the
flowers close in dull
weather. It grows to 6 in
(15 cm) tall and spreads
to 12 in (30 cm), and has
fleshy light green leaves
to 3 in (7 cm) long with
glistening surface cells.
ZONES 9–11.

DOROTHEANTHUS
ICE PLANT, LIVINGSTONE DAISY

A genus of about 10 species of succulent
annuals from South Africa, these mat-
forming plants bear masses of daisy-like
flowers in bright shades of red, pink, white
or bicolored with dark centers in summer.
Ideal for borders and massed displays.

CULTIVATION
Marginally frost hardy, grow in well-drained
soil in a sunny position. Deadhead to
improve appearance and prolong flowering.
In frost-prone areas plant out once the danger
of frost has passed. Propagate from seed.

D

DORYANTHES

The 2 species of *Doryanthes* are large evergreen perennials indigenous to the east coast of Australia. Somewhat resembling agaves in growth habit, they have loose rosettes of sword-shaped leaves and bear large red flowers with spreading petals, at the end of very tall stalks. The nectar attracts birds. Although requiring up to 10 years to bloom, they are popular in warm climates.

CULTIVATION

Frost tender, they do best in full sun or part-shade in warm, frost-free conditions in light, humus-rich, well-drained soil. Water well during the growing season. Propagate from seed or by division.

Doryanthes excelsa *(left)*

GYMEA LILY

The larger and more common of the 2 species, *Doryanthes excelsa* is one of the largest lilies in the world. The large rounded head of deep red, torch-like flowers is borne terminally on a stem that can reach 20 ft (6 m) tall, arising from a rosette of sword-shaped leaves that can spread to about 8 ft (2.4 m) wide. It makes a spectacular feature plant for a large garden. ZONES 9–11.

Doryanthes palmeri *(above)*

This species forms a dense rosette of lance-shaped, bright green leaves up to 10 ft (3 m) long. The flower stalk, up to 18 ft (5 m) tall, carries numerous scarlet, funnel-shaped flowers with white throats. They are arranged along the upper part of the stalk and appear in spring. ZONES 9–11.

Draba sachalinensis (right)

From the far northeast of Asia, this is a tufted perennial with velvety mid-green obovate to spoon-shaped leaves. Its small white flowers are borne in dense racemes up to 8 in (20 cm) tall. ZONES 5–9.

DRABA

Draba is a mainly Arctic and alpine genus of perennial or occasionally annual tufted or cushion plants. There are about 300 species and they range through the northern temperate regions as well as some of the mountains of South America. Some of the very tight cushion-forming species are much prized by alpine plant enthusiasts.

CULTIVATION

Most are frost hardy but they do require ample light, good drainage and protection from winter wet. They are handsome plants in rock gardens, troughs or individually in shallow terracotta pots. Propagate from seed, cuttings or by careful division.

Draba aizoides (center)

YELLOW WHITLOW GRASS

A variable species native to the UK and the mountains of central and southern Europe, this tufted plant usually grows 4 in (10 cm) tall by 10 in (25 cm) wide. Its bright yellow flowers are borne in late spring. This is one of the most easily grown species. ZONES 5–9.

Draba rigida var. bryoides (right)

syn. *Draba bryoides*

From Turkey and Armenia this species makes tufts about 3 in (8 cm) each way. Its bright yellow flowers are produced on stems up to 4 in (10 cm) long. It forms tight rosettes of minute dark green leaves with inrolled margins. ZONES 6–9.

D

Dracocephalum forrestii (left)

This clump-forming perennial from western China grows 18 in (45 cm) tall by 12 in (30 cm) wide. Its stems are erect and densely leafy. It produces deep purple-blue flowers with a white hairy exterior from late summer until mid-autumn. ZONES 4–9.

DRACOCEPHALUM

DRAGON'S HEAD

Related to mints, this genus consists of 50 or more species mainly from temperate Asia but with a few native to Europe and North Africa and one to North America. *Nepeta* is its closest ally, but in general appearance *Dracocephalum* shows parallels with salvias. The common name is merely a translation of the botanical name (of Greek origin) and refers to a fancied resemblance of the flower to a miniature dragon's head. The plants include annuals and perennials and, like most other members of the mint family, have stems that are squarish in cross-section and leaves that are aromatic when crushed and are arranged in strictly opposite pairs. The stems terminate in whorls of 2-lipped flowers, mostly blues and purples, the upper lip hooded and the lower 3-lobed.

CULTIVATION

They are frost hardy and easily cultivated in a temperate climate in reasonably fertile soil with ample moisture in spring and summer. A sunny but sheltered position suits them best. Propagate by division of established clumps.

DROSERA
SUNDEW, DAILY DEW

This genus of carnivorous perennials consists of around 100 species; more than half of these are indigenous to Australia, and the rest are widely distributed throughout the world. They usually grow in highly acidic, damp to wet soils. Sticky glandular hairs on the leaf surfaces attract and catch insects, closing over the prey and slowly absorbing its nutrients. The fork-leafed sundews are among the easiest to cultivate and include the very attractive 'Marston Dragon' with narrow green leaves glistening with red glandular hairs.

D

CULTIVATION

Due to their wide distribution, great differences in hardiness exist. Some species require heated greenhouse conditions if taken from their tropical home; others are very cold tolerant. Grow in damp to wet conditions in a nutrient-deficient mix of peat moss and sand. Most like plenty of light. Propagate from seed, by division or root cuttings.

Drosera aliciae
(below)

This is a South African species with a rosetting habit to 2 in (5 cm) across and dark green leaves with bright red glandular hairs. Flowers are pink and produced on fine stems up to 18 in (45 cm) tall.
ZONES 9–11.

Drosera capensis
(left)
CAPE SUNDEW

This species grows to 6 in (15 cm) tall, with small rosettes of narrow linear leaves covered in sensitive, red, glandular hairs which secrete fluid. In summer many small, purple flowers are produced on leafless stems. Water only with rainwater as it is very sensitive to the impurities found in tapwater. ZONES 9–11.

Drosera binata
(right)
FORKED SUNDEW

A native of southeastern Australia, this erect growing sundew has once- or twice-forked leaves to 24 in (60 cm) long. They are pale green to reddish and are covered in glandular hairs. Numerous white or pink flowers are borne on erect stems to 30 in (75 cm) tall from spring to mid-autumn. ZONES 9–11.

Drosera regia (right)

GIANT SUNDEW

As its common name and the specific epithet *regia* imply, this South African species is among the largest in the genus. It produces rosettes of strappy leaves up to 28 in (70 cm) long, wider in the center than the ends. Its flower stems are up to 28 in (70 cm) high and bear 1½ in (35 mm) wide, pale pink to purple flowers in summer. The species produces rhizomes, around 2 in (5 cm) long, that are usually at soil level and covered in dead foliage.
ZONES 9–11.

Drosera 'Marston Dragon' (below)

Possibly a hybrid of *Drosera binata*, this cultivar is notable for its large size, up to 24 in (60 cm) wide, and the large number of traps it carries. Its stems bend down under the weight of the traps and sprawl over the ground. The young growth and the traps are tinted pinkish red. ZONES 9–10.

Drosera cuneifolia (right)

This South African species has 1 in (25 mm) wide basal rosettes of foliage and small purple flowers on stems 2–10 in (5–25 cm) tall. The leaves are a rounded wedge shape with short stems and are edged with fine hairs. *Drosera cuneifolia* flowers in summer. ZONES 9–11.

D

D

DROSOPHYLLUM
PORTUGUESE SUNDEW

The sole species in this genus is a carnivorous perennial native to Portugal, southern Spain and Morocco. It traps its prey using sticky hairs that cover the foliage. These hairs then secrete a digestive solution. Its flowers appear in spring and summer and are quite showy, being held clear of the foliage.

CULTIVATION

Usually found in dry areas in the wild, in cultivation Portuguese sundew does best in well drained gritty soil with added leaf mold for humus. It can be grown in sun or partial shade and is among the simpler carnivorous plants to grow.

Drosophyllum lusitanicum
(below)

This native of Portugal, southern Spain and Morocco is a woody stemmed carnivorous perennial up to 12 in (30 cm) high. Its stems, which are sometimes branched are covered with old dry leaves that hang on long after they have died. When alive, the leaves are around 10 in (20 cm) long by just over 1 in (25 mm) wide. They are covered in sticky hairs that entrap insects that are then digested by a fluid excreted from the hairs. In spring and summer, branched stems carry sprays of bright yellow 5-petalled flowers up to 1 in (25 mm) wide.
ZONES 9–11.

Dryas octopetala var.
argentea (above)

DRYAS
MOUNTAIN AVENS

A small genus of 3 species from alpine and
Arctic regions of the northern hemisphere,
Dryas species make dense mats of evergreen foliage somewhat like
tiny oak leaves; these often turn dark bronze in winter. Although
the foliage and stems hug the ground, the showy flowers and seed
heads sit up well above them.

CULTIVATION
Completely cold tolerant they may be less than satisfactory in
warm climates. They make attractive rock garden or ground cover
plants and are also useful between paving slabs. Grow in full sun or
part-shade in a well-drained, humus-rich soil. Propagate from seed
or cuttings.

Dryas octopetala
'Minor' *(right)*

Dryas octopetala
(above)
MOUNTAIN AVENS
This lovely European
alpine plant can make
evergreen mats up to
4 in (10 cm) tall in
flower with a spread
exceeding 3 ft (1 m).
It has dark green
scalloped leaves to
1½ in (4 cm) long.
The pure white flowers,
1½ in (4 cm) across
and with a boss of
golden stamens in the
center, are produced in
late spring and early
summer and followed
by equally ornamental
fluffy silver seed heads.
***Dryas octopetala* var.
*argentea*** (syn. *lanata*)
has felted leaves on
both sides; **'Minor'** has
smaller flowers and
leaves. ZONES 2–9.

D

DUCHESNEA
INDIAN STRAWBERRY, MOCK STRAWBERRY

There are 6 species of these perennial plants, closely related to and very similar in appearance to the true strawberries. The leaves are divided into 3 to 5 leaflets and the plant spreads vegetatively with long fine stolons that produce more rosettes. Native to eastern and southern Asia, they differ from strawberries in having yellow flowers instead of white flowers and the red fruits are dry and unpalatable.

CULTIVATION
These frost-hardy plants can be quite aggressive so they should be placed with care; they are probably best as ground covers in less cultivated parts of the garden. They prefer part-shade and are not really fussy about the soil. Propagate by division.

Duchesnea indica (above)
syns *Fragaria indica, Potentilla indica*

A semi-evergreen trailing perennial, this species grows to a height of 4 in (10 cm) and multiplies rapidly by runners to an indefinite spread. It is useful as a ground cover and for bed edges, hanging baskets and pots. It has dark green leaves and bright, 1 in (25 mm) wide, yellow flowers from spring to early summer. Ornamental, strawberry-like small red fruits appear in late summer. ZONES 5–11.

DYMONDIA

A South African genus of one species, rather like a gazania in miniature, this mat-forming perennial is ideal for rock gardens, borders, edging and as a ground cover in warm gardens.

CULTIVATION

In frost-prone climates grow in hanging baskets and containers. In warmer areas plant in the rock garden or in paving crevices in well-drained, moderately fertile soil in full sun. Propagate from seed or by division.

Dymondia margaretae *(below)*

This prostrate ground-covering perennial will spread to 20 in (50 cm) in diameter. The linear dark green leaves to 2 in (5 cm) or less long have 2 or 3 teeth and silvery undersides. Very small bright yellow daisy-like flowerheads on very short stalks are produced in spring.
ZONES 8–11.

D

E

Echinacea purpurea (left)
syn. *Rudbeckia purpurea*
PURPLE CONEFLOWER

This showy, summer-flowering perennial has dark green, lance-shaped leaves and large, daisy-like, rosy purple flowers with high, orange-brown central cones. The flowerheads, about 4 in (10 cm) wide, are borne singly on strong stems and are useful for cutting. Of upright habit, it grows to 4 ft (1.2 m) tall and spreads about 18 in (45 cm). **'Robert Bloom'** has dark pink flowers with orange-brown centers, while **'White Swan'** has large, pure white flowers with orange-brown centers. ZONES 3–10.

Echinacea pallida (below left)
PINK CONEFLOWER

This species is an upright perennial to 4 ft (1.2 m) differing from *Echinacea purpurea* in that its petals are longer and tend to hang down. The petal (ray floret) color is usually a pink-mauve, although purple and white forms are known. ZONES 5–9.

ECHINACEA
CONEFLOWER

The 9 coneflower species, all native to the USA, share their common name with their close cousins the rudbeckias. They are clump-forming plants with thick edible roots. The daisy-like flowerheads are usually mauve-pink or purple, with darker and paler garden forms available. The dried root and rhizome of *Echinacea angustifolia* and *E. purpurea* are used in herbal medicine and allegedly increase the body's resistance to infection.

CULTIVATION
Very frost hardy, these plants like full sun and fertile soil, and resent disturbance—divide them only to increase stock, otherwise leave them alone and mulch each spring. Deadhead regularly to prolong flowering. Propagate by division or from root cuttings from winter to early spring.

Echinops ritro *(right)*

This perennial is a useful plant for the herbaceous border, and its globe-like, spiky flowers can be cut and dried for winter decoration. It has large, deeply cut, prickly leaves with downy undersides, silvery white stems and round, thistle-like, purplish blue flowerheads in summer. Of upright habit, it grows 30 in (75 cm) tall and wide. ZONES 3–10.

E

ECHINOPS
GLOBE THISTLE

This genus, related to thistles, contains about 120 species of erect perennials, biennials and annuals. The perennials are most commonly grown in gardens. They are native to southern Europe, central Asia as well as some of the mountainous areas of tropical Africa. The cultivated species are considered bold, attractive additions to mixed or herbaceous borders and many are used in dried flower arrangements. The foliage is usually gray-green and thistle-like though usually not as spiny. The ball-shaped flowerheads can be blue, blue-gray or white, the rich blues being the most favored, and up to 2 in (5 cm) in diameter. Most cultivated species grow to 4 ft (1.2 m) or more.

Echinops bannaticus

Native to southeastern Europe, this perennial grows to 4 ft (1.2 m) tall and bears spherical, blue-toned flowers during mid- to late summer. It has downy stems and gray-green leaves up to 10 in (25 cm) long. 'Taplow Blue' is taller and produces vivid blue flowers. ZONES 3–10.

CULTIVATION
These plants are usually fully frost hardy and heat tolerant, requiring nothing more than a sunny aspect with a well-drained soil of any quality. Like most herbaceous perennials, cut them to the ground in autumn or early winter. Propagate by division or from seed.

Echinops bannaticus
'Taplow Blue' *(right)*

E

ECHIUM

Indigenous to the Mediterranean, Canary Islands and Madeira in western Europe, the 40 or so species of annuals, perennials and shrubs in this genus are grown for their spectacular bright blue, purple or pink flowers that appear in late spring and summer. The hairy leaves form rosettes at the bases of the flowering stems. They look best in mixed borders. Ingestion of the plants can cause stomach upsets.

CULTIVATION

Very frost hardy to frost tender, *Echium* species require a dry climate, full sun and a light to medium, well-drained soil. They become unwieldy in soil that is too rich or damp. Prune gently after flowering to keep them compact. Coastal planting is ideal. Propagate from seed or cuttings in spring or summer. In mild climates they self-seed readily.

Echium plantagineum (top)
syn. *Echium lycopsis*

This annual or biennial to 24 in (60 cm) and native to warm, dry areas of Europe produces a basal rosette of bristly leaves up to 6 in (15 cm) long. The flower stems produced in late spring and summer form a panicle of rich blue-purple, occasionally red flowers. This is an attractive bedding plant but it tends to self-seed in dry climates; in southern Australia it has become a notorious weed known as Paterson's curse. ZONES 9–10.

Echium pininana (left)

Indigenous to La Palma in the Canary Islands, this biennial species bears striking tapered spires of funnel-shaped, lavender-blue flowers, soaring to 10 ft (3 m) or more in height. The leaves appear in the first year, the flowers the next, and after flowering the plant dies. ZONES 9–10.

E

Echium wildpretii
(right & below left)
syn. *Echium bourgaeanum*
TOWER OF JEWELS

A striking biennial from the
Canary Islands, this evergreen
plant makes a rosette of narrow,
silvery leaves and, in its second
season, bears a single, bold
spike of small, funnel-shaped,
rich coral flowers. It has an
erect habit, growing to 6 ft
(1.8 m) or more high and
about 24 in (60 cm) wide.
ZONES 9–10.

Echium vulgare *(right)*
VIPER'S BUGLOSS

This spectacular European
biennial to 3 ft (1 m) tall has
erect leafy stems. The funnel-
shaped flowers, borne in
spikes or panicles, are usually
a rich violet, although white
and pink forms exist. A dwarf
form is available with white,
blue, pink or purple flowers.
ZONES 7–10.

EICHHORNIA
WATER HYACINTH

This is a genus of 7 species of aquatic perennials native to tropical America. They form rosettes of stalked, broadly oval or heart-shaped leaves and terminal spikes of showy, funnel-shaped flowers. They grow floating in water, with no need to anchor their roots; a raft of connected plants can rapidly cover a large area of water, choking rivers and blocking sunlight to other marine life. Grow only where they can be controlled and never in open water-courses.

CULTIVATION
Reasonably frost hardy, they thrive in warm, slowly moving water in full sun. Propagate by division.

Eichhornia crassipes (above)

This species from South America spreads to around 18 in (45 cm). The pale violet flowers are marked with bright blue and gold, and occur in upright terminal spikes. The rounded, glossy green leaves are arranged in rosettes. Its cultivation is prohibited in most warmer countries. ZONES 9–12.

ELEGIA
CAPE REED

This genus consists of 32 species restricted to the Fynbos (a type of heath-like vegetation) region of southern Africa. Fynbos is typified by poor soils, wet periods and hot, dry, fire-prone seasons. In their native home, many species have been used as thatching and for making brooms. They are also becoming very popular in the florist trade as foliage; the strong, fine stems of *Elegia grandispicata* makes excellent accent

foliage as does *E. persistens* with its terminal ochre-colored bracts. Some species can exceed 10 ft (3 m), although most are smaller. Most are soft rush-like plants that look good by ponds or among rocks. Some species may have weed potential in Mediterranean climates.

CULTIVATION

Most are sun-loving plants requiring nothing more than some moisture and good drainage in a frost-free climate. Cut back any old stems that are dying off. Propagate from seed or by division of young plants.

Elegia capensis
(above)
BESEMRIET, BERGBAMBOES

This is possibly the most attractive and one of the easiest species to grow. It has fluffy, branching, green stems that perform the function of leaves (the leaves are attractive bronze bracts that run up the stems at the nodes). These stems are usually about 5 ft (1.5 m) tall, although they can reach nearly 10 ft (3 m) under ideal conditions. Tiny brown flowers are produced at the ends of the stems. ZONES 9–10.

Elegia cuspidata
(left)
BLOMBIESIES

This species rarely exceeds 3 ft (1 m) tall. The sturdy upright stems support dense bronze flowerheads surrounded by papery brown bracts. ZONES 9–10.

E

ENSETE

At one time the 7 species of this remarkable genus of gigantic tropical herbs were included in the banana genus *Musa,* of which they are undoubtedly the closest relatives. They are native to tropical Africa and Asia and have a non-branching underground stem, which results in only a single, trunk-like false stem being produced. The flowering stem grows through the middle of the crown of large spreading leaves, to produce a pendulous spike of flowers half-hidden among large bracts. After the small banana-like fruits mature the whole plant dies. They make dramatic, yet short-lived ornamentals.

CULTIVATION
Frost-tender, they should be grown in full sun or part-shade in a rich, moist but well-drained soil and given shelter from winds. Propagate from seed in spring; germination can be erratic without the provision of a warm seed-bed.

Ensete ventricosum
(above)
ABYSSINIAN BANANA, WILD BANANA

Native to tropical Africa, this large leafy perennial to 30 ft (9 m) tall has huge leaves up to 12 ft (3.5 m) long with a bright red midrib. In late spring, flowers surrounded by deep red bracts droop in spikes to 10 ft (3 m) long. The fruit are not edible. ZONES 10–12.

EPILOBIUM
syn. *Chamaenerion*

WILLOW HERB

This is a large genus of about 200 species of annuals, biennials, perennials and subshrubs in the evening primrose family, widely distributed throughout the temperate and cold zones of both hemispheres. Most species are invasive, but some are valued in cultivation for their pretty deep pink or white flowers produced over a long period from summer to autumn.

CULTIVATION
Plant in sun or shade in moist, well-drained soil. They are mostly quite frost hardy. Remove spent flowers to prevent seeding. Propagate from seed in spring or autumn, or from cuttings.

Epilobium angustifolium (below)
syn. *Chamaenerion angustifolium*

FIREWEED, ROSE BAY WILLOW HERB

This is a tall, vigorous perennial to 5 ft (1.5 m) found throughout the northern and mountainous parts of Eurasia and North America, most wide-spread in areas that have been recently burned or logged. Drifts of rose-pink flowering spikes are produced in late summer. It will spread indefinitely unless confined by pruning or containing the root system, and self-seeds freely. ZONES 2–9.

E

EPIMEDIUM

BARRENWORT

This genus of about 40 species comes mainly from temperate Asia with a few species extending to the Mediterranean. Among the most useful low-growing perennials for shady situations, the barrenworts produce elegant foliage. Sometimes evergreen, the compound leaves are composed of heart-shaped leaflets. Delightful sprays of delicate, often spurred flowers appear in late spring or early summer just above the foliage. Slowly spreading to form a broad mound or mat, they serve well as ground covers in open woodland or in the foreground of borders and rockeries. A number of cultivars are available. 'Enchantress' has large pale pink flowers and foliage that is copper-tinted when young.

CULTIVATION

Frost hardy, most are tolerant of dry conditions, especially in the shade. All prefer a woodland environment and well-drained soil. Old leaves are best cut back in early spring to display the new foliage and flowers. Propagate from ripe seed or by division in autumn.

Epimedium 'Enchantress' *(above)*

Epimedium alpinum *(below)*

An evergreen, low-growing perennial from southern Europe, this plant makes a good ground cover under azaleas and rhododendrons. The finely toothed, glossy leaves are bronze-red when young, turning to mid-green with age. In spring it bears racemes of pendent yellow and crimson flowers. It grows to a height of 10 in (25 cm) and spread of 12 in (30 cm). It prefers cooler climates. ZONES 5–9.

Epimedium grandiflorum
syn. *Epimedium macranthum*

BISHOP'S HAT, LONGSPUR EPIMEDIUM

This species from northern China, Korea and Japan is deciduous, except in mild climates. It has toothed leaflets often edged with red. Spidery pink or purple flowers with white spurs are held above the foliage on 12 in (30 cm) slender stems in spring. It is best displayed as a clump rather than as a ground cover. **'Rose Queen'** bears clusters of cup-shaped rose-pink flowers with long, white-tipped spurs. **'White Queen'** has large pure white flowers. ZONES 4–9.

Epimedium grandiflorum 'Rose Queen' *(above)*

Epimedium grandiflorum 'White Queen' *(right)*

Epimedium diphyllum *(right)*

From Japan, this dainty semi-evergreen plant to 12 in (30 cm) tall and wide has leaves divided into 2 leaflets. The small, bell-shaped, pure white, spurless flowers are borne in spring. Purple flowering forms are also known. ZONES 5–9.

E

Epimedium pinnatum
subsp. *colchicum* (below)

Epimedium pinnatum (left)

Native to northeastern Turkey, this carpeting perennial grows to about 12 in (30 cm) high and wide. The leaflets are 3 in (8 cm) long and are somewhat leathery, evergreen and with spiny edges. The bright yellow flowers with purplish brown spurs are produced in late spring and early summer. **Epimedium pinnatum subsp. colchicum,** the Persian epimedium, has showy panicles of larger, yellow flowers with short brown spurs. ZONES 6–9.

Epimedium × versicolor

This hybrid of *Epimedium grandi-florum* and *E. pinnatum* is the best known of the epimediums. It is a carpeting perennial to 12 in (30 cm) high and wide. The green, heart-shaped leaves are tinted reddish when young. Clusters of pendent, pink and yellow flowers with red spurs are produced in spring. 'Sulphureum' has sulfur yellow flowers and reddish, bronze-tinted young foliage. As summer advances it turns green, then russet again in autumn. ZONES 5–9.

Epimedium × versicolor
'Sulphureum' (left)

Epimedium × *youngianum* *(right)*

This hybrid between *Epimedium diphyllum* and *E. grandiflorum* is possibly of wild origin. It forms attractive, neat clumps 18 in (45 cm) high and 30 in (75 cm) wide. The leaves can have up to 9 leaflets and are tinted red in spring and autumn. The flowers come in colors varying from white through to pink-mauve and may have spurs or may not. **'Niveum'** is a lovely, white-flowered form with bronze-tinged foliage in spring. **'Roseum'** (syn. 'Lilacinum') has soft pink-mauve flowers. ZONES 5–9.

Epimedium × *youngianum* 'Niveum' *(right)*

Epimedium × *youngianum* 'Roseum' *(below)*

E

EPISCIA

From the jungles of tropical America and the West Indies, the 6 species of this genus are related to the African violet and make ideal plants for hanging baskets. Long runners bear tufts of ornamental leaves, which are hairy and produced in whorls or rosettes; they cascade down the sides of the pot or basket, and given the right conditions produce long-lasting, colorful flowers. The flowers, either solitary or in small racemes, have 5 lobes and appear from spring to autumn.

CULTIVATION

Plant in African violet mix or porous, peaty, indoor plant mix, in bright indirect light. Poor light may result in few flowers. They require constant warmth and humidity, so are well suited to a sunny bathroom or conservatory. Keep moist at all times, but take care not to over-water as it leads to rotting. Pinch back stems after flowering to encourage branching, and repot every year in spring. Propagate in summer by laying runners in compost, from cuttings or by division.

Episcia dianthiflora
(left)
LACE FLOWER VINE

A native of Central America and Mexico, this evergreen, low-creeping perennial has rooting stems that provide an easy means of propagation. Its small leaves, to 2 in (5 cm) long, are dark green often with red veins. Its pure white flowers have purple spotting at the base and inside the spur. The edges of the petals are deeply and attractively fringed.
ZONES 10–12.

Episcia cupreata
'Mosaica' *(above)*

Episcia cupreata
(top)
FLAME VIOLET

This evergreen creeping perennial, native to northern South America, grows to a height of about 6 in (15 cm). The attractive, felted, bronze leaves have silver veins. It intermittently produces tubular, scarlet flowers with yellow centers. **'Mosaica'** has dark, almost black leaves with an embossed appearance. **ZONES 10–12.**

E

EQUISETUM
HORSETAIL, SCOUR RUSH

Some 25 species of rush-like perennials belong to this ancient group of plants, distantly related to the ferns. They occur mainly in the northern hemisphere although a few cross the Equator to Africa and South America. The cylindrical stems are usually erect and may be unbranched or have whorled branches at the nodes. They rarely exceed 10 ft (3 m) tall and grow from vigorous creeping rhizomes. Although quite ornamental, their use in gardens is limited because they can become invasive and are difficult to eradicate. Horsetails

have been used since Roman times to scour pots and medically as a general tonic and an astringent.

CULTIVATION
Most species are very frost hardy. Grow plants in containers and make sure the rhizomes don't escape out the drainage holes. Give them a sunny aspect and plenty of water. Propagation is usually by division.

Equisetum trachyodon (above)
This horsetail is unbranched. It makes an attractive potted specimen and needs shade during the hottest hours. ZONES 5–9.

Equisetum scirpoides (left)
DWARF SCOURING RUSH

This is a fairly small species to 6 in (15 cm) or so tall from Eurasia, Greenland and North America. Its stems are very fine and not usually branched, with 3, or rarely, 4 ridges. This is not a very ornamental species. ZONES 2–9.

E

Eremurus × isabellinus,
'Shelford Desert Candle' *(above)*

EREMURUS
FOXTAIL LILY, DESERT CANDLE

This is a genus of 50 or so species, all native to the cold, high plains of central and western Asia. Among the most dramatic of early summer perennials, they are mainly clump forming with a rosette of strap-shaped leaves. Their flower spikes, each of which can contain hundreds of flowers in pale shades of white, yellow or pink, rise to well over head height. The foliage is luxuriant but low, so the flower stems rise almost naked, which makes them all the more imposing.

CULTIVATION

In the wild these cool- to cold-climate plants are protected from the winter cold by a thick blanket of snow; in milder climates they must be given a winter mulch to ensure the soil does not freeze. The other requirements are sun, a well-drained soil and shelter from strong winds. Propagate from fresh seed in autumn or by careful division after flowering.

Eremurus × isabellinus, Shelford Hybrids

These frost-hardy perennials are grown for their lofty spikes of close-packed flowers, magnificent for floral displays. They produce rosettes of strap-like leaves and in mid-summer each crown yields spikes of blooms with strong stems and hundreds of shallow cup-shaped flowers in a wide range of colors including white, pink, salmon, yellow, apricot and coppery tones. **'Shelford Desert Candle'** is a particularly lovely pure white form. The plants grow to about 4 ft (1.2 m) in height with a spread of 24 in (60 cm). **ZONES 5–9.**

Eremurus × isabellinus,
Shelford Hybrid
cultivar *(left)*

Eremurus stenophyllus *(right)*

This species from southwestern or central Asia has tufted basal leaves that are gray-green in color. The flowers are bright yellow and produced on spikes up to 3 ft (1 m) tall. ZONES 5–9.

Eremurus robustus
(above)

The tallest of the foxtail lilies, this upright perennial from central Asia flowers profusely in early summer. The individual flowers are smallish stars in palest peach-pink and are produced by the hundreds in spires that can reach nearly 10 ft (3 m) in height. They need to be staked. ZONES 6–9.

Eremurus spectabilis *(right)*

This is a tufted perennial with strap-like, rough-margined, gray-green leaves. In mid-summer it sends up rigid spikes of sulfur-yellow flowers to 4–6 ft (1.2–1.8 m). The individual blooms are star-shaped and ½ in (12 mm) across. This species ranges from Turkey to Pakistan. ZONES 6–9.

E

E

ERIGERON
FLEABANE

This large genus of about 200 species of
annuals, biennials and perennials, some
evergreen, occurs throughout temperate
regions of the world but predominantly in
North America. Some species were believed
to repel fleas. The mainly erect stems are
capped by masses of pink, white or blue,
daisy-like flowers and are well suited to the
front of a mixed herbaceous border or rock
garden. They flower between late spring and
mid-summer. There are many garden forms; **'Wayne Roderick'** is
but one example.

Erigeron 'Wayne
Roderick' *(above)*

CULTIVATION

Frost hardy, they prefer a sunny position sheltered from strong
winds and moderately fertile, well-drained soil. Do not allow to dry
out during the growing season. Cut back immediately after flowering
to encourage compact growth and prevent unwanted self-seeding.
Some erigerons can become invasive. Propagate from seed or by
division in spring.

Erigeron aureus
'Canary Bird' *(below)*

Erigeron aureus

The wild forms of
Erigeron aureus are
short-lived perennials
from the mountains
of western North
America. The selected
form **'Canary Bird'**
is a much longer
lived plant that
grows to 4 in (10 cm)
tall in flower. Its
flowers are soft to
bright yellow and are
held singly on stems
above its spoon-
shaped, hairy, gray-
green leaves.
ZONES 5–9.

E

Erigeron 'Charity' *(above)*

This perennial cultivar produces a profusion of
pale lilac-pink flowers with yellowy green centers
over a long period in summer. Clump forming, it
grows to a height and spread of about 24 in
(60 cm) and may require support. ZONES 5–9.

Erigeron compositus *(right)*

This tufted perennial to
6 in (15 cm) tall is native
to Greenland and
western North America.
It has rosettes of hairy
leaves that may be
lobed or dissected. Its
summer flowers can be
white, pink, lilac or
blue with a yellow
center. ZONES 5–9.

E

Erigeron foliosus
(left)

This clump-forming species grows to about 8 in (20 cm) in flower and comes from western North America. Its leaves are narrow-oblong and reduce in size up the stem. The flowers are usually blue with a yellow center. ZONES 5–9.

Erigeron formosissimus *(left)*

This clumping perennial from the southern Rocky Mountains has usually basal leaves that vary somewhat in shape. Its daisy flowers can be blue or pink or, rarely, white. ZONES 6–9.

Erigeron 'Dunkelste Aller' *(left)*

'Dunkelste Aller' ('Darkest of All') is a clump-forming peren-nial reaching a height of 24 in (60 cm) and spread of 18 in (45 cm). It produces semi-double, deep purple flowers with yellow centers in summer and has lance-shaped, grayish green leaves. ZONES 5–9.

Erigeron glaucus 'Cape
Sebastian' *(right)*

Erigeron glaucus *(below)*
SEASIDE DAISY, BEACH ASTER

This clump-forming perennial grows
to about 10 in (25 cm) in height with a
spread of about 8 in (20 cm). The spoon-
shaped leaves are glaucous. Lilac-pink
flowers are borne in summer. **'Cape
Sebastian'** has compact growth and
flowers profusely. ZONES 3–10.

Erigeron 'Strahlenmeer' *(below)*
syn. *Erigeron* 'Shining Sea'

Usually regarded as a cultivar of *Erigeron speciosus*,
though possibly a hybrid, this German-raised
perennial grows to around 28 in (70 cm) high
and has soft violet flowers. Its foliage is the same
as that of *E. speciosus*: clumped spatula-shaped
basal leaves up to 6 in (15 cm) long with smaller
leaves on the lower parts of the flower stems.
ZONES 3–9.

E

ERINUS

ALPINE BALSAM, FAIRY FOXGLOVE

This genus contains 2 species of semi-evergreen, small-growing perennials from northern Africa and southern and central Europe. Only one species, *Erinus alpinus,* is usually found in cultivation. They rarely exceed 3 in (8 cm) tall and 4 in (10 cm) wide so make attractive little tufting plants for a sunny rock garden or between paving slabs.

CULTIVATION

Very frost hardy, grow in a sunny or part-shaded, well-drained site and provide adequate water during summer. Although short lived, they will often self-seed into cracks and gaps helping to soften edges. Propagate from seed in autumn.

Erinus alpinus
(above)

This species is native to the European Alps and is ideal for planting in wall crevices and rock gardens. It forms rosettes of soft, medium green leaves and bears a profusion of starry, rosy purple or white flowers in late spring and summer. It grows to 2–3 in (5–8 cm) in height and spread.
ZONES 6–9.

ERIOGONUM
WILD BUCKWHEAT, UMBRELLA PLANT

This is a large genus of the polygonum family, of some 150 species native to North America, mainly the western side. They may be annuals, perennials or small shrubs often with silvery or white leaves. Some of the smaller ones are ideal rock garden plants and many of the taller species make good cut flowers, both fresh and dried. The long-lasting flowers are small but are produced in clusters surrounded by attractive toothed or lobed bracts. Most come from mountain habitats or alkaline desert areas.

CULTIVATION
Due to the wide distribution of the genus their frost tolerance varies, but all like a sunny, well-drained site. If kept dry in winter they will stand more cold than if damp. Cut back immediately after flowering unless seed is required. Propagate from seed in spring or autumn or by careful division in spring or early summer.

Eriogonum nervulosum *(above)*
SNOW MOUNTAIN BUCKWHEAT

This spreading, mat-forming species to about 4–6 in (10–15 cm) tall has small, obovate, fleshy leaves. Tight, hemispherical heads of pale yellow to reddish flowers are produced atop short, leafless stems. This is an unusual ground cover for gravelly soil. ZONES 8–10.

Eriogonum umbellatum *(below)*
SULFUR BUCKWHEAT

This woody-based perennial from the Rocky Mountains in British Columbia is grown for its attractive heads of tiny, bright yellow flowers borne in summer and turning copper with age. It is a useful rock garden plant, growing to a height of 12 in (30 cm) and a spread of 24 in (60 cm). It has a pros-trate to upright form and the dense green leaves have white, downy undersides. In cooler, wetter areas some shelter is required. *Erigonum umbellatum* var. *subalpinum* has creamy yellow flowers that turn dull mauve with age. ZONES 6–9.

E

This charming, brilliant yellow daisy from northwestern North America grows up to 24 in (60 cm) tall. It has erect to spreading stems clothed in white-felted, silvery leaves. The basal leaves are usually entire with the leaves decreasing in size and often becoming dissected as they go up the stems. The flower-heads can be up to 1½ in (35 mm) across and are produced in late spring and summer. **ZONES 5–9.**

ERIOPHYLLUM

This genus of 11 species of yellow-flowered, herbaceous perennials from western North America belongs to the sunflower tribe of the daisy (or Compositae) family. The genus name, latinized Greek for 'woolly leaf', refers to the whitish coating of felty hairs that is a conspicuous feature of the foliage of most species. Stems branch from the base and can form a dense clump, and the narrow leaves, often with toothed margins, are arranged on them in opposite pairs. The long-stalked flowerheads grow terminally on the branches, and both ray florets and disc florets are bright golden yellow.

CULTIVATION

Frost hardy, they like moderately fertile, very well-drained soil and a sunny position and may be short lived in climates with warm, wet summers. Propagate from seed or by division.

E

Erodium chrysanthum (left)

This Greek tufted perennial grows to about 6 in (15 cm) tall and up to 15 in (38 cm) wide. It has soft, silvery green, dissected foliage and produces its soft creamy yellow to sulfur-yellow flowers throughout summer. It is a lovely plant for a sunny rock garden. ZONES 6–9.

ERODIUM
HERONSBILL

This is a cosmopolitan genus of about 60 species of annuals and perennials in the geranium family. The evergreen leaves are often finely divided and quite attractive, and the 5-petalled flowers are quite like those of the true geranium though generally smaller. They are mostly low-growing, clumping plants and are best suited for ground cover, rock gardens or for cracks in a stone wall.

CULTIVATION

Frost hardy, all species prefer full sun, doing well in warm, dry regions. Soil must be well drained and not too fertile. Propagate from cuttings in summer or from seed when ripe.

Erodium cheilanthifolium (above)
syn. *Erodium petraeum* subsp. *crispum*

This tufted perennial to 8 in (20 cm) tall and 12 in (30 cm) across from southern Spain and the mountains of Morocco has crinkled, dissected, gray-green foliage. In summer it produces pale pink to white flowers veined with deep pink and with purple blotches on the base of the 2 upper petals. ZONES 6–9.

E

Erodium × *kolbianum* 'Natasha' *(below)*

This 6 in (15 cm) tall plant has a spread of around 10 in (25 cm). The dainty flowers of **'Natasha'** have more prominent veins and central blotches than the usual type. The leaves are gray-green and somewhat fern-like. ZONES 6–9.

Erodium glandulosum *(above)*

syns *Erodium macradenum, E. petraeum* subsp. *glandulosum*

This clumping perennial from northern Spain has silvery, dissected foliage. In summer it produces its flowers in clusters of up to 5; they are pink with purple markings on the upper 2 petals. It grows to 8 in (20 cm) tall and wide. ZONES 7–9.

Erodium manescaui *(right)*

syn. *Erodium manescavii*

This perennial to 18 in (45 cm) tall produces very few leaves, all basal and up to 12 in (30 cm) long and 4 in (10 cm) wide. They are hairy and lanceo-late with toothed edges. Its flowers are 1½ in (35 mm) across, saucer-shaped and in clusters of up to 20. They are bright magenta with darker markings on the 2 upper petals. This native of the Pyrenees Mountains can self-seed. ZONES 6–9.

Erodium pelargoniiflorum
(below center)

Native to Turkey, this mound-forming, tufted perennial is ideal for rock gardens or alpine houses, reaching a height of about 12 in (30 cm). It has prostrate, woody stems and heart-shaped, lightly lobed, green leaves. Umbels of white, purple-veined flowers are produced from late spring to autumn. It is prone to aphid infestation. ZONES 6–9.

Erodium trifolium var. *montanum*
(below)

A low-growing, compact perennial from higher elevations in the Atlas Mountains of North Africa, this species is suitable for the alpine house, rock or scree garden. The lobed, toothed leaves are dull green and the simple flowers, in 2 shades of pink, appear in clusters atop slender stems. ZONES 7–9.

Erodium × variabile 'Bishop's Form'
(left & bottom right)

As the name would suggest, this is a variable hybrid, its parents being *Erodium corsicum* and *E. reichardii*. This selected form grows up to 24 in (60 cm) tall. Its branched flower stems produce bright pink flowers throughout summer. ZONES 7–9.

E

E

ERYNGIUM
SEA HOLLY

Mostly native to South America and Europe, these 230 species of biennials and perennials are members of the same family as the carrot, and are grown for their interesting foliage and spiny collared flowerheads that usually have a bluish metallic sheen. They flower over a long period in summer and may be cut before they fully open, and dried for winter decoration. The spiny margins of the strongly colored, thistle-like bracts, which surround the central flower, give rise to the common name 'holly'. A number of named hybrids are available including the rather striking '**Jos Eijking**'.

Eryngium 'Jos Eijking'
(above)

CULTIVATION
Mostly frost hardy, they need sun, good drainage and sandy soil. Plants tend to collapse in wet, heavy ground in winter. Propagate species from fresh seed and selected forms by root cuttings in winter or by division in spring.

Eryngium alpinum
(right)

Considered one of the most beautiful of the genus, this perennial species from south-eastern Europe has green, heart-shaped, spiny basal leaves but with upper stems and leaves suffused with a soft blue. The 1½ in (35 mm) conical flowerheads and showy, intricately cut, feathery bracts are purplish blue. It reaches 30 in (75 cm) in height with a spread of 18 in (45 cm) and is superb in the border, where it will tolerate very light shade. ZONES 3–9.

Eryngium amethystinum
(left)

This perennial to 30 in (75 cm) tall comes from Italy and the Balkans. Its leaves are basal to 6 in (15 cm) long, spiny and mid-green. The ovoid flowerheads are amethyst surrounded by silvery blue bracts about 2 in (5 cm) long and are produced on silvery blue stems. ZONES 7–10.

Eryngium bourgatii *(below)*

This striking herbaceous perennial from the eastern Mediterranean has basal leaves that are leathery, gray-green and silver veined. Its flower spikes rise up to 30 in (75 cm) tall and support numerous blue or gray-green flowers surrounded by silvery spiny bracts. **'Othello'** is a compact form that produces shorter flowers on strong, thick stems. ZONES 5–9.

Eryngium bourgatii 'Othello'
(below left)

E

Eryngium proteiflorum
(right)

syn. *Eryngium delaroux*

This very handsome, ever-
green perennial to 3 ft (1 m)
high has tapered leaves to
12 in (30 cm) or more long
and 1 in (25 mm) wide.
These have white spines
along their edges and form a
cluster like the top of a
pineapple. The heads of small
flowers are whitish and
surrounded by masses of
long, narrow, silvery white
bracts to 4 in (10 cm) in
length. This species is less
frost hardy than others.
ZONES 8–11.

Eryngium giganteum   *(below)*
MISS WILLMOTT'S GHOST

This short-lived, clump-forming perennial grows
3–4 ft (1–1.2 m) tall and spreads about 30 in (75 cm).
The leaves are heart-shaped and mid-green, and it
bears large, rounded, blue or pale green thistle heads
surrounded by silvery bracts. It dies after flowering, but
its seeds will thrive in good conditions. ZONES 6–9.

E

Eryngium × *tripartitum* (right)

Of Mediterranean origin, this perennial hybrid is not as spiny as some of the other species. It has coarsely toothed, smooth, dark green, wedge-shaped leaves and bears globular, magenta flowerheads on blue stems from summer through to autumn. Frost hardy, it reaches a height of about 3 ft (1 m) and a spread of about 18 in (45 cm). It requires some support in exposed conditions. ZONES 5–9.

Eryngium variifolium (above)

Distinctive for its variegated white and green foliage which forms an attractive evergreen clump, this species has silvery blue stems to 18 in (45 cm) that are topped by 1 in (25 mm) flowerheads surrounded by similar silvery blue bracts. It is good for the front of the border, where the foliage will provide interest all year round. ZONES 7–10.

ERYSIMUM

syn. *Cheiranthus*

WALLFLOWER

These 80 species of annuals and perennials range in the wild from Europe to central Asia, with a smaller number in North America. Some are suitable for rock gardens, such as the hybrid '**Orange Flame**', others fit nicely into the border, such as '**Winter Cheer**'. Short-lived species are best grown as biennials. Some form woody bases and become leggy after a few years, at which time they are best replaced with younger specimens. A number are fine winter to spring-flowering plants, while some flower all winter or all year in very mild regions. The older types are sweetly scented, while the newer cultivars have no fragrance but bloom well over a long season. Botanists have now placed all species of *Cheiranthus* into this genus.

Erysimum 'Orange Flame' *(below)*

CULTIVATION

Mostly frost hardy, they do best in well-drained, fertile soil in an open, sunny po-sition. Cut back perennials after flowering so only a few leaves remain on each stem. Propagate from seed in spring or cuttings in summer.

Erysimum 'Winter Cheer' *(below)*

Erysimum × allionii

(left)

syn. *Cheiranthus × allionii*

SIBERIAN WALLFLOWER

This slow-growing but short-lived hybrid is a bushy evergreen suitable for rock gardens, banks and borders. It has toothed, mid-green leaves and bears bright yellow or orange flowers in spring, putting on a dazzling display for a long period. It reaches a height and spread of 12–18 in (30–45 cm). ZONES 3–10.

Erysimum 'Bowles' Mauve' *(right)*

syn. *Erysimum* 'E. A. Bowles'

This shrubby evergreen flowers almost continuously in mild climates. The deep rosy purple flowers on elongating stems are nicely set off against the glaucous foliage. Plants develop into mounds 3 ft (1 m) tall and 4 ft (1.2 m) wide. Prune back lightly when flowering slows to encourage another flush of blooms. Flowering ceases in very hot weather, but will continue through winter in spite of occasional light frosts. ZONES 6–11.

Erysimum cheiri *(left)*

syn. Cheiranthus cheiri

ENGLISH WALLFLOWER

This bushy species from southern Europe is grown as an annual or biennial and has been part of the cottage garden for centuries. Cultivars vary in height from 8–24 in (20–60 cm) and spread to 15 in (38 cm). Fragrant, 4-petalled flowers appear in spring, or during winter in mild-winter regions. Colors range from pastel pink and yellow to deep brown, bronze, orange, bright yellow, dark red and scarlet. All have lance-shaped leaves. They do best where summers are cool. **'Monarch Fair Lady'**, to 18 in (45 cm) high, has single, deep orange to bright yellow flowers; **'Orange Bedder'**, to 12 in (30 cm) high, is grown as a biennial and has abundant, scented, brilliant orange flowers. ZONES 7–10.

E

Erysimum 'Jubilee Gold' *(below)*

This is a bushy plant to 15 in (38 cm) high with lance-shaped leaves and golden yellow flowers in short clusters in spring. ZONES 7–10.

Erysimum 'Golden Bedder' *(above)*
syn. *Cheiranthus* 'Golden Bedder'

This is one of the color forms of the Bedder Series, bred for compact shape and available in shades from cream through yellow to orange and red. They can flower for months, often starting in winter in mild climates. 'Golden Bedder' is a rich golden yellow. ZONES 8–10.

Erysimum cheiri 'Monarch Fair Lady' *(below)*

E

Erysimum linifolium (above)

Native to Spain and Portugal, this narrow-leafed, mat-forming perennial grows to about 30 in (75 cm) tall and has long spikes of comparatively small, deep mauve flowers almost all year round in mild climates. Several forms exist including **'Bicolor'**, with pink-mauve as well as white flowers, and **'Variegatum'**, with mauve flowers and white-edged leaves. ZONES 6–10.

Erysimum 'Moonlight' (above)

This is a mat-forming evergreen perennial to 10 in (25 cm) tall and about 18 in (45 cm) wide. It flowers from early spring well into summer and produces short racemes of cheerful sulfur-yellow flowers. Erysimum 'Moonlight' would make a most attractive rock garden plant or subject for the front of a border. ZONES 6–9.

Erysimum mutabile (right)
syn. Cheiranthus mutabilis

This much-branched shrub from the Canary Islands and Madeira grows to 3 ft (1 m) high and has narrow, lance-shaped leaves. In spring the flowers open pale yellow and age to a purplish color. It is marginally frost hardy. ZONES 9–11.

E

Erysimum ochroleucum (below)
syn. *Erysimum decumbens*

This short-lived perennial should be grown as a biennial. It has spreading stems to 12 in (30 cm) or more tall, lance-shaped leaves and bright yellow flowers in spring and summer. **ZONES 6–9.**

Erysimum perofskianum (above)

This biennial or short-lived perennial is usually treated as an annual in gardens. It grows to 15 in (38 cm) tall and about 10 in (25 cm) wide and has dark green, slightly toothed leaves to 4 in (10 cm) long. It produces its orange to orange-red flowers in spikes of up to 40 blooms in summer. This rosette-forming plant is native to Afghanistan and Pakistan. **ZONES 7–9.**

Eschscholzia californica
(bottom far right)

This short-lived perennial, the official floral emblem of California, has cup-shaped flowers that open out from gray-green feathery foliage into vivid shades of orange. Cultivated strains have extended the color range to bronze, yellow, cream, scarlet, mauve and rose. It flowers in spring with intermittent blooms in summer and autumn, although the flowers close on cloudy days. Of rounded habit, it grows to 12 in (30 cm) high with a similar or wider spread. **'Mission Bells Mixed'** is a seedling strain with double and semi-double blooms in both pastel and strong colors; **'Thai Silk Series'** consists of compact plants with large single or semi-double flowers with fluted and striped petals in orange, pink and bronze-red. ZONES 6–11.

Eschscholzia californica (orange) and *E. caespitosa* (yellow) *(above right)*

Eschscholzia caespitosa *(right)*

This fast-growing, slender, erect annual bears cup-shaped, solitary yellow flowers 1 in (25 mm) wide in summer and early autumn. It has bluish green leaves and reaches a height of 6 in (15 cm). ZONES 7–10.

ESCHSCHOLZIA
CALIFORNIA POPPY

This genus from western North America was named by botanist and poet Adelbert von Chamisso (1781–1838) in honor of his friend, Johan Friedrich Eschscholz. It is a genus of 8 to 10 annuals and perennials with deeply dissected leaves. They bear capsular fruits and yellow to orange poppy-like flowers that close up in dull weather.

CULTIVATION

Species of *Eschscholzia* thrive in warm, dry climates but will tolerate quite severe frosts. They do not like transplanting, so should be sown directly where they are to grow. Grow in poor, well-drained soil and deadhead regularly to prolong flowering. The best method of propagation is from seed which should be sown in spring.

ESPELETIA

This genus contains up to 80 species of
perennials, shrubs and trees from South
America. The leaves are often crowded in a
terminal cluster. Daisy-like flowerheads are
generally borne in terminal panicles
or racemes.

CULTIVATION

Frost tender, these plants require a well-
drained soil in an open, sunny position.
Indoors, provide them with adequate air
movement, good light and a fertile, free-
draining potting mixture. Propagate by
division in spring.

Espeletia schultzii
(below)

From Venezuela, this
perennial to 3 ft (1 m)
tall has stems and
oblong leaves covered
in long, felt-like hair.
The yellow daisy-like
flowerheads are also
felty. ZONES 10–12.

Eupatorium fistulosum
JOE PYE WEED

Native to the southeastern states of the USA, this variable perennial grows 3–10 ft (1–3 m) tall and about as wide. It enjoys constantly moist, humus-rich soil and will tolerate periods of wetness. It produces heads of rosy-mauve flowers from mid-summer to early autumn. It can be invasive in rich, moist soil but is easily controlled by division every second year. **'Filigrankuppel'** is an improved flowering form. ZONES 7–10.

Eupatorium fistulosum 'Filigrankuppel' *(right)*

Eupatorium maculatum *(above)*

This perennial has stems marked with purple blotches and serrated, lance-shaped leaves in whorls of three or four. In late summer and autumn rose-purple flowers are produced in rather flattened terminal clusters. ZONES 5–10.

EUPATORIUM

This genus contains about 40 species of perennials and subshrubs, mainly from the Americas but a few from Asia and Europe. Only a few are cultivated for their large terminal panicles of small flowerheads, which come in white or shades of purple, mauve or pink.

CULTIVATION

Mostly quite frost hardy, they need full sun or part-shade and moist but well-drained soil. The shrubs should be pruned lightly in spring or after flowering. Propagate from seed in spring, from cuttings in summer or by division in early spring or autumn.

EUPHORBIA
MILKWEED, SPURGE

The genus is very large, with close to 2000 species, among numerous succulent species that at first sight look remarkably like cacti. There is a great variety of forms, which suggests that the genus should be divided, but the flowers of all species are almost identical. They are very much reduced, consisting of only a stigma and a stamen, always green, and usually carried in small clusters. Many species have showy bracts, these are the most widely cultivated; examples include *Euphorbia cognata* and *E.* 'Excalibur'. Mainly tropical and subtropical, the genus also includes many temperate species.

CULTIVATION
Plant species of *Euphorbia* in sun or part-shade in moist, well-drained soil. Cold tolerance varies greatly depending on the species; the more highly succulent species are generally frost tender. Propagate from cuttings in spring or summer, allowing succulent species to dry and callus before placing in barely damp sand, by division in early spring or autumn or from seed in autumn or spring.

Euphorbia amygdaloides 'Rubra' (below)

Euphorbia characias subsp. *wulfenii* (above right)

Euphorbia characias

This is a sun-loving, frost-hardy shrubby perennial usually up to 3 ft (1 m) tall. It is native to the Mediterranean region from Portugal and Morocco to Turkey. It likes a sunny, well-drained site and where happy, it will self-seed. It has deep brown nectaries giving a brown spot in the center of each yellow-green bract. **Euphorbia characias subsp. *wulfenii*** (syn. *Euphorbia wulfenii*) has blue-green leaves densely clothing the erect stems, which in spring are topped by dome-like chartreuse flowerheads. ZONES 8–10.

Euphorbia amygdaloides
WOOD SPURGE

Native to much of Europe and also Asia Minor, this erect perennial to 3 ft (1 m) high has dark green leaves to 3 in (8 cm) long and flowerheads with yellowish green bracts from mid-spring to early summer. It is generally represented in cultivation by its frost-hardy, selected, colorful varieties and forms. **Euphorbia amygdaloides var. *robbiae*** (syn. *E. robbiae*), Mrs Robb's bonnet, forms spreading rosettes of dark green leaves to 24 in (60 cm) high and wide and bears rounded heads of lime-green floral bracts; '**Rubra**' has light green leaves heavily suffused with burgundy and acid green floral bracts. ZONES 7–9.

Euphorbia griffithii *(right)*

This perennial from the eastern Himalayas, which grows to a height of 3 ft (1 m), produces small, yellow flowers surrounded by brilliant orange-red bracts in summer. The lanceolate, green leaves have prominent pinkish midribs and turn red and yellow in autumn. 'Fireglow' produces orange-red floral bracts in early summer. ZONES 6–9.

Euphorbia griffithii 'Fireglow' *(right)*

Euphorbia glauca

(below right)

MAORI SPURGE, WAINATUA, SHORE SPURGE

This shrubby perennial species is native to New Zealand and is that country's only member of the genus; its Maori name means 'milk of the demons'. It is an erect plant to about 24 in (60 cm) tall with blue-green foliage. Its flowerheads are only fractionally paler in color than the leaves, but it has tiny red nectaries. ZONES 9–11.

E

Euphorbia marginata (left)
SNOW ON THE MOUNTAIN, GHOSTWEED

Native to central areas of North America, this bushy annual makes an excellent foil for brighter flowers. It has pointed, oval, bright green leaves sharply margined with white, and broad, petal-like white bracts surrounding small flowers in summer. *Euphorbia marginata* is fairly fast growing to about 24 in (60 cm) tall with a spread of about 12 in (30 cm). It will endure cold conditions. ZONES 4–10.

Euphorbia palustris (center left)

This bushy, evergreen perennial occurs through most of Europe and western Asia. It grows to about 3 ft (1 m) tall and has mid-green, lance-shaped foliage and flattish heads of deep yellow flowers and bracts in late spring. Frost hardy, this is one of the few euphorbias that will grow well in damp soil. Prune out flowered stems to ground level. ZONES 5–9.

Euphorbia polychroma (below left)
syn. *Euphorbia epithymoides*
CUSHION SPURGE

Native to central and southern Europe, this frost-hardy, clump-forming perennial is grown for its heads of bright chrome-yellow flowers produced from spring to summer. It has softly hairy, deep green leaves and a rounded, bushy habit, reaching a height and spread of about 18 in (45 cm). **'Major'** has yellowish green flowers in loose clusters. ZONES 6–9.

Euphorbia polychroma 'Major' (below)

Euphorbia sikkimensis (top)

This herbaceous perennial from the eastern Himalayas has a somewhat suckering, spreading root system that produces upright stems to 3 ft (1 m) tall. In late winter its foliage is rich burgundy, fading to green as the season progresses although it keeps a lovely pinkish midrib. By mid-summer it produces flat heads of lime-yellow bracts. ZONES 6–9.

Euphorbia schillingii (center)
SCHILLING'S SPURGE

This is a frost-hardy, clump-forming, perennial species to 3 ft (1 m) tall. It is a comparative newcomer to horticulture, discovered in Nepal by Tony Schilling in 1975. It has unbranched, well-clothed stems with foliage of a soft green with a white midrib. The flat flowerheads are produced from mid-summer to mid-autumn. In some climates—usually with dry autumn weather—its foliage will color well before dying. ZONES 5–9.

Euphorbia seguieriana subsp. niciciana (right)
syn. Euphorbia reflexa

This perennial plant has several slender stems arising from a central woody crown. Its foliage is fine and blue-green and in late summer it bears terminal heads of small yellow-green bracts, sometimes ageing reddish. This frost-hardy plant is a good rock garden subject or suits the edge of a border where it can trail out over gravel or paving. It is native to southeastern Europe and southwestern Asia. ZONES 5–9.

E

Eustoma grandiflorum
cultivar *(above)*

EUSTOMA
syn. *Lisianthius*

Belonging to the gentian family, this genus consists of 3 species of annuals, biennials and perennials, ranging in the wild from southern USA to northern South America. One species, *Eustoma grandiflorum,* has very showy, tulip-like flowers that have become popular as cut flowers in recent years, and has been the subject of considerable breeding work. Japanese plant breeders extended the pastel color range to white, pale blue and pink as well as the original violet, and also developed double-flowered strains. Any unopened buds on the spray develop beautifully in water, so these continue the display for an extended period.

CULTIVATION
Usually regarded as frost tender, the plants are easy to cultivate in any warm-temperate climate. Give them sun, perfect drainage and fertile soil, but they rarely perform well after their first year. Propagate from seed in spring or from cuttings in late spring or summer.

Eustoma grandiflorum
syn. *Lisianthus russellianus*

PRAIRIE GENTIAN, TEXAS BLUEBELL, LISIANTHUS

Native to America's Midwest from Nebraska to Texas, this biennial's flowers last up to 3 weeks in water after cutting. It can also be grown as a container plant. It has gray-green leaves and 2 in (5 cm) wide, flared, tulip-like flowers in colors of rich purple, pink, blue or white. Of an upright habit, the plant is slow growing to a height of 24 in (60 cm) and spread of 12 in (30 cm). **ZONES 9–11.**

Exacum affine
(below)
PERSIAN VIOLET, GERMAN VIOLET

This showy miniature has shiny, oval leaves and bears a profusion of small, 5-petalled, saucer-shaped, usually purple-blue flowers with yellow stamens during summer. A biennial usually treated as an annual, *Exacum affine* grows to a height and spread of 8–12 in (20–30 cm). **'Blue Midget'** grows to only half as big and has lavender-blue flowers, while **'White Midget'** has white flowers. ZONES 10–12.

EXACUM

Like *Eustoma*, this genus belongs to the gentian family. It consists of about 25 species of annuals, biennials or perennials, widely distributed through tropical Africa and Asia. They have mostly yellow, white, blue or purple flowers that are often broadly cup-shaped or flat, unlike the tubular flowers of gentians. Only one species, *Exacum affine*, has become widely cultivated. It is a miniature plant from the hot, dry island of Socotra, just off the horn of Africa at the mouth of the Red Sea, and is grown as an indoor plant, popular for its neat, shrub-like habit and long succession of flowers.

CULTIVATION
These plants can only be grown outdoors in warm, frost-free climates, where they do best in a sunny position in rich, moist but well-drained soil. Indoors they like diffused sun and a night temperature not below 50°F (10°C). Propagate from seed in early spring.

FAGOPYRUM
BUCKWHEAT

This small genus of annuals and perennials are grown for their richly flavored, highly nutritious seeds which are processed into grits or flour. It is unsatisfactory for bread, but is used to make pancakes and ordinary cakes particularly in Europe and eastern Asia; it is also used to make buckwheat pasta. In the USA and Canada the flour is used in griddle cakes and in Japan it is made into thin green-brown noodles called soba. The leaves are alternate, and the small white flowers appear in racemes or corymbs.

CULTIVATION

Buckwheat are frost-hardy plants that will grow in poor soil. They mature within 2 months, which makes it possible to harvest 2 crops per season. Propagate from seed in spring and summer.

Fagopyrum esculentum (below)
syn. *Polygonum fagopyrum*
BUCKWHEAT

A native of northern Asia, this annual species grows to 3 ft (1 m) tall. It has reddish stems and short dense racemes of white fragrant flowers followed by triangular fruit that are enclosed in a tough, dark-brown rind. ZONES 3–9.

**Farfugium
japonicum** *(right)*
syns *Farfugium
tussilagineum,
Ligularia tussilaginea*

Native to Japan, this
clump-forming peren-
nial to 24 in (60 cm)
high has glossy, kidney-
shaped leaves on long
stalks, above which
arise downy branched
stems bearing clusters
of flowers from
autumn to winter.
'Aureomaculatum', the
leopard plant, has
variegated leaves with
circular yellow blotches.
ZONES 7–10.

FARFUGIUM

From temperate Asia, and closely allied to *Ligularia,* the 2 species of
evergreen perennials in this genus are grown for their large, leathery
foliage and daisy-like, yellow flowerheads. They are suitable for
containers.

CULTIVATION

These frost-hardy plants do best in part-shade in fertile, moist but
well-drained soil. Propagate from seed in spring, or divide variegated
cultivars in spring.

Farfugium japonicum
'Aureomaculatum'
(right)

F

FASCICULARIA

This genus is made up of 5 species of ever-green, rosette-forming, perennial plants of the bromeliad family. They all originate from Chile and are valued for their spreading leaves which form large rosettes and for their exotic, long-lasting blue flowers, which are followed by scaly fruits.

CULTIVATION

These frost-tender plants are best grown in a greenhouse in cool climates. In warmer areas grow outside in poor, very well-drained soil in full sun. Water moderately during the growing season and sparingly in winter. Propagate from seed or by division in spring or summer.

Fascicularia bicolor (above)
syn. *Fascicularia andina*

So named because of its green and red inner leaves, this vigorous bromeliad is one of the most attractive of Chile's native plants when in full flower. It has compact clusters of narrow, gray-green leaves with serrated edges which form a large rosette. Its inner leaves turn a vivid fiery red in autumn. The flowers are borne in dense corymbs in summer. ZONES 8–11.

Felicia amelloides (below)
BLUE MARGUERITE

This bushy, evergreen perennial has a spreading habit, and grows to 24 in (60 cm) in height and twice as wide. It has roundish, bright green leaves and pale to deep blue flowerheads with bright yellow centers that are borne on long stalks from late spring to autumn. Frost tender, it is fast growing in temperate climates and is suitable for seaside gardens. It is often grown as an annual in cool areas. **'Santa Anita'** has extra large blue flowers and **'Alba'** is a white form. *Felicia pappei* is like a miniature version of *F. amelloides* in growth, foliage and are an even richer, purer blue. It reaches 20 in (50 cm) in height. ZONES 9–11.

FELICIA
BLUE DAISY

This genus, which ranges from southern Africa to Arabia, consists of 80 species of annuals, perennials and evergreen subshrubs. Named after Herr Felix, mayor of Regensburg on the Danube in the 1800s, they are sprawling plants with aromatic foliage. In mild climates, they flower on and off almost all year. The daisy-like, usually blue flowerheads with yellow disc florets are borne in masses.

F

CULTIVATION
They are fully frost hardy to frost tender and require full sun and well-drained, humus-rich, gravelly soil. They do not tolerate wet conditions. In all but the mildest areas, the frost-tender perennial species need protection in winter with open-ended cloches. Deadheading prolongs the flowering season. Prune straggly shoots regularly. Propagate from cuttings taken in late summer or autumn or from seed in spring.

F

Felicia heterophylla (left)

This dome-shaped, mat-forming annual from South Africa grows to 20 in (50 cm) high and wide. It has lance-shaped, gray-green leaves and solitary blue flower-heads in summer. ZONES 9–11.

Felicia petiolata (below)

This mat-forming prostrate perennial with a spread of up to 3 ft (1 m) has small, sparsely lobed leaves and bears solitary white to violet flowerheads in summer. ZONES 9–11.

Ferula communis
(right)

GIANT FENNEL

Found in most parts of the Mediterranean region, this tall robust perennial to 15 ft (4.5 m) high has narrowly lobed leaves and leaf stalks that sheath the stems. The 5-petalled yellow flowers appear in early summer. Plants may take several years to flower. **ZONES 8–10.**

FERULA
GIANT FENNEL

This genus consists of about 170 species of aromatic herbaceous perennials from central Asia to the Mediterranean, with finely cut pinnate leaves and large rounded umbels of greenish white or yellow flowers borne on tall branching stems. These plants are grown for their strong architectural form and are ideal for the back of a border. They should not be confused with culinary fennel (*Foeniculum*).

CULTIVATION
Grow these frost-hardy plants in full sun in fertile, well-drained soil. Plants often die after seeding. Propagate from seed in late summer. They are prone to attack from aphids and slugs.

FILIPENDULA

This is a genus of 10 species of herbaceous
perennials from northern temperate regions.
All except *Filipendula vulgaris* occur
naturally in moist waterside habitats. They
have alternate pinnate leaves and erect
stems bearing large panicle-like clusters of
tiny, 5-petalled flowers with fluffy stamens.
They do well at the back of large perennial
borders and in waterside positions.

CULTIVATION
Grow these fully frost-hardy plants in full
sun or part-shade in any moisture-retentive
but well-drained soil. *Filipendula rubra* and
F. ulmaria will thrive in swampy, boggy
sites. Propagate from seed or by division in
spring or autumn. Check for powdery
mildew.

Filipendula purpurea
'Elegans' *(below)*

Filipendula purpurea
JAPANESE MEADOWSWEET

From Japan, this
upright clump-forming
perennial reaches 4 ft
(1.2 m) high with
deeply divided toothed
leaves. In summer it
bears large terminal
heads composed of
masses of tiny crimson-
purple flowers. This is a
beautiful plant for
growing near a water
feature. **'Elegans'** has
light, greenish yellow
foliage, and *Filipendula
purpurea* f. *albiflora*
has white flowers.
ZONES 6–9.

Filipendula vulgaris *(right)*
syn. *Filipendula hexapetala*
DROPWORT

From Europe and Asia, this species reaches 24–36 in (60–90 cm) high and has fleshy swollen roots. It is grown for its attractive, deeply cut, fern-like foliage, and showy, crowded heads of tiny white flowers; some garden varieties are pink. This species will tolerate fairly dry conditions and must have good drainage. ZONES 3–9.

F

Filipendula ulmaria
syn. *Spiraea ulmaria*
MEADOWSWEET, QUEEN-OF-THE-MEADOW

Native to Europe and western Asia, this clump-forming perennial grows to 6 ft (1.8 m) high. It has pinnate leaves to 12 in (30 cm) long with sharply toothed ovate leaflets. The creamy white flowers are borne in dense heads to 10 in (25 cm) across in summer. **'Aurea'** has golden-green leaves that are yellow when young; the leaves of **'Variegata'** are striped and mostly blotched yellow. ZONES 2–9.

Filipendula ulmaria 'Variegata' *(above)*

Filipendula ulmaria 'Aurea' *(right)*

F

FITTONIA
NERVE PLANT, PAINTED NET LEAF

This genus consists of 2 species of ever-green, creeping perennials from tropical rainforests in South America. They are grown mainly for their leaves, which are opposite, short-stemmed and have brightly colored veins. They are popular conservatory and house plants. Occasionally, white to reddish white, insignificant flowers are borne on short spikes. In warm, frost-free climates they make excellent ground covers or trailing plants.

CULTIVATION
Grow in part-shade and provide a humus-rich, well-drained soil and plenty of water. Where temperatures drop below 50°F (15°C), grow indoors in a good potting mix and keep evenly moist. They make excellent hanging basket subjects. Cut back straggly stems in spring. Propagate from cuttings or by layering stems in summer.

Fittonia verschaffeltii *(above)*

This species reaches about 6 in (15 cm) high with an indefinite spread and has dark green oval leaves with conspicuous red veins. The insignificant flowers are irregular and best removed. ***Fittonia verschaffeltii* var. *argyroneura*** (syn. *F. argyroneura*), the silver net leaf, has rooting stems and mid- to dark green leaves with conspicuous white veins. ZONES 11–12.

FRAGARIA
STRAWBERRY

The dozen or so species in this genus are mostly native to temperate areas of the northern hemisphere. They are low-growing, creeping or tufted perennials popular as ornamental ground covers and for their fleshy red fruit. The palmate leaves are composed of 3 toothed leaflets, and the white or pink, 5-petalled flowers appear in cymes. The strawberry itself is a false fruit; a large fleshy receptacle covered with tiny pips. Modern, more robust cultivars can fruit 6 months, or all year round in a warm climate. There are many named varieties with varying flavors. **'Red Ruby'** is an interesting cultivar with bright pink-red flowers.

CULTIVATION

Grow these frost-hardy plants in containers or beds lined with straw in free-draining, acidic soil. The plants need full sun or light shade and protection from wind; in cold climates grow them in slits in sheets of plastic. Propagate from seed in spring or autumn or by runners and replant with fresh stock every few years. Protect them from snails, strawberry aphids and birds. Botrytis can be a problem in high rainfall areas.

Fragaria 'Red Ruby'
(below)

F

Fragaria 'Pink Panda'
(above)

This spreading, ground cover perennial to 6 in (15 cm) high with an indefinite spread is grown for its pretty bright pink flowers to 1 in (2.5 cm) across, which appear from late spring to autumn. It rarely bears fruit. ZONES 4–10.

Fragaria chiloensis *(left)*
SAND STRAWBERRY

This species grows wild in coastal North and South America and is one of the parents of modern strawberries. It spreads by runners in dense tufts, the lower leaves forming rosettes. It reaches a height of 12 in (30 cm) and spreads to 18 in (45 cm). The 2 in (5 cm) long, obovate, trifoliate leaves are a lustrous deep green, and hairy underneath. ZONES 4–10.

FRANCOA
MAIDEN'S WREATH, BRIDAL WREATH

The 5 species of evergreen perennials that make up this genus from Chile are grown for their flowers, which are used in floral arrangements. The plants form a basal rosette of wavy, lobed leaves, each with a large terminal lobe. The 5-petalled bell-shaped flowers in white, pink or red with darker markings at the base are borne in terminal, spike-like racemes in summer and early autumn.

CULTIVATION
Mostly frost hardy, but in very cold climates plants make good potted specimens for a cool greenhouse. Outdoors grow in humus-rich, moist but well-drained soil in a sheltered sunny or part-shaded position. Water sparingly in winter. Propagate from seed or by division in spring.

Francoa sonchifolia (below)

This species to 3 ft (1 m) tall has oblong to oval, crinkled dark green basal leaves. The pale pink flowers, spotted deep pink within, appear on erect, sparsely branched stems from summer to early autumn. ZONES 7–10.

GAILLARDIA
BLANKET FLOWER

This genus of around 30 species of annuals, perennials and biennials are all native to the USA, with the exception of 2 South American species. The perennials are better suited to cool-temperate climates. All plants bloom for a very long season from summer until the first frosts. The daisy-like flowers are either single, like small sunflowers, or double and as much as 6 in (15 cm) wide. The common name arose because the colors of the flowers resemble the bright yellows, oranges and reds of the blankets traditionally worn by Native Americans. Gaillardias are a colorful addition to the flower border and meadow garden. They are also very good for cutting.

CULTIVATION
Among the hardiest of garden flowers, they tolerate extreme heat, cold, dryness, strong winds and poor soils. Plant in full sun in well-drained soil and stake if necessary. In cool climates, the stems of perennials should be cut back in late summer in order to recover before frosts. Propagate from seed in spring or early summer. Perennials may be divided in spring.

*Gaillardia ×
grandiflora* (left)
These hybrids of
Gaillardia aristata and
G. *pulchella* are the
most commonly grown
of the blanket flowers.
The plants form
mounds up to 3 ft (1 m)
high and wide and have
narrow, slightly lobed,
hairy leaves. The
flowerheads, 3–4 in
(8–10 cm) in diameter,
come in hot colors: red,
yellow, orange and
burgundy. They are
propagated by division
or from cuttings. There
are several named
cultivars: **'Burgunder'**
('Burgundy') has deep
maroon-colored
blooms; **'Dazzler'** has
bright orange-yellow
flowers with maroon
centers; **'Kobold'**
('Goblin') has compact
growth to 12 in (30 cm)
high and rich red
flowers with yellow
tips. ZONES 5–10.

G

Gaillardia × *grandiflora*
'Kobold' *(above)*

Gaillardia × *grandiflora*
'Dazzler' *(below)*

Galium verum (left)
LADY'S BEDSTRAW

This sprawling perennial from temperate Eurasia and North America grows to about 12 in (30 cm) high forming a dense mass of fine foliage up to 4 ft (1.2 m) across. It has linear leaves arranged in whorls and tiny, bright yellow flowers borne in dense terminal heads in summer and early autumn. **ZONES 3–10.**

GALIUM
BEDSTRAW

This genus contains about 400 species of annuals and perennials of cosmopolitan distribution. Some have become naturalized beyond their native regions and are weeds. They have weak sprawling stems and whorls of narrow green leaves. Many species spread by slender, much-branched rhizomes. The small star-shaped flowers are white, pink or yellow.

CULTIVATION
Grow these frost-hardy plants in part-shade in well-drained but moist soil. Propagate from fresh ripe seed or by division in early spring or autumn.

Galium odoratum
(above left & above)
syn. *Asperula odorata*
SWEET WOODRUFF

This delicate European perennial produces a beautiful pattern of whorled leaves, making a dense mass of foliage about 12 in (30 cm) high and greater spread. The tiny white flowers appear in few-flowered clusters in late spring. The fragrant foliage was traditionally added to white wine to produce May wine in Europe. **ZONES 5–10.**

GAURA

Related to the evening primrose *(Oenothera)*, this genus of about 20 species of annuals, biennials, perennials and subshrubs are from North America. They are apt to be weedy, despite their showy flowers and the genus name that translates as 'gorgeous'. They have simple, narrow leaves and clusters of flat, star-shaped, pink or white flowers.

CULTIVATION

They prefer full sun and light, well-drained soil. Cut ruthlessly to the ground when flowering has finished. Propagate from seed in autumn or spring, or from cuttings in summer.

G

Gaura lindheimeri
(right)

Native to the USA–Mexico border region, this clump-forming, long-flowering perennial is useful for back-grounds and mixed flower borders. It has loosely branched stems covered with tiny hairs, and from spring to autumn produces long sprays of beautiful flowers that open white from pink buds. It grows to 4 ft (1.2 m) in height with a spread of 3 ft (1 m). ZONES 5–10.

GAZANIA

From tropical and southern Africa, this genus consists of about 16 species of low-growing annuals and perennials grown for their bright, colorful flowers. The genus name honors the medieval scholar Theodore of Gaza (1398–1478). The leaves are entire or deeply lobed, long and narrow, often dark green on top and white- or silver-gray-felted beneath, or in some

Gazania 'Flore Pleno'
(above)

species silvery haired on both sides. The flowerheads borne singly on short stalks range from cream to yellow, gold, pink, red, buff, brown and intermediate shades, usually with contrasting bands or spots at the petal bases. They appear from early spring until summer. Most modern varieties are hybrids from several South African species; they are marginally frost hardy and useful for coastal areas for bedding, rock gardens, pots and tubs and for binding soil on slopes. Cultivars include **'Double Orange'**, bearing large orange flowers with double centers on short stems just above the leaves; **'Flore Pleno'**, with bright yellow double flowers; and **'Gwen's Pink'**, with salmon-pink single flowers with yellow centers and dark brown rings. Plants in the **Chansonette Series** are strong but low growers, reaching just 8 in (20 cm) in height. There are many color varieties, mostly with contrasting dark centers.

CULTIVATION

Grow in full sun in sandy, fairly dry, well-drained soil. Mulch with compost and water during dry periods. Propagate by division or from cuttings in autumn, or from seed in late winter to early spring.

Gazania 'Gwen's Pink'
(left)

Gazania Sunshine
Hybrid cultivar
(opposite page right)

Gazania rigens var.
leucolaena
(opposite page far right)

G

Gazania krebsiana *(above)*

From South Africa, this stemless perennial has slender lance-shaped leaves with a smooth upper surface and white downy underside. The flowers range from yellow to orange-red with a contrasting darker color around their centers. **ZONES 9–11.**

Gazania rigens

This perennial species grows to a height of 12 in (30 cm) with a similar spread. It is a mat-forming plant with crowded rosettes of mostly unlobed leaves that are green above and whitish beneath. The orange flowerheads have a black eye spot at the petal bases. The leaves of **Gazania rigens var. leucolaena** are silvery green on both sides and the flowers are yellow; *G. r.* var. *uniflora* has flowers that are smaller and short stalked. **ZONES 9–11.**

Gazania, Sunshine Hybrids

These mat-forming perennials may be grown as annuals. The height and spread is around 8 in (20 cm). Its solitary flowers, which are borne in summer, range in color with the disc-florets usually ringed in a darker color. **ZONES 9–11.**

Gentiana asclepiadea *(above)*
WILLOW GENTIAN

The arching stems of this perennial bear slender, willow-like leaves. In early autumn many rich violet-blue flowers appear in the leaf axils on the upper stems. It forms a loose clump 3 ft (1 m) high and 24 in (60 cm) wide. ZONES 6–9.

GENTIANA
GENTIAN

Occurring worldwide, mostly in alpine meadows and occasionally in woodlands, this is a genus of around 400 species of annuals, biennials and perennials, some of them evergreen. Intense deep blues and sky blues are the usual flower colors, but whites, creams, yellows and even red are also found. The mostly trumpet-shaped flowers are borne from spring to autumn. They are useful in rock gardens and sloping hillside gardens.

CULTIVATION
They prefer cooler regions and well-drained, but moisture-retentive soil rich in humus. Some species grow naturally in limestone soil. Plant in either sun or semi-shade. Propagate by division in spring or from fresh seed in autumn. Divide autumn-flowering species every 3 years in early spring, planting out in fresh soil.

Gentiana acaulis *(below)*
syns *Gentiana excisa, G. kochiana*
STEMLESS GENTIAN, TRUMPET GENTIAN

The stemless gentian is an evergreen, rhizomatous perennial from southern Europe. It makes a striking carpet of small, crowded leaves and disproportionately large, vivid blue trumpet flowers with green-spotted throats in spring and early summer. The foliage is only about 1 in (25 mm) high. It needs a deep root run and benefits from a light application of lime. ZONES 3–9.

Gentiana dinarica (below)

From Italy and the Balkans, this small, tufted perennial grows to about 6 in (15 cm) high with a basal rosette of broadly elliptic leaves to 1½ in (35 mm) long. In summer it bears solitary, deep blue, narrowly bell-shaped flowers on stems to 3 in (8 cm) long. ZONES 6–9.

Gentiana bellidifolia (right)

The 'daisy-leafed' gentian is typical of the New Zealand species in having white flowers in clusters. It is variable, reaching 6 in (15 cm) at the most. The flowers appear in summer, and the leaves are usually brown tinted. ZONES 7–9.

Gentiana farreri (below)

This 4 in (10 cm) tall semi-evergreen perennial from the borders of China and Tibet is one of the most beautiful of the Asiatic gentians. It has trailing stems with rosettes of small lance-shaped leaves. The turquoise blue, trumpet-shaped flowers with a white stripe appear in autumn. ZONES 5–9.

G

Gentiana paradoxa (left)

This beautiful perennial species has prostrate stems with linear, lance-shaped, finely pointed leaves up to 2 in (5 cm) long. The trumpet-shaped, bright blue flowers have deep purple and white stripes at the throat. ZONES 6–9.

Gentiana 'Inverleith' (below)

This robust hybrid of *Gentiana farreri* and *G. veitchiorum* has trailing stems with basal rosettes of linear, lance-shaped leaves. The pale blue trumpet-shaped flowers have deep blue stripes and appear in autumn. ZONES 5–9.

Gentiana lutea
(right)

GREAT YELLOW GENTIAN

This robust, erect, clump-forming perennial from the mountains of Europe produces tubular yellow flowers in clusters in the upper axils of tall stems in summer. It grows to 3–6 ft (1–1.8 m) high and 24 in (60 cm) wide and has oval, stem-clasping leaves to 12 in (30 cm) long. This is the main commercial source of gentian root, used medicinally and to flavor vermouth. ZONES 5–9.

Gentiana sino-ornata
'Alba' *(above)*

Gentiana septemfida *(below)*
CRESTED GENTIAN

Native to mountains of western and central Asia, this sun-loving perennial grows about 8 in (20 cm) tall and has paired oval leaves. The rich blue flowers with white throats are borne in terminal clusters of up to 8 in summer. ZONES 3–9.

Gentiana sino-ornata *(right)*

This evergreen perennial from western China flowers in autumn and bears deep blue trumpet flowers that are paler at the base and banded purplish blue. It has a prostrate, spreading habit, reaching 2 in (5 cm) tall and 12 in (30 cm) wide. '**Alba**' has white flowers. ZONES 6–9.

Gentiana verna
SPRING GENTIAN

This spring-flowering perennial to 2 in (5 cm) high has a scattered distribution in mountainous regions in Europe from Ireland to Russia. Often short-lived, it forms compact clumps of basal rosettes of broadly ovate leaves. Short, erect stems bear solitary brilliant blue flowers with a white throat and spreading petals in early spring. '**Angulosa**' has larger, more robust flowers. ZONES 5–9.

Gentiana verna
'Angulosa' *(below)*

G

GERANIUM

CRANESBILL

Over 300 species of annual, biennial and perennial geraniums, some evergreen, grow all over the world mainly in cool-temperate regions. The leaves are on long stalks, broadly circular in outline but usually palmately lobed. They make small, showy clumps with pink to blue or purple and white, 5-petalled flowers. The true geraniums or cranesbills, so-called for the shape of their small, dry fruitlets, are often confused with species of the genus *Pelargonium,* also commonly known as 'geraniums'. Symmetrical flowers are their chief point of distinction from pelargoniums, which produce irregularly shaped or marked flowers. With their attractive flowers they are useful for rock gardens, ground covers and borders. Compact species and hybrids such as '**Brookside**' and Geranium goldmanii are also good for containers.

CULTIVATION

Mostly quite frost hardy, they prefer a sunny situation and damp, well-drained soil. Transplant during winter. Propagate from cuttings in summer or seed in spring, or by division in autumn.

Geranium 'Brookside' *(below)*

Geranium × cantabrigiense
(above)

This hybrid between *Geranium dalmaticum* and *G. macrorrhizum* to 12 in (30 cm) high spreads by runners to 24 in (60 cm) wide. It has aromatic, light green basal leaves and bright purplish pink flowers in summer. '**Biokovo**' has pink-tinged, white flowers. ZONES 5–9.

Geranium endressii *(right)*

From the Pyrenees, this rhizomatous perennial forms clumps to 18 in (45 cm) high and 24 in (60 cm) across. The leaves are deeply lobed and toothed and pale pink flowers, becoming darker with age, are produced from early summer to early autumn. ZONES 5–9.

Geranium cinereum

This small, tufted perennial to 6 in (15 cm) forms a basal rosette of soft, deeply divided leaves. The cup-shaped flowers, white or pale pink often with purple veins, are produced in late spring or early summer. **'Ballerina'** bears purplish pink flowers with distinct purple veins; *Geranium cinereum* **subsp. subcaulescens** has darker green leaves and magenta flowers with a black center. ZONES 5–9.

Geranium clarkei

From the western Himalayas, this perennial is up to 18 in (45 cm) high and has spreading stems and deeply divided leaves. Its saucer-shaped flowers, borne in summer, are white or violet with pink veins. **'Kashmir Purple'** bears lilac-blue flowers with red veins. ZONES 7–9.

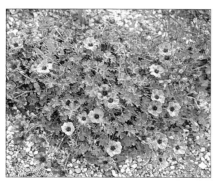

Geranium cinereum subsp. *subcaulescens* *(below)*

Geranium cinereum 'Ballerina' *(above)*

Geranium clarkei 'Kashmir Purple' *(below)*

G

Geranium erianthum *(above)*

This is a clump-forming perennial from north-eastern Asia and north-western North America. It has erect stems to 24 in (60 cm) tall and light green, deeply lobed and toothed leaves, which have a rich autumn coloring. Clusters of saucer-shaped, violet flowers are borne in early summer. ZONES 3–9.

Geranium himalayense *(below)*
syn. *Geranium grandiflorum*

This clump-forming perennial has cushions of neatly cut leaves and grows to 18 in (45 cm) high and 24 in (60 cm) wide. In summer large cup-shaped violet-blue flowers with white centers appear on long stalks. **'Gravetye'** (syn. *Geranium grandiflorum* var. *alpinum*) has lilac-blue flowers with reddish centers and leaves that turn russet before dying down in autumn. **'Plenum'** (syn. 'Birch Double') has double, purplish pink flowers with darker veins. ZONES 4–9.

Geranium himalayense 'Plenum' *(left)*

Geranium himalayense 'Gravetye' *(left)*

Geranium ibericum *(below)*

Although 'ibericum' is normally taken to mean 'Spanish' in Latin, it can also refer to the Caucasus region, where in fact this species comes from. This clump-forming perennial grows to a height and spread of 18 in (45 cm). It has heart-shaped, hairy leaves and produces large sprays of saucer-shaped violet flowers with faint darker veins in early summer. **ZONES 6–9.**

Geranium 'Johnson's Blue' *(above)*

This rhizomatous perennial may be merely a form of *Geranium himalayense*. It has deeply divided leaves and bears cup-shaped lavender-blue flowers with pale centers throughout summer. It has a spreading habit, reaching 18 in (45 cm) tall and 30 in (75 cm) wide. **ZONES 5–9.**

Geranium incanum *(right)*

This South African evergreen perennial grows up to 15 in (38 cm) high and 3 ft (1 m) wide. Its green leaves are deeply cut and feathery with a spicy aroma. The cup-shaped blooms are deep pink with deeper colored veins. It is marginally frost hardy. **ZONES 8–10.**

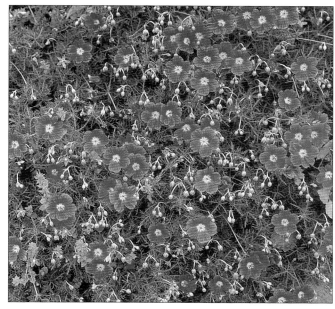

G

Geranium macrorrhizum
(right)

This clump-forming perennial often forms large colonies in its shady mountain habitats of southern Europe. The sticky, deeply lobed leaves are aromatic, often turning red or bronze in autumn. The flowers appear on 12 in (30 cm) stems above the foliage in spring and early summer. Flower color varies from pink or purplish to pure white. It makes an excellent ground cover for a dry, shady site. **'Album'** has white petals with reddish calyces; **'Ingwersen's Variety'** has pale pink flowers and smoother glossy leaves. **'Spessart'** is an attractive German cultivar. ZONES 4–9.

Geranium maculatum *(above)*

Native to eastern American woodlands, this species is best used in woodland gardens as it is less showy and more open in habit than others. It is an erect, clump-forming perennial to 30 in (75 cm) tall with deeply lobed, glossy leaves and bears saucer-shaped, lilac-pink flowers with white centers in late spring to mid-summer. ZONES 6–9.

Geranium macrorrhizum 'Ingwersen's Variety' *(left)*

Geranium × magnificum *(right)*

This vigorous garden hybrid of *Geranium ibericum* and *G. platypetalum* forms clumps to 24 in (60 cm) high. It has hairy deeply cut leaves that color in autumn. Abundant, violet-blue, reddish veined, saucer-shaped flowers appear in mid-summer. Propagate by division or from cuttings. ZONES 5–9.

Geranium malviflorum *(below)*
syn. *Geranium atlanticum* of gardens

From southern Spain and northern Africa, this tuberous perennial to 12 in (30 cm) tall has deeply cut dark green leaves and violet-blue, red-veined, saucer-shaped flowers in spring. It flowers best in a poor soil, although better soil promotes a fine display of foliage. ZONES 9–10.

Geranium maderense *(above)*

Native to Madeira, this short-lived, evergreen, bushy perennial to 5 ft (1.5 m) tall has huge leaves for a geranium, often 12 in (30 cm) or more across. They are divided in a striking snowflake pattern and turn reddish in autumn. Shallowly cup-shaped, pinkish magenta flowers with darker centers are borne in tall panicles from late winter to late summer. Old leaves should not be removed too soon, as the plant props itself on them to resist wind-loosening. ZONES 9–10.

G

Geranium × oxonianum *(right)*

This vigorous upright hybrid of *Geranium endressi* and *G. versicolor* forms clumps to 30 in (75 cm) high; it has light green wrinkled leaves with conspicuous veining. Trumpet-shaped flushed pink flowers with darker veins are produced over a long period from late spring to mid-autumn. **'Claridge Druce'** has mauve-pink darker veined flowers in summer; **'Wargrave Pink'** has bright pink flowers. ZONES 5–9.

Geranium × oxonianum 'Claridge Druce' *(above)*

Geranium × oxonianum 'Wargrave Pink' *(right)*

Geranium phaeum
'Variegatum' *(left)*

Geranium phaeum
'Samobor' *(above)*

G

Geranium phaeum *(below)*
MOURNING WIDOW, DUSKY CRANESBILL

From Europe and western Russia, this clump-forming perennial to 30 in (75 cm) high and 18 in (45 cm) wide has soft green, densely lobed leaves. Its flowers are a deep, brownish purple with a paler center ring, borne in late spring or early summer. **'Lily Lovell'** has large white flowers; ***Geranium phaeum* var. *lividum*** has pale pink or lilac flowers; **'Variegatum'** has leaves with yellow margins and pink splotches. Another cultivar is **'Samobor'**. ZONES 5–10.

Geranium phaeum
'Lily Lovell' *(below)*

Geranium phaeum
var. *lividum* *(above)*

G

Geranium pratense
MEADOW CRANESBILL

From Europe, Siberia
and China, this clump-
forming perennial
species reaches 3 ft
(1 m) in height. It has
hairy stems and the
leaves are deeply lobed
almost to the base.
They become bronze in
autumn. Saucer-shaped,
violet-blue flowers are
carried on erect
branching stems in
summer. **'Plenum
Violaceum'** (syn. 'Flore
Pleno') has double,
deep violet-blue flowers.
ZONES 5–9.

Geranium pratense
'Plenum Violaceum'
(left)

Geranium psilostemon *(right)*
syn. *Geranium armenum*
ARMENIAN CRANESBILL

This robust, clump-forming
perennial grows 2–4 ft (0.6–1.2 m)
high and 24 in (60 cm) wide. It
has lobed, deeply toothed leaves,
often reddish in autumn. Striking,
large, cup-shaped, magenta
flowers with a black eye appear in
summer. ZONES 6–9.

Geranium renardii *(left)*

This clump-forming peren-
nial develops into a neat
mound to 12 in (30 cm) high
and wide. It has lobed,
circular, finely wrinkled
leaves with a velvety underside. The saucer-shaped
white flowers with bold
purple veins are borne in
early summer. ZONES 6–9.

Geranium sanguineum
BLOODY CRANESBILL

In flower color this European species is often less 'bloody' than many other geraniums, but then coiners of English plant names had a weakness for translating the Latin name wherever possible. It is a low-growing perennial of around 8 in (20 cm) tall spreading by rhizomes. The dark green leaves are deeply cut into toothed lobes. Abundant cup-shaped bright magenta flowers with notched petals are produced during summer. **Geranium sanguineum var. striatum** is a pink version; **'Vision'** is a compact form with deep pink flowers. ZONES 5–9.

Geranium sanguineum var. *striatum* *(left)*

Geranium sanguineum 'Vision' *(below)*

Geranium robertianum *(top)*
HERB ROBERT, RED ROBIN

Late in the season, this scrambling annual or biennial, found widespread in regions of the northern hemisphere, takes on an overall red color. The 'Robert' in the name is in fact a corruption of *ruberta*, from the Latin adjective ruber meaning 'red'. Herb Robert derived its traditional uses from the medieval Doctrine of Signatures which stated that a plant's medicinal qualities were revealed in its external features—in this case for diseases of the blood. The plant has deeply cut ferny leaves with a rather strong, not altogether pleasant, scent. Small star-shaped pink or rose flowers are produced from summer to autumn. It is self-seeding, often to the point of being a nuisance. ZONES 6–10.

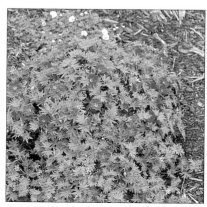

G

Geranium sylvaticum *(below)*
WOOD CRANESBILL

Another well-known European species, this upright, clump-forming perennial to 30 in (75 cm) tall has deeply divided basal leaves from which arise branching stems carrying bluish purple, cup-shaped flowers with white centers from late spring to summer. **'Album'** has white flowers; **'Mayflower'** has rich violet-blue flowers with white centers. ZONES 4–9.

Geranium sylvaticum 'Album' *(below)*

Geranium sylvaticum 'Mayflower' *(above)*

Geranium traversii

From coastal cliffs on the Chatham Islands off southern New Zealand, this perennial of up to 6 in (15 cm) high forms mounds of silvery, gray-green, lobed leaves. The pink or sometimes white saucer-shaped flowers are carried on slender stems above the foliage in summer to autumn. It is ***Geranium traversii* var. *elegans*** rather than the type that is found in cultivation; **'Seaspray'** has small, pale pink flowers on short stems. ZONES 8–9.

Geranium traversii 'Seaspray' *(right)*

GERBERA

This genus of around 40 perennial species is from Africa, Madagascar and Asia. The showy flowerheads, in almost every color except blue and purple, are carried on bare stems 18 in (45 cm) long. Linnaeus named the genus to honor a German colleague, Traugott Gerber. They are ideal rockery plants in frost-free climates. Only one species, *Gerbera jamesonii,* is commonly cultivated, along with its numerous hybrids.

CULTIVATION

They need full sun to part-shade in hot areas, and fertile, well-drained soil. Water well during summer. Gerberas make good greenhouse plants, where they require good light and regular feeding during the growing season. Propagate from seed in autumn or early spring, from cuttings in summer or by division from late winter to early spring.

Gerbera jamesonii 'Brigadoon Red' *(below)*

G

Gerbera jamesonii
BARBERTON DAISY, TRANSVAAL DAISY

Native to South Africa, this is one of the most decorative daisies and is an excellent cut flower. From a basal rosette of deeply lobed, lance-shaped leaves, white, pink, yellow, orange or red flowerheads, up to 3 in (8 cm) wide, are borne singly on long stems in spring and summer. Modern florists' gerberas derive from crosses between *Gerbera jamesonii* and the tropical *G. viridifolia*. Some have flowerheads as much as 12 in (30 cm) across, others in a wide range of colors, as well as double, for example **'Brigadoon Red'**, and quilled forms. **ZONES 8–11.**

Gerbera jamesonii
cultivars *(left & below)*

GEUM
AVENS

This genus of 50 or so herbaceous
perennials is from the temperate and
colder zones of both northern and
southern hemispheres. Species form
basal rosettes of hairy, lobed leaves.
Masses of red, orange and yellow
flowers with prominent stamens are
borne from late spring until early
autumn, and almost all year in frost-
free areas. They suit mixed herbaceous
borders and rock gardens, but may
require a lot of room. *Geum capense*
is suitable for a rock garden.

CULTIVATION
Frost hardy, they prefer a sunny,
open position and moist, well-drained
soil. Propagate from seed or by
division in autumn or spring.

Geum chiloense
'Mrs Bradshaw' *(below)*

Geum chiloense
'Lady Stratheden' *(above)*

Geum chiloense
syns *Geum coccineum* of gardens, *G. quellyon*
SCARLET AVENS

This Chilean native grows to 24 in (60 cm) in
height with a spread of 12 in (30 cm). It forms a
basal rosette of deep green, pinnate leaves to 12 in
(30 cm) long. The vivid scarlet, cup-shaped flowers
appear in terminal panicles in summer. **'Lady
Stratheden'** (syn. 'Goldball') has semi-double,
golden yellow flowers. **'Mrs Bradshaw'** bears
rounded, semi-double, scarlet flowers. ZONES 5–9.

Geum capense *(below)*

Geum montanum
(left)
ALPINE AVENS

From mountainous regions of southern and central Europe, this clump-forming perennial forms mats of up to 6 in (10 cm) high and 12 in (30 cm) wide. The basal leaves are pinnately divided, each with a large, rounded, terminal lobe. Solitary golden-yellow flowers are carried on short stems from spring to early summer. **ZONES 6–9.**

G

Geum triflorum
(left)
PRAIRIE SMOKE, PURPLE AVENS

Geum triflorum, native to northern USA and Canada, is a plant of 12–18 in (30–45 cm) with crowded leaves that have regularly incised margins. In summer it bears sprays of nodding, pinkish white flowers with long protruding styles. The flowers are followed by feathery, smoky gray seed heads that make a striking display in autumn. **ZONES 3–9.**

GILIA

From temperate western regions of both North and South America, this is a genus of about 30 species of annuals, biennials and perennials in the phlox family. The basal leaves are feathery and finely divided, and erect panicles of small, funnel- to trumpet-shaped flowers, often densely clustered, appear in spring and summer.

CULTIVATION

Moderately to very frost hardy, gilias prefer a climate with cool wet winters and hot summers, and well-drained soils in full sun. Water lightly and regularly. They are particularly sensitive to drought and heat and wilt rapidly. Light stakes may be needed for support on windy sites. Propagate from seed in spring directly where they are to grow when the soil has warmed up.

G

Gilia capitata

(right)

QUEEN ANNE'S THIMBLES, BLUE
THIMBLE FLOWER

Native to the west-coastal ranges of Canada, the USA and Mexico, this erect, branching annual to 24 in (60 cm) high has mid-green, fern-like leaves and tiny, soft lavender blue flowers that appear in a pincushion-like mass in summer and early autumn. It is a good cut flower and useful border plant. ZONES 7–9.

GILLENIA

This genus of the rose family consists of
2 species of rhizomatous perennials from
temperate North America. They are clump
forming with stalkless leaves consisting of
3 leaflets and starry, 5-petalled flowers.
After flowering the sepals enlarge and turn
red. They are easy to grow in a shady
position and make good cut flowers.

CULTIVATION

Very frost hardy, they prefer humus-rich,
moist but well-drained soil, preferably in
part-shade. Propagate from seed in spring
or by division in spring or autumn.

Gillenia trifoliata
(below)
INDIAN PHYSIC, BOWMAN'S
ROOT

This species is up to
4 ft (1.2 m) tall and has
reddish stems and
bronze green leaves
composed of 3 oval
toothed leaflets, each
3 in (8 cm) long. Open
panicles of white or
pale pink starry flowers
are produced through-
out summer.
ZONES 3–9.

Glaucidium palmatum var. *leucanthum* (*above*)

Glaucidium palmatum

This clump-forming perennial has a height and spread of 15 in (40 cm). It has light green, palmately lobed leaves with crinkly surfaces and irregularly toothed edges. The large, cup-shaped, 4-petalled lilac or mauve flowers are borne in late spring and early summer. ***Glaucidium palmatum* var. *leucanthum*** (syn. 'Album') has white flowers. ZONES 6–9.

GLAUCIDIUM

This genus of a single species is indigenous to northern Japan. A rhizomatous perennial, its large pink to lilac flowers are somewhat poppy-like but in fact the genus is a relative of *Paeonia*.

CULTIVATION

Plant in rich, peaty soil with plenty of moisture. It prefers part- to deep shade and shelter from drying winds. Propagate from seed in spring or by careful division in early spring.

G

Glechoma hederacea
'Variegata' *(above)*

GLECHOMA

This genus consists of 12 species of low-growing, perennial plants. The stems root at the nodes, often forming extensive mats of coarsely toothed, rounded or broadly oval, soft hairy leaves. Ascending shoots bear pairs of small, tubular, 2-lipped flowers in the leaf axils in summer. They make good carpeting ground covers, but can be very invasive and should be kept away from heavily planted beds. They are good for containers and hanging baskets.

CULTIVATION

They prefer full sun or part-shade and moderately fertile, moist but well-drained soil. Propagate from cuttings in late spring or by division in spring or autumn.

Glechoma hederacea
GROUND IVY, RUNAWAY ROBIN

This prostrate species often forms mats to 6 ft (1.8 m) or more across, producing an unpleasant smell when bruised. The opposite, almost kidney-shaped leaves have scalloped margins. Small violet flowers are borne in late spring and early summer. **'Variegata'** has pretty, soft pale green leaves with white marbling. ZONES 6–10.

GLOBULARIA
GLOBE DAISY

The 20 or so species of this genus of mainly evergreen, tufted or sometimes mat-forming perennials or subshrubs are grown for their neat rounded habit and compact heads of many tiny tubular flowers in shades of blue. Many are suitable for a rock garden or container, such as the tight, cushion-forming 'Hort's Variety'. The bushy subshrubs such as *Globularia* × *indubia* and *G. sarcophylla* are attractive planted among other small shrubs or against low walls.

Globularia sarcophylla
(below)

CULTIVATION
Most cultivated species are only moderately frost hardy. Grow in full sun in well-drained soil. Water sparingly and keep dry in winter. Propagate from seed in autumn or by division in spring and early summer.

G

Globularia × *indubia* *(below)*

Globularia gracilis
(left)

This tufted, upright perennial has dark green, spoon-shaped leaves on long stalks. The lavender-blue flowerheads are borne in summer. **ZONES 7–9.**

G

Globularia punctata *(left)*
syns *Globularia aphyllanthes, G. wilkommii*

Native to Europe, this is a tufted perennial to 12 in (30 cm) high with a basal rosette of long-stalked, somewhat spoon-shaped leaves. Indigo flowerheads are produced in summer. **ZONES 5–9.**

Globularia cordifolia *(below left)*

This evergreen miniature subshrubby perennial, found in central and southern Europe, has creeping woody stems with unusual tiny, spoon-shaped leaves, and produces solitary, stemless, fluffy blue to pale mauve flowerheads from late spring to early summer. It forms a dense mat or hummock, growing to a height of only 1–5 in (2.5–12 cm) and gradually spreading to 8 in (20 cm) or more. **ZONES 6–9.**

GUNNERA

This is a genus of around 45 species of rhizomatous perennials from temperate regions of Africa, Australasia and South America. Occurring in moist habitats, they range in size from small, mat-forming plants to very large clumps with some of the largest leaves of any broad-leaved specimens. They are grown mainly for their striking foliage, although some species have attractive flower spikes and fruits.

CULTIVATION

Most species enjoy moist but well-aerated soil at the edge of a pond or stream. Plant in rich soil in full sun, although they may need shelter from very hot sun (which can scorch the leaves) and wind (which can reduce the leaves to tatters). Propagate from seed in autumn or spring, or by division in early spring. Protect from slugs and snails.

Gunnera tinctoria *(above)*
syn. *Gunnera chilensis*

Next in size to *Gunnera manicata*, this is a slow-growing species from Chile with large, heart-shaped, sharply toothed, deep green leaves up to 5 ft (1.5 m) wide and borne on prickly stalks to 5 ft (1.5 m) in length. Numerous tiny, rusty flowers are borne on erect cylindrical panicles up to 24 in (60 cm) high; they are followed in summer by rounded green fruit suffused with red. **ZONES 6–7.**

Gunnera manicata
(left)
syn. *Gunnera brasiliensis*
GIANT ORNAMENTAL RHUBARB

Native to the high mountain swamps of Brazil and Colombia, this huge plant thrives in boggy soil and is usually grown on the margins of a pond. The massive leaves quickly unfurl in spring to as wide as 8 ft (2.4 m) on prickly stalks about 6 ft (1.8 m) high. Long spikes of greenish red flowers are borne in summer. Give the dormant crown a protective mulch of straw in winter. **ZONES 7–9.**

GUZMANIA

The 120 species in this genus of evergreen, mostly epiphytic bromeliads have lance-shaped leaves that form funnel-shaped rosettes. The flowerheads of tubular white or yellow flowers are usually surrounded by colorful bracts on yellow, orange or bright red stems. Guzmanias are mostly rainforest plants from the American tropics, and are therefore frost tender.

CULTIVATION

They require a position in part-shade in a well-drained compost. Water moderately during the growing season, less at other times, but always keep the leaf vases filled with water. If potting, leave enough room for just one year's growth and then repot. They make good indoor or greenhouse plants where they need plenty of indirect light. Fertilize only when in full growth, during the warmer months. Propagate from seed or offsets in spring or summer.

Guzmania lingulata

Ranging in the wild from Honduras to Bolivia, this is the most commonly grown species. It has basal rosettes of strap-like, apple-green leaves and grows to 12–18 in (30–45 cm) tall. Striking colored bracts surround clusters of tubular, white to yellow flowers in summer. *Guzmania lingulata* var. *minor* grows to 12 in (30 cm) high and across and has creamy yellow flowers and orange-red bracts. It is easily grown in a greenhouse. **'Indiana'** has erect golden yellow bracts tipped with orange-red. ZONES 10–12.

Guzmania 'Squarrosa' *(above)*

This cultivar is a clump-forming epiphyte with rosettes of colorful bronzy leaves that grow up to 3 ft (1 m) in length. The center of the foliage flares a brilliant red for a short period during bloom time. The bright red inflorescence is borne on a short erect stem, and the flowers are white. ZONES 11–12.

Guzmania lingulata 'Indiana' *(left)*

Gypsophila
paniculata *(right)*
BABY'S BREATH

This short-lived peren-
nial, mostly treated as
an annual, has small,
dark green leaves and
sprays of tiny, white
spring flowers. It reaches
a height and spread of
3 ft (1 m) or more.
'Bristol Fairy' has
double white flowers.
'Compact Plena' has
double white or soft
pink flowers. ZONES 4–10.

G

Gypsophila paniculata   *Gypsophila repens*
'Compacta Plena' *(above)*   'Rosea' *(below)*

GYPSOPHILA

Native to Europe, Asia and North Africa,
there are over 100 species of these annuals
and perennials, some of which are semi-
evergreen. They are grown for their masses
of small, dainty, white or pink flowers, often
used by florists as a foil for bolder flowers or
foliage. The narrow leaves are borne in
opposite pairs.

CULTIVATION
Plant in full sun with shelter from strong
winds. Fully frost hardy, they will tolerate
most soils, but do best in deep, well-drained
soil lightened with compost or peat, and
grow well in limy soil. Cut back after
flowering to encourage a second flush.
Transplant when dormant during winter.
Propagate from cuttings in summer or from
seed in spring or autumn.

Gypsophila repens
This prostrate perennial has stems forming low
mounds up to 8 in (20 cm) high and 18 in (45 cm)
wide. It has narrow, bluish green leaves and bears
panicles of star-shaped, white, lilac or pale purple
flowers in summer. It is an ideal plant for trailing
over rocks. **'Dorothy Teacher'** has abundant pale
pink flowers that age to deep pink. **'Rosea'** has
deep pink flowers. ZONES 4–9.

HABERLEA

Of the more than 2000 species of the large African violet and gloxinia family (Gesneriaceae) only a small proportion extend beyond the tropics, and of these a mere half-dozen are native to Europe. The European species are shared among 3 genera, *Ramonda, Jankaea* and *Haberlea,* all perennials and restricted to small regions in the Pyrenees or the Balkans. *Haberlea* consists of 2 species only, occurring in Bulgaria and northern Greece. They are rosette plants that grow on rock ledges and in crevices, resembling some of the smaller *Streptocarpus* species in leaf and flower.

CULTIVATION

They require a climate with warm dry summers and cool wet winters but dislike excessive wetness around the roots at any time. Plant in freely draining crevices in a rock garden or a stone wall, or grow in pots with coarse gravel in an alpine house. Choose an aspect where the roots remain shaded but foliage gets some sun. Propagate from seed, by division of rhizomes, or from leaf cuttings.

Haberlea rhodopensis (left)

This pretty plant grows only to about 4–6 in (10–15 cm) in height, with spatulate, scalloped leaves arising from a short rhizome. In spring and early summer it produces stalked umbels of lilac flowers about 1 in (25 mm) across, the 3 lower petals much longer than the 2 upper. There is also a pure white-flowered form, 'Virginalis'. ZONES 6–9.

HACQUETIA
syn. *Dondia*

There is one species only in this genus: a tiny perennial from the woodlands of eastern Europe. At most it grows to 4 in (10 cm) tall, spreading very slowly into a small mat. The flowers appear in spring before the leaves and the plant is usually grown in rock gardens or in small pots in collections of alpine plants. It requires a cold winter for success.

CULTIVATION

Grow in porous, gritty soil that contains leafmold or other rotted organic matter in part- or dappled shade. Keep moist always but give more water from the time the flower buds appear until the leaves begin to yellow in autumn. Propagate from seed sown as soon as it is ripe or by division of clumps in late winter, before flower buds appear. Divide infrequently as it resents root disturbance.

Hacquetia epipactis
(right)
syn. *Dondia epipactis*

The pinhead-sized, bright yellow flowers of this species are surrounded by glossy green bracts, giving the effect of a most unusual bright green flower. Appearing straight from the ground in earliest spring, they are followed by 3-lobed leaves. This is a most unusual and desirable plant for cooler areas. ZONES 6–9.

HEDYCHIUM
GINGER LILY

Ginger lilies, like frangipanis and hibiscus, are associated with the tropics because of their lush foliage, glamorous flowers and heady scent. Yet, of the 40 species of *Hedychium,* many grow quite high on the mountains, indicating their tolerance for cooler weather. Some recently introduced species are hardy enough to be grown even in temperate gardens. They are perennials that grow from rhizomes to form clumps up to 6 ft (1.8 m) high and 4 ft (1.2 m) wide. For most of the year in warm climates (summer elsewhere) they bear spikes or heads of fragrant flowers that last well and are good for cutting.

CULTIVATION

They prefer humus-rich, moist but well-drained soil in part-shade. They flower in summer, and spent stems should be cut out each season to ensure vigorous growth—or cut blooms for indoors. Propagate from fresh seed or by division.

H

Hedychium coccineum
(right)
RED GINGER LILY

This species from the Himalayas forms a low clump with spreading stems and narrow leaves. Its spectacular erect flower spikes, which carry only a few flowers, can reach 10 in (25 cm) high. The blooms vary from pale coral to a bright red, always with the exaggerated stamen in pink. The cultivar **'Tara'** has brilliant orange flowers and is more frost hardy than the species. ZONES 9–11.

Hedychium gardnerianum (below)
KAHILI GINGER

This species from the Himalayas grows to 8 ft
(2.4 m) tall with long, bright green leaves clasping
the tall stems. This is the most widely cultivated
species; it prefers a warm climate although it will
grow outside in temperate areas that have light,
infrequent frosts. The fragrant, red and pale
yellow flowers
held in dense
spikes, appear
towards the end
of summer. This
species is
considered a
weed in some
regions, such as
in the north of
New Zealand.
ZONES 9–11.

H

H

This upright perennial has sprays of daisy-like, rich orange-red flower-heads with prominent, chocolate-brown central discs. They are borne in summer and early autumn above mid-green foliage. Easily grown, it gives color to borders and is useful for cut flowers. Slow growing to 3 ft (1 m) high and 24 in (60 cm) wide, it enjoys hot summers.
ZONES 5–9.

HELENIUM
SNEEZEWEED, HELEN'S FLOWER

This genus, native to the Americas, consists of about 40 species of annual, biennial or perennial herbs. The mid-green leaves, which are alternate on erect stems, are oval to lance-shaped. The daisy-like flowerheads appear in summer and have yellow, red-brown or orange ray florets and yellow, yellow-green, red or brown disc florets. The flowers make a good border and are ideal for cutting.

CULTIVATION
Frost hardy, heleniums are easy to grow in any temperate climate as long as they get sun. The soil should be moist and well drained. Remove spent flowers regularly to prolong the flowering period. Propagate by division of old clumps in winter or from seed in spring or autumn.

H

Helenium autumnale *(above)*
COMMON SNEEZEWEED

This perennial from North America grows about
5 ft (1.5 m) tall. The flowers occur from late summer to mid-autumn. This species has given rise to
a number of named garden forms, whose flowers
range from yellow to maroon, with many being a
blend of yellow and russet tones. **ZONES 3–9.**

H

Heliamphora heterodoxa (left)

This sun pitcher is from the swampy mountains of Venezuela and grows to about 15 in (38 cm) in height. It has funnels up to 2 in (5 cm) in diameter and white to pink flowers in early winter. There are a number of forms. ZONES 11–12.

HELIAMPHORA

SUN PITCHERS

This genus contains 6 species of rhizomatous, carnivorous plants, allied to sarracenias, and is found on very wet mountains in Venezuela and Guyana. They have funnel-shaped, green to reddish leaves with, in most cases, a small overhanging cap. Each leaf has a nectar-secreting gland designed to attract small insects to their last meal. The flower stems may be up to 24 in (60 cm) tall, each with several delicate white flowers changing to pink with age.

Heliamphora nutans (below)

This is an intriguing sun pitcher with green, basal, pitcher-shaped leaves with red margins and a constriction in the middle. It grows 4–8 in (10–20 cm) high and has large, nodding white to pink flowers on 6–12 in (15–30 cm) stalks. ZONES 11–12.

CULTIVATION

These plants grow naturally in wet, peaty soil and prefer warm, humid conditions, though preferably less than 86°F (30°C); they tolerate a minimum temperature of 40°F (5°C). They are best grown in a pot with a mixture of peat, sand and sphagnum moss placed in a saucer of water. Propagate by division of rhizomes in spring or from seed.

HELIANTHEMUM

ROCK ROSE, SUN ROSE

Helianthemum means flower of sunshine, an appropriate name
for flowers that only open in bright sunlight. Allied to *Cistus,* the
genus contains over 100 species found on rocky and scrubby
ground in temperate zones around the world. Sun roses are sturdy,
short-lived, evergreen or semi-evergreen shrubs or subshrubs.
Their bushy foliage ranges in color from silver to mid-green.
There are many garden forms, mostly of low, spreading habit.
Wild plants have flowers resembling 1 in (25 mm) wide wild roses,
but garden forms can be anything from white through yellow
and salmon-pink to red and orange, and some varieties have
double flowers.

CULTIVATION

Plant in full sun in freely draining, coarse soil with a little peat or
compost added during dry periods. As the flowers fade, they
should be cut back lightly to encourage a second flush of bloom in
autumn. Propagate from seed or cuttings.

Helianthemum
nummularium
(below)

A variable species from
Europe and Turkey,
*Helianthemum
nummularium* has a
neat, prostrate habit. Its
small but profuse
flowers vary in color
from yellow or cream
to pink and orange.
Most of the cultivars
that are traditionally
listed under this name
are in fact of hybrid
origin. ZONES 5–10.

H

HELIANTHUS

This genus of the daisy family includes plants used for livestock fodder, the Jerusalem artichoke with edible tubers, many ornamentals, and one of the world's most important oilseed plants. Consisting of around 70 species of annuals and perennials, all native to the Americas, they have large, daisy-like, usually golden yellow flowerheads, which are on prolonged display from summer to autumn. The plants have hairy, often sticky leaves and tall, rough stems.

CULTIVATION

Frost hardy, they prefer full sun and protection from wind. The soil should be well drained. Fertilize in spring to promote large blooms and water generously in dry conditions. Perennials should be cut down to the base after flowering. Propagate from seed or by division in autumn or early spring.

Helianthus annuus (below)
COMMON SUNFLOWER

This fast-growing, upright annual can reach a height of 10 ft (3 m) or more. Large, daisy-like, 12 in (30 cm) wide, yellow flowerheads with brown centers are borne in summer. They are tall, leggy plants with broad, mid-green leaves. This species produces one of the world's most important oilseeds. It can be a little large for small gardens, but newer varieties have been developed that grow to a more manageable size, about 6 ft (1.8 m). They include **'Autumn Beauty'**, with medium-sized flowers usually brownish red, deep red, light yellow or golden yellow; and **'Teddy Bear'**, a compact grower with double, dark yellow flowers. ZONES 4–11.

H

Helianthus maximilianii *(above)*

Growing to at least 10 ft (3 m) tall, this perennial has rough stems densely covered with spearhead-shaped leaves about 8 in (20 cm) long. Golden yellow flowers 4–6 in (10–15 cm) across appear in summer and autumn. **ZONES 4–9.**

Helianthus × multiflorus *(right)*

This hybrid is a clump-forming perennial to 6 ft (1.8 m) in height and 3 ft (1 m) in spread. The domed flowers can be up to 6 in (15 cm) across and appear in late summer and mid-autumn. The most popular cultivars include **'Capenoch Star'**, **'Loddon Gold'**, **'Soleil d'Or'** and **'Triomphe de Gand'.** **ZONES 5–9.**

H

*Helianthus ×
multiflorus* 'Loddon
Gold' *(above)*

*Helianthus ×
multiflorus*
'Triomphe de Gand'
(left)

HELICHRYSUM
EVERLASTING, PAPER DAISY, STRAWFLOWER

As understood until recently, this is a genus of around 500 species of annuals, perennials and shrubs, their highest concentration being in southern Africa followed by Australia, with smaller numbers in the Mediterranean, west and central Asia, and New Zealand. Belonging to the daisy family, they all have flowerheads with no ray florets or 'petals' but instead papery, mostly whitish bracts that are long-lasting when dried, hence the common names. But study by botanists has shown this to be an unnatural group, and they have been busy carving off both large and small groups of species and renaming them as distinct genera. This study is ongoing, and many species still in *Helichrysum* will eventually be reclassified, particularly among the South African species. The 'true' helichrysums include the Mediterranean and Asian species and an uncertain number from southern Africa; some well-known Australasian species have been reclassified under genera such as *Bracteantha, Ozothamnus* and *Chrysocephalum.*

CULTIVATION
Most species will tolerate only light frosts and are best suited to mild climates with low summer humidity, but a few are more frost hardy. They are mostly rock garden plants, requiring gritty, well-drained soil that is not too fertile and a warm, sunny position. Propagate from seed, cuttings, or rhizome divisions.

Helichrysum argyrophyllum
(below)

This shrubby perennial from eastern South Africa grows to 4 in (10 cm) and is used as a ground cover. It has silvery leaves and clusters of yellow flowers from summer to early winter. The 'petals' are in fact brightly colored bracts surrounding the central florets. ZONES 9–11.

Helichrysum petiolare *(right)*
syn. *Helichrysum petiolatum* of gardens

LICORICE PLANT

This South African evergreen is an excellent foliage plant; its gray, heart-shaped leaves and its stems are covered with cobweb-like white hairs. It is a sprawling subshrub forming dense mounds 24 in (60 cm) or more high and 6 ft (1.8 m) or more wide, with new stems springing from a network of rhizomes. It is well adapted to sun or shade and to dry conditions. The flowers, only occasionally produced, are not showy. '**Limelight**' has pale chartreuse foliage, and '**Variegatum**' has a creamy variegation. Both of these cultivars do better in shade and are superb summer container plants in cold climates. ZONES 9–10.

Helichrysum retortum *(below)*

This prostrate perennial from the Cape region of South Africa can grow to 8 in (20 cm) with a spread of 18 in (45 cm). It has contorted stems with bright, silvery-gray oval leaves and pretty, white papery flowers in spring. It is marginally frost hardy. ZONES 9–11.

HELICONIA
LOBSTER CLAW, FALSE BIRD-OF-PARADISE

From tropical America, Southeast Asia and some Pacific Islands, these beautiful, exotic plants have large leaves and spikes of colorful bracts enclosing relatively insignificant flowers. There are around 100 evergreen perennial species and hybrids in this genus, which is related to bananas and strelitzias. Planted *en masse,* heliconias create an eye-catching show of color all year round. The bracts may be red, yellow or orange, or scarlet tipped with yellow and green, or lipstick red and luminous yellow. The leaves are spoon-shaped and grow to 6 ft (1.8 m) long. Heliconias make excellent cut flowers.

CULTIVATION
Grow only in warm, tropical gardens with a winter minimum of 64°F (18°C). Plant in humus-rich, well-drained soil in filtered sun and with summer humidity. Water well during the growing season. To encourage new growth, remove all dead leaves and flowers. Propagate by division of the rootstock in spring, ensuring there are 2 shoots on each division. Check for spider mites, snails and mealybugs.

Heliconia bihai (right)
syns *Heliconia humilis,*
H. jacquinii
FIREBIRD, MACAW FLOWER

The large, paddle-shaped, green leaves of this species surround a flower stem of pointed, scarlet bracts tipped with green and inconspicuous white flowers. This is the most familiar species and is popular for flower arrangements.
ZONES 11–12.

H

H

Heliconia latispatha (below)

This big, vigorous plant of wide occurrence in tropical America needs plenty of room to spread. It has showy bracts that may be yellow, red or a combination of both. Bracts appear atop tall, erect stems, each pointing in a different direction. In the wild, they are pollinated by hummingbirds. **ZONES 11–12.**

Heliconia collinsiana (left)

COLLINS' HELICONIA, HANGING HELICONIA

Growing to around 12 ft (3.5 m) tall, this heliconia grows into a dense clump of thin stems from which the pendulous flowers hang in long strings. Bracts are 8–10 in (20–25 cm) long, bright red and sheath the golden yellow true flowers. The whole plant is dusted with a staining, powdery bloom. **ZONES 11–12.**

Heliconia psittacorum *(below)*
PARROT FLOWER

Ranging from eastern Brazil to the West Indies, this smaller species is good for mass planting. It has long-stalked, lance-like, rich green leaves. Narrow, pinkish, orange or pale red bracts surrounding yellow or red flowers with green tips are produced in summer. It is usually 3–5 ft (1–1.5 m) tall. ZONES 11–12.

H

Heliconia rostrata *(above)*
FISHTAIL HELICONIA

Possibly the most striking of the heliconias, this species from Peru and Argentina has a large, pendulous cascade of alternating bracts of scarlet tipped with yellow and green. It grows 3–20 ft (1–6 m) in height. ZONES 11–12.

Heliconia wagneriana *(right)*
RAINBOW HELICONIA, EASTER HELICONIA

From steamy Central America, this magnificent heliconia with its cream, red and green bracts cannot fail to impress. They grow at least 12 ft (3.5 m) tall, but the spring flowering season is relatively short for heliconias. ZONES 11–12.

HELIOPSIS

ORANGE SUNFLOWER, OX EYE

The name *Heliopsis* means resembling a sunflower, and these perennials from the North American prairies do look like sunflowers, though on a rather reduced and more manageable scale. There are about 12 species, with stiff, branching stems and toothed, mid- to dark green leaves. The solitary, usually yellow flowers are up to 3 in (8 cm) wide and make good cut flowers.

Heliopsis helianthoides

This species grows to 5 ft (1.5 m) tall and 3 ft (1 m) in spread. It has coarse, hairy leaves and golden yellow flowers in summer. The cultivar **'Patula'** has semi-double orange flowers. **'Light of Loddon'** has rough, hairy leaves and strong stems that carry dahlia-like, bright yellow, double flowers in late summer. It grows to a height of 3 ft (1 m) and a spread of 24 in (60 cm). ZONES 4–9.

CULTIVATION

These plants are easily grown, and will even tolerate poor condi-tions. However, they thrive in fertile, moist but well-drained soil and a sunny position. They are all very frost hardy. Deadhead regularly to prolong the flower display and cut back to ground level after flowering finishes. Propagate from seed or cuttings in spring, or by division in spring or autumn.

Heliopsis helianthoides
'Light of Loddon' *(right)*

HELIOTROPIUM

HELIOTROPE

This genus consists of over 250 species of annuals, perennials, shrubs and subshrubs from most warmer parts of the world. The leaves are simple and usually alternate. The clusters of flowers can be purple, blue, white or yellow and are deliciously scented. They appear in summer and are attractive to butterflies. The smaller varieties make excellent pot plants.

CULTIVATION

Heliotropes grow wild in both subtropical and cooler temperate climates and hence vary in frost hardiness. They prefer moist, well-drained, moderately fertile soil. Cut plants back by about half in early spring to promote bushiness. Propagate from seed in spring or cuttings in early autumn.

Heliotropium arborescens (above)
syn. *Heliotropium peruvianum*

CHERRY PIE, COMMON HELIOTROPE

Traditionally treated as a perennial, this attractive, soft-wooded evergreen shrub bears clusters of fragrant, purple to lavender flowers, with a delicate scent similar to stewed cherries, from late spring to autumn. From the Peruvian Andes, it grows fast to 30 in (75 cm) tall and 3 ft (1 m) wide. It has dark green, wrinkled leaves, golden to lime-green in the cultivar '**Aurea**', and dark purplish green in '**Lord Robert**'. In cold climates it is grown as a conservatory or summer bedding plant. ZONES 9–11.

HELLEBORUS
HELLEBORE

Native to areas of Europe and western Asia, these 15 perennial or evergreen species are useful winter- and spring-flowering plants for cooler climates. They bear beautiful, open flowers in white or shades of green, red and purple and are effective planted in drifts or massed in the shade of deciduous trees. All hellebores are poisonous.

CULTIVATION

Grow in part-shade and moist, well-drained, humus-rich soil, which is not allowed to dry out in summer. Cut off old leaves from deciduous species just as the buds start to appear. Remove flowerheads after seeds drop. A top-dressing of compost or manure after flowering is beneficial. Propagate from seed or by division in autumn or early spring. Check for aphids.

Helleborus foetidus (above)
STINKING HELLEBORE

This clump-forming perennial has attractive, dark green, divided leaves that remain all year. In winter or early spring the clusters of pale green, bell-shaped flowers, delicately edged with red, are borne on short stems. Established plants will often self-seed readily. ZONES 6–10.

Helleborus argutifolius
(right)
syns *Helleborus corsicus,*
H. lividus subsp. *corsicus*
CORSICAN HELLEBORE

This is one of the earliest flowering hellebores, with blooms appearing in late winter and early spring. It is a robust evergreen that bears large clusters of cup-shaped, nodding, 2 in (5 cm) wide, green flowers on an upright spike above divided, spiny-margined, deep green foliage. It has a clump-forming habit, growing to a height of 24 in (60 cm) and a spread of 24–36 in (60–90 cm). This is the most sun- and drought-tolerant species of the genus. ZONES 6–9.

Helleborus lividus
(below)

This species from the islands of the western Mediterranean has deep green or bluish green leaves and bowl-shaped, creamy green flowers from winter to spring. It is slow to establish after being transplanted. **ZONES 7–9.**

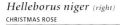

Helleborus orientalis *(above)*
LENTEN ROSE

The most widely grown of the genus, this evergreen, clump-forming species from Greece, Turkey and the Caucasus grows to 24 in (60 cm) high and wide. The large nodding flowers come in a great variety of colors from white, green, pink and rose to purple, sometimes with dark spots. Very frost hardy, it flowers in winter or early spring. The dense foliage fades and can be trimmed back before flowering. **ZONES 6–10.**

Helleborus niger *(right)*
CHRISTMAS ROSE

Popular for its white, mid-winter flowers, often appearing in the snow, this is one of the more temperamental species. It is often worth covering the plant with a cloche before the flowers open, to protect them from the winter weather. The mid-green, deeply lobed leaves are evergreen; mounds are 12 in (30 cm) high with a spread of 12–18 in (30–45 cm). They need steady moisture. **ZONES 3–9.**

H

H

Helleborus 'Queen of the Night'
(left)

Possibly a hybrid between *Helleborus orientalis* and *H. purpurascens*, this plant produces simple, open-faced flowers that are a brownish purple color. ZONES 6–10.

Helleborus purpurascens *(below)*

Flowering from about mid-winter, even in cool climates, this frost-hardy, deciduous perennial from eastern Europe blooms before the new season's leaves appear. Plants grow anywhere up to 12 in (30 cm) tall but often less and the clumps spread at least 12 in (30 cm) across. The compound leaves are big and lobed and the flowers are an odd gray-green-pink combination. ZONES 6–9.

HEMEROCALLIS
DAYLILY

Native to temperate east Asia, these perennials, some of which are semi-evergreen or evergreen, are grown for their showy, often fragrant flowers that come in a vibrant range of colors. Individual blooms last only for a day, but are borne in great numbers on strong stems above tall, grassy foliage and continue to flower from early summer to autumn. The flower size varies from 3 in (8 cm) miniatures to giants of 6 in (15 cm) or more, single or double. Plant heights range from about 24 in (60 cm) to 3 ft (1 m). Grow in a herbaceous border among shrubs or naturalize in grassy woodland areas.

CULTIVATION

Position carefully when planting because the flowers turn their heads towards the sun. Most daylilies are fully hardy. They prefer sun but will grow well and give brighter colors in part-shade. Plant in a reasonably good soil that does not dry out. Propagate by division in autumn or spring, and divide clumps every 3 or 4 years. Cultivars raised from seed do not come true to type. Check for slugs and snails in early spring. Plants may also suffer from aphid or spider mite attack.

Hemerocallis forrestii *(below)*

Collected from the Yunnan Province of China by the plant hunter George Forrest in 1906, this species grows to 18 in (45 cm) with evergreen leaves to 12 in (30 cm). The flower stem rises from the outer foliage and bears 5 to 10 yellow, funnel-shaped flowers. It is less frost hardy than most other species. ZONES 5–10.

Hemerocallis fulva
TAWNY DAYLILY

This clump-forming species to 3 ft (1 m) high and 30 in (75 cm) wide, bears rich orange-red, trumpet-shaped, 3–6 in (8–15 cm) wide flowers from mid- to late summer. It has been in cultivation for centuries, and in China and Japan the flower buds are sold as food. **'Flore Pleno'** (syn. 'Kwanzo') has 6 in (15 cm), double, orange flowers with sepals curved back and a red eye. **'Kwanzo Variegata'** bears similar flowers to 'Flore Pleno' and has leaves with a white margin. ZONES 4–11.

H

Hemerocallis fulva
'Flore Pleno' *(below)*

Hemerocallis Hybrids

Almost all the cultivated species of *Hemerocallis* have played their part in producing the vast range of modern daylily hybrids. Most have been bred for size and texture of blooms, together with rich or delicate coloring, often with an 'eye' of contrasting color in the center; but some others are grown more for the massed effect of smaller or more spidery flowers which can be of great elegance. A recent development is a range of miniatures, in many colors and with either broad or narrow petals: one of the most popular is **'Stella d'Oro'** with clear golden yellow flowers of almost circular outline. ZONES 5–11.

Hemerocallis Hybrid,
'Berlin Lemon' *(below)*

Hemerocallis Hybrid,
'Apricot Queen' *(below)*

Hemerocallis Hybrid,
'Baldone' *(right)*

Hemerocallis Hybrid,
'Bonus' *(left)*

H

Hemerocallis Hybrid,
'Brownie the Gold'
(above)

Hemerocallis Hybrid,
'Gone Native' *(right)*

Hemerocallis Hybrid,
'Grand Prize' *(right)*

Hemerocallis Hybrid,
'Egyptian Ruffles' *(left)*

Hemerocallis Hybrid,
'Grown Fire' *(below)*

Hemerocallis Hybrid,
'Chemistry' *(left)*

Hemerocallis Hybrid,
'Christmas Day' *(below)*

Hemerocallis Hybrid,
'Constant Eye' *(below)*

H

Hemerocallis Hybrid, 'Custom Design' *(above)*

Hemerocallis Hybrid, 'Coquetry' *(right)*

H

Hemerocallis Hybrid,
'High Priestess' *(above)*

Hemerocallis Hybrid,
'Esau' *(left)*

Hemerocallis Hybrid,
'Florisant Snow' *(right)*

Hemerocallis Hybrid, 'Golden Wonder' *(left)*

Hemerocallis Hybrid, 'Holy Mackerel' *(right)*

H

Hemerocallis Hybrid, 'Irish Ranger' *(above)*

Hemerocallis Hybrid, 'Jadis' *(above)*

Hemerocallis Hybrid,
'Silver Threads' *(left)*

Hemerocallis Hybrid,
'Ming Porcelain' *(above)*

Hemerocallis Hybrid,
'Mama Joe' *(left)*

H

Hemerocallis Hybrid,
'Memories' *(left)*

Hemerocallis Hybrid,
'Red Waves' *(below)*

H

Hemerocallis Hybrid,
'Rocket City' *(above)*

Hemerocallis Hybrid,
'Russian Rhapsody'
(left)

Hemerocallis Hybrid,
'Scarlet Pansy' *(left)*

H

Hemerocallis Hybrid,
'Rose Tapestry' *(right)*

Hemerocallis Hybrid,
'Velvet Shadow' *(left)*

Hemerocallis Hybrid,
'So Excited' *(right)*

H

Hemerocallis Hybrid,
'Stella d'Oro' *(left)*

Hemerocallis Hybrid,
'Wynnson' *(right)*

Hemerocallis lilioasphodelus *(left)*
syn. *Hemerocallis flava*
PALE DAYLILY, LEMON DAYLILY

This was one of the first daylilies to be used for breeding. It is found across China, where it forms large, spreading clumps with leaves up to 30 in (75 cm) long. The lemon yellow flowers are sweetly scented and borne in a cluster of 3 to 9 blooms. It has a range of uses in Chinese herbal medicine: some parts may be eaten, while others may be hallucinogenic. ZONES 4–9.

HEPATICA
LIVERLEAF

Hepatica is closely related to *Anemone,* as the flower shape suggests. There are 10 species from North America, Europe and temperate Asia. They are all small, hairy, spring-flowering perennial herbs. The supposed resemblance of their leaves to a liver gave them their common and botanical names: *hepar* is Latin for liver. They have medicinal uses in liver and respiratory complaints, as well as for indigestion. There are a number of garden varieties with white, blue or purple flowers, sometimes double.

CULTIVATION
They occur naturally in woodlands so prefer part-shade and rich, moist but well-drained soil. Propagate from seed or by division, especially for the double varieties.

H

Hepatica nobilis
(right)
syns *Anemone hepatica,*
Hepatica triloba

An inhabitant of mountain woods across much of Europe, this small perennial has solitary blue, pink or white ¹/₂–1¹/₄ in (12–30 mm) flowers on long stalks. It has evergreen leaves with 3 broad, rounded lobes, usually purplish beneath. Although the plant is poisonous, it has been used as a herbal remedy for coughs and chest complaints. ZONES 5–9.

H

Hesperis matronalis *(left)*
DAME'S ROCKET, SWEET ROCKET

Ranging from Europe to central
Asia, *Hesperis matronalis* is
grown for its flowers which
become very fragrant on humid
evenings. It has smooth, narrowly
oval leaves and branching
flowerheads with white to lilac
flowers borne in summer.
Upright in habit, this species
grows 12–36 in (30–90 cm) in
height with a spread of about
24 in (60 cm). Plants lose their
vigor after a time and are best
renewed every 2 to 3 years.
ZONES 3–9.

HESPERIS

From the Mediterranean and temperate Asia, this genus
consists of 60 species of biennials and herbaceous
perennials allied to stocks *(Matthiola)*. They have narrow,
usually undivided leaves that may be toothed or toothless,
and showy pink, purple or white flowers in long racemes.
The flowers of some species are fragrant.

CULTIVATION

The species are readily grown in temperate areas and will
naturalize, but cultivars sometimes prove more difficult.
Frost hardy, they prefer full sun and moist but well-
drained, neutral to alkaline, not too fertile soil. Propagate
from seed or cuttings and check regularly for mildew and
also for attack from slugs and snails.

HETEROCENTRON
syn. *Schizocentron*

About 27 species of shrubby or creeping plants make up this genus which is allied to *Tibouchina*. Originating in Mexico and Central and South America, *Heterocentron* are grown for their showy, 4-petalled, white, pink, mauve or purple flowers which appear from summer to winter.

CULTIVATION
These plants grow well in sun or part-shade in well-drained soil. They are frost tender, and need a minimum temperature of 40°F (5°C). Propagate from cuttings in late winter or early spring.

Heterocentron elegans (above)
syn. *Schizocentron elegans*
SPANISH SHAWL

Native to Central America, *Heterocentron elegans* is a prostrate, evergreen perennial. It is a popular ground cover in areas of warm climate. The foliage is dense, trailing and mid-green, and masses of bright carmine-purple flowers cover the plant in summer. This plant grows to a height of 2 in (5 cm) with an indefinite spread. ZONES 10–11.

H

HETEROTHECA

From the southern parts of the USA and Mexico comes
this genus of around 20 species of annuals and
perennials in the daisy family. The leaves, which may
be silvery or green, smooth edged or toothed, form a
basal clump from which (usually) branched flower stems
arise. Species vary in height from about 8 in (20 cm)
to 5 ft (1.5 m).

CULTIVATION

They are best grown in dry, sandy or gravelly soil in
full sun. Where winters are always frosty, plants may
rot if that season is also rainy and will need some
shelter. In areas with milder winters, rain has no
ill-effect so long as soil drains fast. Propagate annuals
from seed sown in spring; perennial species by division
in spring.

Heterotheca villosa
'San Bruno Mountain'
(left)

Heterotheca villosa
syn. *Chrysopsis villosa*
HAIRY GOLDEN ASTER

A variable perennial from Texas and New Mexico, this species is
sometimes erect, sometimes sprawling, and has hairy, gray-green
leaves and 1 in (25 mm) wide golden yellow flowerheads in
summer and autumn. In hot, dry locations, this species may only
reach a height of 8 in (20 cm) but in better soil with regular
water it may grow over 30 in (75 cm) tall. It is frost hardy. **'San
Bruno Mountain'** is a form selected for attractive foliage and
profusion of flowers. ZONES 5–9.

HEUCHERA
ALUM ROOT, CORAL BELLS

There are about 55 species of these evergreen and semi-evergreen perennials, which are native to North America and Mexico. They form neat clumps of scalloped leaves, often tinted bronze or purple, from which arise stems bearing masses of dainty, nodding, white, crimson or pink bell-shaped flowers often over a long flowering season. They make useful woodland, rock garden, edging plants or can be used as ground covers.

CULTIVATION
Mostly very frost hardy, they grow well in either full sun or semi-shade and like well-drained, coarse, moisture-retentive soil. Propagate species from seed in autumn or by division in spring or autumn. Cultivars can be divided in autumn or early spring. Remove spent flower stems and divide established clumps every 3 or 4 years.

Heuchera × *brizoides* 'June Bride' *(above)*

Heuchera × brizoides *(left)*

This group are all complex hybrids involving *Heuchera sanguinea* and several other species. Highly attractive, they produce mounds of rounded, lobed leaves that are prettily marbled. Above these rise tall, slender, arching stems bearing dainty bell-like flowers in white, as in **'June Bride'**, or shades of pink or red. Foliage mounds are about 12 in (30 cm) tall with flower stems rising at least another 12 in (30 cm). ZONES 3–10.

H

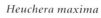

Heuchera maxima
(left)

ISLAND ALUMROOT

Found only on the islands off the southern Californian coast, this species has big, coarse, deeply lobed and cut leaves and bears its small, pinkish white flowers on thick, sturdy stems. It grows well in dry, dappled shade and is marginally frost hardy. ZONES 9–10.

Heuchera micrantha var. diversifolia
'Palace Purple' *(right)*

This cultivar is grown for its striking, purple, palmate leaves and panicles of tiny white flowers in summer. It is clump forming, with a height and spread of about 18 in (45 cm). The leaves last well as indoor decoration. ZONES 5–10.

Heuchera 'Pewter Veil' *(left)*

This beautiful hybrid has silvery green leaves with a contrasting network of deep green veins. Pinkish red flowers appear on stout, red stems. ZONES 5–10.

Heuchera pilosissima *(right)*
SHAGGY ALUMROOT

Compact and free flowering, this Californian species has maple-like lobed and toothed leaves that are rather hairy to the touch. In late spring, pink or white flowers are generously borne on the tall stems typical of the genus.
ZONES 6–10.

H

Heuchera sanguinea
(left)
CORAL BELLS

This is the most commonly grown species, and occurs naturally from Arizona to New Mexico. It grows to 18 in (45 cm) tall and has sprays of scarlet or coral red flowers above toothed, deeply lobed leaves. British and American gardeners have developed cultivars with a wider color range, from pale pink to deep red, and slightly larger flowers. **Bressingham hybrids** are a typical example.
ZONES 6–10.

Heuchera villosa *(right)*

From the mountains of eastern USA, this species has glossy, bronze-green leaves with pointed, triangular lobes. The flowers are usually white but may be pink.
ZONES 5–10.

× HEUCHERELLA

This hybrid genus is the result of a cross between *Heuchera* and
Tiarella, both members of the saxifrage family. Plants are evergreen, clumping or ground-covering perennials with tall, airy stems
of dainty pink or white flowers. These are produced over a long
season beginning in late spring. The leaves are rounded, lobed and
have distinct veins. When young they are bronze-red, turning green
during summer then reddish in autumn.

CULTIVATION

Heucherellas are easy to grow and enjoy leafy, rich, moist but well-
drained soil. Where summers are mild, full sun is best, but in hotter
areas dappled or part-shade suits them and they will do reasonably
well in full shade that is not too dark. Propagation by division is
easy and this should be done in autumn or winter in mild areas,
spring in cooler places.

× *Heucherella tiarelloides*

Growing about 12 in (30 cm) tall with flower
stems rising a further 12–15 in (30–38 cm), this
fully hardy perennial spreads by creeping stolons.
The leaves are lobed and toothed and form a
dense, rounded mound. Small pink flowers appear
on red stems. In the cultivar **'Bridget Bloom'** the
flowers are a soft, pastel pink and very freely
produced. ZONES 5–9.

× *Heucherella
tiarelloides* 'Bridget
Bloom' *(above)*

HIBISCUS

While the genus name conjures up the innumerable cultivars of *Hibiscus rosa-sinensis*, the genus of around 220 species is quite diverse, including hot-climate evergreen shrubs and small trees and also a few deciduous, temperate-zone shrubs and some annuals and perennials. The leaves are mostly toothed or lobed and the flowers, borne singly or in terminal spikes, are of characteristic shape with a funnel of 5 overlapping petals and a central column of fused stamens.

CULTIVATION

Easy to grow, the shrubby species thrive in sun and slightly acid, well-drained soil. Water regularly and feed during the flowering period. Trim after flowering to maintain shape. Propagate from seed or cuttings or by division, depending on the species. Check for aphids, mealybugs and white fly. The *H. rosa-sinensis* cultivars make greenhouse subjects in frosty climates, and compact-growing cultivars are gaining popularity as house plants.

Hibiscus moscheutos *(left)*
COMMON ROSE MALLOW, SWAMP ROSE MALLOW

This herbaceous perennial grows to 8 ft (2.4 m) high and 3–5 ft (1–1.5 m) wide. Single, hollyhock-like flowers, 4–8 in (10–20 cm) wide, are carried on robust, unbranched stems in late summer and autumn. Colors vary from white to pink, some with deeper throat markings. The leaves are large, toothed and softly hairy beneath. A range of lower-growing cultivars with dramatic large flowers have been bred, including 'Southern Belle', with rose pink blooms up to 10 in (25 cm) across.
ZONES 5–9.

HOSTA
PLANTAIN LILY

Natives of Japan and China, the 40 species in this genus of easily grown, frost-hardy perennials are valued for their decorative foliage. They all produce wide, handsome leaves, some being marbled or marked with white and others a bluish green. All-yellow foliage forms are also available. They do well in large pots or planters, are excellent for ground cover, and add an exotic touch planted on the margins of lily ponds or in bog gardens. Tall stems to about 18 in (45 cm) tall, bear nodding, white, pink or shades of purple and blue, bell- or trumpet-shaped flowers during warmer weather. Both the leaves and the flowers are popular for floral arrangements.

CULTIVATION
They grow well in shade and rich, moist, neutral, well-drained soil. Feed regularly during the growing season. Propagate by division in early spring, and guard against snails and slugs.

Hosta crispula (left)
This handsome species has elongated, lanceolate, distinctly pleated leaves. They are gray-green with creamy white margins. Pale lavender flowers are produced in early summer but it is the foliage that is the chief attraction. ZONES 6–10.

Hosta 'Birchwood Parky's Gold' (right)
syn. *Hosta* 'Golden Nakaiana'
The big leaves of this hybrid open yellowish green but turn golden with age and as summer progresses. It is a strong-growing plant up to 18 in (45 cm) tall that slowly spreads to form large colonies. Mauve flowers are produced in late spring or summer. ZONES 6–10.

Hosta 'Eric Smith' *(left)*

This hybrid has big, rounded leaves with a blue-green bloom and is best grown where summers are mild with cool nights. ZONES 6–10.

Hosta fluctuans 'Sagae' *(below)*

H

Hosta fluctuans
KURONAMI-GIBOSHI

This Japanese species has very unusual foliage. The leaves, up to 10 in (25 cm) long, taper markedly from a broad base and are wavy and twisted. They are a deep olive shade on their upper surface with noticeably gray undersides. The flower scape is blue-green, around 3 ft (1 m) tall and carries pale violet flowers. **'Sagae'** or **'Sagae-giboshi'** is a Japanese form that has leaves with creamy white edges. ZONES 7–10.

Hosta fortunei 'Aureomarginata' *(below)*

Hosta fortunei

This strong-growing perennial has given rise to many hybrids. It has ovate or broad lanceolate, pleated and pointed leaves that are a dull mid-green. In summer, tall flower stems are produced from which hang lavender flowers. Plants grow at least 18 in (45 cm) tall but spread nearly twice as wide. **'Albomarginata'** has gray-green leaves with creamy yellow to white margins; **'Albopicta'** has leaves marbled or irregularly marked in 2 shades of green; **'Aurea'** is a luminous golden green; and **'Aureomarginata'** has leaves edged with yellow. ZONES 6–10.

Hosta fortunei 'Aurea'
(right)

Hosta fortunei
'Albomarginata' *(above)*

H

Hosta fortunei
'Albopicta' *(right)*

Hosta 'Frances Williams' *(right)*

This large-growing vigorous variegated hybrid was raised by F. & C. Williams in 1986. Although it is slow to propagate, it has quickly become one of most popular hostas. It has large gray-green, heart-shaped, puckered leaves heavily edged with pale greenish yellow. The flowers are lavender. **ZONES 6–10.**

H

Hosta 'Gold Edger' *(left)*

'Gold Edger' forms a 12 in (30 cm) tall mound of broad, yellowish green leaves and produces tall spikes of almost white flowers in summer. **ZONES 6–10.**

Hosta 'Golden Sculpture' *(left)*

This big-leafed plant with quilted foliage is a combination of yellow and green overlaid with a powdery bloom. It is a vigorous grower. **ZONES 6–10.**

Hosta 'Halcyon' *(right)*

Striking gray-blue leaves make 'Halcyon' an arresting sight, especially when contrasted against green or yellow foliage. Its summer flowers are a dusty mauve color.
ZONES 6–10.

Hosta 'Golden Tiara' *(below)*

'Golden Tiara' forms a dense mound of dull green leaves edged in golden green. As a bonus, it produces unusual striped purple flowers in summer. A compact plant, it rarely exceeds 12 in (30 cm) in height. **ZONES 6–10.**

Hosta 'Honeybells' *(left)*

'Honeybells' has oval to heart-shaped leaves, about 10 in (25 cm) long, with strong veins. The short-lived white flowers, opening from mauvish buds, are borne in late summer. Some are pleasantly scented in the evening. ZONES 6–10.

Hosta 'Hydon Sunset' *(above)*

The leaves of this hybrid open lime green but age to yellow, creating a dense clump of various shades of yellow-green. The flowers are a deep lavender purple. ZONES 6–10.

Hosta 'June' *(below)*

'June' has similar gray-blue leaves to its parent *Hosta* 'Halcyon', overlaid with splashes of yellow and green. ZONES 6–10.

H

H

Hosta lancifolia *(above)*
NARROW LEAFED PLANTAIN LILY

This smaller-leafed species forms a clump to 18 in
(45 cm) high and 30 in (75 cm) wide. It has narrow,
lance-shaped, glossy mid-green leaves. It bears
racemes of trumpet-shaped, pale lilac flowers in
late summer and early autumn. **ZONES 6–10.**

Hosta 'Krossa Regal' *(below)*

This hybrid has beauti-
ful powdery gray-green
leaves that are upward
folded, wavy edged and
distinctly pleated.
ZONES 6–10.

Hosta 'Pearl Lake'
(above)

The 4 in (10 cm) long
leaves of this hybrid are
plain gray-green with a
slight powdery bloom.
The lavender-blue
flowers are are quite
showy. **ZONES 6–10.**

Hosta 'Royal Standard'
(left)

This *Hosta plantaginea* hybrid was registered in 1986 by Wayside Gardens. It forms clumps of deep green glossy foliage with fragrant, white, lily-like flowers on 24 in (60 cm) stems from late summer. One of the few hostas grown as much for its flowers as its foliage. The only drawback is that it needs reasonably mild late summer and early autumn weather to perform well. **ZONES 8–10.**

H

Hosta plantaginea
(right)

AUGUST LILY, FRAGRANT PLANTAIN LILY

Popular for its pure white, fragrant flowers on 30 in (75 cm) stems, this species has mid-green leaves forming a mound 3 ft (1 m) across. It flowers in late summer. **ZONES 3–10.**

Hosta sieboldiana *(left)*

This robust, clump-forming plant grows to 3 ft (1 m) high and 5 ft (1.5 m) wide. It has puckered, heart-shaped, bluish gray leaves and bears racemes of mauve buds, opening to trumpet-shaped white flowers in early summer. **'Frances Williams'** has heart-shaped, puckered blue-green leaves with yellowish green margins. ***Hosta sieboldiana* var. *elegans*** also has heart-shaped, puckered leaves. ZONES 6–10.

Hosta tokudama *(right)*

This very slow-growing perennial, native to Japan, has racemes of trumpet-shaped, pale mauve flowers that are borne above cup-shaped blue leaves in mid-summer. Clump forming, it reaches a height of 18 in (45 cm) and a spread of 30 in (75 cm). There are several cultivars available: **'Aureonebulosa'** has leaves splashed with green and yellow; **'Flavocircinalis'** has heart-shaped leaves with creamy margins. ZONES 6–10.

Hosta tokudama
'Aureonebulosa' *(left)*

H

Hosta undulata (above)
WAVY LEAFED PLANTAIN LILY

Hosta undulata has creamy
white, wavy or twisted
leaves that are splashed
and streaked green along
their edges. Mauve flowers
on tall stems in summer
complete this attractive
and desirable specimen.
ZONES 6–10.

Hosta 'Wide Brim'
(right)

This hybrid has dark
green heavily puckered
leaves with a broad white
margin. Its flowers are pale
lavender. It was registered
in 1979 by the well-known
hosta authority Paul Aden.
ZONES 6–10.

HOUTTUYNIA

There is only one species in this genus, a wide-spreading, creeping herbaceous perennial native to eastern Asia. It grows in moist or wet, part- or fully shaded areas. It is a good ground cover in moist, woodland gardens or beside ponds and can also grow in shallow water or boggy ground. The wild form has dark green, heart-shaped, red-margined, plain green leaves, and in summer bears spikes of tiny yellowish flowers with 4 pure white bracts at the base of each spike.

CULTIVATION

Grow this frost-hardy plant in moist, leafy rich soil. In cooler climates the plant will tolerate sun so long as the ground is moist, but in hotter places some shade is desirable. Where winters are always cold, reduce water in winter or cover the roots with a thick layer of straw. Propagate from ripe seed or from cuttings in late spring and early summer, or by division in spring.

Houttuynia cordata (below)

Ranging from the Himalayas to Japan, this water-loving deciduous perennial makes a good ground cover but may become invasive. It is a vigorous plant, growing to 12 in (30 cm) in height with an indefinite spread. It grows from underground runners that send up bright red branched stems bearing aromatic green leaves. However, the most popular form, **'Chameleon'** (syns 'Tricolor', 'Variegata') is strikingly variegated in red, cream, pink and green. ZONES 5–11.

HUNNEMANNIA

MEXICAN TULIP POPPY, GOLDEN CUP

This genus consists of one species of poppy found in dry, elevated
parts of Mexico. It has an upright habit and is fast growing to a
height of 24 in (60 cm) with a spread of 8 in (20 cm). It has
decorative, oblong, finely dissected, bluish green leaves and bears
rich, glowing yellow, single or semi-double, 3 in (8 cm) wide,
poppy-like flowers in summer and early autumn.

CULTIVATION

Grow in full sun in free-draining, sandy or gravelly soil. Plants
do not enjoy cold, wet winters although they can withstand
considerable frost in their native range where winter days are
sunny. In the UK and similar cool, rainy climates they are often
grown as annuals, the seed sown under glass in late winter or early
spring. Deadhead plants regularly to prolong flowering and
provide support in exposed areas. Water liberally during hot
weather.

Hunnemannia
fumariifolia (above)

One of the best yellow-
flowered perennials,
this relative of the
California poppy
(*Eschscholzia californica*)
is grown as an annual
in frost-prone areas.
ZONES 8–10.

HYPERICUM
ST JOHN'S WORT

This is a large and varied genus of 400 species of annuals, perennials, shrubs and a few small trees, some evergreen but mostly deciduous, grown for their showy flowers in shades of yellow with a central mass of prominent golden stamens. They are found throughout the world in a broad range of habitats. Species range in size from tiny perennials for rockeries to over 10 ft (3 m) tall.

CULTIVATION
Mostly cool-climate plants, they prefer full sun but will tolerate some shade. They do best in fertile, well-drained soil, with plentiful water in late spring and summer. Remove seed capsules after flowering and prune in winter to maintain a rounded shape. Cultivars are propagated from cuttings in summer, and species from seed in autumn or from cuttings in summer. Some species are susceptible to rust.

Hypericum cerastoides (above)
syn. *Hypericum rhodoppeum*

This densely mounding perennial has oval, gray-green leaves and terminal clusters of bright yellow, cup-shaped flowers in late spring and early summer. It has an upright, slightly spreading habit and grows to 12 in (30 cm) tall with a 18 in (45 cm) spread. Frost hardy, it is useful in rock gardens. ZONES 6–9.

HYSSOPUS
HYSSOP

This genus of aromatic culinary and medicinal herbs belongs to the mint family and includes about 5 species of herbaceous perennials and shrubs. All are found in poor soils around the northern Mediterranean coasts and also in Asia Minor. The leaves vary with species from linear to ovate and may be green or blue-green in color. The flowers are small, tubular with protruding stamens, and usually a shade of blue although they may also be white or pink.

CULTIVATION

All species do best in full sun and although they will grow in dry sandy soil, in gardens they look much better when grown in friable, fertile loam though good drainage is essential. Ensure adequate water particularly in autumn and winter. Propagate from cuttings taken in early summer or from seed sown in autumn. Prune by shearing plants all over.

H

Hyssopus officinalis (left)
HYSSOP

This bushy perennial herb grows to 24 in (60 cm) and has narrow, pointed, dark green leaves. Spikes of small violet-blue flowers, which are attractive to bees and butterflies, are borne in late summer. White and pink flowering forms are also available. Fully frost hardy, hyssop is evergreen in mild climates; in cool areas it dies down for the winter. The slightly bitter leaves are used in small quantities with fatty meats and fish. The essential oil made from the leaves has antiseptic properties and is used in the manufacture of perfumes. ZONES 3–11.

IJK

IBERIS

This genus consists of around 50 species of annuals, perennials and evergreen subshrubs, which are mainly from southern Europe, northern Africa and western Asia. Highly regarded as decorative plants they are excellent for rock gardens, bedding and borders. The showy flowers are borne in either flattish heads in colors of white, red and purple, or in erect racemes of pure white. *Iberis spathulata* is an alpine perennial endemic to the Pyrenees.

Iberis spathulata (below)

CULTIVATION

Fully to marginally frost hardy, they require a warm, sunny position and a well-drained, light soil, preferably with added lime or dolomite. Propagate from seed in spring or autumn—they may self-sow, but are unlikely to become invasive—or cuttings in summer.

Iberis amara cultivar (left)

Iberis amara
CANDYTUFT, HYACINTH-FLOWERED CANDYTUFT

This frost-hardy, fast-growing and erect bushy annual has lance-shaped, mid-green leaves and reaches a height of 12 in (30 cm), with a spread of 6 in (15 cm). It produces large racemes of small, fragrant, pure white flowers in early spring and summer. Various strains are available. The **Hyacinth-flowered Series** has large fragrant flowers in varying shades of pink; these are sometimes used as cut flowers. ZONES 7–11.

Iberis umbellata
(right)
GLOBE CANDYTUFT

Native to the Mediterranean region, this upright bushy annual has lance-shaped, mid-green leaves. Flattish heads of small, mauve, lilac, pink, purple, carmine or white flowers are produced in late spring and summer. *Iberis umbellata* grows to a height of 6–12 in (15–30 cm) and a spread of 8 in (20 cm). It is frost hardy and is a useful cut flower. The **Fairy Series** has flowers in shades of pink, red, purple or white which appear in spring. Bushes in this series grow to a height and spread of 8 in (20 cm). Lightly trim after flowering. ZONES 7–11.

Iberis pruitii
(below right)
syn. *Iberis jordanii*

A short-lived perennial or occasionally an annual, this species is native to the Mediterranean. It grows to about 6 in (15 cm) tall with a spread of 8 in (20 cm). *Iberis pruitti* has slightly fleshy, dark green rosette-forming leaves and produces tight clusters of lilac to white flowers in summer. It is frost hardy, but is susceptible in wet winter conditions. ZONES 7–11.

Iberis sempervirens
(right)
CANDYTUFT, EVERGREEN CANDYTUFT

A low, spreading, evergreen perennial, this species from southern Europe is ideal for rock gardens. It has narrow, dark green leaves and dense, rounded heads of unscented white flowers in spring and early summer. It is frost hardy, and grows 6–12 in (15–30 cm) high with a spread of 18–24 in (45–60 cm). The cultivar **'Snowflake'** is most attractive, with glossy, dark green leaves and semi-spherical heads of white flowers. Lightly trim after flowering. ZONES 4–11.

I

Impatiens glandulifera (left)
syn. *Impatiens roylei*

POLICEMAN'S HELMET,
HIMALAYAN BALSAM

A native of the Hima-
layas, this plant has
naturalized in both the
UK and northern
North America. A frost-
hardy annual with a
strong self-seeding
tendency, it grows to
about 6 ft (1.8 m) tall.
It has thick fleshy
stems, particularly at
the bottom, and
produces masses of
flowers during sum-
mer. Its flowers are
rose-purple to lilac or
even white with a
yellow-spotted interior.
ZONES 6–10.

IMPATIENS

This large genus of around 850 species of succulent-stemmed
annuals, evergreen perennials and subshrubs is widely distributed,
especially in the subtropics and tropics of Asia and Africa. They are
useful for colorful summer bedding displays and for indoor and
patio plants. The flowers come in an ever-increasing range of
colors. Many hybrid strains are perennial in mild climates, but in
colder climates are usually grown as annuals. Their botanical name,
Impatiens, refers to the impatience with which they grow and
multiply.

CULTIVATION
Frost hardy to frost tender, they will grow in sun or part-shade:
many species do well under overhanging trees. They prefer a moist
but freely drained soil, and need protection from strong winds. Tip
prune the fast-growing shoots to encourage shrubby growth and
more abundant flowers. Propagate from seed or stem cuttings in
spring and summer.

Impatiens, New Guinea Hybrids

Hybrids from a New Guinean species, members of
this group of fast-growing perennials are also
grown as annuals in cool climates. They are frost
tender and grow to a height and spread of 12–18 in
(30–45 cm). The leaves are oval, pointed and bronze
green, or may be variegated with cream, white or
yellow. The flat, spurred flowers are pink, orange,
red or cerise, sometimes with white markings.
Cultivars include **'Cheers'**, with its coral flowers
and yellow leaves; **'Concerto'**, with crimson-
centered deep pink flowers; **'Tango'**, with deep
orange flowers; and **'Red Magic'**, which has scarlet
flowers and bronze-red leaves. They do well in
brightly lit positions indoors in cooler climates, or
on enclosed verandahs or patios in warmer areas.
'Toga' has blueish pink flowers. ZONES 10–12.

Impatiens, New Guinea Hybrid, 'Toga' *(below)*

Impatiens, New Guinea Hybrid, 'Concerto' *(above)*

Impatiens pseudoviola (left)

This semi-trailing East African species is a perennial. It produces white flowers suffused with rose pink, with violet-rose central stripes on the wing petals. **'Woodcote'** is a shrubby, pale pink-lilac form. ZONES 10–12.

Impatiens pseudoviola 'Woodcote' (below)

I

Impatiens usambarensis ×
walleriana (above)

Impatiens
usambarensis

This tropical African
species gets its name from
the Usambara Mountains
on the borders of Kenya
and Tanzania, where it
was first discovered. It is
related to the better known
Impatiens walleriana, and
has been used in the
breeding of the many
colorful 'busy lizzie'
hybrids in this group.
I. u. × *walleriana*, seen
here, displays just one of
the many possible color
outcomes in such crosses.
ZONES 10–12.

Impatiens repens *(below)*
GOLDEN DRAGON

This evergreen, creeping perennial is native to Sri Lanka.
It bears golden, hooded flowers with a large hairy spur
in summer; these stand out against the small, kidney-
shaped leaves with red stems. *Impatiens repens* is frost
tender, and grows to a height of 2 in (5 cm). This species
is especially suited to hanging baskets. **ZONES 10–12.**

INCARVILLEA

This genus of the bignonia family
(Bignoniaceae) consists of 14 species native
to central and East Asia, including the
Himalayas. They are suitable for rock gardens
and the taller species are more at home in
herbaceous borders. Some species are
annuals, although those in cultivation are
usually perennial. From mountain habitats,
some of the shorter growing types from
higher altitudes have, strangely enough, the
largest and most exotic flowers. Most species
have flowers in shades of magenta and deep
rose pink, although 1 or 2 have flowers in
shades of yellow or white.

CULTIVATION

Most species of *Incarvillea* are frost hardy,
but do not tolerate overly wet or waterlogged
soil in winter. They usually require an
aspect that has rich, moisture-retentive,
well-drained soil, in a position that receives
ample sun except in the very hottest part
of the day. These plants prefer cold to
temperate climates. Propagation is usually
by seed in autumn or spring; division in
spring or autumn is possible, but difficult,
as mature plants resent disturbance.

Incarvillea delavayi *(above)*
PRIDE OF CHINA, HARDY GLOXINIA

This fleshy-rooted, clump-forming perennial is
useful for rock gardens and borders. It has handsome, fern-like foliage and erect stems bearing
large, trumpet-shaped, rosy purple flowers in
summer. It grows to a height of 24 in (60 cm) with
a spread of 12 in (30 cm), but dies down early in
autumn. It is very frost hardy, but should be
protected with a compost mulch during cold
winters. ZONES 6–10.

Incarvillea arguta *(left)*

This hardy species from the Himalayas and western and southwestern
China grows to about 3 ft (1 m) tall
with a spread of 12 in (30 cm). It is
more suitable for a border than a
rock garden, although it will grow
in a crevice in a wall. It will flower
in the first year from seed and
although perennial is sometimes
treated as an annual. Its 1½ in
(35 mm) long trumpet-shaped
flowers are usually deep pink or
sometimes white, and are produced
through summer. ZONES 8–10.

Inula helenium
(left)
ELECAMPANE, SCABWORT

Believed to have originated in central Asia, this plant has become widely naturalized. It is one of the largest *Inula* species at 8 ft (2.4 m) tall with a spread of 3 ft (1 m). As it is rhizomatous, it is also one of the most invasive. It produces its large, yellow daisy-like flowers in summer and should be planted with due deference to its invasive potential. *Inula helenium* was used in medicine as a tonic, astringent, demulcent and diuretic. Because of this, it is often planted in herb gardens.
ZONES 5–10.

INULA

Native to Asia, Africa and Europe, this genus of about 90 species in the daisy family are mostly herbaceous perennials, although some are subshrubs, biennials or annuals. The different species vary in size from quite tiny plants suited to the rock garden up to towering perennials that can exceed 10 ft (3 m) tall. Often in the case of the larger species, the leaves can also be impressive if somewhat rank. Inulas are well known for their fine-petalled, invariably yellow daisies, some species of which are quite large and showy. Several species have been cultivated since ancient times and the name *Inula* was used by the Romans.

CULTIVATION

Inulas are frost-hardy plants. They will grow in any deep, fertile, well-drained or moist soil, but not one that is wet. They prefer a sunny to part-shaded aspect. Propagation is usually from seed or by division in either spring or autumn.

IPOMOEA
syns *Calonyction, Mina, Pharbitis, Quamoclit*
MORNING GLORY

This large genus of some 300 mostly climbing, evergreen shrubs, perennials and annuals is widespread throughout the tropics and warm-temperate regions of the world. It includes sweet potato and some of the loveliest of the tropical flowering vines. Most species have a twining habit and masses of funnel-shaped flowers, which in many species wither by midday. The flowers are usually short-lived, lasting only one day (or night), but bloom prolifically and in succession. They are useful for covering sheds, fences, trellises and banks, and may also be grown in containers.

CULTIVATION
Marginally frost hardy to frost tender, they are best suited to warm coastal districts or tropical areas. They prefer moderately fertile, well-drained soil and a sunny position. Care should be taken when choosing species, as some can become extremely invasive in warm districts. Propagate in spring from seed that has been gently filed and pre-soaked to aid germination, or from cuttings in summer (for perennial species).

Ipomoea nil *(above)*
syns *Ipomoea imperialis, Pharbitis nil*

This soft-stemmed, short-lived, twining perennial is best treated as an annual. Marginally frost hardy, it grows to 12 ft (3.5 m) in height. Its stems are covered with hairs, and the leaves are heart-shaped. Large, trumpet-shaped flowers appear from summer through to early autumn in a variety of shades. **'Scarlett O'Hara'** is a cultivar with dark crimson blooms.
ZONES 9–12.

Ipomoea × multifida *(right)*
syn. *Ipomoea × sloteri*
CARDINAL CLIMBER

This is a hybrid of *Ipomoea coccinea* and *I. quamoclit* of garden origin. A frost-tender annual climber with slender twining stems, it reaches 10 ft (3 m) in height. The foliage is mid-green and divided into several lobes. Its tubular flowers, produced during summer, are crimson-red with white throats. ZONES 9–12.

Ipomoea tricolor
'Heavenly Blue' *(below)*

Ipomoea tricolor
syns *Ipomoea rubrocaerulea, I. violacea, Pharbitis tricolor*

This Mexican perennial vine is more often grown as an annual. It can reach a height of 10 ft (3 m) with a spread of 5 ft (1.5 m), and has cord-like, twining stems and heart-shaped, light green leaves. From summer to early autumn, *Ipomoea tricolor* bears large, blue to mauve, funnel-shaped flowers that open in the morning and gradually fade during the day. Widening to a trumpet as they open, the flowers can reach 6 in (15 cm) across. The cultivar **'Heavenly Blue'** is particularly admired for its color, as is the very similar **'Clarke's Himmelblau'**. ZONES 8–12.

IRESINE

Belonging to the amaranthus family, these tropical perennials from the Americas and Australia—some 80 species in all—are sometimes treated as annuals. They vary in habit from upright to ground-hugging. The flowers are insignificant and not the reason for which these plants are grown. It is for their often brilliantly colored leaves that they merit attention.

CULTIVATION

These frost-tender plants only make permanent garden plants in tropical to warm-temperate climates, where there is no incidence of frost. In cooler areas they can be grown in greenhouses and planted out once all chance of frost has passed. They prefer good loamy, well-drained soil and must be kept moist during the growth period. They also need bright light, with some direct sun, to retain the brilliant color in their leaves. Tips should be pinched out in the growing season to encourage bushy plants. Propagate from cuttings in spring.

Iresine herbstii
'Brilliantissima' *(below)*

Iresine herbstii *(above left)*
syn. *Iresine reticulata*
BEEFSTEAK PLANT, BLOODLEAF

Native to Brazil, this species makes an attractive tropical bedding or pot plant. Although perennial, it is often treated as an annual that is overwintered as struck cuttings in a greenhouse in cold areas. It grows to 24 in (60 cm) tall with a spread of 18 in (45 cm), but usually much less if grown as an annual. It has red stems and rounded, purple-red leaves up to 4 in (10 cm) long, with notches at the tips and yellowish red veins. Garden forms have a range of color, from bright green leaves with bright yellow veins, through to cultivars such as 'Brilliantissima', with its rich purple-green leaves and beetroot-pink veins. ZONES 10–12.

IRIS

This wide-ranging genus of more than 200 species, native to the temperate regions of the northern hemisphere, is named for the Greek goddess of the rainbow, and is valued for its beautiful and distinctive flowers. Each flower has 6 petals: 3 outer petals, called 'falls', which droop away from the center and alternate with the inner petals, called 'standards'. There are many hybrids. Irises are divided into 2 main groups: **rhizomatous and bulbous.**

Rhizomatous irises have sword-shaped leaves, are sometimes evergreen, and are subdivided into 3 groups: **bearded** (or flag) irises, with a tuft of hairs (the 'beard') on the 3 lower petals; **beardless** irises, without the tuft; **crested** or Evansia irises, with a raised crest instead of a beard.

The bearded types include the rare and beautiful **Oncocyclus** and **Regelia** irises, native to the eastern Mediterranean and Central Asia. Therefore they need cold winters and hot, dry summers to flourish. Hybrids between these 2 groups are called **Regeliocyclus** irises, while hybrids between either of them and other bearded irises are called **Arilbred** irises. But the main group of bearded irises consists of numerous species with thick, creeping rhizomes, mainly from temperate Eurasia, and countless hybrids bred from these: both species and hybrids can be subdivided into the 3 classes **Tall Bearded, Intermediate Bearded** and **Dwarf Bearded** irises, depending mainly on the plant's height but some other characteristics as well. Tall bearded irises are the most popular class of irises, with by far the largest number of hybrid cultivars.

The beardless irises mostly have long, narrow leaves and include several identifiable groups of species and hybrids. Most notable are the East Asian **Laevigatae** or **Water** irises, including the large-flowered '**Kaempferi**' irises derived from *I. ensata,* the **Louisiana** irises from southeastern USA and their hybrids, the **Pacific Coast** irises from the west side of North America, also with many hybrids, and the Eurasian **Spuria** and **Siberian** irises, consisting of numerous species and a scattering of hybrids.

The bulbous irises are also divided into 3 groups, the **Juno, Reticulata** and **Xiphium** irises. The first 2 consist of beautiful, but mostly difficult bulbs, from west and central Asia. The Xiphium irises, though, are centered on the Mediterranean and are more easy to grow; they have given rise to a group of bulbous hybrids including the so-called **English, Spanish** and **Dutch** irises. It is the latter that are commonly seen in florist shops.

CULTIVATION

Growing conditions vary greatly. As a rule, rhizomatous irises, with the exception of the crested or Evansia irises, are also very frost hardy and prefer a sunny position; some of the beardless types like very moist soil. Bulbous irises are also very frost hardy, and prefer a sunny position with ample moisture during growth, but very little during their summer dormancy. Bulbous irises should be planted in autumn and are prone to virus infection and so need to be kept free of aphids, which will spread the infection. Propagate irises by division in late summer after flowering or from seed in autumn. Named cultivars should only be divided.

Iris bracteata *(above)*
SISKIYOU IRIS

So called because its leaves on the flowering stems are short and bract-like, this native of Oregon inhabits dry conifer forests. Its flowers are usually predominantly cream or yellow, but some plants with reddish toned flowers exist. The falls are flared with reddish veins, and its standards are erect. The flowers are held on stems 12 in (30 cm) tall. Although frost hardy, this species is not easy to grow; it resents being lifted and divided, so is best raised from seed. ZONES 7–9.

Iris cristata *(below)*
CRESTED IRIS

A woodland crested or Evansia iris native to southeastern USA, this rhizomatous species grows 4–9 in (10–22.5 cm) in height. In spring, it bears faintly fragrant, pale blue to lavender or purple flowers held just above the foliage; each fall has a white patch with an orange crest. It prefers a moist soil in part-shade, making it suitable as a ground cover in shaded gardens; it spreads slowly by rhizomes. **'Alba'** is a vigorous cultivar with white flowers. ZONES 6–9.

Iris cristata 'Alba' *(left)*

Iris ensata *(right)*
syn. *Iris kaempferi*
JAPANESE FLAG, HIGO IRIS

Native to Japan and cultivated there for centuries, this beardless iris grows to 3 ft (1 m) tall. It has purple flowers that appear from late spring to early summer, with yellow blotches on each fall. The leaves have a prominent midrib. The many cultivars bear huge flowers, up to 10 in (25 cm) wide, in shades of white, lavender, blue and purple, often blending 2 shades, and some with double flowers. These plants prefer part-shade in hot areas, rich, acid soil and plenty of moisture. They can even grow in shallow water provided they are not submerged during the winter months. The foliage dies down in winter. **'Exception'** has particularly large falls and deep purple flowers; **'Mystic Buddha'** has purple-blue flowers with red edging. ZONES 4–10.

Iris ensata 'Exception'
(right)

Iris douglasiana *(below)*
DOUGLAS IRIS

One of the chief parents of the Pacific Coast irises, this evergreen, rhizomatous beardless species comes from the coastal mountain ranges of California. It reaches 10–30 in (25–75 cm) in height and its branched stems produce 1 to 3 flowers in early spring. The flowers are variable in color, from rich blue-purple to almost white, while the leathery, dark green leaves are stained with maroon at the base. It readily hybridizes with other species from its region. ZONES 8–10.

I

Iris germanica var.
biliottii *(left)*

Iris germanica
'Florentina' *(below)*

Iris germanica *(above)*
COMMON FLAG, GERMAN IRIS

The putative ancestor of the
modern bearded irises, this
rhizomatous, bearded species is
easy to grow in just about any
temperate climate. Its creeping
rhizomes multiply rapidly into
large clumps. The sparsely
branched stem produces up to
6 yellow-bearded, blue-purple
to blue-violet flowers in spring.
Iris germanica var. *biliottii*
(syn. *Iris biliottii*) occurs
naturally in the Black Sea region
of Turkey. It grows to about 3 ft
(1 m) tall and, like *I. germanica*,
has scented flowers. This variety
has reddish purple falls with
standards of a more blue-purple
shade, and the beard is white
with yellow tips. Another form
of *I. germanica* is '**Florentina**',
which has scented white flowers
with a bluish flush and yellow
beards. Its bracts are brown and
papery during flowering.
'**Florentina**' is cultivated in Italy,
for its perfume (orris root),
which is released when the
roots are dried. It is an early-
flowering variety that prefers
a position in full sun.
ZONES 4–10.

Iris innominata *(below)*
DEL NORTE COUNTY IRIS

Native to the northwest coast of the
USA, this rhizomatous, beardless iris
is one of the parent species of the
Pacific Coast Hybrids. It reaches
6–10 in (15–25 cm) in height. Its
evergreen, narrow, deep green leaves
are up to 12 in (30 cm) long and are
purple at their bases. The unbranched
stems bear 1 or 2 flowers in early
summer. They range in color from
bright yellow to cream, and from
pale lavender-blue to purple. The
falls may be veined with brown or
maroon. **ZONES 8–10.**

Iris japonica *(top right & right)*
syn. *Iris fimbriata*
CRESTED IRIS

This is the best known of the crested
or Evansia species. It grows to
18–32 in (45–80 cm) in height,
forming large clumps of almost evergreen, glossy mid-green leaves. In
late winter and spring, it bears sprays
of 2¹/₂ in (6 cm) wide, ruffled, pale
blue or white flowers; each fall has a
violet patch around an orange crest.
It prefers an acidic soil, a lightly
shaded position, and a mild climate.
It must be kept shaded from
afternoon sun. **ZONES 8–11.**

Iris lutescens
syn. *Iris chamaeiris*

Iris lutescens is a variable rhizomatous, dwarf bearded iris from southwestern Europe similar to *I. pumila*. It is fast growing and can have foliage that is less than ¹/₂ in (12 mm) to more than 1 in (2.5 cm) wide and up to 12 in (30 cm) long. The flowers, borne in early spring, can be yellow, violet blue, white or bicolored; the beard is yellow. This is an easy-to-grow and showy species, but it does need winter cold to flower well. **'Caerulea'** is a bluish version of *I. lutescens*. ZONES 5–9.

Iris lutescens 'Caerulea'
(above)

Iris lactea *(below)*

This widespread beardless species allied to *Iris ensata* is found from central Russia to Korea and the Himalayas. It has stiff, upright, gray-green leaves up to about 2 in (5 cm) wide which can overtop the 12 in (30 cm) tall flower spikes. These are produced in early summer and have 1 or 2 fragrant pale lavender-blue or rarely white flowers. This strong plant will cope with both frost and heat, but is one of the less spectacular irises. ZONES 4–9.

Iris maackii *(left)*

This little known and comparatively newly described species from China is related to *Iris laevigata*. The flowers are more than 2 in (5 cm) wide and completely yellow. It should prove to be a hardy and dainty iris, growing up to about 12 in (30 cm) tall. ZONES 4–9.

Iris missouriensis

(center)
syn. *Iris tolmeiana*
MISSOURI FLAG,
ROCKY MOUNTAIN IRIS

A widespread rhizomatous, beardless iris extending through western and central North America from Mexico to British Columbia, this is a very frost-hardy and easy-to-grow plant, although quite variable in appearance. It reaches 30 in (75 cm) in height. It likes moist soil up until it flowers in early spring and drier conditions during summer. This species can make substantial clumps with slender leaves. Its flowers vary in color from very pale blue through to deep blue or lavender, with some white forms. The falls, veined with deep purple, usually have a yellow blaze. ZONES 3–9.

Iris orientalis *(right)*

syn. *Iris ochroleuca*
SWAMP IRIS

This 4 ft (1.2 m) tall, almost evergreen, rhizomatous beardless iris from western Asia has mid-green leaves and white and yellow flowers in early summer. **Iris orientalis var. monnieri** is an all-yellow form. Although these plants will grow in damp ground, they are perfectly happy in any rich, well-watered garden soil in a sunny position. ZONES 6–9.

Iris munzii *(right)*
MUNZ'S IRIS

One of the largest flowering of the Pacific Coast irises, this species grows up to 30 in (75 cm) tall. Blooms up to 3 in (8 cm) wide are borne in summer. The flowers vary in color from pale blue through lavender to dark red-purple, with the veins often darker. This species is not very frost hardy. ZONES 8–10.

I

Iris pallida *(left)*
DALMATIAN IRIS

This bearded iris from the Dalmatian region of Croatia has fragrant, pale blue flowers with yellow beards, which are borne on 4 ft (1.2 m) high stems in late spring. It is often grown as a source of orris (also obtained from *I. germanica* 'Florentina'), a volatile substance that develops in the dried and aged rhizomes and is used in perfumes, dental preparations and breath fresheners. **'Variegata'** (syn. 'Aurea Variegata') has handsome leaves striped in gray-green and cream. ZONES 5–10.

Iris pallida 'Variegata' *(above)*

Iris pseudacorus 'Variegata' *(right)*

Iris pseudacorus *(left)*
WATER FLAG, YELLOW FLAG

A robust beardless iris from Europe, the water flag has handsome, mid-green leaves and profuse bright yellow flowers on 3 ft (1 m) stems which are borne in early spring. The flowers usually have brown or violet veining, with a darker yellow patch on the falls. It prefers to grow in shallow water and rich soil; plant in autumn in a box of rich earth and place in a sunny position in the garden pond. The cultivar **'Variegata'** has yellow- and green-striped foliage during the spring months, often turning green in summer; it is less vigorous than the species. ZONES 5–9.

Iris setosa subsp. *canadensis* (right)

This subspecies of a more widely spread species is found from Newfoundland to Ontario and south to Maine in North America. It grows to 24 in (60 cm) tall, although it is often shorter. A beardless iris, it flowers from late spring to early summer. Its flowers are usually solitary and are lavender-blue in color. This is a tough, easy-to-grow plant ideal for rock gardens. ZONES 3–9.

Iris 'Roy Davidson' (center)

This beardless iris is a hybrid of *Iris pseuda-corus* and as such is a suitable plant for a boggy site, although it is equally happy in moist garden conditions. It grows to slightly more than 3 ft (1 m) tall and has yellow flowers very like its parent, except that they last longer and are about 4 in (10 cm) across. ZONES 5–9.

Iris pumila

This dainty little bearded iris is distributed throughout central and eastern Europe and Turkey, varying considerably over its range. It has thick fleshy rhizomes and, in flower, rarely exceeds 6 in (15 cm) in height. The color also varies greatly and may be white, yellow, violet, purple or blue, with yellow or blue beards on the falls. It prefers a sunny position and well-drained, slightly alkaline soil. 'Purpurea' is a deep purple form. ZONES 4–9.

Iris pumila 'Purpurea' (below)

Iris sibirica 'Perry's Blue' *(left)*

Iris sibirica 'Vi Luihn' *(left)*

Iris sibirica *(above)*
SIBERIAN FLAG

Despite the name, this well-known species has a natural distribution across temperate Eurasia from France to Lake Baikal. It is one of the most popular beardless irises, usually found in gardens in one of its cultivars rather than its wild form. The plants make strongly vertical clumps of slender bright green leaves 2–4 ft (0.6–1.2 m) high. In late spring or early summer, flowering stems rise above the foliage with narrow-petalled, blue, purple or white flowers, often veined in a deeper color. It prefers full sun to very light shade (particularly in hot areas), a moderately moist, rich soil that may be slightly acid and water during the hottest periods. It will grow in a wet soil and does best in cold winter climates. Some of the available cultivars include **'Cleave Dodge'**, with mid-blue flowers; **'Perry's Blue'**, which has rich lilac-blue flowers with yellow markings and netted brown towards the base of the falls; **'Ruby'**, which has purplish blue flowers; **'White Swirl'**, which has pure white flowers with yellow at the base and flared, rounded petals; and **'Vi Luihn'**, with flowers in a rich violet shade. ZONES 4–9.

Iris sibirica 'Cleave Dodge' *(left)*

Iris tenax *(right)*
syn. *Iris gormanii*
OREGON IRIS

This is a deciduous beardless Pacific
Coast iris from Oregon and Washington
which grows to about 15 in (30 cm) tall.
Its dark green foliage is stained pink at
the base. It flowers from mid-spring into
summer; the blooms are about 3½ in
(9 cm) across and can be blue, lavender,
yellow or white, and often have yellow
and white markings on the falls. This
species is relatively easy to grow and
prefers sun or part-shade. ZONES 8–10.

Iris tectorum *(left)*
JAPANESE ROOF IRIS, WALL FLAG

So-called because in Japan this species was said to have
been grown on thatched roofs in times of hardship when
all available ground was needed for food crops. Originally
native to China, it is a hardy crested or Evansia iris with
thick rhizomes and broad, bright green leaves in fans to
12 in (30 cm) long. The flowers, produced in spring and
early summer, are about 4 in (10 cm) across and are lilac-
blue with darker veins and blotches, and a white crest on
each fall. It prefers part-shade in a sheltered position with
protection from afternoon sun. It also has a white form
called 'Alba'. ZONES 5–10.

Iris unguicularis *(right)*
syn. *Iris stylosa*
WINTER IRIS, ALGERIAN IRIS

This evergreen, beardless species from
northern Africa is notable for bearing its
flowers deep down among the clumps of
grassy, dark green leaves, on stems no
more than 8 in (20 cm) long. The flowers
are typically pale blue, but white and
darker blue to purple varieties are also
available; the falls have yellow centers. It
blooms from autumn to spring and the
flowers are primrose-scented. Although
moderately frost hardy, it does best in a
warm, sheltered, sunny position, in
slightly alkaline soil. To make the flowers
more conspicuous cut the tough foliage
back early each winter. ZONES 7–10.

Iris, Bearded Hybrids

Often classed under *Iris germanica* or
I. pallida, which are only 2 of their ancestral
species, the bearded irises are among the
most widely grown of late-spring flowers,
with fat creeping rhizomes, sword-shaped,
grayish foliage and stems bearing several
large flowers. They are available in an
enormous range of colors—everything but
true red—with many varieties featuring
blended colors, contrasting standards and
falls, or a broad band of color around
basically white flowers (this pattern is
called 'plicata'). Some of the newer varieties,
described as 'remontant', flower a second
time in late summer or autumn, though
rather erratically. All prefer a temperate
climate, sun and mildly alkaline, well-
drained soil, and flower most freely if not
over-watered in summer. Bearded irises are
subdivided into 3 groups:

Dwarf Bearded, which grow 6–15 in
(15–40 cm) tall and flower earlier than the
others.

Intermediate Bearded, about 24 in (60 cm)
tall, which flower a fortnight or so later
than the dwarf varieties. **'Sunny Dawn'** is
typical, with yellow flowers with red beards.

Tall Bearded irises are the last to bloom
and grow to 3 ft (1 m) tall or slightly higher.
Representative Tall Bearded cultivars include
'Blue Shimmer' which has white flowers
with lilac-blue stitching; **'Dancer's Veil'**, to
3 ft (1 m) tall, has white flowers with
plicata edges in blue-violet; **'Light Beam'**
has yellow standards and white falls edged
with yellow; and **'Orange Celebrity'** is
renowned for its ideal form and brilliant
yet delicate colors, including apricot and
pink shades with a flaming orange beard.
'Cannington Skies' has mid-blue standards
and falls. **'Supreme Sultan'** has butterscotch-
yellow standards and crimson-brown falls.
'Sun and Sand' has apricot-yellow
standards and yellow falls. **'White City'** has
pure white flowers. ZONES 5–10.

Iris, Bearded Hybrid, 'Dancer's Veil' *(left)*

Iris, Bearded Hybrid,
'Light Beam' *(right)*

Iris, Bearded Hybrid,
'Sunny Dawn' *(below)*

Iris, Bearded Hybrid,
'White City' *(below)*

Iris, Bearded Hybrid,
'Blue Shimmer' *(below)*

I

Iris, Bearded Hybrid,
'Supreme Sultan' *(left)*

Iris, Bearded Hybrid,
'Sun and Sand'
(below left)

Iris, Bearded Hybrid,
'Cannington Skies'
(below)

Iris, Louisiana Hybrids

This extremely colorful group of rhizomatous, beardless hybrid irises include *Iris fulva* and *I. brevicaulis* among their ancestral species. They are evergreen with fine strap-like foliage and can build into substantial clumps; divide after 2 to 3 years. The Louisiana hybrids are not fully frost hardy in very cold climates, but are becoming increasingly popular in Australia and southern parts of the USA. Although basically swamp or water irises, they will happily grow in the garden if kept very well watered. They do best in a sunny position with average to damp, humus-rich garden soil. This group rarely exceeds 3 ft (1 m) in height and is usually much shorter. Some of the available hybrids include **'Art World'**, with mauve-pink duo-toned flowers; **'Bluebonnet Sue'**, with rich violet-blue blooms; **'Guessing Game'**, with a pale mauve flower with darker violet veins and irregular markings; **'Insider'**, a new Australian hybrid which has yellow-edged reddish brown standards and falls of reddish brown with yellow spray patterning; and **'Vermilion Treasure'**, with a red-violet flower with lighter spray patterning. ZONES 7–10.

Iris, Louisiana Hybrid, 'Guessing Game' *(below)*

Iris, Louisiana Hybrid, 'Bluebonnet Sue' *(above)*

Iris, Louisiana Hybrid, 'Insider' *(below)*

Iris, Louisiana Hybrid, 'Vermilion Treasure' *(left)*

Iris, Louisiana Hybrid, 'Art World' *(above)*

Iris, Spuria Hybrids

While *Iris spuria* (from northern Africa and southern France), *I. sibirica* (from eastern Europe) and their allied species are beautiful plants in their own right, they have been much hybridized. The more common hybrids bear numerous 4 in (10 cm) wide flowers on 4 ft (1.2 m) long stems in early summer. Colors are mainly in the white to blue range, with some yellow and white forms. All prefer sun, rich soil and lavish watering while they are growing and flowering. **'Clarke Cosgrove'** is mauve-blue with a yellow splash. ZONES 4–9.

Iris, Louisiana Hybrid, 'Impressioned' *(above)*

Iris, Spuria Hybrid, 'Clarke Cosgrove' *(left)*

Jeffersonia diphylla (right)

RHEUMATISM ROOT,
TWIN LEAF

This North Ameri-
can species grows in
rich woodland from
Ontario to Tennessee.
Slow-growing, its
attractive kidney-
shaped, deeply
incised leaves are
about 6 in (15 cm)
across and gray
tinted. The dainty,
white, cup-shaped
flowers are 1 in
(25 mm) wide and
produced in late
spring or early
summer; they have
prominent yellow
stamens. The plant
increases in height
after flowering and
can reach 18 in
(45 cm) with a simi-
lar spread by the
time it sets seed. Do
not disturb its roots.
ZONES 5–9.

JEFFERSONIA

TWIN LEAF

This genus of just 2 species of herbaceous
perennials is named after Thomas Jefferson, the
third president of the USA. The species are dainty
woodland plants—one from North America, the
other from northeast Asia. Although they are
part of the *Berberis* family, this fact is not at all
obvious to most gardeners. The rounded, mid-
green leaves consist of 2 even lobes, hence the
common name.

CULTIVATION

As much as possible, try to simulate their
natural woodland homes. They are fully hardy
plants and prefer a cool, part-shaded position
and humus-rich soil; top-dress with leafmold
regularly. Propagation is usually from fresh seed
in autumn or by careful division in late winter
or early spring.

JOVIBARBA

This small genus of 5 species of evergreen, succulent perennials has a rosette-forming habit much like the closely related *Sempervivum* genus. Some species have attractive colored leaves, which are the reason why these plants are grown; all have pale yellow flowers, but these are insignificant. The rosettes die after flowering, but the gaps are soon filled with new growth.

CULTIVATION

Unlike many succulents, these plants are fully frost hardy and only require a well-drained, sunny aspect in temperate to cold climates to succeed. Some shade is necessary in warmer areas. They are ideal in rock gardens, troughs or in dry stone walls packed with a little soil. Propagate from offsets in summer. Simply remove a rosette with a piece of stem; once planted, it will quickly take root.

J

Jovibarba hirta
(left)
syn. *Jovibarba globifera*

The rosettes of this mat-forming species are usually about 2 in (5 cm) across. If the plants become dry, their leaves will curl up; otherwise, they radiate outwards. The thick, fleshy leaves are mid-green and often tipped red or reddish brown; star-shaped flowers are borne in summer. *Jovibarba hirta* subsp. *arenaria* has smaller rosettes—usually only about 1 in (25 mm) across, with occasional red tips on the leaves. These plants dislike winter-wet conditions.
ZONES 7–10.

Keckiella antirrhinoides var. antirrhinoides (left)
syn. *Penstemon antirrhinoides*

BUSH SNAPDRAGON, SNAP-
DRAGON KECKIELLA, YELLOW
PENSTEMON

This species is a large, well-branched, spreading to erect shrub reaching 5–8 ft (1.5–2.4 m) tall and wider. Leafy clusters of bright, yellow, snap-dragon-like flowers appear from scarlet buds in spring. The bush snapdragon prefers hot locations; it sheds many leaves during the hot dry months. ZONES 9–11.

K

KECKIELLA

This is a small group of 7 species of shrubs formerly in the genus *Penstemon*. Keckiellas are grown for their brightly colored, tubular flowers which attract birds. Found mostly in the California chaparral community, they also are native to Arizona and Baja, Mexico.

CULTIVATION
All keckiellas need well-drained soils and part-shade to full sun. Only occasional watering is required in summer. Shrubby keckiellas tend to become scraggly and require pruning to promote compact growth. Propagation is from seed or cuttings.

Keckiella corymbosa (below)
syn. *Penstemon corymbosa*
RED-FLOWERED ROCK PENSTEMON

Summertime clusters of tubular, wide-mouthed, scarlet flowers grace this sprawling, much-branched shrub, which grows up to 18 in (45 cm) tall and wider. Native to rocky slopes in northwest and central western California, it tolerates abundant winter rains when planted in well-drained soils; it is an excellent rock garden plant. ZONES 8–11.

K

KIRENGESHOMA

This aristocrat from the cool forests of Japan and Korea is represented by only one species, although the Korean form which differs little from the Japanese one is sometimes accorded species status. An upright perennial, it has arching, usually black stems with large, lobed, soft green leaves and flowers in summer.

CULTIVATION

This fully frost-hardy perennial suits cool to cold areas in part-shade. It also requires a moist, humus-rich, lime-free soil and complements plants such as hostas and rodgersias. Propagation is from seed or by careful division in autumn or spring.

Kirengeshoma palmata *(above)*
YELLOW WAXBELLS

This unusual perennial thrives in cool, moist conditions. In late summer to autumn, it bears sprays of pale yellow, narrow, shuttle-cock-shaped flowers on arching stems 3 ft (1 m) high, forming a clump about the same distance across. ZONES 5–10.

KNAUTIA

Consisting of 60 species of annuals and perennials, this genus is found extensively throughout temperate Eurasia, from the Mediterranean to Siberia. Their flowers are very like the related *Scabiosa,* but few are ornamental enough to be grown in gardens except for the 2 described here. These have a rosette of basal leaves through which the flower stems grow; these are branched and support some leaves.

CULTIVATION

Occurring in meadows, hedgerows and open woodland, these frost-hardy plants prefer sun or part-shade. Although often found growing in limy soil in their natural habitat, they will grow happily in any well-drained loam, but require staking. Propagate from seed in autumn or by basal cuttings in spring.

Knautia macedonica (right)

A showy species from the central Balkans to Romania, this makes an attractive subject for herbaceous borders. Erect branched stems to 30 in (75 cm) come from basal rosettes of lyre-shaped foliage. The flowers are usually deep purple-red, and occasionally pale pink or white. The darker shades are the best. ZONES 6–10.

K

KNIPHOFIA
RED-HOT POKER, TORCH LILY, TRITOMA

This genus of 68 species of stately perennials, some of which are evergreen, are native to southern and eastern Africa. They are upright, tufted plants with long leaves. In summer, they carry showy, brightly colored, tubular flowers in dense spikes on tall bare stems; some cultivars flower in winter and early spring. Originally the flowers were mostly flame colored (the common name, red-hot poker, dates from the days of coal fires), but due to the work of German plant breeder Max Leichtlin (1831–1910) and others, the flowers can also be pink, orange or yellow. They range from head-high to miniature types, which grow to 24 in (60 cm) or less, and are attractive to nectar-feeding birds.

CULTIVATION
Frost hardy to somewhat frost tender, they require an open position in full sun, well-drained soil and plenty of water in summer. In areas with winter temperatures below 5°F (−15°C), they can be carefully lifted and stored indoors to be planted again in spring, although heavy mulching is preferable. They will tolerate wind and coastal conditions. From spring onwards, fertilize monthly. Remove dead flower stems and leaves in late autumn. Propagate species from seed or by division in spring; cultivars by division in spring.

Kniphofia 'Atlanta'
(below)

One of many fine hybrids and selected forms, 'Atlanta' grows to 4 ft (1.2 m) tall. It has gray-green leaves and orange-red flowers fading to lemon yellow. ZONES 7–10.

Kniphofia caulescens (right)

This majestic, frost-hardy evergreen grows on mountainsides up to altitudes of 10,000 ft (3,000 m). The 12 in (30 cm) rust-colored stems are topped with cream to coral pink flowers that fade to yellow; these appear from late summer to mid-autumn. The narrow leaves are blue green. It reaches 4 ft (1.2 m) in height. ZONES 7–10.

Kniphofia ensifolia
(below right)
WINTER POKER

This moderately frost-hardy evergreen perennial forms a dense clump, growing to 5 ft (1.5 m) tall with a spread of 24 in (60 cm). It has slender, sword-shaped, mid-green leaves and bears torches of prolific, lemon-yellow flowers in late autumn and winter. ZONES 8–10.

Kniphofia 'Cobra'
(far right)

'Cobra' is a compact form with relatively short-stemmed, pale orange flowers that age to cream. ZONES 7–10.

K

Kniphofia 'Erecta'
(below)

'Erecta' is an unusual
deciduous form with orange-
red flowers that point
upwards when open. It
grows to 3 ft (1 m) and
flowers from late summer to
mid-autumn. ZONES 7–10.

Kniphofia 'John Benary' *(above)*
'John Benary' grows to 5 ft (1.5 m)
tall and has loose spikes of deep
scarlet flowers. ZONES 7–10.

Kniphofia 'Gold Crest' *(right)*
This cultivar forms a clump of bright
green, grassy foliage with fine-
stemmed, somewhat loose flowerheads that open orange and age to
bright yellow. ZONES 8–10.

Kniphofia 'Little Maid' *(right)*

'Little Maid' is a dwarf form that reaches a height of 24 in (60 cm). It has buff-tinted, soft yellow flowers opening from pale green buds. ZONES 7–10.

Kniphofia × *praecox* *(below)*
RED-HOT POKER

This South African perennial is the most common species in the wild and reaches up to 5 ft (1.5 m) tall when in bloom. Its slender leaves, up to 24 in (60 cm) long, are heavily keeled and serrated. Vivid red or yellow flowers appear in early summer. It is able to survive long dry periods and enjoys full sun. ZONES 7–10.

K

Kniphofia 'Lemon Green' *(left)*

Yellow green in bud, the flowers of this form open soft yellow and become brighter with age. ZONES 8–10.

Kniphofia 'Royal Standard' *(below)*

This upright perennial reaches 4 ft (1.2 m) in height with a spread of 24 in (60 cm). Moderately frost hardy, it has grass-like leaves and bears terminal spikes of scarlet buds, which open to lemon-yellow flowers in late summer. In cold areas, use a winter mulch to protect the crowns. ZONES 7–10.

K

Kniphofia 'Star of Baden-Baden' *(above)*

Forming large clumps with age, this cultivar has 5 ft (1.5 m) flower stems with flowerheads that are mainly bright orange-red except for the oldest flowers, which fade to yellow. ZONES 7–10.

Kniphofia tuckii (right)

This species closely resembles *Kniphofia ensifolia*, the winter poker, with its heads of greenish white flowers from reddish buds. However, it is not as tall, reaching only 4 ft (1.2 m) in height. ZONES 7–10.

Kniphofia 'Underway' (above)

'Underway' has slightly blue-green foliage with small flowerheads that open rusty orange and fade to buff yellow. ZONES 8–10.

Kniphofia triangularis (right)
syns *Kniphofia galpinii* of gardens, *K. macowanii*, *K. nelsonii*

This poker from South Africa grows to about 3 ft (1 m) tall and is usually deciduous. Its flowers are a rich orange, yellowing slightly with age. This species has probably contributed the coral shade to the gene pool of hybrids. ZONES 7–10.

K

Kniphofia uvaria var. *maxima* *(left)*

K

Kniphofia uvaria

This tall perennial, the source of many hybrids, grows to 4 ft (1.2 m) high and 18 in (45 cm) wide. It has thick, strongly channeled leaves. In late summer and autumn, it bears dense racemes of tubular scarlet flowers becoming orange-yellow with age. It is fully frost hardy. ***Kniphofia uvaria* var. *maxima*** is slightly larger, reaching 6 ft (1.8 m) in height. It also has larger, rich orange-red flowers which fade slightly with age.
ZONES 5–10.

Kniphofia 'Yellow Hammer' *(below)*

This pale yellow *Kniphofia* hybrid, one of the best of the shorter-growing plants, raises its 3 ft (1 m) flower stems in summer. The flowers are excellent for cutting.
ZONES 7–10.

KOHLERIA

This attractive genus of the African violet family consists of about 50 species of rhizome-forming perennials or subshrubs from tropical regions of the Americas. Their tubular flowers are usually felty, pendulous, single or in clusters, in an outrageous array of gaudy colors. The entire plant, including the flowers, is covered in bristles.

CULTIVATION

These plants are tropical and frost tender; in all but tropical climates they are treated as plants for heated greenhouses or as indoor plants. In the tropics, give them a moist shaded site in which to grow. Water sparingly in winter. Propagation is by division of clumping species in spring or soft cuttings from shrubby types.

Kohleria eriantha
(below)

This robust, shrubby perennial, to 4 ft (1.2 m) or more tall, has a rhizomatous root system. Its foliage is avate to lance shaped and up to 5 in (12 cm) long. In summer, it produces brilliant orange to orange-red pendulous trumpets, either singly or in clusters of 3 to 4. ZONES 10–11.

K

LAMIUM
syns *Galeobdolon, Lamiastrum*
DEADNETTLE

This genus of over 50 species of annuals and rhizomatous perennials, native to Europe, Asia and North Africa, belongs to the mint family, not the nettle family as the common name would seem to indicate. They include some common weeds and hedgerow plants and a few that are cultivated for ornament. Some have astringent properties and have been used in folk medicine, or have been grown as pot herbs in parts of Europe. Some are an important source of nectar for bees. They have leaves with toothed margins, arranged in opposite pairs and sometimes splashed with paler gray-green or white. Short spikes or axillary whorls of white, yellow, pink or purple, 2-lipped flowers are produced. The upper lip curves over in a helmet-like shape.

CULTIVATION
Lamiums are frost hardy and grow well in most soils. Flower color determines planting season and light requirement. White- and purple-flowered species are planted in spring and prefer full sun; the yellow-flowered ones are planted in autumn and prefer shade. They often have invasive habits and need plenty of room. Propagate from seed or by division in early spring.

L

Lamium album
(below left)
WHITE DEADNETTLE,
ARCHANGEL

Ranging right across Europe and northern Asia, this species has foliage that superficially resembles that of the common nettle *(Urtica urens)*. An erect perennial of 12–24 in (30–60 cm) high, it produces whorls of pure white flowers from late spring to early autumn. It became known as archangel because it flowers around the 8th of May, the feast day of the Archangel Michael in the old calendar. It is sometimes known to flower in mid-winter. ZONES 4–10.

Lamium galeobdolon

syns *Galeobdolon luteum, G. argentatum, Lamiastrum galeobdolon*

YELLOW ARCHANGEL

This perennial species from Europe and western Asia spreads both by rhizomes and surface runners to form extensive, loose mats of foliage usually about 12 in (30 cm) deep, spreading over moist, shady areas beneath trees. Its leaves are variably splashed with silvery gray and in summer it bears leafy spikes of bright yellow flowers each about $^3/_4$ in (18 mm) long. **'Florentinum'** has leaves splashed with silver that become purple-tinged in winter. **'Hermann's Pride'** is densely mat forming and has narrow leaves streaked and spotted with silver. ZONES 6–10.

Lamium galeobdolon
'Hermann's Pride'
(above)

Lamium garganicum *(below)*

The specific name refers to the Garganian Promontory which extends into the Adriatic from Italy, whence this species extends eastward to Turkey and Iraq. It is a mound-forming perennial up to 18 in (45 cm) tall with toothed, heart-shaped leaves and produces pink, red, purple or, rarely, white flowers in early summer. ZONES 6–10.

L

L

Lamium maculatum
'Roseum' *(above)*

Lamium maculatum
'Golden Anniversary'
(left)

Lamium maculatum
'White Nancy'
(below left)

Lamium maculatum
'Beacon's Silver' *(below)*

Lamium maculatum
SPOTTED DEADNETTLE

Its wild forms often regarded almost as weeds, this semi-evergreen perennial is native to Europe and western Asia. It is also naturalized in North America. A variable species, it may have erect stems to 24 in (60 cm) tall, or have a lower, more spreading habit. The strongly toothed leaves have a central blotch or stripe of pale silvery green, and leafy whorled spikes of very pale pink to deep rose flowers appear in spring and summer. The cultivars are more desirable garden plants, mostly with a compact, mat-forming habit and not more than 6 in (15 cm) high. **'Beacon's Silver'** has purplish flowers with silvery green leaves edged dark green; **'Golden Anniversary'** has leaves with bright golden-yellow edges and a splash of silver in the center; **'Pink Pewter'** has silvery leaves that highlight the beautiful pink flowers; **'Roseum'** has silver-striped foliage and pinkish lilac flowers; and **'White Nancy'** has silvery green leaves and white flowers.
ZONES 4–10.

LATHRAEA

The name of this genus comes from the Greek *lathraios*, meaning hidden, because most of the plant is underground. In fact the 7 species of this Eurasian genus are parasites, lacking chlorophyll of their own and attaching to the roots of trees and shrubs. The fleshy, ivory to mauve leaves are borne in 4 rows on subterranean rhizomes; the interesting fleshy flowers are borne on stems arising from the rhizome and, together with the capsular fruits that succeed them, are the only parts of the plant normally visible.

CULTIVATION

These frost-hardy plants can sometimes be induced to grow in a woodland setting if the right host genera are present. Scatter seed among the tree roots in shade, in moist but well-drained soil with a mulch of leaves in autumn.

Lathraea clandestina (below)
PURPLE TOOTHWORT
This parasitic plant from southwestern Europe bears dense clusters of showy purplish flowers with hooded apices just 2 in (5 cm) above the soil. The scale-like leaves are kidney-shaped and white. The host trees for this species are poplars, willows and alders. ZONES 6–10.

L

Lathyrus nervosus
(below right)
syn. *Lathyrus*
magellanicus of gardens
This perennial climber
from temperate South
America can grow to a
height of 10 ft (3 m)
and has conspicuously
veined, leathery leaves.
The racemes of fragrant,
purplish blue flowers
are borne in summer.
ZONES 8–10.

Lathyrus vernus
'Cyaneus' *(below)*

LATHYRUS

Closely allied to the garden peas *(Pisum)* and vetches *(Vicia)*, this genus of 150 or so species of annuals and perennials are mainly tendril climbers, and some of them are edible. They are native mainly to temperate northern hemisphere regions, but with a significant number also in Andean South America. The leaves are pinnate with the uppermost pair of leaflets usually modified into tendrils. The pea-shaped flowers come in a wide range of colors, from red, mauve and white to blue and even pale yellow. Flat seed pods follow the flowers. *Lathyrus odoratus*, the sweet pea, has a proud place in the history of science: it was one of the chief plants used by Gregor Mendel (1822–84) in his hybridizing experiments that laid the foundations for the science of genetics.

CULTIVATION

These frost-hardy plants need fertile, well-drained soil and full sun. Stake or train on wires and deadhead regularly. Propagate annuals from seed in early summer or early autumn, and perennials from seed in autumn or by division in spring. They may be affected by mildew and botrytis.

Lathyrus vernus
SPRING VETCH

This 24 in (60 cm) high European and west Asian perennial pea is an excellent rockery or bright woodland plant. It doesn't really climb, but instead scrambles over the ground and any low vegetation. The flowers, which open from late winter and continue well into spring, are purple-red when first open, passing through mauve to blue-green as they age. **'Cyaneus'** is a cultivar with purplish blue flowers. ZONES 4–10.

L

Lathyrus odoratus
(right)

SWEET PEA

Native to Italy, the wild form has been much improved by gardeners. It is a vigorous, climbing annual, grown for its abundant, sweetly scented flowers. The 1¹/₂ in (35 mm) wide flowers, in colors of white, cream, pink, blue, mauve, lavender, maroon and scarlet, bloom several to the stem from late winter to early summer and make excellent cut flowers. The plant grows to 6 ft (1.8 m) or more in height, although there are dwarf, non-climbing cultivars available. The climbers will need a good support, such as wire netting or lattice, and are ideal for covering sunny walls or fences. Over many years of development, sweet peas have become less scented and mixed color seedling strains, for example **'Carnival'**, tended to predominate. With the resurgence of interest in cottage gardens, breeders mainly in the UK and New Zealand, have developed a range of very fragrant cultivars in single colors. These include **'Apricot Sprite'**, deep apricot fading with age; **'Bandaid'**, with pale pink flowers; **'Elegance'**, with pure

white flowers; **'Esther Ranson'**, with mauve flowers; **'Felicity Kendall'**, with deep purplish pink flowers; **'Hampton Court'**, with purple to mauve flowers; **'Katherine'**, with bright red-pink flowers; **'Kiri Te Kanawa'**, with pinkish purple flowers; and **'Lucy'**, with apricot-pink flowers. The **Knee-hi Group,** although a little taller than the name suggests, to around 24–30 in (60–75 cm) high, is a bushy strain that flowers heavily in colors from white through red to blue. Cultivars in the **Supersnoop Group** have no tendrils and may be grown as bushes rather than as climbers. ZONES 4–10.

Lathyrus odoratus cultivar *(right)*

Lathyrus odoratus 'Hampton Court' *(below)*

L

LAVATERA

Closely related to the mallows and holly-hocks, this genus of 25 species of annuals, biennials, perennials and softwooded shrubs has a scattered, patchy distribution around temperate regions of the world, mostly in Mediterranean or similar climates. Some of them favor seashores. A few species are cultivated for their colorful mallow flowers, generally produced over a long season. These plants are upright in habit with simple to palmately lobed leaves, often downy to the touch. The shrubs and perennials in this genus are not very long-lived.

CULTIVATION

Moderately to very frost-hardy, these plants prefer a sunny site in any well-drained soil. Prune after a flush of blooms to encourage branching and more flowers. Propagate annuals, biennials and perennials in spring or early autumn from seed sown *in situ* (cuttings do not strike well), and shrubs from cuttings in early spring or summer.

Lavatera trimestris
ANNUAL MALLOW

This shrubby annual, native to the Mediterranean, is grown mainly for its silken, trumpet-shaped, brilliant white or pink flowers. The flowers are 3 in (8 cm) wide and appear from summer to early autumn. They are short lived but are borne in profusion, benefiting from regular deadheading. The annual mallow has an erect, branching habit and is moderately fast growing to a height of 24 in (60 cm) and a spread of 18 in (45 cm). '**Mont Blanc**' (syn. *Lavatera* 'Mont Blanc') has pure white flowers; '**Silver Cup**' has lovely dark pink flowers. ZONES 8–11.

Lavatera trimestris 'Mont Blanc' *(above)*

Lavatera trimestris 'Silver Cup' *(left)*

Leontopodium ochroleucum var. campestre *(left)*
syn. *Leontopodium palibinianum*

This species from Asia is a loosely tufted perennial growing 6–15 in (15–38 cm) tall. It has attractive yellowish, nearly white bracts that almost enclose the inconspicuous disc florets. ZONES 4–9.

LEONTOPODIUM

EDELWEISS

Occurring wild in the mountains of Europe and temperate Asia, this genus consists of about 35 species of short-lived, downy perennials in the daisy family. Their distinctive feature is the flowerheads, with a central disc of rather inconspicuous cream florets surrounded by a ring of overlapping, pointed bracts of unequal length and coated with sparse to dense white wool. The simple, lance-shaped leaves are also covered with white hairs, which protect the plant from cold and from intense ultraviolet sunlight. They are suitable for rock gardens in cool to cold climates.

CULTIVATION

Plant in full sun or part-shade (in hot climates) in gritty, well-drained soil. They are very frost hardy but need shelter from winter rain. Propagate from fresh seed or by division in spring.

Leontopodium alpinum *(below)*

Much loved by the Swiss, the European edelweiss is often regarded as a symbol of the Alps. It reaches a height and spread of around 8 in (20 cm). Each silvery white flowerhead is 2–3 in (5–8 cm) across, the bracts so thickly felted they look like strips of flannel. It blooms in spring or early summer. ZONES 5–9.

L

Leucanthemum vulgare *(above)*
syn. *Chrysanthemum leucanthemum*
OX-EYE DAISY, MOON DAISY

This native of Europe and temperate Asia is like a
small version of the Shasta daisy, though the
pretty white flowerheads, borne in early summer,
are no more than 2 in (5 cm) in diameter.
A clump-forming perennial up to 30 in (75 cm)
tall, it is freely self-seeding and has become
abundantly naturalized in parts of North America,
Australia and New Zealand. ZONES 3–10.

LEUCANTHEMUM

There are about 25 species of annuals or
perennials in this genus from Europe and
temperate Asia. They were previously
included in *Chrysanthemum* by many
botanists, though some botanists always
treated them as a distinct genus. They are
clump-forming plants with variably toothed
or lobed leaves that are neither grayish
hairy nor aromatic, unlike those of other
chrysanthemum relatives. Long-stalked,
daisy-like flowerheads arise from leafy
stems, with white or yellow ray florets and
yellow disc florets. While mostly vigorous,
adaptable plants, some do not do well in
warmer climates.

CULTIVATION

Largely undemanding, these plants grow
well in a perennial border or garden bed in
full sun or morning shade in moderately
fertile, moist but well-drained soil.
Propagate from seed, cuttings or by
division.

*Leucanthemum
paludosum*
syn. *Chrysanthemum
paludosum*

This southern European
annual grows to 6 in
(15 cm) in height. It
has pale yellow or
white-tinged yellow
flowers. **'Show Star'** has
bright yellow flowers
and wavy edged leaves.
ZONES 7–11.

*Leucanthemum
paludosum* 'Show Star'
(left)

Leucanthemum × *superbum* *(below)*
syns *Chrysanthemum maximum* of gardens, *C.* × *superbum*

SHASTA DAISY

Growing to a height and spread of 2–3 ft (60–90 cm), this robust perennial has large, daisy-like, white flowerheads with pale golden centers. These may be 3 in (8 cm) across and are carried high above the dark, shiny, toothed leaves in summer and early autumn. The Shasta daisies were once thought to be *Leucanthemum maximum,* a native of the Pyrenees, but are now believed to be hybrids between that species and the Portuguese *L. lacustre.* They were first noticed naturalized on the slopes of Mount Shasta in Washington State, USA and attracted the attention of the famous plant breeder Luther Burbank. There are now many cultivars, always white-flowered, but including doubles as well as singles, some

with fringed petals. **'Aglaia'** grows to 12 in (30 cm) tall and is noted for its semi-double flowers that last through summer; **'Esther Read'** grows to 3 ft (1 m) tall with a profusion of semi-double flowers; **'Wirral Pride'** reaches 30 in (75 cm) in height with double white flowerheads; and **'Wirral Supreme'** is noted for its anemone-centered double flowers. **'Tinkerbell'** and **'Snow Lady'** are low-growing forms with single flowers. ZONES 5–10.

Leucanthemum × *superbum* cultivar *(above right)*

Leucanthemum × *superbum* 'Wirral Pride' *(right)*

Leucanthemum × *superbum* 'Tinkerbell' *(right)*

Lewisia columbiana (left)

Named after the Columbia River region from whence it originates, this evergreen species forms a clump of narrow, fleshy basal leaves. The foliage clump is around 6 in (15 cm) high with an 8 in (20 cm) spread and in summer it produces heads of pink-veined white to pale pink flowers on 12 in (30 cm) stems. ZONES 5–9.

Lewisia 'Ben Chase'
(left)

LEWISIA
BITTER ROOT

This genus, which honors the explorer Meriwether Lewis (1774–1838), contains about 20 species of small perennials with deep tap roots, leathery leaves and starry flowers, all native to the Rocky Mountains of the USA. The roots are endowed with wonderful powers of survival: Lewis returned to civilization in 1806 and it is said that a botanist in London, studying his dried plant specimens nearly 5 years later, found that one was trying to grow. He planted it and it duly revived, and the following summer bore its beautiful pink flowers. Hybrid lewisias such as 'Ben Chase', flower over a long period in summer in a range of colors—pink, white, apricot, red or flame.

CULTIVATION
Give them a cool climate, full sun or part-shade in warm climates and excellent drainage, so there will be no chance of winter-wet rotting the roots. Propagate herbaceous species from seed in spring or autumn, and evergreen species from seed in spring or offsets in summer.

Lewisia tweedyi
(right)

Growing to 8 in (20 cm) tall and 12 in (30 cm) wide, this evergreen species has succulent stems, small fleshy leaves and pale to peach-pink open-faced flowers from spring to summer. ZONES 5–9.

Lewisia cotyledon 'Pinkie' *(below)*
Lewisia cotyledon var. *howellii* *(bottom right)*

Lewisia cotyledon
(below)

This evergreen, which hybridizes readily, has rosettes of fleshy, toothed leaves and bears clusters of white to yellow, apricot and pink to purple flowers on upright stems. It grows to a height of 12 in (30 cm). *Lewisia cotyledon* var. *howellii* spreads to 6 in (15 cm). '**Pinkie**', with pink flowers grows 1 in (25 mm) tall and 2 in (5 cm) wide.
ZONES 6–10.

LIATRIS
BLAZING STAR

These 40 species of perennials come from the central and eastern regions of North America. In summer they sprout tall, cylindrical spikes of fluffy flowers from a knobby rootstock that remains visible during the rest of the year. They belong to the daisy or composite family, but their spike-like inflorescences, crowded with small flowerheads opening from the top downward, are so unlike those of other daisies that it is hard to recognize their affinity.

CULTIVATION
These plants will grow in most soils and conditions including damp places such as stream banks and ditches. However, they do best in climates with low humidity. They thrive with minimum care and attention, making excellent border plants. Propagation is from seed or by division of old clumps in winter.

Liatris punctata
(below)
SNAKEROOT

Ranging from eastern Canada to New Mexico, this species reaches nearly 3 ft (1 m) in height and has purple, occasionally white, flowers in autumn. Flowering is prolonged by cutting and the stems make an attractive indoor display. They perform best in fertile, well-drained soil.
ZONES 3–10.

Liatris spicata *(right)*
syn. *Liatris callilepis* of gardens
GAY FEATHER, SPIKE GAY FEATHER

This low-growing species is a desirable cut flower and good for attracting bees or butterflies. The flowers are lilac-purple, although they can occur in pink and white. They are produced in crowded, fluffy spikes—like a feather duster—in late summer, and open from the top downwards, which is the opposite of most flower spikes. It grows to a height of 24 in (60 cm), with thickened, corm-like rootstocks and basal tufts of grassy, mid-green foliage. **'Floristan'** is a seedling strain growing to 5 ft (1.5 m) tall, and is available in 2 colors: deep violet (**'Floristan Violett'**) and white (**'Floristan Weiss'**). **'Kobold'** is a dwarf cultivar reaching 15 in (38 cm) and producing bright purple flowers. ZONES 3–10.

Liatris spicata
'Floristan Violett' *(left)*

Liatris spicata 'Kobold'
(below)

L

Libertia peregrinans (left)

This New Zealand species is remarkable for its long, branching rhizomes that send up sparse tufts of narrow, strongly veined leaves at intervals. These turn a striking orange-brown shade in autumn and winter. It reaches 30 in (75 cm) in height and has a yellowish bronze-green flowering stem with white flowers with orange-brown anthers. ZONES 8–10.

LIBERTIA

These 20 species of perennials in the iris family have tufts of grass-like leaves springing from rhizomes that may be very short or long creeping. They are found on both sides of the Pacific Ocean in New Zealand, Australia, New Guinea and the Andes of South and Central America. They grow easily in a temperate climate, producing erect, wiry stems bearing clusters of small, white, iris-like flowers in spring and summer.

CULTIVATION

Moderately frost hardy, they require a sheltered, sunny or part-shaded position and well-drained, peaty soil with plenty of moisture in spring and summer. Propagate by division in spring, or from seed in spring or autumn. Some species naturalize freely.

LIGULARIA

There are at least 150 species of perennials in this genus, which is closely related to *Senecio,* found mainly in temperate eastern Asia, though a smaller number occur in northern Asia and Europe. Many species are large-leaved, clump-forming plants that produce tall spires of daisy-like flower-heads, mostly in shades of yellow or orange. The cultivated ligularias are stately plants and vigorous growers, adapted to moist, sheltered sites such as stream banks and woodland glades. They flower mainly in summer and early autumn. The spring foliage is almost as ornamental as the summer blooms.

CULTIVATION

Quite frost hardy, they prefer moist, well-drained soil in either sun or part-shade. Propagate by division in spring or from seed in spring or autumn. They are prone to attack by slugs and snails.

Ligularia dentata *(above)*
syns *Ligularia clivorum, Senecio clivorum*

This compact species from China and Japan is grown for its striking foliage and showy flower-heads. It grows to a height of 4 ft (1.2 m) and a spread of 3 ft (1 m). It has kidney-shaped, long-stalked, leathery, brownish green leaves and bears clusters of large, 3 in (8 cm) wide, orange-yellow flowerheads on long branching stems in summer. It will grow happily at the edge of ponds. Cultivars worth growing are **'Othello'** and **'Desdemona'**, which has green leaves heavily overlaid with bronze and maroon. **'Gregynog Gold'** has round green leaves and orange flowers. ZONES 4–9.

Ligularia stenocephala *(right)*

This species from Japan, China and Taiwan grows to 5 ft (1.5 m). It has dark purple stems and slender racemes of yellow flowers in summer. The leaves are triangular and toothed. ZONES 5–10.

LIMONIUM

STATICE, SEA LAVENDER

This genus of around 150 species scattered around the world's temperate regions mostly in saline coastal and desert environments, with major concentrations in the Mediterranean, central Asia and the Canary Islands. They include evergreen and deciduous subshrubs, perennials, biennials and annuals. Some of the latter are grown as border plants and are popular for their many-colored heads of small papery flowers, which can be cut and dried for decoration. The flowers should be cut just as they open and hung upside down to dry in a cool, airy place. The tapered, almost stalkless leaves appear in basal rosettes.

CULTIVATION

Statices are easily grown in full sun and well-drained, sandy soil. Their tolerance to sea spray and low rainfall make them a good choice for seaside and low-maintenance holiday-house gardens. Plants will benefit from light fertilizing in spring, while the flowerheads are developing. Propagate by division in spring, from seed in early spring or autumn or from root cuttings in late winter. Transplant during winter or early spring.

Limonium perezii
(below)

Limonium perezii comes from the Canary Islands and is a species of more or less shrubby habit with glossy leaves. The leafless flower stems bear many small flowers, whose insignificant white petals make less impact in the garden than the long-lasting, deep mauve-blue calyces. It grows about 24 in (60 cm) tall and flowers in summer. ZONES 9–11.

L

Limonium sinuatum, Petite Bouquet Series cultivar *(below)*

Limonium latifolium *(above)*
syn. *Limonium platyphyllum*

From eastern Europe, this tall-stemmed perennial bears clusters of lavender-blue or white flowers over summer. Clump forming and large leafed, it grows 24 in (60 cm) tall and spreads 18 in (45 cm). The dried flower stems have a delicate appearance. ZONES 5–10.

Limonium gmelinii *(above)*

This robust perennial from eastern Europe and Siberia grows to 24 in (60 cm) tall in any deep, well-drained soil in full sun. It has leaves in spikelets and lilac tubular flowers. ZONES 4–10.

Limonium sinuatum
syn. *Statice sinuata*

This Mediterranean species is a bushy, upright perennial almost always grown as an annual. It produces dense rosettes of oblong, deeply waved leaves and bears masses of tiny papery flowers on winged stems. It flowers in summer and early autumn and is fairly slow growing, reaching a height of 18 in (45 cm) with a spread of 12 in (30 cm). One of the most popular cut flowers, seedling strains are available in a rainbow of colors. The **Petite Bouquet Series** are dwarf plants to 12 in (30 cm) in height and with golden or lemon yellow, white, cream, salmon-pink, purple or blue spikelets. ZONES 9–10.

Limonium minutum *(above)*

This spreading perennial from southern Europe reaches 4 in (10 cm) tall and is suited to rockeries. It has tiny rosettes of leaves and lilac flowers. ZONES 8–10.

Linaria alpina *(left)*

This trailing perennial from Europe grows to about 3 in (8 cm) in height with a 6 in (15 cm) spread. It has violet, yellow, white or pink flowers and narrow blue-gray leaves. ZONES 4–10.

L

LINARIA
EGGS AND BACON, TOADFLAX

Native mainly to the Mediterranean region and western Europe, these 100 species of adaptable annuals, biennials and perennials are related to snapdragons and have naturalized in many places. They grow to 18 in (45 cm) with masses of tiny snapdragon-like blooms in many colors. The erect stems have stalkless, usually gray-green leaves. They are ideally suited to rock gardens, borders and cottage gardens.

CULTIVATION

They require rich, well-drained, preferably sandy soil, moderate water and full sun. Seed sown directly in autumn or very early spring will germinate in 2 weeks. Seedlings need to be thinned to a 6 in (15 cm) spacing and weeded to ensure there is no over-shadowing. Cutting back after the first flush will produce more flowers.

Linaria vulgaris
(above)

A 3 ft (1 m) tall perennial that occurs wild in the Mediterranean and much of Europe, this species has reddish brown stems, numerous pale blue-green leaves and yellow flowers appearing in summer and autumn. It can be grown from seed and will self-seed. It has traditional uses as a medicinal herb. ZONES 4–10.

Linaria purpurea
'Canon J. Went' *(right)*

Linaria purpurea
(below)

PURPLE TOADFLAX

This perennial from
Europe is naturalized in
some areas and grows
to 3 ft (1 m). It bears
violet-tinged purple
flowers in summer.
'Canon J. Went' is a tall
cultivar of the species
with tiny pale pink
flowers. **ZONES 6–10.**

L

LINDERNIA

A genus of annuals and perennials from most warmer parts of the world, *Lindernia* consists of about 50 species. Related to the snapdragons and toadflaxes, they have colorful flowers on erect racemes or arising singly from leaf axils, and fruits that are narrow capsules.

CULTIVATION
They grow well in moist soil, some liking almost boggy situations, in full sun. Propagate from fresh seed.

Lindernia americana (below)
This species from North America has bright green, rounded, fleshy leaves. Long-tubed, violet-like flowers are borne in the leaf axils and open from spring. **ZONES 9–11.**

LINDHEIMERA
STAR DAISY

This genus consists of a single species of annual from the limestone soils of Texas, USA. It grows to just over 24 in (60 cm) tall, and has yellow flowers suitable for cutting and bright green, bract-like leaves that obscure the seed heads.

CULTIVATION
Grow this plant in moderately fertile, well-drained soil in full sun. Propagate from seed sown direct.

Lindheimera texana *(above)*

This frost-hardy annual is grown for its dainty, daisy-like yellow flowers, borne in late summer and early autumn. It is moderately fast growing, with hairy stems and pointed to oval, serrated, hairy fresh green leaves. Of an erect, branching habit, it grows from 12–24 in (30–60 cm) in height with a spread of 12 in (30 cm). ZONES 6–10.

L

Linum doerfleri (above)

LINUM
FLAX

This genus contains 200 species of annuals, biennials, perennials, subshrubs and shrubs, some of which are evergreen, and are distributed widely in temperate regions. It includes the commercial flax, *Linum usitatissimum,* grown for fiber and oilseed. Several ornamental species are valued for their profusely blooming, 5-petalled flowers, which can be yellow, white, blue, red or pink. They are useful plants in a rock garden or border. *Linum doerfleri* is a yellow-flowered species.

CULTIVATION

They are mostly quite frost hardy, although some need shelter in cool climates. Grow in a sunny spot in humus-rich, well-drained, peaty soil. After perennial species flower, prune them back hard. Propagate the annuals, biennials and perennials from seed in autumn and perennials by division in spring or autumn. Most self-sow readily. Transplant from late autumn until early spring.

Linum capitatum
(above)

This European rhizo-matous perennial grows to about 18 in (45 cm) high. When in flower, it forms a basal clump of foliage from which emerge leafy flower stems bearing heads of 5 or more flowers. ZONES 7–10.

Linum campanulatum
(left)

This small southern European perennial is reminiscent of some of the oxalises or of California poppy (Esch-scholzia californica). It has small, slightly glaucous leaves and during summer produces small, 3- to 5-flowered heads of yellow to orange flowers. ZONES 7–10.

Linum flavum
GOLDEN FLAX, YELLOW FLAX

A 12–24 in (30–60 cm) tall, somewhat woody perennial with a strongly erect habit, this southern European species has dark green, pointed or blunt-ended leaves about 1 in (25 mm) long. The golden yellow, trumpet-shaped flowers, many to each stem, appear in summer. **'Compactum'** is a dwarf variety growing just 6–8 in (15–20 cm) tall. ZONES 5–10.

Linum flavum
'Compactum' *(above)*

Linum narbonense
(right)

A perennial native of the Mediterranean region, this is the most handsome of all the blue flaxes. It has violet, funnel-shaped flowers borne on slender stems, which last for many weeks in summer. It has soft, green leaves and forms clumps 18 in (45 cm) high and wide. ZONES 5–10.

Linum perenne subsp.
lewisii *(left)*

L

Linum perenne
(above & left)
syn. *Linum sibiricum*

Of wide occurrence in
Europe and temperate
Asia, this is a vigorous,
upright perennial that
forms a shapely, bushy
plant 24 in (60 cm)
high with a spread of
12 in (30 cm). It has
slender stems with
grass-like leaves and
clusters of open, funnel-
shaped, light blue
flowers are borne
throughout summer.
'Alba' is a pure white
form. Prairie flax
(Linum perenne subsp.
lewisii) is a more
compact plant than the
species but has slightly
longer leaves.
ZONES 7–10.

LIRIOPE

This genus contains 5 species of clump-forming, rhizomatous, evergreen perennials native to Vietnam, China, Taiwan and Japan. Some cultivars are so dark in leaf they are practically black, a most unusual color for the designer to play with. They do not creep, and for ground cover have to be planted 6 in (15 cm) apart. *Liriope* flowers range from white through to pale purple.

CULTIVATION

Grow in full sun or part-shade in well-drained soil. In early spring, cut back shabby leaves just before the new ones appear. Propagate from seed in autumn or by division in early spring.

Liriope muscari
(right)
syns *Liriope platyphylla, L. graminifolia*

This clumping, evergreen perennial is a useful ground cover or path edging. It has grass-like, shining, dark green leaves and bears erect spikes of rounded, bell-shaped, violet flowers in late summer. It grows to a height of 12–24 in (30–60 cm) with a spread of 18 in (45 cm). The flower spikes are held just above the foliage. **'Lilac Beauty'** comes from China and Japan and is a larger example of the species. Its leaves are 1 in (25 mm) wide and 12–18 in (30–45 cm) long with stiff lilac flowers rising above the foliage. **'Majestic'** has large violet-blue flowers. **'Variegata'** is the most common of the variegated forms. Its leaf margins are lined with cream, and it has lovely lilac flowers. ZONES 6–10.

Liriope muscari
'Variegata' *(below)*

Liriope muscari
'Lilac Beauty' *(below)*

LITHODORA

This genus of 7 species of dwarf evergreen subshrubby perennials and shrubs from Europe, Turkey and North Africa is well suited to rockeries. Most are known for their 5-lobed, funnel-shaped intense blue flowers, borne over a long season in small sprays at the growth tips. The deep green leaves are hairy.

CULTIVATION

Most species prefer well-drained, alkaline soil; water lightly even in summer. They do well in full sun if grown in not too hot an area. Shearing after flowering will promote a compact habit and encourage dense flowering the following year. Propagate from cuttings of last year's growth and strike in a mix of peat and sand.

Lithodora 'Star'
(below)
syn. *Lithospermum* 'Star'

This shrub grows to 12 in (30 cm) in height and has star-shaped, lilac flowers with a purple stripe down the center of each lobe.
ZONES 7–10.

LOBELIA

This genus of 370 species of annuals, perennials and shrubs is widely distributed in temperate regions, particularly the Americas and Africa. Growth habits vary from low bedding plants to tall herbaceous perennials or shrubs. They are all grown for their ornamental flowers and neat foliage and make excellent edging, flower box, hanging basket and rock garden specimens. Some are suitable in wild gardens or by the side of water.

CULTIVATION

These frost-hardy to somewhat frost-tender plants are best grown in well-drained, moist, light loam enriched with animal manure or compost. Most grow in sun or part-shade but resent wet conditions in winter. Prune after the first flush of flowers to encourage repeat flowering, and fertilize weekly with a liquid manure in this season. Propagate annuals from seed in spring, perennial species from seed or by division in spring or autumn, and perennial cultivars by division only. Transplant from late autumn until early spring.

Lobelia × *speciosa* (right)

This is one of a group of hybrid lobelias derived from the American species *Lobelia cardinalis, L. splendens* and *L. siphilitica,* noted for their tall spikes of flowers that range in color from pink to mauve, red or purple. ZONES 4–10.

Lobelia cardinalis (below)
CARDINAL FLOWER

This clump-forming perennial from eastern North America is useful for growing in wet places and beside streams and ponds. From late summer to mid-autumn it produces spikes of brilliant, scarlet-red flowers on branching stems above green or deep bronze-purple foliage. It grows to a height of 3 ft (1 m) and a spread of 12 in (30 cm). ZONES 3–10.

Lobelia erinus *(left)*
EDGING LOBELIA

This slow-growing, compact annual is native to
South Africa and grows to a height of 4–8 in
(10–20 cm) and spread of 4–6 in (10–15 cm). It
has a tufted, often semi-trailing habit, with dense,
oval to lance-shaped leaves tapering at the base.
It bears small, 2-lipped pinkish purple flowers
continuously from spring to early autumn.
'Cambridge Blue' is a popular hybrid along with
'Colour Cascade', with a mass of blue to violet to
pink and white flowers. **'Crystal Palace'** is a very
small variety with dense foliage, and is smothered
in deep violet-blue flowers. **'Tim Riece'** is pale
violet-blue. ZONES 7–11.

Lobelia erinus
'Tim Riece' *(left)*

Lobelia erinus
'Crystal Palace' *(below)*

Lobelia × gerardii *(right)*

This hybrid between the North American species
Lobelia cardinalis and *L. siphilitica* is a robust
perennial that can grow as tall as 5 ft (1.5 m). It
has pink, violet or purple flowers and makes a
beautiful garden specimen. **'Vedrariensis'**, its
best-known cultivar, produces racemes of violet-
blue flowers in late summer. Its leaves are dark
green and lance-shaped. These hybrids prefer to
grow in moist but well-drained soil in full sun.
ZONES 7–10.

Lobelia tupa *(below)*

This vigorous, upright perennial from Chile is a
rather coarse plant with large, light gray-green
leaves and grows to about 6 ft (1.8 m) in height. In
late summer and autumn the stems terminate in
striking many-flowered erect racemes of tubular,
2-lipped flowers in shades from scarlet to deep,
dull scarlet. ZONES 8–10.

Lobelia splendens *(above)*
syn. *Lobelia fulgens*
SCARLET LOBELIA

Native to southern USA and Mexico, *Lobelia
splendens* bears tubular, 2-lipped, scarlet flowers in
one-sided racemes in late summer. It has lance-
shaped, mid-green leaves that are sometimes
flushed red, and grows 3 ft (1 m) tall. ZONES 8–10.

L

Lobularia maritima
syn. *Alyssum maritimum*
SWEET ALYSSUM, SWEET ALICE

This fast-growing, spreading annual is a popular edging, rock garden or window box plant. It produces masses of tiny, honey-scented, 4-petalled white flowers over a long season, from spring to early autumn. Lilac, pink and violet shades are also available. It has a low, rounded, compact habit with lance-shaped, grayish green leaves, and grows to a height of 3–12 in (8–30 cm) and a spread of 8–12 in (20–30 cm). **'Violet Queen'** is the darkest of the garden varieties. ZONES 7–10.

Lobularia maritima cultivars *(left & below left)*

Lobularia maritima 'Violet Queen' *(below)*

LOBULARIA

This genus consists of 5 species of frost-hardy, dwarf plants from the Mediterranean and the Canary Islands. They are useful for rockeries, window boxes and borders. Although there are both annual and perennial forms, the annuals are most commonly grown. They bear tiny, 4-petalled, fragrant flowers in compact, terminal racemes in summer and early autumn.

CULTIVATION
Grow in full sun in fertile, well-drained soil. Continuous flowering can be encouraged by regular deadheading. Propagate from seed in spring or, if outdoors, from late spring to autumn.

Lotus berthelotii (right)
CORAL GEM, PARROT'S BEAK, PELICAN'S BEAK

Native to the Cape Verde and Canary Islands, this semi-evergreen, trailing perennial is suitable for hanging baskets, ground cover or for spilling over rockeries, banks or the tops of walls. It has hairy, silvery branches of fine needle leaves, and clusters of 1 in (25 mm), pea-like, orange to scarlet flowers that cover the plant in spring and early summer. It grows to 8 in (20 cm) tall with an indefinite spread. Frost tender, it suits warm coastal gardens. Tip prune young shoots to encourage dense foliage. **ZONES 10–11.**

Lotus maculatus
(left)

This trailing perennial from the Canary Islands grows to 8 in (20 cm) high and has silver needle-like leaves and claw-like tawny yellow flowers. It also has trailing, cascading fruit. **'Gold Flame'** has golden yellow to orange flowers. **ZONES 10–11.**

LOTUS

This legume genus of 150 species from temperate regions worldwide includes summer-flowering annuals, short-lived perennials and deciduous, semi-evergreen and evergreen subshrubs. They are grown for their foliage and pea-like flowers, which come in a range of colors. They should not be confused with the aquatic plants (*Nelumbo* and *Nymphaea*) commonly known as lotus.

CULTIVATION
Fully frost hardy to frost tender, they prefer moderately fertile, well-drained soil in full sun. Propagate from cuttings in early summer or from seed in autumn or spring.

Lotus maculatus
'Gold Flame' *(above)*

LUNARIA
HONESTY

Allied to stocks *(Matthiola)*, the origin of the common name for this genus of 3 species of annuals, biennials and perennials is uncertain. It could be from the way the silver lining of the seed pods is concealed in the brown husk like a silver coin, the reward of virtue that does not flaunt itself. Sprays of honesty have been popular as dried flower arrangements since the eighteenth century.

CULTIVATION
Plant in full sun or part-shade in fertile, moist but well-drained soil. Propagate perennials from seed or by division in autumn or spring, biennials from seed. They self-seed quite readily.

L

Lunaria rediviva (below)
PERENNIAL HONESTY

This perennial grows to 3 ft (1 m) high with a spread of 12 in (30 cm). It has hairy stems, heart-shaped leaves and pale violet flowers; the fruit are silver pods. ZONES 8–10.

Lunaria annua
(left & below left)
syn. *Lunaria biennis*

This fast-growing biennial, native to southern Europe and the Mediterranean coast, is grown for its attractive flowers and curious fruit. It has pointed, oval, serrated, bright green leaves and bears heads of scented, 4-petalled, rosy magenta, white or violet-purple flowers throughout spring and early summer. These are followed by circular seed pods with a silvery, translucent membrane. Erect in habit, it grows to a height of 30 in (75 cm) and a spread of 12 in (30 cm). ZONES 8–10.

LUPINUS
LUPIN, LUPINE

This legume genus of 200 species of annuals, perennials and semi-evergreen and evergreen shrubs and subshrubs, is mainly native to North America, southern Europe and North Africa. They are popular for their ease of culture, rapid growth and long, erect spikes of showy pea-flowers in a range of colors including blue, purple, pink, white, yellow, orange and red. Apart from being ornamentals, they are used for animal fodder, as a 'green manure' crop because of their nitrogen-fixing capacity. A few species are grown for grain, used as food by both humans and livestock. The compound leaves are distinct among legumes in being palmate, with 5 or more leaflets radiating from a common stalk, rather than the usual pinnate arrangement. *Lupinus purpurescens* is a seldom cultivated species, at one time grown for medicinal purposes.

CULTIVATION
Most lupins prefer climates with cool wet winters and long dry summers. They should be planted in full sun and in well-drained, moderately fertile, slightly acidic, sandy soil. They like plenty of water in the growing season and should be mulched in dry areas. Spent flowers should be cut away to prolong plant life and to prevent self-seeding. The foliage adds nitrogen to the soil when dug in. Propagate species from seed in autumn and Russell hybrids from cuttings or by division in early spring. Watch for slugs and snails.

Lupinus hartwegii *(above)*
HAIRY LUPIN

Native to Mexico, this fast-growing annual has a compact, erect growth habit and reaches 30 in (75 cm) in height with a spread of 15 in (38 cm). It has hairy, dark green leaves, and slender spikes of flowers in shades of blue, white or pink are borne abundantly in late winter, spring and early summer. ZONES 7–11.

L

Lupinus purpurescens
(right)

Lupinus, Russell Hybrids

George Russell was a gardener fond of growing lupins, and over the years selected the best seedlings from open-pollinated plants of *Lupinus polyphyllus*. Around 1937, a colorful selection of his perennial lupins was released and rapidly became popular, known as 'Russell lupins'. It is thought that they are hybrids, the other major parent being the annual *L. hartwegii*. This fine strain of strong-growing lupins bears long spikes of large, strongly colored flowers in cream, pink, orange, blue or violet, some varieties bicolored, in late spring and summer. They produce a magnificent clump of deeply divided, mid-green leaves, growing to a height of 3 ft (1 m). **'Blue Jacket'** has dark blue-purple flowers; **'Noble Maiden'**, one of the Band of Nobles series, has cream flowers; **'Polar Princess'** has white flowers; and the blooms of **'Troop the Colour'** are bright red. There are also dwarf strains, such as the 24 in (60 cm) high **'Lulu'**. ZONES 3–9.

Lupinus 'Troop the Colour' *(above)*

Lupinus 'Noble Maiden' *(below)*

Lupinus 'Polar Princess' *(right)*

Lupinus 'Blue Jacket'
(above)

Lupinus texensis
(right)
TEXAS BLUE BONNET

A bushy annual reaching a height of 12 in (30 cm), this species has bright green leaves divided into 5 small leaflets that are hairy on the undersides, and bears dark blue and white flowers in late spring. Easily grown, it thrives in poor soil and is quick to flower from seed. This is the state flower of Texas, beyond which it does not occur wild. **ZONES 8–10.**

L

LYCHNIS
CAMPION, CATCHFLY

Native to temperate regions of the northern hemisphere, these 15 to 20 species of biennials and perennials include some that have been cultivated for many centuries. They are grown for their summer flowers that range in color from white through pinks and oranges to deep red. All have flat 5-petalled flowers, but in many species the petals are notched or deeply forked or sometimes divided into narrow teeth. The genus is related to *Silene,* and the boundary between the 2 genera has shifted with varying botanical opinion.

CULTIVATION

They are frost hardy and easily grown in cool climates, preferably in sunny sites and in any well-drained soil. The higher mountain species do best in soil that is protected from being excessively warmed by the sun. Remove spent stems after flowering and deadhead frequently to prolong the flowering period. Propagate by division or from seed in autumn or early spring. Some species self-seed readily.

Lychnis chalcedonica (below)
MALTESE CROSS

This perennial species from far eastern Europe has been a favorite with gardeners since the seventeenth century. Its color is such a dazzling orange-red that its garden companions should be chosen with care. It flowers for a rather short season in early summer, grows about 4 ft (1.2 m) tall, and takes its common name from the shape of the flower. White and pink varieties and one with double flowers exist, but these are fairly rare. ZONES 4–10.

Lychnis × arkwrightii 'Vesuvius' (left)
syn. *Lychnis × haageana* 'Vesuvius'

This hybrid is probably a cross between *Lychnis fulgens* and *L. sieboldii* and is a singularly striking perennial in all respects. Often short-lived, it is nonetheless worth growing for its deep bronze green foliage and its large, vivid orange flowers. It reaches around 24 in (60 cm) high and blooms from mid-summer. It is a spectacular plant to contrast against light green foliage and pale flowers. ZONES 6–10.

Lychnis coronaria (below)
ROSE CAMPION, DUSTY MILLER, MULLEIN PINK

This clump-forming perennial, sometimes grown as a biennial, is a striking plant that grows to a height of 30 in (75 cm) and a spread of 18 in (45 cm). It forms a dense clump of silvery white, downy leaves and many-branched gray stems that carry large, deep rose-pink to scarlet flowers throughout summer. **'Alba'** is a white-flowered cultivar. In ancient times the flowers were used for garlands and crowns. It is drought tolerant, requires little or no cultivation or watering, and often self-seeds. **ZONES 4–10.**

Lychnis coronaria 'Alba'
(above)

Lychnis viscaria
GERMAN CATCHFLY

This perennial is widely distributed through Europe and western Asia. Growing to 18 in (45 cm) tall and with a similar spread, it is a densely clumping plant with bronze stems and narrow dark green leaves with sticky hairs. It produces spike-like panicles of mauve to magenta flowers in early summer. **'Splendens Plena'** (syn. 'Flore Pleno') has larger, bright magenta double flowers. **ZONES 4–9.**

Lychnis flos-jovis
(below)

FLOWER OF JOVE, FLOWER OF JUPITER

This perennial species from the Alps grows to a height of 18 in (45 cm). It has tufts of ground-hugging leaves, from the midst of which the flower stems arise to carry the blooms in clusters in summer. The leaves are gray and downy and the flowers are bright pink. **ZONES 5–9.**

Lychnis viscaria
'Splendens Plena' *(right)*

Lycopodium phletmaria (left)
LAYERED TASSEL FERN

This elegant species is widely distributed in rainforests of tropical Asia and the South Pacific. It features small, shiny, lacquered leaves that line the long, pendent stems in 4 rows. In this and many related species the ends of the stems branch into groups of fine, elongated strobili-like green tassels, earning this group the name tassel ferns. They form large clumps of hanging stems that look good in baskets. **ZONES 11–12.**

L

LYCOPODIUM
CLUBMOSS

Widespread throughout most moister regions of the world, the 100 or more species in this genus are an ancient group of plants whose larger ancestors, along with those of the horsetails *(Equisetum)*, dominated the world's vegetation around 250 million years ago. Considered more primitive than the ferns but more advanced than the mosses, they range from tiny thread-stemmed plants that grow in boggy ground below heath, to large epiphytes that form curtains of ferny foliage on the limbs of tropical rainforest trees. All share similar cord-like stems clothed with overlapping, bright green or golden-green scale-like leaves. Club mosses do not flower but instead bear tiny spore capsules between the scales of delicate small cones (strobili).

CULTIVATION
Only the epiphytic species are cultivated to any extent, mainly by fern enthusiasts. Outdoors in the tropics they prefer part-shade and a permanently moist niche in the fork of a tree. Elsewhere they require a greenhouse or conservatory maintained at high humidity, and can make dramatic specimens in hanging baskets. Hang in positions with some air movement; they are sensitive to excess water around the roots. Propagate from cuttings or by layering fertile stem tips.

LYSICHITON
syn. *Lysichitum*
SKUNK CABBAGE

This unusual genus of the arum family is composed of 2 species of rhizomatous perennials, one from northeastern Asia, the other from western North America. They flower in spring as or before the new foliage develops. The stout-stemmed, pointed, heart-shaped leaves are quite large, sometimes as much as 4 ft (1.2 m) long when fully expanded. The spathes, white or yellow depending on the species, are around 15 in (38 cm) long and partially enclose the flower spike (spadix). The flowers have a musky smell that is nowhere near as bad as the common name suggests.

CULTIVATION
Skunk cabbages are frost-hardy plants suited only to cool climates. They normally grow in damp or boggy ground and are best positioned at the edges of ponds or streams. Propagate from seed or by division.

Lysichiton americanus *(left)*
YELLOW SKUNK CABBAGE

This species ranges in the wild from coastal Alaska to northern California and east to Montana. It has large butter-yellow spathes that appear in mid-spring before the leaves, though still present when the leaves have expanded, making a dramatic contrast. It grows to a height of around 3 ft (1 m). ZONES 5–9.

Lysichiton camtschatcensis *(right)*
WHITE SKUNK CABBAGE

As the name suggests, this species occurs on the Kamchatka Peninsula of far eastern Siberia, but its range includes other nearby parts of Siberia and northern Japan. The name skunk cabbage is not at all apt for this species, as its pure white spathes are odorless or even slightly sweet-scented. They appear before the leaves in early spring and stand about 24 in (60 cm) high. The conspicuously veined leaves are up to 3 ft (1 m) long. ZONES 5–9.

LYSIMACHIA
LOOSESTRIFE

Ranging through temperate and subtropical regions of the northern hemisphere, this genus of mainly evergreen perennials and shrubs of the primula family consists of around 150 species, of which about 130 are found in China. There are also a few species in Africa, Australia and South America. They vary greatly in growth habit from low, creeping plants to stately clumps with tall, spike-like racemes of crowded flowers. The 5-petalled flowers are mostly yellow or white, less commonly pink or purple. The botanical name is Latinized Greek for 'ending strife' and the English common name is a version of the same, though why these plants deserve such a name is now unclear.

CULTIVATION
They prefer slightly acidic soil with a good mix of organic matter and medium to moist conditions in sun or part-shade. Some species are marsh plants that grow best at the edge of a pond or stream. Propagate from seed or cuttings, or by division.

Lysimachia clethroides (below)
JAPANESE LOOSESTRIFE

This somewhat hairy perennial from China, Korea and Japan grows to 3 ft (1 m) high making a broad, leafy clump of erect stems. In summer it produces tapering terminal spikes, gracefully nodding in bud but becoming erect with maturity, of crowded starry white flowers. ZONES 4–10.

Lysimachia congestiflora (left)

A spreading perennial ground cover sometimes treated as an annual, this species roots at the nodes as it spreads and eventually covers an area over 3 ft (1 m) wide. A native of the damp meadows and streamsides of China and nearby parts of the Himalayan region, Thailand and Vietnam, it is prized for its bright golden yellow flowers, which are produced in globular terminal clusters in late summer. Where it occurs naturally it is used in herbal medicines to treat fractures, bruises and strains. ZONES 7–10.

Lysimachia ephemerum (right)

A native of south-western Europe, this handsome summer-flowering perennial has stems up to 3 ft (1 m) tall, rather narrow gray-green leaves and erect, tapering spikes of ¹/₂ in (12 mm) wide, starry white flowers at the stem tips.
ZONES 6–10.

Lysimachia vulgaris (right)
YELLOW LOOSESTRIFE

This perennial is a common wildflower in Europe and western Asia, growing in wet meadows and along streams. It has creeping rhizomes with erect stems that can be 4 ft (1.2 m) or more in height, with broad green leaves in whorls of three or four. The starry golden yellow flowers, about ³/₄ in (18 mm) wide, are borne in loose terminal spikes in summer.
ZONES 5–10.

L

Lysimachia nummularia
CREEPING JENNY, MONEYWORT

Native to much of Europe and also Turkey and the
Caucasus, this vigorous creeping perennial has
become widely naturalized in North America.
Various medicinal properties were attributed to it
by herbalists. The prostrate stems take root
wherever they touch damp ground, forming a
dense, rapidly spreading mat usually no more than
3 in (8 cm) deep. The deep yellow bowl-shaped
flowers are up to 1 in (25 mm) wide, borne singly
on short stalks from the leaf axils over a long
summer period. **'Aurea'**, golden creeping Jenny, is a
popular cultivar with pale yellow-green leaves and
stems; when grown in shade it turns an interesting
lime green. Both green and gold forms are useful
ground cover plants for moist or even boggy soil
and can tolerate occasional light foot traffic.
ZONES 4–10.

Lysimachia
nummularia 'Aurea'
(left)

Lysimachia punctata
(above & below left)
GOLDEN LOOSESTRIFE, GARDEN
LOOSESTRIFE

A vigorous clump-
forming perennial, this
species is native to
central and southern
Europe and Turkey. It
grows erect to a height
of 3 ft (1 m) with broad
mid-green leaves in
whorls of 4, grading into
floral bracts on the
upper stems which carry
in summer a massed
display of brilliant
yellow starry flowers,
each about 1 in (25 mm)
across. Golden loose-
strife looks best planted
in large groups. It is
suitable for bedding,
large rock gardens, or
pool and streamside
plantings. ZONES 5–10.

LYTHRUM
LOOSESTRIFE

This genus of annuals, perennials and subshrubs shares the common name 'loosestrife' with *Lysimachia*, though the 2 genera are quite unrelated; however, the long, erect flower spikes of some *Lythrum* species and their boggy habitats are like those of some lysimachias. There are around 35 species, scattered through all continents except South America. They vary from small creeping plants with stems rooting in the mud of ditches, to plants 6 ft (1.8 m) or more tall with showy spikes of pink to purple flowers.

CULTIVATION
These plants will grow in most soil conditions as long as moisture is adequate, and in bogs and other wetlands some species can be quite invasive. Propagation is very easy from seed or by division.

Lythrum virgatum
(below left)

This species extends in the wild from central Europe through central Asia as far as northern China. It is a handsome, vigorous perennial growing to as much as 6 ft (1.8 m) tall, with pretty pinkish red flowers arranged rather loosely in erect spikes. Like the similar *Lythrum salicaria*, it has become a weed in North America. ZONES 4–10.

Lythrum salicaria *(right)*
PURPLE LOOSESTRIFE

This perennial always grows in wet ground, often spreading into the shallow water at the edges of ponds. Erect stems arise from a knotty rhizome 3–6 ft (1–1.8 m) tall depending on soil moisture and fertility. It produces showy long spikes of pink to magenta flowers from mid-summer to autumn. In some areas it is detested as a weed, displacing native wildflowers. Purple loosestrife was used in folk medicine for centuries: its tannins have coagulent properties, hence staunching the flow of blood, and it was also used to treat cholera. There are a number of garden forms, with flowers in the deep rose red to deep pink range, some double-flowered. **'Feuerkerze'** ('Firecandle') is a cultivar with more reddish flowers. ZONES 3–10.

MALVA
MALLOW

This genus is made up of 30 species of annuals, biennials and perennials that originate in Europe, North Africa and Asia, but have in some cases naturalized elsewhere. The flowers are similar to but smaller than the popular *Lavatera* to which the malvas are related; they are single, 5-petalled flowers in shades of white, pink, blue or purple. Although they may not be quite as showy as those of *Lavatera*, they do make attractive subjects for the border or wild garden.

CULTIVATION

These plants flourish in sunny, well-drained aspects and tend to be more robust and longer lived in not too rich soil. They are fully frost hardy. Cut plants back after the first flowers have faded. Propagate from cuttings or seed in spring; the perennials often self-seed. Watch for rust disease in spring.

Malva moschata
MUSK MALLOW

Useful for naturalizing in a wild garden or odd corner, this perennial has narrow, lobed, divided leaves with a sticky, hairy texture which emit a musky, cheesy odor when crushed. A native of Europe, *Malva moschata* bears profuse spikes of saucer-shaped pink flowers in summer. '**Alba**', a white cultivar, is also very popular. It has a bushy, branching habit and can grow to a height of 3 ft (1 m). ZONES 3–10.

Malva moschata 'Alba'
(left)

MARANTA

This is a genus of 32 species of evergreen rhizomatous perennials from the tropical forests of Central and South America. Apart from the beautifully marked and textured leaves, they are known for their habit of 'going to sleep' at night. The leaves spread by day and stand erect at night. One species, *Maranta arundinacea*, is an important crop plant: it is better known to cooks as arrowroot.

CULTIVATION

Marantas are usually grown in greenhouses or as indoor plants. They like humidity and bright light without direct sunlight. In tropical areas, they make a good ground cover under large trees. Propagation is usually done by dividing established clumps or from basal cuttings struck on bottom heat.

Maranta leuconeura
PRAYER PLANT, TEN COMMANDMENTS

This variable species contains most of the best foliage forms of this genus. It usually grows to about 12 in (30 cm) in height and spread, and produces its inconspicuous white flowers with foliate spots in slender spikes during summer. The dark green leaves are usually about 6 in (15 cm) long. They have silver to pink veins and the reverse side can be purple or gray-green. In the cultivar **'Erythroneura'**, the herringbone plant, the leaves are velvety and very dark black-green with a brilliant green irregular zone along the midrib. It also has bright pink veins and a deep red reverse. **'Kerchoviana'**, known as rabbit tracks, has oval, light green leaves with green to brown blotches on either side of the central vein. Its insignificant white to mauve flowers appear intermittently. ZONES 11–12.

Maranta leuconeura 'Kerchoviana' *(below)*

M

MARRUBIUM

HOREHOUND

This genus of around 40 species of aromatic perennial herbs is found in temperate regions of Europe and Asia, often by the roadside and in wastelands. *Marrubium* is a member of the mint family and characteristically has square branching stems and opposite pairs of toothed, ovate leaves with soft hairs and conspicuous veining. The whorls of small flowers are borne in the leaf axils. The botanical name is believed to have evolved from *marob*, a Hebrew word meaning a bitter juice, as this was one of the bitter herbs eaten by Jews to commemorate the feast of Passover.

CULTIVATION

These fully frost-hardy plants prefer full sun in poor, well-drained soil. Although trouble free, avoid planting them in an over-rich soil and protect from drying winds. Propagate by root division in mid-spring or from seed in late spring.

M

Marrubium kotschyi (below)
syn. *Marrubium astracanicum*

This native of Iraq and Kurdistan grows up to 15 in (38 cm) in height. It has elliptic-toothed leaves and whorls of reddish purple flowers are produced in summer. ZONES 7–10.

Marrubium supinum (left)

A native of mountainous regions in central and southern Spain, this species grows to 18 in (45 cm) in height and has kidney-shaped, toothed leaves and pink or lilac flowers in summer. ZONES 7–10.

MATRICARIA

This extensively revised genus of aromatic annual herbs consists of 5 species, native to the temperate regions of the northern hemisphere. They have finely dissected leaves with numerous linear segments and produce terminal, white daisy-like flower-heads from spring to late summer. They can be grown in a rockery, herb garden or as a border edging. Some species produce good cut flowers and *Matricaria* recutita is valued for its herbal use.

CULTIVATION

These fully frost-hardy plants prefer well-drained, light sandy soil in full sun. Propagate from seed in summer.

Matricaria recutita

(below)
syn. *Matricaria chamomilla*
GERMAN CHAMOMILE

This is an aromatic annual with stems to 24 in (60 cm) and finely divided, light green leaves. It has white daisy-like flowers with golden centers. The flowers appear in summer and autumn. The fully opened flowers can be harvested and dried. This species is used in a similar fashion to *Chamaeleum nobile,* chamomile. Use discarded tea flowers on the compost pile to activate decomposition. ZONES 6–10.

M

Matthiola incana
(left)

Best grown as an
annual, this upright,
bushy plant grows up
to 24 in (60 cm) with
a spread of 12 in
(30 cm). Fully frost
hardy, it has lance-
shaped, gray-green
leaves and fragrant,
3–6 in (8–15 cm) long
spikes of flowers in
shades of pink, purple,
red or white, borne in
spring. Many cultivars
are available.
'Mammoth Column'
reaches 30 in (75 cm)
in height, and produces
a single, 12–15 in
(30–38 cm) tall spike of
scented flowers in spring
in mixed or separate
colors. **ZONES 6–10.**

M

MATTHIOLA
STOCK, GILLYFLOWER

This genus contains some 55 species of annuals, biennials and
subshrubby perennials, very few of which are grown in gardens
with the exceptions of the night-scented stock *Matthiola
longipetala* subsp. *bicornis* and the cultivars of *M. incana*. The
species are native to Europe, central and southwestern Asia and
North Africa. The leaves are usually gray-green and the perfumed
flowers can be produced from spring to autumn. They are attractive
both for bedding out and as cut flowers. Unfortunately, stocks are
prone to quite a few pests and diseases, including downy mildew,
club-root, gray mold and cabbage root fly.

CULTIVATION
Matthiola prefer a sunny aspect in moist but well-drained, neutral
or alkaline soil. Shelter from strong winds and stake some of the
larger forms. Propagate from seed sown *in situ* for night-scented
stock, which should be staggered to prolong flowering season,
or in spring sow seed of *M. incana* types into seed trays and move
to beds later.

Meconopsis betonicifolia *(right)*
syn. *Meconopsis baileyi*

BLUE POPPY, TIBETAN POPPY, HIMALAYAN POPPY

This clump-forming woodland species bears sky blue, saucer-shaped, 2–3 in (5–8 cm) wide satiny flowers with yellow stamens in late spring and early summer. The oblong, mid-green leaves are in basal rosettes. It grows 3–5 ft (1–1.5 m) tall and 18 in (45 cm) wide. It does not bloom in the first season, and dies down completely over winter. **ZONES 7–9.**

MECONOPSIS

This genus consists of about 45 species of annuals, biennials and short-lived perennials. They bear large, exotic flowers with papery petals and a bold, central boss of stamens on tall stems. The flower stalks lengthen after flowering as the fruits develop. The hairy leaves are either simple or pinnate.

M

Meconopsis cambrica *(right)*
WELSH POPPY

Native to western Europe and the UK, this species is more easily grown than *Meconopsis betonicifolia.* The slightly hairy, deeply divided, mid-green leaves form basal rosettes. Lemon yellow or rich orange blooms are freely borne from mid-spring to autumn. It has a spreading habit, reaching 12–18 in (30–45 cm) tall and 12 in (30 cm) wide. Though short lived, it self-seeds readily, given the right conditions. **ZONES 6–10.**

CULTIVATION

Mostly frost hardy, they need a moist but not over-wet, lime-free, humus-rich soil and a cool site in part- or full shade with shelter from strong winds. Propagate from seed in late summer.

Meconopsis grandis (left)
HIMALAYAN BLUE POPPY

This stunning rich blue poppy is more solidly perennial than the better known *Meconopsis betonicifolia*. It has rosettes of irregularly toothed, deciduous green leaves with red-brown or rust colored hairs. The brilliant, early summer flowers can be up to 6 in (15 cm) across on stems up to 4 ft (1.2 m) tall. ZONES 5–9.

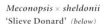

Meconopsis × *sheldonii* 'Slieve Donard' (below)

Meconopsis × sheldonii (above)

These hybrids between *Meconopsis betonicifolia* and *M. grandis* are rosette-forming, hairy perennials with 12 in (30 cm) leaves. They can grow up to 5 ft (1.5 m) tall in good conditions. The blue flowers are borne from late spring to early summer. **'Slieve Donard'** is a vigorous brilliant blue form with long pointed petals, growing to 3 ft (1 m) tall. ZONES 6–9.

Meconopsis pseudointegrifolia (right)

As the name suggests, this species is similar to *Meconopsis integrifolia*. However, it differs in bearing heads of downward-facing blooms at the top of strong stems. The flowers are soft yellow with conspicuous golden stamens and are borne in late spring and early summer. The plant is covered in fine golden brown hairs. ZONES 7–9.

MELISSA
BALM

This genus of 3 species of perennial herbs has representatives from Europe to central Asia. The name *Melissa* is derived from a Greek word meaning bee, owing to the abundance of nectar in the flowers which attracts bees. Borne in opposite pairs on square stems, the crinkled ovate or heart-shaped leaves emit a lemony odor when bruised. Axillary spikes of white or yellowish flowers appear in summer. These quick-growing, decorative foliage plants look good along paths, in herb gardens, among ferns and when grown in pots.

CULTIVATION
Very frost hardy, they prefer full sun or light shade if summers are hot. Slightly moist, well-drained soil is best. Propagate from seed sown in spring. Variegated forms are propagated by root division or from young spring cuttings.

Melissa officinalis
(below)
LEMON BALM, BEE BALM

This perennial to 24 in (60 cm) high is grown for its fresh, lemon-scented and lemon-flavored leaves. Small white flowers appear in late summer and attract pollinating bees into the garden. Lemon balm spreads rapidly, dies down in winter but shoots again in spring. The leaves are valued as a calming herbal tea. They also give a light, lemon flavor to fruit salads, jellies, iced tea and summer drinks, and can be used as a substitute for lemon peel in cooking. ZONES 4–10.

M

MENTHA
MINT

This genus contains 25 species of aromatic, perennial herbs, some evergreen and some semi-evergreen, from Europe, Asia and Africa. Most are cultivated for their fragrance, some for their flavor or ornamental appeal. Several species make attractive ground covers. They vary in size from tiny creeping forms to bushy plants, and vary in flavor from refreshing to very strong.

CULTIVATION

Most are very frost hardy, like sunshine and rich soil and need lots of moisture. They are invasive, spreading rapidly by runners; to keep them under control, try growing them in large pots, watering regularly and repotting annually. Propagate from seed or by root division in spring or autumn.

Mentha arvensis
(below)
CORN MINT, FIELD MINT

This erect hairy perennial reaches up to 24 in (60 cm) in height. It occurs throughout most of Europe on disturbed, often damp ground. The lance-shaped leaves are shallowly toothed. The lilac flowers appear in dense axillary whorls from mid-summer until autumn. This species has the property of being able to prevent milk from curdling and was once cultivated solely for this purpose. ZONES 4–10.

M

Mentha pulegium
(right)

PENNYROYAL, EUROPEAN
PENNYROYAL MINT

A native of Asia and
Europe with small,
elliptical, gray-green,
hairy leaves, this species
has spreading stems
that form a foliage
clump around 4 in
(10 cm) high and 18 in
(45 cm) wide. In sum-
mer and early autumn,
the plant produces
upright spikes with
whorls of white to pale
lilac to soft purple-pink
flowers. Plant in shade
if the soil is inclined to
dry out. Prostrate
dwarf forms grow well
in hanging baskets. It is
renowned for its
curative value in
treating colds, nausea,
headaches, nervous
disorders and various
skin conditions.
ZONES 7–10.

M

Mentha × *piperita* *(above)*
PEPPERMINT

This spreading perennial, grown for its aromatic
foliage and culinary uses, grows to 24 in (60 cm)
high and wide. Using underground stems, it forms
a carpet of oval, toothed, mid-green and reddish
green leaves. Purple flowers appear in spring.
Mentha × *piperita* **f. citrata,** eau de cologne
mint, is too strong and bitter for culinary use but
is grown for its distinctive perfume. ZONES 3–10.

M

MENYANTHES

There is only one species in this genus, with a very wide distribution through Europe, northern Asia, northwestern India and North America. It is an aquatic or marginal water plant with creeping rhizomes to 4 ft (1.2 m) long. This plant has long been used in herbal medicine to relieve gout and fever. The Inuit ground it into a flour and the leaves have been used in Scandinavia to make beer.

CULTIVATION

This plant is fully frost hardy and is happy grown in wet mud in, or on the edge of, water. Propagate from seed sown in wet soil or cuttings of pre-rooted rhizomes in spring.

Menyanthes trifoliata (above)
BOG BEAN

This plant has attractive foliage divided into 3 leaflets of rich green supported by dark-colored stems. The tiny fringed flowers are produced in erect spikes and are white, but pink in bud. This species grows to about 12 in (30 cm) tall and spreads out over a considerable area of water. ZONES 3–10.

Mertensia ciliata
CHIMING BELLS

This species from western USA grows to about 24 in (60 cm) tall. Its leaves are lanceolate and bluish green. The flower stems support nodding, blue, trumpet-shaped flowers, $^1/_3$ in (8 mm) long during summer. **'Blue Drops'** is a selection by the famous British perennial specialist Alan Bloom of Bressingham Gardens. It gives a particularly fine display of bright blue flowers. ZONES 4–10.

Mertensia ciliata
'Blue Drops' *(above)*

MERTENSIA

This genus from northern temperate areas consists of about 50 species of herbaceous perennials. The foliage is usually lanceolate and hairy. They produce terminal panicles of tubular flowers, usually blue, in spring.

CULTIVATION

Some species are small alpines ideal for cool rock gardens; others are taller, making them suitable for most borders and woodland gardens. All species prefer full sun and moisture-retentive soil but in most cases, especially the alpines, sharp drainage is important. All are fully frost hardy. Propagate from seed, although some species can be carefully divided. Check for slugs and snails.

Mertensia pulmonarioides *(above)*
syn. *Mertensia virginica*
VIRGINIA BLUEBELLS

Native to the cooler parts of North America, this perennial is one of the loveliest of all blue spring flowers. It has smooth, oblong, soft blue-green foliage, and bears clusters of rich blue, tubular 1 in (25 mm) long flowers, 20 or more on each stem. It is effective planted with daffodils and polyanthus, and is seen at its best naturalized in woodlands or alongside streams. It grows to a height and spread of around 18 in (45 cm). ZONES 3–9.

M

MEUM
BALDMONEY, SPIGNEL

There is only one species in this genus of the carrot family. It is a clump-forming herbaceous perennial to 24 in (60 cm) tall with attractive foliage and umbels of small white flowers in summer. This plant occurs naturally in western and central Europe.

CULTIVATION

An attractive addition to the perennial border or wild garden, it is simple to grow in any well-drained but moist soil in full sun and does best in temperate to cold climates. It is very frost hardy. Propagate from fresh seed. It will often self-seed if happy.

Meum athamanticum (below)

The pretty soft mid-green basal foliage is the major asset of this plant. In early summer it will start to produce its tiny white or purple-tinged white flowers in small umbels. It spreads to 12 in (30 cm). The foliage is aromatic. ZONES 4–9.

MIMULUS
syn. *Diplacus*
MONKEY FLOWER, MUSK

The 180 or so species of annuals, perennials and shrubs of this genus are characterized by tubular flowers with flared mouths, often curiously spotted and mottled. They have been likened to grinning monkey faces, and come in a large range of colors, including brown, orange, yellow, red, pink and crimson. Mainly native to the cool Pacific coastal areas of Chile and the USA, most species are suited to bog gardens or other moist situations, although some are excellent rock garden plants.

CULTIVATION
Grow these plants in full sun or part-shade in wet or moist soil. Propagate perennials by division in spring and annuals from seed in autumn or early spring.

Mimulus cardinalis *(right)*
CARDINAL MONKEY FLOWER, SCARLET MONKEY FLOWER

From southwestern USA and Mexico, this herbaceous perennial grows at least 3 ft (1 m) tall and 12 in (30 cm) wide. It has sharply toothed, hairy, mid-green leaves and produces racemes of scarlet flowers from summer through to autumn. Found on banks of streams and ponds, it needs a sheltered position as it tends to sprawl if battered by rain and wind. ZONES 7–11.

Mimulus × hybridus Hybrids

These popular hybrids between *Mimulus guttatus* and *M. luteus* blend parental characters in various ways. The funnel-shaped, open-mouthed flowers can be up to 2 in (5 cm) wide and come in red, yellow, cream and white, or mixed variations of these colors, plus red mottling, spotting or freckling. Although reasonably hardy and perennial, they rapidly deteriorate in hot sunlight and become straggly after a few months, and so are treated as annuals. **'Ruiter's Hybrid'** bears orange trumpet-shaped flowers with wavy petal margins. ZONES 6–10.

M

Mimulus × hybridus 'Ruiter's Hybrid' *(below)*

Mimulus luteus
(left)

YELLOW MUSK, GOLDEN
MONKEY FLOWER

A spreading perennial
often grown as an
annual, this plant bears
a profusion of yellow
flowers above mid-
green foliage through-
out summer. It grows
to a height and spread
of 12 in (30 cm). It is
very frost hardy, and
needs part-shade and
moist soil. ZONES 7–10.

M

Mimulus moschatus *(above)*
MONKEY MUSK

This small, creeping, water-loving perennial grows
to a height and spread of 6–12 in (15–30 cm). It
bears pale yellow flowers, lightly dotted with brown,
in summer to autumn. It is very frost hardy. This
plant was once grown for its musk scent, but it has
been mysteriously odorless for many years.
ZONES 7–10.

MIRABILIS
UMBRELLA WORT

This Central and South American genus consists of about 50 species of annuals or herbaceous perennials that make showy garden plants in virtually frost-free climates. Some can become invasive and difficult to eradicate as they can be quite deep rooted. The flowers are often brightly colored and in one case at least are variegated in bold colors like magenta and orange. Most have a pleasant fragrance.

CULTIVATION
In frost-free and dry tropical climates, they are quite easy plants to grow. All that is required is a sunny, well-drained aspect. In colder climates, the tubers of perennial species can be lifted and stored over winter like dahlias. Propagate from seed or by division of the tubers.

Mirabilis jalapa
(above)

MARVEL OF PERU,
FOUR-O'CLOCK FLOWER

This bushy tuberous perennial, native to tropical America, is grown for its fragrant, trumpet-shaped, crimson, pink, white or yellow flowers that open in late afternoon and remain open all night, closing again at dawn. It is good as a pot or bedding plant or as a dwarf hedge. It is summer flowering and grows to around 3 ft (1 m) high with a spread of 24–30 in (60–75 cm).
ZONES 8–11.

MOLTKIA

This genus of 6 species comes from northern Italy to northern
Greece and southwestern Asia. All are perennials or small shrubs
found on rocky, sunny hillsides. They have lance-shaped, hairy,
mid- to dark green leaves. The flowers are usually tubular and
pendulous in shades of blue, purple and occasionally yellow. These
attractive plants can be useful in rock gardens as ground covers or
in the front of perennial borders.

CULTIVATION

They all like full sun and alkaline, well-drained soil, especially in
winter. Some species can be invasive and are best in wilder parts of
the garden. Propagate from seed or cuttings or by layering the
woody species.

M

Moltkia doerfleri
(left)
syn. *Lithospermum
doerfleri*

This is a suckering
herbaceous species to
18 in (45 cm) in height
and spread with
unbranched, erect
stems topped with
drooping clusters of
deep purple flowers
from late spring to
mid-summer. From
Albania, it can be
invasive in gardens and
swamp smaller plants.
ZONES 6–10.

MOLUCCELLA

The origin of this genus name is a puzzle, since none of its 4 species get any closer to the Moluccas than northwestern India, from where they extend to the eastern Mediterranean. They are annuals or short-lived perennials, although it is only the annual species that are usually grown. They are tall, upright, branched plants to 3 ft (1 m) or more with toothed leaves and small white fragrant flowers. It is, however, for the large green calyces that Moluccella species are grown; these are attractive in the garden or as cut flowers, fresh or dried.

CULTIVATION

Marginally frost hardy, these plants prefer full sun and moderately fertile, moist but well-drained soil. Propagate from seed.

Moluccella laevis
(right)
BELLS OF IRELAND,
SHELL FLOWER

This summer-flowering annual, native to Turkey, Syria and the Caucasus, is grown for its flower spikes, surrounded by shell-like, apple green calyces, which are very popular for fresh or dried floral work; the tiny white flowers are insignifi-cant. Its rounded leaves are pale green. This plant is fairly fast growing to a height of 3 ft (1 m) and spread of 12 in (30 cm), and has an erect, branching habit. ZONES 7–10.

M

MONARDA
BERGAMOT, HORSEMINT

This is a genus of 15 species of perennials or annuals from North America with green, sometimes purple-tinged, veined, aromatic leaves. They are much loved by bees and are used for flavoring teas and in potpourris, as well as for their colorful, scented flowers. Plants can be single stemmed or sparsely branching, and bear 2-lipped, tubular flowers from mid-summer to early autumn.

CULTIVATION

They are very frost hardy and are best planted in full sun although some shade is acceptable. They must be well drained, and the annual species do best on sandy soil. The perennials are happy in moist soil and in some climates like a good feed of manure or compost. Annuals are sown directly into their permanent spot, and perennials are usually grown by division of established clumps.

M

Monarda didyma
(left)
BEE BALM, OSWEGO TEA

This plant was used by the Native Americans and early colonists as a herbal tea. With its spidery white, pink or red flowers borne in late summer, it is one of the showiest of the culinary herbs. The young leaves may be used in salads or as a stuffing for roast meat. The species grows 3 ft (1 m) or more tall. 'Aquarius' has deep, purple-lilac flowers with purplish green bracts. 'Cambridge Scarlet' is a vigorous perennial to 3 ft (1 m) with dark green, slightly toothed leaves that when crushed or brushed against emit an exotic, citrus-like scent. 'Croftway Pink' grows to 30 in (75 cm) tall and has rose-pink flowers from mid-summer to early autumn. ZONES 4–10.

Monarda didyma
'Aquarius' *(right)*

Monarda citriodora *(right)*
LEMON MINT

This annual species from central and southern USA and northern Mexico grows to 24 in (60 cm) tall. Its curved tubular flowers are scented and usually white, pink or purplish, and have a hairy mouth. ZONES 5–11.

M

Monarda 'Mahogany' *(right)*

This is a hybrid between *Monarda didyma* and *M. fistulosa*. It is a tall variety that grows to 3 ft (1 m) with handsome wine-red or lilac flowers from midsummer well into autumn. ZONES 4–10.

MONARDELLA

This is a small genus of annuals and perennials from western
North America, some 20 species in all. They are grown for their
highly aromatic foliage, which in some species is used for herbal
teas. The 2-lipped, tubular flowers are formed in terminal clusters
and are most usually red, pink or purple in color.

CULTIVATION

Most like a sunny, sharply drained site and can be attractive in a
rock garden or pot in the alpine house if smaller species are
selected. The taller ones can be used at the front of a dry sunny
border. They have reasonable frost resistance, but do resent
dampness in winter. Propagate from seed or summer cuttings of
perennial species or by division.

Monardella villosa *(above)*
COYOTE MINT

This species is a trailing, woody stemmed,
suckering perennial from California. The flowers
are usually pale pink to rose purple. It can vary in
height from 4 in (10 cm) up to 24 in (60 cm).
ZONES 8–11.

MONOPSIS

This is a genus of 18 species of annuals from tropical and southern Africa that are quite similar to the annual lobelias. They can be used in much the same way in borders of flower beds. The tubular flowers flare at the tips into spreading lobes and are usually in shades of blue or yellow. The tube is split all the way to the base on the top side.

CULTIVATION

They do best in climates with cool summers and prefer full sun or part-shade and well-drained soil of moderate richness. Propagate from seed either planted *in situ* or raised under glass and planted out after frosts are over.

M

Monopsis lutea *(above)*

This spreading, trailing plant has thin wiry stems to 12 in (30 cm) or more long, sometimes taking root from the lower nodes. It has alternate, linear to lance-shaped leaves with toothed margins. In spring and summer, bright yellow flowers are produced towards the ends of the stems. This is a pretty cascading plant for a rock garden or wall. ZONES 10–11.

M

MORINA

This is a small genus of 4 species of prickly, rosette-form perennials that until they flower look for all the world like some species of thistle. The tall flower spikes produce whorls of long tubular curved flowers supported by collars of prickly bracts. These cold-hardy perennials come from mountainous regions of eastern Europe and the Himalayas and make statuesque foliage and flowering plants for the flower border.

CULTIVATION

They prefer full sun and very well-drained soil enriched with compost. Propagate from ripe seed or from root cuttings.

Morina longifolia
(above)
WHORL FLOWER

This is probably the best known species in the genus and grows to 4 ft (1.2 m) or more tall. Its foliage is basal and spiny. The flowers open white and turn deep cerise; after pollination both colors will be seen together. The flowers are supported by bronze-tinged spiny bracts and the calyxes stay ornamental after flowering. **ZONES 6–10.**

MUSA
BANANA, PLANTAIN

Bananas, native to Southeast Asia, are now cultivated throughout the tropics. Since they can ripen in transit, they have become a very familiar fruit in most temperate countries. Nearly all the edible varieties, including red and green fruit, lack seeds entirely. The genus includes several important species, such as *Musa textilis*, which yields strong fiber known as Manila hemp; others are grown for their enormous leaves or colored flowers. The flowers are borne in large spikes, erect or pendulous depending on species, the buds enclosed in large purplish bracts. Female flowers are borne at the base of the spikes, male ones further up. Although they often grow to tree size, they are really giant herbaceous perennials: each 'trunk' is composed of leaf bases and, when the flowering shoot has risen and borne fruit, it dies.

CULTIVATION
Some of the smaller species can be grown as house plants or in greenhouses in temperate climates. Banana crops require fertile, moist soil and full sun. Protect from winds, which will cause new growth to shred. Propagate from ripe seed or by division of clumps.

Musa velutina
(below left & right)

Banana flowers are admired more for their curiosity value than their beauty. This dwarf species grows no higher than 6 ft (1.8 m) with yellow flowers highlighted by red bracts and small, velvety, red, inedible bananas. The fruit unpeel themselves when ripe, hence one common name of self-peeling banana.
ZONES 9–12.

M

MYOSOTIDIUM
CHATHAM ISLAND FORGET-ME-NOT

Though the Chatham Islands lie east of New Zealand, this forget-me-not gives a glimpse of what Antarctic flora might have been like before the continent settled at the South Pole. The scientific name of the only species, *Myosotidium hortensia*, emphasizes the plant's close relationship to the true forget-me-not, *Myosotis*.

CULTIVATION
The instructions that accompanied the plant's introduction to England in 1858 were to give it a cool, rather damp position and mulch it twice a year with rotting fish, a practice that has happily proved unnecessary. Salt tolerant and marginally frost hardy, it requires semi-shade and a humus-rich, moist soil. Propagate by division in spring or from seed in summer or autumn. Once growing well, it should not be disturbed and will naturalize freely.

Myosotidium hortensia (below)

This evergreen, clump-forming perennial is the giant of the forget-me-not family, growing to a height and spread of 24 in (60 cm). It has a basal mound of large, glossy, rich green, pleated leaves, and in spring and summer bears large clusters of bright purple-blue flowers, slightly paler at the edges, on tall flower stems. A white-flowered cultivar is also available. ZONES 9–11.

M

MYOSOTIS

FORGET-ME-NOT

This genus of annuals and perennials includes 34 New Zealand natives among its 50 or so species, but the most commonly cultivated are from the temperate regions of Europe, Asia and the Americas. Their dainty blue (sometimes pink or white) flowers bloom in spring, and most species are useful in rock gardens and borders, or as ground cover under trees and shrubs. The plants fade after flowering. *Myosotis,* from the Greek for 'mouse ear', refers to the pointed leaves. The flowers have long been associated with love and remembrance.

CULTIVATION

Mostly frost hardy, they prefer a semi-shaded setting or a sunny spot protected by larger plants, and fertile, well-drained soil. They are rarely affected by pests or diseases and like fertilizing before the flowering period. Propagate from seed in autumn. Once established, they self-seed freely.

Myosotis sylvatica (center)

GARDEN FORGET-ME-NOT

This European biennial or short-lived perennial is usually grown as an annual for its bright lavender-blue, yellow-eyed flowers in spring and early summer. It forms mounds of fuzzy foliage 18 in (45 cm) tall and 12 in (30 cm) wide, with taller stems uncurling as the flower buds open. There are many named selections, some more compact, some pink or white. **'Blue Ball'** has tiny, deep blue flowers and is good for edging. ZONES 5–10.

Myosotis sylvatica 'Blue Ball' *(below)*

M

Myosotis alpestris (below)

ALPINE FORGET-ME-NOT

This short-lived perennial from Europe (usually grown as an annual or biennial) forms clumps to a height and spread of 4–6 in (10–15 cm). In late spring and early summer, it bears clusters of dainty, bright blue, pink or white flowers with creamy yellow eyes. ZONES 4–10.

MYRIOPHYLLUM
MILFOIL

This genus consists of 45 species, mainly aquatic annuals and perennials with representatives worldwide. They are usually submerged plants rooted in the bottom silt of ponds or slow-moving streams. As their wiry stems elongate they reach the surface, where they float and produce emergent leaves. The submerged leaves are very finely cut, feathery and whorled around the stems, while the emergent leaves are often simple and narrow. Spikes of minute flowers develop in summer, usually at the tips of the emergent stems.

CULTIVATION

Little effort is required in cultivation provided a species appropriate to the climate is chosen. As long as the stems have soil to root in, they should thrive. They prefer sun, but will tolerate part-shade. Hardiness varies with the species. Propagate by breaking off rooted pieces of stem.

Myriophyllum aquaticum (below)
syns *Myriophyllum brasiliense*, *M. proserpinacoides*
PARROT FEATHER, DIAMOND MILFOIL

This perennial species found wild in Australia, New Zealand and South America produces stems up to 6 ft (1.8 m) long often with their tips well up out of the water. The finely dissected foliage appears yellow-green if submerged, blue-green out of the water. Tiny, bright yellow-green flowers appear among the submerged leaves in summer. ZONES 10–12.

M

Myrrhis odorata
(above)

This graceful perennial to 6 ft (1.8 m) high is excellent as a background plant in the herb garden or mixed flower border. It will tolerate shade and can be sited beneath garden trees. It self-seeds readily and the strongest seedlings may be transplanted. ZONES 5–10.

MYRRHIS

SWEET CICELY, MYRRH

This is a genus of only one species, an attractive long-lived perennial in the carrot family, native to southern Europe. It has aromatic, fern-like leaves and fragrant creamy white flowers in flattened heads in early summer, followed by ribbed, shiny brown seeds that have a very brief viability. The leaves and seeds have a sweet aniseed flavor and are cooked with fruit as a sugar substitute. They are also good in raw vegetable juices.

CULTIVATION

Fully frost hardy, they should be grown in part-shade in moist but well-drained, fertile soil. Propagate from fresh seed in autumn or spring or by division in autumn or early spring.

N

NELUMBO
LOTUS

This is a genus of 2 species of deciduous, perennial water plants found in North America, Asia and northern Australia. Lotuses resemble waterlilies, but raise both their leaves and flowers well clear of the muddy water of the ponds and ditches in which they grow, blossoming unsullied. The leaves are waxy and almost circular, while the solitary, fragrant flowers are borne on long stalks. Flowers left on the stem develop into decorative seed pods. When these are dried, they can be used in flower arrangements. Lotus seeds found in Japan, shown by carbon dating to be 2000 years old, have germinated and borne flowers.

CULTIVATION
Frost hardiness varies, some tropical forms of *Nelumbo nucifera* being quite frost tender. They prefer an open, sunny position in 24 in (60 cm) of water. Plant in large pots in heavy loam and submerge. Propagate from seed or by division in spring.

Nelumbo lutea (left)
WATER CHINQUAPIN, AMERICAN LOTUS

This American species, suitable for larger waterscapes, has leaves almost 24 in (60 cm) across emerging 6 ft (1.8 m) or more above the water surface. Pale yellow, 10 in (25 cm) wide summer flowers, held on solitary stalks, are followed by attractive seed heads. ZONES 6–11.

Nelumbo nucifera (left)
SACRED LOTUS, INDIAN LOTUS

The sacred lotus has leaves that emerge 6 ft (1.8 m) or more above the water. The plant spreads to 4 ft (1.2 m) wide. Large, fragrant, pink or white, 10 in (25 cm) wide flowers are borne above large, shield-shaped, pale green leaves. This vigorous plant from Asia and northern Australia grows well in large ponds. Buddha is often depicted in the center of such a lotus. ZONES 8–12.

NEMESIA

This genus of 50-odd species of annuals, perennials and subshrubs comes from South Africa. Their flowering period is short, although if they are cut back hard when flowering slows down they will flower again. The flowers are showy, being trumpet-shaped and 2-lipped, and are borne singly in the upper leaf axils or in terminal racemes. The leaves are opposite and simple.

CULTIVATION

These plants need a protected, sunny position and fertile, well-drained soil. They cannot tolerate very hot, humid climates. Pinch out growing shoots on young plants to ensure a bushy habit. Propagate from seed in early autumn or early spring in cool areas.

Nemesia strumosa *(right)*

This plant is a colorful, fast-growing, bushy annual, popular as a bedding plant. It has lance-shaped, pale green, prominently toothed leaves, and grows to a height of 8–12 in (20–30 cm) and a spread of 10 in (25 cm). Large flowers in yellow, white, red or orange are borne in spring on short terminal racemes. **'Blue Gem'** is a compact cultivar to 8 in (20 cm), with small, clear blue flowers. **'Prince of Orange'** also grows to about 8 in (20 cm), and bears orange flowers with a purple blotch. **'Red and White'** has flowers strikingly bicolored, the upper lip bright red and the lower lip white. ZONES 9–11.

Nemesia caerulea *(below)*
syn. *Nemesia fruticans*

This perennial can grow up to 24 in (60 cm) in height if conditions are to its liking. Becoming slightly woody at the base, it tends to sprawl, branching into erect stems holding small mid-green leaves and terminal heads of soft pink, lavender or blue flowers. **'Elliott's Variety'** is very free-flowering, with bright mauve-blue flowers with a white eye. ZONES 8–10.

Nemesia caerulea
'Elliot's Variety' *(left)*

Nemesia strumosa 'Blue Gem' *(above)*

Nemesia strumosa 'Prince of Orange' *(below)*   *Nemesia strumosa* 'Red and White' *(below)*

Nemophila maculata (right)
FIVE SPOT

Commonly referred to as five spot because each veined, white petal has a prominent deep purple blotch at its tip, this plant grows to 12 in (30 cm) tall. It is used extensively in massed displays as plants hold their profusion of blooms above the ferny foliage over a long period during summer. ZONES 7–11.

Nemophila menziesii (below)
syn. Nemophila insignis
BABY BLUE-EYES

A charming little Californian wildflower, this spreading annual is a useful ground cover under shrubs such as roses, as well as in rock gardens and around edges. It is particularly effective overplanted in a bed with spring bulbs. It bears small, bowl-shaped, sapphire-blue flowers with a well-defined concentric ring of white in the center. It has dainty, serrated foliage, and grows to a height and width of 6–10 in (15–25 cm). These plants dislike heat and transplanting. ZONES 7–11.

NEMOPHILA

This is a group of 11 species of annuals grown for their bright, open, 5-petalled flowers. Originating from western USA, these annuals make good borders and are attractive in window boxes. They produce colorful spring–summer blooms mainly in a range of blues.

CULTIVATION
These quick-growing annuals grow best in full sun or part-shade in friable, moisture-retentive soil. As the foliage is rather soft, provide protection from wind and position plants away from high-traffic pathways. Regular watering will help prolong blooming. Check for aphids. Propagate from seed, which can be sown *in situ* during the autumn months.

N

NEOMARICA

Related to irises, the 15 species in this genus are herbaceous perennials from tropical America and western Africa. The strappy leaves rise from a basal rhizome in fan formation to a height of around 3 ft (1 m). The flowering stems bear masses of short-lived blooms, which have 3 distinct, somewhat flattened outer petals in intense colors. The central segments have interesting markings.

CULTIVATION

They are easily grown plants, but frost tender. Grow in part-shade or full sun in well-drained, humus-rich soil. Water well in summer and ensure the soil does not dry out during the winter months. Propagate by division of the rhizomes, or from seed in spring. Transplant from late autumn until early spring.

Neomarica northiana (below)
WALKING IRIS, APOSTLE PLANT
With long, heavily ribbed leaves up to 24 in (60 cm), this plant from Brazil provides textural interest to warm-climate gardens. Plants flower for a long period during spring and summer, with each stem carrying scented, multi-colored blooms in white, mottled crimson with a violet-blue banding. **ZONES 10–11.**

NEOREGELIA

The 70 or so members of this stemless bromeliad genus vary greatly in size, texture and color. Native to South America, the genus was named after Edward von Regel, Superintendent of the Imperial Botanic Gardens in St Petersburg, Russia. Many species turn a brilliant rose, violet or red color in the center of the rosette when flowering approaches. The flowers may be blue or white and the spined foliage ranges from green to maroon, striped, spotted or marbled. The leaves form a wide funnel-shaped or tube-like rosette, which ranges from 6 in (15 cm) to 5 ft (1.5 m) across.

CULTIVATION

Neoregelias prefer well-drained soil and dislike strong light, but they require some direct light to maintain their color. These plants thrive in a humid atmosphere and are best grown in pots or hanging baskets where they will enjoy good air circulation. Do not allow the center cup to dry out and ensure it stays warm in winter. Propagate from offsets in spring or summer.

Neoregelia carolinae 'Fendleri' *(below)*

N

Neoregelia carolinae *(below right)*
HEART OF FLAME, BLUSHING BROMELIAD

This is the most widely cultivated species of the genus and forms a spreading rosette 15–24 in (38–60 cm) across, composed of light olive green, strap-shaped, saw-toothed leaves. Immediately before flowering, which can be at any time of the year, the youngest inner leaves turn deep red. The cluster of inconspicuous, blue-purple flowers is surrounded by crimson-red bracts. **'Fendleri'** is bright green and has leaves neatly edged with bands of cream. *Neoregelia carolinae* × *concentrica,* an unnamed cross between 2 of the most colorful species, displays the variegation found in some forms of *N. carolinae*, combined with the purple leaf tips of *N. concentrica.* **'Tricolor'** has cream-striped foliage. Its inner leaves turn a rich crimson before producing purple flowers and then the entire plant turns pink. **'Tricolor Perfecta'** is a variety susceptible to cold. ZONES 10–12.

N

Neoregelia carolinae
× *concentrica*
(above)

Neoregelia carolinae
'Tricolor Perfecta'
(above left)

Neoregelia concentrica
'Aztec' *(left)*

Neoregelia concentrica

This Brazilian species has a flat, outstretched funnel-shaped rosette 30–36 in (75–90 cm) across. It has broad, leathery leaves with a center becoming deep purple as the flower buds form. The flowers are blue. **'Aztec'** is possibly of hybrid origin, but shows a strong influence of this species; its leaves are heavily blotched with deep purple. ZONES 10–12.

Neoregelia chlorosticta *(left)*

syn. *Neoregelia sarmentosa* var. *chlorosticta*

This species from Brazil is distinguished by its green-lilac-brown leaf blotching. The flowers are white, opening on short stalks 1 in (25 mm) long. ZONES 10–12.

NEPENTHES

PITCHER PLANT

This genus of nearly 70 species, mainly from Indonesia and tropical Asia, includes some tall climbing perennials, capable of ascending nearly 70 ft (21 m) into any handy tree, but their preference for swampy land means they often have to make do without support. They bear inconspicuous purple or brownish flowers in spikes among the upper leaves; the leaves often terminate in pendulous, colored 'pitchers' with lids strikingly tinted in shades of russet, green or even red and pink. Insects are attracted to them and drown in the liquid held in the pitcher before being absorbed into the plant as food.

CULTIVATION

They require a humid atmosphere, part-shade and moist, fertile soil. Species from tropical lowlands require higher temperatures (minimum winter temperature of 65°F/18°C) than those from the tropical highlands (minimum winter temperature of 50°F/10°C). Propagate from seed in spring or from stem cuttings in spring and summer, although air layering may prove more successful.

Nepenthes
bicalcarata (below)
This native of Borneo has dimorphic pitchers, which means that they occur in two forms. Those found among the climbing stems are predominantly green, bell-shaped or funnel-shaped and around 5 in (12 cm), while those found near the base of the plant are rounded, about 4 in (10 cm) in diameter and may be green, green mottled with red, or red. The lower pitchers also have winged kidney-shaped lids. ZONES 11–12.

N

N

Nepenthes × coccinea *(left)*

A garden crossing of 2 tall perennial climbers, *Nepenthes × coccinea* produces pitchers measuring up to 6 in (15 cm) in length. These are yellow-green in color, mottled with purple-red streaks and blotches. **ZONES 11–12.**

Nepenthes maxima *(right)*

As its name implies, the pitchers on this species are extremely large, often measuring up to 8 in (20 cm) in length. Because this species comes from the high-altitude areas of Indonesia and New Guinea, its temperature requirements are lower than the lowland species. **ZONES 11–12.**

NEPETA

This large genus of more than 200 species of perennial, rarely annual, plants is used extensively in herbaceous borders and for edgings or as ground cover plants. Some species have highly aromatic silver-gray foliage and are naturally compact, while others tend to be taller growing plants and may benefit from staking. Originating from a wide area of Eurasia, North Africa and the mountains of tropical Africa, many species have been extensively hybridized to produce exceptional garden plants.

CULTIVATION

Provide a well-drained soil in a sunny position. Some of the vigorous herbaceous species make good single species ground covers as they have a tendency to overpower less robust plants. However, they can be kept in check by light trimming during the growing season and can be cut back each year to prevent the plants from becoming too straggly. Propagation is by division, from cuttings taken during late spring or from seed.

Nepeta clarkei *(below)*

This species from Pakistan and Kashmir forms large clumps up to 30 in (75 cm) high. The leaves are green and the upright flowering stems hold masses of lilac-blue blooms, each with a white patch on the lower lip. This is a very cold-hardy species. ZONES 3–9.

N

Nepeta cataria
(right)
CATNIP, CATMINT

Catnip is a frost-hardy perennial with branching, upright stems growing up to 3 ft (1 m). It has aromatic, green leaves and whorls of white flowers from late spring through to autumn. Cats are attracted to this plant and will lie in it or play in it and some-times dig it up. A tea made from the leaves is said to be relaxing. ZONES 3–10.

Nepeta racemosa
(below)

syn. *Nepeta mussinii*

Native to the Caucasus region and northern Iran, this species is generally known as *Nepeta mussinii* in gardens, though many plants sold under that name are in fact the hybrid *N. × faassenii*. It is a vigorous perennial up to about 12 in (30 cm) high with gray-green, densely hairy leaves and lavender-blue summer flowers in long racemes. **'Blue Wonder'** is a very free-flowering form of spreading habit with violet-blue flowers; **'Snowflake'** has pure white flowers. ZONES 3–10.

Nepeta racemosa 'Blue Wonder' *(right)*

Nepeta racemosa 'Snowflake' *(left)*

Nepeta nervosa
(right)

This showy species forms a bushy habit to 24 in (60 cm) tall. It has long, narrow, deeply veined leaves and dense spikes of purplish blue flowers, although they can occasionally be yellow in the wilds of its native Kashmir. ZONES 5–9.

Nepeta × faassenii
(right)

CATMINT

This is a bushy, clump-forming perennial, useful for separating strong colors in the shrub or flower border. It is very effective when used with stone, either in walls, paving or rock gardens or as an edging plant. It forms spreading mounds of grayish green leaves that are aromatic when crushed, and the numerous flower stems carry hundreds of small, violet-blue flowers throughout summer. It grows to a height and spread of 18 in (45 cm). Many cultivars are available, including **'Dropmore Blue'**, with upright, tall flower spikes of lavender blue; and **'Six Hills Giant'**, a robust plant growing to around 18 in (45 cm) with gray foliage complemented by tall spikes of lavender-blue blooms that will appear continuously through-out the summer if spent flowers are kept clipped. **'Walker's Blue'** has finer foliage and flowers than the other 2 hybrids. ZONES 3–10.

Nepeta × faassenii
'Dropmore Blue' *(above)*

Nepeta × faassenii
'Six Hills Giant' *(right)*

N

NERTERA

These neat perennial plants, with their prostrate or creeping habit, are native to cool, moist habitats. There are 15 species, all of which form small mats or hummocks of moss-like foliage. It is their bead-like fruits that attract the gardener's interest. Some species make excellent alpine-house plants or they can be used in rock gardens where frosts are only light and infrequent.

CULTIVATION

Nerteras thrive in a cool, sheltered, part-shaded site with gritty, moist but well-drained sandy soil, which can be provided in a sink garden, for example. Water well in summer but keep dryish in winter. Propagate by division or from seed or tip cuttings in spring.

Nertera granadensis (below)
syn. *Nertera depressa*
BEAD PLANT, CORAL MOSS

This carpeting species is grown for the masses of spherical, orange or red, bead-like berries it bears in autumn. It has a prostrate habit, growing to $1/2$ in (12 mm) in height with a spread of 4 in (10 cm), and forms compact cushions of tiny, bright green leaves with extremely small, greenish white flowers in early summer. A variety with purple-tinged foliage is also available. ZONES 8–11.

N

NICOTIANA

FLOWERING TOBACCO

The 67 species of annuals, biennials, perennials and shrubs in this genus from America and Australia include the commercial tobacco plant. Other species are grown for the fragrance of their warm-weather flowers, which usually open at night. The flowers of modern strains remain open all day, but have limited perfume. They are good for cutting, although the plants are sticky to handle.

CULTIVATION

Marginally frost hardy to frost tender, they need full sun or light shade and fertile, moist but well-drained soil. Propagate from seed in early spring. Check carefully for snails and caterpillars.

Nicotiana alata
(right)

syn. *Nicotiana affinis*

A short-lived perennial often grown as an annual, this marginally frost-hardy plant bears clusters of attractive, tubular flowers in white, red or various shades of pink. The flowers open towards evening and fill the garden with scent on warm, still nights. Rosette forming, it has oval leaves and grows to a height of about 3 ft (1 m) with a spread of 12 in (30 cm). It flowers throughout summer and early autumn. **ZONES 7–11.**

Nicotiana langsdorfii *(right)*

This annual species grows to 5 ft (1.5 m) tall and has erect and branching stems that produce masses of fine, tubular lime-green flowers during the summer months. Do not be in a hurry to deadhead the last of the blooms as they may self-seed if conditions are favorable, even though the seeds themselves are extremely small. **ZONES 9–11.**

N

Nicotiana × sanderae

This hybrid is a slow-growing, bushy annual reaching a height of 15 in (38 cm) and spread of 8 in (20 cm). In summer and early autumn, it bears long, trumpet-shaped flowers in shades of white, pink, red, cerise, bright crimson and purple. The flowers stay open during the day and are fragrant in the evening. Many cultivars have been developed from this garden hybrid, including **'Lime Green'**, which has abundant, vivid lime green blooms held over a long summer season. The flowers of **'Falling Star'** range from white to pale pink to deep pink. ZONES 8–11.

Nicotiana × sanderae 'Falling Star'
(above)

Nicotiana sylvestris (left)

This is one of the few summer-flowering annuals that thrive in shade. It is also one of the taller-growing species, with flowers that remain open even in deep shade or on overcast days. It is robust, though tender, and grows to 5 ft (1.5 m) or more, and bears tall, stately flowering stems that arise from a mass of large, bright green lush foliage. The long, tubular, white flowers are particularly fragrant on warm summer evenings, so plant it where the scent can be appreciated. ZONES 8–11.

Nicotiana tabacum (right)
TOBACCO

The flowers of this plant are pretty and offer a pleasant, if faint, perfume. They are rather small, about 1 in (25 mm) wide, and they are borne atop a head-high plant with coarse leaves. The plant is scarcely decorative enough for a flower garden, but the leaves make tobacco. Although different cultivars have been developed for processing into cigarettes, pipe tobacco or cigars, it is the way the leaves are processed that determines their ultimate use. ZONES 8–11.

NIDULARIUM

From the Latin *nidulus,* which means little nest, this genus of bromeliads is characterized by an inflorescence that, in most species, nestles in the rosette. There are 46 species. The flowers vary in color from red to white.

CULTIVATION

These frost-tender plants grow best in moist, rich soil. They prefer warm temperatures in semi-shady to shady positions. Position in an area of bright light for good foliage and color. Water regularly, keeping the rosettes full from spring to the end of summer. Propagate from offsets or seeds.

Nidularium innocentii (below)
syns *Ikaratas innocentii, Regelia innocentii*

The rosette of this stemless bromeliad has a spread up to 24 in (60 cm) across. Its leaves are dark green to reddish brown on the upperside and brown-violet on the underside. White flowers appear on red-brown primary bracts. ZONES 10–12.

N

NIGELLA

Nigellas are a genus of about 15 species of annuals from the Mediterranean region and western Asia. The flowers and ornamental seed pods are attractive and are popular for flower arrangements.

CULTIVATION

Nigella seedlings hate being transplanted, but if seeds are sown where the plants are to grow, and some of the flowers are allowed to go to seed, new plants will come up of their own accord for years. Plant in full sun in fertile, well-drained soil and deadhead to prolong flowering if the seed pods are not needed. Propagate from seed in autumn or spring.

Nigella damascena
(left)
LOVE-IN-A-MIST,
DEVIL-IN-A-BUSH

This fully frost-hardy annual bears spurred, many-petalled, pale to lilac-blue or white flowers in spring and early summer. They are almost hidden by the bright green, feathery foliage, and are followed by rounded, green seed pods that mature to brown. Upright and fast growing, it reaches 24 in (60 cm) in height with a spread of 8 in (20 cm). **'Miss Jekyll'** is a double blue form. ZONES 6–10.

N

Nigella damascena
'Miss Jekyll' *(left)*

NOLANA

Found in Chile, Peru and the Galapagos Islands, this genus consists of 18 species of annuals, perennials and subshrubs. Most are clump forming to semi-trailing and rarely exceed 8 in (20 cm) in height, although they may spread to 18 in (45 cm) or more. The bright green foliage can be slightly succulent, is elliptical and 1–2½ in (2.5–6 cm) long. Long-tubed, bell-shaped flowers, carried singly or in small clusters, develop in the leaf axils near the stem tips. They are up to 1½ in (35 mm) in diameter and appear throughout the growing season. They are generally white to purple with yellow throats.

CULTIVATION

Plant in humus-rich, well-drained soil in sun or part-shade. The semi-trailing types grow well in hanging baskets. Pinch the stem tips back occasionally to keep them bushy. They are only hardy to the lightest frosts. Propagate from seed, layers or tip cuttings.

Nolana paradoxa
(above)

This annual has a dwarf, creeping habit, and is ideal as a colorful ground cover in an open sunny position or for pots and hanging baskets. Low growing, up to 10 in (25 cm) high and 15 in (38 cm) wide, it produces masses of trumpet-shaped, purple-blue flowers, each with a pronounced white throat, over the summer. Many hybrids have evolved: **'Blue Bird'** has flowers in a rich, deep blue shade, again with the white throat.
ZONES 8–11.

NUPHAR
SPATTERDOCK, POND LILY, YELLOW POND LILY

Made up of 25 species of perennial aquatic herbs with creeping rhizomes, these pond lilies from the temperate northern hemisphere have large, floating and submerged leaves. The flowers, usually in yellow or green tones, are held on stalks above the water surface.

CULTIVATION
Requirements are very similar to the hardy species of *Nymphaea* with the additional benefit that they will flower in shade and some are suited to being planted in slow-moving water. They prefer to be planted in pots of rich soil and carefully submerged to around 24 in (60 cm) deep, depending on the species. Propagation is by division and best carried out in spring.

Nuphar lutea (above)
YELLOW POND LILY

This species is native to eastern USA, the West Indies, northern Africa and large tracts of Eurasia. It thrives in deep water and has large orbicular leaves that emerge when the water is shallow or float when planted in deeper ponds. Summer-flowering, deep yellow-orange blooms held just above the surface emit a distinct odor. This is a vigorous species. ZONES 4–11.

Nuphar polysepala (below)
In this species from the USA, the large, round, floating leaves, with their distinct V-shaped lobe, offset the greenish blooms which are tinged with purple-brown. ZONES 4–9.

NYMPHAEA
WATERLILY

This genus of 50 species of deciduous and evergreen perennial aquatic plants with fleshy roots is named after the Greek goddess Nymphe. They are grown for their rounded, floating leaves that are cleft at the base and for their attractive large flowers which come in shades of white and cream, brilliant yellows and oranges, pinks and deep reds, blues and purple. They may be night blooming, depending on species, and sometimes fragrant. The berry-like fruits mature underwater. There are both frost-hardy and tropical varieties.

CULTIVATION

Frost-hardy waterlilies grow in most climates and flower freely throughout summer. Faded foliage should be removed. Divide the tuber-like rhizomes and replant in spring or summer every 3 or 4 years. Tropical waterlilies are all frost tender, and require a very warm, sunny situation. They flower from mid-summer into autumn. In cooler areas, the tubers of tropical waterlilies should be lifted and stored in moist sand over winter. All species need still water and annual fertilizing as they are gross feeders. Propagate from seed or by separating plantlets in spring or early autumn. Check for insects, particularly aphids; goldfish kept in the pool will eat most pests.

N

Nymphaea capensis (right)
CAPE BLUE WATERLILY

This bright blue, fragrant day-opening waterlily from southern and eastern Africa has floating leaves up to 15 in (38 cm) in diameter with acute, overlapping petals. When young, its foliage is spotted with purple below. Some plants cultivated as *Nymphaea capensis* may in fact be *N. caerulea*. ZONES 9–11.

Nymphaea gigantea *(left)*
AUSTRALIAN WATERLILY

This tuberous-rooted plant from the tropical areas of Australia and New Guinea has large leaves, often up to 24 in (60 cm) in diameter. Day-blooming, 12 in (30 cm) flowers range from sky to deeper purple-blue. ZONES 10–12.

Nymphaea, Hardy Hybrid, 'Atropurpurea' *(below)*

Nymphaea, Hardy Hybrid, 'Attraction' *(bottom)*

N

Nymphaea, Hardy Hybrids

These cold-hardy and colorful hybrids have been bred from several European and North American species, principally *Nymphaea alba, N. odorata* and *N. mexicana.* The day-blooming flowers are 3–6 in (8–15 cm) across, mostly in shades of white, yellow, pink or red, set on or just above the surface of the water. **'Atropurpurea'** has reddish purple foliage complementing its dark red, wide-open flowers with golden stamens. **'Attraction'** will grow in quite deep water; its crimson-red flowers with contrasting white sepals deepen to a rich garnet red as they age. **'Aurora'** is smaller, spreading to 30 in (75 cm), and has olive-green leaves blotched with purple; its semi-double flowers are star-shaped, 2 in (5 cm) wide and they turn from cream to yellow, to orange, to blood red as they age. **'Escarboucle'**, with masses of blooms and a long flowering season, has wine-crimson flowers with contrasting golden stamens. **'Formosa'** is a profuse bloomer, producing many large flowers in a soft rosy pink shade on opening, becoming deeper in coloring as the flower ages. **'Gladstoniana'** is generally a very hardy and vigorous plant, its deep red foliage contrasting with very large, pure white flowers that have thick and incurving petals. **'Gonnère'**, once known as **'Snowball'**, is a multi-petalled or double hybrid in pure white with a moderately contained leaf spread. **'James Brydon'** flowers in part-shade, its scented blooms opening pink and ageing to rosy red. **'Lucida'** has large green leaves and attractive deep red flowers with paler outer petals, 5–6 in

(12–15 cm) across; **'Mme Wilfon Gonnère'**
produces 6 in (15 cm) wide flowers in 2 shades
of pink; reddish leaves age to bright green.
'Rose Arey' has dark pink, sweetly fragrant
flowers; leaves are reddish purple ageing to
reddish green. The compact-growing **'Paul
Hariot'**, suited to small and medium ponds, has
foliage streaked maroon and flowers that open
pale peach and darken to rich coppery red with
maturity. Other hybrids include **'Caroliniana
Perfecta'**, **'Colonel Welch'**, **'Colossea'** and
'Helvola'. The compact **Laydeckeri hybrids** are
very free flowering yet produce comparatively
little foliage. Colors range from soft rose pink to
deep pink and rosy
crimson, and they have
a spread of around 24 in
(60 cm). **'Fulgens'** has
star-shaped, semi-
double, crimson to
magenta flowers. The
Marliacea hybrids are
among the most
elegant of all the hardy
waterlilies, raised by
M. Latour-Marliac in
the 1880s. They have
dark green leaves and
star-shaped, semi-
double, soft pink flowers
with golden centers,
which appear in
summer. The large
flowers stand slightly
above the water.
'Albida' is a strong-
growing plant bearing
free-blooming white
flowers. **'Chromatella'**
is a very free-flowering
and reliable hybrid,
even flowering in
part-shade; it has
creamy yellow blooms
and foliage marked
with bronze. **'Rosea'**
has pale salmon
flowers, flushed with
pink at the base of the
petals. **ZONES 5–10.**

Nymphaea, Hardy
Hybrid, 'Formosa'
(above right)

Nymphaea, Hardy
Hybrid, 'Gladstoniana'
(right)

Nymphaea, Hardy
Hybrid, 'Caroliniana
Perfecta' *(below)*

N

N

Nymphaea, Hardy Hybrid, 'Rosea' *(above)*

Nymphaea, Hardy Hybrid, 'Colossea' *(above left)*

Nymphaea, Hardy Hybrid, 'Albida' *(top)*

Nymphaea, Hardy Hybrid, 'Colonel Welch' *(left)*

Nymphaea nouchali *(right)*
SHAPLA

This tropical species has a wide distribution from southern Asia to northern Australia. Its flower is the national emblem of Bangladesh and it is used there and in India in perfumery and cosmetics. It is a rather small waterlily with floating leaves normally only 3–6 in (8–15 cm) across, and 3 in (8 cm) wide flowers held at or just above the water surface; they open during the day and have 10 or fewer pointed petals that may be blue, pink or white, with a distinct gap between the petals and the bunch of yellow stamens. ZONES 11–12.

Nymphaea 'Maurice Laydecker' (pink) and *Nymphaea odorata* (white) *(above)*

Nymphaea odorata
POND LILY, WHITE WATERLILY

This native of North and tropical America has white fragrant, many-petalled flowers 3–5 in (8–12 cm) across, appearing by day in summer. The leaves are thick, glossy and mid-green. It spreads to 4 ft (1.2 m). ZONES 3–11.

N

Nymphaea tetragona 'Helvola' *(right)*

This true miniature waterlily bears soft yellow, star-shaped, semi-double flowers 2–3 in (5–8 cm) across. The leaves are handsome, too, being dark olive green splashed with maroon. The species is widely distributed around the temperate northern hemisphere. Plant with around 10 in (25 cm) of water over the crown of the plant. It is the smallest of the miniature waterlilies. ZONES 7–10.

Nymphaea, Tropical
Day-blooming Hybrid,
'St Louis Gold' *(right)*

Nymphaea, TD-bH,
'Pink Platter' *(below left)*

Nymphaea, TD-bH,
'Margaret Randig'
(below right)

Nymphaea, TD-bH,
'Blue Beauty'
(bottom left)

Nymphaea, TD-bH,
'William B. Shaw'
(bottom right)

Nymphaea, Tropical Day-blooming Hybrids

Tropical hybrids can bear day- or night-time flowers. **'Blue Beauty'** is a deciduous or evergreen, day-blooming waterlily with large, brown-speckled, dark green leaves with purplish undersides. Its flowers are rounded, semi-double, 12 in (30 cm) across, and deep purple-blue with yellow centers, and it spreads to 8 ft (2.4 m). **'Margaret Randig'** has mottled purple foliage

N

with fragrant, large, open, sky blue petals with yellow centers and blue-tipped stamens. Bright green leaves mottled with rich brown offset the open, soft pink blooms of **'Pink Platter'**; those of **'St Louis'** are scented and pale yellow. **'St Louis Gold'**, with abundant blooms of deep gold, is a good variety for smaller pools or tubs. Others include **'Bob Trickett'**, **'Lucida'** and **'William B. Shaw'**. ZONES 10–12.

Nymphaea, Tropical Night-blooming Hybrids

Of the night-bloomers, **'H. T. Haarstick'** is notable. Both have tall stems, the former carrying deep red flowers over deep coppery red leaves with very serrated edges, and the latter bearing creamy white flowers over mid-green leaves that also have serrated margins. **'Emily Grant Hutchings'** has enormous deep pink flowers that can reach 12 in (30 cm) across. ZONES 10–12.

Nymphaea, TD-bH, 'St Louis' *(above)*

Nymphaea, TD-bH, 'Bob Trickett' *(left)*

Nymphaea, Tropical Night-blooming Hybrid, 'E. T. Haarstick' *(below left)*

Nymphaea, TN-bH, 'Emily Grant Hutchings' *(below right)*

N

NYMPHOIDES

FAIRY WATERLILY, WATER SNOWFLAKE

Resembling miniature waterlilies, the 20 species of rhizomatous, aquatic perennials in this genus are distributed throughout the world. Their rootstocks embed in the pond bottom while the long-stalked, oval, round or kidney-shaped, wavy-edged leaves float on the surface. The foliage ranges in diameter from 1–6 in (2.5–15 cm), and is usually slightly glossy and olive green, occasionally purple mottled. The ½–1 in (12–25 mm) diameter flowers, with 5 often fimbriated (fringed) petals, may be white or yellow; they appear in summer and are held just above the foliage.

CULTIVATION

Plant in soil with a water depth of 4–18 in (10–45 cm) in full or half-day sun. The runners can spread to 6 ft (1.8 m), so allow room for development. Propagate by dividing the rootstock in late winter or early spring.

Nymphoides peltata *(below)*

WATER FRINGE, YELLOW FLOATING HEART

This is a very hardy species from a vast area of Eurasia and Japan. The small, heart-shaped submerged leaves grow near the very long rhizomes, while surface leaves are bright green with blackish markings on their upper sides and reddish tinges below. The flowers are bright golden yellow. ZONES 6–10.

Nymphoides indica *(left)*

WATER SNOWFLAKE, FALSE INDIAN WATERLILY

These plants are found throughout the tropics with separate subspecies found in different continents. This hardy perennial has rounded surface leaves ranging from 2–8 in (5–20 cm) across with a heart-shaped base. The flowers are white with a deep yellow center and the petals have characteristic fringed margins. ZONES 10–12.

OCIMUM
BASIL

This genus of approximately 35 species of rather frost-tender annuals, perennials and shrubs is native to tropical Asia and Africa. They are now widely cultivated in many other countries for their highly aromatic leaves, which are used for medicinal purposes or to flavor salads, soups, sauces, stews and curries. They have mostly oval leaves in opposite pairs and small tubular flowers borne in whorls towards the ends of the stems in late summer.

CULTIVATION

Grow in a protected, warm, sunny position in a moist but well-drained soil. Regularly pinch back plants to encourage bushy growth and to prevent them going to seed quickly. Propagate from seed in mid-spring. Protect from late frosts and check for chewing insects and snails.

Ocimum tenuiflorum (below)
syn. *Ocimum sanctum*
HOLY BASIL

This flavorsome aromatic herb from India is an important sacred plant in the Hindu religion. It is a short-lived perennial that dies back to a few woody stems near ground level. It grows to about 3 ft (1 m) tall with many upright stems clothed in oval, toothed leaves. Small, not very showy flowers appear on a spike from the tips of the branches. It is not particularly frost hardy and in cooler areas is usually raised as a summer annual. ZONES 10–12.

O

OENANTHE

WATER DROPWORT

Native to very damp areas of the northern hemisphere and tropical Africa, this genus of the carrot family consists of about 30 species of perennials, found mainly in damp habitats such as marshland and water meadows. Tiny white flowers appear in umbels, while the leaves are divided into many small leaflets. Care must be taken with these plants, as some species are quite toxic.

CULTIVATION

These plants can be naturalized in informal situations, requiring moist, fertile soil and doing well in either shade or sun. Propagate from seed or stem tip cuttings or by division or layering.

Oenanthe crocata

(above)

HEMLOCK, WATER DROPWORT

This European species is extremely poisonous and dangerous to livestock, so care should be taken when planting. It grows to a height of 5 ft (1.5 m) with a robust branching habit and has a very strong smell. Terminal heads of white flowers are borne in winter.
ZONES 5–10.

OENOTHERA

EVENING PRIMROSE

Native to temperate regions of both North and South America but widely naturalized elsewhere, this genus consists of more than 120 species of annuals, biennials and perennials. Their short-lived flowers, borne during summer, have 4 delicate petals, yellow, red, white or (less commonly) pink, and a long basal tube. Most species are pollinated by nocturnal insects and only release their fragrance at night. Some do not even open their petals during the day. Evening primrose oil is extracted from the tiny seeds. It contains certain fatty acids believed to be beneficial to health if consumed regularly in modest quantities.

CULTIVATION

They are mostly frost hardy and grow best in a well-drained, sandy soil in an open, sunny situation. They will tolerate dry conditions. Propagate from seed or by division in spring or autumn, or from softwood cuttings in late spring.

Oenothera elata subsp. *hookeri* *(above)*
HOOKER'S EVENING PRIMROSE

This species from western North America grows to a height of 6 ft (1.8 m). An erect perennial or biennial, it bears its lemon-gold turning to red-orange flowers in summer; the flowers open just as the sun sets. ZONES 7–9.

Oenothera biennis
(right)
COMMON EVENING PRIMROSE

A showy plant, this upright, hairy biennial has large, scented yellow flowers in tall spikes, opening in the evening and shrivelling before noon. It is erect and fast growing to a height of 5 ft (1.5 m). ZONES 4–10.

Oenothera fruticosa
SUNDROPS

This biennial or perennial species from eastern North America sometimes grows to a height of 3 ft (1 m), but is usually smaller. It has a reddish, erect, branching stem and narrow leaves. Deep yellow 1–2 in (2.5–5 cm) wide flowers open by day. **Oenothera fruticosa subsp. glauca** has broader, less hairy leaves with red tints when young. **'Fyrverker'** (syn. 'Fireworks') has yellow flowers that open from red buds. **'Sonnenwende'** grows to 2 ft (60 cm) tall. It has red-tinted autumn foliage and orange-red flower buds. ZONES 4–10.

Oenothera fruticosa subsp. glauca (yellow) with Erigeron 'Quakeress' (above)

Oenothera fruticosa 'Sonnenwende' (left)

Oenothera macrocarpa (left)
syn. Oenothera missouriensis
OZARK SUNDROPS, MISSOURI PRIMROSE, FLUTTERMILLS

This perennial is usually almost stemless with large rosettes of narrow tapering leaves. The flowers are large, reaching 4 in (10 cm) in diameter, lemon yellow in color and open in the evening in summer. This plant reaches a height of no more than 6 in (15 cm), but spreads to 24 in (60 cm) or more across, the flowers appearing singly from between the leaves. ZONES 5–9.

O

Oenothera speciosa
WHITE EVENING PRIMROSE,
SHOWY EVENING PRIMROSE

This short-lived, rhizomatous perennial native to southern USA and Mexico bears spikes of profuse, fragrant, saucer-shaped, pink-tinted white blooms. Fresh flowerheads open daily during summer. The small leaves often turn red in hot or cold weather. Clump forming, it grows to 18–24 in (45–60 cm) in height with a spread of 18 in (45 cm) or more. **'Rosea'** (syns 'Childsii', *Oenothera berlandieri*) is lower growing, with flowers edged and heavily veined rose pink, yellow in the center. **'Siskiyou'** is similar but with larger flowers. These pink forms have often been confused with *O. rosea*, which has much smaller flowers. **ZONES 5–10.**

Oenothera speciosa 'Rosea' *(above right)*

Oenothera speciosa 'Siskiyou' *(right)*

Oenothera odorata *(left)*

This perennial, native to South America, was introduced into England by Sir Joseph Banks in 1790. It has erect red-tinted stems with a rosette of narrow leaves at the base. The fragrant yellow flowers appear in summer, turning red with age and opening at dusk. It reaches a height of 24–36 in (60–90 cm) and a spread of 12 in (30 cm). **ZONES 7–10.**

OMPHALODES
NAVELWORT

From Europe, Asia and Mexico, this genus consists of 28 species of forget-me-not–like annuals and perennials that are either evergreen or semi-evergreen. These plants make excellent ground covers, and they are most suited to rock gardens.

CULTIVATION
These plants prefer shade or part-shade with moist but well-drained soil (except for *Omphalodes linifolia*, which prefers a sunny position). They are mostly frost hardy. Propagate from seed in spring or by division in autumn.

Omphalodes cappadocica 'Cherry Ingram' *(below)*

Omphalodes cappadocica 'Starry Eyes' *(bottom)*

Omphalodes cappadocica
(below left)

This spreading perennial from Turkey has creeping underground stems. It produces numerous sprays of flat, bright purple-blue flowers in spring that arise from clumps of densely hairy, oval to heart-shaped leaves that are found at the base of the plant. This plant reaches a height of 6–8 in (15–20 cm) and a spread of 10 in (25 cm) and is fully frost hardy. '**Cherry Ingram**' is a vigorous grower to 10 in (25 cm) in height with purplish blue flowers. '**Starry Eyes**' has relatively big flowers, with each blue petal edged in white giving a starry effect. ZONES 6–9.

Omphalodes verna *(below)*
BLUE-EYED MARY, CREEPING FORGET-ME-NOT

This semi-evergreen thrives in shady conditions. During spring, it produces long, loose sprays of flat, bright blue flowers with white eyes. This plant has heart-shaped, mid-green leaves that form clumps. It reaches a height and spread of 8 in (20 cm). ZONES 6–9.

ONOPORDUM
syn. *Onopordon*

Found naturally in Europe, North Africa and western Asia, this is a genus of about 40 species of large biennial thistles. They have a basal rosette of large, gray-green, lightly felted leaves, deeply toothed, with a spine at the tip of each tooth. The flowerheads are of typical thistle form: globose with a dense tuft of purple florets at the top and covered in spiny bracts. They are borne at the top of branched stems up to 10 ft (3 m) tall, and mature in mid-summer. On drying, they release downy seeds. In the first year the plants form an attractive foliage clump with a few flowerheads. In the second year they grow rapidly to full height, flower heavily then die.

CULTIVATION
Onopordums are easily cultivated in any well-drained soil in full sun with shelter from strong winds. Offsets and seedlings often naturally replace spent plants. They are frost hardy and are propagated from seed.

Onopordum acanthium (right)
SCOTCH THISTLE, COTTON THISTLE

Despite its common name, it is doubtful that this European and west Asian species is a true native of Scotland or indeed of the British Isles, but it is the thistle usually regarded as the one shown on the Scottish royal emblem. It has a thick, downy stem with many wing-like ridges on its numerous branches. Its leaves are large and also downy, with wavy, sharply prickly edges. The flowers appear in late summer and autumn and are light purple in color. It reaches a height of up to 10 ft (3 m) and a spread of 6 ft (1.8 m) or more. ZONES 6–10.

ONOSMA

This genus comprises 150 species of semi-evergreen biennials, perennials and subshrubs, allied to the comfreys (*Symphytum*), cultivated particularly for their gracefully pendent, tubular flowers. The densely tufted leaves are tongue-like with rather stiff, prickly hairs. Native to the Mediterranean region, they are most useful in rock gardens and along banks.

CULTIVATION

They are moderately frost hardy. Full sun is essential, although in warmer climates some shade must be provided for them to flourish. They prefer well-drained soil and dislike wet summers. They can be propagated from cuttings in summer or from seed in autumn.

Onosma tauricum *(below)*
GOLDEN DROP

Nodding spikes of pale yellow flowers are borne on this 12 in (30 cm) tall perennial. The erect stems are sparsely branched and the lower surfaces of the leaves have minute tufts of short, spreading hairs. ZONES 6–9.

Onosma alborosea *(left)*

This semi-evergreen perennial is covered with fine hairs that may be an irritant to some people. The drooping tubular flowers open as white and then turn pink and appear for a long period during summer. Clump forming, it reaches a height of 6–12 in (15–30 cm) and spread of 8 in (20 cm). ZONES 7–9.

O

OPHIOPOGON
MONDO GRASS, SNAKEBEARD, LILYTURF

This genus contains 50 or so species of evergreen perennials. They are valued for their attractive, long-lived clumps of grass-like foliage springing from underground rhizomes. The summer flowers are small and can be white or blue through to purple. The berry-like fruits each contain one seed. They are trouble-free plants that will last indefinitely, providing an attractive ground cover that effectively suppresses leaves.

CULTIVATION
Most are fairly frost hardy and will tolerate sun or part-shade in moist, well-drained soil. Propagate by division of clumps in spring, or from seed in autumn. For a quick ground cover, plant divisions at 8 in (20 cm) intervals.

Ophiopogon japonicus *(below)*
syn. *Liriope japonica*
MONDO GRASS

This fine-leaved species has dark green recurving foliage that arises from deep rhizomes, spreading to form dense, soft mats up to about 8 in (20 cm) deep. Pale purple flowers are hidden among the leaves in mid-summer, followed by bright blue, pea-sized fruit. **'Kyoto Dwarf'** is only 2–4 in (5–10 cm) high, with very short leaves. ZONES 8–11.

O

Origanum 'Barbara Tingey' *(left)*

This cultivar of possible hybrid origin has rounded, felty, blue-tinged leaves that are reddish purple beneath. In summer, pink flowers appear nestled in bracts which are green at first, but age to a purplish pink color. It grows 4–6 in (10–15 cm) tall, but spreads to at least 10–12 in (25–30 cm) across. ZONES 7–9.

Origanum laevigatum *(above)*

This vigorous and ornamental species has spreading woody rhizomes and densely massed evergreen leaves, from which arise numerous flowering stems 18–24 in (45–60 cm) high. Tiny flowers with purple bracts create a cloud of lavender at the top of the stems all summer long, and provide nectar for bees and butterflies. An excellent filler for the perennial border as well as the herb garden, it also makes a delightful addition to dried flower arrangements. **'Hopleys'** and **'Herrenhausen'** are recent cultivars with richer flower color. ZONES 7–11.

ORIGANUM

syn. *Majorana*

MARJORAM, OREGANO

Native to the Mediterranean region and temperate Asia, these perennials and subshrubs in the mint family have aromatic leaves and stalked spikes or heads of small tubular flowers with crowded, overlapping bracts. Some species are grown as culinary herbs, while others are grown for their decorative pink flowerheads. With arching or prostrate stems arising from vigorously spreading rhizomes, they make useful plants for trailing over rocks, banks and walls.

CULTIVATION

These plants like full sun and a moderately fertile, well-drained soil. Trim excess growth regularly and propagate from seed in spring or by root division in autumn or spring.

Origanum vulgare
COMMON OREGANO, WILD MARJORAM

The common oregano has a sharper, more pungent flavor than marjoram. It has a sprawling habit and grows to 24 in (60 cm) high with dark green, oval leaves and small, white or pink flowers in summer. The leaves are used, fresh or dried, in many Mediterranean-inspired dishes. In Italy, oregano is used in pizza toppings and pasta dishes. **'Aureum'** has a less sprawling habit and bright greenish gold leaves. **'Thumble's Variety'** is a low, mound-forming selection with yellow-green leaves. ZONES 5–9.

Origanum libanoticum *(right)*

From Lebanon, this 24 in (60 cm) tall species produces nodding spikes of quite large pink flowers with dull pink bracts in summer. ZONES 8–10.

Origanum vulgare 'Aureum' *(above right)*

Origanum vulgare 'Thumble's Variety' *(right)*

O

ORONTIUM

GOLDEN CLUB

The single species in this genus is an unusual member of the arum family from eastern USA. An aquatic perennial, it has thick rhizomes and broad spatulate leaves on long-stalked spadices of minute flowers surrounded by a membranous spathe that shrivels at an early stage.

CULTIVATION

This very frost-hardy plant will overwinter in any pond or slow-moving stream with water over 6 in (15 cm) deep that does not freeze solid. The roots need to be in soil, either in silt at the pond bottom or in tubs. The foliage is best in sun or morning shade. Propagate by breaking up the rhizome in late winter as dormancy finishes.

Orontium aquaticum *(below & bottom)*

This species has simple, leathery leaves up to 10 in (25 cm) long that may be submerged, floating or held erect above the water surface. The leaves have metallic blue-green upper surfaces, purple undersides and stalks up to 15 in (38 cm) long. Flower spikes appear in summer and are short lived; the papery spathe is insignificant and quickly withers, but the bright yellow spadix, around 6 in (15 cm) long, is held above the surface on a long stem. ZONES 7–9.

ORTHOPHYTUM

This bromeliad genus is endemic to eastern Brazil and consists of about 17 species, all terrestrial and forming rosettes of stiff, prickly edged leaves, spreading by stolons and sometimes forming extensive mats. The flowering stems may rise well above the leaf rosettes with interesting broad bracts, or the flowers may be in stemless clusters in the center of the rosette.

CULTIVATION

These plants are frost tender and should be grown in fertile, well-drained soil in full sun. Water moderately in the growing season and keep dry in winter. Propagate from seed in early spring. They are susceptible to aphids while flowering.

Orthophytum gurkenii *(below)*

This curious bromeliad has purple-bronze leaves strikingly barred with rows of silvery scales. The erect flowering stem bears bracts like the leaves but broader, and the upper bracts have brilliant green bases the same color as the small tubular flowers. ZONES 9–12.

Orthophytum navioides *(right)*

Found in the wild in rocky crevices, this species has long narrow leaves edged with very short, delicate spines. The white flowers are borne in a dense hemispherical cluster in the center of the rosette, the inner leaves turning deep reddish purple at flowering time. It is easy to grow but needs strong light. ZONES 9–12.

O

*Orthrosanthus
multiflorus* (left)

This native of south-
western Australia
makes an erect tufted
plant with narrow,
grass-like leaves and
spikes of starry blue to
purple flowers which
appear in spring. It
reaches a height of
24 in (60 cm) and a
spread of 12 in (30 cm).
ZONES 9–10.

ORTHROSANTHUS

Found in the mountains of Central and South America and the
sandy plains of southern Australia, the 7 species of this genus of
the iris family are grass-like perennials with short, woody rhizomes
and flattened fans of sword-shaped leaves up to 18 in (45 cm) long.
Blue or yellow 6-petalled flowers up to 2 in (5 cm) in diameter
open in spring and summer. In some species, the flowers have dark
veining. They are carried in clusters of 2 to 8 blooms on wiry stems.

CULTIVATION
Plant in moist, well-drained soil in sun or part-shade. Light frosts
are tolerated, but *Orthrosanthus* species are best grown in a mild,
frost-free climate. They are often short lived. Propagate from seed
or by division of the rhizomes in late winter.

OSTEOSPERMUM

This genus of 70 or so species of evergreen shrubs, semi-woody perennials and annuals is mostly indigenous to South Africa. Allied to *Dimorphotheca,* they have irregularly toothed leaves and produce a profusion of large, daisy-like flowerheads in the white, pink, violet and purple range. Most of the commonly grown osteospermums are cultivars of uncertain origin, suspected to be hybrids. Tough plants, they are useful for rock gardens, dry embankments or the front rows of shrub borders, particularly as temporary filler plants.

CULTIVATION

Osteospermums are marginally to moderately frost hardy and do best in open, well-drained soil of medium fertility. An open, sunny position is essential. Light pruning after flowering helps maintain shape and extends the ultimate lifespan. Propagate from cuttings of non-flowering shoots or from seed in summer.

Osteospermum fruticosum cultivar *(below)*

Osteospermum fruticosum
syn. *Dimorphotheca fruticosa*

FREEWAY DAISY, TRAILING AFRICAN DAISY

This perennial has prostrate or trailing stems that spread to cover large areas when planted along freeways in coastal California. Masses of palest lilac daisies are borne on stalks up to 12 in (30 cm) above the ground; the heaviest bloom is in winter, with some blossoms year-round. Named selections are available with pure white, burgundy or purple flowers. ZONES 9–11.

O

Osteospermum 'Pink Whirls' *(left)*

This new, pink-flowering cultivar has a slight constriction in each petal on some flowerheads, although others may have more normal petals. It reaches a height of about 18 in (45 cm) and spread of 3 ft (1 m). ZONES 8–10.

Osteospermum 'Whirligig' *(below)*
syn. *Osteospermum* 'Starry Eyes'

This somewhat bizarre cultivar has white petals above and gray-blue beneath, each with their edges pinched together in the outer part, but remaining flat right at the tip; the effect is curious but quite decorative. It reaches a height of about 24 in (60 cm) with a spreading habit. ZONES 8–10.

O

Oxalis articulata
(right)

This Paraguayan species has numerous fleshy, caterpillar-like rhizomes which readily disperse when soil is disturbed. In some mild, moist climates it has become a minor nuisance. The 3-lobed, hairy edged leaves are long stalked and the rose-pink flowers are borne above the foliage in dense, showy sprays in summer and autumn. ZONES 8–11.

Oxalis massoniana
(below)

Its orange-toned flowers make *Oxalis massoniana* something of a novelty. From southern Africa, it was named after Francis Masson, a Scot who made notable collections in South Africa in the late eighteenth century. ZONES 9–10.

OXALIS
WOOD-SORREL

This is a genus of 500 or so species of bulbous, rhizomatous and fibrous-rooted perennials and a few small, weak shrubs. Most are native to South Africa and South America. Some have become garden and greenhouse weeds which, though pretty in flower, have given a bad name to the genus; the species listed here are more restrained in growth and make choice additions to the garden. The leaves are always compound, divided into 3 or more heart-shaped or more deeply 2-lobed leaflets in a palmate arrangement (like clover). The funnel-shaped flowers are usually pink, white or yellow, and are carried in an umbel-like cluster on slender stalks.

CULTIVATION

Most species grow from bulbs or corms, which multiply readily. A position in sun or part-shade suits most, along with a mulched, well-drained soil and moderate water. Propagate by division of the bulbs or from seed in autumn.

Oxalis oregana *(below)*
REDWOOD SORREL

This species from western USA and Canada spreads by creeping rhizomes and forms large, dense mats in moist, shady woodlands and forests. It grows 10 in (25 cm) high and has 1 in (25 mm) or more long, broadly heart-shaped dark green leaflets. Rosy pink to white flowers are borne on solitary stems from spring to autumn. ZONES 7–10.

P

Paeonia bakeri
(below)

This species grows to
24 in (60 cm) tall with
leaves composed of two
sets of three, 3–4 in
(8–10 cm) long leaflets.
The leaves are dark
green above, blue-green
below. The flowers,
over 4 in (10 cm) in
diameter, open from
late spring and have
rounded purple-red
petals and bright
golden anthers.
ZONES 5–9.

Paeonia 'Skylark Saunders' *(right)*

This hybrid has
beautiful single pale
pink flowers with
prominent golden
stamens. **ZONES 7–9.**

Paeonia 'Ludovica'
(bottom)

This semi-double
hybrid has reddish pink
to salmon pink flowers
with conspicuous
golden stamens. It
flowers very early.
ZONES 7–9.

PAEONIA
PEONY

There are 33 species in this genus of beautiful perennials and shrubs. The genus name
goes back to classical Greek and arose from
the supposed medicinal properties of some
species. Peonies are all deciduous and have
long-lived, rather woody rootstocks with
swollen roots, and large compound leaves
with the leaflets usually toothed or lobed.
Each new stem in spring terminates in one
to several large, rose-like flowers. Their
centers are a mass of short stamens that
almost conceal the 2 to 5 large ovaries,
which develop into short pods containing
large seeds. The flowers are mostly in shades
of pink or red, but there are also white and
yellow-flowered species. The great majority
of peonies are herbaceous, dying back to the
ground in autumn, but there is a small
group of Chinese species, known as the 'tree
peonies' that have woody stems, although
no more than about 8 ft (2.4 m) in height,
so strictly they are shrubs. Cultivars of this
tree peony group produce the largest and
most magnificent of all peony flowers, some
approaching a diameter of 12 in (30 cm),
mostly double and often beautifully frilled
or ruffled.

Paeonia 'Sophie' *(above)*

This hybrid peony, popular in Germany, has single soft crimson red flowers and a few similarly colored central petaloids with golden stamens. ZONES 7–9.

Paeonia lactiflora 'Yangfeichuyu' *(above)*

Paeonia lactiflora 'Sarah Bernhardt' *(below)*

Paeonia lactiflora Hybrids

CULTIVATION

Most peonies will only succeed in climates with a cold winter, allowing dormancy and initiation of flower buds, but new foliage and flower buds can be damaged by late frosts. They appreciate a sheltered position in full or slightly filtered sunlight, but with soil kept cool and moist. Mulch and feed with well-rotted manure when leaf growth starts, but avoid disturbing roots. Pruning of the tree peonies should be minimal, consisting of trimming out weaker side shoots. Propagate from seed in autumn, or by division in the case of named cultivars. Tree peony cultivars are best propagated from basal suckers, but few are produced. Hence, plants on their own roots are very expensive. A faster and cheaper method is to graft them onto herbaceous rootstocks, but the resulting plants are often short lived.

These herbaceous Chinese peonies are derived mainly from *Paeonia lactiflora*. They have handsome foliage, which is maroon tinted when it first appears in spring, and usually scented flowers in a huge range of colors and forms. **'Beacon Flame'** has deep red, semi-double flowers. **'Bowl of Beauty'** grows to 3 ft (1 m) tall and between late spring and mid-summer bears dense clusters of slender, creamy white petaloids nesting in the center of broad, pink outer petals. **'Coral Charm'** has deep apricot buds fading to soft orange-pink as they mature. **'Cora Stubbs'** has broad outer petals and smaller central ones in contrasting

P

tones. **'Duchesse de Nemours'** is a fairly tall grower with fragrant, white to soft yellow flowers with frilled incurving petals. **'Félix Crousse'** is a deep pink double with a red center. **'Festiva Maxima'** has large, fully double, scented flowers with frilled petals that are white with red flecks. **'Inspecteur Lavergne'** is late-flowering and fully double red. **'Kelway's Glorious'** has highly scented, creamy white, double flowers. **'Miss America'** has large, highly scented white flowers with gold stamens. **'Monsieur Jules Elie'** has very deep cerise-pink single flowers. **'President Roosevelt'** is a luxuriant 'rose' or 'bomb' double peony. **'Sarah Bernhardt'** has scented, double, rose pink flowers with silvery margins. **'Whitleyi Major'** has single, ivory-white flowers with yellow stamens. Others include **'Moonstone'**, **'Scarlett O'Hara'** and **'Yangfeichuyu'**. ZONES 6–9.

Paeonia lactiflora 'Moonstone' *(above)*

Paeonia lactiflora 'Cora Stubbs' *(above left)*

Paeonia lactiflora 'Bowl of Beauty' *(left)*

Paeonia lactiflora
'President Roosevelt'
(right)

Paeonia lactiflora
'Kelway's Glorious'
(below)

Paeonia lactiflora
'Scarlett O'Hara'
(above right)

Paeonia lactiflora
cultivar *(right)*

P

Paeonia mascula
subsp. *russii (left)*

Paeonia mascula

Found from the north-west Balkans to the Himalayas, this herbaceous perennial is a very variable species. It usually has very stout stems 10–24 in (25–60 cm) tall. The leaves vary considerably, some forms having broad leaflets, others narrow and some with serrated edges. The flowers are deep pink, red or white, more than 4 in (10 cm) wide and open early. **Paeonia mascula** subsp. *russii* from Greece and the islands of the Mediterranean differs from the species in having broader, more rounded leaves with hairy undersides. ZONES 8–10.

Paeonia mollis

(above)

Of unknown origin and considered to be a garden variety rather than a true species, this 18 in (45 cm) tall herbaceous peony has biternate (made up of two, 3-leaflet sections) leaves with lobed leaflets up to 4 in (10 cm) long. Its 3 in (8 cm) wide, deep pink or white flowers open from early summer. ZONES 6–9.

Paeonia mlokosewitschii

(below)

CAUCASIAN PEONY

From late spring to mid-summer, this European peony bears big, open, pale to bright yellow flowers atop soft green leaves that have hairy undersides and are sometimes tinged purple at the edges. An erect, herbaceous perennial, it grows to 30 in (75 cm) high and wide, enjoys semi-shade and is resistant to frost. The seed pods split open to reveal black seeds on a red background. ZONES 6–9.

P

Paeonia officinalis
'Rosea' *(below)*

Paeonia officinalis
(above)

Of European origin,
this herbaceous peren-
nial reaches a height
and spread of 24 in
(60 cm) and from
spring to mid-summer
bears single, purple or
red, rose-like flowers.
Although poisonous,
it has been used medi-
cinally. Of similar size,
'Rubra Plena' bears
flowers that consist of
clusters of many small,
mid-magenta petals.
The more compact
'China Rose' bears
darker green foliage
and salmon-pink
flowers with yellow-
orange anthers. **'Rosea'**
has deep pink flowers.
ZONES 8–10.

Paeonia officinalis
cultivar *(left)*

P

Paeonia officinalis
'Rubra Plena' *(left)*

Paeonia peregrina
(left)

Native to southern
Europe, this 18 in
(45 cm) herbaceous
species has sticky stems
and leaves made up of
15 to 17 leaflets. The
leaves have a blue-green
tinge. Cup-shaped, 4 in
(10 cm) wide, deep red
flowers with golden
anthers open from late
spring. **'Sunshine'** (syn.
'Otto Froebel') is an
early-flowering cultivar
with vivid deep orange-
red flowers.
ZONES 8–10.

P

Papaver alpinum *(right)*

A short-lived perennial, this tuft-forming semi-evergreen alpine poppy (a miniature Iceland poppy) grows to 8 in (20 cm) high with a spread of 4 in (10 cm) and has fine, grayish leaves. It bears white or yellow flowers in summer. This species prefers a little lime in the soil. Use on banks or in rock gardens. ZONES 5–10.

PAPAVER
POPPY

The 50 or so annual, biennial or perennial species of the genus *Papaver* are mainly from the temperate parts of Eurasia and Africa, with a couple from eastern USA. Their characteristic cupped petals and nodding buds that turn skywards upon opening make them popular bedding flowers. Several of their close relatives take their name in common usage, such as the tree poppy *(Romneya)*, the Californian poppy *(Eschscholzia)* or the blue poppy *(Meconopsis)*.

CULTIVATION
Poppies are fully frost hardy and prefer little or no shade and deep, moist, well-drained soil. Sow seed in spring or autumn; many species self-seed readily.

Papaver atlanticum *(center)*

This perennial from Morocco has a woody rhizome and 6 in (15 cm) long, toothed-edged, downy leaves. The flowers are borne on 18 in (45 cm) stems and are pale orange to red, around 4 in (10 cm) wide, and open in summer. **'Flore Semi-Pleno'** has semi-double flowers on slightly shorter stems than the species. ZONES 6–10.

Papaver atlanticum
'Flore Semi-Pleno'
(right)

P

Papaver
bracteatum (right)

Occurring naturally
from the Caucasus to
the Himalayas, this
summer-flowering
species is very similar
to *Papaver orientale*. It
is a perennial with 3 ft
(1 m) tall flower stems
and 18 in (45 cm) long
pinnate leaves. The
foliage and stems are
covered with white
hairs. The flowers,
usually red with purple
centers, are 4 in (10 cm)
wide. ZONES 5–10.

Papaver
commutatum
(below)

A close relative of the
blood-red *Papaver
rhoeas*, this annual
species can be massed
in a garden to create an
effect resembling an
Impressionist painting.
The flowers, bright red
on hairy stems, appear
in summer but only last
for about 3 weeks.
ZONES 8–10.

P

Papaver orientale
(center)
ORIENTAL POPPY

This herbaceous peren-
nial is native to south-
west Asia. In summer, it
bears spectacular
flowers as big as peo-
nies in shades of pink
through to red with
dark centers to 4 in
(10 cm) in diameter.
The cultivated varieties,
sometimes double,
come in a wide range of
colors and many feature
a dark basal blotch on
each petal. It has hairy,
lance-like, bluish green
leaves and can become
straggly. According to
the variety, it grows
from 18 in (45 cm) to
more than 3 ft (1 m)
tall. **'Cedric Morris'** is
a big-flowered form
with individual blooms
up to 6 in (15 cm)
across. Its shell-pink
flowers have frilly
petals, each with an
almost black blotch at
the base. **'Mrs Perry'**
has large, coral pink
flowers. **'Feuerriese'**
(syn. 'Fire Giant') is a
30 in (80 cm) tall
German Foerster
cultivar with brick red
flowers on stiffly erect
stems. Other cultivars
include **'China Boy'**
and **'Rosenwelle'**.
ZONES 3–9.

Papaver cruceum
(left)
syn. *Papaver nudicaule*
of gardens
ICELAND POPPY

This tuft-forming
perennial from North
America and Asia
Minor is almost always
grown as an annual. It
is good for rock gardens
and for cutting. Large
scented flowers, borne
in winter and spring,
are white, yellow,
orange or pink, and
have a crinkled texture.
The leaves are pale
green, and the stems
are long and hairy.
It grows 12–24 in
(30–60 cm) tall with a
6–8 in (15–20 cm)
spread. ZONES 2–10.

Papaver orientale
'Feuerriese' and
Delphinium elatum
hybrid *(below)*

P

Papaver orientale
'Rosenwelle' *(left)*

Papaver rhoeas *(below)*
CORN POPPY, FIELD POPPY, FLANDERS POPPY

The cupped flowers on this fast-growing annual
are small, delicate, scarlet and single. The cultivated
varieties (**Shirley Series**) come in reds, pinks,
whites and bicolors. They have a pale heart instead
of the black cross that marks the center of the wild
poppy. The leaves are light green and lobed. This
species grows to 24 in (60 cm) high with a 12 in
(30 cm) spread. Double-flowered strains are also
available. **'Mother of Pearl'** has gray, pink or
blue-purple flowers. ZONES 5–9.

Papaver orientale
'China Boy' *(above)*

Papaver somniferum *(above)*
OPIUM POPPY

The grayish green leaves on this fast-growing annual from the Middle East are lobed and elliptical with serrated edges. It blooms in summer, to display big flowers in white, pink, red or purple, usually as doubles. Opium poppies are cultivated for the milky sap produced in their seed capsules, which is the source of the narcotic drug opium and its derivatives. The flowers of **'Hungarian Blue'** are more intense in color than those of the wild plants. ZONES 7–10.

Papaver rhoeas 'Mother of Pearl' *(below)*

Papaver somniferum 'Hungarian Blue' *(below right)*

P

PARIS
syn. *Daiswa*

This genus consists of 20 species of herbaceous, rhizomatous perennials and is closely related to the trilliums. It is found from Europe to eastern Asia. They form clumps and their leaves are carried in whorls at the top of stems up to 3 ft (1 m) long. Unlike trilliums, the 1–4 in (2.5–10 cm) long, oval to lance-shaped leaves are not always in 3s, but in groups of 4 to 12 depending on the species. The flowers, borne singly at the stem tips in spring and summer, have 4 to 6 petals and sepals that are usually green or yellow-green.

CULTIVATION
Plant in cool, moist, woodland conditions in dappled shade. Most species are vigorous and are not difficult to cultivate. They are very frost hardy. Propagate from seed or by dividing established clumps. Divide only every 3 to 4 years or the plants may be weakened.

Paris lanceolata
(below)

This species has long, narrow leaves that form a very distinct collar around a central stem. At its tip, the stem carries a flower with golden anthers and petals reduced to filaments. ZONES 7–10.

P

Paris japonica *(left)*
syn. *Kinugasa japonica*

This Japanese species has stems up to 30 in (75 cm) tall and whorls of 8–12 in (20–30 cm) long elliptical leaves. The flowers are borne singly on 1–3 in (2.5–8 cm) pedicels at the stem tips and have white sepals up to 2 in (5 cm) long. The petals are much reduced or absent. The flowers are followed by small, fleshy red fruit. ZONES 8–10.

Paris polyphylla
(right)

syn. *Daiswa polyphylla*

This Chinese species grows to 3 ft (1 m) tall with 6 in (15 cm) leaves. The flowers have very narrow, almost filamentous petals up to 4 in (10 cm) long. Although scarcely a feature, they are yellow-green while the center of the flower is purple with brown stigmas. The flowers are followed by red fruit. *Paris polyphylla* var. *yunnanensis,* from Yunnan Province has slightly broader petals. ZONES 7–10.

Paris tetraphylla
(below)

syn. *Paris quadrifolia*

This very frost-hardy species from Eurasia, which grows to 15 in (38 cm) in height, bears its star-shaped, green and white flowers in late spring. The mid-green leaves are from 2–6 in (5–15 cm) long. ZONES 8–10.

Paris polyphylla var. *yunnanensis (right)*

Parnassia grandifolia *(above)*
This species from central and southeastern USA grows to 24 in (60 cm) tall. It has rounded 1½–4 in (3.5–10 cm) long leaves on 1½–6 in (3.5–15 cm) stems. Its flowers are white with very narrow petals. ZONES 6–10.

PARNASSIA
BOG STAR, PARNASSUS GRASS

This is a genus of around 15 species of perennials found over much of the northern temperate zone. They have long-stemmed, kidney-shaped to near round, 1–4 in (2.5–10 cm) long leaves in basal rosettes. The wiry flower's stem, which grows up to 24 in (60 cm) tall, bears a single, 5-petalled, 1–1½ in (25–35 mm) wide flower backed by a single bract. The flowers open in summer.

CULTIVATION
Plant in moist, well-drained soil in sun or part-shade and do not allow to become dry in summer. Some species are very difficult to cultivate and will only grow well in naturally damp, grassy meadows or damp, peaty soil. All species are very hardy. Propagate from seed in autumn or by very careful division of established clumps.

PAROCHETUS

SHAMROCK PEA, CLOVER PEA, BLUE PEA

This genus contains a single species of prostrate perennial with clover-like, trifoliate leaves. The leaflets are about ½ in (12 mm) long. For most of the year it looks exactly like a small patch of clover. However, from late summer to winter, depending on the climate, it is studded with ½–1 in (12–25 mm) wide bright blue, pea-like flowers borne singly or in pairs.

CULTIVATION

It is an excellent plant for rockeries, in an alpine house or in a hanging basket. It prefers to grow in moist, humus-rich soil in sun or part-shade. Although it tolerates only light frosts, in the right conditions it can spread quickly. Propagate from seed or by division.

Parochetus communis (above)

From the mountains of southwest China, Southeast Asia and the Himalayas to Sri Lanka and tropical Africa, this deciduous species grows to a height of 4 in (10 cm) with a 12 in (30 cm) spread. The flowers are borne late in the growing season. ZONES 9–11.

P

PARONYCHIA
WHITLOW WORT

This widespread genus consists of around 50 species of usually mat- or clump-forming, dianthus- or thyme-like annuals or perennials. Most occur naturally in the Mediterranean region and have wiry stems and tiny linear to rounded leaves, often in pairs. The minute flower inflorescences, in themselves quite inconspicuous, smother the plants in early summer and are highlighted by the surrounding silvery bracts.

CULTIVATION
These are very much plants for well-drained, sunny positions and are at home in rockeries or alpine houses. Most are quite frost hardy, but suffer if kept wet and cold in winter. Propagate from seed or by layering (they are often self-layering) or by division.

Paronychia argentea (above)

This species from southern Europe, North Africa and southwest Asia forms a mat of wiry stems with rounded leaves. In summer, it is smothered in small, dull yellow inflorescences partially covered by silvery bracts. ZONES 7–11.

Paronychia capitata (below)

This Mediterranean species is very similar to *Paronychia argentea*. However, its leaves are linear to lance-shaped rather than rounded and its bracts are an even brighter silver. ZONES 5–10.

PELARGONIUM

The widely grown hybrid pelargoniums are
popularly known as 'geraniums', but should
not be confused with members of the genus
Geranium of the same plant family. The
genus *Pelargonium* consists of perhaps
280 species, the vast majority endemic to
South Africa and adjacent Namibia, but a
sprinkling of species are found elsewhere in
the world including other parts of Africa,
southwest Asia, Arabia, Australia, New
Zealand and some Atlantic Ocean islands.
Although pelargoniums are mostly soft-
wooded shrubs and subshrubs, some are
herbaceous perennials or even annuals;
there is also a large but little known group
of species that have succulent stems, leaves
or roots and are grown by collectors. The
leaves of pelargoniums are often as broad as
they are long and are variously toothed,
scalloped, lobed or dissected, depending on
species; they are usually aromatic, containing a wide range of essential oils, and may
secrete resin droplets which give the leaves
a sticky feel. Flowers of the wild species
have the 2 upper petals differently colored

Pelargonium zonale (above)

This South African species is rarely seen in gardens,
being best known for its genetic contribution to
the Zonal pelargonium hybrids. ZONES 9–11.

or marked from the 3 lower ones, a feature
that distinguishes pelargoniums from
true geraniums. Their seeds are plumed
like thistledown, another distinguishing
feature.

Only a few groups of hybrid pelargoniums are widely grown in gardens and as
indoor plants, originating in the early
nineteenth century from a small number of
South African shrub species. The common
garden and pot 'geraniums' are the **Zonal
pelargoniums,** once known botanically as
Pelargonium × hortorum. They have almost
circular leaves with scalloped margins, often
with horseshoe-shaped zones of brown, red
or purple, and flower almost continuously.
Somewhat similar are the **Ivy-leafed
pelargoniums,** with their semi-scrambling
habit and leaves that are fleshier with more
pointed lobes; these are also the subject of
intensive breeding, and are tending to

P

merge with zonals in some of their characteristics. Another major group is the **Regal pelargoniums,** sometimes known as the **Martha Washington geraniums** or *Pelargonium × domesticum;* these have woody stems and sharply toothed and creased leaves, and the large flowers come in a range of gaudy colors and patterns. There are some smaller groups of hybrids bred for their flowers, most significant being the Unique and **Angel pelargoniums.** And then there is a large and varied group, grown primarily for their foliage, known as the **Scented-leafed pelargoniums:** these are mostly shrubby and usually have deeply lobed or dissected leaves that give off a quite remarkable range of odors when bruised or crushed, depending on the variety. They include both species and hybrids, and some also have quite pretty flowers. Some of these are grown commercially for 'geranium oil', used in perfumery.

CULTIVATION

These frost-tender plants are often treated like annuals for summer bedding in colder climates. In warmer climates with long hours of daylight they flower almost all the time, although they do not do well in extreme heat and humidity. Plant in pots or beds. The site should be sunny with light, well-drained, neutral soil. If grown in pots, fertilize regularly and cull dead heads. Avoid over-watering; Zonals in particular rot at the base if soil remains wet, although stems re-root higher up (but weaker plants result). Propagate from softwood cuttings from spring to autumn.

Pelargonium crispum (below)
LEMON GERANIUM, FINGER-BOWL GERANIUM

A distinctive species from South Africa's south-west Cape Province, *Pelargonium crispum* is an erect, few-branched shrubby perennial to 3 ft (1 m) high, its straight stems regularly lined with small lobed leaves with crinkled margins, lemon-scented when bruised. The scattered pink flowers appear large in proportion, up to 1 in (25 mm) across with darker markings. **'Variegatum'** (syn. 'Prince Rupert Variegated') is a widely grown form with cream-edged leaves. **'Prince Rupert'** is a vigorous, larger-leafed form. ZONES 9–11.

Pelargonium tricolor (above)

This species is a sprawling, wiry-stemmed shrubby perennial about 12 in (30 cm) tall. It has narrow, hairy, gray-green leaves with a few deeply cut teeth, and are seldom more than 1½ in (35 mm) long. The distinctive flowers are pansy-like, 1½ in (35 mm) wide; the upper petals are red with a black base and the lower petals are white.

Pelargonium, Ivy-leafed Hybrids

These are derived mainly from the South African *Pelargonium peltatum*, which has a scrambling or trailing habit with fleshy, pointed-lobed, hairless leaves and small pink flowers. The many cultivars retain the leaf characteristics, but have larger flowers in conspicuous long-stalked heads, often double and in a wide range of colors. Easily grown, they tolerate wetter conditions than the Zonals, and are especially suited to hanging baskets and the tops of retaining walls. Recent developments include variegated leaves and compact or miniature plants. Hybridization of Ivy-leafed and Zonal pelargoniums has resulted in plants with leaves like the former, and flowers more like the latter. The popular **'Blooming Gem'** has bright pink flowers. The **Cascade Series** of miniature Ivy-leafed pelargoniums have small leaves and masses of small flowers. It includes **'Laced Red Cascade'**, with red flowers flecked with white, and **'Chic'**, with deep pink, double flowers. **'Galilee'**, one of the best known Ivy-leafed cultivars, is compact and has leaves that may be variegated with cream or cream and pink; its densely massed double flowers are flesh pink. ZONES 9–11.

Pelargonium, Ivy-leafed
Hybrid, 'Blooming Gem'
(above)

Pelargonium cucullatum *(above)*
WILDEMALVA

This South African species is one of the original parents of the Regal pelargonium hybrids; like many other significant species it is restricted in the wild to the southwest Cape Province. It makes a very attractive shrubby perennial of sprawling habit to around 3 ft (1 m) in height; the downy gray-green leaves are sharply toothed and lobed and somewhat cupped. In spring and summer, it bears clusters of bright reddish mauve flowers with darker veins, up to 2 in (5 cm) in diameter. ZONES 9–11.

Pelargonium 'Splendide' *(below)*

Believed to be a hybrid between the South African species *Pelargonium tricolor* and *P. ovale*, this subshrubby 6–12 in (15–30 cm) tall plant, often sold as *P. tricolor* **'Arborea'**, has knotted woody stems with toothed, long-stalked, oval, hairy, gray-green leaves. It produces branched flowering stems ending in 2- to 3-flowered clusters of striking bicolored flowers. They have red upper petals, dark purple at the base, and pure white lower petals, about 1½ in (35 mm) wide. **'Pretty Lady'** is similar. ZONES 9–11.

P

Pelargonium odoratissimum (left)
APPLE GERANIUM

A strong, sweet smell of apples comes off the small, roughly heart-shaped, lobed, gray-green leaves of this very bushy, many-branched geranium. It reaches a height and spread of 12 in (30 cm). The flowers are small and white, sometimes with red veins in the upper petals. In warm-temperate climates, flowers may be borne almost continuously, although it dislikes hot, humid conditions. ZONES 10–11.

Pelargonium, Scented-leafed Hybrids

This varied group of hybrids derives from quite a few wild South African species. Most have dense branches and shallowly to deeply lobed or dissected leaves that in some are quite hairy. The range of essential oils in the leaves is very large, their scents ranging through peppermint, eucalyptus, lemon, cloves, aniseed, apple, rose and even coconut. Often a hot day will bring out the aroma, but it is released most strongly when the foliage is bruised or crushed. Some have quite showy flowers, in others they are small but still pretty. **'Fragrans'** (apple geranium) is a bushy, many-branched shrub reaching 12 in (30 cm) high and wide. A strong spicy smell like green apples comes off the small, roughly heart-shaped, lobed, gray-green leaves. Its flowers are small and white, sometimes with red veining on the upper petals. ZONES 8–11.

Pelargonium,
Scented-leafed Hybrid,
'Fragrans' (left)

Pelargonium peltatum (left)
IVY-LEAFED GERANIUM

From coastal areas of South Africa's Cape Province, this species has trailing or scrambling stems up to 3 ft (1 m) long. Its bright green leaves have 5 sharp lobes, the shape reminiscent of ivy leaves, and are up to 3 in (8 cm) across. The flowers of the original wild form are pale pink and have quite narrow petals, appearing mainly in spring and summer. This species is the chief ancestor of the Ivy-leafed hybrids. ZONES 9–11.

P

PENSTEMON

This large genus consists of 250 species of deciduous, evergreen or semi-evergreen subshrubs and perennials, mostly native to Central and North America. The leaves appear in opposite pairs or whorls, while the flowers have 2 lobes on the upper lip and 3 on the lower. Hybrids are valued for their showy flower spikes in blues, reds, whites, and bicolors. Tall varieties suit sheltered borders, and dwarf strains brighten up bedding schemes. 'Bev Jensen' is red and 'Holly's White' is a favorite in the USA.

CULTIVATION

These marginally to very frost-hardy plants do best in fertile, well-drained soil and full sun. Cut plants back hard after flowering. They can be propagated from seed in spring or autumn, by division in spring, or from cuttings of non-flowering shoots in late summer (the only method for cultivars).

Penstemon 'Alice Hindley' *(below)*
syn. *Penstemon* 'Gentianoides'

This cultivar was raised in 1931. It is tall, around 4 ft (1.2 m) and has pale mauve flowers with a white mouth. Each bloom is a little under 2 in (5 cm) long. The only drawbacks with this impressive plant are that it is inclined to be rather sparsely foliaged and that it often needs staking. ZONES 8–10.

Penstemon 'Andenken an Friedrich Hahn'
(above)
syn. *Penstemon* 'Garnet'

This very frost-hardy perennial, which grows to 30 in (75 cm) with a 24 in (60 cm) spread, bears its dark pink flowers from mid-summer to autumn. ZONES 7–10.

Penstemon barbatus *(right)*
syn. *Chelone barbata*
CORAL PENSTEMON, BEARD-LIP PENSTEMON

The scarlet flowers on this semi-evergreen, very frost-hardy perennial are tubular with 2 lips. They bloom on racemes from mid-summer to early autumn above narrow, lance-shaped, green leaves. The plant grows to 3 ft (1 m) high, with a spread of 12 in (30 cm). ZONES 3–10.

**Penstemon
'Bev Jensen'** *(right)*

This cultivar grows to
about 28 in (70 cm)
high in flower and has
mauve to pale purple
flowers with light
throats. ZONES 8–10.

**Penstemon
campanulatus** *(below)*

This frost-hardy, semi-evergreen perennial from Mexico
and Guatemala is 12–24 in
(30–60 cm) tall with narrow,
serrated, 3 in (8 cm) long
leaves. Its flowers are funnel-
to bell-shaped, reddish
purple to violet and are
carried on a lax inflorescence.
They open from early
summer. ZONES 9–11.

**Penstemon
cardwellii** *(above)*

From northwestern
USA, this very frost-
hardy evergreen
perennial forms broad
4–8 in (10–20 cm) high
clumps with 1/2–2 in
(1.2–5 cm) long,
elliptical, serrated-
edged leaves. Its flowers
are 1–1 1/2 in (25–35 mm)
long, bright purple and
open in summer.
ZONES 8–10.

**Penstemon
'Blue of Zurich'** *(left)*
syn. *Penstemon*
'Zuriblau'

This 18 in (45 cm) tall
cultivar has particularly
bright blue flowers.
ZONES 8–10.

P

Penstemon digitalis
(below)

Native to eastern North
America, this very frost-hardy
perennial species is usually
seen with white or pale
lavender flowers, neither
particularly exciting.
'Husker's Red', however, is
notable for its deep reddish
purple foliage. A robust
plant, it reaches a height of
30 in (75 cm) and spread of
24 in (60 cm), and is
attractive to hummingbirds.
ZONES 3–9.

Penstemon
'Firebird' *(left)*
syn. *Penstemon*
'Schoenholzen'

This cultivar grows to
around 30 in (75 cm)
and has vivid orange-
red flowers. **ZONES 7–10.**

Penstemon digitalis
'Husker's Red' *(right)*

Penstemon
'Cherry Ripe' *(above)*
This is a 4 ft (1.2 m) tall
hybrid with narrow,
warm red blooms on
wiry stems. **ZONES 7–10.**

P

P

Penstemon 'Evelyn'
(above left)

This is a 30 in (75 cm) tall perennial hybrid with very narrow leaves and masses of slightly curved pale pink flowers. It was raised by the famous Slieve Donard nursery of Northern Ireland and is very frost hardy. ZONES 7–10.

Penstemon 'Connie's Pink'
(above)

This 4 ft (1.2 m) tall hybrid has fine wiry stems with a coating of hairs. Its flowers are rose pink and rather narrow. ZONES 7–10.

Penstemon 'White Bedder' *(above)*
syns *Penstemon* 'Burford White', *P.* 'Royal White', *P.* 'Snow Storm'

This frost-hardy, 30 in (75 cm) tall perennial has white flowers with a pale yellow-cream tinge and an occasional hint of pale pink. The buds are often pink tinted. ZONES 7–10.

Penstemon glaber
(left)

This perennial grows to about 24 in (60 cm) tall. Its leaves are 1½–4 in (3.5–10 cm) long and lance-shaped. The inflorescence is up to 10 in (25 cm) long and is composed of 1–1½ in (25–35 mm) flowers that are purple-red at the base and white near the tips. It blooms from late summer. ZONES 3–10.

Penstemon × gloxinioides *(right)*
BORDER PENSTEMON

This name applies to a group of hybrids raised in the middle of the nineteenth century from *Penstemon cobaea* and *P. hartwegii*. They have some of the largest and showiest flowers of any penstemons, mainly in rich reds and pinks and usually with a white throat. However, they are often short lived and not so cold hardy as other penstemons, and have declined in popularity. **ZONES 7–9.**

Penstemon heterophyllus *(below)*
FOOTHILL PENSTEMON, BLUE BEDDER PENSTEMON

From California, this very frost-hardy, summer-flowering species grows to about 18 in (45 cm) tall. Its leaves are 1–2 in (2.5–5 cm) long, lance-shaped and slightly blue-green. The 1–1½ in (25–35 mm) long flowers vary from deep violet-pink to near blue. **ZONES 8–10.**

Penstemon 'Hidcote Pink' *(right)*

Up to 4 ft (1.2 m) tall, this narrow-leafed perennial has gray-green foliage and rose-pink flowers with deep pink streaks. It is very frost hardy. **ZONES 7–10.**

P

Penstemon hirsutus *(below)*

A penstemon from the northeastern and central states of the USA, this species reaches about 24 in (60 cm) in height and has hairy stems and rather narrow, dark green leaves. The flowers, crowded at the ends of the stems in summer, are pale purple outside with a coating of fine fuzzy hairs, and white in the throat. *Penstemon hirsutus* var. *pygmaeus* is a loosely mat-forming plant no more than 4 in (10 cm) high with short, spreading flowering stems and purple-flushed foliage; it is popular as a rock garden plant. ZONES 3–9.

Penstemon 'Pennington Gem' *(below)*

This 30 in (75 cm) tall, frost-hardy perennial has deep pink, white-throated flowers with a few purple-red stripes. ZONES 7–10.

P

Penstemon hirsutus
var. *pygmaeus (above)*

Penstemon pinifolius *(opposite page, left)*

This sprightly evergreen species is best suited to a
well-drained rock garden. A moderately frost-
hardy native of southwest USA and Mexico, it
thrives in heat and needs little water beyond the
normal rainfall. The flowers are typically 2 lipped
and bright orange-red, and are produced for
much of the summer. The leaves are needle-like.
ZONES 8–11.

Penstemon serrulatus *(below)*

CASCADE PENSTEMON

Found from Oregon to southern Alaska, this
12–30 in (30–75 cm) tall, very frost-hardy species
has broad, lance-shaped, 1–4 in (2.5–10 cm) long
leaves with serrated edges. The flowers, in dense
clusters, are less than 1 in (25 mm) long, tubular-
to bell-shaped, deep blue to purple and open from
late summer. **ZONES 5–10.**

Penstemon 'Stapleford Gem'

(above)

A very frost-hardy
strong grower to 4 ft
(1.2 m) tall, this peren-
nial has flowers in a
glowing shade of
purple-pink. The color
varies somewhat with
the climate and soil pH.
ZONES 7–10.

Penstemon 'Thorn'

(left)

This hybrid grows to
3 ft (1 m) in height and
has narrow pink and
white flowers.
ZONES 7–10.

P

PENTAPHRAGMA

This genus of about 25 species from the rainforests of Southeast Asia is related to the bellflowers *(Campanula)* but the relationship would only be evident to a botanist. They evergreen perennials have fleshy, creeping stems, broad, simple leaves that are often one-sided at the base, and dense clusters of rather insignificant circular flowers in the leaf axils. Foliage of some species is gathered by local people for use as a green vegetable.

CULTIVATION

These plants are seldom cultivated except in botanical gardens, and outside the wet tropics would need a heated greenhouse.

Pentaphragma horsfieldii *(below)*

Native to Java, Sumatra and the Malay Peninsula, this low-growing plant has creeping stems and broad, heavily veined green leaves. The tightly clustered small flowers are fleshy, disc-shaped and cream in color, changing to green as they age. ZONES 11–12.

PENTAS

This genus of around 40 species of biennials, perennials and subshrubs is found in tropical parts of Arabia and Africa. They have bright green, lance-shaped, 3–8 in (8–20 cm) long leaves, sometimes coated with a fine down or tiny hairs. The small, starry, long-tubed flowers are massed in flat-topped heads and appear throughout the warmer months. They are usually bright pink, but also occur in red and purple shades and white.

CULTIVATION

Although very frost tender and only suitable for outdoor cultivation in very mild climates, they are easily grown as house plants. The new dwarf strains can be treated as bedding or pot annuals. Plant in moist, well-drained soil in full sun or part-shade and pinch back regularly to maintain a compact habit and to encourage bloom. Deadhead as required and trim lightly in early spring. Water well when in full growth. Propagate from seed in spring or from softwood cuttings in summer. Watch for aphids and red spider mites.

Pentas lanceolata
(below)
syn. *Pentas carnea*
EGYPTIAN STAR, STAR CLUSTER
This erect, straggling shrubby perennial grows to a height of 2–3 ft (0.6–1 m) with a slightly wider spread. It is grown for its clusters of tubular, red, pink, lilac or white flowers, among bright green, hairy leaves during spring and summer. ZONES 10–12.

PEPEROMIA
RADIATOR PLANT

This genus from tropical and subtropical regions worldwide contains 1000 species of evergreen or succulent perennials. Ideal in terrariums or dish gardens, they have diverse and beautifully marked and shaped, fleshy, usually long-stalked leaves. Long-stemmed spikes of minute, greenish white to cream flowers appear erratically in late summer.

CULTIVATION
Frost tender, these make good house plants. Peperomias like bright light, but not direct sun, especially near a window, with high humidity in summer. Keep moist in warm weather, and be sure to water them from below as the leaves mark easily. In winter, allow the plants to dry out between waterings. Use a half-strength, soluble fertilizer once a month in spring and summer. Peperomias are easily propagated from leaf or stem cuttings in spring or summer, and should be repotted annually. Watch for mealybugs, spider mites and white fly.

Peperomia argyreia (left)
WATERMELON PEPEROMIA
Found in northern South America, this is a compact, nearly stemless perennial with rosettes of glossy, rounded, 3–4 in (8–10 cm) long, gray-striped leaves on long red stems. The flower spikes are small, but extend beyond the foliage. ZONES 11–12.

Peperomia caperata
EMERALD RIPPLE
This perennial species has oval, deeply corrugated and veined, heart-shaped, dark green, sometimes purplish leaves. They are pale green underneath and about 1½ in (35 mm) across, carried on pinkish stems. Tight clusters of white flower spikes appear irregularly. **'Silver Ripples'** has silver-gray markings on the ridges of the corrugations. ZONES 11–12.

Peperomia caperata 'Silver Ripples' (left)

PERICALLIS
CINERARIA

This genus has about 15 species of perennials and subshrubs closely allied to *Senecio,* where they were once included. They are distributed throughout the mid-latitude islands of the Atlantic Ocean. Best known in cultivation for the florist's cineraria *(Pericallis × hybrida),* the wild species are nowhere near as fancy. The leaves, which form basal rosettes in the perennials, are usually oval to lance-shaped, 2–6 in (5–15 cm) long, with finely toothed edges and covered in small hairs. The flowers are usually pink, mauve or purple, ½–2 in (1.2–5 cm) wide and carried in open heads.

CULTIVATION

Although easily cultivated in any moist, well-drained soil in part- to full shade, few species will tolerate anything other than very light frosts. The florist's strains are often used as winter-flowering house plants. Propagate from seed or cuttings or by division, depending on the growth form.

Pericallis × hybrida
(below)
syns *Senecio cruentus,*
S. × hybrida

This hybrid reaches 12 in (30 cm) tall and wide. It is a multi-purpose bloomer for grouping or for formal bedding in part-shaded spots. It is ideal for window boxes, for containers on balconies or in courtyards. The color of the daisy-like flowers ranges from pink, red, purple and crimson through to white, as well as the traditional blue. They are very tolerant of heat, salt air and poor soil, but suffer in high humidity or excessive rain. ZONES 9–11.

P

Pericallis × hybrida
(above, above left & left)

Pericallis lanata (left)
syn. *Senecio heritieri*

This 3 ft (1 m) tall species from Tenerife in the
Canary Islands has flexible stems that may be
upright or spreading. Its leaves, which are hairy
and up to 6 in (15 cm) long, are usually oval and
finely toothed, but sometimes have 5 to 7 deep
lobes. The flowers may be borne singly or in loose
heads and are white and purple, up to 1¹/₂ in
(35 mm) wide and sweetly scented. **ZONES 9–11.**

P

P

PEROVSKIA

Found in western Asia and the Himalayan region, the 7 species of deciduous shrubby perennials in this genus have gray-white stems and aromatic leaves that are covered with gray felt when young. As they mature, the deeply lobed, 2–3 in (5–8 cm) long leaves lose their felting and become gray-green. They form large clumps to 3–5 ft (1–1.5 m) tall and are topped in late summer with 12–18 in (30–45 cm) panicles of tiny purple-blue flowers.

CULTIVATION

They are very easily grown in any well-drained, rather dry soil in a sunny position. It is often best to contain their growth by planting them beside a path, wall or border edge. If allowed free rein, smaller, less vigorous plants may be smothered. They are very frost hardy and may be propagated from seed, or by cuttings of non-flowering stems.

Perovskia atriplicifolia (above)
RUSSIAN SAGE

This tall, tough species produces soft, gray-green foliage that beautifully complements the haze of pale lavender-blue flowers, which appear on panicles in late summer and autumn. The plants are upright to 5 ft (1.5 m), with a spread of 3 ft (1 m) or more. They are long lived. ZONES 6–9.

PERSICARIA
syns *Aconogonon, Bistorta, Tovara*

KNOTWEED

This genus of 50 to 80 species of annuals, perennials or subshrubs have strong wiry stems with variously shaped leaves 1½–10 in (3.5–25 cm) long. The foliage often has purple-gray markings and may develop red and gold tints in autumn. The flowers, usually pink or cream, are small and are sometimes borne in showy panicles or spikes.

CULTIVATION
Most are vigorous and very frost hardy, easily cultivated in any well-drained soil in sun or part-shade. Some may become invasive: the stronger growers are best contained. Propagate from seed in spring or by division in spring or autumn.

Persicaria amplexicaulis
syns *Bistorta amplexicaulis, Polygonum amplexicaule*

BISTORT, MOUNTAIN FLEECE

Persicaria amplexicaulis is a clump-forming, leafy, semi-evergreen perennial from the Himalayas. It has oval to heart-shaped mid-green leaves and grows to a height and spread of 4 ft (1.2 m). Its profuse spikes of small, rich red flowers are borne from summer to autumn. *P. amplexicaulis* 'Firetail' is a low grower with vivid crimson flowers. 'Inverleith' is a dwarf cultivar with short spikes of deep crimson flowers. ZONES 5–9.

Persicaria amplexicaulis 'Firetail' *(left)*

Persicaria amplexicaulis 'Inverleith' *(left)*

P

Persicaria bistorta
syn. *Polygonum bistorta*
BISTORT, SNAKEWEED

A vigorous perennial with heavy rootstock, *Persicaria bistorta* is found from Europe to western Asia. This species grows to around 24 in (60 cm) tall. Its leaves are oblong with wavy margins and grow 4–8 in (10–20 cm) long. The flowers open in summer and are white or pink. **'Superba'** is a tall form which has densely packed spikes of pink flowers. ZONES 4–9.

Persicaria campanulata *(right)*
syn. *Polygonum campanulatum*
LESSER KNOTWEED

This Himalayan species is a spreading perennial that forms a clump of unbranched wiry stems. Its leaves are 1½–4 in (3.5–10 cm) long and are lance-shaped, bright green on top with pale gray to pink undersides. The flowering stems are erect, 2–4 ft (0.6–1.2 m) tall with pink or white flowers from late summer. **'Rosenrot'** is an upright grower with deep pink flowers. ZONES 8–10.

Persicaria campanulata 'Rosenrot' *(above)*

Persicaria bistorta 'Superba' *(below)*

Persicaria filiformis (left)
syn. *Polygonum filiforme*

Up to 4 ft (1.2 m) tall, *Persicaria filiformis* comes from Japan, the Himalayas and northeastern USA. It has 3–6 in (8–15 cm) long elliptical leaves with a covering of short, rough hairs and often marked with rows of chocolate-brown flecks. The flower spikes are slender and the green-white or pale pink flowers are not particularly showy. ZONES 5–10.

Persicaria macrophylla (left)
syn. *Polygonum macrophyllum*

This spreading Himalayan and western Chinese semi-evergreen perennial rarely exceeds 6 in (15 cm) in height, but has leaves up to 4 in (10 cm) long. The foliage forms a basal clump that slowly enlarges and spreads. The pink or red flowers open in summer. ZONES 5–9.

Persicaria orientale (left)
syn. *Polygonum orientale*
PRINCE'S FEATHER, PRINCESS FEATHER

From eastern and Southeast Asia and Australia, this species is an annual that reaches 5 ft (1.5 m) tall. Its leaves are large, up to 8 in (20 cm) long, and are roughly an elongated heart shape. The flowers open from late summer and are bright pink to purple-pink or white and are borne in large, slightly pendulous, branched spikes. ZONES 8–11.

P

PETUNIA

'*Petun*' means 'tobacco' in a South American Indian dialect, and petunias are indeed relatives of the tobaccos *(Nicotiana)*. Their leaves have a similar narcotic effect on humans, and both genera belong to the same family as potatoes (Solanaceae). There are around 35 species in the genus, occurring in warmer parts of South America. They include annuals, biennials and shrubby perennials. The leaves are dark green, rather hairy and smooth-edged and the trumpet-shaped flowers are white, purple, red, blue, pink or mixed hues. It is doubtful whether any other group of garden annuals has been the subject of such intense selection by plant breeders over such a long period as the petunias. Interestingly, from what has been revealed of their work, it seems to have been concentrated almost entirely on the one hybrid combination, *Petunia × hybrida*.

Petunia × hybrida, Surfinia Series, 'Pink Vein' *(above)*

CULTIVATION

The garden petunias are frost-tender plants always grown as annuals. They are popular worldwide as bedding plants and for window boxes, hanging baskets and planters. Fairly fast growing, they like well-drained, fertile soil and a sunny location and thrive where summers are hot, although they do need shelter from wind. Flowers of some of the larger **Grandiflora hybrids** are damaged by rain, but others, mainly the **Multiflora hybrids,** are more resistant. Sow seed under glass in early spring, or plant purchased seedlings at beginning of summer. Fertilize every month until flowering is well advanced. Pinch back hard to encourage branching and deadhead regularly. Watch for cucumber mosaic and tomato spotted wilt.

P

Petunia × *hybrida*
'Shihi Purple' *(left)*

Petunia × *hybrida*

Believed to have originated as a cross between the white-flowered *Petunia axillaris* and the pink to purple-flowered *P. integrifolia*, the garden petunia was a well-known summer bedding plant in Europe by the middle of the nineteenth century. From an early stage, the garden petunias were divided into 4 groups of cultivars and seedling strains, designated by Latin names, and this classification still survives. The 2 most important groups are the **Grandiflora** and **Multiflora** petunias, both with plants around 12 in (30 cm) tall at maturity. Flowers of the former are very wide and shallow, scattered over the somewhat sprawling plants, while Multifloras are more compact in growth with densely massed and somewhat narrower blooms. The **Nana Compacta** petunias are generally less than 6 in (15 cm) high, of compact habit, and with profuse small flowers. The **Pendula** petunias have prostrate, trailing stems and are grown mainly in hanging baskets. It is the Grandiflora petunias that are now the most popular, with a dazzling range of newer F1 hybrids, although they are more easily rain damaged and susceptible to disfiguring botrytis rot. They include the **Cascade** and **Supercascade**

Petunia × *hybrida*,
Celebrity Series,
'Pink Morn' *(left)*

Petunia × *hybrida*
cultivars
(below left & below right)

Petunia × *hybrida*
'Flamingo' *(right)*

Series (or Magic Series), available in a wide range of colors, with single flowers and somewhat trailing stems suitable for hanging baskets. **'Giants of California'** is not so profusely blooming, but individual blossoms are very large with ruffled edges and are white, pink or mauve. The Multifloras have smaller blooms but are more prolific flowerers. They include the **Plum Series**, with delightfully veined flowers and **Bonanza Series** with frilly, trumpet-shaped double flowers in a multitude of colors. The **Celebrity Series**, including cultivars such as **'Pink Morn'**, also covers a wide color range, and are mainly in pastel shades. They can be distinguished by their light-throated flowers. The **Madness Series** have small single-color flowers. **'Purple Wave'** is a seedling strain with prolific flowers of a single, magenta-purple color. It has a cascading growth habit and is similar to the vegetatively propagated **'Colorwave'** petunias. **Surfinia Series** petunias are extremely vigorous disease-resistant trailing plants that are smothered throughout the warmer months with rain-tolerant blooms. Other petunia cultivars include **'Flamingo'**, **'Frenzy Rose'**, **'Pink Flamingo'**, and **'Shihi Purple'**. ZONES 9–11.

Petunia × *hybrida*
'Frenzy Rose' *(below)*

Petunia × *hybrida*
cultivar *(below right)*

Petunia × *hybrida,*
Madness Series, 'Purple
Wave' *(right)*

P

Petunia integrifolia, Million Bells Series, 'Terracotta' *(left)*

Petunia integrifolia *(below)*
syn. *Petunia violacea*

Sometimes sold as **'Burgundy Pet'**, this Argentinian species is a short-lived shrubby perennial that produces masses of small, dark-throated, rose purple flowers on sprawling plants. It is a weather- and disease-tolerant species that is being increasingly used in hybridizing. Some very free-flowering cultivars recently released under the trade name Million Bells may belong to this species. **ZONES 9–11.**

Petunia × hybrida, Surfinia Series, 'Blue Vein' and *Petunia integrifolia*, Million Bells Series, 'Blue' *(below)*

Petunia × *hybrida*
'Pink Flamingo' *(below)*

Petunia × *hybrida*,
'Surfinia Series, 'White'
(below right)

Petunia × *hybrida*, Surfinia Series,
'Hot Pink' and *Petunia integrifolia*,
Million Bells Series, 'Trailing Pink' *(above)*

PHACELIA
SCORPION WEED

This is a genus of around 150 species of annuals, biennials and perennials native to the Americas. They are generally shrubby, but vary considerably in size, ranging from as little as 6 in (15 cm) to over 5 ft (1.5 m) tall. The young shoots and leaves are sometimes downy and the leaves are often toothed or lobed, sometimes to the point of being pinnate. They all have clusters of small 5-petalled flowers at the stem tips. The flowers are usually in blue or purple shades, often with white centers, and can be quite striking. *Phacelia bolanderi* is a delicate shade of lilac.

Phacelia grandiflora *(below)*

This species from southern California is a 3 ft (1 m) tall annual with serrated-edged, elliptical leaves up to 8 in (20 cm) long. Its flowers are 1½ in (35 mm) wide and are mauve to white. ZONES 8–11.

CULTIVATION

Most species are very easily grown in any light but moist, well-drained soil in full sun. They are fully frost hardy. Propagate the annuals and biennials from seed, the perennials from seed or cuttings.

Phacelia bolanderi
(below)

PHLOMIS

This is a genus of around 150 species of often downy-leaved perennials, subshrubs and shrubs found from the Mediterranean region to China. Although variable, in most cases their leaves are large, over 4 in (10 cm) long, and densely covered with hair-like felting. Typical of members of the nettle family, the leaves occur in whorls on upright stems. The tubular flowers, borne on upright verticillasters, curl downwards and have 2 lips at the tip, the upper lip hooded over the lower. They occur in clusters of 2 to 40 blooms, depending on the species, and are usually in shades of cream, yellow, pink, mauve or purple.

CULTIVATION

Hardiness varies, though most will tolerate moderate frosts. Species with heavily felted foliage suffer in prolonged wet weather and are best grown in exposed positions where the foliage dries quickly after rain. Plant in moist, well-drained soil in full sun or part-shade. Propagate from seed or from small cuttings of non-flowering shoots, or by division where possible.

Phlomis tuberosa
(right)

This 5 ft (1.5 m) tall species develops small tubers on its roots. Its leaves are an elongated heart shape, up to 10 in (25 cm) long with toothed edges. They have a covering of fine hairs, but are not felted. The flowers open in summer, are pink to purple and quite small, but there are up to 40 in each whorl. ZONES 7–10.

Phlomis russeliana *(below)*

This easily grown perennial thrives in any ordinary soil given a reasonable amount of sun. The large, heart-shaped, fresh green leaves make excellent ground cover if planted in quantity, forming clumps around 12 in (30 cm) high and up to 24 in (60 cm) across. In summer, it bears stout stems 3 ft (1 m) high topped with several whorls of hooded, butter yellow flowers. ZONES 7–10.

P

Phlox adsurgens 'Wagon Wheel' *(below)*

Phlox adsurgens
WOODLAND PHLOX

This prostrate to slightly mounding
perennial is native to Oregon and northern
California. Its leaves are rounded, shiny,
usually less than 1 in (25 mm) long and
slightly hairy. Sprays of bright pink flowers
up to 1 in (25 mm) wide open from late
spring. It prefers a cool, lightly shaded
position. **'Wagon Wheel'** is a popular
cultivar with drooping stems of large
flowers with strappy petals. ZONES 6–10.

PHLOX

This genus contains more than 60 species of evergreen and semi-evergreen annuals and perennials,
mostly native to North America. They are grown
for their profuse, fragrant flowers and the symmetry
of the flower clusters. The name *phlox* means
'flame', appropriate for these brightly colored,
showy flowers popular in bedding and border
displays. *Phlox purpurea* × *lutea* has deep pink
flowers with pale yellow centers.

CULTIVATION
Perennials are easily grown in any temperate
climate, and need a lot of water while they grow.
Annuals grow in almost any climate. Plant in
fertile, moist but well-drained soil in a sunny or
part-shaded position. Propagate from seed or
cuttings or by division. Watch out for red spider
mite, eelworm and powdery mildew.

Phlox douglasii 'Waterloo' *(below)*

Phlox douglasii

This evergreen perennial, occurring naturally from Washington to California in the USA, bears white, lavender-blue or pink flowers and grows to 8 in (20 cm) in height. **'Boothman's Variety'** is a dwarf form with blue-centered lavender flowers. **'Crackerjack'** is a compact cultivar with crimson to magenta flowers. **'Red Admiral'** is a strong-growing yet compact form with vivid crimson flowers. **'Rosea'** forms a neat mat with silver-pink flowers. **'Waterloo'** has deep crimson flowers. **'Rose Cushion'** is a very compact plant that covers itself with dusky pink flowers. ZONES 5–10.

Phlox purpurea × lutea
(above)

Phlox douglasii 'Rose Cushion' *(right)*

Phlox douglasii 'Rosea' *(below)*

P

Phlox maculata
MEADOW PHLOX

Phlox maculata is a perennial that grows to 3 ft (1 m) tall and bears scented, white, pink or purple flowers in mid-summer. **'Alpha'** is around 30 in (75 cm) tall with deep pink flowers. **'Miss Lingard'** is up to 3 ft (1 m) tall with fragrant white flowers that sometimes have a central pink ring. **'Omega'** is around 30 in (75 cm) tall with fragrant white, lilac-centered flowers. ZONES 5–10.

Phlox maculata 'Omega' *(above)*

Phlox maculata 'Alpha' *(left)*

Phlox drummondii 'Sternenzauber' *(left)*

Phlox drummondii
ANNUAL PHLOX

This bushy annual grows quickly to 15 in (38 cm) tall and half that in spread. In summer and autumn, it bears closely clustered, small, flattish flowers with 5 petals in reds, pinks, purples and creams. It has lanceolate, light green leaves and is frost resistant. **'Sternenzauber'** (syn. 'Twinkle') bears star-like flowers that have pointed petals. There are dwarf strains that grow to 4 in (10 cm). ZONES 6–10.

Phlox paniculata
(right)

SUMMER PHLOX, PERENNIAL PHLOX

This tall perennial to 3 ft (1 m) bears long-lasting flowerheads of many small flowers in summer. **'Amethyst'** has violet flowers. **'Brigadier'** has very deep green leaves and pink flowers suffused with orange. **'Bright Eyes'** has pink flowers with red eyes. **'Eventide'** has light mauve or lavender blue flowers. **'Fujiyama'** has pure white flowers on stems up to 30 in (75 cm) tall. **'Graf Zeppelin'** has white flowers with pinkish red centers. **'Mother of Pearl'** has white to pale pink flowers suffused pink on stems up to 30 in (75 cm) tall. **'Prince of Orange'** has deep pink flowers flushed with orange on stems up to 3 ft (1 m) tall. **'Prospero'** is an award-winning cultivar with white-edged, mauve flowers. **'Sir John Falstaff'** has salmon-pink flowers. **'Snow Hare'** has snow white flowers. **'White Admiral'** bears pure white flowers. **'Windsor'** has deep pink flowers. ZONES 4–10.

Phlox paniculata
'Prince of Orange'
(right)

Phlox paniculata
'Graf Zeppelin' *(below)*

P

Phlox paniculata
'Snow Hare' *(above)*

Phlox paniculata
'Mother of Pearl' *(left)*

Phlox paniculata
'Amethyst' and
P. p. 'Europa' *(below)*

P

Phlox subulata
MOSS PHLOX

Throughout spring, this prostrate alpine perennial produces masses of 1 in (25 mm) wide, star-shaped flowers in blue, mauve, carmine, pink and white, the petals being notched and open. Its fine-leaved foliage grows carpet-like to 4 in (10 cm) high with a spread twice that. Fully frost hardy and evergreen, it is suitable for sunny rock gardens. **'Greencourt Purple'** has a rich color and likes a little shade. **'McDaniel's Cushion'** (syn. 'Daniel's Cushion') is best in small groups among shrubs or taller perennials. **'Maischnee'** (syn. 'May Snow') is a beautiful snow white form. **'Marjorie'** has glowing deep pink flowers. **'Oakington Blue Eyes'** forms large mats and is smothered with light blue flowers. ZONES 3–10.

Phlox pilosa subsp. ozarkana (right)
PRAIRIE PHLOX

This form of a perennial widespread in the USA grows to 24 in (60 cm) tall with lance-shaped leaves up to 6 in (15 cm) long. The spring flowers, in large panicles, are up to 1 in (25 mm) wide, white, purple or pink. ZONES 5–10.

Phlox subulata
'McDaniel's Cushion'
(above)

Phlox subulata
'Greencourt Purple'
(right)

P

PHORMIUM
NEW ZEALAND FLAX

Valued for the dramatic effect of their stiff, vertical leaves, these 2 species of large, clumping plants from New Zealand grow well in most conditions. In summer, they produce panicles of flowers that attract nectar-feeding birds. The large, arching, striped leaves appear in clumps and can be anything from dark green to green-yellow. There are many cultivars with variegated or brightly colored foliage. They range in height from 3 ft (1 m) to 6 ft (1.8 m). The fiber of these flaxes has been used commercially, but is now largely confined to traditional Maori crafts.

CULTIVATION
They make splendid container plants as well as useful garden specimens in almost any climate. They are fairly frost hardy, and respond well to generous watering and permanently moist conditions. Propagate from seed or by division in spring.

Phormium 'Apricot Queen' *(below)*

This form has dark green, arching leaves to 4 ft (1.2 m) long with apricot striping and bronze edges. The young foliage is creamy yellow. ZONES 8–11.

Phormium cookianum *(right)*
syn. *Phormium colensoi*

Found throughout New Zealand in a wide range of conditions, this species has leaves 2–5 ft (0.6–1.5 m) long and up to 2½ in (6 cm) wide. Its flowers are yellow to red-brown with yellow interiors, and are carried on stiffly erect stems that extend well above the foliage clump. '**Dark Delight**' has deep wine-red leaves up to 4 ft (1.2 m) long. '**Duet**' is a 12 in (30 cm) tall dwarf cultivar with cream and green foliage. '**Maori Maiden**' (syn. 'Rainbow Maiden') is an upright grower with 3 ft (1 m) long bronze leaves striped red. '**Sundowner**' has extremely long leaves, almost 6 ft (1.8 m), that are bronze-green with cream or pinkish edges. '**Tricolor**' is an evergreen, upright perennial with bold spiky leaves prettily striped with red, yellow and green, and panicles of tubular, pale yellowish green flowers. ZONES 8–11.

Phormium cookianum 'Duet' *(left)*

Phormium cookianum 'Maori Maiden' *(right)*

P

Phormium cookianum
'Sundowner' *(left)*

Phormium tenax *(left)*

The larger of the flax species, this
has olive green, strap-like leaves
6–10 ft (1.8–3 m) tall in clumps
about 6 ft (1.8 m) across. It grows
well by the sea. Hybrids of
Phormium tenax and *P. cookianum*
are often more compact than their
parents, and their foliage varies
from bronze or purplish chartreuse
to pink and salmon. The leaves may
be variegated with vertical stripes
of 2 or more colors. **'Bronze Baby'**
has wide, fibrous, copper-toned
leaves with sharply pointed tips. In
summer, it bears tubular, bronze-
red flowers on a strong stem from
the base of the clump. **'Dazzler'** has
red leaves edged with plum-purple.
'Purpureum' has stiff, pointed,
plum-purple to dark copper leaves
and in summer bears reddish
flowers on purplish blue stems.
'Variegatum' has foliage marked
with a lighter colored stripe.
'Tom Thumb' has green leaves with
bronze margins growing to 24 in
(60 cm). **'Coffee'** is another
popular cultivar. ZONES 8–11.

Phormium tenax
'Bronze Baby' *(left)*

Phormium tenax
'Coffee' *(above)*

Phormium tenax
'Purpureum' *(above)*

Phormium tenax
'Variegatum' *(below)*

Phormium
'Rainbow Warrior'
(right)

This is a recently
released cultivar that
makes a luxuriant
clump of foliage. It has
long arching and
drooping leaves that are
predominantly pinkish
red and irregularly
striped with bronze
green. ZONES 8–11.

PHUOPSIS

This is a genus of just one species, a small clump- or mat-forming perennial native to the Caucasus and northern Iran. Its whorled foliage is reminiscent of the closely related woodruff *(Galium odoratum)* with tiny, narrow leaves in starry clusters at intervals along the 6–8 in (15–20 cm) stems. Its flowers are bright pink, ½ in (12 mm) long, 5-petalled tubes with a protruding style. They are massed in rounded heads of 30 to 50 blooms and open in summer.

CULTIVATION

This plant is very frost hardy and is best grown in gritty, humus-rich, moist soil in sun or part-shade. Propagate from seed or cuttings of non-flowering shoots or by division.

Phuopsis stylosa
(below)

This charming little plant is most at home in a corner of a rockery that doesn't get too hot and dry in summer. Remove the heads of small pink flowers as they deteriorate and the display should last well into autumn. ZONES 7–9.

PHYSALIS
GROUND CHERRY

This is a genus of about 80 species of annuals and perennials with a widespread distribution, especially in the Americas. Most form a clump of upright leafy stems 2–4 ft (0.6–1.2 m) tall. The leaves are variable in shape, usually lance-shaped, oval or deltoid (like a poplar leaf), often with lobes or shallow-toothed edges. The flowers are small, usually white or yellow blotched purple, and are backed by calyces that enlarge to enclose the fruit as they develop. The fruit are yellow, orange or red berries, and are often edible. They are ripe when the calyces start to dry out.

CULTIVATION
Hardiness varies, but most species tolerate moderate frosts. They prefer moist, well-drained soil and a position in sun or part-shade. Propagate from seed or by division.

Physalis alkekengi
(*right*)
CHINESE LANTERN, WINTER CHERRY

This 24 in (60 cm) tall perennial found from southern Europe to Japan is most notable for the vivid orange calyx that surrounds the ripening fruit, giving rise to one of its common names. The narrow leaves, about 3 in (8 cm) long, are mid-green. The flowers are small and white with yellow centers. The fruiting stems are often used fresh in floral arrangements or dried for winter decoration. ***Physalis alkekengi* var. *franchetii*** has minute, creamy white flowers. ZONES 6–10.

Physalis alkekengi var.
franchetii *(left)*

Physalis peruviana
(above right & right)
CAPE GOOSEBERRY, GROUND
CHERRY

This perennial South
American species grows
to around 3 ft (1 m)
tall. It is often treated as
an annual and is grown
for its crop of bright
yellow to purple, edible
berries. Its leaves are
oval to heart-shaped
and up to 4 in (10 cm)
long. The yellow-
blotched purple flowers
are ¹/₂ in (12 mm) wide
and are quickly
enveloped by the calyces.
ZONES 8–11.

P

PHYSOSTEGIA
OBEDIENT PLANT, FALSE DRAGON HEAD

This is a North American genus of some 12 species of rhizomatous perennials. They are vigorous growers and quickly develop in spring to form clumps of unbranched, upright stems clothed in narrow, lance-shaped, long leaves with toothed edges. Plant size varies from 2–6 ft (0.6–1.8 m) tall and the leaves are 2–6 in (5–15 cm) long. From mid-summer, spikes of flowers develop at the stem tips. The flowers are tubular to bell-shaped with 2 upper lobes and 3 lower lobes. They are usually less than ½ in (12 mm) long and in shades of lavender, pink or purple and white. If a flower is moved, it will not spring back into position but will stay put, owing to a stalk with a hinge-like structure.

CULTIVATION
Obedient plants prefer moist, well-drained soil in sun or very light shade. They are very easy to grow and can be slightly invasive. Hardiness varies, though all species tolerate at least moderate frosts. Propagate from seed, from small basal cuttings or by division.

Physostegia virginiana 'Summer Spire' *(above left)*

Physostegia virginiana (above)

The showy flowers of this herbaceous perennial, which bloom in erect terminal spikes late in summer, are tubular, have 2 lips and are available in pale pink, magenta ('**Vivid**') or white. It grows to 3 ft (1 m) and gives a striking display suitable for a mixed border. '**Summer Snow**' has white flowers. '**Summer Spire**' is around 24 in (60 cm) tall with deep pink flowers.
ZONES 3–10.

PHYTEUMA
HORNED RAMPION

This Eurasian genus of around 40 species of small perennials is instantly recognizable for the unusually structured flowerheads. The plants vary in size from 4–30 in (10–75 cm) tall. Their basal leaves are usually heart-shaped, while the upper leaves are oval to lance-shaped. The leaves are sometimes sharply toothed. The flowers are borne on rounded heads and are tubular, often swelling at the base, with scarcely open tips from which the stigma protrudes; they are usually in lavender, blue or purple shades tinged with white.

CULTIVATION
The small alpine species should be grown in light, gritty soil with added humus in a rockery or alpine house; the large species will grow in a normal perennial border, but take care that they do not become overgrown by more vigorous plants. Plant in sun or part-shade. Propagate from seed or by division where possible.

Phyteuma comosum (below)
syn. *Physoplexis comosa*

Native to the European Alps, this tufted perennial rarely exceeds 4 in (10 cm) in height. It has toothed, heart-shaped leaves and heads of violet-blue flowers. A favorite of alpine enthusiasts, it requires a gritty soil with added humus for moisture retention. ZONES 6–9.

P

Phyteuma comosum
(right)

Phyteuma
spicatum *(right)*
SPIKED RAMPION

Up to 30 in (75 cm)
tall, this European
species is suitable for
general garden use. Its
lower leaves are heart-
shaped, toothed and
around 4 in (10 cm)
long. The upper leaves
are more oval in shape
and are less sharply
toothed. The densely
packed flowerheads are
backed by narrow leafy
bracts and the flowers
are white, cream or
blue. **ZONES 6–10.**

PHYTOLACCA
POKEWEED, POKEBERRY

The 35 species in this genus are native to warm-temperate and tropical areas of the Americas, Africa and Asia. Taller plants can grow to 50 ft (15 m). These perennials, evergreen trees and shrubs are valued for their general appearance and decorative, though often poisonous, rounded berries. The leaves can be quite large and have colored stems and attractive hues in autumn; the white flowers are small and are arranged in clusters.

CULTIVATION
They prefer rich soil in a sheltered position in full sun to part-shade and need adequate moisture to thrive. Propagate from seed in spring or autumn.

Phytolacca
americana *(above)*
This soft-wooded shrub from North America is often treated as an herbaceous perennial. The white flowers in summer are followed by purple-blue berries in autumn. All parts of the plant are poisonous. ZONES 2–11.

PILEA

This is a genus of around 600 species of annuals and perennials that are widely distributed in the tropics with the exception of Australia. They may be creeping or erect and are usually small, though the larger species can reach 6 ft (1.8 m) tall. The foliage is variable: many have simple lance-shaped leaves, others have heart-shaped peperomia-like foliage and a few have tiny, clustered, moss-like leaves. The flowers are tiny, cream to pink structures that are easily overlooked. They are sometimes followed by seed pods that forcibly eject their seed when ripe.

CULTIVATION

All frost tender, pileas are widely grown as house plants. The smaller species prefer warm, humid conditions and are ideal for terrariums and heated greenhouses. In subtropical or tropical gardens grow in moist, well-drained, humus-rich soil in part-shade. Propagate from seed or cuttings or by division.

Pilea involucrata (below)
FRIENDSHIP PLANT

From Central and South America, this trailing species that sometimes mounds to 12 in (30 cm) tall has hairy, toothed-edged, 2½ in (6 cm) long, oval leaves. The foliage has a puckered surface and is usually bronze-green above and reddish beneath. There are several cultivated forms with varying leaf colors, shapes and sizes. ZONES 10–12.

P

Pilea nummulariifolia (right)

Usually seen spilling from a hanging basket, this trailing perennial from tropical South America and the West Indies has 1 in (25 mm) long, rounded leaves with toothed edges. In summer it produces small cream flowers in the leaf axils and at the stem tips. ZONES 10–12.

PILOSELLA

This is a genus of some 20 species of small, rosette-forming, dandelion-like perennials from Eurasia and North Africa. At least one species, *Pilosella aurantiaca,* is a serious weed in the western USA and New Zealand. The clump of basal leaves is composed of simple, hairy, oblong, lance- or spatula-shaped leaves, 1–8 in (2.5–20 cm) long depending on the species. Loose, open heads of small yellow or orange daisy-like flowerheads are carried on wiry stems up to 24 in (60 cm) tall. Most species flower continuously through summer.

CULTIVATION

They are not difficult to cultivate in any light, well-drained soil in full sun and are really plants that are more likely to pop up by chance than to be actively cultivated. Most species are very frost hardy. Propagate from seed or by division.

Pilosella laticeps
(below)

The species name means 'wide head' and aptly describes the showy golden flowerheads of this uncommon species, larger than those of most other pilosellas. It shows promise as a rock garden and ground cover plant; the spatula-shaped leaves are glossy deep green above and whitish beneath. The plant spreads to form a mat of foliage 24 in (60 cm) or more across. ZONES 8–10.

PINGUICULA

BUTTERWORT

This widely distributed genus consists of about 45 species of carnivorous perennials. Their 1–2½ in (2.5–6 cm), pointed oval leaves in basal rosettes develop from overwintering buds. The leaves are succulent and their sticky surface traps small insects. The leaf coating also contains an anesthetic that immobilizes the insects, and the leaf edges curl in to trap them. After closing, the leaf secretes a substance to digest the prey and extract its nutrients. In summer the long-spurred, 1–2½ in (2.5–6 cm) long flowers, usually purple, are borne singly on 2–12 in (5–30 cm) stems.

Pinguicula gypsicola (below)

This Mexican species has lance-shaped, 2–3 in (5–8 cm) long leaves and dark-veined lavender to purple flowers on stems up to 5 in (12 cm) high.
ZONES 10–12.

CULTIVATION

Growing naturally in wet, mossy bogs, these plants are not easy to cultivate outside their natural environment. Bell jars and terrariums can provide the necessary humidity, but keeping the soil damp but not putrid is difficult. Frost hardiness varies considerably with the species. Propagate from seed or by division.

P

Pinguicula moranensis (right)

This Mexican species has 2–4 in (5–10 cm) long, rounded leaves. Its flowers are on 4–8 in (10–20 cm) stems and are 1½–2 in (3.5–5 cm) wide, crimson or pink with a red throat.
ZONES 10–11.

PISTIA

WATER LETTUCE, SHELL FLOWER

The sole species in this genus is an aquatic perennial, widespread in the tropics and a noxious weed in some areas. The name water lettuce is an apt description: the 6 in (15 cm) wide, floating rosettes of ribbed, wedge-shaped leaves resemble blue-green lettuce heads. The base of the leaves is spongy, which keeps them buoyant, and the fine roots that emerge from the base of the rosette extract nutrients directly from the water. Although connected by stolons, the rosettes can survive independently. The arum-like inflorescence is enclosed in a leaf-like spathe that makes it inconspicuous.

CULTIVATION

Apart from needing warm subtropical to tropical conditions, water lettuce is easily grown in any pond or slow-moving water. It multiplies rapidly and can quickly clog streams. It is usually self-propagating.

Pistia stratiotes

(above)

Forming large clumps of felted rosettes, this species is an aggressive colonizer that can easily smother a small pond. Although it does not oxygenate the water, fish will feed on its roots. It also helps to shade the surface and keep the water cool. **ZONES 10–12.**

P

Pitcairnia ringens
(right)

This is one of the *Pitcairnia* species adapted to drier environments. It has underground growing points which produce sparse tufts of short, narrowly lance-shaped leaves and spreading spikes about 18 in (45 cm) tall of progressively opening scarlet flowers about 2 in (5 cm) long. **ZONES 10–12.**

P

PITCAIRNIA

This genus of bromeliads is native to Central and South America, Mexico and the West Indies. Mostly rock dwellers or ground dwellers, they are occasionally epiphytic. They produce clumps of somewhat grass-like foliage and spikes of variously colored tubular flowers with recurved petals. The 260 species vary widely in their styles of growth but all of them require a rest period with minimum water in cold months.

CULTIVATION
Some species like full sun while the evergreen species prefer a part-shaded position. The leaf-dropping species need plenty of water and fertilizer as soon as the first regrowth appears. Generally it is a frost-tender genus. All prefer well-drained soil. Propagate from seed or by division of the rhizomes.

PLATYCODON
BALLOON FLOWER, CHINESE BELLFLOWER

The sole species in this genus is a semi-tuberous perennial with flower stems up to 30 in (75 cm) tall. It is native to China, Japan, Korea and eastern Siberia. In spring it forms a clump of 2–3 in (5–8 cm) long, toothed-edged, elliptical to lance-shaped light blue-green foliage. The leafy flower stems develop quickly from mid-summer, and are topped with heads of inflated buds that open into broad, bell-shaped, white, pink, blue or purple flowers up to 2 in (5 cm) wide.

CULTIVATION
Very frost hardy and easily grown in any well-drained soil in full sun, this plant may take a few years to become established. Propagate from seed or by division. Because it resents disturbance, divide it as little as possible.

Platycodon grandiflorus var. *mariesii* (below)

Platycodon grandiflorus

On this species, balloon-like buds open out into 5-petalled summer flowers like bells, colored blue, purple, pink or white. The serrated, elliptical leaves with a silvery blue cast form in a neat clump up to 24 in (60 cm) high and half that in spread. **'Fuji Blue'** is very erect to 30 in (75 cm) tall with large blue flowers. ***Platycodon grandiflorus* var. *mariesii*** is more compact than the species, and grows to 18 in (45 cm) tall and with glossy, lance-shaped leaves. **ZONES 4–10.**

Platycodon grandiflorus 'Fuji Blue' *(above)*

Platycodon grandiflorus cultivar *(right)*

P

*Plectranthus
neochilus* (above)

This is one of a group
of species allied to
Plectranthus caninus
that range from south-
eastern Africa to
southern Arabia. Its
flowers are pale lavender
on short dense spikes
that terminate in a
group of purplish bud
bracts, cast off as flowers
open. The fleshy leaves
have a strong musky
smell. They have a mat-
forming habit of growth
and are fairly drought
tolerant. ZONES 10–12.

PLECTRANTHUS

This genus contains more than 350 species of annuals, perennials
and shrubs. Most are rather frost tender and several species are
grown as house plants, others as garden ornamentals or herbs.
They generally have succulent or semi-succulent stems. The leaves,
too, are often fleshy and frequently oval to heart-shaped. The
flowers are small and tubular, sometimes borne in showy spikes
that extend above the foliage.

CULTIVATION

Plant in moist, well-drained soil in part-shade. Protect from frost
and prolonged dry conditions. Propagate from seed or cuttings or
by layering. Many species are spreading and will self-layer.

PODOPHYLLUM

Although the 9 perennials in this genus have a superficial resemblance to trilliums, they are actually in the berberis family. Native to eastern North America, East Asia and the Himalayas, they have stout rhizomes that in early spring sprout large, peltate leaves up to 12 in (30 cm) across. The leaflets are broad with toothed edges and often lobed. Cup-shaped, upward-facing, 6- to 9-petalled flowers soon follow. They are around 2 in (5 cm) wide, white or soft pink and are often followed by red berries up to 2 in (5 cm) across.

CULTIVATION

These essentially woodland plants prefer moist, humus-rich, well-drained soil and dappled shade. Most tolerate hard frosts provided the rootstock is insulated. Propagate from seed or by division.

Podophyllum
peltatum (below)
MAY APPLE

This is a popular eastern American wildflower, appearing before the leaves on deciduous forest trees. Deeply lobed, peltate leaves around 12 in (30 cm) long shelter creamy white blossoms resembling single roses, almost hidden under the leaves. Edible yellow fruit follow. It spreads rampantly to form a bold ground cover, so it is not for the small garden. Propagate by dividing the rhizomes in early spring.
ZONES 3–9.

POGOSTEMON

PATCHOULI

Famed for their aromatic oils, which are used in perfumes and aromatherapy, the patchouli plants are native to tropical East Asia. They are shrubby with upright stems and have large, nettle-like leaves that are roughly heart-shaped with shallowly lobed edges. Their flowers are white, mauve or pink, and are carried on a typical mint-family verticillaster (whorled flower stem).

CULTIVATION

All species have tropical origins and demand warm, frost-free conditions. They prefer moist, humus-rich, well-drained soil in sun or part-shade. Propagate from seed or cuttings.

Pogostemon cablin

Native to Indonesia, the Philippines and Malaysia, this is the species most often cultivated. It has narrow leaves and hairy stems. Because it seldom flowers, seeds are rarely available so it is usually grown from cuttings. **Pogostemon heyneanus,** often grown as a substitute for *P. cablin,* has smooth stems and slightly bronze new growth, and flowers reliably. **ZONES 11–12.**

Pogostemon heyneanus (left)

POLEMONIUM

JACOB'S LADDER

This genus of around 25 species of annuals and perennials is distributed over the Arctic and temperate regions of the northern hemisphere. They form clumps of soft, bright green, ferny, pinnate leaves from which emerge upright stems topped with heads of short, tubular, bell-or funnel-shaped flowers usually in white or shades of blue or pink. Completely dormant in winter, they develop quickly in spring and are in flower by early summer.

CULTIVATION

Most species are very frost hardy and easily cultivated in moist, well-drained soil in sun or part-shade. Propagate annuals from seed and perennials from seed or cuttings of young shoots or by division. Some species self-sow freely.

Polemonium
'Brise d'Anjou' *(left)*

This cultivar of uncer-tain origin but clearly part of the *Polemonium caeruleum* complex, is distinguished by its neatly variegated foliage—the upper and lower edge of each leaflet has a narrow pale yellow stripe. ZONES 3–9.

Polemonium
boreale *(right)*
NORTHERN JACOB'S LADDER
Found north of the Arctic tree line, this perennial species has basal leaves made up of 13 to 23, ¹/₂ in (12 mm) leaflets. Its flower stems are 3–12 in (8–30 cm) tall, and the blue to purple flowers are about ¹/₂ in (12 mm) long. It is a dwarf species for rock gardens or alpine troughs. ZONES 3–9.

Polemonium caeruleum (right)

Yellowy orange stamens provide a colorful contrast against the light purplish blue of this perennial's bell-shaped flowers when they open in summer. The flowers cluster among lance-shaped leaflets arranged in many pairs like the rungs of a ladder. The plant grows in a clump to a height and spread of up to 24 in (60 cm) or more. The stem is hollow and upright. A native of temperate Europe, it suits cooler climates. **ZONES 2–9.**

Polemonium delicatum (below)
SKUNKLEAF JACOB'S LADDER

This native of the Mid-west and western USA has leaves less than 4 in (10 cm) long made up of 5 to 11, ½–1 in (12–25 mm) long leaflets. The flowers are also small, blue to violet and open in summer. It is an excellent rockery species. **ZONES 6–9.**

P

Polemonium reptans
'Blue Pearl' *(right)*

Polemonium reptans

GREEK VALERIAN, CREEPING
POLEMONIUM

This large perennial species from eastern USA forms a 12–24 in (30–60 cm) high foliage clump with leaves composed of 7 to 19 leaflets. The inflorescence is inclined to be lax and the flowers, which are bright blue, are large: ½–1 in (12–25 mm) in diameter. Low-growing and spreading forms have given rise to several cultivars. **'Blue Pearl'** grows to 10 in (25 cm) tall and has bright blue flowers. ZONES 4–9.

P

Polemonium 'Sapphire' *(right)*

A cultivar probably derived from *Polemonium reptans*, *P.* 'Sapphire' forms a compact clump of foliage with flower stems 12–15 in (30–38 cm) tall. The flowers are light blue and about ½ in (12 mm) wide. ZONES 4–9.

POLYGONATUM

SOLOMON'S SEAL

The 30 or so species in this genus of forest-floor perennials are distributed all over the temperate zones of the northern hemisphere. The most likely explanation of the common name is that the scars left on the creeping rhizomes, after the flowering stems die off in autumn, are thought to resemble the 6-pointed star associated with kings Solomon and David. King Solomon is thought to have first discovered the medicinal qualities of the plants, which are credited with healing wounds. The distilled sap of the rhizomes is still used in the cosmetics industry. The plants' fresh greenery and delicate white flowers make them favorites for planting in woodland gardens.

CULTIVATION

They need rich, moist soil and a shady spot. Cut back to the rhizome in autumn as they are completely dormant in winter. Propagate from seed or by division of the rhizomes in spring or autumn.

Polygonatum falcatum (below)

With stems to 3 ft (1 m) long and long, rather narrow leaves, this Japanese and Korean species is not as attractive as some of the others. Its flowers tend to be small and are carried singly rather than in small clusters. The stems are red tinted. ZONES 6–9.

Polygonatum × *hybridum* (right)

This hybrid species does best in cool to cold areas. In spring, the white, green-tipped, tubular flowers hang down from the drooping 3 ft (1 m) stems at the leaf axils. It is difficult to grow from seed. ZONES 6–9.

Polygonatum multiflorum (below)

This Eurasian species has arching 3 ft (1 m) stems with large, broad leaves that point upwards very distinctly. Its flowers are cream with green tips in 2- to 5-flowered clusters. It has vigorous rhizomes and can be invasive. Although often found on limestone soil in the wild, it does not seem fussy about soil type. ZONES 4–9.

P

Polygonatum odoratum (right)

From Europe, Russia, Japan and the Caucasus, this perennial to 3 ft (1 m) tall has long, hairless leaves in 2 rows. The fragrant, tubular, white flowers have green tips and appear in late spring and early summer. They are followed by rounded black fruit. ZONES 4–9.

PONTEDERIA
PICKEREL WEED

The 5 or so aquatic perennials in this genus are all native to river shallows in North and South America. They have distinctive, lance-shaped leaves and bell-shaped, usually blue flowers in terminal spikes. The Latin name has nothing to do with ponds; it honors Guilio Pontedera (1688–1757), who was a professor of botany at the University of Padua in Italy.

CULTIVATION

Easily grown, pickerel weed flourishes in almost any climate, from cold to subtropical. Plant it in full sun in up to 10 in (25 cm) of water. Only the spent flower stems need pruning, to encourage successive batches of flowers from spring to autumn. Propagate from seed or by division in spring.

Pontederia cordata
(left)
PICKEREL RUSH

This species grows on the east coast of North America. A very frost-hardy, marginal water plant, it grows to 30 in (75 cm) with a 18 in (45 cm) spread. Its tapered, heart-shaped leaves are dark green and shiny. In summer, it produces intense blue flowers in dense, terminal spikes. ZONES 3–10.

PORTEA

This bromeliad genus has 7 species of rock or ground dwellers native to Brazil. Generally they are large rosette-forming perennials with stiff-spined green leaves that vary in height from 30 in (75 cm) to over 6 ft (1.8 m) when in flower.

CULTIVATION

Plants enjoy bright light and warm conditions. Plant in humus-rich, loamy soil. Some species are cold sensitive. Propagate from offsets or seed.

Portea petropolitana
(right & above right)
syns *Aechmea petropolitana, Portea gardneri, Streptocalyx podantha*

This is a large species with varying lengths of branches and flower stalks. The plant is stemless, with thick, heavily spined leaves, and reaches over 3 ft (1 m) in height when in bloom. Narrow, blue-violet flowers are 1¹/₂ in (35 mm) long and the inflorescences upright in length to 15 in (38 cm) long.
ZONES 9–12.

PORTULACA

There are about 100 species of semi-succulent annuals or perennials in this genus, indigenous to the warm, dry regions of the world. The fleshy leaves vary in color from white to green or red, but it is for their cup-shaped flowers that they are grown, which are white, yellow, apricot, pink, purple or scarlet and resembling roses in form.

CULTIVATION

They are easily grown in all climates. In cooler areas they should not be planted out until the danger of frost has passed. Because they are plants of the deserts they need sun, well-drained soil and only occasional watering. Propagate from seed in spring or cuttings in summer. Check for aphids.

Portulaca grandiflora (above)
ROSE MOSS, SUN PLANT

Native to South America and one of the few annual succulents, this low-growing plant reaches 8 in (20 cm) high and spreads to 6 in (15 cm). It has small, lance-shaped, fleshy, bright green leaves like beads on their reddish stems. Its large, open flowers, usually double and borne in summer, are 3 in (8 cm) wide and come in bright colors including yellow, pink, red or orange. The flowers close at night and on cloudy days. It is suitable as a ground cover or in a rockery or border.
ZONES 10–11.

POTENTILLA
CINQUEFOIL

This genus of approximately 500 perennials, annuals, biennials and deciduous shrubs is indigenous mainly to the northern hemisphere, from temperate to arctic regions. Most species have 5-parted leaves (hence the common name cinquefoil), and range from only 1 in (25 mm) or so tall to about 18 in (45 cm). They bear clusters of 1 in (25 mm), rounded, bright flowers in profusion through spring and summer. Some *Potentilla* species are used medicinally: the root bark of one species is said to stop nose bleeds and even internal bleeding.

CULTIVATION
Plant all species in well-drained, fertile soil. Lime does not upset them. Although the species all thrive in full sun in temperate climates, the colors of pink, red and orange cultivars will be brighter if protected from very strong sun. Perennials are generally frost hardy. Propagate by division in spring, or from seed or by division in autumn. Shrubs can be propagated from seed in autumn or from cuttings in summer.

Potentilla cuneata
(above)

This Himalayan perennial develops a woody base and can form a rather upright mound or be a low, spreading plant. Its leaves are trifoliate, up to 6 in (15 cm) long, leathery, deep green above and blue-green below. The flowers are bright yellow, 1 in (25 mm) wide and carried singly. ZONES 5–9.

P

Potentilla alba (left)

This low, spreading perennial from Europe rarely exceeds 4 in (10 cm) high. It has hand-shaped basal leaves with 5 leaflets, each up to 2¹/₂ in (6 cm) long. The young growth has a dense covering of fine hairs that gives it a silver sheen. The white flowers are 1 in (25 mm) wide, in clusters of up to 5 blooms. ZONES 5–9.

Potentilla megalantha (left)

This perennial from Japan forms a mound of foliage about 12 in (30 cm) wide. Its leaves are trifoliate with hairy undersides. Its 1¹/₂ in (35 mm) wide, bright yellow flowers are carried singly and are produced in summer. ZONES 5–9.

Potentilla nepalensis (left)

A profusion of flowers in shades of pink or apricot with cherry red centers appears throughout summer on the slim branching stems of this Himalayan perennial. With bright green, strawberry-like leaves, this species grows to 12 in (30 cm) or more high and twice that in width. 'Miss Willmott' is a 18 in (45 cm) high cultivar with deep pink flowers. ZONES 5–9.

P

Potentilla nepalensis
'Miss Willmott' *(right)*

Potentilla
neumanniana *(right)*
syn. *Potentilla verna*

This herbaceous,
mat-forming perennial
grows to 4 in (10 cm)
in height. Golden
yellow flowers to 1 in
(25 mm) are borne
from spring onwards.
ZONES 5–9.

Potentilla × tonguei *(right)*

This hybrid derives from the Himalayan *Potentilla*
nepalensis crossed with **P. anglica,** a European
species. It is a sprawling perennial with attractive
leaves and abundant 1 in (25 mm) wide, tangerine-
colored flowers in summer. If spent flower stalks
are trimmed, the plant usually responds with
more flowers. ZONES 5–9.

PRATIA

This genus includes 20 species of evergreen perennials. They have multiple branching stems and little toothed leaves. A profusion of starry flowers is followed by globular berries. Most are carpet forming and make excellent rockery specimens, but tend to overrun the garden.

CULTIVATION

Ranging from very frost hardy to frost hardy, these plants generally enjoy damp but porous soil, total sun or part-shade and protection from the elements. Water liberally during the growth period and sparingly in winter. Some species are susceptible to slugs if over-moist. Propagate by division or from seed in autumn.

Pratia perpusilla
(below)

The specific name of this coastal New Zealand species is Latin for 'extremely small'. Its prostrate stems which root at the nodes are very thin and weak, and the narrow, toothed, slightly hairy leaves are little more than $1/8$ in (3 mm) long. The $1/4$ in (6 mm) long white flowers are held just above the foliage on very slender stems. ZONES 8–10.

PRIMULA
PRIMROSE

This well-known and much-loved genus of perennials has about 400 species, found throughout the temperate regions of the northern hemisphere, although most densely concentrated in China and the Himalayas. They also occur on high mountains in the tropics, extending as far south as Papua New Guinea. They are mainly rhizomatous, though some have poorly developed rhizomes and are short lived (*Primula malacoides*, for example). The foliage is usually crowded into a basal tuft or rosette, and the leaves are mostly broadest toward their tips, with toothed or scalloped margins. The flowering stems vary in form, but most often carry successive whorls or a single umbel of flowers. In a few species, the flowers are tightly crowded into a terminal head or a short spike, or they emerge singly or in small groups from among the leaves on short stalks. Flower shape, size and color vary so much that it is hard to generalize, though basically all have tubular flowers that open into a funnel or flat disc with five or more petals that are often notched at their tips.

CULTIVATION
Primulas like fertile, well-drained soil, part-shade and ample water. Propagate from seed in spring, early summer or autumn, by division or from root cuttings. Remove dead heads and old foliage after blooming. There is a primula for virtually every position and purpose.

Primula beesiana *(above)*

This candelabra-style primrose from western China has tapering, toothed-edged leaves, which together with their stems are up to 6 in (15 cm) long. The 24 in (60 cm) flower stems hold 5 to 7 whorls of yellow-eyed red-purple flowers. This deep-rooted species is not a bog plant but does require deep watering. ZONES 5–9.

Primula species *(right)*

Primula allionii
(left)

From the coastal ranges of France and Italy comes this low, evergreen perennial. The leaves, produced in basal rosettes, are sticky, hairy, gray-green and have toothed edges. In winter or early spring stems of up to 5 white, pink or rose flowers, each about 1 in (25 mm) across, rise above the foliage. Plants grow 4–6 in (10–15 cm) tall with a spread of about 8 in (20 cm). **ZONES 7–9.**

P

Primula auricula (left)

This small, central European perennial has yellow flowers in spring and furry leaves (hence the old common name, bear's ear—*auricula* means a 'little ear'). Garden varieties come in a wide range of colors. In the mid-eighteenth century a mutation resulted in flowers in shades of gray, pale green and almost black with centers covered with a white powder called 'paste'. Such flowers, called show auriculas, were once great favorites, but now have few devotees. **ZONES 3–9.**

Primula capitata
subsp. *mooreana*
(right)

This northern Indian subspecies differs from the species in having white powdering on the underside of the foliage and a slightly different leaf shape. Its leaves are up to 6 in (15 cm) long and it has drumstick heads of violet flowers on 12 in (30 cm) stems. ZONES 5–9.

Primula bulleyana

This western Chinese candelabra primrose is very similar to *Primula beesiana* except that its leaves have reddish midribs and its flowers are bright yellow. It dies down completely over winter. **'Ceperley Hybrid'** has yellow, orange and pink flowers. ZONES 6–9.

Primula bulleyana
'Ceperley Hybrid'
(right)

P

Primula cockburniana *(right)*

Native to China, this candelabra primrose has relatively few 6 in (15 cm) toothed-edged leaves and 12–15 in (30–38 cm) stems with 3 to 5 whorls of orange-red flowers. It is less robust than other candelabra primroses but makes up for that with its vivid color. ZONES 5–9.

Primula denticulata *(left)*
DRUMSTICK PRIMROSE

The botanical name of this very frost-hardy Himalayan perennial refers to the toothed profile of the mid-green, broadly lanceolate leaves. A neat and vigorous grower, it reaches a height and spread of 12 in (30 cm). In early to mid-spring its open, yellow-centered flowers of pink, purple or lilac crowd in rounded terminal clusters atop thick hairy stems. **Primula denticulata subsp. *alba*** has white flowers usually on slightly shorter stems than the species. ZONES 6–9.

Primula denticulata
subsp. *alba (below)*

Primula forrestii *(right)*

This Chinese species is often found growing in soil pockets among limestone rocks. It has woody rhizomes and 1½–3 in (3.5–8 cm) leaves with toothed edges and powdering on the undersides. The flowers are bright yellow and are carried in polyanthus-like heads on 6–8 in (15–20 cm) stems. **ZONES 6–9.**

Primula elatior *(below)*
OXLIP

This European species has 2–8 in (5–20 cm) long leaves with finely hairy undersides. Its 4–12 in (10–30 cm) flower stems carry a heavy crop of long-tubed, 1 in (25 mm) wide yellow to orange-yellow flowers. **ZONES 5–9.**

P

Primula sinopurpurea *(below)*

This late-flowering Chinese species has very distinctive, nearly smooth-edged, narrow, bright green leaves that are 2–12 in (5–30 cm) long. It produces its purple-pink flowers when the stems are around 12 in (30 cm) tall, but the stem continues to grow as the seed matures and eventually reaches 30 in (75 cm). **ZONES 5–9.**

Primula florindae *(below)*

TIBETAN PRIMROSE

In spring this perennial carries up to 60 bright yellow flowers to an umbel, hanging like little bells against a backdrop of broad, mid-green leaves with serrated edges. It grows 24–36 in (60–90 cm) high and likes wet conditions, thriving by the edge of a pond or stream. **ZONES 6–9.**

Primula malacoides *(left)*

FAIRY PRIMROSE

This is a native of China. Small, open flowers bloom in spiral masses on this frost-tender perennial, sometimes grown as an annual. The single or double flowers range from white to pink to magenta. Its oval, light green leaves and erect stem have a hairy texture. It reaches a height and spread of 12 in (30 cm) or more. **ZONES 8–11.**

Primula frondosa
(right)

This species has 4 in (10 cm) long, toothed-edged leaves with powdering on the undersides. Its flower stems are 2–6 in (5–15 cm) tall and carry as few as 1 or as many as 30, ½ in (12 mm) wide yellow-eyed lilac to purple flowers. **ZONES 5–9.**

Primula juliae *(below)*

This low-growing, rosette-forming miniature primrose has 4 in (10 cm) long, dark green leaves. It bears bright purple, yellow-centered flowers and has given rise to a series of garden varieties. **ZONES 5–9.**

P

Primula poissonii (left)

This is a Chinese species with rather open rosettes of 6–8 in (15–20 cm) long, blue-green leaves. Its flower stems are up to 18 in (45 cm) tall with 2 to 6 whorls of yellow-eyed deep pink to crimson flowers. It blooms late, prefers wet soil and can be somewhat sparse. ZONES 6–9.

Primula japonica (below)
JAPANESE PRIMROSE

Forming a clump up to 24 in (60 cm) high and 18 in (45 cm) across, this fully frost-hardy perennial flowers in tiers on tall, sturdy stems like a candelabra. Its shiny flowers are borne in spring and early summer, and range through pink, crimson and purple to nearly pure white, usually with a distinct eye of another color. The leaves are elliptical, serrated and pale green. This species does best in a moist situation. **'Postford White'** offers a white, flattish round flower. ZONES 5–10.

P

Primula pulverulenta *(right)*

This is a Chinese candelabra primrose with deep green, wrinkled leaves 12 in (30 cm) or more long. Its flower stems are 3 ft (1 m) tall, white powdered with whorls of 1 in (25 mm) wide flowers. The flowers are white, pink or red with a contrasting eye. ZONES 6–9.

Primula obconica *(below)*
POISON PRIMROSE

Dense flower clusters grow in an umbellate arrangement on hairy, erect stems of this perennial. Native to China, it grows to 12 in (30 cm) high and wide and flowers from winter through spring. The yellow-eyed, flattish flowers, 1 in (25 mm) across, range from white to pink to purple. The light green leaves are elliptical and serrated. ZONES 8–11.

P

Primula, Polyanthus Group *(left)*
syn. *Primula × polyantha*

These fully frost-hardy perennials, sometimes grown as annuals, reach 12 in (30 cm) in spread and height. Large, flat, scented flowers in every color but green bloom on dense umbels from winter to spring. Polyanthus are cultivars derived from *Primula vulgaris* crossed with *P. veris*, and have been grown since the seventeenth century. **'Garryarde Guinevere'** has pink flowers and bronze foliage. ZONES 6–10.

Primula 'Garryarde Guinevere' *(left)*

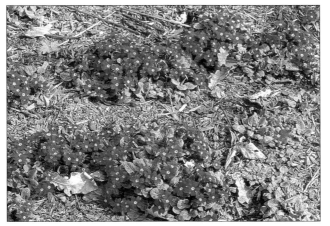

Primula 'Wanda'
(left)

This little plant disappears entirely over winter and begins to burst into flower as the new foliage develops. The leaves are deep green, heavily crinkled and about 3 in (8 cm) long. The short-stemmed flowers are deep magenta to purple with a yellow eye. It is an easily grown plant that quickly forms a small clump. ZONES 6–9.

P

Primula polyneura
(right)

This Chinese species has rounded, light green, softly hairy leaves 2–10 in (5–25 cm) wide on wiry stems. Its flower stems are 8–18 in (20–45 cm) tall with 1, 2 or several whorls of deep pink to purple-red flowers. It spreads freely. ZONES 5–9.

Primula sieboldii *(left)*

This species from Japan and northeast Asia has large, scalloped-edged leaves 4–15 in (10–38 cm) long. Its flowers, which may be white, pink or purple, are carried in 6- to 20-flowered heads on 6–15 in (10–38 cm) stems. There are several cultivated forms, grown mainly in Japan. ZONES 5–9.

P

Primula veris *(right)*
COWSLIP

A European wildflower of open woods and meadows, this species blooms a little later than the common primrose does. It is easily distinguished by the clusters of flowers carried on 6 in (15 cm) tall stalks and its sweeter scent. This plant is easy to grow. ZONES 5–9.

Primula vialii *(left)*

This 24 in (60 cm) tall perennial species from Yunnan Province in China is remarkable for carrying its purple flowers in short spikes, quite unlike any other primula. The buds are bright crimson, giving the inflorescence a two-toned effect. The foliage is lush and bright green. It needs a cool, moist climate. ZONES 7–9.

Primula vulgaris *(below left)*
ENGLISH PRIMROSE, COMMON PRIMROSE

This common European wildflower likes its cultivated conditions to resemble the cool woodland of its native environment. Low growing to 8 in (20 cm) and usually frost hardy, it produces a carpet of bright flowers in spring. The flattish flowers are pale yellow with dark eyes (but the garden forms come in every color), and bloom singly on hairy stems above rosettes of crinkled, lance-shaped, serrated leaves. Both the leaves and the flowers are edible. **'Gigha White'** has white flowers with yellow centers. ZONES 6–9.

Primula vulgaris
'Gigha White' *(below)*

*Protasparagus
densiflorus* 'Myersii'
(right)

*Protasparagus
densiflorus*
syn. *Asparagus
densiflorus*
EMERALD ASPARAGUS FERN

Although frequently
used as an indoor
plant, this South
African species is hardy
to about 25°F (–4°C)
and can be grown
outdoors in many areas.
It produces sprays of
24–36 in (60–90 cm)
long, wiry, rather spiny
stems covered with very
fine, almost needle-like
bright green leaves.
Small but fragrant
white flowers are
followed by bright red
berries. '**Myersii**', the
foxtail fern, has mainly
upright stems with
dense foliage cover,
which gives them a
tapering, cylindrical
shape. '**Sprengeri**' is a
sprawling perennial
with bright green leaves
and bears abundant
tiny, white, heavily
scented flowers, usually
followed by red berries.
ZONES 9–11.

PROTASPARAGUS
syn. *Asparagus*
ASPARAGUS FERN

Primarily native to southern Africa, these tuberous perennials have
now been separated from the true rhizomatous asparagus, although
some botanists disagree with this reclassification. Widely grown as
garden plants in warm-temperate to tropical areas, they are popular
house plants everywhere. Grown primarily for their sprays of
fern-like foliage, they may be shrubby or semi-climbing. Their
stems are often protected by small but vicious thorns. The tiny
white, cream or green flowers are inconspicuous but the red or
black berries can be a feature.

CULTIVATION
They are undemanding plants that are tolerant of neglect, hence
their popularity as house plants. Grow in moist, well-drained,
humus-rich soil in sun or part-shade. Propagate from seed or by
division, but do not divide into very small pieces as plants so
treated seldom recover quickly.

P

PRUNELLA
SELF-HEAL

This is a genus of 7 species of semi-evergreen perennials from Europe, Asia, North Africa and North America. They form low, spreading clumps and bear opposite pairs of ovate to oblong, sometimes deeply lobed leaves. Erect flowering stems bear whorled spikes of 2-lipped tubular flowers in shades of white, pink or purple.

CULTIVATION
Most species spread from creeping stems that readily take root at the nodes, making them excellent ground covering plants for creating large drifts. They are fully frost hardy and will grow in sun or part-shade in moist, well-drained soil. Propagate from seed or by division in spring or autumn.

Prunella
grandiflora *(below)*
LARGE SELF-HEAL

Purple, 2-lipped flowers grow in erect spikes above leafy stubs in spring and summer. A native of Europe, it is good for ground cover or rock gardens, having a spread and height of 18 in (45 cm). **'Loveliness'** has soft mauve flowers. ZONES 5–9.

Prunella grandiflora
'Loveliness' *(below)*

P

PSYLLIOSTACHYS

STATICE

This genus of 6 to 8 species of annuals was once included with *Statice (Limonium)*, but is now classified separately. Rarely over 15 in (38 cm) tall in flower, the plants form a clump of basal leaves, sometimes hairy, that are often deeply cut so they are almost pinnate. The tiny, papery flowers are white, pink or mauve, and borne on upright spikes that only rarely branch. They are dried or used fresh in floral arrangements.

CULTIVATION

Plant in moist, well-drained soil in full sun and allow to dry off after flowering. Propagate from seed.

Psylliostachys suworowii (below)
syn. *Limonium suworowii*

RUSSIAN STATICE, RAT'S TAIL STATICE

Native to Iran, Afghanistan and central Asia, this species has sticky 2–6 in (5–15 cm) leaves and relatively large pink flowers on wavy, 6 in (15 cm) spikes. ZONES 6–10.

P

P

PTILOTUS

This is a genus of around 100 species of annuals, perennials and subshrubs from Australasia. Their leaves are often rather thick and heavy and are stemless. The foliage tends to be red tinted and frequently has wavy edges. The flowers are tiny, usually a shade of green, pink or purple, and are carried on shaggy spikes up to 6 in (15 cm) long.

CULTIVATION

Apart from being frost tender, they are easily cultivated in any well-drained soil in full sun. Propagate the annuals from seed, the perennials and shrubs from seed or cuttings.

Ptilotus manglesii (above)

This is an Australian species that flowers from late winter to early summer when it is covered in rounded, 4 in (10 cm) spikes of pink to purple flowers. Sometimes grown as an annual, it is a short-lived spreading perennial that grows to around 12 in (30 cm) high. The leaves vary in shape: the basal leaves are oval and up to 3 in (8 cm) long, while the upper leaves are narrow. ZONES 9–11.

Pulmonaria longifolia
'Lewis Palmer' *(above)*

Pulmonaria longifolia

This European species has particularly large leaves. They are up to 20 in (50 cm) long, but only 3 in (8 cm) wide, and usually white-spotted. There is a sparse covering of fine hairs on both the upper and lower surfaces of the leaves. The flowers are blue to violet and start to open early in spring, well before the foliage is fully grown. **'Lewis Palmer'** has wider, faintly spotted leaves and pink-tinted pale blue flowers. ZONES 6–9.

PULMONARIA
LUNGWORT

This is a Eurasian genus that consists of 14 species of perennial, rhizomatous, forget-me-not-like plants. The common name refers to their former medicinal use, not their appearance. The most common species are low, spreading plants 6–10 in (15–25 cm) high with a spread of 24 in (60 cm) or more. The simple, oval to lance-shaped leaves are sometimes slightly downy and often spotted silver-white. From very early spring, small deep blue, pink or white flowers open from pink or white buds.

CULTIVATION
These woodland plants are easily grown in cool, moist, humus-rich soil in light shade. All are very frost hardy. Propagate from seed or cuttings or by division.

Pulmonaria
'Mawson's Blue' *(left)*
syn. *Pulmonaria* 'Mawson's Variety'

'Mawson's Blue' is a deep blue-flowered deciduous perennial with narrow 12 in (30 cm) unspotted leaves and very bristly flower stems. It grows to a height of 15 in (38 cm) with an 18 in (45 cm) spread. ZONES 5–9.

Pulmonaria officinalis
JERUSALEM COWSLIP, COMMON LUNGWORT

Often recommended by herbalists as a treatment for coughs, bronchitis and other breathing disorders, this evergreen perennial is widely grown as an ornamental. It has heavily white-spotted 4–6 in (10–15 cm) long leaves and deep blue flowers on stems up to 12 in (30 cm) tall. **'Sissinghurst White'** is an early-blooming, white-flowered cultivar that does not develop pink tints as the flowers age; it grows up to 12 in (30 cm) tall with large leaves. ZONES 6–9.

Pulmonaria officinalis 'Sissinghurst White' *(left)*

Pulmonaria saccharata

JERUSALEM SAGE, BETHLEHEM SAGE

This evergreen perennial has heavily spotted, hairy, 10 in (25 cm) leaves and has given rise to numerous cultivars with flowers in white and all shades of pink and blue. **'Highdown'** is 12 in (30 cm) tall with silver-frosted leaves and pendulous clusters of blue flowers. The cultivars of the **Argentea Group** have silver leaves and red flowers that age to dark purple. ZONES 3–9.

Pulmonaria saccharata 'Highdown' *(right)*

Pulmonaria rubra

RED LUNGWORT

This evergreen perennial has leaves up to 18 in (45 cm) long, only rarely spotted and relatively hairless. The flower stems are covered with fine bristles and bear purple to blue flowers. Near red-flowered forms occur and there are several cultivars in shades of pink and white. **'Redstart'** is up to 15 in (40 cm) high with bright green foliage and large pinkish red flowers. ZONES 6–9.

Pulmonaria rubra 'Redstart' *(right)*

P

PULSATILLA
PASQUE FLOWER

This genus contains 30 species of spring-flowering, deciduous perennials from Eurasia and North America. They form mounds of very finely divided, almost ferny foliaged rosettes. The leaves and flower stems are covered with downy silver-gray hairs. The general effect is that of a hairy anemone with large flowers. The flower color range includes white, pink, purple and red.

CULTIVATION

Most often grown in rockeries, these very frost-hardy plants are also suitable for borders and troughs and prefer a moist, gritty, scree soil in sun or part-shade. They do best with cool to cold winters and cool summers and tend to be short lived in mild areas. Propagate from seed or by division.

Pulsatilla halleri subsp.
slavica (below)

Pulsatilla halleri

This species has white, lavender or purple flowers that open from purple-pink to purple buds. Its new growth is a light green and very hairy. The first flowers are usually open before the early leaves are fully unfurled. The whole plant is covered in fine hairs and has a very silky feel. *Pulsatilla halleri* subsp. *slavica* has deep violet flowers and woolly foliage that is less finely divided than that of the species. ZONES 5–9.

Pulsatilla alpina
subsp. *apiifolia*
(right)

This is a yellow-flowered
form of a normally
white-flowered species
found through much of
southern Europe and
the Caucasus. It usually
occurs on slightly acid
soil and has flower stems
to 18 in (45 cm) tall
with 2 in (5 cm) wide
flowers. ZONES 5–9.

Pulsatilla
bungeana *(right)*

This Siberian species is
very small with flower
stems scarcely 2 in
(5 cm) high. Its flowers
are upward facing,
bell-shaped and violet-
blue when young. They
are a little over ¹/₂ in
(12 mm) wide.
ZONES 4–9.

P

Pulsatilla montana (above)

This species from Switzerland, Romania and Bulgaria has very finely divided leaves, each of the 3 main leaflets having up to 150 lobes. The flowers are 1¹/₂ in (35 mm) wide, deep blue to purple, and bell-shaped. They are carried on 6 in (15 cm) stems that continue to grow after flowering and reach 18 in (45 cm) tall when the seed ripens. ZONES 6–9.

Pulsatilla vulgaris (left)
syns Anemone pulsatilla, A. vulgaris

Nodding, 6-petalled flowers bloom in spring on this species from Europe. The yellow centers of the flowers are a stark color contrast to the petals, which can range through white, pink and red to purple. The finely divided leaves are pale green and very hairy. Reaching 10 in (25 cm) in height and spread, the species is good in a sunny rock garden. Avoid disturbing the roots. **'Alba'** has pure white flowers and needs protection from sun and frost for the flowers to last. **'Rode Klokke'** (syn. 'Rote Glocke') is a free-flowering form with dark red blooms. **'Rubra'** has purplish red or rusty flowers. ZONES 5–9.

Pulsatilla vulgaris
'Alba' *(right)*

Pulsatilla vulgaris
'Rubra' *(right)*

P

PUYA

This large genus of terrestrial bromeliads from South America consists of 170 species. They include the largest of all bromeliads, some species growing to about 20 ft (6 m). They are cultivated in gardens as shrubs. The leaves stand out boldly from a basal rosette and they often have hollow stems. Large blue, purple or yellow flowers are held on unbranched spikes or in dense panicles. The fruit are capsules that enclose winged seeds.

CULTIVATION

These plants can grow in a wide range of soils provided they are well drained, and prefer a sunny position. As with all members of the bromeliad family, keep them away from footpaths because the leaves bear sharp spines along their margins. Prune to remove damaged foliage and propagate by division of offsets or from seed. In cool climates they can be grown in a greenhouse.

Puya alpestris
(above)

Although plants are often sold under this name, those in cultivation are usually *Puya berteroniana*. The true species is a native of southern and central Chile. It grows 4–5 ft (1.2–1.5 m) tall with spine-edged leaves up to 24 in (60 cm) long. The leaves form dense rosettes from which emerge strong flower stems topped with pyramidal heads of tubular blue green flowers. ZONES 8–9.

Puya berteroniana
(right)

This species from Chile has blue-green foliage. The stems are prostrate, and the 3 ft (1 m) long narrow leaves are strap-like and arching. During summer, metallic blue flowers with vivid orange stamens form dense panicles up to 6–10 ft (1.8–3 m) tall at the ends of long stems. The rosette of leaves dies after flowering, leaving offsets to carry on. This plant benefits from mulch to prevent water evaporation from its roots. **ZONES 9–10.**

Puya mirabilis
(right)

Native to Argentina and Bolivia, this species has 24–30 in (60–75 cm) long leaves that are silvery brown with fine spines along the edges. Its flower stems are around 5 ft (1.5 m) tall and the flowers are green to white. **ZONES 9–10.**

P

Q R

QUESNELIA

This bromeliad genus con-
sists of 15 species of stemless,
evergreen perennials found
originally in rocky outcrops
in eastern Brazil. Some species
are also epiphytic. They have
a medium-sized rosette of
lance-shaped, stiff, spiny
leaves. The inflorescences,
which are either upright or
hanging, are composed of
tubular or ovoid flowers that
appear among showy bracts.

CULTIVATION

These frost-tender plants
prefer part-shade and coarse,
humus-rich, moist but
well-drained soil. They need
the protection of a greenhouse
where temperatures drop
below 55°F (13°C). Water
moderately, but reduce
watering levels over the
winter period. Propagate
from seed or offsets.

Quesnelia liboniana
(above)

This species features navy blue
flowers and orange-red bracts.
It is a stemless plant that grows
to 30 in (75 cm) high. The
foliage forms a tube-shaped
rosette composed of light
green leaves with gray scales
on the undersides and spines
on the leaf edges. ZONES 11–12.

Q

RAMONDA

This genus from Spain, the Pyrenees and the
Balkans contains 3 species of evergreen perennials
that have rosettes of hairy, usually wrinkled leaves
with toothed, wavy edges. Doing well in rock gardens
or in cracks in stone walls, they are also grown for
their brightly colored, 4- to 5-petalled flowers,
which appear in late spring and early summer.

CULTIVATION

Excessive water in the leaf rosettes may cause rotting,
so these plants are best grown on an angle in part-
shade and very well-drained, humus-rich soil.
Propagate from seed or cuttings.

Ramonda nathaliae (right)

This species, which
reaches a height and
spread of 4 in (10 cm),
bears panicles of flat,
4-petalled, deep
purple flowers with
orange-yellow centers.
The mid- to dark
green leaves, hairier
on the undersides
than on top, grow to
2 in (5 cm) in length.
ZONES 6–9.

R

Ranunculus acris
'Flore Pleno' (above)

RANUNCULUS

BUTTERCUP

This genus of some 400 annuals and perennials is distributed throughout temperate regions worldwide. They are grown for their colorful flowers, which are bowl- or cup-shaped, 5-petalled and yellow, white, red, orange or pink. The name derives from the Latin for 'frog', due to the tendency of some species to grow in bogs or shallow water. Two species of buttercups are popular folk cures for arthritis, sciatica, rheumatism and skin conditions, including the removal of warts.

CULTIVATION

Most species of *Ranunculus* are easy to grow and thrive in well-drained soil, cool, moist conditions and sunny or shady locations. They are mostly fully frost hardy. Propagate from fresh seed or by division in spring or autumn. Water well through the growing season and allow to dry out after flowering. Keep an eye out for powdery mildew and for attacks by slugs, snails and aphids.

Ranunculus acris
MEADOW BUTTERCUP

This clump-forming perennial from Europe and western Asia has wiry stems with lobed and cut leaves. Panicles of saucer-shaped, bright yellow flowers appear in mid-summer. It grows from 8–36 in (20–90 cm) in height. **'Flore Pleno'** has double, rosetted, golden yellow flowers. ZONES 5–9.

Ranunculus cortusifolius (below)

Found on the Atlantic islands of the Azores, Canaries and Madeira, this species has thick, rounded, leathery basal leaves with toothed edges and shallow lobes. The flower stems, up to 4 ft (1.2 m) tall, bear reduced leaves and many-flowered corymbs of 2 in (5 cm) wide bright yellow flowers. ZONES 9–10.

Ranunculus ficaria
(below)

LESSER CELANDINE, PILEWORT

From southwestern Asia, Europe and north-western Africa, this perennial has single, almost cup-shaped, bright yellow flowers that appear in spring. It reaches only 2 in (5 cm) in height, and has glossy green leaves with silver or gold markings; the leaves die down after the flowers appear. **'Albus'** has single, creamy white flowers with glossy petals. **'Brazen Hussy'** has deep bronze-green leaves and shiny, deep golden yellow flowers with bronze undersides. ZONES 5–10.

Ranunculus gramineus *(above)*

With hairy, bluish green leaves shaped like grass, this clump-forming perennial from south-western Europe has a compact spread and grows 18 in (45 cm) tall. In late spring and early summer it produces yellow, cup-shaped flowers. Plant it in rich soil. ZONES 7–10.

Ranunculus lyallii *(below)*

MT COOK LILY, GIANT MOUNTAIN BUTTERCUP, MOUNTAIN LILY

Native to New Zealand's South Island, this thicket-forming perennial grows to 3 ft (1 m) tall. Its broad, leathery leaves can reach 8 in (20 cm) wide and are lustrous deep green. Glossy, white, cup-shaped flowers appear in clusters in summer. Moderately frost hardy, it can be difficult to grow. ZONES 7–9.

RAOULIA
VEGETABLE SHEEP

This is a genus of about 20 species of evergreen perennials or subshrubs confined to New Zealand. They mostly form slow-growing, ground-hugging carpets of downy leaves and in summer bear small white or pale yellow, papery textured daisies. They are excellent foliage plants for rock gardens or raised beds.

CULTIVATION
Most require a cool-temperate climate, moist, acidic, sharply drained soil and protection from heavy winter rain (otherwise they will rot). They prefer an open, sunny position or part-shade in warmer areas. Propagate from fresh seed or by division in spring.

Raoulia haastii
(right)

This frost-hardy perennial grows to only ½ in (12 mm) in height with a 12 in (30 cm) spread. The pale green, silky leaves overlap slightly in dense cushions. Yellow flowerheads appear in spring.
ZONES 7–9.

Raoulia australis
(above)
syn. Raoulia lutescens
GOLDEN SCABWEED

Suitable for rock gardens, this prostrate, mat-forming perennial native to New Zealand lays down a solid carpet of silvery leaves ½ in (12 mm) deep over a 10 in (25 cm) spread. In summer it produces minuscule flowerheads of fluffy yellow blooms.
ZONES 7–9.

Raoulia eximia
(left)

This perennial makes tight hummocks of growth 3 ft (1 m) across and completely covered with gray hairs. In late spring or summer it bears yellowish white flowerheads. It grows to only 2 in (5 cm) in height. ZONES 7–9.

R

Rehmannia elata *(above & below)*
syn. *Rehmannia angulata* of gardens
CHINESE FOXGLOVE

This is the best known *Rehmannia*. It bears semi-pendent, tubular, bright pink flowers from summer to autumn and grows to 3 ft (1 m) high. Though perennial, it is only short lived. ZONES 9–10.

REHMANNIA

From China, these perennials are sometimes classed with the foxgloves and the snap-dragons, or grouped as cousins of the the African violet. The uncertainty is due to the 2-lipped flowers, which look a bit like foxgloves, snapdragons and African violets. They all have an attractive shape and delicate color, usually some shade of cool pink with pink and gold at their throats. The leaves are large, oblong, veined and hairy, and form basal rosettes.

CULTIVATION

Plant in a warm-temperate climate (or a mildly warmed greenhouse in cool climates) in a sheltered spot in full sun and in rich, leafy soil. Propagate from seed in winter or cuttings in late autumn. Watch for attack by slugs and snails.

R

REINECKEA

From Japan and China and allied to *Ophiopogon,* this genus contains a single species, an evergreen, rhizomatous perennial that has arching, glossy green leaves and small, scented flowers.

CULTIVATION

This frost-hardy plant prefers part-shade and moist but well-drained, humus-rich soil. Propagate from seed or by separation of the rhizomes. It may be prone to attack by snails and slugs.

Reineckea carnea
(above)

This species, which reaches 8 in (20 cm) in height with a 15 in (38 cm) spread, produces its almost cup-shaped, white or pink flowers to $^{1}/_{2}$ in (12 mm) wide in late spring. If the summer months are warm, round berries will appear in autumn. ZONES 7–10.

R

Reseda odorata

(center right)

COMMON MIGNONETTE

From northern Africa, this moderately fast-growing annual is renowned for the strong fragrance of its flowers. The conical heads of tiny greenish flowers with touches of red, have dark orange stamens, but are otherwise unspectacular. They appear from summer to early autumn. The plants grow to 24 in (60 cm) high and about half that in spread. ZONES 6–10.

RESEDA

MIGNONETTE

This genus from Asia, Africa and Europe contains about 60 species of erect or spreading, branching annuals and perennials. They bear star-shaped, greenish white or greenish yellow flowers in spike-like racemes from spring to autumn. These are attractive to bees. Mignonette used to be a favorite with perfumers and the plant is still cultivated in France for its essential oils.

CULTIVATION

Plant in full sun or part-shade in well-drained, fertile, preferably alkaline soil. Deadheading will prolong flowering. Propagate from seed in late winter.

Reseda luteola

(below right)

WELD, WILD MIGNONETTE, DYER'S ROCKET

This biennial or short-lived perennial from Europe and central Asia yields a yellow dye that has been used as a paint pigment and in textile making. Weld grows to 4 ft (1.2 m) tall with narrow bright green leaves; almost half its height is made up of narrow, sometimes branched flower spikes, composed of whorls of small pale yellow to yellow-green flowers. The flowers appear in the second summer of growth, the first season being spent developing the large tap root. ZONES 6–10.

R

RHEUM

This genus contains 50 species of rhizomatous perennials, including
the edible rhubarb and several ornamental plants. From eastern
Europe and central Asia to the Himalayas and China, they are
grown for their striking appearance and for their large basal leaves,
which are coarsely toothed and have prominent midribs and veins.
The minute, star-shaped flowers appear in summer and are followed
by winged fruits.

Rheum palmatum
'Atrosanguineum'
(below)

CULTIVATION
These very frost-hardy plants prefer full sun
or part-shade and deep, moist, humus-rich
soil. Propagate from seed or by division, and
watch out for slugs and crown rot.

Rheum officinale *(below)*
Sometimes used in weight control drugs and
herbal medicine, this species from western China
and Tibet can grow to 10 ft (3 m) tall. Its leaves are
kidney-shaped to round, 5-lobed and up to 30 in
(75 cm) wide. In summer it produces large
branched heads of white to greenish white flowers.
ZONES 7–10.

Rheum palmatum
CHINESE RHUBARB

This species bears
panicles of small, dark
red to creamy green
flowers that open early
in summer. It has deep
green leaves with
decoratively cut edges,
and reaches up to 8 ft
(2.4 m) in height and
6 ft (1.8 m) in spread.
'Atrosanguineum' has
dark pink flowers and
crimson leaves that
fade to dark green.
ZONES 6–10.

R

**Rhodanthe
chlorocephala
subsp. *rosea* *(right)***
syns *Helipterum roseum,
Acroclinium roseum*

This annual grows to a
height of 24 in (60 cm)
and a spread of 6 in
(15 cm). The flower-
heads are composed of
white to pale pink
bracts surrounding a
yellow center, and close
in cloudy weather. It is
widely grown for cut
flowers. ZONES 9–11.

**Rhodanthe 'Paper
Star'** *(below)*

This cultivar has profuse
white flowerheads.
While not very long
lasting as a cut flower, it
is an impressive, long-
flowering garden
specimen of semi-pros-
trate habit. ZONES 7–11.

RHODANTHE
STRAWFLOWER

The 40 species of erect annuals, perennials and subshrubs in this
genus all come from arid areas of Australia. Their daisy-like, everlasting, pink, yellow or white summer flowers are keenly sought for
cut flowers and in dried arrangements. They have alternate,
mid-green to gray-green leaves.

CULTIVATION
These marginally frost-hardy plants
prefer full sun and well-drained soil of
poor uality. The flowerheads can be cut
for drying and hung upside down in a
dark, cool place. Propagate from seed.

R

Rhodiola heterodonta *(left)*
syn. *Sedum heterodontum*

This rhizomatous, clump-forming species from Afghanistan, the Himalayas and Tibet grows to a height and spread of 15 in (38 cm). It bears flattish heads of yellow to orange-qred or greenish flowers in spring to early summer and has thick, un-branched stems with oval, toothed, blue-green leaves.
ZONES 5–10.

RHODIOLA

Similar to *Hylotelephium* and the larger *Sedum* species, this genus includes around 50 species of fleshy leafed, rhizomatous perennials widely distributed in the northern hemisphere. The plants are composed of a mass of thickened stems clothed with simple, often toothed, gray-green leaves. The individual, star-shaped flowers, in shades of yellow, orange, red, occasionally green or white, appear in dense, rounded heads.

CULTIVATION

Most are very frost-hardy and undemanding. Plant in an area that remains moist in summer but which is not boggy in winter. A sunny

R

rockery is ideal. Propagate by division in spring or take cuttings of the young growth. They may be attacked by aphids.

Rhodiola kirilowii *(left)*
syn. *Sedum kirilowii*

Found from central Asia to Mongolia, this species has heavy, branched rhizomes from which develop stout, upright stems that grow to 3 ft (1 m) tall. The narrow to lance-shaped leaves are unusually large, some-times over 10 ft (3 m) long. The flowers are yellow-green to rusty red, and open from early summer.
ZONES 5–10.

Rhodiola rosea (below)
syn. *Sedum rosea*

ROSEROOT

The tightly massed heads of pink buds produced by
this perennial in late spring or early summer open
to small, star-shaped flowers in pale purple, green
or yellow. The saw-edged, elliptical leaves are fleshy.
This species grows into a clump 12 in (30 cm) in
height and spread. The name comes from the scent
of the fleshy roots, used in making perfume. It is a
highly sociable species that occurs right around
the temperate northern hemisphere. ZONES 2–9.

Rhodiola purpureoviridis (above)
syn. *Sedum purpureoviride*

This dense species has rounded, ovate leaves with
densely hairy, toothed margins. The flowering
stems grow to 18 in (45 cm) and bear pale green-
yellow flowers in early summer. It comes from
western China and Tibet. ZONES 6–10.

Rhodiola stephanii (right)
syn. *Sedum stephanii*

This rhizomatous,
branching species
from eastern Siberia
has bright yellow-
green, deeply toothed
leaves. The flowering
stems, to 10 in
(25 cm) in length,
bear their creamy
white flowers in
summer. ZONES 5–10.

R

RODGERSIA

Native to Burma, China, Korea and Japan, this genus consists of 6 species of moisture-loving perennials. They have handsome foliage and flowers, but tend to be grown more for their bold leaves than for their plumes of fluffy flowers, borne in mid- to late summer. The stems unfurl in mid-spring and spread out to form a fan of leaves on top of stout stems.

CULTIVATION

Their liking for moist soil makes them excellent plants for marshy ground at the edge of a pond or in a bog garden in sun or part-shade. They do best in a site sheltered from strong winds, which can damage the foliage. Propagate by division in spring or from seed in autumn.

Rodgersia aesculifolia (below)

This Chinese species has lobed, 10 in (25 cm) wide leaves that are borne on hairy stalks, forming a clump 24 in (60 cm) high and wide. The large, cone-shaped clusters of small, starry flowers are cream or pale pink, and are borne on stout stems up to 4 ft (1.2 m) tall. ZONES 5–9.

Rodgersia pinnata
(above)

This rhizomatous, clump-forming plant produces bold, dark green leaves arranged in pairs. Star-shaped, yellowish white, pink or red flowers are borne in panicles on reddish green stems in mid- to late summer. It reaches a height of 4 ft (1.2 m) and a spread of 30 in (75 cm). **'Superba'** has bright pink flowers and purplish bronze leaves. **'Serenade'** has pale pink flowers. ZONES 6–9.

Rodgersia pinnata
'Serenade' *(above)*

R

Rodgersia sambucifolia *(above)*

This clump-forming, rhizomatous species from western China has emerald-green, occasionally bronze-tinted leaves with large leaflets. It reaches 3 ft (1 m) high and wide and bears sprays of creamy white flowers above the foliage in summer. ZONES 6–10.

Rodgersia podophylla *(left)*

Suited to pond surrounds, this rhizomatous species has green, copper-tinted leaves comprising 5 to 9 large leaflets. It bears multi-branched panicles of cream, star-shaped flowers. It tolerates full shade but does better in part-shade, and grows 3–4 ft (1–1.2 m) tall by 30 in (75 cm) wide. ZONES 5–9.

ROMNEYA
TREE POPPY

The 2 species in this genus from North America are summer-flowering, woody based perennials and deciduous subshrubs. They have blue-green foliage composed of alternate leaves and poppy-like, 6-petalled flowers with glossy yellow stamens.

CULTIVATION

They prefer a warm, sunny position and fertile, well-drained soil. They are difficult to establish (although once established they may become invasive), and they resent transplanting. Protect the roots in very cold areas in winter. Propagate from seed or cuttings.

Romneya coulteri (below)
CALIFORNIA TREE POPPY,
MATILIJA POPPY

This shrubby Californian perennial produces large, sweetly scented, poppy-like white flowers highlighted with fluffy gold stamens. The silvery green leaves are deeply divided, their edges sparsely fringed with hairs. Fully frost hardy, it forms a bush up to 8 ft (2.4 m) high with a spread of 3 ft (1 m). *Romneya coulteri* var. *trichocalyx* has pointed, rather bristly sepals. ZONES 7–10.

R

ROSCOEA

These 18 species of tuberous perennials from China and the Hima-layas are related to ginger *(Zingiber)*, but in appearance are more reminiscent of irises. They are grown for their orchid-like flowers, which have hooded upper petals, wide-lobed lower lips and 2 nar-rower petals. The leaves are lance-shaped and erect. They are most suitable for open borders and rock and woodland gardens.

CULTIVATION

They prefer part-shade and cool, fertile, humus-rich soil that should be kept moist but well drained in summer. Provide a top-dressing of leafmold or well-rotted compost in winter, when the plants die down. Propagate from seed or by division.

Roscoea cautleoides (left)

Bearing its yellow or orange flowers in summer, this frost-hardy species from China grows to 10 in (25 cm) tall with a 6 in (15 cm) spread. The glossy leaves are lance-shaped and erect and wrap into a hollow stem-like structure at their base. ZONES 6–9.

R

Rosmarinus officinalis
'Prostratus' *(right)*

Rosmarinus officinalis

Widely grown as a culinary herb, this species is also ornamental. It is upright with strong woody branches densely clothed with narrow, 1 in (25 mm), deep green leaves. Simple, lavender-blue to deep blue flowers smother the bush in autumn, winter and spring. **'Benenden Blue'** has vivid blue flowers; **'Huntingdon Carpet'** is a low spreader with bluish flowers; **'Lockwood de Forest'** has deep blue flowers and a spreading habit; **'Majorca Pink'** is an upright grower with soft pink flowers; **'Miss Jessop's Upright'** grows vigorously to 6 ft (1.8 m); **'Prostratus'** (syn. *Rosmarinus lavandulaceus* of gardens), a ground cover form, is ideal for spilling over walls or covering banks; and **'Tuscan Blue'** bears dark blue flowers. ZONES 6–11.

ROSMARINUS

ROSEMARY

Some botanists recognize up to 12 species in this genus, but most suggest there is only one, an evergreen native to the Mediterranean. It has been valued for centuries for its perfume and for medicinal and culinary uses. A small shrub rarely growing more than 4 ft (1.2 m) tall, it has narrow, needle-like leaves that are dark green and aromatic. The blue flowers are held in short clusters.

CULTIVATION

Rosmarinus prefers a sunny site and thrives in poor soil if it is well drained; it is salt tolerant. Prune regularly to keep it compact and promote new growth. It can be grown as a specimen shrub or as a low hedge. Propagate from seed or cuttings in summer.

R

Rudbeckia fulgida
BLACK-EYED SUSAN, ORANGE
CONEFLOWER

This rhizomatous perennial, to 3 ft (1 m) tall, has branched stems, mid-green, slightly hairy leaves with prominent veins, and daisy-like, orange-yellow flowers with dark brown centers. *Rudbeckia fulgida* var. *deamii* has very hairy stems and is free flowering; *R. f.* var. *speciosa* has elliptic to lance-shaped basal leaves and toothed stem leaves; *R. f.* var. *sullivantii* 'Gold-sturm' (syn. *R.* 'Goldsturm') grows to 24 in (60 cm) tall and has crowded stems that bear lanceolate leaves. ZONES 3–10.

Rudbeckia fulgida var. *deamii* (above)

Rudbeckia fulgida var. *speciosa* (below)

RUDBECKIA
CONEFLOWER

This popular genus from North America has about 15 species of annuals, biennials and perennials. The plants in this genus have bright, daisy-like, composite flowers with prominent central cones (hence the common name). The single, double or semi-double flowers are usually in tones of yellow. The cones, however, vary from green through rust, purple and black. Species range in height from 24 in (60 cm) to 10 ft (3 m). A number of rudbeckias make excellent cut flowers.

CULTIVATION
Coneflowers prefer loamy, moisture-retentive soil in full sun or part-shade. Propagate from seed or by division in spring or autumn. They are moderately to fully frost hardy. Aphids may be a problem.

Rudbeckia fulgida var. *sullivantii* 'Goldsturm' (left)

R

Rudbeckia hirta 'Toto'
(left)

Rudbeckia hirta
(below right)
BLACK-EYED SUSAN

The flowerheads on this biennial or short-lived perennial are bright yellow, with central cones of purplish brown, and its lanceolate leaves are mid-green and hairy. It reaches 12–36 in (30–90 cm) tall, with a spread of 12 in (30 cm). **'Irish Eyes'** is noteworthy for its olive green center. **'Marmalade'** has large flowerheads with golden orange ray florets. Many dwarf cultivars such as **'Becky Mixed'** are available in a range of colors from pale lemon to orange and red. They are usually treated as annuals. **'Toto'** is a compact strain that flowers heavily and is very even in size and flower distribution. It is ideal for massed plantings. **ZONES 3–10.**

R

Rudbeckia laciniata (left)
CUTLEAF CONEFLOWER

This species is a splendid summer-flowering perennial that can reach 10 ft (3 m) tall, though 6 ft
(1.8 m) is more usual. The drooping ray florets
give the flowerhead an informal elegance. **'Golden
Glow'** is a striking, if somewhat floppy, double
cultivar. **'Goldquelle'** grows to around 30 in (75 cm)
tall and has large, yellow, double flowers. ZONES 3–10.

Rudbeckia laciniata
'Goldquelle' *(right)*

Rudbeckia subtomentosa (left)
SWEET CONEFLOWER

Found naturally in the
central United States,
sweet coneflower has
branched stems up to
28 in (70 cm) tall with
mid-green leaves up to
6 in (15 cm) long. The
leaves are covered in
fine gray hairs. The
flower heads, composed
of yellow ray florets
around a purple-brown
disc, are carried in-
dividually and are up to
3 in (8 cm) wide. Sweet
coneflower is so called
because of the honeyed
scent of its blooms,
which open in autumn.
ZONES 5–10.

RUMEX
DOCK, SORREL

Chiefly found in northern hemisphere temperate regions, this genus comprises around 200 species of annual, biennial and perennial herbs, usually with a deep tap root. Many species have been introduced to other parts of the world and have become invasive weeds. Docks are erect plants, usually with a basal rosette of simple leaves and with or without stem leaves. Flowers are borne in whorls in spikes or panicles, followed by small, oval, pointed fruits. A few species are cultivated for their ornamental foliage or as herbs mainly used as a vegetable.

CULTIVATION
Most docks thrive in full sun in moderately fertile, well-drained soil. They are marginally to fully frost hardy. Propagation is from seed sown in spring or by division in autumn; broken pieces of root will also sprout. Protect young plants from slugs and snails.

Rumex patienta
(right)
PATIENCE DOCK, PATIENCE HERB, SPINACH DOCK

This vigorous Eurasian perennial is up to 7 ft (2 m) high when in flower. Its basal leaves are 6–18 (15–45 cm) long, oval to lance-shaped and wavy. Their size is enhanced by the 12 in (30 cm) stems on which they are carried. The flower stem develops rapidly and starts to bloom around mid-summer.
ZONES 6–9.

R

S

SAGITTARIA
ARROWHEAD, WAPATO, DUCK POTATO

About 20 species of submerged or partially emergent temperate and tropical aquatic perennials, some tuberous, make up this genus. The emersed leaves are often linear to oval, but a few species have sagittate (arrowhead-shaped) leaves, hence the common name. They are usually about 10–12 in (25–30 cm) long. The submerged leaves are ribbon like, up to 4 ft (1.2 m) long including the petioles, and may form dense underwater meadows. In summer showy, purple-spotted white flowers open. They are 3-petalled, borne on branched stems that extend above the foliage and are ½–2 in (1.2–5 cm) wide.

CULTIVATION
Emergent species generally grow in ponds and fully submerged species prefer streams. All are bottom rooting and require a soil base and a position in full sun. Frost hardiness varies considerably according to the species. Propagate from seed or by division of the roots or tubers.

Sagittaria lancifolia 'Rubra' *(left)*

Sagittaria lancifolia

With this species from North Carolina down to northern South America and the West Indies, most leaves are above the water, the whole plant growing to 6 ft (1.8 m). The leaves may be linear, oval or elliptical and up to 15 in (38 cm) long, leathery and pale green. The white flowers may be 2 in (5 cm) wide in several whorls. **'Gigantea'** is larger in all aspects, while **'Rubra'** has a reddish tint to its leaves and flowers. ZONES 9–12.

S

SAINTPAULIA
AFRICA1N VIOLET

Natives of eastern Africa, saintpaulias were originally collected in
the late nineteenth century by Baron von Saint-Paul. There are
20 species of these low-growing, evergreen perennials and several
thousand varieties. Some of these are the most popular flowering
indoor plants because of their attractive foliage, compact nature,
long flowering periods and wide range of flower colors. Cultivars
include '**Chimera Monique**', with purple and white flowers;
'**Chimera Myrthe**', with crimson and white flowers; '**Nada**', with
white flowers; and '**Ramona**', with flowers a rich crimson. The
flowers are 5-petalled and the succulent leaves are usually hairy.

CULTIVATION
Although African violets have a reputation for being difficult to
grow, in the right conditions this is generally not so. They do
demand certain soil, so plant them in commercial African violet
mix. Constant temperature, moderate humidity and bright, indirect light ensure prolonged flowering; in winter they may also need
artificial light. Use room temperature water, allow the surface soil
to dry out a little between waterings, and avoid splashing the leaves.
They bloom best when slightly potbound, so repot when very leafy
and no longer flowering well. Propagate from leaf cuttings rooted
in water or stuck in a layer of pebbles on top of a moist sand and
peat mixture. African violets are vulnerable to cyclamen mite,
mealybug and powdery mildew.

S

Saintpaulia 'Chimera Myrthe' *(above)*

Saintpaulia 'Nada' *(left)*

Saintpaulia 'Ramona' *(below)*

S

Saintpaulia ionantha
(below)

COMMON AFRICAN VIOLET

This species has clusters of tubular, semi-succulent violet-blue flowers, growing on stems above the leaves. The green leaves, with reddish green undersides, are scalloped, fleshy and hairy. Thousands of cultivars are available, now far removed from the species. The flowers can be single or double, usually 1½ in (35 mm) across, and come in shades from white through mauve and blue to purple, and pale and deep pink to crimson. **ZONES 11–12.**

Saintpaulia ionantha **hybrids** *(top & bottom)*

Saintpaulia magungensis *(above)*

This plant from Tanzania has purple flowers ³/₄ in (18 mm) across in groups of 2 or 4, held just above the leaves. Branched stems up to 6 in (15 cm) long bear leaves with petioles (leaf stems) up to 2 in (5 cm) long. The leaves are oval or round, about 2½ in (6 cm) across, with a wavy edge and both long and short hairs on the upper surface. **ZONES 10–12.**

S

Salpiglossis sinuata
(left & below)

PAINTED TONGUE

Offering a variety of flower colors including red, orange, yellow, blue and purple, this annual from Peru and Argentina blooms in summer and early autumn. The 2 in (5 cm) wide, heavily veined flowers are like small flaring trumpets, while the lanceolate leaves are light green. A fast grower, it reaches a height of 18–24 in (45–60 cm) and a spread of at least 15 in (38 cm). It is frost tender and dislikes dry conditions. **ZONES 8–11.**

SALPIGLOSSIS

These species from the southern Andes are not seen very often in gardens as they can be tricky to grow, but patient gardeners who live in mild climates with fairly cool summers will be rewarded by a short but beautiful display of flowers like petunias (they are related). They come in rich shades of crimson, scarlet, orange, blue, purple and white, all veined and laced with gold. There are 2 species of annuals and perennials providing color in borders or as greenhouse plants in cold climates.

CULTIVATION

Plant in full sun in rich, well-drained soil. Deadhead regularly. *Salpiglossis* species are best sown in early spring directly in the place they are to grow, as seedlings do not always survive transplanting. They are prone to attack by aphids.

SALVIA
SAGE

The largest genus of the mint family, *Salvia* consists of as many as 900 species of annuals, perennials and soft-wooded shrubs, distributed throughout most parts of the world except very cold regions and tropical rainforests. Their tubular, 2-lipped flowers are very distinctive. The lower lip is flat but the upper lip helmet- or boat-shaped; the calyx is also 2-lipped and may be colored. The flowers come in a wide range of colors, including some of the brightest blues and scarlets of any plants, though yellows are rare. Many beautiful sage species are grown as garden plants, including some with aromatic leaves grown primarily as culinary herbs, but even these can be grown for their ornamental value alone. The genus name goes back to Roman times and derives from the Latin *salvus,* 'safe' or 'well', referring to the supposed healing properties of *Salvia officinalis.*

CULTIVATION

Most of the shrubby Mexican and South American species will tolerate only light frosts, but some of the perennials are more frost hardy. Sages generally do best planted in full sun in well drained, light-textured soil with adequate watering in summer. Propagate from seed in spring, cuttings in early summer, or division of rhizomatous species at almost any time. Foliage of many species is attacked by snails, slugs and caterpillars.

Salvia argentea (right)
SILVER SAGE

Silver sage is a biennial or short-lived perennial native to southern Europe and North Africa. It has large, silver-felted leaves forming a flat basal rosette that builds up in autumn and winter to as much as 3 ft (1 m) wide before sending up 3 ft (1 m) panicles of small white flowers in spring and summer. Its main attraction is its foliage, which can be maintained for longer if inflorescence buds are removed. Allow to seed in the second or third year to maintain a supply of replacement seedlings. ZONES 6–9.

S

Salvia blepharophylla (left)
EYELASH LEAFED SAGE

This Mexican species is a subshrubby perennial of similar style to the better-known *Salvia greggii* and *S. microphylla*. It is almost evergreen and spreads by creeping rhizomes, reaching about 15 in (38 cm) in height and somewhat greater spread, with rich green foliage. Through summer and autumn it produces a succession of bright red flowers suffused with paler orange or pink. It likes part-shade and moist soil. ZONES 8–11.

Salvia cacaliifolia (left)
GUATEMALAN BLUE SAGE

From the highlands of Mexico, Guatemala and Honduras, this is one of the most distinctive sages: its name signifies a resemblance between its leaves and those of *Cacalia,* a genus allied to *Senecio*. It is a perennial to about 3 ft (1 m) high with stems springing from a creeping rootstock, bearing pairs of glossy bright green triangular leaves that are about as broad as long, with 3 sharp points. In summer and autumn it produces a profusion of small deep blue flowers on branched spikes. ZONES 8–10.

Salvia austriaca (left)
AUSTRIAN SAGE

From eastern Europe, this is one of a large group of cold-hardy perennial sages with basal rosettes of closely veined, jaggedly toothed or lobed leaves, and long, erect spikes of smallish flowers in regular whorls. In *Salvia austriaca* the stalked leaves may be over 12 in (30 cm) long and the pale yellow flowers with protruding stamens are borne in summer on spikes to 3 ft (1 m) tall. ZONES 6–10.

S

Salvia confertiflora *(right)*
SABRA SPIKE SAGE

From Brazil, this perennial plant can reach a height of
6 ft (1.8 m). It has large, 8 in (20 cm) wide, mid-green
oval leaves with downy undersides. The flower spikes
are in 12 in (30 cm) unbranched heads with red flowers
and deep red calyces during late summer and autumn.
ZONES 9–11.

Salvia coccinea
'Coral Nymph'
(below)

Salvia chamaedryoides *(above)*
GERMANDER SAGE

From Texas and Mexico, this tiny
leafed perennial is suitable for the
rock garden, being multi-branched
and very compact. The foliage is
gray-blue and masses of small deep
violet-blue flowers appear in summer. It grows to 12 in (30 cm) high
and 24 in (60 cm) wide. **ZONES 8–11.**

Salvia coccinea
RED TEXAS SAGE

This compact, bushy, short-lived
perennial from South America is
treated as an annual in colder
climates. It has small mid-green
leaves and an abundance of scarlet
flowers from early summer to late
autumn. It is normally grown in full
sun, but when placed in light shade
and protected from frost it can
survive another season or two. Many
forms are known, including a pure
white and a lovely salmon pink and
white bicolor. **'Coral Nymph'** is a
compact form with coral pink
flowers; **'Lady in Red'** is also compact, growing just 15 in (38 cm) tall
with bright red flowers. **ZONES 8–11.**

S

Salvia dolomitica (left)

This native of South Africa is still rare in cultivation. It has gray-green foliage, grows to around 4 ft (1.2 m) tall and spreads slowly by rhizomes to eventually form a dense thicket of stems. Its flowers are dusky lavender-pink and appear in spring. The calyces are purple-red and last well after the flowers have fallen. ZONES 9–11.

Salvia elegans 'Scarlet Pineapple' (above)

Salvia darcyi (left)
DARCY SAGE

This rare perennial from high in the mountains of northeastern Mexico is a recent discovery only named in 1994, although introduced to cultivation in the USA about 5 years earlier. Growing to about 3 ft (1 m) high, it is a little like *Salvia coccinea* but its rich scarlet flowers are larger, about 1¹/₂ in (35 mm) long, and borne in greater profusion in erect panicles. It flowers in summer and early autumn and dies back in winter. Easily grown in fertile soil with ample water in summer, *S. darcyi* is proving an outstanding ornamental. ZONES 8–10.

Salvia elegans
PINEAPPLE-SCENTED SAGE

This open-branched perennial or subshrub from Mexico and Guatemala can reach 6 ft (1.8 m) in milder areas and is grown for its light green foliage. It has a distinctive pineapple scent and flavor. Its whorls of small bright red flowers are borne in late summer and autumn. The leaves are used fresh but sparingly in fruit salads, summer drinks and teas. The flowers are delicious, and may be added to desserts and salads for color and flavor.
'Scarlet Pineapple' (syn. *Salvia rutilans*) is more floriferous with larger scarlet flowers which, in milder areas, will persist to midwinter and are most attractive to honey-eating birds. ZONES 8–11.

S

Salvia farinacea
MEALY-CUP SAGE

This species is grown as an annual in regions that have cold winters and is at its best when mass planted. It is a short-lived perennial in warmer climates, although if planted in a little shade to protect it from hot afternoon sun and pruned hard in mid-autumn it can live up to 5 years. Growing to 24–36 in (60–90 cm), it bears lavender-like, deep violet-blue flowers on slender stems. It is a good cut flower and comes from Texas and Mexico. **'Blue Bedder'** is an improved cultivar; **'Strata'** has blue and white flowers; and **'Victoria'** has deep blue flowers. **'Argent'** (syn. 'Silver') has silvery white flowers. ZONES 8–11.

Salvia farinacea 'Victoria' *(above)*

Salvia farinacea 'Argent' *(left)*

Salvia farinacea 'Strata' *(right)*

S

Salvia forsskaolii *(right)*
syn. *Salvia forskaohlei*

This highly variable perennial from southeastern Europe has slightly hairy basal leaves with small flowers on single 30 in (75 cm) long stems. The flower color will vary from violet to pinkish magenta with white or yellow markings on the lower lip. It is fully frost hardy but prefers drier winters. ZONES 7–10.

Salvia gesneriiflora (above)

This erect Colombian and Mexican perennial usually grows to 24 in (60 cm) high, though reportedly can reach 25 ft (8 m). It has oval or heart-shaped leaves about 4 in (10 cm) long that are bright green and finely hairy. It produces its large orange-red flowers from spring to autumn. Each flower is 2 in (5 cm) long but presents no difficulty to nectar-seeking birds. A light pruning is necessary before winter. ZONES 8–11.

Salvia guaranitica
(below left)
ANISE SCENTED SAGE

Plant this tall-growing perennial from Brazil, Uruguay and Argentina with care, as it has a tendency to 'gallop' in its second or third season, choking less valiant plants. Its deep violet-blue flowers are held aloft on strong 6 ft (1.8 m) stems from mid-summer to late autumn. **'Argentine Skies'** was selected for its pale blue flowers, and **'Purple Splendour'** for its intense blackish purple flowers. ZONES 9–11.

Salvia greggii
(above)
FALL SAGE, CHERRY SAGE, AUTUMN SAGE

This species, which can reach 3–4 ft (1–1.2 m) in height, is native from Texas into Mexico and is a long-flowering addition to dryish gardens in California and southwestern USA. The leaves are small and aromatic; above the foliage rise slender stems with broad-lipped sage blossoms in red, orange, salmon, pink, pale yellow, white and blends. The flowers are produced from spring through autumn in coastal areas, and in autumn and winter in the desert. Many hybrids and named selections are available. ZONES 9–10.

Salvia guaranitica
'Purple Splendour' (left)

Salvia multicaulis
(right)

This low-growing shrubby or mat perennial from southwestern Asia produces erect hairy stems to 18 in (45 cm) tall. The white-felted leaves are mainly basal, oval, 1½ in (35 mm) long and wavy. The hairy calyx can be lime green or purple, the flowers violet or white and up to ¾ in (18 mm) long. It is spring and summer flowering and needs full sun in cultivation. **ZONES 8–11.**

Salvia indica *(right)*

This plant from the Middle East forms an erect branched species to 5 ft (1.5 m) tall with heart-shaped hairy leaves to 12 in (30 cm). Masses of white and blue or lilac flowers are held by heel-shaped ½ in (12 mm) calyces during spring and summer. **ZONES 9–11.**

Salvia involucrata
ROSELEAF SAGE

This is a charming tall perennial that remains evergreen in mild climates but even so, is best cut back to the ground every year to promote flowering. From the highlands of central Mexico, it has erect cane-like stems to about 5 ft (1.5 m) high, and broad, long-stalked leaves that often develop red veining. The loose flower spikes terminate in groups of large mauve to magenta bracts, which are shed one by one to reveal a trio of developing flowers of the same or deeper color; each flower is up to 2 in (5 cm) long, tubular but swollen in the middle, and the small upper lip is covered in velvety hairs. It blooms over a long summer–autumn season, and appreciates sun and rich, well drained soil. In the UK, it has been known as **'Bethellii'**, a superior selection from the wild. **ZONES 9–10.**

Salvia involucrata 'Bethellii' *(right)*

S

Salvia officinalis
'Purpurascens' and
Verbena tenuisecta (red)
(left)

Salvia officinalis
(below)
COMMON SAGE, GARDEN SAGE

From Spain, the Balkans
and North Africa, com-
mon sage is a decorative,
frost-hardy, short-lived
perennial that grows to
30 in (75 cm) high and
wide, with downy gray-
green oval leaves and
short racemes of purple
flowers in summer. Its
culinary merits are well
known, and it has
entered folklore over
the centuries for its real
and supposed medicinal
qualities. **'Purpurascens'**
has gray-green leaves
invested with a purplish
hue and pale mauve
flowers; **'Tricolor'** is a
garish combination of
green, cream and
beetroot red leaves;
'Berggarten' is a lower-
growing form with
larger leaves and blue
flowers. **ZONES 5–10.**

Salvia pratensis (below)
MEADOW CLARY, MEADOW SAGE

This tough, reliable and fully frost-hardy sage
from Europe and Morocco bears oval to oblong
basal leaves and shorter leaves along its 3 ft
(1 m) flowering stems; the flowers are rather
sparsely distributed along these stems. The
commonly grown form has violet-purple
flowers but in the wild it is immensely variable,
from the white and pale blue **'Haematodes'**
through to deeper blues and darker purples and
even **'Rosea'** with rose-pink flowers, and
'Rubicunda' with rose-red flowers. **ZONES 3–9.**

Salvia nemorosa (below)
syn. *Salvia virgata* var.
nemorosa

Many slender, erect spikes
of pinkish purple or white
flowers bloom in summer
on this neat, clump-
forming perennial. Grow-
ing 3 ft (1 m) high with an
18 in (45 cm) spread, this
frost-hardy species has
rough leaves of narrow
elliptical shape. It is widespread from Europe to
central Asia. **ZONES 5–10.**

Salvia sclarea (right)
BIENNIAL CLARY, CLARY SAGE

This native of southern Europe and Syria is a
biennial and grows 3 ft (1 m) tall. Clary sage has
been used medicinally and as a flavoring for
beverages. Moderately fast growing and erect, it
has long, loose, terminal spikes of tubular, greenish
white tinged with purple flowers in summer, and
velvety, heart-shaped leaves. **Salvia sclarea var.
turkestanica** has pink stems and white, pink-
flecked flowers. ZONES 5–10.

Salvia spathacea
(right)
PITCHER SAGE,
HUMMINGBIRD SAGE,
CRIMSON SAGE

This woody perennial
with hairy stems up
to 3 ft (1 m) tall has
leaves which vary
from oval to heart-
or arrowhead-shaped
with a white felt
beneath. Many
magenta flowers
about 1¼ in (30 mm)
long are held above
the bush. It comes
from California.
ZONES 8–11.

Salvia puberula (right)

This species is closely allied to *Salvia
involucrata* and comes from the same
highland region of Mexico. It is a
perennial of much the same size and
growth habit, and the long-pointed
leaves are somewhat more downy.
The flowers also are very similar but a
deeper magenta color and the
inflorescence is shorter and has
smaller bud bracts. It has been grown
in southern USA and makes a fine
ornamental, blooming mainly in
autumn. ZONES 8–10.

S

Salvia splendens 'Salsa Burgundy' *(above)*

Salvia splendens 'Van Houttei' *(below)*

Salvia splendens
SCARLET SAGE

This native of Brazil, which is grown as an annual, produces dense terminal spikes of scarlet flowers in summer through early autumn. The leaves are toothed and elliptical. It grows 3–4 ft (1–1.2 m) tall and wide. In hotter climates, give some shade; it is moderately frost hardy. **'Salsa Burgundy'** has deep burgundy flowers, while **'Van Houttei'** has a deep dull red calyx with large lighter red flowers; both prefer a little shade. ZONES 9–12.

S

Salvia × sylvestris

This leafy perennial to 12–36 in (30–90 cm) high is a hybrid between *Salvia pratensis* and *S. nemorosa*. It has hairy oblong heart-shaped leaves 2–4 in (5–10 cm) long. The summer flowers are purplish violet in long-branched heads. It comes from western Asia and Europe but is naturalized in North America. There are many cultivars, some of uncertain origin. **'Blau-hügel'** ('Blue Mound') is compact with clear blue flowers; **'Ostfriesland'** ('East Friesland') is deep purple; **'Mainacht'** is lower growing with blackish purple tones; and **'Wesuwe'** is an early bloomer with dark violet flowers. ZONES 5–10.

Salvia × sylvestris 'Wesuwe' *(right)*
Salvia × sylvestris 'Mainacht' *(below left)*
Salvia × sylvestris 'Ostfriesland' *(below right)*

S

Salvia viridis *(left)*

This is an erect annual or biennial plant with oval or oblong leaves up to 2 in (5 cm) long. The green or purple calyx bears 1/2 in (12 mm) flowers which may be white to lilac to purple. It occurs around the Mediterranean and flowers in summer. There are several named color forms available. ZONES 7–11.

Salvia taraxacifolia *(above)*

This perennial from Morocco with upright stems reaching only 18 in (45 cm) has ferny leaves that are white underneath and form rosettes. The flowers, which appear from spring to summer, may be white or pale pink with a yellowish blotch on the lower lip and purple specks on the upper. Each flower attains a length of 1 1/4 in (30 mm). ZONES 9–11.

Salvia uliginosa *(left)*
BOG SAGE

Long racemes of sky blue flowers appear in summer on this upright branching perennial from South America. The leaves are toothed, elliptical to lance-shaped and up to 3 in (8 cm) long, smooth or only slightly hairy. Growing to 3–6 ft (1–1.8 m), it has slender curving stems. In good or moist soil it sends out underground rooting shoots and may become invasive. ZONES 8–11.

S

SAMBUCUS

ELDERBERRY, ELDER

This genus includes about 25 species of perennials, deciduous shrubs and soft-wooded trees. Although most are rarely cultivated because of their tendency to be somewhat weedy and invasive, some species are useful for their edible flowers and berries, and are attractive in foliage and flower. Most have pinnate leaves and, in late spring and early summer, bear large radiating sprays of tiny white or creamy flowers followed by clusters of usually purple-black, blue or red berries.

CULTIVATION

Usually undemanding, *Sambucus* thrive in any reasonably well-drained, fertile soil in sun or shade. Prune out old shoots and cut young shoots by half. Propagate from seed in autumn, or cuttings in summer or winter.

Sambucus ebulus

(right)

DWARF ELDER, DANE'S ELDER, DANEWORT, WALLWORT

From Europe, North Africa, Turkey and Iran, this is a herbaceous perennial growing up to 5 ft (1.5 m) high with strong creeping underground stems. The leaflets, usually 9 to 13, are elliptic, toothed and slightly hairy. It produces flat heads up to 4 in (10 cm) across of white-tinged pink flowers in summer, followed by black fruit. It is considered too invasive for a small garden. ZONES 5–10.

S

SANGUINARIA

BLOODROOT, RED PUCCOON

The single species of the genus is a widespread woodland plant
from eastern North America, from Nova Scotia through to Florida.
It is a low-growing perennial herb grown for its spring display of
cup-shaped flowers.

CULTIVATION

It prefers sandy soil but will tolerate clay
soil if not too wet. Bloodroot does well in
sun or part-shade, and especially under
deciduous trees. Propagation is by division
in late summer when the leaves have died
back.

**Sanguinaria
canadensis** *(above)*

This perennial has a
long stout horizontal
rootstock. Each bud on
the stock sends up a
heart-shaped leaf with
scalloped edges on
stalks 6 in (15 cm)
long. Each leaf is up to
12 in (30 cm) across.
The solitary white or
pink-tinged flowers are
up to 3 in (8 cm) across,
single, with 8 to 12 petals
and many yellow
central anthers. They
appear in the folds of
the leaves in spring
before the gray leaves
fully expand, and last
for about 3 weeks.
Sanguinaria canadensis
var. *grandiflora* has
larger flowers; the
double form '**Flore
Pleno**' has more but
narrower petals.
ZONES 3–9.

Sanguinaria canadensis
'Flore Pleno' *(left)*

S

Sanguisorba minor
(right)
syn. *Poterium
sanguisorba*
GARDEN BURNET,
SALAD BURNET

This perennial to 24 in
(60 cm) has 6 to
10 rounded toothed
leaflets on each leafstalk.
The flowers occur in
terminal oblong heads
to 1 in (25 mm). They
are white, the upper
ones female, the lower
ones male, with the
middle section com-
prised of both. It occurs
across Europe, western
Asia and North Africa
in dry rocky areas,
often on limestone. It
is often seen in herb
gardens where fresh
leaves are picked for
soups and salads. It has
a taste rather like
cucumber and is
excellent in cold drinks.
ZONES 5–9.

SANGUISORBA
syn. *Poterium*
BURNET

This is a genus of about 18 species found over the northern
temperate zones. They may be rhizomatous perennials or small
shrubs, and all have coarsely ferny leaves.
The flowerheads resemble small
bottlebrushes, and often only the lower half
of the bottlebrush has male and female
parts to the flowers.

CULTIVATION
They prefer full sun or part-shade and
moderately fertile, moist but well-drained
soil that should not be allowed to dry out
in summer. Propagate from seed or by
division.

Sanguisorba canadensis *(above)*
CANADIAN BURNET

A native of eastern North America, this vigorous
perennial loves full sun and moist soil. The handsome, pinnate leaves form a clump around 18 in
(45 cm) wide, above which are borne masses of
white flowers in late summer. It grows to 6 ft
(1.8 m) in height. ZONES 4–9.

S

Sanguisorba officinalis (above)
GREATER BURNET, BURNET BLOODWORT

The creeping rhizomes of this perennial carry erect stems, sometimes reddish, up to 4 ft (1.2 m) tall. The basal leaves are large with many leaflets up to 2 in (5 cm) long. The ³/₄ in (18 mm) long, dark reddish purple flowers appear in summer and autumn. It comes from China, Japan, North America and western Europe. ZONES 4–9.

Sanguisorba tenuifolia (below left)

This burnet, at 4 ft (1.2 m) one of the taller species, is found principally in Japan, but also occurs in China and Manchuria. It forms clumps of deeply serrated foliage composed of 11–21 leaflets up to 3 in (8 cm) long. The flowers, which open in summer, are carried in cylindrical 3 in (8 cm) long spikes and are usually white, though pink or purple flowers are not uncommon. Plant in partial shade. ZONES 4–9.

SANVITALIA

CREEPING ZINNIA

From southwestern USA and Mexico come these 7 species of annuals or short-lived perennials of the daisy family. The ovate leaves come in pairs and the small white or yellow flowers have a dark purplish black or white center. They make good ground covers, rock garden plants and hanging basket specimens.

CULTIVATION

Plants do best in full sun in humus-rich, well-drained soil. They are grown as annuals, sown *in situ* or in small pots for replanting with minimal root disturbance. Propagate from seed.

Sanvitalia procumbens

A native of Mexico, this summer-flowering, fully frost-hardy annual produces masses of bright yellow flower-heads like 1 in (25 mm) daisies with blackish centers. It is a prostrate species with mid-green, ovate leaves, growing to 8 in (20 cm) high and spreading at least 15 in (38 cm). Many cultivars are available. **'Aztec Gold'** is a good example. ZONES 7–11.

Sanvitalia procumbens
'Aztec Gold' and
Gazania 'Orange Magic'
(right)

S

SAPONARIA
SOAPWORT

The common name of this genus of
20 species of annuals and perennials comes
from the old custom of using the roots for
washing clothes. They contain a glucoside
called saponin, which is just as good as any
detergent for dissolving grease and dirt and
which, being edible, has been used as an
additive to beer to ensure that it develops a
good head when poured. These are good
plants for rock gardens, banks and for
trailing over walls.

CULTIVATION
Fully frost-hardy, they need sun and
well-drained soil. Propagate from seed in
spring or autumn or from cuttings in early
summer.

Saponaria × olivana (above)
This soapwort forms a
tight compact cushion
to 3 in (8 cm) and
bears profuse pale pink
blooms in summer. It
needs very good
drainage. ZONES 5–10.

Saponaria ocymoides (left)
ROCK SOAPWORT
This alpine perennial
from Europe forms a
thick carpet from which
profuse terminal
clusters of small,
flattish flowers, colored
pink to deep red,
bloom in late spring
and early summer. It
has sprawling mats of
hairy oval leaves.
ZONES 4–10.

S

SARMIENTA

The single species in this genus from southern Chile is a wiry stemmed, evergreen creeper or climber with smooth paired fleshy leaves. The flowers appear from the leaf axils on stalks; they are tubular with a central ballooning before narrowing again at the mouth with 5 small spreading lobes.

CULTIVATION

This plant needs well-drained, peaty soil in a protected shady place and abundant water. Propagate from seed in spring or cuttings in late summer.

Sarmienta scandens (above)
syn. *Sarmienta repens*

Smooth obovate to elliptic leaves 1 in (25 mm) long are toothed at the tip on this wiry clambering perennial. The numerous flowers on long fine stalks are bright scarlet and about ¾ in (18 mm) long. ZONES 5–9.

S

Sarracenia alata
(left)

YELLOW TRUMPETS

This species from
southern USA produces
erect, trumpet-like,
yellowish green pitchers
up to 30 in (75 cm) tall.
The upper part of the
trumpet and the
adjacent part of its lid
are often a dull red
color. The nodding
spring flowers are
greenish yellow and up
to $2^{1}/_{2}$ in (6 cm) across.
ZONES 8–11.

SARRACENIA

PITCHER PLANT

The *Sarracenia* genus consists of about 8 insectivorous evergreen or
perennial species from the eastern part of North America; although
they cover a wide area, they prefer to grow in peat bogs or in the
sodden ground at the edges of pools. All the species have curious,
many-petalled flowers whose styles develop into a sort of umbrella
that shelters the stamens. The flowers are usually purple-red or
greenish yellow or a blend of these colors, and the same tints are
found in the modified leaves, called pitchers, which are nearly as
decorative as the flowers. Insects are attracted to the foliage colors
and slide down the slippery sides, drowning in the rainwater that
accumulates at the bottom.

CULTIVATION

These moderately to fully frost-hardy plants need sun or part-shade
and moist, peaty soil. Keep very wet during the growth period, and
cool and moist in winter. Propagate from seed or by division in spring.

Sarracenia purpurea *(right)*
COMMON PITCHER PLANT,
HUNTSMAN'S CUP, INDIAN CUP,
SWEET PITCHER PLANT

This species is wide-spread in eastern North America, from New Jersey to the Arctic. It grows to 6 in (15 cm) in height. The pitchers are slender at the basal rosette, rapidly becoming swollen higher up. They are usually green with purple tints and the lid stands erect. The flowers appear in spring; they are purple or greenish purple and up to 2¹/₂ in (6 cm) wide. It has become naturalized in Europe, particularly Ireland. ZONES 6–10.

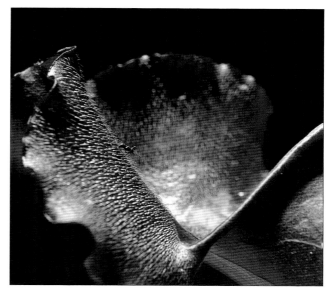

Sarracenia leucophylla *(right)*
syn. *Sarracenia drummondii*

This semi-evergreen perennial bears purple-red flowers in spring and has erect, slender pitchers up to 4 ft (1.2 m) long with narrow wings and erect lids with wavy margins. These are usually white and have light purple-red netting, gradually merging into green bases. ZONES 7–11.

S

SAUSSUREA

This genus consists of 300 species of perennials from Europe, Asia and North America. Most are not particularly ornamental, but some species from the high Himalayas have adapted to the harsh conditions by covering themselves with downy hairs. The leaves are simple and alternate, and the flowerheads appear in rosettes but usually die down as the seeds are released.

CULTIVATION

They do best in full sun in humus-rich, moist but very well-drained soil in areas with cool, moist summers. Water well during growth, but protect them from winter wet. Propagate from seed or by division.

Saussurea stella
(above)

This plant is from damp grassland and bog tussocks up to 13,000 ft (4000 m) in the Himalayas. It is a flat rosette of dark green, 8 in (20 cm) long leaves with purple flowers in the center.
ZONES 7–9.

S

Saxifraga 'Glassel Crimson' *(above)*

SAXIFRAGA

SAXIFRAGE

Both the foliage and blooms on these perennials, biennials and annuals are equally appealing. The genus comprises some 440 species of evergreens and semi-evergreens. Their natural territory includes temperate, alpine and subarctic regions, mostly in the northern hemisphere, but many garden hybrids have been cultivated. They serve well in rock gardens and as ground cover. The flowers are mostly white, sometimes spotted with pink, but other colors are also available. The genus name combines two Latin terms, 'rock' and 'to break', suggestive of either the hardiness of their rooting system or their reputed medicinal effect on bladder stones. Many cultivars are available. **'Glassel Crimson'** has two-tone crimson flowers with a yellow eye; **'Nona McGrory'** has beautiful pale pink spotted with deeper pink.

Saxifraga 'Nona McGrory' *(below)*

CULTIVATION

Soil and light requirements vary greatly depending on the species; they also vary from being very frost hardy to marginally frost hardy. Propagate from seed in autumn, by division or from rooted offsets in winter.

S

Saxifraga bronchialis

This plant forms a tuft to 8 in (20 cm) tall, with stiff linear leaves to ¹/₂ in (12 mm) long. The flowers are cream, spotted with red. It comes from North America and Asia. *Saxifraga bronchialis* subsp. *vespertina* is found in China, Mongolia and Siberia and bears greenish white flowers spotted with reddish pink. ZONES 4–9.

Saxifraga bronchialis subsp. *vespertina* *(above)*

Saxifraga × apiculata *(right)*

This perennial is a hybrid between *Saxifraga marginata* and **S. sancta.** It forms tight rosettes to 4 in (10 cm) high with small lance-shaped leaves and small yellow flowers of 10 to 12 per head. **'Alba'** has white flowers. **'Gregor Mendel'** has soft lemon flowers. Other hybrids are known and all, to various degrees, have a white encrustation to the leaves. They need some protection from heat and are intolerant of drying out. ZONES 6–9.

Saxifraga 'Apple Blossom' *(left)*

The parentage of this plant is unknown. It forms a rounded clump up to 3 in (8 cm) tall and spreads to 24 in (60 cm). The toothed oval green leaves make a dense wall, while the ¹/₂ in (12 mm) pale pink flowerbuds, opening to white, are held above the foliage; they appear from spring to early summer. ZONES 7–9.

S

Saxifraga burseriana
BURSER'S SAXIFRAGE

This is a slow-growing evergreen perennial from the eastern Alps that is woody at its base and forms a series of dense conical cushions rather than rosettes with grayish green to silver leaves. The crimson flowers are solitary on 2 in (5 cm) tall stems. Plant in full sun in moderately fertile, well-drained soil. **'Gloria'** is made distinctive by brilliant red flower stems and larger white flowers with deep yellow centers. ZONES 6–9.

Saxifraga cotyledon
GREAT ALPINE ROCKFOIL

Found from Scandinavia and Iceland to the Pyrenees and the Alps, this rosette-forming species has central rosettes up to 5 in (12 cm) wide with smaller daughter rosettes around them. The leaves are finely toothed and secrete a chalky coating from the limestone on which they grow. The flower stems are branching and up to 28 in (70 cm) tall, carrying 8–40 tiny white flowers per branch. **'Southside Seedling'** has red flowers spotted and edged with white. ZONES 6–9.

Saxifraga burseriana 'Gloria' *(above)*

Saxifraga cotyledon
'Southside Seedling' *(right)*

S

Saxifraga exarata subsp. *moschata*
(left)

syn. *Saxifraga moschata*

This is a delightful downy-leafed cushion-forming plant from central and southern Europe with many round-petalled flowers on 4 in (10 cm) stems. The colors range from white or creamy yellow to pink through to strong carmine pink or red. The tricky combination of full sun and moist soil with perfect drainage in winter will keep it robust and healthy. ZONES 6–9.

Saxifraga *longifolia* *(right)*
PYRENEAN SAXIFRAGE

This species forms a tight rosette of long narrow leaves with heavily lime encrusted margins. It bears a single panicle to 18 in (45 cm) long. This is multi-stemmed, each stem holding a ball-shaped head of tiny, round-petalled white flowers in spring. It is unfortunately monocarpic, so must be grown from seed as it dies after flowering. 'Tumbling Waters' is a particularly fine form. ZONES 6–9.

Saxifraga marginata
var. *rocheliana* *(right)*

Saxifraga *marginata*

This species from southern Italy, Romania and the Balkans forms dense cushions of tiny lime-secreting leaves. The tiny white flowers are carried in panicles of up to 12 blooms on hairy, 1–5 in (25 mm–12 cm) high stems. *S. marginata* var. *rocheliana* has larger leaves on short stems. ZONES 7–10.

Saxifraga rotundifolia (right)
ROUND-LEAFED SAXIFRAGE

This species from southwest France to northern
Turkey grows from a stout rhizome and forms
loose clumps of open rosettes of scalloped
roundish leaves. It flowers on a sparsely leafed
stem 10 in (25 cm) tall, forming an open truss of
small white, often purple-spotted flowers shading
to yellow at the center. It is best grown in moist
soil in light shade. ZONES 6–9.

Saxifraga paniculata
'Rosea' (below right)

Saxifraga paniculata
var. baldensis (right)

Saxifraga paniculata (bottom)
syn. *Saxifraga aizoon*
LIVELONG SAXIFRAGE

This summer-flowering
evergreen perennial
from central Europe
bears terminal clusters
of 5-petalled white,
pale pink or yellow
flowers, often with
spots of reddish purple.
The bluish green leaves
form a rosette below
the flower stems.
Saxifraga paniculata
grows to a height and
spread of 8–10 in
(20–25 cm). Grow in
full sun in well-drained,
alkaline soil. Many
forms have variations
in flower size and color.
'Rosea' has bright pink
flowers. **'Minima'** has
very small foliage and
flowers. *Saxifraga
paniculata* var.
baldensis has very
small rosettes of leaves
and red-tinged flower
stems. ZONES 3–9.

S

Saxifraga 'Ruth Draper' *(above)*

Ruth Draper was a British comedienne of
the 1930s, famous for her monologue,
'You should have seen my garden last week'.
Her namesake is a pretty example of a
mossy saxifrage, a group that likes a moist
and lightly shaded position. It bears large,
cup-shaped, purple-pink flowers in early
spring and grows to 2 in (5 cm) in height.
ZONES 6–9.

Saxifraga sempervivum *(left)*

An evergreen perennial with short leaves,
this species from the Balkans and northwestern Turkey forms open cushions with
minimal lime encrustations. It has tiny
reddish purple flowers, 15 to 20 per panicle
on a 4 in (10 cm) leafy purple flower stem.
Grow in full sun in well-drained soil.
ZONES 7–9.

S

Saxifraga stolonifera
syn. *Saxifraga sarmentosa*

MOTHER OF THOUSANDS, STRAWBERRY BEGONIA

Geranium-like leaves are a feature of this perennial, which has rounded, glossy leaves that are olive green with silver veins, purplish pink on the undersides. In spring through early summer, oddly petalled white flowers are borne in delicate panicles on thin, erect stalks. One petal on the tiny flowers seems to outgrow its 4 companion petals. Frost tender, it grows to a height of 6–8 in (15–20 cm) and spreads to 12 in (30 cm) by runners. **'Tricolor'** has deeply cut, green leaves patterned with red and white. ZONES 5–10.

Saxifraga umbrosa *(below)*

This species from the Pyrenees forms a spreading leafy rosette of gray-green foliage with small white flowers on multiple 8 in (20 cm) stems. It is best in humus-rich soil and, in full sun or part-shade in hotter areas, it will flower freely from late spring to early summer. Other forms with shell-pink flowers are recorded. ZONES 7–9.

Saxifraga stolonifera
'Tricolor' *(above)*

SCABIOSA
SCABIOUS, PINCUSHION FLOWER

This genus of 80 annuals, biennials and perennials from temperate climates, bears tall-stemmed, honey-scented flowers ideal for cutting. The blooms, bearing multiple florets with protruding filaments giving a pincushion effect, range from white, yellow, red, blue and mauve to deep purple.

CULTIVATION
Best in full sun in well-drained, alkaline soil. Propagate annuals from seed in spring, and perennials from cuttings in summer, seed in autumn or by division in early spring.

Scabiosa caucasica *(above)*

This perennial bears summer flowerheads in many hues with centers often in a contrasting color. It reaches a height and spread of 18–24 in (45–60 cm). **'Clive Greaves'** has lilac-blue flowers; **'Miss Wilmott'** has white flowers; **'Staefa'** is a strong grower with blue flowers; and **'Mrs Isaac House'** has creamy white flowers. ZONES 4–10.

Scabiosa anthemifolia *(below)*

This is an annual or short-lived perennial with arching stems up to 30 in (75 cm) long bearing 2½ in (6 cm) flowers in shades of mauve, violet or rose. It comes from South Africa. ZONES 7–11.

Scabiosa columbaria 'Butterfly Blue' *(above)*

Scabiosa columbaria

This biennial or perennial grows to 24 in (60 cm) tall with a spread of 3 ft (1 m). Slender, erect, hairy stems produce globular heads of reddish purple to lilac-blue flowers in 1½ in (35 mm) wide heads during summer and autumn. **'Butterfly Blue'** is a lower growing, dense, fuzzy leafed cultivar with lavender-blue pincushion flowers over a very long period. ZONES 6–10.

Scabiosa caucasica 'Staefa' *(left)*

Scabiosa caucasica 'Mrs Isaac House' *(above)*

SCAEVOLA

FAN FLOWER

This genus from Australia and the Pacific region contains 96 species of mainly temperate origin. Most are evergreen perennials, shrubs, subshrubs and small trees, with a number of ground-covering varieties that have proved adaptable to a wide range of garden conditions, including seaside gardens. Most have leaves that are fleshy, often hairy and occasionally succulent, borne on stout, sometimes brittle stems. Fan-shaped flowers, while generally fairly small at ½–1 in (12–25 mm) across, are profuse and are held on the plant for long periods. The flower color ranges from white to blue, mauve and deep purple.

CULTIVATION

Species of *Scaevola* tolerate a wide range of soils but prefer them light and well drained; they do best in sun or part-shade. Propagate from seed or cuttings in spring or summer.

Scaevola aemula 'Diamond Head' *(below)*

Scaevola aemula
'Blue Wonder' *(left)*

Scaevola aemula

(below)
syn. *Scaevola humilis*
FAIRY FAN FLOWER

The thick, coarsely toothed, dark green leaves on this perennial herb grow along spreading stems to form ground-hugging cover not more than 18 in (45 cm) high with a similar spread. Spikes of large, purple-blue flowers with yellow throats continue to elongate as new flowers open, blooming from early spring to late summer. Native to the sandy coast and near coastal woodlands of Australia, it resists dry conditions, frost and salt spray. **'Blue Wonder'** bears lilac-blue flowers almost continuously in great profusion. Another similar cultivar is **'Diamond Head'**. ZONES 9–11.

SCHIZANTHUS
POOR MAN'S ORCHID, BUTTERFLY FLOWER

This genus contains 12 to 15 species of annuals from the Chilean mountains. Although the blooms do look like miniature orchids, *Schizanthus* are in fact related to petunias. They come in shades of pink, mauve, red, purple and white, all with gold-speckled throats. They grow to about 3 ft (1 m) high and 12 in (30 cm) wide. Most of the flowers seen in gardens are hybrids, and give a colorful display over a short spring to summer season. '**Swingtime**' is a popular cultivar which flowers profusely in varying shades of red.

CULTIVATION
These subtropical mountain plants do not like extremes of heat or cold. They grow best outdoors in a mild, frost-free climate. In colder climates they need the controlled, even temperature of a greenhouse. Grow in full sun in fertile, well-drained soil and pinch out growing tips of young plants to ensure bushy growth. Propagate from seed in summer or autumn.

Schizanthus
'Swingtime' *(below)*

S

Schizanthus × wisetonensis *(above)*

This erect species bears tubular to flared, 2-lipped, white, blue, pink or reddish brown flowers often flushed with yellow from spring to summer. It has lance-shaped, light green leaves and grows to 18 in (45 cm) high with a spread of 12 in (30 cm). Most garden strains are derived from this species. **ZONES 7–11.**

Schizanthus hookeri *(left)*

This species grows to 18 in (45 cm) in height with divided leaves and large pink, violet or purple flowers, whose upper lips are yellow blotched. **ZONES 7–11.**

S

SCHIZOSTYLIS

A single species of grassy leafed rhizomatous perennial makes up this genus. It is widely distributed in South Africa where it grows beside streams. The long-flowering stems terminate in clusters of bowl-shaped 6-petalled flowers in deep scarlet and pink; it is an excellent cut flower.

CULTIVATION

Frost hardy, it prefers full sun and fertile, moist soil with shelter from the cold in cool-temperate climates. Divide every couple of years when it becomes crowded or propagate from seed in spring.

Schizostylis coccinea
CRIMSON FLAG

This variable species can fail in prolonged dry conditions. The sword-shaped leaves are green and are untidy unless pruned regularly and protected from thrips and slugs. It is valued for its late summer and autumn display which in some climates, conditions and seasons can extend into winter and beyond. The flowers are usually scarlet. It is a dainty plant reaching a height of 24 in (60 cm) and spread of 12 in (30 cm). Several named varieties are available in shades of pink, including the rose pink **'Mrs Hegarty'**, the salmon pink **'Sunrise'** and the crimson **'Grandiflora'** (syns 'Gigantea', 'Major'). **'Viscountess Byng'** has pale pink flowers with narrow petals. ZONES 6–10.

Schizostylis coccinea 'Grandiflora' *(left)*

Schizostylis coccinea 'Mrs Hegarty' *(above)*

Schizostylis coccinea 'Viscountess Byng' *(below left)*

Schizostylis coccinea 'Sunrise' *(below)*

S

Scutellaria costaricana (left)

An erect perennial to 3 ft (1 m) tall with dark purple stems, this species has slender oval leaves and 2½ in (6 cm) tubular flowers that are bright orange-scarlet with a golden yellow lip. It comes from Costa Rica. ZONES 9–12.

Scutellaria austinae (below)

Found in rocky areas of the pine forests and chaparrals and coastal ranges of California, this spreading, rather sticky stemmed rhizomatous perennial grows to as much as 12 in (30 cm) high when in flower. Its stems are covered in short hairs and narrow lance-shaped leaves. The flowers, which open in early summer are violet-blue and around 1 in (25 mm) long. ZONES 8–11.

SCUTELLARIA
SKULLCAP, HELMET FLOWER

The name of this genus comes from the Latin *scutella,* meaning a small shield or cup, which is a rough description of the pouch of the upper calyx. There are some 300 known species that consist mainly of summer-flowering perennials, most on a rhizomatous root system, though a few are annuals and rarely subshrubs. Most species occur in temperate regions throughout the northern hemisphere.

CULTIVATION

They are easily grown in full sun in most reasonable garden soil. None would be happy with parched soil in summer, but they are content with ordinary watering throughout dry weather. Propagation is by division in winter or from seed sown fresh in autumn. Cuttings may be taken in summer.

Scutellaria incana *(right)*

This is a rounded perennial to 4 ft (1.2 m) in
height with lightly serrated oval leaves and
large panicles of grayish blue flowers in summer.
A light prune will sometimes produce a second
flush of flowers in autumn. It is widespread
throughout northeastern USA. ZONES 5–9.

Scutellaria orientalis 'Alpina' *(above)*

This is a quickly
spreading perennial
with slightly hairy, oval,
light green leaves on
gray-green stems. It has
upright clusters of
golden flowers with
brownish lips, 4 to
6 flowers per stem. It is
best used as a ground
cover and comes from
southern Europe
to central Asia.
ZONES 7–10.

Scutellaria indica var.
parvifolia *(right)*

Scutellaria indica *(below right)*

This is an upright,
slowly spreading per-
ennial around 12 in
(30 cm) high with light
gray-green oval leaves
and clumped heads of
soft blue-gray, tubular
flowers. **Scutellaria
indica var. parvifolia**
(syn. *S. i.* var. *japonica*)
is lower growing to 4 in
(10 cm) and clumps
more rapidly. It has
crowded heads of blue-
mauve, shortish tubular
flowers in late spring.
If deadheaded
immediately it will
reflower in late summer.
ZONES 5–10.

S

SEDUM
STONECROP

This large genus contains about 400 species of succulent annuals, biennials, perennials, subshrubs and shrubs native to the northern hemisphere. Quick-growing plants, they vary widely in habit from carpet forming to upright up to 3 ft (1 m) tall. Their lush, whole leaves may be tubular, lanceolate, egg-shaped or elliptical, and the 5-petalled flowers appear in terminal sprays. Excellent as hanging basket or pot plants.

CULTIVATION
They range from frost tender to fully frost hardy. Fertile, porous soil is preferred; some types, however, are extremely robust and will grow in most soil types. They need full sun. Propagate perennials, shrubs and subshrubs from seed in spring or autumn, or by division or from cuttings in spring through mid-summer. Propagate annuals and biennials from seed sown under glass in early spring or outdoors in mid-spring.

Sedum ewersii
(below)
syn. *Hylotelephium ewersii*

This plant from the northern Himalayas, Mongolia, central Asia and China has branching, spreading low stems up to 12 in (30 cm) high with oval gray-green leaves up to 1 in (25 mm) long. The pink flowers persist from late spring to early autumn. ZONES 4–9.

Sedum 'Herbstfreude' *(left)*
syn. *Hylotelephium* 'Autumn Joy', *Sedum* 'Autumn Joy'

This plant forms a small clump which grows to 24 in (60 cm) tall. It has toothed fleshy leaves. Large heads of pink flowers appear in autumn. These fade to copper tones and then finally turn red. In cold climates it dies back to the ground in winter. ZONES 5–10.

Sedum
'Mohrchen' *(right)*

This ia an upright-
stemmed hybrid that
reaches about 18 in
(45 cm) tall in flower.
The stems are
purple-red with
brownish red leaves
with shallowly
toothed edges. The
flower clusters are
deep red and open
from late summer.
Valuable not just for
its show of late
flowers, but also
throughout the sum-
mer for its foliage.
ZONES 4–10.

Sedum spectabile
(above)
syn. *Hylotelephium
spectabile*
SHOWY SEDUM, ICE PLANT

Spoon-shaped, fleshy, gray-
green leaves grow in clusters on the erect branching
stems of this succulent
perennial from China and
Korea. Butterflies flock to
the flattish heads of small,
pink, star-like flowers,
which bloom in late sum-
mer. It grows to a height
and spread of 18 in (45 cm)
and is resistant to both
frost and dry conditions.
'Brilliant' bears profuse
heads of bright rose-pink
flowers. **'Stardust'** has rich
green leaves. **ZONES 5–10.**

S

Sedum telephium *(above)*
syn. *Hylotelephium telephium*

ORPINE, LIVE-FOREVER

Found from eastern Europe to Japan, this semi-succulent deciduous perennial is a very reliable plant for late season color. Its flowering stems are up to 24 in (60 cm) tall and carry heads of densely packed small reddish purple flowers that open from late summer until well into autumn. The leaves are oblong, 1–3 in (25 mm–8 cm) long with shallow teeth around the edges. ZONES 4–10.

Sedum spurium *(right)*

This summer-flowering, evergreen perennial from Turkey and northern Iran bears small blooms in big, rounded flowerheads; colors range from white to purple. Hairy stems carrying saw-edged, elliptical leaves spread widely into a carpet 4 in (10 cm) tall, suitable for covering banks and slopes. **'Schorbuser Blut'** ('Dragon's Blood') is a creeping cultivar with plum-toned leaves and magenta flowers; **'Sunset Cloud'** has deep pinkish orange flowers. *Sedum stoloniferum* is similar to *S. spurium* but its stems lie close to the ground and the flowers are pink. ZONES 7–10.

SELAGINELLA

LITTLE CLUB MOSS, SPIKE MOSS

There are about 700 species of evergreen, rhizomatous perennials in this genus, which occur mainly in tropical and warm-temperate zones. They are grown for their attractive branching foliage. Many are suitable for hanging baskets or for pots in greenhouses in cooler areas.

CULTIVATION

These frost-tender plants prefer part-shade and moderately fertile, moist but well-drained soil. Propagate from spores or by division.

Selaginella martensii
(below)

Overlapping bright green leaves on 6 in (15 cm) high stems trail and root from the nodes on this species. Some forms have a white variegation. It comes from Central America. **ZONES 9–11.**

Selaginella kraussiana *(above)*
SPREADING CLUB MOSS, TRAILING SPIKE MOSS, KRAUSS'S SPIKE MOSS

The trailing branched stems of this species form a bright green feathery mesh up to 1 in (25 mm) high. Dwarf plants are available, as well as the golden '**Aurea**' and the green and yellow '**Variegata**'. **ZONES 9–11.**

S

Sempervivum arachnoideum (left)
COBWEB HOUSELEEK

The web of white hairs covering the green, triangular-leafed rosettes of this species no doubt inspired its name. Through summer it produces pink to crimson flowers in loose terminal clusters. A native of the European Alps, it grows to a height of 3 in (8 cm) and spread of 12 in (30 cm). ZONES 5–10.

SEMPERVIVUM

This is a genus of about 40 evergreen, perennial succulents originating in Europe and western Asia. They almost all have small yellow, pink or white, star-shaped flowers in summer, but their chief beauty resides in the symmetry of their rosettes of leaves and the way they spread to form carpets of foliage. This makes them ideal for rock gardens, walls and banks, and like all succulents they do not mind dry conditions. They take their common name from a custom dating from Roman times, which was to grow them on the roofs of houses—it was said that no witch could land her broomstick on a roof on which houseleeks were growing.

CULTIVATION

Plant in full sun in gravelly, well-drained soil. Flowering does not begin for several years; the rosettes die after flowering leaving offsets, from which they can be propagated.

Sempervivum tectorum 'Purple Beauty' *(above)*

Sempervivum tectorum
COMMON HOUSELEEK, ROOF HOUSELEEK, HENS AND CHICKENS

The rosettes of this species are reddish tipped, sometimes red throughout. The flowers are purple to rosy red and appear in one-sided terminal clusters on 12 in (30 cm) high stems in summer. It reaches 4–6 in (10–15 cm) high and 18 in (45 cm) wide. Applying bruised leaves to the skin has a cooling effect and is said to relieve burns, insect bites, skin problems and fever; the juice is used on warts and freckles. **'Commander Hay'** from the UK has large rosettes of red and green; **'Purple Beauty'** has dark violet leaves; and **'Magnificum'** has large rosettes and pink flowers. ZONES 4–10.

SENECIO

This large genus of vigorous leafy plants includes some 1000 species from all over the world. Plants range from annuals, biennials and perennials to evergreen tree-like shrubs and climbers, some of the species being succulent. The daisy-like flowers, usually yellow but sometimes red, orange, blue or purple, are arranged in small to large clusters at the tops of the plants. Some species contain alkaloids and are poisonous to humans and animals.

CULTIVATION

Reasonably fertile, well-drained soil suits these frost-tender to fully frost-hardy plants, as well as a sunny location. Regular tip pruning encourages a bushy habit. Propagate shrubs from cuttings in summer, annuals from seed in autumn and perennials by division in spring.

Senecio elegans
(below)

WILD CINERARIA

This marginally frost-hardy, hairy annual is native to South Africa and has an erect habit, growing to 24 in (60 cm) tall. Its branching stems are covered with variable dark green leaves that range from entire to pinnate, up to 3 in (8 cm) long. In spring to summer daisy-like purplish pink flowers appear in dome-shaped terminal clusters. ZONES 9–11.

S

Shortia galacifolia
(left)

OCONEE BELLS

The rather round leaves of this perennial from eastern USA are 2 in (5 cm) in diameter, glossy green, toothed and becoming bronzed in winter. Single white or blue flowers occur on 4 in (10 cm) stalks, each flower reaching 1 in (25 mm) across. ZONES 5–9.

Shortia soldanelloides var. *ilicifolia* *(below)*

SHORTIA

There are 6 species of these evergreen stemless plants with creeping roots. They come from eastern Asia and North America. The long-stalked leaves form a rosette, each leaf being round or heart-shaped and rather glossy. The flowers may be white, blue or pink, either single or in small heads and rather nodding.

CULTIVATION

Species of *Shortia* need a deeply shady spot with humus-rich, moist but well-drained soil. Propagation is by division or from rooted runners.

Shortia soldanelloides
FRINGED GALAX, FRINGEBELL

This mat-forming perennial from Japan has rounded leaves 2 in (5 cm) in diameter and with coarse teeth. Deep pink, white or bluish flowers occur in groups of 4 to 6 on 3 in (8 cm) stalks; each flower is 1 in (25 mm) across with the petals fringed. It comes from Japan. **Shortia soldanelloides var. *ilicifolia*** has leaves which have only a few coarse teeth. ZONES 7–9.

Sidalcea malviflora
(right)
CHECKERBLOOM

This erect perennial plant grows to 4 ft (1.2 m) tall with spreading fibrous roots. It has lobed leaves and loose heads of pink or white flowers resembling hollyhocks during spring and summer. Most cultivars included under this name are now believed to be hybrids with other species. ZONES 6–10.

SIDALCEA
PRAIRIE MALLOW, CHECKER MALLOW

These 20 to 25 species of upright annuals or perennials with lobed, rounded leaves are found in open grasslands and mountain forests of western USA. Pink, purple or white flowers have a silky appearance and feel, and last well when cut.

CULTIVATION
They prefer cool summers and mild winters in good, deep, moisture-retentive soil. They will tolerate a little shade in hot climates. If cut back after flowering they will produce a second flush of blooms. Propagate from seed or by division.

Sidalcea 'Rose Queen' *(below)*
syn. *Sidalcea malviflora* 'Rose Queen'

Large, deep pink, cupped flowers are borne in spikes in summer on this fully frost-hardy perennial. The divided leaves form a basal clump with a spread of 24 in (60 cm). The overall height of this plant is 4 ft (1.2 m) and tall plants may need staking. **'William Smith'** is similar but grows only 3 ft (1 m) tall and produces flowers in 2 tones of deep pink. ZONES 6–10.

Sidalcea campestris *(left)*
MEADOW SIDALCEA

This hairy stemmed perennial grows up to 6 ft (1.8 m) tall. The pale pink or white flowers are 3 in (8 cm) across. It comes from northwestern USA. ZONES 7–10.

S

SILENE
CAMPION, CATCHFLY

This genus contains over 500 species of annuals, biennials and deciduous or evergreen perennials. They all feature 5-petalled summer flowers, baggy calyces and a multitude of small, elliptical, often silky leaves. Some of the species do well potted and others make good ground covers, with numerous stems forming a mound. Many of the weedier species open their flowers only at night, when they can be quite pretty, though all that is seen during the day are shrivelled petals. Some exude gum from their stems; passing flies get stuck to this, hence the common name catchfly.

CULTIVATION
Widely distributed throughout temperate and cold climates of the northern hemisphere, these marginally to fully frost-hardy plants like fertile, well-drained soil and full or part-sun. Propagate from seed in spring or early autumn or from cuttings in spring.

Silene acaulis (above)
MOSS CAMPION

This is a mat-forming evergreen perennial with masses of small leaves and shortly stalked pink flowers in summer. It comes from subarctic regions of Europe, Asia and North America, but is often poorly flowering in cultivation. It reaches a height of only 2 in (5 cm) with an 8 in (20 cm) spread. ZONES 2–9.

Silene armeria (below)

This European annual or biennial has pink, bell-shaped flowers with 5 notched petals. Growing to a height of 12 in (30 cm) with a spread of 6 in (15 cm), it has slender, erect, branching stems and linear leaves. ZONES 6–10.

Silene coeli-rosa
(right)
syns *Agrostemma coeli-rosa, Lychnis coeli-rosa, Viscaria elegans*

ROSE OF HEAVEN

This upright annual from the Mediterranean bears pinkish purple flowers in summer. Its lance-shaped, green leaves have a grayish cast. It grows rapidly to 18 in (45 cm) high and 6 in (15 cm) wide. **'Blue Angel'** has bright mid-blue flowers with slightly darker centers. **ZONES 6–11.**

Silene coeli-rosa 'Blue Angel' *(below)*

S

Silene fimbriata *(above & left)*

This hairy perennial to 24 in (60 cm) tall with upright leafy stems has loose heads of large white flowers and a persistent light green inflated calyx. It comes from Turkey. **ZONES 6–10.**

Silene keiskei var. minor *(below)*

This evergreen perennial from Japan reaches 4 in (20 cm) tall and 8 in (20 cm) wide, on slender stems with hairy, dark green leaves. Sprays of dark rose-pink flowers appear in late summer. **ZONES 6–10.**

Silene laciniata *(left)*

INDIAN PINK, MEXICAN CAMPION

This 3 ft (1 m) tall perennial comes from California and northern Mexico. The flowers are held in small heads and are bright crimson in color. **ZONES 7–11.**

Silene pendula
NODDING CATCHFLY

This fast-growing, bushy annual from the Mediterranean bears clusters of pale pink flowers in summer and early autumn. It has oval, hairy, mid-green leaves and grows to 8 in (20 cm) high and wide. **'Compacta'** is dense and grows to just 4 in (10 cm). **ZONES 7–11.**

Silene pendula 'Compacta' *(right)*

Silene schafta 'Shell Pink'
(right)

Silene schafta

This is a hairy clump-
forming, semi-evergreen
perennial from western
Asia. The deep purplish
red flowers appear in late
summer and autumn on
stems 10 in (25 cm) high.
'Shell Pink' has very pale
pink, nearly white flowers.
ZONES 6–10.

Silene vulgaris   *(below)*
BLADDER CAMPION, MAIDEN'S TEARS

This perennial has stems up to 24 in (60 cm) tall,
oval leaves and white flowers with 2-lobed petals;
the flowers are either solitary or in heads. It is
found throughout northern Africa, temperate Asia
and Europe. However, most plants sold as Silene
vulgaris are, in fact, *S. uniflora*. ZONES 5–10.

Silene uniflora   *(above)*
syn. *Silene vulgaris* subsp. *maritima*
SEA CAMPION

This deep-rooted perennial bears a multitude of
white flowers like pompons on branched stems in
spring or summer. Its calyces are greenish and
balloon like, and its lanceolate leaves have a grayish
cast. Reaching about 8 in (20 cm) in height and
spread, it can be grown on top of walls, in beds or
containers and grows wild on cliffs along the
European seaboard. **'Flore Pleno'** has double white
flowers with deeply cut petals. ZONES 3–10.

Silene uniflora 'Flore
Pleno' *(left)*

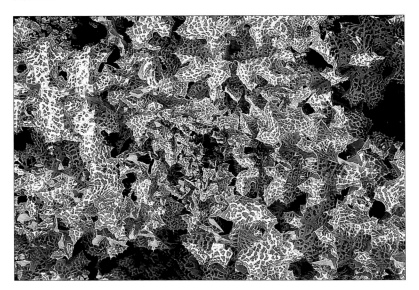

SILYBUM

Two erect annuals or biennials make up this genus from the Mediterranean, southwest Europe, central Asia and Africa. They are grown for their rosettes of intensely spiny, glossy dark green foliage, and the rounded, single, purple-pink flowerheads which are surrounded by thorny bracts.

CULTIVATION

Fully frost hardy, they prefer full sun and poor to moderately fertile, well-drained soil. Propagate from seed and watch out for slugs and snails.

Silybum marianum
(above)
BLESSED THISTLE, HOLY THISTLE
Viciously spiny dark green foliage marbled with white forms a rosette of dissected leaves on this biennial. Single stalks produce a head of flowers up to 4 ft (1.2 m) tall in the summer of the second year. It has become naturalized in California and the pampas of Argentina. **ZONES 7–11.**

S

SINNINGIA

This genus of about 40 species of tuberous perennials and deciduous or evergreen shrubs includes the flower-shop gloxinias. The flowers can be as much as 4 in (10 cm) across and come in the richest shades of blue, violet, pink or red, usually with mottled throats and their petals edged in white or a pale color. They make spectacular pot plants, each plant carrying as many as 20 flowers at the center of a rosette of coarsely velvety leaves. They are useless as garden plants because when rain fills the trumpets they collapse.

CULTIVATION

They are best in a humid atmosphere with bright light and indirect sun, and moist, peaty soil. The leaves die down after flowering, when the tubers can be dried out and stored in a frost-free area. Propagate from seed in spring or from stem cuttings in late spring or summer.

Sinningia speciosa
(below)

FLORIST'S GLOXINIA, VELVET SLIPPER PLANT

This perennial is valued for its large, trumpet-shaped, summer flowers in white, red, blue, purple and pastels. Nearly stemless with long, velvety leaves, it grows to a height and spread of 12 in (30 cm). The **Fyfiana Group** has large open flowers in various colors; the **Maxima Group** has nodding flowers. ZONES 11–12.

S

SISYRINCHIUM

The genus includes 90 marginally to fully frost-hardy species of annuals and rhizomatous perennials. They often self-destruct in seasons of prolific blooming, because the flower stem kills off the leaf stem from which it sprouts. *Sisyrinchium platense* was first collected in the River Plate region of Argentina.

CULTIVATION

Establish them in poor to moderately fertile, moist but well-drained soil. Although tolerant of part-shade, they prefer sun. They readily self-seed, otherwise they can be propagated by division in late summer.

Sisyrinchium 'Californian Skies' *(right)*

Often listed as a cultivar of *Sisyrinchium bellum*, but possibly a hybrid, 'California Skies' is a slowly spreading, grassy leafed perennial with branched stems of pale blue flowers in early summer. It is very like *S. bellum* but with flowers of a lighter, less mauve shade of blue. ZONES 8–11.

Sisyrinchium platense *(below)*

S

Sisyrinchium idahoense *(below)*

Winged unbranched stems grow to 18 in (45 cm) on this semi-evergreen perennial from western USA. The flowers are violet-blue with a yellow center, rarely white. ZONES 3–9.

Sisyrinchium graminoides *(right)*
syn. *Sisyrinchium angustifolium*
BLUE-EYED GRASS

This semi-evergreen perennial blooms in spring, producing terminal clusters of small pale to dark purple flowers like irises, with yellow throats. The stalks are flattened and winged. ZONES 3–10.

Sisyrinchium striatum *(right)*
syn. *Phaiophleps nigricans*
SATIN FLOWER

Long, narrow and sword-shaped, the leaves on this fully frost-hardy, evergreen perennial are gray-green. In summer it bears slender spikes of small cream flowers, striped purple. The species, which originates in Chile and Argentina, grows 18–24 in (45–60 cm) high with a 12 in (30 cm) spread. There is an attractive variegated form. ZONES 8–10.

S

Smilacina racemosa (left)
FALSE SOLOMON'S SEAL, FALSE SPIKENARD

Red fleshy fruit appear on this North American and Mexican species after it blooms in spring through mid-summer, producing lemon-scented white flowers in feathery sprays above fresh green, elliptical leaves. It grows to 3 ft (1 m) high with a spread of 24 in (60 cm). ZONES 4–9.

Smilacina stellata (below)
STAR-FLOWERED LILY OF THE VALLEY, STARFLOWER

This species has stems up to 24 in (60 cm) long that produce lance-shaped 6 in (15 cm) long folded leaves which are finely hairy underneath. Up to 20 white flowers are crowded on a 2 in (5 cm) wide head. The berries are at first green with black stripes, later becoming dark red. It comes from North America and Mexico. ZONES 3–9.

SMILACINA
FALSE SOLOMON'S SEAL

The 25 species in this genus occur in North and Central America and over much of temperate and subtropical Asia. These very attractive perennials with their plumes of white flowers in early summer bear a genus name meaning 'like a *Smilax*', which is a closely related though mainly tropical genus from the roots of which sarsaparilla is made. The common name suggests that their rhizomes might be confused with those of another cousin, *Polygonatum multiflorum* (Solomon's seal). However, while both sarsaparilla and the 'true' Solomon's seal are used medicinally, *Smilacina* species are not. They colonize rapidly, adorning gardens with their luxuriant foliage and pretty flowers.

CULTIVATION
These fully frost-hardy plants prefer dappled or deep shade and humus-rich, moist but well-drained neutral to acid soil. Propagate from seed in autumn or by division in autumn or spring.

S

SOLANUM
syn. *Lycianthes*

There are over 1400 species in this genus including trees, shrubs, annuals, biennials, perennials and climbers from a range of habitats worldwide. Some are evergreen, others semi-evergreen or deciduous. The genus includes important food plants like the potato and eggplant (aubergine), though many species are dangerously poisonous. Ornamental species are grown for their flowers and fruits. The leaves are arranged alternately, while the showy flowers are solitary or in clusters, star-shaped to bell-shaped, ranging in color from white and yellow to blue and purple. The fruits are berries that contain many seeds.

Solanum
pyracanthum (below)
This perennial from tropical Africa grows to 5 ft (1.5 m) tall. The lobed leaves are spiny along the central vein. The flowers are violet. ZONES 10–12.

CULTIVATION

These warm-climate plants have a wide range of requirements; most prefer full sun and rich, well-drained soil. They are commonly grown from seed in spring or cuttings in summer. They are prone to attack by spider mite, white fly and aphids.

Solanum
pseudocapsicum (left)
JERUSALEM CHERRY, WINTER CHERRY, CHRISTMAS CHERRY

This frost-tender, evergreen Mediterranean native produces starry white flowers in summer, followed by small scarlet berries that are poisonous. It grows sedately into a bushy, velvety leafed shrub about 4 ft (1.2 m) high and wide and is perhaps best grown as an annual, even in wild areas, in which case it should grow to 24 in (60 cm) tall. Several varieties with differently colored fruit are available. The species is related to the potato, eggplant and tomato, as well as to some other less edible plants. ZONES 9–11.

S

Soldanella caucasica
'Alba' *(left)*

SOLDANELLA
SNOWBELL

The soldanellas are elegant relatives of the primrose. They come from the mountains of Europe and flower at the end of spring. There are 10 species of evergreen perennials, all rather alike and interbreeding freely both in the wild and in gardens much to the irritation of those who like to be certain of their plants' names. They have nodding to pendent purple to white flowers and leathery leaves and are good plants for rock gardens and tubs. A good example is *Soldanella caucasica* 'Alba'.

CULTIVATION
These plants are mostly fully frost hardy, although the flower buds may be destroyed by frost. They need part-shade and humus-rich, well-drained, peaty soil. Propagate from seed in spring or by division in late summer. Watch out for slugs.

Soldanella hungarica (below)

Found on the Balkan Peninsula and the mountains of eastern central Europe, this delicate little alpine is a superb plant for a cool rockery. It has 1 in (25 mm) wide, rounded, kidney-shaped leaves that are deep green above, purplish below. The flowers, carried singly or in twos or threes, on hairy 4 in (10 cm) high stems, are ½ in (12 mm) long and lavender to pale purple in color with narrow petals. ZONES 6–9.

Soldanella montana (right)

Growing to about 12 in (30 cm) tall, this mound-forming species comes from the Alps but prefers the alpine woodlands to the bare rocks higher up. It flowers in early spring, often before the snows have not quite melted, producing long, pendent, bell-shaped, lavender-blue blossoms with fringed mouths. It has shallow-toothed, rounded leaves. ZONES 6–9.

S

SOLENOSTEMON
COLEUS, FLAME NETTLE, PAINTED NETTLE

This genus comprises 60 species of low shrubby perennials, often hairy and with variegated leaves from tropical Africa and Asia. The stems are 4-angled and the opposite leaves are often toothed. The flowers are small with an elongated lower lip.

CULTIVATION
These frost-tender plants are easily grown in milder climates with adequate summer moisture and protection from hot sun. They prefer humus-rich, moist but well-drained soil and need pinching back to promote bushiness. Propagate from seed or cuttings.

Solenostemon scutellarioides
(below)
syns *Coleus blumei* var. *verschaffeltii, C. scutellarioides*

Native to Southeast Asia, this bushy, fast-growing perennial is grown as an annual in more temperate climates. The leaves are a bright mixture of pink, green, red or yellow and are a pointed, oval shape with serrated edges. It grows 24 in (60 cm) high and 12 in (30 cm) wide.
ZONES 10–12.

Solidago 'Baby Gold'
(right)
syn. *Solidago* 'Golden Baby'

Some garden hybrids are valuable for their bright color in early autumn. This one is an upright plant with feathery spikes of golden flowers. Reaching 3 ft (1 m) in height, it has lance-shaped, green leaves. ZONES 5–10.

SOLIDAGO
GOLDENROD

The goldenrods are a genus of about 100 species of woody based perennials, almost all indigenous to the meadows and prairies of North America, with a few species in South America and Eurasia. They are related to the asters and, like them, flower in autumn. Their effect is quite different, however, as the individual flowers are very much smaller and are bright yellow. Most of the species are too weedy to be allowed into even the wildest garden, but some are worth cultivating for their big flower clusters and there are some very attractive hybrids.

CULTIVATION
These fully frost-hardy plants grow well in sun or shade in any fertile, well-drained soil. Most species self-seed, or they can be propagated by dividing the clumps in autumn or spring.

S

Solidago 'Golden Wings' *(above)*

This perennial grows to 5 ft (1.5 m) high with a spread of 3 ft (1 m). It has downy, lance-shaped leaves with serrated margins, and produces small, bright yellow flowers in feathery panicles early in autumn. ZONES 5–10.

Solidago sphacelata *(below)*

FALSE GOLDENROD

This species grows 24–36 in (60–90 cm) tall and has serrated, heart-shaped leaves. It eventually forms a large clump but is not invasive. The yellow flowers are borne on narrow arching stems from late summer. ZONES 4–9.

Solidago virgaurea *(left)*

This 3 ft (1 m) tall plant from Europe blooms in summer and autumn, with dense heads of yellow flowers. **Solidago virgaurea subsp. minuta** only grows to 4 in (10 cm) high. ZONES 5–10.

SONERILA

These evergreen perennials and small shrubs come from Southeast Asia and southern China, and over 175 species are known. The leaves are oval, sometimes toothed with 3 to 5 veins, dark green, spotted, and bristly. The flowers appear in racemes or corymbs and are anything from star- to cup-shaped.

CULTIVATION

They are usually grown as greenhouse plants outside the tropics; outdoors they prefer dappled shade and humus-rich, moist but well-drained soil. Propagate from cuttings.

Sonerila margaritacea
'Argentea' *(left)*

Sonerila margaritacea
var. *victoriae (below)*

Sonerila margaritacea

This 10 in (25 cm) high plant comes from Malaysia and Java. The arching or hanging stems are scarlet, and the leaves are dark polished green with white spots in lines in between the veins. Underneath the veins are purple. The rose-colored flowers are in heads of 8 to 10 and up to ³/₄ in (18 mm) across. **'Argentea'** has purple-red foliage with silver markings, a striking contrast. **Sonerila margaritacea var. victoriae** is similar but with wider leaves and wider petals.
ZONES 10–12.

S

SPATHIPHYLLUM

Most of the 36 species of this genus of evergreen, rhizomatous perennials come from tropical America, with some native to Malaysia. They
are lush, with dark green, oval leaves that stand erect or arch slightly.
The beautiful white, cream or green flowers resemble arum lilies and
bloom reliably indoors. A NASA study of 'sick building syndrome'
found spathiphyllums to be among the top 10 plants for their ability
to 'clean' the air in offices.

CULTIVATION

Grow in loose, fibrous, porous potting soil in filtered light away from
the sun. To simulate tropical conditions, increase the humidity by
placing the plant on a tray of pebbles. Water or mist regularly and
sponge any dust from the leaves. Keep the soil moist but not soggy,
and allow it to dry out a little in winter. Feed every 4 to 6 weeks with
half-strength soluble fertilizer in spring and summer. Propagate by
division in spring or summer. They are generally pest free. Too much
light may turn the foliage yellow.

S

Spathiphyllum 'Sensation' (left)

This is the largest of the
Spathiphyllum cultivars.
It has dark green foliage
with prominent ribbing
and large, well-shaped
white flowers, ageing to
green. It is a very
attractive plant even
when not in bloom.
ZONES 11–12.

Spathiphyllum
'Mauna Loa' *(right)*
PEACE LILY

The leathery, lance-shaped, glossy, mid-green leaves of this perennial reach lengths of 12 in (30 cm). Oval, white, papery spathes surrounding white spadices are borne intermittently, and turn green with age. It is the best known of a fairly numerous group of large-flowered cultivars. Others include **'Clevelandii'**, which is shorter, and **'Aztec'**. **ZONES 11–12.**

Spathiphyllum wallisii *(left)*
WHITE SAILS

This is a dwarf species that bears clusters of glossy green, lance-shaped leaves on reed-like stems, which grow to 12 in (30 cm). A white spathe encloses tiny, creamy white spadices of fragrant flowers tightly packed around an upright spike. The color changes to green with age. **ZONES 11–12.**

SPEIRANTHA

This genus consists of only one species, a perennial related to *Convallaria*. From thick spreading rhizomes, stemless leaves form a basal rosette. White flowers are followed by berries.

CULTIVATION

This plant prefers part-shade and moderately fertile, moist, humus-rich soil enriched with leafmold. Propagate from ripe seed or by division.

Speirantha convallarioides

(above)

This species has stemless leaves 6 in (15 cm) long and 1¼ in (30 mm) wide, tapering to a blunt point. The flower stalk is 4 in (10 cm) tall and carries a loose head of 25 white flowers in spring and summer. This plant for shady places comes from China. **ZONES 8–10.**

STACHYS
BETONY, WOUNDWORT, HEDGE NETTLE

This genus of the mint family contains about 300 species of annuals, perennials and evergreen shrubs. They have long been used in herb gardens and many of them have supposed medicinal value. They come from a range of habitats mostly in northern temperate regions. Many species are aromatic, and most are attractive to bees and butterflies. They bear tubular, 2-lipped, purple, red, pink, yellow or white flowers.

CULTIVATION
They all like well-drained, moderately fertile soil in full sun. Propagate from seed or cuttings or by division.

Stachys albotomentosa
(below)

The specific name of this Mexican species means white felting, which is an apt description of the foliage as it is covered in a dense coating of fine white hairs. A perennial, it grows to around 18 in (45 cm) tall and produces salmon-pink flowers from early summer until cut back by cold. In its homeland the flowers are very attractive to hummingbirds.
ZONES 9–11.

S

Stachys byzantina
'Cotton Boll' *(left)*

Stachys byzantina
'Silver Carpet' *(above)*

Stachys byzantina
'Big Ears' *(below left)*

Stachys byzantina
'Primrose Heron' *(below)*

Stachys byzantina *(below right)*
syns *Stachys lanata, S. olympica*
LAMBS' EARS, LAMBS' TAILS, LAMBS' TONGUES

The leaves give this perennial its common names:
they are lance-shaped and have the same white,
downy feel of a lamb. Unfortunately, the leaves
turn to mush in very cold, humid or wet weather.
It makes a good ground cover or border plant,
growing 12–18 in (30–45 cm) high, with a 24 in
(60 cm) spread. Mauve-pink flowers appear in
summer. **'Silver Carpet'** seldom flowers, remaining
more compact than the species; **'Cotton Boll'**
(syn. 'Sheila McQueen') has flowers that look like
cottonwool balls; **'Primrose Heron'** has yellowish
green leaves; and **'Big Ears'** (syn. 'Countess Helen
von Stein') is a large-growing cultivar that bears
tall spikes of purple flowers. ZONES 5–10.

Stachys macrantha
(right)

This perennial has erect
stems up to 24 in
(60 cm) tall bearing
heads of hooded,
purple-pink flowers
from early summer to
early autumn. The
basal leaves are long
and heart-shaped,
wrinkled and rough
with hairs. ZONES 5–10.

Stachys coccinea (below)
SCARLET HEDGE NETTLE

This long-flowering perennial native to southwest
USA and Mexico bears red flowers, although pink
and white forms are now available. The flowers are
almost irresistible to hummingbirds. Flowering
continues from spring through autumn on plants
that grow 12–36 in (30–90 cm) tall and 18 in
(45 cm) wide. ZONES 6–10.

S

STEIRODISCUS

This genus consists of 5 annuals from South Africa with spirally arranged, toothed, divided leaves. Yellow or orange daisy flowers appear in summer.

CULTIVATION

Frost tender, they prefer full sun and well-drained, humus-rich soil. Propagate from seed or cuttings.

Steirodiscus tagetes
(above)

This species grows to 12 in (30 cm) in height with wiry branching stems and 2 in (5 cm) long divided leaves. The bright yellow or orange flowers are $^{3}/_{4}$ in (18 mm) wide. **'Gold Rush'** is a larger yellow form. **ZONES 9–11.**

Steirodiscus tagetes 'Gold Rush' *(left)*

S

Stokesia laevis
(above)
syn. *Stokesia cyanea*

This fully frost-hardy perennial has evergreen rosettes of narrow, mid-green, basal and divided leaves. The blue-mauve or white blooms have a shaggy appearance reminiscent of cornflowers, and are borne freely on erect stems. **ZONES 7–10.**

STOKESIA

STOKES' ASTER

This genus of a single perennial species native to the southeastern states of the USA was named after Englishman Dr Jonathan Stokes (1755–1831). One of the most attractive late-flowering perennials, it grows to about 18 in (45 cm) high and flowers from late summer to autumn if the spent flower stems are promptly removed. It is very good for cutting.

CULTIVATION

Plant in full sun or part-shade and fertile, well-drained soil. Water well in summer. Propagate from seed in autumn or by division in spring.

S

STRELITZIA

BIRD OF PARADISE

These 5 species of clump-forming perennials have exotic flowers that resemble the head of a bird. Each bloom consists of several spiky flowers arising from a boat-like bract. The leaves are large and dramatic. Strelitzias form large clumps of evergreen banana-like foliage. They occur naturally in South Africa but are grown in warm climates around the world. In cool areas they are enjoyed as greenhouse specimens. The fruits are capsules.

CULTIVATION

They need full sun or part-shade and prefer well-drained soil enriched with organic matter and dryish conditions in cooler months. New plants can be produced by dividing a clump, but this is hard work as the clump and roots are very dense. They can also be propagated from seed or suckers in spring.

Strelitzia juncea

(above)

syn. *Strelitzia reginae* var. *juncea*

Botanists have long disputed whether this should be treated as a species distinct from *Strelitzia reginae* or as a variety of that species. Its appearance is dramatically different with tall, rush-like, straight leaf stalks to 6 ft (1.8 m) high, lacking any leaf blade. The flowerheads are identical with those of *S. reginae*, but their stems are much shorter than the leaf stalks. ZONES 9–12.

Strelitzia nicolai *(right)*
WILD BANANA, GIANT BIRD OF PARADISE

The erect, woody, palm-like stems on this tree-sized species reach a height of 20 ft (6 m) and the clump spreads over 12 ft (3.5 m). It has large, dull green leaves over 5 ft (1.5 m) long on lengthy stalks. The flowers appear in summer near the top of the plant from the leaf axils. These striking flowers are greenish blue and white, and open a few at a time from a reddish brown bract. ZONES 10–12.

Strelitzia reginae
'Mandela's Gold' *(below)*

Strelitzia reginae *(below)*
CRANE FLOWER, BIRD OF PARADISE

This shrub-sized species has blooms of bright orange and blue sitting in a pointed green bract edged with red. The main flowering season is spring to summer. It grows to 6 ft (1.8 m) high and spreads over 3 ft (1 m), forming an erect clump of leaves and smooth flower stalks arising from underground stems. The spoon-like leaves are grayish green. **'Mandela's Gold'** has yellow-orange and purplish blue blooms. ZONES 10–12.

S

STREPTOCARPUS

This genus consists of 130 species of annuals, perennials and rarely subshrubs from tropical Africa, Madagascar, Thailand, China and Indonesia. There are 3 main groups: shrubby bushy species with vigorous growth; rosetted plants; and single-leafed species producing one very large leaf up to 3 ft (1 m) long. They all bear tubular flowers with 5 lobes and hairy, veined, crinkly leaves. An example of the rosette species is *Streptocarpus capensis*.

CULTIVATION

Frost tender, they prefer part-shade and leafy, humus-rich, moist but well-drained soil. Seeding will be prevented if flowers are deadheaded and stalks are removed. Propagate from seed or cuttings or by division.

Streptocarpus capensis (above)

Streptocarpus caulescens (left)

A native of Tanzania and Kenya, this upright fleshy stemmed perennial grows to around 24 in (60 cm) tall and has elliptical 2¹/₂ in (6 cm) long leaves that are covered in soft hairs. Its flowers, usually violet, are just under 1 in (25 mm) in diameter and are borne in sprays of 6–12 blooms. They open from autumn. ZONES 10–12.

S

Streptocarpus Hybrids

Most *Streptocarpus* hybrids have *S. rexii* as a major parent. They are generally plants with a rosette growth habit and large, showy, trumpet-shaped flowers in bright colors with a white throat. **'Bethan'** bears multitudes of lilac-purple flowers; **'Blue Heaven'** has flowers that are a strong mid-blue to pale purple; **'Falling Stars'** has many small sky-blue to lilac flowers; **'Gloria'** has pinkish flowers; **'Ruby'** has crimson-red flowers; and **'Susan'** has deep red flowers with yellow centers. ZONES 10–11.

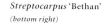

Streptocarpus 'Falling Stars' *(left)*

Streptocarpus 'Gloria' *(center left)*

Streptocarpus 'Blue Heaven' *(bottom left)*

Streptocarpus 'Ruby' *(above)*

Streptocarpus 'Susan' *(below)*

Streptocarpus 'Bethan' *(bottom right)*

S

STROMANTHE

This genus of some 13 species of evergreen, rhizomatous perennials in the arrowroot family is found from Central America to southern Brazil. They often develop short trunks or sturdy, trunk-like stems. The leaves, enclosed in a petiole sheath before expanding, are oblong, heavily veined and 4–18 in (10–45 cm) long depending on the species. They are usually dark green above with purplish undersides. Inflorescences of small white, pink or mauve flowers appear in summer. Leafy bracts enclose the flowers and are occasionally brightly colored. Small, ridged fruits follow the flowers.

CULTIVATION

Plant in moist, humus-rich, well-drained soil in light to moderate shade. Principally tropical plants, they will not tolerate frosts and prefer a mild, humid climate. Propagate from seed or by division where possible, or by removing rooted basal offsets.

Stromanthe sanguinea (above)

This is an erect species from Brazil to 5 ft (1.5 m). The oblong 18 in (45 cm) leaves are dark green above and purple underneath. The stem-leaf sheaths are papery and broad and pink or red. White flowers occur in panicles and have red bracts and orange-red calyces. ZONES 10–12.

S

STYLIDIUM
TRIGGER PLANT

About 140 species of annuals, perennials and subshrubs make up this genus, most native to Australia, but some ranging as far as Southeast Asia. The leaves may be grass-like and basal, or short and narrow on wiry stems. Some species are clump forming, others shrubby, and at least one is a low-growing climber. All share a similar flowering habit with small, lobelia-like, white, pink or yellow flowers. Each flower has an irritable style that snaps over to deposit and receive pollen from visiting insects, hence the common name trigger plant.

CULTIVATION
These are tropical plants and few will tolerate anything other than very light frosts. Plant in well-drained, humus-rich soil with a sunny aspect or cultivate in a greenhouse. Propagate from seed or cuttings or by division.

Stylidium graminifolium
(right)
GRASS TRIGGER PLANT

This is a variable species from eastern Australia growing in habitats ranging from coastal to alpine. It forms a clump of grassy leaves, from which arise several stems 12–36 in (30–90 cm) tall; each stem bears a long, gradually opening spike of flowers ranging in color from palest pink to magenta, the latter color most often associated with the alpine forms.
ZONES 9–11.

S

STYLOPHORUM
WOOD POPPY

This genus consists of 3 poppy-like perennials from eastern Asia and eastern North America. They form low rosettes of deeply lobed foliage: the basal leaves, which have long petioles, are about 18 in (45 cm) long, while the leaves higher in the rosette have shorter petioles and are correspondingly smaller. Simple 4-petalled, bright yellow flowers up to 2 in (5 cm) in diameter are carried in clusters at the top of leafy stems barely higher than the foliage rosette. They appear in spring and summer.

CULTIVATION

Woodland conditions with cool, moist, humus-rich soil in dappled shade are ideal. However, with occasional watering they can be grown in perennial borders with a sunny exposure. Propagate from seed or by dividing established clumps in late winter.

Stylophorum diphyllum (below)
CELANDINE POPPY

This hairy plant grows to 12 in (30 cm) in height and has deeply toothed leaves. The simple flower stalks give rise to a cluster of bracts holding yellow flowerheads up to 2 in (5 cm) across. It comes from eastern USA. ZONES 7–10.

S

SWAINSONA
PEA, DESERT PEA

This genus of around 50 species of perennials, annuals and subshrubs or trailing plants is endemic to Australia with one species from New Zealand. Most species are found in dry to arid areas, with some occupying moister sites in cooler regions. The leaflets are mostly gray to gray-green, with the pea-shaped flowers in extended racemes ranging in color from white to blue, mauve and dramatic scarlet.

CULTIVATION
Frost tender, they prefer full sun and moderately fertile, very well-drained soil. Propagate from seed or cuttings.

Swainsona formosa
(above)

syns *Clianthus dampieri, C. formosus*
STURT'S DESERT PEA

Native to the dry outback of Australia, this slow-growing, trailing annual has unusually large and showy, brilliant red, black-blotched spring flowers and small, grayish leaves. It grows to a height of 6 in (15 cm) and spread of 3 ft (1 m). ZONES 9–11.

S

Symphytum asperum (left)
PRICKLY COMFREY

This thick-rooted perennial from Europe, Turkey and Iran has oval, heart-shaped or oblong leaves covered with stiff prickly hairs. The flower stems grow up to 5 ft (1.5 m) tall and are openly branched with few hairs. There are many flowers in the head; they open a rose color, soon changing to lilac or blue, and are $^1/_2$ in (12 mm) long. It has become naturalized in North America where it has been grown as a fodder plant.
ZONES 5–10.

SYMPHYTUM
COMFREY

This genus comprises 25 to 35 species of hairy perennials from damp and shaded places in Europe, North Africa and western Asia. They grow rapidly and may become invasive in the garden. The leaves are alternate and rather crowded at the base of the plant. The flowers are held in shortly branched heads of pink, blue, white or cream. Each flower consists of a tube terminating in 5 triangular lobes.

CULTIVATION
They are easily grown in sun or part-shade in moist, well-dug soil with added manure. Propagate from seed, cuttings, or by division.

Symphytum × uplandicum
RUSSIAN COMFREY

This coarse, hairy perennial hybrid between *Symphytum asperum* and *S. officinale* grows to 6 ft (1.8 m) tall. Leaves are oblong and run a short distance down the stem. Flowers are ³/₄ in (18 mm) long, rosy at first then becoming purple or blue. **'Variegatum'** has attractive cream leaf variegation, but flower color is poor and flowers are often removed. **ZONES 5–10.**

Symphytum × uplandicum 'Variegatum' *(right)*

Symphytum 'Goldsmith' *(above)*
syn. *Symphytum* 'Jubilee'

'Goldsmith' grows to 12 in (30 cm) and has leaves edged and blotched with cream and gold; the flowers are blue, pink or white. **ZONES 5–10.**

Symphytum caucasicum *(right)*

This is a smaller, softly hairy branched perennial growing to 24 in (60 cm). The leaves are hairy on both sides and oval to oblong up to 8 in (20 cm) long; they run back a short way down the stem. The flowers are at first red-purple, changing to blue, and ³/₄ in (18 mm) long in terminal paired heads. It occurs naturally in the Caucasus and Iran. **ZONES 5–10.**

S

T

TACCA

This genus of 10 species of rhizomatous perennials is widespread throughout tropical Southeast Asia and Africa. They have basal leaves close to the ground, from which rise a scape with greenish yellow flowers surrounded by bracts. The strange, almost bizarre flowers have earned members of this genus names such as bat flowers, cats' whiskers and devil's tongue.

CULTIVATION

These frost-tender plants can be grown outdoors in the tropics and subtropics, but elsewhere require the protection of a greenhouse. They need a humid atmosphere, some shade and a peaty soil. Water amply in summer, but allow to dry out almost totally in winter. Propagate by division of the rhizomes or from seed, if available, in spring.

Tacca integrifolia (right)
BAT PLANT, BAT FLOWER

Found naturally in Southeast Asia and from eastern India to southern China, this upright species has lance-shaped leaves up to 24 in (60 cm) long. The flowers, which open in summer and are carried in racemes of up to 30 blooms, are purple-red to brown and are backed by 4 green to purple-tinted bracts. Filaments up to 8 in (20 cm) long hang from the flowers. ZONES 10–12.

T

Tagetes 'Disco Orange' *(right)*

Judging by the cultivar name, it's a safe bet that 'Disco Orange' first appeared sometime in the 1970s. It is a cheerful dwarf marigold suitable for the front of a summer border, and produces single, weather-resistant flowerheads from late spring to early autumn.
ZONES 9–11.

TAGETES
MARIGOLD

These annuals were rare at the time of their discovery in the seventeenth century; today, they are among the most familiar of summer plants and are useful as bedding plants or for edging. The single or double flowers come in cheerful shades of orange, yellow, mahogany, brown and red and contrast brightly with the deep green leaves. Some of the 50 or so species have aromatic foliage, hence *Tagetes minuta's* common name of stinking Roger. It is also said that the roots exude substances fatal to soil-borne pests, leading to their extensive use as companion plants.

CULTIVATION

These fast-growing plants thrive in warm, frost-free climates, but the young plants may need to be raised in a greenhouse in cooler climates. Grow in full sun in fertile, well-drained soil. Deadhead regularly to prolong flowering. Propagate from seed in spring after the danger of frost has passed. They may be prone to attack by slugs, snails and botrytis.

Tagetes lemmonii *(below)*
MOUNTAIN MARIGOLD

Native to Arizona and adjacent regions of Mexico, this species is unusual in being a shrub of 3–5 ft (1–1.5 m) in height, of somewhat sprawling habit. The leaves are light green and pinnately divided into narrow segments; they are very aromatic, giving off a smell like ripe passionfruit when brushed against. In autumn and winter it bears small golden yellow flowerheads, sometimes continuing through most of the year (encouraged by cutting back in early summer). A popular species in southwestern USA, it likes full sun and a sheltered position.
ZONES 9–11.

T

Tagetes erecta and *Tagetes tenuifolia* (orange) *(above)*

Tagetes erecta 'Marvel Gold' *(below)*

Tagetes erecta
(above)

AFRICAN MARIGOLD, AMERICAN MARIGOLD, AZTEC MARIGOLD

The aromatic, glossy dark green leaves of this bushy annual from Mexico have deeply incised margins. With its upstanding, branching stems, it grows to 18 in (45 cm) in height and spread. Orange or yellow daisy-like flowers bloom in summer and early autumn. The flowers can be as large as 4 in (10 cm) across. **'Crackerjack'** has double flowers and grows to a height of 24 in (60 cm). This species is used as a culinary and medicinal herb. **'Marvel Gold'** bears large pompons of golden yellow. ZONES 9–11.

Tagetes tenuifolia
SIGNET MARIGOLD

More delicate in its lacy foliage than other *Tagetes* species, the signet marigold grows to a height and spread of only 8 in (20 cm), making it suitable for edgings and bedding. The summer and early autumn flowers are also small and are soft yellow or orange. **'Tangerine Gem'** bears small, single, rich orange flowerheads. ZONES 9–11.

Tagetes patula *(below)*
FRENCH MARIGOLD

This fast-growing, bushy annual reaches 12 in (30 cm) in height and spread. It was introduced to European gardens from its native Mexico via France—hence its common name. The double flowerheads, produced in summer and early autumn, resemble carnations. They bloom in red, yellow and orange. The leaves are deep green and aromatic. **'Dainty Marietta'** is an all-yellow cultivar with single flowerheads; **'Naughty Marietta'** bears single, golden yellow flowerheads with dark red-brown markings on the petal bases; and **'Honeycomb'** has large, mahogany-red flowers edged with gold. ZONES 9–11.

Tagetes tenuifolia
'Tangerine Gem' *(above)*

Tagetes patula 'Dainty
Marietta' *(below)*

T

TANACETUM
syn. *Pyrethrum*

In classical Greek mythology, immortality came to Ganymede as a result of drinking tansy, a species of this genus of rhizomatous perennial daisies. Even in recent times, it has been used (despite being potentially quite poisonous even when applied externally) for promoting menstruation and treating hysteria, skin conditions, sprains, bruises and rheumatism. Confined mainly to temperate regions of the northern hemisphere, the 70 or so species of this genus, relatives of the chrysanthemum, are today more appreciated for their daisy-like flowers and their foliage, which is often white-hairy and in many cases finely dissected. The leaves of many of the perennials are also strongly aromatic.

CULTIVATION
Moderately to very frost hardy, they prefer full sun in well-drained, dryish soil; in fact, any soil that is not wet and heavy. Do not overwater. A second flowering may be encouraged if faded flowers are cut back. These plants spread readily and need to be kept under control. Propagate by division in spring or from seed in late winter or early spring.

Tanacetum argenteum (above)
syn. *Achillea argentea*

This usually evergreen perennial has a mat-forming habit. It reaches 10 in (25 cm) in height with a spread of 8 in (20 cm). Very frost hardy, it is prized for its fine, silvery green foliage. Masses of small, white, daisy-like flowers are produced in summer. ZONES 5–10.

Tanacetum balsamita
syns *Balsamita major*,
Chrysanthemum balsamita
CAMPHOR PLANT, ALECOST, COSTMARY

This tough, frost-hardy perennial with strong rhizomatous roots can become somewhat invasive. It grows to 5 ft (1.5 m) tall and produces heads of white flowers with bright yellow disc florets from late summer. The leaves can be used sparingly in salads and as a flavoring in meat and vegetable dishes. The name 'alecost' comes from its former use as a spicy additive to beer. It also has antiseptic properties. *Tanacetum balsamita* var. *tomentosum* has leaves densely covered with fine hairs on their undersides. It is commonly known as the camphor plant because of its strongly camphor-scented foliage, which the parent species lacks. ZONES 6–10.

Tanacetum balsamita var.
tomentosum (below)

T

Tanacetum coccineum (right)
syns *Chrysanthemum coccineum, Pyrethrum roseum*

PAINTED DAISY, PYRETHRUM

This frost-hardy, erect perennial has dark green, feathery, scented leaves that are finely dissected. Its single, or sometimes double, long-stalked flowerheads may be pink, red, purple or white, and appear from late spring to early summer. The species grows 2–3 ft (60–90 cm) tall with a spread of 18 in (45 cm) or more. **'Brenda'** has striking magenta single flowers. **'Eileen May Robinson'** is one of the best single pinks. **'James Kelway'** has deep crimson-pink flowers. It is a native of western Asia. **ZONES 5–9.**

Tanacetum corymbosum (right)

This dense, clump-forming species from southern and central Europe and central Russia grows to a height of 3 ft (1 m) with a spread of 12 in (30 cm). The leaves are finely cut and the flowers white. **ZONES 2–10.**

Tanacetum niveum (right)

SILVER TANSY

Growing to about 24 in (60 cm) with a spread of up to 3 ft (1 m), this attractive species has deeply divided gray-green leaves. In mid-summer it produces an abundant display of small white flowerheads with yellow centers. A fine ornamental species, it will often self-seed when grown in a border. **ZONES 7–10.**

T

Tanacetum parthenium
syn. *Chrysanthemum parthenium*

FEVERFEW

Feverfew is one of those aromatic plants with a long history of medicinal use. It was once used to dispel fevers and agues, and as an antidote for over-indulgence in opium. These days it is admired for its pretty clusters of single or double, 1/2 in (12 mm) wide, white-petalled, daisy-like flowers. These are borne over a long period in summer. Frost hardy, it has yellow-green leaves up to 3 in (8 cm) long. This species reaches 24 in (60 cm) in height with a spread of 18 in (45 cm). Although perennial, it is short lived, and many gardeners prefer to sow it afresh each spring. **'Aureum'** has bright golden foliage. **'Golden Moss'** is a dwarf cultivar with a height and spread of 6 in (15 cm). It has golden, moss-like foliage and is often grown as an edging or bedding plant. **'Snowball'** has pompon flowers and grows to 12 in (30 cm) tall. ZONES 6–10.

Tanacetum parthenium 'Aureum' *(top)*

Tanacetum parthenium 'Golden Moss' *(center)*

Tanacetum parthenium 'Snowball' *(left)*

Tanacetum ptarmiciflorum
(below left)

syn. *Chrysanthemum ptarmiciflorum*

DUSTY MILLER, SILVER LACE

This bushy perennial from the Canary Islands spreads from a woody tap root. Its silvery, lanceolate leaves are strongly divided. Marginally frost-hardy and with a maximum height and spread of 15 in (38 cm), it is good for the rock garden. White flowerheads in terminal clusters are borne in summer. It is very useful in floral arrangements. ZONES 9–11.

T

TAPEINOCHILOS

INDONESIAN GINGER

Ranging in the wild from Southeast Asia to northern Australia, members of this genus are plants of the forest floor. There are some 15 tropical species in this genus and, like *Costus* and *Heliconia* species, they make their dramatic statement not so much from the insignificant flowers but from the brilliantly colored bracts that surround them. Unfortunately their splendor is often hidden beneath the handsome foliage. These evergreen perennials make excellent cut flowers, but their short stems and cultivation requirements have cost them popularity.

CULTIVATION

These frost-tender plants need heat and humidity to thrive. In cooler climates they are happy in a well-warmed green-house. Plant in part-shade in humus-rich soil. Propagate from seed or bulbils, or by division in spring.

Tapeinochilos ananassae (right)
syn. *Tapeinochilos queenslandiae*

As the botanical name suggests, this species resembles a hard, scarlet pineapple *(Ananas)*, but without the deep green fronds at the top. The flower spike rises about 15 in (38 cm) directly from the ground and is overtopped by the considerably taller stems, which carry the foliage. The scarlet bracts almost hide the small, tubular, yellow flowers. This species is native to eastern Indonesia, New Guinea and northeastern Australia. ZONES 11–12.

T

TELLIMA
FRINGECUPS

Native to North America, this genus consists
of only one species. An evergreen perennial,
it makes an ideal ground cover in cool part-
shaded woodland gardens or under shrubs
in sunnier positions.

CULTIVATION
Very frost hardy, it does best in reasonably
well-drained soil. Propagate by division in
spring or from seed in autumn.

Tellima grandiflora *(above)*

This clump-forming perennial has heart-shaped,
purple-tinted green leaves. Semi-evergreen, they
form a neat clump around 24 in (60 cm) high.
Racemes of small, bell-shaped, creamy flowers are
borne in spring on 24 in (60 cm) stems, well above
the foliage. **'Rubra'** (syn. 'Purpurea') has reddish
purple leaves underlaid with dark green and
pink-tinged cream flowers. It can be grown as a
ground cover and in woodland gardens.
ZONES 6–9.

T

Thalia dealbata
(right)

This aquatic, deciduous perennial from the southeast of North America grows to 6 ft (1.8 m) in height with a spread of 24 in (60 cm) or more. It carries leaves that are broadly elliptical to lanceolate, and have a mealy whitish coating. Its stems are erect and unbranching. The flowers, which occur in tall spikes, are violet and waxy, their 6 petals forming a narrow tube; they are borne in summer and are followed by decorative seed heads. ZONES 9–10.

THALIA
WATER CANNA

The 7 species of this American genus honor a German botanist, Johann Thal, who lived from 1542 to 1583. Deciduous or perennial marginal water plants, they are grown for their spikes of tubular flowers and their oval, long-stalked, blue-green leaves.

CULTIVATION
Grow these frost-tender plants in baskets of fertile, loamy soil or in deep, humus-rich mud in up to 20 in (50 cm) of water and in full sun; some species tolerate cool water. Pick off spent foliage. Propagate from seed or by division in spring.

T

THALICTRUM
MEADOW RUE

Over 300 species make up this genus of perennials known for their fluffy, showy flowers. The branches of their slender, upstanding stems often intertwine. The leaves are finely divided. Blooming in spring and summer, the flowers have no petals, but instead have 4 or 5 sepals and conspicuous stamen tufts. They serve well in borders, particularly as a contrast to perennials with bolder blooms and foliage, and in the margins of bush gardens.

CULTIVATION
Grow these frost-hardy plants in sun or part-shade in any well-drained soil. Some species need cool conditions. Propagate from fresh seed in autumn or by division in spring.

Thalictrum aquilegiifolium
(above)
GREATER MEADOW RUE

This clump-forming Eurasian perennial grows to 3 ft (1 m) tall and has a spread of 18 in (45 cm). Pink, lilac or greenish white flowers in fluffy clusters on strong stems appear in summer. Each gray-green leaf comprises 3 to 7 small, elliptical, toothed leaflets in a feather-like arrangement, resembling the leaves of some *Aquilegia* species. ZONES 6–10.

T

Thalictrum kiusianum (right)

This mat-forming perennial species from Japan grows to 6 in (15 cm) tall with a spread of 12 in (30 cm). It produces clusters of tiny purple flowers from spring to summer and has small, fern-like, 3-lobed leaves. There is also a white-flowered form. This species prefers shade and moist, sandy, peaty soil. It is particularly suitable for peat beds and rock gardens. ZONES 8–10.

Thalictrum delavayi (below)
syn. *Thalictrum dipterocarpum* of gardens
LAVENDER SHOWER

Rather than fluffy heads, this graceful, clump-forming perennial bears a multitude of nodding, lilac flowers in loose panicles, with prominent yellow stamens. The flowers are borne from the middle to the end of summer. The finely divided leaves give the mid-green foliage a dainty appearance. Reaching 4 ft (1.2 m) high, this species has a spread of 24 in (60 cm). **'Hewitt's Double'** has rounded, pompon-like, mauve flowers. ZONES 7–10.

T

THLADIANTHA

Related to the cucumbers, the 23 species in this East Asian and African genus are annual or perennial trailers or climbers. They have simple oval or trifoliate leaves and bell-shaped yellow flowers borne singly or in small clusters; these are followed by small, sometimes ribbed fruits.

CULTIVATION

Except for a few species, they are only moderately frost hardy. They prefer moist, humus-rich soil and a position in full sun. Propagate from seed or cuttings, or by layering.

Thladiantha dubia

(right)

Among the hardier species, this summer-flowering native of Korea and northeastern China climbs by means of tendrils and has 2–4 in (5–10 cm) heart-shaped leaves.
ZONES 7–11.

THYMUS

THYME

This genus consists of over 300 evergreen species of herbaceous perennials and subshrubs, ranging from prostrate to 8 in (20 cm) high. Chosen for their aromatic leaves, these natives of southern Europe and Asia are frequently featured in rockeries, between stepping stones or for a display on banks. Some species are also used in cooking. The flowers are often tubular and vary from white through pink to mauve. Historically, thyme has been associated with courage, strength, happiness and well-being.

Thymus × *citriodorus* *(left)*
syn. *Thymus serpyllum* var. *citriodorus*
LEMON-SCENTED THYME
This delightful rounded, frost-hardy shrub grows 12 in (30 cm) high and has tiny oval lemon-scented leaves and pale lilac flowers. The leaves are used fresh or dry in poultry stuffings or to add lemon flavor to fish, meat and vegetables. **'Anderson's Gold'** is a yellow-foliaged spreader that is inclined to revert to green; **'Argenteus'** has silver edges to the leaves; **'Aureus'** has golden variegated leaves; **'Doone Valley'** is prostrate with gold variegated leaves that develop red tints in winter; and **'Silver Queen'** has silvery white foliage. ZONES 7–10.

CULTIVATION
These plants are mostly frost hardy. For thick, dense plants, the flowerheads should be removed after flowering. Plant out from early autumn through to early spring in a sunny site with moist, well-drained soil. Propagate from cuttings in summer or by division.

Thymus species *(below)*

T

Thymus caespititius (left)

syn. *Thymus micans*

This species is found naturally on dry, stony slopes in the Azores, northwestern Spain and Portugal. An evergreen, mat-forming subshrub, this moderately frost-hardy plant has slender woody stems and minute hairy, aromatic midgreen leaves. Small lilac or lilac-pink flowers are produced in late spring and summer. It grows to little more than 2 in (5 cm) high.
ZONES 7–10.

Thymus camphoratus (right)

This Portuguese species has camphor-scented foliage, as its name suggests. It is a small, wiry stemmed shrub around 18 in (45 cm) high with slightly hairy leaves and purple flowers. ZONES 7–10.

Thymus pannonicus (left)

This species usually behaves as an herbaceous perennial, although in mild climates it may be evergreen. It is a low spreader or trailer with pink flowers and is native to southwestern and central Europe.
ZONES 5–10.

T

Thymus polytrichus
'Porlock' *(above)*

Thymus serpyllum
'Annie Hall' *(right)*

Thymus serpyllum
WILD THYME, CREEPING THYME,
MOTHER OF THYME

This species grows to
10 in (25 cm) with a
spread of 18 in (45 cm),
forming a useful ground
cover. Its creeping stem
is woody and branching,
and the scented, bright
green leaves are elliptical
to lanceolate. The
bluish purple flowers
are small and tubular
with 2 lips, and are
borne in spring and
summer in dense
terminal whorls. It is
very frost hardy and
will take moderate foot
traffic. **'Annie Hall'** has
rounded leaves and
mauve flowers;
'Coccineus Minor', has
crimson-pink flowers;
and **'Pink Ripple'**, has
bronze-pink flowers.
ZONES 3–9.

Thymus serpyllum
'Pink Ripple' *(right)*

Thymus polytrichus
syn. *Thymus praecox*
CREEPING THYME, WILD THYME

This evergreen creeping perennial grows to ½ in
(12 mm) high, with prostrate woody stems covered
in minute oval to oblong aromatic green leaves.
The flowers are produced in clusters in summer;
they are small, 2-lipped, and may be purple, mauve
or white. This species is fully frost hardy. **'Porlock'**
has rounded dark green leaves and fragrant pink
flowers. ZONES 5–10.

T

TIARELLA
FOAMFLOWER

The foamflowers are a genus of 5 species of forest-floor perennials, all of which are native to North America. They resemble their relatives, the heucheras, and can be hybridized with them. They all grow from thick rootstocks, with their decorative leaves growing close to the ground. The airy sprays of small white flowers are borne on bare stems about 12 in (30 cm) tall; pale pink forms occur rarely.

CULTIVATION
Very frost hardy, they are easy to grow in cool-temperate climates, and make good ground covers for a woodland-style garden. Plant in part- to deep shade in moist, well-drained soil. Propagate from seed or by division in early spring.

Tiarella cordifolia
(below)
FOAMFLOWER, COOLWORT

This vigorous spreading evergreen blooms profusely in early to late spring, producing terminal spikes of tiny, creamy white flowers with 5 petals. Its leaves are mostly pale green, lobed and toothed, with dark red marbling and spots; the basal leaves take on an orange-red hue in winter. When in flower, it has a height and spread of 12 in (30 cm) or more. ZONES 3–9.

Tiarella polyphylla (right)

This perennial species is native to China and the Himalayas. It grows to a height of 18 in (45 cm) with a similar spread. It has a stout, erect stem and heart-shaped leaves about 2 in (5 cm) in length. In late spring and summer, 5-petalled pink or white flowers are borne in terminal clusters. ZONES 7–10.

Tiarella wherryi (right)

An almost evergreen perennial, this slow-growing, clump-forming species reaches 8 in (20 cm) high and wide. The late spring flowers make a decorative mass of soft pink or white star shapes and last quite well when cut. The hairy, green leaves turn crimson in autumn. ZONES 6–10.

T

TILLANDSIA
AIR PLANT

This genus contains more than 350 species of evergreen, mainly epiphytic bromeliads from the Americas. They are grown for their foliage and unusual flowers, which are usually carried on spikes, heads or panicles and range in color from white to purple and green to red. Plants vary from 2½ in (6 cm) to more than 12 ft (3.5 m) high. The leaves may be gray, green or red-brown and are covered with microscopic silver scales.

CULTIVATION

All species are frost tender. Generally, the stiff, silver-leaved varieties are hardier and are grown in full sun, while the softer, green-leaved prefer part-shade. Plant in well-drained sphagnum moss or on slabs of bark or driftwood. Equal parts of bark and coarse sand can be used. They are often placed high up in hanging baskets to catch rising heat. Mist regularly and water moderately in summer, and sparingly at other times. Propagate from offsets or by division in spring to summer.

Tillandsia aeranthos
(left)

From the Latin meaning 'air blooming', this epiphyte is often confused with its close relative *Tillandsia bergeri*. It is a bromeliad with dark purple to red flowers. The plant is rosette-shaped and has a spread of 4–6 in (10–15 cm). The leaves are narrow and taper to a point. ZONES 9–11.

Tillandsia argentea
(below)

This small bromeliad grows 4–6 in (10–15 cm) wide, with a bulbous base and heavily scaled, silver, thread-like leaves. The leaves are arranged spirally around the short stem so that they resemble an onion. The red to violet flowers, held almost perpendicularly, are offset by red stems and red and green bracts. It grows best when mounted on trees or driftwood in filtered sunlight. Ensure good air circulation and a moderately humid atmosphere. ZONES 10–12.

Tillandsia bergeri *(left)*

Native to Argentina, this epiphyte grows in thick clumps with an average height of 4 in (10 cm) and a spread of 6 in (15 cm) and requires frequent watering. Its leaf blades are slightly channelled and thickly scaled. The flowers grow to 1½ in (35 mm) long with blue petals that turn to pink as they fade. Both leaves and flowers are arranged spirally. **ZONES 9–11.**

Tillandsia caulescens *(below left)*

This species from Bolivia and Peru grows to 18 in (45 cm) high. It has compact, spiralled, gray-green foliage, red bracts and white to purple flowers; these are 1 in (25 mm) long with recurved tips to the petals. In its native habitat, it is epiphytic on trees or cliffs at high altitudes. It is easy to grow. **ZONES 10–12.**

Tillandsia cyanea *(right)*
PINK QUILL

The dense rosettes of grass-like, arching leaves on this species are usually deep green, but often reddish brown when young. In summer to autumn the spectacular, paddle-shaped flowerheads rise on tall stems from among the foliage. They consist of overlapping pink or red bracts with deep violet-blue flowers. It needs maximum humidity and is best in a compost of tree fern fiber, peat and sand. **ZONES 9–11.**

T

Tillandsia flabellata (right)

Native to the cloud forests of
Mexico and Guatemala, this is a
very decorative plant when in
flower. The foliage is rosette-
shaped and either red or green;
the bracts are pointed and bright
red. Its long, narrow bloom spikes
grow upright in a fan-like
arrangement to a height of 15 in
(38 cm). The flowers are blue
with petals up to 2 in (5 cm) long,
fused into a tube. It needs a
moderately humid atmosphere.
ZONES 10–12.

Tillandsia ionantha (right)

This small stemless bromeliad
from Mexico usually grows in
thick clumps. It has a tight, bulb-
like rosette with narrow, densely
scaly, triangular leaves. When in
flower, the inner rosette complements the white-tipped, violet
blooms by turning brilliant red. It
likes moderately damp conditions
and its size makes it suitable for
terrariums; it can be grown outdoors in summer. ZONES 9–11.

Tillandsia lindenii (left)

This species grows in a typical rosette.
The arching leaves are thin, smooth,
pointed, and marked with red-
brown lines. In autumn, a large
flower spike of crimson or pink-
tinted bracts overlaps dense clusters
of pansy-shaped, deep blue or
purple-blue flowers rising just above
the leaves. ZONES 10–12.

T

Tillandsia stricta *(right)*
syns *Tillandsia krameri, T. meridionalis, T. stricta* var. *krameri*

This epiphytic species may have a short stem or be stemless, and usually grows in thick clumps. The foliage is green and covered in silver-gray scales on both sides. The flowers form a rigid, upright, sometimes one-sided rosette; the bracts are bright carmine and the petals blue with flared tips. It prefers a moderately damp and shady position, but is easy to grow. When in flower, it is one of the most beautiful species of the entire genus. ZONES 9–11.

Tillandsia usneoides *(right)*
SPANISH MOSS, GRAY BEARD

This remarkable epiphytic and rootless plant hangs in pendulous festoons from the branches of other plants. Inconspicuous flowers in summer are almost hidden by the fine, curled leaves, which are densely covered in silvery white scales. It is widely distributed from the Deep South of the USA to northern South America. ZONES 8–11.

TITHONIA
MEXICAN SUNFLOWER

This genus of 10 species consists mainly of tall, somewhat woody annuals, biennials and perennials. Originating in Central America and the West Indies, they are related to sunflowers and bear large, vivid yellow, orange or scarlet daisy-like flowerheads in summer and autumn. The leaves are often hairy on the undersides and sharply lobed.

CULTIVATION
Marginally frost hardy, these plants thrive in hot, dry conditions, but require a plentiful supply of water. They grow best in well-drained soil and need full sun. They may need staking. Deadhead regularly to promote a longer flowering season and prune hard after flowering to encourage new growth. Propagate from seed sown under glass in late winter or early spring.

Tithonia diversifolia (below)
TREE MARIGOLD

A very large, robust perennial or shrub growing to 15 ft (4.5 m) tall, this species has large, oval to oblong, hairy leaves with lobed margins. It is best suited to the rear of a shrub border where it can supply visual impact during the late summer months with its large, orange-yellow flowerheads. Dead flowers may be difficult to remove because of its height; the seed heads themselves are of interest. ZONES 9–11.

T

Tithonia rotundifolia *(above)*

This bulky annual needs plenty of room in the garden as it can easily grow to 5 ft (1.5 m) tall with a spread of 3 ft (1 m). Its leaves are heart-shaped. It is great for hot color schemes, both in the garden and as a cut flower, with its 4 in (10 cm) wide, zinnia-like flowers of orange or scarlet. **'Torch'** bears bright orange or red flowerheads and grows to 3 ft (1 m). **ZONES 8–11.**

Tithonia rotundifolia
'Torch' *(left)*

TOLMIEA
PIGGYBACK PLANT, YOUTH-ON-AGE, MOTHER-OF-THOUSANDS

A relative of *Heuchera* and *Saxifraga,* this genus consists of a single species of evergreen perennial from the west coast of North America. Its dark green leaves are very like those of some heucheras, heart-shaped and coarsely toothed, but the plant's most distinctive feature is the production, on some leaves, of a plantlet at the point where the leaf joins its stalk. As the leaves age and droop, these plantlets take root and grow, which allows the plant to spread quite extensively over the shaded forest floor of its normal habitat. The slender, erect flowering stems bear inconspicuous flowers, again very like those of some heucheras.

CULTIVATION
It is a popular indoor plant as well as being a useful ground cover for shade in regions of mild, moist climate. It adapts well to hanging baskets, making a ball of luxuriant foliage. Keep soil moist but not soggy and water sparingly in winter. Feed every 2 months in the warmer season with half-strength soluble fertilizer. Attacks by spider mites cause browning of the leaves, and require immediate treatment. It is easily propagated by detaching well-developed plantlets.

Tolmiea menziesii
(above)

The pale green leaves of this perennial are speckled with gold and somewhat hairy, 2–4 in (5–10 cm) long, and arise in dense clumps from short surface rhizomes. In late spring and early summer it produces sparse flowering stems 12–24 in (30–60 cm) tall bearing dull red-brown flowers with tiny narrow petals. ZONES 7–10.

T

TORENIA
WISHBONE FLOWER

This genus of 40 to 50 species of erect to spreading, bushy annuals and perennials comes from tropical African and Asian woodlands. They have oval to lance-shaped, entire or toothed, opposite leaves. In summer, they bear racemes of trumpet-shaped, 2-lipped flowers with 2-lobed upper lips and 3-lobed lower lips.

CULTIVATION

Torenias prefer a warm, frost-free climate. In cooler climates, they should not be planted out until the last frost. They make attractive pot plants and in cool climates are grown in greenhouses. Grow in fertile, well-drained soil in part-shade in a sheltered position. Pinch out the growing shoots of young plants to encourage a bushy habit. Propagate from seed in spring.

Torenia fournieri
Summer Wave Series
'Large Blue' *(right)*

Torenia fournieri
(below)
BLUEWINGS

This branching annual has light to dark green, ovate or elliptical leaves with toothed edges. Frost tender, it grows fairly rapidly to a height of 12 in (30 cm) and a spread of 8 in (20 cm). Its flowers, borne in summer and early autumn, are pansy-like and a deep purplish blue with a touch of yellow, turning abruptly paler nearer the center. Red, pink and white varieties are also available. **Summer Wave** is a trailing, long-flowering strain with large light or dark blue flowers. **'Large Blue'** is an example. ZONES 9–12.

TOWNSENDIA

This North American genus comprises around 20 species of annual, biennial and perennial daisies. They form mats of narrow or spatula-shaped leaves, often silvery to gray-green in color. Most species are less than 6 in (15 cm) high and less than 18 in (45 cm) wide. The ½–1½ in (12–35 mm) diameter flowers, which open in spring and summer, resemble a single-flowered Michaelmas daisy. They are white, pink, mauve or purple, with a yellow central disc.

CULTIVATION

Most species are extremely hardy alpines that prefer to grow in well-drained soil that stays moist in summer. Plant in sun or morning shade. Despite their hardiness, they tend to be short lived and often do better in alpine houses, where they are protected from cold, wet conditions that may cause rotting. Propagate from seed.

Townsendia exscapa (above)

Probably the most widely cultivated species and a favorite of rockery enthusiasts, this little white-flowered, silver-leafed daisy occurs naturally from central Canada to Mexico. It demands perfectly drained soil and shelter from winter rain, protection it receives in the wild from a covering of snow. ZONES 3–9.

TRADESCANTIA
syns *Rhoeo, Setcreasea, Zebrina*
SPIDERWORT

This genus consists of 50 or more species of perennials, some of them evergreen, from North and South America. Some are rather weedy, but the creeping species (wandering Jew) make useful ground covers and are grown for their attractive foliage. Some of the upright species are cherished for their pure blue flowers, a color not easy to find for the late-summer garden. Most of the trailing types are rather frost tender and are usually grown as greenhouse pot plants. In mild winter climates they make good ground cover, admired for their richly toned foliage.

CULTIVATION
Grow in full sun or part-shade in fertile, moist to dry soil. Cut back ruthlessly as they become straggly. Propagate by division or from tip cuttings in spring, summer or autumn.

Tradescantia, Andersoniana Group, 'J. C. Weguelin' *(above right)*

Tradescantia, Andersoniana Group, 'Jazz' *(right)*

Tradescantia, Andersoniana Group, 'Alba' *(left)*

Tradescantia, Andersoniana Group

This group covers a range of plants formerly listed under *Tradescantia × andersoniana* or *T. virginiana.* They are mainly low-growing perennials with fleshy, strap-like leaves and heads of 3-petalled flowers. Although the foliage clump seldom exceeds 18 in (45 cm) high, the flower stems can reach 24 in (60 cm). There are many hybrids in a range of white, mauve, pink and purple flower shades. Those of **'Alba'** are white; **'J. C. Weguelin'** has lavender-blue flowers; **'Jazz'** has magenta flowers; and **'Red Cloud'** is cerise-red. ZONES 7–10.

T

Tradescantia,
Andersoniana
Group, 'Red
Cloud' *(left)*

Tradescantia cerinthoides *(left)*
syn. *Tradescantia blossfeldiana*
FLOWERING INCH PLANT

Native to southeastern Brazil, this
species has glossy deep green, oval
leaves up to 6 in (15 cm) long that
are purple and hairy on the undersides. From spring to autumn it bears
heads of purple-pink flowers. It is a
sprawling plant of up to about 24 in
(60 cm) in height. ZONES 7–11.

Tradescantia fluminensis 'Variegata'
(below)

Tradescantia fluminensis
syn. *Tradescantia albiflora*
WANDERING JEW

This is a frost-tender, evergreen perennial with
trailing rooting stems and oval fleshy leaves about
1.5 in (35 mm) long that clasp the stem. The
leaves are a glossy green with purple undersides.
Tiny white flowers are produced intermittently,
enclosed in leaf-like bracts. It is invasive.
'Variegata' has glossy green leaves irregularly
striped with white, cream and yellow; they are
tinged with purple on the undersides. ZONES 9–12.

Tradescantia pallida
syn. *Setcreasea purpurea*

This species from eastern Mexico forms a dense clump of foliage and has small pink flowers in summer. The slightly succulent, lance-shaped, 3–6 in (8–15 cm) long leaves often develop red tints if grown in full sun. **'Purple Heart'** (syn. 'Purpurea') has purple foliage. ZONES 8–11.

Tradescantia pallida 'Purple Heart' *(above)*

Tradescantia spathacea 'Vittata' *(below)*

Tradescantia sillamontana
(above)

syns *Tradescantia pexata, T. velutina*

This evergreen erect perennial has oval, stem-clasping leaves that are densely covered in fine white hairs. It produces clusters of small purplish pink flowers in spring and summer. It has a height and spread of 12 in (30 cm) and is frost tender. ZONES 9–11.

Tradescantia spathacea
syns *Rhoeo discolor, R. spathacea*
BOAT LILY, MOSES-IN-THE-CRADLE

This evergreen, clump-forming, frost-tender species reaches 18 in (45 cm) high and 10 in (25 cm) wide. It bears rosettes of fleshy, lance-shaped, glossy leaves to 12 in (30 cm) long with purple undersides. Tiny white flowers, held in leaf-like bracts, appear throughout the year. **'Vittata'** has yellow-striped leaves. ZONES 9–11.

T

TRAGOPOGON

Widely distributed over Europe and temperate Asia, this genus consists of over 100 species of annuals, biennials and perennials belonging to the daisy family. They have solitary or sparsely branched stems, grass-like leaves and terminal, star-shaped flowerheads that are followed by large heads of thistle down.

CULTIVATION
Most species are frost hardy and adaptable to most soils. All prefer a sunny position. Propagate from seed sown in spring.

Tragopogon dubius
(below)
GOATSBEARD

This European species is an erect biennial herb that grows to 3 ft (1 m) tall. It has basal grass-like leaves that half sheathe the base of the stem. The lemon-yellow, star-shaped flowerheads open in the morning and close during the day.
ZONES 5–10.

Tricyrtis hirta *(above)*

This upright species bears 2 in (5 cm) wide, star-shaped white flowers spotted with purple from late summer to autumn. The branching stems are about 3 ft (1 m) long. ZONES 5–9.

TRICYRTIS

TOAD LILIES

The common name of this genus of about 20 species seems to have biased gardeners against the toad lilies—no one thinks of toads as attractive—but these clumping rhizomatous summer-flowering perennials from the woodlands of Asia are really quite attractive in their quiet colorings and markings. The flowers, which are star-, bell- or funnel-shaped, with opened-out tips, are held in the axils of the leaves. The leaves are pointed and pale to dark green, appearing on erect or arching, hairy stems.

CULTIVATION

Grow these very frost-hardy plants in part-shade in humus-rich, moist soil; in areas with cool summers, they need a warm spot. Propagate from seed in autumn or by division in spring.

Tricyrtis suzukii *(above)*

The flowers in this species from Taiwan are white with purple spots, but otherwise it is similar to *Tricyrtis formosana.* It is seldom found in cultivation. ZONES 7–10.

T

Trifolium pratense *(left)*
RED CLOVER

This coarse, erect or decumbent perennial is up to 24 in (60 cm) tall. From late spring to early autumn it bears large, globose heads of pink to purple flowers. Native to Europe, it is a popular pasture clover. It is occasionally sold in cultivated forms and its flowers are popular with apiarists. ZONES 6–10.

TRIFOLIUM
CLOVER

This large genus of annuals, biennials or perennials consists of about 230 species, some of which are semi-evergreen. Widespread throughout temperate and subtropical regions, they are absent from Australia. Species have rounded, usually 3-parted leaves and heads of pea-like flowers. The individual blooms are often very small, making the head resemble a single bloom. Many species become invasive, but have agricultural uses; others are suitable for banks or in rock gardens.

Trifolium repens *(below)*
WHITE CLOVER

This European species has low creeping stems which root at the nodes. The trifoliate leaves have leaflets with serrated margins and a whitish mark at the base. The white or green flowers are produced in globular terminal clusters from spring to autumn and into winter in warmer climates. **'Purpurascens Quadrifolium'** is grown for its bronze-green 4-parted foliage that is variably edged with bright green. Although unwelcome in fine turf, white clover is an important pasture plant and honey source. ZONES 4–10.

CULTIVATION
All species are very frost hardy. Clovers will grow in sun or part-shade. Propagate from seed in autumn or by division in spring. Most species self-seed readily.

T

Trifolium repens
'Purpurascens
Quadrifolium' *(above)*

T

Trifolium uniflorum *(left)*

This is a low-growing creeping and clump-forming species from the eastern Mediterra-nean. It has trifoliate leaves and the lilac flowers are borne in terminal clusters in summer. ZONES 7–10.

TRILLIUM
WAKE ROBIN, WOOD LILY

Among North America's most beautiful wildflowers, this genus in the lily family contains 30 species of rhizomatous, deciduous perennials; they also occur naturally in northeastern Asia. Upright or nodding, solitary, funnel-shaped flowers with 3 simple petals are held just above a whorl of 3 leaves. The numerous species are found in woodland habitats, flowering in spring before the deciduous leaves which remain green until autumn. They make good ornamentals in wild gardens and shady borders.

CULTIVATION
Very frost hardy, they prefer a cool, moist soil with ample water and shade from the hot afternoon sun. Slow to propagate from seed in autumn or by division in summer, they are long lived once established.

Trillium albidum (above)
Native to western USA, this species has 8 in (20 cm) leaves, grows to over 18 in (45 cm) tall and is similar to *Trillium chloropetalum*. Its flowers are white flushed pink and are up to 4 in (10 cm) long. ZONES 6–9.

Trillium cernuum (below)
NODDING WOOD LILY, NODDING TRILLIUM

This species from eastern USA and Canada grows to no more than 2 in (5 cm) high and frequently less. It has almost stalkless foliage, 2–6 in (5–15 cm) long and narrower at the tips, and produces 2 or 3 stems in spring. These stems carry small, drooping white flowers, rarely pink, up to 1 in (25 mm) long and with the same diameter. ZONES 6–9.

Trillium chloropetalum *(above & right)*
GIANT TRILLIUM

The giant trillium is found from California to
Washington in western USA, in wooded or
streamside situations. Growing up to 24 in
(60 cm) tall, its flowers may be green, white, pink
or maroon, with the 3 petals held upright. This
species is more tolerant of dry shade than others.
ZONES 6–9.

Trillium cuneatum *(left)*
WHIPPORWILL FLOWER

Native to southern USA, this species bears reddish
brown to maroon flowers in early spring. It grows
to a height of 12–24 in (30–60 cm). It prefers a soil
that is slightly alkaline. ZONES 6–9.

T

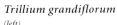

Trillium grandiflorum
(left)
SNOW TRILLIUM, WAKE-ROBIN

This showy, clump-forming
trillium is the easiest to grow,
reaching 12–18 in (30–45 cm)
in height. The pure white
flowers, borne in spring, fade to
pink as they age. The double-
flowered white form, **'Flore
Pleno'**, is beautiful but rare,
and has arching stems and oval,
dark green leaves. **ZONES 3–9.**

Trillium luteum *(below)*
syns *Trillium sessile* var. *luteum,*
Trillium viride
WOOD TRILLIUM

From Appalachian woodlands
of eastern USA, this species is
distinguished by its rather
pointed leaves that are spotted
and splashed with paler green,
and small, stalkless yellow-
green flowers that do not open
very widely. **ZONES 6–9.**

Trillium grandiflorum
'Flore Pleno' *(below)*

Trillium sessile (left)
TOAD-SHADE, WAKE-ROBIN

This upright, clump-forming perennial reaches 12–15 in (30–38 cm) in height with a spread of 12–18 in (30–45 cm). It has deep green leaves marbled with pale green, gray and maroon. They bear stalkless, maroon flowers with lance-shaped petals in late spring. **Trillium sessile var. californicum** bears white flowers. ZONES 4–9.

Trillium rugelii
(below)
SOUTHERN NODDING TRILLIUM

Trillium sessile var. *californicum* (right)

Endemic to Tennessee, USA, this trillium is now regarded as rather rare and endangered in the wild. However, it is becoming more common in cultivation. ZONES 5–9.

T

Trollius chinensis
(left)
syn. *Trollius ledebourii*
CHINESE GLOBE FLOWER

This is one of the lesser known but still very desirable species. It grows 2–3 ft (60–90 cm) tall and bears its shining flowers in spring above handsomely slashed foliage. The flower color varies from light to deep yellow. It is a fast grower, but is not invasive. ZONES 5–9.

TROLLIUS
GLOBE FLOWER

The perennial globe flowers resemble their cousins the buttercups in their bright yellow flowers and their liking for wet ground, but they are much more sedate in their habits—no chance of the garden being taken over here. The flowers are also often bigger—to about 3 in (8 cm)—and their larger number of petals gives them the appearance of being double. From Europe and temperate Asia, any of the 30 species is worth growing. Spring is the main flowering season, but do not be surprised to see some autumn flowers, too.

CULTIVATION
Very frost hardy, they can be grown in regular flowerbeds in moist soil provided they are watered generously, but the boggy edge of a pond or stream suits them better. They are among the few water's edge plants that actually prefer a little shade. Propagate from seed in spring or autumn or by division in early autumn or early spring.

Trollius europaeus
(below left)
COMMON GLOBE FLOWER

The stem on this clump-forming perennial from northern and central Europe is smooth, hollow and upstanding, branching at the apex. Its spring flowers are yellow and terminal; the 5 to 15 petal-like sepals forming a rounded shape 2 in (5 cm) across. Each mid-green leaf has 3 to 5 lobes arranged palmately, with each lobe deeply incised. This species grows to a height of 24 in (60 cm) with an 18 in (45 cm) spread. ZONES 5–9.

TROPAEOLUM
NASTURTIUM

The 87 species of annuals, perennials and twining climbers in this genus from Chile to Mexico are admired for their brightly colored flowers. In warm areas, nasturtiums can survive for several years, self-sowing freely and flowering all year. The flowers can be single or double, about 2 in (5 cm) across, and come in red, orange, russet, yellow, cream and even blue. In the nineteenth century a white cultivar was bred, only to be lost.

CULTIVATION
Frost hardy to frost tender, most species prefer moist, well-drained soil in full sun or part-shade. Propagate from seed, basal stem cuttings or tubers in spring. Check for aphids and cabbage moth caterpillars.

Tropaeolum majus
GARDEN NASTURTIUM, INDIAN CRESS

The stem is trailing and climbing on this vigorous, bushy annual. Its leaves are rounded and marked with radial veins. It blooms in summer and autumn; its 5-petalled flowers are spurred, open and trumpet-shaped, and come in many shades from deep red to pale yellow. It grows to a spread of 3 ft (1 m) and a height of up to 18 in (45 cm). The hot-tasting leaves and flowers of this species are sometimes added to salads. There are several varieties with single or double flowers, and a compact or trailing habit. The **Alaska Hybrids** have single flowers in a range of colors and variegated leaves. **'Crimson Beauty'** has rich red flowers. ZONES 8–11.

Tropaeolum majus Alaska Hybrids *(left)*

Tropaeolum majus cultivar
(below left)

Tropaeolum majus 'Crimson Beauty' *(below)*

T

TUSSILAGO

This genus of about 15 species of perennials from cooler parts of the northern hemisphere is a rather humble relative of the more stately ligularias. Only one species is known in cultivation, and that is grown more for its medicinal uses than for any ornamental qualities—it has been renowned for centuries as a cough remedy, hence the genus name, from the Latin *tussis,* cough, and *-ago,* act upon. They are plants with long-running rhizomes that send up widely spaced tufts of often almost circular leaves. The flowerheads are borne on stems separate from the leafy shoots and often appearing before the leaves; they are daisy-like with numerous narrow ray-florets and a small central disc.

CULTIVATION

These plants are easily grown in a temperate climate, preferring heavy soils and damp ground, and where conditions suit them they may become invasive. They will thrive in full sun or part-shade. Propagate from seed or by division of rhizomes.

Tussilago farfara
(above & below left)
COLTSFOOT

Of wide occurrence in Europe, temperate Asia and North Africa, coltsfoot grows on moist banks, screes or river gravels. Its distinctively shaped leaves (hence the common name) are glossy green above and white-felted beneath, mostly 4–8 in (10–20 cm) across. From early spring onward tight groups of scaly flowering stems about 6 in (15 cm) high emerge from the ground, each stem bearing a gold flower-head up to 1 1/2 in (35 mm) across; the leaves emerge while later flowerheads are opening; they are commonly dried and then smoked like tobacco as a remedy for coughs and chest complaints. ZONES 3–9.

T

TWEEDIA

This genus of one species of straggling perennial is grown for its clear pale blue, star-shaped flowers, which are long lasting and cut well. White- and pink-flowered forms, usually sold as 'Alba' and 'Rosea' are occasionally offered. The seed pods are filled with seeds that have downy 'parachute' tufts.

CULTIVATION

Plant in full sun in a well-drained soil that is a little on the dry side. It is slightly frost hardy but otherwise undemanding. Propagate from seed.

Tweedia caerulea *(above)*
syn. *Oxypetalum caeruleum*

This perennial to 3 ft (1 m) has heart-shaped, gray-green, downy leaves. The summer flowers age to purple and are followed by 6 in (15 cm) long, boat-shaped, green seed pods. ZONES 9–11.

T

UV

URSINIA

Native to southern Africa and Ethiopia, this genus contains up to 40 species of annuals, perennials, subshrubs and shrubs. The plants have pinnate, fern-like foliage. They bear open, terminal clusters of yellow, white, orange or occasionally red flowers with purple or yellow centers.

CULTIVATION

Ranging from marginally frost hardy to frost tender, they require warm, dry climates, full sun and well-drained, moderately fertile soil. Propagate from cuttings or seed in spring. Protect from aphids.

Ursinia calenduliflora (below)
SPRINGBOK ROCK URSINIA

This South African annual grows to 15 in (38 cm) tall. *Ursinia calenduliflora* has pinnate, 2½ in (6 cm) long leaves which consist of narrow to rounded leaflets. The daisy-like flowers, 2½ in (6 cm) in diameter, are yellow and are frequently marked with dark purple near the base. ZONES 9–11.

Ursinia cakilefolia (above)

Indigenous to the Cape Province area, this sun-
loving annual grows to a height of 18 in (45 cm)
and bears deep yellow or orange flowerheads,
about 2 in (5 cm) across, with a darker central
disc. The collar at the base of the flower is rigid
and purple-tipped. The leaves are somewhat fleshy
and coarsely divided and the stems are straw
colored. ZONES 9–11.

Ursinia sericea
(right)

This species grows to
about 30 in (75 cm) in
height and bears large
yellow flowers in
summer. The leaves are
tapered, hairy and
about 3 in (8 cm) long.
ZONES 9–11.

U

UTRICULARIA
BLADDERWORT

This large genus with worldwide distribution consists of more than 200 species of annual or perennial carnivorous plants including terrestrial, epiphytic and aquatic forms. A peculiarity of all species is that they do not possess any kind of root, but instead form long, occasionally branching stems or stolons. Most are found growing in water or wet places, some with submersed stems and leaves; some tropical species are epiphytic. The most remarkable feature of each plant are the stalked and bladder-like traps scattered on the stems or leaves of the plant, ingeniously adapted to catch tiny aquatic creatures. The 2-lipped, spurred flowers vary in size, form and color.

CULTIVATION
The diversity of these variably frost-hardy to frost-tender species necessitates different treatments. The aquatic species are best grown in aquaria or shallow pans of water with sphagnum moss; terrestrial species can be grown in pots of peat moss. They require full sun if grown outdoors. Propagate by division in spring and summer.

Utricularia sandersonii (left)
RABBIT EARS

This small perennial species grows naturally among moss-covered rocks in the Cape Province to Natal area of South Africa. The leaves are light green to pale yellow and fan-shaped. The flowers, which appear throughout the year, are white with mauve veins and a yellow center. This terrestrial bladderwort is one of the prettiest and easiest to grow, and multiplies freely. ZONES 9–11.

Utricularia reniformis (right)
Growing either in soil or as an epiphyte, this Brazilian perennial is notable for its large, heavily built, spreading stolons. Its insect traps are found on the branches of the stolons and are sometimes obscured from view by the 6 in (15 cm) long, leathery, kidney-shaped leaves. The flower scapes grow to as much as 3 ft (1 m) tall and have 1–1½ in (25–35 mm) wide, purple-edged violet flowers. ZONES 10–12.

U

UVULARIA
BELLWORT, MERRY-BELLS

The 5 species of rhizomatous perennials in this genus are native to eastern North America. These herbaceous woodland plants are usually found growing in moist but well-drained leafy soil in the shade of deciduous trees. The stems are either simple or branched, erect to arching and the leaves are perfoliate in some species. The pendulous, bell-shaped flowers are borne either solitary and terminal, or in axillary clusters. They usually come in shades of yellow and appear in spring.

CULTIVATION
Very frost hardy, they can be grown in rock gardens and beside water features provided they are in at least part-shade and the acidic soil contains plenty of organic matter. Propagate by division in late winter or early spring or from ripe seed.

Uvularia perfoliata
(above)

This species has markedly stem-clasping leaves, glabrous and paler underneath, and reaches a height of about 24 in (60 cm). The flowers are up to 2 in (5 cm) long, pale yellow with rather twisted, upturned segments and are carried conspicuously above the leaves in spring. It forms a clump that can be easily divided for propagation.
ZONES 4–9.

U

Valeriana officinalis *(left)*
CAT'S VALERIAN, COMMON VALERIAN, GARDEN HELIOTROPE

This clump-forming, fleshy perennial, which is attractive to cats, grows to 4 ft (1.2 m) tall with a spread of 3 ft (1 m). It occurs naturally throughout Europe and eastwards to Russia and western Asia. It bears rounded flowerheads of white to dark pink flowers in summer on erect, hollow, hairy stems. The leaves are opposite with serrated margins. ZONES 3–9.

VALERIANA
VALERIAN

This genus consists of more than 150 species of herbaceous perennials, herbs and subshrubs, but few of the plants are of any ornamental value. Those that are may be good border and rock garden plants. The name derives from the Latin *valere,* meaning 'keep well', in recognition of the medicinal properties of some species: before modern tranquilizers were introduced, the root from *Valeriana officinalis* was used to treat nervous conditions.

CULTIVATION
Very frost hardy, they will thrive in almost any soil, in sun or part-shade. Propagate from seed or by division of established plants in autumn.

Valeriana arizonica *(right)*

A low-growing plant with a creeping rhizome, this species is a native of Arizona and can grow up to 12 in (30 cm) in height. It has fleshy leaves and clusters of rounded flowerheads of tiny pink flowers appearing in late spring. ZONES 7–10.

VANCOUVERIA

There are 3 species in this genus of graceful, creeping, woodland plants with slender rhizomes. These perennial herbs and shrubs are native to western North America and are related to *Epimedium.* The leaves are rounded and often 3 lobed; the flowering stem, 8–16 in (20–40 cm) long, is normally leafless. The small pendulous flowers are white or yellow, and borne in spring or summer.

CULTIVATION

Useful as a ground cover in cool shaded areas, these frost-hardy plants usually prefer a cool position in peaty soil. Propagate by division, or from fresh ripe seed in spring.

Vancouveria hexandra *(below)*

This deciduous perennial reaches a height of 18 in (45 cm) and a spread of up to 3 ft (1 m). It is distributed from Washington to California, and is found in shady woods. The white flowers are tinged with pink and borne in pendent clusters in mid-summer. The leaves are divided into almost hexagonal leaflets and are thin but not leathery. ZONES 5–9.

Vancouveria planipetala *(right)*
REDWOOD IVY, INSIDE-OUT FLOWER

This plant is found growing in the redwood forests of North America in sunny or part-shaded positions which are sheltered in winter. It grows to 18 in (45 cm) in height with a 3 ft (1 m) spread. The stems are creeping, prostrate and branching. The evergreen leaves are thick and leathery with a wavy margin. The flower stem is leafless, up to 18 in (45 cm) tall, and the flowers are white, tinged with lavender and borne in spring. ZONES 7–9.

V

VERATRUM

This genus consists of about 45 species of perennial herbs found in Europe, Siberia and North America. They grow from a thick rhizome, which is poisonous, and from this arises erect, leafy stems which make arching mounds of foliage. The leaves are large, pleated and very decorative. The flowers, often on tall, leafless stalks, are broadly bell-shaped in terminal panicles. The powdered rhizome of *Veratrum album,* called hellebore powder, was once used to destroy caterpillars.

CULTIVATION

Very frost hardy, these are easy plants to grow given a rich, moist soil. When the plants need to be divided, this should be done in autumn as they start into growth very early in spring. They can also be propagated from seed in autumn. Protect from snails. All species are poisonous.

Veratrum nigrum (below)
BLACK FALSE HELLEBORE

This species is a rare perennial from southern Europe and Asia. It carries long, narrow, terminal spikes of small, purplish brown flowers with 6 petals that bloom from late summer. The large, pleated, elliptical leaves are arranged spirally into a sheath around the stout, erect stems. It grows to a height of 6 ft (1.8 m) and half as wide. **ZONES 6–9.**

Veratrum album
(left)
WHITE FALSE HELLEBORE, EUROPEAN WHITE HELLEBORE

This clump-forming perennial grows to 6 ft (1.8 m) tall with a spread of 24 in (60 cm). The large, striking leaves are clear green and appear to be folded like a fan. The leafless flower stalk bears dense terminal panicles of pale green to almost white bell-shaped flowers in late summer. This species does best when grown in a shaded, protected position. **ZONES 5–9.**

V

Verbascum bombyciferum
(right)

This biennial from Asia Minor has silvery gray, furry, large leaves and grows 6 ft (1.8 m) tall. It bears golden yellow, cup-shaped flowers in summer, sometimes in terminal spikes. ZONES 6–10.

VERBASCUM
MULLEIN

This genus consists of semi-evergreen to evergreen perennials, biennials and shrubs from Europe and the more temperate zones of Asia. Including some very large and some very coarse species, the genus offers much variety in the foliage with leaves ranging from glossy to velvety. They develop large, often complex, basal rosettes. Many of the 250 or so species are scarcely better than weeds. However, several are desirable in the garden for their stately habit, gray foliage and long summer-flowering season. The flowers do not open from the bottom up as, for example, delphiniums or foxgloves do, but a few at a time along the spike.

CULTIVATION

These plants are fully to moderately frost hardy but will not tolerate winter-wet conditions. Establish all species in well-drained soil and an open, sunny location, although they do tolerate shade. Propagate from seed in spring or late summer or by division in winter. Some species self-seed readily.

V

Verbascum dumulosum (above)

This evergreen, low-spreading perennial from southwest Turkey grows 6–12 in (15–30 cm) tall with a spread of about 18 in (45 cm). The gray-green leaves are felty in texture. In late spring is produces a succession of bright yellow flowers, each with 5 lobes, on short clusters. It will not tolerate wet soil. ZONES 8–10.

Verbascum chaixii (left)

This species from southern Europe can be relied on to live long enough to form clumps. The flowers, borne on 3 ft (1 m) tall stems in summer, are normally yellow. The white form **'Album'** is usually finer. ZONES 5–10.

Verbascum chaixii 'Album' (left)

Verbascum 'Letitia' *(right)*

This small-growing hybrid between *Verbascum dumulosum* and *V. spinosum* has slender, felted, silver-gray foliage. From mid-spring onwards, it produces masses of delicate lemon-yellow flowers on short, branched stems. It is ideal for a rock garden or as a container plant in a sunny position. The flowers are sterile, so propagation is by division. **ZONES 8–10.**

Verbascum nigrum
(right)

BLACK MULLEIN, HAG TAPER

Native to Morocco, this semi-evergreen, clump-forming perennial is very frost hardy and grows to a height and spread of about 3 ft (1 m). Long spikes of yellow flowers with purple centers appear from summer through to autumn. Its mid-green leaves taper to a point and carry a dense layer of hairs. Black mullein is used as a herbal remedy for colic, coughs and spitting blood. So-called witches of the Middle Ages were thought to use the plant in their love potions and brews, hence the common name hag taper. **ZONES 5–10.**

V

Verbascum phoeniceum
(left)

PURPLE MULLEIN

A native of Europe, this species
forms basal rosettes of dark
green, broad leaves from
which rise branching stems
bearing clusters of violet, pink
or purple flowers. It is reliably
perennial and self-sows quite
prolifically when in a warm,
well-drained situation. This
species is one of the parents of
the many beautiful garden
hybrids. It grows to a height of
2–4 ft (0.6–1.2 m) and can
make a strong focal point in a
border. **ZONES 6–10.**

Verbascum thapsus
(left)

This species has soft,
velvety, pale green leaves
and yellow, stalkless
flowers produced in
dense, terminal spikes
in summer. It grows on
freely draining hillsides,
often in very poor soil.
The flowers, once dried,
form an ingredient in
herbal teas and cough
mixtures. **ZONES 3–9.**

V

VERBENA

Originating in Europe, South America and North America, this genus of 250 or more species of biennials and perennials is characterized by small, dark, irregularly shaped and toothed leaves. They bloom in late spring, summer and autumn. An agreeably spicy aroma is associated with most verbenas.

CULTIVATION

Marginally frost hardy to frost tender, they do best where winters are not severe. Establish in medium, well-drained soil in full sun or at most part-shade. Propagate from seed in autumn or spring, stem cuttings in summer or autumn, or by division in late winter. They can also be propagated in spring by division of young shoots.

Verbena bonariensis (left)

This tall South American perennial is often grown as an annual, primarily for its deep purple flowers which top the sparsely foliaged 4–5 ft (1.2–1.5 m) stems from summer to autumn. The deeply toothed leaves cluster in a mounded rosette, which easily fits in the front or middle of a border; the floral stems give a vertical line without much mass. Frost hardy, it self-seeds readily and survives with only minimal water, even in dry areas. ZONES 7–10.

Verbena canadensis (left)
ROSE VERBENA, CREEPING VERVAIN

This native of eastern North America is a trailing or sprawling, short-lived perennial easily grown as an annual. It grows to 18 in (45 cm) in height with a spread of 24 in (60 cm). The dark purplish pink flowers appear from summer through autumn. ZONES 5–10.

V

Verbena × *hybrida* *(right & center)*
GARDEN VERBENA

This trailing perennial bears slightly hairy leaves
and blooms from summer to autumn. Its fragrant
flowers appear in dense clusters 1 in (25 mm)
across, many showing off white centers among the
hues of red, mauve, violet, white and pink. It is
suitable for use in summer beds and containers.
Avoid being heavy handed with fertilizers or the
plants will yield more leaves than flowers.
'**Homestead Purple**' is a sturdy cultivar with rich
red-purple flowers. '**La France**' has bright pink
flowerheads. '**Silver Ann**' has heads of light pink

flowers with darker
blooms at the center.
'**Sissinghurst**' has mid-
green leaves and bears
stems of brilliant pink
flowerheads in sum-
mer, and it reaches a
height of 6–8 in
(15–20 cm). The
Tapien Series verbenas
are a seedling strain
renowned for their
depth and intensity of
flower color. They are
strong growing, heat-
and disease-resistant
trailers for hanging
baskets. The **Temari
Series** verbenas are a
Japanese-raised strain
with large flower
clusters. The name
means 'handful of
flowers', which is exactly
what you get with each
head of bloom. Other
cultivars include
'**Patio Blue**' and '**Patio
Purple**'. ZONES 9–10.

Verbena × *hybrida*
'**Homestead Purple**'
(right)

V

Verbena × *hybrida*
'La France' *(right)*

Verbena × *hybrida*
'Silver Ann' *(below)*

Verbena × *hybrida*
'Sissinghurst' *(below)*

V

*Verbena ×
hybrida*
'Patio Blue'
and 'Patio
Purple' *(left)*

Verbena × hybrida
'Tapien Blue' and
'Tapien Pink' *(left)*

V

Verbena × hybrida
'Temari Scarlet' *(right)*

Verbena laciniata *(below)*
syn. *Verbena erinoides*

This marginally frost-hardy, prostrate South American perennial grows to only 12–18 in (30–45 cm) tall, but spreads widely. It bears finely divided, gray-green leaves and abundant heads of blue, magenta or violet flowers. Trim back after flowering and avoid mildew by not over-watering. **ZONES 8–10.**

Verbena × hybrida, Temari Series *(above)*

Verbena × hybrida 'Temari Violet' *(right)*

V

Verbena tenuisecta
(below)

MOSS VERBENA

Native to Chile and Argentina, this evergreen perennial gets its common name from its dense, prostrate habit and minute, finely divided, vivid green foliage that forms a flat, moss-like ground covering. Through late spring and summer, it bears masses of flowers in shades of white, blue and purple in small, rounded inflorescences. It requires a hot, dry position and is frost tender. ZONES 9–11.

Verbena peruviana 'Red Cascade' *(below)*

Verbena peruviana
syn. *Verbena chamaedrifolia*

This low, creeping perennial has stems rooting at the nodes and oval, toothed, mid-green leaves forming a carpet. Heads of small, tubular, intense scarlet flowers with spreading petals appear in summer and autumn. It reaches a height of 3 in (8 cm) with a spread of about 3 ft (1 m). Propagate from cuttings. **'Red Cascade'** has particularly bright flowers. ZONES 9–11.

Verbena rigida *(above right)*
syn. *Verbena venosa*

A South American native, this tuberous-rooted perennial is an excellent species for seaside cultivation. It reaches a height of 18–24 in (45–60 cm) with a spread of 12 in (30 cm). The dense spikes of pale violet to magenta flowers are borne from mid-summer. **'Silver Jubilee'** bears a mass of red flowers right through the growing season. ZONES 8–10.

Verbena rigida 'Silver Jubilee' *(right)*

V

VERONICA

SPEEDWELL

Saint Veronica was the woman who, pious legend relates, wiped the face of Christ with her veil and was rewarded with having his image imprinted on it. Her connection with this flower is that the savants of the Middle Ages thought they could see a face in it. They must have peered rather closely, because veronica flowers are not exactly large—½ in (12 mm) wide is big for the genus. The shrubby species are now given a genus of their own, *Hebe*, and all the remaining 200 or so are herbaceous perennials. They range from prostrate, creeping plants suitable for the rock garden to 6 ft (1.8 m) high giants. Small as the flowers are, they make quite an impact, being gathered in clusters of various sizes and coming in great abundance in summer. Blue is the predominant color, although white and pink are also common. For example, **'Pretty in Pink'** bears spikes of deep pink flowers.

Veronica 'Pretty in Pink' *(below)*

CULTIVATION

Fully to moderately frost hardy, these plants are easy to grow in any temperate climate, and are not fussy about soil or position. Propagate from seed in autumn or spring, from cuttings in summer or by division in early spring or early autumn.

V

Veronica austriaca *(left)*
syn. *Veronica teucrium*

Distributed from southern Europe to northern Asia, this species grows in grassland and open woods. This clump-forming perennial grows to 10–18 in (25–45 cm) tall with long, slender stems bearing bright blue, saucer-shaped flowers in late spring. The leaves vary in shape from broadly oval to narrow and are either entire or deeply cut. Propagate by division in autumn or from softwood cuttings in summer. **'Crater Lake Blue'** is 12 in (30 cm) tall and has deep blue flowers; **'Royal Blue'** is taller with royal blue flowers. In late summer, **Veronica austriaca subsp. *teucrium*** bears 12 in (30 cm) high flower stems, comprising many tiny blooms in deep true blue; it prefers full sun and well-drained soil. ZONES 6–10.

Veronica austriaca 'Crater Lake Blue' *(left)*

Veronica austriaca 'Royal Blue' *(below)*

V

Veronica gentianoides (right)
GENTIAN SPEEDWELL

This mat-forming perennial has wide, dark green leaves from which rise spikes of pale blue or white flowers in late spring. It reaches 18 in (45 cm) in height and spread. ZONES 4–9.

Veronica cinerea (left)

This mat-forming, many-branched perennial from Turkey has small, narrow or occasionally oval leaves with the margins inrolled and silver gray in color. The flowers are borne on trailing stems in summer and are purplish blue with white eyes. Growing to 6 in (15 cm) tall, it makes a good plant for a sunny rock garden. ZONES 5–9.

V

Veronica longifolia
(left)

BEACH SPEEDWELL

From northern and
central Europe and
Asia, this perennial
plant grows up to 3 ft
(1 m) tall. Its narrow,
tapering leaves are
arranged in whorls and
toothed on the edges.
The flowers are lilac
blue and closely packed
on a long, erect inflor-
esence. **'Rosea'** has pink
flowers and branched
stems. ZONES 4–9.

Veronica peduncularis

Ranging from the
Ukraine and the
Caucasus to western
Asia, this spreading and
mounding perennial
has tiny oval leaves and
2–4 in (5–10 cm) sprays
of pink-veined blue,
white or pink flowers
from late spring to
early summer. **'Georgia
Blue'** (syn. 'Oxford
Blue') is a vigorous
grower with bright blue
flowers. ZONES 6–9.

Veronica longifolia
'Rosea' *(left)*

Veronica peduncularis
'Georgia Blue' *(below)*

V

Veronica prostrata
(right)

syn. *Veronica rupestris*

This perennial from Europe and parts of Asia has woody, branching stems and variable foliage, although all are tooth edged. The flowers are small and blue with widely flared petals, occurring in upright spikes in spring and early summer. This species spreads widely into a mat of indefinite coverage; however, it only reaches 12 in (30 cm) in height. ZONES 5–9.

Veronica spicata   *(below)*
DIGGER'S SPEEDWELL, SPIKE SPEEDWELL

This very frost-hardy European perennial reaches a height of 24 in (60 cm) and a spread of up to 3 ft (1 m). Its stems are erect, hairy and branching. Spikes of small, star-shaped, blue flowers with purple stamens bloom in summer. The leaves are mid-green, linear to lanceolate. **Veronica spicata subsp. *incana*** is notable for its spreading clumps of silvery, felty leaves and deep violet-blue flowers; **'Floristan'** is similar. **'Blaufuchs'** is bright lavender blue; **'Blue Peter'** has dark blue flowers in very compact spikes; **'Heidekind'**, a compact form to 12–15 in (30–38 cm) tall, has hot pink flowers and silver-gray foliage; **'Red Fox'** has crimson flowers; and **'Rosea'** is a pink-flowered form. ZONES 3–9.

Veronica spicata subsp. *incana*   *(below)*

Veronica spicata
'Blaufuchs' *(left)*

Veronica spicata
'Blue Peter' *(below)*

Veronica spicata
subsp. *incana*
'Floristan' *(left)*

Veronica 'Waterperry'
(above)

The spreading 4 in (10 cm) high perennial has wiry reddish stems clothed with small, heart-shaped, deep green leaves rather like pansy foliage. The leaves develop purple tones in winter. From early summer, or year-round in mild areas, 'Waterperry' is covered in sprays of small lavender blue flowers. Provided it has good drainage and does not dry out in summer, it is easily grown in sun or partial shade. ZONES 8–11.

Veronica spuria *(above)*

This erect species from southeast Europe grows 12–36 in (30–90 cm) tall and has dense and downy foliage. The leaves are arranged in whorls and are slightly toothed. The flowers, produced in summer, are blue and in large terminal panicles. ZONES 3–9.

V

VERONICASTRUM
CULVER'S PHYSIC

This genus consists of 2 species of tall, slender, perennial herbs closely related to *Veronica*, found in eastern North America and East Asia. Formerly used medicinally, they are now grown as ornamentals only. Pale blue or white flower spikes open in summer.

CULTIVATION

Plant in a humus-rich, moist soil and do not allow to dry out in summer. Any exposure from full sun to part-shade will do. Propagate from seed or by division.

Veronicastrum virginicum *(below & below left)*
BLACK ROOT, CULVER'S ROOT, BOWMAN'S ROOT

Native to the USA, this perennial prefers moist, swampy soils in a protected, shaded position. Although frost hardy, it does not tolerate dry conditions. This plant grows to about 5 ft (1.5 m), and has slender, erect stems and lance-shaped, finely serrated leaves. The tubular, purplish blue or white flowers are produced in summer.
ZONES 3–9.

V

Victoria amazonica × cruziana
'Longwood Hybrid' *(above)*

VICTORIA
GIANT LILY, ROYAL WATERLILY

This genus of just 2 species of rhizomatous, deep-water aquatic annuals or perennials comes from tropical South America. Their strong rhizomes support huge floating leaves and bear nocturnal, waterlily-like flowers. Joseph Paxton (1801–65), gardener to the Duke of Devonshire, was the first to make them flower in Britain, and based his design for the Crystal Palace on the structure of its leaves—so strong they could bear the weight of his 7-year-old daughter.

CULTIVATION
These frost-tender plants need at least 3 ft (1 m) of water in which to grow and a position in full sun. Plant them in containers of rich loamy soil with added organic matter. Propagate from seed in early spring.

Victoria amazonica
syn. *Victoria regia*
AMAZON WATERLILY

This is the largest known waterlily, with leaves reaching to 6 ft (1.8 m) across. It grows quickly, achieving its huge size just 7 months after planting from seed. The flat, prickly leaves have upturned margins of 2–4 in (5–10 cm). Leaf size is determined by the depth of the water in which the plant is growing—the deeper the water, the bigger the leaves. The flowers, white outside and pink inside, have as many as 60 petals each; they are more than 12 in (30 cm) wide. Only one flower blooms at a time. '**Longwood Hybrid**', a hybrid between *Victoria amazonica* and *V. cruziana*, has white flowers that age to pink. ZONES 11–12.

V

VIOLA

VIOLET, HEARTSEASE, PANSY

This well-known and much-loved genus of annuals, perennials and subshrubs consists of as many as 500 species. They are found in most temperate regions of the world including high mountains of the tropics, though with the greatest concentrations of species in North America, the Andes and Japan. Most are creeping plants, either deciduous or evergreen, with slender to thick rhizomes and leaves most often kidney-shaped or heart-shaped, though in some species they are divided into narrow lobes. Flowers of the wild species are seldom more than 1 in (25 mm) across and characteristically have 3 spreading lower petals and 2 erect upper petals, with a short nectar spur projecting to the rear of the flower. Many species also produce *cleistogamous* flowers, with smaller petals that do not open properly, and are able to set seed without cross-pollination.

A few Eurasian species have been hybridized extensively to produce the garden pansies, violas and violettas, with showy flowers in very bright or deep colors. These are nearly always grown as annuals, though potentially some are short-lived perennials.

CULTIVATION

Most of the cultivated Viola species will tolerate light frosts at least, and many are fully frost hardy. The more compact perennial species suit rock gardens where they do best in cooler, moister spots, while the more spreading species make effective ground covers beneath trees and taller shrubs, requiring little or no attention. Pansies and violas *(Viola × wittrockiana)* are grown as annuals or pot plants in full sun, but appreciate shelter from drying winds. Sow seed in late winter or early spring, under glass if necessary, planting out in late spring in soil that is well-drained but not too rich. Water well and feed sparingly as flowers develop. Propagate perennial species by division or from cuttings.

V

Viola cornuta
(opposite page)
HORNED VIOLET

Native to the Pyrenees, this is a broad-faced violet with a short spur at the back, in shades of pale blue to deeper violet and borne in spring and summer. The plants spread by rhizomes, sending up flowering stems to 6 in (15 cm) long. The horned violet is one of the major parent species of pansies and violas. **'Minor'** has smaller leaves and flowers. ZONES 6–9.

Viola cornuta 'Minor'
(right)

Viola cornuta
(right & below)

V

Viola elatior *(left)*

This species is found in the damp meadows and marshy areas of central and eastern Europe and northwest China. It has long, tapered leaves and grows up to 18 in (45 cm) tall. The stems are erect and tufted; the large flowers are lilac blue and appear in early summer. The plants grow well in leafy, peaty soil in sun or part-shade. **ZONES 5–9.**

Viola hederacea *(right)*
syns *Erpetion reniforme, Viola reniformis*
AUSTRALIAN NATIVE VIOLET

The small, scentless flowers borne on short stems on this creeping evergreen perennial from southeastern Australia are mostly white with a lilac blotch in the throat; they appear from spring to autumn. Its stems are prostrate, suckering and mat forming, spreading widely and growing 2–4 in (5–10 cm) in height. Its leaves are kidney-shaped with irregular edges. **ZONES 8–10.**

Viola labradorica *(left)*
LABRADOR VIOLET

Native to North America through to Greenland, this low-growing, spreading species has light purple flowers in spring. It does well in shady places, but can become invasive. **ZONES 2–9.**

Viola odorata *(right)*
SWEET VIOLET

A sweet perfume wafts from the flowers of this much-loved species, which are the well-known florists' violets. It is a spreading, rhizomatous perennial from Europe, which grows 3 in (8 cm) tall and may spread indefinitely on cool, moist ground. Its dark green leaves are a pointed kidney shape with shallowly toothed edges. Spurred, flat-faced flowers in violet, white or rose appear from late winter through early spring. It boasts many cultivars. ZONES 6–10.

Viola, Perennial Cultivars

Primarily of *Viola lutea, V. amoena* and *V. cornuta* parentage, these hardy perennial plants are long flowering, year round in mild climates. **'Hunter-combe Purple'** has creamy centered purple flowers; **'Jackanapes'** has brown upper petals and yellow lower petals; **'Maggie Mott'** has bright purple-blue flowers; **'Nellie Britten'** (syn. 'Haslemere') has lavender-pink flowers; and **'Magic'** is rich purple with a small eye of dark purple and yellow. ZONES 6–10.

Viola, Perennial Cultivar, 'Huntercombe Purple' *(right)*

V

Viola, Perennial Cultivar, 'Jackanapes' *(above)*   *Viola*, Perennial Cultivar, 'Magic' *(below)*

V

Viola septentrionalis

(left)

NORTHERN BLUE VIOLET

This spring-flowering perennial from North America bears large flowers with a spur, in hues usually of bluish purple but sometimes white. The hairy green leaves are pointed and oval to heart-shaped and have toothed edges. The plant has creeping and suckering stems and grows 6–8 in (15–20 cm) high and wide. **ZONES 7–10.**

Viola riviniana

DOG VIOLET

Found in Europe, Iceland, North Africa and Madeira, this tufted little violet produces colonies from sucker shoots. The flowers are blue-violet, scentless and are borne from spring through summer. The leaves are long-stemmed and rounded. **'Purpurea'** has purple-green leaves and purple flowers; it reaches 2–4 in (5–10 cm) in height, with a spread of 10 in (25 cm). **ZONES 5–10.**

Viola riviniana 'Purpurea' *(above)*

V

Viola sororia *(above)*
syn. *Viola papilionacea*
WOOLLY BLUE VIOLET

This stemless, herbaceous perennial has
scalloped, thickly hairy leaves 4 in (10 cm)
long. It bears short-spurred white flowers
heavily speckled with violet blue from
spring to summer; the flowers are sometimes deep violet blue. **'Freckles'** has
white flowers speckled with violet-purple.
Both the species and the cultivar reach
4–6 in (10–15 cm) in height. *Viola
sororia* var. *priceana* has grayish white
flowers with violet-blue stems.
ZONES 4–10.

Viola sororia
'Freckles' *(right)*

Viola tricolor 'Bowles'
Black' *(right)*

Viola tricolor *(right)*
**WILD PANSY, JOHNNY JUMP UP,
LOVE-IN-IDLENESS**

Of wide occurrence in
Europe and temperate
Asia, this annual,
biennial or short-lived
perennial produces
neat flowers in autumn
and winter in mild
climates if cut back in
late summer. They have
appealing faces, in
shades of yellow, blue,
violet and white. It has
lobed, oval to lance-
shaped leaves. It grows
to a height and spread
of 6 in (15 cm) and
self-seeds readily. *Viola
tricolor* **'Bowles' Black'**
is a striking cultivar
with black velvety
petals and a yellow
center. **ZONES 4–10.**

V

Viola × *wittrockiana* (below)
PANSY, VIOLA

This hybrid group of compactly branched perennials are almost always grown as biennials or annuals. Offering flowers of a great many hues, the numerous cultivars bloom in late winter through spring and possibly into summer in cooler climates. The flowers are up to 4 in (10 cm) across and have 5 petals in a somewhat flat-faced arrangement. The mid-green leaves are elliptical, with bluntly toothed margins. The plants grow slowly, reaching about 8 in (20 cm) in height and spread. This is a complex hybrid group, including both pansies and violas, the latter traditionally distinguished by the flowers lacking dark blotches, but there are now intermediate types with pale-colored markings. Hybrids in the **Imperial Series** are large-flowered pansies. **'Gold Princess'** is a good example, producing bicolored flowers in golden yellow and red. The **Joker Series** are of an intermediate type, with a range of very bright contrasting colors such as orange and purple. The **Accord Series** of pansies covers most colors and has a very dark central blotch. **'Padparadja'** has vibrant orange flowers. **'Magic'** has purple flowers with a bright face. Other seedling strains include the **Universal, Princess** and **Sky Series**. ZONES 5–10.

Viola × *wittrockiana*
(above & right)

Viola × *wittrockiana*
'Jolly Joker' (below)

Viola × wittrockiana
'Accord Red Blotch'
(left)

Viola × wittrockiana
'Princess Deep
Purple' *(right)*

Viola × wittrockiana
'Universal Orange'
(below)

V

Viola × *wittrockiana*
'Sky Clear Purple' *(above)*

Viola × *wittrockiana*
'Universal True Blue'
(above)

Viola × *wittrockiana*
'Penny Azure Wing'
(right)

V

VRIESEA

Native to Central and South America, this genus consists of around 250 species of epiphytes. They are among the most popular bromeliads, and are closely related to *Tillandsia*. The smooth-margined leaves are often coated in mealy scales and have colored cross-bandings. The spectacular flower spikes vary in shape, with petals free or fused into a tube. They can be red, orange or yellow. Different species flower at different times of the year. Many hybrid cultivars have been developed, for example 'Christine'.

CULTIVATION

These plants are frost tender. Plant in part-shade in well-drained orchid medium. Water moderately during growth periods, always ensuring the rosette centers are filled with water. Propagate from offsets or seed from spring to summer.

Vriesea 'Christine'
(above)

Vriesea carinata (left)
LOBSTER CLAWS

The striking flattened spike of crimson and gold bracts gives this Brazilian bromeliad its common name. It grows to 10 in (25 cm) and has soft, arching, light green leaves. An excellent pot plant, be aware that this species needs a big pot as it has a larger root system than most bromeliads. ZONES 11–12.

V

Vriesea splendens
(right)
syns *Tillandsia splendens, Vriesea speciosa*

FLAMING SWORD

This very striking bromeliad earned its common name from its sword-shaped flower spike of bright red or orange. It has medium-sized, soft green leaves with purple-black bands and a 18 in (45 cm) high inflorescence. ZONES 11–12.

V

WXYZ

WACHENDORFIA
RED ROOT

Only a couple of the 25 or so species of this genus of cormous perennials from South Africa are cultivated outside their own country. Wachendorfias have basal tufts of long, narrow, pleated leaves and bear erect spikes of starry, golden flowers in spring and summer. Their common name comes from the red sap of the corms, used as a dye, and the bright red-orange color of the roots themselves.

CULTIVATION
Only moderately frost hardy, they thrive when grown outdoors in warm, near frost-free climates. They require a moist but well-drained soil in a sunny position and are ideal for bog gardens. They spread readily throughout the garden by seed. Propagate from seed or by division in spring.

Wachendorfia thyrsiflora
(above & left)
RED ROOT

This is the best known species. It grows to 7 ft (2 m) and bears thick, straight spikes of bright yellow flower clusters in spring and early summer. The narrow, lance-shaped leaves are pleated, strong and strap-like, and up to 3 ft (1 m) long. It tolerates light frost. ZONES 8–11.

W

Wahlenbergia communis
(right)
syn. *Wahlenbergia bicolor*
TUFTED BLUEBELL, GRASS-LEAF BLUEBELL

This tufted perennial is native to Australia where it occurs in all mainland states, sometimes in fairly arid areas. It grows up to 30 in (75 cm) high and has linear leaves to 3 in (8 cm) long, sometimes with small teeth. Masses of star-shaped, light blue flowers are borne in spring and summer. ZONES 8–11.

WAHLENBERGIA
BLUEBELLS

This is a genus of about 200 species of annuals or perennials with a wide distribution, mostly in the southern hemisphere. They have variable foliage and the flowers range from wide open stars to tubular bells, all with 5 prominent lobes, in shades of blue, purple or white. They are usually small in stature and are suitable for a rock garden or border.

CULTIVATION
Unless otherwise stated, the species described are fully frost hardy. Grow in a well-drained, humus-rich soil in full sun or light shade. Propagate from seed or by division in spring.

Wahlenbergia albomarginata
(above)
NEW ZEALAND BLUEBELL

This tufted perennial to 8 in (20 cm) high forms basal rosettes of lance-shaped oval or spoon-shaped hairy leaves. Underground rhizomes spread to form new rosettes and these may develop into mat-like colonies. The nodding, usually solitary bell-shaped pale blue to white flowers with spreading lobes are borne on fine stems in summer. This marginally frost-hardy, short-lived plant grows best in part-shade. ZONES 7–10.

W

Wahlenbergia gloriosa (left)

ROYAL BLUEBELL, AUSTRALIAN BLUEBELL

This perennial with spreading rhizomes and erect stems to about 8 in (20 cm) high is a native of Australian alpine regions and is the floral emblem of the Australian Capital Territory. It has dark green, lance-shaped leaves to 1½ in (35 mm) long with wavy, toothed margins and bears a profusion of royal-blue or purple, bell-shaped flowers on separate fine stems in summer. ZONES 8–10.

Wahlenbergia stricta (left)
syn. *Wahlenbergia consimilis*

TALL BLUEBELL

This tufted perennial herb to 3 ft (1 m) tall has a wide distribution throughout southern Australia and is quite common in open forests and grasslands. The basal obovate leaves with wavy margins become linear up the stem. Lower stems and leaves have spreading, long white hairs. Small, blue star-shaped flowers are borne in spring and summer. **'Tasmanian Sky'** has light purple flowers. ZONES 9–10.

W

WALDSTEINIA

Found over much of the northern temperate zone, the 6 species in this genus are clump-forming, rhizomatous perennials. They are semi-evergreen, creeping ground covers with 3-part leaves resembling those of their close allies, the strawberries. The hairy leaves are usually bright green with bronze tints if grown in the sun. In spring and summer, bright yellow 5-petalled flowers are borne singly or in clusters of up to 8 blooms.

CULTIVATION

Most species are quite frost hardy and easily grown in any well-drained soil in sun or part-shade. Propagate by division or by self-rooted offsets from the runners.

Waldsteinia ternata (right)
syn. *Waldsteinia trifoliata*

Native to central Europe through Russia to China and Japan, this herbaceous or semi-evergreen creeping perennial grows to a height of about 6 in (15 cm). Golden yellow, buttercup-like flowers appear from late spring, mostly on the new growth. Each bloom is about 1/2 in (12 mm) across. It spreads quite fast and makes a thick ground cover in moist soil in part-shade beneath trees. In ideal conditions, *Waldsteinia ternata* can become invasive. ZONES 3–9.

W

WELWITSCHIA

This bizarre genus consists of a single species, native to the desert regions of southern Angola and Namibia. It is a gymnosperm, occasionally cultivated for its curiosity value. Its short, hollow, woody stems terminate in a 2-lobed disc-like apex. From opposite sides of the disc sprout 2 long strap-like leaves. These 2 leaves persist for the full lifetime of the plant, splitting lengthwise with age. Male or female cones are borne on separate plants on branched stalks that arise from the center of the disc.

CULTIVATION

This is a very slow-growing frost-tender plant requiring dry, hot conditions and adequate soil depth for a long tap root. It needs full sun and perfect drainage. Water moderately during the growing season and keep completely dry during winter. Propagation is from seed.

Welwitschia mirabilis
(above & left)
syn. *Welwitschia bainesii*

This species' leaves are leathery and long, up to 8 ft (2.4 m), and 3 ft (1 m) wide, splitting with age into multiple strips. Scarlet cones are set in groups of up to 20 on stalks up to 12 in (30 cm) long, each female cone bearing many winged seeds under its scales. Male cones are smaller and insignificant. It is adapted to desert conditions. ZONES 9–10.

W

WITTROCKIA

This small genus of 7 species of bromeliads is found only in southern coastal mountains of Brazil. They are epiphytic, terrestrial or rock-dwelling plants that form stemless rosettes. Most species have colorful thinly textured linear leaves with a few marginal spines. Spikes of flowers nestled in the heart of the plant have colorful bracts and blue or white petals.

CULTIVATION

In warm, frost-free areas they may be grown outdoors in an open, well-drained soil in filtered shade. When grown as pot plants in a greenhouse, use an open, porous bromeliad potting mix. Indoors they need warm humid conditions and bright, filtered light. Propagation is from seed or offsets.

Wittrockia superba (above)
syns *Nidularium karatas, N. superbum, Canistrum cruentum*

In its natural habitat this rosette-forming bromeliad, to 3 ft (1 m) high and across, grows on trees, on rocks or in leaf litter on the ground. The long stiff leaves are a glossy green with red tips and sharp terminal spines. The flowers, arranged in a cone-shaped spike, are nestled in the heart of the plant. These are blue and white, surrounded by red bracts and are produced in summer. ZONES 11–12.

W

WULFENIA

This is a genus of about 6 species of small evergreen tufted perennials, native to southeastern Europe, western Asia and the Himalayas. Leaves are usually rough-textured with scalloped margins, set from a basal point on long stalks. Flowers are borne on spike-like racemes from the base of the plant—these are blue to purple, tubular in shape with 4 lobes. The fruits are capsules.

CULTIVATION

Fully frost hardy and suited to cold climates, plants resent high humidity and excessive moisture in winter. They prefer full sun and moist, but well-drained soil. Propagate from seed or by division in spring.

Wulfenia carinthiaca (above)

Native to the Alps and the Balkan Peninsula, this species has a height and spread of about 8 in (20 cm). Leaves are in a basal rosette and are lance-shaped to oval, about 7 in (18 cm) long, toothed, dark green and hairy underneath. The top quarter of the flower stem is a one-sided spike of tubular flowers; violet blue with rounded lobes, which are borne in summer. ZONES 5–9.

W

XERANTHEMUM
IMMORTELLE

The 5 or 6 annuals included in this genus are natives of the Mediterranean region, extending to Iran. They are known as immortelles or everlasting flowers because their dried flowerheads retain their color and form for many years. The upright, branching stems have narrow, hoary leaves. The flowerheads are solitary on long stems and the small fertile flowers are surrounded by papery bracts which may be white, purple or pink.

CULTIVATION
Moderately frost hardy, they grow best in a sunny position in fertile, well-drained soil. Propagate in spring from seed sown *in situ*.

Xeranthemum annuum
IMMORTELLE

A good source of dried flowers, this annual blooms in summer, producing heads of purple, daisy-like flowers; whites, pinks and mauves, some with a 'double' appearance are also available. The leaves are silvery and lance-shaped and the plants grow to around 24 in (60 cm) high and 18 in (45 cm) wide. **Mixed Hybrids** include singles and doubles in shades of pink, purple, mauve, red or white. ZONES 7–10.

Xeranthemum annuum
Mixed Hybrids *(below)*

X

XERONEMA

There are only 2 species in this genus and it has never been common, either in the wild or in gardens. Found naturally in New Caledonia and on the Poor Knights Islands northeast of New Zealand, they are striking plants that appeal to all who see them. There is nothing quite like their brilliant red flowers borne on one-sided racemes among iris-like, leathery, sword-shaped leaves.

CULTIVATION

Although able to be grown from seed or by careful division, tissue culture propagation has been the key to success and plants are now readily available to gardeners. It needs a frost-free climate and, even in a rich soil, can take a few years to settle down to flowering. Plant in a humus-rich soil with added pumice or scoria to ensure good drainage.

Xeronema callistemon *(below)*
POOR KNIGHTS LILY

The unique and beautiful flowers of this perennial are a rare sight. A vivid red in color, their long stamens are massed to create a 6 in (15 cm) brush. They are held horizontally to provide a perch for the honey-eating birds that pollinate them. They are strictly greenhouse plants in areas with cool-temperate climates. **ZONES 10–11.**

Yucca whipplei
(left)

OUR LORD'S CANDLE, CANDLE
YUCCA

This is distinguished
from most other yuccas
by its very narrow,
gray-green leaves which
form a nearly perfect
sphere. Native to the
coastal lower ranges of
California, in late sum-
mer and autumn it
sends up a straight,
flowering spike to 12 ft
(3.5 m) high that is
densely covered in
creamy white flowers,
sometimes tinged with
purple. It is very tole-
rant of dry conditions.
ZONES 8–11.

YUCCA

The 40 or so species of unusual evergreen
perennials, shrubs and trees in this genus
are found in drier regions of North America.
Often slow growing, they form rosettes of
stiff, sword-like leaves usually tipped with a
sharp spine; as the plants mature, some
species develop an upright woody trunk,
often branched. Yuccas bear showy, tall
panicles of drooping, white or cream, bell-
to cup-shaped flowers. The fruits are either
fleshy or dry capsules, but in most species
are rarely seen away from the plants' native
lands as the flowers must be pollinated by
the yucca moth.

CULTIVATION
Yuccas do best in areas of low humidity;
they prefer full sun and sandy soil with
good drainage. Depending on the species,
they are frost hardy to frost tender.
Propagate from seed (if available), cuttings
or suckers in spring.

Yucca baccata (above)
BLUE YUCCA, BANANA YUCCA,
DATIL YUCCA

Yucca baccata comes from
southwestern USA and
northern Mexico and grows to
5 ft (1.5 m) in height. Its twisted
leaves are flexible near the base
and are dark green tinged with
yellow or blue. The pendent
flowers are bell-shaped, white
or cream and often tinged with
purple. ZONES 9–11.

Y

ZANTEDESCHIA

ARUM LILY, CALLA LILY, PIG LILY

Indigenous to southern and eastern Africa, this well-known genus of the arum family consists of 6 species of tuberous perennials. The inflorescence consists of a showy white, yellow or pink spathe shaped like a funnel, with a central finger-like, yellow spadix. The leaves are glossy green and usually arrow-head-shaped.

CULTIVATION

Consisting of both evergreen and deciduous species, this genus includes frost-tender to moderately frost-hardy plants. Most are intolerant of dry conditions, preferring well-drained soil in full sun or part-shade, although *Zantedeschia aethiopica* will grow as a semi-aquatic plant in boggy ground that is often inundated. Propagate from offsets in winter.

Zantedeschia aethiopica *(left)*

WHITE ARUM LILY,
LILY OF THE NILE

Although normally deciduous, in summer and early autumn this species can stay ever-green if given enough moisture. It can also be grown in water up to 6–12 in (15–30 cm) deep. *Zantedeschia aethiopica* reaches 24–36 in (60–90 cm) in height and spread, with large clumps of broad, dark green leaves. The large flowers, produced in spring, summer and autumn, are pure white with a yellow spadix. **'Crowborough'** is more cold tolerant and better suited to cool climates such as the UK and the northwest USA. It grows to about 3 ft (1 m) tall. **'Green Goddess'** has interesting green markings on the spathes. ZONES 8–11.

Zantedeschia aethiopica 'Green Goddess' *(below)*

Zantedeschia elliottiana
(left)
GOLDEN ARUM LILY

This summer-flowering species has a yellow spathe surrounding a yellow spadix, sometimes followed by a spike of bright yellow berries that are attractive to birds. It grows 24–36 in (60–90 cm) tall with a spread of 24 in (60 cm). The heart-shaped, semi-erect leaves have numerous white spots or streaks.
ZONES 8–11.

Zantedeschia rehmannii *(right)*
PINK ARUM LILY, PINK CALLA

The spathe on this summer-flowering plant is mauve to rose-purple with paler margins, enclosing a yellow spadix. Its green, unmarked leaves are semi-erect and not arrowhead-shaped as in other species. It grows 15 in (38 cm) tall and 12 in (30 cm) wide. Marginally frost hardy, it likes well-composted soil, a protected location and part-shade.
ZONES 8–11.

Z

Zantedeschia, New Zealand Mixed Hybrids

These hybrids of *Zantedeschia rehmannii* and *Z. elliottiana* have flowers in a range of colors from red, pink and bronze to orange. Some have spotted leaves. Although there are miniatures, most reach a height of 24 in (60 cm) or more with a spread of 8 in (20 cm). Not as easy to grow as their parents, they need warmth and very rich soil. The flowers of **'Brigadier'** are washed a reddish orange; and the orange-red tones of **'Mango'** varies with cultivation, a slightly alkaline soil giving richer color than an acid one. The 'flower' is about 6 in (15 cm) wide and the leaves are spotted. ZONES 8–11.

Zantedeschia, New Zealand Mixed Hybrid, 'Brigadier' *(left)*

Zantedeschia, New Zealand Mixed Hybrid, 'Mango' *(below)*

ZAUSCHNERIA

From southwestern USA and Mexico, this genus consists of about 4 species of shrubby perennials. Although very similar, for horticultural purposes they can be considered variations on *Zauschneria californica*. They are grown for their masses of orange to scarlet, tubular flowers. Some botanists now believe these species belong in the *Epilobium* genus.

CULTIVATION

These plants are marginally frost hardy. Grow in full sun in well-drained soil in a warm, sheltered position. Propagate from seed or by division in spring, or from side-shoot cuttings in summer.

Zauschneria californica (bottom)
syn. *Epilobium canum* subsp. *canum*
CALIFORNIAN FUCHSIA

The common name refers both to the species' Californian origin and to its flowers, which are indeed like the related fuchsias. These are bright red, appearing in terminal spikes on erect, slender stems in late summer and early autumn. This evergreen shrub has lance-like, 1 in (25 mm) long leaves, is highly variable and grows 12–24 in (30–60 cm) tall and 3–6 ft (1–1.8 m) wide. It needs only occasional water and is hardy to around 15°F (–9°C). *Zauschneria californica* subsp. *cana* (syn. *Zauschneria cana*), a small suckering shrub, reaches 24 in (60 cm) high. It has felty gray foliage and its larger flowers are a brilliant vermilion red. *Z. c.* subsp. *canum* 'Dublin' (syn. 'Glasnevin'), more compact to 12 in (30 cm) tall with bright orange-red flowers, was selected at Glasnevin Gardens in Ireland. ZONES 8–10.

Zauschneria septentrionalis
(below)
syn. *Epilobium septentrionale*
HUMBOLDT COUNTY FUCHSIA

Native to western North America, this species is more or less mat-forming and grows to 8 in (20 cm) tall. The leaves are gray-white and felted; the flowers are bright orange-red. ZONES 8–10.

ZINNIA
ZINNIA

This genus of 20 species of erect to spreading annuals, perennials and subshrubs has daisy-like, terminal flowerheads in many colors including white, yellow, orange, red, purple and lilac. Found throughout Mexico and Central and South America, some are grown for cut flowers and in mixed borders.

CULTIVATION
These plants are marginally frost hardy and are best in a sunny position in fertile soil that drains well. They need frequent deadheading. Propagate from seed sown under glass early in spring.

Zinnia elegans *(right & below)*
YOUTH-AND-OLD-AGE

This sturdy Mexican annual is the best known of the zinnias. The wild form has purple flowerheads, and blooms from summer to autumn. It grows fairly rapidly to 24–30 in (60–75 cm), with a smaller spread. Garden varieties offer hues of white, red, pink, yellow, violet, orange or crimson in flowers up to 6 in (15 cm) across. '**Envy**' has pale green semi-double flowers. The **Dreamland series** is compact and heavy flowering, which is typical of F1 Hybrid bedding zinnias. '**Dreamland Ivy**' has pale greenish yellow flowers. The **Thumbelina series** has 2 in (5 cm) wide flowerheads on plants that are only 6 in (15 cm) high. ZONES 8–11.

Zinnia elegans 'Dreamland Ivy'
(above)

Zinnia elegans 'Thumbelina'
(right)

Zinnia elegans 'Envy'   *(below)*

Z

Zinnia haageana
syns *Zinnia mexicana,*
Z. angustifolia

This Mexican annual
reaches 24 in (60 cm)
in height with a spread
of 8 in (20 cm). The
small but profuse yellow,
orange and bronze
flowerheads, more than
1½ in (35 mm) wide,
appear in summer and
early autumn. **'Chip-
pendale Daisy'** grows
to 24 in (60 cm) tall
and has simple, single,
2 in (5 cm) wide red
flowers with gold petal
tips. **'Old Mexico'** is an
old but valuable cultivar
that is drought resistant.
ZONES 8–11.

Zinnia haageana 'Chippendale
Daisy' *(above)*

Zinnia peruviana *(below)*

This species ranges in the wild from
Arizona to Argentina. An erect-growing,
summer-flowering annual, it reaches a
height of 3 ft (1 m). The hairy stems are
green, changing to yellow or purple. Its
flowerheads are yellow to scarlet.
ZONES 8–11.

Zinnia haageana
cultivar *(above)*

Reference Table

This table provides information to help you choose annuals and perennials. Information on plant type, climate zones, color of flowers, planting time and flowering season will help you find the annuals and perennials best suited to your purposes.

Plant Type

The reference table uses the following symbols for plant type:

- A for annuals;
- B for biennials; and
- P for perennials.

As the classification of some plants is not clear cut, the following combinations are also used:

- A(P) or B(P), meaning annuals or biennials that can live on to become short-lived perennials;
- P(A) or B(A), meaning perennials or biennials that are usually treated as annuals;
- A(B), meaning annuals that can live on to become biennials; and
- P(B), meaning perennials that are usually treated as biennials

Climate Zones

These match the climate zones given in the main text for each plant. An explanation of climate zones can be found on pages 31–33.

NAME	TYPE	ZONES	COLOR	PLANTING TIME	FLOWERING SEASON
Abelmoschus moschatus	P	8–12	red, pink or white	spring	summer–autumn
Acaena argentea	P	7–10	purple	spring	summer
Acaena novae-zelandiae	P	5–10	red	spring	summer
Acanthus hungaricus	P	7–10	white	autumn–winter	summer–autumn
Acanthus mollis	P	7–10	white	autumn–winter	summer–autumn
Acanthus spinosus	P	7–10	white	autumn–winter	summer–autumn
Achillea 'Coronation Gold'	P	4–10	yellow	winter	summer–autumn
Achillea filipendulina & cultivars	P	3–10	yellow	winter	summer–autumn
Achillea 'Great Expectations'	P	2–10	yellow	winter	summer–autumn
Achillea 3 kellereri	P	5–10	white	winter	summer
Achillea 'Lachsschönheit'	P	3–10	salmon pink	winter	summer–autumn
Achillea millefolium & cultivars	P	3–10	white to pink & red tones	winter	summer
Achillea 'Moonshine'	P	3–10	yellow	winter	summer–autumn
Achillea ptarmica	P	3–10	white	winter	summer
Achillea 'Schwellenberg'	P	3–10	yellow	winter	summer–autumn
Achillea 'Taygetea'	P	4–10	yellow	winter	summer–autumn
Achillea tomentosa	P	4–10	yellow	winter	summer
Acinos alpinus	P	6–9	violet & white	spring	summer
Aciphylla aurea	P	7–9	yellow-green	spring	summer
Aciphylla hectori	P	7–9	pale yellow to white	spring	summer
Aciphylla montana	P	7–9	pale yellow	spring	summer
Aconitum carmichaelii	P	4–9	violet-blue	winter–spring	late summer–autumn
Aconitum 'Ivorine'	P	4–9	pale ivory yellow	winter–spring	autumn
Aconitum napellus	P	5–9	violet blue to purple	winter–spring	autumn
Aconitum vulparia	P	4–9	pale yellow	winter–spring	summer
Acorus gramineus	P	3–11	foliage plant	most of the year	summer
Acorus gramineus 'Ogon'	P	3–11	foliage plant	most of the year	summer
Actaea alba	P	3–9	white	late autumn–winter	late spring–early summer
Actaea rubra	P	3–9	white tinted mauve	late autumn–winter	late spring–early summer
Actinotus helianthi	B	9–10	pink & green, white bracts	spring–summer	late spring–summer
Adenophora uehatae	P	5–9	pale mauve-blue	winter–spring	summer
Adonis annua	A	6–9	red	autumn–spring	summer

NAME	TYPE	ZONES	COLOR	PLANTING TIME	FLOWERING SEASON
Adonis vernalis	P	3–9	yellow	late summer–autumn	spring
Aechmea chantinii	P	11–12	red & yellow	most of the year	summer
Aechmea chantinii 'Black'	P	11–12	red & yellow	most of the year	summer
Aechmea fasciata	P	10–12	mauve-blue, pink bracts	most of the year	summer
Aechmea nidularioides	P	10–12	yellow flowers, red bracts	most of the year	summer–autumn
Aechmea pineliana	P	10–12	yellow flowers, red bracts	most of the year	winter–spring
Aechmea 'Royal Wine'	P	11–12	dark blue	most of the year	variable
Aechmea 'Shining Light'	P	11–12	red flowers, red bracts	most of the year	summer
Aegopodium podagraria	P	3–9	white	winter	summer
Aethionema grandiflorum	P	7–9	pink	autumn–winter	spring
Aethionema 'Mavis Holmes'	P	7–9	pink	autumn–winter	spring
Agapanthus africanus	P	8–10	blue	autumn–spring	summer–autumn
Agapanthus campanulatus	P	7–11	light purple-blue	autumn–spring	summer
Agapanthus 'Irving Cantor'	P	8–11	purple-blue	autumn–spring	late spring–autumn
Agapanthus 'Loch Hope'	P	8–11	purple–blue	autumn–spring	late spring–autumn
Agapanthus praecox	P	9–11	lavender blue	autumn–spring	late spring–autumn
Agastache foeniculum	P	8–10	purple	late autumn–spring	summer
Agastache rugosa	P	8–10	pink or mauve & white	late autumn–spring	summer
Ageratina altissima	P	6–9	white	most of the year	late summer
Ageratina ligustrina	P	9–11	white flowers, pink bracts	most of the year	late summer–autumn
Ageratina occidentalis	P	6–9	white, pink or purple	most of the year	late summer
Ageratum houstonianum	A	9–12	dusky blue, pink or white	spring–summer	spring–autumn
Aglaonema 'Parrot Jungle'	P	10–12	foliage plant	most of the year	summer
Aglaonema 'Silver Queen'	P	10–12	foliage plant	most of the year	summer
Agrimonia eupatoria	P	6–10	yellow	winter	late spring
Agrostemma githago	A	8–10	deep pink	spring or autumn	summer
Ajania 'Bess', *A.* 'Benny'	P	4–10	yellow	winter–early spring	autumn
Ajania pacifica	P	4–10	yellow	winter–early spring	autumn
Ajania pacifica 'Silver and Gold'	P	4–10	yellow	winter–early spring	autumn
Ajuga pyramidalis	P	5–9	blue or mauve	most of the year	summer to autumn
Ajuga pyramidalis 'Metallica Crispa'	P	5–9	purple-blue	most of the year	summer to autumn
Ajuga reptans & cultivars	P	3–10	deep blue	most of the year	late spring to autumn
Alcea rosea	B	4–10	all except true blue	winter–spring	summer–autumn
Alchemilla conjuncta	P	5–9	yellow-green	late autumn–winter	late spring–summer

NAME	TYPE	ZONES	COLOR	PLANTING TIME	FLOWERING SEASON
Alchemilla mollis	P	4–9	yellow-green	late autumn–winter	late spring–summer
Alchemilla rohdii	P	6–9	yellow-green	late autumn–winter	late spring–summer
Alchemilla speciosa	P	4–9	yellow-green	late autumn–winter	late spring–summer
Alonsoa warscewiczii	P	9–11	pink, orange or red	spring	spring–autumn
Alpinia galanga	P	11–12	white & pink	winter	summer
Alpinia purpurata	P	11–12	white flowers, red bracts	winter	most of the year
Alpinia zerumbet	P	10–12	white, gold & red	winter	mainly spring–summer
Alstroemeria aurea	P	7–9	orange & bronze shades	early spring	spring–summer
Alstroemeria haemantha	P	7–9	orange to red	early spring	summer
Alstroemeria hybrids	P	7–10	all except true blue	early spring	summer–autumn
Alstroemeria psittacina	P	8–10	red & green	early spring	summer–early autumn
Alyssum chalcidicum	P	7–10	yellow	spring–early summer	spring
Alyssum murale	P	7–9	yellow	spring	spring
Amaranthus caudatus	A	8–11	red	spring	summer–autumn
Amaranthus tricolor & hybrids	A	8–11	red (mainly foliage plants)	spring	summer
Ammi majus	P	6–10	white	winter–early spring	summer–autumn
Amsonia tabernaemontana	P	3–9	pale blue	winter–early spring	late spring–summer
Anagallis monellii	P	7–10	blue or red	winter–early spring	summer
Anagallis tenella	P	8–10	pale pink or white	winter–early spring	summer
Anaphalis javanica	P	9–10	white	winter–early spring	summer
Anaphalis triplinervis	P	5–9	white	winter–early spring	summer
Anaphalis triplinervis 'Sommerschnee'	P	5–9	white	winter	summer
Anchusa azurea & cultivars	P	3–9	blue to purple tones	winter–early spring	spring–summer
Anchusa capensis	A(B)	8–10	blue	early spring	spring–summer
Anchusa capensis 'Blue Angel'	A(B)	8–10	blue	winter	spring–summer
Anchusa granatensis	P	6–9	reddish-purple	spring	spring–summer
Androsace sarmentosa	P	3–8	pink	spring	late spring–summer
Androsace sarmentosa 'Brilliant'	P	3–8	mauve-pink	spring	late spring–summer
Anemone appenina	P	6–9	blue	autumn–winter	spring
Anemone blanda	P	6–9	white, pink or blue	autumn–winter	late winter–spring
Anemone blanda 'Radar'	P	6–9	magenta with white center	autumn–winter	late winter–spring
Anemone b. 'White Splendour'	P	6–9	white	autumn–winter	late winter–spring
Anemone hupehensis	P	6–10	white, pink or mauve	winter–spring	late summer–autumn
Anemone × *hybrida*	P	6–10	white or pink shades	winter–spring	late summer–autumn

NAME	TYPE	ZONES	COLOR	PLANTING TIME	FLOWERING SEASON
Anemone × hybrida 'Honorine Jobert'	P	6–10	white	winter–spring	late summer–autumn
Anemone nemorosa	P	5–9	white	autumn–winter	spring
Anemone nemorosa 'Robinsoniana'	P	5–9	lavender blue	autumn–winter	spring
Anemone rivularis	P	6–9	white tinted blue	winter	spring–early summer
Anemone sylvestris	P	4–9	white	winter	spring–early summer
Anemone trullifolia	P	5–9	white, pale blue or yellow	winter–early spring	summer
Anemonella thalictroides	P	4–9	white to pale mauve	autumn	spring–early summer
Anemopsis californica	P	8–11	white	winter–spring	spring–autumn
Angelica pachycarpa	P	8–10	green	winter	summer
Angelica sylvestris	P	7–10	green	winter	summer
Anigozanthos, Bush Gems Series	P	9–11	yellow, orange, red & green	spring	spring–summer
Anigozanthos flavidus	P	9–11	greenish yellow	spring	spring–early summer
Anigozanthos humilis	P	9–11	cream to yellow & red	spring	late winter–spring
Anigozanthos manglesii	P	9–10	green & red	spring	spring–early summer
Anigozanthos 'Red Cross'	P	9–11	red	spring	spring–summer
Anigozanthos 'Regal Claw'	P	9–11	orange & red	spring	spring–summer
Antennaria dioica	P	5–9	white, pink or yellow	winter–early spring	summer
Antennaria dioica 'Australis'	P	5–9	white	winter–early spring	summer
Anthemis cretica	P	5–9	white & yellow	most of the year	spring–summer
Anthemis 'Moonlight'	P	5–10	yellow	most of the year	late spring–summer
Anthemis tinctoria	P	4–10	yellow	most of the year	spring–summer
Anthericum liliago	P	7–10	white	late winter–spring	summer
Anthericum liliago 'Major'	P	7–10	white	late winter–spring	summer
Anthurium andraeanum	P	11–12	red	spring	variable
Anthurium scherzerianum	P	10–12	red	spring	mainly summer–autumn
Anthyllis montana	P	7–9	pink & white	spring	late spring–summer
Anthyllis vulneraria	P	7–9	cream tinted purple	spring	late spring–summer
Antirrhinum hispanicum	P	7–10	mauve-pink	spring	late spring–summer
Antirrhinum majus seed strains	P(A)	6–10	all except true blue	most of the year	spring–summer
Aponogeton distachyos	P	8–10	white	winter–early spring	late spring–autumn
Aquilegia atrata	P	3–9	violet–purple	autumn–spring	spring–early summer
Aquilegia caerulea	P	3–9	dusky blue & white	spring	late spring–early summer
Aquilegia canadensis	P	3–9	red & yellow	late winter–spring	late spring–early summer

NAME	TYPE	ZONES	COLOR	PLANTING TIME	FLOWERING SEASON
Aquilegia chrysantha	P	3–10	yellow or white	late winter–spring	late spring–early summer
Aquilegia 'Crimson Star'	P	3–10	red & white	late winter– early spring	late spring– early summer
Aquilegia elegantula	P	5–9	pale orange or yellow	late winter–spring	late spring–early summer
Aquilegia flabellata	P	5–9	purple-blue & white	late winter–spring	late spring–early summer
Aquilegia formosa	P	5–9	orange-red	late winter–spring	late spring–early summer
Aquilegia, McKana Hybrids	P	3–10	most colors	late winter–spring	late spring–early summer
Aquilegia vulgaris	P	3–10	most colors	late winter–spring	late spring–early summer
Aquilegia vulgaris 'Nora Barlow'	P	3–10	pink & greenish-white	late winter–spring	late spring–early summer
Arabis blepharophylla	P	7–10	pink to purple	most of the year	spring
Arabis caucasica	P	4–10	white	most of the year	spring
Arctotheca calendula	P	8–11	light yellow	most of the year	spring–autumn
Arctotheca populifolia	P	9–11	yellow	most of the year	summer–autumn
Arctotis cumbletonii	P	9–11	golden yellow	most of the year	spring–summer
Arctotis fastuosa	P	9–11	orange & purple	most of the year	spring–summer
Arctotis hirsuta	P	9–11	orange, yellow or white	most of the year	spring–summer
Arctotis hybrids	P	9–11	most colors except blue	most of the year	spring–summer
Arenaria balearica	P	7–9	white & green	most of the year	spring–early summer
Arenaria montana	P	4–9	white & yellow-green	most of the year	spring–early summer
Arenaria tetraquetra	P	6–9	white	most of the year	spring
Argemone mexicana	A	8–11	yellow	spring	late spring–summer
Aristea ecklonii	P	9–11	purple–blue	autumn or spring	summer
Aristolochia clematitis	P	5–9	yellow	winter–spring	late spring–early summer
Armeria alliacea	P	5–9	purple-pink	autumn or spring	late spring–early summer
Armeria leucocephala	P	7–9	white, pink shades or red	autumn or spring	late spring–summer
Armeria maritima	P	4–9	pink shades or white	autumn or spring	spring–summer
Artemisia absinthium	P	4–10	yellow (foliage plant)	spring–summer	late summer
Artemisia arborescens	P	8–11	yellow (foliage plant)	spring–summer	late summer–autumn
Artemisia caucasica	P	5–9	yellow (foliage plant)	spring–summer	late summer
Artemisia dracunculus	P	6–9	insignificant	spring–summer	late summer
Artemisia ludoviciana	P	4–10	greyish cream (foliage plant)	spring–summer	summer
Arthropodium cirrhatum	P	8–10	white	autumn–early spring	summer–autumn
Arthropodium milleflorum	P	8–11	pale pink to lilac	autumn–early spring	late spring–summer
Aruncus dioicus	P	3–9	greenish white to cream	winter	summer
Aruncus dioicus 'Kneiffii'	P	3–9	cream	winter	summer

NAME	TYPE	ZONES	COLOR	PLANTING TIME	FLOWERING SEASON
Asarum arifolium	P	7–9	purple-brown (foliage plant)	late winter–early spring	late spring–early summer
Asarum canadense	P	3–8	purple-brown (foliage plant)	late winter–early spring	late spring–early summer
Asarum caudatum	P	6–9	purple-brown (foliage plant)	late winter–early spring	late spring–early summer
Asarum europaeum	P	6–9	purple-brown (foliage plant)	late winter–early spring	late spring–early summer
Asarum maximum	P	7–9	purple-brown (foliage plant)	late winter–early spring	late spring–early summer
Asarum muramatui	P	7–9	purple-brown (foliage plant)	late winter–early spring	late spring–early summer
Asclepias speciosa	P	2–9	pink & white	spring–summer	summer
Asperula arcadiensis	P	5–9	pink to pale purple	late winter–early summer	summer
Asperula setosa	A	5–9	lilac	late winter–spring	summer
Asphodeline lutea	P	6–10	yellow	winter–early spring	summer
Asphodelus aestivus	P	6–10	white to pale pink	summer	spring
Asphodelus albus	P	5–10	white striped pink	summer	spring
Astelia nervosa	P	9–10	creamy brown	winter	summer
Aster alpinus	P	3–9	white & pink or blue shades	autumn–winter	late spring–early summer
Aster amellus	P	4–9	pink or purple-blue	winter–early spring	late summer–autumn
Aster amellus cultivars	P	4–9	pink, mauve, blue or purple	winter–early spring	late summer–autumn
Aster 'Coombe's Violet'	P	4–9	light purple	winter–early spring	late summer–autumn
Aster divaricatus	P	3–9	white	winter–early spring	summer–autumn
Aster ericoides	P	4–10	white & pink or yellow	winter–early spring	summer–autumn
Aster ericoides 'White Heather'	P	4–10	white	winter–early spring	summer–autumn
Aster linosyris	P	4–10	yellow	winter–early spring	late summer
Aster novae-angliae	P	4–9	pink or mauve	winter–early spring	late summer–autumn
Aster novae-angliae cultivars	P	4–9	pink, mauve, blue or purple	winter–early spring	late summer–autumn
Aster novi-belgii	P	4–9	pink, mauve, blue or purple	winter–early spring	late summer–autumn
Aster sedifolius	P	5–9	pink, violet or purple	winter–early spring	late spring–autumn
Aster umbellatus	P	3–9	white	winter–early spring	summer
Astilbe, Arendsii Hybrids	P	6–10	white, cream, pink & red	winter–early spring	summer
Astilbe 'Betsy Cuperus'	P	6–10	pale peach pink	winter–early spring	summer
Astilbe chinensis	P	5–10	white flushed pink	winter–early spring	summer
Astilbe chinensis 'Pumila'	P	5–10	white flushed pink	winter–early spring	summer
Astilbe chinensis var. *davidii*	P	5–10	pinkish purple	winter–early spring	summer

NAME	TYPE	ZONES	COLOR	PLANTING TIME	FLOWERING SEASON
Astilbe 'Serenade'	P	5–10	pinkish red	winter–early spring	summer
Astilbe 'Straussenfeder'	P	6–10	rose pink	winter–early spring	summer
Astragalus angustifolius	P	7–9	light purple	spring–autumn	summer
Astrantia major	P	6–9	pink & white	winter–early spring	late spring–summer
Astrantia major 'Sunningdale Variegated'	P	6–9	pink & white	winter–early spring	late spring–summer
Aubrieta × cultorum	P	4–9	white & pink or purple shades	late winter–summer	spring
Aubrieta deltoidea	P	4–9	mauve-pink	late winter–summer	spring
Aubrieta gracilis	P	5–9	purple	late winter–summer	summer
Aurinia saxatilis	P	4–9	pale- to golden-yellow	spring–summer	spring–early summer
Baptisia alba	P	7–10	white	autumn–winter	summer
Baptisia australis	P	3–10	purple-blue	autumn–winter	summer
Begonia 'Cleopatra'	P	10–12	pale pink	winter	spring–summer
Begonia fuchsioides	P	10–12	pale pink to coral	summer	winter
Begonia × hiemalis	P	10–11	white, yellow, orange, red, pink	summer	winter
Begonia 'Pink Shasta'	P	10–12	salmon pink	winter	spring–autumn
Begonia, Semperflorens-cultorum Group	P(A)	9–11	white or pink & red shades	spring	summer–early autumn
Bellis perennis	P	3–10	white	most of the year	late winter–early summer
Bellis perennis 'Medicis White'	P	3–10	white	autumn–winter	late winter–early summer
Bellis perennis 'Pomponette Series'	P	3–10	white or pink & red shades	autumn–winter	late winter–early summer
Bergenia hybrids	P	4–9	white or pink to red shades	late spring	spring
Bergenia cordifolia	P	3–9	mauve-pink	late spring	spring
Bergenia purpurascens	P	5–9	pink to purple-red	late spring	spring
Bergenia × schmidtii	P	5–10	rose pink	late spring	spring
Bergenia stracheyi	P	6–9	white to deep pink	late spring	spring
Bidens aequisquamea	P	8–10	deep pink	most of the year	late spring–autumn
Bidens ferulifolia & hybrids	P	8–10	bright yellow	most of the year	late spring–autumn
Billbergia amoena	P	11–12	blue-green flowers, pink bracts	after flowering	variable
Billbergia nutans	P	10–12	green flowers, pink bracts	autumn–early winter	spring
Blandfordia grandiflora	P	9–11	pink to red & yellow	winter	early summer
Boltonia asteroides	P	4–9	white or pink & mauve tones	winter–early spring	late summer–autumn
Borago officinalis	A	5–10	purple-blue	spring	late spring–summer

NAME	TYPE	ZONES	COLOR	PLANTING TIME	FLOWERING SEASON
Boykinia jamesii	P	5–8	pink to purple-red	late winter	spring–summer
Brachycome hybrids	P	9–11	white & pink or purple	spring or autumn	late spring–summer
Brachycome iberidifolia	A	9–11	white, blue, pink or purple	spring	summer–early autumn
Brachycome multifida	P	9–11	mauve-pink	spring or autumn	late spring–summer
Bracteantha bracteata & strains	A(P)	8–11	cream, yellow, bronze, pink, red	spring–autumn	summer–early autumn
Bromelia balansae	P	10–12	purple flower, white bracts	spring	late summer
Brunnera macrophylla	P	3–9	light blue	autumn–winter	spring
Bulbinella floribunda	P	8–10	golden yellow	winter	late spring–summer
Bulbinella hookeri	P	8–10	golden yellow	winter	late spring–summer
Calamintha nepeta	P	7–10	pale mauve	winter–early spring	summer
Calathea burle-marxii	P	11–12	pale violet	early spring	variable
Calathea makoyana	P	11–12	white (foliage plant)	early spring	variable
Calathea veitchiana	P	11–12	white spotted violet	early spring	variable
Calathea zebrina	P	10–12	white & violet	winter	spring
Calceolaria, Herbeohybrida Group	B(A)	9–11	yellow, orange or red	most of the year	most of the year
Calceolaria tomentosa	P	9–10	yellow	late spring–summer	summer
Calendula arvensis	A	6–10	yellow	late winter–spring	spring–autumn
Calendula officinalis & cultivars	A	6–10	yellow, apricot or orange tones	autumn	winter–spring
Callistephus chinensis	A	6–10	white, pink, mauve, purple, red	spring	summer
Caltha palustris & cultivars	P	3–9	golden yellow	autumn–winter	spring
Campanula 'Birch Hybrid'	P	4–9	purple-blue	autumn–winter	late spring–summer
Campanula 'Burghaltii'	P	4–9	mauve–light purple	winter	summer
Campanula carpatica	P	3–9	white or blue to purple tones	winter	late spring–summer
Campanula glomerata	P	3–9	purple-blue	winter	early summer & autumn
Campanula isophylla & cultivars	P	8–10	white or purple-blue tones	winter–early spring	summer
Campanula lactiflora	P	5–9	lilac-blue, white or pink	winter–early spring	summer
Campanula latifolia	P	5–9	purple, lilac or white	winter–early spring	summer
Campanula medium	B	6–10	white or pink & blue tones	spring	spring–early summer
Campanula persicifolia	P	3–9	purple-blue or white	winter–early spring	summer
Campanula portenschlagiana	P	5–10	violet to purple	winter–early spring	late spring–summer
Campanula rapunculoides	P	4–10	violet blue	winter–early spring	summer
Campanula rotundifolia	P	3–9	lilac-blue or white	winter–early spring	early summer

NAME	TYPE	ZONES	COLOR	PLANTING TIME	FLOWERING SEASON
Campanula takesimana	P	5–9	lilac-pink to purple-red	winter–early spring	late spring–summer
Campanula takesimana 'Alba'	P	5–9	white	winter–early spring	late spring–summer
Campanula vidalii	P	9–11	pink shades or white	spring	early summer
Canistrum lindenii	P	11–12	white flowers, green bracts	autumn–winter	summer
Canna × *generalis* hybrids	P	9–12	yellow, orange or red tones	late winter–spring	summer–autumn
Canna indica	P	9–12	yellow or dark red	late winter–spring	summer
Cardamine raphanifolia	P	7–9	pinkish purple	winter–early spring	late spring–summer
Carthamus tinctorius	A	7–11	orange-yellow	spring	summer
Catharanthus roseus	P	9–12	white or pink & purple tones	most of the year	most of the year
Celmisia asteliifolia	P	6–9	white	autumn or spring	summer
Celmisia hookeri	P	7–9	white	autumn or spring	summer
Celmisia semicordata	P	7–9	white	autumn or spring	summer
Celosia argentea & seed strains	A	10–12	yellow, orange & red tones	spring	summer
Celosia spicata & seed strains	A	10–12	purple-pink	spring	summer
Cenia turbinata	P(A)	8–10	yellow	autumn	spring
Centaurea cineraria	P	7–10	lilac-pink	autumn or spring	summer
Centaurea cyanus	A	5–10	white or pink, blue, purple	spring	summer
Centaurea dealbata	P	4–9	white or pink to purple shades	autumn or spring	late spring–summer
Centaurea hypoleuca	P	5–9	pink shades	autumn or spring	early summer & autumn
Centaurea h. 'John Coutts'	P	5–9	deep rose pink	autumn or spring	early summer & autumn
Centaurea macrocephala	P	4–9	yellow	autumn or spring	summer
Centaurea montana	P	3–9	violet	late autumn–spring	summer
Centranthus ruber	P	5–10	white or pink to red shades	winter–early spring	late spring–autumn
Cerastium alpinum	P	2–8	white	winter–early spring	summer
Ceratostigma plumbaginoides	P	6–9	blue	winter–early summer	late summer–autumn
Chelidonium majus & 'Flore Pleno'	P	6–9	golden yellow	autumn	mid spring–mid autumn
Chelone lyonii	P	6–9	deep pink	autumn or early spring	summer
Chelone obliqua	P	6–9	rosy purple	autumn or early spring	late summer–autumn
Chiastophyllum oppositifolium	P	7–9	golden yellow	autumn or summer	late spring–early summer
Chrysanthemum carinatum	A	8–10	yellow, orange, red or white	spring	summer
Chrysanthemum coronarium	A	7–11	yellow shades	spring	summer
Chrysanthemum × *grandiflora* hybrids	P	8–11	white, yellow or pink shades	most of the year	most of the year

NAME	TYPE	ZONES	COLOR	PLANTING TIME	FLOWERING SEASON
Chrysanthemum segetum	A	7–10	yellow shades	spring	summer–autumn
Chrysocephalum apiculatum	P	8–11	golden yellow	most of the year	mainly spring & summer
Chrysocephalum baxteri	P	8–10	white, cream or pale pink	most of the year	most of the year
Chrysogonum virginianum	P	6–9	yellow	late winter–spring	summer–autumn
Chrysosplenium davidianum	P	5–9	yellow	late winter–spring	late spring–early summer
Cimicifuga japonica & var. *acerina*	P	5–9	white	autumn or spring	summer–autumn
Cimicifuga simplex	P	3–9	white	winter–spring	autumn
Cineraria saxifraga	P	9–11	yellow	most of the year	spring–autumn
Cirsium occidentale	B	9–11	red flowers, white bracts	spring	spring–summer
Clarkia amoena	A	7–11	white or pink & red tones	autumn or spring	summer
Clarkia unguiculata	A	7–11	white, pink, purple, orange, red	autumn or spring	summer
Clematis integrifolia	P	3–9	purple or lavender shades	winter	summer
Clematis mandshurica	P	7–9	white	winter	summer
Cleome hassleriana	A	9–11	pink & white	spring	summer–early autumn
Clintonia andrewsiana	P	7–9	carmine red	winter–spring	spring–early summer
Clintonia borealis	P	3–9	creamy white	winter–spring	spring–early summer
Clintonia umbellulata	P	4–9	white	winter–spring	spring–early summer
Clivia miniata	P	10–11	deep orange	summer	spring–early summer
Codonopsis clematidea	P	5–9	white to violet	winter–spring	summer
Codonopsis convolvulacea	P	5–9	pale lavender & purple	winter–spring	summer
Columnea arguta	P	11–12	bright red & yellow	spring–autumn	most of the year
Consolida ajacis	A	7–11	white or blue, pink & purple	autumn or spring	late spring–summer
Convallaria majalis	P	3–9	white or pale pink	winter	spring
Convolvulus althaeoides	P	8–10	bright pink	spring–autumn	late spring–summer
Convolvulus cneorum	P	8–10	white & yellow	spring–autumn	spring–summer
Convolvulus tricolor & cultivars	A	8–11	blue or purple & white	spring	summer
Coreopsis auriculata & cultivars	P	4–9	deep yellow	autumn or spring	summer
Coreopsis grandiflora	P	6–10	golden yellow	autumn or spring	late spring–summer
Coreopsis lanceolata & cultivars	P	3–11	golden yellow	autumn or spring	spring–early summer
Coreopsis tinctoria	A	4–10	bright yellow & red	autumn or spring	summer–autumn
Coreopsis verticillata	P	6–10	bright yellow	autumn or spring	late spring–early autumn
Coreopsis verticillata 'Moonbeam'	P	6–10	light lemon yellow	autumn or spring	late spring–early autumn

NAME	TYPE	ZONES	COLOR	PLANTING TIME	FLOWERING SEASON
Coronilla varia	P	6–10	pink to lilac-pink	most of the year	summer
Corydalis flexuosa	P	5–9	bright blue	winter	spring–early summer
Corydalis lutea	P	6–10	yellow	winter	spring–early summer
Corydalis solida	P	6–9	pink to purple-red	autumn–winter	spring
Corydalis wilsonii	P	7–9	yellow	autumn–winter	spring
Cosmos atrosanguineus	P	8–10	deep red-brown	early spring	summer–autumn
Cosmos bipinnatus seed strains	A	8–11	white, pink, purple or red tones	spring	summer–autumn
Costus speciosus	P	11–12	white to pale pink with yellow	spring	most of the year
Crambe cordifolia	P	6–9	white	autumn–spring	late spring–summer
Crambe maritima	P	5–9	white	autumn–spring	late spring–summer
Cryptanthus bivittatus	P	10–12	white (foliage plant)	most of the year	spring–early summer
Cryptanthus bivittatus 'Pink Starlight'	P	10–12	white (foliage plant)	most of the year	spring–early summer
Cryptanthus zonatus	P	10–12	white (foliage plant)	most of the year	spring–early summer
Ctenanthe lubbersiana	P	10–12	white (foliage plant)	early spring	variable
Ctenanthe oppenheimiana	P	10–12	white (foliage plant)	early spring	variable
Cynoglossum amabile	A(B)	5–9	blue, white or pink	autumn or spring	spring–early summer
Cynoglossum amabile 'Firmament'	A(B)	5–9	bright blue	autumn or spring	spring–early summer
Dahlia hybrids	P	7–11	all except true blue	early spring	summer–autumn
Darmera peltata	P	5–9	pale pink or white	winter	spring
Datura innoxia	P	9–11	white	spring	summer–autumn
Datura stramonium	A	7–11	white or purple	spring	summer–autumn
Delphinium, Belladonna Group	P	3–9	white or blue	late winter–spring	summer–autumn
Delphinium cardinale	P	8–9	orange-red & yellow	spring	summer
Delphinium, Elatum Hybrids	P	3–9	white, pink, blue, purple	late winter–spring	summer–autumn
Delphinium grandiflorum	P	3–9	bright blue	late winter–spring	summer
Delphinium grandiflorum 'Blue Butterfly'	P	3–9	bright blue	late winter–spring	summer
Delphinium, Pacific Hybrids	P(B)	7–9	white, pink, blue, purple	spring	summer–autumn
Delphinium semibarbatum	P	6–9	soft yellow	spring	spring–summer
Dianella caerulea	P	9–11	mauve-blue or white	autumn–spring	spring–early summer
Dianthus, Alpine Pinks	P	4–9	white, pink, red, mauve-purple	late winter–spring	late spring–summer
Dianthus barbatus	P(B)	4–10	white, pink, red or purple tones	autumn–spring	late spring–summer

NAME	TYPE	ZONES	COLOR	PLANTING TIME	FLOWERING SEASON
Dianthus caryophyllus	P	8–10	white, pink or mauve tones	late winter–spring	summer
Dianthus chinensis	A	7–10	white, pink, red or mauve tones	late winter–spring	late spring–summer
Dianthus erinaceus	P	7–9	pink	late winter–spring	summer
Dianthus giganteus	P	5–9	purple–pink	late winter–spring	summer
Dianthus gratianopolitanus	P	5–9	purple-pink	late winter–spring	late spring–autumn
Dianthus, Modern Pinks	P	5–10	white, pink, red, mauve-purple	late winter–spring	late spring–early autumn
Dianthus, Old Fashioned Pinks	P	5–9	white, pink, red, mauve-purple	late winter–spring	late spring–early summer
Dianthus pavonius	P	4–9	pale pink	late winter–spring	summer
Dianthus, Perpetual-flowering Carnations	P	8–11	all except true blue	spring	late spring–autumn
Dianthus plumarius	P	3–10	white, pink, red, mauve–purple	late winter–spring	summer
Dianthus, seedling strains	P(A)	5–9	white, pink, red, mauve-purple	spring	late spring–autumn
Dianthus superbus	P	4–10	purple-pink	late winter–spring	summer
Dianthus s. 'Rainbow Loveliness'	P	4–10	mauve & pink shades	late winter	spring
Diascia barberae	P	8–10	salmon pink	autumn or spring	late spring–autumn
Diascia barberae 'Ruby Fields'	P	8–10	deep salmon pink	autumn or spring	summer–autumn
Diascia 'Blackthorn Apricot'	P	8–10	apricot pink	autumn or spring	summer–autumn
Diascia fetcaniensis	P	8–10	rose pink	autumn or spring	summer–autumn
Diascia 'Rupert Lambert'	P	8–10	deep pink	autumn or spring	summer–autumn
Diascia stachyoidese	P	8–10	deep rose pink	autumn or spring	summer
Diascia vigilis	P	8–10	pink	autumn or spring	summer–early winter
Dicentra formosa	P	3–9	pink & red	winter	spring–summer
Dicentra formosa 'Alba'	P	3–9	white	winter	spring–summer
Dicentra spectabilis	P	2–9	pink & white	winter–early spring	late spring–early summer
Dicentra spectabilis 'Alba'	P	2–9	white	winter–early spring	late spring–early summer
Dichorisandra reginae	P	11–12	purple	early spring–summer	summer–autumn
Dichorisandra thyrsiflora	P	10–12	purple	early spring–summer	autumn
Dicliptera suberecta	P	8–11	orange-red	spring	summer–autumn
Dictamnus albus	P	3–9	white, pink or lilac	summer	early summer
Dierama pendulum	P	8–10	pink or magenta shades	early spring	summer
Dierama pendulum 'Album'	P	8–10	white	early spring	summer
Dietes bicolor	P	9–11	pale yellow & brown	early spring	spring–early autumn

NAME	TYPE	ZONES	COLOR	PLANTING TIME	FLOWERING SEASON
Dietes iridioides	P	8–11	white & golden yellow	early spring	spring–early autumn
Digitalis ferruginea	B(P)	7–10	golden brown	winter–early spring	late spring–summer
Digitalis grandiflora & cultivars	B(P)	4–9	pale yellow	winter–early spring	summer
Digitalis lanata	B(P)	4–9	cream & pale brown	winter–early spring	summer
Digitalis lutea	P	4–9	white to soft yellow	winter–early spring	summer
Digitalis × *mertonensis*	P	4–9	salmon- to deep pink	winter–early spring	late spring–summer
Digitalis purpurea	P	5–10	white, pale yellow, pink to purple	winter–early spring	late spring–summer
Digitalis purpurea f. *albiflora*	P	5–10	white	winter–early spring	late spring–summer
Dimorphotheca pluvialis	A	8–10	white & brownish purple	autumn or spring	late winter–early summer
Dionaea muscipula	P	8–10	white (foliage plant)	spring	late spring–summer
Dionysia involucrata	P	4–9	violet to violet-purple	spring	early summer
Dipsacus fullonum	B	4–10	mauve-pink	spring	summer
Dipsacus sativus	B	5–10	mauve-pink	spring	summer
Disporum flavens	P	5–9	light yellow	late winter–spring	spring
Disporum smilacinum	P	5–9	white	late winter–spring	spring
Dodecatheon jeffreyi	P	5–9	red-purple	autumn–winter	late spring–early summer
Dodecatheon meadia	P	3–9	white or rose pink	autumn–winter	late spring–early summer
Dodecatheon pulchellum	P	4–9	deep cerise to lilac	autumn–winter	late spring–early summer
Dodecatheon p. 'Red Wings'	P	4–9	magenta	autumn–winter	late spring–early summer
Doronicum columnae 'Miss Mason'	P	5–9	bright yellow	winter–early spring	spring
Doronicum orientale 'Magnificum'	P	4–9	bright yellow	winter–early spring	spring
Doronicum pardalianches	P	5–9	bright yellow	winter–early spring	spring
Dorotheanthus bellidiformis	A	9–11	white, yellow, pink or red	spring	summer
Doryanthes excelsa	P	9–11	deep red	winter–early spring	spring
Doryanthes palmeri	P	9–11	deep red	winter–early spring	spring
Draba aizoides	P	5–9	bright yellow	spring	late spring
Draba rigida var. *bryoides*	P	6–9	bright yellow	spring	late spring
Draba sachalinensis	P	5–9	white	spring	late spring
Dracocephalum forrestii	P	4–9	violet-blue to purple	late winter–spring	summer
Drosera aliciae	P	9–11	pink	most of the year	summer
Drosera binata	P	9–11	white or pink	most of the year	summer
Drosera capensis	P	9–11	purple	most of the year	summer
Drosera cuneifolia	P	9–11	purple	most of the year	summer

NAME	TYPE	ZONES	COLOR	PLANTING TIME	FLOWERING SEASON
Drosera regia	P	9–11	pale pink to purple	most of the year	summer
Drosophyllum lusitanicum	P	9–11	bright yellow	spring	spring–summer
Dryas octopetala & varieties	P	2–9	white	autumn or spring	spring–early summer
Duchesnea indica	P	5–11	yellow	late winter–early spring	spring–early summer
Dymondia margaretae	P	8–11	yellow	late winter–spring	spring
Echinacea pallida	P	5–9	mauve-pink, white or purple	winter–early spring	summer
Echinacea purpurea	P	3–10	purplish-pink	winter–early spring	summer
Echinops bannaticus	P	3–10	mauve-blue	winter–early spring	summer
Echinops bannaticus 'Taplow Blue'	P	3–10	bright blue	winter–early spring	summer
Echinops ritro	P	3–10	purple-blue	winter–early spring	summer
Echium pininana	B	9–10	lavender-blue	spring	late spring–early summer
Echium plantagineum	A(B)	9–10	purple-blue to pinkish-red	spring	late spring–summer
Echium vulgare	B	7–10	violet blue or white or pink	spring	late spring–summer
Echium wildpretii	B	9–10	coral red	spring	late spring–summer
Eichhornia crassipes	P	9–12	violet with blue & gold	most of the year	spring–autumn
Elegia capensis	P	9–10	brown (foliage plant)	late winter–early spring	summer
Elegia cuspidata	P	9–10	brown (foliage plant)	late winter–early spring	summer
Ensete ventricosum	P	10–12	red	spring	late spring
Epilobium angustifolium	P	2–9	deep rose pink	autumn or spring	late summer–autumn
Epimedium alpinum	P	5–9	yellow & crimson	autumn–winter	spring
Epimedium diphyllum	P	5–9	white or purple	autumn–winter	spring
Epimedium 'Enchantress'	P	5–9	pale pink	autumn–winter	spring
Epimedium grandiflorum	P	4–9	pink to reddish-purple	autumn–winter	spring
Epimedium g. 'Rose Queen'	P	4–9	rose pink	autumn–winter	spring
Epimedium g. 'White Queen'	P	4–9	white	autumn–winter	spring
Epimedium pinnatum	P	5–9	yellow	autumn–winter	spring
Epimedium pinnatum ssp. *colchicum*	P	5–9	yellow	autumn–winter	spring
Epimedium × *versicolor*	P	5–9	yellow & red	autumn–winter	spring
Epimedium × *versicolor* 'Sulphureum'	P	5–9	yellow	autumn–winter	spring
Epimedium × *youngianum*	P	5–9	white or mauve-pink	autumn–winter	spring
Epimedium × *youngianum* 'Niveum'	P	5–9	white	autumn–winter	spring

NAME	TYPE	ZONES	COLOR	PLANTING TIME	FLOWERING SEASON
Epimedium × *youngianum* 'Roseum'	P	5–9	mauve-pink	autumn–winter	spring
Episcia cupreata	P	10–12	red	spring	spring–autumn
Episcia cupreata 'Mosaica'	P	10–12	red	spring	spring–autumn
Episcia dianthiflora	P	10–12	white	spring	spring–autumn
Equisetum scirpoides	P	2–9	buff (foliage plant)	winter–early spring	early summer
Equisetum trachyodon	P	5–9	buff (foliage plant)	winter–early spring	early summer
Eremurus × *isabellinus*, Shelford Hybrids	P	5–9	white, pink, apricot, yellow tones	late summer–autumn	early summer
Eremurus robustus	P	6–9	pale peach pink	late summer–autumn	early summer
Eremurus spectabilis	P	5–9	bright yellow	late summer–autumn	early summer
Eremurus stenophyllus	P	5–9	bright yellow	late summer–autumn	early summer
Erigeron aureus	P	5–9	soft yellow	early spring	summer
Erigeron aureus 'Canary Bird'	P	5–9	soft to bright yellow	early spring	summer
Erigeron 'Charity'	P	5–9	pale lilac pink	early spring	summer
Erigeron compositus	P	5–9	white, pink, lilac or blue	early spring	summer
Erigeron 'Dunkelste Aller'	P	5–9	deep purple	early spring	summer
Erigeron foliosus	P	5–9	lavender-blue	early spring	summer
Erigeron formosissimus	P	6–9	blue, pink or white	early spring	summer
Erigeron glaucus & cultivars	P	3–10	lilac-pink	early spring	summer
Erigeron 'Wayne Roderick'	P	5–9	soft pink	early spring	summer
Erinus alpinus	P	6–9	rosy purple or white	autumn or spring	late spring–summer
Eriogonum nervulosum	P	8–10	pale yellow to red	most of the year	summer
Eriogonum umbellatum	P	6–9	bright yellow	most of the year	summer
Eriophyllum lanatum	P	5–9	bright yellow	late winter–spring	late spring–summer
Erodium cheilanthifolium	P	6–9	white to pink with deep pink	spring–early summer	summer
Erodium chrysanthum	P	6–9	cream to sulfur yellow	spring–early summer	summer
Erodium glandulosum	P	7–9	pale pink with purple	spring–early summer	summer
Erodium × *kolbianum* 'Natasha'	P	6–9	pink & purple-red	spring–early summer	summer
Erodium manescaui	P	6–9	bright magenta	spring–early summer	summer
Erodium pelargoniiflorum	P	6–9	white & purple	spring–early summer	late spring–autumn
Erodium trifolium var. *montanum*	P	7–9	pink & dark pink	spring–early summer	summer
Erodium × *variabile* 'Bishop's Form'	P	7–9	bright pink	spring–early summer	summer
Eryngium alpinum	P	3–9	purple-blue	winter–early spring	summer–autumn

NAME	TYPE	ZONES	COLOR	PLANTING TIME	FLOWERING SEASON
Eryngium amethystinum	P	7–10	purple & silver-blue	winter–early spring	summer–autumn
Eryngium bourgatii & cultivars	P	5–9	silver-blue to gray-green	winter–early spring	summer–autumn
Eryngium giganteum	P	6–9	pale silvery blue-green	winter–early spring	summer
Eryngium 'Jos Eijking'	P	7–9	silver-blue	winter–early spring	summer–autumn
Eryngium proteiflorum	P	8–11	silver-white	winter–early spring	summer–autumn
Eryngium × tripartitum	P	5–9	magenta	winter–early spring	summer–autumn
Eryngium variifolium	P	7–10	silver-blue	winter–early spring	summer–autumn
Erysimum 3 allionii	P	3–10	yellow or orange	autumn–spring	spring–early summer
Erysimum 'Bowles' Mauve'	P	6–11	rosy purple	most of the year	autumn–early summer
Erysimum cheiri	A(B)	7–10	most except true blue	autumn–spring	late winter–early summer
Erysimum cheiri 'Monarch Fair Lady'	A(B)	7–10	bright yellow to orange	autumn–spring	late winter–early summer
Erysimum 'Golden Bedder'	A(B)	8–10	yellow to orange	most of the year	winter–early summer
Erysimum 'Jubilee Gold'	P	7–10	golden yellow	autumn–winter	spring
Erysimum linifolium	P	6–10	deep mauve	most of the year	autumn–early summer
Erysimum 'Moonlight'	P	6–9	sulfur yellow	most of the year	spring–early summer
Erysimum mutabile	P	9–11	pale yellow to purple	most of the year	autumn–early summer
Erysimum ochroleucum	P	6–9	bright yellow	most of the year	spring–summer
Erysimum 'Orange Flame'	P	6–11	deep orange	most of the year	autumn–early summer
Erysimum perofskianum	B(P)	7–9	orange to orange-red	winter–spring	summer
Erysimum 'Winter Cheer'	P	6–11	cream, yellow & purple-pink	most of the year	autumn–early summer
Eschscholzia caespitosa	A	7–10	yellow	spring	summer–autumn
Eschscholzia californica	P	6–11	orange or yellow, pink, red tones	spring	summer–autumn
Espeletia schultzii	P	10–12	yellow	spring	spring–summer
Eupatorium fistulosum	P	7–10	mauve-pink	spring or late autumn	summer–autumn
Eupatorium maculatum	P	5–10	rose-purple	spring or late autumn	summer–autumn
Euphorbia amygdaloides	P	7–9	green	autumn–early spring	spring–early summer
Euphorbia characias	P	8–10	green	autumn–early spring	spring
Euphorbia glauca	P	9–11	blue-green	autumn or early spring	spring–early summer
Euphorbia griffithii	P	6–9	orange & yellow	autumn–early spring	summer
Euphorbia griffithii 'Fireglow'	P	6–9	orange-red & yellow	autumn–early spring	summer
Euphorbia marginata	A	4–10	green & white	early spring	summer

NAME	TYPE	ZONES	COLOR	PLANTING TIME	FLOWERING SEASON
Euphorbia palustris	P	5–9	yellow-green	autumn–early spring	late spring
Euphorbia polychroma	P	6–9	yellow	autumn–early spring	spring–early summer
Euphorbia polychroma 'Major'	P	6–9	yellow-green	autumn–early spring	spring–early summer
Euphorbia schillingii	P	5–9	green	autumn–early spring	summer–autumn
Euphorbia seguieriana ssp. *niciciana*	P	5–9	yellow to red	autumn–early spring	late summer
Euphorbia sikkimensis	P	6–9	yellow-green	autumn–early spring	summer–autumn
Eustoma grandiflorum	B	9–11	white, pink, blue or purple	spring	summer
Exacum affine	B(A)	10–12	purple-blue	spring	summer
Fagopyrum esculentum	A	3–9	white	spring–summer	summer
Farfugium 'Aureomaculatum'	P	7–10	bright yellow	early spring	autumn
Farfugium japonicum	P	7–10	bright yellow	early spring	autumn
Fascicularia bicolor	P	8–11	pale blue-green	spring–summer	late summer–autumn
Felicia amelloides	P	9–11	light sky blue	spring	spring–autumn
Felicia heterophylla	A	9–11	blue	spring	summer
Felicia petiolata	P	9–11	white to violet	spring	summer
Ferula communis	P	8–10	yellow	summer	early summer
Filipendula purpurea	P	6–9	purple-red	autumn–spring	summer
Filipendula ulmaria & cultivars	P	2–9	creamy white	autumn–spring	summer
Filipendula vulgaris	P	6–9	white	autumn–spring	summer
Fittonia verschaffeltii	P	11–12	greenish white (foliage plant)	summer	variable
Fragaria chiloensis	P	4–10	white	autumn–spring	spring–summer
Fragaria 'Pink Panda'	P	4–10	bright pink	autumn–spring	spring–autumn
Fragaria 'Red Ruby'	P	4–10	red	autumn–spring	spring–autumn
Francoa sonchifolia	P	7–10	pale pink	early spring	summer–early autumn
Gaillardia × *grandiflora*	A(P)	5–10	yellow, orange, red, burgundy	spring	summer–autumn
Gaillardia × *grandiflora* 'Dazzler'	A(P)	5–10	yellow-orange & maroon	spring	summer–autumn
Gaillardia × *grandiflora* 'Kobold'	A(P)	5–10	yellow & red	spring	summer–autumn
Galium odoratum	P	5–10	white	autumn or spring	late spring
Galium verum	P	3–10	yellow	autumn or spring	summer–early autumn
Gaura lindheimeri	P	5–10	white & pink	most of the year	spring–autumn
Gazania 'Flore Pleno'	P	9–11	bright yellow	autumn–spring	early spring–summer

NAME	TYPE	ZONES	COLOR	PLANTING TIME	FLOWERING SEASON
Gazania 'Gwen's Pink'	P	9–11	pink & red-brown	autumn–spring	early spring–summer
Gazania krebsiana	P	9–11	yellow to orange-red	autumn–spring	early spring–summer
Gazania rigens	P	9–11	orange & brown-black	autumn–spring	early spring–summer
Gazania, Sunshine Hybrids	P	9–11	cream, yellow, orange, pink	autumn–spring	summer
Gentiana acaulis	P	3–9	deep blue	early spring	spring–early summer
Gentiana asclepiadea	P	6–9	violet blue	early spring	autumn
Gentiana bellidifolia	P	7–9	white to cream	early spring	summer–early autumn
Gentiana dinarica	P	6–9	deep blue	early spring	summer
Gentiana farreri	P	5–9	sky blue & white	early spring	autumn
Gentiana 'Inverleith'	P	5–9	light blue & dark blue	early spring	autumn
Gentiana lutea	P	5–9	yellow	early spring	summer
Gentiana paradoxa	P	6–9	deep blue, white & purple	early spring	late summer
Gentiana septemfida	P	3–9	dark blue to purple-blue	early spring	late summer–early autumn
Gentiana sino-ornata	P	6–9	dark blue	early spring	autumn
Gentiana sino-ornata 'Alba'	P	6–9	white	early spring	autumn
Gentiana verna	P	5–9	bright deep blue	early spring	spring
Gentiana verna 'Angulosa'	P	5–9	bright deep blue	early spring	spring
Geranium 'Brookside'	P	4–9	bright purple	most of the year	spring
Geranium × *cantabrigiense*	P	5–9	purplish pink	most of the year	spring–summer
Geranium cinereum	P	5–9	white or pink with purple	most of the year	late spring–early summer
Geranium cinereum 'Ballerina'	P	5–9	pink with purple veins	most of the year	late spring–early summer
Geranium clarkei	P	7–9	white or violet with pink	most of the year	summer
Geranium endressii	P	5–9	pale pink	most of the year	early summer–early autumn
Geranium erianthum	P	3–9	violet	most of the year	early summer
Geranium himalayense	P	4–9	violet-blue & white	most of the year	late spring–summer
Geranium himalayense 'Gravetye'	P	4–9	lavender blue & purple-red	most of the year	late spring–summer
Geranium himalayense 'Plenum'	P	4–9	purplish pink	most of the year	late spring–summer
Geranium ibericum	P	6–9	violet	most of the year	early summer
Geranium incanum	P	8–10	deep pink	spring	summer–autumn
Geranium 'Johnson's Blue'	P	5–9	purplish blue	most of the year	late spring–summer
Geranium macrorrhizum	P	4–9	pink, purple or white	most of the year	spring–early summer
Geranium m. 'Ingwersen's Variety'	P	4–9	pale pink	most of the year	spring–early summer
Geranium maculatum	P	6–9	lilac-pink & white	most of the year	late spring–summer

NAME	TYPE	ZONES	COLOR	PLANTING TIME	FLOWERING SEASON
Geranium maderense	P	9–10	magenta pink	late winter–early spring	spring–summer
Geranium malviflorum	P	9–10	violet-blue & purple-red	spring	spring
Geranium × oxonianum	P	5–9	pink with dark veins	most of the year	late spring–autumn
Geranium × oxonianum 'Claridge Druce'	P	5–9	mauve-pink with dark veins	most of the year	late spring–autumn
Geranium × oxonianum 'Wargrave Pink'	P	5–9	bright pink	most of the year	late spring–autumn
Geranium phaeum & varieties	P	5–10	brownish purple, pink or white	most of the year	late spring–early summer
Geranium pratense & cultivars	P	5–9	violet-blue	most of the year	summer
Geranium psilostemon	P	6–9	magenta	most of the year	summer
Geranium renardii	P	6–9	white with purple veins	most of the year	early summer
Geranium robertianum	P	6–10	pink shades	most of the year	summer–autumn
Geranium sanguineum & varieties	P	5–9	pink to magenta	most of the year	summer
Geranium sylvaticum & varieties	P	4–9	white to purple & white	most of the year	late spring–summer
Geranium traversii & varieties	P	8–9	white to pale pink	most of the year	summer–autumn
Gerbera jamesonii cultivars	P	8–11	white, yellow, orange, pink, red	most of the year	spring–summer
Geum chiloense	P	5–9	bright red	autumn or spring	late spring–summer
Geum chiloense 'Lady Stratheden'	P	5–9	golden yellow	autumn or spring	late spring–summer
Geum chiloense 'Mrs Bradshaw'	P	5–9	bright red	autumn or spring	late spring–summer
Geum montanum	P	6–9	golden yellow	autumn or spring	summer
Geum triflorum	P	5–9	white to pale pink	autumn or spring	summer
Gilia capitata	A	7–9	lavender blue	spring	summer–early autumn
Gillenia trifoliata	P	3–9	white to pale pink	spring	summer
Glaucidium palmatum	P	6–9	lilac to mauve	early spring	late spring–early summer
Glaucidium palmatum var. leucanthum	P	6–9	white	early spring	late spring–early summer
Glechoma hederacea	P	6–10	mauve (foliage plant)	autumn–spring	late spring–early summer
Glechoma hederacea 'Variegata'	P	6–10	mauve (foliage plant)	autumn–spring	late spring–early summer
Globularia cordifolia	P	6–9	blue to mauve	spring	late spring–early summer
Globularia gracilis	P	7–9	lavender blue	spring	summer
Globularia × indubia	P	5–9	mauve	spring	spring–early summer
Globularia punctata	P	5–9	purple-blue	spring	summer
Globularia sarcophylla	P	6–9	mauve	spring	spring–early summer
Gunnera manicata	P	7–9	greenish-red (foliage plant)	winter–early spring	summer

NAME	TYPE	ZONES	COLOR	PLANTING TIME	FLOWERING SEASON
Gunnera tinctoria	P	7–9	red-brown (foliage plant)	winter–early spring	late spring–early summer
Guzmania lingulata	P	11–12	white to yellow flowers, red bracts	spring–summer	summer
Guzmania lingulata 'Indiana'	P	11–12	white to yellow flowers, orange-red bracts	spring–summer	summer
Guzmania 'Squarrosa'	P	11–12	white flowers, red bracts	spring–summer	summer
Gypsophila paniculata	P	4–10	white	spring–autumn	late spring–summer
Gypsophila paniculata 'Compacta Plena'	P	4–10	white to pale pink	spring–autumn	late spring–summer
Gypsophila repens	P	4–9	white, lilac or pale purple	spring–autumn	summer
Haberlea rhodopensis	P	6–9	lilac or white	most of the year	spring–early summer
Hacquetia epipactis	P	6–9	yellow flowers, green bracts	winter	early spring
Hedychium coccineum	P	9–11	coral to red	winter–early spring	mainly summer
Hedychium gardnerianum	P	9–11	red & pale yellow	winter–early spring	mainly summer
Helenium autumnale	P	3–9	yellow & red to maroon	winter–early spring	late summer–autumn
Helenium 'Moerheim Beauty'	P	5–9	brownish orange-red	winter–early spring	summer–autumn
Heliamphora heterodoxa	P	11–12	white to pink	spring	early winter
Heliamphora nutans	P	11–12	white to pink	spring	early winter
Helianthemum nummularium	P	5–10	cream, yellow, pink, orange	spring–summer	late spring–summer
Helianthus annuus	A	4–11	cream, yellow, russet red	spring	summer–autumn
Helianthus maximilianii	P	4–9	bright yellow	autumn–spring	summer–autumn
Helianthus × *multiflorus* & cultivars	P	5–9	bright yellow	autumn–spring	late summer–autumn
Helichrysum argyrophyllum	P	9–11	yellow	most of the year	summer–early winter
Helichrysum petiolare	P	9–10	cream (foliage plant)	spring–summer	late winter–spring
Helichrysum retortum	P	9–11	white	most of the year	spring
Heliconia bihai	P	11–12	white flowers, red bracts	spring	variable, mainly summer
Heliconia collinsiana	P	11–12	yellow flowers, red bracts	spring	variable, mainly summer
Heliconia latispatha	P	11–12	yellow flowers, red & yellow bracts	spring	variable, mainly summer
Heliconia psittacorum	P	11–12	yellow flowers, orange bracts	spring	summer
Heliconia rostrata	P	11–12	cream flowers, red & yellow bracts	spring	variable, mainly summer
Heliconia wagneriana	P	11–12	cream flowers, cream & red bracts	spring	spring
Heliopsis helianthoides	P	4–9	golden yellow	autumn–spring	summer
Heliopsis h. 'Light of Loddon'	P	4–9	bright yellow	autumn–spring	summer
Heliotropium arborescens	P	9–11	lavender to purple-blue	spring	late spring–autumn

NAME	TYPE	ZONES	COLOR	PLANTING TIME	FLOWERING SEASON
Helleborus argutifolius	P	6–9	green	autumn	late winter–early spring
Helleborus foetidus	P	6–10	green	autumn	winter–early spring
Helleborus lividus	P	7–9	creamy green	autumn	winter–early spring
Helleborus niger	P	3–9	white tinted pink	autumn	winter–early spring
Helleborus orientalis	P	6–10	white, green, pink to purple	autumn	late winter–early spring
Helleborus purpurascens	P	6–19	pink & green	autumn	winter–early spring
Helleborus 'Queen of the Night'	P	6–10	deep brownish purple	autumn	winter–early spring
Hemerocallis forrestii	P	5–10	yellow	autumn–spring	summer
Hemerocallis fulva	P	4–11	orange-red	autumn–spring	summer
Hemerocallis fulva 'Flore Pleno'	P	4–11	orange-red	autumn–spring	summer
Hemerocallis hybrids	P	5–11	cream, yellow, pink, orange, red	autumn–spring	summer–autumn
Hemerocallis lilioasphodelus	P	4–9	bright yellow	autumn–spring	summer
Hepatica nobilis	P	5–9	blue, pink or white	autumn	spring
Hesperis matronalis	B(P)	3–9	white to lilac	spring	summer
Heterocentron elegans	P	10–11	carmine-purple	spring	summer
Heterotheca villosa	P	5–9	yellow	spring	summer–autumn
Heuchera × *brizoides*	P	3–10	white, pink or red	autumn or spring	spring–summer
Heuchera × *brizoides* 'June Bride'	P	3–10	white	autumn or spring	spring–summer
Heuchera maxima	P	9–10	pinkish white	autumn or spring	spring–summer
Heuchera 'Palace Purple'	P	5–10	white	autumn or spring	summer
Heuchera 'Pewter Veil'	P	5–10	pinkish red	autumn or spring	spring–summer
Heuchera pilosissima	P	6–10	pink or white	autumn or spring	late spring
Heuchera sanguinea	P	6–10	coral to scarlet	autumn or spring	spring–summer
Heuchera villosa	P	5–10	white or pink	autumn or spring	spring–summer
× *Heucherella tiarelloides*	P	5–9	bright pink	autumn–spring	spring–summer
× *Heucherella t.* 'Bridget Bloom'	P	5–9	light pink	autumn–spring	spring–summer
Hibiscus moscheutos	P	5–9	white to pink	spring	summer–autumn
Hosta 'Birchwood Parky's Gold'	P	6–10	mauve (foliage plant)	late winter–spring	late spring–summer
Hosta crispula	P	6–10	lavender (foliage plant)	late winter–spring	early summer
Hosta 'Eric Smith'	P	6–10	lavender (foliage plant)	late winter–spring	early summer
Hosta fluctuans & cultivars	P	6–10	pale violet (foliage plant)	late winter–spring	summer
Hosta fortunei & cultivars	P	6–10	lavender (foliage plant)	late winter–spring	summer
Hosta 'Frances Williams'	P	6–10	white (foliage plant)	late winter–spring	early summer

NAME	TYPE	ZONES	COLOR	PLANTING TIME	FLOWERING SEASON
Hosta 'Gold Edger'	P	6–10	white to lavender (foliage plant)	late winter–spring	summer
Hosta 'Golden Sculpture'	P	6–10	lavender (foliage plant)	late winter–spring	early summer
Hosta 'Golden Tiara'	P	6–10	purple (foliage plant)	late winter–spring	summer
Hosta 'Halcyon'	P	6–10	dusky mauve (foliage plant)	late winter–spring	summer
Hosta 'Honeybells'	P	6–10	white & mauve (foliage plant)	late winter–spring	late summer
Hosta 'Hydon Sunset'	P	6–10	lavender-purple (foliage plant)	late winter–spring	summer
Hosta 'June'	P	6–10	dusky mauve (foliage plant)	late winter–spring	summer
Hosta 'Krossa Regal'	P	6–10	lavender (foliage plant)	late winter–spring	summer
Hosta lancifolia	P	6–10	pale lilac (foliage plant)	late winter–spring	late summer–autumn
Hosta 'Pearl Lake'	P	6–10	lavender-blue (foliage plant)	late winter–spring	summer
Hosta plantaginea	P	3–10	white (foliage plant)	late winter–spring	late summer–early autumn
Hosta 'Royal Standard'	P	3–10	white (foliage plant)	late winter–spring	early summer
Hosta sieboldiana	P	6–10	white (foliage plant)	late winter–spring	early summer
Hosta tokudama & cultivars	P	6–10	pale mauve (foliage plant)	late winter–spring	summer
Hosta undulata	P	6–10	mauve (foliage plant)	late winter–spring	summer
Hosta 'Wide Brim'	P	6–10	mauve (foliage plant)	late winter–spring	summer
Houttuynia cordata	P	5–11	yellow & white (foliage plant)	spring–summer	summer
Hunnemannia fumariifolia	P	8–10	yellow	spring	summer–autumn
Hypericum cerastoides	P	6–9	bright yellow	spring–summer	late spring–early summer
Hyssopus officinalis	P	3–11	violet-blue, white or pink	spring–summer	late summer
Iberis amara	A	7–11	white or pink	spring	spring–summer
Iberis pruitii	A(P)	7–11	white to lilac	spring	summer
Iberis sempervirens	P	4–11	white	late winter–spring	spring–early summer
Iberis umbellata	A	7–11	white, mauve, pink to carmine	spring	late spring–summer
Impatiens glandulifera	A	6–10	lilac to purple or white	spring	summer
Impatiens, New Guinea Hybrids	P(A)	10–12	pink, orange, red or cerise	spring	late spring–autumn
Impatiens pseudoviola	P	10–12	rose-pink & violet	spring	late spring–autumn
Impatiens p. 'Woodcote'	P	10–12	pale lilac-pink	spring	late spring–autumn
Impatiens repens	P	10–12	golden yellow	spring	late spring–autumn
Impatiens usambarensis	P(A)	10–12	vermilion to deep red	spring	late spring–autumn

NAME	TYPE	ZONES	COLOR	PLANTING TIME	FLOWERING SEASON
Impatiens usambarensis × *walleriana*	P(A)	10–12	most except true blue	spring	late spring–autumn
Incarvillea arguta	P	8–10	deep pink or white	spring	summer
Incarvillea delavayi	P	6–10	purplish pink	spring	summer
Inula helenium	P	5–10	yellow	autumn–spring	summer
Ipomoea × *multifida*	A	9–12	crimson & white	spring	summer
Ipomoea nil	P(A)	9–12	white, pink, mauve to crimson	spring	summer–autumn
Ipomoea tricolor	P(A)	9–12	mauve to blue	spring	summer–autumn
Iresine herbstii & cultivars	P(A)	10–12	cream (foliage plant)	spring	late spring–summer
Iris, Bearded Hybrids	P	5–10	most except true red	early summer	late spring–early summer
Iris bracteata	P	7–9	cream to yellow, red veining	spring	early summer
Iris cristata	P	6–9	lavender to purple	spring	early summer
Iris cristata 'Alba'	P	6–9	white	spring	early summer
Iris douglasiana	P	8–10	white to deep purple-blue	spring	spring–early summer
Iris ensata	P	4–10	white, lavender, blue, purple	winter–spring	late spring–early summer
Iris ensata 'Exception'	P	4–10	deep purple	winter–spring	late spring–early summer
Iris germanica	P	4–10	violet to purple-blue	early summer	late spring–early summer
Iris germanica 'Florentina'	P	4–10	white flushed blue	early summer	late spring–early summer
Iris germanica var. *biliottii*	P	4–10	purple & reddish purple	early summer	late spring–early summer
Iris innominata	P	8–10	cream, gold, lavender or purple	winter–spring	late spring–early summer
Iris japonica	P	8–11	white or pale blue with violet	winter	late winter–early spring
Iris lactea	P	4–9	pale lavender or white	early summer	late spring–early summer
Iris, Louisiana Hybrids	P	7–10	most except true red	late winter–spring	late spring–early summer
Iris lutescens	P	5–9	yellow, violet-blue or white	winter	early spring
Iris maackii	P	4–9	light yellow	early summer	spring–early summer
Iris missouriensis	P	3–9	violet to purple-blue	winter	spring
Iris munzii	P	8–10	pale blue, lavender, purple-red	winter–early spring	summer
Iris orientalis	P	6–9	white & golden yellow	winter	early summer
Iris pallida & cultivars	P	4–10	pale blue to violet	early summer	late spring–early summer
Iris pseudacorus & cultivars	P	5–9	yellow	autumn	late spring–early summer
Iris pumila	P	4–9	white, yellow violet or purple	early summer	spring
Iris pumila 'Purpurea'	P	4–9	deep purple	early summer	spring

NAME	TYPE	ZONES	COLOR	PLANTING TIME	FLOWERING SEASON
Iris 'Roy Davidson'	P	5–9	golden yellow	autumn	late spring–early summer
Iris setosa ssp. canadensis	P	3–9	lavender-blue	autumn–winter	late spring–early summer
Iris sibirica & cultivars	P	4–9	white, violet to purple-blue	winter	late spring–early summer
Iris, Spuria Hybrids	P	4–9	white, yellow, blue to	late winter–spring	summer
Iris tectorum	P	5–10	lilac blue & white, dark veins	late autumn–winter	spring–early summer
Iris tenax	P	8–10	white, yellow, lavender to blue	late autumn–winter	spring–summer
Iris unguicularis	P	7–10	violet, purple-blue or white	late summer–early winter	autumn–spring
Jeffersonia diphylla	P	5–9	white	late winter–spring	late spring–early summer
Jovibarba hirta	P	7–10	brown (foliage plant)	late spring–summer	summer
Keckiella antirrhinoides var. anti.	P	9–11	yellow & orange-red	spring	spring
Keckiella corymbosa	P	8–11	bright scarlet	spring	summer
Kirengeshoma palmata	P	5–10	pale yellow	winter–early spring	late summer–autumn
Knautia macedonica	P	6–10	reddish purple	winter–early spring	summer–auutmn
Kniphofia caulescens	P	7–10	coral pink to yellow	spring	summer–autumn
Kniphofia ensifolia	P	8–10	yellow	spring	autumn–winter
Kniphofia hybrids	P	7–10	cream, yellow & orange tones	spring	late spring–autumn
Kniphofia × praecox	P	7–10	orange and/or yellow	spring	summer
Kniphofia triangularis	P	7–10	orange to yellow	late winter–spring	summer
Kniphofia tuckii	P	7–10	pale yellow & red	spring	autumn–winter
Kniphofia uvaria	P	7–10	orange-red & yellow	spring	late summer–autumn
Kohleria eriantha	P	10–11	orange to orange-red	spring	summer–autumn
Lamium album	P	4–10	white	early spring	late spring–early autumn
Lamium galeobdolon	P	6–10	yellow (foliage plant)	early spring	summer
Lamium garganicum	P	6–10	pink, purple or white	early spring	early summer
Lamium maculatum	P	4–10	pink shades	early spring	spring–summer
Lamium maculatum cultivars	P	4–10	white or pink to purple shades	early spring	spring–summer
Lathraea clandestina	P	6–10	purple pink	autumn	summer
Lathyrus nervosus	P	8–10	purple-blue	autumn or spring	summer
Lathyrus odoratus & cultivars	A	4–10	most except true yellow	autumn or spring	summer
Lathyrus vernus	P	4–10	reddish-purple to blue	autumn	late winter–spring
Lavatera trimestris	A	8–11	white or pink shades	spring	late spring–autumn
Lavatera trimestris 'Mont Blanc'	A	8–11	white	spring	late spring–autumn

NAME	TYPE	ZONES	COLOR	PLANTING TIME	FLOWERING SEASON
Lavatera trimestris 'Silver Cup'	A	8–11	deep pink	spring	late spring–autumn
Leontopodium alpinum	P	5–9	silvery white	spring	spring–early summer
L. ochroleucum var. *campestre*	P	4–9	cream to pale yellow	spring	spring–early summer
Leucanthemum paludosum	A	7–11	pale yellow or cream	spring	summer
Leucanthemum p. 'Show Star'	A	7–11	bright yellow	spring	summer
Leucanthemum × superbum	P	5–10	white	late winter–spring	summer–autumn
Leucanthemum × superbum cultivars	P	5–10	white to creamy yellow	late winter–spring	summer–autumn
Leucanthemum vulgare	P	3–10	white	late winter–spring	early summer
Lewisia 'Ben Chace'	P	5–9	pink	spring	summer
Lewisia columbiana	P	5–9	white to pale pink	spring	summer
Lewisia cotyledon	P	6–10	white, yellow, pink, purple tones	spring	summer
Lewisia cotyledon var. *howellii*	P	6–10	pinkish purple	spring	early summer
Lewisia cotyledon 'Pinkie'	P	6–10	pink	spring	summer
Lewisia tweedyi	P	5–9	pale to peach pink	spring	spring–summer
Liatris punctata	P	3–10	purple or white	winter–early spring	autumn
Liatris spicata	P	3–10	purple, pink or white	winter–early spring	late summer–autumn
Liatris spicata 'Floristan Violett'	P	3–10	deep violet	winter–early spring	late summer–autumn
Liatris spicata 'Kobold'	P	3–10	bright purple	winter–early spring	late summer–autumn
Libertia peregrinans	P	8–10	white	winter–early spring	spring–early summer
Ligularia dentata	P	4–9	orange-yellow	late winter–spring	summer
Ligularia stenocephala	P	5–10	yellow	late winter–spring	summer
Limonium gmelinii	P	4–10	lilac	winter–early spring	late spring–summer
Limonium latifolium	P	5–10	lavender-blue or white	winter–early spring	summer
Limonium minutum	P	8–10	lilac	winter–early spring	late spring–summer
Limonium perezii	P	9–11	mauve to purple & white	winter–early spring	summer
Limonium sinuatum	P(A)	9–10	lilac to purple	early spring	summer–early autumn
Limonium s. Petite Bouquet Series	P(A)	9–10	most except true red	early spring	summer–early autumn
Linaria alpina	P	4–10	white, yellow, violet or pink	autumn or spring	spring–summer
Linaria purpurea	P	6–10	violet tinged purple	autumn or spring	summer
Linaria purpurea 'Canon J. Went'	P	6–10	pale pink	autumn or spring	summer
Linaria vulgaris	P	4–10	yellow	autumn or spring	summer–autumn
Lindernia americana	P	9–11	purple & white	spring	spring–summer

NAME	TYPE	ZONES	COLOR	PLANTING TIME	FLOWERING SEASON
Lindheimera texana	A	6–10	yellow	spring	late summer–early autumn
Linum campanulatum	P	7–10	yellow–orange	autumn–spring	summer
Linum capitatum	P	7–10	deep golden yellow	autumn–spring	summer
Linum flavum	P	5–10	golden yellow	autumn–spring	summer
Linum narbonense	P	5–10	violet	autumn–spring	summer
Linum perenne & varieties	P	7–10	light blue, blue or white	autumn–spring	summer
Liriope muscari & varieties	P	6–10	violet-blue to purple	early spring	late summer
Lithodora 'Star'	P	7–10	lilac striped purple	spring	spring–early summer
Lobelia cardinalis	P	3–10	bright red	autumn–spring	late summer–autumn
Lobelia erinus	A	7–11	white, pink, blue or purple	spring	spring–autumn
Lobelia erinus 'Crystal Palace'	A	7–11	deep violet-blue	spring	spring–autumn
Lobelia erinus 'Tim Riece'	A	7–11	pale violet-blue	spring	spring–autumn
Lobelia × *gerardii*	P	7–10	pink, violet or purple	autumn–spring	late summer
Lobelia × *speciosa*	P	4–10	pink, mauve, red or purple	autumn–spring	late summer–autumn
Lobelia splendens	P	8–10	bright red	late winter–spring	late summer
Lobelia tupa	P	8–10	scarlet to brick red	late winter–spring	late summer–autumn
Lobularia maritima	A	7–10	white	spring	spring–autumn
Lobularia maritima cultivars	A	7–10	white, cream, pink to purple	spring	spring–autumn
Lotus berthelotii	P	10–11	red	spring–early summer	spring–early summer
Lotus maculatus	P	10–11	brownish yellow	spring–early summer	spring–early summer
Lotus maculatus 'Gold Flame'	P	10–11	golden yellow to orange	spring–early summer	spring–early summer
Lunaria annua	B	8–10	white or magenta to purple	autumn or spring	spring–early summer
Lunaria rediviva	P	8–10	pale violet	autumn or spring	spring–early summer
Lupinus hartwegii	A	7–11	blue, white or pink	late summer–autumn	late winter–early summer
Lupinus hybrids	P	3–9	most colors	autumn–early spring	late spring–summer
Lupinus texensis	A	8–10	blue & white	autumn or spring	late spring–early summer
Lychnis × *arkwrightii* 'Vesuvius'	P	6–10	deep orange	late winter–spring	summer
Lychnis chalcedonica	P	4–10	orange-red	late winter–spring	summer
Lychnis coronaria	P(B)	4–10	pink to scarlet	late winter–spring	summer
Lychnis coronaria 'Alba'	P(B)	4–10	white	late winter–spring	summer
Lychnis flos-jovis	P	5–9	bright pink	late winter–spring	summer
Lychnis viscaria	P	4–9	mauve to magenta	late winter–spring	summer
Lychnis viscosa 'Splendens Plena'	P	4–9	bright magenta	late winter–spring	summer
Lycopodium phlegmaria	P	11–12	foliage plant	most of the year	not applicable
Lysichiton americanus	P	5–9	soft yellow	winter–early spring	spring–early summer

NAME	TYPE	ZONES	COLOR	PLANTING TIME	FLOWERING SEASON
Lysichiton camtschatcensis	P	5–9	white	winter–early spring	spring
Lysimachia clethroides	P	4–10	white	late winter–early spring	summer
Lysimachia congestiflora	P	7–10	golden yellow	spring	late summer
Lysimachia ephemerum	P	6–10	white	late winter–early spring	summer
Lysimachia nummularia & cultivars	P	4–10	bright yellow	late winter–early spring	late spring–early autumn
Lysimachia punctata	P	5–10	golden yellow	late winter–early spring	summer–early autumn
Lysimachia vulgaris	P	5–10	bright to golden yellow	late winter–early spring	summer–early autumn
Lythrum salicaria	P	3–10	pink to magenta	winter–early spring	summer–autumn
Lythrum virgatum	P	4–10	pink, mauve, crimson	winter–early spring	summer–autumn
Malva moschata	P	3–10	pink	spring	summer
Malva moschata 'Alba'	P	3–10	white	spring	summer
Malva moschata 'Husker's Red'	P	3–10	crimson	spring	summer
Maranta leuconeura & cultivars	P	11–12	white (foliage plant)	spring	summer
Marrubium kotschyi	P	7–10	reddish-purple	spring	summer
Marrubium supinum	P	7–10	pink or lilac	spring	summer
Matricaria recutita	A	6–10	white & golden yellow	spring	summer–autumn
Matthiola incana strains	B	6–10	white, pink, mauve to purple	autumn–spring	mid-winter–early summer
Meconopsis betonicifolia	P(B)	7–9	sky blue	spring	late spring–early summer
Meconopsis cambrica	A, B or P	6–10	bright yellow	spring	spring–autumn
Meconopsis grandis	P	5–9	deep sky blue	spring	late spring–early summer
Meconopsis pseudointegrifolia	P	7–9	soft yellow	spring	late spring–early summer
Meconopsis × sheldonii	P	6–9	sky blue	spring	late spring–early summer
Melissa officinalis	P	4–10	white	late winter–spring	late summer
Mentha arvensis	P	4–10	lilac	autumn or spring	summer–autumn
Mentha × piperita	P	3–10	purple	autumn or spring	spring
Mentha pulegium	P	7–10	white, pale lilac to purple	autumn or spring	summer–autumn
Menyanthes trifoliata	P	3–10	white	spring	summer
Mertensia ciliata	P	4–10	blue	autumn–spring	late spring–summer
Mertensia ciliata 'Blue Drops'	P	4–10	bright blue	autumn–spring	late spring–summer
Mertensia pulmonarioides	P	3–9	bright blue	autumn–spring	spring
Meum athamanticum	P	4–9	white or purple-pink	spring	summer

NAME	TYPE	ZONES	COLOR	PLANTING TIME	FLOWERING SEASON
Mimulus cardinalis	P	7–11	yellow & red	spring	summer–autumn
Mimulus × hybridus hybrids	P(A)	6–10	cream, yellow, orange or red	spring	late spring–summer
Mimulus × hybridus 'Ruiter's Hybrid'	P(A)	6–10	orange	spring	late spring–summer
Mimulus luteus	P	7–10	bright yellow	spring	summer
Mimulus moschatus	P	7–10	yellow spotted red-brown	spring	summer–autumn
Mirabilis jalapa	P	8–11	white, yellow, pink to crimson	spring	summer
Moltkia doerfleri	P	6–10	deep purple	spring	late spring–summer
Moluccella laevis	A(B)	7–10	white flowers, green calyces	spring	summer
Monarda citriodora	A	5–11	white or pink to purple	spring	summer–autumn
Monarda didyma	P	4–10	white, pink, mauve or red	late winter–spring	summer–autumn
Monarda didyma 'Aquarius'	P	4–10	lilac-purple	late winter–spring	summer–autumn
Monarda 'Mahogany'	P	4–10	lilac to wine red	late winter–spring	summer–autumn
Monardella villosa	P	8–11	pale pink to rose purple	most of the year	summer
Monopsis lutea	A	10–11	bright yellow	spring	spring–summer
Morina longifolia	P	6–10	white to cerise	spring	summer
Musa velutina	P	9–12	yellow flowers, red bracts	spring	summer
Myosotidium hortensia	P	9–11	purple-blue or white	late winter–spring	spring–early summer
Myosotis alpestris	P(A)	4–10	blue, pink or white	autumn–spring	late spring–early summer
Myosotis sylvatica	B(P)	5–10	blue, pink or white	autumn–spring	spring–early summer
Myosotis sylvatica 'Blue Ball'	B(P)	5–10	blue	autumn–spring	spring–early summer
Myriophyllum aquaticum	P	10–12	yellow	most of the year	summer
Myrrhis odorata	P	5–10	white	autumn or spring	early summer
Nelumbo lutea	P	6–11	pale yellow	spring	summer
Nelumbo nucifera	P	8–12	pink or white	spring	summer
Nemesia caerulea	P	8–10	pink, lavender or blue	spring	summer
Nemesia caerulea 'Elliot's Variety'	P	8–10	mauve-blue	spring	summer
Nemesia strumosa & seed strains	A	9–11	white, yellow, red or orange	spring–summer	spring–autumn
Nemophila maculata	A	7–11	white & purple	autumn or spring	summer
Nemophila menziesii	A	7–11	blue & white	autumn or spring	summer
Neomarica northiana	P	10–11	creamy white, crimson, violet	autumn–spring	spring–summer
Neoregelia carolinae & cultivars	P	10–12	blue-purple (foliage plant)	spring–autumn	summer
Neoregelia chlorosticta	P	10–12	white (foliage plant)	spring–autumn	summer

NAME	TYPE	ZONES	COLOR	PLANTING TIME	FLOWERING SEASON
Neoregelia concentrica & cultivars	P	10–12	blue (foliage plant)	spring–autumn	summer
Nepenthes bicalcarata	P	11–12	brownish purple (foliage plant)	spring–summer	summer
Nepenthes × *coccinea*	P	11–12	brownish purple (foliage plant)	spring–summer	summer
Nepenthes maxima	P	11–12	brownish purple (foliage plant)	spring–summer	summer
Nepeta cataria	P	3–10	white	spring–summer	spring–autumn
Nepeta clarkei	P	3–9	lilac & white	spring–summer	summer
Nepeta × *faassenii* & cultivars	P	3–10	lavender-blue	spring–summer	summer
Nepeta nervosa	P	5–9	purplish-blue or yellow	spring–summer	summer
Nepeta racemosa	P	3–10	lavender-blue	spring–summer	summer
Nepeta racemosa 'Blue Wonder'	P	3–10	deep violet-blue	spring–summer	summer
Nepeta racemosa 'Snowflake'	P	3–10	white	spring–summer	summer
Nertera granadensis	P	8–11	greenish-white	spring	early summer
Nicotiana alata	P(A)	7–11	white, pink or red	spring	summer–autumn
Nicotiana langsdorfii	A	9–11	lime green	spring	summer
Nicotiana × *sanderae*	A	8–11	white, pink, crimson to red	spring	summer–autumn
Nicotiana × *sanderae* 'Falling Star'	A	8–11	white or pale to deep pink	spring	summer–autumn
Nicotiana sylvestris	P	8–11	white	spring	summer
Nicotiana tabacum	A(B)	8–11	greenish white to rose red	spring	summer
Nidularium innocentii	P	10–12	white or red	spring to early summer	variable
Nigella damascena	A	6–10	white, blue or purple tones	autumn or spring	spring–early summer
Nigella damascena 'Miss Jekyll'	A	6–10	blue	autumn or spring	spring–early summer
Nolana paradoxa	A	8–11	purple-blue & white	spring	summer
Nuphar lutea	P	4–11	deep yellow-orange	spring	summer
Nuphar polysepala	P	4–11	greenish yellow tinted purple	spring	summer
Nymphaea capensis	P	9–11	bright blue	spring	summer–autumn
Nymphaea gigantea	P	10–12	sky blue to purple-blue	spring	summer–autumn
Nymphaea, Hardy Hybrids	P	5–10	all except true red	spring	late spring–autumn
Nymphaea nouchali	P	11–12	blue, pink or white	spring	summer–autumn
Nymphaea odorata	P	3–11	white	spring	summer–autumn
Nymphaea tetragona 'Helvola'	P	7–10	soft yellow	spring	summer–autumn
Nymphaea, Tropical Day Hybrids	P	10–12	all except true red	spring	summer–autumn

NAME	TYPE	ZONES	COLOR	PLANTING TIME	FLOWERING SEASON
Nymphaea, Tropical Night Hybrids	P	10–12	all except true red	spring	summer–autumn
Nymphoides indica	P	10–12	white & yellow	late winter–early spring	summer
Nymphoides peltata	P	6–10	golden yellow	late winter–early spring	summer
Ocimum tenuiflorum	P(A)	10–12	pale mauve	spring	summer
Oenanthe crocata	P	5–10	white	late winter–spring	summer
Oenothera biennis	B	4–10	bright yellow	spring	summer
Oenothera elata ssp. *hookeri*	B(P)	7–9	yellow to orange-red	spring	summer
Oenothera fruticosa & forms	B(P)	4–10	bright to deep yellow	spring	summer
Oenothera macrocarpa	P	5–9	bright yellow	spring	summer
Oenothera odorata	P	7–10	yellow to orange-red	spring	summer
Oenothera speciosa & cultivars	P	5–10	white to pink shades	spring	summer
Omphalodes cappadocica	P	6–9	purple-blue	autumn–spring	spring
Omphalodes c. 'Cherry Ingram'	P	6–9	purple-blue	autumn–spring	spring
Omphalodes c. 'Starry Eyes'	P	6–9	purple-blue edged white	autumn–spring	spring
Omphalodes verna	P	6–9	blue & white	autumn–spring	spring
Onopordum acanthium	B	6–10	light purple	spring	late summer–autumn
Onosma alborosea	P	7–9	white to pink	summer–autumn	summer
Onosma tauricum	P	6–9	pale yellow	summer–autumn	summer
Ophiopogon japonicus	P	8–11	pale purple	autumn	summer
Origanum 'Barbara Tingey'	P	7–9	pink flowers, purple-pink bracts	autumn or spring	summer
Origanum laevigatum	P	7–9	lavender flowers, purple bracts	autumn or spring	summer
Origanum libanoticum	P	8–10	pink flowers, pink bracts	autumn or spring	summer
Origanum vulgare & cultivars	P	7–10	white flowers	autumn or spring	summer
Orontium aquaticum	P	7–9	cream to yellow	late winter	summer
Orthophytum gurkenii	P	9–11	green flowers, green bracts	summer	variable
Orthophytum navioides	P	9–12	white flowers, red-purple bracts	summer	variable
Orthrosanthus multiflorus	P	9–10	blue to purple	late winter	spring
Osteospermum fruticosum & cultivars	P	8–10	white. pink, burgundy to purple	spring	winter–spring
Osteospermum 'Pink Whirls'	P	8–10	pink	spring	summer
Osteospermum 'Whirligig'	P	8–10	white & purplish gray	spring	summer
Oxalis articulata	P	8–11	rose pink	autumn–early winter	summer–autumn

NAME	TYPE	ZONES	COLOR	PLANTING TIME	FLOWERING SEASON
Oxalis massoniana	P	9-10	soft orange	autumn–early winter	late summer–autumn
Oxalis oregana	P	7–10	rose pink or white	autumn–early winter	spring–autumn
Paeonia bakeri	P	5–9	bright purple-red	late winter–spring	late spring
Paeonia lactiflora hybrids	P	6–9	white, cream, pink, mauve, red	late winter–spring	late spring–summer
Paeonia mascula & subspecies	P	8–10	pink, white or red	late winter–spring	late spring
Paeonia mlokosewitschii	P	6–9	pale to bright yellow	late winter–spring	late spring–early summer
Paeonia mollis	P	6–9	deep pink or white	late winter–spring	early summer
Paeonia officinalis & cultivars	P	5–9	white, cream, pink, mauve, red	late winter–spring	late spring–summer
Paeonia peregrina	P	8–10	deep red	late winter–spring	late spring
Papaver alpinum	P(A)	5–10	white or yellow	spring	summer
Papaver atlanticum & cultivars	P	6–10	pale orange to red	spring	summer
Papaver bracteatum	P	5–10	red	autumn or spring	summer
Papaver commutatum	A	8–10	bright red	spring	summer
Papaver nudicaule	A	2–10	white, yellow, orange, pink, red	spring	summer
Papaver orientale & cultivars	P	3–9	white, yellow, orange, pink, red	spring	summer
Papaver rhoeas & seed strains	A	5–9	white, pink, red to purple	spring	summer
Papaver somniferum & seed strains	A	7–10	white, pink, red or purple	spring	summer
Paris japonica	P	8–10	white flushed pink	late winter–early spring	spring–summer
Paris lanceolata	P	7–10	golden anthers, green sepals	late winter–early sprinmg	spring–summer
Paris polyphylla	P	7–10	yellow-green	late winter–early spring	spring–summer
Paris polyphylla var. *yunnanensis*	P	7–10	white	late winter–early spring	spring–summer
Paris tetraphylla	P	8–10	green & white	late winter–early spring	late spring
Parnassia grandifolia	P	6–10	white	late winter–spring	late spring–summer
Parochetus communis	P	9–11	bright blue	spring	late summer–autumn
Paronychia argentea	P	7–11	yellow	spring	summer
Paronychia capitata	P	5–10	yellow	spring	summer
Pelargonium crispum	P	9–11	pink (foliage plant)	spring–summer	summer
Pelargonium cucullatum	P	9–11	reddish-mauve	spring	spring–summer
Pelargonium, Ivy-leaved Hybrids	P	9–11	white, pink, mauve, purple, red	spring–summer	spring–autumn

NAME	TYPE	ZONES	COLOR	PLANTING TIME	FLOWERING SEASON
Pelargonium odoratissimum	P	10–11	white (foliage plant)	spring	summer
Pelargonium peltatum	P	9–11	pink	spring–summer	spring–autumn
Pelargonium, Scented-leafed Hybrids	P	9–11	white, pink or purple	spring–summer	summer
Pelargonium 'Splendide'	P	9–11	red & white	spring	spring–autumn
Pelargonium tricolor	P	9–11	white & red	spring	summer
Pelargonium, Zonal Hybrids	P	9–11	white, pink, mauve, purple, red	spring–summer	spring–autumn
Pelargonium zonale	P	9–11	red	spring	summer
Penstemon barbatus	P	3–10	purple-pink	spring–summer	summer–autumn
Penstemon campanulatus	P	9–11	reddish purple to violet	spring–summer	summer–autumn
Penstemon cardwellii	P	8–10	bright purple	spring–summer	summer
Penstemon cultivars	P	7–10	white, pink, mauve, purple, red	spring–summer	summer–autumn
Penstemon digitalis	P	3–9	white or pale lavender	spring–summer	summer–autumn
Penstemon glaber	P	3–10	purple-red & white	spring–summer	late summer–autumn
Penstemon × gloxinioides	P	7–9	pink or red with white	spring–summer	summer–autumn
Penstemon heterophyllus	P	8–10	violet-pink to blue	spring–summer	summer
Penstemon hirsutus	P	3–9	pale purple	spring–summer	summer
Penstemon pinifolius	P	8–11	orange-red	spring–summer	summer–autumn
Penstemon serrulatus	P	5–10	deep blue to purple	spring–summer	late summer–autumn
Pentaphragma horsfieldii	P	11–12	cream to green	summer	summer
Pentas lanceolata	P(A)	10–12	pink, lilac, white or red	spring	spring–summer
Peperomia argyreia	P	11–12	creamy white (foliage plant)	spring–summer	variable
Peperomia caperata & cultivars	P	11–12	creamy white (foliage plant)	spring–summer	variable
Pericallis × hybrida	P(A)	9–11	most except yellow shades	autumn–spring	winter–early summer
Pericallis lanata	P	9–11	purple & white	spring	spring
Perovskia atriplicifolia	P	6–9	lavender-blue	late winter–spring	late summer–autumn
Persicaria amplexicaulis & cultivars	P	5–9	red & crimson shades	autumn–spring	summer–autumn
Persicaria bistorta	P	4–9	white or pink	autumn–spring	summer
Persicaria bistorta 'Superba'	P	4–9	soft pink	autumn–spring	summer
Persicaria campanulata	P	8–10	white or pink	autumn–spring	late summer–autumn
Persicaria campanulata 'Rosenrot'	P	8–10	deep pink	autumn–spring	late summer–autumn
Persicaria filiformis	P	5–10	greenish white to pale pink	autumn–spring	summer–autumn

NAME	TYPE	ZONES	COLOR	PLANTING TIME	FLOWERING SEASON
Persicaria macrophylla	P	5–9	pink or red	autumn–spring	summer
Persicaria orientale	P	8–11	pink, purple-pink or white	autumn–spring	late summer–autumn
Petunia × hybrida	P(A)	9–11	most colors	spring–summer	late spring–autumn
Petunia integrifolia & seed strains	P	9–11	crimson to purple tones	spring–summer	late spring–early winter
Phacelia grandiflora	A	8–11	mauve to white	spring–early summer	summer–autumn
Phlomis russeliana	P	7–10	yellow	late winter–spring	summer
Phlomis tuberosa	P	7–10	pink to light purple	late winter–spring	summer
Phlox adsurgens & cultivars	P	6–10	bright pink	late winter–early spring	late spring–early summer
Phlox douglasii	P	5–10	lavender, pink to crimson or white	late winter–early spring	late spring–early summer
Phlox drummondii & seed strains	A	6–10	most colors except true yellow	spring	summer
Phlox maculata & cultivars	P	5–10	white, pink or purple	late winter–early spring	summer
Phlox paniculata & cultivars	P	5–10	pink, purple, red shades or white	late winter–early spring	summer–autumn
Phlox pilosa ssp. *ozarkana*	P	5–10	white, pink or purple	late winter–early spring	spring
Phlox subulata & cultivars	P	3–10	pink, purple, red shades or white	late winter–early spring	spring–early summer
Phormium cookianum cultivars	P	8–11	red-brown to yellow (foliage plant)	late winter–spring	summer
Phormium cultivars	P	8–11	red-brown to yellow (foliage plant)	late winter–spring	summer
Phormium tenax cultivars	P	8–11	red-brown to yellow (foliage plant)	late winter–spring	summer
Phuopsis stylosa	P	7–9	pink	spring	summer–autumn
Physalis alkekengi	P	6–10	white	spring	summer–early autumn
Physalis alkekengi var. *franchetii*	P	6–10	creamy white	spring	summer–early autumn
Physalis peruviana	P(A)	8–11	purple & yellow	spring	summer–early autumn
Physostegia virginiana	P	3–10	pink, magenta or white	spring	late summer–autumn
Physostegia v. 'Summer Spire'	P	3–10	deep pink	spring	late summer–autumn
Phyteuma comosum	P	6–9	violet-blue	late winter–early spring	summer
Phyteuma spicatum	P	6–10	white, cream or blue	late winter–early spring	summer
Phytolacca americana	P	2–11	white	winter–early spring	summer
Pilea involucrata	P	10–12	greenish white (foliage plant)	spring–summer	summer
Pilea nummulariifolia	P	10–12	cream (foliage plant)	spring–summer	summer

NAME	TYPE	ZONES	COLOR	PLANTING TIME	FLOWERING SEASON
Pilosella laticeps	P	8–10	yellow	spring–early summer	summer
Pinguicula gypsicola	P	10–12	violet & purple shades	spring–summer	variable
Pinguicula moranensis	P	10–11	crimson or pink with red	spring–summer	variable
Pistia stratiotes	P	10–12	cream (foliage plant)	spring–summer	summer
Pitcairnia ringens	P	10–12	scarlet	spring–summer	summer
Platycodon grandiflorus & cultivars	P	4–10	blue, pink, purple shades or white	late winter–spring	summer
Plectranthus neochilus	P	10–12	pale lavender, purple bracts	spring	summer
Podophyllum peltatum	P	3–9	cream	late winter–spring	spring
Pogostemon cablin	P	11–12	pale lavender (foliage plant)	spring–summer	summer
Pogostemon heyneanus	P	11–12	pale lavender	spring–summer	summer
Polemonium boreale	P	3–9	blue to purple	winter–early spring	late spring–summer
Polemonium 'Brise d'Anjou'	P	3–9	lavender (foliage plant)	winter–early spring	late spring–summer
Polemonium caeruleum	P	2–9	blue to purple	winter–early spring	summer
Polemonium delicatum	P	6–9	blue to lavender	winter–early spring	summer
Polemonium reptans & cultivars	P	4–9	lavender to blue	winter–early spring	late spring–summer
Polemonium 'Sapphire'	P	4–9	light blue	winter–early spring	late spring–summer
Polygonatum falcatum	P	6–9	white	late winter–spring	spring
Polygonatum × *hybridum*	P	6–9	white	late winter–spring	spring
Polygonatum multiflorum	P	4–9	cream & green	late winter–spring	spring
Polygonatum odoratum	P	4–9	white & green	late winter–spring	spring–early summer
Pontederia cordata	P	3–10	blue	late winter–spring	summer
Portea petropolitana	P	9–12	violet-blue flowers, red-brown bracts	spring–summer	summer
Portulaca grandiflora	A	10–11	yellow, orange, pink or red	spring–early summer	summer–autumn
Potentilla alba	P	5–9	white	autumn or spring	summer
Potentilla cuneata	P	5–9	bright yellow	autumn or spring	summer
Potentilla megalantha	P	5–9	bright yellow	autumn or spring	summer
Potentilla nepalensis	P	5–9	pink to apricot & red	autumn or spring	summer
Potentilla nepalensis 'Miss Willmott'	P	5–9	cerise-red	autumn or spring	summer
Potentilla neumanniana	P	5–9	bright yellow	autumn or spring	spring–summer
Potentilla × *tonguei*	P	5–9	orange & red	autumn or spring	summer
Pratia perpusilla	P	8–10	white	spring	summer
Primula allionii	P	7–9	pink to light rose-red	spring	winter–early spring

NAME	TYPE	ZONES	COLOR	PLANTING TIME	FLOWERING SEASON
Primula auricula & cultivars	P	3–9	pale yellow, green, pink, maroon	late winter spring	spring
Primula beesiana	P	5–9	purple-red & yellow	late winter–spring	spring
Primula bulleyana	P	6–9	bright yellow	late winter–spring	spring
Primula capitata ssp. *mooreana*	P	5–9	violet to purple	late winter–spring	spring
Primula cockburniana	P	5–9	orange-red	late winter–spring	spring
Primula denticulata	P	6–9	purple, lilac or pink	late winter–spring	spring
Primula denticulata ssp. *alba*	P	6–9	white	late winter–spring	spring
Primula elatior	P	5–9	yellow to orange	late winter–spring	spring
Primula florindae	P	6–9	bright yellow	late winter–spring	spring
Primula forrestii	P	6–9	bright yellow	late winter–spring	spring
Primula frondosa	P	5–9	lilac to purple with yellow	late winter–spring	spring
Primula 'Garryarde Guinevere'	P	5–9	pink	late winter–spring	spring
Primula japonica	P	5–10	white, pink, crimson or purple	late winter–spring	spring
Primula juliae	P	5–9	purple & yellow	winter–spring	late winter–spring
Primula malacoides	P(A)	8–11	white, pink or magenta	autumn–early spring	winter–spring
Primula obconica	P(A)	8–11	white, pink or purplish tones	autumn–winter	winter–early spring
Primula poissonii	P	6–9	pink to crimson with yellow	late winter–spring	spring–early summer
Primula, Polyanthus Group	P(A)	6–10	all colors	autumn–spring	winter–spring
Primula polyneura	P	5–9	pink to purple-red	late winter–spring	spring
Primula pulverulenta	P	6–9	white, pink or red	late winter–spring	spring
Primula sieboldii	P	5–9	white, pink or purple	late winter–spring	spring
Primula sinopurpurea	P	5–9	purple-pink	late winter–spring	spring
Primula veris	P	5–9	soft yellow to light orange	late winter–spring	spring
Primula vialii	P	5–9	purple flowers, crimson buds	late winter–spring	spring
Primula vulgaris & seed strains	P	6–9	all colors	autumn–spring	winter–spring
Primula vulgaris 'Gigha White'	P	6–9	white & yellow	autumn–spring	winter–spring
Primula 'Wanda'	P	6–9	purple & yellow	winter–spring	late winter–spring
Protasparagus densiflorus	P	9–11	white (foliage plant)	spring	summer
Prunella grandiflora	P	5–9	pink to deep purple	most of the year	spring–early autumn
Prunella grandiflora 'Loveliness'	P	5–9	soft mauve	most of the year	spring–early autumn
Psylliostachys suworowii	A	6–10	pink to carmine	spring	summer
Ptilotus manglesii	P(A)	9–11	pink to purple	summer–autumn	late winter–early summer

NAME	TYPE	ZONES	COLOR	PLANTING TIME	FLOWERING SEASON
Pulmonaria longifolia	P	6–9	violet to blue-violet	winter–early spring	spring
Pulmonaria longifolia 'Lewis Palmer'	P	6–9	soft blue tinted pink	winter–early spring	spring
Pulmonaria 'Mawson's Blue'	P	5–9	deep blue	winter–early spring	spring
Pulmonaria officinalis	P	6–9	deep blue	winter–early spring	spring
Pulmonaria rubra	P	6–9	blue, purple-blue, pink or white	winter–early spring	spring
Pulmonaria rubra 'Redstart'	P	6–9	deep pinkish red	winter–early spring	spring
Pulmonaria saccharata	P	3–9	white, pink or blue	winter–early spring	spring
Pulmonaria saccharata 'Highdown'	P	3–9	deep blue	winter–early spring	spring
Pulsatilla alpina ssp. *apiifolia*	P	5–9	yellow	late winter–early spring	spring
Pulsatilla bungeana	P	4–9	light violet-blue	late winter–early spring	spring
Pulsatilla halleri	P	5–9	purple-pink to purple	late winter–early spring	spring
Pulsatilla halleri ssp. *slavica*	P	5–9	dark violet	late winter–early spring	spring
Pulsatilla montana	P	6–9	deep blue to purple	late winter–early spring	spring
Pulsatilla vulgaris & cultivars	P	5–9	purple, pink, red or white	late winter–early spring	spring
Puya alpestris	P	8–9	deep greenish blue	late winter–spring	summer–early autumn
Puya berteroniana	P	9–10	deep greenish blue	late winter–spring	summer–early autumn
Puya mirabilis	P	9–10	green to white	late winter–spring	summer
Quesnelia liboniana	P	11–12	blue flowers, orange-red bracts	spring	summer
Ramonda nathaliae	P	6–9	purple & yellow	early spring	late spring–early summer
Ranunculus acris & cultivars	P	5–9	bright yellow	winter–early spring	summer
Ranunculus cortusifolius	P	9–10	bright yellow	winter–early spring	summer
Ranunculus ficaria	P	5–10	bright yellow or cream to bronze	winter–early spring	spring
Ranunculus gramineus	P	7–10	bright yellow	winter–early spring	spring–summer
Ranunculus lyallii	P	7–9	white	early spring	late spring–early summer
Raoulia australis	P	7–9	yellow (foliage plant)	spring	summer
Raoulia eximia	P	7–9	cream (foliage plant)	spring	summer
Raoulia haastii	P	7–9	yellow (foliage plant)	spring	late spring
Rehmannia elata	P(B)	9–10	deep pink	late winter–spring	summer–autumn
Reineckea carnea	P	7–10	white or pink	winter–early spring	late spring

NAME	TYPE	ZONES	COLOR	PLANTING TIME	FLOWERING SEASON
Reseda luteola	B(P)	6–10	pale yellow to yellow-green	winter–early spring	summer
Reseda odorata	A	6–10	green tinted red	spring	summer–autumn
Rheum officinale	P	7–10	white to greenish white	winter–early spring	summer
Rheum palmatum	P	6–10	cream to pink or red	winter–early spring	summer
Rheum palmatum 'Atrosanguineum'	P	7–10	dark pinkish red	winter–early spring	summer
Rhodanthe chlorocephala ssp. *rosea*	A	9–11	white to deep pink	spring	late spring–summer
Rhodanthe 'Paper Star'	P	7–11	white	most of the year	most of the year
Rhodiola heterodonta	P	5–10	yellow to orange-red or greenish	late winter–early spring	spring–early summer
Rhodiola kirilowii	P	5–10	yellow-green to rusty red	late winter–early spring	summer
Rhodiola purpureoviridis	P	6–10	light greenish yellow	late winter–early spring	early summer
Rhodiola rosea	P	2–9	pale purple, green or yellow	late winter–early spring	spring–early summer
Rhodiola stephanii	P	5–10	creamy white	late winter–early spring	summer
Rodgersia aesculifolia	P	5–9	cream to pale pink	winter–early spring	late spring–summer
Rodgersia pinnata & cultivars	P	6–9	cream, pink or red	winter–early spring	summer
Rodgersia podophylla	P	5–9	cream	winter–early spring	late spring–summer
Rodgersia sambucifolia	P	6–10	cream to very pale pink	winter–early spring	summer
Romneya coulteri	P	7–10	white	late winter–spring	summer
Roscoea cautleoides	P	6–9	yellow to orange	late winter–early spring	late spring–summer
Rosmarinus officinalis & cultivars	P	6–11	lavender to deep blue	most of the year	autumn to early summer
Rudbeckia fulgida & varieties	P	3–10	golden yellow & brown	late winter–spring	summer
Rudbeckia hirta	B(P)	3–10	bright yellow & purplish brown	late winter–spring	summer
Rudbeckia hirta 'Toto'	B(P)	3–10	golden yellow	late winter–spring	summer
Rudbeckia laciniata & cultivars	P	3–10	bright yellow	late winter–spring	summer–early autumn
Rudbeckia subtomentosa	P	5–10	yellow & purple-brown	late winter–spring	late summer–autumn
Rumex patienta	P	6–10	green flushed pinkish red	late winter–spring	summer
Sagittaria lancifolia & cultivars	P	9–12	white	spring	summer
Saintpaulia ionantha cultivars	P	11–12	white or mauve, purple, pink shades	spring–summer	most of the year

NAME	TYPE	ZONES	COLOR	PLANTING TIME	FLOWERING SEASON
Saintpaulia ionantha hybrids	P	11–12	white or mauve, purple, pink shades	spring–summer	most of the year
Saintpaulia magungensis	P	10–12	purple	spring–summer	most of the year
Salpiglossis sinuata	A	8–11	white, gold, orange, purple, red	spring–early summer	summer–autumn
Salvia argentea	B(P)	6–9	white (foliage plant)	spring	spring–summer
Salvia austriaca	P	6–10	pale yellow	late winter–spring	summer
Salvia blepharophylla	P	8–11	red suffused orange or pink	spring	summer–autumn
Salvia cacaliifolia	P	8–10	deep blue	spring	summer–autumn
Salvia chamaedryoides	P	8–11	deep violet-blue	late winter–spring	summer
Salvia coccinea	P(A)	8–11	white or salmon pink to red	spring	early summer–late autumn
Salvia coccinea 'Coral Nymph'	P(A)	8–11	coral pink	spring	early summer–late autumn
Salvia confertiflora	P	9–11	deep brownish red	spring	late summer–autumn
Salvia darcyi	P	8–10	rich scarlet	late winter–spring	summer–early autumn
Salvia dolomitica	P	9–11	dusky lavender pink	late winter–spring	spring
Salvia elegans & cultivars	P	8–11	bright red	late winter–spring	summer–autumn
Salvia farinacea & cultivars	P(A)	8–11	white, pink & blue to purple tones	spring–early summer	summer–autumn
Salvia forsskaolii	P	7–10	violet to pinkish magenta and white	late winter–spring	summer
Salvia gesneriiflora	P	8–11	orange-red	spring	spring–autumn
Salvia greggii	P	9–10	red, orange, pink, yellow or white	spring	spring–autumn
Salvia guaranitica	P	9–11	deep violet blue	late winter–spring	summer–late autumn
Salvia guaranitica 'Purple Splendour'	P	9–11	deep purple	late winter–spring	summer–late autumn
Salvia indica	P	9–11	white & blue or lilac	spring	spring–summer
Salvia involucrata & cultivars	P	9–10	deep pink	spring	summer–autumn
Salvia multicaulis	P	8–11	violet or white	spring	spring–summer
Salvia nemorosa	P	5–10	pinkish purple or white	winter–spring	summer
Salvia officinalis & cultivars	P	5–10	bluish mauve (foliage plant)	late winter–spring	summer
Salvia pratensis	P	3–9	violet-purple or white to pale blue	winter–spring	spring–summer
Salvia puberula	P	8–10	magenta	spring	late summer–autumn
Salvia sclarea	B	5–10	greenish white tinged purple	late winter–spring	summer
Salvia spathacea	P	8–11	magenta	spring	summer

NAME	TYPE	ZONES	COLOR	PLANTING TIME	FLOWERING SEASON
Salvia splendens & cultivars	P	9–12	red to scarlet tones	spring	summer–autumn
Salvia × *sylvestris* & cultivars	P	5–10	blue to deep purple tones	late winter–spring	late spring–summer
Salvia taraxacifolia	P	9–11	white to pale pink with yellow	spring	spring–summer
Salvia uliginosa	P	8–11	sky blue	late winter–spring	summer–early autumn
Salvia viridis	A(B)	7–11	white to lilac or purple	spring	summer
Sambucus ebulus	P	5–10	white tinged pink	winter–early spring	summer
Sanguinaria canadensis & cultivars	P	3–9	white or white tinted pink	late summer–autumn	spring
Sanguisorba canadensis	P	4–9	white	late winter–spring	summer
Sanguisorba minor	P	5–9	white	late winter–spring	summer
Sanguisorba officinalis	P	4–9	reddish purple	late winter–spring	summer–autumn
Sanguisorba tenuifolia	P	4–9	white to purple	late winter–spring	summer
Sanvitalia procumbens & cultivars	A	7–11	bright yellow	spring	summer
Saponaria × *olivana*	P	5–10	pale pink	spring	summer
Saponaria ocymoides	P	4–10	pink to deep red	late winter–spring	late spring–early summer
Sarmienta scandens	P	5–9	bright red	late winter–spring	summer
Sarracenia alata	P	8–11	light yellow tinted pink	spring	spring
Sarracenia leucophylla	P	7–11	purple	late winter–spring	spring
Sarracenia purpurea	P	6–10	purple or greenish purple	late winter–spring	spring
Saussurea stella	P	7–9	purple	spring	summer
Saxifraga × *apiculata*	P	6–9	yellow	winter–spring	spring
Saxifraga 'Apple Blossom'	P	7–9	pale pink to white	winter–spring	spring–summer
Saxifraga bronchialis	P	4–9	cream spotted red	winter–spring	spring–early summer
Saxifraga bronchialis ssp. *vespertina*	P	4–9	greenish white spotted deep pink	winter–spring	spring–early summer
Saxifraga burseriana	P	6–9	crimson	winter–spring	spring–early summer
Saxifraga cotyledon	P	6–9	white sometimes spotted red	winter–spring	spring–early summer
Saxifraga exarata ssp. *moschata*	P	6–9	white or cream to pink & red	early spring	spring–early summer
Saxifraga longifolia	P	6–9	white	autumn	spring
Saxifraga marginata	P	7–9	white	winter–spring	spring–early summer
Saxifraga paniculata	P	3–9	white to cream or yellow	winter–spring	summer
Saxifraga paniculata 'Rosea'	P	3–9	bright pink	winter–spring	summer
Saxifraga paniculata var. *baldensis*	P	3–9	white tinged red	winter–spring	summer

NAME	TYPE	ZONES	COLOR	PLANTING TIME	FLOWERING SEASON
Saxifraga rotundifolia	P	6–9	white, often spotted purple	winter–spring	spring–early summer
Saxifraga 'Ruth Draper'	P	6–9	purple-pink	winter–early spring	spring
Saxifraga sempervivum	P	7–9	reddish purple	winter–spring	spring
Saxifraga stolonifera & cultivars	P	5–10	white	winter–spring	spring–early summer
Saxifraga umbrosa	P	7–9	white	winter–spring	spring–early summer
Scabiosa anthemifolia	A(P)	7–11	mauve, violet or rose	spring	summer
Scabiosa caucasica	P	4–10	mauve-blue, pink, to reddish purple	late winter–spring	summer
Scabiosa caucasica 'Staefa'	P	4–10	blue	late winter–spring	summer
Scabiosa columbaria	B(P)	6–10	reddish purple to lilac-blue	late winter–spring	summer–autumn
Scaevola aemula & cultivars	P	9–11	mauve-blue to purple with yellow	late winter–spring	early spring–late summer
Schizanthus hookeri	A	7–11	pink or violet to purple with yellow	spring	spring–summer
Schizanthus × *wisetonensis* strains	A	7–11	white, pink, blue to red with yellow	spring	spring–summer
Schizostylis coccinea	P	6–10	bright red	late winter–spring	late summer–autumn
Schizostylis coccinea cultivars	P	6–10	white or pink to red shades	late winter–spring	late summer–autumn
Scutellaria austinae	P	8–11	violet-blue	late winter–spring	summer
Scutellaria costaricana	P	9–12	orange-red & gold	spring	summer
Scutellaria incana	P	5–9	grayish blue	late winter–spring	summer–autumn
Scutellaria indica	P	5–10	blue–gray	late winter–spring	late spring–late summer
Scutellaria indica var. *parvifolia*	P	5–10	blue–gray & white	late winter–spring	late spring–late summer
Scutellaria orientalis 'Alpina'	P	7–10	golden yellow	spring	summer
Sedum ewersii	P	4–9	pink	winter–early spring	late spring–early autumn
Sedum 'Herbstfreude'	P	5–10	pink to brick red	winter–early spring	autumn
Sedum 'Mohrchen'	P	4–10	deep red	winter–early spring	late summer–early autumn
Sedum spectabile	P	5–10	pink	winter–early spring	late summer–early autumn
Sedum spurium	P	7–10	white, pink or red to purple	winter–early spring	summer
Sedum telephium	P	6–10	purple-red	winter–early spring	late summer–early autumn
Selaginella kraussiana	P	9–11	foliage plant	most of the year	not applicable
Selaginella martensii	P	9–11	foliage plant	most of the year	not applicable
Sempervivum arachnoideum	P	5–10	deep pink to crimson	late winter–spring	summer
Sempervivum tectorum	P	4–10	purple to rosy red	late winter–spring	summer

NAME	TYPE	ZONES	COLOR	PLANTING TIME	FLOWERING SEASON
Senecio elegans	A	9–11	bright purple-pink	spring	spring–summer
Shortia galacifolia	P	5–9	white, pink or blue	late winter–spring	spring–early summer
Shortia soldanelloides	P	7–9	white, pink or blue	late winter–spring	spring–early summer
Sidalcea campestris	P	6–10	pale pink or white	late winter–spring	summer
Sidalcea malviflora	P	6–10	pink or white	late winter–spring	late spring–summer
Sidalcea 'Rose Queen'	P	7–10	deep pink	late winter–spring	summer
Silene acaulis	P	2–9	pink	spring–early summer	summer
Silene armeria	A(B)	6–10	pink	spring–early summer	summer
Silene coeli-rosa	A	6–11	pinkish purple	spring–early summer	summer
Silene coeli-rosa 'Blue Angel'	A	6–11	light sky blue	spring–early summer	summer
Silene fimbriata	P	6–10	white	spring–early summer	summer
Silene keiskei var. *minor*	P	6–10	deep rose pink	spring–early summer	late summer–autumn
Silene laciniata	P	7–11	bright crimson	spring–early summer	summer–early autumn
Silene pendula	P	7–11	pale pink	spring–early summer	summer
Silene schafta	P	6–10	purple-red	spring–early summer	late summer–autumn
Silene schafta 'Shell Pink'	P	6–10	soft pink	spring–early summer	late summer–autumn
Silene uniflora & cultivars	P	3–10	white	spring–early summer	spring–summer
Silene vulgaris	P	5–10	white	spring–early summer	spring–summer
Silybum marianum	A(B)	7–11	purple-pink	spring	spring–summer
Sinningia speciosa	P	11–12	white, pink, blue, purple, red	spring–summer	summer
Sisyrinchium 'California Skies'	P	5–10	violet blue	autumn–spring	late spring–summer
Sisyrinchium graminoides	P	3–10	purple shades with yellow	autumn–spring	late spring–summer
Sisyrinchium idahoense	P	3–9	violet-blue with yellow	autumn–spring	late spring–summer
Sisyrinchium striatum	P	8–10	cream to pale yellow	late winter–spring	summer
Smilacina racemosa	P	4–9	white	autumn–early spring	summer
Smilacina stellata	P	3–9	white	autumn–early spring	summer
Solanum pseudocapsicum	P(A)	9–11	white	spring	summer
Solanum pyracanthum	P	10–12	violet	spring–early summer	summer
Soldanella hungarica	P	6–9	lavender to pale purple	early spring	spring
Soldanella montana	P	6–9	lavender	autumn or early spring	spring
Solenostemon scutellarioides	P(A)	10–12	white-cream (foliage plant)	spring–early summer	summer
Solidago 'Baby Gold'	P	5–10	golden yellow	winter–early spring	autumn
Solidago 'Golden Wings'	P	5–10	bright yellow	winter–early spring	autumn

NAME	TYPE	ZONES	COLOR	PLANTING TIME	FLOWERING SEASON
Solidago sphacelata	P	4–9	golden yellow	winter–early spring	late summer–autumn
Solidago virgaurea	P	5–10	bright yellow	winter–early spring	summer–autumn
Sonerila margaritacea & cultivars	P	10–12	pink to rose shades	spring	summer
Spathiphyllum cultivars	P	11–12	cream flowers, white spathes	spring–summer	most of the year
Spathiphyllum wallisii	P	11–12	cream flowers, white spathes	spring–summer	most of the year
Speirantha convallarioides	P	8–10	white	autumn–early spring	late spring–early summer
Stachys albotomentosa	P	9–11	salmon pink	spring	summer–autumn
Stachys byzantina	P	5–10	mauve-pink	late winter–spring	summer
Stachys byzantina cultivars	P	5–10	pink to purple shades	late winter–spring	summer
Stachys coccinea	P	6–10	red, pink or white	late winter–spring	spring–autumn
Stachys macrantha	P	5–10	purple-pink	late winter–spring	summer–early autumn
Steirodiscus tagetes & cultivars	A	9–11	yellow to orange	spring	summer
Stokesia laevis	P	7–10	white, lilac to blue	spring	late spring–summer
Strelitzia juncea	P	9–12	orange & blue	late winter–spring	spring–summer
Strelitzia nicolai	P	10–12	greenish blue & white	late winter–spring	summer
Strelitzia reginae	P	10–12	orange & blue	late winter–spring	spring–summer
Strelitzia reginae 'Mandela's Gold'	P	10–12	yellow-orange & purple-blue	late winter–spring	spring–summer
Streptocarpus caulescens	P	10–11	violet	spring–early summer	autumn
Streptocarpus hybrids	P	10–11	white, pink, mauve, purple, crimson	spring–early summer	variable, mainly spring–summer
Stromanthe sanguinea	P	10–12	white flowers, red bracts	spring	summer
Stylidium graminifolium	P	9–11	pale pink to magenta	spring	summer
Stylophorum diphyllum	P	7–10	yellow	late winter–early spring	spring–summer
Swainsona formosa	A	9–11	bright red with black	winter–spring	late winter–summer
Symphytum 'Goldsmith'	P	5–10	blue, pink or white	winter–early spring	summer
Symphytum asperum	P	5–10	rose to lilac	winter–early spring	summer
Symphytum caucasicum	P	5–10	red-purple to blue	winter–early spring	summer
Symphytum × *uplandicum*	P	5–10	rose to purple or blue	winter–early spring	summer
Tacca integrifolia	P	10–12	purple-red	spring	summer
Tagetes erecta seed strains	A	9–11	yellow or orange	spring–summer	summer–autumn
Tagetes lemmonii	A(P)	9–11	golden yellow	spring–summer	variable, mainly summer
Tagetes patula seed strains	A	9–11	yellow, orange or red	spring–summer	summer–autumn

NAME	TYPE	ZONES	COLOR	PLANTING TIME	FLOWERING SEASON
Tagetes tenuifolia seed strains	A	9–11	yellow or orange	spring–summer	summer–autumn
Tanacetum argenteum	P	5–10	white	late winter–early spring	summer
Tanacetum balsamita & varieties	P	6–10	white	late winter–early spring	summer
Tanacetum coccineum	P	5–9	pink, red, purple or white	late winter–early spring	late spring–early summer
Tanacetum corymbosum	P	2–10	white	late winter–early spring	summer
Tanacetum niveum	P	7–10	white	late winter–early spring	summer
Tanacetum parthenium & cultivars	P	6–10	white (also foliage plant)	late winter–early spring	summer
Tanacetum ptarmiciflorum	P	9–11	white	late winter–early spring	summer
Tapeinochilos ananassae	P	11–12	yellow flowers, scarlet bracts	spring	summer
Tellima grandiflora	P	6–9	cream	late autumn–early spring	spring
Thalia dealbata	P	9–10	violet	late winter–spring	summer
Thalictrum aquilegiifolium	P	6–10	pink, lilac or greenish white	winter–early spring	summer
Thalictrum delavayi	P	7–10	lilac	winter–early spring	summer
Thalictrum kiusianum	P	8–10	purple or white	winter–early spring	late spring–summer
Thladiantha dubia	P	7–11	yellow	spring	summer
Thymus caespititius	P	7–10	lilac to lilac-pink	late winter–spring	late spring–summer
Thymus camphoratus	P	7–10	purple	late winter–spring	summer
Thymus × *citriodorus*	P	7–10	lilac	late winter–spring	summer
Thymus pannonicus	P	5–10	pink	late winter–spring	summer
Thymus polytrichus	P	5–10	purple, mauve or white	late winter–spring	summer
Thymus polytrichus 'Porlock'	P	5–10	pink	late winter–spring	summer
Thymus serpyllum & cultivars	P	7–10	pink to purple shades	late winter–spring	spring–summer
Tiarella cordifolia	P	3–9	creamy white	late winter–early spring	spring
Tiarella polyphylla	P	7–10	pink or white	late winter–early spring	late spring–summer
Tiarella wherryi	P	6–10	soft pink or white	late winter–early spring	late spring
Tillandsia aeranthos	P	9–11	purple flowers, red bracts	spring–summer	summer–autumn
Tillandsia argentea	P	10–12	red or violet flowers, red & green bracts	spring–summer	summer–autumn

NAME	TYPE	ZONES	COLOR	PLANTING TIME	FLOWERING SEASON
Tillandsia bergeri	P	9–11	blue flowers, red bracts	spring–summer	summer–autumn
Tillandsia caulescens	P	10–12	white to purple flowers, red bracts	spring–summer	summer–autumn
Tillandsia cyanea	P	9–11	violet-blue flowers, pink bracts	spring–summer	summer–autumn
Tillandsia flabellata	P	10–12	blue flowers, red bracts	spring–summer	summer–autumn
Tillandsia ionantha	P	9–11	white & violet flowers, red bracts	spring–summer	summer–autumn
Tillandsia lindenii	P	10–12	blue or purple flowers, red bracts	spring–summer	autumn
Tillandsia stricta	P	9–11	blue flowers, carmine bracts	spring–summer	summer–autumn
Tillandsia usneoides	P	8–11	greenish yellow (foliage plant)	spring–summer	summer
Tithonia diversifolia	P	9–11	yellow to orange-yellow	spring	late summer–autumn
Tithonia rotundifolia & seed strains	A	8–11	orange to orange–red	spring–early summer	late summer–autumn
Tolmiea menziesii	P	7–10	red-brown (foliage plant)	late winter–spring	summer
Torenia fournieri & seed strains	A	9–12	blue, purple pink, red, white	spring–early summer	summer–early autumn
Townsendia exscapa	P	3–9	white	spring	spring–early summer
Tradescantia, Andersoniana Group	P	7–10	white, mauve, pink to purple	late winter–spring	spring–autumn
Tradescantia cerinthoides	P	7–11	purple-pink	late winter–spring	spring–autumn
Tradescantia fluminensis & cultivars	P	9–12	white (foliage plant)	spring	late spring–summer
Tradescantia pallida & cultivars	P	8–11	pink (foliage plant)	late winter–spring	summer
Tradescantia sillamontana	P	9–11	purple-pink	late winter–spring	spring–autumn
Tradescantia spathacea & cultivars	P	9–11	white	late winter–spring	variable
Tragopogon dubius	B	5–10	yellow	spring	summer
Tricyrtis hirta	P	5–9	white spotted purple	late winter–spring	late summer–autumn
Tricyrtis suzukii	P	7–10	white spotted purple	late winter–spring	late summer–autumn
Trifolium pratense	P	6–10	pink to purple	autumn or spring	spring–autumn
Trifolium repens & cultivars	P	4–10	white or green	autumn or spring	spring–autumn
Trifolium uniflorum	P	7–10	lilac	autumn or spring	summer
Trillium albidum	P	6–9	white flushed pink	autumn, late winter–spring	spring
Trillium cernuum	P	6–9	white or pink	autumn, late winter–spring	spring

NAME	TYPE	ZONES	COLOR	PLANTING TIME	FLOWERING SEASON
Trillium chloropetalum	P	6–9	green, white, pink or maroon	autumn, late winter–spring	spring
Trillium cuneatum	P	6–9	red-brown to maroon	autumn, late winter–spring	early spring
Trillium grandiflorum & cultivars	P	3–9	white to pink	autumn, late winter–spring	spring
Trillium luteum	P	6–9	yellow-green	autumn, late winter–spring	spring
Trillium rugelii	P	5–9	white	autumn, late winter–spring	spring
Trillium sessile	P	4–9	maroon	autumn, late winter–spring	spring
Trillium sessile var. *californicum*	P	4–9	white	autumn, late winter–spring	spring
Trollius chinensis	P	5–9	golden yellow	autumn or spring	spring–early summer
Trollius europaeus	P	5–9	golden yellow	autumn or spring	spring–early summer
Tropaeolum majus & cultivars	A	8–11	cream, yellow, orange & red	spring	summer–autumn
Tussilago farfara	P	3–9	golden yellow	winter	spring–early summer
Tweedia caerulea	P	9–11	blue, also white or pink	spring	summer–autumn
Ursinia cakilefolia	A	9–11	deep yellow–orange	spring	summer
Ursinia calenduliflora	A	9–11	golden yellow with purple	spring	summer
Ursinia sericea	P	9–11	yellow	spring	summer
Utricularia reniformis	P	10–12	purple edged violet	spring–early summer	summer
Utricularia sandersonii	P	9–11	mauve & yellow	spring–early summer	most of the year
Uvularia perfoliata	P	4–9	pale yellow	late winter–early spring	spring
Valeriana arizonica	P	7–10	pink	autumn or spring	late spring
Valeriana officinalis	P	3–9	white to deep pink	autumn or spring	summer
Vancouveria hexandra	P	5–9	white tinged pink	late winter–early spring	summer
Vancouveria planipetala	P	7–9	white tinged lavender	late winter–early spring	spring
Veratrum album	P	5–9	pale green to white	late winter–spring	late summer
Veratrum nigrum	P	6-9	purplish brown	late winter–spring	late summer
Verbascum bombyciferum	P	6–10	golden yellow	early spring	summer
Verbascum chaixii	P	5–10	bright yellow	early spring	summer
Verbascum chaixii 'Album'	P	5–10	white	early spring	summer
Verbascum dumulosum	P	8–10	bright yellow	early spring	late spring–early summer
Verbascum 'Letitia'	P	8–10	bright yellow	early spring	spring–summer

NAME	TYPE	ZONES	COLOR	PLANTING TIME	FLOWERING SEASON
Verbascum nigrum	P	5–10	bright yellow with purple	early spring	summer–autumn
Verbascum phoeniceum	P	6–10	violet, pink or purple	early spring	spring–summer
Verbascum thapsus	B	3–9	bright yellow	early spring	summer
Verbena bonariensis	P	7–10	deep purple	spring–early summer	summer–autumn
Verbena canadensis	P(A)	5–10	purplish pink	spring–early summer	summer–autumn
Verbena × *hybrida*	P	9–10	red, purple, pink, mauve, white	spring–early summer	summer–autumn
Verbena laciniata	P	8–10	blue, magenta or violet	spring–early summer	summer–autumn
Verbena peruviana & cultivars	P	9–11	vivid red	spring–early summer	summer–autumn
Verbena rigida	P	8–10	pale violet to magenta	spring–early summer	summer–autumn
Verbena rigida 'Silver Jubilee'	P	8–10	red	spring–early summer	spring–autumn
Verbena tenuisecta	P	9–11	purple-pink edged white	spring–early summer	late spring–summer
Veronica austriaca	P	6–10	bright blue	late winter–early spring	late spring
Veronica austriaca cultivars	P	6–10	blue shades	late winter–early spring	late spring
Veronica cinerea	P	5–9	purplish blue & white	late winter–early spring	summer
Veronica gentianoides	P	5–9	pale blue or white	late winter–early spring	late spring
Veronica longifolia	P	4–9	lilac blue	late winter–early spring	late spring
Veronica longifolia 'Rosea'	P	4–9	pink	late winter–early spring	late spring
Veronica peduncularis	P	6–9	pink & blue, white or pink	late winter–early spring	late spring–early summer
Veronica peduncularis 'Georgia Blue'	P	6–9	bright blue	late winter–early spring	late spring–early summer
Veronica prostrata	P	5–9	blue	late winter–early spring	spring–early summer
Veronica spicata	P	3–9	blue	late winter–early spring	summer
Veronica spicata varieties	P	3–9	lavender, blue, pink or white	late winter–early spring	summer
Veronica spuria	P	3–9	blue	late winter–early spring	summer
Veronica 'Waterperry'	P	8–11	lavender blue	spring	variable, mainly summer
Veronicastrum virginicum	P	3–9	purplish blue or white	late winter–early spring	summer
Victoria amazonica	P	11–12	pink & white	spring–early summer	summer

NAME	TYPE	ZONES	COLOR	PLANTING TIME	FLOWERING SEASON
Victoria amazonica × *cruziana* 'Longwood Hybrid'	P	11–12	white turning pink	spring–early summer	summer
Viola cornuta & cultivars	P	6–9	pale blue to deep violet	late winter–early spring	spring–summer
Viola elatior	P	5–9	lilac blue	late winter–early spring	early summer
Viola hederacea	P	8–10	pale blue to deep violet	late winter–early spring	spring–summer
Viola labradorica	P	6–9	white & lilac	winter–early spring	spring–autumn
Viola odorata	P	6–10	violet, white or rose pink	autumn–early spring	late winter–early spring
Viola, Perennial Cultivars	P	6–10	all colors	most of the year	most of the year
Viola riviniana	P	5–10	violet-blue	late winter–early spring	spring–summer
Viola riviniana 'Purpurea'	P	5–10	purple	late winter–early spring	spring–summer
Viola septentrionalis	P	7–10	bluish purple or white	late winter–early spring	spring–summer
Viola sororia	P	4–10	white to deep violet blue	late winter–early spring	spring–summer
Viola sororia 'Freckles'	P	4–10	white flecked violet-purple	late winter–early spring	spring–summer
Viola tricolor	B(P)	4–10	yellow, blue, violet or white	most of the year	late summer–early winter
Viola tricolor 'Bowles' Black'	P	4–10	black with yellow	most of the year	late summer–early winter
Viola × *wittrockiana* hybrid seedlings	P(A)	5–10	all colors	all except midsummer	all except midsummer
Vriesea carinata	P	11–12	golden yellow flowers, red bracts	spring–summer	late autumn
Vriesea 'Christine'	P	11–12	orange-yellow flowers, red bracts	spring–summer	mainly summer
Vriesea splendens	P	11–12	yellow flowers, purple-green bracts	spring–summer	mainly summer
Wachendorfia thyrsiflora	P	8–11	bright yellow	late winter–early spring	spring–early summer
Wahlenbergia albomarginata	P	7–10	pale blue to white	spring	summer
Wahlenbergia communis	P	8–11	light blue	spring	spring–summer
Wahlenbergia gloriosa	P	8–10	deep blue to purple-blue	spring	summer
Wahlenbergia stricta	P	9–10	blue to light purple	spring	spring–summer
Waldsteinia ternata	P	3–9	golden yellow	late winter–early spring	late spring–summer
Welwitschia mirabilis	P	9–10	scarlet cones	spring	variable
Wittrockia superba	P	11–12	blue flowers, red bracts	spring–summer	summer

NAME	TYPE	ZONES	COLOR	PLANTING TIME	FLOWERING SEASON
Wulfenia carinthiaca	P	5–9	deep violet-blue	spring	summer
Xeranthemum annuum	A	7–10	white, pink or mauve	spring	summer
Xeranthemum annuum, Mixed Hybrids	A	7–10	pink, purple, mauve, red or white	spring	summer
Xeronema callistemon	P	10–11	bright red	spring	spring
Yucca baccata	P	9–11	white or cream tinged purple	late winter–spring	late summer
Yucca whipplei	P	8–11	cream, sometimes tinged purple	late winter–spring	late summer–autumn
Zantedeschia aethiopica	P	8–11	yellow flowers, white spathe	winter–early spring	late spring–early winter
Zantedeschia a. 'Green Goddess'	P	8–11	yellow flowers, green spathe	winter–early spring	late spring–autumn
Zantedeschia elliottiana	P	8–11	yellow flowers, yellow spathe	winter–early spring	summer–autumn
Zantedeschia, New Zealand Hybrids	P	8–11	yellow, orange, pink, red spathes	winter–early spring	summer
Zantedeschia rehmannii	P	8–11	yellow flowers, deep pink spathes	winter–early spring	summer–autumn
Zauschneria californica	P	8–10	bright red	late winter–early summer	late summer–early autumn
Zauschneria septentrionalis	P	8–10	orange-red	late winter–early summer	late summer–early autumn
Zinnia elegans seed strains	A	8–11	all except true blue	spring	summer–autumn
Zinnia haageana seed strains	A	8–11	yellow, orange & bronze	spring	summer–autumn
Zinnia peruviana	A	8–11	yellow to orange or scarlet	spring	summer–early autumn

Index to Common Names and Synonyms

WORLD
WHISKEY

EDITOR-IN-CHIEF

CHARLES MACLEAN

WRITTEN BY

**DAVE BROOM, TOM BRUCE-GARDYNE,
IAN BUXTON, CHARLES MACLEAN, PETER MULRYAN,
HANS OFFRINGA, GAVIN D. SMITH**

REVISED BY

GAVIN D. SMITH

DK

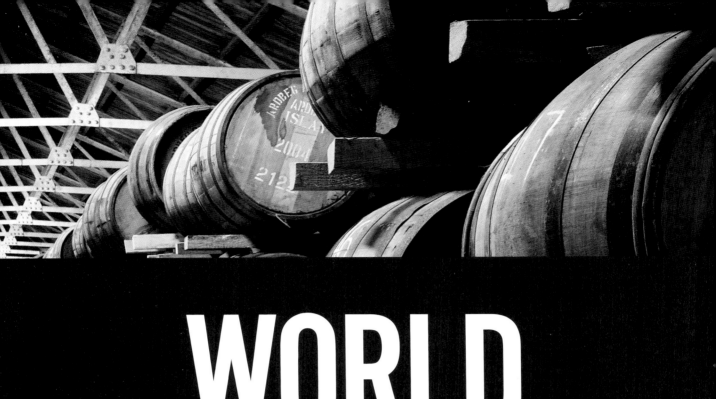

WORLD
WHISKEY

DK UK

EDITOR Toby Mann
SENIOR DESIGNER Kathryn Wilding
US CONSULTANT Aaron Barker
US EDITORS Lori Cates Hand, Rachel Bozek
JACKET DESIGNER Harriet Yeomans
SENIOR PRE-PRODUCTION PRODUCER Tony Phipps
SENIOR PRODUCER Che Creasey
CREATIVE TECHNICAL SUPPORT Sonia Charbonnier
MANAGING EDITOR Angela Wilkes
MANAGING ART EDITOR Marianne Markham
ART DIRECTOR Maxine Pedliham
US PUBLISHER Mike Sanders
PUBLISHING DIRECTOR Mary-Clare Jerram

DK INDIA

SENIOR EDITOR Bushra Ahmed
EDITOR Shreya Sengupta
SENIOR ART EDITOR Ivy Roy Sengupta
ART EDITOR Sourabh Challariya
PRE-PRODUCTION MANAGER Sunil Sharma
DTP DESIGNER Rajdeep Singh
MANAGING EDITOR Glenda Fernandes
MANAGING ART EDITOR Navidita Thapa

First American Edition, 2009
This edition published in the United States in 2016 by DK
Publishing, 1450 Broadway, Suite 801, New York, NY 10018

Copyright © 2009, 2016 Dorling Kindersley Limited
DK, a Division of Penguin Random House LLC
21 22 23 24 25 10 9 8 7 6 5 4 3
015-262225-Nov/2016

A catalog record for this book is available from the Library
of Congress.
ISBN 978-1-4654-5359-4

DK books are available at special discounts when purchased in
bulk for sales promotions, premiums, fund-raising, or educational
use. For details, contact: DK Publishing Special Markets, 1450
Broadway, Suite 801, New York, NY 10018

SpecialSales@dk.com

Printed and bound in Malaysia

For the curious
www.dk.com

CONTENTS

INTRODUCTION

Global interest in and enthusiasm for whiskey has never been greater. In recent years, many new distilleries have opened in Australia, Europe, Taiwan, and Japan, as well as in Scotland. Most of these are small concerns, designed to meet local demand, but some are major production sites. Several leading malt distilleries have recently expanded capacity, and in Europe a handful of liqueur distillers are now producing whiskey as well.

What has prompted this expansion and confident investment? Two factors: first, the interest in single malts, which continues to grow in every market, and second the anticipated demand from emerging markets in China, India, Russia, and Brazil.

The burgeoning interest in single malts is proved not only by the year-on-year rise in sales, but also the phenomenal enthusiasm for whiskey festivals around the world—from Finland to New Zealand, San Francisco to Moscow. Once a taste for whiskey is developed, the passion for information about this beguiling subject is inexhaustible.

It is important to remember that the whiskey made today cannot be sold as "whiskey" until it has matured for at least two years in the US and at least three years in Scotland—and is often aged for far longer periods. The distiller must, therefore, peer into the future, gauge the likely demand in 5, 10, 15, or 20 years, in various markets, and gear production accordingly.

From time to time they get it wrong, and, to a large extent, the availability today of some very fine old whiskeys, both single malts and blended, is a reflection of over-production in the early 1980s. The point remains, though, that the excellence of the spirit will always be recognized. Fashions in drinks may come and go, but, for the discriminating consumer, whiskey goes on forever!

The book you are holding offers a superb catalog of the aforementioned whiskeys that are available around the world today. Not only does it cover the output of major and lesser-known whiskey distilleries, but it also includes a wide selection of blended whiskeys. The main section of the book—Whiskeys Worth the Wait—is broken down into countries. It catalogs in A–Z format first the key whiskey-making nations of Scotland, Ireland, the US, Canada, and Japan, followed by whiskeys from other parts of Europe, South Asia, Australasia, and Africa. Secreted within this listing of world whiskeys are features on the production processes and the varied types of whiskey made, examinations of particular distilleries to divulge the secrets of their whiskey-making, and tours that will guide you to the whiskey regions of Scotland, Ireland, the US, and Japan. For no experience adds more to the enjoyment of whiskey than visiting a working distillery, to savor the aromas, appreciate the skill, dedication, and time that goes into making this profound spirit, and, of course, to sample a dram right at its source.

Charles MacLean

MAKING WHISKEY

Whiskey is both a simple product and an endlessly ponderable drink. It is made from just grain, water, and yeast, and yet the spectrum of aromas and tastes that emerge from a mature whiskey can be wondrous and beguiling. How can such basic ingredients produce such an array of flavors? The answer lies in all the small variations in the whiskey-making process: the grain(s) used, how the barley is malted, the shape of the stills, the angle of the lyne arms, the length of maturation, and types of casks used. But to understand those nuances, first you need to be familiar with the basics—the principal stages of whiskey making.

The first step is choosing the grain. Barley is the most commonly used grain in whiskey making. It is the sole grain in Scotch malt, and a percentage of malted barley is used in almost all whiskey. Corn, wheat, and rye are the other grains used in whiskey making. Corn is the principal grain for making bourbon and Tennessee whiskey, and rye grain is the key ingredient in rye whiskey. The term "grain whiskey" refers to whiskey made principally from grains other than barley for primary use in making blended whiskey. The main grains used for making grain whiskey are either corn or wheat. For more on whiskey types, *see pp. 12–13*.

1 MALTING

Barley goes through a malting process to activate enzymes and maximize its starch content, which is later converted to sugar and then alcohol. If peat is burned while drying the grains, the whiskey will have a smoky flavor. Some distilleries have their own floor maltings *(above)*, but most use independent maltsters. *(See also pp. 38–39)*

2 MASHING

At the distillery, the malt is milled to produce a coarse flour called grist. The grist is then mixed with hot water in a mash tun *(above)* to extract soluble sugars. The sugar-laden water, known as wort, is piped off for use. Other unmalted grain can be combined with the grist in the mash tun for making non-malt whiskeys.

3 FERMENTING

The wort is mixed with yeast and heated in a washback *(above)*. The yeast feeds off the sugars in the wort, so producing alcohol and carbon dioxide. This process, known as fermentation, lasts between 48 and 74 hours, and results in what is effectively a strong and rather tart beer, called wash.

4 DISTILLING

The next stage is for the wash to be distilled. Whether using a column still for continuous distillation or a pot still for batch distillation, the purpose is the same: to extract alcohol spirit from the wash. The essential process is simple: the wash is boiled and, as alcohol boils at a lower temperature than water, the alcohol is driven off the wash as vapor; this vapor is then condensed into liquid. With pot still distillation, the spirit is condensed either in a shell-and-tube condenser *(as above)* or an old-fashioned worm tub *(see p.167)*, which produces a heavier, oilier style of spirit. Most whiskey is distilled twice—the first time in a wash still (known as a "beer still" in the US), the second time in a spirit (or "low wines") still. But Irish whiskey is traditionally triple-distilled to create an even purer spirit.

5 THE CUT

A spirit safe *(above)* is used at distilleries using pot still distillation to enable the distillers to assess the spirit. The first and last parts of the "run" during the second distillation are not pure enough for use. Known as the "foreshots" and the "feints," respectively, they will go back for redistillation along with the "low wines" from the first distillation. The desired and usable part of the distillation, however, is the middle section, and this is known as the "middle cut," or just "the cut". This usable spirit, which is called "new make," is drinkable and exhibits some of the characteristics that will be in the final whiskey. However, it will not have achieved any depth of flavor or color yet, and cannot legally be called whiskey.

6 FILLING INTO CASKS

The new make will have its strength slightly reduced to about 63 or 64% ABV—the optimum strength to begin maturation. The spirit is then piped from a holding tank into oak casks *(above)*. In the US, the spirit is filled into new, charred barrels; in Scotland, it is filled into used casks.

7 MATURATION

The process that turns raw, clear, new make into the richly hued, complex-tasting drink we know as whiskey is maturation. The length of time for maturation varies, depending on climatic conditions, the size and type of the casks used, and legal requirements—at least three years for Scotch. *(See also pp.66–67 and 72–73)*

8 BLENDING

The majority of whiskey sold is blended whiskey—a mix of malt whiskey and grain whiskey. As many as 40 or more whiskeys may be combined in a blend, and the art of the blender *(above)* is to marry flavors so that they balance and unify. Blends tend to be tailored to specific tastes and markets. *(See also p.78)*

9 BOTTLING

The bottling of whiskey is often carried out at automated plants *(above)*, but sometimes the bottling and labeling is done by hand. Most whiskey is reduced with water to a bottling strength of 40 or 43% ABV, but cask strength bottlings are released at the strength they came out of the cask (in the region of 53–65% ABV).

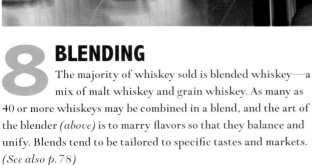

WHISKEY TYPES

There are several distinct types of whiskey, and the variations depend upon the type and proportion of grains used and the methods employed in making the whiskey. Barley, corn, wheat, and rye are the principal grains, while the variations in methods that lead to different classifications of whiskey include the way of distilling (batch or continuous distillation) and the process and period of maturation. American whiskeys are mostly aged in new oak, while Scotch and Irish whiskeys employ reused casks.

MALT Made solely from malted barley in copper pot stills, this is the "original" whisky of the Scottish Highlands. It has also been made in Japan since the 1920s, and is now made in Canada, parts of Asia, and (in small amounts) in almost every European country. "Single malt" is the product of an individual distillery. In Scotland it must be matured for a minimum of three years. *(See p.26)*

GRAIN Distilled in a continuous still, grain whiskey is typically made from wheat or corn (maize), along with unmalted and malted barley. Though mostly used for blending, some is bottled as grain whiskey. *(See p.163)*

BLENDS A mix of malt whisky and grain whiskey, blends typically have a proportion of 40 percent malt to 60 percent grain. More malt is used in deluxe blends, less in standard blends. They account for 92% of all Scotch. *(See p.78)*

BLENDED MALT While single malt is the product of just one distillery, a blended malt is a mix of malt whiskeys from more than one. *(See p.172)*

PURE POT STILL WHISKEY Made from a mix of malted and unmalted barley, pure pot still whiskey is unique to Ireland. *(See p.190)*

TENNESSEE WHISKEY Made much in the same way as bourbon, with a mashbill of at least 51 percent corn, Tennessee whiskey has the distinction of undergoing filtration through a deep bed of sugar-maple charcoal. This is known as the Lincoln County Process. *(See p.228)*

BOURBON For a whiskey to be deemed bourbon, it must contain at least 51 percent corn in the mashbill, the remainder being made up of barley, wheat, or rye. It has to be matured in new, charred white-oak casks for a minimum of two years. *(See p.221)*

RYE Although relatively uncommon today, rye is the original American whiskey. It must contain at least 51 percent rye and be matured in new, charred white oak for at least two years. Canada produces a lot of rye whiskey, though the process and classification is different to that of US rye. *(See pp.260 and 268)*

ALL ABOUT...
APPRECIATING WHISKEY

Whiskey is one of the world's most versatile drinks, and may be enjoyed in a variety of ways. But when it comes to appreciating fully its flavors and complexity, only a little water should be added. Flavor is a combination of aroma and taste, and to properly appreciate whiskey, you must have a glass that will present the aroma to its best advantage *(see pp.156–157)*. The addition of a dash of still water (how much depends on the individual whiskey and personal preferences) disturbs the molecules in the liquid and tends to increase the aroma; by contrast, ice closes it down. Here are some pointers on the best way to appreciate whiskey and some of the key flavors associated with the drink.

TASTING

When tasting whiskey, use a clean glass for each drink, have a small jug of water to use when diluting the spirit slightly, and drink more water between each tasting to cleanse the palate. It's a good idea to keep notes as you go *(see p.334)*.

1. Appearance Consider the whiskey's color *(see p.73)*. Swirl the spirit in the glass and look at the "legs" that trickle down the inside. If they are slow-running and thick, it indicates good body, while skinny, fast-running legs suggest a thinner texture to the whiskey.

2. Aroma Swirl the liquid and sniff it. Note first the physical effects (if any)—prickle, sharpness, warming, cooling. Then try to put words to the smells. Add a drop of water and repeat.

3. Taste By all means taste the whiskey straight, but its character can best be appreciated once a little water has been added. Note the texture or "mouthfeel"—smooth, oily, waxy, drying, acerbic, and so on. Then consider the balance of the four primary tastes: sweetness, acidity, dryness, saltiness. Does the overall taste remind you of anything? Finally, how long is the finish, and does it leave a pleasant aftertaste?

4. Development After 10 minutes or so, sniff and taste the whiskey again to see if it has changed.

A glass that narrows toward the rim is ideal for appreciating whiskey, as it concentrates the all-important aromas

FLAVORS

Whiskey should smell and taste of whiskey, but when we are appreciating it to the full, we go beyond this simple description to isolate and identify what the smells and tastes remind us of. Here are some of the key flavor groups:

CEREAL

As you might expect, this flavor comes from the grain. You can taste it in whiskeys such as Knockando (p.124), Tullibardine (p.176), and McDowell's (p.322).
• cookies • breakfast cereals
• bran • new leather • malt extract
• corn mash

FRUITY

The fresh, fruity flavors develop in the spirit itself while being fermented and distilled. Dried and cooked fruit flavors come from the wood in which the whiskey is matured. Glenmorangie (p.100), Yoichi (p.294), and Yamazaki (p.297) are examples of whiskeys that offer different fruity flavors.
• fresh fruit (apples, pears, peaches)
• citrus fruits (oranges, lemons, tangerines)
• tropical fruits (pineapples, lychees, bananas) • dried fruits (raisins, candied peel, figs, prunes, fruitcake)
• stewed fruits • hard candy
• solvent (nail-polish remover)

FLORAL

Scottish Lowland malts are the archetypal floral whiskeys. The flavor is well suited to aperitif-style whiskeys, such as the younger offerings from Auchentoshan (p.30) and Glenkinchie (p.97).
• florist's shop • scented flowers (rose, lavender, heather) • grass (clippings, dried grass, flower stems) • artificial perfume (air fresheners, violet candy)

SMOKY

Peated malt gives us the smokiest flavored whiskeys, as exemplified by Islay malts such as Lagavulin (p.126) but also Talisker (p.164) and Longrow (p.135).
• smoked meat, fish, cheese • charred sticks
• bonfires, burning leaves • peat smoke
• tobacco • soot, coal • tar • creosote

MEDICINAL

The medicinal tang is not a taste for everyone, but those who like it tend to really like it and head for the malts of Islay. Taste it in any Laphroaig (p.128), in Benriach's Curiositas (p.42), and in Ardbeg's 10-year-old (p.24).
• bandages • hospitals • mouthwash
• coal tar soap • iodine (sea salt)
• antiseptic (antiseptic cream, ointment)

WOODY

The influence of the cask is two-fold. The first flavor influence is in woody notes, as can be found in Balvenie (p.36) and Glenrothes (p.104).
• new wood (sap, pine, bark, fresh oak)
• scented wood (sandalwood, cedar, cigar boxes) • pencil shavings • sawdust

WOOD EXTRACTIVE

The second influence of the cask comes in the form of vanillins and tannins within the wood. Vanillins are particularly strong in American oak, and all bourbons feature these notes. European oak is richer in tannins, giving spicier and winey influences.

Tamdhu (p.168) displays the former; Glenfiddich Solera (p.88) the latter.
• vanilla (vanilla pods and essence, ice cream, custard, cake mix, pastry)
• coconut (dried coconut, gorse bushes, suntan oil) • caramel (toffee, fudge, cotton candy) • honey • spicy (nutmeg, clove, cinnamon, ginger) • winey (sherry, prune juice, port, rum)

OILY

The heavier spirits tend to have an oily character, which you'll find in Dalmore (p.70) and Jura (p.120). It also characterizes pure pot still Irish whiskey, like Redbreast (p.212), which use unmalted as well as malted barley.
• butter, fat • cream • crème brûlée
• lubricating oil • grease (roasting pans)
• unscented soap • cheese • leather polish, furniture polish

SULFURY

Subtle sulfury notes can be found in great whiskeys, such as Aberlour a'bunadh (p.21) and Macallan (p.136).
• rubber • struck matches • yeast
• cooked vegetables

Some of the most clearly discernable flavors in whiskey—from sweet vanillins to fragrant spices such as cinnamon, cloves, and nutmeg—derive from the cask in which the spirit was matured.

WHISKEYS WORTH THE WAIT

KEY
NATIONS

SCOTLAND • IRELAND • USA
CANADA • JAPAN

RYE QUAICH CEREALS BLENDS PEAT FE
LENMORANGIE WHEAT HIGHLAND HOG
PETARD RIEDEL TENNESSEE YEAST D
MATURATION BOURBON GRAIN PINC
FASHIONED MALTING SCOTCH DIST
COPITA SWING MASH TUN POT STI
PATENT ISLAY SINGLE MALT OLD
DS PEAT FERMENTATION BLEN
AND HOGSHEADS STARCH CO
ST DRAM RYE QUAICH CE
PINCH GLENMORANGIE W
PETARD RIEDEL TENNES
MATURATION BOURBON
FASHIONED MALTING SC
COPITA SWING MASH T
PATENT ISLAY SINGLE
DS PEAT FERMENTATION
AND HOGSHEADS STARCH
ST DRAM RYE QUAICH C
PINCH GLENMORANGIE W
FASHIONED MALTING SC

Scapa Highland Park

Wolfburn JOHN O'GROATS

Old Pulteney

Clynelish

Abhainn
Dearg

Harris

ULLAPOOL

Balblair Glenmorangie

Invergordon Teaninich Inchgower
Dalmore Benromach Aultmore
Glen Ord Royal Knockdhu
Brackla Strathisla
INVERNESS Strathmill
Glentauchers
Talisker Balmenach Glendronach
Ardmore Glen Garioch
SKYE Tomatin
ABERDEEN

Speyside Royal
Dalwhinnie Lochnagar

CENTRAL
SPEYSIDE

Ben Nevis Fettercairn

Ardnamurchan FORT WILLIAM

Tobermory Blair Athol Glencadam
Edradour Arbikie
MULL HIGHLANDS Aberfeldy

Oban DUNDEE
Glenturret PERTH Eden Mill
Tullibardine Strathearn Kingsbarns
Deanston Daftmill

Jura Loch Lomond Glengoyne
Auchentoshan EDINBURGH Glenkinchie
Glasgow
ISLAY GLASGOW Strathclyde

Arran LOWLANDS

Glen Scotia CAMPBELTOWN ISLAY
Springbank Ailsa Bay
Glengyle Girvan Bunnahabhain
Caol Ila
PORT
ASKAIG
Kilchoman
DUMFRIES Bruichladdich Bowmore
Annandale
STRANRAER PORT ELLEN Ardbeg
Bladnoch Lagavulin
Laphroaig

miles
0   50
0   50
kilometers

miles
0   5
0   5
kilometers

CENTRAL SPEYSIDE

Roseisle · ● LOSSIEMOUTH

Glenburgie
Glen · Linkwood
Moray · Benriach
Miltonduff · Longmorn · Glen
Glenlossie · Glen Elgin · Keith
Glen Grant · Auchroisk
Glenrothes · Speyburn
Dalmunach · Macallan · Glen Spey
Cardhu · Craigellachie
Tamdhu · Balvenie
Knockando · Aberlour · Kininvie
Dailuaine · Glenfiddich
Glenallachie · Glendullan
Benrinnes
Glenfarclas · Ballindalloch · Mortlach
Cragganmore · Dufftown
Tormore · Allt-a-Bhainne

Glenlivet

Tomintoul
Braeval

miles
0 — 5
0 — 5
kilometers

N
W · E
S

This map shows the location of active distilleries in Scotland, which in most cases have the same names as the Scottish whisky brands. It does not include the names of blended whiskies or independent bottlings that cannot be pinpointed geographically. The Speyside region has about 50 distilleries—the world's greatest concentration of whisky distilleries. Another major whisky region of Scotland is called simply the Highlands, which encompasses a huge area stretching roughly from Loch Lomond up to the north coast of mainland Scotland. Further south is the Lowlands region, which has a sprinkling of distilleries. Whiskies from the Islands region are sometimes called the maritime malts. The island of Islay to the west forms its own whisky region, with a clutch of distilleries that make good use of the island's peat. To the southeast of Islay, Campbeltown had a big whisky industry in the 19th century, though only three distilleries survive today.

SCOTLAND

BRUICHLADDICH—ISLAY

GLENKINCHIE—LOWLANDS

FETTERCAIRN—HIGHLANDS

TALISKER—ISLANDS

GLENLIVET—SPEYSIDE

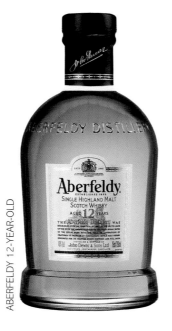

ABERFELDY 12-YEAR-OLD

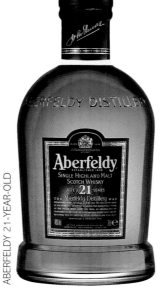

ABERFELDY 21-YEAR-OLD

ABERLOUR 12-YEAR-OLD

100 PIPERS

Owner: Chivas Brothers

Created in 1965 by Seagram, and named after an old Scots song, 100 Pipers was originally a contender in the "value" sector of the Scotch whisky market, where it was an immediate success. The blend contains Allt-a-Bhainne and Braeval, and probably some Glenlivet and Longmorn as well. Seagrams developed the brand very effectively and it has continued to prosper under the new owners, Chivas Brothers (themselves owned by Pernod Ricard). It is one of the best-selling whiskies in Thailand, a dynamic market for Scotch, and is growing rapidly in many countries, especially Spain, Venezuela, Australia, and India.

100 PIPERS

BLEND 40% ABV
Pale in color. A light and very mixable whisky, with a smooth yet subtly smoky taste.

ABERFELDY

Aberfeldy, Perthshire
www.aberfeldy.com

Plenty of malt distilleries claim to be the spiritual home of a particular blend, and celebrate the fact with a plaque on the wall or a large sign by the entrance. In its life-long bond with Dewar's White Label, Aberfeldy takes this a whole lot further: an impressive, fully interactive visitor's center was opened in 2000 and the distillery effectively became the Dewar's World of Whisky.

Although visitors get to see the nuts and bolts of malt whisky distilling, the main emphasis is on the art of blending and the role of Tommy Dewar (1864–1930), arguably the greatest whisky baron of them all.

The distillery was built by John Dewar & Sons in 1898 with the express purpose of supplying malts for the company's blends. The site was chosen for its good, consistent

source of water and for the rail link to Perth, where the company was based. It was also a tribute to the original John Dewar, who was born in a bothy nearby and, according to legend, had walked from here to Perth in 1828.

Having spent most of the 20th century as part of DCL (now Diageo), Aberfeldy was bought by Bacardi as part of a billion-pound deal involving five malt distilleries and the gin brand Bombay Sapphire.

ABERFELDY 12-YEAR-OLD

SINGLE MALT: HIGHLANDS 40% ABV
The standard expression has a clean, apple-scented nose with a medium-bodied fruity character in the mouth.

ABERFELDY 21-YEAR-OLD

SINGLE MALT: HIGHLANDS 40% ABV
Launched in 2005, the 21-year-old has greater depth and richness than the 12-year-old, with a sweet, heathery nose and a slight spicy catch on the finish.

ABERLOUR

Aberlour, Banffshire
www.aberlour.com

Although Aberlour is not so well-known in its homeland, it is extremely popular in France, and it can claim to be one of the top ten best-selling malts in the world. As part of the old Campbell Distillers, it has been owned by the French group Pernod Ricard since 1975. Its malt is used in a great number of blends, particularly in Clan Campbell, but up to half the production is bottled as a single malt in a wide range of age statements and finishes.

The village of Aberlour lies a short distance from the Spey, and had only recently been founded when James Gordon and Peter Weir established a distillery on the main street in 1826. It survived for 50 years, but was then gutted by a fire. As a result, a new Aberlour Distillery was built in 1879,

ABERLOUR A'BUNADH

ABERLOUR 10-YEAR-OLD

a couple of miles upstream, by James Fleming, who already owned Dailuaine *(see p.69)*. What you see today is a classic late-Victorian distillery, designed by Charles Doig after another bad fire in 1898.

ABERLOUR 12-YEAR-OLD DOUBLE CASK MATURED

SINGLE MALT: SPEYSIDE 43% ABV
Soft nose of cloves, nutmeg, and banana. The spicy pear and dark berry palate leads to a slightly bitter oak finish, with sherry and a wisp of smoke.

ABERLOUR A'BUNADH

SINGLE MALT: SPEYSIDE 60% ABV
A'bunadh (a-boon-ahh), "the origin" in Gaelic, is a cask strength, non-chill filtered malt matured in Oloroso casks. It has a sumptuous character of fruitcake and spice.

ABERLOUR 10-YEAR-OLD

SINGLE MALT: SPEYSIDE 40% ABV
Matured mainly in ex-bourbon casks, this has a caramel sweetness from the wood and a gentle nutty, spicy flavor.

ALLT-A-BHAINNE

Glenrinnes, Dufftown, Banffshire
Owner: Pernod Ricard

The building of Allt-a-Bhainne in 1975 is a testament to the post-war success of Chivas Regal. Having taken the US, Seagram's flagship Scotch was busy conquering Asia and Latin America. As sales boomed, so did demand for the malts needed for the blend. This primary blend-supplying role for the distillery has never changed, nor is it likely to under its present owner, Pernod Ricard, which is on a mission to make its Chivas Regal the world's number one 12-year-old blend. To date, there have been very few independent bottlings of the malt.

DEERSTALKER 18-YEAR-OLD

SINGLE MALT: SPEYSIDE 46% ABV
The nose is initially slightly astringent, with malt and brittle toffee. Light-bodied, with pears and ripe apples on the palate, leading to a medium-length finish.

ANCNOC VINTAGE 2000

ANCNOC 12-YEAR-OLD

ANCNOC 18-YEAR-OLD

ANCNOC

Knockdhu Distillery, Knock,
Huntly, Aberdeenshire
www.ancnoc.com

Named after the nearby "Black Hill," the springs of which supply its water, anCnoc is the core expression of Knockdhu Distillery.

With its solitary pair of stills and a capacity of just 200,000 gallons (900,000 liters) of spirit a year, Knockdhu Distillery is no giant. Yet, from this tiny acorn, planted in 1893, grew the mighty oak that is now Diageo. It was the first—and for years the only—distillery built by the Distillers Company (DCL), who preferred to grow by acquisition. It was not until 1967 that the company built its second distillery, Clynelish.

Knockdhu was closed in 1983 and brought back to life six years later by its new owner, Inver House, which has been at pains to preserve the character of the distillery, keeping the wooden washbacks and the old stone-built dunnage warehouses. The traditional worm tubs for condensing the spirit have also been retained; they add a slight sulfury, meaty character to the new make.

ANCNOC VINTAGE 2000

SINGLE MALT: SPEYSIDE 46% ABV
Toffee, vanilla, plums, spicy orange, and chocolate on the nose. Cocoa, vanilla, nutty sherry, nutmeg, and black pepper on the smooth palate.

ANCNOC 12-YEAR-OLD

SINGLE MALT: SPEYSIDE 40% ABV
A relatively full-bodied Speyside malt, with notes of lemon peel and heather-honey on the nose, a fairly luscious mouthfeel, and some length on the finish.

ANCNOC 18-YEAR-OLD

SINGLE MALT: SPEYSIDE 46% ABV
Apples, butterscotch, malt, and honey on the nose, with soft cinnamon spice. Supple on the palate, with stewed fruits, toffee, cinnamon, and developing black pepper notes.

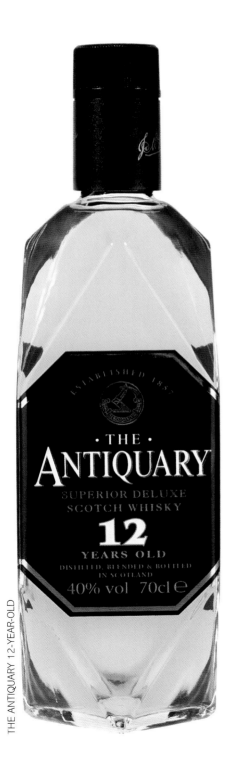

THE ANTIQUARY 12-YEAR-OLD

THE ANTIQUARY 21-YEAR-OLD

THE ANTIQUARY

Owner: Tomatin Distillery
www.tomatin.com

Introduced in 1857 by John and William Hardie, The Antiquary got its name from a novel by Sir Walter Scott. For many years, it was the product of William Sanderson (of VAT 69 fame), but was sold in 1996. Today it is owned by The Tomatin Distillery Company, itself a subsidiary of Takara Shuzo Co.

Packaged in a decanter-like bottle, The Antiquary was a prized luxury blend in its heyday, but sales gradually ebbed, prompting the sale of the name and the recipe. The current owners offer 12- and 21-year-old expressions, and appear to be making energetic efforts to re-establish the brand. New packaging, reminiscent of the old bottle, has been introduced, and The Antiquary features strongly in Tomatin's marketing.

Befitting the blend's deluxe status, The Antiquary has at its heart a very high malt-to-grain ratio, including some of the finest malts from Speyside and Highland distilleries and more than a splash of Tomatin. Islay seems to feature more strongly than previously.

THE ANTIQUARY 12-YEAR-OLD
BLEND 40% ABV

Subtle fruitiness concealing a hint of apples. Outstanding smoothness, depth of flavor, and a long aftertaste. Recent batches may vary somewhat. Other tasters have reported a striking peat influence, new to the blend.

THE ANTIQUARY 21-YEAR-OLD
BLEND 43% ABV

The subtle maltiness with muted peaty notes allows the heather, dandelion, and blackcurrant notes to flourish. A dash of Islay malt creates a truly exceptional dram, as well-balanced as it is rich and smooth. A stand-out blend that deserves to be more widely enjoyed.

ARDBEG 10-YEAR-OLD

SINGLE MALT: ISLAY 46% ABV

This non-chill filtered malt has notes of creosote, tar, and smoked fish on the nose. Any sweetness on the tongue quickly dries to a smoky finish.

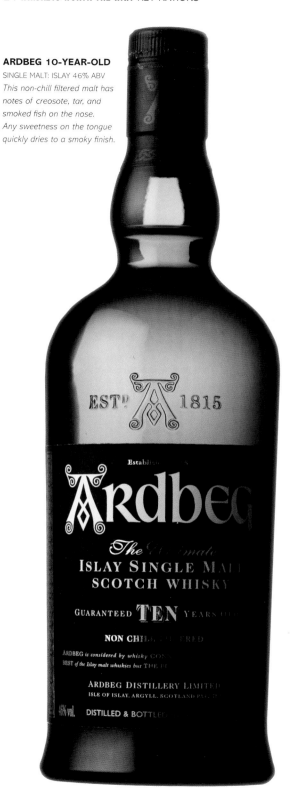

ARDBEG BLASDA

SINGLE MALT: ISLAY 40% ABV

The Gaelic name translates as "sweet and delicious," a reference to a much gentler style than usual, made from malt peated at only 8ppm, one-third Ardbeg's usual levels.

ARDBEG UIGEADAIL

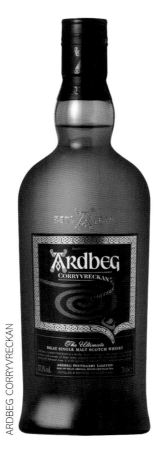

ARDBEG CORRYVRECKAN

ARDBEG PERPETUUM

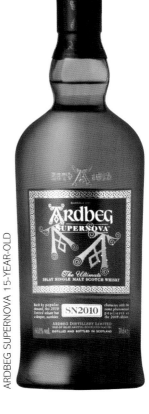

ARDBEG SUPERNOVA 15-YEAR-OLD

ARDBEG

Port Ellen, Islay
www.ardbeg.com

If Islay is the spiritual home of Scotland's pungent, peat-smoked whiskies, then Ardbeg is undoubtedly one of the island's leading disciples. The distillery was first licensed in 1815 in the parish of Kildalton, on Islay's southern coast just beyond Lagavulin and Laphroaig. "Its isolation tends to heighten the romantic sense of its position," wrote the whisky writer Alfred Barnard in the 1880s. Yet, by then, it was fully part of the whisky industry, supplying "pure Islay malt" to the blenders via Buchanan's in Glasgow.

Reliance on the blending market left Ardbeg in a vulnerable position, however, and when "the whisky loch" became full to the brim in the early 1980s, the distillery was mothballed. Its then owners, Allied Distillers, had decided to mainly concentrate on Laphroaig, which it also owned. The staff, who once numbered 60, were laid off and, despite being cranked back to life at the end of the decade, the distillery had an uncertain future.

In 1997, Ardbeg was rescued by Glenmorangie, who paid a reported £7 million and then spent a further £1.4 million on upgrading the distillery. At first, the years of non-production caused problems but, as the gaps in the

inventory receded, the distillery was finally able to release a standard 10-year-old bottling. Since then, there has been a raft of new bottlings, which have added to Ardbeg's growing cult status among fans of Islay's smoky malt whiskies.

ARDBEG UIGEADAIL

SINGLE MALT: ISLAY 54.2% ABV
Named after Loch Uigeadail—Ardbeg's water source—this has a deep gold color and a molasses-like sweetness on the nose, with savory, smoky notes following through on the tongue.

ADBEG CORRYVRECKAN

SINGLE MALT: ISLAY 57.1% ABV
Peat smoke, tar, freshly dug soil, and medicinal on the nose. A mouth-coating,

silky palate, with rich, sweet peat notes, as well as lemon and salt. Peppery peat in the finish.

ARDBEG PERPETUUM

SINGLE MALT: ISLAY 47.4% ABV
Fragrant, leathery peat smoke on the nose, with white pepper, cinnamon, lime, and milk chocolate. Full and peppery on the palate, with vanilla and orchard fruit sweetness, plus treacle and a hint of contrasting ozone.

ARDBEG SUPERNOVA
15-YEAR-OLD

SINGLE MALT: ISLAY 60.1% ABV
Brine, smoked fish in butter, apricots, ginger, antiseptic, and cigar smoke on the nose. The palate is sweet, with fierce bonfire smoke, lemon, orange peel, oak, almonds, and finally peat ash.

The stills at Bunnahabhain on Islay have been left to form a patina on their surface—the natural effect of salty sea air interacting with the copper. It emphasizes that these are no-nonsense, working stills, producing very fine spirit.

WHISKEY STYLES
MALT

The original Scotch whisky—or *uisge beatha* ("water of life" in Gaelic)—from the 15th century or earlier would have been a single malt. That is, a distillation made from barley and the product of just one distillery (or, more likely, pot still on a farm) rather than a blend or vatting of whiskies of different kinds or different provenances. However, it would have been rather different from the malt we know today. It would not have been aged in oak casks but instead drunk almost hot from the still.

The invention of the continuous still in the 19th century created a seismic shift for whisky. It led to the development of blended whisky *(see p. 78)*, and the international success of blends all but eclipsed the category of single malt whisky, which became virtually unheard of. The resurrection of single malts was led by Glenfiddich in the 1960s, though the real boom in interest has been far more recent. Today you can find single malts from many parts of the world, including pretty much every one of the 90 or so active malt distilleries in Scotland. You can also find bottlings from many of the so-called "silent distilleries"—those that are either mothballed and may one day produce again or have closed entirely (stocks can be eked out for decades after a closure). Even in cases where the distillery has yet to bottle its own malt, the whiskies are usually available somewhere thanks to independent bottlers *(see pp. 86–87)*, who buy selected casks from distilleries and usually bottle them as single-cask releases.

By law, a single malt can only come from a single distillery, and to protect the category, the Scotch whisky industry has outlawed the use of potentially misleading terms like "pure malt." Today any vatting of malts from different distilleries has to be called a blended malt *(see p. 172)*.

THE ARRAN MALT 10-YEAR-OLD

THE ARRAN MALT 12-YEAR-OLD

THE ARRAN MALT 18-YEAR-OLD

THE ARDMORE

Kennethmont, Aberdeenshire
www.ardmorewhisky.com

Ardmore owes its existence to Teacher's Highland Cream. The blend was well-established in Scotland, particularly in Glasgow, where it was sold through Teacher's Dram Shops, and sales were growing abroad. To keep up with demand, Adam Teacher decided to build a new distillery in 1898 and found the ideal spot near Kennethmont, beside the main Aberdeen-to-Inverness railway. Famed for producing the smokiest malt on Speyside, Ardmore released a 12-year-old in 1999 to celebrate its centenary. The distillery is now owned by Beam Suntory Inc.

THE ARDMORE LEGACY

SINGLE MALT: HIGHLAND 40% ABV
Vanilla, caramel, and sweet peat smoke on the nose, while on the palate vanilla and honey contrast with quite dry peat notes, plus ginger, and dark berries.

THE ARRAN MALT

Lochranza, Isle of Arran
www.arranwhisky.com

Arran lies across the water from Alloway, Robert Burns' birthplace. This bond with Scotland's national bard has been kept alive by the Isle of Arran Distillery, which has produced a range of blends in his honor *(see p.152)*. It was founded by Harold Currie in 1993, a time when the mainstream whisky industry was closing distilleries as fast as it could. Arran has survived, however, and in 2006 released its first official bottling of a 10-year-old. Since then there have been various limited editions and wood finishes. In 2008, the first 12-year-old expression was released, with the first bottling of an 18-year-old following in 2015.

When the distillery opened in 1993, it marked the return of distilling on the Isle of Arran after a hiatus of some 156 years. That's legal distilling, at least, for there is thought to have been as many as 50 distilleries quietly going about their business in an illegal fashion during much of the 19th century.

Whatever the case, the rebirth of legal distilling on Arran was marked by an impromptu fly-past by two golden eagles during the opening ceremony, and a pair of the birds can often be observed soaring above the distillery today.

Arran's whisky-making resources are somewhat modest— four pine washbacks and a solitary pair of stills—but plans for expansion are already under way. A racked ware-house has recently been added, as an addition to the original dunnage warehouse, and a milling machine has been installed so that the distillery can now produce its own grist on site (previously, it had bought in its malt already ground).

Arran uses water from Loch na Davie, which is located in the hills above Lochranza on the north coast of Arran. The island itself is positioned right in the Gulf Stream, and the warm waters and climate system associated with it are said to be beneficial factors in speeding up the period of maturation at Arran.

THE ARRAN MALT 10-YEAR-OLD

SINGLE MALT: ISLANDS 46% ABV
Bottled without chill-filtering, this has fresh bread and vanilla aromas, with citrus notes that carry through onto the tongue.

THE ARRAN MALT 12-YEAR-OLD

SINGLE MALT: ISLANDS 46% ABV
This expression has an orange peel and chocolate sweetness and a rich, creamy texture thanks to the influence of sherry wood.

THE ARRAN MALT 18-YEAR-OLD

SINGLE MALT: ISLANDS 46% ABV
Floral and fragrant on the nose, with soft fruits and marzipan. Viscous and full on the palate, with fruit spices, vanilla, sweet sherry, orange marmalade, and finally raisins.

AUCHENTOSHAN
AMERICAN OAK

SINGLE MALT: LOWLANDS 40% ABV
*An initial note of rosewater,
then vanilla, developing musky
peaches, and icing sugar. Spicy
fresh fruit on the palate, chili
notes, and more vanilla.*

AUCHENTOSHAN
12-YEAR-OLD

SINGLE MALT: LOWLANDS 40% ABV
*This expression replaced the old
10-year-old and has a dense,
spicy character thanks to the
use of sherry casks.*

AUCHENTOSHAN 18-YEAR-OLD

AUCHENTOSHAN 21-YEAR-OLD

AUCHENTOSHAN SPRINGWOOD

AUCHENTOSHAN THREE WOOD

AUCHENTOSHAN

Dalmuir, Clydebank, Glasgow
www.auchentoshan.com

While Glenkinchie sits among the barley fields of East Lothian just south of Edinburgh, Scotland's other main Lowlands distillery lies west of Glasgow by the Erskine Bridge and the Clyde River.

Auchentoshan stands on the site of a monastery that was dissolved in 1560. Whether the monks moved on from the monastic tradition of making beer to distilling spirits is unknown, but if they did, the roots of Auchentoshan whisky would be very old indeed.

There used to be a distillery called Duntocher here, which was first mentioned in 1800. This may

have evolved into Auchentoshan, which was licensed in 1823 by a man named Thorne. With its solitary pair of stills, it produced a modest 50,000 gallons (225,000 liters) a year until it acquired a third still. Ever since, Auchentoshan, with its triple-distilled malt, has been almost unique in Scotland. This being the standard style of Irish whiskey, it soon caught on among the burgeoning Irish community in Glasgow, who arrived seeking work and respite from the potato famine back home.

Having grown up in open countryside, the distillery was gradually swallowed up into a suburb of Clydebank. This area was a key target for the Luftwaffe during World War II and, on 13th and 14th of March, 1941, up to

200,000 bombs fell on the area, badly damaging the distillery. Since then, Auchentoshan has drawn its cooling water from a pond created in a giant bomb crater. The rest is piped from Loch Katrine in the Highlands.

Auchentoshan joined forces with the Islay distillery Bowmore in 1984, becoming Morrison Bowmore, which is now part of the Japanese Suntory group. In the past decade, the range of single malts has been greatly expanded.

AUCHENTOSHAN 18-YEAR-OLD

SINGLE MALT: LOWLANDS 43% ABV
This is a classic nutty, spicy malt with plenty of age and complexity on the palate and some fruity sherry notes on the nose.

AUCHENTOSHAN 21-YEAR-OLD

SINGLE MALT: LOWLANDS 43% ABV
Despite its age, the oldest standard expression of Auchentoshan is surprisingly crisp and refreshing, with a nutty, honeyed, malty flavor.

AUCHENTOSHAN SPRINGWOOD

SINGLE MALT: LOWLANDS 40% ABV
Matured in oak bourbon casks, its floral nose has canned peaches and whipped cream. The clean palate starts citric, with emerging fruit, honey, and spice.

AUCHENTOSHAN THREE WOOD

SINGLE MALT: LOWLANDS 43% ABV
This is matured in three different types of cask, and sherry clearly has a big influence on the color and sweet, candied-fruit flavors.

AULTMORE 12-YEAR-OLD

AULTMORE 18-YEAR-OLD

AUCHROISK

Mulben, Banffshire
www.malts.com

This modern distillery lies on the main road between Craigellachie and Keith. The site was bought by IDV in 1970 for £5 million, and Auchroisk (which means "ford of the red stream" in Gaelic) was up and running four years later. The principal role of the distillery was to supply malt for the J&B blend, but, after a decade, it was decided to release a distillery bottling as well. This was called the Singleton of Auchroisk. The name was soon abandoned, however, and replaced by a 10-year-old in the Flora & Fauna range and occasional Rare Malt series bottlings.

AUCHROISK FLORA & FAUNA 10-YEAR-OLD

SINGLE MALT: SPEYSIDE 43% ABV
An aromatic Speyside with a wisp of smoke and citrus notes, combined with malty flavors that dry on the finish.

AULTMORE

Keith, Banffshire
Owner: John Dewar & Sons (Bacardi)

Alexander Edward was a seasoned distiller who had helped run Benrinnes with his father before establishing the Craigellachie Distillery with Peter Mackie, the whisky baron and founder of the White Horse blend.

In 1895, at the peak of the late-Victorian whisky boom, Edward built a third distillery on the flat farmland between Keith and the sea. It was some distance from the glens but, in good Speyside tradition, he called it the Aultmore-Glenlivet Distillery and promptly doubled its capacity. He also bought Oban and was then in a position to offer the big blenders a choice of Speyside or West Coast malt.

In 1923, Aultmore was sold to John Dewar & Sons. Within three years, it was part of the mighty DCL. Today there is little trace of its Victorian roots, and Aultmore sits wrapped in its concrete cladding like a light industrial unit from the 1970s, when it underwent a major refurbishment.

In 1991 a 12-year-old bottling of Aultmore was released as part of the Flora & Fauna range. A 21-year-old expression was added in 1996. Two years on, the distillery was one of five sold to the Bacardi company. Over 2014 and 2015 the range was revamped and expanded.

AULTMORE 12-YEAR-OLD

SINGLE MALT: SPEYSIDE 46% ABV
A nose of peaches and lemonade, freshly mowed grass, linseed, and milky coffee. Very fruity on the palate, mildly herbal, with toffee and light spices.

AULTMORE 18-YEAR-OLD

SINGLE MALT: SPEYSIDE 46% ABV
Vanilla, newly cut hay, and contrasting lemon notes on the nose, while the nicely textured palate offers more lemon, along with orange and malt.

BALMENACH

Cromdale, Grantown-on-Spey, Morayshire
www.inverhouse.com

In 1824 James McGregor, like many illicit distillers, decided to come in from the cold and take out a license for his farm distillery near Grantown-on-Spey. It was owned by the family for 100 years until they sold out to DCL. Apart from during World War II, the distillery was in constant production until 1993, when its whisky was available as part of the Flora & Fauna range. In 1997, Balmenach was sold to Inver House, who fired up the stills the following year. A full distillery bottling has had to wait, owing to a dearth of inherited stocks.

BALMENACH GORDON & MACPHAIL 1990

SINGLE MALT: SPEYSIDE 43% ABV
Citrus, grass, and malt on the nose, slight smoke on the palate. Opens up with water.

BALBLAIR 90

BALBLAIR 03

BALBLAIR 99

BALBLAIR

Edderton, Tain, Ross-shire
www.balblair.com

While late-18th-century Scotland was awash with distilleries, both legal and illicit, Balblair is one of only a handful that has survived to this day. It was founded by John Ross in 1790 on the Dornoch Firth, north of Inverness, and sourced its water from the Ault Dearg burn, as it still does today. The first recorded sale was for a gallon of whisky on January 25, 1800.

Balblair remained in family hands for over 100 years. It was then taken over by Alexander Cowan, of Balnagowan, who was forced to close the distillery in 1911. It did not reopen until after World War II, when it was bought by Robert Cumming, who sold it on to the Canadian distiller Hiram Walker in 1970.

Since 1996, the distillery has been owned by Inver House

Distillers, who began with a core range called Elements. This was succeeded by a range of vintage malts in a similar style to Glenrothes bottlings, right down to the bulbous bottle shape.

BALBLAIR 90

SINGLE MALT: HIGHLANDS 46% ABV
The nose is rich, sherried, and spicy, with leather and fruit. Smooth and full on the palate, with honey and spicy sherry. Drying oak in the persistently spicy finish.

BALBLAIR 03

SINGLE MALT: HIGHLANDS 46% ABV
Canned peaches and apricot jam on the nose, with honey and caramel. Early malt, then zesty lemon on the palate, with freshly cut grass and hazelnuts. Finally, white pepper and cocoa powder.

BALBLAIR 99

SINGLE MALT: HIGHLANDS 46% ABV
Floral on the nose, with ripe apples, light sherry, and furniture polish. The palate is sweet and rounded, with fruitcake, honey, and warm leather.

BALLANTINE'S
21-YEAR-OLD

BLEND 43% ABV

The sought-after older expressions of Ballantine's are deep in color, with traces of heather, smoke, licorice, and spice on the nose. The 21-year-old has a complex, balanced palate, with sherry, honey, and floral notes.

BALLANTINE'S
30-YEAR-OLD

BLEND 43% ABV

Ballantine's flagship 30-year-old is one of the world's most prestigious blends. It is characterized by great depth and range, and has a complex mix of vanilla and honey.

BALLANTINE'S FINEST

BALLANTINE'S 12-YEAR-OLD

BALLANTINE'S 17-YEAR-OLD

BALLANTINE'S

www.ballantines.com

Ballantine's is now part of Chivas Brothers, the Scotch whisky arm of Pernod Ricard, the world's number two wines and spirits company after Diageo. The Ballantine's range is arguably the most extensive in the world today, and includes Ballantine's Finest (the standard bottling), as well as Ballantine's 12-year-old, 17-year-old, 21-year-old, and 30-year-old.

Ballantine's was a pioneer in developing aged blends. The flagship 30-year-old was first blended in the late 1920s from special stocks of malt and grain Scotch set aside for many years with the vision of creating

a super-premium product. This remarkable foresight enabled the brand to establish a strong position at the top of the market, which has stood it in good stead despite various changes of ownership.

Relatively hard to find in the UK, Ballantine's Finest has long been popular in Europe, while the older, more premium expressions enjoy huge success in China, Japan, South Korea, and Asian duty-free markets. The range now sells nearly 6.5 million 2-gallon (9-liter) cases a year, making it the world's second biggest Scotch whisky by volume and the top-selling super-premium brand in Asia.

The blend is noted for its complexity, with over 40 different malts and grains being used.

The two Speyside single malts Glenburgie and Miltonduff form the base for the blend, but malts from all parts of Scotland are also employed. For maturation, Ballantine's principally favors the use of ex-bourbon barrels, for the vanilla influences and sweet creamy notes they characteristically bring to the blend.

The Glenburgie Distillery has been completely remodeled and modernized and is today Ballantine's spiritual home. Recently, there has been an emphasis on entering the various Ballantine's expressions into international competitions, and a series of major awards suggests the owners have renewed confidence in the quality of this long-established brand.

BALLANTINE'S FINEST

BLEND 40% ABV

A sweet, soft-textured blend, with the Speyside malts giving chocolate, vanilla, and apple notes.

BALLANTINE'S 12-YEAR-OLD

BLEND 40% ABV

Golden-hued, with a honey sweetness on the nose, and vanilla from the oak. Creamy texture and balanced palate, with floral, honey, and oaky vanilla notes. Some tasters detect a hint of salt.

BALLANTINE'S 17-YEAR-OLD

BLEND 43% ABV

A deep, balanced, and elegant whisky with a hint of wood and vanilla. The body is full and creamy, with a vibrant, honeyed sweetness and hints of oak and peat smoke on the palate.

THE BALVENIE DOUBLEWOOD 12-YEAR-OLD

THE BALVENIE PORTWOOD 21-YEAR-OLD

THE BALVENIE CARIBBEAN CASK 14-YEAR-OLD

THE BALVENIE

Dufftown, Keith, Banffshire
www.thebalvenie.com

Having spent 16 years as a book-keeper at Mortlach Distillery in Dufftown, William Grant finally took the plunge to go solo in 1886 and set up Glenfiddich. Within six years he was converting Balvenie Castle (actually a derelict Georgian wreck) next door into another distillery, using second-hand stills from Lagavulin and Glen Albyn. His decision to expand came partly as a result of a request from an Aberdeen blender who desperately needed 400 gallons (1,800 liters) of Glenlivet-style whisky a week. Glenlivet itself was closed at the time, after being damaged by a fire in 1891. People congratulated

Grant on his romantic idea of turning a "castle" into a distillery, although one customer in Liverpool warned that he was simply adding to the overproduction in the whisky industry—a warning that proved prescient when a slump hit the trade in the early 20th century.

Despite being physically overshadowed by Glenfiddich, Balvenie is no boutique distillery: it can produce 1.5 million gallons (6.8 million liters) a year and has built up an impressive range of single malts, the first of which was officially released in 1973. One early expression came wrapped in black leatherette with gold lettering. Recent packaging has been much more restrained. This is in keeping with Balvenie's carefully crafted image as an artisan distillery

that claims to grow some of its own barley, and in contrast to Glenfiddich. It has also retained its floor maltings to satisfy part of its requirements, and employs a team of coopers and a coppersmith.

The coopers are kept busy by repairing and reconditioning the wide variety of casks employed to mature the varied expressions of Balvenie. Indeed, the distillery's attention to maturation and different wood finishes rivals even that of Glenmorangie.

THE BALVENIE DOUBLEWOOD 12-YEAR-OLD

SINGLE MALT: SPEYSIDE 40% ABV
After a decade in American oak, Doublewood spends two years in ex-sherry casks to give it a smooth, confected, slightly nutty character.

THE BALVENIE PORTWOOD 21-YEAR-OLD

SINGLE MALT: SPEYSIDE 40% ABV
The nose is soft, warming, and creamy, with ripe fruits, vanilla, and a smoky, musky red wine note. Full-bodied, rich, and silky on the palate; subtly spiced, drying steadily to nutty oak, with fruity wine notes on the finish.

THE BALVENIE CARIBBEAN CASK 14-YEAR-OLD

SINGLE MALT: SPEYSIDE 43% ABV
Toffee, orchard fruits, and white rum on the nose, while the rounded palate yields sugary malt, more fruit, vanilla, and soft oak. The finish is medium in length, with gently spiced oak.

THE BALVENIE SINGLE BARREL 12-YEAR-OLD

SINGLE MALT: SPEYSIDE 47.8% ABV

Maple, honey, vanilla, pine, and oak on the aromatic nose. Vanilla, honey, milk chocolate, newly planed oak, and apple on the full palate, which closes with sweet spices.

THE BALVENIE 30-YEAR-OLD

SINGLE MALT: SPEYSIDE 47.3% ABV

The nose features caramel, nutmeg, figs, Jaffa oranges, and spicy oak, while the rich palate offers honey, spice, ripe plums, and supple oak.

ALL ABOUT...
MALTING

Malt is derived from grains of barley. It is the core ingredient of malt whiskey and is vital to almost all whiskies, as a proportion of barley malt is used to produce most types, including grain, rye, and bourbon whiskies. Barley corns are mainly starch. To make alcohol from them, the starch must be converted into sugar and fermented with yeast. Malting prepares the starches in the grain for conversion. It does this by breaking down the tough cell walls and proteins that bind the starch cells, and by activating the enzymes that will later convert the starches into sugar, when the malt is ground into grist and mixed with hot water during "mashing" *(see p.8.)*

FROM BARLEY TO MALT ▶
The malting process starts with raw grains of barley (1). The grains are encouraged to germinate and produce shoots, at which point they are called green malt (2). The green malt is kilned to halt the germination when the starch levels are at their maximum; starch in the resulting malt grain (3) is converted into sugar and then into alcohol through the processes known as mashing and fermentation.

FLOOR MALTINGS ▶
Once the barley has been steeped in water over the course of two days, it will begin to germinate. The traditional method is for the damp barley to be spread out on a cement floor, to a depth of about 2 ft (60 cm). The barley generates heat, so it has to be regularly turned with wooden shovels, to prevent the rootlets from matting.

▲ DRUM MALTINGS
These days, most distilleries buy their malt from large industrial maltings. Here, the wet grain is cast into large germination drums *(above)* instead of being laid out on a floor. Cool, humid air is blown through the malt to control the temperature and, every now and again, the drums are turned by motors so the rootlets do not become matted together.

KILNING ▶
Once the barley has begun to germinate, its growth must be stopped. This is done by spreading the green malt over a perforated metal floor above a kiln, and blowing hot air through the grain. It is important that the air is not too hot, or vital enzymes in the malt will be damaged. Moisture is reduced to 4.5 percent during kilning, which takes about 30 hours.

▲ 1 BARLEY
The most common form used for Scotch malt is plump "two-row" barley.

▲ 2 GREEN MALT
The barley is steeped in water to stimulate germination.

▲ 3 MALT
Once kilned, the grain is more friable and crisp, and rich in starch.

▲ PEAT REEK
If a peaty, smoky flavor is desired in the whiskey, peat turfs will be burned during the early hours of kilning. The fragrant peat smoke sticks to the husks of the green malt while it is still damp, so the fires are kept low and cool. *(See also pp.44–45.)*

FROM GRAIN TO GLASS ▶
Once malted, the barley will have shrunk slightly; the grains are not as hard as raw barley, and their moisture content will have reduced from 12 to 4%. When you bite into a malted grain, it has a sweet taste. The malt flavor is often not at all obvious in malt whiskies, but in some, such as Ardmore and Glenfarclas, the taste can be more easily discerned.

BELL'S ORIGINAL

BELL'S SPECIAL RESERVE

BELL'S DECANTER

BELL'S

www.bells.co.uk

"Several fine whiskies blended together please the palates of a greater number of people than one whisky unmixed," wrote the first Arthur Bell, and his confidence in his products led him to appoint a London agent as early as 1863.

Bell's acquired the Blair Athol and Dufftown distilleries in 1933, adding Inchgower three years later. Today the company is owned by Diageo, which has taken a number of steps to consolidate Bell's position. Visitor facilities at the Blair Athol Distillery (the source of the single malt at the heart of the blend) have been enhanced and the blend itself has undergone continuous change and evolution.

After 14 years of being sold as an 8-year-old, Bell's has been non-aged since 2008. But, in keeping with the spirit of Arthur Bell himself, great emphasis is laid on the skill of the blenders, and the

company insists that, in blind tests they conducted, experienced drinkers prefer the new version.

The famous and very collectable Bell's decanters are limited-edition releases. They were first produced in the 1930s and a decanter decorated with jolly festive imagery (*see above*) has been released each Christmas since 1988. They are also brought out to commemorate historic moments, such as the marriage of Prince Charles and Diana in 1981.

BELL'S ORIGINAL
BLEND 40% ABV
As well as Blair Athol, Dufftown and Inchgower are important components here, along with Glenkinchie and Caol Ila. Medium-bodied blend, with a nutty aroma and a lightly spiced flavor.

BELL'S SPECIAL RESERVE
BLEND 40% ABV
Special Reserve has smoky hints from the Islay malts, tempered with warm pepper and a rich honey complexity.

BEN NEVIS MCDONALD'S TRADITIONAL

BEN NEVIS SHERRY CASK

BEN NEVIS

Lochy Bridge, Fort William
www.bennevisdistillery.com

It is hard to believe that Scotland's most northerly distillery on the west coast once employed 230 people, when it was owned by the MacDonald family in the 19th century. Not all of them were making whisky, as there were workshops and a sawmill too, as well as a farm with 200 head of cattle that fed on the distillery's rich draff. Sitting by Loch Linnhe on the edge of Fort William, Ben Nevis even had its own small fleet of steamers to ferry the whisky down the loch.

It was founded in 1825 by "Long John" MacDonald, who was the inspiration for the once-popular blend of that name. The brewing company Whitbread briefly owned the distillery during the 1980s, before it left the drinks business to concentrate on hotels. Ben Nevis is currently owned by Nikka.

Despite gaps in its inventory due to periodic closures during the 1970s and '80s, a number of older single malts have been released alongside the various Dew of Ben Nevis blends. Since the mid-1990s, the core single malt has been the 10-year-old, augmented in 2011 by the McDonald's Traditional. Additionally, single cask and wood-finished releases appear occasionally.

BEN NEVIS 10-YEAR-OLD

SINGLE MALT: HIGHLANDS 46% ABV
A big, mouth-filling West Highlands malt with a sweet smack of oak and an oily texture that finishes dry.

BEN NEVIS MCDONALD'S TRADITIONAL

SINGLE MALT: HIGHLANDS 46% ABV
Initial starch on the nose, then buttery smoked haddock, a hint of chili, sherry, and gentle wood smoke. Spicy on the palate, with hazelnuts, peat, and stewed fruit. Lingering, spicy cigarette ash in the finish.

BEN NEVIS 10-YEAR-OLD

**BENRIACH CURIOSITAS
10-YEAR-OLD**

SINGLE MALT: SPEYSIDE 40% ABV
*A bittersweet whisky with
a dense peaty flavor. Beneath
the smoke, there are flavors
of tea cookies, cereal, and
some citrus notes.*

**BENRIACH
12-YEAR-OLD**

SINGLE MALT: SPEYSIDE 40% ABV
*More classically Speyside in
character than the 10-year-
old, with a heathery nose,
creamy vanilla ice cream
flavor, and a hint of honey.*

BENRIACH 16-YEAR-OLD

BENRIACH 20-YEAR-OLD

BENRIACH AUTHENTICUS 21-YEAR-OLD

BENRIACH 30-YEAR-OLD

BENRIACH

Longmorn, Elgin, Morayshire
www.benriachdistillery.co.uk

Of all the Speyside distilleries built on the crest of the great speculative wave that ended the chapter on whisky-making in the 19th century, few crashed so badly as BenRiach.

BenRiach opened in 1897 and, after repossession by the bank two years later, became part of the Longmorn Distilleries Company. It made whisky until 1903 and then shut down for most of the 20th century, although Longmorn, just next door, continued to make use of its floor maltings as well as its warehouses to mature its spirit.

Then, in 1965, after a major refurbishment, its solitary pair of stills was fired up again by its new owners, Glenlivet. It subsequently became part of Seagram, who, having no distillery on Islay, decided to produce a powerful peat-smoked malt at BenRiach in 1983. There were still some stocks of this peated BenRiach left when the distillery's new owners took over in 2004. This led to the Curiositas and Authenticus bottlings—the only commercially available Speyside single malts distilled from peated malted barley.

The new owners were a South African consortium led by Billy Walker, the former head of Burn

Stewart Distillers. They paid Chivas Brothers a reported £5.4 million. The deal included around 5,000 casks dating back to 1970. There were no holes in the inventory due to years of non-production and there were plenty of different casks and different levels of peating to play with. This has allowed Billy Walker and his colleagues to dramatically expand the range of BenRiach malts available.

BENRIACH 16-YEAR-OLD

SINGLE MALT: SPEYSIDE 40% ABV
A nutty, spicy Speysider, with a honeyed texture in the mouth and perhaps the faintest wisp of smoke.

BENRIACH 20-YEAR-OLD

SINGLE MALT: SPEYSIDE 40% ABV
The long years in oak have given this expression a dry, woody flavor, with sharp citrus notes and a clean finish.

BENRIACH AUTHENTICUS 21-YEAR-OLD

SINGLE MALT: SPEYSIDE 46% ABV
The 21-year-old big brother to the 10-year-old Curiositas. A mix of peat, oak, raisins, honey, and spices.

BENRIACH 30-YEAR-OLD

SINGLE MALT: SPEYSIDE 50% ABV
A sumptuous, full-bodied malt, full of raisins, candied fruit, dark chocolate, and spice, which linger on the finish.

ALL ABOUT...
PEAT

Peat is decayed vegetation, decomposed over thousands of years by water and partially carbonized by chemical changes. The vegetation itself varies from place to place, but usually includes mosses, sedges, heather, and rushes. For peat to develop, the climate must be cool and damp, the drainage poor, and the ground poorly aerated. As it decomposes, the vegetation becomes waterlogged and sinks, piling up and being compressed and carbonized. Once the surface turf is cut away, and a trench (or "bank") dug, the peat is revealed. Once dug out, the peat is laid out on the bank to dry.

▲ **PEAT WATER**
The water on Islay (and in many other places in the Highlands) flows through peat and is the color of tea.

THE PEATING TRADITION ▶
After the Little Ice Age, which began around 1300, there were few trees left in the Scottish Highlands, but there were huge tracts of peat bog. Peat was the fuel in the Highlands, and remains so to this day in some places, for domestic fires as well as for drying malt and firing stills.

▲ **CUTTING TOOLS**
All that is needed to "win" peat, as the expression goes, is a peat spade (to cut the turf), a tool called a fal (with a "finger," to cut the peats themselves), and a fork to lift the peats onto the bank where they will dry. A small amount of peat is still dug by hand today, but most is now extracted by machine.

PEAT BOGS ▶
Some peat bogs are thought to be as much as 10,000 years old, and they can be up to 30 ft (9 m) deep. Vast swaths of Islay are covered with peat bogs.

◄ PEAT ON THE FIRE
During the kilning of the barley, peat is often burned on the kiln fire. This is best done during the early stages of drying the green malt *(see p.39)*, while it is still damp and sticky.

▲ FRAGRANT SMOKE
The peat smoke adheres to the husks of the grains, which are laid out on a perforated floor above the kiln. It only sticks while the malt is still damp, so the peat fire must be kept cool and smoldering.

SMOKY FLAVORS ►
The chemicals that impart smoky or medicinal flavors to malt, and the whisky made from it, are called phenols, and are measured in parts per million (ppm). Heavily peated whiskies such as Lagavulin and Laphroaig peat to around 35ppm phenols, and Ardbeg to around 50ppm. Peated to an extraordinary 167ppm phenols, Bruichladdich's limited release Octomore is currently the most heavily peated whisky.

BENROMACH 10-YEAR-OLD

BENROMACH 15-YEAR-OLD

BENROMACH 100 PROOF

BENROMACH

Forres, Morayshire
www.benromach.com

With just a single pair of stills and a maximum production of 110,000 gallons (500,000 liters) of pure alcohol a year, Benromach was always something of a pint-sized distillery. It was founded in 1898 and changed hands no fewer than six times in its first 100 years. At one point, it found itself part of National Distillers of America, sharing a stable with bourbon brands such as Old Crow and Old Grand-Dad. Then, like so many dispossessed distilleries, Benromach became part of the giant DCL who, as UDV, mothballed the distillery in 1983, along with many others. This time the stills were ripped out and the warehouses knocked down, and it seemed Benromach would never produce whisky again.

Luckily, it was not just the whisky industry that was in depression, otherwise some wily property developer would doubtless have snapped up the site. Benromach's savior was the famous firm of independent bottlers Gordon & MacPhail of Elgin, who bought the distillery in 1993. A new pair of stills was installed, and the first spirit flowed from it in 1998, when Prince Charles officially opened the new Benromach.

In line with many Speyside single malts of old, there is an element of peatiness about the spirit.

BENROMACH PEAT SMOKE

BENROMACH ORGANIC

BENROMACH 35-YEARS-OLD

BENROMACH 10-YEAR-OLD

SINGLE MALT: SPEYSIDE 43% ABV

Smoky on the nose, with wet grass, butter, ginger, and brittle toffee. Mouth-coating, spicy, malty, and nutty on the palate, with citrus fruits, raisins, and soft wood smoke.

BENROMACH 15-YEAR-OLD

SINGLE MALT: SPEYSIDE 43% ABV

Nutty and spicy on the nose, with dried fruits, sherry, and orange. More orange on the palate, with ginger and milk chocolate, leading into smoky, spicy oak.

BENROMACH 100 PROOF

SINGLE MALT: SPEYSIDE 57% ABV

Fragrant sherry, malt, vanilla, chili, and dried fruits on the nose. Voluptuous in the mouth, with rich malt, smoky sherry, orange, and pepper. Long and smoky finish.

BENROMACH PEAT SMOKE

SINGLE MALT: SPEYSIDE 46% ABV

Sweet peat and cigarette smoke over fresh, fruity notes on the nose. Big-bodied, smoky, fruity, malty, and delightfully balanced on the palate. The long finish tastes a bit fishy.

BENROMACH ORGANIC

SINGLE MALT: SPEYSIDE 43% ABV

The first single malt officially certified by the UK's Soil Association has a sweet American oak character with notes of toffee and orange zest.

BENROMACH 35-YEARS-OLD

SINGLE MALT: SPEYSIDE 43% ABV

The nose is warm and floral, with sherry, cocktail cherries, and faint smoke in time. Smooth, spicy, and lightly smoky on the palate, with orchard fruits, then orange gummy candy, drying to spicy tannins.

BENRINNES

Aberlour, Banffshire
www.malts.com

The original Benrinnes Distillery was founded in 1826 at Whitehouse Farm on lower Speyside by Peter McKenzie, but was swept away in a flood three years later. In 1834 a new distillery called the Lyne of Ruthrie was built a few miles away and, despite bankruptcies and a bad fire in 1896, it has survived as Benrinnes. What you see today is a modern post-war distillery, which was completely rebuilt in the mid-1950s. It has six stills that operate a partial form of triple distillation, with one wash still paired with two spirit stills.

SINGLE MALT: SPEYSIDE 43% ABV

SINGLE MALT: SPEYSIDE 43% ABV
The only official distillery bottling is fairly sumptuous, with some smoke and spicy flavors and a creamy mouthfeel.

BLACK BOTTLE

Owner: Burn Stewart Distillers
www.blackbottle.com

Black Bottle was created in 1879 by C., D., & G. Grahams, a firm of Aberdeen tea blenders. Grahams ran the company for almost 90 years before it was eventually sold in 1964. The Black Bottle brand changed hands several times before being bought in 2003 by Burn Stewart Distillers as part of their purchase of the Bunnahabhain distillery. In 2013, Burn Stewart relaunched the brand, giving less prominence to malts from Islay by including more Speyside-style characteristics, taking it closer to its northeastern roots.

BLACK BOTTLE

BLEND 40% ABV
Fresh oak, light smoke, honey, and a hint of sherry on the nose. Caramel, berry fruits, honey, and more light smoke on the palate, with plain chocolate and drying oak.

BLACK & WHITE

Owner: Diageo

A fondly regarded brand from the Buchanan's stable, Black & White originally went by the name Buchanan's Special. The story goes that, in the 1890s, James Buchanan supplied his whisky to the House of Commons in a very dark bottle with a white label. Apparently incapable of memorizing the name, British parliamentarians simply called for "Black and White." Buchanan adopted the name and subsequently adorned the label with two dogs—a black Scottish terrier and a white West Highland terrier. Today it is marketed by Diageo in France, Brazil, and Venezuela, where it continues to enjoy a popularity long since lost in its homeland.

BLACK & WHITE

BLEND 40% ABV
A high-class, traditional-style blend. Layered hints of peat, smoke, and oak.

BLAIR ATHOL

Pitlochry, Perthshire
www.malts.com

In 1798 John Stewart and Robert Robertson took out a license for their Aldour Distillery on the edge of Pitlochry. In an area crawling with illicit stills, life was tough for legitimate, tax-paying distilleries, and Aldour soon closed. It was resurrected in 1826 by Alexander Connacher, who re-named it Blair Athol. Within 30 years, some of the malt was being sold to the Perth blender Arthur Bell & Sons, who finally bought the distillery in 1933. Except for the 12-year-old and the occasional rare malt, nearly every drop goes into blends, particularly Bell's.

BLAIR ATHOL FLORA & FAUNA 12-YEAR-OLD

SINGLE MALT: HIGHLANDS 43%
Smooth, well-rounded flavors, with spice and candied fruit, and a trace of smoke on the finish.

BLADNOCH 15-YEAR-OLD

BLADNOCH 18-YEAR-OLD

BLADNOCH

Bladnoch, Wigtown, Wigtownshire
www.bladnoch.com

The most southerly distillery in Scotland, Bladnoch has a capacity of just 22,000 gallons (100,000 liters) a year, a figure capped by its previous owners, UDV. This classic doll's house distillery was founded by Thomas and John McClelland in 1817 on the banks of the Bladnoch River and remained in the family's hands until 1911, when it was bought by an Irish company. In 1937 it went bust, and was bought and sold six times over the next few years, spending long periods lying idle in between. Finally, it was taken over by Guinness UDV (now Diageo) in 1985. With the next big whisky slump, its solitary pair of stills went cold once more in 1993, seemingly for good. But just a year later it was bought by Raymond Armstrong from Northern Ireland. The deal brokered was that Bladnoch would never produce whisky again but, by 2000, Diageo had relented and the distillery is now allowed to produce the equivalent of 250,000 bottles a year. Under the Armstrong regime, Bladnoch distilled and bottled both unpeated and peated expressions at a variety of ages. In 2015, the distillery was acquired by Australian entrepreneur David Prior, after a six-year period of silence.

BLADNOCH 15-YEAR-OLD
SINGLE MALT: LOWLANDS 55% ABV
A light, crisp, aperitif-style whisky with a trace of green apples.

BLADNOCH 18-YEAR-OLD
SINGLE MALT: LOWLANDS 55% ABV
This smooth Lowlands malt is bottled at full cask strength without chill-filtration, but is in short supply.

BOWMORE LEGEND
SINGLE MALT: ISLAY 40% ABV
*Dry and bracing, with
a faint citrus flavor that
develops into a smoky finish.*

BOWMORE 12-YEAR-OLD
SINGLE MALT: ISLAY 40% ABV
*Gently aromatic, with a mix of
citrus fruits and smoke on the
nose, which carries through
to the tongue, together with
some dark chocolate.*

BOWMORE 15-YEAR-OLD

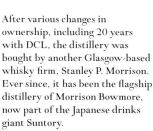

BOWMORE SMALL BATCH

BOWMORE 18-YEAR-OLD

BOWMORE 25-YEAR-OLD

BOWMORE

Bowmore, Isle of Islay
www.bowmore.com

The oldest surviving distillery on Islay was founded in 1779 by John Simpson, who, as a farmer, distiller, builder, quarry-owner, and part-time postmaster, was a man of many parts. Quite how much time he devoted to Bowmore is unclear, but the distillery remained small for years. When it was bought by the Glasgow firm of W. & J. Mutter in 1837, it was producing just 800 gallons (3,640 liters) a year. Within 50 years, annual production had soared to 200,000 gallons (900,000 liters). This was filled into casks and shipped to Mutter's bonded warehouse beneath Glasgow's Central Station.

After various changes in ownership, including 20 years with DCL, the distillery was bought by another Glasgow-based whisky firm, Stanley P. Morrison. Ever since, it has been the flagship distillery of Morrison Bowmore, now part of the Japanese drinks giant Suntory.

Bowmore stands on the shores of Loch Indaal. With the salty sea breeze blowing right into the warehouses, some of it is bound to seep into the casks. As with most Islay distilleries, the majority of the spirit is tankered off the island to mature on the mainland. The distillery has two pairs of stills, six Oregon-pine washbacks, and its own floor maltings, which can supply up to 40 percent of Bowmore's needs. Whether using

its own malt, which is peated to around 25 ppm, improves the flavor of Bowmore would be hard to prove, but to see the whole process, from the freshly steeped barley to the peat-fired kiln and its dense blue smoke, certainly makes a visit to the Bowmore Distillery that much more special.

BOWMORE 15-YEAR-OLD

SINGLE MALT: ISLAY 43% ABV
The deep mahogany color comes from two years in Oloroso casks, which also give a raisin-like sweetness to Bowmore's signature note of smoke.

BOWMORE SMALL BATCH

SINGLE MALT: ISLAY 40% ABV
Floral and delicate, with coconut and vanilla on the nose, then soft peat smoke emerges. Vanilla, honey,

fudge, and sweet smoke on the palate, with a hint of oak toward the close.

BOWMORE 18-YEAR-OLD

SINGLE MALT: ISLAY 43% ABV
A mellow, more autumnal take on the 15-year-old expression, with a waxy, orange-peel flavor mixed with smoke and burned sugar.

BOWMORE 25-YEAR-OLD

SINGLE MALT: ISLAY 43% ABV
The stewed fruit and molasses flavors from the wood subsume the drier, smokier elements of Bowmore, thanks to a heavy sherry influence.

ALL ABOUT...
POT STILLS

To create an acceptable whiskey, the still must be made from copper. The reason for this is that copper purifies the spirit. It acts as a catalyst to extract foul-smelling sulfur compounds and heavy oils, and it assists in creating desirable fragrant and fruity flavors. It follows that the more contact the alcohol vapor has with copper, the purer and lighter the spirit will be. As the vapor rises during the distillation, much of it condenses in the still and trickles back to be boiled up again. This is called "reflux," and leads to greater purity. The amount of reflux depends upon a number of factors. The size and shape of the still is vital, but so is the depth to which it is filled. Typically, this won't exceed two-thirds of the still's capacity; a high fill makes for less reflux. How fast the stills are operated is another factor, with a speedy operation leading to less reflux. The temperature of the distillate is important too—the warmer the spirit, the greater the copper uptake in the condensers. The pitch of the lyne arms connecting the head of the still to the condenser is also crucial, with different angles affecting the purity of the spirit.

▲ **SQUAT STILLS**
These act like a reverse boil-ball and create a similarly complex spirit, without the same level of copper contact as onion stills.

▲ **ONION OR PLAIN STILL**
Large and tall onion-shaped stills afford the greatest copper contact and tend to produce the purest spirit. They are the traditional still shape, and the most common in Scotch malt distilling.

▲ **BOIL-BALL STILL**
These generally take longer to complete a distillation, because of condensation in the ball. But such condensation does not lead to increased reflux, so these stills tend to make a heavier, more complex spirit.

▲ **LAMP GLASS STILL**
The tight neck of the lamp glass still restricts and slows the upward flow of the spirit vapor. It acts like a reverse boil-ball to create a similarly complex spirit, without the same level of copper contact as onion stills.

▲ ASCENDING LYNE ARMS

The more the lyne arm angles upward, the more reflux is created, making for a lighter spirit. The lyne arms here rise up from the stills to connect to a series of shell-and-tube condensers. Shell-and-tube are the most common form of condensers used in the industry today, and allow more contact between the spirit and copper than traditional "worm tub" condensers.

▲ DESCENDING LYNE ARM

A descending lyne arm encourages the vapor to pass quickly to the condenser, reducing reflux. Where these are found on wash stills, the chance of "carry over" is increased, where liquid rather than vapor makes its way into the condenser, spoiling the spirit.

▲ TALL STILLS

Tall-necked stills make for increased reflux, whereby part of the spirit vapor condenses on the sides of the still and trickles back down to be re-distilled. The spirit therefore has more contact with copper, which leads to greater purity and delicacy, but to less "character" than the spirit from squat stills.

BRUICHLADDICH THE CLASSIC LADDIE

BRUICHLADDICH PORT CHARLOTTE PC12

BRUICHLADDICH ISLAY BARLEY 2009

BRUICHLADDICH

Bruichladdich, Isle of Islay
www.bruichladdich.com

Islay's most westerly distillery stands on the shores of Loch Indaal, across the water from Bowmore. It was built in 1881 by three brothers—Robert, William and John Gourlay Harvey, who were also the owners of Dundashill in Glasgow, the largest malt distillery in Scotland at the time. Unlike older distilleries on Islay, it was purpose-built and boasted state-of-the-art cavity walls and its own steam generator.

After a promising start supplying blends with a pungent top dressing of Islay malt, Bruichladdich fell into disuse from 1929 to 1937, the first of many closures that have dogged the distillery. After repeated sales, it passed in the 1970s to the owners of Whyte & Mackay, who closed it down in 1994, seemingly for good. Then, days before Christmas 2000, it was rescued by a private consortium led by the independent bottler Murray McDavid. The old Victorian decor has been lovingly preserved, and no computers are used in the production. The whisky is bottled on site and even uses barley grown on the island.

In recent years, Bruichladdich's core range was joined by a heavily peated whisky, called Port Charlotte after a nearby village, and the intensely smoky Octomore, which took its name from an old Islay distillery that closed in 1852. In 2003, Bruichladdich became the first distillery on Islay to bottle its whiskies on the island. From the heavily sherried Blacker Still and the pink-hued Flirtation, to 3D, Infinity, and The Yellow Submarine, the range of bottlings has been staggering. To date, over 200, many of them in very limited quantities, have been released.

In 2012, Remy Cointreau acquired the distillery, since which date the number of expressions available has been significantly reduced.

BRUICHLADDICH
THE CLASSIC LADDIE

SINGLE MALT: ISLAY 46% ABV
Chocolate, icing sugar, and contrasting rock salt on the nose, with kiwi fruit and vanilla on the palate, plus spicy, brine notes.

BRUICHLADDICH
PORT CHARLOTTE PC12

SINGLE MALT: ISLAY 58.7% ABV
Apple turnovers, soft caramel, and progressively developing wood smoke on the nose. Sweet peat on the oily palate, with ripe bananas and ultimately licorice.

BRUICHLADDICH
ISLAY BARLEY 2009

SINGLE MALT: ISLAY 50% ABV
Vanilla, honey, red apples, and an earthy malt note on the nose. Lemon contrasts with vanilla and honey on the gingery palate, closing with cinnamon and dried fruits.

BRUICHLADDICH
OCTOMORE 7.1

SINGLE MALT: ISLAY 59.5% ABV

The nose opens with a big hit of peat, followed by brine and orchard fruits. The palate is slick and full, with sweet peat, caramel, ripe apples, and developing oak.

BRUICHLADDICH
THE SCOTTISH BARLEY

SINGLE MALT: ISLAY 50% ABV

Baked apples and linseed on the nose after a slightly metalic opening. The body is oily, and rich fruit notes open the palate, with vanilla, spicy hard toffee, and brine.

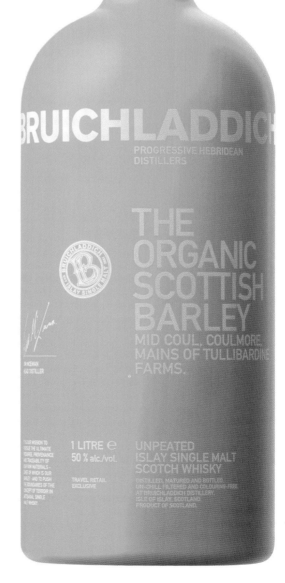

BUNNAHABHAIN TOITEACH

BUNNAHABHAIN 25-YEAR-OLD

BRAEVAL

Chapeltown of Glenlivet,
Ballindalloch, Banffshire

In the early 1970s, when global sales of blended Scotch were booming, the Braeval Distillery was built to help supply the malt to meet demand. Edgar Bronfmann, heir apparent to the Seagram empire, flew in to cut the turf in 1972 and, within a year, the distillery was in production. A century earlier, such a distillery would have created a whole community, with houses, shops, and perhaps even a school. But today's fully computerized Braeval needs a staff of one. Only independent bottlings of the malt exist. Gordon & MacPhail's goes by the name of Braes of Glenlivet.

BRAES OF GLENLIVET
GORDON & MACPHAIL 1975

SINGLE MALT: SPEYSIDE 43% ABV
Floral and vanilla flavors combine to great effect. The finish offers a dry, light touch.

BUCHANAN'S

Owner: Diageo

James Buchanan was one of the most notable whisky barons—the Victorian entrepreneurs who brought Scotch to world attention, amassing personal fortunes along the way. Starting as an agent in 1879, he soon began trading on his own and rapidly saw his whisky adopted in the House of Commons. Today, the Buchanan's brand is showing signs of prospering once again under its owners, Diageo. Mainly seen in Venezuela, Mexico, Colombia, and the US, Buchanan's is positioned as a premium-style blend. There are two expressions: a 12-year-old and the Special Reserve at 18 years old.

BUCHANAN'S 12-YEAR-OLD

BLEND 40% ABV
Rich on the nose, with sherry and spice. Thinner on the palate, with bitter, dried-lemon notes. Winey, with a touch of dry wood.

BUNNAHABHAIN

Port Askaig, Islay
www.bunnahabhain.com

Before the distilleries of Islay found fame for the heavily peat-smoked character of their single malts, their market was not the whisky drinker, but the big blending houses. Many of these used Islay malts as a top dressing, to add a smoky intensity to their blends. The trouble was they only required limited quantities, as too much would leave their whiskies unbalanced. With this in mind, Bunnahabhain, the most northerly distillery on the island, used unpeated or lightly peated malt.

It was founded in 1881 on a shingle beach near Port Askaig. Before the distillery was built, a road had to be laid, along with a pier, cottages for the workforce, and a school for their children. The whole venture cost £30,000, yet the business was making a profit of £10,000 by its second year. The distillery was once part of Edrington. As a consequence, its malt was overshadowed by its stablemates—Macallan and Highland Park. Since 2003, however, it has belonged to Burn Stewart, who are investing heavily in Bunnahabhain's single malts.

The core range consists of the 12-, 18-, and 25-year-old. Heavily peated variants are also now available, and a bottling strength of 46.3% without chill filtration is in place across the range.

BUNNAHABHAIN TOITEACH

SINGLE MALT: ISLAY 46% ABV
The nose offers hot peat, caramel, and lively spices, while peat features strongly on the palate, along with caramel, dried fruits, brine, and finally, smoky oak.

BUNNAHABHAIN 25-YEAR-OLD

SINGLE MALT: ISLAY 46.3% ABV
A relatively fulsome malt with aromas of polished leather and crème caramel. On the palate there is ripe European oak. The texture is luscious and creamy.

**BUNNAHABHAIN
12-YEAR-OLD**

SINGLE MALT: ISLAY 46.3% ABV
*A clean, refreshing whisky
with a scent of ozone and
sea spray, which gives way
to a nutty, malty sweetness
in the mouth.*

**BUNNAHABHAIN
18-YEAR-OLD**

SINGLE MALT: ISLAY 46.3% ABV
*With its richer sherry influence,
this has less of the malty distillery
character than the 12-year-old.
Instead it has a broader texture
and woody flavor.*

CAOL ILA 12-YEAR-OLD

CAOL ILA CASK STRENGTH

CAOL ILA DISTILLERS EDITION 1995

CAOL ILA

Port Askaig, Islay
www.malts.com

Just as Ardbeg played second fiddle to Laphroaig when both were owned by Allied Domecq, the same was true of Diageo's Caol Ila and Lagavulin. For years the largest distillery on Islay—with a capacity to produce 800,000 gallons (3.6 million liters) of spirits a year—had a very low profile. This is beginning to change, as its owners are now promoting Caol Ila as a top-quality single malt.

The distillery was built in 1846 by Hector Henderson, who was forced to sell up six years later to Norman Buchanan, the owner of the Jura Distillery across the water. After just five years, he sold out to the big Glasgow blender Bulloch Lade, who reconstructed Caol Ila on a larger scale in 1879.

In 1972 the distillery was effectively demolished. When it reopened two years later, the only

original building still standing was the warehouse. As demand for Lagavulin began to outstrip supply, Caol Ila's malts were finally given the attention they deserved.

CAOL ILA DISTILLERS EDITION 1995

SINGLE MALT: ISLAY 43% ABV
Sweet, smoky, and malty, with aromatic spices (cinnamon), especially in the lingering finish. The most rounded expression of the core range.

CAOL ILA 12-YEAR-OLD

SINGLE MALT: ISLAY 43% ABV
Balancing the scent of tar and peat is a malty sweetness and some citrus aromas. Oily textured, with flavors of molasses and smoke.

CAOL ILA CASK STRENGTH

SINGLE MALT: ISLAY 55% ABV
Paler in color than other expressions of Caol Ila, the cask-strength version has a strong, assertive character that starts smooth and sweet and dries to a smoky finish.

CARDHU 12-YEAR-OLD

CARDHU AMBER ROCK

CAMERON BRIG

Cameronbridge Distillery,
Winygates, Leven, Fife

Greatly misunderstood, little
drunk in their own right, and sadly
misrepresented, grain whiskies
are Scotch's poor relation. Yet, they
are the essential component and
base of all blends and, when found
as a single grain bottling, the source
of much pleasure. Cameron Brig is
made at Diageo's Cameronbridge
Distillery in Fife, a massive complex
of giant continuous stills. The sheer
scale of grain whisky production
offends some purists but, at its
best, good grain whisky is very
good indeed. You would not expect
anything less from Diageo in its
only offering in this category, and
Cameron Brig won't disappoint.

CAMERON BRIG

SINGLE GRAIN 40% ABV
*Light nose of apples with spicy bourbon
notes. Smooth, fruity palate has grain,
nuts, coffee, and a hint of pepper.*

CARDHU

Knockando, Aberlour, Morayshire
www.malts.com

Having made whisky on the side
for over a decade, John Cumming
decided to take out a license for
his Cardhu Distillery in 1824.
It remained a small farm distillery
until his daughter-in-law,
Elizabeth Cumming, rebuilt it in
the 1880s. Soon after, it was sold
to Johnnie Walker and became the
spiritual home of the blend.

However, at some point in the
1990s, a wrench was thrown into
the works. The owners, Diageo,
had tried to steer Spain's whisky
drinkers on to Johnnie Walker
Black Label as an alternative to
Chivas Regal, but the Spanish, it
seemed, wanted a bottle that had
"malt" on the label. Spanish sales
of Cardhu 12-year-old grew by
100,000 cases between 1997 and
2002, but supply was becoming
a serious issue. Rather than tame
demand by putting up the price,

Diageo took the decision to
re-christen the whisky as Cardhu
Pure Malt, which would allow
them to add in other malts.

Whether Spanish consumers
were bothered is unclear, but
the industry certainly was. After
much outrage, and even questions
in Parliament, Diageo was forced
to withdraw the brand in March
2003 and revert to selling
Cardhu as a genuine 12-year-old
single malt.

CARDHU 12-YEAR-OLD

SINGLE MALT: SPEYSIDE 40% ABV
*This heathery, pear-drop-scented malt is
on the lighter side of Speyside, with a
light to medium body and a malty, slightly
nutty flavor that finishes fairly short.*

CARDHU AMBER ROCK

SINGLE MALT: SPEYSIDE 40% ABV
*Stewed apples, dried fruit, and icing
sugar on the nose. Mouth-coating, with
summer fruits, vanilla, and peppery
spice on the palate. Drying oak and
light licorice in the finish.*

CATTO'S

Owner: Inver House Distillers
www.cattos.com

James Catto, an Aberdeen-based
whisky blender, set up in
business in 1861. His whiskies
achieved international distribution
on the White Star and P&O
shipping lines.

After the death of James
Catto's son Robert in World
War I, the company passed to the
distillers Gilbey's. More recently,
it was acquired by Inver House
Distillers. Catto's is a deluxe, fully
matured, and complex blend. Two
versions are available: a non-age
standard bottling and a 12-year-
old expression with a yellow-gold,
straw-like appearance that belies
its complexity and warm finish.

CATTO'S

BLEND 40% ABV
*The standard Catto blend is aromatic
and well-rounded in character, with
a smooth, mellow finish.*

The Four Ale Bar at the Canny Man's pub in Edinburgh is stocked with several hundred malts as well as numerous objects collected over the course of its nearly 145-year history.

CHIVAS REGAL 25-YEAR-OLD

CHIVAS REGAL 12-YEAR-OLD

CHIVAS REGAL 18-YEAR-OLD

CHIVAS REGAL

Owner: Chivas Brothers
www.chivas.com

Chivas Regal is one of the top five best-selling blends in the world and among the few truly global brands in terms of distribution. Chivas Brothers was founded in the early 19th century and prospered, due in part to some favorable royal connections. The business is owned today by the French multinational Pernod Ricard.

At the heart of Chivas Regal blends are Speyside single malt whiskies, in particular Strathisla Distillery's rich and full single malt. To safeguard the supply of this critically important ingredient, Chivas Brothers bought the distillery in 1950. It maintains attractive visitor facilities there.

Chivas Regal 18 was launched in 1997 and is a super-premium blend. Strathisla 18-year-old contributes to its memorable, warm finish, but is not available commercially anywhere in the world. Chivas Regal 25 represents a further move upmarket, although supplies of it are strictly limited.

CHIVAS REGAL 25-YEAR-OLD

BLEND 40% ABV

The flagship blend, Chivas Regal 25-year-old is classy and rich. A luxury blend for indulgent sipping. Well-mannered, balanced, and stylish.

CHIVAS REGAL 12-YEAR-OLD

BLEND 40% ABV

An aromatic infusion of wild herbs, heather, honey, and orchard fruits. Round and creamy on the palate, witha full, rich taste of honey and ripe apples and notes of vanilla, hazelnut, and butterscotch. Rich and lingering.

CHIVAS REGAL 18-YEAR-OLD

BLEND 40% ABV

An intense dark amber color. Multi-layered aromas of dried fruits, spice, and toffee. Exceptionally rich and smooth, with a velvety chocolate palate, floral notes, and a wisp of mellow smokiness.

CLAN CAMPBELL

Owner: Chivas Brothers

Launched as recently as 1984, Clan Campbell is a million-case-selling brand from Chivas Brothers, the whisky arm of drinks giant Pernod Ricard. It is not available in the UK, but is a leader in the important French market, and may also be found in Italy, Spain, and some Asian countries. Despite its relative youth, its origins are now inextricably entwined with Scottish heritage, thanks to clever marketing and a link to the Duke of Argyll, head of the clan. Indeed, what is claimed to be the oldest whisky-distilling relic in Scotland, a distiller's worm was luckily found on Campbell lands.

CLAN CAMPBELL

BLEND 40% ABV

The malt component of Clan Campbell comes largely from Speyside (Aberlour and Glenallachie especially). A smooth, light whisky with a fruity finish.

CLAN MACGREGOR

Owner: William Grant & Sons
www.williamgrant.com/clanmacgregor.php

This budget-priced blend is sold largely in North America and from Venezuela to the Middle East to Thailand, but not by and large in its Scottish homeland. Sales approach an impressive 1.5 million cases a year and it is one of the world's fastest-growing whisky brands.

Owned by William Grant & Sons, it is primarily a mix of Grant's own malts (Glenfiddich, Balvenie, and Kininvie) and grain whisky from its substantial Girvan operation. The label proudly carries the badge, motto, and personal crest of the 24th clan chief, Sir Malcolm MacGregor of MacGregor.

CLAN MACGREGOR

BLEND 40% ABV

A blend of grain whiskies and some Speyside malt. Light in style, fragrant, with just a little fruitiness.

THE CLAYMORE

Owner: Whyte & Mackay

A claymore is a Highland broadsword. The name was deemed appropriate by DCL (forerunner of drinks giant Diageo) when, in 1977, it attempted to recover some of the market share it had lost when it withdrew Johnnie Walker Red Label from the UK market. Competitively priced, The Claymore was an immediate success. In 1985, the brand was sold to Whyte & Mackay. It continued to sell well for some time, but in recent years has declined and is now principally seen as a low-priced secondary brand. Dalmore is believed to be the main malt whisky in the blend.

THE CLAYMORE

BLEND 40% ABV

The nose is heavy and full, with silky mellow tones. Well-balanced and full-bodied on the palate. Polished finish.

CLUNY

Owner: Whyte & Mackay

Although it is produced by Whyte & Mackay, Cluny is supplied in bulk to Heaven Hill Distilleries, which has bottled the whisky in the US since 1988. Today it is one of America's top-selling domestically bottled blended Scotch whiskies.

Cluny contains over 30 malts from all regions of Scotland (Isle of Jura, Dalmore, and Fettercairn single malts among them), along with grain whisky that is almost certainly largely sourced from Whyte & Mackay's Invergordon plant. Cluny is sold primarily on its competitive price. Under Whyte & Mackay's new Indian ownership, it may be a candidate for further international development.

CLUNY

BLEND 40% ABV

Subtle sweet-and-sour nose, with a slight metallic, bitter tang on the palate.

CRAGGANMORE 12-YEAR-OLD

CRAGGANMORE DISTILLERS EDITION 1992

CLYNELISH

Brora, Sutherland
www.malts.com

A large box-shaped distillery dating from 1967, Clynelish has six stills and a capacity of 750,000 gallons (3.4 million liters). Within its grounds is a much older distillery that ran alongside it until 1983. This was Brora, founded in 1819 by the Marquis of Stafford. Known briefly as Old Clynelish, Brora made a heavily peated malt during the 1970s to ensure a supply of Islay-style malts for blends like Johnnie Walker Black Label. In 1983 Brora closed for good, leaving just Clynelish. There have been various rare malts and independent bottlings from Douglas Laing and Caidenheads among others.

CLYNELISH 14-YEAR-OLD

SINGLE MALT: HIGHLANDS 46% ABV
A mouthfilling malt, quite fruity with a creamy texture, a wisp of smoke, and a firm, dry finish.

CRAGGANMORE

Ballindalloch, Morayshire
www.malts.com

When Diageo launched its Classic Malts to showcase the great malt whisky regions of Scotland, deciding which malts to pick must have been challenging, especially on Speyside, where there were so many distilleries to choose from. But most agree that the decision to run with Cragganmore was a good one.

This was a well-conceived distillery from the start. It was built in 1869 by John Smith, a highly experienced distiller who had been involved in Glenfarclas, Macallan, and Glenlivet. He had a reliable source of pure water from the Craggan burn, which also provided the distillery with power. He had nearby access to peat and barley, and he was close to Ballindalloch station. By laying a short stretch of track, Cragganmore became the first distillery in Scotland to have its

own railway siding, to bring in supplies and carry off the freshly filled casks of whisky. It was a model that was widely copied on Speyside, where distilleries sprang up beside the track like farmsteads in the American Midwest.

Part of Cragganmore's famed complexity as a single malt may come from the unusual flat-topped stills and the use of worm tubs to create a heavier spirit.

CRAGGANMORE 12-YEAR-OLD

SINGLE MALT: SPEYSIDE 40% ABV
With its floral, heathery aromas, Cragganmore smells typically Speyside, but there is a robust woody complexity with a trace of smoke on the palate.

CRAGGANMORE DISTILLERS EDITION 1992

SINGLE MALT: SPEYSIDE 40% ABV
This is double-matured, with the final part of its maturation being in a port cask. This results in a cherry and orange sweetness that dies away into a lightly smoky finish.

COMPASS BOX

www.compassboxwhisky.com

Compass Box is the brainchild of ex-Diageo marketing executive John Glaser. The company was formed in 2000 and describes itself as an "artisanal whisky maker," which may seem disingenuous since it isn't a distiller but a blender, albeit a highly innovative and experimental one. From time to time this brings it into conflict with the industry's establishment. The company's technique of inserting additional oak staves into a barrel to produce Spice Tree led to pressure from the Scotch Whisky Association and the eventual withdrawal of the product. For all this, the company has been highly influential and in its short life has won more than 60 medals and awards. Its limited release "small batch" whiskies sell out quickly.

There are two main ranges: Signature and Limited Release. The former is regularly available and comprises the company's three most popular products: Oak Cross, The Peat Monster, and Asyla. The Limited Release range is indeed very limited: Optimism, for example, was restricted to just 163 bottles.

COMPASS BOX OAK CROSS

BLENDED MALT 43% ABV
Notes of clove and vanilla on the palate accent a sweet maltiness and subtle fruit character.

COMPASS BOX THE PEAT MONSTER

BLENDED MALT: ISLAY / SPEYSIDE 46% ABV
Rich and loaded with flavor: a bacon-fat smokiness, full-blown peat, hints of fruit and spice. A long finish, echoing peat and smoke for several minutes.

COMPASS BOX ASYLA

BLEND 40% ABV
A frequent award-winner. Sweet, delicate, and very smooth on the palate, with flavors of vanilla cream, cereals, and a subtle apple-like character.

COMPASS BOX OAK CROSS

COMPASS BOX THE PEAT MONSTER

COMPASS BOX ASYLA

ALL ABOUT...
CASKS

"The wood makes the whisky" has long been a saying in Scotland, but it is only over the past 25 years that scientists have discovered why the cask is so important. Oak is the best wood (and incorporated into the legal definition of most whiskeys). Most is *Quercus alba* (American white oak), some *Quercus robur* (European oak), and a very small amount of *Quercus mongolica* (Japanese oak). Each type matures its contents slightly differently. The oak cask performs three vital functions: it removes harshness and unwanted flavors (charring plays an important role in this); it adds desirable flavors—vanilla and coconut in the case of American oak, astringency, and dried fruit notes in the case of European oak; and, being semiporous, it allows the spirit to "breathe" and interact with the surrounding air to oxidize, develop mellowness, increase complexity, and add fruitiness.

▲ **INTERACTION WITH WOOD**
The vast majority of the character of mature whisky develops during its aging in oak casks, so the types of casks used are vitally important.

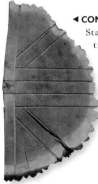

◄ **CONSTRUCTION OF A CASK**
Stave blanks are cut from the tree trunk in a pattern called "quarter-sawing," which cuts across the grain so the staves won't leak. The blanks are shaped so they fit snugly. Hoops hold them in place while they are heated (traditionally by fire) to bend the wood into the right shape.

AMERICAN BARRELS ▶
By law, to be called bourbon or rye whiskey, the spirit must be matured in new white-oak barrels, which hold 44 gallons (200 liters). Maturation lasts for at least two years. The barrels have a second life in Scotland and other countries where they are exported to be used for maturation. Most Scotch is matured in bourbon casks.

◄ SHERRY BUTTS
Butts and puncheons hold 110 gallons (500 liters) and are usually made from European oak. They are seasoned with sherry for one or two years before being filled with whisky.

▼ MAKING HOGSHEADS
The majority of casks used by the whiskey industries of Scotland, Japan, and Ireland began life as American barrels. Having been used to mature American whiskey, the barrels are taken apart and transported in bundles to be "remade" as hogsheads, which contain around 55 gallons (250 liters) by cannibalizing one barrel in five. A hogshead cask will then be used several times for maturing whiskey.

▲ TOASTING AND CHARRING
Burning the inside of the cask causes essential chemical changes within the surface of the wood, without which the spirit will not mature. European oak casks are generally lightly "toasted" to activate the changes; American barrels are more heavily burned, so the surface blisters.

▲ CASK FINISHING
This is the process in which whisky is aged in one cask, then re-racked into another for the final year or two of its maturation to add an extra layer of flavors. The "finishing cask" is most often a wine, sherry, or—as in the case of the Glenmorangie Quinta Ruban single malt *(right)*—a port cask.

CUTTY SARK 12-YEAR-OLD

CUTTY SARK 18-YEAR-OLD

CRAIGELLACHIE

Craigellachie, Banffshire

Although the name of John Dewar & Sons is writ large above the modern, plate-glass still house that sits on the main road out of Craigellachie, the distillery was originally tied to White Horse. Peter Mackie, the man behind the famous blend, built Craigellachie in 1891 in partnership with Alexander Edward. Of all the Victorian whisky barons, Mackie was the most connected to malt distilling, having served as an apprentice at Lagavulin, whose whisky was also part of White Horse. Since 1998, Craigellachie has been owned by Bacardi.

CRAIGELLACHIE 13-YEAR-OLD

SINGLE MALT: SPEYSIDE 46% ABV

The nose is fresh and fruity, with just a hint of spent matches and a nutty, savory note. Oily and sweet on the early palate, with more savory notes coming through in time, plus a hint of charcoal.

CRAWFORD'S

Owner: Whyte & Mackay / Diageo

Crawford's 3 Star was established by Leith firm A. & A. Crawford, and by the time the company joined the Distillers Company (DCL) in 1944 the blend was a Scottish favorite. Although its popularity continued, it was not of strategic significance to its owners, hence the decision to license the brand to Whyte & Mackay in 1986. Whyte & Mackay are today owned by the Indian UB Group, so the future of this venerable label may lie on the subcontinent. Diageo, successors to DCL, retain the rights to the name Crawford's 3 Star Special Reserve outside the UK. Benrinnes single malt *(see p.48)* has been a long-time component in the Crawford's blend.

CRAWFORD'S 3 STAR

BLEND 40% ABV

Spirity, fruity, fresh-tasting blend, with a smack of citrus, a sweet center, and a dry, slightly sooty finish.

CUTTY SARK

Owner: Berry Bros. & Rudd

Cutty Sark is blended and bottled in Glasgow by Edrington (proprietors of The Famous Grouse). The first very pale-colored whisky in the world, Cutty Sark was created in 1923 for Berry Bros & Rudd Ltd., a well-established London wine and spirit merchants who are still the brand owner. The company was looking to innovate with its whisky and decided to produce an original style. The result was a naturally light-colored blend of quality and character, with a name inspired by the fastest and most famous of all the Scottish-built clipper ships.

One of the acclaimed blended whiskies of the world, Cutty Sark uses some 20 single malt whiskies, many from Speyside distilleries such as Glenrothes and Macallan. Maturation and marriage both contribute to the distinguishing qualities of the blend. The wood for the oak casks is carefully chosen to bring out the characteristic flavor and aroma of each whisky in the Cutty Sark blend and to impart color gently during the long maturation. There is a non-age expression and a deluxe range at 12, 15, 18, and 25 years old.

CUTTY SARK 12-YEAR-OLD

BLEND 43% ABV

Elegant and fruity, with a subtle vanilla sweetness. Here the malts used are between 12 and 15 years old.

CUTTY SARK 18-YEAR-OLD

BLEND 43% ABV

Balance of vanilla sweetness and bitter and spicy notes—lemon peel, wood, and coal smoke. A dry, wood influence on the finish.

CUTTY SARK ORIGINAL

BLEND 40% ABV

Light and fragrant aroma, with hints of vanilla and oak. Sweet and creamy, with a vanilla note, and a crisp finish.

DAILUAINE

Carron, Banffshire
www.malts.com

Under the shadow of Benrinnes, a local farmer called William Mackenzie built Dailuaine in 1854. His son Thomas later went into partnership with James Fleming to form Dailuaine-Talisker Distilleries Ltd. In 1889 Dailuaine was rebuilt and became one of the biggest distilleries in Scotland. The architect Charles Doig erected his first pagoda roof here, to draw smoke from the kiln through the malt. The idea caught on at other distilleries. With all but 2 percent of Dailuaine used as fillings, single malt bottlings are relatively rare.

DAILUAINE GORDON & MACPHAIL 1993

SINGLE MALT: SPEYSIDE 43% ABV
Sweet and malty, with spicy notes of licorice and aniseed. Oaky, toasty notes too. Creamier with a little water.

DALLAS DHU

Forres, Morayshire

This late-Victorian distillery, founded in 1898 by the Master Distiller Alexander Edward, was one of many owned by the Distillers Company (DCL) to be shut down in 1983 to await its fate. With just two stills and a waterwheel that had provided the power right up until 1971, Dallas Dhu never fully embraced the 20th century. However, while its stills have never been fired up again, it has lived on as a museum run by Historic Scotland. Thousands of visitors have taken the tour and tried a drop of the malt in a blend called Roderick Dhu. Rumors of its restart persist.

DALLAS DHU RARE MALTS 21-YEAR-OLD

SINGLE MALT: SPEYSIDE 61.9% ABV
Full-bodied, almost Highland character on the nose, with a trace of smoke and a robust, malty flavor.

**THE DALMORE
12-YEAR-OLD**

SINGLE MALT: HIGHLANDS
40% ABV
*The well-established
12-year-old has moved
upmarket in its packaging
and price. It has a gentle
flavor of candied peel
and vanilla fudge.*

**THE DALMORE
15-YEAR-OLD**

SINGLE MALT: HIGHLANDS
40% ABV
*This has the characteristic
rich, fruity sherry
influence, but with rather
more spice—cloves,
cinnamon, and ginger.*

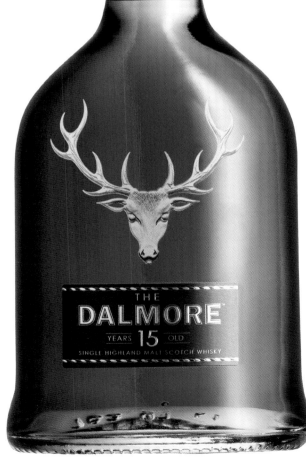

THE DALMORE GRAN RESERVA

THE DALMORE 40-YEAR-OLD

THE DALMORE 1974

THE DALMORE 1263 KING ALEXANDER III

THE DALMORE

Alness, Ross-shire
www.thedalmore.com

While the Whyte & Mackay blend has a long association with Glasgow, its heart lies in the Highlands, in Dalmore on the banks of the Cromarty Firth. The distillery became part of Whyte & Mackay in 1960, and The Dalmore is now the company's flagship single malt.

The name Dalmore is a fusion of Norse and Gaelic and means "the big meadowland." Founded in 1839 by Alexander Matheson, the distillery stands facing the Black Isle, where some of Scotland's best barley is grown. With ample supplies of grain, plenty of local peat, and water from the Alness River, the site was well-chosen.

Matheson soon let others run the distillery for him, among them the Mackenzie brothers, who eventually bought Dalmore in 1891. They were actively involved for a century and today their family motto, *"I shine, not burn,"* has been adopted by the brand. According to legend, the Mackenzie clan saved King Alexander III from being gored to death by a stag in 1263. In gratitude, the king granted the Mackenzies the right to bear the head of a 12-point stag on their coat of arms. This has become Dalmore's official crest.

For years, the only distillery bottling of Dalmore was a 12-year-old single malt, but in time a 21- and 30-year-old were added, together with Gran Reserva (formerly known as the Cigar Malt) in 2002. That year also saw a 62-year-old expression bought at auction for a record-breaking £25,877. Since then, the core range has swelled alongside limited-release bottlings. Many of these have played on different cask maturation, a subject that clearly fascinates Whyte & Mackay's Master Blender, Richard Paterson.

THE DALMORE
GRAN RESERVA
BLENDED MALT: HIGHLANDS 40% ABV
A blend of Dalmore malts. Subtly smoky, with traces of burned sugar.

THE DALMORE 40-YEAR-OLD
SINGLE MALT: HIGHLANDS 40% ABV
After years in American oak casks, this Dalmore was poured into second-fill Matusalem Oloroso sherry butts and then Amoroso sherry wood.

THE DALMORE 1974
SINGLE MALT: HIGHLANDS 45% ABV
Smooth and full-bodied, with sherry notes, bananas, dark chocolate, orange, coffee, and walnuts, and a long finish.

THE DALMORE
1263 KING ALEXANDER III
SINGLE MALT: HIGHLANDS 40% ABV
To make this vatting of different-aged Dalmore malts, Richard Paterson used French wine barrels, sherry butts, port pipes, and bourbon casks.

ALL ABOUT...
MATURATION

Whiskey consultant Dr. Jim Swan likens the change in the character of spirit during maturation to the transformation of a caterpillar into a butterfly: the new-make spirit is the caterpillar, the butterfly is the mature whiskey, the cask the chrysalis. The process of ageing in oak wood rounds off, fills out, and mellows the harsh characteristics of the new spirit and develops a huge range of additional aromas and tastes. However, advanced age is not necessarily a good thing: long maturation in an over-active cask can lead to the spirit being dominated by wood-derived flavors. Moreover, a long period in an exhausted cask will not mature the whiskey successfully, for the wood will be unable to transform undesirable and immature characteristics of the spirit.

▲ NEW MAKE

Fresh off the still, new make—it cannot be called "whiskey" until it has matured for 3 years (2 years in the US)—is crystal clear, fiery, and estery (acetone). It can be quite fruity and drinkable—some is even bottled—but it offers only the merest indication of how the mature whiskey will taste.

◄ HOGSHEADS

American whiskey is mostly matured in new oak, while Scotch is always matured in re-used casks. The most commonly used cask for maturing Scotch is an ex-bourbon cask, which is remade into what is known as a hogshead, or a "hoggie" *(see p.66).*

BUTTS ►

Sherry butts and puncheons are also traditionally used in whiskey maturation. They are usually made from European oak—though American oak is used as well—and have previously been used to hold sherry *(see p.66).*

DUNNAGE WAREHOUSE ►

Cool, damp, earth-floored, and with casks racked three-high, dunnage warehouses are the traditional Scottish warehouse. During maturation in such a warehouse, the spirit's strength reduces but its volume stays high.

▲ RACKED WAREHOUSE

Ubiquitous in North America but also common elsewhere (including Scotland), racked warehouses allow for the storage of casks up to 80-high. In the US, the atmosphere can be warm—even hot—close to the roof, and dry. The volume of liquid in the cask reduces in these conditions, but the strength remains high.

TIME IN CASK ▶

The length of maturation is the single most influential factor in the flavor of the mature whiskey. There is no optimum time—this depends on the history of the cask *(see pp. 66–67)*. Each is unique, and whiskeys of the same vintage and distillery are nevertheless still discernably distinct from one cask to the next.

▲ TAKING SAMPLES

Samples are drawn with a simple tubular instrument called a valinch. Some distilleries draw samples intermittently to monitor the progress of the spirit's maturation.

THE WHISKEY'S HUE ▶

The whiskey draws color from the wood: the more tannic the wood, the deeper the tint. European oak, being more tannic, gives an umbrageous, "polished mahogany" hue, while American oak (less tannic) tints the liquid golden. The more times a cask has been filled, the less color it will impart and the less impact it will have on the spirit it carries.

DEWAR'S 12-YEAR-OLD

DEWAR'S 18-YEAR-OLD

DALWHINNIE

Dalwhinnie, Inverness-shire
www.malts.com

Founded in 1897, Dalwhinnie used to claim to be the highest distillery in Scotland, at 1,073 ft (327 m) above sea level, but it has since been eclipsed by Braeval. Its other claim to fame holds good, however: with a mean annual temperature of just 43°F (6°C), Dalwhinnie remains the coldest distillery in the country. In 1905 it became Scotland's first American-owned distillery, bought by the New York company Cook & Bernheimer, and the Stars and Stripes were raised above the owners' warehouse in Leith. Since 1926 it has been part of DCL (now Diageo), supplying blends such as Black & White.

DALWHINNIE 15-YEAR-OLD

SINGLE MALT: HIGHLANDS 43% ABV
Sweet, aromatic, and subtly infused with smoke, this complex malt is thick on the tongue.

DEANSTON

Deanston, Perthshire
www.deanstonmalt.com

Many distilleries evolved from illicit stills on the farm, others from breweries or malt mills, but only Deanston is a former cotton mill. It was founded in 1785 by Richard Arkwright, one of the pioneers of the Industrial Revolution. The conversion to whisky-making took place in 1965, in a joint venture with Brodie Hepburn, who also owned Tuillibardine. Deanston was soon producing a single malt—Old Bannockburn was released in 1971. Having spent most of the 1980s in mothballs, the distillery was bought in 1990 by Burn Stewart, now owned by South African Distell Group.

DEANSTON 12-YEAR-OLD

SINGLE MALT: HIGHLANDS 46% ABV
A relatively light-bodied Highland malt, with a nutty flavor and hints of vanilla and sherry.

DEWAR'S

www.dewars.com

When it was bought by Bacardi in 1988, the whole Dewar's enterprise was reinvigorated. The brand was repackaged, with considerable investment made throughout the business, from distilling to warehousing and bottling. New products were developed to augment the standard White Label—one of the biggest selling Scotch blends in the US. First of these was a 12-year-old expression, Special Reserve, followed by the 18-year-old Founder's Reserve bottling, and finally an ultra-premium non-age style known as Signature.

The main single malt in the Dewar's blends is Aberfeldy (a visitor's center at the latter distillery celebrates the firm's long history), although the group's other single malts—Aultmore, Craigellachie, Royal Brackla and, to a lesser extent, MacDuff *(see Glen Deveron, p. 80)*—are also used.

Dewar's is not widely available in the UK, but is a dominant presence in the US. It is also important in some European markets and is developing a following in Asia. Bacardi has expanded global distribution for Dewar's and greatly expanded its profile through increased advertising and marketing. Standards of production have been kept high, and some would say that the blend quality has improved, especially in the new products.

DEWAR'S 12-YEAR-OLD

BLEND 40% ABV
Sweetish and floral. A full and rich blend, with honey and caramel, and licorice notes in the long finish.

DEWAR'S 18-YEAR-OLD

BLEND 43% ABV
In the 18-year-old expression, the Dewar's nose is more delicately perfumed, with notes of pear and lemon zest. Soft on the palate, but drying, with a slightly spicy finish.

DEWAR'S WHITE LABEL

BLEND 40% ABV

Sweet and heathery on the nose. Medium-bodied, fresh, malty, and vaguely spicy, with a clean, slightly dry finish.

DEWAR'S SIGNATURE

BLEND 43% ABV

A limited-edition blend, with a heavy share of old Aberfeldy malt. Silky textured and mellow, with rich fruit and dark honey to the fore.

DIMPLE 12-YEAR-OLD

DIMPLE 15-YEAR-OLD

DIMPLE

Owner: Diageo

Launched to marked success in 1890, Haig's Dimple brand is today part of the Diageo stable. However, despite its long and distinguished history, it is rarely seen in the UK, and is sold mainly in Korea, Greece, Germany, the US, and Mexico.

John Haig began operations in 1627, when there are records of distilling on the family's farm in Stirlingshire. The family united through marriage with the powerful Stein family, also distillers on a prodigious scale, and eventually founded a large grain distillery at Cameronbridge, which is still in business today.

Dimple has always been a deluxe blend, noted for its distinctive packaging introduced by G.O. Haig in the 1890s. It stood out in particular for the wire net over the bottle, originally applied by hand and intended to prevent the cork popping out in warm climates or

during sea transport. It was the first bottle of its type to be registered as a trademark in the United States, although this was done only in 1958.

Shortly after World War I, the British military leader Field Marshal Douglas Haig returned to head the family firm. Years spent dominating the UK followed thanks to strong but simple advertising ("Don't be vague, ask for Haig"). Today there are three expressions —at 12-, 15-, and 18-year-old.

DIMPLE 12-YEAR-OLD

BLEND 40% ABV
Aromas of fudge, with woody notes. Hints of mint, and an initial richness on the palate, with candy apples and caramel; spiciness and dried fruits too.

DIMPLE 15-YEAR-OLD

BLEND 43% ABV
In this blend, there are hints of smoke, chocolate, and cocoa, completed by a long, rich finish.

DUFFTOWN

Dufftown, Keith, Banffshire
www.malts.com

This epicenter of Speyside whisky-making was bound to have a distillery named after it, although it took until 1896, by which point there were already five distilleries in town. Within a year, Dufftown was owned outright by Peter Mackenzie, who also owned Blair Athol. He was soon selling whisky to the blender Arthur Bell & Sons, who eventually bought Dufftown in 1933. Now part of Diageo, Dufftown continues to supply malt for the Bell's blend and, until recently, had produced little in the way of its own single malt.

SINGLETON OF DUFFTOWN

SINGLE MALT: SPEYSIDE 40% ABV
A sweet and eminently drinkable, introductory malt. If this recently launched 12-year-old takes off, there should be plenty available—it comes from one of Diageo's biggest distilleries.

EDRADOUR

Pitlochry, Perthshire
www.edradour.com

With a production of just 21,000 gallons (95,000 litres) of pure alcohol a year, this picturesque distillery would have been one of many farm distilleries in the Perthshire hills when it was founded in 1825. Today it feels much more special, and a world apart from the large-scale malt distilleries of Speyside. It became part of Pernod Ricard in 1975 but, as the French group expanded to become a huge global player in the whisky industry, tiny Edradour began to look increasingly out of place. In 2002 it was finally sold to Andrew Symington, owner of independent bottler Signatory.

EDRADOUR 10-YEAR-OLD

SINGLE MALT: HIGHLANDS 40% ABV
Clean peppermint nose, with a trace of smoke. Richer, nutty flavors and a silky texture on the tongue.

THE FAMOUS GROUSE
MELLOW GOLD

BLEND 40% ABV

Subtle sherry, vanilla, almonds, and dried fruits on the nose. Vanilla, brittle toffee, sultanas, figs, and mildly spicy sherry on the palate, which closes with Jaffa oranges and ginger.

THE FAMOUS GROUSE MELLOW GOLD

THE FAMOUS GROUSE ORIGINAL

THE FAMOUS GROUSE SMOKY BLACK

THE FAMOUS GROUSE

Owner: Edrington
www.thefamousgrouse.com

The best-selling blend in Scotland was created by the Victorian entrepreneur Matthew Gloag in 1896. At first, it was known simply as The Grouse Brand, but it evolved to become The Famous Grouse. The company was passed down through the generations until 1970, when death duties forced the family to sell out to Highland Distillers, today part of the powerful Edrington. Sales developed well ahead of the market over the next 20 years and The Famous Grouse increased its visibility. Today, with sales of nearly 3 million cases a year, it is firmly established in the top ten global brands.

Edrington also owns some of Scotland's finest single malt distilleries—Highland Park, Macallan, and Glenrothes. Naturally, high proportions of these whiskies are in The Famous Grouse blend.

The last decade has seen a number of interesting innovations, including The Black Grouse, now rebranded as "Smoky Black." It contains more strongly flavored Islay malt in the blend. Snow Grouse is a grain whisky, sold initially in duty-free outlets. The company recommends it is drunk cold from the freezer, like vodka. A creamy mouth-coating effect results.

THE FAMOUS GROUSE ORIGINAL

BLEND 40% ABV

Oak and sherry on the nose, well balanced with a citrus note. Easy-going, and full of bright Speyside fruit. Clean and medium-dry finish.

THE FAMOUS GROUSE SMOKY BLACK

BLEND 40% ABV

Cream teas, peaches, apples, and jammy aromas. Soft peat and smoke notes on the palate (more so with water), plus vanilla, pepper, and spices, then a gentle finish.

WHISKEY STYLES
BLENDS

A blended whiskey (usually called simply a "blend") is a mixture of one or more single malts and one or more single grain whiskies. The advent of blending in the mid-19th century proved to be the making of the Scotch whiskey industry. Drinkers rapidly adopted the lighter, cheaper, and more palatable blends over the then highly variable and strongly flavored "single whiskeys" and Irish whiskey.

Today, more than 90 percent of all Scotch whiskey is a blend, with brands such as Johnnie Walker, Chivas Regal, Dewar's, Ballantines, and Cutty Sark dominating world markets. In the UK, The Famous Grouse and Bells vie for top spot. Blending was made possible by the invention of the continuous still by Aeneas Coffey and by legislative changes that permitted blending under bond (that is, before the payment of tax on the alcohol). The growth in the popularity of blends was also greatly assisted by the collapse of France's brandy production, following the phylloxera infestation of European vineyards in the 1880s. As a result, whiskey was increasingly drunk instead of brandy.

The first blends were produced in about 1853 by Andrew Usher, an Edinburgh whiskey merchant. His Old Vatted Glenlivet is often cited as the first blend, and it achieved rapid popularity. Charles Mackinlay and W. P. Lowrie were also early pioneers, as were many well-known whiskey houses in the industry today, such as Johnnie Walker, Dewar's, and Buchanan's.

The master blenders are important figures in the distilling business. They are responsible for the selection of the whiskies for a blend—a process described by Whyte & Mackay's Richard Paterson as "90 percent down to instinct and a 'feel-good' factor."

FETTERCAIRN

Fettercairn, Laurencekirk, Kincardineshire

While the northeastern flank of the Grampians is full of distilleries spilling down to the Spey, the southern slopes are now depleted. Fettercairn stands as their sole survivor. The distillery was established in 1824 as a farm distillery on the Fasque Estate, which was soon bought by Sir John Gladstone, father of the Victorian prime minister William Gladstone. It remained in family hands until 1939, since when it has been bought, sold, and mothballed several times. Today Fettercairn is part of Whyte & Mackay, but their main priorities are in the shape of Dalmore and Jura.

FETTERCAIRN FIOR

SINGLE MALT: HIGHLANDS 43% ABV
Weighty, smoky nose of sherry, ginger, orange, and toffee. Palate has smoke, treacle, orange, chocolate, and nuts.

GIRVAN

Grangestone Industrial Estate, Girvan, Ayrshire

The distillery at Girvan was established in 1964 by William Grant & Sons in response to a perceived threat to their grain-whiskey supplies. Today it includes a grain-whiskey distilling complex, a gin distillery, and the Ailsa Bay single malt distillery. Until 2013, Girvan was rarely bottled by the proprietors as a single grain, but now several expressions of Girvan Patent Still are available. Older expressions are generally dominated by the corn component and are greatly softened by age to provide a delicate and refined whiskey of some subtlety and delightful complexity.

GIRVAN PATENT STILL NO. 4 APPS

SINGLE GRAIN 42% ABV
The nose yields citrus fruit and brittle toffee, while the palate is glossy, with spicy fruit. Faint spice and watery toffee in the finish.

GLENALLACHIE

Aberlour, Banffshire

This modern gravity-flow distillery was established by a subsidiary of the giant Scottish & Newcastle Breweries in 1967. The architect was William Delmé-Evans, who had earlier designed and part-owned Tullibardine and Jura. With the capacity to produce 615,000 gallons (2.8 million liters) of pure alcohol a year, there should be plenty available for a single malt. And yet, so far there have only been a few independent bottlings and a 16-year-old cask strength expression from the distillery's current owners, Chivas Brothers (Pernod Ricard).

GLENALLACHIE 16-YEAR-OLD 1990

SINGLE MALT: SPEYSIDE 56.9% ABV
A dark, heavily sherried whiskey matured in first-fill Oloroso casks, which can be hard to find.

GLENBURGIE

Glenburgie, Forres, Morayshire

Glenburgie began life as the Kilnflat Distillery in 1829. It was renamed Glenburgie in 1878 and, after various changes in ownership, became part of Canada's Hiram Walker in the 1930s. From then on, the primary role of this distillery was to supply whiskey for Ballantine's Finest. Yet, as early as 1958, long before most of Speyside began thinking of single malt, Glenburgie released its own bottling under the name Glencraig. In 2004, its then owners, Allied Distillers, demonstrated their faith in Glenburgie by investing £4.3 million. The distillery was completely rebuilt. Only the stills and milling equipment were kept.

GLENBURGIE 10-YEAR-OLD

SINGLE MALT: SPEYSIDE 40% ABV
The nose offers fudge, vanilla, honey, malt, and soft oak flavors. Has a creamy mouthfeel.

GLENDRONACH 12-YEAR-OLD

GLENDRONACH 18-YEAR-OLD

GLENCADAM

Brechin, Angus
www.glencadamdistillery.co.uk

With the demise of Lochside in 2005, Glencadam became the only distillery left in Angus. It was founded in 1825 by George Cooper and, despite various changes in ownership, remained in private hands until 1954, when it became part of Hiram Walker and later Allied Distillers. While there was some safety in numbers on Speyside, Glencadam looked increasingly isolated. When it shut down in 2000—a victim of overproduction in the industry—its prospects looked bleak. But it slipped back into independent hands in 2003 when bought by Angus Dundee.

GLENCADAM 10-YEAR-OLD

SINGLE MALT: HIGHLANDS 46% ABV
The nose is fresh and grassy, with citrus notes and a trace of spicy oak. Rounded on the palate, citrusy and crisp. Well-balanced, with a long finish.

GLEN DEVERON

Macduff Distillery, Banff, Aberdeenshire

While the single malt is Glen Deveron (named after the water source—the Deveron River in eastern Speyside), the distillery is called Macduff. It was founded in 1962 by a consortium led by the Duff family. Much of the malt was used in blends, particularly William Lawson, whose owners bought the distillery in 1972. Since then it has changed hands twice, increased its number of stills to five, and now belongs to Bacardi. Various age statements are produced, and, just to confuse matters, there are occasional independent bottlings under the name Macduff.

GLEN DEVERON 10-YEAR-OLD

SINGLE MALT: HIGHLANDS 40% ABV
Although it is described as a "Pure Highland Single Malt" on the bottle's label, in style this is a classic, clean, gentle Speyside whisky.

GLENDRONACH

Forgue, Huntly, Aberdeenshire

This distillery is the spiritual sister to Ardmore, and fellow contributor to the Teacher's blend. Although William Teacher & Sons did not buy Glendronach until 1960, the firm had sourced Glendronach malts for years. After Teacher's was swallowed up by Allied Distillers, Glendronach was picked, in 1991, to be one of the "Caledonian Malts" —the company's belated riposte to UDV's Classic Malts. A decade later, after five years in mothballs, the distillery reopened. In 2008, the BenRiach Distillery Co. acquired Glendronach, and set about restoring the single malt to its former sherried glory.

Accordingly, some £3 million was invested over a five-year period in ex-sherry casks, sourced directly from Spain, and a three- year program was undertaken to rerack around 50 percent of the entire inventory into fresh, Oloroso sherry casks. Today, all spirit distilled is filled into either ex-Pedro Ximinez or ex-Oloroso casks.

Cask-finished variants have been added to the portfolio along with a peated edition, and vintage and single cask bottlings have become a regular part of the Glendronach release strategy. In April 2016, Glendronach was acquired by Brown-Forman. Marketing and production changes may be in store.

GLENDRONACH 12-YEAR-OLD

SINGLE MALT: SPEYSIDE 40% ABV
This dense, heavily sherried malt replaced the 15-year-old and is best suited to after-dinner sipping.

GLENDRONACH 18-YEAR-OLD

SINGLE MALT: SPEYSIDE 46% ABV
A medium-bodied single malt with red currants, soft fudge, and a hint of cinnamon on the nose. Cedar spice and red berry fruit on the palate. Long, oaky spice finish.

Macallan still has in use 16 traditional dunnage warehouses with earth floors and thick stone walls. The atmosphere is cool and damp all year round, and the air is rich with aromas of whisky and oak.

The landscape of Islay is low-lying and boggy, with plenty of peaty earth and peaty rivulets. Like much of Scotland's coastal peat, Islay's has a slightly sandy texture and sweet, citrus, and maritime characteristics from the mix of sphagnum moss and bog myrtle that produced it.

GLENFARCLAS 10-YEAR-OLD

GLENFARCLAS 105

GLENFARCLAS 12-YEAR-OLD

GLENFARCLAS 15-YEAR-OLD

GLENFARCLAS 21-YEAR-OLD

GLENFARCLAS 25-YEAR-OLD

GLENFARCLAS 30-YEAR-OLD

GLENFARCLAS

Ballindalloch, Banffshire
www.glenfarclas.co.uk

The oldest family-owned distillery in Scotland has belonged to the Grants since 1865, when John Grant and son George took over the tenancy of Rechlarich farm, near Ballindalloch. The small distillery on site was immediately sublet to John Smith, of Glenlivet. Five years later, when Smith left to set up Cragganmore, it was back with the Grants. It gradually assumed importance in the family business, and went on to become the Glenfarclas-Glenlivet Distillery Company in partnership with the Pattison Brothers of Leith, whose bankruptcy at the end of

the 19th century almost dragged the distillery down with it.

Surrounded by 32 large dunnage warehouses, Glenfarclas is no boutique distillery. It boasts a modern mill and six stills. It also claims to be the first malt distillery to have offered a cask strength expression—Glenfarclas 105 was released in 1968. At the time, the industry doubted that single malts, let alone something that was 60 percent alcohol, would catch on.

Since 2007, single cask bottlings from as early as 1952 have been offered in the Family Casks range. The house style is a robust, outdoors take on Speyside, with a greater affiliation to sherry butts than bourbon barrels.

GLENFARCLAS 10-YEAR-OLD

SINGLE MALT: SPEYSIDE 40% ABV
This rich, malty whisky with a smoky, aromatic nose is a nod to the Highlands.

GLENFARCLAS 105

SINGLE MALT: SPEYSIDE 60% ABV
A cask strength 10-year-old. Water dampens the fiery edge and brings out a sweet, nutty-spicy character.

GLENFARCLAS 12-YEAR-OLD

SINGLE MALT: SPEYSIDE 43% ABV
A distinct sherry nose, with spicy flavors of cinnamon and stewed fruit.

GLENFARCLAS 15-YEAR-OLD

SINGLE MALT: SPEYSIDE 46% ABV
The 15-year-old expression was once described by writer Dave Broom as "George Melly in a glass",

for its fruity, over-the-top exuberance. It is intensely perfumed, sherried, and powerful.

GLENFARCLAS 21-YEAR-OLD

SINGLE MALT: SPEYSIDE 43% ABV
A ripe, truffly nose. There is plenty of sherry influence on this earthy, leathery malt.

GLENFARCLAS 25-YEAR-OLD

SINGLE MALT: SPEYSIDE 43% ABV
A fruity, toffee-scented whisky with a smooth, spicy character and a taste of ginger and burned sugar.

GLENFARCLAS 30-YEAR-OLD

SINGLE MALT: SPEYSIDE 43% ABV
The wood is more obvious here: oaky, spicy, and nutty. Slight peatiness in the long finish.

ALL ABOUT...
INDEPENDENT BOTTLERS

Whiskey is either bottled by the brand owner (proprietary bottlings) or by other companies, clubs, or individuals—these are known as independent bottlings. The former are subject to rigorous quality controls; the latter may be more variable, although the "indies" mentioned here all have high reputations for the quality of their goods. Proprietors also have huge stocks to draw from, while independents select and buy individual casks from distilleries or brokers, and sometimes have their own casks filled by distillers.

ADELPHI The original Adelphi Distillery was in Glasgow, and ceased production in 1902. Ninety years later the name was revived by the great-grandson of the last owner, to select and bottle around 50 top-quality single cask malt whiskies each year.

GORDON & MACPHAIL Established in Elgin in 1895, Gordon & MacPhail has been bottling single malts for longer than any other company. The business is still family owned and managed, and still operates from the original shop (*see p. 93*). The Connoisseur's Choice range was launched in 1956, and the company currently offers around 300 bottlings.

SIGNATORY Based in Leith, the port of Edinburgh, and founded in 1988 by Andrew and Brian Symington, Signatory lists some 50 single malts from operating, mothballed, and closed distilleries, which they bottle at natural strength and at 43% ABV. Andrew Symington bought Edradour Distillery in 2002.

Single Cask

NUMBER
ONE
DRINKS
COMPANY

Distilled at
Hanyu Distillery

Distilled 1990
Bottled 2007
Cask No .... #9511
Number of bottles 374bts
Cask Type... Bourbon hogshead,
        finished in Japanese oak

Volume
700ml

Japanese Single Malt Whisky
www.onedrinks.co.uk

Alc/vol
55.5%

CADENHEAD Established in Aberdeen in 1842, Cadenhead is Scotland's oldest firm of independent bottlers. In 1972, the business was bought by J. & A. Mitchell, owners of Springbank Distillery, and Cadenhead is now based in Campbeltown, with outlets in Edinburgh and London.

NUMBER ONE DRINKS COMPANY This company was founded in 2006 to select and bottle casks of distinguished Japanese single malt whiskey, and to distribute them throughout Europe via specialist retailers and bars.

DEERSTALKER The Deerstalker independent bottling brand is owned by Glasgow-based Aberko Ltd. The company offers 10- and 12-year-old single malts from unspecified Speyside distilleries, as well as single cask bottlings in its Limited Release range. To date, these have included Allt-a-Bhainne, Braeval, and Auchroisk single malts.

DEERSTALKER
LIMITED RELEASE

SPEYSIDE SINGLE MALT
SCOTCH WHISKY

DUNCAN TAYLOR The company has been filling its own casks and laying down whisky since the 1960s. When Euan Shand bought the company and its stocks in 2001, he acquired one of the world's largest privately held collections of rare Scotch casks.

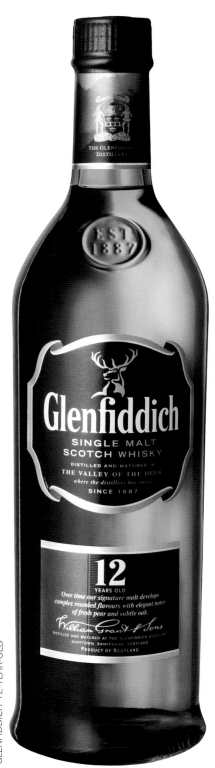

GLENFIDDICH 12-YEAR-OLD

GLENFIDDICH

Dufftown, Keith, Banffshire
www.glenfiddich.com

It was no impulsive decision when William Grant decided to abandon a 16-year career at Mortlach Distillery in 1886 to go it alone. With a wife and nine children to support on a salary of £100 a year, plus the £7 he received as the precentor of the Free Church of Dufftown, he had to scrimp and save until he raised the funds to start Glenfiddich. Using stones from the bed of the Fiddich River, and second-hand stills from neighboring Cardhu, he was able to produce his first spirit on Christmas Day 1887. From these humble beginnings, Glenfiddich has grown into the biggest malt distillery in the world.

In 1899, the distillery almost collapsed when its biggest customer, Pattison Brothers of Leith, went bankrupt. The fact that it survived engendered a spirit of self-reliance in William Grant & Sons. By the time William Grant died in 1923, his firm was already producing its own blends, which were sold as far afield as Australia and Canada. In the same spirit, the company pioneered today's market for single malts in the 1960s. Such whiskies existed, but there was no big brand before Glenfiddich.

To meet demand, Glenfiddich underwent a dramatic expansion in 1974, when 16 new stills were added. Today it has no fewer than 31 stills and a capacity of 3.1 million gallons (14 million liters) of pure alcohol a year. This makes it the most productive malt distillery in Scotland, with significantly greater capacity than Diageo's new Roseisle Distillery (the main purpose of which is to supply malt for blending). Having enjoyed the status of being the world's best-selling single malt since 1963, Glenfiddich was finally overtaken by The Glenlivet in 2014.

The Glenfiddich range includes expressions from a soft 12-year-old up to a luscious, creamy 30-year-old with a trace of ginger.

GLENFIDDICH 12-YEAR-OLD

SINGLE MALT: SPEYSIDE 40% ABV
A gentle aperitif-style whisky with a malty, grassy flavor and a little vanilla sweetness. Quite soft.

GLENFIDDICH 15-YEAR-OLD SOLERA RESERVE

SINGLE MALT: SPEYSIDE 40% ABV
After 15 years in American oak, this is finished off in Spanish casks for an extra-soft layer of fresh fruit and spice.

GLENFIDDICH 18-YEAR-OLD SOLERA RESERVE

SINGLE MALT: SPEYSIDE 40% ABV
A big step up from the 12-year-old, with ripe tropical fruit flavors, a pleasant oaky sweetness, and a trace of sherry.

GLENFIDDICH 21-YEAR-OLD CARIBBEAN RUM CASK

SINGLE MALT: SPEYSIDE 40% ABV
Rich, toffee-flavored malt with flavors of bananas, caramel, spice, and chocolate orange.

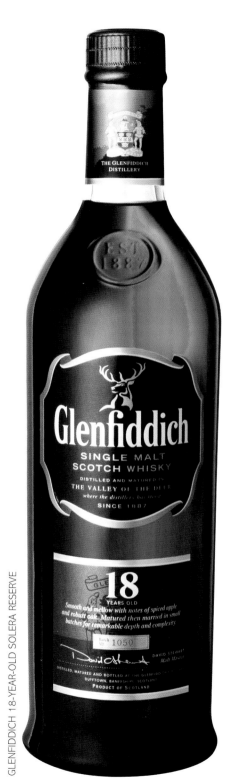

GLENFIDDICH 15-YEAR-OLD SOLERA RESERVE

GLENFIDDICH 18-YEAR-OLD SOLERA RESERVE

GLENFIDDICH 21-YEAR-OLD CARIBBEAN RUM CASK

GLEN ELGIN 12-YEAR-OLD

GLEN ELGIN 16-YEAR-OLD

GLEN GARIOCH FOUNDER'S RESERVE

GLENDULLAN

Dufftown, Keith, Banffshire
www.malts.com

There were already six distilleries
in Dufftown when the Aberdeen-
based blenders William Williams
& Sons decided to build a seventh.
Work on Glendullan began in 1897,
and within five years its whisky
had secured a royal warrant
from the new king, Edward VII.
The distillery has been in almost
continual production ever since.
In the 1960s, a modern distillery
was erected next door. Although
both facilities continued in
tandem for 20 years, now the
modern distillery carries on
alone. Since 2007, Singleton of
Glendullan bottlings have been
available in the US.

GLENDULLAN FLORA & FAUNA 12-YEAR-OLD

SINGLE MALT: SPEYSIDE 43% ABV
*A crisp, aperitif-style malt with a
sweeter palate than you would expect.*

GLEN ELGIN

Longmorn, Morayshire
www.malts.com

Although Cragganmore's position
as the Speyside among the original
Classic Malts is well-deserved,
Glen Elgin must have been a strong
contender. It has always been
considered a top-rated malt by
blenders, and has long been
a key component of White Horse.

The distillery was founded in
1898 by James Carle and William
Simpson, a former manager of
Glenfarclas, when demand for
Speyside malt from the blenders
was at its peak. It was the last
distillery to be built on Speyside
for 60 years. Within two years,
however, the speculative boom had
turned to bust and the industry
entered a prolonged slump.

During its first three decades,
production at Glen Elgin was
intermittent, as the distillery
passed from one owner to the next.
Since 1930, Glen Elgin has been

part of what is now Diageo.
In the 1960s the number of stills
was increased from two to six.
The old worm tubs, which add
weight and body to the new
make, were retained. In 1977
a first distillery bottling of Glen
Elgin was released. The stills at
Glen Elgin were fired up again
in May 1990, only to go cold five
months later. Production resumed
once again in September 1995.

GLEN ELGIN 12-YEAR-OLD

SINGLE MALT: SPEYSIDE 43% ABV
*This is one of the most floral and
perfumed Speyside malts, with a nutty,
honey-blossom aroma and a balanced
flavor that goes from sweet to dry.*

GLEN ELGIN 16-YEAR-OLD

SINGLE MALT: SPEYSIDE 58.5% ABV
*A recent limited edition, the 16-year-old
is a non-chill filtered, cask-strength malt
with a deep mahogany color and a ripe,
fruitcake flavor from its years in
European oak.*

GLEN GARIOCH

Oldmeldrum, Inverurie, Aberdeenshire
www.glengarioch.com

Three centuries old and still going
strong—quite an achievement for
this small Aberdeenshire distillery
on the road between Banff and
Aberdeen. It was founded by
Thomas Simpson in 1797, yet the
first distillery bottling of Glen
Garioch (pronounced *glen geerie*)
as a single malt was not until
1972. It survived the long years
in between thanks to its popularity
among blenders.

One such was William
Sanderson of Aberdeen, who
came across Glen Garioch when
it belonged to a firm of blenders
in Leith. In 1886 he bought a half
share in the distillery, and by
1921 his son, together with other
investors, had full control of the
business. After numerous changes
in ownership since, and extended
periods of lying idle, Glen Garioch
is now part of Morrison Bowmore,

GLEN GARIOCH 12-YEAR-OLD

GLEN GARIOCH VIRGIN OAK

which bottles most of the distillery's limited production as a single malt.

GLEN GARIOCH FOUNDER'S RESERVE

SINGLE MALT: HIGHLANDS 48% ABV
Pears, peaches, and apricots on the nose, plus butterscotch and vanilla. Relatively full-bodied, with a palate of vanilla, malt, melon, and subtle smoke.

GLEN GARIOCH 12-YEAR-OLD

SINGLE MALT: HIGHLANDS 48% ABV
The nose yields peaches, pineapple, malt, vanilla, and light sherry. Full-bodied with orchard fruits on the palate, plus spicy toffee and ultimately drying oak.

GLEN GARIOCH VIRGIN OAK

SINGLE MALT: HIGHLANDS 48% ABV
Ripe peaches on the nose, spicy oak, vanilla, and developing floral notes. The palate yields malt, milk chocolate, nougat, orange, and a hint of cloves.

GLENGLASSAUGH

Portsoy, Banffshire
www.glenglassaugh.com

Glenglassaugh was founded by Aberdeenshire entrepreneur James Moir in the 1870s at a cost of £10,000. Although it was also renovated and expanded, it was sold for only £15,000 20 years later, when it was bought by the blender Robertson & Baxter, now called Edrington. The distillery has had periodic bursts of production, but has spent much of its life in mothballs. When its stills went cold before the millennium, many feared that Glenglassaugh was doomed. It was rescued by a private consortium, however, and was reopened in 2008. Glenglassaugh is now owned by Brown-Forman.

GLENGLASSAUGH EVOLUTION

SINGLE MALT: HIGHLANDS 57.2% ABV
The nose offers toffee, ginger, peaches, and vanilla. Orchard fruits, caramel, and coconut on the palate.

WHISKY TOUR: SPEYSIDE

Speyside boasts the greatest concentration of distilleries in the world and thus is a "must see" for all whisky lovers. The concept of the distillery tour was also pioneered here, when William Grant & Sons first opened Glenfiddich to the public in 1969. Its competitors laughed, but soon opened their own centers. Today, Speyside hosts two whisky festivals each year, in May and September, with special events and tastings. Discount bus and taxi travel is available during festival times. Two accommodation options favored by whisky fans are the Highlander Inn in Craigellachie and The Mash Tun in Aberlour.

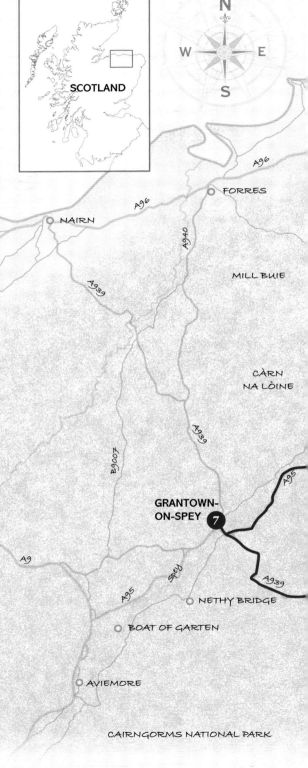

SCOTLAND

TOUR STATISTICS		
DAYS: 3	**LENGTH:** 90 miles (145 km)	**DISTILLERIES:** 5
TRAVEL: Car, or bus and taxi	**REGION:** Banffshire and Moray, Scotland	

DAY 1: GLENFIDDICH, THE BALVENIE

1 Begin at Dufftown's **Glenfiddich,** the ultimate home of whisky tourism. The makers of the world's most popular single malt offer a free tour or, like a number of their competitors, an option with extended tastings at extra cost. You need to pre-book for the extended tour, which lasts for two and a half hours. (*www.glenfiddich.com*)

GLENFIDDICH STILLS

2 After lunch at the Glenfiddich café, you can stroll down the hill to sister distillery **The Balvenie** (*www.thebalvenie. com*). The three-hour guided tour here, which must also be pre-booked, includes the floor maltings and tastings of exclusive vintages. You can also bottle your own whisky straight from the cask. If time permits after the tour, head to Dufftown's well-stocked Whisky Shop.

THE BALVENIE

DAY 2: COOPERAGE, ABERLOUR, THE MACALLAN, CARDHU

3 Start the day at the **Speyside Cooperage.** There you can watch a film about cask-making and see the the coopers at work from a viewing gallery. *(www.speysidecooperage.co.uk)*

4 **Aberlour** Distillery is the next stop and, again, pre-booking is advisable. The tour culminates in a tasting and the chance to bottle your own. *(www.aberlour.com/distillery)*

ABERLOUR CASKS

5 Head over the Spey, pausing to admire the Thomas Telford bridge (1812), then take the B9102 to **The Macallan.** Its "Precious Tour" is the one to pre-book for its tutored nosing and tasting of a range of Macallan whiskies. *(www.themacallan.com)*

6 **Cardhu** Distillery is further along the B9102, which you can visit without pre-booking. The malt made here is used in Johnnie Walker blends. *(www.discovering-distilleries.com/cardhu)*

DAY 3: GRANTOWN-ON-SPEY, THE WHISKY CASTLE, THE GLENLIVET, GORDON & MACPHAIL

7 **Grantown-on-Spey** is the gateway to the Cairngorms National Park. It's a handy place to pick up provisions, and has a good little whisky shop on the High Street called the Wee Spey Dram.

8 Head east from Grantown to get to Tomintoul, where **The Whisky Castle** shop has an excellent selection of Scotch malts. *(www.whiskycastle.com)*

9 Pre-register on **The Glenlivet** website as a "Guardian" to gain access to a secret room where you can enjoy some unusual drams. The free tour is a good introduction to the oldest legal distillery in Speyside; better still is its three-day Whisky School. *(www.theglenlivet.com)*

SHOP SIGN

THE WHISKY CASTLE

10 The final stop on this tour is a place of pilgrimage for serious whisky fans: the **Gordon & MacPhail** shop in Elgin. Here you'll find all your favorites, some rare bottles, and exceptional value in G&M's own bottlings from their vast stock of whiskies laid down over many years. *(www.gordonandmacphail.com)*

GORDON & MACPHAIL

LOSSIEMOUTH

FINISH

10 GORDON & MACPHAIL

A96

A98

A96

Spey

A941

MORAY

A95

THE MACALLAN

CRAIGELLACHIE

B9102

5

SPEYSIDE COOPERAGE

3

2 THE BALVENIE

6 CARDHU

1 GLENFIDDICH

A920

A95

4 ABERLOUR

DUFFTOWN

START

A941

BANFFSHIRE

9 THE GLENLIVET

B9008

CAIRNGORMS NATIONAL PARK

8 THE WHISKY CASTLE

A939

miles
0   5
0   5
kilometres

GLENGOYNE 12-YEAR-OLD CASK STRENGTH

GLENGOYNE 10-YEAR-OLD

GLENGOYNE 18-YEAR-OLD

GLENGOYNE 21-YEAR-OLD

GLENGOYNE

Drumgoyne, Stirlingshire
www.glengoyne.com

The Campsie Fells were once a hotbed of whisky smuggling. Before the Excise Act of 1823, there were at least 18 illicit distillers in this corner of Stirlingshire. Among them was probably George Connell, who finally took out a license for his Burnfoot Distillery in 1833. It went on to become Glenguin and eventually Glengoyne in 1905.

By then the distillery was owned by the blending house of Lang Brothers, who were bought out in the 1960s by Robertson & Baxter, now Edrington. In 2001, it released a novel expression of Glengoyne, involving the first ever use of Scottish oak casks.

Two years later, the distillery was sold to the blender and bottler Ian MacLeod & Co. The number of single malts has grown dramatically and includes single cask bottlings alongside the core range.

GLENGOYNE 12-YEAR-OLD CASK STRENGTH

SINGLE MALT: HIGHLANDS 57.2% ABV
Non-chill filtered and bottled at cask strength, it has a lightly sweet nose, with notes of heather, pear drops, and marzipan. Malty, cereal palate, seasoned with black pepper.

GLENGOYNE 10-YEAR-OLD

SINGLE MALT: HIGHLANDS 40% ABV
This unpeated whisky has a clean, grassy aroma, with a nutty sweetness that comes through on the palate.

GLENGOYNE 18-YEAR-OLD

SINGLE MALT: HIGHLANDS 43% ABV
Milk chocolate, vanilla, melon, and grapefruit on the nose. The palate is rich, with cinnamon and ginger, almonds, and orange marmalade.

GLENGOYNE 21-YEAR-OLD

SINGLE MALT: HIGHLANDS 43% ABV
This is a rich, after-dinner malt, with notes of brandy butter, cinnamon, and sweet spice.

The Spey gives its name to Scotland's best-known and most productive whisky region, Speyside. Winter is traditionally the season for whisky-making here.

GLEN GRANT SINGLE MALT

GLEN GRANT 12-YEAR-OLD NON-CHILL FILTERED

GLEN GRANT 18-YEAR-OLD

GLEN GRANT

Rothes, Morayshire
www.glengrant.com

There is something solid and baronial about the Glen Grant Distillery on Speyside. It was the first of the five distilleries in the town of Rothes, built in 1840 from red sandstone, with a pair of pepperpot turrets.

It was founded by James Grant, a lawyer in Elgin, and his brother, John, a grain merchant who is said to have learned about whisky-making from supplying all the illicit distillers in the area.

It was a very good site for a distillery, with the Glen Grant burn supplying water for the mash and to power the machinery. There were plentiful supplies of grain too, from the barley fields of nearby Moray. And, from 1858, when the first train steamed into Rothes, there was also the railway to carry off the filled casks and bring back the empties.

In 1872, James Grant's son took over the business. Known to all as "The Major," permanently clad in tweed and with a bristling walrus mustache, he was very much the quintessential Victorian gent. After dining, he would take guests to a narrow ravine in the garden and unlock a safe secreted in the rock to produce a tray of glasses and a bottle of Glen Grant. For anyone requiring water, they had only to dip their glass into the fast-flowing waters of the nearby stream.

The distillery remained in family hands until 1977 when it was sold to Seagrams. Soon afterward, an Italian visitor persuaded the owners to sell him some cases of Glen Grant 5-year-old, which went on to become Italy's biggest-selling brand of Scotch. Having passed through the hands of Pernod Ricard in 2001–2006, it is now with the Italian Campari group. Though it receives little attention at home, it is one of the top five best-selling malts in the world.

GLEN GRANT 10-YEAR-OLD

SINGLE MALT: SPEYSIDE 40% ABV
A relatively dry nose with the scent of orchard fruit. Light to medium body with a cereal, nutty flavor.

GLEN GRANT 12-YEAR-OLD NON-CHILL FILTERED

SINGLE MALT: SPEYSIDE 48% ABV
Malt, caramel, and bright, fresh fruits on the vibrant nose. The palate is nicely textured, with sweet apple, more caramel, and light spices.

GLEN GRANT 18-YEAR-OLD

SINGLE MALT: SPEYSIDE 43% ABV
The nose is fresh and fruity, but with added depth and greater fragrance compared to younger expressions. Full and rich on the fruity palate, with milk chocolate, sweet spices, brittle toffee, and a hint of creamy oak.

GLEN KEITH

Keith, Banffshire

Having bought Strathisla in 1950, Seagram built Glen Keith on the site of an old grain mill seven years later. Both are in Keith and were part of Seagram's whisky arm, Chivas Brothers (now part of Pernod Ricard). Both also shared a simple function—to supply the company's best-selling brands. Glen Keith began life using triple distillation and later pioneered the use of computers in its whisky-making at a time when some distilleries had only recently joined the national power grid.

Glen Keith was mothballed in 2000, but reopened in 2013 after major refurbishment.

GLEN KEITH 19-YEAR-OLD CASK STRENGTH

SINGLE MALT: SPEYSIDE 56.3% ABV
Banana-toffee pie, ginger, and raisins on the nose. The viscous palate yields sherry, fudge, and white pepper.

GLENKINCHIE 12-YEAR-OLD

GLENKINCHIE 20-YEAR-OLD

GLENKINCHIE DISTILLERS EDITION 1991

GLENKINCHIE

Pencaitland, Trenent, East Lothian
www.malts.com

Robert Burns described the rolling farmland south of Edinburgh as "the most glorious corn [grain] country I have ever seen," and it was here at Pencaitland that John and George Rate founded Glenkinchie in 1825. It was originally the Milton Distillery and struggled in its early years, spending much of the second half of the 19th century as a saw mill. In 1881 it was rescued by an Edinburgh brewer and a couple of wine merchants, who transformed it into a highly efficient whisky-making machine, with everything from mechanical rakes in the mash tun to its own railway siding. The grain came from the surrounding fields, and the draff was fed to the Aberdeen Angus cattle on site.

In modern times the most important date was probably 1988, when the Glenkinchie 10-year-old was picked as one of the original Classic Malts by Diageo.

GLENKINCHIE 12-YEAR-OLD

SINGLE MALT: LOWLANDS 43% ABV
The nose reveals a sweet, grassy aroma with a faint wisp of smoke. In the mouth it has a firm, cereal flavor and a touch of spice at the end.

GLENKINCHIE 20-YEAR-OLD

SINGLE MALT: LOWLANDS 58.4% ABV
Aged in bourbon casks and then reracked into brandy barrels, the 20-year-old has a luscious, mouth-coating texture and plenty of spicy, stewed fruit flavors.

GLENKINCHIE
DISTILLERS EDITION 1991

SINGLE MALT: LOWLANDS 43% ABV
The malty flavor of tea cookies is well balanced by the drier, oaky flavors from the wood, and these linger to a long, slow finish.

THE GLENLIVET XXV

SINGLE MALT: SPEYSIDE 43% ABV

This 25-year-old is a sumptuous after-dinner malt of real complexity, with flavors of candied orange peel and raisins and an intense nutty, spicy character.

THE GLENLIVET FOUNDER'S RESERVE

SINGLE MALT: SPEYSIDE 40% ABV

The nose is fresh and floral, with ripe pears, pineapple, tangerines, honey, and vanilla. Medium-bodied, with gingersnaps, soft toffee, and tropical fruit on the smooth, softly spiced palate.

THE GLENLIVET FRENCH OAK RESERVE 15-YEAR-OLD

THE GLENLIVET 18-YEAR-OLD

THE GLENLIVET ARCHIVE 21-YEAR-OLD

THE GLENLIVET

Ballindalloch, Banffshire
www.theglenlivet.com

In the early 19th century, before the Excise Act lured so many distillers to come in from the cold and take out a license, Glenlivet was a one-industry glen dedicated to making moonshine after the harvest. It was said that there were at least 200 illicit stills in this small corner of Speyside. Doubtless among them was George Smith, who made whisky on the side at his Upper Drummin farm. In 1824 he established Glenlivet as a licensed distillery there. But breaking ranks with the smuggling fraternity meant that, from then on, Smith had to carry hair-trigger revolvers for his protection.

Smith began supplying Andrew Usher in Edinburgh, who bottled a prototype blend, Old Vatted Glenlivet, in 1853. As blended Scotch took off toward the end of the 19th century, demand for "Glenlivet-style" malts to feed the blends also soared. This encouraged distillers all down the Spey to bolt the magic name "Glenlivet" to their distillery and hope the blenders beat a path to their door.

Glenlivet's current owner—the French giant Pernod Ricard, who bought it from Seagram in 2001, along with Chivas Regal and a host of other whisky brands and distilleries—set about restoring its good name: although always strong in the US, Glenlivet had been somewhat neglected in other markets.

The core range of malts has been dusted off, expanded, and repackaged, while new expressions such as Nadurra Cask Strength Glenlivet have been launched in duty-free markets and regular retail.

During 2009 and 2010, the capacity of Glenlivet was dramatically increased to 2.3 million gallons (10.5 million liters) per year, as Pernod's whisky division, Chivas Brothers, sought to overtake Glenfiddich as the world's best-selling single malt. That ambition was finally achieved in 2014.

THE GLENLIVET FRENCH OAK RESERVE 15-YEAR-OLD

SINGLE MALT: SPEYSIDE 40% ABV
A smoother, richer take on the 12-year-old, with a malty, strawberries-and-cream flavor laced with a little spice.

THE GLENLIVET 18-YEAR-OLD

SINGLE MALT: SPEYSIDE 43% ABV
Far more depth and character than the standard 12-year-old. Honeyed, fragrant, and dries to a long, nutty finish.

THE GLENLIVET ARCHIVE 21-YEAR-OLD

SINGLE MALT: SPEYSIDE 43% ABV
A distinctly smooth and richly fruity whisky. Malty, toasty flavors, an almond sweetness, and a touch of fresh orange. A long, slightly smoky finish.

GLENMORANGIE ORIGINAL

GLENMORANGIE 18-YEAR-OLD

GLENMORANGIE 25-YEAR-OLD

GLENLOSSIE

Elgin, Morayshire
www.malts.com

Glenlossie was built in 1876 by John Duff, the former manager of Glendronach. For a century it was a single entity, and part of DCL from 1919. Its role was simply to pump out malt whisky for blends. Yet, within the industry, the quality of Glenlossie was appreciated and it was one of only a dozen to be designated "top class." It now shares its site with Mannochmore, a new distillery built in 1971.

Glenlossie has produced a 10-year-old since 1990, although there have been a fair number of independent bottlings from Gordon & MacPhail among others.

GLENLOSSIE FLORA & FAUNA 10-YEAR-OLD

SINGLE MALT: SPEYSIDE 43% ABV
Grassy, heathery, with a smooth, mouth-coating texture and a long spicy finish.

GLENMORANGIE

Tain, Ross-shire
www.glenmorangie.com

The "Glen of Tranquillity," to use the single malt's old slogan, has been bustling with activity since the French luxury goods group LVMH bought Glenmorangie for £300 million in 2004. The distillery started life as an old farm distillery, but was taken over and licensed in 1843 by William Matheson, who was already involved with Balblair. It remained a rustic operation for years. In the 1880s Alfred Barnard described Glenmorangie as "the most ancient and primitive we have seen" and "almost in ruins".

Outside investors were brought in just in time and the distillery was rebuilt. For much of the 20th century its key role was to supply malt for blends such as Highland Queen and James Martin's. In the 1970s, though, Glenmorangie started laying down casks for a 10-year-old single malt. In

hindsight, it was the best decision the company ever took—by the late 1990s, this had become the best-selling single malt in Scotland. Glenmorangie's stills are tall and thin, and produce a light, very pure spirit. The real skill of the distillery has been in the way it has combined this elegant spirit with wood—indeed, Glenmorangie has been a pioneer of wood finishes.

After endless experiments with increasingly exotic barrels, it became an expert in how a particular cask could twist and refocus a mature malt before bottling.

GLENMORANGIE ORIGINAL

SINGLE MALT: HIGHLANDS 40% ABV
This is the ever-popular 10-year-old, dressed up in new packaging. It has honeyed flavors with a hint of almonds.

GLENMORANGIE 18-YEAR-OLD

SINGLE MALT: HIGHLANDS 43% ABV
A rich, well-rounded whisky, with dried fruit notes and a distinctive nuttiness from its finishing in sherry butts.

GLENMORANGIE 25-YEAR-OLD

SINGLE MALT: HIGHLANDS 43% ABV
Packed with flavor, this produces dried fruit, berries, chocolate, and spice. An intense and complex whisky.

GLENMORANGIE NECTAR D'OR

SINGLE MALT: HIGHLANDS 46% ABV
Here, the Glenmorangie honeyed floral character is given a twist of spice and lemon tart from Sauternes casks.

GLENMORANGIE QUINTA RUBAN

SINGLE MALT: HIGHLANDS 46% ABV
The slight reddish-amber tint and Portuguese name are a clue: this malt is finished off in port pipes to give it a fruity, mint-chocolate character.

GLENMORANGIE LASANTA

SINGLE MALT: HIGHLANDS 46% ABV
The facelift and fancy Latin name were not the only changes Glenmorangie made to its finely balanced sherry finish: it is now bottled non-chill filtered.

GLENMORANGIE NECTAR D'OR

GLENMORANGIE QUINTA RUBAN

GLENMORANGIE LASANTA

GLEN MORAY CLASSIC PEATED

GLEN MORAY CLASSIC

GLEN MORAY 12-YEAR-OLD

GLEN MORAY

Bruceland Road, Elgin
www.glenmoray.com

The trouble with being the little brother of two far more famous siblings is that you are liable to feel unloved at times. Being in the same family as Glenmorangie and Ardbeg must have been tough for the small distillery of Glen Moray. Even its lead role in the premium blend of Bailie Nicol Jarvie went unnoticed. So, when Glenmorangie's parent company, LVMH, announced it was selling Glen Moray to the French group La Martiniquaise, no one was surprised.

Glen Moray began life as a brewery and was converted into a distillery in 1897. It struggled for the first couple of decades, until it was bought by the blenders Macdonald & Muir, who were the owners until 2004, when it was sold to LVMH. Before then, Glen Moray followed the lead of Glenmorangie and released a range of special wine finishes, including Chenin Blanc and Chardonnay. These have since been abandoned and replaced with three or four core expressions and a raft of limited releases.

GLEN MORAY CLASSIC PEATED

SINGLE MALT: SPEYSIDE 40% ABV
Light-bodied, with fruity peat, vanilla, and black pepper. Drying in the medium-length finish, with citrus fruit and a hint of licorice.

GLEN MORAY CLASSIC

SINGLE MALT: SPEYSIDE 40% ABV
The distillery also produces this introductory single malt without an age statement. It has a pale straw color and some light grassy notes.

GLEN MORAY 12-YEAR-OLD

SINGLE MALT: SPEYSIDE 40% ABV
This is a classic light Speyside malt, with cotton-candy aromas and notes of heather honey. There is a faint taste of dried fruit and orange peel on the tongue.

Traditional methods persist in the cooperage, and straw remains the best material for creating a watertight seal for the ends of the casks.

THE GLENROTHES 1975

THE GLENROTHES 1978

THE GLENROTHES 1994

THE GLENROTHES

Rothes, Morayshire
www.theglenrothes.com

After Dufftown, Rothes is the second busiest whisky town on Speyside. Not that you would know it, driving through this small town by day: the distilleries are tucked discreetly out of sight, including Glenrothes, which sits quietly in a dip beside the Rothes burn.

The distillery was built in 1878 as a joint venture between James Stuart of Macallan and two local bankers—Robert Dick and Willie Grant. Before building finished, Stuart had pulled out and a banking crisis that year almost destroyed the plans entirely.

After this shaky start, Glenrothes began to build a reputation among blenders for the quality of its malt, and became a key filling in Cutty Sark, which, for a brief period, was the best-selling Scotch whisky in the

U.S. It was also supplying other blends, and it seemed as if there was never any to spare—until 1987, when the first single malt, a 12-year-old, was released. At first, Glenrothes failed to stand out from the crowd: it had entered the 12-year-old stakes late in the day and there was plenty of competition, particularly on Speyside.

This all changed with the launch of the highly acclaimed Glenrothes Vintage malt in 1994. The brand owners, wine merchants Berry Bros. & Rudd, realized that if vintage variation was appreciated by wine-lovers, the same might be true of malt-whisky-lovers. In 2004, Glenrothes Select Reserve was released to provide continuity between vintages.

To date, the oldest vintage released has been the 1972, and the core range now includes the Select Reserve and the Alba

THE GLENROTHES 1987

THE GLENROTHES 1991

THE GLENROTHES SELECT RESERVE

Reserve, along with the Vintage Single Malt, which contains a vatting of ten different vintages from 1989 to 2007.

THE GLENROTHES 1994

SINGLE MALT: SPEYSIDE 43% ABV

A satisfyingly complex malt with a fruity, toffee-scented bouquet that leads to a soft citrus flavor and long, gentle finish.

THE GLENROTHES 1975

SINGLE MALT: SPEYSIDE 43% ABV

Increasingly hard to find, this vintage offers big, rich flavors—stewed fruits, toffee, bitter chocolate, and orange peel. Medium-sweet satisfying finish.

THE GLENROTHES 1978

SINGLE MALT: SPEYSIDE 43% ABV

A very rare expression, released in 2008, with a concentrated plum pudding and molasses character, a silky, honeyed texture and great length.

THE GLENROTHES 1987

SINGLE MALT: SPEYSIDE 43% ABV

Fruit, vanilla, and floral notes hit the nose. The palate is juicy, with an orange zestiness balancing the sweetness, and a long, sweetish finish.

THE GLENROTHES 1991

SINGLE MALT: SPEYSIDE 43% ABV

A nose of ripe berry fruits and vanilla, with some butterscotch and coconut flavors that last long on the palate.

THE GLENROTHES SELECT RESERVE

SINGLE MALT: SPEYSIDE 43% ABV

Like non-vintage Champagne, this is a vatting of different ages to produce a complex whisky with notes of hard candy, ripe fruit, vanilla, and spice. Sweeter on the nose than in the mouth.

GLEN ORD

Muir of Ord, Ross-shire

Despite its name, Glen Ord is not in a valley, but on the fertile flatlands of the Black Isle, north of Inverness. It was founded in 1838, close to the alleged site of the Ferintosh Distillery, which was established in the 1670s. In 1923 Glen Ord was bought by John Dewar & Sons, shortly before they joined the DCL.

With 14 stills and a 2.4-million-gallon (11-million-liter) production, it has plenty to spare for a single malt. Confusingly, this has been called Ord, Glenordie, and Muir of Ord at various times. Recent bottlings are the Singleton of Glen Ord, aiming at the Asian market.

THE SINGLETON OF GLEN ORD 12-YEAR-OLD

SINGLE MALT: HIGHLANDS 40% ABV
The nose is nutty, with honey, milk chocolate, and Turkish delight. Relatively light-bodied, with cinnamon, sherry, toffee, apples, and a hint of milky coffee.

GLEN SCOTIA

Campbeltown, Argyll
www.glenscotia.com

Strung out at the far end of the Mull of Kintyre, Campbeltown's rise and fall as "whiskyopolis" has been well-documented—as has the story of the Springbank Distillery's survival and subsequent cult status. Meanwhile, the much lesser known Glen Scotia also survived. With its single pair of stills, Campbeltown's "other" distillery was founded in the 1830s by the Galbraith family, who retained control for the rest of the century. After various owners followed, it was bought by Loch Lomond Group, part of Exponent Private Equity, in 2014.

GLEN SCOTIA DOUBLE CASK

SINGLE MALT: CAMPBELTOWN 46% ABV
Sweet on the nose, with brambles, red currants, vanilla, and toffee. More vanilla on the smooth palate, with ginger, spicy sherry, and finally a suggestion of sea salt.

GLEN SPEY

Rothes, Aberlour, Banffshire
www.malts.com

James Stuart was an established distiller with Macallan and the key partner in building the Glenrothes Distillery in 1878, although he quickly pulled out of that venture. A few years later, he decided to convert an oat mill he owned into Glen Spey, on the opposite bank of the Rothes Burn from Glenrothes. The project inevitably led to disputes over water rights. In 1887, Glen Spey was sold to the London-based gin distiller Gilbey's, who later merged with Justerini & Brooks. Its J&B blend has contained Glen Spey ever since. The current owners, Diageo, have just one malt bottling in their Flora & Fauna range.

GLEN SPEY FLORA & FAUNA 12-YEAR-OLD

SINGLE MALT: SPEYSIDE 43% ABV
A light, grassy nose and brisk, nutty flavor. Very dry, with a short finish.

GLENTAUCHERS

Mulben, Keith,
Banffshire

Many late-Victorian distilleries sprang up in the hope of finding a market among whisky blenders but, in 1897, Glentauchers was built to supply Buchanan's blend, which evolved into the top-selling Black & White. The distillery was a joint venture between James Buchanan and the Glasgow-based blender W. P. Lowrie. They chose an ideal site, right by a main road that connected to the east-coast rail line from Aberdeen to Inverness. Now owned by Pernod Ricard, Glentauchers has the same principal role it always had—supplying malt for blends.

GLENTAUCHERS GORDON & MACPHAIL 1991

SINGLE MALT: SPEYSIDE 43% ABV
This 16-year-old Gordon & MacPhail bottling has a sweet, sherried character, with a subtle smoky flavor.

THE GLENTURRET 10-YEAR-OLD

THE GLENTURRET PEATED

GRAND MACNISH ORIGINAL

GRAND MACNISH 12-YEAR-OLD

THE GLENTURRET

Crieff, Perthshire
www.theglenturret.com

This small Perthshire distillery, first licensed in 1775, claims to be the oldest working distillery in Scotland. It was certainly one of the first local farm distilleries to go legal, and this must have made life tough for the first few decades, given that most of the competition would have been untaxed.

Today Glenturret is known as the spiritual home of The Famous Grouse (see p.77). This fact is hard to escape as a 17-ft (5m) sculpture of the bird stands in the parking lot of the distillery.

Though Glenturret malt may have gone into the Grouse blend for years, most visitors would have been unaware of the fact until fairly recently. The only animal they would have been told about was Towser, the distillery cat, who won a place in The Guinness Book of Records

for killing nearly 30,000 mice between 1963 and 1984.

All changed when Glenturret's owners, Edrington, built a visitor center at the distillery, from which a number of tour options are available. On top of that, the last couple of years have seen a concerted effort to reestablish Glenturret as a premium single malt in its own right. Glenturret single malt is promoted using the slogan "By Hand and by Heart"—the distillery is the last in Scotland with a hand-operated mash tun.

THE GLENTURRET 10-YEAR-OLD

SINGLE MALT: HIGHLANDS 40%
Replacing the 12-year-old, this floral, vanilla-scented malt is now the main Glenturret expression.

THE GLENTURRET PEATED

SINGLE MALT: HIGHLANDS 46% ABV
Furniture polish, pineapple, and rosehip on the nose. Smooth, fruity palate of chocolate, vanilla, and allspice, finishing with slightly bitter orange.

GRAND MACNISH

Owner: MacDuff International
www.macduffint.co.uk

The long history of this brand dates back to Glasgow and 1863, when the original Robert McNish (an "a" crept into the brand name some time later), a grocer and general merchant, took up blending. The pioneering family firm was driven forward by his two sons, who greatly expanded the business and developed sales in the whisky boom of the 1890s.

Things grew harder after World War I, and the family eventually sold out to Canadian Industrial Alcohol (later Corby Distilleries) in 1927. Further changes of ownership ensued, but today the Grand Macnish has returned to Glasgow in the custody of MacDuff International, which appears to be developing an international profile for the brand and its distinctively "retro" dimpled bottle.

Two blended expressions are available: Grand Macnish Original, which still uses up to 40 whiskies in the blend, as was Robert McNish's practice, and a 12-year-old, described by the company as "more mature, fruity, and malty" than its younger sibling. The distinctive bottle gives Grand Macnish splendid "on shelf" presence, and the label is graced by the McNish clan motto, "*Forti nihil difficile*" ("To the strong, nothing is difficult").

GRAND MACNISH ORIGINAL

BLEND 40% ABV
Old leather and ripe fruits, giving way to a brandy-like aroma. Noticeably sweet on the palate, with strong vanilla (wood) influences. A sustained and evolving finish, with some gentle smoke.

GRAND MACNISH 12-YEAR-OLD

BLEND 40% ABV
The extra age shows here in a fuller, rounder flavor with greater intensity and a more sustained finish.

GRANT'S SIGNATURE

GRANT'S ALE CASK RESERVE

GRANT'S SHERRY CASK RESERVE

GRANT'S

www.grantswhisky.com

This staunchly independent company has prospered on Speyside since 1887, when the original William Grant and family opened the Glenfiddich Distillery. Grant had served a long apprenticeship in rival distilleries and shrewdly applied his knowledge when setting up his own business.

The company remains in private hands and is renowned for its focus on whisky and its determination to pass this down the generations. Today, it is famous for Glenfiddich and its sister single malt, Balvenie, but it also produces a third malt, Kininvie, which is reserved for blending. In addition, it built a grain distillery at Girvan in 1963. Chosen for ease of access to North American grain supplies, the site has been expanded massively, and, in 2008, a new

single malt distillery, Ailsa Bay, was opened there. A number of distinct styles of spirit are produced, though its output was primarily intended for blending purposes.

The first Ailsa Bay single malt was released in 2016, and it is a heavily peated whisky, comprising spirit matured in four different types of cask, namely refill American oak, first-fill bourbon, new oak, and Baby Bourbon casks from the Hudson Distillery in New York State.

Grant's Family Reserve blend broke through the 1 million case barrier as long ago as 1979 and, since then, has continued to grow at an exceptional rate, keeping up with demand from the world's Scotch whisky drinkers. Grant's now sells around 4 million cases of whisky a year and is one of the world's top five Scotch whisky brands, enjoyed in over 180 countries. The fact that the

GRANT'S FAMILY RESERVE

GRANT'S 25-YEAR-OLD

HAIG GOLD LABEL

HAIG CLUB

company is privately owned, and therefore not subject to pressures from shareholders, has enabled Grant's blenders to work with a remarkable depth of mature stock, some dating back as far as 40 years or more.

The blended range of whiskies continues to evolve, while still remaining true to the distinctive triangular bottle that marks out the products of this respected firm.

GRANT'S SIGNATURE

BLEND 40% ABV

Soft citrus fruits, barley, vanilla, and almonds on the nose. Nutty spices, milky coffee, and caramel shortcake on the palate. Coffee turns to cocoa powder in the finish, accompanied by light oak notes.

GRANT'S ALE CASK RESERVE

BLEND 40% ABV

Grant's has ventured into special wood finishes with great success. This is the only Scotch whisky to be finished in barrels that have previously held beer,

and the ale casks give the whisky a uniquely creamy, malty, and honeyed taste.

GRANT'S SHERRY CASK RESERVE

BLEND 40% ABV

Prepared in the same way as the ground-breaking ale cask version, but here the whisky is finished in Spanish Oloroso sherry casks instead, giving it a distinctively warm, rich, and fruity palate.

GRANT'S FAMILY RESERVE

BLEND 40% ABV

An unmistakably Speyside nose, with fluting malty notes. A firm mouthfeel, with banana-vanilla sweetness balancing sharper malty notes. Clean, but very complex with a long, smooth finish.

GRANT'S 25-YEAR-OLD

BLEND 40% ABV

Mellow on the nose; warm, floral, and peachy, with butter, vanilla, worn leather, and a whiff of smoke. Fresh fruits, spice, discreet vanilla, ginger, and oak on the palate.

HAIG

Owner: Diageo
www.haigwhisky.com

The distinguished name of Haig can trace its whisky-making pedigree back to the 17th century, when distilling began on the family farm. The first record that the Haigs were making whisky dates from 1655, when Robert Haig was obliged to appear before the local church council for the serious misdemeanor of distilling on a Sunday. The company developed extensive interests in grain whisky distilling and was an early pioneer of blending. By 1919, however, it was absorbed into the DCL, where it continued to be a powerful force. The company's Dimple brand (*see p. 76*) was a highly successful deluxe expression, and Haig was once the best-selling whisky in the UK. But its glory days are far behind it: today, under the control of Diageo, it is found mainly in

Greece and the Canary Islands. During its heyday, the ubiquitous blend was advertised for many years with the tagline "Don't be vague—ask for Haig."

HAIG GOLD LABEL

BLEND 40% ABV

Some sweetness on the nose, with faint smoky notes. Light and delicate, with soft wood notes and some spice on the finish, where a hint of smoke returns.

HAIG CLUB

SINGLE GRAIN 40% ABV

Gentle on the early nose, with apricots, hot metal, and subtle spices. Relatively viscous and fruity on the palate, with toffee, honey, gingerbread, and a hint of cloves.

ALL ABOUT...
WHISKEY COCKTAILS

When it comes to whiskey, cocktails can be a thorny subject, with some traditionalists condemning them as an "adulteration" of the finest of all drinks. They're missing out: the interplay of flavors from the whiskey and its accompanying ingredients can be sublime. What's more, a decent whiskey has the strength and character to maintain its identity in the mix, and delicate layerings of flavors can be achieved. Bartenders today are experimenting with big, characterful malts—even peaty expressions from Islay have their place. Balance of flavors is key, but the results can be astounding. Here are seven using whiskeys from around the globe.

MINT JULEP Roughly tear 12–15 mint leaves and place in a julep glass. Add some crushed ice, 1oz (30ml) Buffalo Trace bourbon, and ½ oz (15ml) sugar syrup, and stir well. Add 5 more torn mint leaves and another 1oz (30ml) bourbon, and stir well. Add 5 more torn mint leaves, fill the glass with crushed ice, and stir well. Top with more crushed ice, garnish with a sprig of mint, and serve with two short straws.

PEAT COLLINS Chill a collins glass with ice cubes. Put 2oz (60ml) Laphroaig 10-year-old into the mixing glass, add ½oz (15ml) freshly squeezed lime juice, ½oz (15ml) sugar syrup, a dash of orange bitters, and shake well. Double-strain the Peat Collins into the collins glass, add a couple of dashes of soda water, and stir well. Top with crushed ice and a twist of orange zest.

RYE MANHATTAN Chill a martini glass with crushed ice. Half-fill a mixing glass with ice cubes, add a dash of Angostura bitters, 2oz (60ml) Sazerac rye whiskey, and 1oz (30ml) Antica Formula sweet red vermouth. Fill with more ice cubes and stir for 20 seconds. Discard the crushed ice from the martini glass and double-strain the Rye Manhattan into it. Garnish with a maraschino cherry.

ROB ILA Chill a coupette glass with crushed ice. Fill the mixing glass with ice cubes, add 2oz (60ml) Caol Ila Distillers Edition, ½oz (15ml) Muscat de Beaumes de Venise, a dash of orange bitters, and ½oz (15ml) Drambuie, and stir well for 30 seconds. Discard the ice and double-strain the Rob Ila into it. Run a piece of lemon peel round the rim and garnish with a twist of zest.

BLACK SOUR Put three cardamom seeds in the mixing glass and crush well. Add half a cored Bartlett pear and mash to a pulp. Add 1½oz (45ml) Bushmills Black Bush, ½oz (15ml) crème de pêche, 2 good dashes of Angostura bitters, 1oz (30ml) freshly squeezed lemon juice, 1oz (30ml) sugar syrup, and a dash of egg white, and shake well. Double-strain into a chilled old-fashioned glass, top with crushed ice, and garnish with fanned Bartlett pear.

YAMAZAKI MARTINI Chill a small martini glass with crushed ice. Fill a mixing glass with ice cubes, add 2oz (60ml) Yamazaki 12-year-old, a dash of Angostura bitters, ½oz (15ml) orgeat (almond) syrup, ½oz (5ml) sugar syrup, ½oz (15ml) freshly squeezed lime juice, and a dash of egg white, and shake well. Discard the ice from the martini glass and double-strain the Yamazaki Martini into it.

ALBANNACH RENAISSANCE Fill a mixing glass with ice cubes, add 1½oz (45ml) Ardbeg Renaissance, ½oz (15ml) Aperol, ½oz (15ml) lime juice, ½oz (15ml) sugar syrup, and dashes of orange bitters, grapefruit juice, and egg white. Cover and shake till frothy. Double-strain into a chilled rocks glass, squeeze in the juice from a small piece of orange peel, and garnish with a twist of orange zest.

**HIGHLAND PARK
12-YEAR-OLD**

SINGLE MALT: ISLANDS 40% ABV
*This whisky has been praised
for its all-around quality.
There are soft heather-honey
flavors, some richer spicy
notes, and an enveloping
wisp of peat smoke that
leaves the finish quite dry.*

**HIGHLAND PARK
15-YEAR-OLD**

SINGLE MALT: ISLANDS 40% ABV
*Sweetly aromatic, with ripe
fruits and almond notes.
The fruit is more caramelized
on the palate, which fades
to a dry, smoky finish.*

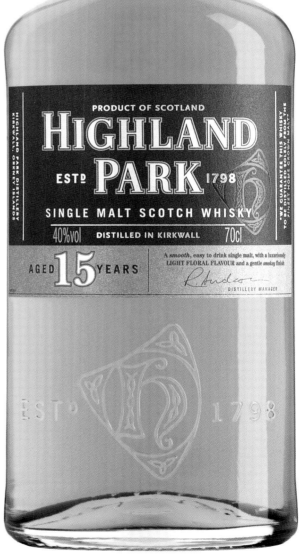

HIGHLAND PARK 18-YEAR-OLD

HIGHLAND PARK 21-YEAR-OLD

HIGHLAND PARK 25-YEAR-OLD

HIGHLAND PARK 30-YEAR-OLD

HIGHLAND PARK

Kirkwall, Orkney
www.highlandpark.co.uk

Unless, and until, a distillery is built on Shetland, Highland Park will remain Scotland's most northerly distillery. Today its far-flung island location is a great asset for the marketing of Highland Park whiskies but, for much of its history, the distance from its core market—the big blenders on the mainland—represented a major challenge for the distillery. It survived, and now produces a Highland malt that is highly regarded. Highland Park was first licensed to David Robertson in 1798 and stands near the island's

capital, Kirkwall, on the site of an illicit distillery run by Magnus Eunson, a notorious smuggler. Eunson was finally arrested by John Robertson, an excise officer, who took over the distillery in 1826. In 1895 it was bought by James Grant of Glenlivet, who expanded the number of stills to four. Since 1937 it has been part of Highland Distilleries (now Edrington), which began to invest seriously in single malts from Highland Park in the late 1970s. To this day, a proportion of the barley is malted using the distillery's original floor maltings. The malt is then dried in a kiln, using local peat, which has a slightly sweeter aroma than that from Islay.

The range starts with the no-age-statement (NAS) Dark Origins and stretches to a 50-year-old. There have also been many limited edition and travel retail-exclusive releases in recent years.

HIGHLAND PARK 18-YEAR-OLD

SINGLE MALT: ISLANDS 43% ABV
This is a touch sweeter than the 12-year-old, with notes of heather, toffee, and polished leather. The flavor of peat smoke comes through stronger on the finish than on the palate.

HIGHLAND PARK 21-YEAR-OLD

SINGLE MALT: ISLANDS 47.5% ABV
The nose offers brittle toffee, spicy malt, and contrasting heather and smoke notes. Rich and full-bodied

in the mouth, with caramel, stewed fruits, and milk chocolate, plus a hint of gentle smoke.

HIGHLAND PARK 25-YEAR-OLD

SINGLE MALT: ISLANDS 48.1% ABV
As suggested by its deep amber color, this whisky had plenty of contact with European oak. In fact, half of it was matured in first-fill sherry butts. Despite its age, it has a rich, nutty flavor, with dried fruits and scented smoke.

HIGHLAND PARK 30-YEAR-OLD

SINGLE MALT: ISLANDS 48.1% ABV
The flagship of the range. Caramel sweetness, aromatic spices, dark chocolate, and orange notes. A long, drying, smoky finish, tinged with salt.

HANKEY BANNISTER

Owner: Inver House Distillers

Messrs. Hankey and Bannister went into partnership in 1757 and were wine merchants to the great and the good, including the Prince Regent and William IV. Today the company is owned by Inver House Distillers, giving it access to a range of single malts from some of Scotland's distinguished but lesser-known distilleries, such as Balblair, Balmenach, and Knockdhu. Although managed in Scotland, Inver House is owned by Thai Beverage, and key markets for Hankey Bannister include Latin America, Australia, and South Africa, but it is exported to a total of 47 countries worldwide.

The 12-year-old was awarded a silver medal at the 2007 International Wine and Spirit Competition while, in June 2008, the 40-year-old received the coveted accolade of World's Best Scotch Blended Whisky at the World Whiskies Awards. This rare blend is characterized by the presence of whiskies such as Glen Flagler, Garnheath, and Killyloch, whose distilleries are no more.

HANKEY BANNISTER 21-YEAR-OLD

BLEND 43% ABV

A fresh and quite youthful nose. Soft and smooth, creamy toffee, with the vanilla house style coming through. Greater depth on the palate, with malty overtones and a warm finish.

HANKEY BANNISTER ORIGINAL BLEND

BLEND 40% ABV

Light on the nose, with grain and hints of lemon and pepper. Creamy mouthfeel, with more grain, lemon, and soft toffee.

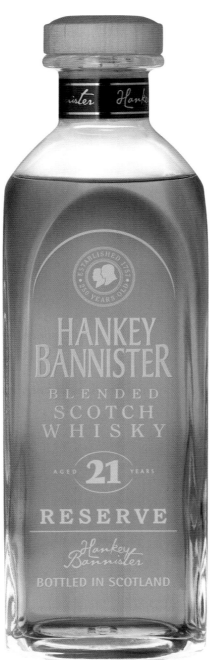

HANKEY BANNISTER 21-YEAR-OLD

HANKEY BANNISTER ORIGINAL BLEND

HAZELBURN

Well Close, Campbeltown
www.springbankwhisky.com

Springbank Distillery is the great survivor of the Campbeltown whisky boom, which saw a staggering 34 distilleries in town in the 19th century. Today, Springbank is a miniature malt-whisky industry on its own, with three separate distillations under one roof: Springbank itself, the pungently smoky Longrow, and the light, gentle Hazelburn. As well as using no peat in its malt, Hazelburn—which was named after an old, abandoned distillery in Campbeltown—is triple-distilled. The first spirit was produced in 1997 and bottled as an 8-year-old in 2005. The oldest expression currently available is a 12-year-old.

HAZELBURN 8-YEAR-OLD

SINGLE MALT: CAMPBELTOWN 46% ABV
Lowland in style, clean and refreshing, with a subtle, malty flavor.

INCHGOWER

Buckie, Banffshire
www.malts.com

This is Speyside, but only just—the Inchgower Distillery sits near the mouth of the Spey and the fishing port of Buckie. It was established in 1871 by Alexander Wilson, using equipment from the disused Tochieneal Distillery, which had been founded in 1824 by his father, John Wilson, a short distance down the coast at Cullen. It remained a family business until 1930, when the stills went cold. Six years on, the local town council bought it for just £1,000, selling it on to Arthur Bell & Sons in 1938. Bell's blends swallow up most of the malt.

INCHGOWER FLORA & FAUNA 14-YEAR-OLD

SINGLE MALT: SPEYSIDE 43% ABV
Brisk and fresh, with a floral nose, sweet-and-sour flavor, develping into a very short finish.

INVER HOUSE GREEN PLAID

Owner: Inver House Distillers

Controlled today by Thai Beverage, Inver House is one of the smaller but more dynamic Scotch whisky companies and, in 2008, was named International Distiller of the Year by *Whisky Magazine*. Its Green Plaid label was originally launched in 1956 in the US, where it remains among the top ten best-selling whiskies. More than 20 malts and grains are used to blend Green Plaid, which is available as a competitively priced non-aged version and as 12- and 21-year-olds. Inver House's Speyburn, anCnoc, Balblair, Old Pulteney, and Balmenach single malts undoubtedly feature strongly in the blend.

INVER HOUSE GREEN PLAID

BLEND 40% ABV
A light, pleasant, undemanding dram, with notes of caramel and vanilla.

INVERGORDON

Cottage Brae, Invergordon, Ross-shire
www.whyteandmackay.com

Located on the shores of the Moray Firth, the Invergordon grain distillery is owned by Whyte & Mackay. It was established in 1961 and expanded in 1963 and 1978. The distillery issued its pioneering official bottling of Invergordon Single Grain as a 10-year-old in 1991, but this was subsequently withdrawn. As a consequence, the only supplies now available are independent bottlings, many of which are very highly regarded by independent tasters.

INVERGORDON WEMYSS APPLEWOOD BAKE 1988

SINGLE GRAIN 46% ABV
Cider-like notes on the nose, with grapes and walnuts. Pears, vanilla, and milk chocolate on the palate, which is quite short with a peppery oak finish.

ISLAY MIST

Owner: MacDuff International

Created in 1922 for the 21st birthday of the son of the Laird of Islay House, Islay Mist is a highly awarded blend of single malts from the Hebridean island. The strongly flavored Laphroaig is predominant, but is tempered with Speyside and Highland malts. Naturally, Islay Mist is favored by lovers of peat-flavored whiskies, but it also offers an excellent alternative to less characterful blends. It is produced by MacDuff International, and is available in Peated Reserve, Deluxe, 12-, and 17-year-old.

ISLAY MIST DELUXE

BLEND 40% ABV
A great smoky session whisky that some will find easier to drink than full-on Islay malt. Sweet and complex under all the peat.

J&B RARE

J&B

Owner: Diageo

A Diageo brand widely sold in Spain, France, Portugal, Turkey, South Africa, and the US, J&B is one of the world's top-selling blended whiskies. In fact, nearly two bottles are sold every second.

The founding firm dates from 1749. In 1831, it was bought by the entrepreneurial Alfred Brooks, who renamed it Justerini and Brooks. The company began blending in the 1880s, and developed J&B Rare in the 1930s, when the end of Prohibition in the US created a demand for lighter-colored whisky with a more delicate flavor. It was an immediate success, achieving sales in excess of 3 million cases a year by the 1970s.

J&B has long been a favorite with writers and film stars: Truman Capote, Graham Greene, and Bret Easton Ellis have all been connected with the brand. J&B have attempted several innovative

J&B JET

J&B ULTIMA

JAMES MARTIN'S 20-YEAR-OLD

JAMES MARTIN'S 30-YEAR-OLD

expressions, including the -6°C in 2006, an almost clear blend aimed at younger vodka drinkers, and the Urban Honey "spirit drink" launched in 2014.

J&B RARE

BLEND 40% ABV

Top-class single malts such as Knockando, Auchroisk, and Glen Spey are at its heart; delicate smokiness suggests an Islay influence. Apple and pear sweetness, vanilla notes, and honey hint against a background of restrained peat. A highly distinctive blend.

J&B JET

BLEND 40% ABV

A very mellow, smooth whisky, with Speyside malt at its core.

J&B ULTIMA

BLEND 43% ABV

With a blending of whiskies from no fewer than 128 malt and grain distilleries, this is about as rich and complex a blend as it's possible to get. Increasingly rare, though, as J&B has discontinued this bottling.

JAMES MARTIN'S

Owner: Glenmorangie

This brand exhibits something of a split personality: Martin's VVO (very, very old—a generous description of the blend) remains a low-price contender in parts of the US, where it was once a significant seller; in Portugal, however, the older expressions of Martin's are highly regarded as a prestigious, premium style.

The name relates to the Leith blenders MacDonald Martin Distillers (now Glenmorangie, and thus part of the French luxury goods house LVMH) and dates back to 1878, when the original James Martin set up in business. Given LVMH's influence over Glenmorangie, and its wish to concentrate on prestige products, the future of the VVO style may be in some doubt. It is certainly years since it received any meaningful marketing, trading largely on price. In their stylish

Art Deco bottles, the older expressions may have brighter prospects. They are certainly better suited to the new corporate strategy, and the product was always highly regarded, as it contained a healthy proportion of Glenmorangie single malt with some richer components.

Currently there are 12- and 20-year-old versions of James Martin's. The 30-year-old version appears to have been withdrawn, presumably owing to a shortage of aged stocks—but bottles can still be bought from specialist retailers.

JAMES MARTIN'S 20-YEAR-OLD

BLEND 40% ABV

Citrus on the nose initially, then honey, vanilla, and a rich mead liqueur. With water, hints of coconut and vanilla appear. Very soft on the palate at the start, with cereal (grain) notes to the fore. Complex, lively spice and soft, sweet grain notes. Well-balanced with a soft finish.

JOHN BARR

Owner: Whyte & Mackay

Introduced into the UK by DCL to compensate for its withdrawal of Johnnie Walker (the result of a spat with the EU over pricing), John Barr was intended to make up for lost sales. The range echoes Johnnie Walker quite shamelessly, with Red, Black, and Gold being the main variants. Today the brand is owned by Whyte & Mackay and is seen principally in the US, where it competes largely on price. The Whyte & Mackay single malts Jura, Tamnavulin, and Fettercairn appear to play a large part in the blend, along with a good measure of Invergordon grain.

JOHN BARR

BLEND 40% ABV

The nose is firm, with luscious, creamy, round tones. Positive and full-flavored, with an almost spicy richness.

JOHNNIE WALKER BLACK LABEL

JOHNNIE WALKER GREEN LABEL

JOHNNIE WALKER GOLD LABEL RESERVE

JOHNNIE WALKER BLUE LABEL

JOHNNIE WALKER

Owner: Diageo

While the original firm, then called simply "Walker's," can be traced back to the purchase of a Kilmarnock grocery store in 1820, it did not enter the whisky business in a serious way until the 1860s. Then, with the legalization of blending, John Walker's son and grandson progressively launched and developed their range of whiskies. These were based around the original Walker's Old Highland blend, which was launched in 1865 and is the ancestor of today's Black Label. Having been renamed

"Johnnie Walker" in 1908, the firm joined DCL in 1925 and, by 1945, was the world's best-selling brand of Scotch.

Total sales of Johnnie Walker whiskies amount to around 19 million cases a year, and its Red Label is the most successful brand of Scotch whisky in the world. There has been significant growth in Scotch's developing markets (China, Asia, and Russia), where the brand is seen as a symbol of Western affluence and success.

The range comprises Johnnie Walker Red, Black, Double Black, Gold, Platinum, and Blue. From time to time the firm also releases a number of one-off, limited, or regional expressions, including

Swing, Quest, Honour, Excelsior, Old Harmony, and 1805.

From the early 1990s, the brand positioned itself upmarket. Blue Label, launched in 1992, set new price records for blended whisky. The King George V Edition followed, costing three times more than the Blue, then the ultra-exclusive 1805, sold at £1,000 a glass.

JOHNNIE WALKER
BLACK LABEL

BLEND 40% ABV

The flagship, classic blend, recognizable by the smoky kick contributed by Talisker and Diageo's Islay malts, Caol Ila and Lagavulin. Glendullan and Mortlach add some Speyside malt; the grain component is from Cameron Brig.

JOHNNIE WALKER
GREEN LABEL

BLENDED MALT 43% ABV

Complex, rich, and powerful. Pepper and oak, fruit aromas, a malty sweetness, and some smoke.

JOHNNIE WALKER
GOLD LABEL RESERVE

BLEND 40% ABV

A floral, honey, and banana nose, with a vanilla, butterscotch, and lightly spiced oak palate. The body is smooth, and the medium-length finish has brittle toffee.

JOHNNIE WALKER
BLUE LABEL

BLEND 40% ABV

Smooth and mellow, with traces of spice, honey, and the signature hint of smoke.

**JOHNNIE WALKER
PREMIER**
BLEND 43% ABV
*A complex blend of 28
different single malt and
grain whiskies. Rich, with
a subtle oak finish. Sweet
and dark, with dried fruits,
treacle toffee, and chocolate.*

**JOHNNIE WALKER
SWING**
BLEND 43% ABV
*Notes of sherry wood
and vanilla, with an almost
perfumed sweetness. Fresh,
light, smooth, and intensely
fruity, with traces of oak
and a hint of smoke.*

JURA SUPERSTITION

JURA 10-YEAR-OLD

JURA 16-YEAR-OLD

JURA

Isle of Jura, Argyllshire
www.jurawhisky.com

When the Indian tycoon Vijay Mallya bought Whyte & Mackay in May 2007, part of the appeal was sentimental: included in the sale was Jura—an island distillery off the northeast tip of Islay, which his father found irresistible. "I remember hearing the name 40 years ago," Mallya told reporters. "It was his favorite whisky and now it's part of Whyte & Mackay. I hope he would be proud." In 2014, Whyte & Mackay Distillers and the Jura brand were acquired by Emperador Inc.

The original Jura Distillery was licensed in 1831 and later leased to James Ferguson, who rebuilt it in

1875. However, the terms of the lease were so harsh that his family abandoned Jura in 1901, ripping out the equipment as they did so. For the next 20 years the landlord and local laird, Archibald Campbell, pursued them in court, while removing the distillery roof to avoid paying taxes.

In the late 1950s two estate owners on Jura resurrected the distillery in a joint venture with Scottish & Newcastle breweries. They hired the leading distillery architect, William Delmé-Evans, and his design, completed in the early 1960s, still stands.

The profile of the whisky also changed when the distillery was resurrected. Gone was the strong, phenolic malt of the past, and in came something more Highland

in style, with less peat and a more subtle touch. Employing large stills (nearly as tall as those at Glenmorangie) to create a cleaner style of spirit, Jura was able to produce a softer malt whisky— one that would be distinct from those of its peaty neighbors, over on Islay.

Having said that, in recent years Jura has produced an interesting array of limited-edition bottlings, some of which have used various sherry cask finishes and some of which have actually been quite heavily peated. A whisky called Earth (from the Elements series) was one such bottling.

Jura's core range consists of 10-year-old, Origin, 16-year-old, Diurach's Own, Superstition, and the peated Prophecy.

JURA SUPERSTITION

SINGLE MALT: ISLANDS 43% ABV
A mix of heavily peated, young Jura with older whisky, to produce an intensely smoky, smooth-textured malt.

JURA 10-YEAR-OLD

SINGLE MALT: ISLANDS 40% ABV
A lightly peated island malt that seems to have improved in recent years.

JURA 16-YEAR-OLD

SINGLE MALT: ISLANDS 40% ABV
A slightly spicy, cereal nose with a nutty flavor that dries on the finish.

KILKERRAN WORK IN PROGRESS 6 BOURBON MATURED

KILKERRAN WORK IN PROGRESS 6 SHERRY MATURED

KILKERRAN

Glengyle Road, Campbeltown
www.kilkerransinglemalt.com

Glengyle is Campbeltown's newest distillery in the sense that it first produced spirit during 2004. However, the original Glengyle operated between 1872 and 1925—a period when Campbeltown was still a major player in the Scotch whisky world. The malt whisky it produces is named Kilkerran, as "Glengyle" was already registered as a blend by Loch Lomond.

Glengyle was revived by Springbank owner Hedley Wright, and features a pair of modified stills formerly used by the Ben Wyvis malt distillery at Invergordon in the late seventies. The first permanent expression of Kilkerran will be a 12-year-old, but since 2009, the distillery has released annual limited batches of "Work in Progress." In 2014, "Work in Progress 6" featured both sherry cask-matured and bourbon cask-matured bottlings.

KILKERRAN WORK IN PROGRESS 6 BOURBON MATURED

SINGLE MALT: CAMPBELTOWN 46% ABV
Lemongrass, a pinch of salt, wood smoke, and ginger snaps on the nose. Tropical fruits on the soft, oily palate, with a slight underpinning of nutty, spicy smoke. Drying in the mellow finish.

KILKERRAN WORK IN PROGRESS 6 SHERRY MATURED

SINGLE MALT: CAMPBELTOWN 46% ABV
Initially savory on the nose, slightly earthy, with sherry, new leather, and a hint of chlorine. Spicy and zesty, with developing stewed fruits, dark chocolate, and deep sherry notes on a mildly smoky palate.

WHISKY TOUR: ISLAY

"Peat freaks" adore the Islay taste, and tourism to this Hebridean island is booming, particularly during the annual Feis Ile (the Islay Malt and Music Festival) at the end of May. The easiest way to reach Islay is to fly from Glasgow, but you will need to rent a car to get around; the Caledonian MacBrayne ferry from Kennacraig allows you to bring your own vehicle but is a longer journey (four hours). For accommodation, there are converted distillery cottages at Bowmore and Bunnahabhain available to rent, hotels in Bowmore and Port Charlotte, and plenty of B&B and efficiency options too. A four-day itinerary should take in all eight distilleries.

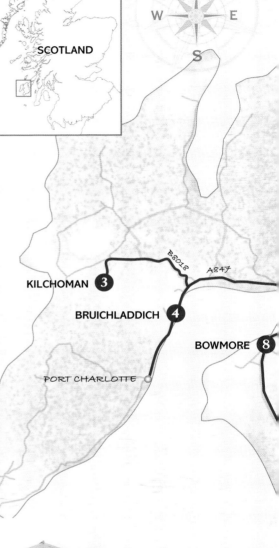

TOUR STATISTICS		
DAYS: 4	**LENGTH:** 60 miles (96 km)	**DISTILLERIES:** 8
TRAVEL: Car, walking	**REGION:** Islay, Scotland	

DAY 1: CAOL ILA, BUNNAHABHAIN

1 Arriving in Port Askaig by ferry, the logical place to stay is the charming, family-run Port Askaig Hotel on the coast *(www.portaskaig.co.uk)*. From there you can walk to **Caol Ila**, a large Diageo distillery that is the most highly productive on the island. *(www.discovering-distilleries.com/caolila)*

2 It's a car trip or hike along the coastal path from Port Askaig to **Bunnahabhain.** This distillery makes the most lightly peated of all Islay whiskies. It is possible to rent one of the distillery cottages and soak up the tranquillity of Bunnahabhain Bay, with its captivating views of Jura. *(www.bunnahabhain.com)*

WASHBACKS AT CAOL ILA

BUNNAHABHAIN DISTILLERY

Map labels:

Port Askaig - Colonsay ferry

JURA

BUNNAHABHAIN ❷

CAOL ILA

❶

PORT ASKAIG

○ FEOLIN FERRY

START

FINISH

A846

Port Askaig - Kennacraig ferry

BRIDGEND

A846

ISLAY

B8016

846

○ KILDALTON

Port Ellen - Kennacraig ferry

ARDBEG

❼

❺ ❻ LAGAVULIN

LAPHROAIG

PORT ELLEN

miles
0   2

0   2
kilometres

DAY 2: KILCHOMAN, BRUICHLADDICH

❸ Tiny **Kilchoman** is Islay's newest and smallest distillery. It's also a farm with a friendly café. Like other Islay distilleries, it sells special bottlings that may not be available elsewhere. This is a great spot for lunch and the dishes use locally sourced ingredients. Alternatively, in good weather, you can picnic at nearby Machir Bay. *(www.kilchomandistillery.com)*

❹ A short drive back over the hill brings you to **Bruichladdich** *(www.bruichladdich.com)*, which produces a huge array of whiskies. The distillery is just outside Port Charlotte, where you can learn about illicit whisky production in the Museum of Islay Life *(www.islaymuseum.org)*, then enjoy dinner at the Port Charlotte Hotel *(www.portcharlottehotel.co.uk)*.

BRUICHLADDICH

DAY 3: LAPHROAIG, LAGAVULIN, ARDBEG

❺ Spend today taking in three distilleries and some ancient history. The Kildalton distilleries, as these three are known, are renowned for their strong peaty character, and **Laphroaig** is reputedly Prince Charles's favorite dram. The distillery tour includes the splendidly maintained maltings. *(www.laphroaig.com)*

❻ From Laphroaig, take a five-minute stroll to **Lagavulin** to compare these two strongly peated single malts with their assertive flavors. *(www.discovering-distilleries.com/lagavulin)*

❼ The last distillery of the day is **Ardbeg** *(www.ardbeg.com)*, where lunch at the Old Kiln Café is not to be missed. If you're interested in history, drive a few miles further on the tiny road to Kildalton where there's a very fine 8th-century cross.

MODEL IN LAGAVULIN'S DRAM ROOM

DAY 4: BOWMORE

❽ Spend your last morning in the little town of Bowmore, where you can visit the floor maltings, history of distillery exhibition, and visitor center at **Bowmore** Distillery *(www.bowmore.com)*. Repair to the Harbour Inn *(www.harbour-inn.com)* for a final lunch of local produce before catching the afternoon ferry from Port Askaig back to the mainland.

BOWMORE WAREHOUSE

KILCHOMAN

Rockside Farm, Bruichladdich, Islay
www.kilchomandistillery.com

Whisky-making began here in 2005, and this is as quintessential a farm distillery as you'll find. The barley is grown on Rockside Farm, and malting, fermenting, distilling, and maturing all take place on-site; a dam on the farm creates a supply of fresh water.

Having started out selling new-make spirit, Kilchoman released its first 3-year-old single malt in 2009, followed by several limited bottlings before the first "core" expression—Machir Bay—appeared in 2012. Loch Gorm and 100% Islay are also regularly produced.

KILCHOMAN MACHIR BAY

SINGLE MALT 46% ABV
A nose of sweet peat and vanilla, undercut by brine, wood smoke, kelp, and black pepper. Smooth on the palate, with citrus fruit, peat smoke, and antiseptic, leading to a long, sweet, chilli, and nut finish.

KNOCKANDO

Knockando, Morayshire
www.malts.com

Knockando was launched as a single malt in the late 1970s and had some success in Spain, although most of the production went into J&B. The name is an anglicized version of Cnoc-an-Dhu, which is Gaelic for the "dark hillock" that stands close by the distillery, guarding a bend in the Spey.

The distillery was set up by John Thomson in 1898 close to Cardhu, on the old Strathspey railway line, where it had its own station. Although it was one of the first to have electric light, it was only run on a seasonal basis and soon fell victim to the speculative crash that hit the industry at the beginning of the 20th century. Knockando was snapped up by London gin distillers Gilbey's, who, via a series of acquisitions, became part of what is now

KNOCKANDO 21-YEAR-OLD

LANGS SUPREME

LANGS 12-YEAR-OLD

Diageo. In 1968, the floor maltings were stopped and the old malt barns converted to host meetings for J&B salesman around the world.

As a single malt, Knockando was originally sold not by age statement, but by vintage in all its markets except the US. It has proved popular in Spain and France.

KNOCKANDO 12-YEAR-OLD

SINGLE MALT: SPEYSIDE 43% ABV
This very gentle, grassy malt has a cereal character and a light, creamy texture.

KNOCKANDO 18-YEAR-OLD

SINGLE MALT: SPEYSIDE 43% ABV
A slightly fuller expression of this gentle Speyside malt, with a smooth, mellow texture.

KNOCKANDO 21-YEAR-OLD

SINGLE MALT: SPEYSIDE 43% ABV
Sweet on the nose, with oak and nuts (almonds) on the palate, matched by berry fruits, leading on to a smoky, oaky finish.

LABEL 5

Owner: La Martiniquaise

The Label 5 brand is owned by La Martiniquaise, a French producer with significant blending and distilling facilities in Scotland, as well as interests in rum and other spirits. Founded in 1934 as a blending house, the company now owns Glen Moray single malt and is building new grain and single malt facilities at its central Scotland base.

Label 5 is its leading brand, and sells well over 1 million cases in the price-competitive "value" category, mainly in France, although it is available in more than 50 countries worldwide. A 12-year-old deluxe version is also available.

LABEL 5 CLASSIC BLACK

BLEND 40% ABV
Delicate, malty, and smoky, with hints of flowers and fruit. Smooth, robust, and balanced on the palate, with subtle oak notes.

LANGS

Owner: Ian MacLeod
www.ianmacleod.com

At the heart of this long-established blend is Glengoyne single malt, from the distillery just outside Glasgow. This was bought in 1876 by two local merchants, Alexander and Gavin Lang. In 1965 the brand and distillery were sold to their rivals, Robertson & Baxter, who invested in the distillery and developed the brand with some success. Sales also grew steadily in Europe and the Far East and, in 1984, HM The Queen Mother awarded Langs her royal warrant.

But in 2003, Robertson & Baxter decided they could take Langs no further. The sale to Ian MacLeod marked an important transition for that business, from blender and bottler to full-blown distiller.

Since the acquisition, Ian MacLeod has invested in both the Glengoyne Distillery, with

its range of alternative visitor experiences, and in presenting Langs in new packaging. Today, the principal Langs products are Langs Select 12-year-old and Langs Supreme, both blends noted for their relatively high malt content. Langs Select was awarded a gold medal by Scottish Field magazine's *Merchants' Challenge*, beating some very well-known names.

LANGS SUPREME

BLEND 40% ABV
A rich malt aroma on the nose, well-matured, with just a hint of sherry. A full-flavored, medium-sweet blend, with the Glengoyne heart evident.

LANGS SELECT 12-YEAR-OLD

BLEND 40% ABV
Rhubarb and cooking apples on the nose, with a good helping of vanilla. Sweet, soft, and delicate. Richer on the palate, with lots of fruity notes and a lemon-tart sweetness that build toward a spicy finish with hints of peat smoke.

LAGAVULIN 16-YEAR-OLD

LAGAVULIN 12-YEAR-OLD

LAGAVULIN 21-YEAR-OLD

LAGAVULIN

Port Ellen, Isle of Islay
www.malts.com

Lagavulin is said to have evolved into a distillery from various illicit smuggling botheys in 1816. In 1836 its lease was taken over by Alexander Graham, who sold the island's whiskies through his shop in Glasgow. Peter Mackie, the nephew of Graham's partner, worked for the business and went on to create the famous White Horse blend based on Islay malt. When neighboring Laphroaig refused to supply him, he decided to build Malt Mill Distillery in the grounds of Lagavulin, which he inherited after his uncle's death. Malt Mill was demolished in the

1960s, but Lagavulin rode on the back of the White Horse until its iconic 16-year-old became a founding member of the "Classic Malts" in 1988.

During the slump in demand for Scotch in the 1980s, Lagavulin was working a two- to three-day week. Sixteen years down the line, the managers were having to juggle the short supply with booming demand. Having been the top-selling Islay malt, low stocks pushed it into third place behind Laphroaig and Bowmore. To try and meet demand, production at Lagavulin was cranked up to a seven-day week, and less and less was made available for blends. It is said that over 85 percent of Lagavulin is now bottled as

LAGAVULIN 25-YEAR-OLD

LAGAVULIN 1976 37-YEAR-OLD

LAGAVULIN DISTILLERS EDITION

a single malt. The core range comprises the 12-year-old Cask Strength, 16-year-old, and Pedro Ximinez sherry cask-finished Distillers Edition. In recent years, 21- and 37-year-olds have also been bottled as limited editions.

LAGAVULIN 16-YEAR-OLD

SINGLE MALT: ISLAY 43% ABV
The long-time stalwart of the "Classic Malts" has an intensely smoky nose with the scent of seaweed and iodine and a sweetness in the mouth that dries to a peaty finish.

LAGAVULIN 12-YEAR-OLD

SINGLE MALT: ISLAY 56.4% ABV
An initial sweetness gives way to scented smoke and a malty, fruity flavor ahead of the dry, peaty finish.

LAGAVULIN 21-YEAR-OLD

SINGLE MALT: ISLAY 56.5% ABV
Pungent and smoky on one hand, with a sherried, golden-syrup warmth on the other. The two sides live in harmony.

LAGAVULIN 1976 37-YEAR-OLD

SINGLE MALT: ISLAY 51% ABV
Earthy, savory, and smoky on the nose, with old leather, sea salt, almonds, and honey. Oak, brine, more leather, and earthy notes on the palate, with kelp, dried fruits, and lingering sweet peat smoke.

LAGAVULIN DISTILLERS EDITION

SINGLE MALT: ISLAY 43% ABV
A richer, fuller-flavored take on the 16-year-old, still with plenty of dense smoke and seaweed.

LAPHROAIG 10-YEAR-OLD CASK STRENGTH

LAPHROAIG 18-YEAR-OLD

LAPHROAIG 25-YEAR-OLD

LAPHROAIG SELECT

LAPHROAIG

Port Ellen, Isle of Islay
www.laphroaig.com

In June 2008, Prince Charles returned to visit the home of his favorite Islay malt after 14 years. This time he came with his wife, Camilla, and did not crash-land on Islay's tiny airstrip, as he had the last time (he made the mistake of landing with a strong tail wind, and the plane came to a halt nose-down in the peat bog).

Laphroaig has always reveled in its pungent smokiness—a mix of hemp, carbolic soap, and bonfire that is about as a far from the creamy, cocktail end of whisky as it is possible to get. Its intense medicinal character is said

to be one reason it was among the few Scotch whiskies allowed into the US during Prohibition—it was accepted as a "medicinal spirit," and could be obtained with a prescription from a doctor.

Laphroaig was founded in 1810 by Alexander and Donald Johnston, although official production did not begin for five years. Living beside the equally famous Lagavulin has not always been easy, and there were the usual fights over water access, but today the feeling is more one of mutual respect.

Laphroaig is one of the very few distilleries to have retained its floor maltings, which supply about a fifth of its needs. The reason may be more to do with

marketing than anything else, but it makes for an interesting distillery visit.

Although Allied Distillers could appear ambivalent about its commitment to Scotch, there were never any doubts about its proud flagship distillery. Just before Allied was bought out in 2005, and Laphroaig became part of Fortune Brands, it released its first Quarter Cask expression: by increasing the proportion of wood to whisky for the final seven months before bottling, the whole process of maturation is speeded up.

Quarter Cask is now offered alongside 10-year-old, 10-year-old Cask Strength, Select, Triple Wood, and 18- and 25-year-old expressions.

LAPHROAIG 10-YEAR-OLD CASK STRENGTH

SINGLE MALT: ISLAY 57.3% ABV
Tar, seaweed, and salt, and some sweet wood too. Iodine and hot peat rumble through a long, dramatic finish.

LAPHROAIG 25-YEAR-OLD

SINGLE MALT: ISLAY 50.9% ABV
A spicy, floral character, with smoke and sea spray taking over only in the finish. Also available in cask strength.

LAPHROAIG SELECT

SINGLE MALT: ISLAY 40% ABV
Nose of pipe tobacco, peat, and, in time, a medicinal note and smoky peaches. Thin on the peaty palate, with dark berries and contrasting hints of vanilla.

LAPHROAIG
QUARTER CASK

SINGLE MALT: ISLAY 48% ABV

The Quarter Cask is at the heart of Laphroaig's core range. Small casks speed up the maturation process and lead to a sweet, woody taste that succumbs to a triumphal burst of peat smoke.

LAPHROAIG
10-YEAR-OLD

SINGLE MALT: ISLAY 40% ABV

The 10-year-old is also very popular. Beneath the dense peat smoke and salty sea spray is a refreshing, youthful malt with a sweet core.

THE SECRETS OF...
LAPHROAIG

The malt from this great Islay distillery delights in its tough, uncompromising image, and for years it was promoted as a whisky that people would either love or hate.

Laphroaig is one of the smokiest, most pungent malts around, and, as a result, you almost expect the distillery to be perched on a cliff-top, battered by the ocean waves. It is a coastal distillery, but its position is a little more serene, in a quiet bay on the southern shore of the island.

The signature note of Laphroaig is apparent before you step inside. As one of the very few distilleries to have retained its floor maltings, you can see and smell the plumes of peat smoke wafting from the pagoda roof above the kiln. While the maltings provide only some of the malt needed, they do make visiting the distillery particularly interesting. Until 50 years ago, this was how all malt whisky was made.

Other factors that make Laphroaig special include the long years in wood and a unique set of stills. The dominant note remains the same today as it was in the 19th century. Then, when the whisky writer Alfred Barnard asked about the influence of the sea air, he was told it had no effect whatsoever. It was all because of peat.

▲ A SEASIDE LOCATION
It is tempting to relate the maritime character of Laphroaig to the distillery's dramatic position by the sea. Though hard to prove, the whisky does have a distinct taste of seaweed.

▼ SOFT, PEATY WATER
An abundant supply of water is vital for any distillery, yet many believe the character of the water has a minimal effect on the whisky's flavor. Laphroaig's whisky-makers disagree, and say the soft, peaty water from Loch Kilbride is an important factor.

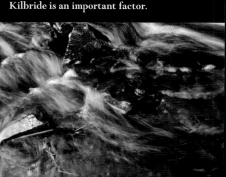

▲ TURNING THE WET BARLEY
Having been steeped in water, the wet barley is spread across a stone floor, about 6in (15cm) deep. It is turned regularly with wooden shiels (broad shovels) to prevent the shoots from matting together as the barley starts to germinate. After six days, this "green" malt is ready for the kilns.

▼ A UNIQUE SET OF STILLS

Laphroaig has three wash stills and four spirit stills in two different sizes, which is very unusual. Another uncommon feature of the stills is the way the lyne arms slope upward rather than downward. This increases reflux during the long, slow distillation.

▼ PEATING BEFORE KILNING

The green malt is spread on a wire mesh suspended 15 ft (5 m) above a kiln, filled with peat. The kiln is fired up, and dense smoke immediately begins to impregnate the grains of malt. Unlike any other Scotch malt distillery, Laphroaig peats the malt first and then dries it afterward. It is maintained that this gives the whisky a much wider range of smoke flavors.

◄ CASKING STRENGTH

The middle cut from the spirit stills comes in at a strength of 68% ABV which is then reduced to 63.5% ABV before filling into casks. This is thought to be the most desirable strength for the maturation process.

LONG YEARS IN WOOD ►

The casks used at Laphroaig are almost entirely from Maker's Mark (see pp. 244–245), its sister distillery in the US. Maturation is said to account for a third of the character of the whisky. Recently, the distillery began using quarter casks to increase the ratio of wood to whisky and speed up the process.

LINKWOOD FLORA & FAUNA 12-YEAR-OLD

THE LAST DROP

www.lastdropdistillers.com

This unusual super-premium blend is the brainchild of three industry veterans—Tom Jago, James Espey, and Peter Fleck. Allegedly, a random discovery of very old whiskies pre-vatted at 12 years of age and then allowed to mature for a further 36 years in sherry casks, The Last Drop would appear to have been something of an accident and cannot be repeated. Included in the blend are whiskies from long-lost distilleries, the youngest reputed to have been distilled in 1960. Savor the tasting notes—at £1,000 or so a bottle and with only 1,347 bottles available, it may be the closest you'll get to tasting it.

THE LAST DROP

BLEND 54.5% ABV
Exceptionally complex nose, with figs, chocolate, and vanilla. An unusual combination of new-mown hay, dried fruit, herbs, and butter cookies.

LAUDER'S

Owner: MacDuff International

Between 1886 and 1893, Lauder's Royal Northern Cream scooped up a total of six gold medals in international competitions—a tribute to the meticulous research and repeated trials undertaken by the original proprietor, Archibald Lauder, a Glasgow publican. The development of the blend is said to have taken him two years. Today Lauder's is once again blended in Glasgow, by MacDuff International, and Lauder's Bar on Sauchiehall Street remains to commemorate Lauder himself. His blend has largely slipped from public view in its homeland, but is imported by Barton Brands of Chicago to the US, where it remains popular among value-conscious consumers.

LAUDER'S

BLEND 40% ABV
A light and fruity blend designed for session drinking and mixing.

LEDAIG

Tobermory Distillery,
Tobermory, Isle of Mull

Tobermory, the capital of Mull and the island's main port, was originally called Ledaig, and this was the name chosen by John Sinclair when he began distilling here in 1798. Quite when the Ledaig Distillery became Tobermory is unclear, as it has had an incredibly interrupted life, spending more time in mothballs than in production. In recent years the distillery adopted a similar approach to Springbank, producing a heavily peated robust West Coast malt called Ledaig and a lightly peated malt called Tobermory. At present, 10- and 18-year-old expressions of Ledaig are available, along with 10- and 15-year-old Tobermorys *(see p.170).*

LEDAIG 10-YEAR-OLD

SINGLE MALT: ISLANDS 43% ABV
Slightly medicinal, but full of dry, slightly dusty peat smoke.

LINKWOOD

Elgin, Morayshire
www.malts.com

From the outset, Linkwood was a well-conceived, almost self-sufficient distillery. It was named after Linkwood House on the Seafield Estate, where the estate manager, Peter Brown, decided to build a distillery in 1821. It was surrounded by barley fields to supply the grain, and cattle to feed on the spent draff. What you see today dates back to the 1870s, when Brown's son William demolished the original Linkwood and built a new distillery on the same site. It remained in private hands until 1933, when it became part of DCL. As a supplier of a "top dressing" malt used in many blends, Linkwood was highly regarded, and DCL paid a hefty £80,000 for it, around £4.3 million in today's money.

In 1960 the number of stills was tripled to six, with the new stills

LINKWOOD RARE MALTS 26-YEAR-OLD

LOCH FYNE PREMIUM SCOTCH

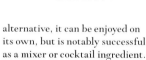

LOCH FYNE LIVING CASK

housed in a separate building. Between 2011 and 2013, much of the existing distillery was demolished, and replaced with new structures housing six stills. Linkwood now has a capacity of 1.2 million gallons (5.6 million liters) of spirit per year.

LINKWOOD FLORA & FAUNA 12-YEAR-OLD

SINGLE MALT: SPEYSIDE 43% ABV
This standard expression is on the lighter side of the Speyside style, with a fresh, grassy, green-apple fragrance and faint notes of spice. In the mouth it has a delicate sweet-and-sour flavor and a slow finish.

LINKWOOD RARE MALTS 26-YEAR-OLD

SINGLE MALT: SPEYSIDE 56.1% ABV
Bright and breezy for a 26-year-old. Lightly smoky with caramelized sugar notes. Spicy and warm in the finish.

LOCH FYNE

Owner: The Whisky Shop
www.lochfynewhiskies.com

Created by Professor Ronnie Martin, a former production director at United Distillers (now Diageo), Loch Fyne is the exclusive and eponymous house blend of Loch Fyne Whiskies of Inverary. It is blended and bottled under license for this famous Scottish whisky specialist. The label, incidentally, honours the long-lost Highland distillery Glendarroch.

Slightly sweet and smoky, Loch Fyne is an easy-drinking, well-flavored blend, which the proprietors describe as "one to drink and enjoy rather than concentrate on". It has been praised by leading critics and won awards in international competition.

Also available is a full-strength 12-year-old liqueur, which comes in a 23 oz (70 cl) decanter. Created for whisky-lovers on the look-out for a sophisticated and complex

alternative, it can be enjoyed on its own, but is notably successful as a mixer or cocktail ingredient.

In addition to this, Loch Fyne has an ongoing whisky project in the shape of the Living Cask. Inspired by the way whisky was kept and drunk prior to the ubiquity of bottles, this is a cask used simultaneously for maturing and serving. The cask is filled with a vatting of malt whiskies, and tapped halfway down for drawing off bottlings. When about half the contents has been used, it is filled to the top again, so creating an everchanging blended malt, which can be bought in 7 oz (20 cl) sample bottles at cask strength.

LOCH FYNE PREMIUM SCOTCH

BLEND 40% ABV
Apple dumplings on the nose, enlivened by orange and tangerine notes. Subtle, with nutty, oil-related aromas and hints of smoke. The palate is smooth and well-balanced: acidic, salty, sweet, and dry. The finish is surprisingly warming.

LOCH LOMOND

Alexandria, Dumbartonshire
www.lochlomondgroup.com

Within the confines of the Loch Lomond Distillery, on the southern end of Loch Lomond, all manner of Scotch whiskies are produced, although originally it was just malt. The distillery was built in 1965 as a joint venture between Barton Brands of America and Duncan Thomas. Twenty years later, it was bought by Alexander Bulloch and his company, Glen Catrine Bonded Warehouse Ltd. and is now owned by Exponent Private Equity. Today, grain whisky is produced alongside the malt. The distillery's stills have rectifying columns that can be adjusted to produce a lighter or heavier spirit.

LOCH LOMOND

SINGLE MALT: HIGHLANDS 40% ABV
With no age statement and a competitive price, this is likely to be a fairly young single malt. It has a light, fresh flavor and no great influence of wood.

LONGMORN 16-YEAR-OLD

LONGMORN CASK STRENGTH

LONGMORN BITTER SWEET BARLEY 1997 (WEMYSS)

LONG JOHN

Owner: Chivas Brothers

Despite reasonably healthy sales in France, Scandinavia, and some Spanish-speaking markets, Long John appears very much the poor relation in the Chivas Brothers' stable, dominated as it is by Chivas Regal and Ballantine's. The brand has passed through a number of owners since it was founded in the early 19th century by the eponymous Long John MacDonald.

In the past, Long John has produced and marketed 12- and 15-year-old expressions, but today, the concentration is on the standard non-age version.

LONG JOHN 12-YEAR-OLD

BLEND 40% ABV
A deluxe blend, Long John 12-year-old is a dark, traditional style of whisky, noted for its distinctive character. The blend is said to contain 48 different malts, including Laphroaig and Highland Park.

LONGMORN

Elgin, Morayshire

John Duff was 52 when he went into partnership with George Thomson and Charles Shirres in 1894. Together, they built Longmorn, in a village of the same name just south of Elgin. The distillery occupies the site of an old chapel (Longmorn means "place of the holy man" in Gaelic) and, with its four stills, it was conceived on a grand scale at a cost of £20,000 (around £2 million in today's money). Yet within five years Duff had bought out his partners and built another distillery, BenRiach, next door. While BenRiach has often struggled, Longmorn has been in almost continuous production since the start. It seems this classic, floral Speyside malt was just what the blenders wanted.

In 1970, Longmorn formed a small group with Glenlivet and Glen Grant, which had become

part of Seagram by the end of the decade. Aside from independent expressions, a distillery bottling appeared in Seagram's Heritage Selection of malts in 1994.

Since 2000, Longmorn has been owned by Chivas Brothers, the whisky arm of drinks giant Pernod Ricard, which has replaced the existing 15-year-old with one a year older and clearly aimed at the super-premium category of malts.

Meanwhile, its valuable blending role sees it featured in several of Chivas Brothers' high-end blends, including the Royal Salute range and Chivas Regal 18-year-old.

In 2012, Longmorn underwent major expansion work, with a new lauter mash tun being fitted, along with three additional stainless steel washbacks. The four pairs of stills have been adapted to save energy in line with Chivas Brothers' overall policy in that area, and capacity has been extended by around 30 percent to 990,000 gallons (4.5 million liters) per year.

LONGMORN 16-YEAR-OLD

SINGLE MALT: SPEYSIDE 48% ABV
Its cereal aroma is sweetened with coconut from ageing in bourbon casks. The mouthfeel is smooth and silky and dries on the tongue to give a crisp, slightly austere finish.

LONGMORN CASK STRENGTH

SINGLE MALT: SPEYSIDE 56.9% ABV
The nose is floral, with rose water, soft toffee, lemon, and sweet oak. Rich on the palate, with more rose and lemon, plus milk chocolate. Creamy and sweet in the finish.

LONGMORN BITTER SWEET BARLEY 1997 (WEMYSS)

SINGLE MALT: SPEYSIDE 46% ABV
Notably fruity on the nose, with sweet barley notes, figs, and hazelnuts. Vanilla, ripe peach, and coconut feature on the warming palate, closing with spiced cookies.

LONGROW

Springbank Distillery,
Well Close, Campbeltown, Argyll
www.springbankwhisky.com

After being Scotland's most famous whisky town, Campbeltown suffered a swift and brutal demise. As blenders began to source their malt from Speyside, it turned to the US, until Prohibition shut that market down in 1919. From over a dozen distilleries, only Springbank and Glen Scotia were left by 1935.

In 1973, Springbank decided to distil a pungent, heavily smoked whisky alongside its main malt. The new whisky was christened Longrow after a distillery that had once stood next door. It was released as an experiment in 1985 and finally became a regular fixture in 1992.

Today, the core range includes Longrow, Longrow Red, and Longrow 18-year-old, the last released in small amounts from time to time. Various limited-release expressions have been added, including one finished in old Barolo casks.

LONGROW PEATED

SINGLE MALT: CAMPBELTOWN 46% ABV
The nose offers vanilla, brine, and peat smoke, while the relatively light palate features early orchard fruits and milk chocolate before more brine and smoke appear and really make their presence felt.

LONGROW RED

SINGLE MALT: CAMPBELTOWN 52.9% ABV
Smoked fish, coal tar soap, citrus fruit, and new leather on the peaty nose. Mouth-coating, with rich peat on the palate, plus fruity spice, red currants, and licorice, leading into a long finish.

LONGROW 18-YEAR-OLD

SINGLE MALT: CAMPBELTOWN 46% ABV
The nose is oily, with sherry, brine, figs, and spicy peat. Citrus fruit and earthy peat on the full, oily palate, with smoked fish and barbecue notes.

THE MACALLAN GOLD

THE MACALLAN

Easter Elchies, Craigellachie, Morayshire
www.themacallan.com

The Macallan stands on the west bank of the Spey, just across the river from Craigellachie and well beyond the bustle of Dufftown and the Speyside whisky trail. The signpost to the distillery is discreet, and visitors tend to come privately, by appointment.

It was first licensed in 1824 as the Elchies Distillery by Alexander Reid, a tenant farmer on Easter Elchies farm. It was a small-scale operation, run as a sideline to the main business of farming. At certain times of year, however, there would have been a good passing trade of cattle drovers on their way to and from the big markets to the south. Being close to a ford through the river, the farm became a good stopping place for them to rest, swap stories, and buy whisky.

Annual production at Macallan was still only 40,000 gallons (180,000 liters) when it was sold to Roderick Kemp in 1892. The distillery was expanded and remained in family control until 1996, when it was bought by Highland Distillers (now part of Edrington), for £180 million. Ironically, Highland had made an unsolicited bid for Macallan back in 1898. Its offer then was a modest £80,000, which was turned down flat.

In the intervening years, the distillery was rebuilt in the 1950s and the number of stills grew to 21. More importantly, The Macallan 10-year-old, launched in 1978, established itself as one of the leading single malts on Speyside. The distillery had always made a virtue of its use of sherry casks, which were carefully selected and shipped in from Spain. A deep amber color and fruitcake character came to symbolize the whisky. So the launch of the Fine Oak series in 2004, which uses bourbon casks alongside sherry butts, marked a radical departure.

In 2012, Macallan began to phase in a new core range to replace Sherry Oak and Fine Oak, all expressions being without age statements. They are Gold, Amber, Sienna, and Ruby.

THE MACALLAN GOLD

SINGLE MALT: SPEYSIDE 40% ABV
The nose offers apricots and peaches, fudge, and a hint of leather. Medium-bodied, with malt, walnuts, and spices on the palate. Quite oaky in the medium-length finish.

THE MACALLAN FINE OAK 10-YEAR-OLD

SINGLE MALT: SPEYSIDE 40% ABV
With less sherry influence than the standard 10-year-old, more of the fresh, brisk, malty distillery character comes through.

THE MACALLAN 25-YEAR-OLD

SINGLE MALT: SPEYSIDE 43% ABV
Spicy citrus notes accompany the ripe dried-fruit character from the sherry casks, which lead to a little wood-smoke on the tongue.

THE MACALLAN 30-YEAR-OLD

SINGLE MALT: SPEYSIDE 43% ABV
A big, post-prandial malt with a sweet, sherried nose and spicy flavors of orange peel, cloves, and dates that linger on the finish.

THE MACALLAN FINE OAK 10-YEAR-OLD

THE MACALLAN 25-YEAR-OLD

THE MACALLAN 30-YEAR-OLD

THE SECRETS OF...
MACALLAN

Of everything that goes into making malt whisky, the greatest impact comes from wood, and this is something that Macallan understood and appreciated long before many of its rivals.

Maturation is something that the Speyside distillery has always taken very seriously, and the insistence on expensive sherry butts rather than far cheaper bourbon barrels goes way back. The rich, nutty flavor from the sherry casks remains the signature tune to The Macallan, though The Fine Oak range, launched in 2004, now provides a partly bourbon-matured alternative.

Yet, while maturation may be the biggest single influence on the whisky, the casks can only work their magic on what the distillery provides in terms of new make spirit. The unique character of this is determined by a host of factors—from the choice of barley, to the shape of the stills, to the speed of distillation.

Among the most important choices is selecting the final "cut"—that part of the spirit between the foreshots and the feints that is kept. The Macallan prides itself on one of the finest cuts of any distillery in Scotland: Just 16 percent of what flows from the spirit still is filled into casks.

▲ A FARM DISTILLERY
Long before the distillery was founded in 1824, local farmers were distilling whisky from the barley in surrounding fields. This would have been offered to the drovers who stopped here on their way to market.

▲ DOUGLAS FIR WASHBACKS
Macallan has used stainless-steel washbacks for many years, but, as part of a recent expansion, a new set of six Douglas fir washbacks were built, so now fermentation is carried out in both wood and metal.

SQUAT STILLS ▶
The seven wash stills at the distillery work in tandem with 14 spirit stills—these being the smallest on Speyside. Their unique shape and size helps maximize the contact between the liquid and the copper. This strips out some of the heavier sulfur compounds, leaving the new make spirit clean and fruity.

◄ THE LONG SLEEP

Having been diluted to a strength of 69.8% ABV with water from the estate, the spirit is filled into casks and left to slumber. A quarter of the 140,000 casks are stored in Macallan's 16 traditional dunnage warehouses, which are cool and damp, with earth floors and stone walls. The rest of the casks are kept in five modern-racked warehouses that have recently been built on site.

▲ SHERRY AND BOURBON

Although most of the casks in Macallan's warehouses are sherry butts, you can also find puncheons, barrels, and ex-bourbon hogsheads shipped over from Kentucky. The sherry casks are a mixture of European and American oak.

▲ THE FLAVOR PROFILE

The key flavors of The Macallan can be explored in an interactive display at the distillery's visitor center. Traditional Macallan takes a floral, quite fruity Speyside spirit and coats it with a rich layer of spicy sherry flavors. The relatively new Fine Oak range has a fresher, more delicate flavor, with the distillery character more pronounced.

MANNOCHMORE FLORA & FAUNA 12-YEAR-OLD

MANNOCHMORE RARE MALTS 22-YEAR-OLD

MACARTHUR'S

Owner: Inver House Distillers

The MacArthur clan of Argyllshire fought nobly alongside Robert the Bruce in the struggle for Scottish independence and subsequently gave their name to this standard blend. Like so many others, it has its roots in the upsurge of blending from independent merchants in the late-Victorian era and can be traced to the 1870s. Today it is owned by Inver House Distillers, who describe it as having a "light, smooth flavor with toffee and vanilla from cask ageing" MacArthur's is not to be confused with single malts bottled independently under the label James MacArthur.

MACARTHUR'S

BLEND 40% ABV
Fragrant, barley-malt nose with sweet, citrus aftertones. A medium-bodied, uncomplicated whisky, softly aromatic, with a smooth, mellow palate and a fresh, lingering finish.

MAC NA MARA

Owner: The Gaelic Whisky Co.
www.gaelicwhisky.com

Despite its Irish-sounding name, which means "son of the sea" in Gaelic, Mac Na Mara hails from the Isle of Skye whisky company Pràban na Linne (also known as the Gaelic Whisky Company).

A lighter blended whisky with some West Coast character, it was first introduced in 1992 and became popular in France, where the company enjoys its strongest following. A Rum Finish version is also offered from time to time. Unusually for a blended whisky, this is non-chill filtered and aged for a further 12 months in Guyanan rum casks for a sweet finish.

MAC NA MARA

BLEND 40% ABV
A light and essentially undemanding blended whisky with a biscuit-like nose, a citrus tang, and a creamy finish.

MANNOCHMORE

Elgin, Morayshire
www.malts.com

This modern distillery was part of the Haig empire—a separate fiefdom within the Distillers Company Limited. It was built in 1971 as one of a cluster of distilleries between Elgin and Rothes. Nearby are Longmorn and BenRiach, while almost next door is Glenlossie, which has operated in tandem with Mannochmore from the start, sharing the same workforce and warehouses.

From conception, Mannochmore's simple role in life was supplying malt for Haig, then the top-selling blend in the UK. Fourteen years later it fell victim to the chronic oversupply in the industry and was mothballed, as the big distillers sought to drain the whisky loch. It was back in production by 1989 and launched its first official malt as part of the Flora & Fauna range three years later.

Mannochmore is famous for launching Loch Dhu in 1996. With its distinctive dark color, it was only produced for four years, but has become something of a cult since, particularly in Denmark. There has been the odd independent bottling, including, in 2014, a 1994 distillation from Gordon & MacPhail, and a 1999 14-year-old from Douglas Laing.

MANNOCHMORE FLORA & FAUNA 12-YEAR-OLD

SINGLE MALT: SPEYSIDE 43% ABV
This is very much an aperitif-style malt, with a light, floral nose but, in the mouth, a more luscious, spicy character, with hints of licorice and vanilla, comes through.

MANNOCHMORE RARE MALTS 22-YEAR-OLD

SINGLE MALT: SPEYSIDE 60.1% ABV
Distilled in 1974, this limited edition exudes fragrant, flowery aromas. Herbaceous and peppery, with a touch of peat in the mix.

MCCLELLAND'S HIGHLAND

MCCLELLAND'S SPEYSIDE

MCCLELLAND'S ISLAY

MCCLELLAND'S LOWLAND

MCCLELLAND'S

Owner: Morrison Bowmore
www.mcclellands.co.uk

The range of McClelland's single malts offers a chance to explore Scotland and four of its key whisky-distilling regions. It was first launched in 1986, with a Highland, Lowland, and Islay expression. These proved so successful that a Speyside expression was introduced in 1999. According to the company, each one is carefully selected to reflect the true essence and character of the region in which it is produced.

The brand currently claims to be number four in the US market, where it competes against the likes of Glenlivet, Glenfiddich, and The Macallan. McClelland's is also distributed to global markets, including Taiwan, Austria, South Africa, Japan, Canada, France, Russia, and the Netherlands.

MCCLELLAND'S LOWLAND

SINGLE MALT: LOWLANDS 40% ABV
A richly floral nose with hints of nutmeg, ginger, and citrus fruits. Very clean and delicate on the palate, with floral notes.

MCCLELLAND'S HIGHLAND

SINGLE MALT: HIGHLANDS 40% ABV
Delicate wood notes on the nose, with sweet buttercream and fresh vanilla. Some initial sweetness, giving way to fresh fruit and lime hints.

MCCLELLAND'S SPEYSIDE

SINGLE MALT: SPEYSIDE 40% ABV
Fresh mint, cut pine, hints of dark chocolate, and sweet malt on the nose. Initially sweet, developing nutty flavors and floral hints.

MCCLELLAND'S ISLAY

SINGLE MALT: ISLAY 40% ABV
The nose is unmistakably Islay: wood smoke and cinders, tar, vanilla, and citrus hints. Forceful sea salt, burnt oak, and peat smoke, with vanilla undertones on the palate.

MORTLACH RARE OLD

MILLBURN

Inverness, Inverness-shire

It was Millburn's misfortune to be located on the outskirts of Inverness on the road to Elgin. When the whisky industry suffered one of its big periodic downturns in the 1980s, the distillery was in the wrong place at the wrong time—not remote enough to simply be mothballed when there was the prospect of redevelopment instead. And so it shut down for good in 1985 and was turned into a steakhouse; today, it's a hotel and restaurant called The Auld Distillery. Brand owner Diageo released several expressions in its Rare Malts series.

MILLBURN RARE MALTS 25-YEAR-OLD

SINGLE MALT: SPEYSIDE 61.9% ABV

This Rare Malts bottling is a big, meaty whisky that is dry and chewy in the mouth, with damp wood, smoke, and orange skins.

MILTONDUFF

Miltonduff, Elgin, Morayshire

Miltonduff was one of supposedly more than 50 illicit stills in Elgin until it took out a license in 1824. In 1936, it was bought by George Ballantine & Son. From 1964 until 1981, the distillery had a pair of Lomond stills, allowing it to produce different styles of whisky, such as the single malt Mosstowie. These are now increasingly rare. Pernod Ricard bought Miltonduff in 2005, and uses much of the 1.3 million-gallon (5.8 million-liter) production to supply malt for its Ballantine's Finest blend. An official 16-year-old cask strength malt is now available, with several more bottlings existing among independents.

MILTONDUFF 16-YEAR-OLD CASK STRENGTH

SINGLE MALT: SPEYSIDE 52.9% ABV

Soft nose, with vanilla and citrus, continuing through the cinnamon and toffee palate. Lengthy finish.

MONKEY SHOULDER

Owner: William Grant & Sons

The name may seem contrived, but this blended malt from William Grant & Sons refers to a condition known among workers in the maltings—turning the damp grain by hand, they often incurred a repetitive strain injury.

Three metal monkeys decorate the shoulder of the bottle and just three single malts go into the blend—Glenfiddich, Balvenie, and Kininvie. At the launch, great play was made of the whisky's mixability, and you're as likely to encounter it on a cocktail menu as you are in your local liquor store.

MONKEY SHOULDER

BLEND 40% ABV

Banana, honey, pears, and allspice on the nose. Vanilla, nutmeg, citrus hints, and generic fruit on the palate. A dry finish, then a short burst of menthol.

MORTLACH

Dufftown, Keith, Banffshire
www.mortlach.com

Long before the distillery building boom on Speyside, James Findlater became the first licensed distiller in Dufftown in 1823. By the end of the century, the town had no fewer than six distilleries. Mortlach changed hands at regular intervals, and was briefly a brewery and even a temporary home for the Free Church of Scotland at one point. In 1897, the number of stills was doubled to six, making this one of the largest distilleries in the Highlands. It became part of DCL (now Diageo) in 1925, which used its malt in blends, especially Johnnie Walker. The first official bottling as a single malt was not until 1995, when a 22-year-old Rare Malt was released.

The six stills are configured in a uniquely complex manner, with a fifth of the spirit being triple-distilled in an intermediate

MORTLACH 25-YEAR-OLD

OBAN 14-YEAR-OLD

OBAN DISTILLERS EDITION 1992

SINGLE MALT: HIGHLANDS 43% ABV
A 15-year-old malt, aged in different casks during maturation. Spicy and oaky flavors dominate from the strong sherry-wood effect—the result of finishing in Montilla Fino casks.

still called "Wee Witchie." This process is intended to add richness and depth to the spirit, which is then condensed in traditional worm tubs outside, to create a more robust style of whisky.

Mortlach is ever-popular with blenders, but 2014 saw the single malt given a greatly enhanced profile, with the release of four new expressions, namely Rare Old, Special Strength, 18-year-old, and 25-year-old.

MORTLACH RARE OLD

SINGLE MALT: SPEYSIDE 43.4% ABV
Fresh on the nose, with peaches and apricots, milk chocolate, and finally caramel. Fruit carries over, from the nose to the nutty palate, with cinnamon spice.

MORTLACH 25-YEAR-OLD

SINGLE MALT: SPEYSIDE 43.4% ABV
A hint of fresh soil on the nose, with apples, and a slight meatiness. Malt, muted spices, and interplay between sweet and savory on the palate. Gentle oak finish.

OBAN

www.malts.com

Oban Distillery dates back to 1793, when Oban itself was a tiny West Coast fishing village. The town (dubbed "Gateway to the Isles") now surrounds the distillery and prevents any expansion. Due to its small capacity of 150,000 gallons (700,000 liters), Oban was never closed during periods of overproduction, and so it has been in almost continuous production since it was built.

Oban has been one of Diageo's "Classic Malts" since 1990, and is only sold in selected markets. Alongside the official no-age Little Bay and 14-year-old statements, double-matured Distillers Edition malts are released from time to time.

OBAN 14-YEAR-OLD

SINGLE MALT: HIGHLANDS 43% ABV
The brisk, maritime distillery character is mellowed by the years in wood. It has a rich, dried-fruit character.

ALL ABOUT...
BOTTLES

It was only in the late 1880s, with the invention of mechanical glass-blowing, that whiskey began to be filled into glass bottles. Prior to this, it was sold in bulk, by the small cask, or the stoneware jar. The advantage of the sealed bottle—until 1913 the seal was always a driven cork, requiring a corkscrew—was that it prevented, or at least discouraged, adulteration. Such bottles as were used for whiskey prior to the 1880s were recycled wine bottles, made from dark glass—clear glass was taxed at 11 times the rate of dark glass.

STANDARD LIQUOR BOTTLE This shape became the standard bottle for Scotch whisky in the 1890s, although earlier bottles tend to be heavier and of very dark green glass.

PETARD In its shape and use of a small, hand-written label, The Glenrothes petard derives its look from a lab sample bottle. The color of the liquid is allowed to shine through, and this design embodies integrity. Introduced in 1994, it quickly became known as the "petard" or "grenade."

EMBOSSED Heavily embossed bottles speak of luxury and are especially popular in Asia. Crown Royal was introduced to mark the State Visit of Britain's King George VI to Canada in 1939. The bottle is further "ennobled" by coming in a purple velvet bag.

PINCH George Ogilvy Haig introduced this unusual shape in 1893 for his Dimple brand of Scotch. In the US it was sold as Pinch, and the bottle shape was the first to be patented under US law, in 1958.

SWING Sir Alexander Walker, Johnnie Walker's grandson, created the deluxe blend Swing specifically for luxurious transatlantic liners. The bottle has a rounded base, so it "swings" with the motion of the ship and remains perpendicular!

TRIANGULAR William Grant & Sons introduced this supremely ergonomic shape for their brand Standfast in the mid-1950s, and adopted it in 1964 for Glenfiddich. The innovative shape was created by the modernist designer Hans Schleger.

CERAMIC Such vessels hark back to the stoneware jars of the late 19th century. Arthur Bell & Sons have been issuing commemorative bell-shaped Christmas decanters annually since 1988. They have become collectors' items, and some are now very valuable.

WAX-SEALED MAKER'S MARK In the late 19th century, some blenders dipped the neck of the bottle in sealing wax, having driven home the cork. This was common practice with port, and made the bottle "tamper-proof." Marge Samuels, wife of the owner of Maker's Mark, applied it to this brand in the 1950s.

GRAND OLD PARR 12–YEAR-OLD

OLD PARR SPRING

OLD PARR SUMMER

OLD PARR WINTER

OLD PARR

Owner: Diageo

"Keep your head cool by temperance and your feet warm by exercise. Rise early, go soon to bed, and if you want to grow fat [prosperous], keep your eyes open and your mouth shut." So said the original "Old Parr," one Thomas Parr, who lived from 1483 to 1635, making him 152 years old when he died. If that seems improbable, his tomb can be inspected in Poets' Corner, Westminster Abbey.

In 1871, Old Parr's name was borrowed by two famous blenders of their day, the Greenlees brothers, for their deluxe whisky. Now under the stewardship of industry giants Diageo, the brand has gone on to success in Japan, Venezuela, Mexico, and Colombia. The square brown bottle appears unchanged in years, and Old Parr whisky has a loyal band of followers who appreciate its distinctive, old-fashioned style.

Old Parr 18-year-old was awarded the title of "World Whisky of the Year" by one popular guide in 2007. By tradition, Cragganmore is the mainstay of the blend.

A few years ago, Old Parr launched a limited-edition series that it called the Four Seasons. Comprising blends of carefully selected casks to obtain four styles of whisky with very different characteristics, the series has become something of a collector's item, with the Autumn expression in particular having become extremely rare.

GRAND OLD PARR 12-YEAR-OLD

BLEND 43% ABV

Pronounced malt, raisin, and orange notes on the nose, with some apple and dried-fruit undertones, and perhaps a hint of peat. Forceful on the palate, with flavors of malt, raisin, burned caramel, and brown sugar.

OLD PULTENEY 12-YEAR-OLD

OLD PULTENEY 17-YEAR-OLD

OLD PULTENEY 21-YEAR-OLD

OLD PULTENEY

Pulteney Distillery, Wick, Caithness
www.oldpulteney.com

Wick, in the far northeast corner of Scotland, is just a short distance from John o' Groats, commonly regarded as Britain's most northerly point. Wick was a tiny village when Sir William Johnstone Pulteney decided to turn it into a major fishing port in the early 1800s. In 1826, with the trade in herring booming, James Henderson built Pulteney in his honor.

The business of fishing, gutting, and packing the herring into barrels was thirsty work, and the town's only distillery thrived. The setting appeared perfect, but dwindled the herring fleet gradually and, in 1922, at the high-water mark of the temperance movement, the town voted to go dry. The distillery closed in 1930 and did not reopen until 1951—by which time the town was no longer a haven of sobriety.

The solitary wash still comes with a giant ball, to increase reflux, and a truncated top, supposedly lopped off to fit the still room. Pulteney's malts are marketed today as "Old Pulteney."

OLD PULTENEY 12-YEAR-OLD

SINGLE MALT: HIGHLANDS 40% ABV
Launched by Inver House in 1997, two years after buying the distillery, this is a brisk, salty, maritime malt with a woody sweetness from aging in bourbon casks.

OLD PULTENEY 17-YEAR-OLD

SINGLE MALT: HIGHLANDS 46% ABV
The non-chill filtered big brother of the 12-year-old is partly matured in sherry wood, to add fruity, butterscotch notes to the flavor, which is long with a medium-full body in the mouth.

OLD PULTENEY 21-YEAR-OLD

SINGLE MALT: HIGHLANDS 46% ABV
The sherry influence comes from the American oak used in the cask. The result is a rich, creamy, honey-scented malt that dries on the finish.

OLD SMUGGLER

Owner: Gruppo Campari

Reputedly, and appropriately, a big favorite during Prohibition, Old Smuggler was first developed by James and George Stodart in 1835. Although the firm is today largely forgotten, history records that it was the first to marry its whisky in sherry butts. The brand is now owned by Gruppo Campari, who acquired it along with its sister blend Braemar and the flagship Glen Grant Distillery from Pernod Ricard in 2006. It continues to hold a significant position in the US and Argentina, where it is the second-best-selling whisky, and is reported to be developing strong sales in Eastern Europe.

OLD SMUGGLER

BLEND 40% ABV

Decent Scotch with no offensive overtones and some smoke hints. Blended for value, and for drinking with a mixer.

PASSPORT

Owner: Chivas Brothers

Passport was developed by Seagram and acquired by Pernod Ricard in 2002. Like many brands that are invisible in the UK, it enjoys conspicuous success elsewhere: Passport's main strongholds are the US, South Korea, Spain, and Brazil, where its fruity taste lends itself to being served on the rocks, in mixed drinks and in cocktails. Packaged in a distinctive retro, rectangular green bottle, Passport is "a unique Scotch whisky, inspired by the revolution of 1960s Britain, with a young and vibrant personality." Such distinguished and famous malts as Glenlivet are found in the blend.

PASSPORT

BLEND 40% ABV

A fruity taste and a deliciously creamy finish. It can be served straight or, more usually, mixed over ice. Medium-bodied, with a soft and mellow finish.

PIG'S NOSE

Owner: Spencerfield Spirits
www.spencerfieldspirit.com

Should you visit one of the UK's many agricultural or county fairs, you may well encounter this whisky being sold from the back of an old horse box. Do not walk away: Pig's Nose has been re-blended by Whyte & Mackay's superstar master blender, Richard Paterson, and launched back on to the market in smart new livery. Brother to the better-known blended malt Sheep Dip *(see p.155)*, Pig's Nose is a full-flavored and drinkable blend that more than lives up to the claim that "our Scotch is as soft and smooth as a pig's nose."

PIG'S NOSE

BLEND 40% ABV

The nose is delicate and refined, with soft and sensual floral notes supported by complex fruit flavors. On the palate, there is a forceful array of malty flavors from Scotland's four distilling regions.

PINWINNIE ROYALE

Owner: Inver House Distillers

Pinwinnie Royale stands out from the crowd, its label hinting at an early ecclesiastical manuscript and regal connections, though there is little to support these romantic suppositions. Given its place in the Inver House stable, it would seem likely that Old Pulteney, Speyburn, anCnoc, and Balblair single malts are to be found in the blend, with the emphasis on the lesser-known names. As well as the standard expression, there is a 12-year-old version, which mixes a light Speyside fruitiness with drier background wood notes, and a buttery texture.

PINWHINNIE ROYALE

BLEND 40% ABV

Young, spirity fruitiness on the nose, smooth-textured but spicy in the mouth, with burned, sooty notes in the finish.

POIT DHUBH

Owner: The Gaelic Whisky Co.
www.gaelicwhisky.com

Pràban na Linne (known also as the Gaelic Whisky Co.) was established by Sir Iain Noble in 1976 to create employment in the south of Skye. The business has grown steadily since. Poit Dhubh (pronounced *Potch Ghoo*) is a non-chill filtered blended malt supplied as 8-, 12-, and 21-year-olds. A limited edition 30-year-old was bottled for the company's 30th anniversary. Poit Dhubh makes much play of the possible bootleg nature of its whisky, stating, "We are unwilling either to confirm or deny that Poit Dhubh comes from an illicit still." This is, of course, complete fantasy.

POIT DHUBH 8-YEAR-OLD

BLENDED MALT 43% ABV

Dried fruits and a light spiciness give a bittersweet character, with dry, woody notes and a trace of peat.

PORT ELLEN

Port Ellen, Isle of Islay

Of all Islay malts, Port Ellen has possibly the largest cult following, owing to its rarity, which has increased every year since the distillery shut down in 1983. It was founded in 1825 by Alexander Kerr Mackay, and remained in family hands until the 1920s, when it became part of DCL (Distillers Company Ltd.). Its misfortune was to be part of the same stable as Laphroaig and Caol Ila: when the downturn came, it was the weakest link. Today it remains active as a maltings plant, supplying Islay's distilleries with most of their malt.

PORT ELLEN DOUGLAS LAING 26-YEAR-OLD

SINGLE MALT: ISLAY 50% ABV

Matured in refill bourbon casks, this bottling has a sweet and fruity nose, with some new leather. Sweetness on the palate, but overwhelmed by peat smoke. A long, tarry finish, with a dab of salt.

PRIME BLUE

Owner: Morrison Bowmore

Prime Blue is a blended malt available largely in Taiwan, where the market has developed in sensational style during the last decade. The color blue is said to convey nobility and royalty, and the brand name was reputedly chosen to reflect sophistication in the whisky's taste. At their peak, sales exceeded 1 million cases a year, although the market for this style in the Far East has declined somewhat in recent years and competition in Taiwan and elsewhere has intensified.

PRIME BLUE

BLENDED MALT 40% ABV

Aromas of vanilla and malted barley are soon followed by light cocoa, and then heathery, floral notes. Initially fruity on the palate, followed by a malty sweetness, and a long finish.

QUEEN ANNE

Owner: Chivas Brothers

A good example of an "orphan brand" that has found its way into the portfolio of a larger company and appears to lack any clear role and purpose, Queen Anne was once a leading name from the distinguished Edinburgh blenders Hill, Thomson & Co. It was first produced in 1884 and blended by one William Shaw. Today it belongs to Chivas Brothers. Like so many once-famous and proud brands, Queen Anne has been left bereft and isolated by consolidation in the Scotch whisky industry, steadfastly clinging on in one or more regions where once it was loved and popular.

QUEEN ANNE

BLEND 40% ABV

Not especially characterful, as the flavors are so tightly integrated that it is difficult to discern individual aromas or tastes. A standard blend for mixing.

Hogsheads are assembled from the broken down staves of bourbon barrels. They are about 20 percent bigger than barrels and, once reassembled, are steam heated to expand the oak and make the joints watertight.

ROBERT BURNS BLEND

ROBERT BURNS SINGLE MALT

ROBERT BURNS

Owner: Isle of Arran Distillers
www.arranwhisky.com

With the Scotch whisky industry generally apt to employ Scottish imagery and heritage associations at the drop of a tam-o'-shanter, it is a surprise to find that no one had previously marketed a brand named after Scotland's national bard. Independent distiller Isle of Arran has worked with the World Burns Federation to fill this gap, and now produces an officially endorsed Burns Collection of blended whiskies and malts.

Naturally, the Robert Burns brand contains a significant proportion of Arran single malt, and is claimed by the company to "capture the character of our beautiful island of clear mountain water and soft sea air". Sadly, it seems that the poet never actually visited the Isle of Arran, although he would have been able to see it from his Ayrshire home.

Isle of Arran Distillers (*see The Arran Malt, p.29*) is one of the few remaining independent distilleries in Scotland. It was set up in 1995 by Harold Currie, who was previously managing director of Chivas Brothers.

ROBERT BURNS BLEND

BLEND 40% ABV
Hints of oak on the nose give way to sherry, almonds, toffee, and ripe fruits. Plenty of toffee, cake, and dried fruits on the palate, with a light to medium, spicy finish.

ROBERT BURNS SINGLE MALT

SINGLE MALT 40% ABV
A nose of green apples, the acidity tempered by a note of vanilla. Apple and citrus notes on the palate, balanced by vanilla again. An aperitif whisky that is light in style and finish.

ROSEBANK

Camelon, Falkirk

Few distilleries have managed to stay in continuous production. Many closed during the 1980s and '90s when the industry was dealing with oversupply. Whether a distillery survived when demand picked up depended largely on location. Rosebank, near Falkirk, was mothballed in 1993 and has since been redeveloped. Founded in 1840, it was chosen to be part of The Ascot Malt Cellar in 1982. Unfortunately for Rosebank, when this became the "Classic Malts" series, Glenkinchie was picked to represent the Lowlands rather than Rosebank.

ROSEBANK DOUGLAS LAING 16-YEAR-OLD

SINGLE MALT: LOWLANDS 50% ABV
This independent bottling from Douglas Laing is part of its Old Malt Cask collection. Despite its strength and age, it is fresh and citrussy.

ROYAL BRACKLA

Cawdor, Nairn, Nairnshire

Brackla was founded between the River Findhorn and the Murray Firth by Captain William Fraser in 1812. He was soon complaining that, although he was surrounded by whisky-drinkers, he could only sell 100 gallons (450 liters) a year. By way of compensation, he secured the first royal warrant for a distillery in 1835. Whether he would recognize Royal Brackla today seems unlikely: it was fully modernized in the 1970s and 1990s and now belongs to Bacardi, who launched 12-, 16-, and 21-year-old expressions in 2015.

ROYAL BRACKLA 12-YEAR-OLD

SINGLE MALT: HIGHLANDS 40% ABV
Ripe peaches, spice, walnuts, malt, honey, vanilla, and a slightly herbal note on the nose. Spice, sweet sherry, and mildly smoky orchard fruit on the full palate, closing with cocoa and ginger.

ROYAL LOCHNAGAR

Ballater, Aberdeenshire
www.malts.com

This charming distillery sits alone on Deeside as the only whisky-making business in the area. It was founded by John Begg in 1845 as New Lochnagar, to distinguish it from a distillery of the same name that had stood on the other bank, only to be washed away in the great Muckle Spate of 1829. Begg wasted no time in asking his new neighbors at Balmoral—Queen Victoria and Prince Albert—to look around his distillery in 1848. By the end of the year, Lochnagar had become Royal Lochnagar.

Begg prospered until he sold out to John Dewar & Sons in 1916, by which point the malt had become a key component in VAT 69.

With a production of just 90,000 gallons (400,000 liters) from its single pair of stills, it is a fairly pocket-sized distillery and, being so far from any others, it must have felt vulnerable at times. Yet in recent years its owner, Diageo, has lavished lots of money and attention on Royal Lochnagar. A Distillers Edition expression featuring a Moscatel finish was launched in 2008, and, in 2013, a Triple Matured bottling was released exclusively to Friends of the Classic Malts.

ROYAL LOCHNAGAR
12-YEAR-OLD

SINGLE MALT: HIGHLANDS 40% ABV
A subtle, leathery nose with a flavor that becomes drier and more acidic before a spicy, sandalwood finish.

ROYAL LOCHNAGAR
DISTILLERS EDITION 2000

SINGLE MALT: HIGHLANDS 48% ABV
Pears poached in dessert wine on the malty, gingery nose. The rich palate offers ripe peaches, figs, ginger, and cloves, closing with nutty spice.

ROYAL SALUTE 21-YEAR OLD

ROYAL SALUTE, THE HUNDRED CASK SELECTION

ROYAL SALUTE 38-YEAR-OLD

ROYAL SALUTE

www.royalsalute.com

Originally produced by Seagram in 1953 to commemorate the coronation of Queen Elizabeth II, Royal Salute claims to be the first super-premium whisky. Today it remains market leader in the over 21 years category.

Historically, Chivas Brothers were noted for their exceptional stocks of rare, aged whiskies, and these formed the basis for the Royal Salute expressions. The company is now controlled by Pernod Ricard, whose blenders, led by the highly respected Colin Scott, have access to single malts from such well-known distilleries as Glenlivet, Aberlour, Strathisla, and Longmorn.

Given the veneration and respect accorded to age by consumers in the Far East, it is no surprise that Royal Salute is particularly successful in Asia, especially in China (where Chivas has invested

much effort), Taiwan, Korea, and Vietnam. Duty-free shops also provide a major source of sales.

The various expressions have won an impressive range of medals, including major awards at the International Wine and Spirit Competition.

ROYAL SALUTE 21-YEAR-OLD

BLEND 40% ABV

Soft, fruity aromas balanced with a delicate floral fragrance and mellow, honeyed sweetness.

ROYAL SALUTE, THE HUNDRED CASK SELECTION

BLEND 40% ABV

Elegant, creamy, and exceptionally smooth, with a mellow, oaky, slightly smoky finish.

ROYAL SALUTE 38-YEAR-OLD

BLEND 40% ABV

Rich notes of cedarwood and almond, with a sherried oakiness. Dried fruits linger with an assertive spiciness. An experience, even for the connoisseur.

SCAPA

St. Ola, Orkney
www.scapamalt.com

Founded in 1885 on the "Mainland," as Orcadians call the largest of the Hebridean islands, Scapa kept going more or less continuously until 1994, when it was shut down. Although production resumed three years later, it was only on a seasonal basis, using staff from its neighbor, Highland Park. For years it seemed there was only room for one viable distillery on Orkney—that being Highland Park—but Scapa's rescue came in the form of Allied Domecq, and over £2 million was lavished on it in 2004. The company has since been bought by Chivas Brothers.

SCAPA 16-YEAR-OLD

SINGLE MALT: ISLANDS 40% ABV
The nose offers apricots and peaches, nougat, and mixed spices. Medium-bodied, with caramel and spice notes on the palate, leading to a gingery, buttery finish.

SCOTTISH LEADER

Owner: Burn Stewart Distillers
www.scottishleader.com

The owner describes Scottish Leader as "An international award-winning blend with a honey rich smooth taste profile. It has a growing presence in a number of world markets." The blend's heart is Deanston single malt, from the Perthshire distillery of the same name. Although it was initally targeted at the value-conscious supermarket buyer, Scottish Leader has subsequently been repackaged and moved somewhat upmarket. Today, there are Original, Signature, Supreme, and 12-year-old expressions.

SCOTTISH LEADER

BLEND 40% ABV
A standard blend in which the flavor characteristics are tightly integrated. Not much to mark it out, but okay for mixing or drinking on the rocks.

SHEEP DIP

Owner: Spencerfield Spirits
www.spencerfieldspirit.com

Sheep Dip is one of the better blended malts. The brand has been around since the 1970s but, under the ownership of Whyte & Mackay, was largely ignored. In 2005, it was taken on by Alex and Jane Nicol, who aim to rebuild the former glory of so-called "orphan brands." Since then, they've introduced new packaging, appointed a global network of agents and, most important of all, reformulated the whisky under the guidance of master blender Richard Paterson. It seems to be working. The whiskies are aged between 8 and 12 years in quality first-fill wood, producing a great dram.

SHEEP DIP

BLENDED MALT 40% ABV
The nose is delicate and refined. Great finesse on the palate, then a majestic assertion of pure malty flavors.

SOMETHING SPECIAL

Owner: Chivas Brothers

It's quite a name to live up to, but "something special" is a justifiable claim for this premium blend, which, with sales of over half a million cases, is the third best-selling whisky in South America. The blend dates back to 1912, when it was created by the directors of Hill Thompson & Co. of Edinburgh. The primary component is drawn from Speyside malts, especially the highly regarded Longmorn, which is at the heart of the blend. A 15-year-old version was launched in 2006. The distinctive bottle is said to have been inspired by an Edinburgh diamond-cutter.

SOMETHING SPECIAL

BLEND 40% ABV
A distinctive blend of dry, fruity, and spicy flavors, with a subtle, smoky, sweetness on the palate.

ALL ABOUT...
WHISKEY GLASSES

The traditional whiskey glass is a cut crystal "Old-fashioned" glass. It was invented for drinking brandy and soda (with ice) in the 1840s, and was adopted 30-odd years later for drinking blended Scotch (with soda and ice) or an "Old-fashioned" cocktail, which consists of sugar syrup, Angostura bitters, ice cubes, and bourbon or rye whiskey. Fine for drinking long, it is hopeless for appreciating the aroma and taste of malt whiskey—or indeed of any whiskey worthy of consideration. For this, you need a glass that will present the aroma to the best advantage.

COPITA Also known as a *catavino*—and adopted and adapted from sherry glasses—the copita is the industry standard glass for the organoleptic assessment of whiskey. It has a bowl, so you can swirl the liquid and release its aroma, and the rim narrows, so the aroma is presented to the nose extremely well.

THE RIEDEL "GLAS" Founded in Austria in 1756, and still managed by descendants of the founder, Riedel is the world's leading manufacturer of glasses designed specifically for wines and spirits. Georg Riedel, the current president of the company, created this glass in 1992, but now admits that it was his one failure. Its straight sides do not gather the aroma, although the lip presents the spirit nicely on the palate.

THE GLENCAIRN GLASS The malt whisky industry wanted something more robust than a copita, so Glencairn Crystal in Glasgow came up with a stocky glass, reminiscent of a pot still. It is widely used in the whiskey world.

THE GLENMORANGIE GLASS This small, elegant glass was first adopted and promoted by Glenmorangie. It is standard practice in the whiskey trade to place a cover on the glass, to hold in the aromas—usually a watch glass is used. Glenmorangie went further with this charming little lid.

THE SINGLE MALTS OF SCOTLAND GLASS Developed by The Whiskey Exchange, London, to showcase their range of malts of the same name, this glass is good for both nosing and tasting.

OLD-FASHIONED GLASS Often made of crystal, an old-fashioned glass is designed for a long drink with lots of ice. Since the liquid will "sweat," coasters should be provided. A smaller version is called a "jigger" and is used as a measure.

QUAICH The Celtic *quaich* ("koo-ayk") is a very ancient drinking vessel. The shape is thought to have evolved from that of a scallop shell. Early examples are wooden, but today they are typically of silver or pewter. The Scotch whisky industry's most exclusive club is The Keepers of the Quaich.

SPRINGBANK 10-YEAR-OLD

SPRINGBANK 15-YEAR-OLD

SPEY

Glen Tromie, Kingussie, Inverness-shire
www.speysidedistillery.com

With a production of just 130,000 gallons (600,000 liters), the Speyside distillery, named after Scotland's biggest malt whisky region is no giant. Nor is it all that old. Despite its rustic appearance—only a discreet modern smoke stack belies its youth—Speyside was commissioned in 1962 by the blender and bottler George Christie. Built stone-by-stone, it was not finished until 1987. In 2012, the distillery was acquired by Harvey's of Edinburgh, and, since 2015, its single malt has been marketed as Spey.

SPEY 12-YEAR-OLD

SINGLE MALT: SPEYSIDE 40% ABV
Fresh and relatively light on the nose, with roasted barley, cooking apples, and nutty vanilla. More vanilla on the palate, along with walnuts, dried fruit, and brittle toffee.

SPEYBURN

Rothes, Aberlour, Morayshire
www.speyburn.com

Whether she knew it or not, Queen Victoria's loyal subjects at the newly built Speyburn Distillery near Rothes labored through the night to produce a whisky for her Diamond Jubilee of 1897. It was mid-December and, though the windows were not yet in place and snow was swirling in from outside, the distillery manager ordered the stills to be fired up. Speyburn has retained its Victorian charm and, since 1991, has been owned by Inver House.

SPEYBURN 10-YEAR-OLD

SINGLE MALT: SPEYSIDE 40% ABV
Despite older expressions, including a recently released 25-year-old Solera, the core expression remains the 10-year-old, which has a flavor of vanilla fudge and a sweet, lingering finish.

SPRINGBANK

Campbeltown, Argyll
www.springbankwhisky.com

Springbank was officially founded in 1828, at a time when there were no fewer than 13 licensed distillers in Campbeltown. Although this end of the Mull of Kintyre stills feels pretty cut off by car, it was always a short hop across the Firth of Clyde to Glasgow by ship. And, as the second city of the empire boomed, distilleries like Springbank were on hand to quench its ever-growing thirst. In the other direction there was the US but, when that went dry during Prohibition, and the big blenders turned ever more to Speyside, Campbeltown's demise was swift.

Yet Springbank survived. Much of this must have been down to its continuity: the distillery was originally owned by the Reid family, who sold out to their in-laws, the Mitchells, in the mid-19th century. The Mitchells are still in charge, and have built up a real cult following for their innovative range of single malts.

The distillery itself is quirky in the extreme, and Springbank malts all its own barley requirements in a house on a traditional malting floor. It then mashes in a cast iron open mash tun, and the wash still is both directly fired and internally steam-heated. Finally, the mature spirit is bottled on site.

SPRINGBANK 10-YEAR-OLD

SINGLE MALT: CAMPBELTOWN 46% ABV
A complex cocktail of flavors, from ripe citrus fruit to peat smoke, vanilla, spice, and a faint underlying salty tang.

SPRINGBANK 15-YEAR-OLD

SINGLE MALT: CAMPBELTOWN 46% ABV
Sweet toffee and candied peel on the nose give way to more exotic sweet-and-sour flavors in the mouth.

**SPRINGBANK 12-YEAR-OLD
CASK STRENGTH 2014 RELEASE**

SINGLE MALT: CAMPBELTOWN 54.3% ABV
*Christmas cake aromas, with vanilla
and sherry on the nose, plus a maritime
note. The palate is viscous and earthy,
with soft peat smoke, plus spice, ginger,
caramel, and light sherry.*

SPRINGBANK 18-YEAR-OLD

SINGLE MALT: CAMPBELTOWN 46% ABV
*The nose is rich, with sweet sherry,
angelica, and apricots, while the
palate is rounded and confident,
offering fresh fruit, smoke, molasses,
and licorice, leading into a slowly
drying finish.*

Standing on the shore of Loch Indaal, Bowmore is Islay's oldest distillery. It was founded in 1779 by a local farmer *(see p. 51)*, who in its early years complained of having an insufficient supply of barley due to the number of illicit distillers on the island.

STEWARTS CREAM OF THE BARLEY

Owner: Chivas Brothers

First produced around 1831, this old-established brand is today a bestseller in Ireland. For many years it enjoyed great popularity in Scotland, too, not least because of its widespread distribution in public house chain of Allied, the owner at the time. Single malt from Glencadam used to be at the heart of the blend. With changes in ownership, Glencadam is now in other hands, but the blend reputedly still contains a healthy proportion of up to 50 different single malts.

STEWARTS CREAM OF THE BARLEY

BLEND 40% ABV
A malty, sweet, soft, and slightly spirity nose. The fruitiness of a young spirit on the palate—raw and a little smoky. Peppery, drying, charred-wood finish.

STRATHCLYDE

Owner: Chivas Brothers

Strathclyde first opened in the Gorbels district of Glasgow in 1928, constructed by Long John blended whisky owners Seager Evans & Co. The distillery eventually passed to Allied Domecq, whose investment in the facility increased capacity to 8.6 million gallons (39 million liters) a year. The facility uses two of its column stills for grain whisky, and the other five for grain neutral spirit. Very little Strathclyde is bottled as grain whisky, although a 2001 13-year-old Cask Strength is now available. Strathclyde is considered the most ''meaty'' of the grain whiskies.

STRATHCLYDE CASK STRENGTH 13-YEAR-OLD

SINGLE GRAIN 64.4% ABV
Citrus, toffee, and banana, on the nose. Fudge and brandy on the palate, before drying rapidly.

STRATHISLA

Keith, Banffshire
www.maltwhiskydistilleries.com

In 1786, Alexander Milne and George Taylor founded the Milltown Distillery in Keith. The whisky it produced was known as Strathisla and, in 1951, this was adopted as the name for the distillery. Over the years, Strathisla has survived fires, explosions, and bankruptcy, to become the oldest and possibly most handsome distillery in the Highlands, with a high-gabled roof and two pagodas. Bought by Chivas Brothers in 1950, it has been the spiritual home of Chivas Regal ever since.

STRATHISLA 12-YEAR-OLD

SINGLE MALT: SPEYSIDE 43% ABV
A rich, sumptuous nose and a spicy, fruitcake character, thanks to the influence of sherry. It is medium-bodied, with a slight smoky note on the finish.

STRATHMILL

Keith, Banffshire
www.malts.com

With its twin pagoda roof, this handsome late-Victorian distillery was built in 1891 as the Glenisla-Glenlivet Distillery. Four years later it was bought by Gilbey's, the London-based gin distiller, and rechristened Strathmill—a reference to the fact that it stood on the site of an old corn mill. A single malt expression was released as early as 1909, but Strathmill's long-term role in life was—and is—to supply malt for blended Scotch, particularly J&B.

STRATHMILL FLORA & FAUNA 12-YEAR-OLD

SINGLE MALT: SPEYSIDE 43% ABV
On the lighter, more delicate side of Speyside, Strathmill has a nutty, malty character with notes of vanilla from the wood. It is quite soft and medium-sweet on the tongue.

WHISKEY STYLES
GRAIN WHISKEY

Unlike malt whiskey, which is made in pot stills, grain whiskey is made using a continuous still (also known as a Coffey or Patent still). It is distilled from a mixture of malted barley and other unmalted cereals, such as wheat or corn. Barley is malted in the conventional way (*see pp.38–39*) and mixed with hot water in a mash tun with the unmalted cereals, which have been cooked under pressure to soften the starch and make it soluble. The resulting sugary liquid (or wort) is then fermented with yeast to produce the wash, ready for distilling.

In the continuous still, the wash passes through two columns fitted with metal plates. Heated wash is pumped into the top of the first column (the analyzer), where it meets steam rising up through the column. As alcohol boils at a lower temperature than water, the alcohol can be extracted as vapor. It is then pumped to the base of the second column (the rectifier). The temperature of the column is highest at the base and coolest at the top, so the higher the vapor rises, the greater its alcohol content. The distiller can draw off the resulting grain whiskey at the desired strength from one of the plates, where the vapor condenses. Virtually pure alcohol (about 96% ABV) is collected at the top of the column and water discharged at the base. This kind of still can be operated for several weeks continuously.

Like malt whiskey, grain whiskey is filled into oak casks and matured in warehouses for many years. It tends to be milder in flavor and aroma than malt, and is predominantly used in blending (*see p.78*). However, a tiny amount is sold as grain whiskey. Cameron Brig bottles a single grain 12-year-old and Compass Box sells a delicately flavored blended grain, called Hedonism.

TALISKER 10-YEAR-OLD
SINGLE MALT: ISLANDS 45.8% ABV
An iconic West Coast malt with a pungent, slightly peaty character that has a peppery catch on the finish.

TALISKER 18-YEAR-OLD
SINGLE MALT: ISLANDS 45.8% ABV
Age has softened the youthful vigor of the 10-year-old, and given it a fine scent of leather and aromatic smoke and a creamy, mouth-filling texture.

TALISKER DISTILLERS EDITION 1996

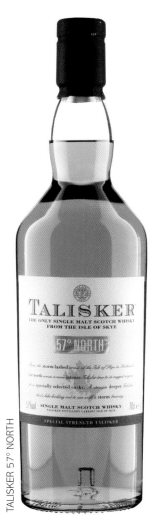

TALISKER 57° NORTH

TALISKER 25-YEAR-OLD

TALISKER 30-YEAR-OLD

TALISKER

Carbost, Isle of Skye
www.discovering-distilleries.com

The Scotch Whisky Industry Record of 1823 lists seven licensed distilleries on Skye, of which none has survived. There were doubtless many illicit stills in operation, but these have all long gone, leaving only Talisker, founded in 1830 by Hugh and Kenneth MacAskill, still going strong. Given Skye's size and proximity to the mainland, it seems odd that it has only one distillery when Islay has so many.

Talisker struggled through the 19th century, being sold in 1857 for just £500. Things picked up when Aberdeen entrepreneur

Roderick Kemp became a co-partner in 1880. As demand from the blenders increased, small steamers began to call at the distillery to discharge grain and load up with casks.

In 1898, Talisker teamed up with Dailuaine, then the largest distillery in the Highlands. In 1916, the venture was bought by a consortium involving Dewar's, the Distillers Company, and John Walker & Sons. Ever since, Talisker has been a key component in Johnnie Walker Black Label.

Until 1928 Talisker was triple-distilled, like an Irish whiskey, which explains why two wash stills are paired to three spirit stills. The lyne arms have a unique

U shape to increase reflux and produce a cleaner spirit, although the fact that this is then condensed in worm tubs seems contradictory, as worm tubs tend to produce a heavier, more sulfurous spirit. Whatever the rationale, it seems to work, and Talisker has won countless awards. The owners have delighted fans by releasing a whole raft of ages and special editions—more than any other Diageo malt.

TALISKER DISTILLERS EDITION 1996

SINGLE MALT: ISLANDS 45.8% ABV
With a maturation that ends in Amoroso sherry casks, it has a peppery, spicy character, softened by a luscious, dried-fruit richness in the mouth.

TALISKER 57° NORTH

SINGLE MALT: ISLANDS 57% ABV
Named in reference to the latitude of the distillery, this is rich, fruity, smoky, peppery, and spicy, with a long finish.

TALISKER 25-YEAR-OLD

SINGLE MALT: ISLANDS 54.2% ABV
A brooding, complex malt, with notes of seaweed and smoke giving way to a leathery, more fruity richness.

TALISKER 30-YEAR-OLD

SINGLE MALT: ISLANDS 49.5% ABV
A highly sophisticated Talisker that's sweet, spicy, fruity, and floral, with understated peat smoke and leather.

THE SECRETS OF...
TALISKER

Distilling whisky on Skye never took off as it did on Islay, possibly because it was always too wet and infertile to grow the barley to kick-start a whisky industry on the island.

In Talisker's case there was also the local minister to contend with and his weekly sermon on the evils of strong drink. In the 1850s his prayers were answered when the distillery was sold for a pittance—half what it cost to build.

From this shaky start, Talisker has risen to cult status among its devotees. Its single malts, with their brooding, pungent character that seems to explode with a peppery catch on the finish, have grown evermore popular and garnered many prestigious awards.

Somehow the physical isolation of Talisker, on the shores of Loch Harport, must play a part in its distinctive taste. Unlike on Speyside, where there were always neighboring distilleries to learn from, Talisker had to work things out for itself. One can imagine early distillers playing with the shape of the lyne arms, adjusting the peating of the barley, the shape of the stills, and the speed of distillation to achieve a desired effect. The result is the Talisker we can taste today, a whisky like no other in Scotland.

▲ SWEET ISOLATION
Though Skye is connected to the mainland by a bridge, Talisker still feels cut off. It sits by the shore of Loch Harport, beneath the blackened, serrated peaks of the Cuillins.

▼ THE WASH STILLS SET-UP
In 1960, Talisker almost burned down when the door to a wash still was left open, and the volatile liquid ignited. They were replaced with stills of exactly the same shape and size. Quite what their unique shape, with their curious U-shaped lyne arms, give to the final character of the whisky is hard to gauge, but the master distiller at the time did not take any chances.

▲ SUGAR LEVELS IN THE WASH
Samples are taken to find the specific gravity of the wash before fermentation. By checking sugar levels before the yeast enzymes have started their work, the distiller can predict the final alcoholic strength of the wash. The other, less scientific, check is simply to sniff the air and make sure it is sweet and malty.

INCREASED REFLUX ▶

Having three spirit stills for just two wash stills is said to be a hangover from the old days, before 1928, when Talisker was triple distilled, like an Irish whiskey. This must have stripped out much of its character. The lyne arms are flat, rather than tilting down, to increase reflux.

▼ OLD-STYLE WORM TUBS

There is no doubt that having traditional, old-style worm tubs to condense the spirit impacts on the character of the new make. Though the famous U-shaped lyne arms will have increased the amount of copper contact, the use of worm tubs works the other way, ensuring a heavier, more sulfurous spirit. It may appear counter-intuitive, but it certainly seems to work.

▲ THE DUNNAGE WAREHOUSE

While much Talisker is shipped off the island for maturation on the mainland, some casks are matured on site. The old-fashioned dunnage warehouses have a glorious musty smell of damp earth, wood, and sweet, spirity vapors. How much the scent of sea air and seaweed actually penetrates the casks is hard to say, but Talisker does have an unmistakable maritime character.

TAMDHU 10-YEAR-OLD

TAMDHU BATCH STRENGTH (BATCH 1)

THE TALISMAN

Tomatin Distillery, Inverness-shire
www.talismanwhisky.co.uk

The Talisman is the house blend from Tomatin Distillery (*see p.170*). As you might expect, given this, there is a high proportion of Tomatin malts in what is a superior blend. It offers surprises, too: there are complex and smooth aromas, with subtle peaty and savory overtones, and the grain marries well with the malt. If you like your blend smooth but with a bit of bite, this could be the one for you.

THE TALISMAN

BLEND 40% ABV
A complex aroma on the nose: fruits and maltiness with some pleasing grain or cereal highlights. Honey and vanilla with hints of apple on the palate. Subtle peaty notes linger to give a long finish.

TAMDHU

Knockando, Aberlour, Morayshire
Owner: Ian Macleod Distillers
www.tamdhu.com

For all the misty-eyed romance about Speyside's early roots as a region teeming with smugglers and illicit stills, the railways, which arrived in the second half of the 19th century, had a far greater impact. Before the opening of the Strathspey line in 1863, the region was simply too cut off to flourish. But once the rails were laid, distilleries began popping up. One such was Tamdhu, founded in 1896 between Cardhu and Knockando. In fact, Knockando's old station was used as the reception center of Tamdhu Distillery.

Tamdhu is a large setup, with nine pine washbacks, three pairs of stills, and a mix of dunnage and racked warehousing on site. The former Saladin maltings, which were an interesting feature of

Tamdhu, are now disused. The distillery was closed in 2010, and, in 2011, owner Edrington sold the mothballed distillery to Ian Macleod Distillers, with production resuming the following year. A 10-year-old with a strong sherry cask maturation influence is now the principal expression.

TAMDHU 10-YEAR-OLD

SINGLE MALT: SPEYSIDE 40% ABV
Soft sherry notes on the nose, new leather, almonds, marzipan, and a hint of peat. Citrus fruit, gentle spice, and more sweet sherry on the leathery palate, which closes with black pepper.

TAMDHU BATCH STRENGTH (BATCH 1)

SINGLE MALT: SPEYSIDE 58.8% ABV
Vanilla, toffee, milk chocolate, and sweet sherry on the nose. The palate offers orange marmalade, vanilla, malt, cinnamon, and pepper, finishing with sherry and nutmeg.

TAMNAVULIN

Ballindalloch, Banffshire

In 1966, Invergordon Distillers, now part of Whyte & Mackay, decided to build a big new distillery in a picturesque corner of Upper Speyside by the River Livet. Its six stills could pump out as much as 880,000 gallons (4 million liters) of pure alcohol a year. Yet, in 1995, Tamnavulin closed down—the owners, it seemed, had decided to focus their attention on their other distilleries, Dalmore and Jura in particular. The UB Group bought Whyte & Mackay in 2007, and now Tamnavulin is back up and running.

TAMNAVULIN 12-YEAR-OLD

SINGLE MALT: SPEYSIDE 40% ABV
A light, aperitif-style malt, with a dry, cereal character and minty nose. This standard release of the so-called "Stillman's Dram" is joined by occasional older expressions.

TEANINICH FLORA & FAUNA 10-YEAR-OLD

TEANINICH GORDON & MACPHAIL 1991

TEACHER'S

Owner: Beam Suntory
www.teacherswhisky.com

This venerable brand can be dated to 1830, when William Teacher opened a grocery shop in Glasgow. Like other whisky entrepreneurs, he soon branched out into the spirits trade. His sons took over, and blending became increasingly important. In 1884 the trademark Teacher's Highland Cream was registered, and this single brand eventually came to dominate the business. The whisky was always forceful in character, built around single malts from Glendronach and Ardmore. Today it continues to prove popular in South America.

TEACHER'S HIGHLAND CREAM

BLEND 40% ABV

Full-flavored, oily, with fudge and caramel notes on the nose, toffee and licorice on the palate. A well-rounded, smooth texture and quite a quick finish that leaves the palate refreshed.

TEANINICH

Alness, Ross-shire
www.malts.com

Distillery visitors to the Highland village of Alness, just north of Inverness, rarely notice Teaninich as they make their way to its more famous neighbor Dalmore. And yet Teaninich has been quietly distilling away with barely a break since 1817, when it was set up by Captain Hugh Munro, who named it after his Highland estate beside the River Alness.

Teaninich, it seems, was run as a hobby until 1852, when it was leased out to Robert Pattison of Leith, whose family firm almost brought down the entire whisky industry when it collapsed in 1899. Despite this, the distillery has been in almost continual production, stopping during World War II and briefly again in the 1980s. By then there were two still rooms working in tandem. These were known as Side A and Side B—not the most

poetic of names, but then no one was interested in marketing Teaninich as a single malt to whisky-drinkers—its role was to supply the spirit for blending.

In 1992, Teaninich's owners, UDV (now Diageo), released a 10-year-old expression. Seven years later it decommissioned Side B. The distillery crushes its malted barley with an Asnong hammer mill, as opposed to the more traditional roller mills. Whether this affects the flavor of the malt is hard to say.

TEANINICH FLORA & FAUNA 10-YEAR-OLD

SINGLE MALT: HIGHLANDS 43% ABV

The only official distillery bottling is polished and grassy, with a predominantly malty flavor.

TEANINICH GORDON & MACPHAIL 1991

SINGLE MALT: HIGHLANDS 46% ABV

A deep amber, fruitcake-flavored malt, with notes of mint, tobacco, cloves, and wood smoke.

TÉ BHEAG

Owner: The Gaelic Whisky Co.
www.gaelicwhisky.com

Although it is blended and bottled elsewhere in Scotland, this is another brand from the Pràban na Linne company on Skye (The Gaelic Whisky Company). Té Bheag (pronounced *Chey Vek*) means "the little lady" and is the name of the boat in the logo. It is also colloquial Gaelic for a "wee dram." The blend is popular in France and has won medals in international competition. Té Bheag is non-chill filtered, and Islay, Island, Highland, and Speyside malts aged from 8–11 years are used in the blend.

TÉ BHEAG

BLEND 40% ABV

The nose is fresh, with a citrus note, good richness, a delicate peatiness, and a touch of cereal. Weighty on the palate, with a good touch of licorice, a toffee-like richness, and some peat.

TOBERMORY 10-YEAR-OLD

TOBERMORY 15-YEAR-OLD

TOMATIN LEGACY

TOMATIN 30-YEAR-OLD

TOBERMORY

Tobermory, Isle of Mull
www.tobermorydistillery.com

If Islay to the south can boast eight working distilleries (at the last count), it seems only fair that Mull should have at least one. And yet the very survival of Tobermory has been something of a miracle, given that it has spent much of its life lying idle.

Tobermory was founded as the Ledaig Distillery by John Sinclair in 1798. For Sinclair, whisky was a sideline to his main business of dealing in kelp, and, when he died in 1837, the distillery died with him, remaining shut for the next 40 years. It was bought by the Distillers Company in 1916, but became an early casualty of the Depression and closed in 1930.

Once the place had been gutted, few believed whisky would ever be made here again. Then, in 1972, the site was bought and restored by a consortium that included a shipping company and the famous sherry house of Domecq. The new Ledaig distillery company soon collapsed but, having installed new stills and other whisky-making equipment, Tobermory's future was finally made secure. Production resumed in 1989 and, in 1993, the distillery was bought by its current owner, Burn Stewart.

TOBERMORY 10-YEAR-OLD

SINGLE MALT: ISLANDS 46.3% ABV
This fresh, unpeated, maritime malt claims to have a slight smoky character, thanks to the water from Mull's peat lochans. If true, the effect is subtle.

TOBERMORY 15-YEAR-OLD

SINGLE MALT: ISLANDS 46.3% ABV
The nose has rich fruitcake notes and a trace of marmalade, thanks to aging in sherry casks. The spicy character comes through on the tongue. It is non-chill filtered.

TOMATIN

Tomatin, Inverness-shire
www.tomatin.com

With 23 stills and a capacity of 2.6 million gallons (12 million liters) of pure alcohol, Tomatin was the colossus of the malt whisky industry in 1974 at the time of its expansion.

Founded in 1897, it took a while to reach its super-size status. Its two stills were increased to four as recently as 1956; thereafter expansion was rapid until it peaked in the 1970s, just in time for the first big post-war slump. Tomatin struggled on as an independent distillery until 1985, when the liquidators arrived. A year later it was sold to two of its long-standing customers—Takara Shuzo and Okara & Co—thus becoming the first Scottish distillery in Japanese hands. With 11 fewer stills, production has been cut back to 1.1 million gallons (5 million liters), which still allows plenty of capacity for bottling as a single malt. Tomatin's principal bottlings include 12-, 18-, and 30-year-olds, and Legacy, the no-age-statement, while several expressions of peated Tomatin have been released since 2013 under the Cù Bòcan label.

TOMATIN LEGACY

SINGLE MALT: HIGHLANDS 43% ABV
The fragrant nose offers malt, honey, pepper, and faint treacle. The palate is fresh and fruity, with pineapple, pepper, and a suggestion of chile in the drying finish.

TOMATIN 30-YEAR-OLD

SINGLE MALT: HIGHLANDS 43% ABV
A voluptuous after-dinner dram with a big, sherried nose and impressive legs.

TOMATIN 12-YEAR-OLD

SINGLE MALT: HIGHLANDS 40% ABV
*A mellow, soft-centered
Speyside-style malt, which
replaced the old core 10-year-old
expression back in 2003.*

TOMATIN 18-YEAR-OLD

SINGLE MALT: HIGHLANDS 43% ABV
*The deep amber hue betrays
a strong sherry influence that
brings out a fruity, cinnamon
flavor in the malt.*

WHISKEY STYLES
BLENDED MALT

In 1853 Andrew Usher, an Edinburgh-based wine and spirit merchant, launched the world's first modern brand of Scotch whisky—Old Vatted Glenlivet. Assuming there was no grain spirit in the mix, this would now be called a "Blended Malt," defined by the Scotch Whisky Association (SWA) as "a blend of Single Malt Scotch Whiskies which have been distilled at more than one distillery."

This definition was hammered out when Diageo decided to relaunch the Speyside whisky as a "Pure Malt" in 2002. No longer a "single malt," it meant other malts could be added to Diageo's Cardhu to satisfy surging demand in Spain and perhaps challenge Glenfiddich for pole position among malts. Glenfiddich's owners, William Grant & Sons, were alarmed and led a campaign that provoked the biggest storm in the whisky industry in recent years. There were cries of betrayal, questions in Parliament, and eventually an embarrassing climbdown by Diageo in March 2003.

While Cardhu reverted to being a single malt, the industry had to decide what to call such whiskies in the future. Within the trade they had always been known as vatted malts, though this was thought to have industrial connotations. "Pure malt" sounded better to marketing folk, though it was no longer politically acceptable within the industry. Eventually, having studied Roget's Thesaurus for many months, the committee responsible came up with "blended malt," though many still question whether this will only confuse consumers even more.

TOMINTOUL 10-YEAR-OLD

TOMINTOUL 16-YEAR-OLD

TOMINTOUL PEATY TANG

TOMINTOUL

Kirkmichael, Ballindalloch, Grampian
www.tomintoulwhisky.com

Of all the Speyside distilleries that bolted the magic word "Glenlivet" on to their names in the hope of added luster, Tomintoul-Glenlivet has the best case, being a virtual next-door neighbor. Tomintoul stands 1,165ft (350m) up, beside the Avon River, the largest tributary of the Spey River. It opened in 1964—a time of great confidence in the industry, with booming sales of blended Scotch, particularly in export markets such as the US. Tomintoul's role in life was simply to supply malt for these blends. This role continues under Angus Dundee, who bought the distillery in 2000, when it was in need of malt for its own blends (see p.23). And yet, while single malts account for a small fraction of the 600,000 gallons (3.3 million liters) produced each year, the number of expressions has

increased greatly. Peaty Tang, for example, is a vatting of young unpeated malt and even younger peated malt. The distillery's oldest expression is a 40-year-old released in 2015.

TOMINTOUL 10-YEAR-OLD

SINGLE MALT: SPEYSIDE 40% ABV
First launched in 2002, this delicate, aperitif-style malt has some vanilla from the wood and a light cereal character.

TOMINTOUL 16-YEAR-OLD

SINGLE MALT: SPEYSIDE 40% ABV
The extra years give this expression a more nutty, spicy character, with notes of orange peel on the nose, as well as more depth and a more rounded texture.

TOMINTOUL PEATY TANG

SINGLE MALT: SPEYSIDE 40% ABV
The peaty character of this malt comes through on the nose, though not so much as to set off the smoke alarm or swamp the underlying cereal character.

ALL ABOUT...
LIQUEURS

The earliest way of drinking whiskey was probably to mix the spirit with honey, herbs, and fruits. From as early as the late 14th century, and increasingly during the 16th century, recipe books were available for preparing medicines at home, which involved distilled spirits compounded with many varieties of herbs. An alfresco hunting feast enjoyed by James V, King of Scots, in 1531 includes, among many other drinks, *Hippocras aquavitae*—a mix of spirits with sugar and spices, strained through a "Hippocrates sleeve," named after the patron of physicians. By the 18th century, when whiskey drinking was more widespread, it was commonly served as a "toddy" or a "punch," mixed with sugar, lemons, and spices such as cloves and cinnamon—no doubt to cover the variable quality of the whiskey itself.

DRAMBUIE Supposedly made from a recipe gifted by Bonnie Prince Charlie to Captain John McKinnon in 1746, Drambuie began to be made commercially in the 1880s. The recipe is still a family secret, handed down through the female line. It has a honeyed sweetness, a floral heathery note, and a little spiciness.

BAILEYS Launched in 1974, this mix of Irish whiskey and cream has for many years been the best-selling liqueur (and one of the top-selling premium spirits) in the world. It is the single most successful spirit to be launched anywhere in the world in the last 50 years. As well as whiskey and cream, there's a touch of vanilla and chocolate in the blend of this silky liqueur.

GLAYVA Created by Ronald Morrison before World War I, and named by his Gaelic-speaking warehouseman (*gle mhath*), pronounced "glay-va," is Gaelic for "very good"). Almond essence and tangerine are discernable in the flavor, and some mildly warming spices. The liqueur makes a good base for fruity cocktails.

IRISH MIST Claiming to be made to an ancient recipe for a drink known as "heather wine," and using Irish whiskey, honey, and herbs in the blend, Irish Mist is now sold in 60 countries.

JACQUIN'S ROCK AND RYE Made with rock candy, Kentucky Rye whiskey, and candied oranges (which are suspended in the bottle), this liqueur was first introduced in Philadelphia in the 1930s. The flavor is caramel-like, with hints of cherry.

SOUTHERN COMFORT This blend of whiskey, sugar, and assorted fruits was invented by New Orleans bar tender Martin Wilkes Heron in 1874. He later patented the drink in Memphis, Tennessee, in 1889. It is produced at various strengths.

ORANGERIE Created by John Glaser, the talented and passionate owner of Compass Box, this is an "infusion" of Navalino orange zest, cassia bark, cloves, and blended Scotch. Clean and fresh on the palate, Orangerie is not as sweet as most liqueurs.

TULLIBARDINE 225 SAUTERNES FINISH

TULLIBARDINE 228 BURGUNDY FINISH

TULLIBARDINE SOVEREIGN

TULLIBARDINE

Blackford, Perthshire
www.tullibardine.com

With its box shape, corrugated roof, and tall metal chimney, Tullibardine is no homely Victorian distillery. It was designed in 1949 by William Delmé-Evans, and survived through various changes in ownership until it was bought by Whyte & Mackay in 1993. The company promptly mothballed the distillery a year later and, as each year passed, the chances of resuscitation appeared to fade.

Then, in 2003 a rescue package was agreed, and Tullibardine was bought by an independent consortium that began distilling again. The new owners released a wide range of expressions, including many cask finishes, and, in 2011, the French family drinks company Picard Vins & Spiritueux purchased Tullibardine, going on to launch an entirely new product range in 2013. Two years later, the oldest cask of whisky in the Tullibardine warehouse—dating from 1952—was bottled as the first release in the Custodian Collection.

TULLIBARDINE 225 SAUTERNES FINISH

SINGLE MALT: HIGHLANDS 43% ABV
Citrus fruits, vanilla, white pepper, and a slightly herbal note on the nose. Citrus fruits carry over onto the malty palate, with orange, milk chocolate, and enduring spice.

TULLIBARDINE 228 BURGUNDY FINISH

SINGLE MALT: HIGHLANDS 43% ABV
A hint of charred oak on the nose, with vanilla, milk chocolate, and sweet chili. Sweet and spicy on the palate, with hazelnuts, apples, and allspice, leading to a lengthy finish.

TULLIBARDINE SOVEREIGN

SINGLE MALT: HIGHLANDS 43% ABV
The floral nose features fudge, vanilla, and freshly cut, sweet grass, while the palate is fruity and malty with cocoa, vanilla, and a spicy finish.

TORMORE

Advie, Grantown-on-Spey, Morayshire
www.tormoredistillery.com

Built on a grand scale in 1958, Tormore symbolizes the whisky industry's self-confidence at a time when global demand for blended Scotch was growing strongly.

With its copper-clad roof and giant chimney stack, the distillery towers up beside the A95 in Speyside. It seems no expense was spared by the architect, Sir Albert Richardson, a past president of the Royal Academy.

Tormore is now owned by Chivas Brothers (Pernod Ricard), who released 14- and 16-year-old variants in 2014.

TORMORE 14-YEAR-OLD

SINGLE MALT: SPEYSIDE 43% ABV
Tangy berry fruits, vanilla, spice, and almonds on the nose. The palate is smooth and citric, with toffee, ginger, and a closing note of pepper.

VAT 69

Owner: Diageo

At its peak, VAT 69 was the tenth-best-selling whisky in the world, and references to it crop up in films and books from the 1950s and 60s. It was launched in 1882 and was once the flagship brand of the independent South Queensferry blenders William Sanderson & Co, its name coming from the fact that VAT 69 was the finest of 100 possible blends tested. Today its current owner, Diageo, gives precedence to Johnnie Walker and J&B, and it might not be unreasonable to suggest that—despite sales of more than 1 million cases a year in Venezuela, Spain, and Australia—VAT 69's glory days are behind it.

VAT 69

BLEND 40% ABV
A light and well-balanced standard blend with a noticeably sweet impact of vanilla ice cream initially and a pleasantly malty background.

WHITE HORSE

Owner: Diageo

In its heyday, White Horse was one of the world's top ten whiskies, selling more than 2 million cases a year.

Its guiding genius was "Restless Peter" Mackie, described in his day as "one-third genius, one-third megalomaniac, and one-third eccentric". He took over the family firm in 1890 and established an enviable reputation as a gifted blender and entrepreneur.

White Horse is still marketed in more than 100 countries. A deluxe 12-year-old version, White Horse Extra Fine, is occasionally seen.

WHITE HORSE

BLEND 40% ABV
Complex and satisfying, White Horse retains the robust flavor of Lagavulin, assisted by renowned Speysiders such as Aultmore. With its long finish, this is a stylish, intriguing blend of crisp grain, clean malt, and earthy peat.

WILLIAM LAWSON'S FINEST

WILLIAM LAWSON'S SCOTTISH GOLD 12-YEAR-OLD

WINDSOR 12-YEAR-OLD

WINDSOR 17-YEAR-OLD

WILLIAM LAWSON'S

Owner: John Dewar & Sons (Bacardi)

Although the brand name of Lawson's dates back to 1849, the "home" distillery today is Macduff, built in 1960 by a consortium of blenders in northeast Scotland and subsequently sold to Martini.

Lawson's is managed alongside its big brother, Dewar's, and, although dwarfed by it and virtually invisible in the UK, the brand sells well over 1 million cases a year in France, Belgium, Spain, and parts of South America. It is well known in Europe for its iconoclastic advertising and provocative TV commercials.

Glen Deveron single malt from Macduff features heavily in the blend. Macduff employs the highest percentage of sherry wood of any whisky in the Dewar's group, and this contributes to the Lawson house style—a full flavor and rich golden color. In recent years the standard expression,

William Lawson's Finest, has been moved into line with other standard blends and is competitive on price while remaining good value for money. The range also comprises the 12-year-old Scottish Gold and two premium styles: an 18-year-old Founder's Reserve and limited quantities of the 21-year-old Private Reserve.

WILLIAM LAWSON'S FINEST

BLEND 40% ABV

The nose is slightly dry, with delicate oak notes. The palate is well-balanced, with hints of a crisp candy-apple flavor. A medium- to full-bodied whisky that punches above its weight.

WILLIAM LAWSON'S SCOTTISH GOLD 12-YEAR-OLD

BLEND 40% ABV

Fuller-flavored than the standard Lawson's expression, suggesting a higher malt content.

WINDSOR

Owner: Diageo

According to its owner Diageo, Windsor is "the largest selling super premium Scotch whisky in the world." As such, the brand has fallen prey to counterfeiting in the highly competitive South Korean market. Drinkers here look for a small, bar-shaped weight that signals the whisky's authencity— once the cap is twisted and opened, the weight is separated and falls into the bottle.

The name Windsor is an overt link to the British royal family, and the packaging strongly confirms the brand's luxury position. Although Windsor was originally developed in a partnership between Seagram and local producer Doosan, Diageo acquired the Seagram interest and launched Windsor 17 as the first super premium whisky in 2000. The Korean market at the time was dominated by 12-year-old premium products. Windsor 17's sweeping

popularity posed a strong threat to its competitors, many of whom have since emulated the older style.

Buoyed by the success of Windsor 17, Diageo recently unveiled a 21-year-old variant, aimed at encouraging further trading up to even more premium blends. The company currently supplies Windsor products to China and Japan, and has plans to expand into other Asian countries.

Do not confuse Windsor with its Canadian namesake (see p.277).

WINDSOR 12-YEAR-OLD

BLEND 40% ABV

Vanilla, wood, and light fresh fruit on the nose. Green apples on the palate, with honey, more vanilla, and spiciness that mellows into a smooth finish.

WINDSOR 17-YEAR-OLD

BLEND 40% ABV

A rich vanilla crème brûlée nose, with fruit and a background layer of malt. Fresh fruit and honey on the palate, with creamy vanilla oak notes.

Quarter casks like these at the Speyside Cooperage accelerate the rate of maturation through increased interaction between the wood and the spririt. Laphroaig uses them to good effect to bottle a relatively young whisky.

**WHYTE & MACKAY
30-YEAR-OLD**

BLEND 40% ABV

*The flagship of the Whyte &
Mackay range is a big, rich, oaky
whisky with a deep mahogany
hue. The sherry influence is
strong, with a pepperiness
mellowed by the sweeter flavors.*

**WHYTE & MACKAY
OLD LUXURY**

BLEND 40% ABV

*A rich bouquet, with malty
notes and a subtle sherry
influence. It all blends
smoothly on the palate.
Mellow and silky textured.
Warming finish.*

WHYTE & MACKAY SPECIAL

WHYTE & MACKAY THE THIRTEEN

WHYTE & MACKAY SUPREME

WHYTE & MACKAY

www.whyteandmackay.com

The Glasgow-based firm of Whyte & Mackay started blending in the late-19th century. Its flagship Special brand quickly established itself as a Scottish favorite, and remains so to this day among value-conscious consumers. Having been through a bewildering number of owners and a management buyout in recent years, the company was acquired in May 2007 by the Indian conglomerate UB Group, which sold it to Emperador Inc. in 2014.

One constant through all these changes has been Whyte & Mackay's

highly regarded master blender, Richard Paterson, who joined the firm in 1970 and has received a great number of awards. As well as creating the "new" 40-year-old, Paterson has overseen several aged innovations. The range today includes the Special (which is actually the standard blend) and five expressions aged at 13, 19, 22, 30, and 40 years old. The company defends the unusual age declarations on the grounds that "the extra year gives the whisky a chance to marry for a longer period, giving it a distinct graceful smoothness." A number of own-label customers are also supplied by Whyte & Mackay.

Historically, the company's main market has been the UK, although

the older styles, especially the 13-year-old, are popular in Spain, France, and Scandinavia. Sales in India are expected to grow since the launch of the locally bottled Whyte & Mackay range in 2008.

The backbone of the blends emanates from Speyside and the Highlands, although small amounts from Islay, Campbeltown, and the Lowlands are also used. Dalmore and—to a lesser extent—Isle of Jura are the company's flagship single malts, and Dalmore's influence can be clearly felt in the premium blends. Great stress is laid on marrying, the company having long been an adherent to this time-consuming process. All the blends are noticeably smooth and well balanced.

WHYTE & MACKAY SPECIAL
BLEND 40% ABV
The nose is full, round, and well-balanced. On the palate, honeyed soft fruits in profusion; smooth and rich, with a long finish.

WHYTE & MACKAY THE THIRTEEN
BLEND 40% ABV
Full, firm, and rich nose, with a slight hint of sherry wood. "Marrying" for a full year before bottling gives great backbone. A well-integrated blend.

WHYTE & MACKAY SUPREME
BLEND 40% ABV
Aged for 22 years, the Supreme is velvet textured, with a soft maltiness and sherry wood notes on nose and palate.

TULLAMORE D.E.W.

Bushmills

LONDONDERRY

Northern
Ireland

BELFAST

OMAGH

Echlinville

DOWNPATRICK

SLIGO

Cooley

The Shed

WESTPORT

IRELAND

Kilbeggan
(used by Cooley)

DUBLIN   Teeling

Tullamore D.E.W.   TULLAMORE

Clonminch

Glendalough   WICKLOW

GALWAY

CARLOW

LIMERICK

CLONMEL

WATERFORD

Dingle

CORK   Midleton

West Cork
Distillers

miles
0   25

0   25
kilometres

TYRCONNEL—COOLEY

POWERS—MIDLETON

U ntil comparatively recently, modern-day whiskey-making in Ireland centered on just three producers: Bushmills, Midleton, and Cooley. Now, however, we are seeing the development of a vibrant craft distilling movement, with several new entrants to the distilling ranks, while William Grant & Sons Ltd. has constructed an entirely new, large-scale distillery in which to produce its Tullamore D.E.W. brand. Bushmills and Midleton have a long history and are the only distilleries to have survived from Ireland's golden age of whiskey distilling in the 19th century. Other famous whiskey names from the 19th century, such as Jameson and Powers, which used to be made at distilleries in Dublin, were closed as independent operations, but live on as brands from Midleton. The modern Midleton plant, near Cork in the Republic of Ireland, has been in operation since the mid-1970s and produces a wide range of whiskeys. By contrast, the Bushmills Distillery, in Northern Ireland, makes only single malt whiskey—this is mixed with grain whiskey bought in from Midleton for Bushmills blends. Cooley dates only from 1987, and has revived the Locke's and Tyrconnell names in its whiskey ranges.

LOCKE'S—COOLEY

CONNEMARA—COOLEY

GREEN SPOT—MIDLETON

BUSHMILLS

JAMESON—MIDLETON

BUSHMILLS ORIGINAL

BLEND 40% ABV

*A fruity, easy-to-drink,
vanilla-infused mouthful.
Its clean, clear character
makes it very approachable.
A lovely entry to the world
of Irish whiskey.*

BUSHMILLS BLACK BUSH

BLEND 40% ABV

*A living legend, Black Bush is
the lovable rogue of the family.
It is a very classy glassful of
honey nut scrumptiousness with
an extremely silky mouthfeel.
The benchmark for Irish blends.*

BUSHMILLS MALT 10-YEAR-OLD

BUSHMILLS MALT 16-YEAR-OLD

BUSHMILLS MALT 21-YEAR-OLD

BUSHMILLS

2 Distillery Road, Bushmills,
County Antrim
www.bushmills.com

Old Bushmills has the amazing ability to be all things to all men: a thoroughly modern distillery housed in a beautiful Victorian building; a boutique distillery that nevertheless produces global brands; and a working distillery that welcomes the public.

Bushmills produces only malt whiskey, so the grain used in its blends is made to order in the Midleton Distillery. Unusually, Old Bushmills doesn't have a problem selling single malts and blends under the same name: it

is a distillery that isn't afraid to push the boundaries. An example of this is the whiskey Bushmills produced to celebrate the 400th anniversary of its original license to distil. Only a company as quixotic as Bushmills would choose a blended whiskey for such an occasion—and one bottled at 46% ABV too. Bushmills 1608 was the result, and at the heart of this limited-edition whiskey was spirit made using crystal malt—the kind of malt mostly found only in breweries. Its effect on the blend was to give it an almost spicy intensity, which was complemented by some fine sherry notes from the Oloroso casks.

BUSHMILLS MALT 10-YEAR-OLD

SINGLE MALT 40% ABV

As you'd expect from a triple-distilled, peat-free whiskey, this charmer appeals to just about everyone. There's a hint of sherry wood, but it is the classy malt that's showcased here—sweet with hints of fudgy chocolate. A classic and very approachable Irish malt.

BUSHMILLS MALT 16-YEAR-OLD

SINGLE MALT 40% ABV

This malt isn't just a straight aging of the classic 10-year-old. Instead, it's a pretty much half-and-half mix of bourbon- and sherry-cask-matured malt, married for a further nine months in port pipes. The three woods bring their own

magic to bear, and produce a riot of dried-fruit flavors cut with almonds and the ever-present honey.

BUSHMILLS MALT 21-YEAR-OLD

SINGLE MALT 40% ABV

This is the rarest of all Bushmills whiskeys—only 900 cases of the 21-year-old malt are produced each year, and then only when stocks of suitably matured whiskey become available.

This bottling is made from sherry- and bourbon-matured whiskey, which is then finished for another two years in Madeira drums. As you'd expect after 21 years, the malt is almost chewy, with chocolate notes and a sweetness that has mellowed almost to raisin pastry. Delicious.

THE SECRETS OF...
BUSHMILLS

Old Bushmills has been around for a very long time. Distilling on this site goes back to 1608 and possibly even further, though the current distillery was built in the Victorian period.

With its twin pagoda roof, the Victorian distillery is a classic of its type. What is really remarkable about Bushmills, though, is that, while production here has expanded time and again, somehow the place has never lost its charm.

Bushmills has survived for this long because it does what it does very well indeed. The equipment may change over time, but the distillery's attention to consistency means that the single malt produced today doesn't taste much different from what was being made here when America was still a colony.

Over the centuries various people and companies have owned this little corner of County Antrim; while they have come and gone, the whiskey has kept on going. In a world of change, this place is truly remarkable.

▲ **THE WATER SOURCE**
The picturesque lake in front of the distillery nicely frames the buildings. More importantly, however, it is where St. Columb's Rill is pooled. This is the distillery water source, and so this water will one day get turned into whiskey.

▲ **REVITALIZED MASH HOUSE**
Bushmills' mash house was refitted with a new stainless-steel mash tun and washbacks in 2007. This is part of Diageo's investment in the distillery, with a view to greatly increasing sales of Bushmills over the forthcoming years. The mash house is full of wonderful yeasty and malty aromas; in the stills house, the aromas are more fruity

◄ CASK SELECTION

Bushmills mostly uses a mix of bourbon and sherry casks for maturation, and the master blender takes regular trips to Spain and Portugal to select casks being seasoned with sherry. Once the new oak has been mellowed by the sherry and has absorbed some of its fruity flavors, it is ready to mature Bushmills whiskey.

▼ WOOD FINISHES

Bushmills was one of the pioneers of exotic wood finishes. The light style of the spirit produced here lends itself nicely to ageing in Port, Madeira, or Oloroso sherry casks. This is best experienced by sampling the 16- and 21-year-old malts. Bushmills 16 is finished in port pipes for the final months of maturation; Bushmills 21 is finished in Madeira casks for about two years.

◄ TRIPLE DISTILLATION

Bushmills has four wash stills and five spirit stills, and uses triple distillation to produce a very light and pure spirit—the traditional Irish way. The distillery produces two kinds of spirit: one is unpeated; the other is given a light peating. The two types of spirit are matured in separate casks, and can be used in combination to produce the final whiskey.

MALTS AND BLENDS ►

Bushmills is highly regarded for the quality of its single malts, but it also pays close attention to the standard of its blends. Grain whiskey from Midleton Distillery is used for Bushmills blends, and, significantly, the malt and grain are "married" in casks for a period so that the flavors fully integrate.

CLONTARF

www.clontarf1014.com

Clontarf is owned by Castle Brands Inc. The name commemorates the battle of Clontarf in 1014, when Irish high king Brian Boru achieved a remarkable victory for the Irish over Viking raiders. There is no distillery in Clontarf (near Dublin), and so Castle Brands sources its spirit from third-party distillers.

CLONTARF SINGLE MALT

SINGLE MALT 40% ABV

Sweet and thin with some nice mouthfeel. Cereal notes with hints of honey, but a bit one-dimensional.

COLERAINE

Coleraine Distillery Ltd., Hawthorn Office Park, Stockman's Way, Belfast

Never underestimate the selling power of nostalgia: the sole reason this blend is still produced is because whiskey drinkers are very brand loyal, and the name Coleraine still has resonance some three decades after the distillery fell silent. It once produced a single malt of some repute, then in 1954 it started to make grain whiskey for Bushmills, before it was eventually wound down in the 1970s. The reputation of the distillery was such, however, that customers still look out for the name, and so a brand and blend were created to fill a niche. Though the company is called Coleraine Distillery, the whiskey is produced elsewhere.

COLERAINE

BLEND 40% ABV

Light, sweet, and grainy. Probably best suited to drinking with a mixer.

CONNEMARA

Cooley Distillery, Riverstown, Cooley, County Louth
www.kilbeggandistillingcompany.com

Connemara is one of the few whiskeys the Cooley Distillery produces that has no heritage. Names like Millars, Tyrconnell, and Locke's have been around in one form or another for a century or more, but here a totally new brand was created for a totally new whiskey. So what's new? Well, it's a peated malt. Nothing too radical if this were Scotland, but in Ireland it caused quite a stir. In the eyes of the Irish whiskey industry—and many a traditionalist—Irish whiskey was a triple-distilled and unpeated drink. Then along came Cooley's John Teeling, who started making Irish whiskey that was double-distilled and peated.

It's not surprising that when Irish Distillers tried to take over Cooley a few years back, IDL boss Richard Burrows was adamant that brands such as Connemara would have no future. Yet, Connemara has gone from being a curiosity to winning gold medals. In December 2011, Beam Inc. acquired Cooley from the Teeling family, and early in 2014, Suntory took over Beam, creating Beam Suntory Inc., with the Irish operation being renamed the Kilbeggan Distilling Company. Several expressions of Connemara have been offered, but today, only the flagship Original variant is produced.

CONNEMARA ORIGINAL

SINGLE MALT 40% ABV

A smoldering turf fire on the nose, with marshmallows, honey, and floral notes. Spicy malt, sweet smoke, and peppery, drying oak on the palate.

KILBEGGAN WHISKEY *(SEE P.198)*

KILBEGGAN 8-YEAR-OLD *(SEE P.198)*

TYRCONNELL WHISKEY *(SEE P.214)*

COOLEY

Riverstown, Cooley, County Louth
www.kilbeggandistillingcompany.com

In the 1930s, the Irish Government went into the distilling business. It wasn't out to make whiskey; it was simply looking for a way of using up blighted potatoes. Five industrial alcohol factories were built to produce power methylated spirit (PMS), which was then mixed with gasoline to make it go further.

By the 1980s, PMS was a thing of the past, and the last of these distilleries on the Cooley Peninsula was being sold for scrap. In 1988 Dr. John Teeling bought the Cooley Distillery unseen: he reckoned the scrap value alone was greater than the £106,000 the government wanted. But Teeling didn't do the sensible thing and sell off the scrap. Instead he opened a distillery.

On July 17, 1992, as the first cask of Cooley whiskey was tapped, Teeling's dream of taking on Irish Distillers had turned into a

nightmare: the company was strapped for cash, and Teeling was looking to offload the loss-making distillery. But the only interested buyers were arch-rivals Irish Distillers, who intended to close the place down. Not surprisingly, its offer was blocked by Ireland's Competition Authority, which ruled that any takeover by Irish Distillers would be anti-competitive. By 1994, Teeling was stuck with a distillery that he couldn't sell and neither could afford to run.

How he, Master Distiller Noel Sweeney, and his team turned Cooley around is nothing short of remarkable. They pre-sold whiskey to the American and German markets, and expanded into the retailer own-brand business. Eventually, with the launch of the Tyrconnell single malt and Kilbeggan blend, Cooley started to sell whiskey under its own label. Today, the Cooley operation is in the hands of Beam Suntory Inc.

WHISKEY STYLES
IRISH WHISKEY

Ireland produces four different styles of whiskey, and it is a unique combination. Pure pot still is the style of whiskey that is as Irish as leprechauns. You just don't get it anywhere else. Pot still whiskey is made from both malted and unmalted barley in a pot still. It's a full-flavored whiskey, which in the Victorian era accounted for just about all the whiskey made in the country.

Nowadays, it is only produced in Midleton and there are just two expressions of pure pot still currently produced, Redbreast and Green Spot. However it can be found in the makeup of the most popular Irish whiskeys, including Jameson, Paddy, and most obviously in Powers Gold Label.

Single malt whiskey is made purely from malted barley. It's a popular style that is produced everywhere from Japan to Scotland. In Ireland it is made by Bushmills and Cooley, and both companies market it at various different ages. Bushmills 10-year-old or The Tyrconnell would be good examples. Most Irish single malts are unpeated, but Connemara bucks the trend, with a classic Irish peated malt.

Produced in a continuous still, grain whiskey is usually made from corn in Ireland. It is lighter in flavor than either malt or pot still whiskey. Midleton and Cooley both make grain whiskey. The former uses grain in Jameson and Paddy for example; Cooley blends its grain—though it also bottles an 8-year-old single grain called Greenore. Irish whiskey brands like Jameson, Powers, Paddy, Black Bush, and Kilbeggan are blends. In Ireland, that means a mixture of grain with either or both pot still and single malt.

CRAOI NA MONA

Cooley Distillery, Riverstown,
Cooley, County Louth
Owner: Berry Bros. & Rudd

Craoi na Mona is Gaelic for "heart of peat." Produced by Cooley, though not one of its own brands, this whiskey can be found in places as diverse as Moscow and London, but so far it hasn't been spotted in Dublin. Given the huge rise in the popularity of Irish whiskey recently, it's not surprising that so many drinks companies are trying to cut themselves a slice of the action. The Craoi Na Mona brand is owned by leading London wine merchants Berry Bros. & Rudd, and at 10 years of age, is part of their Berrys' Own Selection range.

CRAOI NA MONA

SINGLE MALT 40% ABV
Sweet and young, this is a decidedly immature peated malt.

CRESTED TEN

Midleton Distillery, Midleton,
County Cork

Launched in 1963, Crested Ten was Jameson's first venture into distillery bottling. The fact that it came at least a century after the Scots started branding and distillery bottling shows how far behind the times the Irish industry was and how close it came to vanishing entirely. Crested Ten is a whiskey you'll see lurking on a top shelf in many Irish pubs. It's never on an optic, probably because it's no good with mixers. Instead, you'll have to ask for it by name. Soon it will be rebranded as Jameson Crested.

CRESTED TEN

BLEND 40% ABV
An old-fashioned Irish whiskey with plenty of pot-still character and its Oloroso maturation in evidence. This is a great big hug of a drink that will reward those brave enough to take it from the top shelf. Have it neat, cut with just a splash of water.

DUNGOURNEY 1964

Midleton Distillery, Midleton,
County Cork

No one is quite sure how, but for 30 years some of the last pot still to be produced at the old Midleton Distillery lay undiscovered in the corner of a warehouse at Dungourney. In 1994 the remarkable survivor was bottled and named after the river it had come from some three decades before.

Dungourney 1964 is a time machine: one sniff and you are transported back to the days when Jameson, Powers, and Paddy came from competing distilleries.

DUNGOURNEY 1964

IRISH POT STILL WHISKEY 40% ABV
The mushroom edge to the nose gives a hint of age, but the body is still firm. They made whiskey differently back then, which is why this tastes slightly oily, but the tell-tale, almost minty, kick of pure pot still whiskey is still evident.

DUNVILLE'S

Echlinville Distillery, Kircubbin,
County Down
www.echlinville.com

Echlinville became the first new Northern Irish distillery in over 125 years when it opened in 2013. The plan is to produce spirit for use in the Feckin Irish Whiskey blends, founded by distillery owner Shane Braniff, who has also revived the old Dunville's brand. At one time, Dunville's Royal Irish Distillery was the biggest in Belfast, but Dunville & Co. went into liquidation in 1936.

DUNVILLE'S VERY RARE 10-YEAR-OLD

SINGLE MALT 46% ABV
Finished in Pedro Ximénez sherry casks, this expression has cut grass, orchard fruits, and vanilla on the nose, with a soft, sweet, lightly spiced palate.

FECKIN IRISH WHISKEY

www.feckinirishwhiskey.com

As Irish whiskey sales continue to buck the trend and sail upward, it's not surprising that bright entrepreneurs continue to pour new products onto the market. From its name to the label, this offering is aimed at the younger end of the spectrum, and there's not a tweed jacket in sight. "Feck," by the way, is a very mild and very Irish swear word that was popularized on the British TV show *Father Ted*.

FECKIN IRISH WHISKEY

BLEND 40% ABV

Made using whiskey from the Cooley Distillery, this is light, approachable, and totally inoffensive. It's clearly a young whiskey and lacks much in the way of depth.

GLENDALOUGH

Glendalough Distillery, Glendalough, County Wicklow
www.glendaloughdistillery.com

Glendalough distillery was established in 2013, purchasing a still made in Germany's Black Forest region. The company had actually already been trading for two years at that point, offering a range of poteen and whiskeys sourced from other distillers.

Glendalough currently markets 7- and 13-year-old single malts, and an innovative single grain whiskey, matured initially for three years and six months in ex-Bourbon barrels, and then finished for six months in Spanish Oloroso sherry casks.

GLENDALOUGH SINGLE GRAIN DOUBLE BARREL

SINGLE GRAIN 42% ABV

Light on the nose, with Christmas pudding aromas. The palate features honey, vanilla, dried fruit, and a hint of pepper. Ginger and almonds in the finish.

GREEN SPOT

Midleton Distillery, Midleton, County Cork

In the days before distillers in Ireland spent millions on building brands, they simply used to make the stuff, leaving the filthy job of selling the whiskey to bonders like Mitchell's. This, of course, was a terrible business plan: it allowed the Scots to build global brands, while the Irish were obsessed with an ever-shrinking domestic market. By the time the Irish got back into the race in the 1960s, Irish whiskey had a miserable 1 percent of the global whiskey market. Green Spot is the last bonder's own label. Owned by Mitchell's of Dublin, it's a pure pot still whiskey, made in Midleton.

GREEN SPOT

PURE POT STILL 40% ABV

Green Spot is matured for just six to eight years, but a glass of this is still bracing stuff, with a wonderful lightly sherried finish. One of a kind.

INISHOWEN

Cooley Distillery, Riverstown, Cooley, County Louth
www.killbeggandistillingcompany.com

Inishowen is the kind of concept an accountant would come up with. It's brand economics by numbers. The Scotch industry is worth billions, with blended Scotch making up 90 percent of sales. So if an Irish brand could create a similar product, it would have to be a sure-fire success—wouldn't it? There's nothing much wrong with Inishowen—it is well-made and nicely blended—it's just that it will never be... well, Scotch.

INISHOWEN

BLEND 40% ABV

You won't find any other blended Irish whiskey that has a nose like this: it's both peaty and floral. However, it's the fine grain whiskey and not the malt that gives Inishowen some real charm.

THE IRISHMAN

Walsh Whiskey Distillery
Royal Oak, County Carlow
www.irishmanwhiskey.com

The Irishman whiskey was launched in 2007 by Bernard and Rosemary Walsh, who had previously specialized in bottling an Irish coffee recipe under the Hot Irishman label. Whiskey was supplied by Irish Distillers, but, in 2013, the Walshes revealed plans to build their own distillery at Royal Oak, County Carlow.

The Irishman range now includes the Single Malt, the 12-year-old Single Malt, the Founder's Reserve, and The Irishman Rare Cask Strength.

THE IRISHMAN FOUNDER'S RESERVE

BLEND 40% ABV
Cooking apples, vanilla, and black pepper on the nose. Rich mouthfeel with cinnamon, peaches, caramel, and spicy oak.

THE IRISHMAN SINGLE MALT

SINGLE MALT 40% ABV
Bushmills tends to keep all the best whiskey for itself, which means the Irishman malt has great cereal character but will never be anything outstanding. There is a hint of sherry on the palate.

THE IRISHMAN CASK STRENGTH

PURE POT STILL/MALT BLEND 56% ABV
A limited-release, cask-strength version of the Irishman 70. The whiskey has a rich, sherried nose. Chocolate notes are in evidence here, alongside rum and raisin, and dark brown sugar. The blend is fresh and vigorous on the palate, with spice and notes of orange zest. The chile-pepper heat creates a lingering finish.

The old Jameson Distillery at Bow Street in Dublin is where the famous Irish whiskey was made until the mid-1970s, when production moved to the new Midleton Distillery. Today, it is a visitor center.

JAMESON

BLEND 40% ABV

This whiskey has a malty smell, which is promising, but the drink itself is a major let-down. The grain is unruly and overwhelms the pot still, leaving some citrus notes. There is a gently buzz of sherry, but nothing more.

JAMESON GOLD RESERVE

BLEND 43% ABV

This is a viscous, oily, syrupy mouth-coater of a whiskey. Finer, lighter flavors find it hard to fight their way through the fug of sugars. The finish is buzzy and long, in rather the same way as a cough medicine.

JAMESON SPECIAL RESERVE 12-YEAR-OLD

JAMESON LIMITED RESERVE 18-YEAR-OLD

JAMESON RAREST VINTAGE RESERVE

JAMESON

Midleton Distillery,
Midleton, County Cork
www.jamesonwhiskey.com

This is the biggest selling Irish whiskey of them all. Jameson is a global brand and can be found in just about every bar in the world. However, if the founder of the company, John Jameson, was around today, he certainly wouldn't recognize the whiskey that now bears his name. The modern standard blend is a 50:50 blend of medium-bodied pot still and grain whiskey. It's a light, approachable spirit that lacks character. Beyond the standard bottling, though, are some

cracking whiskeys. Gold Reserve was originally launched as a premium, duty-free blend, but it is now widely available. Some of the whiskeys used in it are more than 20 years old, but they are cut with younger pot still whiskey, matured in first-fill oak casks. This is the only Irish whiskey to feature virgin wood, and it lends the blend a really sweet, vanilla-like flavor.

Jameson's Special Reserve 12-year-old is a full-bodied whiskey, with plenty of malt from the whiskey and spicy oak after 12 years in Oloroso sherry butts. This whiskey has won several awards and collected Gold at the San Francisco World Spirits Competition in 2007.

Six extra years in the cask doesn't change the flavor profile of the 18-year-old premium offering too much, but what it does do is double the price. The Limited Reserve blend is hand-picked by a Jameson master blender from a limited, but excellent selection of sherry casks.

JAMESON SPECIAL RESERVE 12-YEAR-OLD

BLEND 40% ABV

This world-beating whiskey tweaks the nose firmly with hints of leather and spice. It has an incredible, silky quality, quite unlike the monotone, regular Jameson. Dried fruits wrapped in milk chocolate round off a master-class in how to make a great whiskey.

JAMESON LIMITED RESERVE 18-YEAR-OLD

BLEND 40% ABV

The pot still here has taken old age well. The body of the whiskey is firm and yielding and the Oloroso wood has to be very fine not to dominate a blend this old. Sweet almond and spiced fudge notes compliment the oiliness of the pot still.

JAMESON RAREST VINTAGE RESERVE

BLEND 40% ABV

An exceptional blending of choice, aged grain, pot still from bourbon wood, and some pot still aged in port pipes. Sweet fruits on the nose, coupled with pot still spice. Rich fruit, oak, and caramel flavors, and a long fruity, spicy finish.

KILBEGGAN 8-YEAR-OLD

KILBEGGAN

BLEND 40% ABV

This whiskey has improved over the past decade. It is a grainy blend, with strong notes of honey and oatmeal. The end note is a pleasing combination of coffee and dark chocolate. Dollar for dollar, Kilbeggan is one of the best Irish whiskeys that money can buy.

KILBEGGAN

The Old Kilbeggan Distillery, Main Street, Kilbeggan, County Westmeath
www.kilbeggandistillingcompany.com

Kilbeggan has been home to many distilleries, and if you visit the town you can understand why: there's plenty of fresh water (and plenty of rain), and County Westmeath is good barley-growing country. Yet, in the mid-1950s the most famous of the distilleries, John Locke & Sons, fell silent. Although the two remaining Locke family members—sisters Flo and Sweet—had warehouses full of raw ingredients, they had no interest in whiskey-making. With post-war whiskey prices on the rise, they decided to sell the distillery to an international consortium. However, when the deposit of £75,000 never materialized, questions began to be asked. It was rumored that various members of the government were involved in a shady deal to sell the distillery to foreigners. Accusations of bribery went as high as the Taoiseach, Eamon de Valera, but nothing was ever proven. In the end, the sale fell through, but a year later, the Locke scandal was a factor in the government's subsequent downfall.

Having been part of the Teeling family's Cooley-centred operation for some years, Kilbeggan is now owned by Beam Suntory Inc., and a Kilbeggan blend and a Kilbeggan 8-year-old single grain are available.

KILBEGGAN 8-YEAR-OLD

SINGLE GRAIN 40% ABV

Lemon and vanilla on the nose, with a smooth palate of vanilla and honey, which ultimately becomes drier.

KNAPPOGUE CASTLE 1994

KNAPPOGUE CASTLE 1995

KNAPPOGUE CASTLE

Bushmills Distillery, 2 Distillery Road,
County Antrim

After World War II, the owner of
Knappogue Castle, near the city
of Limerick, took to buying casks
of Irish whiskey—particularly
from the Tullamore Distillery—
which he'd store in a cellar in the
family pile. These whiskeys would
then be bottled and given away to
family and friends over time. The
last of these original casks filled
with Tullamore whiskey was
bottled in 1987, when the spirit
was 36 years old.

This particular whiskey is
obviously extremely rare now.
It is not only its age that makes
it rather special, though. It is
also that this bottling perfectly
captures the flavor of a dying age
and a whiskey industry that then
looked to be heading the same
way. However, fast-forward to
the 1990s, and the story begins
to take on a more upbeat air, when
the son of the castle's owner, Mark
Andrews, decides to follow in his
father's footsteps and bottle single
vintages of his own, also labeled
Knappogue Castle.

The range now includes a
12-year-old (triple-distilled single
malt) and 14- and 16-year-old
Twin Wood expressions.

KNAPPOGUE CASTLE 1995

SINGLE MALT 40% ABV

*This whiskey clearly originates from
a Bushmills malt, and a seriously classy
one to boot. There are strong notes
of toasted nuts here, while a juicy,
honey sweetness lingers on the palate.
However, like many of the independent
Bushmills offerings, the whiskey
is still a bit too young to display the
full potential of its characteristics.*

WHISKEY TOUR: IRELAND

In 1887, when the Victorian travel and drinks writer Alfred Barnard visited Ireland, he had 28 different distilleries to visit. Nowadays, the range is markedly more limited, but every bit as enjoyable. Several historic whiskey distilleries have facilities for tourists, and there are other attractions along with the beautiful Irish landscape to further entice the visitor on a whiskey tour of the country.

TOUR STATISTICS

DAYS: 4	**LENGTH:** 375 miles (600 km)	**DISTILLERIES:** 1 working, 3 converted
TRAVEL: Car, tram, walking	**REGION:** Northern Ireland and Republic of Ireland	

DAY 1: GIANTS CAUSEWAY, BUSHMILLS

1 The North Antrim coast is stunning. Start your journey at the magnificent **Giants Causeway**, a World Heritage Site near the town of Bushmills, where extraordinary hexagonal basalt columns stretch out along the rugged coast.

2 Of all the distilleries in Ireland that are open to the public, **Bushmills** (*www.bushmills.com*) is the only one that is still in production. Enjoy the tour, sample some fine whiskeys, then stroll to the nearby Bushmills Inn (*www.bushmillsinn.com*) for some superb food and a good night's sleep. Rooms in the Mill House are best.

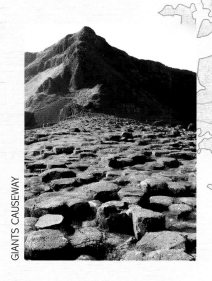

GIANTS CAUSEWAY

DAY 2: COOLEY, OLD JAMESON DISTILLERY

3 Although Cooley Distillery is not open to the public, the hilly Cooley Peninsula and its attractive seaside town of Greenore are worth taking in on the way to Dublin.

4 Avoid the Dublin traffic by taking the LUAS tram from Junction 9 of the M50 to Smithfield in the city center. This is near the Old Jameson Distillery, which offers guided tours and the chance to sample Jameson whiskey. (*www.jamesonwhiskey.com*)

COOLEY DISTILLERY

GALWAY

LIMERICK

CORK **7** **8**

THE JAMESON EXPERIENCE

FINISH

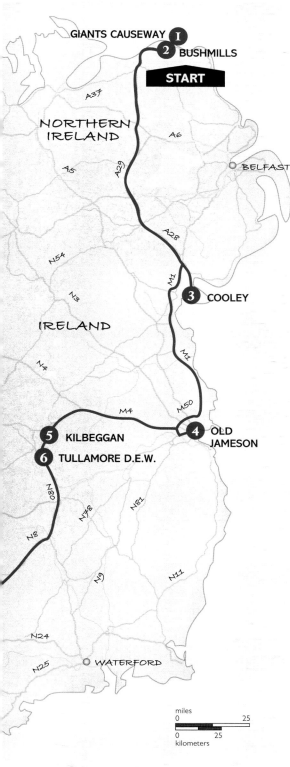

GIANTS CAUSEWAY **1**

2 BUSHMILLS

START

NORTHERN IRELAND

BELFAST

IRELAND

3 COOLEY

4 OLD JAMESON

5 KILBEGGAN

6 TULLAMORE D.E.W.

WATERFORD

miles
0   25
0   25
kilometers

DAY 3: KILBEGGAN, TULLAMORE D.E.W.

5 Take Junction 7 of the M50 and head west out of Dublin to the old Locke's building at **Kilbeggan**. The original distillery fell silent in 1957, but the site has been revived by locals and now houses the Kilbeggan micro-distillery and a whiskey museum with working waterwheel, restaurant, shop, and whiskey bar. Cooley leases warehouses at this site and brings casks of its whiskey here for maturation. (*www.kilbeggandistillery.com*)

KILBEGGAN

TULLAMORE D.E.W.

6 The vibrant town of Tullamore is home to the **Tullamore D.E.W.** visitor center. This building used to be a bonded warehouse for storing whiskey casks before they were shipped downstream to Dublin. It is now the setting for an exhibition about traditional whiskey-making. Although now distilled at Clonminch, on the outskirts of the town, Tullamore whiskey is, of course, available for tasting and purchase at the visitor center. (*www.tullamoredew.com*)

DAY 4: CORK, THE JAMESON EXPERIENCE AT MIDLETON

7 The cross-country trip from Tullamore to Cork traverses the boggy heart of Ireland—a bleak landscape that is strangely beautiful at any time of the year. The city of **Cork** is a food haven, where you can visit the historic English Market to buy a picnic lunch and eat it in nearby Bishop Lucey Park. Alternatively, the Market Café is a great place to try local specialities such as tripe, pigs' feet, and Irish Stew. For a drink, stop at the South County Bar & Café (*www.thesouthcounty.com*), in Douglas Village, a suburb of Cork. It's a traditional, family-run pub, with its own "whiskey corner" to celebrate Irish whiskey.

POT STILL AT MIDLETON

8 **The Jameson Experience** (*www.jamesonwhiskey.com*) is set in the beautifully restored 18th-century distillery at Midleton, and boasts the world's largest pot still, which now stands outside the buildings. For refreshment, try the restaurant at nearby Ballymaloe House, which is overseen by Darina Allen, the doyen of Irish foodies. (*www.ballymaloe.ie*)

KNOCKEEN HILLS POTEEN—FARMER'S STRENGTH

KNOCKEEN HILLS POTEEN—GOLD STRENGTH

LOCKE'S 8-YEAR-OLD

LOCKE'S BLEND

KNOCKEEN HILLS

www.irish-poteen.com

Poteen (or poitín) is a clear spirit that was traditionally distilled in homemade pot stills throughout Ireland. It was originally made with malted barley or any other available grain, though potatoes were also used. Poteen is synonymous with illegal spirit, and the reason for this can be traced back to the 1660s. This was when the English government in Ireland first started taxing the ancient art of distilling. *Uisce beatha* became the legal, duty-paid whiskey; *uisce poitín* the illegal version. Over the intervening 300 years, its love-hate relationship with the law has been celebrated in story and song. This is a rich folk heritage for drinks companies to draw upon.

In 1997 the government removed their previous objection to the term being used to describe a white spirit on which duty had been paid. Hackler from Guinness

was soon out of the trap and it quickly went the way of Guinness Light. One of the few to survive—and indeed to thrive—is Knockeen Hills. Its spirit is bottled at three strengths: triple-distilled at 60% and 70% ABV, and quadruple-distilled at 90% ABV. It should not be drunk neat.

KNOCKEEN HILLS POTEEN —FARMER'S STRENGTH

POTEEN 60% ABV

Clean, fresh, and fruity on the nose. Creamy textured, with tantalizing sweet and juicy fruit notes on the palate. Crisp, mouth-cleansing finish.

KNOCKEEN HILLS POTEEN —GOLD STRENGTH

POTEEN 70% ABV

Stronger on the nose than the 60. With a large measure of water (almost 50-50), it becomes fruity, with tangerine-skin aromas and a sweet perfumed note. Warming in the mouth, sweet and sour on the palate, with a dry, fruit-tinged finish.

LOCKE'S

Cooley Distillery, Riverstown,
Cooley, County Louth
www.killbeggandistillingcompany.com

Locke's Distillery in the town of Kilbeggan is an oasis of calm in the Irish midlands. The ancient stone walls filter what traffic noise there is, while the inner courtyard still echoes to the sound of a blacksmith and the trickle of whiskey-making.

It's hard to believe that, just 25 years ago, this truly remarkable distillery was almost derelict. Since the early 1950s, when the Locke's whiskey business initially folded, the abandoned distillery buildings had been used to house pigs and farm machinery. In the late 1970s, the local community got together and restored the distillery. Shortly after the renovation was completed, fate decided to smile upon Kilbeggan. John Teeling was setting up a new distillery in County Louth and wanted to age his maturing stocks at Locke's. A deal was done

in which Cooley bought the rights to the Locke's brand, leased the buildings and, after decades of dusty silence, whiskey barrels once more trundled into the stone warehouses.

In 2007, to celebrate the distillery's 250th anniversary, a micro-distillery was opened at Locke's. The first of its spirit came of age in 2010.

LOCKE'S 8-YEAR-OLD

SINGLE MALT 40% ABV

This malt is a vatting of Cooley's unpeated malt, with a top dressing of peated malt. It is not a bad whiskey; but it's just a bit dull. More Daniel O'Donnell than Shane McGowan, as it were.

LOCKE'S BLEND

BLEND 40% ABV

This is a pleasant enough dram. It would be particularly good in a hot whiskey, where its limited range doesn't have to sing out. Taken neat, Locke's can be a tad monosyllabic, in thaqt it only really has a malty note.

MICHAEL COLLINS SINGLE MALT

MICHAEL COLLINS BLEND

MICHAEL COLLINS

Owner: Beam Suntory

General Michael Collins was one of the founding fathers of the modern Irish state. Numerous movies have been made about his life, with everyone from Brendan Gleeson to Liam Neeson playing "the big fellow," as he was known. Almost everyone in Ireland knows just about everything there is to know about Collins, and yet most people have never heard of this whiskey.

The reason for this is that the whiskey was initially formulated for the American market by Cooley Distillery in conjunction with US importer Sidney Frank. However, it can now be bought on both sides of the Atlantic.

Unusually for an Irish whiskey, the Michael Collins malt is double-distilled and has a light peating too. The blend is a mix of the malt and a younger grain whiskey, which is subsequently put into bourbon casks for maturation.

MICHAEL COLLINS SINGLE MALT
SINGLE MALT 40% ABV
This is like a cream soda for adults—but in a good way. It is soft and drinkable, with plenty of biscuity flavors. Vanilla notes emerge, as a result of the bourbon casking, with a hint of light smoke. This is a vatting of peated and unpeated malt, and a really classy one at that.

MICHAEL COLLINS BLEND
BLEND 40% ABV
The blend is a lot less impressive than the malt. It is thin, with the scent of woody embers at its core, but it lacks a decent finish.

Bushmills in County Antrim is the only working distillery in Ireland that is open to the public. It is also the world's oldest surviving distillery, dating back to 1608.

YELLOW SPOT 12-YEAR-OLD

GREEN SPOT CHÂTEAU LÉOVILLE BARTON

MIDLETON

Midleton, County Cork
www.irishdistillers.ie

Midleton is Ireland's largest distillery. It is home to Jameson, Powers, Paddy, and all of the Irish Distillers' portfolio of whiskeys, as well as their gins and vodkas. The place looks like an enormous petro-chemical plant, but it can still make some sublime spirits.

The history of distilling on this site goes back as far as 1825, when the Murphy brothers went into the drinks business. One branch of the family started to make a stout, which still bears their name, and the other side of the family went into the whiskey business.

With its proximity to fine fields of barley and a large harbor on its coast, County Cork enjoys a long tradition of distilling. In 1867, five of the local operations joined forces to form Cork Distilleries Company (CDC) and, gradually, all production was centralized at the Midleton plant.

In 1966, CDC, along with Jameson and Powers, were among the founding members of Irish Distillers. As before, all production was eventually moved over to Midleton Distillery. But by 1975, the old Victorian building could no longer cope with the demands of production, and a new state-of-the-art plant was built to the rear of the original Victorian buildings.

The company also produces the only regular bottlings of pure pot still whiskey in the world. Having

MIDLETON VERY RARE

MIDLETON MASTER DISTILLER'S PRIVATE COLLECTION 1973

MIDLETON DAIR GHAELACH GRINSELL'S WOOD

POWER'S JOHN'S LANE 12-YEAR-OLD

previously offered only Redbreast and Green Spot pure pot still malts, Irish Distillers set out to raise the profile of what it termed "single pot still whiskeys" on a grand scale, launching a number of new expressions and building a dedicated new pot still stillhouse at Midleton. The result is that Power's Signature Release and John's Lane Release have been bottled, along with a Green Spot Château Léoville Barton (finished in ex-Bordeaux wine casks), a 12-year-old Yellow Spot, and, most radical of all, Midleton Dair Ghaelach, the first Irish whiskey to be finished in virgin Irish oak casks. The Redbreast range has also been expanded.

Among all the spirits produced at Midleton, there is just one regularly appearing whiskey that carries the actual Midleton moniker. Launched in 1984,

Midleton Very Rare is aimed at the premium market and the price reflects whatever that market can bear. A new vintage is released late every year and, although they vary slightly, the house style is essentially the same. The constituent whiskeys are aged for between 12 and 25 years in seasoned bourbon casks. The spirit in these bottlings was mostly distilled at the new plant, but the oldest vintages were made at the old Midleton Distillery—now beautifully restored to house the Jameson Experience *(see p.209).*

YELLOW SPOT 12-YEAR-OLD

SINGLE POT STILL 46% ABV

Sweet and oily on the nose, with vanilla and peaches in syrup, icing, sugar, and Madeira. Very spicy on the palate, mouth-coating, with citrus fruits, roasted coffee beans, and toasted oak.

GREEN SPOT CHÂTEAU LÉOVILLE BARTON

SINGLE POT STILL 46% ABV

Fragrant nose, with caramel, rose petals, apple pie, and white pepper. Smooth and oaky on the palate, with cereal, plums, berries, vanilla, honey, and hot spices.

MIDLETON VERY RARE

BLEND 40% ABV

The nose is a skilful balancing act; classy oak and bold cereal notes dance on a high wire made of pure beeswax. The body is full and yielding, and the nish breaks on the tongue in waves of silky, walnut whip. You get a classy ball of malt for your money, and so you should. Note that there is a little variation in the whiskey from year to year.

MIDLETON MASTER DISTILLER'S PRIVATE COLLECTION 1973

PURE POT STILL 56% ABV

Even rarer than Midleton Very Rare, this whiskey was distilled in 1973 and is a

bottling of pure pot still whiskey from the old Midleton Distillery. It was produced as a 30-year-old in an edition of 800 bottles, and its taste is said to be spicy, fruity, and honeyed, with some dry, sherry nuttiness.

MIDLETON DAIR GHAELACH GRINSELL'S WOOD

SINGLE POT STILL 58.2% ABV

Oily on the nose, with freshly sawed timber, bananas, cinnamon, nutmeg, and ginger. Viscous and spicy on the palate, nutty, with pineapple, cloves, and tingling oak. Very spicy in the drying finish.

POWER'S JOHN'S LANE 12-YEAR-OLD

SINGLE POT STILL 46% ABV

Vanilla, new leather, nougat, and carnations on the slightly salty nose. Sunflower oil and, ultimately, a whiff of molasses. Full-bodied in the mouth, with an oily texture. Palate of dried fruits, spices, and nuts.

THE SECRETS OF...
MIDLETON

The town of Midleton is an easy 30-minute drive from Cork city. It's a pleasant market town and on a clear day, with the wind in a certain direction, comes the curious scent of whiskey.

Set back slightly from the main thoroughfare, hugging the bank of the Dungourney River, lie the imposing Victorian buildings of Midleton Distillery. This is the original Cork Distilleries Company (CDC) plant that ceased production in the early 1970s. Nowadays, it houses an impressive visitor center, the Jameson Experience.

Behind the old distillery, lies the new one. In 1966, the remaining Irish distilleries—Powers and Jameson in Dublin, and CDC in Cork—came together to form Irish Distillers. When the two Dublin-based distilleries closed, all production shifted to the new state-of-the-art plant at Midleton. This is now where everything from Jameson whiskey to Cork Dry Gin are produced. You shouldn't be put off by its industrial scale, though, for Midleton has exacting standards and produces fantastic whiskeys, including bottlings of the two remaining Irish pot still whiskeys, Redbreast and Green Spot. It all comes down to the basics: a good water source and local barley.

▲ **THE WHISKEY'S SOURCE**
Dungourney River runs right past the distillery. In fact the river is the reason the factory is sited where it is. The old Midleton distillery was powered by a giant waterwheel *(see bottom right)*. That may have changed, but the new distillery still uses the Dungourney for its whiskey.

◀ **LOCAL BARLEY**
Midleton uses locally grown barley for its malt. The malt used to produce its great whiskeys is dried by warm air and not with peat smoke, as is common in Scotland. This means that there is nothing to mask the wonderful malty, biscuity taste of fine Irish barley.

THREE MASH PROCESS ▶
The malt (or a mixture of malt and barley if pot still whiskey is being produced) is ground into a coarse flour called grist and dumped into a large tub known as a mash tun, or locally as a kieve. Hot water is added, and the mixture is stirred to help convert the starch in the grain into sugar. At Midleton, this process is repeated three times, with the barley water being drained off after each mashing. The final barley water is held and used in the first mashing of the next batch of grist. This ensures a certain continuity between batches.

◄ CHOICE WOOD

Midleton has a very strict wood policy: only the finest American oak barrels are used, while the sherry wood comes from oak butts that are built and seasoned to order in Jerez, Spain. They will be used to mature sherry for one or two years before being brought over to Midleton to age the whiskey. The distillery is currently building new warehousing to cope with its maturing stocks.

◄ BOTTLING

Jameson is the biggest-selling whiskey that Midleton produces, and the vast majority of it is bottled near Dublin. But there is a second line close to Midleton, at the old North Mall Distillery in the heart of Cork. This old distillery no longer produces whiskey, but does at least keep a connection to the industry by bottling some of the output from Midleton.

▼ THE JAMESON EXPERIENCE

The old Midleton Distillery now houses a visitor center, where you can be taken on a tour of the buildings and the grounds, sample some whiskeys, and become an expert on the characteristics of Irish whiskey (see also p.201).

▲ PRODUCTION VARIATIONS

There isn't a distillery in the world that can produce the range of whiskeys that comes out of Midleton. Many pure pot still, malt, and grain variations are stored in tanks under the plant. These can then be combined in different quantities and matured in different woods to produce myriad whiskey types and styles.

Without barley, there would be no whiskey; it's as simple as that. Midleton Distillery in County Cork sits among scenic, rolling fields of barley. The distillery makes great use of this local supply.

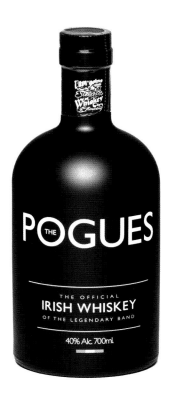

POWERS GOLD LABEL

POWERS GOLD LABEL 12-YEAR-OLD

PADDY

Midleton Distillery, Midleton,
County Cork
www.paddy.ie

There was a time when Irish whiskey was sold anonymously from casks in pubs. What whiskey a pub stocked was down to the owner and his relationship with the agent for the distillery.

Paddy Flaherty was an agent for the Cork Distilleries Company of Midleton in the 1920s and '30s. You knew when he was in town, as he'd buy everyone drinks at the bar, and the whiskey he sold—the CDC's Old Irish Whiskey—became so synonymous with the man himself that it was simply known as Paddy's whiskey.

PADDY

BLEND 40% ABV

This is a malty dram, which is both solid and well matured. It offers a satisfying, spicy, peppery kick.

THE POGUES

West Cork Distillers, Market Street,
Skibbereen, County Cork
www.thepoguesirishwhiskey.com

The official Irish whiskey of legendary band The Pogues, this blend is produced by West Cork Distillers in Skibbereen. It was launched during 2015, and, according to the whiskey's promoters, it is "Sunlight and barley held together with water and left in an oak barrel for three years and a day. This whiskey is a measure of who we are, made with the sole intention of spreading that same raucous joy."

THE POGUES

BLEND 40% ABV

The nose is floral and nutty, with almonds and malt. Sweet, smooth, and malty on the palate, with milk chocolate, spice, and citrus fruit.

POWERS

Midleton Distillery, Midleton,
County Cork
www.irishdistillers.ie

For longer than anyone could remember, Jameson and Powers used to stare each other down across the narrow strip of Dublin water they call the Liffey. The Powers family (on Dublin's south side) had been in the business since 1817, and a member of the family sat on the board of Irish Distillers until it was incorporated into the Pernod Ricard group, some 171 years later.

The Powers family had always embraced innovation. They pioneered the production of Irish gin and vodka, and moved into distillery bottling before anyone else in the country. They also invented the miniature, or, as it is known, the "baby Powers."

Incidentally, the picture of the three swallows on the Powers label is an example of typical Dublin wit.

It has long been held that the only way to enjoy a Powers is not to sip it slowly, but to lower the glass in "three swallows." As well as the famous blends, Powers John's Lane Release *(see p.207)* and Signature Release pot still whiskeys are now available.

POWERS GOLD LABEL

BLEND 40% ABV

This whiskey is something really special. Powers Gold Label is an upfront, take-no-prisoners experience. This isn't another bland, global brand; this is a real, solid whiskey. The nose is classically Irish—at once bracing and brittle. At its core, this whiskey is pure pot still, cut with just enough good grain. Powers Gold Label is an utterly captivating blend.

POWERS GOLD LABEL 12-YEAR-OLD

BLEND 40% ABV

An older, more layered expression of the same Powers formulation. Spice, honey, crème brûlée, with soft wood tones and sweet, fresh fruits.

TEELING SINGLE GRAIN

TEELING SINGLE MALT

TEELING SMALL BATCH

REDBREAST

Midleton Distillery, Midleton,
County Cork
www.irishdistillers.ie

Redbreast was the name that
wine merchants Gilbey's gave
to the Jameson whiskey that they
matured and bottled. The bonder
trade was finally phased out in 1968,
but Redbreast was so popular that
it was allowed to continue well
into the 1980s. In the 1990s, Irish
Distillers bought the brand from
Gilbey's and relaunched the drink
as a 12-year-old pure pot still,
part-matured in sherry wood.
There are also now 12-year-old
cask strength and 15- and
21-year-old versions.

REDBREAST 12-YEAR-OLD

PURE POT STILL 40% ABV

*This is, without doubt, one of the
world's finest whiskeys. Flavors range
from ginger to cinnamon, peppermint
to linseed, and licorice to camphor.
A sherry note sets off an elegant finish.*

TEELING

Teeling Distillery,
13-17 Newmarket, Dublin 8
www.teelingwhiskey.com

When the €10 million Teeling
Distillery opened for business on
St. Patrick's Day (March 17) 2015,
it was the first time since 1974 that
whiskey had been produced in
the city of Dublin. The venture
is headed by brothers Jack and
Stephen Teeling, whose father John
established the Cooley distillery
in County Louth in 1987. In 2011,
the family sold the Cooley to Beam
Inc. for $16 billion. However, the
Teeling siblings wanted to continue
in the Irish Whiskey business, and
their new Dublin distillery is the
ultimate result.

Teeling is situated in The
Liberties, a historic district of the
city. This area was home to no fewer
than 37 distilleries during the early
19th century, but is now best
known for the vast St. James's Gate
Guinness Brewery and adjacent

Storehouse—named Europe's
leading tourist attraction in 2015.

The Teelings wanted to create a
modern, city-based distillery, and
were inspired by Anchor Distilling
in San Francisco and the London
Distillery Company. The Teeling
Distillery in Dublin occupies two
adjoining converted warehouses
and is equipped with a four-ton
Steinecker full-lauter mash tun,
six washbacks, two pine and four
stainless steel, holding a combined
total of 24,000 gallons (110,000
liters), and three pot stills fabricated
by Frilli. The annual output is
currently 44,000 to 55,000 gallons
(200,000 to 250,000 liters).

Although primarily producing
pot still single malt whiskey, the
Teelings want to devote 25 percent
of their distilling time to
experimentation. They may, in
time, produce an Irish rye and a
heavily-peated single malt.
In addition to their Single Grain,
Single Malt, and Small Batch
expressions, all based on spirits

sourced from Cooley, the Teelings
also offer The Revival—a limited
edition, 15-year-old single malt
specially selected to celebrate the
opening of the new distillery—
and a 21-year-old single malt
finished in Sauternes casks.

TEELING SINGLE GRAIN

SINGLE GRAIN 46% ABV

*Sweet on the nose, with spicy fruit
notes. Notably spicy in the mouth,
with red berries and drying tannins.*

TEELING SINGLE MALT

SINGLE MALT 46% ABV

*This expression comprises a vatting
of five different wine cask–finished
Irish malt whiskeys. Lemon, toffee, and
melon on the lively nose, with a palate
of vanilla, spicy dry fruits, and cloves.*

TEELING SMALL BATCH

BLEND 46% ABV

*Finished in ex-rum casks, it has vanilla
and spice on the nose, with sweet rum
in the background. Smooth and sweet,
with light, spicy wood notes.*

TULLAMORE D.E.W.

TULLAMORE D.E.W. 10-YEAR-OLD

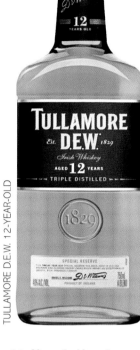

TULLAMORE D.E.W. 12-YEAR-OLD

TULLAMORE D.E.W.

www.tullamoredew.com

Tullamore is a sizable market town. It is situated pretty much smack-dab in the middle of Ireland. Although Tullamore itself is largely built on bogland, some great barley-producing counties lie nearby that once provided the grain for both this distillery and the operation at Locke's Distillery in nearby Kilbeggan.

In 1901, the worldwide sales of Irish whiskey peaked at 10 million cases, and two years later the Williams family gained control of Tullamore Distillery. In fact, D.E. Williams is the man whose name is still associated with whiskey in Tullamore; as in Tullamore D.E.Williams.

In 1954, the distillery closed and the brand was sold to Powers. It was then absorbed by Irish Distillers and ultimately ended up in the hands of William Grant & Sons Ltd. in 2010. Grant's reunited the brand with its original home, building a large new distillery on the outskirts of Tullamore. After Jameson, Tullamore D.E.W. is the world's second-best-selling Irish whiskey.

TULLAMORE D.E.W.

BLEND 40% ABV

This whiskey is fairly one-dimensional. It has a characteristic bourbon burn, with not much else to recommend it.

TULLAMORE D.E.W. 10-YEAR-OLD

BLEND 40% ABV

There's malt, spice, and vanilla on the nose, and a hint of oakiness and spice on the palate. The finish is long and dry, with a citric tang.

TULLAMORE D.E.W. 12-YEAR-OLD

BLEND 40% ABV

A considerable step up from the other Tullamore blends, the 12-year-old is reminiscent of a premium Jameson. The precious trinity of pot still, sherry, and oak is very much in evidence.

TYRCONNELL SINGLE MALT

SINGLE MALT 40% ABV
Cooley's best-selling malt, and it's easy to see why. This has the loveliest nose of any Irish whiskey, releasing jasmine, honeysuckle, and malted-milk cookies.

TYRCONNELL 10-YEAR-OLD PORT CASK

THE TYRCONNELL

www.kilbeggandistillery.com

Once very popular in the US, the original Old Tyrconnell whiskey is now remembered by few. In 1925, civil unrest in Ireland and Prohibition in the US pushed the Watt Distillery, where Old Tyrconnell was produced, into the hands of the Scottish United Distillers Company. UDC closed the many Irish distilleries it bought to protect its core Scotch brands, bringing the Irish industry to its knees. However, Tyrconnell was the first brand Cooley's John Teeling brought back to life when he bottled his first single malt in 1992. The brand is now owned by Beam Suntory Inc.

TYRCONNELL 10-YEAR-OLD PORT CASK

SINGLE MALT 46% ABV
Port changes the nose slightly, spicing things up. The body has aromas of fig pastry and plum pudding.

WRITERS TEARS

Walsh Whiskey, Equity House, Deerpark Business Park, Dublin Rd., Co. Carlow
www.walshwhiskey.com

Writers Tears is a pot still-blended Irish whiskey produced by the Walsh family, which is also responsible for The Irishman range. It was introduced in 2009, and contains only pot still whiskey and malt whiskey, with no grain whiskey component.

The Walsh family is currently engaged in the construction of a new distillery in County Carlow, which will be equipped with both pot and column stills, and will have the capacity to distill up to 8 million bottles of whiskey per year.

WRITERS TEARS POT STILL BLEND

BLEND 40% ABV
Soft on the nose, with honey and citrus fruits. Mellow and easy-drinking, with malt, caramel, and apple notes on the long, warming palate.

THE WILD GEESE CLASSIC BLEND

THE WILD GEESE RARE IRISH

THE WILD GEESE SINGLE MALT

THE WILD GEESE

www.thewildgeese-irishwhiskey.com

With victory at the Battle of Kinsale, the English crown finally wrestled power from the native Gaelic chieftains, and in 1608 these Irish nobles fled the country. However, this didn't end the conflict in Ireland. The term "Wild Geese" refers to those Irish nobles and soldiers who left to serve in continental European armies from the early 17th century to the dawn of the 20th century. Most of those families remained in Europe. Some, like the Hennessys, started producing cognac. Others, such as the Lynchs, went on to make wine.

The name "Wild Geese" has come down through history to embrace all the men and women who left Ireland in the last 400 years—not just the nobles. The idea of diaspora and immigration has, of course, been a poignant theme in Irish culture and remains so today. Wild Geese raises a glass to this part of Irish history, and they've certainly produced a good whiskey for the job.

THE WILD GEESE CLASSIC BLEND

BLEND 40% ABV

A boiled-sweet nose. The malt doesn't have much impact here, leaving the grain to carry things to the finish.

THE WILD GEESE RARE IRISH

BLEND 43% ABV

A rich and malty blend, with some spiciness and lemon notes in the body. You'll find a little dry oak in the finish.

THE WILD GEESE SINGLE MALT

SINGLE MALT 43% ABV

This whiskey is predominantly malty, with a caramel sweetness. There is also a little oakiness and a hint of spice.

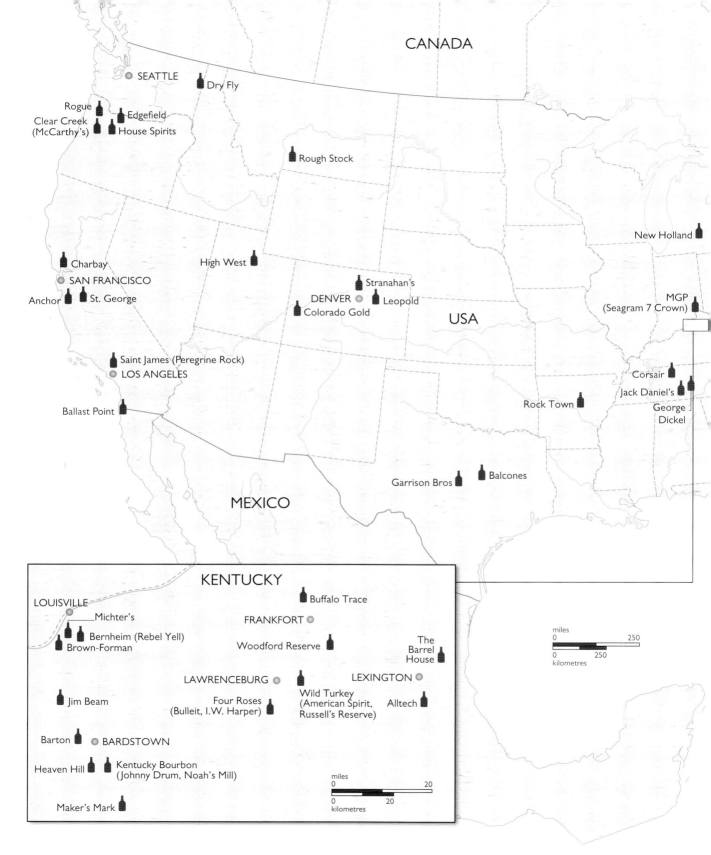

CANADA

SEATTLE ● Dry Fly

Rogue
Clear Creek
(McCarthy's)   Edgefield
House Spirits

Rough Stock

New Holland

Charbay
● SAN FRANCISCO
Anchor   St. George

High West

Stranahan's
DENVER ●   Leopold
Colorado Gold

USA

MGP
(Seagram 7 Crown)

Saint James (Peregrine Rock)
● LOS ANGELES

Corsair
Jack Daniel's
George
Dickel

Ballast Point

Rock Town

MEXICO

Garrison Bros   Balcones

KENTUCKY

LOUISVILLE
Michter's
Bernheim (Rebel Yell)
Brown-Forman

Buffalo Trace

FRANKFORT ●

Woodford Reserve

The
Barrel
House

Jim Beam

LAWRENCEBURG ●

LEXINGTON ●

Four Roses
(Bulleit, I.W. Harper)

Wild Turkey
(American Spirit,
Russell's Reserve)

Alltech

Barton   ● BARDSTOWN

Heaven Hill   Kentucky Bourbon
(Johnny Drum, Noah's Mill)

Maker's Mark

miles
0   20
0   20
kilometres

miles
0   250
0   250
kilometres

Nashoba Valley

BOSTON

Tuthilltown
(Hudson)

Triple Eight
(The Notch)

NEW YORK

New York
Distilling Company

Belmont Farm
(Virginia Lightning)

Copper Fox
(Wasmund's)

Mount Vernon

A. Smith Bowman
(Virginia Gentleman)

Piedmont (Catdaddy)

N
W E
S

The limestone soil of Kentucky yields rich crops of corn, and it is no coincidence that Kentucky and the surrounding whiskey-producing states of the US partly overlie the same limestone shelf. Kentucky is the heartland of American whiskey, and is where most of the US's large-scale commercial distilleries are located, including Jim Beam, Buffalo Trace, Heaven Hill, Barton, and Brown-Forman. To the south, Tennessee has its own legally defined whiskey style and is the home of two other big names in American whiskey: Jack Daniel's and George Dickel. Today, international spirit companies own many of these major distilleries and brands. Besides this core of large-scale distillers, however, the US has seen an explosion of craft distilling during the last couple of decades, with 769 distilleries now operational across the country at last count. They are often eager to experiment with recipes and production practices, injecting new and dynamic life into the exciting world of American whiskey.

WILD TURKEY

BUFFALO TRACE

CATDADDY

OLD POTRERO

MELLOW CORN

1776

www.jamesepepper.com

1776 was the year the US declared its independence, and the year in which Elijah Pepper of Culpeper, Virginia, settled at Old Pepper Springs in Kentucky. By 1780, he was a well-established distiller, and today the site where he began distilling is home to the Woodford Reserve Distillery. Three generations of the Pepper family were involved in distilling, and in more recent years, the Georgetown Trading Co. has been custodian of the Pepper distilling legacy. Both 1776 Bourbon and 1776 Rye are available.

1776 STRAIGHT BOURBON WHISKEY

BOURBON 50% ABV

Vanilla, spicy rye, and citrus fruit on the nose. Honey and vanilla on the palate, with chocolate, tangerines, and then cinnamon in the lengthy finish.

AMERICAN SPIRIT

Wild Turkey Distillery, US Highway 62 East, Lawrenceburg, Kentucky
www.wildturkeybourbon.com

American Spirit is distilled at the Wild Turkey Distillery *(see p.262)* by Austin Nichols & Co, and was introduced in September 2007. According to Eddie Russell, who developed this expression with his father, Master Distiller Jimmy Russell, the name "American Spirit" seemed to suggest itself.

AMERICAN SPIRIT 15-YEAR-OLD

BOURBON 50% ABV

Richly aromatic and characterful on the nose, silky smooth in the mouth, with vanilla, brittle toffee, molasses, stewed fruits, spice, and a little mint. The finish is lengthy and spicy, with gentle oak and a final menthol note.

ANCIENT AGE

Buffalo Trace, 1001 Wilkinson Boulevard, Frankfort, Kentucky
www.buffalotrace.com

Ancient Age was, from 1969 to 1999, the name of what is now the Buffalo Trace Distillery *(see p.223)*. The brand was introduced in the 1930s shortly after the end of Prohibition, initially being distilled in Canada. After World War II it was reformulated as a straight Kentucky-made bourbon, and went on to become one of the best-known brands produced by its proprietors.

ANCIENT AGE 10-YEAR-OLD

BOURBON 40% ABV

This 10-year-old bourbon is complex and fragrant on the nose, with spices, fudge, oranges, and honey. Medium-bodied and, after a slightly dry opening, the oily palate sweetens with developing vanilla, cocoa, and a lightly charred note.

BAKER'S

Jim Beam Distillery, 149 Happy Hollow Road, Clermont, Kentucky
www.jimbeam.com

Baker's is one of three whiskeys that were introduced in 1992 as Beam's Small Batch Bourbon Collection. It is named after Baker Beam, the former Clermont Master Distiller and grand-nephew of the legendary Jim Beam himself. He is also a cousin of the late Booker Noe, the high-profile distiller who instigated small-batch bourbon distilling.

Baker Beam's namesake whiskey is distilled using the standard Jim Beam formula, but is aged for longer and offered at a higher bottling strength.

BAKER'S 7-YEAR-OLD

BOURBON (53.5% ABV)

Baker's is a fruity, toasty expression of the Jim Beam formula: medium-bodied, mellow, and richly flavored, with notes of vanilla and caramel.

BALCONES

Balcones Distilling,
212 S. 17th Street, Waco, Texas
www.balconesdistilling.com

Balcones was established in 2008
by Chip Tate, but he has since
parted company with the venture
and plans to create a new distillery
in the near future. From the outset,
Balcones was synonymous with
the more experimental side of
micro-distilling, producing products
such as the "Texas Scrub Oak
Smoked" corn whiskey Brimstone,
and Baby Blue, made from roasted
heirloom blue corn. The innovative
company's best-seller is its Texas
Single Malt whiskey.

BALCONES TEXAS SINGLE MALT

SINGLE MALT 53% ABV
Toffee, honey, and creamy vanilla on the
nose. Malt, honey, apples, and cinnamon
on the palate, with closing spicy oak.

BARTON

300 Barton Road, Bardstown, Kentucky
Owner: Sazerac

Very Old Barton is distilled in the
Barton 1792 distillery at Bardstown,
and the brand is now owned by
Sazerac Company Inc. of New
Orleans. Bardstown is in the true
heartland of bourbon, and once
boasted more than 20 distilleries.
Barton's whiskeys are typically
youthful, dry, and aromatic.

In addition to the Barton-
named brands, the company also
owns Kentucky Gentleman *(see*
p.242), Kentucky Tavern *(p.242)*,
Ridgemont *(p.252)*, Ten High
(p.256), and Tom Moore *(p.256)*.

VERY OLD BARTON

BOURBON 43% ABV
The nose is rich, syrupy, and spicy, with
a prickle of salt. Big-bodied in the mouth,
it is fruity and spicy, with spices and ginger
in the drying finish.

BASIL HAYDEN'S

Jim Beam Distillery, 149 Happy Hollow
Road, Clermont, Kentucky
www.basilhaydens.com

Basil Hayden's was one of the
three whiskeys that made up
Beam's pioneering Small Batch
Bourbon Collection, introduced
in 1992. Basil Hayden was
an early Kentucky settler from
Maryland who began making
whiskey in the late 18th century
near Bardstown, and it is claimed
that the recipe for this particular
expression dates from that period.

BASIL HAYDEN'S 8-YEAR-OLD

BOURBON 40% ABV
The nose is light, aromatic, and spicy,
with flavors of soft rye, wood-polish,
spices, pepper, vanilla, and a hint
of honey on the comparatively dry
palate. The finish is long, with notes
of peppery rye.

BERNHEIM

Heaven Hill Distillery, 1701 West
Breckinridge Street, Louisville, Kentucky
www.bernheimwheatwhiskey.com

The Bernheim brand takes its
name from Heaven Hill's Bernheim
Distillery in Louisville, Kentucky,
where Heaven Hill whiskeys have
been produced since the plant was
acquired in 1999.

Launched in 2005, Bernheim
is the only straight wheat whiskey
on the US market.

Heaven Hill father and son Master
Distillers Parker and Craig Beam
developed the wheat formula with
a minimum of 51 percent winter
wheat, and the recipe also includes
corn and malted barley.

BERNHEIM ORIGINAL

WHEAT WHISKEY 45% ABV
Bernheim exhibits light fruit notes on the
spicy nose, with freshly sawn wood, toffee,
vanilla, sweetish grain, and a hint of mint
on the palate. A long, elegant, honeyed,
and spicy finish.

EARLY TIMES (SEE P.224)

OLD FORESTER (SEE P.248)

BLANTON'S

Buffalo Trace, 1001 Wilkinson
Boulevard, Frankfort, Kentucky
www.buffalotrace.com

Colonel Albert Bacon Blanton
worked for no fewer than 55 years
at what is now the Buffalo Trace
Distillery, starting as office boy in
1897 and graduating to distillery
manager in 1912. When he retired
in 1955 the distillery was renamed
Blanton's in his honor. This single
barrel expression was created in
1984 by Master Distiller Elmer T.
Lee, who worked with Blanton
during the 1950s.

BLANTON'S SINGLE BARREL

BOURBON 46.5% ABV
*The nose of Blanton's is soft,
with toffee, leather, and a hint of
mint.Full-bodied and rounded on
the palate, this is a notably sweet
bourbon, embracing vanilla, caramel,
honey, and spices. The finish is long
and creamy, with a hint of late spice.*

BOOKER'S

Jim Beam Distillery, 149 Happy Hollow
Road, Clermont, Kentucky
www.bookersbourbon.com

A brand created by the global Jim
Beam company, Booker's is named
after Jim Beam's grandson, Booker
Noe. Booker was a sixth-generation
Master Distiller and the man
credited with the introduction of
"small batch" bourbon in 1992.
On its website, Booker's declares
that of the few batches they release
every year, "each varies in age and
proof because reaching Booker's
standards is a mix of art, science
and Mother Nature. It tells us
when it's ready, and then we'll
let you know."

BOOKER'S 2015 BATCH 06
NOE'S SECRET

BOURBON 64.05% ABV
*Richly aromatic nose of vanilla, corn,
and cinnamon. Caramel and more
vanilla on the palate, with big spice
notes, char, oak, and raspberries.*

BROWN-FORMAN

850 Dixie Highway,
Louisville, Kentucky
www.brown-forman.com

The Brown-Forman Distillery is
situated in the area of Louisville
known as "Distillery Row." Half
a dozen once operated here, but
today only Brown-Forman and
Bernheim (see p.219) survive.

The Brown-Forman Corporation
has its origins in a blending and
bottling operation established by
George Garvin Brown and his
half-brother John Thompson Street
Brown in 1870. Their practice of
selling whiskey in sealed bottles
was a major innovation that
overcame problems of adulteration,
but the Browns were also forward-
thinking in acquiring whiskeys
from a variety of distillers and
blending them to achieve ongoing
consistency. Their whiskey brand
was originally called Old Forrester
(later changed to Forester). When
John Brown left the company, he

was replaced by accountant George
Forman, whose name was added
to the company title in 1890.

The firm's Louisville facility
was established in 1935 as
the Old Kentucky Distillery.
Brown-Forman acquired it in
1940 and subsequently rebuilt
the plant, renaming it the
Early Times Distillery. Brown-
Forman's other distillery in
Louisville, Old Forester Distillery,
closed in 1979, after which
production of Old Forester
bourbon was moved to the Early
Times Distillery.

Today it is simply the Brown-
Forman Distillery. Early Times
Kentucky Whisky (see p.224)
and Old Forester Kentucky
Straight Bourbon Whisky (p.248)
are now its principal output
(Brown-Forman favors the Scottish
spelling of "whisky" for some of
its output). The Brown-Forman
Corporation also owns the Jack
Daniel's (p.236) and Woodford
Reserve distilleries (p.264).

WHISKEY STYLES
BOURBON

Bourbon enjoys a global reputation as the quintessential US whiskey, and boasts a long and colorful heritage. It takes its name from Bourbon County in Kentucky, which in turn was named in honor of the French royal House of Bourbon when the former Western Virginian county of Kentucky was subdivided in the 1780s.

Distilling probably began in the area when settlers of Scottish, Irish, and German origin arrived during the late 18th century. The "invention" of bourbon is often credited to the Baptist minister, entrepreneur, and distiller Elijah Craig, who is said to have pioneered the use of charred casks for maturation at the distillery he founded in 1789. In reality, however, no one person created bourbon, which evolved from the distilling practices of many individuals. It is also a common misconception that bourbon must be distilled in Kentucky. In fact, it can be produced anywhere in the United States where it is legal to distill spirits. However, in practice, some 95 percent of all bourbon is distilled and matured in its "home" state.

The legally binding modern definition of bourbon dates from May 1964, when the US Congress recognized it as a "distinctive product of the United States", and created the Federal Standards of Identity for Bourbon. By law, the type must be produced from a mash of not less than 51 percent corn grain, and is usually made using between 70 and 90 percent corn, with some barley malt plus rye and/or wheat in the mashbill. It has to be distilled to no more than 80% ABV and casked at 62.5% ABV or less. Legally, bourbon must be matured in new, charred, white-oak barrels for a minimum of two years.

Among the most notable bourbon brands on the market are Jim Beam *(see p.240)*, Buffalo Trace *(p.223)*, Maker's Mark *(p.244)*, Wild Turkey *(p.262)*, and Woodford Reserve *(p.264)*.

A misty morning dawns at Buffalo Trace in Frankfort, Kentucky. The distillery's water towers are an iconic landmark in the heartland of Bourbon Country.

BUFFALO TRACE KENTUCKY STRAIGHT BOURBON

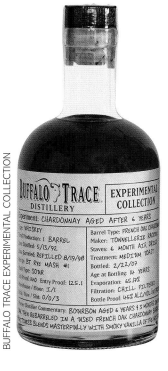

BUFFALO TRACE EXPERIMENTAL COLLECTION

BUFFALO TRACE

Buffalo Trace Distillery, 1001 Wilkinson Boulevard, Frankfort, Kentucky
www.buffalotrace.com

Formerly known as Ancient Age *(see p.218)*, Buffalo Trace is located at a crossing point where, in the past, herds of migrating buffalo forded the Kentucky River. The trail they followed was known as the Great Buffalo Trace.

A distillery was first established here in 1857 by the Blanton family. Later, it was run by "bourbon aristocrat" Edmund Haynes Taylor and the pioneering George T. Stagg. Then Albert Bacon Blanton steered and grew the company through flood, Prohibition, and war. He and Stagg have exclusive bourbons named after them *(see pp.220 and 231)*.

Buffalo Trace boasts the broadest age-range of whiskey in the US (from 4 to 23 years) and is the only US distillery using five recipes—a wheat whiskey, a rye whiskey, two rye bourbons, and a barley.

The Buffalo Trace Experimental Collection of cask strength, wine-barrel-aged whiskeys was launched in 2006. It included a "Fire Pot Barrel" for which the barrel was heated to 102°F (39°C) prior to filling, to give a greater "burn" than usual. Subsequent releases in the Experimental Collection have included a 10-year-old Chardonnay, a 14- and a 16-year-old Cabernet Franc, and a 6-year-old Zinfandel.

BUFFALO TRACE KENTUCKY STRAIGHT BOURBON

BOURBON 45% ABV
Aged a minimum of nine years, it has aromas of vanilla, gum, mint, and molasses. Sweet, fruity, and spicy on the palate, with emerging brown sugar and oak. The finish is long, spicy, and fairly dry, with developing vanilla.

BULLEIT

Four Roses Distillery, 1224 Bonds Mill Road, Lawrenceburg, Kentucky
www.bulleit.com

Bulleit Bourbon originated in the 1830s with tavern-keeper and small-time distiller Augustus Bulleit, but production ceased after his death in 1860. However, the brand was revived, using the original recipe, in 1987 by his great-great-grandson Tom Bulleit. Seagram subsequently took over the label and from there it passed to Diageo. Although it is distilled by Four Roses *(see p.228)*, brand owner Diageo has created the Bulleit Experience at the silent Stitzel-Weller Distillery in Louisville. *(www.bulleitexperience.com)*.

BULLEIT BOURBON

BOURBON 40% ABV
Rich, oaky aromas lead into a mellow flavor, focused around vanilla and honey. The medium-length finish features vanilla and a hint of smoke.

CATDADDY

Piedmont Distillers, 203 East Murphy Street, Madison, North Carolina
www.catdaddymoonshine.com

Piedmont is the only licensed distillery in North Carolina, and its Catdaddy Moonshine celebrates the state's great heritage of illicit distilling. In 2005, ex-New Yorker Joe Michalek established Piedmont in Madison. It is the first legal distillery in the Carolinas since before Prohibition. "According to the lore of moonshine, only the best moonshine earns the right to be called the Catdaddy," says Joe Michalek. "True to the history of moonshine, every batch of Catdaddy is born in an authentic copper pot still."

CATDADDY CAROLINA MOONSHINE

CORN WHISKEY 40% ABV
Triple-distilled from corn in small batches, Catdaddy is sweet and spicy, with notes of vanilla and cinnamon.

CHARBAY

Domaine Charbay, 4001 Spring
Mountain Road, St. Helena, California
www.charbay.com

The father-and-son partnership
of Miles and Marko Karakasevic
are 12th and 13th generation wine-
makers and distillers. Charbay
whiskeys are distilled in a 3,750
liter (1,000-gallon) copper
alembic Charentais pot still. Many
innovative whiskeys have emerged
from the still, including R5 Lot
No. 3, double-distilled from Bear
Republic IPA, and Whiskey S
(Lot 211A), produced from Bear
Republic Stout. Whiskey Release
III was distilled using Pilsner.

CHARBAY WHISKEY RELEASE III
6-YEAR-OLD

AMERICAN WHISKEY 66.2% ABV
*This "hop-flavored whiskey" offers
an herbal, lager-like nose, with lemon
and cloves, plus a note of vanilla.
Big fruit, spice, and herbal notes in
the full palate, with developing oak.*

EAGLE RARE

Buffalo Trace Distillery, 1001 Wilkinson
Boulevard, Frankfort, Kentucky
www.eaglerare.com

The Eagle Rare brand was
introduced in 1975 by Canadian
distilling giant Joseph E. Seagram
& Sons Inc. In 1989 it was acquired
by the Sazerac company of New
Orleans. In its present incarnation,
Eagle Rare is part of Sazerac's
Buffalo Trace Antique Collection,
which is updated annually.

In addition to the popular
10-year-old expression, Eagle
Rare also releases small quantities
of a 17-year-old variant in the
autumn of each year.

EAGLE RARE 10-YEAR-OLD

BOURBON 45% ABV
*Stewed fruits, spicy aok, new leather,
brittle toffee, and orange on the nose.
Rounded on the palate, with dried
fruits, spicy cocoa, almonds, and
a lengthy finish.*

EARLY TIMES

Brown-Forman Distillery, 850 Dixie
Highway, Louisville, Kentucky
www.earlytimes.com

Early Times takes its name
from a settlement near Bardstown
where it was created in 1860. It
cannot be classified as a bourbon
because some spirit is put into used
barrels, and bourbon legislation
dictates that all spirit of that name
must be matured in new barrels.

This version of Early Times
was introduced in 1981 to compete
with the increasingly popular,
lighter-bodied Canadian whiskies.
The Early Times mashbill is made
up of 79 percent corn, 11 percent
rye, and 10 percent malted barley.

EARLY TIMES

KENTUCKY WHISKEY 40% ABV
*Quite light on the nose, with nuts
and spices. The palate offers more
of the same, together with honey
and butterscotch notes, leading into
a medium-length finish.*

EDGEFIELD

2126 Southwest Halsey Street,
Troutdale, Oregon
www.mcmenamins.com

Operated by the McMenamin's
hotel and pub group, Edgefield
Distillery is located in a former
dry store for root vegetables on the
beautiful Edgefield Manor Estate
at Troutdale. The distillery has
been in production since February
1998 and features a 12-ft (4-m)
tall copper and stainless-steel still.
According to Mcmenamin's, it
resembles a hybrid of a 19th-
century diving suit and oversized
coffee urn, a design made famous
by Holstein of Germany, the world's
oldest surviving still manufacturer.

EDGEFIELD HOGSHEAD

OREGON WHISKEY 46% ABV
*Hogshead whiskey has banana and
malt on the sweet, floral nose, with
vanilla and caramel notes on the
palate, plus barley, honey, and oak
in the medium-length finish.*

EVAN WILLIAMS BLACK LABEL

EVAN WILLIAMS SINGLE BARREL 1998 VINTAGE

ELIJAH CRAIG

Heaven Hill Distillery, 1701 West Breckinridge Street, Louisville, Kentucky www.heavenhill.com

The Reverend Elijah Craig (1743–1808) was a Baptist minister who is widely viewed as the "father of bourbon," having reputedly invented the concept of using charred barrels to store and mature the spirit he made. There seems to be no hard evidence that he was the first person to make bourbon, but the association between a "man of God" and whiskey was seen as a useful tool in the struggle against the temperance movement.

ELIJAH CRAIG 12-YEAR-OLD

BOURBON 47% ABV

A classic bourbon, with aromas of caramel, vanilla, spice, and honey, plus a bit of mint. Full-bodied, rounded on the mellow palate, with caramel, malt, corn, rye, and a little smoke. Sweet oak, licorice, and vanilla dominate the finish. and vanilla dominate the finish.

ELMER T. LEE

Buffalo Trace Distillery, 1001 Wilkinson Boulevard, Frankfort, Kentucky www.buffalotrace.com

Elmer T. Lee is a former Master Distiller at Buffalo Trace *(see p.223),* having joined what was then the George T. Stagg Distillery in the 1940s. During his time there, the name changed first to the Albert B. Blanton Distillery (1953), then to the Ancient Age Distillery (1962), and finally to the Buffalo Trace Distillery in 2001.

Lee is credited with creating the first modern single barrel bourbon in 1984.

ELMER T. LEE SINGLE BARREL

BOURBON 45% ABV

Aged from six to eight years, this expression offers citrus, vanilla, and corn merging on the fragrant nose, with a full and sweet palate, where honey, lingering caramel, and cocoa notes are also evident.

EVAN WILLIAMS

Heaven Hill Distillery, 1701 West Breckinridge Street, Louisville, Kentucky www.evanwilliams.com

The second biggest-selling bourbon after Jim Beam, Evan Williams takes its name from the person considered by many experts to be Kentucky's first distiller.

Evan Williams was born in Wales but emigrated to and settled in Virginia, moving to what would become Kentucky (but was then Fincastle County of Virginia) in around 1780. Subsequently, he set up a small distillery on the Ohio River at the foot of what is now Fifth Street in Louisville.

According to an article in the *Louisville Courier-Journal* for April 29, 1889, Williams was a member of the early Board of Trustees of Louisville, and tradition says he never attended a meeting of the board without bringing a bottle of his whiskey, and that what he brought was always drunk by the members before the meeting adjourned. He was apparently censured every time for doing so, but still he never left with a full jug.

EVAN WILLIAMS BLACK LABEL

BOURBON 43% ABV

The nose is quite light, yet aromatic, with vanilla and mint notes. The palate is initially sweet, with caramel, malt, and developing leather and spice notes.

EVAN WILLIAMS SINGLE BARREL 1998 VINTAGE

BOURBON 43.3% ABV

This is the world's only vintage-dated single barrel bourbon, selected by Master Distillers Parker and Craig Beam. The latest release, distilled in 1998, offers an aromatic nose of cereal, dried fruit, caramel, and vanilla. The palate comprises maple, molasses, cinnamon, nutmeg, and berry notes. There is a whiff of smoke, plus almonds and honey in the spicy finish.

WHISKEY TOUR: KENTUCKY

The state of Kentucky is the bourbon-producing heartland of the US and home to many of the best-known names in American whiskey. Most of the state's distilleries offer visitor facilities, allowing guests to study the production and maturation of this historic spirit. A tour embracing these distilleries and associated attractions not only provides an opportunity to make a real connection with bourbon and its fascinating heritage, but also offers a great way to experience the beauty of Kentucky and its hospitality.

USA

TOUR STATISTICS

DAYS: 5	LENGTH: 85 miles (137 km)	DISTILLERIES: 8
TRAVEL: Car	REGION: Northern Kentucky, US	

DAY 1: BUFFALO TRACE, WOODFORD RESERVE

BARRELS AT WOODFORD RESERVE

1 Frankfort, the state capital, has a range of hotels and restaurants, and is the home of **Buffalo Trace**. The distillery has a large visitors' center and offers tours throughout the year. (*www.buffalotrace.com*)

2 **Woodford Reserve** lies near the attractive town of Versailles, in Kentucky's famous "bluegrass" horse-breeding country. Its copper pot stills are the highlight of the distillery tour. (*www.woodfordreserve.com*)

DAY 2: WILD TURKEY, FOUR ROSES

3 Spectacularly situated on a hill above the Kentucky River, **Wild Turkey**'s Boulevard Distillery allows visitors into its production areas at most times of the year. (*www.wildturkeybourbon.com*)

4 **Four Roses** Distillery is a striking structure, built in the style of a Spanish Mission. Tours are available from fall to spring (the distillery is closed throughout the summer). You can also pre-arrange to visit Four Roses' warehouse at Cox's Creek. (*www.fourrosesbourbon.com*)

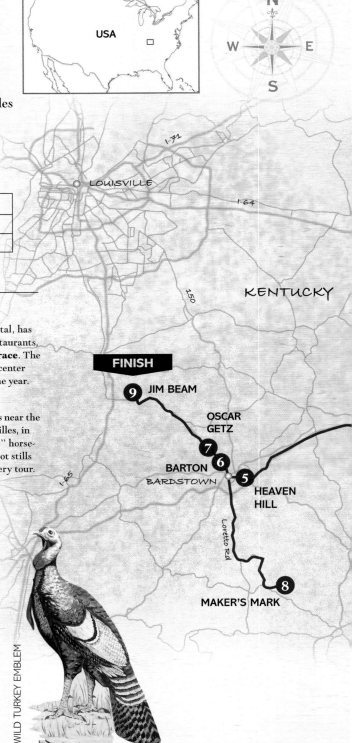

WILD TURKEY EMBLEM

FINISH

9 JIM BEAM

OSCAR GETZ

7

6

5

BARTON

BARDSTOWN

HEAVEN HILL

Loretto Rd

8

MAKER'S MARK

LOUISVILLE

KENTUCKY

DAY 3: HEAVEN HILL, BARTON, OSCAR GETZ

5 Bardstown is renowned as the "World Capital of Bourbon," and makes an excellent base for visiting the distilleries in the area. Book a room at the Old Talbott Tavern *(www.talbotts. com)*, which is set in a building dating back to the late 1700s and offers a well-stocked bourbon bar. Then head out to the **Heaven Hill** Bourbon Heritage Center, which includes a tour of a bourbon-aging rackhouse and the chance to taste two Heaven Hill whiskeys. *(www.heavenhill.com)*

HEAVEN HILL, BARDSTOWN

6 The **Barton 1792 Distillery** in downtown Bardstown traditionally maintained a low profile compared to its neighbors, but nowdays comprehensive tours of the production areas are available, together with a state-of-the-art visitor center. *(www.1792bourbon.com)*

7 A few blocks from Tom Moore, the **Oscar Getz Whiskey Museum** houses a collection of whiskey artifacts, including rare antique bottles, a moonshine still, advertising art, novelty whiskey containers, and Abraham Lincoln's original liquor license. *(www.whiskeymuseum.com)*

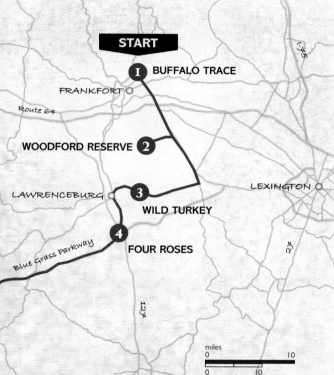

START

1 BUFFALO TRACE

FRANKFORT

Route 64

WOODFORD RESERVE **2**

LAWRENCEBURG

3

WILD TURKEY

LEXINGTON

4

FOUR ROSES

Blue Grass Parkway

127

miles
0 — 10
0 — 10
kilometers

DAY 4: MAKER'S MARK

8 The historic **Maker's Mark** Distillery stands on the banks of Hardin's Creek, near Loretto, in Marion County. The distillery grounds are notable as they act as an arboretum, being home to some 275 species of trees and shrubs. Guided tours of the distillery are available daily. *(www.makersmark.com)*

MAKER'S MARK

JIM BEAM'S CLERMONT DISTILLERY

DAY 5: JIM BEAM

9 **Jim Beam**'s Clermont Distillery offers tours of the site grounds, a working rackhouse, and the Hartmann Cooperage Museum. The American Outpost is an on-site visitors' center, with a film about the bourbon-making process at Jim Beam and displays of whiskey memorabilia that take in more than two centuries of bourbon history. *(www.jimbeam.com)*

WHISKEY STYLES
TENNESSEE WHISKEY

Whiskey-making in Tennessee dates back at least as far as the 18th century. During the late 19th century there were said to be some 700 stills in operation in the state, but Tennessee went "dry" in 1910 and distilling remained illegal until 1938.

Tennessee whiskeys are essentially bourbon-style spirits that undergo filtration through a thick layer of sugar-maple charcoal before the spirit is casked. The same legal criteria that apply to bourbon, in terms of strength and maturation period (*see p.221*), also apply to Tennessee whiskey, but formal adoption of the classification of Tennessee whiskey as a distinct style can be dated to 1941, when the charcoal filtration process was recognized in a United States tax authority letter to Jack Daniel Distillers. This defining aspect is known as the Lincoln County Process in reference to Lincoln County, Tennessee, where Jack Daniel's was founded.

Jack Daniel's (*see p.236*) is undoubtedly the best-known Tennessee whiskey. The distillers like to emphasize that their product has the distinctive classification of Tennessee whiskey—it is not a bourbon, although it has some of the characteristics of bourbon. The difference, according to Jack Daniel's, is that their whiskey is trickled very slowly through 10 feet (3 meters) of hard maple charcoal, right after distillation. The company claims that this extra step in the whiskey-making process provides the special character known only to Tennessee whiskey. The charcoal mellowing process is said to remove some of the congeners and harsh fusel oils that are present in any grain alcohol.

The use of charcoal leaching was actually pioneered in 1825 by Alfred Eaton of Tullahoma, close to where the George Dickel Distillery operates today. Along with Jack Daniel, George Dickel (*see p.230*) is the only surviving, licensed, full-scale distillery left in Tennessee.

FOUR ROSES SINGLE BARREL

FOUR ROSES SMALL BATCH

EZRA BROOKS

www.ezrabrooks.com

The Ezra Brooks brand was introduced in 1957 by Frank Silverman to take advantage of a shortage of Jack Daniel's (and its early presentation was markedly similar). The whiskey is sourced from the Hoffman Distilling Co. in Lawrenceburg, Kentucky, though the Ezra Brooks website claims it is from the Medley Distillery set up during 1901 in Owensboro, Kentucky. David Sherman Coporation (now Luxco Inc.) acquired the brand in 1993. The signature sour mash bourbon is produced at the Heaven Hill distillery, and an Ezra Brooks cinnamon liqueur is also now available.

EZRA BROOKS BOURBON

BOURBON 40% ABV
Sweet nose of vanilla, corn, and coconut. The palate offers stewed fruit, cream, and a hint of oak. Milky coffee finish.

FOUR ROSES

1224 Bond Mills Road,
Lawrenceburg, Kentucky
www.fourrosesbourbon.com

Built to a striking Spanish Mission-style design in 1910, Four Roses Distillery near Lawrenceburg takes its name from the brand first trademarked by Georgia-born Paul Jones, Jr., in 1888. Legend has it that the southern belle with whom he was in love wore a corsage of four red roses to signify her acceptance of his marriage proposal, hence the name he gave to his bourbon.

In 2002, after a period of almost 60 years under the ownership of the Seagram organization, when it had become a bestseller in the booming European and Asian market, the Four Roses trademark brand, production, bottling, and warehousing facilities were bought by Tokyo-based Kirin Brewery Company. In addition to its own Four Roses whiskeys, the distillery now produces a number of other well-known brands, including Bulleit Bourbon *(see p.223)* and I. W. Harper President's Reserve Bourbon.

FOUR ROSES SINGLE BARREL

BOURBON (VARIABLE ABV)
Offers a rich, complex nose, comprising malt, fruits, spices, and fudge. Long and mellow in the mouth, with vanilla, oak, and a hint of menthol. The finish is long, spicy, and decidedly mellow.

FOUR ROSES SMALL BATCH

BOURBON 45% ABV
Mild and refined on the nose, with nutmeg and restrained honey. Bold and rich on the well-balanced palate, with spices, fruit, and honey flavors. The finish is long and insinuating, with developing notes of vanilla.

GARRISON BROTHERS

Garrison Brothers Distillery,
1827 Hye Albert Road, Hye, Texas
www.garrisonbros.com

The oldest legal distillery in Texas, Garrison Brothers has produced nothing but bourbon since it opened in 2005. The distillery uses organic yellow corn from the Texas Panhandle, organic winter wheat from the Garrison ranch, and two-row winter barley from the Pacific Northwest and Canada. Grain is ground daily, and the sweet mash is cooked one batch at a time. The distillery receives many visitors, and its whiskey has won several major awards.

GARRISON BROTHERS TEXAS STRAIGHT BOURBON

BOURBON 47% ABV
Rich aromas of honey and vanilla on the nose, continuing onto the palate of apple, cinnamon, and black pepper.

GEORGE DICKEL NO. 12

GEORGE DICKEL BARREL SELECT

GEORGE DICKEL NO. 8

GEORGE DICKEL

1950 Cascade Hollow Road,
Normandy, Tennessee
www.georgedickel.com

Along with Jack Daniel's, George
Dickel is the last licensed, full-scale
distillery in the state of Tennessee,
though there were around 700
operating there a century ago.

The distillery uses the spelling
"whisky" because founder George
A. Dickel insisted that the spirit he
made was as smooth as the finest
Scotch. Dickel, who was German
by birth, was a Nashville merchant
before he founded Cascade Hollow
distillery in the 1870s. He used
pure water from the nearby
Cascade Springs source.

The year 1910 saw the arrival
of Prohibition in Tennessee, and
the Dickel operation was moved
to Kentucky and subsequently
acquired by Schenley Distilling Co.
In 1958, Schenley decided that
George Dickel should return to
its roots, and a new distillery was
built close to the original Cascade
Hollow location, and using recipes
from Dickel's own notes. Dickel is
now owned by the Diageo group.

GEORGE DICKEL NO. 12
TENNESSEE WHISKEY 45% ABV
*The nose is aromatic, with fruit, leather,
butterscotch, and a whiff of charcoal
and vanilla. The palate is rich, with rye,
chocolate, fruit, and vanilla. The finish
offers vanilla toffee and drying oak.*

GEORGE DICKEL BARREL SELECT
TENNESSEE WHISKEY 43% ABV
*Aromas of rich corn, honey, nuts,
and caramel lead into a full body
with soft vanilla, spices, and roast
nuts. The long, creamy finish boasts
almond and spices.*

GEORGE DICKEL NO. 8
TENNESSEE WHISKEY 40% ABV
*Sweet on the nose, with chocolate,
cocoa, and vanilla. The palate is quite
sweet and well rounded, with fresh
fruit and vanilla notes. The short
finish features spices and charcoal.*

GEORGE T. STAGG

Buffalo Trace Distillery, 1001 Wilkinson Boulevard, Frankfort, Kentucky
www.buffalotracedistillery.com

Part of the Buffalo Trace Antique Collection, George T. Stagg takes its name from the one-time owner of what is now the Buffalo Trace Distillery. In the early 1880s the distillery was owned by Edmund Haynes Taylor, Jr. During tough economic times he obtained a loan from his friend Stagg—who later foreclosed on Taylor, taking over his company in the process.

GEORGE T. STAGG
2008 EDITION

BOURBON 72.4% ABV

Distilled in the spring of 1993, this high-strength whiskey boasts a rich nose of butterscotch, marzipan, sweet oak, and cherries. The palate features corn, coffee beans, leather, spice, and oak, with a long toffee and spice finish.

GEORGIA MOON

Heaven Hill Distillery, 1701 West Breckinridge Street, Louisville, Kentucky
www.heavenhill.com

Corn whiskey is distilled from a fermented mash of not less than 80 percent corn, and no minimum maturation period is specified. One of the best-known examples is Heaven Hill's Georgia Moon. With a label that promises that the contents are fewer than 30 days old, and available bottled in a mason jar *(see p.233)*, Georgia Moon harks back to the old days of moonshining.

GEORGIA MOON

CORN WHISKEY 40% ABV

The nose commences with an initial tang of sour liquor, followed by the smell of sweet corn. The palate suggests cabbage water and plums, along with developing sweeter, candy-corn notes. The finish is short. Drinkers should not expect anything sophisticated.

HANCOCK'S RESERVE

Buffalo Trace Distillery, 1001 Wilkinson Boulevard, Frankfort, Kentucky
www.buffalotrace.com

This whiskey, which is usually created from barrels of spirit aged for around 10 years, takes its name from Hancock Taylor, great-uncle of US president Zachary Taylor, and an early surveyor of Kentucky. He was shot and killed by Native Americans in 1774, and it is said that his deathbed will was one of the first legal documents executed in the region.

HANCOCK'S RESERVE
PRESIDENT'S SINGLE BARREL

BOURBON 44.45% ABV

Oily on the nose, with licorice, caramel, and spicy rye. Sweet in the mouth, with malt, fudge, and vanilla notes. Drying in the finish, with oak notes, but the whiskey's residual sweetness remains to the end.

I.W. HARPER

Four Roses Distillery, 1224 Bond Mills Road, Lawrenceburg, Kentucky
www.iwharper.com

The historic and once best-selling I.W. Harper brand was established by Jewish businessman Isaac Wolfe Bernheim (1848–1945), a major figure in the bourbon business at the turn of the 20th century. It was made at the Bernheim Distillery *(see p.219)* in Louisville. It is now produced in no-age-statement (NAS) and 15-year-old formats for current owners Diageo by Four Roses Distillery and is one of the leading bourbons on the Japanese market.

I.W. HARPER

BOURBON 43% ABV

A big-bodied bourbon in which pepper combines with mint, oranges, caramel, and quite youthful charring on the nose, while caramel, apples, and oak feature on the elegant palate. The finish is dry and smoky.

HEAVEN HILL

BERNHEIM ORIGINAL *(SEE P.221)*

PARKER'S HERITAGE *(SEE P.251)*

HEAVEN HILL

1701 West Breckinridge Street,
Louisville, Kentucky
www.heavenhill.com

Heaven Hill is the US's largest independent producer of distilled spirits to remain in family ownership and the last family-owned distillery in Kentucky. A Heaven Hill distillery had been built in 1890, but the present one was established in 1935, soon after the repeal of Prohibition, by five Shapira brothers, who built their distillery just south of Bardstown. Their descendants control the firm to this day.

The Shapira brothers were experts in the dry-goods business, but had no practical knowledge of bourbon distillation. However, they employed Joe Beam, a cousin of legendary Jim Beam, who proved adept at making fine spirit.

More recently, Parker Beam has flown the flag for Heaven Hill as a high-profile Master Distiller,

starting work at the distillery in 1960, and succeeding his father, Earl, as Master Distiller in 1975. Parker's son, Craig, is a seventh-generation Master Distiller, following in the footsteps of his now-retired and hugely respected father.

On November 7, 1996, the distillery and warehouses were almost completely destroyed by fire, and more than 90,000 US gallons (350,000 liters) of maturing spirit was lost. As a result, the company purchased Diageo's technologically advanced Bernheim Distillery in Louisville, and all production was moved to that site. For most of its existence, Heaven Hill has concentrated on its flagship bourbon labels: Evan Williams *(see p.225)* and Elijah Craig *(p.225)*. Its speciality is older, higher proof bourbons that are traditional in character, full-bodied, and complex. As part of its notably diverse portfolio, Heaven Hill also produces

Bernheim Original *(see p.219)*, Pikesville *(p.252)*, Parker's *(p.249)*, and Rittenhouse Rye *(p.253)*. Additionally, it is the only remaining national producer of corn whiskeys, such as Mellow Corn *(see p.246)* and Georgia Moon *(p.231)*. Heaven Hill is also a major supplier of "own-label" whiskey to other customers.

HEAVEN HILL
BOURBON 40% ABV
An excellent and competitively priced "entry-level" bourbon, it has a nose of oranges and cornbread, a sweet, oily mouth-feel, and vanilla and corn featuring on the well-balanced palate.

HENRY MCKENNA

Heaven Hill Distillery, 1701 West
Breckinridge Street, Louisville, Kentucky
www.heavenhill.com

Irish-born Henry McKenna emigrated to Fairfield, Kentucky, where, in 1855, he began to distill a whiskey that soon became very popular. McKenna died in 1893, and, later, Prohibition saw the closure of his distillery. However, McKenna's family reopened the plant after Prohibition was repealed in 1933, and later sold it to Seagram's. The brand was eventually discontinued, and the name was purchased by Heaven Hill.

HENRY MCKENNA SINGLE BARREL 10-YEAR-OLD
BOURBON 50% ABV
Nose boasts citrus, charcoal, vanilla, and caramel. Contrasts continue to the palate, where spices and charred oak vie pleasingly with mint and honey.

WHISKEY STYLES
CORN WHISKEY

Corn whiskey is distilled from a fermented mash of not less than 80 percent corn at less than 80 percent ABV. It is the one American whiskey that does not have to be aged in new, charred-oak barrels, and no minimum maturation period is specified. It is often sold new and clear and, when maturation does take place, it tends to be for a period of months rather than years.

Corn whiskey was a favorite illicitly distilled, "moonshine" product. The story is told of a well-known early 20th-century North Carolina moonshiner by the name of Quill Rose who, when asked by a judge whether aging would not be beneficial to the liquor, is supposed to have replied, "Your honor has been misinformed. I have kept some for a week one time and I couldn't tell it was a bit better than when it was new and fresh." The growth in production of corn whiskey dates back to the years following the imposition of the first tax on spirits in North America during 1791, and the subsequent Whiskey Rebellion of 1794 by distillers and their supporters, who refused to pay the tax, assaulted excise officers, and marched on Pittsburgh in protest. The rebellion came to an end after 13,000 troops were assembled and marched down the Monongahela River under the command of President George Washington.

After the rebellion had been suppressed, many disgruntled distillers of mainly rye whiskey subsequently moved south and west from Maryland, Pennsylvania, and Virginia into Indiana, Illinois, Kentucky, and Tennessee. As these were great corn-producing states, it was inevitable that this migration led to a growth in whiskeys made from corn rather than rye.

Today, the best-known commercial brands of corn whiskey include Georgia Moon *(see p.231)* and Mellow Corn from Heaven Hill *(p.246)*, while a number of micro-distillers also produce corn whiskeys.

Woodford Reserve *(see p.264)* may have the smallest distillery in Kentucky, but its triple-distilled bourbons are held in high regard. The distillery is operated by the Brown-Forman Corporation.

HUDSON MANHATTAN RYE

HUDSON NEW YORK CORN

HIGH WEST

27649 Old Lincoln Highway,
Wanship, Utah
www.highwest.com

High West was established by
David Perkins during 2007 in Park
City, Utah. However, since 2015,
distillation has taken place in a
1,600-US-gallon (6,000-liter) pot
still at Blue Sky Ranch, Wanship,
a facility described by its owners
as "…the world's only distillery-
dude-ranch…!" High West makes
a variety of whiskeys, including
Valley Tan Utah oat whiskey and the
Bourbon and rye "blend" Bourye.
The distillery is best known for
its ryes, especially those released
under the Rendezvous label.

HIGH WEST RENDEZVOUS RYE

RYE WHISKEY 46% ABV
*Rendezvous Rye is a blend of 16- and
6-year-old rye. The nose offers pepper
and spice, vanilla, and toffee, with an
intense, sweet, fruity, smoky palate and
a long, spicy, caramel-coated finish.*

HIRSCH RESERVE

Distribution: Preiss Imports

Hirsch Reserve is a drop of US
whiskey history. The spirit itself
was distilled in 1974 at Michter's
Distillery, the last surviving one
in Pennsylvania. Michter's closed
in 1988, but one Adolf H. Hirsch
had acquired a considerable stock
of the spirit some years previously
and, after it had been matured
for 16 years, it was put into
stainless steel tanks to prevent
further aging. This whiskey is
now available from Preiss Imports
but, once gone, is gone forever.

HIRSCH RESERVE

BOURBON 45.8% ABV
*Caramel, honey, and rye dominate the
complex nose, with a whiff of smoke
also coming through. Oily corn, honey,
and oak on the rich palate, with rye
and more oak in the drying finish.*

HUDSON

Tuthilltown Distillery, 14 Gristmill Lane,
Gardiner, New York
www.tuthilltown.com

In 1825, New York State had more
than 1,000 working distilleries
and produced a major share of
the nation's whiskey. These days,
Tuthilltown is New York's only
remaining distillery. Based in a
converted granary, the distillery
adjoins a gristmill, which dates
back to 1788 and is listed on the
National Register of Historic Places.

Tuthilltown Distillery was
founded in 2001 by Brian Lee
and Ralph Erenzo, and is now
equipped with a 106-US-gallon
(400-liter) pot still that was
installed in 2005. Tuthill Spirits
produces a quartet of "Hudson"
bottlings, including a rich and
full-flavored four-grain whiskey
and a rich, caramel single malt,
which is intended to be an
American "re-interpretation"
of traditional Scottish whiskies.

The distillery also produces Old
Gristmill Authentic American
Corn Whiskey. In 2010, William
Grant & Sons Ltd. acquired the
Hudson Whiskey brand, while
Tuthilltown Distillery remains
independent.

HUDSON MANHATTAN RYE

RYE WHISKEY 46% ABV
*The first whiskey to be distilled in
New York State for more than 80 years.
Floral notes and a smooth finish on the
palate, with a recognizable rye edge.*

HUDSON NEW YORK CORN

BOURBON 46% ABV
*Made with 100 percent New York
State corn, this is the first bourbon ever
to be made in New York, and the first
pot-distilled whiskey to be produced
legally in New York since Prohibition.
It is a mildly sweet, smooth spirit with
subtle hints of vanilla and caramel.*

THE SECRETS OF...
JACK DANIEL'S

The story of Jack Daniel's, America's best-selling whiskey, begins with the birth of Jasper "Jack" Newton Daniel in Lincoln County, Tennessee, in 1846.

Legend has it that Jack did not get along with his stepmother and, at the age of just six, left home to live first with an elderly neighbor and his family, and then with local farmer and Lutheran lay preacher Dan Call, of Louse Creek, who also ran a whiskey still. It was one of Call's slaves, Nearest Green, who taught Jack the art of distilling.

Pressure from his congregation eventually forced Call to choose religion over whiskey-making, so young Jack took over the business and, by 1860, the precocious teenager owned the still.

Jack Daniel's Tennessee whiskey has come a long way from those modest beginnings, and enjoys an iconic status as one of the world's highest-profile drink brands. It is distilled in Lynchburg, to which, every year, hundreds of thousands of visitors flock in pilgrimage. However, while they can purchase any number of souvenirs bearing the Jack Daniel's name, they cannot buy the whiskey itself. Lynchburg is situated in Moore County, which is officially "dry."

Despite an image in which the figure of its founder plays a major part, since 1956 Jack Daniel's has belonged to Brown-Forman *(see p.220)*, which also owns Kentucky distilleries producing Old Forester *(p.248)*, Early Times *(p.224)*, and Woodford Reserve *(p.264)*.

▲ THE REAL JACK DANIEL
"Mr. Jack" is a flamboyant figure in the history of American whiskey. He was reputedly quite a ladies' man, although he never married, and the brand name Old No. 7 is sometimes said to have referred to the number of his girlfriends.

▲ A TENNESSEE INSTITUTION
Licensed in 1886, the Jack Daniel Distillery is the oldest registered distillery in the US. Lem Motlow was Jack's nephew, who joined him in 1887 and inherited the business. The sign remains unchanged.

JACK DANIEL DISTILLERY
Lem Motlow, Prop. Inc.
DSP Tennessee - 1
Distiller

There is no set schedule to determine when the whiskey is ready, as maturation can vary from barrel to barrel, and by the relative positions of barrels in the warehouses. A panel of experts regularly noses the maturing spirit to decide when it's ready for bottling.

▲ NEW HAND-MADE CASKS

Jack Daniel is the only distillery to craft its own barrels by hand using new white oak. The interiors are then charred to caramelize the wood's natural sugars. As a result, the whiskey matured in these casks is deeply mellow, amber-hued, and aromatic.

◄ THE CHARCOAL ELEMENT

Jack Daniel creates its own charcoal by burning sugar maple wood in the rickyard, to be used in Tennessee whiskey's signature Lincoln County Process. This is a method of mellowing, in which the spirit is filtered slowly through 10 ft (3 m) of charcoal before being matured, resulting in a very smooth whiskey.

▲ MR. JACK'S GRAVE

Jack Daniel died in 1911, having been unfortunate enough to contract blood poisoning after kicking his safe door in frustration when he forgot the combination. He is buried in Lynchburg's cemetery, close to his beloved distillery. The chairs are said to have been placed there for grieving Lynchburg ladies.

JACK DANIEL'S SINGLE BARREL

GENTLEMAN JACK

JACK DANIEL'S OLD NO. 7

JACK DANIEL'S

280 Lynchburg Road,
Lynchburg, Tennessee
www.jackdaniels.com

Jack Daniel's has become an iconic brand worldwide, and is America's best-selling whiskey. Its founder, Jasper Newton "Jack" Daniel reputedly started to make whiskey as a child, and by 1860 was running his own distilling business at the tender age of 14.

Today, the Jack Daniel Distillery at Lynchburg, Tennessee, is owned by the Brown-Forman Corporation *(see p.220)* and is a major visitor attraction. Along with its fellow Tennessee distiller George Dickel *(p.230)*, Jack Daniel's uses a version of the Lincoln County Process of charcoal mellowing prior to the spirit being put into barrels.

JACK DANIEL'S OLD NO. 7

TENNESSEE WHISKEY 40% ABV
Jack Daniel's presents a powerful nose of vanilla, smoke, and licorice. On the palate it offers oily cough syrup and

molasses, with a final kick of maple syrup and burnt wood lingering in the surprisingly long finish. Not particularly complex, but decidedly muscular and certainly distinctive.

JACK DANIEL'S SINGLE BARREL

TENNESSEE WHISKEY 47% ABV
Introduced in 1997, Single Barrel is charming and smooth on the nose, with notes of peach, vanilla, nuts, and oak. The comparatively dry palate offers depth, richness, and elegance, with oily corn, licorice, malt, and oak. Malt and oak are also highlighted in the lengthy finish, along with a touch of rye spice.

GENTLEMAN JACK

TENNESSEE WHISKEY 40% ABV
After aging for about four years, this is charcoal-mellowed once before barrelling. The result is a nose that is more mellow, muted, and fruity than that of Old No.7. The palate also yields more fruit, plus notes of caramel, licorice, vanilla, and a whiff of smoke.

Jim Beam (*see overleaf*) is a global company with industrial-scale distilleries, but its American Outpost in Clermont, Kentucky, evokes the older traditions of whiskey.

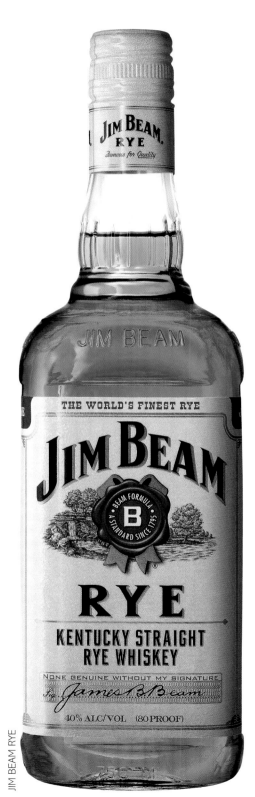

JIM BEAM WHITE LABEL 4-YEAR-OLD

JIM BEAM RYE

JIM BEAM

Jim Beam Distillery, 149 Happy
Hollow Road, Clermont, Kentucky
www.jimbeam.com

Jim Beam is the best-selling bourbon
brand in the world. Its origins date
back to the 18th century, when
German-born farmer and miller
Jacob Boehm traveled west into
Bourbon County, Kentucky, from
Virginia, carrying with him his
copper pot still. He is reputed to
have sold his first barrel of whiskey
for cash in 1795, and subsequently
moved his distilling operation into
Washington County when he
inherited land there from his
father-in-law.

Jacob had two sons, John and
David, and during David Beam's
time at the helm, the distillery
adopted the name Old Tub. In
1854, his son, also David, moved
the venture to Nelson County,
where the Clear Springs Distillery
was established close to a railroad.

Jim (James Beauregard) Beam
himself was Jacob Boehm's great-
grandson. He joined the family
business at the age of 16, in 1880,
and trade prospered in the years
before Prohibition forced the closure
of Clear Springs.

Jim Beam founded the present
Clermont Distillery close to Clear
Springs soon after the repeal of
Prohibition in 1933, despite being
70 years old at the time. He died in
1947, five years after "Jim Beam"
first appeared on the bottle label,
and two years after the firm had
been sold to Harry Blum of Chicago,
previously a partner in the company
for several years.

The Beam family connection,
however, carries on to this day
through Fred Noe, great-grandson
of Jim and a seventh-generation
Beam family member. Fred's father
was Booker Noe, acknowledged as
one of the true greats of bourbon

distilling, and the man principally responsible for developing "small batch bourbon." Clermont, near the bourbon capital of Bardstown, remains the principal Jim Beam distillery, but its output is boosted by that of the nearby Boston distillery, which dates from 1953.

In addition to Jim Beam brands, a range of specialist whiskeys is also produced, including Baker's Kentucky *(see p.218)*, Booker's Kentucky *(p.220)*, Basil Hayden's *(p.219)*, Knob Creek *(p.243)*, Old Crow *(p.247)*, Old Grand-Dad *(p.248)*, and Old Taylor *(p.249)*. Additionally, Beam Suntory Inc. operates the Maker's Mark Distillery *(p.244)* at Loretto.

JIM BEAM WHITE LABEL 4-YEAR-OLD

TENNESSEE WHISKEY 40% ABV
Vanilla and delicate floral notes on the nose. Initially sweet, with restrained vanilla, then drier, oaky notes develop, fading into furniture polish and soft malt in the finish. Once described, with some justification, as "a mellow baritone of a spirit".

JIM BEAM RYE

RYE WHISKEY 40% ABV
Light, perfumed, and aromatic on the nose, with lemon and mint, Jim Beam Rye is oily in the mouth, with soft fruits, honey, and rye on the palate, drying and spicy in the finish.

JIM BEAM BLACK LABEL 6-YEAR-OLD

BOURBON 43% ABV
The nose offers caramel, vanilla, and ripe oranges, while the palate is smooth, with honey, fudge, and citrus fruits.

JIM BEAM DEVIL'S CUT

BOURBON 45% ABV
Freshly planed wood and spicy vanilla on the nose, with vanilla and oak majoring on the palate, plus more vanilla and spice.

JIM BEAM BLACK LABEL 6-YEAR-OLD

JIM BEAM DEVIL'S CUT

JEFFERSON'S

McLain & Kyne Ltd. (Castle Brands),
Louisville, Kentucky
www.jeffersonsbourbon.com

The Louisville company of McLain
& Kyne Ltd. was formed by Trey
Zoeller to carry on the distilling
traditions of his ancestors. McLain
& Kyne specializes in premium,
very small batch bourbons, most
notably Jefferson's and Sam
Houston (see p.254).

JEFFERSON'S SMALL BATCH 8-YEAR-OLD
BOURBON (VARIABLE ABV)
*This bourbon has been aged in the heart
of metal-clad warehouses to accentuate
the extreme temperatures of Kentucky,
forcing the bourbon to expand deep
into the barrel and extract desirable
flavors from the wood. The nose is
fresh, with vanilla and ripe peach notes,
while the smooth, sweet palate boasts
more vanilla, caramel, and berries.
The finish is very delicate, with toasted
vanilla and cream.*

JOHNNY DRUM

Kentucky Bourbon Distillers, 1869
Loretto Road, Bardstown, Kentucky
www.kentuckybourbonwhiskey.com

Johnny Drum is said to have been
a Confederate drummer boy during
the Civil War, and later a pioneer
farmer and distiller in Kentucky.

Johnny Drum bourbon was
formerly produced in the Willett
Distillery near Bardstown, but
this closed in the early 1980s when
the last of the Willett family
members retired. The plant was
acquired by Kentucky Bourbon
Distillers Ltd., for whom a
range of whiskeys is distilled
under contract.

JOHNNY DRUM
BOURBON (VARIABLE ABV)
*Smooth and elegant on the nose,
with vanilla, gentle spices, and
smoke. This is a full-bodied bourbon,
well-balanced and smooth in the mouth,
with vanilla and a hint of smoke. The
finish is lingering and sophisticated.*

KENTUCKY GENTLEMAN

Barton Distillery, 300 Barton Road,
Bardstown, Kentucky
www.sazerac.com

Kentucky Gentleman is offered
both as a blended whiskey and
as a straight bourbon.

According to its producers,
the blended version is created
from a blend of Kentucky straight
bourbon whiskey and spirits from
the finest grains.

The popular straight expression
enjoys a notably loyal following
in the southern states, particularly
Florida, Alabama, and Virginia.

KENTUCKY GENTLEMAN
BOURBON 40% ABV
*Made with a higher percentage of rye
than most Barton whiskeys, this offers
caramel and sweet oak aromas, and is
oily, full-bodied, spicy, and fruity in the
mouth. Rye, fruits, vanilla, and cocoa
figure in the lingering, flavorful, and
comparatively assertive finish.*

KENTUCKY TAVERN

Barton Distillery, 300 Barton Road,
Bardstown, Kentucky
www.sazerac.com

The Kentucky Tavern brand has
been established for over a century,
and was the leading whiskey
produced by the Louisville-based
Glenmore Distilleries Company.
It was named after a bar and
restaurant situated on the east
side of Louisville.

In 1992, Glenmore was
acquired by United Distillers,
which has since been amalgamated
with Diageo, and the Kentucky
Tavern brand was subsequently
sold to Sazerac Company Inc.

KENTUCKY TAVERN
BOURBON 40% ABV
*Assertive and oaky on the nose,
with apples and honey. Spices,
oak, more apples, and a note
of rye contribute to the palate,
while the medium-length finish
is peppery and oaky.*

GEORGIA PEACH

NEW YORK APPLE

KESSLER

Jim Beam Distillery,149 Happy Hollow Road, Clermont, Kentucky
www.jimbeam.com

One of the best-known and most highly regarded blended American whiskeys, Kessler traces its origins back to 1888, when it was first blended by one Julius Kessler, who traveled from saloon to saloon across the West, selling his whiskey as he went. Kessler Whiskey was acquired by The Seagram Company during the mid-1930s, eventually passing to Beam Inc., which was then purchased by Suntory Holdings in 2014. Kessler is now produced by Beam Suntory, and is the second-best-selling American blended whiskey.

KESSLER

BLEND 40% ABV
Lives up to its "Smooth as silk" slogan Light, fruity nose and sweet palate with enough complexity of licorice and leather achieved by the blend's four-year aging.

KNOB CREEK

Jim Beam Distillery,149 Happy Hollow Road, Clermont, Kentucky
www.knobcreek.com

Knob Creek is the Kentucky town where Abraham Lincoln's father, Thomas, owned a farm and worked at the local distillery. This bourbon is one of three introduced in 1992, when Jim Beam launched its Small Batch Bourbon Collection. It is made to the same high-rye formula as the Jim Beam-distilled Basil Hayden's *(see p.219)* and Old Grand-Dad *(p.248)* brands.

Several new bottles have been added to the Knob Creek range since its launch, including, in 2012, Knob Creek Straight Rye Whiskey — the brand's first expression not to carry an age statement.

KNOB CREEK 9-YEAR-OLD

BOURBON 50% ABV
Nutty nose of sweet, tangy fruit and rye. Malt, spice, and nuts on the fruity palate, drying finish with notes of vanilla.

LEOPOLD BROTHERS

5258 Joliet Street, Denver, Colorado
www.leopoldbros.com

Leopold Bros. is a family owned and operated small batch distillery based in Denver, Colorado, the home state of brothers Scott and Todd Leopold. Scott takes care of the business side of the company, while Master Distiller Todd Leopold makes liqueurs, vodka, gin, rum, absinthe, and flavored whiskeys in the distillery's 48-US-gallon (180-liter) copper pot still. The distillery specializes in small batch blends, so all blends are made using artisan processes and the bottles are subsequently hand-numbered.

Unusual blends include a whiskey made from the juice of Rocky Mountain peaches and another flavored whiskey made in a similar fashion from blackberries. These fruit whiskies are matured in used, charred bourbon barrels, so that the sweetness of the fruit is balanced by the smoothness of a bourbon finish.

Leopold Bros. now also produces a "Small Batch Whiskey," made from rye and American corn.

GEORGIA PEACH

FLAVORED WHISKEY 30% ABV
Peach juice is blended with small batch whiskey, and matured in bourbon barrels. The result is a peachy-sweet spirit with oak, vanilla, and raisins.

NEW YORK APPLE

FLAVORED WHISKEY 40% ABV
Blended with apples grown in New York State, this whiskey is racked into used bourbon barrels for additional aging. According to its producers, the barrels add the oak, raisin, and vanilla finish, while the mix of the sweet and tart apples balances perfectly with the charred oak finish.

THE SECRETS OF...
MAKER'S MARK

The Maker's Mark Distillery stands on the banks of Hardin's Creek, near Loretto in Marion County, Kentucky. Established in 1805, its modern history dates from 1953.

That was the year Taylor William Samuels, Sr., bought the dilapidated distillery known as Happy Hollow. His great-great-great-grandfather had been a Kentucky whiskey-maker in the 1780s, and Taylor was in possession of the secret family recipe for bourbon. However, one of his first acts on taking over at Happy Hollow was symbolically to burn the recipe, declaring: "Nothing that we need! To craft a truly new and soft-spoken bourbon, we will have to start from scratch."

By this, Samuels meant a more mellow whiskey than was the norm at the time. He achieved this using corn and malted barley, coupled with red winter wheat, rather than the usual rye. He used the spelling "whisky" from the outset, in honor of his Scottish ancestry.

Long acknowledged as one of Kentucky's great bourbons, in 1981 Maker's Mark passed out of family ownership. It is now part of Beam Suntory Inc., which also owns Jim Beam (see p.240).

▲ MASHBILL
The grain recipe, or mashbill, for Maker's Mark comprises 70 percent corn, 16 percent red winter wheat, and 14 percent malted barley, producing a comparatively soft, gentle spirit—the "soft-spoken bourbon" that T. W. Samuels had envisioned from the beginning.

▼ COPPER POT STILLS
The "distiller's beer" is initially distilled in a five-story column still, after which it undergoes a secondary distillation in copper pot stills in order to remove any remaining impurities, leaving a clear 65% ABV spirit.

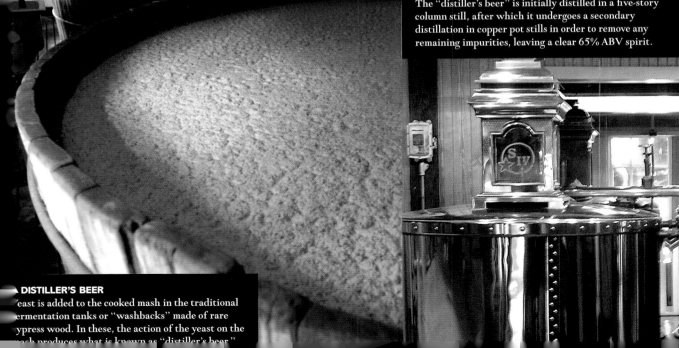

▲ DISTILLER'S BEER
Yeast is added to the cooked mash in the traditional fermentation tanks or "washbacks" made of rare cypress wood. In these, the action of the yeast on the mash produces what is known as "distiller's beer."

◄ CHARRING THE CASKS

Barrels undergo a "charring" stage, in which their interiors are seared with fire. By law, bourbon must be matured in new, charred white-oak barrels. The layer of char on the wood facilitates the maturation process.

▼ RICK HOUSES

At Maker's Mark, barrels of spirit are stored in three-story warehouses or "rick houses," and are periodically moved around within each warehouse to ensure consistency of maturation.

▲ MONITORING THE CASKS

The new make is put into oak barrels for maturation. A watchful eye is kept on the spirit while it's maturing to ensure that it is bottled at the peak of perfection. As part of this process, each barrel is sampled five times during the maturation period.

◄ DIPPING IN WAX

After being machine-filled, each bottle of Maker's Mark is labeled by hand and then its neck is dipped into hot wax for a few seconds to create the brand's characteristic red wax seal.

CREATING THE SEAL ►

This was the brainchild of Marge Samuels, wife of T. W. "Bill" Samuels. She collected antique cognac bottles, many of which were sealed with wax. She also designed the "Maker's Mark" symbol itself.

MAKER'S MARK

Maker's Mark Distillery, 3350 Burks
Springs Road, Loretto, Kentucky
www.makersmark.com

Maker's Mark Distillery is located
on the banks of Hardin's Creek,
near Loretto. Established in 1805,
it is the US's oldest working
distillery remaining on its original
site. The Maker's Mark brand was
developed during the 1950s by Bill
Samuels, Jr., and is now owned
by Fortune Brands Inc. The use
of the Scots spelling of "whisky,"
rare among US brands, is a nod
to the Samuels' Scottish ancestry.

MAKER'S MARK

BOURBON 45% ABV

*A subtle, complex, and clean nose,
with vanilla and spice, a delicate floral
note of roses, plus lime and cocoa
beans. Medium in body, it offers a palate
of fresh fruit, spices, eucalyptus, and
ginger cake. The finish features more
spices, fresh oak with a hint of smoke,
and a final flash of peach cheesecake.*

MCCARTHY'S

Clear Creek Distillery, 2389 NW Wilson
Street, Portland, Oregon
www.clearcreekdistillery.com

Steve McCarthy established
Clear Creek Distillery in 1986,
and has been distilling whiskey
for over two decades. He is of
the opinion that, since it is made
from peat-malted barley brought
in from Scotland, "our whiskey
would be a single malt Scotch if
Oregon were Scotland."

MCCARTHY'S OREGON

SINGLE MALT 40% ABV

*McCarthy's is initially matured in former
sherry casks for two or three years, then
for six to twelve months in barrels made
from air-dried Oregon oak. Kippery and
spicy on the nose, with a hint of sulfur,
peat, and vanilla. It is big-bodied and
oily, smoky-sweet on the meaty palate,
and with dry oak, malt, spice, and salt
in the long finish.*

MELLOW CORN

Heaven Hill Distillery, 1701 West
Breckinridge Street, Louisville, Kentucky

According to Heaven Hill, "The
forerunner and kissing cousin to
Bourbon, American straight corn
whiskey is defined by the US
Government as having a recipe
or mashbill with a minimum of
81 percent corn, the rest being
malted barley and rye".

Today, Heaven Hill is the sole
remaining national producer of
this classic whiskey style, bottling
Georgia Moon (*see p.231*) in
addition to Mellow Corn.

MELLOW CORN

CORN WHISKEY 50% ABV

*Wood varnish and vanilla, with floral
and herbal notes on the nose. The
palate is big, oily, and fruity, with
candy apples. More fruit, toffee,
and understated vanilla complete
the finish. Young and boisterous.*

MICHTER'S

Michter's Distillery, 2351 New
Millennium Drive, Louisville, Kentucky
www.michters.com

Michter's whiskey was distilled
in Pennsylvania until 1989, when
its owners were declared bankrupt
and the distillery closed down. The
brand name was resurrected by
businessmen Joseph J. Magliocco
and Dick Newman a few years
later, and production now takes
place in the Michter's Distillery
in the Shively section of Louisville,
Kentucky. A number of ryes and
bourbons are marketed under the
Michter's label, along with an
unblended American whiskey
and a sour mash whiskey.

MICHTER'S US NO.1 BOURBON

BOURBON 45.7% ABV

*Very spicy on the nose, with caramel,
apricots, and cinnamon. Sweet palate
delivery, with more apricots, cloves,
black pepper, and a smoky note.
Spicy oak in the finish.*

NOAH'S MILL

Kentucky Bourbon Distillers Ltd., Nelson County, Kentucky
www.kentuckybourbonwhiskey.com

Like Johnny Drum *(see p.242)*, Noah's Mill was once distilled in the now silent Willett Distillery, which operated in Bardstown from 1935 until the early 1980s. In 1984 the site was bought by Thompson Willett's Norwegian-born son-in-law Even Kulsveen, who runs Kentucky Bourbon Distillers Ltd. and plans to restore the old distillery to production. Noah's Mill is a hand-bottled, small batch bourbon, currently produced under contract.

NOAH'S MILL 15-YEAR-OLD

BOURBON 57.15% ABV
Elegant and well-balanced on the nose, with caramel, nuts, coffee, dark fruits, and oak. Noah's Mill has a rich texture and is notably dry on the palate, with background notes of soft fruit and spice. The finish is long and oaky.

THE NOTCH

Triple Eight Distillery, 5&7 Bartlett Farm Road, Nantucket, Massachusetts
www.ciscobrewers.com

Dean and Melissa Long started up their Nantucket Winery in 1981, and added the Cisco Brewery in 1995. Two years later they founded the region's first micro-distillery, Triple Eight.

The first single malt whiskey was distilled in 2000 and is called The Notch Whiskey, because it is "not Scotch," though it is produced in the Scottish style. It is matured in former bourbon barrels before being finished in French oak Merlot barrels.

THE NOTCH

SINGLE MALT 44.4% ABV
Sweet aromas of almonds and fruit on the nose, backed by vanilla and toasted oak. Mellow honey and pear notes are present on the palate, which also contains a suggestion of Merlot. The finish is lengthy and herbal.

OLD CHARTER

Buffalo Trace Distillery, 1001 Wilkinson Boulevard, Frankfort, Kentucky

The Old Charter brand dates back to 1874, and the name is a direct reference to the Charter Oak tree, where Connecticut's colonial charter was hidden from the English in 1687. The Buffalo Trace Distillery itself dates back to the early 1900s and is listed on the National Register of Historic Places.

OLD CHARTER 8-YEAR-OLD

BOURBON 40% ABV
Initially dry and peppery on the nose, with sweet and buttery aromas following through. Mouth-coating, with fruit, vanilla, old leather, and cloves on the palate. The finish is long and sophisticated.

OLD CROW

Jim Beam Distillery, 149 Happy Hollow Road, Clermont, Kentucky
www.jimbeam.com

Old Crow takes its name from the 19th-century Scottish-born chemist and Kentucky distiller James Christopher Crow. Along with Old Grand-Dad *(see p.248)* and Old Taylor *(p.249)*, this brand was acquired by Jim Beam *(p.240)* from National Distillers in 1987, and the three distilleries associated with these bourbons were closed. All production now takes place at Jim Beam's distilleries in Boston and Clermont.

OLD CROW

BOURBON 40% ABV
Complex on the nose, with malt, rye, and sharp fruit notes combining with gentle spice. The palate follows through with spicy, malty, and citric elements, with citrus and spice notes to the fore.

OLD FORESTER

OLD FORESTER BIRTHDAY BOURBON

OLD FITZGERALD

Heaven Hill Distillery,
1701 West Breckinridge Street,
Louisville, Kentucky
www.heavenhill.com

Old Fitzgerald was named by
John E. Fitzgerald, who founded
a distillery at Frankfort in 1870.
The brand moved to its present
home of Louisville when the
Stitzel brothers, Frederick and
Philip, merged their company with
that of William LaRue Weller
& Sons, and subsequently opened
the new Stitzel-Weller distillery
at Louisville in 1935.

VERY SPECIAL OLD FITZGERALD
12-YEAR-OLD

BOURBON 45% ABV

*A complex and well-balanced bourbon,
made with some wheat in the mashbill,
rather than rye. The nose is rich, fruity,
and leathery, while the palate exhibits
sweet and fruity notes balanced
by spices and oak. The finish is long
and drying, with vanilla fading to oak.*

OLD FORESTER

Brown-Forman Distillery,
850 Dixie Highway,
Louisville, Kentucky
www.oldforester.com

The origins of the Old Forester
brand date back to 1870, when
George Garvin Brown established
a distillery in Louisville, Kentucky
(*see p.220*). The whiskey initially
used the spelling "Forrester," and
there are several theories as to
the choice of name. Some say it
was selected to honor Confederate
army officer General Nathan
Bedford Forrest, and others that
it was inspired by George Garvin
Brown's physician Dr. Forrester.
It has also been suggested that the
name was chosen to appeal to the
many timber workers in the area.

OLD FORESTER

BOURBON 43% ABV

*Complex, with pronounced floral notes,
vanilla, spice, pepper, fruit, chocolate,
and menthol on the nose. Full and fruity*

*in the mouth, where rye and peaches
vie with fudge, nutmeg, and oak. The
finish offers more rye, toffee, licorice,
and drying oak.*

OLD FORESTER
BIRTHDAY BOURBON

BOURBON 47% ABV

*Since September 2002 there has
been an annual release of vintage Old
Forester to commemorate the birthday
of George Garvin Brown. The 2007
expression was distilled in the spring
of 1994, and consists of fewer than
8,500 bottles. According to Brown-
Forman, this vintage strikes a balance
between the previous two: 2005 was
heavy in cinnamon spice while 2006
had a pronounced mint note.*

*The 2007 release is sweet on the
nose, with cinnamon, caramel, and
vanilla, plus a contrasting whiff of mint.
The palate is full and complex, with
caramel, apples, and vanilla oak, and
a lengthy, warm, clean finish.*

OLD GRAND-DAD

Jim Beam Distillery,
149 Happy Hollow Road,
Clermont, Kentucky
www.theoldswhiskeys.com

Old Grand-Dad was established
in 1882 by a grandson of distiller
Basil Hayden (*see p.219*). The
brand and its distillery eventually
passed into the hands of American
Brands (Now Fortune Brands
Inc.) which subsequently closed
the distillery. Production of Old
Grand-Dad now takes place in the
Jim Beam distilleries in Clermont
and Boston.

OLD GRAND-DAD

BOURBON 43–57% ABV

*Made with a comparatively high
percentage of rye, the nose of Old
Grand-Dad reveals oranges and peppery
spices. Quite heavy-bodied, the taste
is full, yet surprisingly smooth, considering
the strength. Fruit, nuts, and caramel
are foremost on the palate, while the
finish is long and oily.*

OLD POTRERO

Anchor Distilling Company,
1705 Marisposa Street,
San Francisco, California
www.anchorbrewing.com

Fritz Maytag is one of the pioneers of the American "micro-drinks" movement, and has been running San Francisco's historic Anchor Steam Brewery since 1965. In 1994 he added a small distillery to his brewery on San Francisco's Potrero Hill. Here, Maytag aims to "re-create the original whiskey of America", by making small batches of spirits in traditional, open pot stills, using 100 percent rye malt.

OLD POTRERO 18TH CENTURY STYLE WHISKEY

SINGLE MALT RYE 62.55% ABV

An award-winning, 18th-century-style whiskey distilled in a small pot still, then aged for a year in new, lightly toasted oak barrels. Floral, nutty nose, with vanilla and spice. Smooth on the palate, with mint, honey, and pepper in the lengthy finish.

OLD TAYLOR

Jim Beam Distillery,
149 Happy Hollow Road,
Clermont, Kentucky
www.jimbeam.com

Old Taylor was introduced by Edmund Haynes Taylor, Jr., who was associated at various times with three distilleries in the Frankfort area of Kentucky, including what is now Buffalo Trace *(see p.223)*. He was the man responsible for the Bottled-in-Bond Act of 1897, which guaranteed a whiskey's quality—any bottle bearing an official government seal had to be 100 proof (50% ABV) and at least four years old. Old Taylor was bought by Fortune Brands in 1987.

OLD TAYLOR

BOURBON 40% ABV

Light and orangey on the nose, with a hint of marzipan; sweet, honeyed, and slightly oaky on the palate.

PARKER'S

Heaven Hill Distillery, 1701 West Breckinridge Street, Louisville, Kentucky
www.heavenhill.com

Parker's Heritage Collection is a limited annual series of rare whiskeys that pays tribute to Heaven Hill's sixth-generation Master Distiller Parker Beam.

The first edition is a cask strength 1996 bourbon that was bottled at barrel-proof, the first such barrel-proof bourbon release by the distillers in the US. The barrels were selected by Parker Beam for their fine nose, robust flavor, and long, smooth finish.

PARKER'S HERITAGE COLLECTION (FIRST EDITION)

BOURBON 61.3% ABV

Honey, vanilla, almonds, leather, and cherries on the nose, while the palate displays spicy fruit and caramel, with leather, pipe tobacco, and oak. The finish is long and fruity, with spice and oak.

PEREGRINE ROCK

Saint James Spirits, 5220 Fourth Street,
Irwindale, California
www.saintjamesspirits.com

Saint James Spirits was founded in 1995 by teacher Jim Busuttil, who learnt the craft of distilling in Germany and Switzerland. He has been making single malt whiskey (note the Scottish spelling) since 1997, and Peregrine Rock is produced from peated Scottish barley in a 40-US-gallon (150-liter) alambic copper pot still and put into bourbon barrels for a minimum period of three years, mimicking the Scottish method.

PEREGRINE ROCK CALIFORNIA PURE

SINGLE MALT 40% ABV

Floral on the nose, with fresh fruits and a hint of smoke. The palate is delicate and fruity, with a citric twist to it, while sweeter, malty, and new-mown-grass notes develop in the slightly smoky finish.

Fermenting liquid in one of the washbacks at the Jack Daniel Distillery in Tennessee—at this stage of the process, the yeast is interacting with the sugars from the wort to create alcohol at a strength of about 8% ABV.

PIKESVILLE

Heaven Hill Distillery, 1701 West
Breckinridge Street, Louisville, Kentucky
www.pikesvillerye.com

Rye whiskeys fall into two
stylistic types, namely the
spicy, tangy Pennsylvania style,
as exemplified by Rittenhouse,
and the Maryland style, which
is softer in character. Pikesville
is arguably the only example
of Maryland rye still being
produced today. This whiskey
takes its name from Pikesville
in Maryland, where it was first
distilled during the 1890s and
last produced in 1972. A decade
later the brand was acquired
by Heaven Hill.

PIKESVILLE SUPREME

RYE WHISKEY 40% ABV

The crisp nose presents bubble gum,
fruit, and wood varnish, while on the
palate there is more bubble gum,
spice, oak, and overt vanilla. The finish
comprises lingering vanilla and oranges.

RAGTIME

New York Distilling Company,
Richardson Street, Brooklyn, New York
www.nydistilling.com

Although the first distilleries
in Brooklyn, New York, were
established in the 18th century,
there was no legal whiskey
distillation in the Big Apple after
Prohibition. That was until 2009
when Tom Potter, cofounder of
Brooklyn Brewery, and Allen Katz,
former chairman of Slow Food USA,
established the New York Distilling
Co. In 2015, it started retailing its
Ragtime Rye alongside its range of
gins. This straight rye has a mashbill
of 72 percent rye, 16 percent corn,
and 12 percent barley, and has been
aged for three years and six months.

RAGTIME RYE

RYE WHISKEY 45.2% ABV

Rye spice, oak, and red berries on the
nose. The palate is full, with peppery rye,
cinnamon, nutmeg, and caramel. Finally
drying, with licorice, spice, and oak.

REBEL YELL

Heaven Hill Distillery, 1701 West
Breckinridge Street, Louisville, Kentucky
www.rebelyellbourbon.com

Made at the Bernheim Distillery
in Louisville, Rebel Yell is distilled
with a percentage of wheat in its
mashbill, instead of rye. Whiskey
was first made to the Rebel Yell
recipe in 1849 and, after enjoying
popularity in the southern states
for many years, the brand was
finally released on an international
basis during the 1980s. In addition
to the standard bottling, the Rebel
Yell range now includes American
Whiskey and Small Batch, a well
as a Small Batch Reserve.

REBEL YELL

BOURBON 40% ABV

A nose of honey, raisins, and butter
leads into a big-bodied bourbon, which
again features honey and a buttery
quality, along with plums and soft
leather. The finish is long and spicier
than might be expected from the palate.

RIDGEMONT

Barton Distillery, 300 Barton Road,
Bardstown, Kentucky
www.1792bourbon.com

The "1792" element of the name
pays homage to the year in which
Kentucky became a state, the 15th
state to become part of the US.
When this bourbon was introduced
to the market in 2004, it was
initially called Ridgewood Reserve
but, after litigation between the
distillers and Woodford Reserve's
owners Brown-Forman, the name
was changed.

1792 RIDGEMONT RESERVE

BOURBON 46.85% ABV

This comparatively delicate and complex
8-year-old, small batch bourbon boasts
a soft nose with vanilla, caramel, leather,
rye, corn, and spice notes. Oily and
initially sweet on the palate, caramel
and spicy rye develop along with a
suggestion of oak. The finish is oaky,
spicy, and quite long, with a hint of
lingering caramel.

RITTENHOUSE RYE

Heaven Hill Distillery, 1701 West Breckinridge Street, Louisville, Kentucky
www.heavenhill.com

Once associated with Pennsylvania, the rye-whiskey making heartland, Rittenhouse Rye now survives in Kentucky, and its mashbill comprises 51 percent rye, 37 percent corn, and 12 percent barley.

Rittenhouse was launched by the Continental Distilling Company of Philadelphia as soon as Prohibition was repealed in 1933, and was later acquired by Heaven Hill, which continued to produce the brand through the lean years when rye whiskey as a style was largely forgotten.

RITTENHOUSE STRAIGHT RYE

RYE WHISKEY 40% ABV
Immediate aromas of rye, with black pepper, spice, and cedar. Oily on the palate, with more spicy rye, ginger, and vanilla, leading to cinnamon notes.

ROCK HILL FARMS

Buffalo Trace Distillery, 1001 Wilkinson Boulevard, Frankfort, Kentucky
www.buffalotrace.com

This single cask brand was first introduced to the Buffalo Trace *(see p.223)* lineup in 1990, and is named after the home farm of the Blanton family. It was Colonel Benjamin Blanton who first made whiskey on the site of what is now Buffalo Trace Distillery, just after the Civil War. The Rock Hill mansion itself survives within the Buffalo Trace complex.

ROCK HILL FARMS

BOURBON 50% ABV
Oak, raisins, and fruity rye on the nose, with a hint of mint. Medium- to full-bodied, bitter-sweet on the palate, with rye fruitiness, fudge, oak, and a long, sweet, rye finish with a suggestion of licorice.

ROCK TOWN

1216 E. 6th Street,
Little Rock, Arkansas
www.rocktowndistillery.com

Founded in 2010 by Phil Brandon, Rock Town is the first legal distillery in the state of Arkansas since Prohibition. All corn, wheat, and rye used in the distilling process is grown within a maximum of 125 miles (200 km) of the distillery. Rye and Hickory-smoked whiskeys are made here, along with Arkansas' first ever bourbon, which is matured in small, newly charred oak barrels that were coopered in Arkansas at Gibbs Brothers Cooperage. All bottling takes place at the distillery.

ROCK TOWN ARKANSAS BOURBON

BOURBON 46% ABV
The nose is smoky and sweet, with roasted corn aromas, while the palate is smooth and sweet, with almonds and graham crackers.

ROGUE SPIRITS

Rogue Brewery, 1339 NW Flanders, Portland, Oregon
www.rogue.com

Dead Guy Ale was created in the early 1990s to celebrate the Mayan Day of the Dead (November 1, or All Souls' Day) and, in 2008, the Oregon-based producers launched their Dead Guy Whiskey. It is distilled using the same four malts used in the creation of Dead Guy Ale, and fermented wort from the brewery is taken to the nearby Rogue House of Spirits, where it is double-distilled in a 150-gallon (570-liter) copper pot still. A brief maturation period follows, using charred American white-oak casks.

DEAD GUY

BLENDED MALT 40% ABV
Youthful on the nose, with notes of corn, wheat, and fresh, juicy orange. The palate is medium-dry, fruity, and lively. Pepper and cinnamon feature in the finish.

RUSSELL'S RESERVE RYE

RUSSELL'S RESERVE 10-YEAR-OLD

RUSSELL'S RESERVE

Wild Turkey Distillery, US Highway 62 East, Lawrenceburg, Kentucky
www.wildturkeybourbon.com

Austin Nicholls' Master Distiller Jimmy Russell and his son Eddie, of Wild Turkey *(see p.262)* fame, developed this small batch rye whiskey, launched in 2007.

Jimmy is one of the great characters of the bourbon world, and now serves as a leading international ambassador for the bourbon industry. James C. Russell, to give him his full name, has been distilling whiskey since the 1950s and both his father and grandfather were also distillers. So, it was no great surprise when his son Eddie joined the company in 1980.

According to Jimmy Russell, "rye whiskey is its own animal and rye fans are a special breed." His son, Eddie Russell, adds that "we knew the whiskey we wanted, but had never tasted

it before. This one really makes the grade—deep character and taste and, at six years, aged to perfection."

RUSSELL'S RESERVE RYE

RYE WHISKEY 45% ABV

Fruity, with fresh oak and almonds on the nose. Full-bodied and robust, yet smooth. Almonds, pepper, and rye dominate the palate, while the finish is long, dry, and characteristically bitter.

RUSSELL'S RESERVE 10-YEAR-OLD

BOURBON 45% ABV

The stable-mate to Russell's Reserve Rye, this bourbon boasts a nose of pine, vanilla, soft leather, and caramel. The palate features more vanilla, along with toffee, almond, honey, coconut, and the appearance of a slightly unusual note of chiles that continues through the lengthy, spicy finish.

SAM HOUSTON

McLain & Kyne Ltd. (Castle Brands), Louisville, Kentucky
www.samhoustonwhiskey.com

McLain & Kyne Ltd. is best known for what it terms "very small batch bourbons", and the firm blends whiskey from as few as eight to 12 barrels of varying ages for their Jefferson's *(see p.242)* and Sam Houston bourbon brands.

Sam Houston was introduced in 1999 and is named after the colorful 19th-century soldier, statesman, and politician Samuel Houston, who became the first president of the Republic of Texas.

SAM HOUSTON AMERICAN STRAIGHT WHISKEY

AMERICAN WHISKEY 43% ABV

Apples and a hint of caramel on the relatively light nose, while the palate is very sweet, with more caramel and emerging black pepper.

SAZERAC RYE

Buffalo Trace Distillery, 1001 Wilkinson Boulevard, Frankfort, Kentucky
www.buffalotrace.com

Sazerac Rye is part of the annually updated Buffalo Trace Antique Collection *(see p.223)* and, having been aged for 18 years, is the oldest rye whiskey currently available. According to Buffalo Trace, the 18-year-old 2008 release is comprised of whiskey that has been aging in its warehouse on the first floor—this location enables the barrels to age slowly and gracefully.

SAZERAC RYE 18-YEAR-OLD

RYE WHISKEY 45% ABV

Rich on the nose, with maple syrup and a hint of menthol, this expression is oily on the palate, fresh, and lively, with fruit, pepper, and pleasing oak notes. The finish boasts lingering pepper, with returning fruit and a final flavor of molasses.

SEAGRAM'S 7 CROWN

Angostura Distillery,
Lawrenceburg, Indiana

One of the best known and most characterful blended American whiskeys, Seagram's 7 Crown has survived the break-up of the Seagram distilling empire and is now produced by Caribbean-based Angostura (of Angostura Bitters fame).

This relative newcomer to the US distilling arena has acquired the former Seagram distillery at Lawrenceburg, where 7 Crown is made, along with the long-shuttered Charles Medley Distillery in Owensboro Kentucky. The Lawrenceburg distillery is the largest spirits facility in the US in terms of production capacity.

SEAGRAM'S 7 CROWN

BLEND 40% ABV

This possesses a delicate nose with a hint of spicy rye, and is clean and well structured on the spicy palate.

ST. GEORGE

St. George Spirits, 2601 Monarch Street, Alameda, California
www.stgeorgespirits.com

St. George Spirits was established by Jörg Rupf in 1982, and the distillery operates two Holstein copper pot stills. A percentage of heavily roasted barley is used, some of which is smoked over alder and beech wood. Most of the single malt whiskey is put into former bourbon barrels and matured for between three and five years, with a proportion matured in French oak and former port casks.

ST. GEORGE SINGLE MALT WHISKEY (LOT 14)

SINGLE MALT 43% ABV

The nose features apples, sweet berry fruits, malt, and cocoa. Milk chocolate, vanilla, dried fruit, and spicy oak on the palate.

STRANAHAN'S

Stranahan's Colorado Whiskey, 2405 Blake Street, Denver, Colorado
www.stranahans.com

Jess Graber and George Stranahan established the Denver distillery, the first licensed distillery in Colorado, in March 2004. Whiskey is produced using a four-barley fermented wash produced by the neighboring Flying Dog Brewery. The distillation takes place in a Vendome still, and the spirit is put into new, charred American oak barrels. It is aged for a minimum of two years, and each bottled batch composed of the contents of between two and six barrels.

STRANAHAN'S COLORADO WHISKEY

COLORADO WHISKEY 47% ABV

The nose is very bourbon-like, with notes of caramel, licorice, spice, and oak. The palate is slightly oily, big, and sweet, with honey and spices. The fairly short finish is quite oaky.

TEMPLETON RYE

East 3rd Street, Templeton, Iowa
www.templetonrye.com

Scott Bush's Templeton Rye whiskey came onto the market in 2006. It is distilled in a 300-gallon (1,150-liter) copper pot still in Indiana before being aged in new, charred-oak barrels. Bush boasts that his rye is flavored to a Prohibition-era recipe.

During the years of the Great Depression a group of farmers in the Templeton area started to distil a rye whiskey illicitly in order to boost their faltering agricultural incomes. Soon, "Templeton Rye" achieved a widespread reputation as a high-quality spirit.

TEMPLETON RYE SMALL BATCH

RYE WHISKEY 40% ABV

Bright, crisp, and mildly sweet on the palate. The finish is smooth, long, and warming.

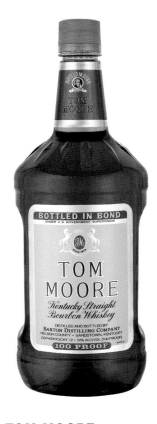

TEN HIGH

Barton Distillery, 300 Barton Road,
Bardstown, Kentucky
www.sazerac.com

Ten High, a long-established name,
was first created in 1879 and is
now a Barton-owned brand. It is
a sour mash, which means that it
is made with a small quantity of
an old batch of mash containing
a certain strain of live yeast,
which ensures a consistent taste—
similar to the process of making
sourdough bread. The whiskey
is matured in white-oak barrels.
The name Ten High comes from
a term used in playing poker.

TEN HIGH KENTUCKY

BOURBON 40% ABV
Grainy and slightly oaky on the nose,
Ten High is notably malty on the palate,
almost like a young malt Scotch,
and has notes of vanilla and caramel.
The finish is quite short and drying.

THOMAS H. HANDY SAZERAC

Buffalo Trace Distillery, 1001 Wilkinson
Boulevard, Frankfort, Kentucky
www.buffalotrace.com

Thomas H. Handy Sazerac is
the newest addition to the Buffalo
Trace Antique Collection. It is
an uncut and unfiltered straight
rye whiskey, named after the
New Orleans bartender who first
used rye whiskey to make the
Sazerac Cocktail.

   According to the distillers,
the barrels are aged six years
and five months on the fifth floor
of Warehouse M—"it's very
flavorful and will remind drinkers
of Christmas cake."

THOMAS H. HANDY SAZERAC 2008 EDITION

RYE WHISKEY 63.8% ABV
Summer fruits and pepper notes
on the nose. The palate is a blend
of soft vanilla and peppery rye; the
finish is long, with oily, spicy oak.

TINCUP

Tincup Whiskey, Denver, Colorado
www.tincupwhiskey.com

Tincup is the latest whiskey venture
of Colorado-based Jess Graber,
cofounder of Stranhan's Whiskey
Distillery. Although Graber has
been distilling whiskey since 1972,
the ex-construction company boss,
firefighter, and rodeo rider more
recently, decided he wanted to offer
the market a bourbon-style whiskey
with a more powerful, spicy flavor.
The result was Tincup, which has a
high rye content in its mashbill, and
is sourced from the MGP Distillery
at Lawrenceburg, Indiana. The
name recalls days when gold
prospectors drank whiskey from
tin cups.

TINCUP AMERICAN WHISKEY

AMERICAN WHISKEY 40% ABV
Lots of spice on the nose, with warm
apple pie, honey, and ginger. Cinnamon,
toffee, and more apple on the palate, with
caramel and lively spice in the finish.

TOM MOORE

Barton Distillery, 300 Barton Road,
Bardstown, Kentucky
www.sazerac.com

This Barton Kentucky straight
bourbon brand takes its name
from the Tom Moore Distillery,
which was established in 1889
by Tom Moore and Ben Mattingly,
just a stone's throw from the
present Barton Distillery.

   The plant was closed during
Prohibition but reopened in 1934
and, a decade later, was acquired
by the Oscar Getz family, who
subsequently established the Barton
Distilling Company. The company
was bought by Sazerac in 2009.

TOM MOORE

BOURBON 50% ABV
Distinct notes of rye and herbs on
the nose, along with vanilla, oak, and
cooked berries. Medium-bodied, the
palate is a blend of sugary sweetness
and spicy rye bitterness. Toffee and
ginger dominate the finish.

WHISKEY STYLES
US MICRO-DISTILLING

The US is currently undergoing a boom in small-scale or "micro" distilling, mirroring the country's earlier rapid growth of micro-brewing operations. Whiskey micro-distilling is a notably vibrant area of the market, where experimentation and innovation with different grains and production techniques are the norm. Distillers often operate outside the legally defined boundaries of bourbon, rye, or corn whiskeys.

A micro-distillery is defined as one manufacturing fewer than 500 barrels of spirits per year. One of the early pioneers of the movement was San Francisco craft brewer Fritz Maytag, who set up the Anchor Distilling Company (*see Old Potrero, p.249*) in 1994. Since then, micro-distilleries have multiplied at a remarkable rate, being established in many states where there has been no distilling since the onset of Prohibition in 1920. Distilling now takes place in no fewer than 47 states, whereas 20 years ago, it was confined to no more than a handful. In the whiskey heartland of Kentucky, there are now ten operational micro-distilleries, while neighboring Tennessee boasts nine.

In Virginia, Mount Vernon Distillery (*www.mountvernon.org*) is a working recreation of the whiskey-making facility established by President George Washington in 1797. Its 18th-century-style stills were installed in reconstructed buildings in 2006. Some of the more recently established US micro-distilleries that are majoring in whiskey include Black Bear (*www.blackbeardistillery.com*) in Colorado, which is ultra-traditional in style and plans to produce an Irish-style whiskey. Bent Brewstillery (*www.bentbrewstillery.com*) in Minnesota is, as the name suggests, a combined brewery and distillery, and some of its single malt whiskey has been aged in a combination of charred oak and charred applewood. California-based Venus Spirits (*www.venusspirits.com*) uses a hand-beaten Spanish alembic still to produce single malt, rye, and bourbon, while Alabama's John Emerald Distilling Company (*www.johnemeralddistilling.com*) makes a single malt using barley flavoured with peach wood and southern pecan during malting. Clearly, the spirit of innovation and experimentation in US micro-distilling is more alive than ever.

VAN WINKLE

2843 Brownsboro Road
Louisville, Kentucky
www.oldripvanwinke.com

Buffalo Trace *(see p.223)* has been in partnership with Julian Van Winkle since 2002, making and distributing his whiskeys. The current expressions were produced at a number of distilleries, and matured at the Van Winkle's now silent Old Hoffman Distillery.

Julian is a grandson of legendary Julian P. "Pappy" Van Winkle Sr., who started working as a sales-man for W. L. Weller & Sons in Louisville in 1893 at the age of 18 and went on to become famous for his Old Fitzgerald bourbon.

Van Winkle specializes in small-batch, aged whiskeys. The bourbons are made with wheat, rather than cheaper rye. This is said to give the whiskeys a smoother, sweeter flavor during the long maturation period favored by Van Winkle. All whiskeys are matured for at least 10 years in lightly charred mountain oak barrels. The range includes the rare 23-year-old and the 107 proof 10-year-old.

OLD RIP VAN WINKLE
10-YEAR-OLD

BOURBON 45% ABV

Caramel and molasses on the big nose, then honey and rich, spicy fruit on the profound, mellow palate. The finish is long, with coffee and licorice notes.

PAPPY VAN WINKLE'S FAMILY
RESERVE 20-YEAR-OLD

BOURBON 45.2% ABV

Old for a bourbon, this has stood the test of time. Sweet vanilla and caramel nose, plus raisins, apples, and oak. Rich and buttery in the mouth, with molasses and a hint of char. The finish is long and complex, with a touch of oak charring.

OLD RIP VAN WINKLE 10-YEAR-OLD

PAPPY VAN WINKLE'S FAMILY RESERVE 20-YEAR-OLD

**PAPPY VAN WINKLE'S
FAMILY RESERVE
15-YEAR-OLD**

BOURBON 53.5% ABV

*A sweet caramel and vanilla
nose, with charcoal and oak.
Full-bodied, round and smooth
in the mouth, with a long and
complex finish of spicy orange,
toffee, vanilla, and oak.*

**VAN WINKLE FAMILY
RESERVE RYE 13-YEAR-OLD**

RYE WHISKEY 47.8% ABV

*An almost uniquely aged rye.
Powerful nose of fruit and spice.
Vanilla, spice, pepper, and cocoa
in the mouth. A long finish pairs
caramel with black coffee.*

WHISKEY STYLES
AMERICAN RYE

The heritage of rye whiskey in North America probably dates back to the 1600s. Its development owes much to Irish and Scottish settlers, who found rye less difficult than barley to grow there. The Irish were already familiar with the use of rye in whiskey making.

Rye whiskey was particularly associated with the states of Pennsylvania and Maryland, with each making a distinctive style of the spirit; however, most rye is now distilled in Kentucky. At one time much more widely consumed in the US than bourbon, rye whiskey never fully recovered from Prohibition. Its distinctive, peppery, slightly bitter character probably worked against it as drinkers developed a taste for blander spirits. However, there has been a slow revival in rye's fortunes, with a number of US micro-distilleries *(see p.257)* producing small quantities of rye for appreciative connoisseurs. For example, in 1996, the pioneering Fritz Maytag of San Francisco's Anchor Brewery began distilling Old Potrero *(see p.249)* from 100 percent malted rye. Moreover, the recreated Mount Vernon Distillery in Virginia *(see p.257)* now distills rye whiskey to a recipe developed by Scottish-born farm manager James Anderson.

By law, rye whiskey has to be made from a mash of no less than 51 percent rye, with the other ingredients usually being corn and malted barley. It has to be distilled to no more than 80% ABV and casked at 62.5% ABV or less. As with bourbon, virgin charred-oak barrels are used for maturation and the minimum maturation period is two years. Leading brands of rye whiskey include Pikesville *(see p.252)*, Rittenhouse *(p.253)*, and Sazerac *(p.254)*. Jim Beam *(p.240)* and Wild Turkey *(p.263)* also produce expressions of rye.

VIRGINIA GENTLEMAN

A. Smith Bowman Distillery, Bowman Drive, Fredericksburg, Virginia
www.asmithbowman.com

The only full-scale distillery in a state that once made more whiskey than Kentucky, and founded by Abram Smith Bowman in 1935, it was acquired in 2003 by Sazerac, which also owns Buffalo Trace *(see p.223)*. Virginia Gentleman's first run is fermented and distilled at Buffalo Trace before a second, slow run through a copper pot doubler still on the Smith Bowman site, where it is also matured in charred white-oak barrels. A higher corn percentage than many bourbons gives it a greater sweetness.

VIRGINIA GENTLEMAN

BOURBON 45% ABV
A light, sweet, toasted nut aroma, and spicy rye, sweet corn, honey, caramel, and cocoa on the palate. A complex finish, with rye, malt, and vanilla.

VIRGINIA LIGHTNING

Belmost Farm of Virginia, 13490 Cedar Run Road, Culpeper, Virginia
www.belmontfarmdistillery.com

For Virginia Lightning, distiller Chuck Miller uses an original, secret family recipe, a blend of corn, wheat, and barley that is mashed and fermented in copper fermentation tanks. Distillation takes place in a 1930s, 2,000-US-gallon (7,600-liter) copper still. Finally, it is passed through a doubler still to increase strength and remove impurities. It is then bottled unaged. Its assertive sister spirit, Kopper Kettle, is charcoal-filtered; oak and apple-wood chips are used to boost maturation before it is barrel-aged for two years.

VIRGINIA LIGHTNING

CORN WHISKEY 50% ABV
Corn and alcohol on the nose, smooth and sugary on the palate, with oily corn, plus a powerful kick in the finish.

WASMUND'S

Copper Fox Distillery, 9 River Lane, Sperryville, Virginia
www.copperfox.biz

In spring 2003, Rick Wasmund purchased an existing Virginia distillery to launch Copper Fox Whiskey, and in 2005 the operation moved to its present, newly built site at Sperryville.

One of the few US distilleries to perform all its own malting, Wasmund malts barley in the traditional Scottish manner and then dries it using apple, cherry, and oak wood. It is distilled in a double pot still in single barrel batches and matured using an original "chip and barrel" aging process, which dramatically speeds up maturation.

WASMUND'S

SINGLE MALT WHISKEY 48% ABV
Honey, vanilla, watermelon, and leather on the nose, and a well-balanced blend of sweet and dry flavors on the palate, with nuts, smoke, spices, and vanilla.

W.L. WELLER

Buffalo Trace Distillery, 1001 Wilkinson Boulevard, Frankfort, Kentucky
www.buffalotrace.com

Distilled by Buffalo Trace, W. L. Weller is made with wheat as the secondary grain, for an extra smooth taste.

William LaRue Weller was a prominent 19th-century Kentucky distiller, whose company ultimately merged with that of the Stitzel brothers in 1935. A new Stitzel-Weller Distillery was subsequently constructed in Louisville.

W. L. WELLER SPECIAL RESERVE

BOURBON 45% ABV
Fresh fruit, honey, vanilla, and toffee characterize the nose, while the palate has lots of flavor, featuring ripe corn and spicy oak. The medium-length finish displays sweet, cereal notes and pleasing oak.

WILD TURKEY 81 PROOF

WILD TURKEY KENTUCKY SPIRIT

WILD TURKEY

Wild Turkey Distillery, US Highway
62 East, Lawrenceburg, Kentucky
www.wildturkeybourbon.com

Wild Turkey's Boulevard Distillery
is situated on Wild Turkey Hill,
above the Kentucky River, near
Lawrenceburg, in Anderson
County. Wild Turkey has been
owned by the Pernod Ricard
Group since 1980, when the
French drinks giant took over the
New-York-based Austin Nichols
Distilling Co. The distillery was
first established in 1905 by the
three Ripy brothers, whose family
had been making whiskey in the
nearby distilling center of Tyrone
since the year 1869.

The Wild Turkey brand itself
was conceived in 1940, when
Austin Nichols' president,
Thomas McCarthy, chose a
quantity of 101 proof straight
bourbon from his company stocks
to take along on a wild turkey

shoot. Today, Wild Turkey is
distilled under the watchful eyes
of legendary Master Distiller
Jimmy Russell, the world's
longest-tenured active Master
Distiller, and his son Eddie,
who is the fourth-generation
Russell to work at the distillery.
In 2015, Eddie was named
Master Distiller in his own
right, after 35 years of working
with the Wild Turkey brand.
The Russells have also created
some other highly regarded
brands, including Russell's
Reserve *(see p.254)* and
American Spirit *(see p.218).*

Wild Turkey is matured in
American oak barrels that are
subjected to the deepest No.4
"Alligator" char, and they are
filled with spirit at a lower proof
than that of some competitors.
This means less water has to be
added before bottling, allowing
more flavors imparted from the
barrel to be retained.

WILD TURKEY 101 PROOF

WILD TURKEY RARE BREED

WILD TURKEY KENTUCKY STRAIGHT RYE

WILD TURKEY 81 PROOF

BOURBON 40.5% ABV

Spicy corn, vanilla, oak, and coffee on the nose. The palate yields big caramel and honey notes, plus cinnamon and allspice.

WILD TURKEY KENTUCKY SPIRIT

BOURBON 50.5% ABV

A single barrel whiskey, each one being personally selected by Jimmy Russell to be fuller-bodied than normal. A fresh, attractive nose, with oranges and notes of rye. Complex palate with almonds, honey, more oranges, and a hint of leather. Long and sweet finish, darkening and becoming more syrupy.

WILD TURKEY 101 PROOF

BOURBON 50.5% ABV

Jimmy Russell maintains that 50.5% (101 proof) is the optimum bottling strength for Wild Turkey. This has a remarkably soft yet rich aroma for such a high-proof whiskey, due in part to its eight years of maturation. Caramel,

vanilla, soft fruits, and a touch of spice on the nose, full-bodied, rich, and robust in the mouth, with more vanilla, fresh fruit, and spice, plus brown sugar and honey. Notes of oak develop in the long, and powerful, yet smooth finish.

WILD TURKEY RARE BREED

BOURBON (VARIABLE ABV)

Launched in 1991, this brand comprises 6- to 12-year-old whiskeys. Aroma and flavor are notably smooth for a bourbon with such a high alcohol content. Complex, initially assertive nose, with nuts, oranges, spices, and floral notes. Honey, oranges, vanilla, tobacco, mint, and molasses make for an equally complex palate. A long, nutty finish, with spicy, peppery rye.

WILD TURKEY KENTUCKY STRAIGHT RYE

RYE WHISKEY 50.5% ABV

This straight rye has a pleasingly firm nose, crammed with fruit. The body is full and rich, and the well-balanced palate offers intense spices and ripe fruit. A profoundly spicy, nutty, finish.

WOODFORD RESERVE MASTER'S COLLECTION 1838 STYLE WHITE CORN

WOODFORD RESERVE DISTILLER'S SELECT

WOODFORD RESERVE

7855 McCracken Pike,
Versailles, Kentucky
www.woodfordreserve.com

Woodford Reserve is unique among bourbon distilleries; it uses a triple distillation method and three copper pot stills for a portion of production.

Woodford Reserve is operated by the Louisville-based Brown-Forman Distiller Corporation, which also owns Jack Daniel's *(see p.236)*, but the distillery's origins can be traced back as far as 1797. Brown-Forman only began to distil there in 1996, when it was known as the Labrot & Graham Distillery. The company subsequently spent $10.5 million restoring the plant, and in 2003 the present Woodford Reserve name was adopted for both the distillery and its whiskey.

In 2005, the first bottling in the Master's Collection range was released under the Four Grain Bourbon name, and two years later,

WOODFORD RESERVE DOUBLE OAKED

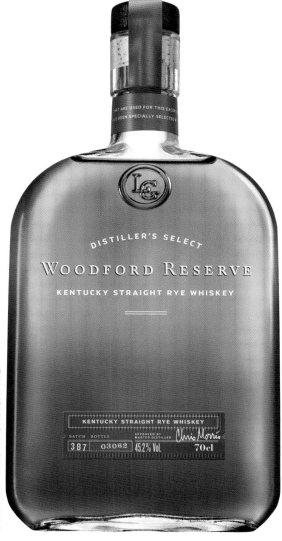

WOODFORD RESERVE STRAIGHT RYE

a Sonoma-Cutrer Finish was added to the line-up. The Master's Collection 1838 Sweet Mash was released in 2008 to commemorate the year the present Woodford Reserve Distillery was constructed, and to also celebrate the historic "sweet mash" method of bourbon production. Other Master's Collection bottlings have subsequently been released, including the 1838 Style White Corn, made from white corn rather than the traditional yellow.

WOODFORD RESERVE MASTER'S COLLECTION 1838-STYLE WHITE CORN

BOURBON 45.2% ABV

Malt, apple, mixed nuts, and popcorn on the soft nose, while the palate yields new leather, more popcorn, spicy lemon, and pepper.

WOODFORD RESERVE DISTILLER'S SELECT

BOURBON 45.2% ABV

Distiller's Select is elegant yet robust on the nose, perfumed, with milk-chocolate raisins,

dried fruit, burned sugar, ginger, and a touch of saddle soap. Equally complex on the palate, Distiller's Select is fragrant and fruity, with raspberries, camomile, and ginger. The finish displays lingering vanilla notes as well as peppery oak.

WOODFORD RESERVE DOUBLE OAKED

BOURBON 45.2% ABV

Oak, caramel, dark berry fruits on the nose, with orange and fudge in the background. Black pepper, vanilla, caramel, and honey on the lingering palate.

WOODFORD RESERVE STRAIGHT RYE

RYE WHISKEY 45.2% ABV

Light on the nose, with rye, black pepper, pears, and fresh oak. Rye, malt, and honey on the peppery palate, with a hint of mint.

NORTHWEST
TERRITORIES

BRITISH
COLUMBIA

ALBERTA

SASKATCHEWAN

MANITOBA

HUDSON
BAY

ONTARIO

EDMONTON

Alberta

CALGARY

Highwood

VANCOUVER

Black Velvet

REGINA

WINNIPEG

Crown Royal

USA

OTTAWA

Canadian Mist

TORONTO

Hiram Walker
(Canadian Club)

Kittling
Ridge

miles
0   300
0   300
kilometres

N
W   E
S

FORTY CREEK

GLEN BRETON

CROWN ROYAL

QUÉBEC

NEWFOUNDLAND
AND LABRADOR

QUÉBEC

NEW
BRUNSWICK   Glenora
            (Glen Breton)
ONTRÉAL
        NOVA
        SCOTIA

The golden age of Canadian whisky was from late-19th to mid-20th centuries, with whisky makers such as Hiram Walker, creator of Canadian Club, and Sam Bronfman at Seagram forming vast commercial empires. These two dominated much of the world market. From this high point, however, Canadian whisky experienced a marked decline in the second half of the 20th century, and it now operates on a far more modest scale. Where once 200 distilleries produced rivers of whisky to serve a seemingly insatiable American market, now Canada has fewer than a dozen distilleries, most of which are owned by US bourbon companies or international spirits producers. Seagram's—a name so closely associated with Canada—is still the brand name for a handful of whiskies, but the Seagram's empire itself is gone. It remains to be seen if the remaining producers can take their nation's whisky industry back to being a major player on the world stage.

ALBERTA

WISER'S

SEAGRAM'S V.O.

CANADIAN CLUB

CANADIAN MIST

WHISKEY STYLES
CANADIAN WHISKY

All Canadian whisky is blended, apart from Glen Breton, a single malt *(see p.275)*. Production is in column stills, but each distillery produces a range of styles, and each blend will use between 15 and 50 different whiskies. As in Scotland, the spirit must be matured for at least three years, although much is aged six to eight years. The base spirit is light and relatively neutral in character, distilled from rye, barley, wheat, or corn. Unlike in the US, there is no constraint upon the mashbill. A proportion of rye or malted rye spirit, which adds spice to the blend and body, is added to the mix, and this provides Canadian whisky with its chief characteristics. It is often described as rye whiskey, but Canadian whisky is of a different style than American rye whisky.

Early immigrants to Canada found a country blessed with the necessities for making whisky. By 1840, there were about 200 distillers in the country. Commercial distilleries usually began as offshoots of grain mills—among them were Hiram Walker, Joseph Seagram, J. P. Wiser, and Gooderham & Worts. Their business was not easy because of a Puritan ethic that constrained the sale of alcohol. Today, liquor stores are run by the state, except in Alberta. Ironically, it was the imposition of Prohibition in the US, between 1920 and 1933, that provided Canadian whisky with the impetus it needed. The major players—Seagram, Schenley, and Hiram Walker—realized that they could build an export market for the future. Today, the US consumes more Canadian whiskey than any other spirit, including American whisky. Indeed, a great deal of Canadian whisky is blended specifically for the US market, having a light and smooth style, the former coming from a very pure base spirit, and the latter from other elements in the blend.

ALBERTA SPRINGS 10-YEAR-OLD

ALBERTA PREMIUM

ALBERTA

1521 34th Avenue Southeast,
Calgary, Alberta
www.albertarye.com

Alberta Distillery was founded
in Calgary in 1946 to take
advantage of the immense prairies
of the Canadian west and the fine
water cascading down from the
Rocky Mountains. It has capacity
to produce over 5 million gallons
(20 million liters) per annum
in its beer, column, and pot stills,
and since 1987 has been owned
by Jim Beam. As well as the
Alberta labels, other brands from
this distillery include Tangle
Ridge and Windsor Canadian
(see p.277).

Rye is at the heart of many
Canadian whiskies, and is
predominant in all the whiskies
that come from Alberta. The bulk
of the distillery's blends are made
up of a base spirit made with
rye rather than corn. This is first
distilled in a beer still, then in
a continuous rectifier. A separate
rye spirit is also made up. This is
distilled once only, leaving oils
and congeners in the spirit to make
it heavy, oily, and rich in flavor.
The two spirits are then blended
together. Maturation takes place
in first-fill bourbon casks, or even
in new white-oak casks.

ALBERTA SPRINGS
10-YEAR-OLD

CANADIAN RYE 40% ABV
*A sweet aroma, with rye bread and
black pepper. The taste is very sweet,
even somewhat cloying, becoming
charred and caramelized.*

ALBERTA PREMIUM

CANADIAN RYE 40% ABV
*Described as "Special Mild Canadian
Rye Whisky." The aroma presents
vanilla toffee, a hint of spice, light citric
notes, and fruitiness. The taste is sweet
above all, with stewed apples, plums,
and marzipan.*

BLACK VELVET

2925 9th Avenue North,
Lethbridge, Alberta
www.blackvelvetwhisky.com

Black Velvet is the third best-selling
Canadian whisky in the US. It
was created by Gilbey Canada
in the 1950s as Black Label, and
made at the Old Palliser Distillery
in Toronto. It was so successful
that, in 1973, the Black Velvet
Distillery was established at
Lethbridge, in the shadow of
the Rockies, only a couple of hours
drive from the US border. In 1999,
both Black Velvet and Palliser were
sold to Barton Brands, now a
division of Constellation Brands.

BLACK VELVET 8-YEAR-OLD

BLEND 40% ABV
*The nose is light, with citrus fruit, while
the soft palate yields orchard fruits,
pepper, oak, and grain.*

CANADIAN MIST

202 MacDonald Road,
Collingwood, Ontario
www.canadianmist.com

Launched in 1965, this whisky
now sells 3 million cases a year in
the US. Its distillery is odd in several
ways: the equipment is all stainless
steel; it is the only Canadian distillery
to use a mash-bill of corn and malted
barley; and it imports its rye spirit
from sister distillery Early Times
(see p.224) in Kentucky. Almost
all the spirit is tankered to
Kentucky for blending. In addition
to the popular Canadian Mist
brand, the 1185 Special Reserve
is also available.

CANADIAN MIST

BLEND 40% ABV
*Lightly fruity on the nose, with vanilla
and caramel notes. Mild, sweet flavor
with traces of vanilla toffee.*

CANADIAN CLUB 1858

CANADIAN CLUB SMALL BATCH SHERRY CASK

CANADIAN CLUB

Hiram Walker Distillery, Riverside Drive East, Walkerville, Ontario
www.canadianclub.com

Canadian Club is the oldest and most influential whisky brand in Canada. Created by businessman Hiram Walker in 1884, it was named simply "Club" and aimed at discerning members of gentlemen's clubs. Unusually, in an era when most whiskies were sold in bulk, it was supplied in bottles, and thus could not be adulterated by the retailer, a practice soon adopted by other Canadian and American distillers. The company has had numerous Royal Warrants, from Queen Victoria to Elizabeth II.

A less lofty customer, Al Capone, smuggled thousands of cases across the border during Prohibition.

In 1927 Hiram Walker & Sons was bought by Harry Hatch, who owned the Gooderham & Worts Distillery in Toronto. The merged company was the largest distiller in the world. Entrepreneur Hatch made a fortune during Prohibition. In 1935, he took a controlling interest in H. Corby (see Wiser's, p.277). Then, in 1937, he bought Ballantine's (p.35) and a clutch of malt whisky distillers, and built the Strathclyde grain distillery. Allied Distillers acquired the company in 1987.

The Canadian Club brands were sold to Fortune Brands, the owner of Jim Beam (see p.240), in 2005.

Canadian Club is always "blended at birth"—that is, the component whiskies are mixed prior to a maturation of at least five years.

CANADIAN CLUB 1858

BLEND 40% ABV

Floral notes on the nose, with dried fruits and rye. The palate is oily, sweet, fruity, and mildly herbal, with white pepper.

CANADIAN CLUB SMALL BATCH SHERRY CASK

BLEND 41.3% ABV

Rye, pine, freshly sawed timber, ginger, and discreet sweet sherry on the nose, while the palate yields vanilla, caramel, black pepper, and light fruit notes.

CANADIAN CLUB SMALL BATCH CLASSIC 12

BLEND 40% ABV

Caramel, orange, and hand-rolling tobacco on the nose, with cereal, honey, and spice. More caramel and oranges on the gently spiced palate, with almonds and dates.

CANADIAN CLUB RESERVE 9-YEAR-OLD

BLEND 40% ABV

Vanilla, maple syrup, rye, and fresh oak on the nose, while the palate soffers spicy rye, butterscotch, and milk chocolate, underpinned by corn notes.

Canada's huge grain silos, standing starkly against the sky, are an icon of the country's landscape and agricultural heritage, including its whisky distilling industry.

CROWN ROYAL BLACK

CROWN ROYAL RYE

CROWN ROYAL DELUXE

CROWN ROYAL

Distillery Road, Gimli, Manitoba
www.crownroyal.com

Crown Royal was created by Sam Bronfman, President of Seagram (*see p. 276*), to mark the state visit to Canada of King George VI and Queen Elizabeth in 1939, with its "crown-shaped" bottle and purple velvet bag. Although it was only available in Canada until 1964, it is now one of the best-selling Canadian whiskies in the US.

Although it has been produced at Gimli Distillery on Lake Winnipeg since 1992, Crown Royal was originally made at Waterloo Distillery, founded in 1857, and sold to the Distillers Corporation in 1928. The driving force behind this company was Sam Bronfman, or "Mr. Sam," a man of energy, daring, ruthlessness, and passion. With the help of his brothers, he built Seagram into the largest liquor company in the world. Prohibition was their big break,

though Sam tended to draw a veil over this period in later life. "We shipped a lot of goods. Of course, we knew where it went, but we had no legal proof. I never went to the other side of the border to count the empty Seagram bottles."

In 2001, the company shed its alcohol interests—Gimli Distillery and Crown Royal went to Diageo.

CROWN ROYAL DELUXE

BLEND 43% ABV

Nose of toffee, vanilla, and cereal. Smooth palate of caramel, peaches, and oak.

CROWN ROYAL BLACK

BLEND 45% ABV

Rum-raisin ice cream sprinkled with black pepper on the nose, while vanilla, caramel, and oak dominate the fruity palate.

CROWN ROYAL NORTHERN HARVEST RYE

BLEND 45% ABV

Rye, cinnamon, and caramel on the nose. Spicy rye, ginger, and black pepper on the sweet palate.

FORTY CREEK

Kittling Ridge Distillery,
Grimsby, Ontario
www.fortycreekwhisky.com

Kittling Ridge was named 2008
Canadian Distillery of the Year
by *Whisky Magazine*. Unusually,
it uses pot stills as well as column
stills, and a mashbill mix of rye,
barley, and corn. Built in 1970,
it is part of a winery and was
originally designed to make eau de
vie. John Hall, its owner since 1992,
brings the skills of a winemaker
to distilling: "I am not so bound
by tradition as inspired by it."
Whisky critic Michael Jackson
called Forty Creek "the most
revolutionary whisky in Canada."

BARREL SELECT

BLEND 40% ABV
*A complex, fragrant nose, with soft
fruit, honeysuckle, vanilla, and some
spice. A similar palate, with traces of
nuts and leather, and a smooth finish
with lingering fruit and vanilla.*

GLEN BRETON

Glenora Distillery, Route 19, Glenville,
Cape Breton, Nova Scotia
www.glenoradistillery.com

This is North America's only malt
whisky distillery. Cape Breton
Island has a strong Scottish
heritage, but the Scotch Whisky
Association has criticized the name
for sounding too much like a Scotch.

Production began in June 1990,
halting within weeks due to lack
of funds. The distillery was later
bought by Lauchie MacLean, who
has re-distilled earlier, inconsistent
spirit, and bottles at 8 or 9 years.

Glenora has its own maltings and
uses Scottish barley that is given a
light peating. The two stills it uses
are made by Forsyths of Rothes.

GLEN BRETON RARE

SINGLE MALT 43% ABV
*Butterscotch, heather, ground ginger,
and honey nose. Light to medium body,
with a creamy mouthfeel and notes
of wood, almonds, caramel, and peat.*

HIGHWOOD

114 10th Avenue Southeast,
High River, Alberta
www.highwood-distillers.com

Unusually for Canada, Highwood,
founded in 1974, is independently
owned. It makes a range of spirits
and is the only distillery in Canada
using just wheat in its column stills
as the base spirit for its blends. In
2005, it bought the Potter's and
Cascadia distilleries. Potter's is
a separate brand from Highwood.
It is mixed with sherry, and this
flavor adds another dimension.

HIGHWOOD

CANADIAN RYE 40% ABV
*A blend of wheat and rye spirits.
The oaky, vanilla-scented nose has
traces of rye spice, orange blossom,
and honey. The palate balances
sweetness with oak tannins and nuts.*

HIRSCH

Distribution: Preiss Imports Inc,
San Diego, California

This whisky is no longer being
made, but is still available via a
US distributor. Although Canadian
whisky is often referred to as
"rye," only a few brands contain
more than 50 percent rye spirit,
which is what makes it a true
rye whisky. Hirsch is one, and
connoisseurs claim it rivals the
best Kentucky ryes.

The whiskies are bottled in
small batches, made in column
stills, aged in ex-bourbon barrels,
selected by Preiss Imports, and
bottled by Glenora Distillers,
Nova Scotia *(see Glen Breton)*.

HIRSCH SELECTION 8-YEAR-OLD

CANADIAN RYE 43% ABV
*Solvent and pine essence, then sweet
maple sap on the nose. The taste is
sweet, with caramel, dry coconut, and
oakwood; full-bodied. A bittersweet
finish with a few earthy notes.*

SEAGRAM'S V.O.

SEAGRAM'S 83

SEAGRAM'S FIVE STAR

SEAGRAM'S

Diageo Canada, West Mall,
Etobicoke, Ontario
www.diageo.com

Joseph Emm Seagram's family emigrated to Canada from Wiltshire, England, in 1837. In 1864, he was appointed manager of a flour mill at Waterloo, Ontario, where he became interested in distilling as a way of using surplus grains. By 1869, he was a partner in the company, and, in 1883, by which time distilling was the core business, he was the sole owner. The brand 83 commemorates this. The V.O. brand stands for 'Very Own'' and was once the best-selling Canadian whisky in the world. It was also Sam Bronfman's favorite tipple (see p.274).

Joseph Seagram's sons sold the company to Bronfman's Distillers Corporation Ltd., which used Seagram's stocks of old whisky to good advantage once Prohibition was repealed in 1933. After further changes of ownership, the Seagram's portfolio, which includes other spirits and wines, was bought out in 2001 by a partnership between Diageo and Pernod Ricard. Diageo now controls the Canadian Seagram's labels, as well as Seagram's 7 Crown (see p.255), which is marketed as an American whiskey.

SEAGRAM'S V.O.

BLEND 40% ABV

The nose presents pear drops, caramel, and some rye spice, along with butter. Light-bodied, sweet, and lightly spicy, with a slightly acerbic mouthfeel.

SEAGRAM'S 83

BLEND 40% ABV

At one time, this was even more popular than V.O. Now it is a standard Canadian: smooth and easy to drink.

SEAGRAM'S FIVE STAR

CANADIAN RYE 40% ABV

A perfectly acceptable budget whisky of good mixing quality.

WISER'S DELUXE

WISER'S SMALL BATCH

TANGLE RIDGE

Alberta Distillery, 1521 34th Avenue
Southeast, Calgary, Alberta

This whisky from the Alberta
Distillery (see p.269) is sweeter
than its stablemates, although,
like the other Alberta whiskies,
it is made exclusively from rye.
Introduced in 1996, it is one of the
new school of premium Canadian
whiskies: aged 10 years in oak, it is
then "dumped" and small amounts
of vanilla and sherry are added.
The spirit is then re-casked for a
time to allow the flavors to marry.

Its name comes from a limestone
wall in the Canadian Rockies that
was discovered by distinguished
explorer, artist, and writer Mary
Schaffer (1861–1939).

TANGLE RIDGE DOUBLE CASK

CANADIAN RYE 40% ABV
*Butterscotch and burned caramel on
the nose, velvet-smooth mouthfeel, and
a very sweet taste, with a hint of sherry.
Lacks complexity, however.*

WINDSOR CANADIAN

Alberta Distillery, 1521 34th Avenue
Southeast, Calgary, Alberta

One might think that this comes
from the Hiram Walker Distillery
at Windsor, Ontario; actually, it
is made at the Alberta Distillery
(see p.269). The name is no doubt
meant to recall the British Royal
Family, but it should not be confused
with the Scotch Windsor (see
p.178). Like other whiskies made
at Alberta, Windsor Canadian is
exclusively rye-based.

WINDSOR CANADIAN

BLENDED CANADIAN RYE 40% ABV
*Honey, peaches, pine nuts, and cloves
on the nose. A medium body and a
sweet taste, with cereal and wood
notes. An unassuming whisky; great
value for money.*

WISER'S

Hiram Walker Distillery, Riverside Drive
East, Walkerville, Ontario
www.wisers.ca

John Philip Wiser may well have
been the first distiller to use the
term "Canadian Whiskey" on his
label, at the Chicago World's Fair
in 1893. He was the son of Dutch
immigrants and, in 1864, he took
over a distillery on the banks of the
St. Lawrence River at Prescott,
Ontario, from a business partner.
By the early 1900s, it was the third
largest distillery in Canada, and its
whiskies were being exported to
China and the Philippines, as well
as the US.

Not long after the death of
J. P. Wiser in 1917, the company
decided to form a merger with
the H. Corby Distillery Company,
which was founded by Henry
Corby in 1859 at Corbyville in
Ontario. Production of Wiser's
brands was moved to here in 1932.
Three years later, Hiram Walker,

Gooderham & Worts acquired
51 percent of the company.
In 1969, Hiram Walker was
bought by Allied Lyons. Corby
Distillery was closed in 1989,
and production of the Corby/
Wiser whiskies moved to the
Hiram Walker Distillery at
Walkerville, which is now
owned by Pernod Ricard, as
are the brands. Today Wiser's
are the fifth best-selling
Canadian whiskies in Canada.

WISER'S DELUXE

BLEND 40% ABV
*A fruity and spicy nose, with cereal
and linseed oil, vanilla, and toffee.*

WISER'S SMALL BATCH

BLEND 43.4% ABV
*A recent addition to Wiser's
range, Small Batch is a full-flavored
Canadian whisky, with vanilla,
oak, and butterscotch on the nose
and in the taste. The slightly higher
strength makes for more flavor
and texture.*

SUNTORY YAMAZAKI

KIRIN KARUIZAWA

NIKKA PURE MALT

HOKKAIDO

Nikka
Yoichi

● SAPPORO

● AOMORI

Nikka Miyagikyo

● SENDAI

HONSHU

Chichibu

● TOKYO

Suntory Hakushu

Kirin Gotemba

KYOTO ●

OSAKA ● Suntory Yamazaki

HIROSHIMA ●

SHIKOKU

FUKUOKA ●

KYUSHU

NAGASAKI ●

N
E
S
W

miles
0   100

0   100
kilometres

NIKKA YOICHI

HANYU

Suntory is Japan's biggest whisky producer and has two large whisky distilleries at Yamazaki and Hakushu. Its main competitor, Nikka, has two distilleries at Yoichi and Miyagikyo. The drinks company Kirin has whisky facilities at Gotemba, while other working distilleries making whisky are Miyashita Shuzo, Shinshu, White Oak, and Chichibu. The rest of Japan's distilleries abandoned whisky-making after the Asian financial crisis of 1997, either closing down or shifting their focus to making *shochu*, the traditional Japanese potato spirit. Nikka's Yoichi Distillery is situated on Hokkaido, Japan's northernmost island, where the climate is similar to that in Scotland. The others are located on Honshu island in central Japan. Unlike distilleries in Scotland and other parts of the whisky-making world, Japanese distillers do not trade whiskies with each other for making blends. Instead, they each produce a range of whiskies to make up their own blends.

SUNTORY HIBIKI

SUNTORY HAKUSHU

NIKKA TAKETSURU

NIKKA MIYAGIKYO

KIRIN FUJI-GOTEMBA

ICHIRO'S MALT—ACE OF DIAMONDS, DISTILLED 1986, BOTTLED 2008

CHICHIBU

Venture Whisky, Saitama Prefecture
www.one-drinks.com

The newest Japanese distillery
was founded in 2007 by Ichiro
Akuto, previously of Hanyu *(see
Hanyu)*. A small plant, it features
what might be the only Japanese
oak washbacks in the world.
Aging takes place in a mix of more
than 20 cask types, including
ex-bourbon, ex-sherry, ex-Madeira,
and ex-cognac casks. Some 10
percent of the barley used is malted
onsite, and batches of peated spirit
are distilled annually. Chichibu
releases are highly prized and
difficult to obtain, even in Japan.

ICHIRO'S MALT CHICHIBU THE PEATED 2015

SINGLE MALT 62.5% ABV
*Warm asphalt, earthy peat, lemon,
new oak, and sea spray on the
nose. The palate is smooth, with
sweet peat, new leather, licorice,
citrus fruit, and plain chocolate.*

GOLDEN HORSE

Toa Shuzo, Chichibu
www.toashuzo.com

The Golden Horse brand is still
owned by Toa Shuzo, the firm
which used to own the Hanyu
distillery *(see Hanyu)*, and the
whiskies are drawn from its
last remaining stocks. There are
bottlings at 8, 10, and 12 years.
They are rarely seen on the
export markets, and, at the time
of writing, it is unclear what
will happen to the Golden Horse
brand once the Toa Shuzo stocks
have disappeared.

GOLDEN HORSE 8-YEAR-OLD

SINGLE MALT 40% ABV
*A quite vibrant nose with light malt
extract notes and some oak. There's
a basic sweetness to this lightly
perfumed malt, which has just a wisp
of smoke on the finish, but a nagging
acidic touch in some bottlings.*

HANYU

Toa Shuzo, Saitama Prefecture
www.one-drinks.com

The Hanyu distillery was built by
the Akuto family in the 1940s for
producing shochu. Full production
of whisky begans in 1980, and
Hanyu enjoyed success until the
financial crisis of 1996 triggered
the end of the whisky boom in
Japan. The distillery had to close
in 2000. When the firm was
bought out in 2003, Ichiro Akuto
(see Ichiro's Malt) was given a
few months to buy back as much
stock as he could before the
distillery was demolished.

HANYU 1988 CASK 9501

SINGLE MALT 55.6% ABV
*Vibrant and intense, with vanilla,
some citrus, and a delicate cocoa-butter
character. The Japanese oak adds a
bittersweet edge. On the palate there's
a rich depth. The finish shows smoke.*

ICHIRO'S MALT

Hanyu Distillery, Saitama Prefecture
www.one-drinks.com

Ichiro's Malt is a range of bottlings
from Ichiro Akuto, who was
the former president of Hanyu
(see Hanyu), and the grandson
of Hanyu's founder, Isouji Akuto.
The whiskies are drawn from
the 400 casks of Hanyu single
malt that Akuto managed to
obtain after the Hanyu distillery
was closed down.

As a young man, Ichiro Akuto
had worked as a brand manager
at Suntory and developed a strong
feel for marketing. The bulk of
Hanyu's remaining stock is being
released by Akuto in a series of
53 whiskies named after playing
cards. This Card Series, as it is
known, is memorable not only for
its distinctive branding but also
for the high quality of many
of its expressions.

Distillation dates for the Card
Series range from 1985 to 2000,

ICHIRO'S MALT—ACE OF SPADES, DISTILLED 1985, BOTTLED 2006

ICHIRO'S MALT DOUBLE DISTILLERIES

with some of the expressions being given secondary maturation in other types of barrel—Japanese oak, cognac, and sherry among them. Other old Hanyu casks were re-racked into either new wood or American oak. Some are still untouched. All of the Card Series bottlings are now extremely rare and highly collectable.

ICHIRO'S MALT—ACE OF DIAMONDS, DISTILLED 1986, BOTTLED 2008

SINGLE MALT 56.4% ABV

Mature nose, with Seville orange, furniture polish, rose, pipe tobacco, and when diluted, sloe and Moscatel. Spicy and chocolatey on the tongue.

ICHIRO'S MALT—ACE OF SPADES, DISTILLED 1985, BOTTLED 2006

SINGLE MALT 55% ABV

The Ace of Spades—sometimes called the Motorhead malt, after the band best known for singing "Ace of Spades"—is one of the oldest in the

Card Series. Bold, rich, and fat with masses of raisin, some tarry notes, and treacle. The palate is chewy and toffee-like, with some prune and a savory finish.

ICHIRO'S MALT DOUBLE DISTILLERIES

BLENDED MALT 46% ABV

The nose is sweet and oaky, with sawdust and hints of sandalwood. Malt and spice on the palate, with developing oak and licorice.

ICHIRO'S MALT & GRAIN

BLEND 46% ABV

Honey, vanilla, malt, and apricots on the nose. The palate offers more honey, plus citrus fruit, ginger, pepper, and sweet hay. Tropical fruits in the peppery finish.

ICHIRO'S MALT & GRAIN

GOTEMBA FUJISANROKU 18-YEAR-OLD

GOTEMBA FUJISANROKU 50°

KIRIN GOTEMBA

Shibanta 970, Gotembashi, Shizuoka
www.kirin.co.jp

Spectacularly situated in the cool foothills of Mount Fuji, 2,000 feet (620 meters) above sea level, Kirin's Gotemba distillery was built in 1973 as part of a joint venture with the former Canadian giant Seagram *(see p.276)*. It contains both a grain-whisky distillery and a malt plant.

The distillery's output is much in line with the light flavors typical of Seagram's house style. In the 1970s this was also the style preferred by the Japanese consumer and was intended to partner Japanese cuisine. That said, the distillery had to supply all the needs of Kirin's blends, so it made three different grain whiskies and three styles of malt, including peated.

Gotemba Distillery is open to the public, but is currently not in production. Its whiskies are available through specialist retailers in Japan and some overseas outlets.

GOTEMBA FUJISANROKU 18-YEAR-OLD

SINGLE MALT 40% ABV

Gotemba's new 18-year-old bottling, Fujisanroku is more floral and restrained than the "old" Fuji Gotemba 18-year-old, with less of the oakiness. Some peach, lily, and a zesty grapefruit note. The honey found in the grain reappears here.

FUJISANROKU TARUJUKU 50°

BLEND 50% ABV

Vanilla and light oak on the slightly spirit-y nose, while the palate is oaky, with malt and allspice, leading to a short finish.

WHISKEY STYLES
JAPANESE WHISKY

The Japanese whisky industry was founded in the 1920s with a partnership between Shinjiro Torii, the owner of a firm importing Scotch, and Masataka Taketsuru, a distiller who had studied whisky-making in Scotland. Torii built Yamazaki *(see p.298)*, Japan's first malt distillery, and employed Taketsuru as his distiller. Torii's company grew to become the drinks giant Suntory. In 1934, Taketsuru founded his own distillery at Yoichi; his company became Suntory's great rival, Nikka.

While Taketsuru preferred a heavier, more Scottish, peaty style that he could develop on Japan's northern island, Hokkaido, Torii continued to develop a light style of whisky in the mild climate of central Japan. These rivals were joined by a handful of other distilleries starting in the 1950s. Like Scotch, the initial success of the Japanese industry was built on blended varieties. By the 1980s, the biggest-selling single whisky brand in the world was Suntory Royal, which was selling more than 15 million cases in its home market. Also like Scotch, the Japanese whisky industry's recent surge has come through the burgeoning interest in single malt and a discovery by whisky lovers around the world of the Japanese purity of flavor.

The Japanese art of distilling is based on an in-depth, quality-driven, scientific knowledge of production. The minutiae of whisky-making—water, barley, yeast types, mashing, fermentation, distillation, and maturation in different oaks—has been investigated by the Japanese in depth. This allows firms to produce a wide range of different flavors of single malt from a single distillery, which, in turn, takes Japanese single malt away from the Scotch model. Most Japanese single malts today are blends of different flavored malts from the same distillery.

Like other whisky bars in Japan, The Crane in Tokyo has a distinctly Scottish feel, though a Japanese barman is more likely to wear a bow tie and hand cut ice than his Scottish counterpart. Japanese whiskies are also based on Scotch models, but have their own character.

KARUIZAWA 1986

KARUIZAWA 1995: NOH SERIES

KARUIZAWA 1971

KIRIN KARUIZAWA

Maseguchi 1795–2, Oaza,
Miyotamachi, Kitasakugun, Nagano
www.kirin.co.jp

Originally a winery, Kirin's second
distillery was converted to whisky
production in the 1950s. Unusually
for most Japanese distilleries, it
made only one style of whisky.
Whereas the majority of Japan's
malts tend to be light and delicate,
Karuizawa has always specialized
in a robust, big-hitting, and smoky
style. To achieve this, it retained
techniques that are rare now even
in Scotland: the heaviness of the
Golden Promise strain of barley
used is accentuated by the small
stills, while maturation in
ex-sherry casks adds a dried-
fruit character.

The distillery is no longer
in production, but, in recent
years, single cask bottlings
of Karuizawa have become
extremely collectible, being
sold at very high prices.

KARUIZAWA 1986: CASK NO. 7387, BOTTLED 2008

SINGLE MALT 60.7% ABV

*Incense on the nose along with wax,
crystallized fruits, dried fig, porcini, cassia,
tamarind paste, smoke, and spice. The
palate needs water to bring forth dried
fruits, rosewood, and coffee.*

KARUIZAWA 1995: NOH SERIES, BOTTLED 2008

SINGLE MALT 63% ABV

*The nose is hugely resinous, mixing
tiger balm, geranium, boot polish, prune,
and heavily oiled woods. There's also
mint chocolate with water. The palate
is lightly astringent and needs a drop
of water to release the tannic grip.
An exotic and floral whisky.*

KARUIZAWA 1971: CASK NO. 6878, BOTTLED 2008

SINGLE MALT 64.1% ABV

*Beeswax and sandalwood becoming
fragrant with tea, molasses, and smoke.
The palate is resinous with walnut, long
pepper, and Bolivar cigar.*

NIKKA COFFEY MALT WHISKY

NIKKA WHISKY FROM THE BARREL

NIKKA PURE MALT RED

NIKKA—GRAIN & BLENDS

Nikka 1, Aobaku, Sendaishi, Miyagiken;
Kurokawacho 7–6, Yoichimachi,
Yoichigun, Hokkaido
www.nikka.com

Japan's second-largest distillery company was founded in 1933 by Masataka Taketsuru. This charismatic distiller had learned the art of whisky-making in Scotland—at Longmorn in Speyside and Hazelburn in Campbeltown. Back in Japan, he initially worked with Shinjiro Torii, helping to establish Yamazaki distillery *(see p.298)*, which is now owned by Suntory. He then went to Hokkaido island in Japan, where conditions were closer to those in Scotland, and founded Yoichi distillery.

Taketsuru's company, Nikka, now part of Asahi Breweries, operates two malt distilleries at Yoichi and Miyagikyo. It also has grain plants and an ever-growing portfolio of styles, including blends and single malts. Like its domestic rivals, it produces all the whiskies for its in-house blends.

In recent years, Nikka has been focusing on the export market. Although its blends are available overseas, the thrust of its commercial push has been through its single-malt range branded as Nikka Miyagikyo *(see p.290)* and Nikka Yoichi *(p.294)*. Its blends include the Pure Malt Series *(opposite)* and Nikka Taketsuru Pure Malt range *(p.291)*.

NIKKA COFFEY MALT WHISKY

MALT WHISKY 45% ABV
Lemon sprinkled with black pepper and background vanilla on the feisty nose. The palate continues those themes, with the addition of milky coffee and prune juice.

NIKKA WHISKY FROM THE BARREL

BLEND 51.4% ABV
Nikka's award-winning blend of malts and grain is given further aging in first-fill bourbon casks. The nose is

NIKKA PURE MALT WHITE

NIKKA PURE MALT BLACK

NIKKA COFFEY GRAIN WHISKY

upfront, and slightly floral, with good intensity, peachiness, and a lift akin to rosemary oil and pine sap. The palate is lightly sweet, with some vanilla, a hint of cherry, and plenty of spiciness on the finish. This is a top blend.

NIKKA PURE MALT SERIES

This trio of "pure" (blended) malts are drawn from the wide range of different styles made at Nikka's two malt distilleries, Yoichi and Miyagikyo.

NIKKA PURE MALT RED

BLENDED MALT 43% ABV
Red is light and fragrant, with faint hints of pineapple, fresh apple, pear, and a gentle almond-like oakiness. This delicacy continues on the palate, along with a light citric finish.

NIKKA PURE MALT WHITE

BLENDED MALT 43% ABV
The smokiest member of the trio, with plenty of salt spray, fragrant dried lavender, and soot on the nose,

and the same herbal, oily note as From The Barrel. The palate is rich and soapy.

NIKKA PURE MALT BLACK

BLENDED MALT 43% ABV
Rich and sweet, with lots of black fruits, dark chocolate, and a little polished oak. More substantial than the Red, with an extra layer of smokiness and greater depth and power on the palate. Peppery on the finish.

NIKKA COFFEY GRAIN WHISKY

SINGLE GRAIN 45% ABV
Sweet-spicy aromas, with vanilla, cereal, and coconut. Tropical fruit, graham crackers, and toffee on the palate, with developing sweet oak.

WHISKY TOUR: JAPAN

Tokyo is a good starting point for the whisky lover. The city has myriad whisky bars and excellent train connections to the distilleries at Chichibu, Hakushu, and Gotemba. Further afield, Suntory's flagship distillery, Yamazaki, is also accessible by train, and can be easily combined with a visit to Kyoto or Osaka.

JAPAN

TOUR STATISTICS		
DAYS: 6	**LENGTH:** 530 miles (850 km)	**DISTILLERIES:** 4
TRAVEL: Shinkansen (bullet trains), local trains	**REGION:** Central Honshu, Japan	

THE STILLROOM AT CHICHIBU

DAY 1: CHICHIBU DISTILLERY

I **Chichibu,** Japan's newest distillery, started by Ichiro Akuto, has no visitor facilities yet, but whisky enthusiasts can arrange a personal tour by contacting the distillery in advance. Chichibu city is 90 minutes by train from Tokyo's Ikebukuro station. A taxi can be taken from the station to the distillery, which is outside the city. *(+81 (0)494 62 4601)*

Shinjiro Torii is revered in Japan as the founder of Suntory, which operates the Yamazaki and Hakushu distilleries on this tour.

MATSUE

Chugoku EXPY

KYOTO

YAMAZAKI

KOBE

OKAYAMA

4

OSAKA

FINISH

Chugoku EXPY

Sanyo EXPY

HIROSHIMA

FUKUOKA

DAY 2: SUNTORY'S HAKUSHU DISTILLERY

3 Situated in the southern Japanese Alps, the Suntory Distillery at **Hakushu** is surrounded by a lovely nature reserve. The nearest station is Kobuchizawa, which is 2 hours 30 minutes by express train (JR Chou Line) from Tokyo's Shinjuku Station. After exploring the distillery and museum you can try some of the hiking trails that run through the forest. It is then best to return to Tokyo to get a fast train connection to Gotemba. *(+81 (0) 551 35 2211)*

HAKUSHU DISTILLERY

DAYS 3–4: KIRIN'S GOTEMBA DISTILLERY

4 The town of **Gotemba** is the start of one of the main routes up Mount Fuji. It is also home to Kirin's Gotemba Distillery. Many visitors come to visit both. They start climbing Fuji in the afternoon to reach the 8th or 9th stage by nightfall, where there are huts for pilgrims. The summit of Fuji is reached at dawn. After descending, it is possible to get a bus back to Gotemba to visit the distillery. Although not the prettiest of distilleries, this has good facilities for visitors and a spectacular view of Fuji from its rooftop terrace. The train from Tokyo's Shinjuku Station takes about 1 hour 40 minutes. *(+81 (0) 550 89 4909)*

MOUNT FUJI AND TRAIN

DAYS 5–6: SUNTORY'S YAMAZAKI DISTILLERY

YAMAZAKI DISTILLERY

5 It is best to take the bullet train to either Kyoto or Osaka to make a base for visiting the Suntory Distillery at **Yamazaki,** the company's original and flagship whisky-making plant. Local trains from either city stop at J. R. Yamazaki station. The distillery is a 10-minute walk from the station. There are extensive visitor facilities, including an impressive tasting bar with exclusive bottlings. The distillery offers well-heeled clients a chance to buy a cask through its Owner's Cask scheme. There is also a traditional Shinto shrine to visit. *(+81 (0) 75 961 1234; www.theyamazaki.jp/en/distillery)*

NIKKA MIYAGIKYO 12-YEAR-OLD

NIKKA MIYAGIKYO 15-YEAR-OLD

NIKKA MIYAGIKYO 10-YEAR-OLD

NIKKA MIYAGIKYO

Nikka 1, Aobaku, Sendaishi, Miyagiken
www.nikka.com

Also known as Sendai after its
nearest main town, Nikka's
Miyagikyo was the second distillery
built by Nikka founder, Masataka
Taketsuru. Today, it has a malt
distillery with eight stills, a
grain plant with two different
set-ups, and extensive warehousing.
Like most Japanese distilleries,
it makes a wide range of spirit
styles. The predominant one—
which is most common in the
single-malt bottlings—is lightly
fragrant and softly fruity. But
there are some peaty examples,
too. The distillery is open to the
public, and is home to Nikka's
Coffey Grain Whisky.

A new release is a Miyagikyo
without an age statement, which
is made to be drunk *mizuwari*-style
(with water). The nose is floral
and light, and the palate shows
a touch of golden raisins.

NIKKA MIYAGIKYO 10-YEAR-OLD

SINGLE MALT 45% ABV
*Typical of the main distillery character,
this has an attractive floral lift: lilies, hot
gorse, lilac, with a touch of anise in the
background. The palate shows balanced,
crisp oak, some butterscotch notes, and
a pinelike finish.*

NIKKA MIYAGIKYO 12-YEAR-OLD

SINGLE MALT 45% ABV
*The extra two years fill out the nose with
flowers, giving way to soft tropical fruits,
such as mango and persimmon, as well
as richer vanilla pod character. Good
structure with a wisp of smoke.*

NIKKA MIYAGIKYO 15-YEAR-OLD

SINGLE MALT 45% ABV
*Bigger, with raisiny ex-sherry cask notes
alongside the toffee and superfruits.
The gentle distillery character is in
evidence, along with a hint of the fresh
floral nature of youth. The richest of
the expressions.*

NIKKA TAKETSURU 17-YEAR-OLD

NIKKA TAKETSURU 21-YEAR-OLD

NIKKA TAKETSURU PURE MALT

NIKKA TAKETSURU

Nikka 1, Aobaku,
Sendaishi, Miyagiken;
Kurokawacho 7–6, Yoichimachi,
Yoichigun, Hokkaido
www.nikka.com

This small range of blended
(vatted) malts is named after
the founder of Nikka, Masataka
Taketsuru. Like the Pure Malt
range, it is made up of component
whiskies from the firm's two sites
although, given the range of malts
produced at each of them, it would
be difficult to guess which element
came from which distillery.

NIKKA TAKETSURU PURE MALT

BLENDED MALT 43% ABV
*Sweet, sherried, and spicy on the nose,
with vanilla, honey, and red berries. Rich,
fruity notes in the mouth, with a hint of
smokiness and a relatively short finish.*

NIKKA TAKETSURU 17-YEAR-OLD

BLENDED MALT 43% ABV
*The biggest-selling expression in
the range, the 17-year-old has all*
*the complexity you would expect from
mature stock. There's more obvious
smoke at work than in the 12-year-old:
some cigar-box aromas, varnish, and
light leather. When diluted, a fresh
tropical-fruit character comes out. This
is what leads on the palate, before the
peat smoke begins to assert itself.
A clean, precise, and complex whisky.*

NIKKA TAKETSURU 21-YEAR-OLD

BLENDED MALT 43% ABV
*With this multi-award winner, the smoke
is immediate while the spirit behind is
thicker, richer, and darker: ripe berries,
cake mix, oak, and a touch of mushroom
or truffle indicative of age. Fruit syrups,
figs, prune, smoke, and multi-layered,
complex whisky.*

Nikka's Miyagikyo Distillery is set among the mountains and cherry orchards of Miyagi Prefecture to the northeast of Tokyo. Company legend has it that master distiller Masataka Taketsuru came here in the 1960s, tasted the water, and pronounced it good.

NIKKA YOICHI 10-YEAR-OLD

NIKKA YOICHI 12-YEAR-OLD

NIKKA YOICHI 20-YEAR-OLD

NIKKA YOICHI

Kurokawacho 7–6, Yoichimachi,
Yoichigun, Hokkaido
www.nikka.com

Although Yoichi's malts are most definitely Japanese, they do have close resemblances to their cousins in Scotland—the whiskies of Islay and Campbeltown in particular. A wide range of styles is made, but Yoichi is famous for its complex, robust, oily, and smoky malts.

The most youthful Yoichi, without an age statement, is intended as an introduction to the distillery and should be drunk *mizuwari*-style (with water) or *sodawari* (with soda). It is crisp and clean with light smoke, a hay-like note, and a sweet spot in the middle of the palate.

NIKKA YOICHI 10-YEAR-OLD

SINGLE MALT 45% ABV
There's a hint of maltiness in here, unusual for a Japanese single malt. Salt spray and light smoke on the nose initially, with some caramelized fruit notes. Yoichi's oiliness coats the tongue while the smoke changes from fragrant to sooty with dried flowers toward the finish.

NIKKA YOICHI 12-YEAR-OLD

SINGLE MALT 45% ABV
The understated qualities have been banished here. This is classic Yoichi—big, deep, robust, and complex. The peatiness adds an earthy character to the coal-like sootiness. Poached pear and baked peach give a balancing sweetness, offset by smoke, licorice, and heather.

NIKKA YOICHI 20-YEAR-OLD

SINGLE MALT 52% ABV
A huge, uncompromising nose, where the oiliness apparent in all the expressions is now to the fore. Deck oil or gun oil, seashores, kippers, and the funky notes of great maturity—leather, cedar, yew, and leaf-mold. Clean turmeric and coriander spiciness. The palate is massive, with decent mouthwatering acidity balancing the dry oak and smoke. Still fresh on the finish.

SUNTORY HAKUSHU 12-YEAR-OLD

SUNTORY HAKUSHU 18-YEAR-OLD

SUNTORY HAKUSHU DISTILLER'S RESERVE

SUNTORY HAKUSHU

Torihara 2913–1, Hakushucho,
Komagun, Yamanashi
www.suntory.co.jp

Located in a forest high in the
Japanese Alps, Hakushu was once
the largest malt distillery in the
world, with two huge stillhouses
producing a vast array of different
makes for the Suntory blenders.
These days, only one of the
stillhouses is operational, but
the ethos of variety is still adhered
to. Nowhere else offers such an
array of shapes and sizes of pot
stills. The Suntory bottlings of
Hakushu as a single malt seem
to echo the location, being light,
gentle, and fresh, though there
are also smoky and heavy versions.

SUNTORY HAKUSHU
12-YEAR-OLD

SINGLE MALT 43.5% ABV

*The best-selling Hakushu, the 12-year-
old nose is very cool, with cut grass
and a growing mintiness. There's a hint
of linseed oil, suggestive of youth.
The palate is sweet but quite slow, with
that minty, grassy character being given
a little depth by apricot fruitiness and
extra fragrance by a camomile note.*

SUNTORY HAKUSHU
18-YEAR-OLD

SINGLE MALT 43% ABV

*Balanced and slightly restrained.
Once again a vegetal note, this
time more like a tropical rain forest.
There's also plum, mango, hay, and
fresh ginger. Good acidity and toasty
oaky finish. There's a general fresh
acidity, cut with a generous delicate
sweetness. The palate is direct and
shows more toasty oak.*

SUNTORY HAKUSHU
DISTILLER'S RESERVE

SINGLE MALT 43% ABV

*This nose is herbal, with wet grass,
pine cones, and cucumber, and the
palate carries on those notes, along
with a waft of smoke and mint.*

SUNTORY HIBIKI 17-YEAR-OLD

SUNTORY HIBIKI 21-YEAR-OLD

SUNTORY HIBIKI 30-YEAR-OLD

SUNTORY HIBIKI

Torihara 2913–1, Hakushucho,
Komagun, Yamanashi
www.suntory.co.jp

Japan's most powerful distiller
was founded in 1923 by Shinjiro
Torii. Its fortunes were built on
blended whiskies based on malts
from its two distilleries: Yamazaki
and Hakushu. Although there is a
move toward single malts globally,
Suntory's blends, such as the
Hibiki range, are still regarded
as very important.

The Hibiki 12-year-old is
the most recent member of the
stable. It has a nose akin to plum,
pineapple, lemon, then fudge
and fresh, sappy oak. It is sweet
and thick on the tongue with
a menthol-like finish.

SUNTORY HIBIKI
17-YEAR-OLD

BLENDED MALT 43% ABV
*This, the original Hibiki, has a soft,
generous nose featuring super-ripe*

*fruits, light peatiness, a hint of heavy
florals (jasmine), and citrus. On the
palate, there's caramel, black cherry,
vanilla, rosehip, and light oak structure.*

SUNTORY HIBIKI 21-YEAR-OLD

BLENDED MALT 43% ABV
*Deep and sensual, with the density
and musty nature of great aged
whiskey. Black butter, sandalwood,
and an intriguing green herbal thread.
Perfumed and hinting at light smoke.
The palate is thick and ripe with plenty
of flowers and dried fruits. Sweet and
long on the tongue.*

SUNTORY HIBIKI 30-YEAR-OLD

BLENDED MALT 43% ABV
*This multi-award winner (it won Best
Blend in the World two years in a row
at the World Whiskies Awards) is huge
in flavor, with a compote of different
fruits: Seville orange, quince paste,
quite assertive wood, and walnuts,
followed by aniseed and fennel, and a
deep spiciness. The palate is sweet and
velvety, with Old English Marmalade to
the fore, along with sweet, dusty spices.*

THE YAMAZAKI DISTILLER'S RESERVE

THE YAMAZAKI 25-YEAR-OLD

THE YAMAZAKI 18-YEAR-OLD

THE YAMAZAKI 12-YEAR-OLD

SUNTORY YAMAZAKI

Yamazaki 5–2–2, Honcho,
Mishimagun, Osaka
www.suntory.co.jp

Yamazaki claims to be the first
malt distillery built in Japan,
and was home to the fathers of
the nation's whiskey industry,
Shinjiro Torii and Masataka
Taketsuru. Like Hakushu, it
produces a huge range of styles.
The official single-malt bottlings
concentrate on the sweet fruity
expression. Single-cask bottlings
have also been released. Most of
the older expressions have been
aged in ex-sherry casks, but there
is the occasional Japanese-oak
release for Japanese malt converts.

THE YAMAZAKI 12-YEAR-OLD

SINGLE MALT ABV 43%

The mainstay of the range, the 12-year-old is crisp, with a fresh nose of pineapple, citrus, flowers, dried herbs, and a little oak. The palate is sweet and filled with ripe soft fruits and a hint of smoke.

THE YAMAZAKI DISTILLER'S RESERVE

SINGLE MALT 43% ABV

Fragrant and delicately fruity, with sandalwood on the nose. Summer fruits, vanilla, and subtle spice on the palate, with nutmeg and cinnamon at the close.

THE YAMAZAKI 25-YEAR-OLD

SINGLE MALT 43% ABV

A huge, concentrated, almost balsamic sherried nose, with sweet raisin, pomegranate, molasses, fig jam, prune, rose petal, musk, leather, and burning leaves. The palate is bitter and quite tannic. It's very dry.

THE YAMAZAKI 18-YEAR-OLD

SINGLE MALT 43% ABV

With age, Yamazaki acquires more influence from oak. The estery notes of younger variants are replaced by ripe apple, violet, and a deep, sweet oakiness. This impression continues on the palate with a mossy, pine-like character and the classic Yamazaki richness in the middle of the mouth. This is an extremely classy whiskey.

THE SECRETS OF ...
YAMAZAKI

When Shinjiro Torii bought land near a small village on the old road between Kyoto and Osaka in 1921 he had a grand vision. There was no reason, he believed, that Japan couldn't make its own whisky. And he would create it here, at Yamazaki.

The only thing missing in his great scheme was someone with whisky-making knowledge. He found this in Masataka Taketsuru, a young scientist who had gone to Scotland to study chemistry, returning home with a Scots wife and a passion for whisky making. Yamazaki began distilling in 1924, and five years later, Japan's first whisky, Shirofuda (White Label), was launched.

Yamazaki is one of the world's most remarkable distilleries, and experimentation has never ceased. This is in part due to the Japanese distillers' idiosyncrasy in using only their own whiskies for their blends. Thus, the more complex the blend,

the more whiskies are required, so constant innovation is essential. Yamazaki is also at the forefront of the new, export-driven Japanese whisky industry. The domestic boom is long over, but distillers are courting a new generation. Though weaned on *shochu* (a traditional spirit), young Japanese, like their international contemporaries, are interested in single malt, individuality, and premium.

Who knows if Torii's vision ran to selling his whiskies in direct competition with Scotch, or if he dreamed that they would one day be seen as the equals of Scottish single malts. The fact is that they are.

▲ PLACE OF POWER
Yamazaki is the place where, in the 16th century, Sen no Rikyu, the creator of *cha-noyu* (tea ceremony), built his first tea house. The waters of three rivers merge here. Torii needed water and wanted humidity to help with maturation; this wooded site also simply felt right to him.

SUNTORY YAMAZAKI DISTILLERY

▲ SUNTORY'S FLAGSHIP
The original rustic wood and slate building is long gone, as are the first stills. Today, the distillery is a rather grand, imposing red brick structure topped with two large pyramids

◄ WASHBACKS

Yamazaki processes unpeated, lightly peated, and heavily peated malt. The two mash tuns produce different types of wort, and various yeast strains are used. Wort and yeast come together in the washbacks, and fermentation begins, although the length varies.

▲ TASTING NEW MAKE

Suntory's most recent preference for direct firing and smaller stills adds weight to the new make spirit. This new make is a medium-bodied, fruity malt with a subtle depth in the middle of the palate. Future bottlings are likely to contain a whiff of smoke.

◄ STILLS

The stillhouse at Yamazaki contains a remarkable collection of stills, which are mostly run in tandem. They include steam-fired stills of differing shapes and sizes. This distillery is renowned for its willingness to experiment; the smaller, direct-fired stills were added in 2005.

▲ MATURATION

A broad range of woods is used for maturation, including new oak, ex-bourbon, and ex-sherry casks. There is even a whisky that has been matured in casks formerly used to age plum liqueur. The official number of Yamazaki whisky varieties has never been revealed.

TENNESSEE YEAST DRA
BOURBON GRAIN PINC
FASHIONED MALTING SCOTCH DI
COPITA SWING MASH TUN POT S
PATENT ISLAY SINGLE MALT
PEAT FERMENTATION BLEND
HOGSHEADS STARCH COFFEY
YEAST DRAM RYE QUAICH CEREALS
GLENMORANGIE WHEAT HI
DISTIL PETARD RIEDEL TENNESSEE
DISTILL MATURATION BOURBON GRA
OLD FASHIONED MALTING SCOTCH DI
COPITA SWING MASH TUN POT S
PATENT ISLAY SINGLE MALT
PEAT FERMENTATION BLEND
HOGSHEADS STARCH COFFEY
DRAM RYE QUAICH CEREALS
GLENMORANGIE WHEAT HI
RIEDEL TENNESSEE
MATURATION BOURBON GRA
ISLAY SINGLE MALT

WHISKEYS WORTH THE WAIT

REST OF
THE WORLD

EUROPE • ASIA
AUSTRALASIA • AFRICA

WHISKEY STYLES
EUROPEAN WHISKY

Outside the key whiskey nations of Scotland and Ireland, there is a smattering of whisky distilleries across Western Europe. Northern countries such as Germany and Sweden have been distilling "aqua vitae" from grains for centuries, mainly in the form of vodka, gin, akvavit, korn, and schnapps. Southern countries such as France have long traditions of distilling fruits into eaux-de-vie.

In recent years, with global interest in whiskey increasing, some of these mostly small-scale, family-owned European distilleries have expanded into whisky-making. In the north, such operations are often an extension of existing beer breweries, whereas in the south, the stills used for brandy may also be used for whisky. For that reason, southern European whiskies often turn out fruitier than their northern counterparts. The use of a range of former wine casks for maturation also adds significantly to the sweet flavors of southern European whiskies.

The output of most European distilleries is small, but with a dedicated local following, so whisky releases can sell out within a few days. Apart from the Swedish Mackmyra, few are available outside their own countries. Other tiny whisky operations include Weutz (Austria), Fisselier (France), Brasch, Gruel, Höhler, Zaiser, and Rabel (Germany), Maison Les Vignettes and Bauernhof (Switzerland).

Further east, Turkey's state-owned brand Tekel cannot technically be called "whisky" because it is made from a mash of malted barley and rice. Kizlyar distillery in Dagestan, Russia, was founded in 2003 and produces single malt, grain, and blended whiskies.

PENDERYN LEGEND

SINGLE MALT 41% ABV

Light on the nose, with tropical fruit, vanilla, and honey, while the palate yields more vanilla, honey, and fruit, notably ripe bananas, leading into a relatively short peppery finish.

PENDERYN LEGEND

PENDERYN PEATED

PENDERYN MYTH

PENDERYN
WALES

Penderyn, near Aberdare
www.welsh-whiskey.co.uk

Currently the only whisky distillery in Wales, Penderyn was named "Microdistillery Whisky of the Year" in 2008 by leading American whiskey magazine *Malt Advocate*. It is indeed micro, producing only one cask a day. After a slow start, the distillery is now acknowledged worldwide as making exquisite whiskies. In his *Whisky Bible 2009*, Jim Murray describes Penderyn as "a prince of a Welsh whisky truly fit for the Prince of Wales." And it was HRH Prince Charles who opened the distillery to the public in June 2008, eight years after the first distillate ran off the single still. Capacity was greatly increased with the introduction of a second still in 2013 and a pair of traditional pot stills the following year. Whisky-

making in Wales started long before that: according to Penderyn, the Welsh may have been making whisky (*"gwirod"*) in the 4th century. It is also said that the American whiskey pioneers Evan Williams and Jack Daniel were from Welsh stock.

The core Penderyn range includes Legend, Peated, and Myth, with the latter undergoing its entire maturation in ex-Bourbon casks.

PENDERYN PEATED

SINGLE MALT 46% ABV

Sweet, aromatic smoke followed by vanilla, green apples, and refreshing citrus notes.

PENDERYN MYTH

SINGLE MALT 41% ABV

Vanilla, apple juice, and coconut milk on the light nose, with a thin palate offering citrus fruits, chocolate ice cream, and spicy notes in the medium to long finish.

THE ENGLISH WHISKY CO. CHAPTER 14

THE ENGLISH WHISKY CO. CHAPTER 15

THE ENGLISH WHISKY CO.

ENGLAND

St. George's Distillery, Harling Road, Roudham, Norfolk
www.englishwhisky.co.uk

According to Alfred Barnard, in his 1887 tome *Distilleries of the United Kingdom and Ireland*, England had at least four distilleries in the 1800s. These had all gone by the turn of the 20th century and it was not until 2006 that pot stills produced malt spirit in England again, thanks to The English Whisky Co. Whisky has been released in sequential chapters, in both unpeated and peated formats, while more mainstream Classic and Peated expressions are also available.

THE ENGLISH WHISKY CO. CHAPTER 14

SINGLE MALT 46% ABV

The nose is floral and fruity, with honey, vanilla, and orange. Oily on the palate, very fruity, vanilla custard, and ultimately a lengthy, drying finish.

THE ENGLISH WHISKY CO. CHAPTER 15

SINGLE MALT 46% ABV

This heavily peated, five-year-old expression features bonfire and citrus notes on the nose, with more citrus fruit on the palate, along with vanilla and chili, leading into a dry, oaky finish.

ADNAMS
ENGLAND

Copper House Distillery, Adnams PLC,
Sole Bay Brewery, Southwold, Suffolk,
www.adnams.co.uk

Adnams Brewery has been a
feature of the Suffolk town of
Southwold since 1872; in 2010,
a license was granted to distill on
the site, and distilling equipment
was subsequently installed in
a redundant brewhouse building.

Adnams released its first two
whiskies in 2013: Triple Grain
No.2 and Single Malt No.1. Both are
produced from local, East Anglian
grains, with the former matured in
American oak barrels and the latter
in French oak casks. Adnams also
distills gin, vodka, and absinthe.

ADNAMS COPPER HOUSE
SINGLE MALT NO.1

SINGLE MALT 43% ABV
*New oak opens the nose, soon followed
by vanilla, honey, and spices. Caramel,
apples, and black pepper on the palate.*

HICKS & HEALEY
ENGLAND

Healey's Cornish Cyder Farm,
Penhallow, Truro, Cornwall
www.thecornishcyderfarm.co.uk

St. Austell Brewery produces the
mash for Healey's whiskey—which
employs the Irish and US spelling.
This is then double distilled in
a small pair of Scottish-made copper
pot stills at the Cornish Cyder Farm,
located near Newquay. The stills
were installed in 2000, and in 2011,
a single cask was bottled, with
its 7-year-old single malt whiskey
subsequently hitting the shelves.
This was the oldest English
whisk(e)y available, and batches
are bottled each year, with a 2004
distillation being released aged eight.

HICKS & HEALEY SINGLE MALT
CORNISH WHISKEY 8-YEAR-OLD

SINGLE MALT 60.2% ABV
*Sweet fruits on the early nose, then malt,
ginger, and vanilla. Baked apple, cinnamon,
and caramel on the spicy palate.*

FRYSK HYNDER
THE NETHERLANDS

Us Heit Distillery, Snekerstraat 43,
8701 XC Bolsward, Friesland
www.usheitdistillery.nl

Us Heit (Frisian for "Our Father")
was founded as a brewery in
1970. In 2002, owner Aart van
der Linde, a whisky enthusiast,
decided to start distilling whisky
with barley from a local mill. It
is the same barley from which Us
Heit beer is made and it is malted
at the distillery. A 3-year-old single
malt, Frysk Hynder, has been
released in limited quantities
every year since 2005. Us Heit
uses different types of cask for
maturing, from ex-bourbon barrels
to wine casks and sherry butts.

FRYSK HYNDER 3-YEAR-OLD
SHERRY MATURED

SINGLE MALT 43% ABV
*Sweet nose, with sherry, soft spice, oak,
and figs. Smooth, sherried palate with
developing dark chocolate and spicy oak.*

MILLSTONE
THE NETHERLANDS

Zuidam, Weverstraat 6, 5111 PW,
Baarle Nassau
www.zuidam.eu

What started as a gin distillery some
50 years ago is now a company with
a second generation of the Zuidam
family at the helm. It produces
beautifully crafted single malts,
alongside excellent young and old
jenevers, as the Dutch call their gin.
The Millstone 5-year-old single malt
whisky was introduced in 2007,
to be followed by an 8-year-old
sibling. Zuidam uses ex-bourbon as
well as ex-sherry casks to mature its
whisky. A 10-year-old expression
is in the making.

MILLSTONE 5-YEAR-OLD

SINGLE MALT 40% ABV
*Delicate tones of fruit and honey
combined with vanilla, wood,
and a hint of coconut. Rich honey
sweetness, delicate spicy notes, and
a long vanilla oak finish.*

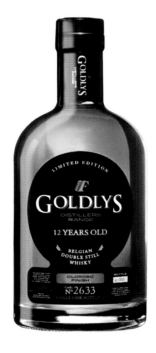

THE BELGIAN OWL
BELGIUM

The Owl Distillery, Rue Sainte
Anne 94, B4460 Grâce-Hollogne
www.belgianwhisky.com

Master Distiller Etienne
Bouillon founded this distillery
in the French-speaking part
of Belgium in 2004. He uses
home-grown barley and first-
fill bourbon casks to produce
a 3-year-old single malt whisky.
The first batch was bottled
in the fall of 2007. The Belgian
Owl Distillery was formerly
known under the names
Lambicool and PUR·E.

BELGIAN SINGLE MALT

SINGLE MALT 46% ABV
*This non-chill filtered malt offers
vanilla, coconut, banana, and
ice cream, topped with fig, followed
by a crescendo of other flavors such
as lemon, apples, and ginger. A long
finish, with ripe fruits and vanilla.*

GOLDLYS
BELGIUM

Graanstokerij Filliers,
Leernsesteenweg 5, 9800 Deinze
www.filliers.be

Flemish distiller Filliers has been
making grain spirits since 1880. In
2008, it surprised the whisky world
by launching two whiskies it had
been maturing for years. Their name
comes from the Lys River, which
is nicknamed the "Golden River"
because of the flax retted (soaked)
in it. Goldlys uses malt, rye, and
corn, and is distilled twice, first
in a column still, then in a pot still
—a similar process to making
bourbon. The spirit is then matured
in ex-bourbon casks, and a number
of "finishes" are available.

GOLDLYS 12-YEAR-OLD
OLOROSO CASK FINISH

DOUBLE STILL WHISKY 43% ABV
*Vanilla, honey, and citrus on the nose.
Oily palate of sherry and raisin leads
to a lengthy finish.*

GOUDEN CAROLUS
BELGIUM

Brouwerij Het Anker, Guido Gezellelaan
49, B-2800 Mechelen
www.hetanker.be

The Belgian beer brewery Het
Anker—makers of the famous
Gouden Carolus Tripel beer—first
ventured into whiskey-making in
2003. The current owner, Charles
Leclef, is the fifth generation of
the de Van Breedam family to own
the company. In 2008, 2,500
bottles of Gouden Carolus Single
Malt were bottled and distributed.

GOUDEN CAROLUS

SINGLE MALT 40% ABV
*Nicely balanced for a young whiskey,
with fruity, woody notes.*

ARMORIK
FRANCE

Distillerie Warenghem, Route de
Guingamp, 22300 Lannion, Bretagne
www.distillerie-warenghem.com

The Warenghem Distillery was
founded in 1900 to produce apple
cider and fruit spirits. It was not
until 99 years later that the owners
decided to start making other
types of spirits, including malted
beers and whisky. There are now
two types of whisky made here:
Armorik, a single malt, and WB
(Whisky Breton), a blend. The
type of casks used for maturation
is not specified.

ARMORIK WHISKY
BRETON CLASSIC

SINGLE MALT 46 % ABV
*Citrus fruits, spicy malt, hazelnuts,
and vanilla on the nose, while the full,
oily palate yields malt, honey, vanilla,
and dried fruits, before a spicy and
slightly salty finish.*

EDDU SILVER

EDDU GOLD

EDDU GREY ROCK

EDDU
FRANCE

Des Menhirs, Pont Menhir, 29700
Plomelin, Bretagne
www.distillerie.bzh

This is from the land of *menhirs*
(standing stones) and Calvados
distilled from apples. The Des
Menhirs Distillery started life as
a manufacturer of apple cider in
1986, but in 1998 branched out
into whisky. Most fruit distillers
that venture into whisky-making
use their existing equipment to
distill whisky on the side. Not so
this company: Des Menhirs built
a separate still for the exclusive
production of whisky, which it
distills not from barley but from
buckwheat (*eddu* in Breton). The
distillery currently carries three
different expressions of its Eddu
whisky—Silver, Gold, and Grey
Rock. The types of cask used are
not specified. In 2006 the distillery
was extended and now houses
a shop as well.

EDDU SILVER
BUCKWHEAT WHISKY 40% ABV
*Aromatic rose and heather on the
nose. Fruity, with a touch of honey,
marmalade, and some nutmeg.
Velvety body, with vanilla and oak
in the finish.*

EDDU GOLD
BUCKWHEAT WHISKY 43% ABV
*Almost identical to its Silver sibling—
with the same flowers and spices—
but higher in alcohol.*

EDDU GREY ROCK
BLEND 40% ABV
*A blended variety containing 30 percent
buckwheat. Orange and apricot flavors
combine with broom flower. A faint sea
breeze is framed by a hint of cinnamon.
Balanced flavors and a long, long finish.*

GLANN AR MOR
FRANCE

Crec'h ar Fur, 22610 Pleubian, Bretagne
www.glannarmor.com

Glann ar Mor means "by the sea" in Breton. The distillery opened in 2005 after eight years of planning. On November 17, 2008, the contents of one cask were emptied and bottled, rendering 305 bottles. The Glann ar Mor distillery now produces an unpeated single malt named Glann ar Mor and a peated single malt named Kornog (meaning "The West Wind" in Breton). Maturation takes place in first-fill Sauternes wine barriques and first-fill bourbon barrels. The company is building a new Scotch distillery at Gartbreck on Islay.

GLANN AR MOR

SINGLE MALT 46% ABV
Fairly complex, with ginger, vanilla, and a whiff of the sea, then grassy and leafy. Big fruit, including ripe apples and pears, framed in fine oak.

GUILLON
FRANCE

Hameau de Vertuelle,
51150 Louvois, Champagne
www.distillerie-guillon.com

The Guillon Distillery is located in the Champagne region of France, and was purpose-built in 1997 to produce whisky. It started distilling in 1999, distinguishing itself by the use of a variety of ex-wine casks for maturation. For the first maturation period, ex-Burgundy casks are used. After that, the whisky is finished for six months in casks that used to contain sweet wines like Banyuls, Loupiac, and Sauternes. Guillon bottles a premium blend at 40% ABV. The various single malts are bottled at 42, 43, and 46% ABV.

GUILLON CUVEE 42

SINGLE MALT 42% ABV
Barley, berry fruits, and a slight hint of smoke on the nose, with more barley plus apples, before a slightly ashy, fiery finish.

P&M
FRANCE

Domaine Mavela, Brasserie Pietra,
Route de La Marana,
20600 Furiani, Corsica
www.corsican-whisky.com

P&M is a fruitful cooperation between two companies on the Mediterranean island of Corsica. Founded as a brewery in 1996, Pietra produces the mash that is distilled at Mavela. The single malt whisky is aged in casks made from oak from the local forest. As well as single malts, P&M also produces a blended variant.

P&M PURE MALT

MALT 42% ABV
This complex, aromatic whisky has a subtle aroma of honey, apricot, and citrus fruit, and a rich flavor.

UBERACH
FRANCE

Bertrand Distillery, 3 rue du Maréchal
Leclerc, BP 21,
67350 Uberach, Alsace
www.distillerie-bertrand.com

The Bertrand brandy and liqueur distillery in Alsace dates from 1874 and has been run by the same family ever since. The Alsace region is blessed with particularly fertile, alluvial soil and the area around the distillery produces a range of fruits that are used in some of Bertrand's spirits. The company also produces beer and two non-filtered whiskies, Uberach Single Malt and Uberach Single Cask.

UBERACH SINGLE MALT

SINGLE MALT 42.2% ABV
Floral, fruity, and spicy, with black tea and hints of plums, as well as wax, and tobacco notes. Aromatic with good balance and an oaky, fruity finish.

WAMBRECHIES
FRANCE

1 Rue de la Distillerie,
59118 Wambrechies,
Nord-Pas-de-Calais
www.wambrechies.com

Wambrechies was founded in 1817 as a *jenever* (gin) distillery and is one of only three stills left in the region. It continues to produce an impressive range of jenevers, as well as one malt whisky and a *jenever* beer. Wambrechie whiskies are bottled at three and eight years old, with the younger whisky consisting of a lighter, floral blend and the older having a deeper, spicy character. They have also released two 12-year-old expressions.

WAMBRECHIES 8-YEAR-OLD

SINGLE MALT 40% ABV
Delicate nose, with aniseed, fresh paint, vanilla, and cereal notes. Smooth on the palate, with a fine malty profile. Spicy finish, with powdered ginger and milk chocolate.

HOLLE
SWITZERLAND

Hollen 52, 4426 Lauwil, Basel
www.single-malt.ch

Until July 1, 1999, it was strictly forbidden in Switzerland to distill spirit from grain, which was considered a food staple. After a change in the law, the Bader family, who had been making fruit spirits for a long time, started to distill from grains, and became the country's first whisky producer.

HOLLE

SINGLE MALT 42% ABV
Delicate aromas of malt, wood, and vanilla, with a flavor of wine. There are two varieties: one is matured in a white-wine cask, the other in a red-wine cask. A cask strength version is bottled at 51.1% ABV.

SINGLE LAKELAND
SWITZERLAND

Zürcher Nägeligässli 7,
2562 Port

The Zürcher Distillery was set up in 1968 by Heinz Zürcher, although he had been distilling and selling spirits since 1959. Whisky was first distilled at Zürcher in 2003. The spirit matures in Oloroso sherry casks for three years. The first bottling was released in 2007. Due to its popularity and low production rates, the single malt sells out very quickly.

SINGLE LAKELAND

SINGLE MALT 42% ABV
DISTILLED 2005 BOTTLED 2008
Perfectly balanced. Flavors of tannin and smoke. Smooth vanilla and cinnamon aromas.

WHISKY CASTLE
SWITZERLAND

Schlossstrasse 17, 5077 Elfingen www.
whisky-castle.com

Käsers Schloss (the Swiss name of the distillery) is owned by Ruedi and Franziska Käser. The couple started producing whisky in 2000 and expanded the business in 2006 to include themed events such as whisky dinners and whisky conferences at their premises. The brand name of their whisky in English is Whisky Castle, and there are a number of expressions, including Double Wood, Terroir, Smoke Barley (aged in new French oak casks), Smoke Rye, Full Moon, and Château (matured in Château d'Yquem wine casks).

WHISKY CASTLE FULL MOON

SINGLE MALT 43% ABV
Made from smoked barley during the full moon, it is a young whiskey with a sweetish aroma and taste.

REISETBAUER 7-YEAR-OLD

SINGLE MALT 43% ABV

Delicate and multi-layered on the nose, with slightly roasted aromas reminiscent of hazelnuts and dried herbs. Pleasant notes of bread and cereals on the palate. Slightly smoky, with fine spice.

REISETBAUER 12-YEAR-OLD

NOCK-LAND
AUSTRIA

Wolfram Ortner, Untertscherner Weg 3, 9546 Bad Kleinkirchheim
www.wob.at

Ortner specializes in luxury products, especially cigars, glasses, and fruit liqueurs. The company started producing Nock-Land whisky in 1996, named after the Nockberg Mountains nearby. Since 2014, two principal expressions have been available, namely Nock-Land Single Malt XV Double Matured (15-year-old) and the 6-year-old Double Matured, which has been finished in charred Limousin oak.

NOCK-LAND WHISKY

MALT 48% ABV

Sweet and malty with heavy notes of spice and tobacco. Rounded off with a faint whiff of honeycomb.

REISETBAUER
AUSTRIA

Axberg 15, 4062 Kirchberg-Thening
www.reisetbauer.at

Han Reisetbauer made his name as a quality distiller of fruit. He started distilling whisky in 1995, claiming to be the first Austrian to do so. Waldviertler Roggenhof Distillery *(see next entry)* makes the same claim.

Reisetbauer grows his own barley, and does his own malting and fermentation. The wash is double distilled, and he uses Trockenbeeremauslee and Chardonnay casks, allowing the spirit to absorb traces of fruit left in the wood, enhancing its flavor. His first bottling was released in 2002.

REISETBAUER 12-YEAR-OLD

MALT 48% ABV

Similar to the 7-year-old, with greater emphasis on fruit notes from the wine barrels used for maturation.

WALDVIERTLER J.H. SPECIAL PURE RYE MALT "NOUGAT"

WALDVIERTLER J.H. SPECIAL SINGLE MALT "KARAMELL"

WALDVIERTLER J.H. ORIGINAL RYE WHISKY

RYE WHISKY 41% ABV
Extremely sweet and dense on the nose, with honey, ripe peaches, and spicy rye. The palate is equally full and sweet, with honey, caramel, and a hint of lemon. An after-dinner dram.

WALDVIERTLER
AUSTRIA

Whiskeydestillerie J. Haider OG,
3664 Roggenreith 3
www.whiskyerlebniswelt.at

The Waldviertler Roggenhof Distillery was founded in 1995 and, like Reisetbauer *(see previous entry)*, claims to be the first whisky distillery in Austria. It produces five different whiskies. Two are single malts—J. H. Single Malt and J. H. Special Single Malt "Karamell." The other three are rye whiskies—J. H. Original Rye, J. H. Pure Rye Malt, and J. H. Special Pure Rye Malt "Nougat."

The company uses casks made from Manharstberger oak trees that grow in the local region. The whiskies are matured for between three and twelve years and offered as single-cask bottlings. Alcohol percentages vary from 41–54% ABV, and the flavors range from light vanilla to caramel, chocolate, and nougat.

Johann Haider, the master distiller and joint owner of Waldviertler Roggenhof, has also created the "Whiskey Experience" on the premises, consisting of an audio-visual tour and a café in which to sample various whiskies in coffee. Seminars are given on Haider's book *Fascination Whiskey*. Other spirits made here include vodka, gin, and brandy, but—unusually for a Continental European distillery—whisky is the main focus.

WALDVIERTLER J.H. SPECIAL PURE RYE MALT "NOUGAT"

RYE WHISKY 41% ABV
A gentle, sweet taste of honey, harmonizing perfectly with the light vanilla taste.

WALDVIERTLER J.H. SPECIAL SINGLE MALT "KARAMELL"

SINGLE MALT 41% ABV
Smoky and dry, with an intense caramel flavor.

HAMMERHEAD
CZECH REPUBLIC

www.stockspirits.com

Hammerhead whisky was distilled during 1989 at the Pradlo Distillery near Plzen, in western Czechoslovakia. The distillery had been making pot-still spirits for many years before experimenting with single malt whisky. This experiment is believed to be the only Bohemian single malt in the world.

Stock Spirits purchased the distillery without knowing of the whisky's existence. It was first bottled in 2011, and further releases have ensued since.

HAMMERHEAD 25-YEAR-OLD

SINGLE MALT 40.7% ABV
A very drinkable whisky made from Czech barley and finished in casks made of Czech oak. It has a nutty, floral nose, spiced palate of dried fruit, and an oaky, licorice finish.

GOLD COCK
CZECH REPUBLIC

Jelinek Distillery,
Razov 472, 76312 Vizovice
www.rjelinek.cz

Jelinek Distillery was founded at the end of the 19th century, and acquired the Gold Cock brand from Tesetice, a Czech distillery that no longer exists. For its two expressions—Red Feathers and a 12-year-old—Jelinek uses Moravian barley and water is sourced from an underground well that is rich in minerals. The type of cask used is not specified.

GOLD COCK RED FEATHERS

BLEND 40% ABV
Light and grainy, slightly metallic, and sweetish.

AMMERTAL
GERMANY

Hotel Gasthof Lamm, Jesinger
Hauptstrasse 55/57, 72070 Tübingen
www.lamm-tuebingen.de

Volker Theurer, the owner of Hotel Gasthof Lamm, is also a distiller and makes a whisky known as Black Horse Original Ammertal for a local market. The mash consists of 70 percent malted barley and 30 percent rye and wheat. It is aged in German oak ex-bourbon barrels and ex-sherry casks and is matured for a minimum of seven years.

ORIGINAL AMMERTAL

BLEND 40% ABV
Slightly nutty with some coffee notes and sweet grains.

BLAUE MAUS
GERMANY

Fleischmann, Bamberger Strasse 2,
91330 Eggolsheim-Neuses
www.fleischmann-whisky.de

The Fleischmann brandy distillery was founded in 1980 on the premises of the original family company— a grocery and tobacco shop. In 1996, after nearly 14 years of experimentation with whisky distillation, the company launched its first whisky expression. There are now eight different single cask malt whiskies available, including Blaue Maus, Grüner Hund, and Old Fahr, along with a single cask grain whisky—Austrasier.

BLAUE MAUS OLD FAHR

SINGLE MALT 40% ABV
The nose offers plain chocolate, ginger, and a slight oiliness. The oiliness continues onto the soft palate, which features contrasting vanilla and drying oak notes, with plain chocolate returning in the finish.

FRÄNKISCHER
GERMANY

Reiner Mösslein, Untere Dorfstrasse 8, 97509 Zeilitzheim
www.weingeister.de

Reiner Mösslein Distillery produces just one malt whisky—Fränkischer—and a variety of schnapps. The whisky is distilled from a blend of home-grown barley and grain. The spirit then matures in charred-oak casks for five years, lending it a smoky aroma.

FRÄNKISCHER 5-YEAR-OLD
GRAIN S 40% ABV
Chocolate and smoke on the nose, leading on to earthy flavors with oaky notes.

GLEN ELS
GERMANY

Hammerschmiede Spirituosen, Elsbach 11A, 37449 Zorge
www.hammerschmiede-spirituosen.de

The Hammerschmiede company was founded in 1984, and its first distillation of single malt whisky took place in autumn 2002. The spirit is stored in a smithy dating from 1250, and matures in Bordeaux and German oak casks that previously contained Amontillado, Fino, Manzanilla, Oloroso, and cream sherries, plus port, Marsala, or Madeira. Glen Els is available only as a single cask expression bottled at cask strength. The distillery operates with relatively small copper pot stills.

GLEN ELS THE JOURNEY
SINGLE MALT 43% ABV
A whiff of smoke on the nose, along with vanilla, toffee, and citrus fruits. The palate is sweet, with more vanilla and fudge, before a gentle smoky note develops.

SLYRS
GERMANY

Bayrischzellerstrasse 13 , 83727 Schliersee, Ortsteil Neuhaus
www.slyrs.de

Slyrs was founded in 1999 and makes a well-regarded whisky, which is distributed by Lantenhammer, a schnapps distillery located in the same Bavarian village. Slyrs is bottled after maturing for an unspecified time in new American white-oak barrels. Sherry cask matured and cask strength expressions have also been released.

SLYRS
SINGLE MALT 43% ABV
Some flowery aromas and spicy notes deliver a nice and easy dram. The taste varies according to the vintage.

BRAUNSTEIN
DENMARK

Braunstein, Carlsensvej 5, 4600 Koge
www.braunstein.dk

A microbrewery located in an old warehouse in Koge harbor, Braunstein was established in 2005 and uses a small still to make spirit from malted barley. The resulting spirit is clean, fresh, and fruity. Maturation takes place in ex-Oloroso sherry casks. A new edition of the whisky is added each year. The distillery also manufactures aquavit, herbal spirits, schnapps, and a beer called BB Amber Lager. Tastings are held each month, and there is a notably active Braunstein Whisky Club.

BRAUNSTEIN
SINGLE MALT (VARIABLE ABV)
Fruits, raisins, and chocolate come to the fore in this single malt that varies in strength from batch to batch.

BOX EXPLORER

BOX MESSENGER
SINGLE MALT 48.4% ABV
Matured in a mix of bourbon and Oloroso sherry casks, with a proportion of peated spirit. Pears, bananas, and vanilla on the nose, with a hint of peat. Pepper and salt on the herbal palate, finishing with banana.

TEERENPELI
FINLAND
Teerenpeli, Hämeenkatu 19, Lahti
www.teerenpeli.com

The first Teerenpeli Brewery was founded in May 1995 in Restaurant Teerenpeli, and the beer won several medals. In 2002 the new brewery and distillery were opened in Restaurant Taivaanranta. The brew house is situated in the dining room, while the fermentation and distilling equipment are in the cellar, along with a visitor center. Casks of Teerenpeli new malt whisky are available for sale to private individuals or corporate groups.

TEERENPELI 3-YEAR-OLD NO. 001
SINGLE MALT 43% ABV
A lot of grain (barley), vanilla, and oak wood with a slightly thick body.

BOX
SWEDEN
Sörviken 140, 872 96 Bjärtrå
www.boxwhisky.se

The Box Distillery came on stream in 2010, situated at the old Box Power Station, constructed in 1912 in the heart of the Ädalen region of Sweden. The distillery has two conventional, Scottish-built pot stills, and produces two styles of spirit—one unpeated, the other peated with imported Islay peat.

Box has issued a number of limited edition bottlings to date, and they have been met with great enthusiasm from Swedish whisky fans. The Pioneer, released in 2014, sold out its 5,000-bottle run in only seven hours.

BOX EXPLORER
SINGLE MALT 48.3% ABV
Light on the nose, with tropical fruit, honey, oak, and sweet peat smoke. Palate has lots of black pepper and peat smoke, with a gingery oak finish.

SPIRIT OF HVEN TYCHO'S STAR SINGLE MALT

SPIRIT OF HVEN SEVEN STARS NO.3 PHECDA'S SINGLE MALT

GOTLAND
SWEDEN

Gotland Whiskey AB, Sockerbruket,
62254 Romakloster
www.gotlandwhisky.se

Many decades ago, Sweden had
a thriving whisky industry, and
recent years have seen the number
of operational distilleries in the
country rise to eight. Gotland was
created in a former sugar factory,
not far from the historic city of
Visby, and the first spirit flowed
from the Scottish-built pot stills in
2012. Local barley is used in whisky
production, with onsite maltings
in operation, and both peated
and unpeated whiskies are being
produced. It is called "Isle of Lime"
because of the large quantity of
limestone found on Gotland island.

GOTLAND ISLE OF LIME

SINGLE MALT 40% ABV
*Light and fruity on the nose, with
vanilla, straw, and a hint of coconut
on the medium-bodied palate.*

HVEN
SWEDEN

Backafallsbyn AB,
Isle of Hven, S:t Ibb
www.hven.com

Spirit of Hven micro-distillery
is located on the island of Hven,
found in the Oresund Strait
between Sweden and Denmark.

Opened in 2008, the Hven
Distillery has only the third
pot still built in Sweden, older
Swedish distilleries often
importing secondhand stills
from Scottish distilleries.

Today, some malting is practiced
onsite, with Swedish peat (and
even seaweed) used in the drying
process. As well as whisky, the
distillery also produces rum, gin,
Calvados, and aquavit.

Among the whiskies currently
available are Urania (made using
barley from Scotland, Belgium,
and Hven, and matured in
casks from America, France,
and Spain), Seven Stars No.2

Merak Single Malt Whisky, and
Sankt Claus (matured in French
oak casks that previously held
Merlot wine).

SPIRIT OF HVEN TYCHO'S
STAR SINGLE MALT

SINGLE MALT 41.8% ABV
*New leather and orchard fruits, peat
smoke, and a slight sea salt on the
nose. More peat on the palate, with
freshly cut hay, orange, and pepper.*

SPIRIT OF HVEN SEVEN STARS
NO.3 PHECDA'S SINGLE MALT

SINGLE MALT 45% ABV
*Barbecue smokiness, brine, and ginger
on the nose, with developing honey
and pepper. The palate is quite oily,
with cinnamon, honey, more smoke,
and increasingly spicy and dry nutty
and oak notes.*

SMÖGEN
SWEDEN

Smögen Whisky AB, Ståleröd Heather
Liden 1 Hunnebostrand,
www.smogenwhisky.se

Smögen, a farm-based distillery
on the west coast of Sweden,
started producing whisky in 2010.
Designed by its owner, lawyer and
whisky aficionado Pär Caldenby,
it has a 200-gallon (900-liter) wash
still and a 130-gallon (600-liter)
spirit still, with an annual capacity
of some 7,700 gallons (35,000
liters). Caldenby imports heavily
peated malt from Scotland.

Smögen's first release, Smögen
Primör, came in 2013. It is a
3-year-old cask strength matured
in European oak and ex-Bordeaux
wine casks.

SMÖGEN PRIMÖR

SINGLE MALT 63.7% ABV
*Earthy nose of sweet smoke, salt,
leather, and cocoa. Sweet peat on
the palate, with berries and spices.*

MACKMYRA SVENSK EK

MACKMYRA BRUKSWHISKY

MACKMYRA SVENSK RÖK

MACKMYRA
SWEDEN

Mackmyra, Kolonnvägen 2, Gävle
www.mackmyra.se

Mackmyra was founded in 1999 by the Swedish engineer Magnus Dardanell and a group of friends. In 2012, a remarkable new 120-foot-tall (37-meter), gravity-fed distillery opened a few miles from the Valbo original, and all commercial distilling now takes place on that site. The first Mackmyra distillery has been retained, however, and is still used for occasional special runs and to host marketing activities.

Having first released a series of six "Preludium" expressions during 2006 and 2007, many other bottlings have followed, and the core range now consists of Brukswhisky, Svensk Ek (matured in Swedish oak barrels), and the smoky Svensk Rök.

Mackmyra matures its spirit in several locations, including in a series of underground warehouses in the old Bodås mine, on Fjäderholmarna (an island near Stockholm), at Häckeberga Castle, and on the historic Gut Basthorst estate in Germany.

MACKMYRA SVENSK EK
SINGLE MALT 46.1% ABV
Toasted oak notes on the nose, with honey and citrus fruits. More honey and citrus notes on the palate, with malt, ginger, pepper, and spicy oak.

MACKMYRA BRUKSWHISKY
SINGLE MALT 41.4% ABV
The nose is light, with pine, cereal, citrus, and spicy toffee. The palate is also light and approachable, with cinnamon, vanilla, raspberries in cream, lively spices, and mild oak.

MACKMYRA SVENS RÖK
SINGLE MALT 46.1% ABV
Peat smoke, citrus fruit, and vanilla on the nose, with a palate displaying sooty peat, more citrus fruit, and a hint of honey, with lingering spiciness.

DYC PURE MALT

DYC FINE BLEND

DYC 8-YEAR-OLD

DYC
SPAIN

Beam Global España SA, Pasaje Molino del Arco, 40194 Palazuelos de Eresma, Segovia
www.dyc.es

The first whisky distillery in Spain was founded in 1959 close to Segovia and started producing whisky in 1963. It stands next to the Eresma River, famous for the excellent quality of its water. The distillery is now owned by Beam Suntory. DYC (which stands for Destilerías y Crianza del Whiskey) comes in four versions. There is an unaged expression, called Fine Blend, and an 8-year-old; these are both blends of various grains. The pure malt, which has no age statement, is a blended malt, and, since 2009, there has also been a 10-year-old single malt.

The spirits mature in American oak barrels and are primarily sold on the home market. The Spanish tend to drink it in a mix with cola and ask at the bar for a "whisky-dyc," pronouncing it "whisky-dick."

DYC 8-YEAR-OLD
BLEND 40% ABV
Floral, spicy, smoky, grassy, with a hint of honey and heather. Smooth, creamy mouthfeel; malty with hints of vanilla, marzipan, apple, and citrus. A bittersweet, long, smooth finish.

DYC PURE MALT
BLENDED MALT 40% ABV
Sophisticated, fragrant bouquet with hints of citrus, sweetness, honey, and vanilla. Full-bodied, rich malt flavor. The finish is long, sophisticated, and subtle, with hints of heather, honey, and fruit.

DYC FINE BLEND
BLEND 40% ABV
Clean, with a hint of fruit, spice, and toasted wood. Malty, spicy, smooth, and creamy mouthfeel. The finish is smoky and spicy.

WHISKEY STYLES
ASIAN WHISKY

India is the largest consumer of whisky in the world. Along with other parts of Asia, its spirits industry was founded by European expatriates in the 18th century. Western spirits such as gin and whisky were known throughout these countries as "locally made foreign liquor" (LMFL). In India, the British Raj named it "Indian-made foreign liquor" (IMFL).

To this day, the raw materials and processes for LMFL/IMFL are not defined by law. However, a brand of "Indian whisky" made from molasses alcohol and whisky essence is not allowed to bear the name "whisky" within the EC and many other export markets. The Thai Mekhong brand used to be described as "whisky," but is now marketed as "rum." Most LMFL and IMFL spirits are made in industrial ethanol plants. However, there are a few grain and pot still malt distilleries in India, Pakistan, Taiwan, and Israel.

Categories of Asian whisky:

Extra Neutral Alcohol (ENA) Made by fermentation and distillation in continuous stills, typically of molasses, rice, millet, buckwheat, or barley. Basic Asian whiskies are made from ENA mixed with whisky essence and other artificial flavorings.

Blended Whisky A mix of ENA whisky and locally produced malt whisky and/or bulk imported whisky. Where an age statement is given, this is the age of the imported whisky. The product does not pass the EC definition as "whisky."

Malt Whiskey Blends of 100 percent malt whiskies, domestic or foreign, qualify as "whisky" in the EC if matured for at least three years.

Single Malt Whisky Made from malted barley in a single distillery. So long as this is matured for at least three years, it meets EC regulations.

MURREE'S CLASSIC 8-YEAR-OLD

MURREE'S RAREST 21-YEAR-OLD

8PM CLASSIC

8PM ROYALE

MURREE
PAKISTAN

Murree Distillery, National
Park Road, Rawalpindi
www.murreebrewery.com

Murree began life in 1860 as
a brewery serving the needs of
British troops stationed in the
Punjab, and today it still makes
the leading brand of beer in
Pakistan. It was built in Ghora
Gali, 6,000 ft (1,830 m) above
sea level in the foothills of the
Western Himalayas, and took its
name from a nearby hill station.
In 1889, the company built another
brewery in Rawalpindi, and
it was here, 10 years later, that
the distillery was installed.

By this time, Rawalpindi was
part of Pakistan, but a dispensation
was granted to the non-Muslim
owners to distill alcoholic drinks
"for visitors and non-Muslims."
This makes it the only distillery
of alcoholic beverages in a Muslim
country; the oldest continuing

industrial enterprise in Pakistan;
and one of the oldest public
companies on the subcontinent.

The barley comes from the UK
and is malted in floor maltings
and Saladin boxes. The four large
open-air wash stills have stainless-
steel pots and copper heads and
condensers. Two spirit stills are
under cover. Some of the spirit
is filled into cask, most into large
vats (some made from Australian
oak), and matured in cellars
equipped with a cooling system.

MURREE'S CLASSIC 8-YEAR-OLD
SINGLE MALT 43% ABV
*A flowery nose and finish, somewhat
green, with a hard-candy taste.
Unlikely to be pure malt whisky.*

MURREE'S RAREST
21-YEAR-OLD
SINGLE MALT 43% ABV
*This is the oldest whisky to have been
produced in Asia and has developed
and deepened the Murree key notes with
a big dose of wood-extractive flavors.*

8PM
INDIA

Owner: Radico Khaitan
www.radicokhaitan.com

Launched as recently as 1999,
8PM had the singular distinction
of selling a million cases in its first
year (it now sells 3 million). The
brand owner is Radico Khaitan,
which describes itself as "one
of India's oldest and largest liquor
manufacturers." It is owned
and managed by veteran distiller
Dr. Lalit Khaitan and his son
Abhishek. The company owns
other whisky brands, including
Whytehall *(see p.324)*, and it
has recently formed a partnership
with Diageo, the world's largest
drinks conglomerate, to produce
Masterstroke *(see p.322).*
The company's headquarters
are at Rampur Distillery, Uttar
Pradesh. Established in 1943,
it is now a gigantic unit with a
capacity of over 20 million gallons
(90 million liters) of alcohol a year

in three distinct operations: a
small malt distillery, a recently
opened grain distillery, and
a molasses distillery making ENA
(see p.318), anhydrous alcohol,
ethanol, and gasohol (which is
mixed with gasoline and used as
fuel). As well as whisky, Radico
Khaitan produces rum, brandy,
gin, and vodka.

8PM CLASSIC
BLEND
*Made from "a mix of quality grains,"
this has a core that promises "thaath"
(boldness, opulence) and "the reach
of a man to the dream world."*

8PM ROYALE
BLEND
*A blend of Indian spirits and mature
Scotch malt whiskies.*

AMRUT PEATED INDIAN SINGLE MALT

AMRUT SINGLE MALT

AMRUT INDIAN SINGLE MALT CASK STRENGTH

AMRUT
INDIA

www.amrutwhisky.co.uk

The family-owned company of Amrut Distilleries was founded in 1948 by Shri J. N. Radhakrishna Jagdale to supply bottled liquor to the Ministry of Defence. He was succeeded in 1976 by his son, Shri Neelakanta Rao Jagdale, the current chairman, who has focused on innovation, product quality, and transparency in the IMFL industry.

In 2002, Amrut experimented with the sale of miniatures in Indian restaurants in the UK. It was very successful in Glasgow, and the brand now features at European whisky fairs.

In Hindu mythology, the *amrut* was a golden pot containing the elixir of life. The whisky of the same name is made from barley grown in the Punjabi foothills of the Himalayas. This is malted in Jaipur and distilled in small

batches 3,000 ft (900 m) above sea level in Bangalore, where it is also matured in ex-bourbon and new oak casks and bottled without chill-filtration.

AMRUT INDIAN SINGLE MALT CASK STRENGTH

SINGLE MALT 61.9% ABV

Lightly fruity and cereal-like, with the bourbon cask introducing toffee. More woody, spicy, and malty with water. Similar in profile to a young Speyside malt.

AMRUT PEATED INDIAN SINGLE MALT

SINGLE MALT 62.78% ABV

Cereal and kippery smoke on the nose; oily, with salt and pepper. The taste is sweet and malty, with a whiff of smoke in the finish.

AMRUT SINGLE MALT

SINGLE MALT 40% ABV

A fresh and fruity nose, with a trace of spice, ginger, and anise. The taste is smooth and sweet, the finish is short.

ANTIQUITY
INDIA

Owner: United Spirits
www.unitedspirits.in

Antiquity is owned by the long-established Indian trading firm Shaw Wallace, now part of United Spirits. It is India's most expensive whisky, and won a gold award at the World Beverage Competition in 2007 in the "Scotch Whisky" category. It is, in fact, a blend of Scotch whisky, Indian malt whisky, and ENA.

United Spirits is the largest spirits company in India, and among the top three in the world. It is also the spirits division of the massive United Breweries Group.

ANTIQUITY
BLEND 42.8% ABV
A mild, biscuity nose, with some well-integrated fruit and floral notes. The taste is sweet overall, with some sulfur traces in the medium-length finish.

ARISTOCRAT
INDIA

Jagatjit Industries,
91 Nehru Place, New Delhi
www.jagatjit.com

Aristocrat comes from Jagatjit Industries—the third largest spirits producer in India, and a leading producer of IMFL from grains rather than molasses. The company was founded in 1944 by L. P. Jaiswal, under the patronage of the Maharaja of Kapurthala, Jagatjit Singh, with the guiding philosophy "Spirit of Excellence." Aristocrat is widely referred to as "AC" ("A" for "Aristo," "C" for "Crat") and a brand with this abbreviated name recently joined the portfolio.

ARISTOCRAT
BLEND 42.8% ABV
This is certainly not a pure malt whisky. Indeed, some commentators believe it might be an IMFL with a dash of malt extract.

BAGPIPER
INDIA

Owner: United Spirits
www.unitedspirits.in

Formerly "The world's no. 1 non-Scotch whisky," Bagpiper occupied fourth place with sales of nearly 11.6 million cases in 2013. An IMFL, probably made from molasses alcohol and concentrates, it was launched by the United Spirits subsidiary Herbertson's in 1987 and, in its first year, sold 100,000 cases. The brand has always been closely associated with Bollywood, India's huge film-production industry, and has successfully won accreditation from many movie stars. The company also broadcasts a weekly *Bagpiper* show on TV, and sponsors talent-spotting programs.

BAGPIPER GOLD
BLEND 42.8% ABV
The premium expression of Bagpiper, but still has a somewhat artificial taste and is best drunk with a mixer like cola.

BLENDERS PRIDE
INDIA

Owner: Pernod Ricard
www.pernod-ricard.com

Since it fell under the ownership of Pernod Ricard, the brand has been neck and neck with Royal Challenge *(see p. 324)* as the bestseller in its sector. It is a premium IMFL (made from Scotch malts and Indian grains), whose name comes from a story about the master blenders who exposed a cask of whisky to the warmth of the sun at regular intervals. The delicate sweetness and aromatic flavor of the blend are testimony to the success of their experiment.

BLENDERS PRIDE
BLEND 42.8% ABV
A smooth and rich mouthfeel, with a sweet taste that gives way to a disappointingly dull finish.

MCDOWELL'S NO. 1 RESERVE

MCDOWELL'S SINGLE MALT

IMPERIAL BLUE
INDIA

Owner: Pernod Ricard
www.pernod-ricard.com

Imperial Blue is Pernod Ricard's second-best-selling brand in India, selling around 11 million cases in 2013. Launched in 1997, it was previously a Seagram's brand, benefitting hugely from Pernod Ricard's acquisition of Seagram in 2001, jumping from producing under half a million cases to over a million by 2002. Imperial Blue hit the headlines in 2008 when some bottles in Andhra Pradesh were found to be understrength. It later transpired that they had been sabotaged by disgruntled workers.

IMPERIAL BLUE

BLEND 42.8% ABV

In spite of the "grain" in its name, Imperial Blue is a blend of imported Scotch malt and locally made neutral spirit. It is light, sweet, and smooth.

MASTERSTROKE
INDIA

Owner: Diageo Radico
www.radicokhaitan.com
www.diageo.com

Masterstroke De Luxe Whiskey, an IMFL priced for the "prestige" category, was launched by Diageo Radico in February 2007. The company is a joint 50:50 venture between Radico Khaitan Ltd. *(see 8PM, p.319)*, "India's fastest-growing liquor manufacturer," and the world's largest drinks company, Diageo. It is their first joint venture.

Within three months the brand was being endorsed by Bollywood superstar Shah Rukh Khan.

MASTERSTROKE

BLEND 42.8% ABV

A rich nose and mouthfeel, lent by a liberal amount of Blair Athol single malt. Well-balanced, with the light finish characteristic of Indian-made foreign liquors.

MCDOWELL'S
INDIA

Owner: United Spirits
www.unitedspirits.in

Scotsman Angus McDowell founded McDowell & Co. in Madras in 1826 as a trading company specializing in liquor and cigars. In 1951 it was acquired by Vitall Mallya, owner of United Breweries. McDowell's No.1 was launched in 1968, and currently sells over 23 million cases a year, making it the second-best-selling Indian-produced whisky in India.

A malt whisky distillery was commissioned by McDowell & Co. at Ponda, Goa, in 1971. It employs the distilling regime used for Scotch malt, with maturation in ex-bourbon casks for around three years. It is claimed that the heat and humidity of Goa leads to a more rapid maturation.

The product is described as "the first-ever indigenously developed single malt whisky in Asia." Three main expressions are available: two blends, called No. 1 Reserve and Signature Rare, and a single malt. McDowell also produces "the world's first diet whisky," as it calls it. This is a blend of "reserve" whisky and garcenia, an Indian herb reputed to control cholesterol levels and burn off fat.

MCDOWELL'S NO.1 RESERVE

BLEND 42.8% ABV

"Blended with Scotch and Select Indian Malts," this has a nose of dried figs and sweet tobacco and, later, prunes and dates. A sweet taste initially, then burned sugar and a short finish.

MCDOWELL'S SINGLE MALT

SINGLE MALT 42.8% ABV

A true single malt, with a fresh cereal and fruity nose and a sweet, pleasantly citric taste, not unlike a young Speyside.

PAUL JOHN BOLD

PAUL JOHN BRILLIANCE

PAUL JOHN EDITED

OFFICER'S CHOICE
INDIA

Owner: Allied Blenders and Distillers
www.abdindia.com/officers_choice

Available in some 18 countries, Officer's Choice has become one of the largest whisky brands in the world since its 1988 launch. Sales have risen at 14 percent per year over the past five years, with sales of 23 million cases between 2014 and 2015. It enjoys a 37 percent share in the Indian whisky market, jostling for a top spot with McDowell's No.1 Reserve. Two "semi-premium" variants of Officer's Choice are also available: Blue, which appeared in 2012, and Black, released two years later. All expressions comprise Indian grain whisky and Scottish blended malts.

OFFICER'S CHOICE
BLEND 42.8% ABV
The nose is spirit-y, with a hint of rum, while the palate yields caramel and cinnamon before a short finish.

PAUL JOHN
INDIA

John Distilleries Pvt. Ltd.,
110, Pantharapalya, Mysore Road,
Bangalore 560 039
www.pauljohnwhisky.com

Paul John single malts are produced on the tropical coast of Goa, using six-row barley grown on the foothills of the Himalayas. Distillation takes place in traditional copper pot stills, which can yield up to 660 gallons (3,000 liters) of spirit per day. Casks are stored in a temperature-controlled cellar, but the climate of Goa means that whiskies mature relatively quickly. The first single malt was distilled in 2007 and the initial release took place in autumn 2012.

Paul John established John Distilleries Ltd. (JDL) in 1992, and, as well as whisky, the company also produces brandy and wine. Its "flagship" brand Original Choice Whisky sells over 10 million cases a year. In recent times, however, there has been a conscious effort to focus on single malts, and a range of peated and unpeated expressions is now available, featuring both single malts and single cask single malts.

PAUL JOHN BOLD
SINGLE MALT 46% ABV
Vanilla, honey, lively spices, and peat on the nose. Honey, oak, spice, and smoke on the full palate.

PAUL JOHN BRILLIANCE
SINGLE MALT 46% ABV
Honey, cinnamon, and spice on the fragrant nose. Sweet, spicy, and smooth on the palate, with a suggestion of milk chocolate.

PAUL JOHN EDITED
SINGLE MALT 46% ABV
The nose is fruity, with honey, coffee, and gentle smoke. Grassy and peaty on the palate, with more coffee coming through.

ROYAL CHALLENGE
INDIA
Owner: United Spirits
www.unitedspirits.in

This "blend of rare Scotch and matured Indian malt whiskies" is owned by Shaw Wallace, a part of United Spirits since 2005. It is described as "the iconic" premium Indian whisky and, until 2008, it was also the best-selling premium Indian whisky, but is now severely challenged by Blenders Pride.

ROYAL CHALLENGE
BLEND 42.8% ABV
A soft, rounded nose, with traces of malt, nuts, caramel, and a light rubber note. These aromas translate well in the taste at full strength. With water, it remains dense and full-bodied but the taste, diluted, is not as heavy. Very sweet, slightly nutty, and mouth-drying, but with a longish finish.

ROYAL STAG
INDIA
Owner: Pernod Ricard
www.pernod-ricard.com

Seagram's Royal Stag broke the million-cases-a-year barrier in 2000. Early the following year it was acquired by Pernod Ricard, when the Seagram empire was carved up between the French company and Diageo. The new owner continued the Seagram name, adopting the brand as its leader in the "prestige" sector of the vigorous Indian market. It also improved the blend, which is a combination of blended Scotch malts and Indian grain whiskies. Sales in 2013 amounted to 14.7 million cases, making it the third-best-selling Indian whisky.

ROYAL STAG
BLEND 42.8% ABV
For a standard blend, this shapes up well: fresh and sweet to start, with spice and cereal notes, and a firm finish.

SIGNATURE
INDIA
Owner: United Spirits
www.unitedspirits.in

The recently introduced Signature Rare Aged Whiskey comes from the McDowell's stable, owned by United Spirits, and has the slogan "Success is Good Fun." It is a blend of Scotch and Indian malt whiskies and is the fastest-growing brand in the company's portfolio, selling over 600,000 cases in 2006–7. It has also won a clutch of international awards, including a gold in the Monde Selection 2006.

SIGNATURE
BLEND 42.8% ABV
A rich nose, with a distinct medicinal note. Straight, the taste is surprisingly sweet, with smoky and medicinal undertones, becoming less sweet with water. Relatively light in body, with a distinct peaty, smoky edge.

WHYTEHALL
INDIA
Owner: Radico Khaitan
www.radicokhaitan.com

Another Radico Khaitan brand *(see 8PM, p.319)*, Whytehall became a part of the portfolio after Radico bought out the stake of its former joint venture partner, Bacardi, in Whytehall India Limited in July 2005.

Whytehall is made in the company's distillery at Hyderabad, and now sells half a million cases per annum. The brand won a silver medal at the International Wine and Spirit Competition 2007 and a gold medal at the Monde Selection in Belgium in 2008.

WHYTEHALL
BLEND 42.8% ABV
A superior IMFL blend of aged Scotch malts and Indian spirits.

KAVALAN PODIUM SINGLE MALT

KAVALAN KING CAR CONDUCTOR SINGLE MALT

KAVALAN CLASSIC SINGLE MALT

KAVALAN CONCERTMASTER PORT CASK FINISH SINGLE MALT

KAVALAN
TAIWAN

Kavalan Distillery, No. 326, Sec. 2, Yuanshan Road, Yuanshan, Yilan
www.kavalanwhisky.com

The distillery is located in north-eastern Taiwan and was created by the King Car Food Industrial Company, with Scottish whisky consultant Dr. Jim Swan playing a significant role in its design. The distillery, completed in March 2006, was equipped with two pairs of copper pot stills, giving an annual capacity of 330,000 gallons (1.5 million liters).

The year 2015 saw capacity dramatically increase to around 990,000 gallons (4.5 million liters) with the addition of six more stills. The intention is for production to increase to 7.8 million gallons (9 million liters) per year.

This expansion is due to the overwhelmingly positive response the whiskies have received since first released in 2008. The distillery visitor center now welcomes more than one million people per year.

Although the Classic Single Malt is the best-selling Kavalan, there is a wide range of other expressions available. Most are around three years of age as Taiwan's sub-tropical climate enhances early maturation and leads to significant spirit losses due to evaporation.

KAVALAN PODIUM SINGLE MALT
SINGLE MALT 46% ABV

The nose is light and fresh, with honey, coconut, and vanilla. Ripe bananas, honey, and ginger on the palate, with spicy oak.

KAVALAN KING CAR CONDUCTOR SINGLE MALT
SINGLE MALT 46% ABV

A fresh nose of banana, apple, and floral notes. More banana on the voluptuous palate, with coconut milk and vanilla.

KAVALAN CLASSIC SINGLE MALT
SINGLE MALT 40% ABV

Vanilla and fruit cocktail on the nose, tropical fruits, spice, vanilla, and soft oak on the palate.

KAVALAN CONCERTMASTER PORT CASK FINISH SINGLE MALT
SINGLE MALT 40% ABV

Port, berry fruits, honey, and milk chocolate on the nose, while tropical fruits and sweet oak develop on the palate.

WHISKEY STYLES
AUSTRALASIAN WHISKY

Australia and New Zealand have a significant number of whisky distilleries producing malt. Some of these malts have been favorably compared with the best from Scotland. Tasmania, in particular, has ideal conditions for whisky production. However, Australasian whiskys can be hard to track down outside the continent, as the markets are mainly domestic.

Until 1938, Australasia was the largest export market for Scotch whisky, and it is hardly surprising that enterprising settlers of Scots descent established distilleries in Australia and New Zealand during the 19th century. Most were illicit farm stills, but there were a couple of short-lived industrial ventures, like the New Zealand Distillery, Dunedin (1867–73), and the Crown Distillery, Auckland, New Zealand (1865–79), which both opened in response to the halving of duties on locally made spirits. They soon closed when duties rose again, following pressure on the government by Scottish banks, which were payrolling the construction of the country's railways.

The first attempt to revive the distilling tradition in New Zealand was Wilson's Willowbank Distillery at Dunedin (1964–95), whose Lammerlaw brand became reasonably well known in Europe and East Asia, as well as in its home market. During the 1990s, however, the focus for revival was in Australia, particularly in Tasmania, where five distilleries opened, and that number has now grown to nine. The reasons for this are a combination of climate— Tasmania has the purest air in the world, and copious clean water dumped on the island by the Roaring Forties—and plenty of fertile country for growing barley. Away from Tasmania, Australia now boasts nine additional distilleries, located in Victoria, Albany, New South Wales, Queensland, and South Australia. These concerns are all "boutique" operations—small by choice and design—but they are now producing malt whiskies with a uniquely Australasian character.

BAKERY HILL PEATED MALT

BAKERY HILL CASK STRENGTH PEATED MALT

BAKERY HILL
AUSTRALIA

28 Ventnor Street,
North Balwyn, Victoria
www.bakeryhilldistillery.com.au

"Single malt whisky is more than a craft, it's our passion." So says David Baker, chemist and founder (together with his wife, Lynn) of Bakery Hill Distillery near Melbourne, Victoria. Their first spirit flowed in 2000.

The barley strains Australian Franklin and Australian Schooner are sourced locally and sometimes malted over locally cut peat. The wash is brewed in 264-gallon (1,000-liter) batches and distilled twice in a single copper pot still. Maturation is on-site in barrels from Jack Daniel Distillery (*see p. 236*). The ambient temperature at Bakery Hill is 50–86°F (10–30°C), so maturation is quicker than in Scotland.

Baker was determined to prove that top-quality malt whisky could be made in Australia, and he has succeeded: his single cask, non-chill filtered malts are already winning awards. Bakery Hill whiskies are now available beyond their Victoria homeland.

BAKERY HILL PEATED MALT
SINGLE MALT 46% ABV
A sweet and oaky balance of peat and malt on the nose. These aromas carry through in the taste.

BAKERY HILL CASK STRENGTH PEATED MALT
SINGLE MALT 59.88% ABV
Intense peatiness on the nose, with dark cherry. The taste is sweet (toffee, honeycomb), with some salt and smoke. It has a good texture.

BAKERY HILL DOUBLE WOOD
SINGLE MALT 46% ABV
Finished in French oak ex-wine casks after ex-bourbon-cask maturation. Apricot, coconut, and plum, then syrup, fruitcake, and cloves. Sweet taste, with orange marmalade and oak.

BAKERY HILL DOUBLE WOOD

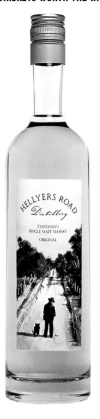

LARK'S SINGLE MALT

LARK'S PM

HELLYERS ROAD
AUSTRALIA

153 Old Surrey Road, Burnie, Tasmania
www.hellyersroaddistillery.com.au

Hellyers Road, opened in 1999, and owned by the Betta Milk Cooperative, now has about 3,000 ex-bourbon casks under maturation; it also produces a Tasmanian barley-based, pot-still vodka. The experience gained in running a milk processing plant has provided owner Laurie House with all the knowledge he needs to run this modern and highly automated plant.

The distillery is named after Henry Hellyer who, in the 1820s, created the first road into the interior of Tasmania, the same road that now leads to the distillery.

HELLYERS ROAD ORIGINAL

SINGLE MALT 46.2% ABV

A light-bodied, pale-colored malt, un-tinted and non-chill filtered. The nose is fresh and citric, with vanilla notes.

LARK
AUSTRALIA

14 Davey Street, Hobart, Tasmania
www.larkdistillery.com

The modern revival of whisky-making in Australia began in Tasmania, with the opening of this small distillery in Hobart in 1992. It was the brainchild of Bill Lark, who, the story goes, was inspired by a bottle of single malt Scotch consumed during a fishing trip with his father-in-law, which prompted the question "why is nobody making malt whisky in Tasmania today?" Lark realized that the island has all the right ingredients: plenty of rich barley fields, abundant pure soft water, peat bogs, and a perfect climate for maturation.

Lark located his distillery on the harborfront at Hobart, and is now assisted by his wife Lyn and daughter Kristy. They use locally grown Franklin barley, 50 percent of it re-dried over peat. The

Distilling Act 1901 required a minimum still capacity of 600 gallons (2,700 liters)—Lark's first task was to have this law amended so that they could use smaller stills. The distillery produces 10 to 12 22-gallon (100-liter) barrels of whisky a month, as well as a range of other spirits, including liqueurs using the indigenous pepperberry spice. The malt is bottled from single casks at three to five years. Unusually, all Lark's products are Kosher Certified.

LARK'S SINGLE MALT

SINGLE MALT 58% ABV

Malty and lightly peated, with peppery notes. A smooth mouthfeel, with rich malt, apples and oak-wood, and some spice in the finish.

LARK'S PM

BLENDED MALT 45% ABV

Sweet and smoky on the nose and in the mouth; clean and lightly spicy. This can be regarded as a well-made "barley schnapps."

LIMEBURNERS
AUSTRALIA

Great Southern Distilling Company, 252 Frenchman Bay Road, Albany, Western Australia
www.distillery.com.au

The Great Southern Distillery was built in 2007, the brainchild of lawyer and accountant Cameron Syme. Its location was chosen for Albany's cool, wet winters and enough breeze to provide 75 percent of its energy needs by wind power. It is close to the Margaret River wineries, which supply the ingredients for schnapps and liqueur-making. Limeburners whisky is offered in single barrel bottlings: the first, M2, launched in April 2008, won an award.

LIMEBURNERS BARREL M11

SINGLE MALT 43% ABV

The fourth bottling (M11), nicknamed "The Dark One," is from a French oak ex-brandy cask, re-racked into a second-fill ex-bourbon barrel.

OVEREEM PORT CASK MATURED—CASK STRENGTH

OVEREEM SHERRY CASK MATURED

OVEREEM BOURBON CASK MATURED—CASK STRENGTH

OVEREEM
AUSTRALIA

Old Hobart Distillery, Blackman's Bay, Tasmania, Australia
www.overeem.co.uk

Overeem single malt whiskies were first produced in Tasmania by businessman and whisky aficionado Casey Overeem, who built the custom Old Hobart Distillery, complete with copper pot still, within walking distance of his family home. He was granted a license to distill in 2005, and started production two years later. Overeem visited no fewer than 15 Scotch whisky distilleries in one trip to the UK to expand his knowledge of the whisky distillation process.

Distillation takes place in a pair of copper pot stills, using a wash with a lightly peated element that is produced to Overeem's specifications at the nearby Lark Distillery. Maturation takes place in ex-bourbon, port, or sherry casks. Since 2014, Lark Distillery Pty. Ltd. has owned Old Hobart Distillery and the Overeem brand.

OVEREEM PORT CASK MATURED—CASK STRENGTH

SINGLE MALT 60% ABV
Summer fruits and vanilla on the softly spicy nose, while the palate offers more vanilla and spice, with licorice and oak.

OVEREEM SHERRY CASK MATURED

SINGLE MALT 43% ABV
The nose yields vanilla, milk chocolate, and spicy raisins, while the palate delivers orange, sweet sherry, caramel, dark chocolate, and cloves.

OVEREEM BOURBON CASK MATURED—CASK STRENGTH

SINGLE MALT 60% ABV
Fresh and green on the early nose, with nutty vanilla and caramel. Big flavors of ripe apple, vanilla, and coconut.

SULLIVANS COVE AMERICAN OAK CASK

SULLIVANS COVE DOUBLE CASK

NANT
AUSTRALIA

The Nant Estate, Bothwell, Tasmania
www.nant.com.au

The Nant estate in Tasmania, founded in 1821, was bought by Keith and Margaret Batt in 2004 with a view to building a distillery on the historic working farm. With the expert guidance of Bill Lark *(see Lark, p.328)*, the distillery went into production in April 2008. The plan is to produce a limited number of casks each year. The barley and water for the distillery come from the estate, while a restored mill provides the grist. There is also an elegant new visitor center.

NANT DOUBLE MALT

BLENDED MALT 43% ABV
This is a vatting of two casks selected from other Tasmanian distilleries, and gives an idea of what Nant's own whisky will taste like in the future. Sweet and fruity, with plums and cream soda, it is medium-bodied and smooth.

SMITH'S
AUSTRALIA

Yalumba, Angaston, South Australia
www.yalumba.com

Samuel Smith arrived in Angaston in 1847, one of the first settlers. He was a brewer by trade and, within two years, had set up the Yalumba Winery, having made a small fortune in the goldfields of Victoria. In the early 1930s the company that bears his name installed a pot still at the winery to make brandy. This was used three times to distill a mash of locally grown barley malt (in 1997, 1998, and 2000). It was matured in a mix of sherry, French wine, bourbon, and new American oak casks. After a period of silence, the still is active again, and a 12-year-old single malt is now available.

SMITH'S ANGASTON

BLENDED MALT 40% ABV
Hay, vanilla, and toffee on the nose; sweet, light and delicate, with vanilla and nuts to taste; clean and sweet in the finish.

SULLIVANS COVE
AUSTRALIA

Tasmania Distillery, Lamb Place, Cambridge, Tasmania
www.sullivanscovewhisky.com

Sullivans Cove was the original British settlement at Hobart, on the island of Tasmania. There was a great deal of distilling taking place on the island— legal and illegal—until a total prohibition on distillation was introduced in 1838. The ban lasted until the early 1990s, when it was overturned.

In 1994, a small distillery was established in what is now Hobart, but the malt whisky produced was named after the area's original name: Sullivans Cove. The distillery changed hands in 2003, when the equipment was moved to Cambridge, on the outskirts of the city of Hobart.

The whisky is now winning awards (a gold and silver in blind tastings by the Whisky Society of Australia in 2007). The spirit is brewed at Cascade Brewery, distilled in a Charentais-style pot still, and bottled from single casks by hand. Like most other Australian distilleries, Tasmania also makes gin, vodka, and liqueurs.

SULLIVANS COVE
AMERICAN OAK CASK

SINGLE MALT 47.5% ABV
The initially sweet nose develops pepper and oaky notes. The palate has malt and vanilla.

SULLIVANS COVE
DOUBLE CASK

SINGLE MALT 40% ABV
Vanilla, orange, lemon, honey, figs, and allspice on the nose. The mildly herbal palate delivers honey, ginger, dried fruits, then white pepper in the finish.

Barley is grown in the foothills of the Stirling Ranges and in other pockets of Australia and New Zealand. Some distilleries, such as Lark, have experimented with new strains of barley that tolerate local conditions better than the strains grown in Europe.

LAMMERLAW
NEW ZEALAND

Bottled by Cadenhead
www.wmcadenhead.com

In 1974, the Wilson Brewery and Malt Extract Company produced New Zealand's first legal whiskey for 100 years. Unfortunately, its pot stills were made from stainless steel, and the spirit was horrible. In 1981, the distillery was acquired by Seagram, who vastly improved quality and produced a 10-year-old single malt—Lammerlaw—named after the nearby mountain range. The distillery was dismantled in 2002, and the casks passed to Milford's owners *(see Milford)*. Cadenhead has bottled Lammerlaw in its World Whiskies series.

CADENHEAD'S LAMMERLAW 10-YEAR-OLD

SINGLE MALT 47.3% ABV
Light-bodied and somewhat "green" and cereal-like, but pleasant to taste.

MACKENZIE
NEW ZEALAND

Southern Distilleries,
Stafford Street, Timaru
www.hokonuiwhiskey.com

The eponymous Mackenzie was a shepherd and sheep-rustler during the 1850s, and gave his name to that part of the Southern Alps between Canterbury and Otago where he operated. He and his dog are commemorated by monuments in the district. Scotch was his drink, and this recreation of his favorite tipple is a blend of Scotch and New Zealand malts from Southern Distilleries, which also makes Old Hokonui *(see entry)*. The process and reduction water used in Mackenzie's creation flows from the Mackenzie Basin.

THE MACKENZIE

BLENDED MALT 40% ABV
A light and refreshing dram, with plain caramel and oak notes.

MILFORD
NEW ZEALAND

The New Zealand Malt Whiskey Company & Preston Associates, 14–16 Harbour St., Oamaru
www.thenzwhisky.com

Milford whisky was originally made at Willowbank Distillery in Dunedin, South Island, which was owned by the Wilson Brewery *(see Lammerlaw)*. The New Zealand Malt Whisky Company now owns the Milford label (and also the less prestigious Prestons label). It has also opened a retail warehouse named Cellar Door at Oamaru, where a wide range of expressions of New Zealand whisky are available.

MILFORD 10-YEAR-OLD

SINGLE MALT 43% ABV
Often compared to a Scottish Lowland malt, Milford's 10-year-old has a light, dry, and fragrant nose; the taste is sweet, then dry, with a slightly woody, short finish.

OLD HOKONUI
NEW ZEALAND

Southern Distilleries,
Stafford Street, Timaru
www.hokonuiwhiskey.com

Southern Distilleries has two small pot stills producing Old Hokonui Moonshine, single malt, and blended malts, using—as the distillers put it—"Murdoch McRae's original 1892 recipe."

McRae was the leading illicit distiller in the district, having learned the craft from his mother, with whom he had arrived from Kintail, Scotland, in 1872. Many of his descendants also became distillers and their story is told with memorabilia in the Hokonui Museum at Gore.

OLD HOKONUI

BLEND 40% ABV
Pale in color, and light-bodied, with a smooth mouthfeel, and an oaky taste with distinct smoky notes.

THREE SHIPS
SOUTH AFRICA

James Sedgwick Distillery, Wellington East, Drakenstein 7655, South Africa
www.threeshipswhisky.co.za

The James Sedgwick Distillery was founded around 1886 and is named after the Yorkshire-born Western Cape-based businessman Captain James Sedgwick. Despite the age of the distillery, whisky has only been produced there since 1990. Today, the distillery is owned by the Distell Group Ltd.

The distillery's Three Ships brand was originally a blend of imported Scotch and native South African whisky, and this tradition has continued in the Select and Premium Select expressions, the latter aged for five years. These blends have now been joined by two newer expressions. First was the limited edition 10-year-old Single Malt—South Africa's first single malt whisky — of which there have been three subsequent releases since its initial launch in 2003. Second was the Special Release, the first blend made entirely of South African whisky that is matured for three years before being finished in bourbon casks for six months.

THREE SHIPS 10-YEAR-OLD
SINGLE MALT 43% ABV

The nose is floral, with just a hint of brine, plus barley and fresh pears. The palate is rounded and malty, with ripe peaches, honey, and soft spices.

Your Tasting Notes...

You can use these pages to make your own notes about the appearance, aroma, taste, and finish of different whiskeys that you have the opportunity to sample.

WHISKEY			
TYPE			
BOTTLER			
AGE			
APPEARANCE			
AROMA			
TASTE			
WITH WATER			
FINISH			
VERDICT	AGAIN & AGAIN SAME AGAIN NEVER AGAIN	AGAIN & AGAIN SAME AGAIN NEVER AGAIN	AGAIN & AGAIN SAME AGAIN NEVER AGAIN

WHISKEY			
TYPE			
BOTTLER			
AGE			
APPEARANCE			
AROMA			
TASTE			
WITH WATER			
FINISH			
VERDICT	AGAIN & AGAIN SAME AGAIN NEVER AGAIN	AGAIN & AGAIN SAME AGAIN NEVER AGAIN	AGAIN & AGAIN SAME AGAIN NEVER AGAIN

Your Tasting Notes...

You can use these pages to make your own notes about the appearance, aroma, taste, and finish of different whiskeys that you have the opportunity to sample.

WHISKEY			
TYPE			
BOTTLER			
AGE			
APPEARANCE			
AROMA			
TASTE			
WITH WATER			
FINISH			
VERDICT	AGAIN & AGAIN SAME AGAIN NEVER AGAIN	AGAIN & AGAIN SAME AGAIN NEVER AGAIN	AGAIN & AGAIN SAME AGAIN NEVER AGAIN

WHISKEY			
TYPE			
BOTTLER			
AGE			
APPEARANCE			
AROMA			
TASTE			
WITH WATER			
FINISH			
VERDICT	AGAIN & AGAIN SAME AGAIN NEVER AGAIN	AGAIN & AGAIN SAME AGAIN NEVER AGAIN	AGAIN & AGAIN SAME AGAIN NEVER AGAIN

Your Tasting Notes...

You can use these pages to make your own notes about the appearance, aroma, taste, and finish of different whiskeys that you have the opportunity to sample.

WHISKEY			
TYPE			
BOTTLER			
AGE			
APPEARANCE			
AROMA			
TASTE			
WITH WATER			
FINISH			
VERDICT	AGAIN & AGAIN SAME AGAIN NEVER AGAIN	AGAIN & AGAIN SAME AGAIN NEVER AGAIN	AGAIN & AGAIN SAME AGAIN NEVER AGAIN

WHISKEY			
TYPE			
BOTTLER			
AGE			
APPEARANCE			
AROMA			
TASTE			
WITH WATER			
FINISH			
VERDICT	AGAIN & AGAIN SAME AGAIN NEVER AGAIN	AGAIN & AGAIN SAME AGAIN NEVER AGAIN	AGAIN & AGAIN SAME AGAIN NEVER AGAIN

GLOSSARY

ABV (alcohol by volume) This is the proportion of alcohol in a drink, expressed as a percentage. Whiskey is most commonly at 40% or 43% ABV.

Analyzer still *see* continuous distillation

Angels' share The expression given for the amount of liquid that evaporates from the cask during the period of *maturation*.

Batch distillation Distillation carried out in batches, as opposed to *continuous distillation*. Each batch may be marginally different, which gives the method an artisanal quality.

Barrel *see* cask

Blended malt A mix of single malt whiskies from more than one distillery.

Blended whiskey A mix of malt whiskies and grain whiskies.

Cask The oak container in which whiskey is matured. There are many different styles and sizes of cask as well as a principle distinction between the type of wood used: American or European oak. In the US, whiskey is most commonly matured in barrels (200 liters/ 53 US gallons). American barrels are reused elsewhere; in Scotland they are often broken down and reassembled as hogsheads (250 liters/55 gallons). Butts and puncheons (both 500 liters/110 gallons) are the largest casks used for maturing whiskey, having first been seasoned with, or used to age, sherry.

Cask finishing The practice of using a different cask (such as port, Madeira, French wine, or rum casks) for the final period of the whiskey's maturation.

Cask strength Whiskey that is bottled straight from the cask rather than first being diluted. It is typically around 57–63% ABV.

Column still Also known as a Coffey, Patent or continuous still, this is the type of still used for *continuous distillation*.

Condenser The vaporized spirit driven off the stills is turned into liquid in a condenser. The traditional type of condenser is a "worm tub"—a tapering coil of copper pipe set in a vat of cold water outside the still house. Worm tubs have largely been superseded by shell-and-tube condensers, usually situated inside the still house.

Continuous distillation The creation of spirit as an ongoing process, as opposed to *batch distillation*. Continuous distillation uses a column still (also known as a Patent or Coffey still) rather than a *pot still*. It has two connected columns: the Rectifier and the Analyzer. The cool wash travels down the Rectifier in a sealed coil, where it becomes heated. It then passes to the head of the Analyzer, down which it trickles over a series of perforated copper plates. Steam enters the foot of the Analyzer and bubbles through the wash, driving off alcoholic vapor, which rises up the Analyzer then passes to the foot of the Rectifier. Again it ascends, to be condensed by the cool wash (which is thus heated) as it rises in a zigzag manner through another series of perforated copper plates. As the vapor rises it becomes purer and of higher strength, until it is drawn off at the "striking plate" at 94% ABV.

Cut points In the process of pot still distillation, the operator divides the run into three "cuts" to separate the usable spirit from rejected spirit, which must be redistilled. The first cut contains the foreshots; the middle cut is the section of usable spirit; the end cut contains the feints or aftershots.

Draff The Scottish name for the remains of the grain after mashing. It is a nutritious cattle fodder, used either wet or dried and pelletized.

Drum maltings Large cylinders in which grain is germinated during the industrial *malting* of barley. The drums are ventilated with temperature-controlled air and rotate so the grains do not stick together.

Dumping Emptying the contents of a cask into a vat, either prior to bottling or before putting into a different kind of cask.

Eau de vie Literally, "water of life," and usually used in reference to grape-based spirits. Compare with *uisge beatha*.

Expression The term given to a particular whiskey in relation to the overall output of a distillery or spirits company. It may refer to the age, as in 12-year-old expression, or to a particular characteristic, such as a cask strength expression.

Feints The final fraction of the spirit produced during a distillation run in batch distilling. Feints (also called tails or aftershots) are aromatically unpleasant, and are sent to a feints and foreshots receiver to be mixed with *low wines* and redistilled with the next run.

Fermenter Another name for *mash tun*.

First fill The first time a cask has been used to hold whiskey other than bourbon, it is referred to as first-fill cask. A first-fill sherry cask will have held only sherry prior to its use for maturing whiskey; a first-fill bourbon cask will have been used once only to hold bourbon prior to its use in maturing whiskey.

Foreshots The first fraction of the distillation run in pot-still distillation. Foreshots (also known as heads) are not pure enough to be used and are returned to a feints and foreshots receiver to be redistilled in the next run.

Grist Ground, malted grain. Water is added to grist to form the *mash*.

Heads *see* foreshots

High wines (US) A mix of spirit that has had its first distillation and the foreshots and feints from the second distillation. With a strength of around 28% ABV, high wines undergo a second distillation to create *new make*.

Independent bottler/bottling A company that releases bottles of whiskey independently of the official distillery bottlings. They buy small quantities of casks and bottle the whiskey as and when they choose.

Kilning In the process of *malting*, kilning involves gently heating the "green malt" to halt its germination and thereby retain its starch content for turning into sugars (in the mashing stage). Ultimately these sugars will be turned into alcohol. Peat may be added to the kiln to produce a smoky-flavored malt.

Lomond still This pot still was designed so that a distillery could vary the character of spirit being produced. The level of *reflux* could be altered by way of an additional condenser on the still, so that a heavy or light style of spirit could be made, as required.

Low wines The spirit produced by the first distillation. It has a strength of about 21% ABV. Compare with *high wines*.

Lyne arm (or "lye pipe") The pipe running from the top of the still to the condenser. Its angle, height, and thickness all have a bearing on the characteristics of the spirit.

Malting The process of deliberately starting and stopping germination in grain to maximize its starch content. As the grain begins to germinate (through the influence of heat and moisture), it becomes "green malt" (grain that has just begun to sprout). The green malt undergoes kilning to produce malt.

Marrying The mixing of whiskies prior to bottling. It most often applies to blends, where whiskies of different types and from several distilleries are combined for a period in vats or casks to blend more fully before the whiskey is bottled.

Mash The mix of grist and water.

Mashbill The mix of grains used in the making of a particular whiskey. In the US, there are specific requirements about the percentage of certain grains for making bourbon, Tennessee whiskey, and rye, for example.

Mash tun The vessel in which the grist is mixed with hot water to convert starch in the grain into sugars, ready for fermentation. The fermentable liquid that results is known as *wort*; the solid residue (husks and spent grain) is *draff*.

Maturation For *new make* to become whiskey, it must go through a period of maturation in oak casks. The length of time varies: in Scotland and Ireland, the minimum period is three years; in the US, the minimum maturation is two years.

Middle cut *see* cut points

New make The clear, usable spirit that comes from the spirit still. It has a strength of about 70% ABV and is diluted to around 63–64% before being put into

casks for maturation. In the US, new make is called white dog.

Peating Adding peat to the kiln ovens when *malting* barley to impart a smoky, phenolic aroma and taste to the whiskey. Barley that has undergone this process is known as peated malt.

Phenols A group of aromatic chemical compounds. In whiskey-making, the term is used to refer to the chemicals that impart smoky and medicinal flavors to malt and the whiskey made from it, which may be described as phenolic. Phenols are measured in parts per million (ppm). Highly phenolic whiskies, such as Laphroaig and Ardbeg, will use malt peated to a level of between 35 and 50ppm.

Poteen *see* uisce poitín

Pot still The large onion-shaped vessels, nearly always made of copper, used for batch distillation. Pot stills vary in size and shape, and these variations affect the style of spirit produced.

ppm *see* phenols

Proof The old term for the alcoholic proportion of a spirit, now superseded by ABV. The American proof figure, which is different to Imperial proof, is twice that of the ABV percentage.

Rectifier *see* continuous distillation

Reflux The process by which heavier alcoholic vapors fall back into the still rather than passing along the *lyne arm* to the *condenser*. By falling back, these vapors are re-distilled, becoming purer and lighter. The size, height, and shape of the still, and how it is operated, contribute to the degree of reflux, and therefore to the lightness and character of the spirit. Long-necked stills have a greater degree of reflux and

produce a more delicate style of spirit than squatter stills, which tend to make heavier, "oilier" whiskies.

Run In batch distillation—as carried out using pot stills—the extent of distillation is referred to as a run. The spirit produced during the run is variable in quality, and is divided by *cut points*.

Saladin box Used in the industrial *malting* of barley, these are large rectangular troughs in which the grains are germinated. Air is blown through the barley in the trough and the grain turned by mechanical screws to prevent the grains from sticking together.

Silent distillery A distillery in which whiskey production has stopped—possibly only temporarily.

Single cask A bottling that comes from just one cask (often bottled at *cask strength*).

Single malt A malt whiskey that is the product of just one distillery.

Spirit safe A glass-fronted cabinet through which the distilled spirit passes and which is used to monitor the purity of the spirit. The stillman operates the spirit safe during a run to assess its quality and make *cut points*.

Spirit still In *batch distillation*, the spirit still is used for the second distillation, in which the spirit from the *wash* still is distilled again to produce *new make*.

Still The vessel in which distillation takes place. There are two basic types: a *pot still* for *batch distillation* and a *column still* for *continuous distillation*.

Triple distillation Most batch distillation involves two distillations: in a wash still and in a *spirits still*. Triple distillation

—the traditional method in Ireland —involves a third distillation, which is said to produce a smoother and purer spirit.

Uisge beatha / uisce beatha The Scottish Gaelic and Irish Gaelic terms, respectively, from which the word whiskey derives. The term means "water of life," and so is synonymous with *eau de vie* and *aqua vita*.

Uisce poitín Historically, the Irish Gaelic term for non-licensed whiskey, usually known as poteen.

Vatting The mixing of whiskey from several casks. This is usually done to achieve a consistency of flavor over time. (*see also* Marrying)

Viscimetric whorls The eddies and vortices observed when water is added to whiskey. The capacity of an individual whiskey to sustain viscimation is termed its viscimetric potential.

Wash The resultant liquid when yeast is added to the *wort*, fermenting into a kind of ale. Wash has an alcoholic strength of about 7% ABV. It passes into a *wash still* for the first distillation.

Wash still In *batch distillation*, the wash still is used for the first distillation, in which the *wash* is distilled.

Washbacks The fermenting vessels in which yeast is added to the *wort* to make *wash*. Called "fermenters" in the US.

Wood finish *see* cask finish

Worm / worm tubs *see* condensers

Wort The liquid produced as a result of mixing hot water with grist in a *mash tun*.

REFERENCE

WHISKEY OWNERSHIP

It can, at times, be difficult to work out exactly which company owns a specific whiskey brand or distillery. As firms have merged or been bought out by larger business groups, the trail is sometimes rather elusive and confusing. Here is a brief summary of the major conglomerations, which elucidates how they have emerged and transformed over time into the key big players in the world of whiskey today: Diageo, Chivas Brothers/Pernod Ricard, United Spirits (the UB group), and Beam Global (itself part of Fortune Brands).

THE RISE OF DIAGEO

The Distillers Company Limited (**DCL**) was founded in 1877 as an amalgamation of six leading grain whiskey distilleries. In 1894 it opened its first malt whiskey distillery (Knockdhu) and, in the early 20th century, began to acquire blending companies and their brands. Following "The Big Amalgamation" in 1925, when the big blending firms Walkers, Dewars, and Buchanans joined DCL, it became the largest distiller in the world at the time.

In 1987, DCL was acquired by Guinness, and the whiskey side of the business was renamed United Distillers. Then, in 1998, Guinness merged with Grand Metropolitan, who had a drinks subsidiary called Independent Distillers & Vintners. The combined operating name for this subsidiary and United Distillers became United Distillers & Vintners (**UDV**).

In the same year (1998) that Guinness merged with Grand Metropolitan, **Diageo** was formed as the holding company. Two years later the corporate structure was simplified and UDV was replaced as the trading entity by Diageo.

Diageo owns a plethora of whiskey brands, including verable old blends such as Buchanan's,

Haig, and Johnnie Walker. It also owns many Scotch whiskey distilleries—its flagships are the 12 that produce the Classic Malts range: Caol Ila, Cardhu, Clynelish, Cragganmore, Dalwhinnie, Glen Elgin, Glenkinchie, Knockando, Lagavulin, Oban, Talisker, and Royal Lochnagar.

CHIVAS & PERNOD RICARD

Founded in Aberdeen in 1801, **Chivas Brothers** was a wine & spirits merchant. It was acquired by the Canadian distiller Seagram in 1949. Seagram went on to acquire or build nine distilleries and a number of leading blends.

In 2001, Seagram decided to divest itself of its alcoholic beverages divisions, which was divided between Diageo and Pernod Ricard. Chivas remains the whiskey arm of Pernod Ricard.

The French distiller **Pernod Ricard** entered the Scotch whiskey industry with the purchase of Aberlour Distillery in 1974, but moved into the "First Division" when it acquired part of the Seagram's drinks empire in 2001. This included The Glenlivet Distillery, together with the Chivas Regal brand, and six of Allied-Domecq's distilleries in 2005, together with Ballantine's. Pernod Ricard owns brands such as Ballantine's, Chivas Regal, Jameson, Paddy, and Powers, and prestigious distilleries such as Glenlivet, Aberlour, Scapa, and Longmorn. In the States, it owns the Wild Turkey brand and, in Canada, Wiser's.

IRISH DISTILLERS

The story of Irish Distillers goes back to 1867, when five small distillers in County Cork amalgamated to form The Cork Distillers Company (**CDC**), which consolidated its production at Midleton Distillery.

That was the status quo until almost 100 years later, when, in 1966, The Irish Distillers Group (**IDG**) was formed by the merger

of Powers, Jameson's, and CDC. Powers and Jameson's historic distilleries in Dublin were closed by the early 1970s, and a large new distillery was built at Midleton in 1975 to accommodate production of all the whiskeys in the IDG stable. IDG was taken over by Pernod Ricard in 1988.

UNITED SPIRITS

Part of the UB Group, **United Spirits** became the third-biggest spirits producer (after Diageo and Pernod Ricard) when it acquired **Whyte & Mackay** in 2007. With this purchase came several Scottish distilleries, including Dalmore and Jura. However, in 2014, Emperador Inc. bought the Whyte & Mackay business from United Spirits.

BEAM SUNTORY INC.

This subsidiary of Suntory Holdings Ltd. owns the Jim Beam brand, as well as Maker's Mark and Canadian Club. Its Scotch whiskey ownership includes Laphroaig and the Teacher's blend.

BACARDI

The famous rum maker **Bacardi** joined the Scotch whiskey industry in 1992 with the acquisition of William Lawson Ltd., owner of Macduff Distillery (*see Glen Deveron*). In 1998, Bacardi acquired John Dewar & Sons, together with four distilleries from Diageo, making it a major player in Scotch whiskey.

ALLIED-DOMECQ

Though now broken up, Allied-Domecq in its 1990s heyday was one of the world's biggest whiskey companies. It began as **Allied Breweries**, which acquired Teacher's in 1976, and changed the name of its spirits division to Allied Distillers when it bought Hiram Walker, owner of Ballantine's brands and distilleries, in 1987. Three years later the company acquired Whitbread's whiskey interests and moved into the big league.

In 1993, with the acquisition of the Spanish distiller and sherry-maker Pedro Domecq, the name was changed to **Allied-Domecq**, which became the third-largest drinks company in the world. Allied-Domecq was broken up in 2005, with Teacher's going to Beam Global and Ballantine's to French drinks giant Pernod Ricard.

WHISKEY RANGES

Throughout this book, and when studying or buying whiskey, three key whiskey ranges are regularly mentioned: Flora & Fauna, Classic Malts, and Rare Malts. Here is a little background information about each of them.

Classic malts A range of six malts was introduced by United Distillers in 1987/88. The malts came from UD's Cragganmore, Dalwhinnie, Glenkinchie, Lagavulin, Oban, and Talisker distilleries. Under the ownership of Diageo, the range has been expanded to 12 of its flagship malts: the six original members of the range, plus Caol Ila, Cardhu, Clynelish, Glen Elgin, Knockando, and Royal Lochnagar.

Flora & Fauna In the early 1990s, UDV introduced the Flora & Fauna range of single malt bottlings from all of its distilleries. Diageo continued to produce the range but recently decided that it will be discontinued.

Rare Malts A selection of small batch bottlings from UDV at natural strength and color, without chill-filtration. They were released between 1995 and 2006, and 36 distilleries were represented in the range.

WHISKEY SHOPS

AUSTRALIA

Scotch Malt Whisky Society in Australia
mail order to members only
www.smws.com.au

Single Malt Whisky Club PTY LTD
Unit M3, 63 Mandoon Road
Girraween, 2145
+ 61 (4)58 109 110
www.singlemalt.com.au

AUSTRIA

Potstill
Laudongasse 18, 1080 Wien
+43 (0)664 118 85 41
www.potstill.org

BELGIUM

Whiskycorner
Kraaistraat 18, 3530 Houthalen
+32 (0)89 386233
www.whiskycorner.be

Jurgen's Whiskyhuis
Gaverland 70, 9620 Zottegem
+32 (0)9 336 51 06
www.whiskyhuis.be

FRANCE

La Maison du Whisky
20 rue d'Anjou, 75008 Paris
+33 (0)1 42 65 03 16
www.whisky.fr

also at 47 rue Jean Chatel
97400 Saint-Denis
+33 (0)2 62 21 31 19

GERMANY

Cadenhead's Whisky Market
Luxemburger Strasse 257
50939 Köln
+49 (0)221 283 1834
www.cadenhead.de

Celtic Whisk(e)y & Versand
Otto Steudel, Bulmannstrasse 26
90459 Nürnberg
+49 (0)911 45097430
celtic.whiskymania.de

Weinquelle Lühmann
Lubeckerstrasse 145
22087 Hamburg
+49 (0)40 256 391
www.weinquelle.com

Whisky & Cigars
Sophienstrasse 8-9
10178 Berlin-Mitte
+49 (0)30 282 03 76
www.whiskyandcigars.de

Whisky Corner
Reichertsfeld 2
92278 Illschwang
+49 (0)96 6695 1213
www.whisky-corner.de

IRELAND

Celtic Whiskey Shop
27–28 Dawson Street
Dublin 2
+353 (0)1 675 9744

Mitchell & Son
The CHQ building
IFSC Docklands
Dublin 1
+353 (01)612 5540
www.mitchellandson.com

also at Glasthule
54 Glasthule Road
Sandycove
County Dublin
+353 (01)230 2301

JAPAN

Shinanoya
Kabukicho 1-12-9, Shinjuku
Kabukicho, Tokyo
+81 (0)3 3204 2365
(more branches throughout Tokyo)

Kawachiya
5-40-15 Nakakasai
Edogawa-ku
Tokyo, 134-0083
+81 (0)3 3680 4321
(more branches throughout Tokyo)

Tanakaya
3-4-14 Mejiro, Toshima-ku, Tokyo
+81 (0)3 3953 8888

NEW ZEALAND

The Whisky Shop
www.whiskyshop.co.nz

RUSSIA

Whisky World Shop
9 Tverskoy Boulevard
123104 Moscow
+7 495 787 9150
www.whiskyworld.ru

UNITED KINGDOM

Berry Brothers & Rudd
3 St. James's Street
London SW1A 1EG
+44 (0)20 7022 8973
www.bbr.com

Cadenheads Whisky Shop and Tasting Room
26 Chiltern Street
London W1U 7QF
+44 (0)20 7935 6999
www.whiskytastingroom.com

Gordon & MacPhail
58–60 South Street, Elgin
Moray IV30 1JY
+44 (0)1343 545110
www.gordonandmacphail.com

Loch Fyne Whiskies
Inveraray, Argyll PA32 8UD
+44 (0)1499 302 219
www.lfw.co.uk

Milroy's of Soho
3 Greek Street
London W1D 4NX
+44 (0)20 7437 2385
shop.milroys.co.uk

Royal Mile Whiskies
379 High Street, Royal Mile
Edinburgh EH1 1PW
+44 (0)131 225 3383
www.royalmilewhiskies.com

also at 3 Bloomsbury Street
London WC1B 3QE

Scotch Malt Whisky Society
mail order to members only
www.smws.com

The Vintage House
42 Old Compton Street
London W1D 4LR
+44 (0)20 7437 2592
www.sohowhisky.com

Whisky Castle
6 Main Street, Tomintoul,
Ballindalloch, Moray, AB37 9EX

+44 (0)1807 580 213
www.whiskycastle.com

The Whisky Exchange
2 Bedford Street, Covent Garden
London WC2E 9HH
+44 (0)20 7100 0088
www.thewhiskyexchange.com

The Whisky Shop
12 branches in England and Scotland
+44 (0)14 1427 2977
www.whiskyshop.com

The Whisky Shop Dufftown
1 Fife Street, Dufftown, Keith,
Moray AB55 4AL
+44 (0)1340 821097
www.whiskyshopdufftown.co.uk

USA

D&M
2200 Fillmore Street
San Francisco, CA 94115
(415) 346 1325
(800) 637 0292
www.dandm.com

Park Avenue Liquor Shop
270 Madison Avenue
New York, NY 10017
(212) 685 2442
www.parkaveliquor.com

Binny's Beverage Depot/ South Loop
1132 South Jefferson Street
Chicago, IL 60607
(312) 768 4440
www.binnys.com

The Whisky Shop
360 Sutter Street
San Francisco, CA, 94108
(415) 989 1030
www.whiskyshopusa.com

WHISKEY WEBSITES

www.maltmadness.com
www.maltmaniacs.net
www.nonjatta.com
www.whiskyadvocate.com
www.whiskycast.com
www.whiskyforum.se
www.whiskymag.com
www.whisky-pages.com
www.youtube.com/user/SingleMaltTv

INDEX

PICTURE CREDITS

Deepak Aggarwal © Dorling Kindersley:
321 Antiquity, Bagpiper, Blenders Pride, 322
Imperial Blue, Masterstroke, McDowell's,
324 Royal Challenge

Alamy Images: 194–5 © FAN Travelstock/
Alamy, 204–5 © David Sanger Photography/
Alamy, 250–1 © Peter Horree/Alamy, 272–3
© Design Pics Inc./Alamy

Paul Bock © Beam Global: 130–1
Laphroaig Distillery

Dave Broom: 288 Chichibu Distillery

Chris Bunting: 280 Golden Horse, 284
The Crane bar, Tokyo

Corbis: 331 © Doug Pearson/JAI/Corbis

Peter Mulryan: 11 bottling line, 208–9
Midleton's water source, local barley, the
mashtun, Jameson bottling line, 210 a field
of barley near Midleton

Peter Anderson © Dorling Kindersley:
25 Ardbeg Corryvreckan, Ardbeg Perpetuum,
Ardbeg Supernova, 30 Auchentoshan American
Oak, 31 Auchentoshan Springwood, 51
Bowmore Small Batch, 59 Cameron Brig, 79
Girvan, Glenburgie, 90–91 Glen Garioch,
102 Glen Moray Classic Peated, 108 Grant's
Signature, 109 Grant's 25-year-old, 113
Highland Park 21-year-old, 136 Macallan
Gold, 193 The Irishman Founder's Reserve,
196 Kilbeggan 8-year-old, 206, 207 Midleton
Dair Ghaelach Grinsell's Wood, Powers John
Lane Releases 12-year-old, 229 Ezra Brooks,
231 I.W. Harper, 235 High West, 246 Michter's,
253 Rittenhouse Rye, 254 Sam Houston, 256
Tincup, 270 Canadian Club Reserve 9-year-old,
281 Ichiro's Double Distilleries, Ichiro's Malt
& Grain, 286 Nikka Coffey Malt Whisky,
287 Nikka Coffey Grain Whisky, 291 Nikka
Taketsuru Pure Malt, 295 Suntory Hakushu
Distiller's Reserve, 297 The Yamazaki Distiller's
Reserve, 305 Adnams, 306 Armorik, 308 Glann
ar Mor, Guillon, 313 Glen Els, 328 Lark's
Single Malt, 329 Overeem Sherry Cask Matured,
Overeem Bourbon Cask Matured, 333

Sachin Singh: 323 Officer's Choice

**Thameside Media/Michael Ellis ©
Dorling Kindersley:** 6, 8–11, 14–15, 26–7,
28, 32 Balmenach, 38–39, 40 Bell's, 41 Ben
Nevis, 44–5, 48 Blair Athol, 49, 56 Braeval, 58

Caol Ila Distillers Edition, 60–1, 68
Crawford's, Cutty Sark, 69 Dailuaine, Dallas
Dhu, 74 Deanston, 76 Dimple, Dufftown,
Edradour, 78, 79 Glenallachie, 80 Glen
Deveron, 81, 82–3, 92–3, 100 Glenlossie,
106 Glen Spey, Glentauchers, 107 Glenturret
10-year-old, 109 Haig Gold Label, 110–1, 115
Inchgower, 118–9, 124–5 Knockando, 122–3,
126 Lagavulin 21-year-old, 129, 132 Lauder's,
133 Linkwood, Loch Fyne Living Cask, Loch
Lomond, 134 Long John, Longmorn 16-year-old,
137 Macallan 10-year-old, 140 Mannochmore,
142 Millburn, 143 Oban Distillers Edition,
146, 149 Poit Dhubh, Port Ellen, Prime Blue,
150–1, 155 Sheep Dip, 156–7, 162 Stewarts
Cream of the Barley, 163, 164–5, 169 Teaninich
G&M, Te Bheag, 172, 174–5, 177 White Horse,
179, 188 Coleraine, 190, 191 Craoi Na Mona,
192 Feckin' Irish, Green Spot, 221, 223 Bulleit,
228, 232 Henry McKenna, 233, 243 Knob Creek,
255 Seagram's 7 Crown, 257, 258–9, 260, 261,
262 Wild Turkey Kentucky Spirit, 263 Wild
Turkey Rare Breed, 268, 275 Glen Breton,
Hirsch, 276 Seagram's, 283, 286–7 Nikka
Whisky From the Barrel, Nikka Pure Malt Red,
Nikka Pure Malt White, Nikka Pure Malt Black,
290, 291 Nikka Taketsuru 17-year-old, Nikka
Taketsuru 21-year-old, 294, 297 The Yamazaki
12-year-old, The Yamazaki 25-year-old, The
Yamazaki 18-year-old, 302, 306 Gouden Carolus,
312 Gold Cock, 313 Slyrs, 318, 320, 326,
332 Lammerlaw; cartography by Rosalyn Ellis,
Nora Zimerman, Steve Crozier.

Cartography (Dorling Kindersley):
Rajesh Kumar Mishra, Suresh Kumar

The Whisky Couple: 226 Wild Turkey sign,
227 Maker's Mark, 237 tasting glasses, 239,
244–5 copper pot stills, 245 rick houses

The Whisky Exchange: 235 Hirsch Reserve

The publishers would like to thank the following
producers for their assistance with the project and
kind permission to reproduce their photographs:

Aberfeldy Distillery; Aberlour Distillery;
Alberta Distillery: Alberta, Tangle Ridge,
Windsor Canadian; Allied Distillers; Anchor
Distilling Company: Old Potrero; Ardbeg
Distillery; Ardmore Distillery; Arran Distillers:
Arran; Auchroisk Distillery; Aultmore
Distillery; Bacardi & Company: Aultmore,

Craigellachie, Dewar's, Royal Brackla, William
Lawson's; Backafallsbyn AB: Hven; Bakery Hill
Distillery; Balblair Distillery; Balcones Distilling;
The Balvenie Distillery Company; Beam Global
España: DYC; Beam Global Distribution (UK):
Ardmore, Laphroaig, Teacher's; Beam Global
Spirits & Wine, Inc. (USA): Baker's® Kentucky
Straight Bourbon Whiskey (53.5% Alc./Vol.
©CST), James B. Beam Distilling Co., Clermont,
KY; Basil Hayden's® Kentucky Straight Bourbon
Whiskey (40% Alc./Vol. ©CST), Kentucky
Springs Distilling Co., Clermont, KY; Clermont
Distillery; Jim Beam® Kentucky Straight
Bourbon Whiskey (40% Alc./Vol. ©2009),
James B. Beam Distilling Co., Clermont, KY;
Jim Beam® Straight Rye Whiskey (40% Alc.
/Vol. ©CST), James B. Beam Distilling Co.,
Clermont, KY; Kessler® American Blended
Whiskey Lightweight Traveler® (40% Alc.
/Vol. 72.5% Grain Neutral Spirits, ©2009),
Julius Kessler Company, Deerfield, IL; Knob
Creek® Kentucky Straight Bourbon Whiskey
(50% Alc./Vol. ©2009), Knob Creek Distillery,
Clermont, KY; Maker's Mark® Bourbon Whisky
(45% Alc./Vol. ©CST), Maker's Mark Distillery,
Inc., Loretto, KY; Old Crow® Kentucky Straight
Bourbon Whiskey (40% Alc./Vol. ©2009),
W.A. Gaines, Div. of The Old Crow Distillery
Company, Frankfort, KY; Old Grand-Dad®
Kentucky Straight Bourbon Whiskey (43%,
50% and 57% Alc./Vol. ©2009), The Old
Grand-Dad Distillery Company, Frankfort,
KY; Old Taylor® Kentucky Straight Bourbon
Whiskey (40% Alc./Vol. ©CST), The Old
Taylor Distillery Company, Frankfort, KY;
Beam Suntory: Ardmore, Laphroaig Select,
Booker's, Canadian Club, Jim Beam Black
6-year-old, Jim Beam Devil's Cut; Belmont
Farm of Virginia: Virginia Lightning; Ben
Nevis Distillery: MacDonald's Traditional;
Benriach Distillery: Benriach, Glenglassaugh;
Benrinnes Distillery; Benromach Distillery;
Berry Brothers & Rudd: Cutty Sark; Bertrand
Distillery: Uberach; Betta Milk Cooperative:
Hellyers Road; Bowmore Distillery; Box
Distillery AB; Braunstein; Brown-Forman
Corporation: Canadian Mist, Early Times,
Old Forester, Woodford Reserve, Jack Daniel's;
Bruichladdich Distillery; Buffalo Trace
Distillery: Ancient Age, Blanton's, Buffalo
Trace, Eagle Rare, Elmer T. Lee, Experimental
Collection, George T. Stagg, Hancock's Reserve,

Old Charter, Rock Hill Farms, Sazerac Rye, Thomas H. Handy, W.L. Weller; Bunnahabhain Distillery; Burn Stewart Distillers: Black Bottle, Deanston, Scottish Leader; The Old Bushmills Distillery Co: Bushmills, The Irishman, Knappogue Castle; Campari Drinks Group: Glen Grant, Old Smuggler, Wild Turkey 81 Proof; Cardhu Distillery; Castle Brands Inc.: Jefferson's; Chichibu Distillery: The Peated 2015; Chivas Brothers: 100 Pipers, Ballantine's, Chivas Regal, Clan Campbell, Long John, Passport, Queen Anne, Royal Salute, Something Special, Stewarts Cream of the Barley, Strathisla, Tormore; Clear Creek Distillery: McCarthy's; Clontarf Distillery; Clynelish Distillery; Compass Box Delicious Whisky; Constellation Spirits Inc.: Very Old Barton®, Kentucky Gentleman®, Kentucky Tavern®, Ridgemont®, Ten High®, Tom Moore®, Black Velvet®; Cooley Distillery: Connemara, Cooley, Inishowen, Kilbeggan, Locke's, Tyrconnell, Wild Geese; Copper Fox Distillery: Wasmund's; Corby Distilleries: Wiser's; Craigellachie Distillery; Cragganmore Distillery; Des Menhirs: Eddu; Deerstalker Whisky: Allt-a-Bhainne; Diageo plc: Bell's, Black & White, Buchanan's, Bulleit Bourbon, Bushmills, Cameron Brig, Caol Ila, Cardhu, Crown Royal, Dalwhinnie, Dimple, Glen Elgin, Glen Ord, Haig Club, J&B, Johnnie Walker, Lagavulin, Linkwood, Mortlach, Oban, Old Parr, Royal Lochnagar, Teaninich, VAT 69, White Horse, Windsor; Diageo Canada: Seagram's; Domaine Charbay: Charbay; Domaine Mavela: P&M; Echlinville Distillery: Dunville's; Edrington: Glenturret Peated, The English Whisky Co.; The Famous Grouse; The Fleischmann Distillery; Four Roses Distillery; The Gaelic Whisky Co.: Mac Na Mara, Poit Dhubh; Garrison Brothers Distillery: Texas Straight Bourbon; George A. Dickel & Co.: George Dickel; Georgetown Trading Co.: 1776; Girvan Distillery; Glan ar Mor; Glencadam Distillery; Glendalough Distillery; Glendronach Distillery; Glendullan Distillery; Glenfarclas Distillery; Glenfiddich Distillery; Glenglassaugh Distillery; Glengoyne Distillery; Glengyle Distillery: Kilkerran; Glenkinchie Distillery; Glenlivet Distillery; The Glenmorangie Company: Glenmorangie, James Martin's; Glen Moray Distillery; Glenora Distillery: Glen Breton; Glenrothes Distillery; Glenturret Distillery; Gotland Whisky AB; Graanstokerij Filliers: Goldlys; Great Southern

Distilling Company: Limeburners; Guillon Distillery; Healeys Cornish Cyder Farm: Hicks & Healey; Heaven Hill Distilleries, Inc.: Bernheim, Elijah Craig, Evan Williams, Heaven Hill, Georgia Moon, Mellow Corn, Old Fitzgerald, Parker's, Pikesville, Rittenhouse Rye; Highland Park Distillery; Highwood Distillers; Holle; Hotel Gasthof Lamm: Ammertal; Ian MacLeod: Glengoyne 18-year-old, Langs, Tamdhu; International Beverage Holdings: anCnoc 2000, anCnoc 18-year-old, Balblair, Hankey Bannister Original Blend; Inver House Distillers: Catto's, Hankey Bannister, Inver House, MacArthur's, Pinwinnie Royale, Speyburn; Isle of Arran: Robert Burns; Jagatjit Industries: Aristocrat; John Distilleries Pvt. Ltd: Paul John; Jura Distillery; Käsers Schloss: Whisky Castle; Kavalan Distillery; Kentucky Bourbon Distillers, Ltd.: Johnny Drum, Noah's Mill; Kilchoman Distillery; Kirin Holdings Company: Kirin Gotemba, Kirin Karuizawa; Kittling Ridge Distillery: Forty Creek; Knockdhu Distillery: anCnoc; Knockeen Hills; La Maison du Whisky: Nikka; La Marttiniquaise: Label 5; Lark Distillery: Lark Overeem Port Cask Matured; Last Drop Distillers; Leopold Bros; Loch Lomond Distillery Group: Glen Scotia; Luxco Spirited Brands: Rebel Yell; Macallan; Macduff International: Grand Macnish, Islay Mist, Lauder's; Mackmyra; McMenamin's Group: Edgefield; Midleton Distillery: Clontarf, Crested Ten, Dungourney, Green Spot, The Irishman, Jameson, Midleton, Paddy, Powers, Redbreast, Tullamore D.E.W.; Morrison Bowmore Distillers: Auchentoshan, Bowmore, Glen Garioch, McClelland's, Yamazaki; Murree Distillery; The Nant Estate; New York Distilling Company: Ragtime Rye ; The New Zealand Malt Whisky Company: Milford; The Nikka Whisky Distilling Co.; Chichibu, Number One Drinks Company: Hanyu, Ichiro's Malt; Old Pulteney Distillery; The Owl Distillery: The Belgian Owl; Pernod Ricard: Glen Keith, Glenlivet Founder's Reserve, Longmorn Cask Strength, Miltonduff, Scapa, Strathclyde; Pernod Ricard USA: American Spirit, Russell's Reserve, Wild Turkey; Piedmont Distillers: Catdaddy; Preiss Imports; Radico Khaitan: 8PM, Whytehall; Reiner Mösslein:Fränkischer; Reisetbauer; Richard Joynson: Loch Fyne; Rock Town Distillery: Rock Town Arkansas Bourbon; Rogue Spirits; Rosebank Distillery;

Saint James Spirits: Peregrine Rock; Scapa Distillery, Smögen Whisky AB; Southern Distilleries: MacKenzie, Old Hokonui; Spencerfield Spirits: Pig's Nose; Speyside Distillery: Spey; Springbank Distillers: Hazelburn, Longrow, Springbank; St George Spirits; Stock Spirits: Hammerhead; Stranahan's Colorado Whiskey; Suntory Group: Suntory Hakushu, Suntory Hibiki; Tasmania Distillery: Sullivan's Cove; Teeling Distillery; Teerenpeli; Templeton Rye; Talisker Distillery; Tobermory Distillery: Ledaig, Tobermory; Tomatin Distillery: The Antiquary, The Talisman, Tomatin; Tomintoul Distillery; Triple Eight Distillery: The Notch; Tullibardine Distillery; Tuthilltown Distillery: Hudson; United Spirits: Signature; Us Heit Distillery: Frysk Hynder; Waldviertler Whiskydestillerie; Walsh Whiskey: Writers Tears; Wambrechies Distillery; Welsh Whisky Company: Penderyn; Wemyss Malts: Invergordon, Longmorn Bitter Sweet Barley 1997; West Cork Distillers: The Pogues; Whyte & Mackay: The Claymore, Cluny, The Dalmore, Fettercairn, John Barr, Tamnavulin, Whyte & Mackay; William Grant & Sons: Balvenie Portwood 21-year-old, Balvenie Caribbean Cask 14-year-old, Balvenie Single Barrel 12-year-old, Blavenie 30-year-old, Clan MacGregor, Glenfiddich, Grant's, Monkey Shoulder; Wolfram Ortner: Nock-Land; Woodford Reserve Distillery: Woodford Reserve Double Oaked, Woodford Reserve Straight Rye, Woodford Reserve Master's Collection 1838 White Corn; Yalumba: Smith's; Zuidam Distillery: Millstone; Zürcher Brewery: Single Lakeland

ACKNOWLEDGMENTS

FIRST EDITION

Thameside Media would like to thank the following people and companies for their help and kind permission to photograph at their premises:

Jane Grimley at Aberfeldy Distillery, Ann Miller at Aberlour Distillery, Michael Heads at Ardbeg Distillery, Rob, Robbie, and Brian at Balvenie and Glenfiddich Distilleries, Adam Holden at Berry Brothers & Rudd, Dave and Heather at Bowmore Distillery, Mark and Duncan at Bruichladdich Distillery, John MacLellan at Bunnhabhain Distillery, Ewan Mackintosh at Caol Ila Distillery, the staff and owners of The Canny Man's in Edinburgh, Stephanie Macleod at Dewar's, Ian and Claire at Gordon & MacPhail, Cathy and Ruth at Kilchoman Distillery, Ruth and Ian (Pinky) at Lagavulin Distillery, Vicky Stevens, Graham Holyoake, and David McLean at Laphroaig Distillery, Margaret and Morag at Macallan Distillery, staff at The Mash Tun in Aberlour, Philip Shorten at Milroy's of Soho, Graham Logie at Port Ellen Maltings, Gary at Speyside Cooperage, The Whisky Shop Dufftown.

Thameside Media would also like to thank the following individuals for their kind assistance with the project: Sukhinder Singh and staff at The Whisky Exchange, London *(www.thewhiskyexchange.com)*, Marisa Renzullo, Casper Morris, Becky Offringa of The Whisky Couple, Aparna Sharma at DK India office.

First edition produced for Dorling Kindersley by **THAMESIDE MEDIA**
www.thamesidemedia.com

DIRECTORS Michael Ellis, Rosalyn Ellis

EDITORS Fay Franklin, Michael Fullalove, Caroline Blake, Zoe Ross

DESIGNERS Nora Zimerman, Kate Leonard, Ian Midson

RETOUCHER Steve Crozier

For **DK**

PROJECT EDITOR Danielle Di Michiel

PROJECT DESIGNER Will Hicks

EDITORIAL ASSISTANCE Andrew Roff

SENIOR JACKET CREATIVE Nicola Powling

MANAGING EDITOR Dawn Henderson

MANAGING ART EDITOR Christine Keilty

PRODUCTION EDITOR Ben Marcus

CREATIVE TECHNICAL SUPPORT Sonia Charbonnier

And a big thank you to Stuart Bale and Luca Saladini at The Albannach bar in London for guidance with, and mixing of, the cocktails featured on pp.110–111.

SECOND EDITION

DK would like to thank Jane Simmonds for proofreading, Marie Lorimer for compiling the index, and Karen Constanti, Bhavika Mathur, Juhi Sheth, Suzena Sengupta, and Vikas Sachdeva for design assistance.

WRITERS

FIRST EDITION

DAVE BROOM

Dave is editor of *Whisky Magazine Japan*, contributing editor to *Whisky Magazine*, a regular columnist on many periodicals, has written a dozen books, and won three Glenfiddich Awards for his writing. He is a respected taster, and in demand as a teacher and lecturer. For the first edition, Dave wrote the section on Japanese whisky.

TOM BRUCE-GARDYNE

Tom is an expert on Scotch malt and has written several books on the subject, including *The Scotch Whisky Book* and *Scotch Whisky Treasures*. He is a regular contributor to *Unfiltered* and *scotchwhisky.com* and wrote a weekly drinks column for *The Herald*. Tom wrote the entries on Scotland's malt whiskies for the first edition.

IAN BUXTON

Elected Keeper of the Quaich (1991)—the Scotch whisky industry's highest accolade—and a Liveryman of the Worshipful Company of Distillers, Ian is a member of *Whisky Magazine*'s "World Whiskies Awards" tasting panel and also Director of the World Whiskies Conference. He writes for *Whisky Magazine*, *Scottish Field*, and *The Times*, among other titles. He recently edited and contributed to the Gedenkschrift for Michael Jackson *Beer Hunter*, *Whisky Chaser*, and is currently working on a history of Glenglassaugh Distillery. Ian wrote the entries on Scotland's blended whiskies for the first edition.

CHARLES MACLEAN

Charlie has been writing about whisky since 1981, and has published 15 books on the subject—*The Times* describes him as "Scotland's leading whisky expert." In 2009, he was elected Master of the Quaich (the whisky industry's highest accolade) and, in 2012, won the Outstanding Achievement Award at the International Wines & Spirits Competition. Visit his website at *whiskymax.co.uk*. Charles is Editor-in-Chief of this book, and also wrote the sections on Canadian, Asian, and Australasian whiskies for the first edition.

PETER MULRYAN

Peter is the author of four books on spirits: *The Whiskeys of Ireland*, *Poteen —Irish Moonshine*, *Bushmills—400 years*, and *Irish Whiskey Guide*. He has contributed to numerous publications, including *Whisky Magazine*, and, as a television producer, specializes in food and drink programs. Peter wrote the section on Irish whiskey for the first edition.

HANS OFFRINGA

An eclectic bilingual author and photographer, among other works, Hans has written and translated more than 20 books on whisky, and numerous articles for various publications across the globe. He is one of very few writers to have been named Kentucky Colonel as well as Keeper of the Quaich. For more information about Hans's work, see *www.thewhiskycouple.com*. Hans wrote the section on European whisky for the first edition.

GAVIN D. SMITH

Gavin is the author of some 25 published books, more than a dozen of which are whisky-related, such as *The A–Z of Whisky* and *Whisky Opus* (with Dominic Roskrow). He regularly contributes to various whisky magazines and websites, including *Whisky Magazine* and scotchwhisky. com, as well as hosting whisky events. Gavin is a Keeper of the Quaich. He wrote the US chapter for the first edition.

SECOND EDITION

All revisions for the second edition were carried out by Gavin D. Smith.